Professional Resources

- **Document/Work Product Templates:** If you need examples of the format and content of software engineering work products, they are provided for you to download.
- **Software Engineering Checklists:** When you conduct a review or assess software engineering work products, it is a good idea to have a checklist to guide your evaluation. A wide variety of checklists are provided, and links to additional checklists are also included.
- **Tiny Tools:** There are lots of little things that lead to success in software engineering work. This collection of simple software engineering tools will help you with some of them.
- **Professional Tools (CASE):** "What is the best CASE tool for our situation?" is a commonly asked question. The SEPA, 6/e, Web site provides you with links to hundreds of CASE tools and more than a few comparisons of these tools.
- **Software Engineering Resources:** If you need to do some research or take an online tutorial, the SEPA, 6/e, Web site contains over 900 pointers to a broad array of software engineering topics.
- **Adaptable Process Model:** The adaptable process model is a comprehensive process template that can be tuned to your organization's needs.
- **Distance Learning:** An Internet-based curriculum, designed for use by individuals, teams, and entire software organizations, is available to supplement SEPA, 6/e. Information about this product is available at the Web site.
- **Industry Commentary:** A collection of short essays, extracted from a number of industry sources, is provided to help spur thoughtful debate.

Student Resources

- **Study Guide:** Need a quick review during exam time? The Study Guide can help by summarizing the key points presented within each SEPA, 6/e, chapter.
- **Self-Tests:** Have you learned the key points as you've read a chapter? Multiple-choice self-tests enable you to test your knowledge of chapter content and tell you where to look for the right answer.
- **Solved Problems:** Do you want to reinforce your understanding of key topics? SEPA, 6/e, presents well over 300 problems for you to solve, and provides solutions for many of them.
- **Web-based Resources:** Need to learn a bit more about a software engineering topic? The SEPA, 6/e, Web site contains over 900 pointers, organized by chapter, to a broad array of software engineering topics.
- **Case Study:** Would you like examples of software engineering work products? The case study provides running examples of all important software engineering work products.
- **Reference Library:** Have you been assigned some in-depth research? The SEPA, 6/e, Web site provides access to over 500 downloadable papers on a broad array of software engineering topics.
- **Supplementary Content:** Need even more information? The site contains a collection of supplementary materials that expand on topics presented within the book.
- **Message Board:** Want to talk with other readers? The message board promotes Q&A among students and others, and provides a useful mechanism for informal communication.

IMPORTANT:

HERE IS YOUR REGISTRATION CODE TO ACCESS YOUR PREMIUM McGRAW-HILL ONLINE RESOURCES.

For key premium online resources you need THIS CODE to gain access. Once the code is entered, you will be able to use the Web resources for the length of your course.

If your course is using **WebCT** or **Blackboard**, you'll be able to use this code to access the McGraw-Hill content within your instructor's online course.

Access is provided if you have purchased a new book. If the registration code is missing from this book, the registration screen on our Website, and within your WebCT or Blackboard course, will tell you how to obtain your new code.

Registering for McGraw-Hill Online Resources

To gain access to your McGraw-Hill web resources simply follow the steps below:

1. USE YOUR WEB BROWSER TO GO TO: **www.mhhe.com/pressman**
2. CLICK ON **FIRST TIME USER**.
3. ENTER THE REGISTRATION CODE* PRINTED ON THE TEAR-OFF BOOKMARK ON THE RIGHT.
4. AFTER YOU HAVE ENTERED YOUR REGISTRATION CODE, CLICK **REGISTER**.
5. FOLLOW THE INSTRUCTIONS TO SET-UP YOUR PERSONAL UserID AND PASSWORD.
6. WRITE YOUR UserID AND PASSWORD DOWN FOR FUTURE REFERENCE. KEEP IT IN A SAFE PLACE.

TO GAIN ACCESS to the McGraw-Hill content in your instructor's **WebCT** or **Blackboard** course simply log in to the course with the UserID and Password provided by your instructor. Enter the registration code exactly as it appears in the box to the right when prompted by the system. You will only need to use the code the first time you click on McGraw-Hill content.

Thank you, and welcome to your McGraw-Hill online resources!

* YOUR REGISTRATION CODE CAN BE USED ONLY ONCE TO ESTABLISH ACCESS. IT IS NOT TRANSFERABLE.

0-07-301871-6 T/A PRESSMAN: SOFTWARE ENGINEERING, 6E

MCGRAW-HILL

ONLINE RESOURCES

REGISTRATION CODE

52TI-AL44-1U1H-STHZ-L45I

Mc Graw Hill Higher Education

Software Engineering

A PRACTITIONER'S APPROACH

Software Engineering

A PRACTITIONER'S APPROACH

SIXTH EDITION

Roger S. Pressman, Ph.D.

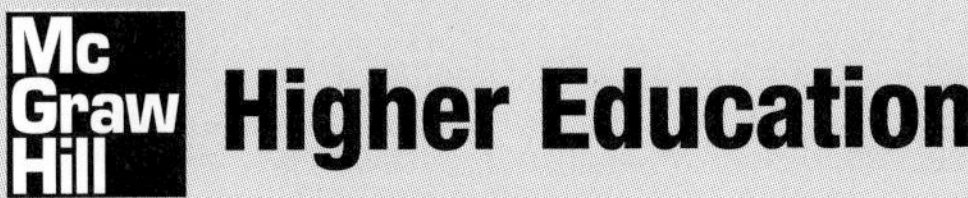

Boston Burr Ridge, IL Dubuque, IA Madison, WI New York San Francisco St. Louis
Bangkok Bogotá Caracas Kuala Lumpur Lisbon London Madrid Mexico City
Milan Montreal New Delhi Santiago Seoul Singapore Sydney Taipei Toronto

The McGraw-Hill Companies

SOFTWARE ENGINEERING: A PRACTITIONER'S APPROACH
SIXTH EDITION

Published by McGraw-Hill, a business unit of The McGraw-Hill Companies, Inc., 1221 Avenue of the Americas, New York, NY 10020.

Some ancillaries, including electronic and print components, may not be available to customers outside the United States.

This book is printed on acid-free paper.

1 2 3 4 5 6 7 8 9 0 DOC/DOC 0 9 8 7 6 5 4

ISBN 0-07-285318-2

Publisher: *Elizabeth A. Jones*
Managing developmental editor: *Emily J. Lupash*
Marketing manager: *Dawn R. Bercier*
Senior project manager: *Gloria G. Schiesl*
Lead production supervisor: *Sandy Ludovissy*
Lead media project manager: *Audrey R. Reiter*
Senior media technology producer: *Eric A. Weber*
Senior designer: *David W. Hash*
Cover image: *Palenque (1980), Color Intaglio, Mauricio Lasansky (artist), Lasansky Corporation © (copyright)*
Compositor: *Carlisle Communications, Ltd.*
Typeface: *8.5/13.5 Leawood*
Printer: *R. R. Donnelley Crawfordsville, IN*

Library of Congress Cataloging-in-Publication Data

Pressman, Roger S.
Software engineering : a practitioner's approach / Roger S. Pressman. — 6th ed.
p. cm. — (McGraw-Hill series in computer science)
Includes index.
ISBN 0-07-285318-2 (alk. paper)
1. Software engineering. I. Title. II. Series.

QA76.758P75 2005
005.1—dc22 2003026394
CIP

www.mhhe.com

To my parents,
who taught me how
to navigate life's many roads.

To Barbara, Mathew, and Michael,
who make the journey worthwhile.

About the Author

Roger S. Pressman is an internationally recognized authority in software process improvement and software engineering technologies. For over three decades, he has worked as a software engineer, a manager, a professor, an author, and a consultant, focusing on software engineering issues.

As an industry practitioner and manager, Dr. Pressman worked on the development of CAD/CAM systems for advanced engineering and manufacturing applications. He has also held positions with responsibility for scientific and systems programming.

After receiving a Ph.D. in engineering from the University of Connecticut, Dr. Pressman moved to academia where he became Bullard Associate Professor of Computer Engineering at the University of Bridgeport and director of the university's Computer-Aided Design and Manufacturing Center.

Dr. Pressman is currently president of R.S. Pressman & Associates, Inc., a consulting firm specializing in software engineering methods and training. He serves as principle consultant and has designed and developed *Essential Software Engineering*, a complete video curriculum in software engineering, and *Process Advisor*, a self-directed system for software process improvement. Both products are used by thousands of companies worldwide. More recently, he has worked in collaboration with QAI India to develop a comprehensive Internet-based "eSchool" in software engineering.

Dr. Pressman has written many technical papers, is a regular contributor to industry periodicals, and is author of six technical books. In addition to *Software Engineering: A Practitioner's Approach*, he has written the award-winning *A Manager's Guide to Software Engineering* (McGraw-Hill); *Making Software Engineering Happen* (Prentice-Hall), the first book to address the critical management problems associated with software process improvement; and *Software Shock* (Dorset House), a treatment that focuses on software and its impact on business and society. Dr. Pressman has been on the Editorial Boards of a number of industry journals, and for many years, was editor of the "Manager" column in *IEEE Software*.

Dr. Pressman is a well-known speaker, keynoting a number of major industry conferences. He is a member of the ACM, IEEE, and Tau Beta Pi, Phi Kappa Phi, Eta Kappa Nu, and Pi Tau Sigma.

On the personal side, Dr. Pressman lives in South Florida with his wife, Barbara. An athlete for most of his life, he is a serious tennis player (NTRP 4.5) and a single-digit handicap golfer. He has written two novels, *The Aymara Bridge* and *The Puppeteer*.

Contents at a Glance

TABLE OF CONTENTS

CHAPTER 8 ANALYSIS MODELING 175

CHAPTER 9 DESIGN ENGINEERING 226

CHAPTER 19 DESIGN MODELING FOR WEB APPLICATIONS 527

CHAPTER 20 TESTING WEB APPLICATIONS 562

CHAPTER 23 ESTIMATION FOR SOFTWARE PROJECTS 642

CHAPTER 24 SOFTWARE PROJECT SCHEDULING 673

CHAPTER 25 RISK MANAGEMENT 694

CHAPTER 26 QUALITY MANAGEMENT 712

PREFACE

When computer software succeeds—when it meets the needs of the people who use it, when it performs flawlessly over a long period of time, when it is easy to modify and even easier to use—it can and does change things for the better. But when software fails—when its users are dissatisfied, when it is error prone, when it is difficult to change and even harder to use—bad things can and do happen. We all want to build software that makes things better, avoiding the bad things that lurk in the shadow of failed efforts. To succeed, we need discipline when software is designed and built. We need an engineering approach.

In the 25 years since the first edition of this book was written, software engineering has evolved from an obscure idea practiced by a relatively small number of zealots to a legitimate engineering discipline. Today, it is recognized as a subject worthy of serious research, conscientious study, and tumultuous debate. Throughout the industry, software engineer has replaced programmer as the job title of preference. Software process models, software engineering methods, and software tools have been adopted successfully across a broad spectrum of industry applications.

Although managers and practitioners alike recognize the need for a more disciplined approach to software, they continue to debate the manner in which discipline is to be applied. Many individuals and companies still develop software haphazardly, even as they build systems to service today's most advanced technologies. Many professionals and students are unaware of modern methods. And as a result, the quality of the software that we produce suffers, and bad things happen. In addition, debate and controversy about the true nature of the software engineering approach continue. The status of software engineering is a study in contrasts. Attitudes have changed, progress has been made, but much remains to be done before the discipline reaches full maturity.

The sixth edition of *Software Engineering: A Practitioner's Approach* is intended to serve as a guide to a maturing engineering discipline. The sixth edition, like the five editions that preceded it, is intended for both students and practitioners, retaining its appeal as a guide for the industry professional and as a comprehensive introduction for the student at the upper-level undergraduate or first-year graduate level.

The sixth edition is considerably more than a simple update. The book has been revised extensively and restructured to emphasize new and important software engineering processes and practices. In addition, a new "support system," illustrated on the next page, provides a comprehensive set of student, instructor, and professional resources to complement the content of the book. These resources are presented as part of a Web site (www.mhhe.com/pressman) specifically designed for *Software Engineering: A Practitioner's Approach.*

The Sixth Edition. The 32 chapters of the sixth edition have been organized into five parts. This has been done to compartmentalize topics and assist instructors who may not have the time to complete the entire book in one term. Part 1, *The Software Process,* presents different views of software process, considering all important process models and addressing the debate between prescriptive and agile process philosophies. Part 2,

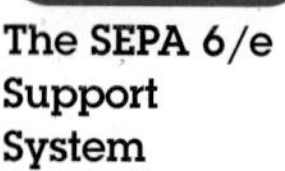

The SEPA 6/e Support System

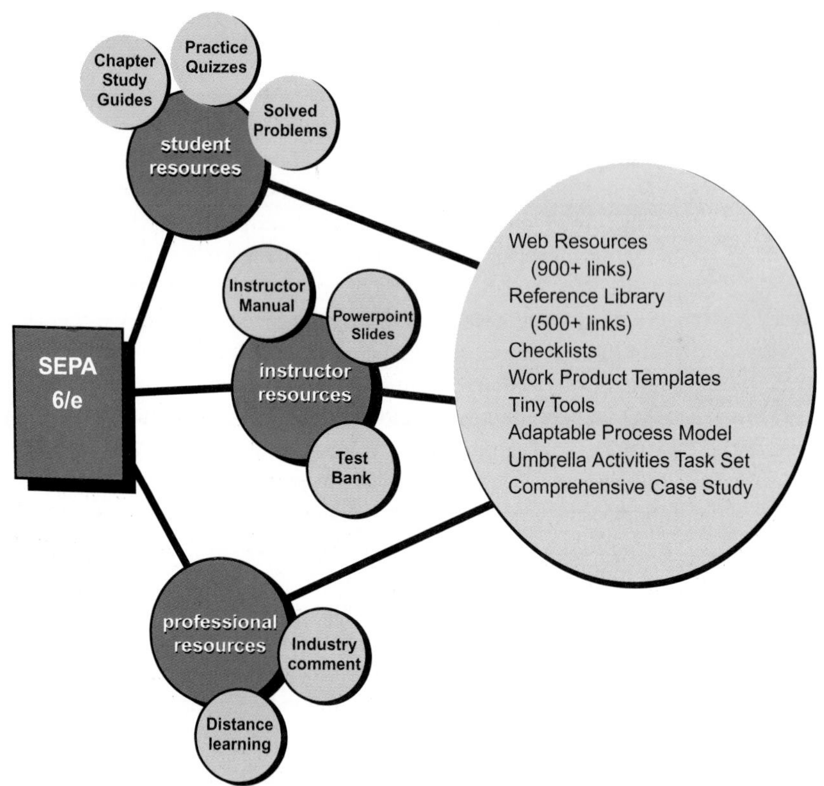

Software Engineering Practice, presents analysis, design, and testing methods with an emphasis on object-oriented techniques and UML modeling. Because object-oriented methods are now widely used throughout the industry, the content of Part 4 of the fifth edition ("object-oriented software engineering") has now been fully integrated into all discussions of software engineering practice in this edition. Part 3, *Applying Web Engineering,* presents a complete engineering approach for the analysis, design, and testing of Web applications. Part 4, *Managing Software Projects,* presents topics that are relevant to those who plan, manage, and control a software project. Part 5, *Advanced Topics in Software Engineering,* presents dedicated chapters that address formal methods, cleanroom software engineering, component-based software engineering, reengineering, and future trends.

In addition to many new and significantly revised chapters, the sixth edition introduces over 120 sidebars that (1) allow the reader to follow a (fictional) project team as it plans and engineers a computer-based system; (2) provide complementary discussions of selected topics; (3) outline "task sets" that describe work flow for selected software engineering activities; and (4) suggest automated tools relevant to chapter topics.

The five-part organization of the sixth edition enables an instructor to "cluster" topics based on available time and student need. An entire one-term course can be built around one or more of the five parts. For example, a "methods course" might emphasize only Parts 1 and 2; a Web development course might emphasize Parts 1 and 3; a "management course" would stress Parts 1 and 4. By organizing the sixth edition in this way, I have attempted to provide an instructor with a number of teaching options. In every case, the content of the sixth edition is complemented by the following elements of the *SEPA, 6/e Support System*.

Student Resources. A wide variety of student resources includes an extensive on-line learning center encompassing study guides, practice quizzes and a variety of Web-based resources including software engineering checklists, an evolving collection of "tiny tools," a complete case study, and work product templates. In addition, over 900 categorized Web references allow a student to explore software engineering in greater detail.

Instructor Resources. A broad array of instructor resources has been developed to supplement the sixth edition. These include a comprehensive on-line *Instructor's Guide* (also downloadable) and supplementary teaching materials including a complete set of over 700 Powerpoint slides that may be used for lectures, a test bank, and sample exams. In addition, a "reference library", containing pointers to over 500 software engineering papers (organized by topic and downloadable in pdf format) can be used in advanced software engineering courses where in-depth discussion of specific topics is required.

The *Instructor's Guide* presents suggestions for conducting various types of software engineering courses, recommendations for a variety of software projects to be conducted in conjunction with a course, and a number of useful teaching aids.

Professional Resources. A collection of resources available to industry practitioners (as well as students and faculty) includes outlines and samples of software engineering documents and other work products, a useful set of software engineering checklists, a catalog of software engineering (CASE) tools, a comprehensive collection of Web-based resources, and an "adaptable process model" that provides a detailed task breakdown of the software engineering process.

When coupled with its on-line support system, the sixth edition of *Software Engineering: A Practitioner's Approach* provides flexibility and depth of content that cannot be achieved by a textbook alone.

Acknowledgments. My work on the six editions of *Software Engineering: A Practitioner's Approach* has been the longest continuing technical project of my life. Even when the writing stops, information extracted from the technical literature continues to be assimilated and organized. For this reason, my thanks to the many authors of books, papers, and articles (in both hardcopy and electronic media) who have provided me with additional insight, ideas, and commentary over the past 25 years.

Special thanks go to Tim Lethbridge of the University of Ottawa who performed an extremely detailed review of the sixth edition, assisted me in the development of UML and OCL examples, and developed the comprehensive case study that accompanies this book. His assistance and comments were invaluable. Special thanks also go to Bruce Maxim of the University of Michigan–Dearborn, who assisted me in developing the Web site that accompanies this book. Bruce is responsible for much of its pedagogical content. Finally, I wish to thank the reviewers of the sixth edition. Their in-depth comments and thoughtful criticism have been invaluable.

Mark Ardis
Rose-Hulman Institute
Xiaoxia Cao
Shanghai University
Nimmagadda Chalamaiah
Jawaharlal Nehru Technological University
Sergiu Dascalu
University of Nevada, Reno
Harry Delugach
University of Alabama, Huntsville
Premkumar Devanbu
University of California, Davis

Lipika Dey
I.I.T., Delhi

Osama Eljabiri
New Jersey Institute of Technology

Gerald Gannon
Arizona State University

David Gustafson
Kansas State University

Qingchun Hu
East China University of Science and Technology

Shi-Ming Huang
National Chung Cheng University

Clinton Jeffery
New Mexico State University

Barbara Jennings
Colorado School of Mines

Venkatesh Kamat
Goa University

Jo Ann Lane
San Diego State University

Minglu Li
Shanghai Jiao Tong University

Robert Lingard
California State University, Northridge

Jiang B. Liu
Bradley University

WY Liu
City University of Hongkong

Banshidhar Majhi
National Institute of Technology

Aditya P Mathur
Purdue University

John D. McGregor
Clemson University

Hong Mei
Peking University

Ahmed Naumaan
University of Minnesota

Joey Paquet
Concordia University

Deepak Phatak
Indian Institute of Technology Bombay

James Purtilo
University of Maryland

Tong Seng, Jon Quah
Nanyang Technological University

K.V.S.V.N. Raju
Andhra University

D Janaki Ram
Indian Institute of Technology, Madras

J.L. Rana
Maulana Azad National Institute of Technology (MANIT)

Ahmed Salem
California State University, Salem

Hee Beng Kuan Tan
Nanyang Technological University

Chris Teng
San Jose State University

Flora Tsai
Nanyang Technological University

David Umphress
Auburn University

Muthanna Gowramma Venkateshmurthy
Visveswaraiah Technological University

Liang Wang
Renmin University of China

Laura Williams
North Carolina State University

Junmin Ye
Central China Normal University

Renkun Ying
Tsinghua University

The content of the sixth edition of *Software Engineering: A Practitioner's Approach* has been shaped by industry professionals, university professors, and students who have used earlier editions of the book and have taken the time to communicate their suggestions, criticisms, and ideas. My thanks to each of you. In addition, my personal thanks go to our many industry clients worldwide, who certainly have taught me as much or more than I could ever teach them.

As the editions of this book have evolved, my sons, Mathew and Michael, have grown from boys to men. Their maturity, character, and success in the real world have been an inspiration to me. Nothing has filled me with more pride. And finally, to Barbara, my love and thanks for encouraging still another edition of "the book."

Roger S. Pressman

WALKTHROUGH

CHAPTER

2 PROCESS: A GENERIC VIEW

KEY CONCEPTS

In a fascinating book that provides an economist's view of software and software engineering, Howard Baetjer, Jr. [BAE98] comments on the software process:

> Because software, like all capital, is embodied knowledge, and because that knowledge is initially dispersed, tacit, latent, and incomplete in large measure, software development is a social learning process. The process is a dialogue in which the knowledge that must become the software is brought together and embodied in the software. The process provides interaction between users and designers, between users and evolving tools, and between designers and evolving tools [technology]. It is an iterative process in which the evolving tool itself serves as the medium for communication, with each new round of the dialogue eliciting more useful knowledge from the people involved.

Indeed, building computer software is an iterative learning process, and the outcome, something that Baetjer would call "software capital," is an embodiment of knowledge collected, distilled, and organized as the process is conducted.

QUICK LOOK

What is it? When you work to build a product or system, it's important to go through a series of predictable steps—a road map that helps you create a timely, high-quality result. The road map that you follow is called a *software process*.

Who does it? Software engineers and their managers adopt the process to their needs and then follow it. In addition, the people who have requested the software have a role to play in the process of defining, building, and testing it.

Why is it important? Because it provides stability, control, and organization to an activity that can, if left uncontrolled, become quite chaotic. However, a modern software engineering approach must be "agile." It must demand only those activities, controls, and documentation that are appropriate for the project team and the product that is to be produced.

What are the steps? At a detailed level, the process that you adopt depends on the software that you're building. One process might be appropriate for creating software for an aircraft avionics system, while an entirely different process would be indicated for the creation of a Web site.

What is the work product? From the point of view of a software engineer, the work products are the programs, documents, and data that are produced as a consequence of the activities and tasks defined by the process.

How do I ensure that I've done it right? There are a number of software process assessment mechanisms that enable organizations to determine the "maturity" of their software process. However, the quality, timeliness, and long-term viability of the product you build are the best indicators of the efficacy of the process that you use.

20

CHAPTER OPENER

Introduces the topics that you will learn and provides basic background.

Quick Look provides an overview of what the chapter is about.

Key Concepts are indexed so that the reader can quickly turn to the concept he or she wants to learn about.

CHAPTER 3 PRESCRIPTIVE PROCESS MODELS 53

developers get to build something immediately. Yet, prototyping can be problematic for the following reasons:

1. The customer sees what appears to be a working version of the software, unaware that the prototype is held together "with chewing gum and baling wire," unaware that in the rush to get it working we haven't considered overall software quality or long-term maintainability. When informed that the product must be rebuilt so that high-levels of quality can be maintained, the customer cries foul and demands that "a few fixes" be applied to make the prototype a working product. Too often, software development management relents.
2. The developer often makes implementation compromises in order to get a prototype working quickly. An inappropriate operating system or programming language may be used simply because it is available and known; an inefficient algorithm may be implemented simply to demonstrate capability. After a time, the developer may become comfortable with these choices and forget all the reasons why they were inappropriate. The less-than-ideal choice has now become an integral part of the system.

ADVICE: *Resist pressure to extend a rough prototype into a production product. Quality almost always suffers as a result.*

Although problems can occur, prototyping can be an effective paradigm for software engineering. The key is to define the rules of the game at the beginning; that is, the customer and developer must both agree that the prototype is built to serve as a mechanism for defining requirements. It is then discarded (at least in part), and the actual software is engineered with an eye toward quality.

SAFEHOME

Selecting a Process Model, Part 1

The scene: Meeting room for the software engineering group at CPI Corporation, a (fictional) company that makes consumer products for home and commercial use.

The players: Lee Warren, engineering manager; Doug Miller, software engineering manager; Jamie Lazar, software team member; Vinod Raman, software team member; and Ed Robbins, software team member.

The conversation:

Lee: So let's recapitulate. I've spent some time discussing the *SafeHome* product line as we see it at the moment. No doubt, we've got a lot of work to do to simply define the thing, but I'd like you guys to begin thinking about how you're going to approach the software part of this project.

Doug: Seems like we've been pretty disorganized in our approach to software in the past.

Ed: I don't know, Doug. We always got product out the door.

Doug: True, but not without a lot of grief, and this project looks like it's bigger and more complex than anything we've done in the past.

Jamie: Doesn't look that hard, but I agree . . . our ad hoc approach to past projects won't work here, particularly if we have a very tight timeline.

Doug (smiling): I want to be a bit more professional in our approach. I went to a short course last week and learned a lot about software engineering . . . good stuff. We need a process here.

Jamie (with a frown): My job is to build computer programs, not push paper around.

Doug: Give it a chance before you go negative on me. Here's what I mean. [Doug proceeds to describe the

PRACTICAL FLAVOR

New Running Case Study "SafeHome" is found throughout the text. These dialogues present real world situations that show you how members of a software team interact and apply key software engineering principles and methods.

Software Tools sidebars help you identify which software tools are appropriate for specific tasks. The sidebars also include a list of representative tools.

SOFTWARE TOOLS

Generalized Analysis Modeling in UML

Objective: Analysis modeling tools provide the capability to develop scenario-based models, class-based models, and behavioral models using UML notation.

Mechanics: Tools in this category support the full range of UML diagrams required to build an analysis model (these tools also support design modeling). In addition to diagramming, tools in this category (1) perform consistency and correctness checks for all UML diagrams; (2) provide links for design and code generation; (3) build a database that enables the management and assessment of large UML models required for complex systems.

Representative Tools[27]

The following tools support a full range of UML diagrams required for analysis modeling:

ArgoUML, an open source tool (argouml.tigris.org).

Control Center, developed by TogetherSoft (www.togethersoft.com).

Enterprise Architect, developed by Sparx Systems (www.sparxsystems.com.au).

Object Technology Workbench (OTW), developed by OTW Software (www.otwsoftware.com).

PowerDesigner, developed by Sybase (www.sybase.com).

Rational Rose, developed by Rational Corporation (www.rational.com).

System Architect, developed by Popkin Software (www.popkin.com).

UML Studio, developed by Pragsoft Corporation (www.pragsoft.com).

Visio, developed by Microsoft (www.microsoft.com).

Visual UML, developed by Visal Object Modelers (www.visualuml.com).

8.9 SUMMARY

The objective of analysis modeling is to create a variety of representations that depict software requirements for information, function, and behavior. To accomplish this, two different (but potentially complementary) modeling philosophies can be applied: structured analysis and object-oriented analysis. Structured analysis views software as an information transformer. It assists the software engineer in identifying data objects, their relationships, and the manner in which those data objects are transformed as they flow through software processing functions. Object-oriented analysis examines a problem domain defined as a set of use-cases in an effort to extract classes that define the problem. Each class has a set of attributes and operations. Classes are related to one another in a variety of different ways and are modeled using UML diagrams. The analysis model is composed of four modeling elements: scenario-based models, flow models, class-based models, and behavioral models.

Scenario-based models depict software requirements from the user's point of view. The use-case—a narrative or template-driven description of an interaction between an actor and the software—is the primary modeling element. Derived during requirement elicitation, the use-case defines the key steps for a specific function or interaction. The

27 Tools noted here do not represent an endorsement, but rather a sampling of tools in this category. In most cases, tool names are trademarked by their respective developers.

FIGURE 8.8 Swimlane diagram for Access camera surveillance—display camera views function

KEY POINT A UML swimlane diagram represents the flow of actions and decisions and indicates which actors perform each.

rectangle. Responsibilities are represented as parallel segments that divide the diagram vertically, like the lanes in a swimming pool.

Three analysis classes—**Homeowner, Interface,** and **Camera**—have direct or indirect responsibilities in the context of the activity diagram represented in Figure 8.7. Referring to Figure 8.8, the activity diagram is rearranged so that activities associated with a particular analysis class fall inside the swimlane for that class. For example, the **Interface** class represents the user interface as seen by the homeowner. The activity diagram notes two prompts that are the responsibility of the interface—*prompt for*

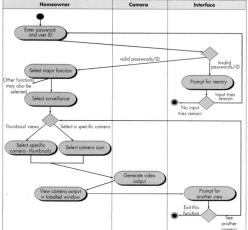

UML Diagrams are used to illustrate important analysis and design methods for both conventional software and Web applications.

Practical advice from the real world of software engineering.

Advice Icons provide pragmatic guidance that can help you make the right decision or avoid common problems while building software.

EXCELLENT PEDAGOGY

Quotes interspersed throughout the book makes reading fun and interesting.

The **KeyPoints Icon** highlights important concepts to remember.

Info sidebars present information that complements and enhances the topic being discussed.

9.3 DESIGN CONCEPTS

A set of fundamental software design concepts has evolved over the history of software engineering. Although the degree of interest in each concept has varied over the years, each has stood the test of time. Each provides the software designer with a foundation from which more sophisticated design methods can be applied.

M. A. Jackson [JAC75] once said: "The beginning of wisdom for a [software engineer] is to recognize the difference between getting a program to work, and getting it right." Fundamental software design concepts provide the necessary framework for "getting it right."

9.3.1 Abstraction

When we consider a modular solution to any problem, many *levels of abstraction* can be posed. At the highest level of abstraction, a solution is stated in broad terms using the language of the problem environment. At lower levels of abstraction, a more detailed description of the solution is provided.

> "Abstraction is one of the fundamental ways that we as humans cope with complexity."
>
> Grady Booch

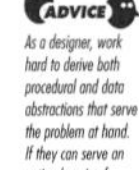

As a designer, work hard to derive both procedural and data abstractions that serve the problem at hand. If they can serve an entire domain of problems, that's even better.

As we move through different levels of abstraction, we work to create procedural and data abstractions. A *procedural abstraction* refers to a sequence of instructions that have a specific and limited function. The name of procedural abstraction implies these functions, but specific details are suppressed. An example of a procedural abstraction would be the word *open* for a door. *Open* implies a long sequence of procedural steps (e.g., walk to the door, reach out and grasp knob, turn knob and pull door, step away from moving door, etc.).[4]

A *data abstraction* is a named collection of data that describes a data object. In the context of the procedural abstraction *open,* we can define a data abstraction called **door.** Like any data object, the data abstraction for **door** would encompass a set of attributes that describe the door (e.g., **door type, swing direction, opening mechanism, weight, dimensions**). It follows that the procedural abstraction *open* would make use of information contained in the attributes of the data abstraction **door.**

9.3.2 Architecture

Software architecture alludes to "the overall structure of the software and the ways in which that structure provides conceptual integrity for a system" [SHA95a]. In its simplest form, architecture is the structure or organization of program components

…tions can be replaced with another, as long as the …ains the same. Therefore, the steps required to …oor were automatic and attached to a sensor.

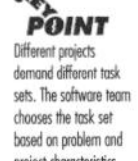

Different projects demand different task sets. The software team chooses the task set based on problem and project characteristics.

design, architectural design, interface design, and component-level design) that create a design model (and/or a design specification).[3]

Referring again to Figure 2.2, each software engineering action is represented by a number of different *task sets*—each a collection of software engineering work tasks, related work products, quality assurance points, and project milestones. The task set that best accommodates the needs of the project and the characteristics of the team is chosen. This implies that a software engineering action (e.g., design) can be adapted to the specific needs of the software project and the characteristics of the project team.

INFO

Task Set

A *task set* defines the actual work to be done to accomplish the objectives of a software engineering action. For example, "requirements gathering" is an important software engineering action that occurs during the **communication** activity. The goal of requirements gathering is to understand what various stakeholders want from the software that is to be built.

For a small, relatively simple project, the task set for requirements gathering might look like this:

1. Make a list of stakeholders for the project.
2. Invite all stakeholders to an informal meeting.
3. Ask each stakeholder to make a list of features and functions required.
4. Discuss requirements and build a final list.
5. Prioritize requirements.
6. Note areas of uncertainty.

For a larger, more complex software project, a different task set would be required. It might encompass the following work tasks:

1. Make a list of stakeholders for the project.
2. Interview each stakeholder separately to determine overall wants and needs.
3. Build a preliminary list of functions and features based on stakeholder input.
4. Schedule a series of facilitated requirements gathering meetings.
5. Conduct meetings.
6. Produce informal user scenarios as part of each meeting.
7. Refine user scenarios based on stakeholder feedback.
8. Build a revised list of stakeholder requirements.
9. Use quality function deployment techniques to prioritize requirements.
10. Package requirements so that they can be delivered incrementally.
11. Note constraints and restrictions that will be placed on the system.
12. Discuss methods for validating the system.

Both of these task sets achieve requirements gathering, but they are quite different in their depth and formality. The software team chooses the task set that will allow it to achieve the goal of each process activity and software engineering action and still maintain quality and agility.

The framework described in the generic view of software engineering is complemented by a number of *umbrella activities.* Typical activities in this category include:

Software project tracking and control—allows the software team to assess progress against the project plan and take necessary action to maintain schedule.

3 It should be noted that "modeling" must be interpreted somewhat differently when the maintenance of existing software is conducted. In some cases, analysis and design modeling do occur, but in other maintenance situations, modeling may be used to help understand the legacy software as well as to represent additions or modifications to it.

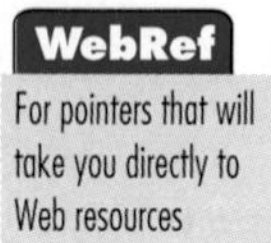

WebRef
For pointers that will take you directly to Web resources

The **WebRef Icon** points readers to where more relevant information can be found on the web.

The **Question Mark Icon** asks common questions that are answered in the body of the text.

END OF CHAPTER MATERIAL

A **Summary** briefly reviews the highlights of each chapter.

Numerous References to significant literature give you a lead on quickly finding more information.

Problems and Points to Ponder are problem sections that reinforce important software engineering concepts.

Further Readings provide pointers to further indepth information.

480 PART THREE APPLYING WEB ENGINEERING

factors. Like other types of software, WebApps can be assessed using a variety of quality criteria that include usability, functionality, reliability, efficiency, maintainability, security, availability, scalability, and time to market.

WebE can be described in three layers—process, methods, and tools/technology. The WebE process adopts the agile development philosophy that emphasizes a "lean" engineering approach that leads to the incremental delivery of the system to be built. The generic process framework—communication, planning, modeling, construction, and deployment—is applicable to WebE. These framework activities are refined into a set of WebE tasks that are adapted to the needs of each project. A set of umbrella activities similar to those applied during software engineering work—SQA, SCM, project management—apply to all WebE projects.

REFERENCES

[AOY98] Aoyama, M., "Web-Based Agile Software Development, *IEEE Computer*, November/December, 1998, pp. 56–65.

[DAR99] Dart, S., "Containing the Web Crisis Using Configuration Management," *Proc. First ICSE Workshop on Web Engineering*, ACM, Los Angeles, May 1999. (*The Proceedings of the First ICSE Workshop on Web Engineering* are published on-line at http://fistserv.macarthur.uws.edu.au/san/icse99-WebE/ICSE99-WebE-Proc/ default.htm).

[FOW01] Fowler M., and J. Highsmith, "The Agile Manifesto," *Software Development Magazine*, August 2001, http://www.sdmagazine.com/documents/s=844/ sdm0108a/0108a.htm.

[MCD01] McDonald, A., and R. Welland, *Agile Web Engineering (AWE) Process*, Department of Computer Science, University of Glascow, Technical Report TR-2001-98, 2001, downloadable from http://www.dcs.gla.ac.uk/~andrew/TR-2001-98.pdf.

[MUR99] Murugesan, S., *WebE Home Page*, http://fistserv.macarthur.uws.edu.au/ san/WebEHome, July, 1999.

[NOR99] Norton, K., "Applying Cross Functional Evolutionary Methodologies to Web Development," *Proc. First ICSE Workshop on Web Engineering*, ACM, Los Angeles, May 1999.

[POW98] Powell, T. A., *Web Site Engineering*, Prentice-Hall, 1998.

[PRE98] Pressman, R. S. (moderator), "Can Internet-Based Applications Be Engineered?" *IEEE Software*, September 1998, pp. 104–110.

[QUI01] Quibeldey-Cirkel, K., "Checklist for Web Site Quality Assurance," *Quality Week Europe*, 2001, downloadable from www.fbi.fh-darmstadt.de/~quibeldey/ Projekte/QWE2001/ Paper_Quibeldey_Cirkel.pdf.

[WEI02] Weinschenk, S., "Psychology and the Web: Designing for People," 2002, http://www.weinschenk.com/learn/facts.asp.

PROBLEMS AND POINTS TO PONDER

16.1. Are there other generic attributes that differentiate WebApps from more conventional software applications? Try to name two or three.

16.2. How do you judge the "quality" of a Web site? Make a prioritized list of 10 quality attributes that you believe are most important.

16.3. Do a bit of research and write a two to three page paper that summarizes one of the technologies noted in Section 16.2.3.

16.4. Using an actual Web site as an example, illustrate the different manifestations of WebApp "content."

SUPPLEMENTS FOR INSTRUCTORS, STUDENTS, AND PROFESSIONALS WWW.MHHE.COM/PRESSMAN

For Instructors:

- **Instructor Guide** provides tips for teaching.
- **PowerPoint Slides**
- **Test Questions**
- **Sample Exams**
- **Problem Solutions**

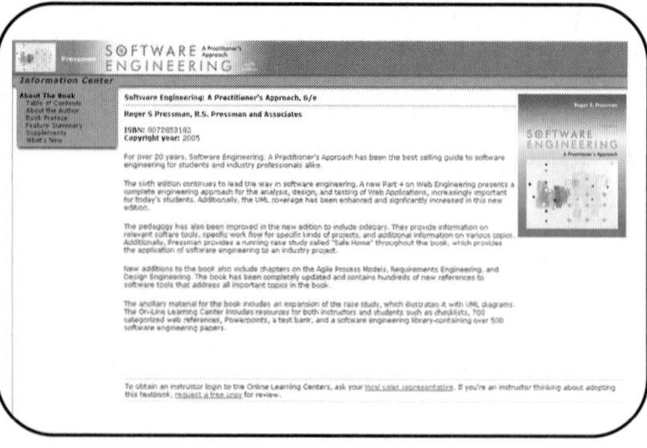

For Students and Professionals

- **Chapter Outlines**
- **Practice Quizzes**
- **Web Resources** provide links to over 900 Web-based software engineering resources.
- **Software Engineering Reference Library** provides access to hundreds of articles on software engineering.
- **Software Engineering Checklists**
- **Adaptable Process Model**
- **Work Product Templates**
- **Tiny Tools** are a collection of simple software engineering tools, which allow practice of techniques learned in the book.
- **Industry Commentary**

CHAPTER 1 Software and Software Engineering

Key Concepts

Have you ever noticed how the invention of one technology can have profound and unexpected effects on other seemingly unrelated technologies, on commercial enterprises, on people, and even on culture as a whole? This phenomenon is often called "the law of unintended consequences."

Today, computer software is the single most important technology on the world stage. And it is also a prime example of the law of unintended consequences. No one in the 1950s could have predicted that software would become an indispensable technology for business, science, and engineering; that software would enable the creation of new technologies (e.g., genetic engineering), the extension of existing technologies (e.g., telecommunications), and the demise of older technologies (e.g., the printing industry); that software would be the driving force behind the personal computer revolution; that shrink-wrapped software products would be purchased by consumers in neighborhood malls; that a software company would become larger and more influential than the vast majority of industrial-era companies; that a vast software-driven network called the Internet would evolve and change everything from library research to consumer shopping to the dating habits of young (and not-so-young) adults.

No one could have foreseen that software would become embedded in systems of all kinds: transportation, medical, telecommunications, military, industrial, entertainment, office machines—the list is almost endless. And if we are to believe the law of unintended consequences, there are many effects that we cannot yet predict.

Quick Look

What is it? Computer software is the product that software professionals build and then support over the long term. It encompasses programs that execute within a computer of any size and architecture, content that is presented as the computer programs execute, and documents in both hardcopy and virtual forms that encompass all forms of electronic media.

Who does it? Software engineers build and support it, and virtually everyone in the industrialized world uses it either directly or indirectly.

Why is it important? Because it affects nearly every aspect of our lives and has become pervasive in our commerce, our culture, and our everyday activities.

What are the steps? You build computer software like you build any successful product, by applying an agile, adaptable process that leads to a high-quality result that meets the needs of the people who will use the product. You apply a software engineering approach.

What is the work product? From the point of view of a software engineer, the work product is the programs, content (data), and documents that are computer software. But from the user's viewpoint, the work product is the resultant information that somehow makes the user's world better.

How do I ensure that I've done it right? Read the remainder of this book, select those ideas which are applicable to the software that you build, and apply them to your work.

And, finally, no one could have foreseen that millions of computer programs would have to be corrected, adapted, and enhanced as time passed and that the burden of performing these "maintenance" activities would absorb more people and more resources than all work applied to the creation of new software.

> **"Ideas and technological discoveries are the driving engines of economic growth."**
>
> **The Wall Street Journal**

As software's importance has grown, the software community has continually attempted to develop technologies that will make it easier, faster, and less expensive to build and maintain high-quality computer programs. Some of these technologies are targeted at a specific application domain (e.g., Web-site design and implementation); others focus on a technology domain (e.g., object-oriented systems or aspect-oriented programming); and still others are broad-based (e.g., operating systems such as LINUX). However, we have yet to develop a software technology that does it all, and the likelihood of one arising in the future is small. And yet, people bet their jobs, their security, and their very lives on computer software. It better be right.

This book presents a framework for those who build computer software—people who must get it right. The framework encompasses a process, a set of methods, and an array of tools that we call *software engineering.*

> **"In modern society, the role of engineering is to provide systems and products that enhance the material aspects of human life, thus making life easier, safer, more secure, and more enjoyable."**
>
> **Richard Fairley and Mary Willshire**

1.1 The Evolving Role of Software

Software is both a product and a vehicle that delivers a product.

Today, software takes on a dual role. It is both a product and a vehicle for delivering a product. As a product, it delivers the computing potential embodied by computer hardware or, more broadly, by a network of computers that are accessible by local hardware. Whether software resides within a cellular phone or operates inside a mainframe computer, it is an information transformer—producing, managing, acquiring, modifying, displaying, or transmitting information that can be as simple as a single bit or as complex as a multimedia presentation. As the vehicle for delivering the product, software acts as the basis for the control of the computer (operating systems), the communication of information (networks), and the creation and control of other programs (software tools and environments).

Software delivers the most important product of our time—information. It transforms personal data (e.g., an individual's financial transactions) so that the data can be more useful in a local context; it manages business information to enhance competitiveness; it provides a gateway to worldwide information networks (e.g., the Internet) and provides the means for acquiring information in all of its forms.

The role of computer software has undergone significant change over a span of little more than 50 years. Dramatic improvements in hardware performance, pro-

WebRef
Take a look back at the software industry at **www.softwarehistory.org.**

found changes in computing architectures, vast increases in memory and storage capacity, and a wide variety of exotic input and output options have all precipitated more sophisticated and complex computer-based systems. Sophistication and complexity can produce dazzling results when a system succeeds, but they can also pose huge problems for those who must build complex systems.

Popular books published during the 1970s and 1980s provide useful historical insight into the changing perception of computers and software and their impact on our culture. Osborne [OSB79] characterized a "new industrial revolution." Toffler [TOF80] called the advent of microelectronics part of "the third wave of change" in human history, and Naisbitt [NAI82] predicted the transformation from an industrial society to an "information society." Feigenbaum and McCorduck [FEI83] suggested that information and knowledge (controlled by computers) would be the focal point for power in the twenty-first century, and Stoll [STO89] argued that the "electronic community" created by networks and software was the key to knowledge interchange throughout the world. All of these writers were correct.

ADVICE
If you have some time, take a look at one or more of these classic books. Pay attention to what these experts got wrong as they predicted future events and technologies. Stay humble: none of us can really know the future of the systems we build.

As the 1990s began, Toffler [TOF90] described a "power shift" in which old power structures (governmental, educational, industrial, economic, and military) disintegrate as computers and software lead to a "democratization of knowledge." Yourdon [YOU92] worried that U.S. companies might lose their competitive edge in software-related businesses and predicted "the decline and fall of the American programmer." Hammer and Champy [HAM93] argued that information technologies were to play a pivotal role in the "reengineering of the corporation." During the mid-1990s, the pervasiveness of computers and software spawned a rash of books by "neo-Luddites" (e.g., *Resisting the Virtual Life,* edited by James Brook and Iain Boal, and *The Future Does Not Compute* by Stephen Talbot). These authors demonized the computer, emphasizing legitimate concerns but ignoring the profound benefits that have already been realized [LEV95].

> **"Computers make it easy to do a lot of things, but most of the things they make it easier to do don't need to be done."**
> **Andy Rooney**

During the later 1990s, Yourdon [YOU96] reevaluated the prospects of the software professional and suggested the "the rise and resurrection" of the American programmer. As the Internet grew in importance, Yourdon's change of heart proved to be correct. As the twentieth century closed, the focus shifted once more, this time to the impact of the Y2K "time bomb." (e.g., [YOU98a], [KAR99]). Although the dire predictions of the Y2K doomsayers were overreactions, their popular writings drove home the pervasiveness of software in our lives.

As the 2000s progressed, Johnson [JOH01] discussed the power of "emergence"—a phenomenon that explains what happens when interconnections among relatively simple entities result in a system that "self-organizes to form more intelligent, more adaptive behavior." Yourdon [YOU02] revisited the tragic events of 9/11 to discuss

WebRef
For commentary on a wide array of software-related topics, visit **www.yourdon.com.**

the continuing impact of global terrorism on the IT community. Wolfram [WOL02] presented a treatise on "a new kind of science" that posits a unifying theory based primarily on sophisticated software simulations. Daconta and his colleagues [DAC03] discussed the evolution of "the semantic Web" and ways in which it will change the way people interact across global networks.

> "For I dipped into the future, far as the human eye could see, Saw the vision of the world and all the wonder that would be."
>
> **Tennyson**

Today, a huge software industry has become a dominant factor in the economies of the industrialized world. The lone programmer of an earlier era has been replaced by teams of software specialists, each focusing on one part of the technology required to deliver a complex application. And yet, the questions that were asked of the lone programmer are the same questions that are asked when modern computer-based systems are built:[1]

- Why does it take so long to get software finished?
- Why are development costs so high?
- Why can't we find all errors before we give the software to our customers?
- Why do we spend so much time and effort maintaining existing programs?
- Why do we continue to have difficulty in measuring progress as software is being developed and maintained?

These questions and many others demonstrate the industry's concern about software and the manner in which it is developed—a concern that has lead to the adoption of software engineering practice.

1.2 SOFTWARE

In 1970, less than 1 percent of the public could have defined what "computer software" meant. Today, most professionals and many members of the public at large feel that they understand software. But do they?

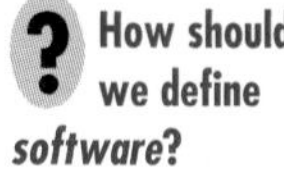
How should we define *software*?

A textbook definition of software might take the following form: *Software is (1) instructions (computer programs) that when executed provide desired features, function, and performance; (2) data structures that enable the programs to adequately manipulate information; and (3) documents that describe the operation and use of the programs.*

---

1 In an excellent book of essays on the software business, Tom DeMarco [DEM95] argues the counterpoint. He states: "Instead of asking why software costs so much, we need to begin asking what have we done to make it possible for today's software to cost so little. The answer to that question will help us continue the extraordinary level of achievement that has always distinguished the software industry."

There is no question that more complete definitions could be offered. But we need more than a formal definition.

To gain an understanding of software (and ultimately an understanding of software engineering), it is important to examine the characteristics of software that make it different from other things that human beings build. Software is a logical rather than a physical system element. Therefore, software has characteristics that are considerably different than those of hardware:

Software is engineered, not manufactured.

1. *Software is developed or engineered; it is not manufactured in the classical sense.*

   Although some similarities exist between software development and hardware manufacturing, the two activities are fundamentally different. In both activities, high quality is achieved through good design, but the manufacturing phase for hardware can introduce quality problems that are nonexistent (or easily corrected) for software. Both activities are dependent on people, but the relationship between people applied and work accomplished is entirely different (see Chapter 24). Both activities require the construction of a "product," but the approaches are different. Software costs are concentrated in engineering. This means that software projects cannot be managed as if they were manufacturing projects.

Software doesn't wear out, but it does deteriorate.

2. *Software doesn't "wear out."*

   Figure 1.1 depicts failure rate as a function of time for hardware. The relationship, often called the "bathtub curve," indicates that hardware exhibits relatively high failure rates early in its life (these failures are often attributable to design or manufacturing defects). Defects are then corrected, and failure rate

FIGURE 1.1

Failure curve for hardware

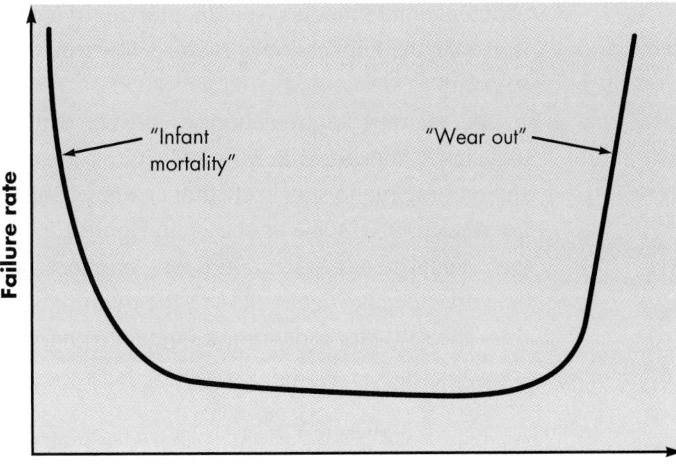

FIGURE 1.2

Failure curves for software

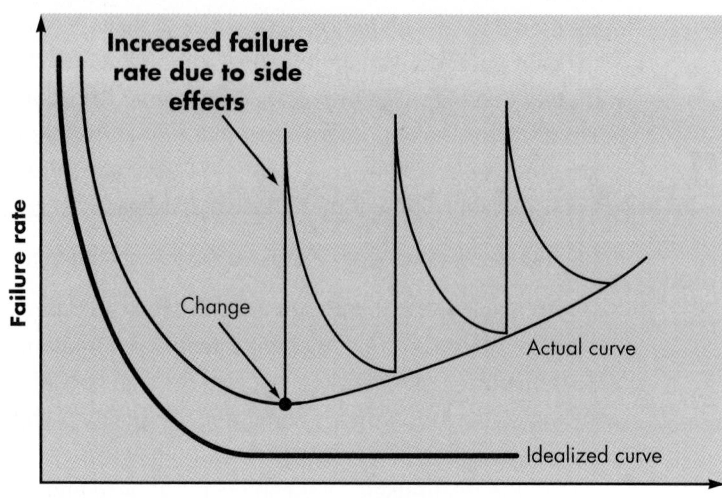

drops to a steady-state level (hopefully, quite low) for some period of time. As time passes, however, the failure rate rises again as hardware components suffer from the cumulative affects of dust, vibration, abuse, temperature extremes, and many other environmental maladies. Stated simply, the hardware begins to *wear out.*

If you want to reduce software deterioration, you'll have to do better software design (Chapters 9–12).

Software is not susceptible to the environmental maladies that cause hardware to wear out. In theory, therefore, the failure rate curve for software should take the form of the "idealized curve" shown in Figure 1.2. Undiscovered defects will cause high failure rates early in the life of a program. However, these are corrected (hopefully, without introducing other errors), and the curve flattens as shown. The idealized curve is a gross oversimplification of actual failure models (see Chapter 26 for more information) for software. However, the implication is clear—software doesn't wear out. But it does *deteriorate!*

Software engineering methods strive to reduce the magnitude of the spikes and slope of the actual curve in Figure 1.2.

This seeming contradiction can best be explained by considering the "actual curve" in Figure 1.2. During its life,[2] software will undergo change. As changes are made, it is likely that errors will be introduced, causing the failure rate curve to spike as shown in Figure 1.2. Before the curve can return to the original steady-state failure rate, another change is requested, causing the curve to spike again. Slowly, the minimum failure rate level begins to rise—the software is deteriorating due to change.

2 In fact, from the moment that development begins and long before the first version is delivered, changes may be requested by the customer.

Another aspect of wear illustrates the difference between hardware and software. When a hardware component wears out, it is replaced by a spare part. There are no software spare parts. Every software failure indicates an error in design or in the process through which design was translated into machine-executable code. Therefore, software maintenance involves considerably more complexity than hardware maintenance.

Most software continues to be custom built.

3. *Although the industry is moving toward component-based construction, most software continues to be custom built.*

Consider the manner in which the control hardware for a computer-based product is designed and built. The design engineer draws a simple schematic of the digital circuitry, does some fundamental analysis to ensure that proper function will be achieved, and then goes to the shelf where catalogs of digital components exist. Each integrated circuit has a part number, a defined and validated function, a well-defined interface, and a standard set of integration guidelines. After each component is selected, it can be ordered off the shelf.

As an engineering discipline evolves, a collection of standard design components is created. Standard screws and off-the-shelf integrated circuits are only two of thousands of standard components that are used by mechanical and electrical engineers as they design new systems. The reusable components have been created so that the engineer can concentrate on the truly innovative elements of a design, i.e., the parts that represent something new. In the hardware world, component reuse is a natural part of the engineering process. In the software world, it has only begun to be achieved on a broad scale.

> **"Ideas are the building blocks of ideas."**
>
> **Jason Zebehazy**

A software component should be designed and implemented so that it can be reused in many different programs. Modern reusable components encapsulate both data and the processing that is applied to the data, enabling the software engineer to create new applications from reusable parts.[3] For example, today's user interfaces are built with reusable components that enable the creation of graphics windows, pull-down menus, and a wide variety of interaction mechanisms. The data structures and processing detail required to build the interface are contained within a library of reusable components for interface construction.

3 Component-based software engineering is presented in Chapter 30.

1.3 The Changing Nature of Software

Today, seven broad categories of computer software present continuing challenges for software engineers:

System software. System software is a collection of programs written to service other programs. Some system software (e.g., compilers, editors, and file management utilities) processes complex, but determinate,[4] information structures. Other systems applications (e.g., operating system components, drivers, networking software, telecommunications processors) process largely indeterminate data. In either case, the systems software area is characterized by heavy interaction with computer hardware; heavy usage by multiple users; concurrent operation that requires scheduling, resource sharing, and sophisticated process management; complex data structures; and multiple external interfaces.

WebRef
One of the most comprehensive libraries of shareware/freeware can be found at **shareware.cnet.com.**

Application software. Application software consists of standalone programs that solve a specific business need. Applications in this area process business or technical data in a way that facilitates business operations or management/technical decision-making. In addition to conventional data processing applications, application software is used to control business functions in real-time (e.g., point-of-sale transaction processing, real-time manufacturing process control).

Engineering/scientific software. Formerly characterized by "number crunching" algorithms, engineering and scientific software applications range from astronomy to volcanology, from automotive stress analysis to space shuttle orbital dynamics, and from molecular biology to automated manufacturing. However, modern applications within the engineering/scientific area are moving away from conventional numerical algorithms. Computer-aided design, system simulation, and other interactive applications have begun to take on real-time and even system software characteristics.

Embedded software. Embedded software resides within a product or system and is used to implement and control features and functions for the end-user and for the system itself. Embedded software can perform limited and esoteric functions (e.g., keypad control for a microwave oven) or provide significant function and control capability (e.g., digital functions in an automobile such as fuel control, dashboard displays, braking systems, etc.).

Product-line software. Designed to provide a specific capability for use by many different customers, product-line software can focus on a limited and esoteric mar-

4 Software is *determinate* if the order and timing of inputs, processing, and outputs is predictable. Software is *indeterminate* if the order and timing of inputs, processing, and outputs cannot be predicted in advance.

ketplace (e.g., inventory control products) or address mass consumer markets (e.g., word processing, spreadsheets, computer graphics, multimedia, entertainment, database management, personal and business financial applications).

Web-applications. "WebApps," span a wide array of applications. In their simplest form, WebApps can be little more than a set of linked hypertext files that present information using text and limited graphics. However, as e-commerce and B2B applications grow in importance, WebApps are evolving into sophisticated computing environments that not only provide standalone features, computing functions, and content to the end user, but also are integrated with corporate databases and business applications.

Artificial intelligence software. AI software makes use of nonnumerical algorithms to solve complex problems that are not amenable to computation or straightforward analysis. Applications within this area include robotics, expert systems, pattern recognition (image and voice), artificial neural networks, theorem proving, and game playing.

> "There is no computer that has common sense."
>
> **Marvin Minsky**

Millions of software engineers worldwide are hard at work on projects in one or more of these categories. In some cases, new systems are being built, but in others, existing applications are being corrected, adapted, and enhanced. It is common for a young software engineer to work on a program that is older than she is! Past generations of software people have left a legacy in each of the categories we have discussed. Hopefully, the legacy left behind by this generation will ease the burden of future software engineers. And yet, new challenges have appeared on the horizon:

Ubiquitous computing. The rapid growth of wireless networking may soon lead to true distributed computing. The challenge for software engineers will be to develop systems and application software that will allow small devices, personal computers, and enterprise system to communicate across vast networks.

Netsourcing. The World Wide Web is rapidly becoming a computing engine as well as a content provider. The challenge for software engineers is to architect simple (e.g., personal financial planning) and sophisticated applications that provide benefit to targeted end-user markets worldwide.

> "You can't always predict, but you can always prepare."
>
> **Anonymous**

Open source. A growing trend that results in distribution of source code for systems applications (e.g., operating systems, database, and development environments) so that customers can make local modifications. The challenge for software engineers is to build source code that is self-descriptive, but, more importantly, to develop techniques that will enable both customers and developers to know what changes have been made and how those changes manifest themselves within the software.

The "new economy." The dot-com insanity that gripped financial markets during the late 1990s and the bust that followed in the early 2000s have lead many business people to believe that the new economy is dead. The new economy is alive and well, but it will evolve slowly. It will be characterized by mass communication and distribution. Andy Lippman [LIP02] notes this when he writes:

> We are entering an era characterized by communications among distributed machines and dispersed people, rather than being mostly about a connection between two individuals or between an individual and a machine. The old approach to telephony was about "connections to"; the next wave is about "connections among." Napster, instant messaging, short message systems, and BlackBerries are examples.

The challenge for software engineers is to build applications that will facilitate mass communication and mass product distribution using concepts that are only now forming.

Each of these "new challenges" will undoubtedly obey the law of unintended consequences and have effects (for business people, software engineers, and end-users) that cannot be predicted today. However, software engineers can prepare by instantiating a process that is agile and adaptable enough to accommodate dramatic changes in technology and business rules that are sure to come in the next decade.

> "[T]he computer itself will make a historic transition from something that is used for analytic tasks . . . to something that can elicit emotion."
>
> **David Vaskevitch**

1.4 Legacy Software

Hundreds of thousands of computer programs fall into one of the seven broad application domains—system software, application software, engineering/scientific software, embedded software, product software, WebApps, and AI applications—discussed in Section 1.3. Some of these are state-of-the-art software—just released to individuals, industry, and government. But other programs are older, in some cases *much* older.

? What is legacy software?

These older programs—often referred to as *legacy software*—have been the focus of continuous attention and concern since the 1960s. Dayani-Fard and his colleagues [DAY99] describe legacy software in the following way:

> Legacy software systems . . . were developed decades ago and have been continually modified to meet changes in business requirements and computing platforms. The proliferation of such systems is causing headaches for large organizations who find them costly to maintain and risky to evolve.

Liu and his colleagues [LIU98] extend this description by noting that "many legacy systems remain supportive to core business functions and are indispensable to the business." Hence, legacy software is characterized by longevity and business criticality.

1.4.1 The Quality of Legacy Software

? What should I do if I encounter a legacy system that exhibits poor quality?

Unfortunately, there is one additional characteristic that can be present in legacy software—*poor quality.*[5] Legacy systems sometimes have inextensible designs, convoluted code, poor or nonexistent documentation, test cases and results that were never archived, a poorly managed change history—the list can be quite long. And yet, these systems support "core business functions and are indispensable to the business" [LIU98]. What can one do?

The only reasonable answer may be to do nothing, at least until the legacy system must undergo some significant change. If the legacy software meets the needs of its users and runs reliably, it isn't broken and does not need to be fixed. However, as time passes legacy systems often evolve for one or more of the following reasons:

? What types of changes are made to legacy systems?

- The software must be adapted to meet the needs of new computing environments or technology.
- The software must be enhanced to implement new business requirements.
- The software must be extended to make it interoperable with more modern systems or databases.
- The software must be re-architected to make it viable within a network environment.

Every software engineer must recognize that change is natural. Don't try to fight it.

When these modes of evolution occur, a legacy system must be reengineered (Chapter 31) so that it remains viable into the future. The goal of modern software engineering is to "devise methodologies that are founded on the notion of evolution;" that is, the notion that "software systems continually change, new software systems are built from the old ones, and . . . all must interoperate and cooperate with each other" [DAY99].

1.4.2 Software Evolution

Regardless of its application domain, size, or complexity, computer software will evolve over time. Change (often referred to as *software maintenance*) drives this process and occurs when errors are corrected, when the software is adapted to a new environment, when the customer requests new features or functions, and when

5 In this case, quality is judged based on modern software engineering thinking—a somewhat unfair criterion since some modern software engineering concepts and principles may not have been well understood at the time that the legacy software was developed.

the application is reengineered to provide benefit in a modern context. Sam Williams [WIL02] describes this when he writes:

> As large-scale programs such as Windows and Solaris expand well into the range of 30 to 50 million lines of code, successful project managers have learned to devote as much time to combing the tangles out of legacy code as to adding new code. Simply put, in a decade that saw the average PC microchip performance increase a hundredfold, software's inability to scale at even linear rates has gone from dirty little secret to an industry-wide embarrassment.

Over the past 30 years, Manny Lehman [e.g., LEH97a] and his colleagues have performed detailed analyses of industry-grade software and systems in an effort to develop a *unified theory for software evolution.* The details of this work are beyond the scope of this book,[6] but the underlying laws that have been derived are worthy of note [LEH97b]:

The Law of Continuing Change (1974). E-type systems[7] must be continually adapted, or else they become progressively less satisfactory.

? Why do legacy systems evolve as time passes?

The Law of Increasing Complexity (1974). As an E-type system evolves its complexity increases unless work is done to maintain or reduce it.

The Law of Self-Regulation (1974). The E-type system evolution process is self-regulating with distribution of product and process measures close to normal.

The Law of Conservation of Organizational Stability (1980). The average effective global activity rate in an evolving E-type system is invariant over product lifetime.

The Law of Conservation of Familiarity (1980). As an E-type system evolves all associated with it, developers, sales personnel, and users, for example, must maintain mastery of its content and behavior to achieve satisfactory evolution. Excessive growth diminishes that mastery. Hence the average incremental growth remains invariant as the system evolves.

The Law of Continuing Growth (1980). The functional content of E-type systems must be continually increased to maintain user satisfaction over the system's lifetime.

The Law of Declining Quality (1996). The quality of E-type systems will appear to be declining unless they are rigorously maintained and adapted to operational environment changes.

The Feedback System Law (1996). E-type evolution processes constitute multilevel, multiloop, multiagent feedback systems and must be treated as such to achieve significant improvement over any reasonable base.

---

6 The interested reader should see [LEH97a] for a comprehensive discussion of software evolution.

7 *E-types systems* are software that has been implemented in a real-world computing context and will therefore evolve over time.

The laws that Lehman and his colleagues have defined are an inherent part of a software engineer's reality. For the remainder of this book, we discuss software process models, software engineering methods, and management techniques that strive to maintain quality as software evolves.

1.5 Software Myths

Software myths—beliefs about software and the process used to build it—can be traced to the earliest days of computing. Myths have a number of attributes that have made them insidious. For instance, myths appear to be reasonable statements of fact (sometimes containing elements of truth), they have an intuitive feel, and they are often promulgated by experienced practitioners who "know the score."

> **"In the absence of meaningful standards, a new industry like software comes to depend instead on folklore."**
>
> **Tom DeMarco**

Today, most knowledgeable software engineering professionals recognize myths for what they are—misleading attitudes that have caused serious problems for managers and technical people alike. However, old attitudes and habits are difficult to modify, and remnants of software myths are still believed.

Management myths. Managers with software responsibility, like managers in most disciplines, are often under pressure to maintain budgets, keep schedules from slipping, and improve quality. Like a drowning person who grasps at a straw, a software manager often grasps at belief in a software myth, if that belief will lessen the pressure (even temporarily).

WebRef
The Software Project Managers Network can help you dispel these and other myths. It can be found at **www.spmn.com.**

Myth: *We already have a book that's full of standards and procedures for building software. Won't that provide my people with everything they need to know?*

Reality: The book of standards may very well exist, but is it used? Are software practitioners aware of its existence? Does it reflect modern software engineering practice? Is it complete? Is it adaptable? Is it streamlined to improve time to delivery while still maintaining a focus on quality? In many cases, the answer to all of these questions is no.

Myth: *If we get behind schedule, we can add more programmers and catch up (sometimes called the* Mongolian horde *concept).*

Reality: Software development is not a mechanistic process like manufacturing. In the words of Brooks [BRO75]: "Adding people to a late software project makes it later." At first, this statement may seem counterintuitive. However, as new people are added, people who were working must spend time educating the newcomers, thereby reducing the amount of time spent on productive development effort. People can be added but only in a planned and well-coordinated manner.

Myth: *If I decide to outsource the software project to a third party, I can just relax and let that firm build it.*

Reality: If an organization does not understand how to manage and control software projects internally, it will invariably struggle when it outsources software projects.

Customer myths. A customer who requests computer software may be a person at the next desk, a technical group down the hall, the marketing/sales department, or an outside company that has requested software under contract. In many cases, the customer believes myths about software because software managers and practitioners do little to correct misinformation. Myths lead to false expectations (by the customer) and, ultimately, dissatisfaction with the developer.

ADVICE

Work very hard to understand what you have to do before you start. You may not be able to develop every detail, but the more you know, the less risk you take.

Myth: *A general statement of objectives is sufficient to begin writing programs—we can fill in the details later.*

Reality: Although a comprehensive and stable statement of requirements is not always possible, an ambiguous statement of objectives is a recipe for disaster. Unambiguous requirements (usually derived iteratively) are developed only through effective and continuous communication between customer and developer.

Myth: *Project requirements continually change, but change can be easily accommodated because software is flexible.*

Reality: It is true that software requirements change, but the impact of change varies with the time at which it is introduced. When requirement changes are requested early (before design or code has been started), cost impact is relatively small.[8] However, as time passes, cost impact grows rapidly—resources have been committed, a design framework has been established, and change can cause upheaval that requires additional resources and major design modification.

ADVICE

Whenever you think that we don't have time for software engineering, ask yourself, will we have time to do it over again?

Practitioner's myths. Myths that are still believed by software practitioners have been fostered by over 50 years of programming culture. During the early days of software, programming was viewed as an art form. Old ways and attitudes die hard.

Myth: *Once we write the program and get it to work, our job is done.*

Reality: Someone once said that the sooner you begin writing code, the longer it'll take you to get done. Industry data indicate that between

8 Many software engineers have adopted an "agile" approach that accommodates change incrementally, thereby controlling its impact and cost. Agile methods are discussed in Chapter 4.

60 and 80 percent of all effort expended on software will be expended after it is delivered to the customer for the first time.

Myth: *Until I get the program running, I have no way of assessing its quality.*

Reality: One of the most effective software quality assurance mechanisms can be applied from the inception of a project—*the formal technical review.* Software reviews (described in Chapter 26) are a "quality filter" that have been found to be more effective than testing for finding certain classes of software errors.

Myth: *The only deliverable work product for a successful project is the working program.*

Reality: A working program is only one part of a software configuration that includes many elements. Documentation provides a foundation for successful engineering and, more importantly, guidance for software support.

Myth: *Software engineering will make us create voluminous and unnecessary documentation and will invariably slow us down.*

Reality: Software engineering is not about creating documents. It is about creating quality. Better quality leads to reduced rework. And reduced rework results in faster delivery times.

Many software professionals recognize the fallacy of software myths. Regrettably, habitual attitudes and methods foster poor management and technical practices, even when reality dictates a better approach. Recognition of software realities is the first step toward formulation of practical solutions for software engineering.

1.6 How It All Starts

Every software project is precipitated by some business need—the need to correct a defect in an existing application; the need to adapt a legacy system to a changing business environment; the need to extend the functions and features of an existing application; or the need to create a new product, service, or system.

At the beginning of a software engineering project, the business need is often expressed informally as part of a simple conversation. The conversation presented in the sidebar (next page) is typical.

With the exception of a passing reference, software was hardly mentioned as part of the conversation. And yet, software will make or break the *SafeHome* product line. The engineering effort will succeed only if *SafeHome* software succeeds. The market will accept the product only if the software embedded within it properly meets the customer's (as yet unstated) needs. We'll follow the progression of *SafeHome* software engineering in subsequent chapters.

SAFEHOME[9]

How a Project Starts

The scene: Meeting room at CPI Corporation, a (fictional) company that makes consumer products for home and commercial use.

The players: Mal Golden, senior manager, product development; Lisa Perez, marketing manager; Lee Warren, engineering manager; Joe Camalleri, executive VP, business development.

The conversation:

Joe: Okay, Lee, what's this I hear about your folks developing a what? A generic universal wireless box?

Lee: It's pretty cool, about the size of a small matchbook. We can attach it to sensors of all kinds, a digital camera, just about anything. Using the 802.11b wireless protocol. It allows us to access the device's output without wires. We think it'll lead to a whole new generation of products.

Joe: You agree, Mal?

Mal: I do. In fact, with sales as flat as they've been this year, we need something new. Lisa and I have been doing a little market research, and we think we've got a line of products that could be big.

Joe: How big. . . , bottom-line big?

Mal: (avoiding a direct commitment): Tell him about our idea, Lisa.

Lisa: It's a whole new generation of what we call "home management products." We call 'em *SafeHome*. They use the new wireless interface, provide homeowners or small business people with a system that's controlled by their PC—home security, home surveillance, appliance and device control. You know, turn down the home air conditioner while you're driving home, that sort of thing.

Lee: (jumping in) Engineering's done a technical feasibility study of this idea, Joe. It's doable at low manufacturing cost. Most hardware is off the shelf. Software is an issue, but it's nothing that we can't do.

Joe: Interesting. Now, I asked about the bottom line.

Mal: PCs have penetrated 60 percent of all households in the USA. If we could price this thing right, it could be a killer-App. Nobody else has our wireless box—it's proprietary. We'll have a two-year jump on the competition. Revenue? Maybe as much as $30–40 million in the second year.

Joe (smiling): Let's take this to the next level. I'm interested.

1.7 SUMMARY

Software has become the key element in the evolution of computer-based systems and products and one of the most important technologies on the world stage. Over the past 50 years, software has evolved from a specialized problem solving and information analysis tool to an industry in itself. Yet we still have trouble developing high-quality software on time and within budget. Software—programs, data, and documents—addresses a wide array of technology and application areas, yet all software evolves according to a set of laws that have remained the same for over 30 years. The intent of software engineering is to provide a framework for building higher quality software.

9 The *SafeHome* project will be used throughout this book to illustrate the inner workings of a project team as it builds a software product. The company, the project, and the people are purely fictitious, but the situations and problems are real.

References

[BRO75] Brooks, F., *The Mythical Man-Month,* Addison-Wesley, 1975.

[DAC03] Daconta, M., L. Obrst, and K. Smith, *The Semantic Web,* Wiley, 2003.

[DAY99] Dayani-Fard, H., et al., "Legacy Software Systems: Issues, Progress, and Challenges," IBM Technical Report: TR-74.165-k, April 1999, available at http://www.cas.ibm.com/toronto/publications/TR-74.165/k/legacy.html.

[DEM95] DeMarco, T., *Why Does Software Cost So Much?,* Dorset House, 1995.

[FEI83] Feigenbaum, E. A., and P. McCorduck, *The Fifth Generation,* Addison-Wesley, 1983.

[HAM93] Hammer, M., and J. Champy, *Reengineering the Corporation,* HarperCollins Publishers, 1993.

[JOH01] Johnson, S., *Emergence: The Connected Lives of Ants, Brains, Cities, and Software,* Scribner, 2001.

[KAR99] Karlson, E., and J. Kolber, *A Basic Introduction to Y2K: How the Year 2000 Computer Crisis Affects YOU,* Next Era Publications, Inc., 1999.

[LEH97a] Lehman, M., and L. Belady, *Program Evolution: Processes of Software Change,* Academic Press, 1997.

[LEH97b] Lehman, M., et al., "Metrics and Laws of Software Evolution—The Nineties View," *Proceedings of the 4th International Software Metrics Symposium (METRICS '97),* IEEE, 1997, can be downloaded from http://www.ece.utexas.edu/~perry/ work/papers/feast1.pdf.

[LEV95] Levy, S., "The Luddites Are Back," *Newsweek,* July 12, 1995, p. 55.

[LIP02] Lippman, A., "Round 2.0," *Context Magazine,* August 2002, http://www.contextmag.com/.

[LIU98] Liu, K., et al., "Report on the First SEBPC Workshop on Legacy Systems," Durham University, February, 1998, available at http://www.dur.ac.uk/ CSM/SABA/legacy-wksp1/report.html.

[OSB79] Osborne, A., *Running Wild—The Next Industrial Revolution,* Osborne/McGraw-Hill, 1979.

[NAI82] Naisbitt, J., *Megatrends,* Warner Books, 1982.

[STO89] Stoll, C., *The Cuckoo's Egg,* Doubleday, 1989.

[TOF80] Toffler, A., *The Third Wave,* Morrow Publishers, 1980.

[TOF90] Toffler, A., *Powershift,* Bantam Publishers, 1990.

[WIL02] Williams, S., "A Unified Theory of Software Evolution," salon.com, 2002, http://www.salon.com/tech/feature/2002/04/08/lehman/index.html.

[WOL02] Wolfram, S., *A New Kind of Science,* Wolfram Media, Inc, 2002.

[YOU92] Yourdon, E., *The Decline and Fall of the American Programmer,* Yourdon Press, 1992.

[YOU96] Yourdon, E., *The Rise and Resurrection of the American Programmer,* Yourdon Press, 1996.

[YOU98a] Yourdon, E., and J. Yourdon, *Time Bomb 2000,* Prentice-Hall, 1998.

[YOU98b] Yourdon, E., *Death March Projects,* Prentice-Hall, 1999.

[YOU02] Yourdon, E., *Byte Wars,* Prentice-Hall, 2002.

Problems and Points to Ponder

1.1. Provide at least five additional examples of how the law of unintended consequences applied to computer software.

1.2. Provide a number of examples (both positive and negative) that indicate the impact of software on our society. Review one of the pre-1990 references in Section 1.1 and indicate where the author's predictions were right and where they were wrong.

1.3. Develop your own answers to the questions asked in Section 1.1. Discuss them with your fellow students.

1.4. Does the definition for software presented in Section 1.2 apply to Web sites? If you answered yes, indicate the subtle difference between a Web site and conventional software, if any.

1.5. Many modern applications change frequently—before they are presented to the end-user and then after the first version has been put into use. Suggest a few ways to build software to stop deterioration due to change.

1.6. Consider the seven software categories presented in Section 1.3. Can the same approach to software engineering be applied for each? Explain your answer.

1.7. Select one of the new challenges noted in Section 1.3 (or an even newer challenge that has arisen since this book was printed) and write a one-page paper that describes the technology and the challenges it poses for software engineers.

1.8. Describe *The Law of Conservation of Organizational Stability* (Section 1.4.2) in your own words.

1.9. Describe *The Law of Conservation of Familiarity* (Section 1.4.2) in your own words.

1.10. Describe *The Law of Declining Quality* (Section 1.4.2) in your own words.

1.11. As software becomes more pervasive, risks to the public (due to faulty programs) become an increasingly significant concern. Develop a realistic doomsday scenario where the failure of a computer program could do great harm (either economic or human).

1.12. Peruse the Internet newsgroup comp.risks and prepare a summary of risks to the public that have recently been discussed. Alternate source: *Software Engineering Notes* published by the ACM.

Further Readings and Information Sources[10]

There are literally thousands of books written about computer software. The vast majority discuss programming languages or software applications, but a few discuss software itself. Pressman and Herron (*Software Shock,* Dorset House, 1991) present an early discussion (directed at the layman) of software and the way professionals build it. Negroponte's best-selling book (*Being Digital,* Alfred A. Knopf, Inc., 1995) provides a view of computing and its overall impact in the twenty-first century. DeMarco [DEM95] has produced a collection of amusing and insightful essays on software and the process through which it is developed. Books by Norman (*The Invisible Computer,* MIT Press, 1998) and Bergman (*Information Appliances and Beyond,* Academic Press/Morgan Kaufmann, 2000) suggest that the widespread impact of the PC will decline as information appliances and pervasive computing connect everyone in the industrialized world and almost every "appliance" that they own to a new Internet infrastructure.

Minasi (*The Software Conspiracy: Why Software Companies Put Out Faulty Products, How They Can Hurt You, and What You Can Do,* McGraw-Hill, 2000) argues that the "modern scourge" of software bugs can be eliminated and suggests ways to accomplish this. Compaine (*Digital Divide: Facing a Crisis or Creating a Myth,* MIT Press, 2001) argues that the "divide" between those who have access to information resources (e.g., the Web) and those who do not is narrowing as we move into the first decade of this century.

A wide variety of information sources on software related topics and management are available on the Internet. An up-to-date list of World Wide Web resources that are relevant to software can be found at our Web site:
http://www.mhhe.com/pressman.

10 The *Further Readings and Information Sources* section presented at the conclusion of each chapter presents a brief overview of print sources that can help to expand your understanding of the major topics presented in the chapter. We have created a comprehensive Web site to support *Software Engineering: A Practitioner's Approach* at http://www.mhhe.com/pressman. Among the many topics addressed within the Web site are chapter-by-chapter software engineering resources to Web-based information that can complement the material presented in each chapter. An Amazon.com link to every book noted in this section is contained within these resources.

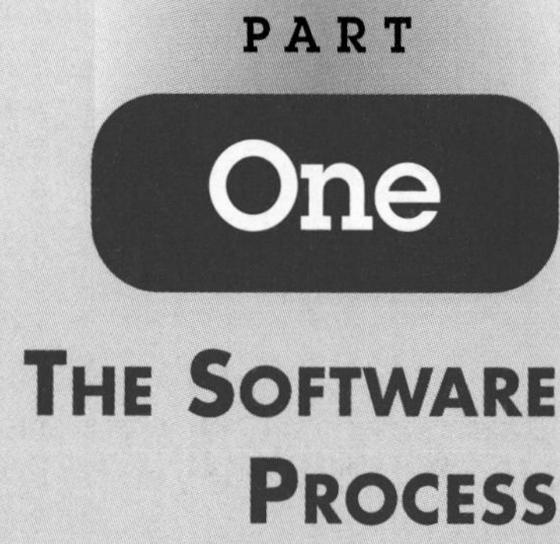

The Software Process

In this part of *Software Engineering: A Practitioner's Approach* you'll learn about the process that provides a framework for software engineering practice. These questions are addressed in the chapters that follow:

- What is a software process?
- What are the generic framework activities that are present in every software process?
- How are processes modeled and what are process patterns?
- What are prescriptive process models and what are their strengths and weaknesses?
- What characteristics of incremental models make them amenable to modern software projects?
- What is the unified process?
- Why is "agility" a watchword in modern software engineering work?
- What is agile software development and how does it differ from more traditional process models?

Once these questions are answered you'll be better prepared to understand the context in which software engineering practice is applied.

CHAPTER

2 PROCESS: A GENERIC VIEW

KEY CONCEPTS

In a fascinating book that provides an economist's view of software and software engineering, Howard Baetjer, Jr. [BAE98] comments on the software process:

> Because software, like all capital, is embodied knowledge, and because that knowledge is initially dispersed, tacit, latent, and incomplete in large measure, software development is a social learning process. The process is a dialogue in which the knowledge that must become the software is brought together and embodied in the software. The process provides interaction between users and designers, between users and evolving tools, and between designers and evolving tools [technology]. It is an iterative process in which the evolving tool itself serves as the medium for communication, with each new round of the dialogue eliciting more useful knowledge from the people involved.

Indeed, building computer software is an iterative learning process, and the outcome, something that Baetjer would call "software capital," is an embodiment of knowledge collected, distilled, and organized as the process is conducted.

QUICK LOOK

What is it? When you work to build a product or system, it's important to go through a series of predictable steps—a road map that helps you create a timely, high-quality result. The road map that you follow is called a *software process*.

Who does it? Software engineers and their managers adapt the process to their needs and then follow it. In addition, the people who have requested the software have a role to play in the process of defining, building, and testing it.

Why is it important? Because it provides stability, control, and organization to an activity that can, if left uncontrolled, become quite chaotic. However, a modern software engineering approach must be "agile." It must demand only those activities, controls, and documentation that are appropriate for the project team and the product that is to be produced.

What are the steps? At a detailed level, the process that you adopt depends on the software that you're building. One process might be appropriate for creating software for an aircraft avionics system, while an entirely different process would be indicated for the creation of a Web site.

What is the work product? From the point of view of a software engineer, the work products are the programs, documents, and data that are produced as a consequence of the activities and tasks defined by the process.

How do I ensure that I've done it right? There are a number of software process assessment mechanisms that enable organizations to determine the "maturity" of their software process. However, the quality, timeliness, and long-term viability of the product you build are the best indicators of the efficacy of the process that you use.

But what exactly is a software process from a technical point of view? Within the context of this book, we define a *software process* as a framework for the tasks that are required to build high-quality software. Is *process* synonymous with software engineering? The answer is yes and no. A software process defines the approach that is taken as software is engineered. But software engineering also encompasses technologies that populate the process—technical methods and automated tools.

More important, software engineering is performed by creative, knowledgeable people who should adapt a mature software process that is appropriate for the products they build and the demands of their marketplace.

2.1 Software Engineering—A Layered Technology

Although hundreds of authors have developed personal definitions of *software engineering,* a definition proposed by Fritz Bauer [NAU69] at the seminal conference on the subject still serves as a basis for discussion:

> [Software engineering is] the establishment and use of sound engineering principles in order to obtain economically software that is reliable and works efficiently on real machines.

Almost every reader will be tempted to add to this definition. It says little about the technical aspects of software quality; it does not directly address the need for customer satisfaction or timely product delivery; it omits mention of the importance of measurement and metrics; it does not state the importance of an effective process. And yet, Bauer's definition provides us with a baseline. What are the "sound engineering principles" that can be applied to computer software development? How do we "economically" build software so that it is "reliable"? What is required to create computer programs that work "efficiently" on not one but many different "real machines"? These are the questions that continue to challenge software engineers.

> **"More than a discipline or a body of knowledge, engineering is a verb, an action word, a way of approaching a problem."**
>
> **Scott Whitmire**

The IEEE [IEE93] has developed a more comprehensive definition when it states:

? How do we define *software engineering?*

> Software Engineering: (1) The application of a systematic, disciplined, quantifiable approach to the development, operation, and maintenance of software; that is, the application of engineering to software. (2) The study of approaches as in (1).

And yet, what is "systematic, disciplined" and "quantifiable" to one software team may be burdensome to another. We need discipline, but we also need adaptability and agility.

FIGURE 2.1
Software engineering layers

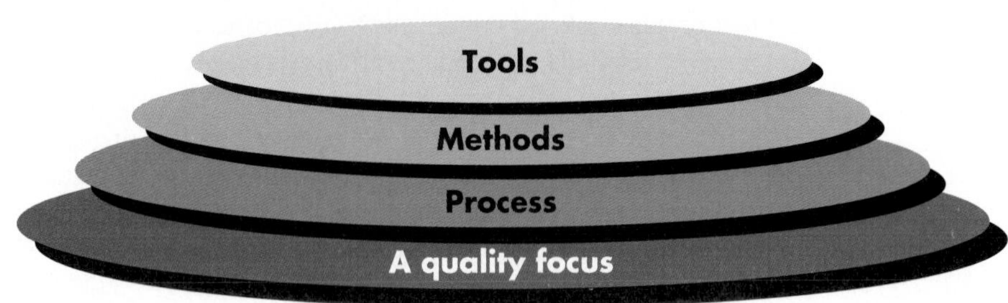

Software engineering is a layered technology. Referring to Figure 2.1, any engineering approach (including software engineering) must rest on an organizational commitment to quality. Total Quality Management, Six Sigma, and similar philosophies foster a continuous process improvement culture, and it is this culture that ultimately leads to the development of increasingly more effective approaches to software engineering. The bedrock that supports software engineering is a *quality focus.*

KEY POINT
Software engineering encompasses a process, methods, and tools.

The foundation for software engineering is the *process* layer. Software engineering process is the glue that holds the technology layers together and enables rational and timely development of computer software. Process defines a framework [PAU93] that must be established for effective delivery of software engineering technology. The software process forms the basis for management control of software projects and establishes the context in which technical methods are applied, work products (models, documents, data, reports, forms, etc.) are produced, milestones are established, quality is ensured, and change is properly managed.

Software engineering *methods* provide the technical "how to's" for building software. Methods encompass a broad array of tasks that include communication, requirements analysis, design modeling, program construction, testing, and support. Software engineering methods rely on a set of basic principles that govern each area of the technology and include modeling activities and other descriptive techniques.

WebRef
Cross Talk is a journal that provides pragmatic information on process, methods, and tools. It can be found at **www.stsc.hill.af.mil.**

Software engineering *tools* provide automated or semiautomated support for the process and the methods. When tools are integrated so that information created by one tool can be used by another, a system for the support of software development, called *computer-aided software engineering,* is established.

2.2 A PROCESS FRAMEWORK

A *process framework* establishes the foundation for a complete software process by identifying a small number of *framework activities* that are applicable to all software projects, regardless of their size or complexity. In addition, the process framework encompasses a set of *umbrella activities* that are applicable across the entire software process.

FIGURE 2.2

A software process framework

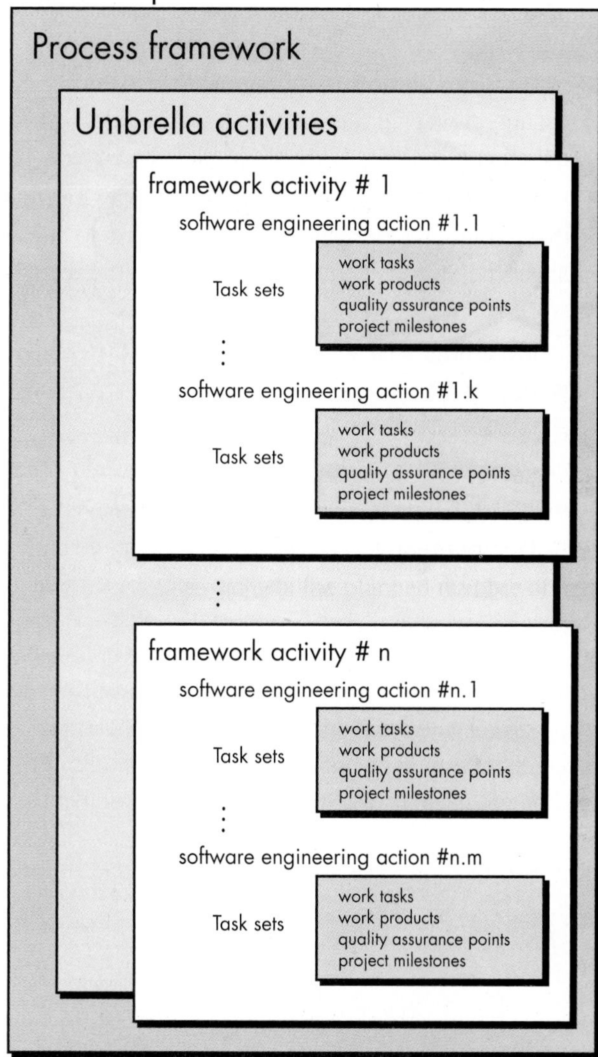

Referring to Figure 2.2, each framework activity is populated by a set of *software engineering actions*—a collection of related tasks that produces a major software engineering work product (e.g., *design* is a software engineering action). Each action is populated with individual *work tasks* that accomplish some part of the work implied by the action.

> "A process defines who is doing *what, when,* and *how* to reach a certain goal."
>
> **Ivar Jacobson, Grady Booch, and James Rumbaugh**

The following *generic process framework* (used as a basis for the description of process models in subsequent chapters) is applicable to the vast majority of software projects:

? **What are the five generic process framework activities?**

Communication. This framework activity involves heavy communication and collaboration with the customer (and other stakeholders[1]) and encompasses requirements gathering and other related activities.

Planning. This activity establishes a plan for the software engineering work that follows. It describes the technical tasks to be conducted, the risks that are likely, the resources that will be required, the work products to be produced, and a work schedule.

Modeling. This activity encompasses the creation of models that allow the developer and the customer to better understand software requirements and the design that will achieve those requirements.

Construction. This activity combines code generation (either manual or automated) and the testing that is required to uncover errors in the code.

Deployment. The software (as a complete entity or as a partially completed increment) is delivered to the customer who evaluates the delivered product and provides feedback based on the evaluation.

These five generic framework activities can be used during the development of small programs, the creation of large Web applications, and for the engineering of large, complex computer-based systems. The details of the software process will be quite different in each case, but the framework activities remain the same.

> "Einstein argued that there must be a simplified explanation of nature, because God is not capricious or arbitrary. No such faith comforts the software engineer. Much of the complexity that he must master is arbitrary complexity."
>
> **Fred Brooks**

Using an example derived from the generic process framework, the *modeling* activity is composed of two software engineering actions—*analysis* and *design.* Analysis[2] encompasses a set of work tasks (e.g., requirements gathering, elaboration, negotiation, specification, and validation) that lead to the creation of the analysis model (and/or requirements specification). Design encompasses work tasks (data

1 A *stakeholder* is anyone who has a stake in the successful outcome of the project—business managers, end-users, software engineers, support people, and so forth. Rob Thomsett jokes that "a stakeholder is a person holding a large and sharp stake. . . . If you don't look after your stakeholders, you know where the stake will end up."

2 Analysis is discussed at length in Chapters 7 and 8.

Different projects demand different task sets. The software team chooses the task set based on problem and project characteristics.

design, architectural design, interface design, and component-level design) that create a design model (and/or a design specification).[3]

Referring again to Figure 2.2, each software engineering action is represented by a number of different *task sets*—each a collection of software engineering work tasks, related work products, quality assurance points, and project milestones. The task set that best accommodates the needs of the project and the characteristics of the team is chosen. This implies that a software engineering action (e.g., design) can be adapted to the specific needs of the software project and the characteristics of the project team.

INFO

Task Set

A *task set* defines the actual work to be done to accomplish the objectives of a software engineering action. For example, "requirements gathering" is an important software engineering action that occurs during the **communication** activity. The goal of requirements gathering is to understand what various stakeholders want from the software that is to be built.

For a small, relatively simple project, the task set for requirements gathering might look like this:

1. Make a list of stakeholders for the project.
2. Invite all stakeholders to an informal meeting.
3. Ask each stakeholder to make a list of features and functions required.
4. Discuss requirements and build a final list.
5. Prioritize requirements.
6. Note areas of uncertainty.

For a larger, more complex software project, a different task set would be required. It might encompass the following work tasks:

1. Make a list of stakeholders for the project.
2. Interview each stakeholder separately to determine overall wants and needs.
3. Build a preliminary list of functions and features based on stakeholder input.
4. Schedule a series of facilitated requirements gathering meetings.
5. Conduct meetings.
6. Produce informal user scenarios as part of each meeting.
7. Refine user scenarios based on stakeholder feedback.
8. Build a revised list of stakeholder requirements.
9. Use quality function deployment techniques to prioritize requirements.
10. Package requirements so that they can be delivered incrementally.
11. Note constraints and restrictions that will be placed on the system.
12. Discuss methods for validating the system.

Both of these task sets achieve requirements gathering, but they are quite different in their depth and formality. The software team chooses the task set that will allow it to achieve the goal of each process activity and software engineering action and still maintain quality and agility.

The framework described in the generic view of software engineering is complemented by a number of *umbrella activities.* Typical activities in this category include:

Software project tracking and control—allows the software team to assess progress against the project plan and take necessary action to maintain schedule.

3 It should be noted that "modeling" must be interpreted somewhat differently when the maintenance of existing software is conducted. In some cases, analysis and design modeling do occur, but in other maintenance situations, modeling may be used to help understand the legacy software as well as to represent additions or modifications to it.

Umbrella activities occur throughout the software process and focus primarily on project management, tracking, and control.

Risk management—assesses risks that may effect the outcome of the project or the quality of the product.

Software quality assurance—defines and conducts the activities required to ensure software quality.

Formal technical reviews—assesses software engineering work products in an effort to uncover and remove errors before they are propagated to the next action or activity.

Measurement—defines and collects process, project, and product measures that assist the team in delivering software that meets customers' needs; can be used in conjunction with all other framework and umbrella activities.

Software configuration management—manages the effects of change throughout the software process.

Reusability management—defines criteria for work product reuse (including software components) and establishes mechanisms to achieve reusable components.

Work product preparation and production—encompasses the activities required to create work products such as models, documents, logs, forms, and lists.

Umbrella activities are applied throughout the software process and are discussed in detail later in this book.

Software process adaptation is essential for project success.

All process models can be characterized within the process framework shown in Figure 2.2. Intelligent application of any software process model must recognize that adaptation (to the problem, project, team, and organizational culture) is essential for success. But process models do differ fundamentally in:

? How do process models differ from one another?

- The overall flow of activities and tasks and the interdependencies among activities and tasks.
- The degree to which work tasks are defined within each framework activity.
- The degree to which work products are identified and required.
- The manner which quality assurance activities are applied.
- The manner in which project tracking and control activities are applied.
- The overall degree of detail and rigor with which the process is described.
- The degree to which customer and other stakeholders are involved with the project.
- The level of autonomy given to the software project team.
- The degree to which team organization and roles are prescribed.

> "I feel a recipe is only a theme which an intelligent cook can play each time with a variation."
>
> **Madame Benoit**

Process models that stress detailed definition, identification, and application of process activities and tasks have been applied within the software engineering community for the past 30 years. When these *prescriptive process models* are applied, the intent is to improve system quality, to make projects more manageable, to make delivery dates and costs more predictable, and to guide teams of software engineers as they perform the work required to build a system. Unfortunately, there have been times when these objectives were not achieved. If prescriptive models are applied dogmatically and without adaptation, they can increase the level of bureaucracy associated with building computer-based systems and inadvertently create difficulty for developers and customers.

? What characterizes an "agile" process?

Process models that emphasize project agility and follow a set of principles[4] that lead to a more informal (but, proponents argue, no less effective) approach to software process have been proposed in recent years. These *agile process models* emphasize maneuverability and adaptability. They are appropriate for many types of projects and are particularly useful when Web applications are engineered.

Which software process philosophy is best? This question has spawned emotional debate among software engineers and will be addressed in Chapter 4. For now, it is important to note that these two process philosophies have a common goal—to create high-quality software that meets the customer's needs—but different approaches.

2.3 The Capability Maturity Model Integration (CMMI)

The Software Engineering Institute (SEI) has developed a comprehensive process meta-model that is predicated on a set of system and software engineering capabilities that should be present as organizations reach different levels of process capability and maturity. To achieve these capabilities, the SEI contends that an organization should develop a process model (Figure 2.2) that conforms to *The Capability Maturity Model Integration* (CMMI) guidelines [CMM02].

WebRef
Complete information on the CMMI can be obtained at **http://www.sei.cmu.ed.u/cmmi/.**

The CMMI represents a process meta-model in two different ways: (1) as a *continuous* model and (2) as a *staged* model. The continuous CMMI meta-model describes a process in two dimensions as illustrated in Figure 2.3. Each process area (e.g., project planning or requirements management) is formally assessed against specific goals and practices and is rated according to the following capability levels:

Level 0: Incomplete. The process area (e.g., requirements management) is either not performed or does not achieve all goals and objectives defined by the CMMI for level 1 capability.

Level 1: Performed. All of the specific goals of the process area (as defined by the CMMI) have been satisfied. Work tasks required to produce defined work products are being conducted.

Level 2: Managed. All level 1 criteria have been satisfied. In addition, all work associated with the process area conforms to an organizationally defined policy; all people doing the work have access to adequate resources to get the job done;

4 Agile models and the principles that guide them are discussed in Chapter 4.

FIGURE 2.3

CMMI process area capability profile [PHI02]

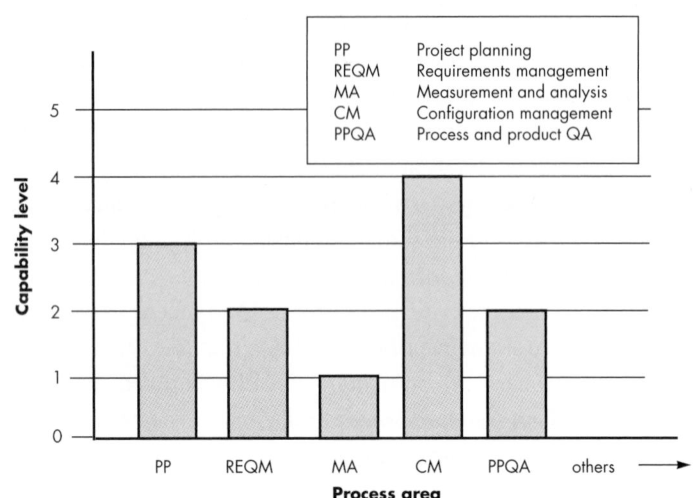

stakeholders are actively involved in the process area as required; all work tasks and work products are "monitored, controlled, and reviewed; and are evaluated for adherence to the process description" [CMM02].

Level 3: Defined. All level 2 criteria have been achieved. In addition, the process is "tailored from the organization's set of standard processes according to the organization's tailoring guidelines, and contributes work products, measures, and other process-improvement information to the organizational process assets" [CMM02].

Level 4: Quantitatively managed. All level 3 criteria have been achieved. In addition, the process area is controlled and improved using measurement and quantitative assessment. "Quantitative objectives for quality and process performance are established and used as criteria in managing the process" [CMM02].

Level 5: Optimized. All capability level 4 criteria have been achieved. In addition, the process area is adapted and optimized using quantitative (statistical) means to meet changing customer needs and to continually improve the efficacy of the process area under consideration" [CMM02].

ADVICE

Every organization should strive to achieve the intent of the CMMI. However, implementing every aspect of the model may be overkill in some situations.

> "Much of the software crisis is self-inflicted, as when a CIO says, "I'd rather have it wrong than have it late. We can always fix it later."
>
> **Mark Paulk**

The CMMI defines each process area in terms of "specific goals" and the "specific practices" required to achieve these goals. *Specific goals* establish the characteristics that must exist if the activities implied by a process area are to be effective. *Specific practices* refine a goal into a set of process-related activities.

For example, **project planning** is one of eight process areas defined by the CMMI for the "project management" category.[5] The specific goals (SG) and the associated specific practices (SP) defined for project planning are [CMM02]:

SG 1 Establish estimates

SP 1.1-1 Estimate the scope of the project

SP 1.2-1 Establish estimates of work product and task attributes

SP 1.3-1 Define project life cycle

SP 1.4-1 Determine estimates of effort and cost

SG 2 Develop a Project Plan

SP 2.1-1 Establish the budget and schedule

SP 2.2-1 Identify project risks

SP 2.3-1 Plan for data management

SP 2.4-1 Plan for project resources

SP 2.5-1 Plan for needed knowledge and skills

SP 2.6-1 Plan stakeholder involvement

SP 2.7-1 Establish the project plan

SG 3 Obtain commitment to the plan

SP 3.1-1 Review plans that affect the project

SP 3.2-1 Reconcile work and resource levels

SP 3.3-1 Obtain plan commitment

WebRef
Complete information as well as a downloadable version of the CMMI can be obtained at **www.sei.cmu.edu/cmmi/.**

In addition to specific goals and practices, the CMMI also defines a set of five generic goals and related practices for each process area. Each of the five generic goals corresponds to one of the five capability levels. Hence, to achieve a particular capability level, the generic goal for that level and the generic practices that correspond to that goal must be achieved. To illustrate, the generic goals (GG) and practices (GP) for the project planning process area are [CMM02]:

GG 1 Achieve specific goals

GP 1.1 Perform base practices

GG 2 Institutionalize a managed process

GP 2.1 Establish an organizational policy

GP 2.2 Plan the process

GP 2.3 Provide resources

---

5 Other process areas defined for "project management" include: project monitoring and control, supplier agreement management, integrated project management for IPPD, risk management, integrated teaming, integrated supplier management, and quantitative project management.

GP 2.4 Assign responsibility

GP 2.5 Train people

GP 2.6 Manage configurations

GP 2.7 Identify and involve relevant stakeholders

GP 2.8 Monitor and control the process

GP 2.9 Objectively evaluate adherence

GP 2.10 Review status with higher level management

GG 3 Institutionalize a defined process

GP 3.1 Establish a defined process

GP 3.2 Collect improvement information

GG 4 Institutionalize a quantitatively managed process

GP 4.1 Establish quantitative objectives for the process

GP 4.2 Stabilize subprocess performance

GG 5 Institutionalize an optimizing process

GP 5.1 Ensure continuous process improvement

GP 5.2 Correct root causes of problems

The staged CMMI model defines the same process areas, goals, and practices as the continuous model. The primary difference is that the staged model defines five maturity levels, rather than five capability levels. To achieve a maturity level, the specific goals and practices associated with a set of process areas must be achieved. The relationship between maturity levels and process areas is shown in Figure 2.4.

INFO

The CMMI—Should We or Shouldn't We?

The CMMI is a process meta-model. It defines (in over 700 pages) the process characteristics that should exist if an organization wants to establish a software process that is complete. The question that has been debated for well over a decade is: Is the CMMI overkill? Like most things in life (and in software), the answer is not a simple yes or no.

The spirit of the CMMI should always be adopted. At the risk of oversimplification, it argues that software development must be taken seriously—it must be planned thoroughly; it must be controlled uniformly; it must be tracked accurately; and it must be conducted professionally. It must focus on the needs of project stakeholders, the skills of the software engineers, and the quality of the end product. No one would argue with these ideas.

The detailed requirements of the CMMI should be seriously considered if an organization builds large complex systems that involve dozens or hundreds of people over many months or years. It may be that the CMMI is just right in such situations, if the organizational culture is amenable to standard process models and management is committed to making it a success. However, in other situations, the CMMI may simply be too much for an organization to successfully assimilate. Does this mean that the CMMI is bad or overly bureaucratic or old fashioned? No, it does not. It simply means that what is right for one company culture may not be right for another.

The CMMI is a significant achievement in software engineering. It provides a comprehensive discussion of the activities and actions that should be present when an organization builds computer software. Even if a software organization chooses not to adopt its details, every software team should embrace its spirit and gain insight from its discussion of software engineering process and practice.

FIGURE 2.4

Process areas required to achieve a maturity level

Level	Focus	Process Areas
Optimizing	*Continuous process improvement*	Organizational Innovation and Deployment Causal Analysis and Resolution
Quantitatively managed	*Quantitative management*	Organizational Process Performance Quantitative Project Management
Defined	*Process standardization*	Requirements Development Technical Solution Product Integration Verification Validation Organizational Process Focus Organizational Process Definition Organizational Training Integrated Project Management Integrated Supplier Management Risk Management Decision Analysis and Resolution Organizational Environment for Integration Integrated Teaming
Managed	*Basic project management*	Requirements Management Project Planning Project Monitoring and Control Supplier Agreement Management Measurement and Analysis Process and Product Quality Assurance Configuration Management
Performed		

2.4 Process Patterns

What is a process pattern?

The software process can be defined as a collection of patterns that define a set of activities, actions, work tasks, work products and/or related behaviors [AMB98] required to develop computer software. Stated in more general terms, a *process pattern* provides us with a template—a consistent method for describing an important characteristic of the software process. By combining patterns, a software team can construct a process that best meets the needs of a project.

> "The repetition of patterns is quite a different thing than the repetition of parts. Indeed, the different parts will be unique because the patterns are the same."
>
> **Christopher Alexander**

Patterns can be defined at any level of abstraction.[6] In some cases, a pattern might be used to describe a complete process (e.g., prototyping). In other situations, patterns can be used to describe an important framework activity (e.g., planning) or a task within a framework activity (e.g., project-estimating).

Ambler [AMB98] has proposed the following template for describing a process pattern:

KEY POINT
A pattern template provides a consistent means for describing a pattern.

Pattern Name. The pattern is given a meaningful name that describes its function within the software process (e.g., **customer-communication**).

Intent. The objective of the pattern is described briefly. For example, the intent of **customer-communication** is "to establish a collaborative relationship with the customer in an effort to define project scope, business requirements, and other project constraints." The intent might be further expanded with additional explanatory text and appropriate diagrams if required.

Type. The pattern type is specified. Ambler [AMB98] suggests three types:

- *Task patterns* define a software engineering action or work task that is part of the process and relevant to successful software engineering practice (e.g., **requirements gathering** is a task pattern).
- *Stage patterns* define a framework activity for the process. Since a framework activity encompasses multiple work tasks, a stage pattern incorporates multiple task patterns that are relevant to the stage (framework activity). An example of a stage pattern might be **communication**. This pattern would incorporate the task pattern **requirements gathering** and others.
- *Phase patterns* define the sequence of framework activities that occur with the process, even when the overall flow of activities is iterative in nature. An example of a phase pattern might be a **spiral model or prototyping**.[7]

Initial Context. The conditions under which the pattern applies are described. Prior to the initiation of the pattern, we ask (1) what organizational or team-related activities have already occurred, (2) what is the entry state for the process, and (3) what software engineering information or project information already exists.

---

6 Patterns are applicable to many software engineering activities. Analysis, design, and testing patterns are discussed in Chapters 7, 9, 10, 12, and 14. Patterns and "antipatterns" for project management activities are discussed in Part 4 of this book.

7 These phase patterns are discussed in Chapter 3.

For example, the **planning** pattern (a stage pattern) requires that (1) customers and software engineers have established a collaborative communication; (2) successful completion of a number of task patterns (specified) for the **customer-communication** pattern has occurred; and (3) project scope, basic business requirements, and project constraints are known.

Problem. The problem to be solved by the pattern is described. For example, the problem to be solved by **customer-communication** might be described in the following manner: *Communication between the developer and the customer is often inadequate because an effective format for eliciting information is not established, a useful mechanism for recording it is not created, and meaningful review is not conducted.*

Solution. The implementation of the pattern is described. This section discusses how the initial state of the process (that exists before the pattern is implemented) is modified as a consequence the initiation of the pattern. It also describes how software engineering information or project information that is available before the initiation of the pattern is transformed as a consequence of the successful execution of the pattern.

Resulting Context. The conditions that will result once the pattern has been successfully implemented are described. Upon completion of the pattern we ask (1) what organizational or team-related activities must have occurred, (2) what is the exit state for the process, and (3) what software engineering information or project information has been developed.

Related Patterns. A list of all process patterns that are directly related to this one are provided—as a hierarchy or in some other diagrammatic form. For example, the stage pattern **communication** encompasses the task patterns **project-team assembly, collaborative-guideline definition, scope-isolation, requirements gathering, constraint-description, and mini-spec/model creation.**

Known Uses/Examples. The specific instances in which the pattern is applicable are indicated. For example, **communication** is mandatory at the beginning of every software project; it is recommended throughout the software project; and it is mandatory once the **deployment** activity is underway.

WebRef
Comprehensive resources on process patterns can be found at **www.ambysoft.com/processPatternsPage.html.**

Process patterns provide an effective mechanism for describing any software process. The patterns enable a software engineering organization to develop a hierarchical process description that begins at a high-level of abstraction (a phase pattern). The description is refined into a set of stage patterns that describe framework activities and then further refined in hierarchical fashion into more detailed task patterns for each stage pattern. Once process patterns have been developed, they can be reused for the definition of process variants—that is, a customized process model can be defined by a software team using the patterns as building blocks for the process model.

INFO

An Example Process Pattern

The following abbreviated process pattern describes an approach that may be applicable when stakeholders have a general idea of what must be done, but are unsure of specific software requirements.

Pattern name. Prototyping.

Intent. The objective of the pattern is to build a model (a prototype) that can be assessed iteratively by stakeholders in an effort to identify or solidify software requirements.

Type. Phase pattern.

Initial context. The following conditions must be met prior to the initiation of this pattern: (1) stakeholders have been identified; (2) a mode of communication between stakeholders and the software team has been established; (3) the overriding problem to be solved has been identified by stakeholders; (4) an initial understanding of project scope, basic business requirements, and project constraints has been developed.

Problem. Requirements are hazy or nonexistent, yet there is clear recognition that there is a problem, and the problem must be addressed with a software solution. Stakeholders are unsure of what they want; that is, they cannot describe software requirements in any detail.

Solution. A description of the prototyping process is presented here. See Chapter 3 for details.

Resulting context. A software prototype that identifies basic requirements (e.g., modes of interaction, computational features, processing functions) is approved by stakeholders. Following this, (1) the prototype may evolve through a series of increments to become the production software or (2) the prototype may be discarded and the production software built using some other process pattern.

Related patterns. The following patterns are related to this pattern: **customer-communication; iterative design; iterative development, customer assessment; requirement extraction.**

Known uses/examples. Prototyping is recommended when requirements are uncertain.

2.5 Process Assessment

Assessment attempts to understand the current state of the software process with the intent of improving it.

The existence of a software process is no guarantee that software will be delivered on time, that it will meet the customer's needs, or that it will exhibit the technical characteristics that will lead to long-term quality characteristics (Chapter 26). Process patterns must be coupled with solid software engineering practice (Part 2 of this book). In addition, the process itself should be assessed to ensure that it meets a set of basic process criteria that have been shown to be essential for a successful software engineering.[8] The relationship between the software process and the methods applied for assessment and improvement is shown in Figure 2.5. A number of different approaches to *software process assessment* have been proposed over the past few decades:

? What formal techniques are availabe for assessing the software process?

Standard CMMI Assessment Method for Process Improvement (SCAMPI) provides a five-step process assessment model that incorporates initiating, diagnosing, establishing, acting, and learning. The SCAMPI method uses the SEI CMMI (Section 2.3) as the basis for assessment [SEI00].

CMM-Based Appraisal for Internal Process Improvement (CBA IPI) provides a diagnostic technique for assessing the relative maturity of a software or-

8 The SEI's CMMI [CMM02] describes the characteristics of a software process and the criteria for a successful process in voluminous detail.

FIGURE 2.5

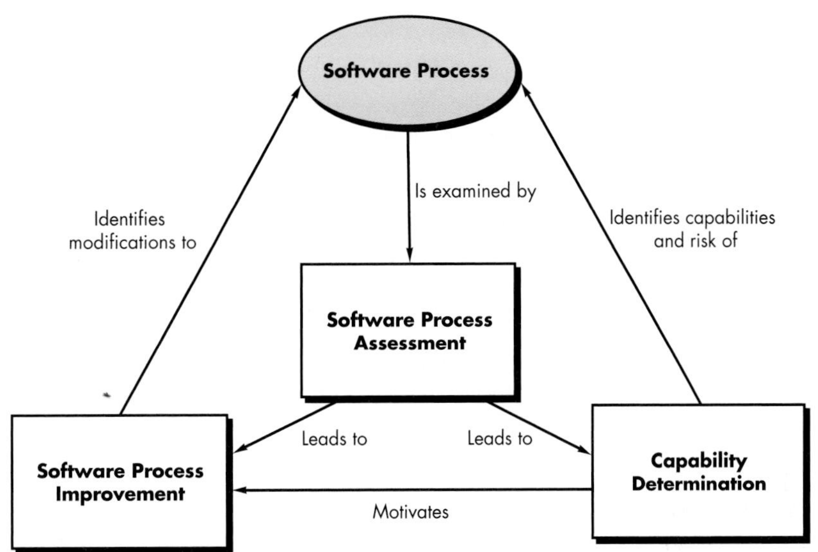

ganization, using the SEI CMM (a precursor to the CMMI discussed in Section 2.3) as the basis for the assessment [DUN01].

SPICE (ISO/IEC15504) standard defines a set of requirements for software process assessment. The intent of the standard is to assist organizations in developing an objective evaluation of the efficacy of any defined software process [SPI99].

ISO 9001:2000 for Software is a generic standard that applies to any organization that wants to improve the overall quality of the products, systems, or services that it provides. Therefore, the standard is directly applicable to software organizations and companies.

Because ISO 9001:2000 is widely used on an international scale, we examine it briefly in the paragraphs that follow.

> "Software organizations have exhibited significant shortcomings in their ability to capitalize on the experiences gained from completed projects."
>
> **NASA**

The International Organization for Standardization (ISO) has developed the ISO 9001:2000 standard [ISO00] to define the requirements for a quality management system (Chapter 26) that will serve to produce higher quality products and thereby improve customer satisfaction.[9]

9 Software quality assurance (SQA), an important element of quality management, has been defined as a umbrella activity that is applied across the entire process framework. It is discussed in detail in Chapter 26.

The underlying strategy suggested by ISO 9001:2000 is described in the following manner [ISO01]:

> ISO 9001:2000 stresses the importance for an organization to identify, implement, manage, and continually improve the effectiveness of the processes that are necessary for the quality management system, and to manage the interactions of these processes in order to achieve the organization's objectives . . .

WebRef
An excellent summary of ISO 9001:2000 can be found at **http://praxiom.com/iso-9001.htm.**

ISO 9001:2000 has adopted a "plan-do-check-act" cycle that is applied to the quality management elements of a software project. Within a software context, "plan" establishes the process objectives, activities, and tasks necessary to achieve high-quality software and resultant customer satisfaction. "Do" implements the software process (including both framework and umbrella activities). "Check" monitors and measures the process to ensure that all requirements established for quality management have been achieved. "Act" initiates software process improvement activities that continually work to improve the process.

For a detailed discussion of ISO 9001:2000 interested readers should see the ISO standards themselves or [CIA01], [KET01], or [MON01] for comprehensive information.

2.6 Personal and Team Process Models

The best software process is one that is close to the people who will be doing the work. If a software process model has been developed at a corporate or organizational level, it can be effective only if it is amenable to significant adaptation to meet the needs of the project team that is actually doing software engineering work. In an ideal setting, each software engineer would create a process that best fits his or her needs, and at the same time meets the broader needs of the team and the organization. Alternatively, the team itself would create its own process, and at the same time meet the narrower needs of individuals and the broader needs of the organization. Watts Humphrey ([HUM97] and [HUM00]) argues that it is possible to create a "personal software process" and/or a "team software process." Both require hard work, training and coordination, but both are achievable.[10]

> **"A person who is successful has simply formed the habit of doing things that unsuccessful people will not do."**
> **Dexter Yager**

WebRef
A wide array of resources for PSP can be found at **www.ipd.uka.de/PSP/.**

2.6.1 Personal Software Process (PSP)

Every developer uses some process to build computer software. The process may be haphazard or ad hoc, may change on a daily basis, may not be efficient, effective or even successful, but a process does exist. Watts Humphrey [HUM97] suggests that in

10 It's worth noting that the proponents of agile software development (Chapter 4) also argue that the process should remain close to the team. They propose an alternative method for achieving this.

order to change an ineffective personal process, an individual must move through four phases, each requiring training and careful instrumentation. The *personal software process* (PSP) emphasizes personal measurement of both the work product that is produced and the resultant quality of the work product. In addition, PSP makes the practitioner responsible for project planning (e.g., estimating and scheduling) and empowers the practitioner to control the quality of all software work products that are developed.

The PSP process model defines five framework activities: planning, high-level design, high-level design review, development, and postmortem.

? **What framework activities are used during PSP?**

Planning. This activity isolates requirements and, based on these, develops both size and resource estimates. In addition, a defect estimate (the number of defects projected for the work) is made. All metrics are recorded on worksheets or templates. Finally, development tasks are identified and a project schedule is created.

High-level design. External specifications for each component to be constructed are developed and a component design is created. Prototypes are built when uncertainty exists. All issues are recorded and tracked.

High-level design review. Formal verification methods (Chapter 26) are applied to uncover errors in the design. Metrics are maintained for all important tasks and work results.

Development. The component level design is refined and reviewed. Code is generated, reviewed, compiled, and tested. Metrics are maintained for all important tasks and work results.

Postmortem. Using the measures and metrics collected (a substantial amount of data that should be analyzed statistically), the effectiveness of the process is determined. Measures and metrics should provide guidance for modifying the process to improve its effectiveness.

PSP emphasizes the need to record and analyze the types of errors you make, so you can develop strategies to eliminate them.

PSP stresses the need for each software engineer to identify errors early and, as important, to understand the types of errors that he is likely to make. This is accomplished through a rigorous assessment activity performed on all work products produced by the software engineer.

PSP represents a disciplined, metrics-based approach to software engineering that may lead to culture shock for many practitioners. However, when PSP is properly introduced to software engineers [HUM96], the resulting improvement in software engineering productivity and software quality are significant [FER97]. However, PSP has not been widely adopted throughout the industry. The reasons, sadly, have more to do with human nature and organizational inertia than they do with the strengths and weaknesses of the PSP approach. PSP is intellectually challenging and demands a level of commitment (by practitioners and their managers) that is not always possible to obtain. Training is relatively lengthy, and training costs are high. The required level of measurement is culturally difficult for many software people.

Can PSP be used as an effective software process at a personal level? The answer is an unequivocal yes. But even if PSP is not adopted in its entirety, many of the personal process improvement concepts that it introduces are well worth learning.

2.6.2 Team Software Process (TSP)

WebRef
Information on building high-performance teams using TSP and PSP can be obtained at **www.sei.cmu.edu/tsp/.**

Because many industry-grade software projects are addressed by a team of practitioners, Watts Humphrey extended the lessons learned from the introduction of PSP and proposed a *team software process* (TSP). The goal of TSP is to build a "self-directed" project team that organizes itself to produce high-quality software. Humphrey [HUM98] defines the following objectives for TSP:

- Build self-directed teams that plan and track their work, establish goals, and own their processes and plans. These can be pure software teams or integrated product teams (IPT) of 3 to about 20 engineers.
- Show managers how to coach and motivate their teams and how to help them sustain peak performance.
- Accelerate software process improvement by making CMM level 5 behavior normal and expected.
- Provide improvement guidance to high-maturity organizations.
- Facilitate university teaching of industrial-grade team skills.

To form a self-directed team, you must collaborate well internally and communicate well externally.

A self-directed team has a consistent understanding of its overall goals and objectives. It defines roles and responsibilities for each team member; tracks quantitative project data (about productivity and quality); identifies a team process that is appropriate for the project and a strategy for implementing the process; defines local standards that are applicable to the team's software engineering work; continually assesses risk and reacts to it; and tracks, manages, and reports project status.

> **"Finding good players is easy. Getting them to play as a team is another story."**
>
> **Casey Stengel**

TSP scripts define elements of the team process and activities that occur within the process.

TSP defines the following framework activities: launch, high-level design, implementation, integration and test, and postmortem. Like their counterparts in PSP (note that terminology is somewhat different), these activities enable the team to plan, design, and construct software in a disciplined manner while at the same time quantitatively measuring the process and the product. The postmortem sets the stage for process improvements.

TSP makes use of a wide variety of scripts, forms, and standards that serve to guide team members in their work. *Scripts* define specific process activities (i.e., project launch, design, implementation, integration and testing, and postmortem) and other more detailed work functions (e.g., development planning, requirements development, software configuration management, and unit test) that are part of the team process. To illustrate, consider the initial process activity—*project launch.*

Each project is "launched" using a sequence of tasks (defined as a script) that enables the team to establish a solid basis for starting the project: The following *launch script* (outline only) is recommended [HUM00]:

WebRef
Information on the software process dashboard—a PSP and TSP support tool—can be found at **processdash.sourceforge.net.**

- Review project objectives with management and agree on and document team goals.
- Establish team roles.
- Define the team's development process.
- Make a quality plan and set quality targets.
- Plan for the needed support facilities.
- Produce an overall development strategy.
- Make a development plan for the entire project.
- Make detailed plans for each engineer for the next phase.
- Merge the individual plans into a team plan.
- Rebalance team workload to achieve a minimum overall schedule.
- Assess project risks and assign tracking responsibility for each key risk.

It should be noted that the launch activity can be applied prior to each TSP framework activity noted earlier. This accommodates the iterative nature of many projects and allows the team to adapt to changing customer needs and lessons learned from previous activities.

TSP recognizes that the best software teams are self-directed. Team members set project objectives, adapt the process to meet their needs, have control over schedule, and through measurement and analysis of the metrics collected, work continually to improve the team's approach to software engineering.

Like PSP, TSP is a rigorous approach to software engineering that provides distinct and quantifiable benefits in productivity and quality. The team must make a full commitment to the process and must undergo thorough training to ensure that the approach is properly applied.

2.7 Process Technology

The generic process models discussed in the preceding sections must be adapted for use by a software project team. To accomplish this, *process technology tools* have been developed to help software organizations analyze their current process, organize work tasks, control and monitor progress, and manage technical quality [NEG99].

Process technology tools allow a software organization to build an automated model of the common process framework, task sets, and umbrella activities discussed in Section 2.2. The model, normally represented as a network, can then be analyzed to determine typical workflow and examine alternative process structures that might lead to reduced development time or cost.

Once an acceptable process has been created, other process technology tools can be used to allocate, monitor, and even control all software engineering tasks defined as part of the process model. Each member of a software team can use such tools to develop a checklist of work tasks to be performed, work products to be produced, and quality assurance activities to be conducted. The process technology tool can also be used to coordinate the use of other computer-aided software engineering tools that are appropriate for a particular work task.

SOFTWARE TOOLS

Process Modeling Tools

Objective: If an organization works to improve a business (or software) process, it must first understand it. Process modeling tools (also called *process technology* or *process management tools*) are used to represent the key elements of a process so that it can be better understood. Such tools can also provide links to process descriptions that help those involved in the process to understand the actions and work tasks that are required to perform it. Process modeling tools provide links to other tools that provide support to defined process activities.

Mechanics: Tools in this category allow a team to define the elements of a unique process model (actions, tasks, work products, QA points), provide detailed guidance on the content or description of each process element, and then manage the process as it is conducted. In some cases, the process technology tools incorporate standard project management tasks such as estimating, scheduling, tracking and control.

Representative Tools:[11]

Igrafx Process Tools, distributed by Corel Corporation (www.igrafx.com/products/process), is a set of tools that enable a team to map, measure, and model the software process

Objexis Team Portal, developed by Objexis Corporation (www.objexis.com), provides full process workflow definition and control.

2.8 Product and Process

If the process is weak, the end product will undoubtedly suffer. But an obsessive over-reliance on process is also dangerous. In a brief essay, Margaret Davis [DAV95] comments on the duality of product and process:

> About every ten years give or take five, the software community redefines "the problem" by shifting its focus from product issues to process issues. Thus, we have embraced structured programming languages (product) followed by structured analysis methods (process) followed by data encapsulation (product) followed by the current emphasis on the Software Engineering Institute's Software Development Capability Maturity Model (process) [followed by object-oriented methods, followed by agile software development].
>
> While the natural tendency of a pendulum is to come to rest at a point midway between two extremes, the software community's focus constantly shifts because new force is applied when the last swing fails. These swings are harmful in and of themselves because they confuse the average software practitioner by radically changing what it means

11 Tools noted here do not represent an endorsement, but rather a sampling of tools in this category. In most cases, tool names are trademarked by their respective developers.

to perform the job, let alone perform it well. The swings also do not solve "the problem," for they are doomed to fail as long as product and process are treated as forming a dichotomy instead of a duality.

There is precedence in the scientific community to advance notions of duality when contradictions in observations cannot be fully explained by one competing theory or another. The dual nature of light, which seems to be simultaneously particle and wave, has been accepted since the 1920s when Louis de Broglie proposed it. I believe that the observations we can make on the artifacts of software and its development demonstrate a fundamental duality between product and process. You can never derive or understand the full artifact, its context, use, meaning, and worth if you view it as only a process or only a product. . . .

All of human activity may be a process, but each of us derives a sense of self-worth from those activities that result in a representation or instance that can be used or appreciated either by more than one person, used over and over, or used in some other context not considered. That is, we derive feelings of satisfaction from reuse of our products by ourselves or others.

Thus, while the rapid assimilation of reuse goals into software development potentially increases the satisfaction software practitioners derive from their work, it also increases the urgency for acceptance of the duality of product and process. Thinking of a reusable artifact as only product or only process either obscures the context and ways to use it or obscures the fact that each use results in product that will, in turn, be used as input to some other software development activity. Taking one view over the other dramatically reduces the opportunities for reuse and, hence, loses the opportunity for increasing job satisfaction.

> **"No doubt the ideal system, if it were attainable, would be a code at once so flexible and minute, as to supply in advance for every conceivable situation a just and fitting rule. But life is too complex to bring the attainment of this idea within the compass of human power."**
>
> **Benjamin Cardozo**

People derive as much (or more) satisfaction from the creative process as they do from the end-product. An artist enjoys the brush strokes as much as the framed result. A writer enjoys the search for the proper metaphor as much as the finished book. A creative software professional should also derive as much satisfaction from the process as the end-product.

The work of software people will change in the years ahead. The duality of product and process is one important element in keeping creative people engaged as the transition from programming to software engineering is finalized.

2.9 Summary

Software engineering is a discipline that integrates process, methods, and tools for the development of computer software. A number of different process models for software engineering have been proposed, but all define a set of framework activities, a collection of tasks that are conducted to accomplish each activity, work products produced as a consequence of the tasks, and a set of umbrella activities that span the entire process. Process patterns can be used to define the characteristics of a process.

The Capability Maturity Model Integration (CMMI) is a comprehensive process meta-model that describes the specific goals, practices, and capabilities that should be present in a mature software process. SPICE and other standards define the requirements for conducting an assessment of software process, and the ISO 9001: 2000 standard examines quality management within a process.

Personal and team models for the software process have been proposed. Both emphasize measurement, planning, and self-direction as key ingredients for a successful software process.

The principles, concepts, and methods that enable us to perform the process that we call *software engineering* are considered throughout the remainder of this book.

References

[AMB98] Ambler, S., *Process Patterns: Building Large-Scale Systems Using Object Technology,* Cambridge University Press/SIGS Books, 1998.

[BAE98] Baetjer, Jr., H., *Software as Capital,* IEEE Computer Society Press, 1998, p. 85.

[CIA01] Cianfrani, C., et al., *ISO 9001: 2000 Explained,* American Society of Quality, 2001.

[CMM02] *Capability Maturity Model Integration (CMMI),* Version 1.1, Software Engineering Institute, March 2002, available at http://www.sei.cmu.edu/cmmi/.

[DAV95] Davis, M., "Process and Product: Dichotomy or Duality," *Software Engineering Notes,* ACM Press, vol. 20, no. 2, April, 1995, pp. 17–18.

[DUN01] Dunaway, D., and S. Masters, *CMM-Based Appraisal for Internal Process Improvement (CBA IPI Version 1.2 Method Description,* Software Engineering Institute, 2001, can be downloaded at http://www.sei.cmu.edu/publications/documents/01.reports/01tr033.html.

[ELE98] El Emam, K., J. Drouin, and W. Melo (eds.), *SPICE: The Theory and Practice of Software Process Improvement and Capability Determination,* IEEE Computer Society Press, 1998.

[FER97] Ferguson, P., et al., "Results of applying the personal software process," *IEEE Computer,* vol. 30 , no. 5, May 1997, pp. 24–31.

[HUM96] Humphrey, W., "Using a Defined and Measured Personal Software Process," *IEEE Software,* vol. 13, no. 3, May/June 1996, pp. 77–88.

[HUM97] Humphrey, W., *Introduction to the Personal Software Process,* Addison-Wesley, 1997.

[HUM98] Humphrey, W., "The Three Dimensions of Process Improvement, Part III: The Team Process," *Crosstalk,* April 1998. Available at http://www.stsc.hill.af.mil/ crosstalk/1998/apr/dimensions.asp

[HUM00] Humphrey, W., *Introduction to the Team Software Process,* Addison-Wesley, 2000.

[IEE93] *IEEE Standards Collection: Software Engineering,* IEEE Standard 610.12-1990, IEEE, 1993.

[ISO00] *ISO 9001:2000 Document Set,* International Organization for Standards, 2000, http://www.iso.ch/iso/en/iso9000-14000/iso9000/iso9000index.html.

[ISO01] "Guidance on the Process Approach to Quality Management Systems," Document ISO/TC 176/SC 2/N544R, International Organization for Standards, May 2001.

[KET01] Ketola, J., and K. Roberts, *ISO 9001: 2000 in a Nutshell,* 2 ed., Paton Press, 2001.

[MON01] Monnich, H., Jr., and H. Monnich, ISO 9001: 2000 for Small- and Medium-Sized Businesses, American Society of Quality, 2001.

[NAU69] Naur, P., and B. Randall (eds.), *Software Engineering: A Report on a Conference Sponsored by the NATO Science Committee,* NATO, 1969.

[NEG99] Negele, H., "Modeling of Integrated Product Development Processes," *Proc. 9th Annual Symposium of INCOSE,* United Kingdom, 1999.

[PAU93] Paulk, M., et al., *Capability Maturity Model for Software,* Software Engineering Institute, Carnegie Mellon University, Pittsburgh, PA, 1993.

[PHI02] Phillips, M., "CMMI V1.1 Tutorial," April 2002, available at http://www.sei. cmu.edu/cmmi/.

[SEI00] *SCAMPI, V1.0 Standard CMMI ® Assessment Method for Process Improvement: Method Description,* Software Engineering Institute, Technical Report CMU/SEI-2000-TR-009, downloadable from http://www.sei.cmu.edu/publications/documents/00.reports/00tr009. html.

[SPI99] "SPICE: Software Process Assessment, Part 1: Concepts and Introduction," Version 1.0, ISO/IEC JTC1, 1999.

Problems and Points to Ponder

2.1. In the introduction to this chapter, Baetjer notes: "The process provides interaction between users and designers, between users and evolving tools, and between designers and evolving tools [technology]." List five questions that (a) designers should ask users; (b) users should ask designers; (c) users should ask themselves about the software product that is to be built; and (d) designers should ask themselves about the software product that is to be built and the process that will be used to build it.

2.2. Figure 2.1 places the three software engineering layers on top of a layer entitled "a quality focus." This implies an organization-wide quality program such as Total Quality Management. Do a bit of research and develop an outline of the key tenets of a Total Quality Management program.

2.3. Is there ever a case when the generic activities of the software engineering process don't apply? If so, describe it.

2.4. Umbrella activities occur throughout the software process. Do you think they are applied evenly across the process, or are some concentrated in one or more framework activities?

2.5. Describe a process framework in your own words. When we say that framework activities are applicable to all projects, does this mean that the same work tasks are applied for all projects, regardless of size and complexity? Explain.

2.6. Try to develop a task set for the *communication* activity.

2.7. Research the CMMI in a bit more detail and discuss the pros and cons of both the continuous and staged CMMI models.

2.8. Download the CMMI documentation from the SEI Web site and select a process area other than project planning. Make a list of specific goals (SG) and the associated specific practices (SP) defined for the area you have chosen.

2.9. Consider the framework activity *communication.* Develop a complete process pattern (this would be a stage pattern) using the template presented in Section 2.4.

2.10. What is the purpose of process assessment? Why has SPICE been developed as a standard for process assessment?

2.11. Do some research on PSP and present a brief presentation that indicates the quantitative benefits of the process.

2.12. The use of "scripts" (a required mechanism in TSP) is not universally praised within the software community. Make a list of pros and cons regarding scripts and suggest at least two situations in which they would be useful and another two situations where they might provide less benefit.

Further Readings and Information Sources

The current state of software engineering and the software process can best be determined from monthly publications such as *IEEE Software, Computer,* and *IEEE Transactions on Software Engineering.* Industry periodicals such as *Application Development Trends* and *Cutter IT Journal* often contain articles on software engineering topics. The discipline is "summarized" every year in the *Proceeding of the International Conference on Software Engineering,* sponsored by the IEEE and ACM, and is discussed in depth in journals such as *ACM Transactions on Software Engineering and Methodology, ACM Software Engineering Notes,* and *Annals of Software Engineering.* Thousands of Web pages are dedicated to software engineering and the software process.

Many books addressing the software process and software engineering have been published in recent years. Some present an overview of the entire process, while others delve into a few important topics to the exclusion of others. Among the more popular offerings (in addition to this book!) are:

Abran, A., and J. Moore, *SWEBOK: Guide to the Software Engineering Body of Knowledge,* IEEE, 2002.

Ahern, D., et al., *CMMI Distilled,* Addison-Wesley, 2001.

Chrisis, B., et al., *CMMI: Guidelines for Process Integration and Product Improvement,* Addison-Wesley 2003.

Christensen, M., and R. Thayer, *A Project Manager's Guide to Software Engineering Best Practices,* IEEE-CS Press (Wiley), 2002.

Glass, R., *Fact and Fallacies of Software Engineering,* Addison-Wesley, 2002.

Hunter, R., and R. Thayer (eds), *Software Process Improvement,* IEEE-CS Press (Wiley), 2001.

Persse, J., *Implementing the Capability Maturity Model,* Wiley, 2001.

Pfleeger, S., *Software Engineering: Theory and Practice,* 2nd ed., Prentice-Hall, 2001.

Potter, N., and M. Sakry, *Making Process Improvement Work*, Addison-Wesley, 2002.

Sommerville, I., *Software Engineering,* 6th ed., Addison-Wesley, 2000.

On the lighter side, a book by Robert Glass (*Software Conflict,* Yourdon Press, 1991) presents amusing and controversial essays on software and the software engineering process. Yourdon (*Death March Projects,* Prentice-Hall, 1997) discusses what goes wrong when major software projects fail and how to avoid these mistakes.

Garmus (*Measuring the Software Process,* Prentice-Hall, 1995) and Florac and Carlton (*Measuring the Software Process,* Addison-Wesley, 1999) discuss the use of mea-surement as a means for statistically assessing the efficacy of any software process.

A wide variety of software engineering standards and procedures have been published over the past decade. The IEEE *Software Engineering Standards* contains many different standards that cover almost every important aspect of the technology. The ISO 9001:2000 document set provides guidance for software organizations that want to improve their quality management activities. Other software engineering standards can be obtained from the Department of Defense, the FAA, and other government and nonprofit agencies. Fairclough (*Software Engineering Guides,* Prentice-Hall, 1996) provides a detailed reference to software engineering standards produced by the European Space Agency (ESA).

A wide variety of information sources on software engineering and the software process are available on the Internet. An up-to-date list of World Wide Web references that are relevant to the software process can be found at the SEPA Web site:
http://www.mhhe.com/pressman.

CHAPTER

3 PRESCRIPTIVE PROCESS MODELS

KEY CONCEPTS

Prescriptive process models were originally proposed to bring order to the chaos of software development. History has indicated that these conventional models have brought a certain amount of useful structure to software engineering work and have provided a reasonably effective roadmap for software teams. However, software engineering work and the product that it produces remain on "the edge of chaos" [NOG00].

In an intriguing paper on the strange relationship between order and chaos in the software world, Nogueira and his colleagues [NOG00] state:

> The edge of chaos is defined as "a natural state between order and chaos, a grand compromise between structure and surprise" [KAU95]. The edge of chaos can be visualized as an unstable, partially structured state. . . . It is unstable because it is constantly attracted to chaos or to absolute order.
>
> We have the tendency to think that order is the ideal state of nature. This could be a mistake. Research . . . supports the theory that operation away from equilibrium generates creativity, self-organized processes, and increasing returns [ROO96]. Absolute order means the absence of variability, which could be an advantage under unpredictable environments. Change occurs when there is some structure so that the change can be organized, but not so rigid that it cannot occur. Too much chaos, on the other hand, can make coordination and coherence impossible. Lack of structure does not always mean disorder.

QUICK LOOK

What is it? Prescriptive process models define a distinct set of activities, actions, tasks, milestones, and work products that are required to engineer high-quality software. These process models are not perfect, but they do provide a useful roadmap for software engineering work.

Who does it? Software engineers and their managers adapt a prescriptive process model to their needs and then follow it. In addition, the people who have requested the software have a role to play as the process model is followed.

Why is it important? Because it provides stability, control, and organization to an activity that can, if left uncontrolled, become quite chaotic. Some have referred to prescriptive process models as "rigorous process models" because they often encompass the capabilities suggested by the CMMI (Chapter 2). However, every process model must be adapted so that it is used effectively for a specific software project.

What are the steps? The process guides a software team through a set of framework activities that are organized into a process flow that may be linear, incremental, or evolutionary. The terminology and details of each process model differ, but the generic framework activities remain reasonably consistent.

What is the work product? From the point of view of a software engineer, the work products are the programs, documents, and data that are produced as a consequence of the activities and tasks defined by the process.

How do I ensure that I've done it right? There are a number of software process assessment mechanisms that enable organizations to determine the "maturity" of their software process. However, the quality, timeliness, and long-term viability of the product you build are the best indicators of the efficacy of the process that you use.

The philosophical implications of this argument are significant for software engineering. If prescriptive process models[1] strive for structure and order, are they inappropriate for a software world that thrives on change? Yet, if we reject conventional process models (and the order they imply) and replace them with something less structured, do we make it impossible to achieve coordination and coherence in software work?

There are no easy answers to these questions, but there are alternatives available to software engineers. In this chapter we examine the prescriptive process approach in which order and project consistency are dominant issues. In Chapter 4 we examine the agile process approach in which self-organization, collaboration, communication, and adaptability dominate the process philosophy.

3.1 Prescriptive Models

A prescriptive process model populates a process framework with explicit task sets for software engineering actions.

Every software engineering organization should describe a unique set of framework activities (Chapter 2) for the software process(es) it adopts. It should populate each framework activity with a set of software engineering actions, and define each action in terms of a task set that identifies the work (and work products) to be accomplished to meet the development goals. It should then adapt the resultant process model to accommodate the specific nature of each project, the people who will do the work, and the environment in which the work will be conducted. Regardless of the process model that is selected, software engineers have traditionally chosen a generic process framework that encompasses the following framework activities: communication, planning, modeling, construction, and deployment.

> "There are many ways of going forward, but only one way of standing still."
>
> **Franklin D. Roosevelt**

In the sections that follow, we examine a number of prescriptive software process models. We call them "prescriptive" because they prescribe a set of process elements—framework activities, software engineering actions, tasks, work products, quality as-

1 Prescriptive process models are often referred to as "conventional" process models.

Even though a process is prescriptive, don't assume that it is static. Prescriptive models should be adapted to the people, the problem, and the project.

surance, and change control mechanisms for each project. Each process model also prescribes a *workflow*—that is, the manner in which the process elements are interrelated to one another.

All software process models can accommodate the generic framework activities that have been described in Chapter 2, but each applies a different emphasis to these activities and defines a workflow that invokes each framework activity (as well as software engineering actions and tasks) in a different manner.

3.2 The Waterfall Model

There are times when the requirements of a problem are reasonably well understood—when work flows from communication through deployment in a reasonably linear fashion. This situation is sometimes encountered when well-defined adaptations or enhancements to an existing system must be made (e.g., an adaptation to accounting software that has been mandated because of changes to government regulations). It may also occur in a limited number of new development efforts, but only when requirements are well-defined and reasonably stable.

The *waterfall model,* sometimes called the *classic life cycle,* suggests a systematic, sequential approach[2] to software development that begins with customer specification of requirements and progresses through planning, modeling, construction, and deployment, culminating in on-going support of the completed software.

The waterfall model is the oldest paradigm for software engineering. However, over the past two decades, criticism of this process model has caused even ardent supporters to question its efficacy [HAN95]. Among the problems that are sometimes encountered when the waterfall model is applied are:

? Why does the waterfall model sometimes fail?

1. Real projects rarely follow the sequential flow that the model proposes. Although the linear model can accommodate iteration, it does so indirectly. As a result, changes can cause confusion as the project team proceeds.

FIGURE 3.1 The waterfall model

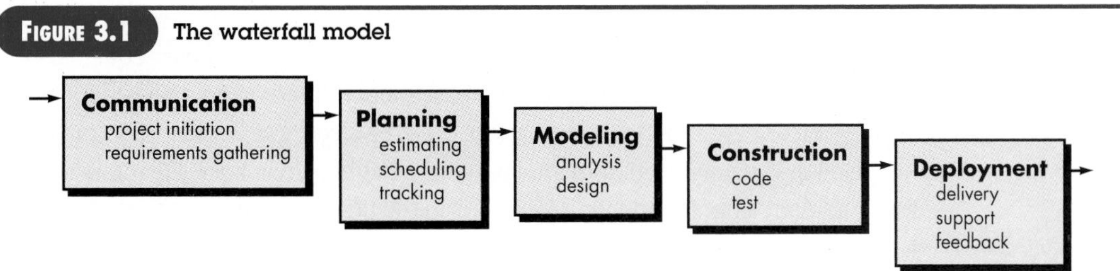

2 Although the original waterfall model proposed by Winston Royce [ROY70] made provision for "feedback loops," the vast majority of organizations that apply this process model treat it as if it were strictly linear.

2. It is often difficult for the customer to state all requirements explicitly. The waterfall model requires this and has difficulty accommodating the natural uncertainty that exists at the beginning of many projects.
3. The customer must have patience. A working version of the program(s) will not be available until late in the project time-span. A major blunder, if undetected until the working program is reviewed, can be disastrous.

In an interesting analysis of actual projects, Bradac [BRA94] found that the linear nature of the waterfall model leads to "blocking states" in which some project team members must wait for other members of the team to complete dependent tasks. In fact, the time spent waiting can exceed the time spent on productive work! The blocking state tends to be more prevalent at the beginning and end of a linear sequential process.

Today, software work is fast-paced and subject to a never-ending stream of changes (to features, functions, and information content). The waterfall model is often inappropriate for such work. However, it can serve as a useful process model in situations where requirements are fixed and work is to proceed to completion in a linear manner.

3.3 Incremental Process Models

There are many situations in which initial software requirements are reasonably well-defined, but the overall scope of the development effort precludes a purely linear process. In addition, there may be a compelling need to provide a limited set of software functionality to users quickly and then refine and expand on that functionality in later software releases. In such cases, a process model that is designed to produce the software in increments is chosen.

> "Too often, software work follows the first law of bicycling: No matter where you're going, it's uphill and against the wind."
>
> **Author unknown**

3.3.1 The Incremental Model

The incremental model delivers a series of releases, called *increments,* that provide progressively more functionality for the customer as each increment is delivered.

The *incremental model* combines elements of the waterfall model applied in an iterative fashion. Referring to Figure 3.2, the incremental model applies linear sequences in a staggered fashion as calendar time progresses. Each linear sequence produces deliverable "increments" of the software [MCD93]. For example, word-processing software developed using the incremental paradigm might deliver basic file management, editing, and document production functions in the first increment; more sophisticated editing, and document production capabilities in the second increment; spelling and grammar checking in the third increment; and advanced page layout capability in the fourth increment. It should be noted that the process flow for any increment may incorporate the prototyping paradigm discussed in Section 3.4.1.

When an incremental model is used, the first increment is often a *core product.* That is, basic requirements are addressed, but many supplementary features (some

FIGURE 3.2
The incremental model

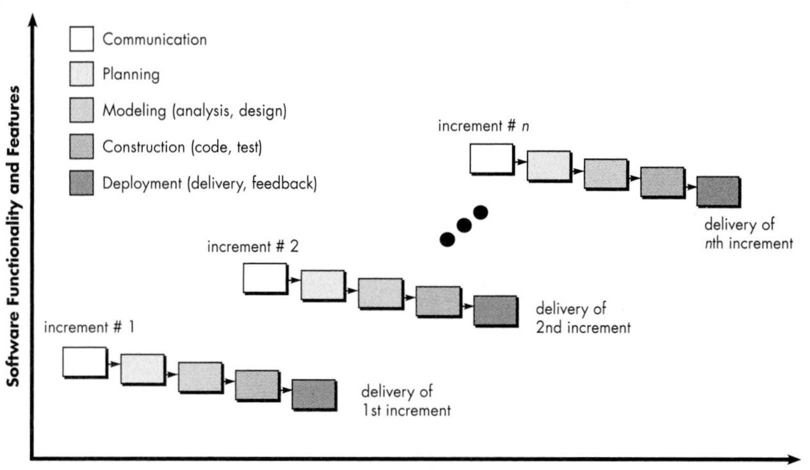

known, others unknown) remain undelivered. The core product is used by the customer (or undergoes detailed evaluation). As a result of use and/or evaluation, a plan is developed for the next increment. The plan addresses the modification of the core product to better meet the needs of the customer and the delivery of additional features and functionality. This process is repeated following the delivery of each increment, until the complete product is produced.

If your customer demands delivery by a date that is impossible to meet, suggest delivering one or more increments by that date and the rest of the software (additional increments) later.

The incremental process model, like prototyping and other evolutionary approaches, is iterative in nature. But unlike prototyping, the incremental model focuses on the delivery of an operational product with each increment. Early increments are "stripped down" versions of the final product, but they do provide capability that serves the user and also provides a platform for evaluation by the user.[3]

Incremental development is particularly useful when staffing is unavailable for a complete implementation by the business deadline that has been established for the project. Early increments can be implemented with fewer people. If the core product is well received, additional staff (if required) can be added to implement the next increment. In addition, increments can be planned to manage technical risks. For example, a major system might require the availability of new hardware that is under development and whose delivery date is uncertain. It might be possible to plan early increments in a way that avoids the use of this hardware, thereby enabling partial functionality to be delivered to end-users without inordinate delay.

3.3.2 The RAD Model

Rapid Application Development (RAD) is an incremental software process model that emphasizes a short development cycle. The RAD model is a "high-speed" adaptation

3 It is important to note that an incremental philosophy is also used for all "agile" process models discussed in Chapter 4.

of the waterfall model, in which rapid development is achieved by using a component-based construction approach. If requirements are well understood and project scope is constrained,[4] the RAD process enables a development team to create a "fully functional system" within a very short time period (e.g., 60 to 90 days) [MAR91].

Like other process models, the RAD approach maps into the generic framework activities presented earlier. *Communication* works to understand the business problem and the information characteristics that the software must accommodate. *Planning* is essential because multiple software teams work in parallel on different system functions. *Modeling* encompasses three major phases—business modeling, data modeling and process modeling—and establishes design representations that serve as the basis for RAD's construction activity. *Construction* emphasizes the use of preexisting software components and the application of automatic code generation. Finally, *deployment* establishes a basis for subsequent iterations, if required [KER94].

The RAD process model is illustrated in Figure 3.3. Obviously, the time constraints imposed on a RAD project demand "scalable scope" [KER94]. If a business application can be modularized in a way that enables each major function to be completed

FIGURE 3.3
The RAD model

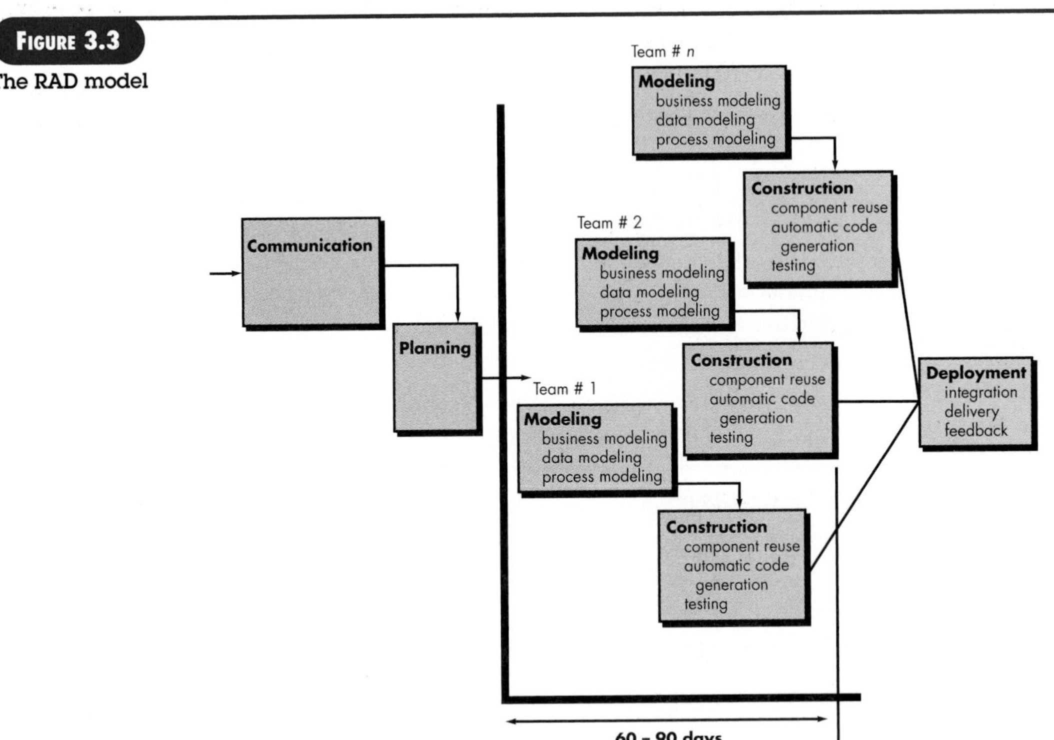

4 These conditions are by no means guaranteed. In fact, many software projects have poorly defined requirements at the start. In such cases prototyping or evolutionary approaches (Section 3.4) are much better process options. See [REI95].

in less than three months (using the approach described above), it is a candidate for RAD. Each major function can be addressed by a separate RAD team and then integrated to form a whole.

What are the drawbacks of the RAD model?

Like all process models, the RAD approach has drawbacks [BUT94]: (1) for large, but scalable projects, RAD requires sufficient human resources to create the right number of RAD teams; (2) if developers and customers are not committed to the rapid-fire activities necessary to complete the system in a much abbreviated time frame, RAD projects will fail; (3) if a system cannot be properly modularized, building the components necessary for RAD will be problematic; (4) if high performance is an issue, and performance is to be achieved through tuning the interfaces to system components, the RAD approach may not work; and (5) RAD may not be appropriate when technical risks are high (e.g., when a new application makes heavy use of new technology).

3.4 Evolutionary Process Models

Evolutionary process models produce an increasingly more complete version of the software with each iteration.

Software, like all complex systems, evolves over a period of time [GIL88]. Business and product requirements often change as development proceeds, making a straight-line path to an end product unrealistic; tight market deadlines make completion of a comprehensive software product impossible, but a limited version must be introduced to meet competitive or business pressure; a set of core product or system requirements is well understood, but the details of product or system extensions have yet to be defined. In these and similar situations, software engineers need a process model that has been explicitly designed to accommodate a product that evolves over time.

Evolutionary models are iterative. They are characterized in a manner that enables software engineers to develop increasingly more complete versions of the software.

3.4.1 Prototyping

Often, a customer defines a set of general objectives for software, but does not identify detailed input, processing, or output requirements. In other cases, the developer may be unsure of the efficiency of an algorithm, the adaptability of an operating system, or the form that human-machine interaction should take. In these, and many other situations, a *prototyping paradigm* may offer the best approach.

When your customer has a legitimate need but is clueless about the details, develop a prototype as a first step.

Although prototyping can be used as a standalone process model, it is more commonly used as a technique that can be implemented within the context of any one of the process models noted in this chapter. Regardless of the manner in which it is applied, the prototyping paradigm assists the software engineer and the customer to better understand what is to be built when requirements are fuzzy.

The prototyping paradigm (Figure 3.4) begins with communication. The software engineer and customer meet and define the overall objectives for the software, identify whatever requirements are known, and outline areas where further definition is

FIGURE 3.4

The prototyping model

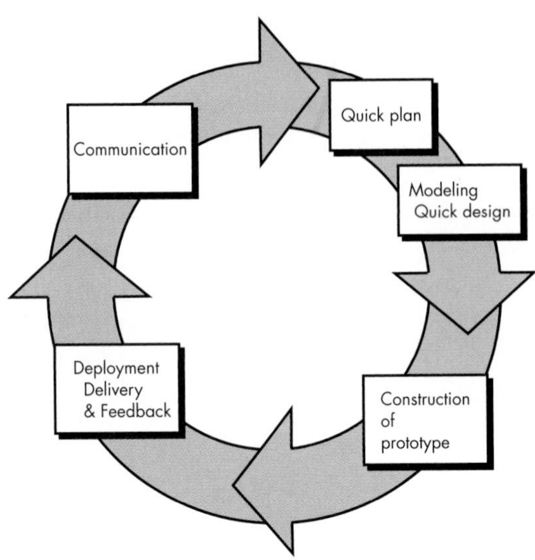

mandatory. A prototyping iteration is planned quickly and modeling (in the form of a "quick design") occurs. The quick design focuses on a representation of those aspects of the software that will be visible to the customer/end-user (e.g., human interface layout or output display formats). The quick design leads to the construction of a prototype. The prototype is deployed and then evaluated by the customer/user. Feedback is used to refine requirements for the software. Iteration occurs as the prototype is tuned to satisfy the needs of the customer, while at the same time enabling the developer to better understand what needs to be done.

Ideally, the prototype serves as a mechanism for identifying software requirements. If a working prototype is built, the developer attempts to make use of existing program fragments or applies tools (e.g., report generators, window managers, etc.) that enable working programs to be generated quickly.

But what do we do with the prototype when it has served the purpose described above? Brooks [BRO75] provides one answer:

> In most projects, the first system built is barely usable. It may be too slow, too big, awkward in use or all three. There is no alternative but to start again, smarting but smarter, and build a redesigned version in which these problems are solved. . . . When a new system concept or new technology is used, one has to build a system to throw away, for even the best planning is not so omniscient as to get it right the first time. The management question, therefore, is not whether to build a pilot system and throw it away. You will do that. The only question is whether to plan in advance to build a throwaway, or to promise to deliver the throwaway to customers.

The prototype can serve as "the first system," the one that Brooks recommends we throw away. But this may be an idealized view. It is true that both customers and developers like the prototyping paradigm. Users get a feel for the actual system, and developers get to build something immediately. Yet, prototyping can be problematic for the following reasons:

1. The customer sees what appears to be a working version of the software, unaware that the prototype is held together "with chewing gum and baling wire," unaware that in the rush to get it working we haven't considered overall software quality or long-term maintainability. When informed that the product must be rebuilt so that high-levels of quality can be maintained, the customer cries foul and demands that "a few fixes" be applied to make the prototype a working product. Too often, software development management relents.
2. The developer often makes implementation compromises in order to get a prototype working quickly. An inappropriate operating system or programming language may be used simply because it is available and known; an inefficient algorithm may be implemented simply to demonstrate capability. After a time, the developer may become comfortable with these choices and forget all the reasons why they were inappropriate. The less-than-ideal choice has now become an integral part of the system.

ADVICE

Resist pressure to extend a rough prototype into a production product. Quality almost always suffers as a result.

Although problems can occur, prototyping can be an effective paradigm for software engineering. The key is to define the rules of the game at the beginning; that is, the customer and developer must both agree that the prototype is built to serve as a mechanism for defining requirements. It is then discarded (at least in part), and the actual software is engineered with an eye toward quality.

SAFEHOME

Selecting a Process Model, Part 1

The scene: Meeting room for the software engineering group at CPI Corporation, a (fictional) company that makes consumer products for home and commercial use.

The players: Lee Warren, engineering manager; Doug Miller, software engineering manager; Jamie Lazar, software team member; Vinod Raman, software team member; and Ed Robbins, software team member.

The conversation:

Lee: So let's recapitulate. I've spent some time discussing the *SafeHome* product line as we see it at the moment. No doubt, we've got a lot of work to do to simply define the thing, but I'd like you guys to begin thinking about how you're going to approach the software part of this project.

Doug: Seems like we've been pretty disorganized in our approach to software in the past.

Ed: I don't know, Doug. We always got product out the door.

Doug: True, but not without a lot of grief, and this project looks like it's bigger and more complex than anything we've done in the past.

Jamie: Doesn't look that hard, but I agree . . . our ad hoc approach to past projects won't work here, particularly if we have a very tight timeline.

Doug (smiling): I want to be a bit more professional in our approach. I went to a short course last week and learned a lot about software engineering . . . good stuff. We need a process here.

Jamie (with a frown): My job is to build computer programs, not push paper around.

Doug: Give it a chance before you go negative on me. Here's what I mean. [Doug proceeds to describe the process framework described in Chapter 2 and the prescriptive process models presented to this point.]

Doug: So anyway, it seems to me that a linear model is not for us . . . assumes we have all requirements up front and knowing this place, that's not likely.

Vinod: Yeah, and that RAD model sounds way too IT-oriented . . . probably good for building an inventory control system or something, but it's just not right for *SafeHome*.

Doug: I agree.

Ed: That prototyping approach seems OK. A lot like what we do here anyway.

Vinod: That's a problem. I'm worried that it doesn't provide us with enough structure.

Doug: Not to worry. We've got plenty of other options, and I want you guys to pick what's best for the team and best for the project.

3.4.2 The Spiral Model

The *spiral model,* originally proposed by Boehm [BOE88], is an evolutionary software process model that couples the iterative nature of prototyping with the controlled and systematic aspects of the waterfall model. It provides the potential for rapid development of increasingly more complete versions of the software. Boehm [BOE01] describes the model in the following manner:

> The spiral development model is a *risk-driven process model* generator that is used to guide multi-stakeholder concurrent engineering of software intensive systems. It has two main distinguishing features. One is a *cyclic* approach for incrementally growing a system's degree of definition and implementation while decreasing its degree of risk. The other is a set of *anchor point milestones* for ensuring stakeholder commitment to feasible and mutually satisfactory system solutions.

Using the spiral model, software is developed in a series of evolutionary releases. During early iterations, the release might be a paper model or prototype. During later iterations, increasingly more complete versions of the engineered system are produced.

KEY POINT The spiral model can be adapted to apply throughout the entire life cycle of an application, from concept development to maintenance.

A spiral model is divided into a set of framework activities defined by the software engineering team. For illustrative purposes, we use the generic framework activities discussed earlier.[5] Each of the framework activities represent one segment of the spiral path illustrated in Figure 3.5. As this evolutionary process begins, the software team performs activities that are implied by a circuit around the spiral in a clockwise direction, beginning at the center. Risk (Chapter 25) is considered as each revolution is made. *Anchor point milestones*—a combination of work products and conditions that are attained along the path of the spiral—are noted for each evolutionary pass.

The first circuit around the spiral might result in the development of a product specification; subsequent passes around the spiral might be used to develop a prototype and then progressively more sophisticated versions of the software. Each pass

5 The spiral model discussed in this section is a variation on the model proposed by Boehm. For further information on the original spiral model, see [BOE88]. More recent discussion of Boehm's spiral model can be found in [BOE98].

FIGURE 3.5

A typical spiral model

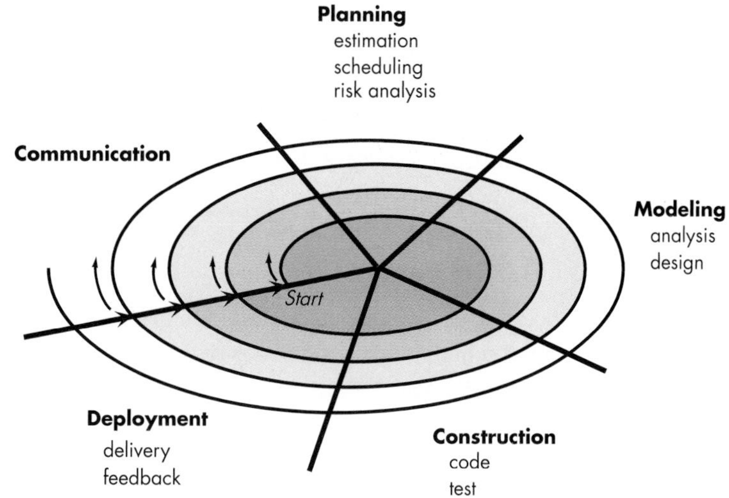

through the planning region results in adjustments to the project plan. Cost and schedule are adjusted based on feedback derived from the customer after delivery. In addition, the project manager adjusts the planned number of iterations required to complete the software.

WebRef
Useful information about the spiral model can be obtained at **www.sei.cmu.edu/cbs/spiral2000/.**

Unlike other process models that end when software is delivered, the spiral model can be adapted to apply throughout the life of the computer software. Therefore, the first circuit around the spiral might represent a "concept development project" which starts at the core of the spiral and continues for multiple iterations[6] until concept development is complete. If the concept is to be developed into an actual product, the process proceeds outward on the spiral and a "new product development project" commences. The new product will evolve through a number of iterations around the spiral. Later, a circuit around the spiral might be used to represent a "product enhancement project." In essence, the spiral, when characterized in this way, remains operative until the software is retired. There are times when the process is dormant, but whenever a change is initiated, the process starts at the appropriate entry point (e.g., product enhancement).

If your management demands fixed-budget development (generally a bad idea), the spiral can be a problem: as each circuit is completed, project cost is revisited and revised.

The spiral model is a realistic approach to the development of large-scale systems and software. Because software evolves as the process progresses, the developer and customer better understand and react to risks at each evolutionary level. The spiral model uses prototyping as a risk reduction mechanism but, more importantly, enables the developer to apply the prototyping approach at any stage in the evolution of the product. It maintains the systematic stepwise approach suggested by the classic life cycle but incorporates it into an iterative framework that more realistically reflects the real world. The spiral model demands a direct consideration of technical

6 The arrows pointing inward along the axis separating the *deployment* region from the *communication* region indicate a potential for local iteration along the same spiral path.

risks at all stages of the project and, if properly applied, should reduce risks before they become problematic.

But like other paradigms, the spiral model is not a panacea. It may be difficult to convince customers (particularly in contract situations) that the evolutionary approach is controllable. It demands considerable risk assessment expertise and relies on this expertise for success. If a major risk is not uncovered and managed, problems will undoubtedly occur.

3.4.3 The Concurrent Development Model

The *concurrent development model,* sometimes called *concurrent engineering,* can be represented schematically as a series of framework activities, software engineering actions and tasks, and their associated states. For example, the *modeling* activity defined for the spiral model is accomplished by invoking the following actions: prototyping and/or analysis modeling and specification and design.[7]

The concurrent model is often more appropriate for system engineering projects (Chapter 6) where different engineering teams are involved.

Figure 3.6 provides a schematic representation of one software engineering task within the modeling activity for the concurrent process model. The activity—*modeling*—may be in any one of the states[8] noted at any given time. Similarly, other activities or tasks (e.g., communication or construction) can be represented in an analogous manner. All activities exist concurrently but reside in different states. For example, early in a project the *communication* activity (not shown in the figure) has completed its first iteration and exists in the **awaiting changes** state. The *modeling* activity which existed in the **none** state while initial communication was completed, now makes a transition into the **under development** state. If, however, the customer indicates that changes in requirements must be made, the *modeling* activity moves from the **under development** state into the **awaiting changes** state.

The concurrent process model defines a series of events that will trigger transitions from state to state for each of the software engineering activities, actions, or tasks. For example, during early stages of design (a software engineering action that occurs during the modeling activity), an inconsistency in the analysis model is uncovered. This generates the event *analysis model correction* which will trigger the analysis action from the **done** state into the **awaiting changes** state.

The concurrent process model is applicable to all types of software development and provides an accurate picture of the current state of a project. Rather than confining software engineering activities, actions, and tasks to a sequence of events, it defines a network of activities. Each activity, action, or task on the network exists simultaneously with other activities, actions, or tasks. Events generated at one point in the process network trigger transitions among the states.

7 It should be noted that analysis and design are complex actions that require substantial discussion. Part 2 of this book considers these topics in detail.

8 A *state* is some externally observable mode of behavior.

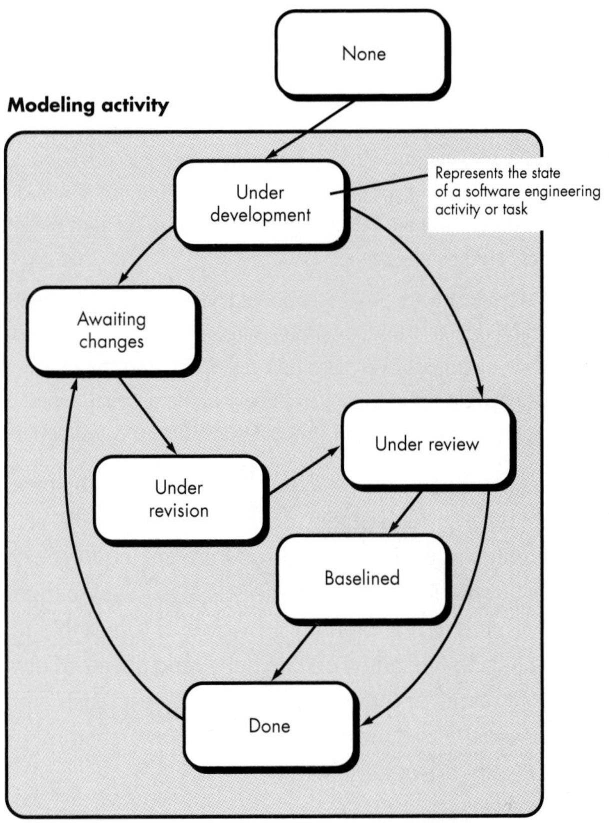

FIGURE 3.6 One element of the concurrent process model

3.4.4 A Final Comment on Evolutionary Processes

We have already noted that modern computer software is characterized by continual change, by very tight timelines, and by an emphatic need for customer/user satisfaction. In many cases, time-to-market is the most important management requirement. If a market window is missed, the software project itself may be meaningless.[9]

> "I'm only this far and only tomorrow leads my way."
>
> **Dave Matthews Band**

Evolutionary process models were conceived to address these issues, and yet, as a general class of process models, they too have weaknesses. These are summarized by Nogueira and his colleagues [NOG00]:

9 It is important to note, however, that being the first to reach a market is no guarantee of success. In fact, many very successful software products have been second or even third to reach the market (learning from the mistakes of their predecessors).

> Despite the unquestionable benefits of evolutionary software processes, we have some concerns. The first concern is that prototyping [and other more sophisticated evolutionary processes] poses a problem to project planning because of the uncertain number of cycles required to construct the product. Most project management and estimation techniques are based on linear layouts of activities, so they do not fit completely.
>
> Second, evolutionary software processes do not establish the maximum speed of the evolution. If the evolutions occur too fast, without a period of relaxation, it is certain that the process will fall into chaos. On the other hand, if the speed is too slow then productivity could be affected. . . .
>
> Third, software processes should be focused on flexibility and extensibility rather than on high quality. This assertion sounds scary. However, we should prioritize the speed of the development over zero defects. Extending the development in order to reach high quality could result in a late delivery of the product, when the opportunity niche has disappeared. This paradigm shift is imposed by the competition on the edge of chaos.

Indeed, a software process that focuses on flexibility, extensibility, and speed of development over high quality does sound scary. And yet, this idea has been proposed by a number of well-respected software engineering experts (e.g., [YOU95], [BAC97]).

The intent of evolutionary models is to develop high-quality software[10] in an iterative or incremental manner. However, it is possible to use an evolutionary process to emphasize flexibility, extensibility, and speed of development. The challenge for software teams and their managers is to establish a proper balance between these critical project and product parameters and customer satisfaction (the ultimate arbiter of software quality).

SAFEHOME

Selecting a Process Model, Part 2

The scene: Meeting room for the software engineering group at CPI Corporation, a company that makes consumer products for home and commercial use.

The players: Lee Warren, engineering manager; Doug Miller, software engineering manager; Ed and Vinod, members of the software engineering team.

The conversation:

(Doug describes evolutionary process options.)

Ed: Now I see something I like. An incremental approach makes sense and I really like the flow of that spiral model thing. That's keepin' it real.

Vinod: I agree. We deliver an increment, learn from customer feedback, replan, and then deliver another increment. It also fits into the nature of the product. We can have something on the market fast and then add functionality with each version, er, increment.

Lee: Wait a minute, did you say that we regenerate the plan with each tour around the spiral, Doug? That's not so great, we need one plan, one schedule, and we've got to stick to it.

Doug: That's old school thinking, Lee. Like Ed said, we've got to keep it real. I submit that it's better to tweak the plan as we learn more and as changes are requested.

10 In this context, software quality is defined quite broadly to encompass not only customer satisfaction, but also a variety of technical criteria discussed in Chapter 26.

It's way more realistic. What's the point of a plan if it doesn't reflect reality?

Lee (frowning): I suppose so, but senior management's not going to like this . . . they want a fixed plan.

Doug (smiling): Then you'll have to reeducate them, buddy.

3.5 Specialized Process Models

Special process models take on many of the characteristics of one or more of the conventional models presented in the preceding sections. However, specialized models tend to be applied when a narrowly defined software engineering approach is chosen.[11]

3.5.1 Component-Based Development

Commercial off-the-shelf (COTS) software components, developed by vendors who offer them as products, can be used when software is to be built. These components provide targeted functionality with well-defined interfaces that enable the component to be integrated into the software.

WebRef
Useful information on component-based development can be obtained at **www.cbd-hq.com.**

The *component-based development* model (Chapter 30) incorporates many of the characteristics of the spiral model. It is evolutionary in nature [NIE92], demanding an iterative approach to the creation of software. However, the model composes applications from prepackaged software components.

Modeling and construction activities begin with the identification of candidate components. These components can be designed as either conventional software modules or object-oriented classes or packages[12] of classes. Regardless of the technology that is used to create the components, the component-based development model incorporates the following steps (implemented using an evolutionary approach):

- Available component-based products are researched and evaluated for the application domain in question.
- Component integration issues are considered.
- A software architecture (Chapter 10) is designed to accommodate the components.
- Components (Chapter 11) are integrated into the architecture.
- Comprehensive testing (Chapters 13 and 14) is conducted to ensure proper functionality.

---

11 In some cases, these specialized process models might better be characterized as a collection of techniques or a methodology for accomplishing a specific software development goal. However, they do imply a process.

12 Object-oriented technology is discussed through Part 2 of this book. In this context, a class encapsulates a set of data and the procedures that process the data. A package of classes is a collection of related classes that work together to achieve some end result.

The component-based development model leads to software reuse, and reusability provides software engineers with a number of measurable benefits. Based on studies of reusability, QSM Associates, Inc. reports that component-based development leads to a 70 percent reduction in development cycle time; an 84 percent reduction in project cost; and a productivity index of 26.2, compared to an industry norm of 16.9 [YOU94]. Although these results are a function of the robustness of the component library, there is little question that the component-based development model provides significant advantages for software engineers.

3.5.2 The Formal Methods Model

The *formal methods* model (Chapter 28) encompasses a set of activities that leads to formal mathematical specification of computer software. Formal methods enable a software engineer to specify, develop, and verify a computer-based system by applying a rigorous, mathematical notation. A variation on this approach, called *cleanroom software engineering* [MIL87, DYE92], is currently applied by some software development organizations and is discussed in Chapter 29.

> **"It is easier to write an incorrect program than understand a correct one."**
>
> **Alan Perlis**

When formal methods are used during development, they provide a mechanism for eliminating many of the problems that are difficult to overcome using other software engineering paradigms. Ambiguity, incompleteness, and inconsistency can be discovered and corrected more easily—not through *ad hoc* review, but through the application of mathematical analysis. When formal methods are used during design, they serve as a basis for program verification and therefore enable the software engineer to discover and correct errors that might otherwise go undetected.

Although not a mainstream approach, the formal methods model offers the promise of defect-free software. Yet, concern about its applicability in a business environment has been voiced:

? If formal methods can demonstrate software correctness, why is it they are not widely used?

- The development of formal models is currently quite time-consuming and expensive.
- Because few software developers have the necessary background to apply formal methods, extensive training is required.
- It is difficult to use the models as a communication mechanism for technically unsophisticated customers.

These concerns notwithstanding, the formal methods approach has gained adherents among software developers who must build safety-critical software (e.g., developers of aircraft avionics and medical devices) and among developers who would suffer severe economic hardship should software errors occur.

3.5.3 Aspect-Oriented Software Development

WebRef
A wide array of resources and information on AOP can be found at **aosd.net.**

Regardless of the software process that is chosen, the builders of complex software invariably implement a set of localized features, functions, and information content. These localized software characteristics are modeled as components (e.g., object-oriented classes) and then constructed within the context of a system architecture. As modern computer-based systems become more sophisticated (and complex), certain "concerns"—customer required properties or areas of technical interest—span the entire architecture. Some concerns are high-level properties of a system (e.g., security, fault tolerance). Other concerns affect functions (e.g., the application of business rules), while others are systemic (e.g., task synchronization or memory management).

When concerns cut across multiple system functions, features, and information, they are often referred to as *crosscutting concerns. Aspectual requirements* define those crosscutting concerns that have impact across the software architecture. *Aspect-oriented software development* (AOSD), often referred to as *aspect-oriented programming* (AOP), is a relatively new software engineering paradigm that provides a process and methodological approach for defining, specifying, designing, and constructing *aspects*—"mechanisms beyond subroutines and inheritance for localizing the expression of a crosscutting concern" [ELR01].

KEY POINT
AOSD defines "aspects" that express customer concerns that cut across multiple system functions, features, and information.

Grundy [GRU02] provides further discussion of aspects in the context of what he calls *aspect-oriented component engineering* (AOCE):

> AOCE uses a concept of horizontal slices through vertically-decomposed software components, called "aspects," to characterize cross-cutting functional and non-functional properties of components. Common, systemic aspects include user interfaces, collaborative work, distribution, persistency, memory management, transaction processing, security, integrity and so on. Components may provide or require one or more "aspect details" relating to a particular aspect, such as a viewing mechanism, extensible affordance and interface kind (user interface aspects); event generation, transport and receiving (distribution aspects); data store/retrieve and indexing (persistency aspects); authentication, encoding and access rights (security aspects); transaction atomicity, concurrency control and logging strategy (transaction aspects); and so on. Each aspect detail has a number of properties, relating to functional and/or non-functional characteristics of the aspect detail.

A distinct aspect-oriented process has not yet matured. However, it is likely that such a process will adopt characteristics of both the spiral and concurrent process models (Sections 3.4.2 and 3.4.3). The evolutionary nature of the spiral is appropriate as aspects are identified and then constructed. The parallel nature of concurrent development is essential because aspects are engineered independently of localized software components and yet, aspects have a direct impact on these components. Hence, it is essential to instantiate asynchronous communication between the software process activities applied to the engineering and construction of aspects and components.

A detailed discussion of aspect-oriented software development is best left to books dedicated to the subject. The interested reader should see [GRA03], [KIS02], or [ELR01].

Software Tools

Process Management

Objective: To assist in the definition, execution, and management of prescriptive process models.

Mechanics: Process management tools allow a software organization or team to define a complete software process model (framework activities, actions, tasks, QA checkpoints, milestones, and work products). In addition, the tools provide a roadmap as software engineers do technical work and a template for managers who must track and control the software process.

Representative Tools[13]

GDPA, a research process definition tool suite, developed at Bremen University in Germany (www.informatik.uni-bremen.de/uniform/gdpa/home.htm), provides a wide array of process modeling and management functions.

SpeeDev, developed by SpeeDev Corporation (www.speedev.com), encompasses a suite of tools for process definition, requirements management, issue resolution, project planning, and tracking.

Step Gate Process, developed by Objexis (www.objexis.com), encompasses many tools that assist in workflow automation.

A worthwhile discussion of the methods and notation that can be used to define and describe a complete process model can be found at http://205.252.62.38/English/D-ProcessNotation.htm.

3.6 The Unified Process

In their seminal book on the *Unified Process,* Ivar Jacobson, Grady Booch, and James Rumbaugh [JAC99] discuss the need for a "use-case driven, architecture-centric, iterative and incremental" software process when they state:

> Today, the trend in software is toward bigger, more complex systems. That is due in part to the fact that computers become more powerful every year, leading users to expect more from them. This trend has also been influenced by the expanding use of the Internet for exchanging all kinds of information. . . . Our appetite for ever-more sophisticated software grows as we learn from one product release to the next how the product could be improved. We want software that is better adapted to our needs, but that, in turn, merely makes the software more complex. In short, we want more.

In some ways the Unified Process (UP) is an attempt to draw on the best features and characteristics of conventional software process models, but characterize them in a way that implements many of the best principles of agile software development (Chapter 4). The Unified Process recognizes the importance of customer communication and streamlined methods for describing the customer's view of a system (i.e., the use-case[14]). It emphasizes the important role of software architec-

---

13 Tools noted here do not represent an endorsement, but rather a sampling of tools in this category. In most cases, tool names are trademarked by their respective developers.

14 A *use-case* (Chapters 7 and 8) is a text narrative or template that describes a system function or feature from the user's point of view. A use-case is written by the user and serves as a basis for the creation of a more comprehensive analysis model.

ture and "helps the architect focus on the right goals, such as understandability, reliance to future changes, and reuse" [JAC99]. It suggests a process flow that is iterative and incremental, providing the evolutionary feel that is essential in modern software development.

In this section we present an overview of the key elements of the Unified Process. In Part 2 of this book, we discuss the methods that populate the process and the complementary UML[15] modeling techniques and notation that are required as the Unified Process is applied in actual software engineering work.

3.6.1 A Brief History

During the 1980s and into the early 1990s, object-oriented (OO) methods and programming languages[16] gained a widespread audience throughout the software engineering community. A wide variety of object-oriented analysis (OOA) and design (OOD) methods were proposed during the same time period, and a general purpose object-oriented process model (similar to the evolutionary models presented in this chapter) was introduced. Like most "new" paradigms for software engineering, adherents of each of the OOA and OOD methods argued about which was best, but no individual method or language dominated the software engineering landscape.

During the early 1990s James Rumbaugh [RUM91], Grady Booch [BOO94], and Ivar Jacobson [JAC92] began working on a "unified method" that would combine the best features of each of their individual methods and adopt additional features proposed by other experts (e.g., [WIR90]) in the OO field. The result was UML—a *unified modeling language* that contains a robust notation for the modeling and development of OO systems. By 1997, UML became an industry standard for object-oriented software development. At the same time, the Rational Corporation and other vendors developed automated tools to support UML methods.

UML provides the necessary technology to support object-oriented software engineering practice, but it does not provide the process framework to guide project teams in their application of the technology. Over the next few years, Jacobson, Rumbaugh, and Booch developed the *Unified Process,* a framework for object-oriented software engineering using UML. Today, the Unified Process and UML are widely used on OO projects of all kinds. The iterative, incremental model proposed by the UP can and should be adapted to meet specific project needs.

An array of work products (e.g., models and documents) can be produced as a consequence of applying UML. However, these are often pared down by software engineers to make development more agile and more responsive to change.

---

15 UML (the Unified Modeling Language) has become the most widely used notation for analysis and design modeling. It represents a marriage of three important object-oriented notations.

16 If you are unfamiliar with object-oriented methods, a brief overview is presented in Chapters 8 and 9. For a more detailed presentation see [REE02], [STI01], or [FOW99].

3.6.2 Phases of the Unified Process[17]

WebRef
Useful white papers on the UP can be found at **www.rational.com/products/rup/whitepapers.jsp.**

We have discussed five generic framework activities and argued that they may be used to describe any software process model. The Unified Process is no exception. Figure 3.7 depicts the "phases" of the Unified Process (UP) and relates them to the generic activities that have been discussed in Chapter 2.

POINT
UP *phases* are similar in intent to the generic framework activities defined in this book.

The *inception* phase of the UP encompasses both customer communication and planning activities. By collaborating with the customer and end-users, business requirements for the software are identified, a rough architecture for the system is proposed, and a plan for the iterative, incremental nature of the ensuing project is developed. Fundamental business requirements are described through a set of preliminary use-cases that describe what features and functions are desired by each major class of users. In general, a use-case describes a sequence of actions that are performed by an *actor* (e.g., a person, a machine, another system) as the actor interacts with the software. Use-cases help to identify the scope of the project and provide a basis for project planning.

Architecture at this point is nothing more than a tentative outline of major subsystems and the function and features that populate them. Later, the architecture will be refined and expanded into a set of models that will represent different views of the system. Planning identifies resources, assesses major risks, defines a schedule, and establishes a basis for the phases that are to be applied as the software increment is developed.

The *elaboration* phase encompasses the customer communication and modeling activities of the generic process model (Figure 3.7). Elaboration refines and expands the preliminary use-cases that were developed as part of the inception phase and expands the architectural representation to include five different views of the software—the use-case model, the analysis model, the design model, the implementation model, and the deployment model. In some cases, elaboration creates an "executable architectural baseline" [ARL02] that represents a "first cut" executable system.[18] The architectural baseline demonstrates the viability of the architecture but does not provide all features and functions required to use the system. In addition, the plan is carefully reviewed at the culmination of the elaboration phase to ensure that scope, risks, and delivery dates remain reasonable. Modifications to the plan may be made at this time.

WebRef
Illuminating discussion and commentary on the UP can be found at **www.unifiedprocess.org.**

The *construction* phase of the UP is identical to the construction activity defined for the generic software process. Using the architectural model as input, the construction phase develops or acquires the software components that will make each

17 The Unified Process is sometimes called the *Rational Unified Process* (RUP) after the Rational Corporation, a primary contributor to the development and refinement of the process and a builder of complete environments (tools and technology) that support the process.

18 It is important to note that the architectural baseline is not a prototype (Section 3.4.1) in that it is not thrown away. Rather, the baseline is fleshed out during the next UP phase.

FIGURE 3.7

The Unified Process

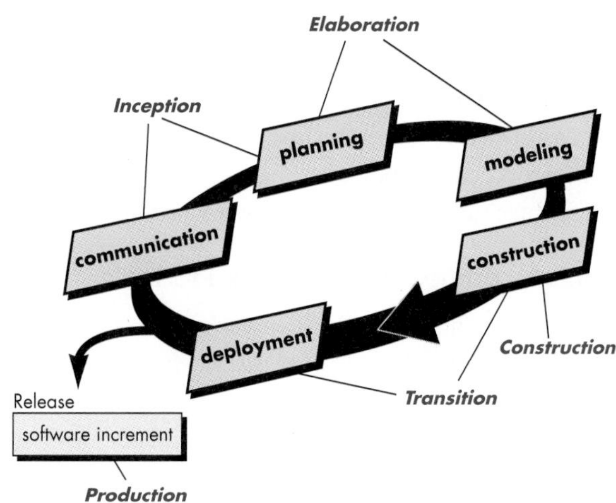

use-case operational for end-users. To accomplish this, analysis and design models that were started during the elaboration phase are completed to reflect the final version of the software increment. All necessary and required features and functions of the software increment (i.e., the release) are then implemented in source code. As components are being implemented, unit tests are designed and executed for each. In addition, integration activities (component assembly and integration testing) are conducted. Use-cases are used to derive a suite of acceptance tests that are executed prior to the initiation of the next UP phase.

The *transition* phase of the UP encompasses the latter stages of the generic construction activity and the first part of the generic deployment activity. Software is given to end-users for beta testing[19], and user feedback reports both defects and necessary changes. In addition, the software team creates the necessary support information (e.g., user manuals, trouble-shooting guides, and installation procedures) that is required for the release. At the conclusion of the transition phase, the software increment becomes a usable software release.

The *production* phase of the UP coincides with the deployment activity of the generic process. During this phase, the on-going use of the software is monitored, support for the operating environment (infrastructure) is provided, and defect reports and requests for changes are submitted and evaluated.

It is likely that at the same time the construction, transition, and production phases are being conducted, work may have already begun on the next software increment. This means that the five UP phases do not occur in a sequence, but rather with staggered concurrency.

---

19 *Beta testing* is a controlled testing action (Chapter 13) in which the software is used by actual end-users with the intent of uncovering defects and deficiencies. A formal defect/deficiency reporting scheme is established, and the software team assesses feedback.

A software engineering workflow is distributed across all UP phases. In the context of UP, a *workflow* is analogous to a task set (defined in Chapter 2). That is, a workflow identifies the tasks required to accomplish an important software engineering action and the work products that are produced as a consequence of successfully completing the tasks. It should be noted that not every task identified for a UP workflow is conducted for every software project. The team adapts the process (actions, tasks, subtasks, and work products) to meet its needs.

3.6.3 Unified Process Work Products

Figure 3.8 illustrates the key *work products* produced as a consequence of the four technical UP phases. During the inception phase, the intent is to establish an overall "vision" for the project, identify a set of business requirements, make a business case for the software, and define project and business risks that may represent a threat to success. From the software engineer's point of view, the most important work product produced during the inception is the *use-case model*—a collection of use-cases that describe how outside actors (human and nonhuman "users" of the software) interact with the system and gain value from it. In essence, the use-case model is a collection of usage scenarios described with standardized templates that imply software features and functions by describing a set of preconditions, a flow of events or a scenario, and a set of post-conditions for the interaction that is depicted. Initially, use-cases describe requirements at the business domain level (i.e., the level of abstraction is high). However, the use-case model is refined and elaborated as each UP phase is conducted and serves as an important input for the creation of subsequent work products. During the inception phase only 10 to 20 percent of the use-case model is completed. After elaboration, between 80 and 90 percent of the model has been created.

The elaboration phase produces a set of work products that elaborate requirements (including nonfunctional[20] requirements) and produce an architectural description and a preliminary design. As the software engineer begins object-oriented analysis, the primary objective is to define a set of analysis classes that adequately describe the behavior of the system. The UP *analysis model* is the work product that is developed as a consequence of this activity. The classes and analysis packages (collections of classes) defined as part of the analysis model are refined further into a *design model* which identifies design classes, subsystems, and the interfaces between subsystems. Both the analysis and design models expand and refine an evolving representation of software architecture. In addition, the elaboration phase revisits risks and the project plan to ensure that each remains valid.

The construction phase produces an *implementation* model that translates design classes into software components that will be built to realize the system, and a *deployment* model maps components into the physical computing environment. Finally,

20 Requirements that cannot be discerned from the use-case model.

FIGURE 3.8

Major work products produced for each UP phase

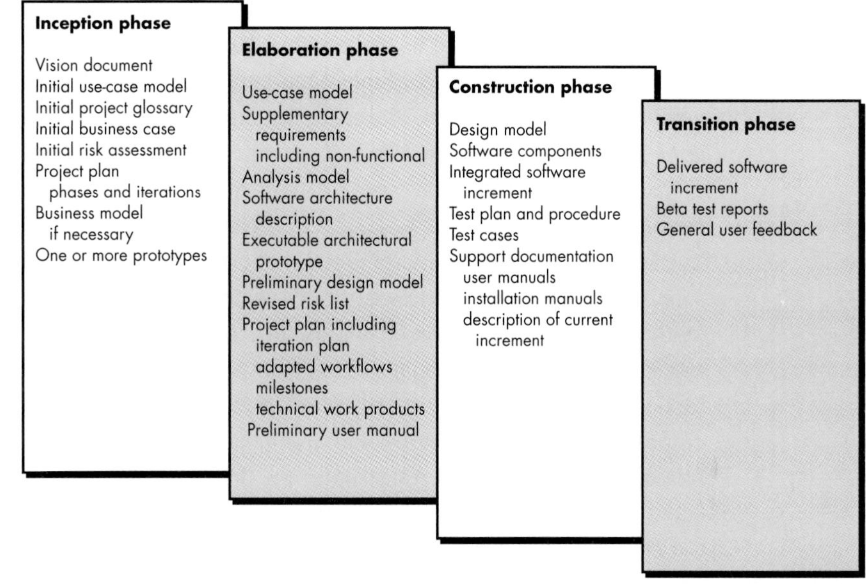

a *test* model describes tests that are used to ensure that use-cases are properly reflected in the software that has been constructed.

The transition phase delivers the software increment and assesses work products that are produced as end-users work with the software. Feedback from beta testing and qualitative requests for change are produced at this time.

3.7 SUMMARY

Prescriptive software process models have been applied for many years in an effort to bring order and structure to software development. Each of these conventional models suggests a somewhat different process flow, but all perform the same set of generic framework activities: communication, planning, modeling, construction, and deployment.

The waterfall model suggests a linear progression of framework activities that is often inconsistent with modern realities (e.g., continuous change, evolving systems, tight timelines) in the software world. It does, however, have applicability in situations where requirements are well-defined and stable.

Incremental software process models produce software as a series of increment releases. The RAD model is designed for larger projects that must be delivered in tight time frames.

Evolutionary process models recognize the iterative nature of most software engineering projects and are designed to accommodate change. Evolutionary models, such as prototyping and the spiral model, produce incremental work products (or working versions of the software) quickly. These models can be adopted to apply across all software engineering activities—from concept development to long-term system maintenance.

The component-based model emphasizes component reuse and assembly. The formal methods model encourages a mathematically based approach to software development and verification. The aspect-oriented model accommodates cross-cutting concerns that span the entire system architecture.

The Unified Process is a "use-case driven, architecture-centric, iterative and incremental" software process designed as a framework for UML methods and tools. The Unified Process is an incremental model in which five phases are defined: (1) an *inception* phase that encompasses both customer communication and planning activities and emphasizes the development and refinement of use-cases as a primary model; (2) an *elaboration* phase that encompasses the customer communication and modeling activities focusing on the creation of analysis and design models with an emphasis on class definitions and architectural representations; (3) a *construction* phase that refines and then translates the design model into implemented software components; (4) a *transition* phase that transfers the software from the developer to the end-user for beta testing and acceptance; and (5) a *production* phase in which on-going monitoring and support are conducted.

References

[AMB02] Ambler, S., and L. Constantine, *The Unified Process Inception Phase,* CMP Books, 2002.

[ARL02] Arlow, J., and I. Neustadt, *UML and the Unified Process,* Addison-Wesley, 2002.

[BAC97] Bach, J., "Good Enough Quality: Beyond the Buzzword," *IEEE Computer,* vol. 30, no. 8, August 1997, pp. 96–98.

[BOE88] Boehm, B., "A Spiral Model for Software Development and Enhancement," *Computer,* vol. 21, no. 5, May 1988, pp. 61–72.

[BOE98] Boehm, B., "Using the WINWIN Spiral Model: A Case Study," *Computer,* vol. 31, no. 7, July 1998, pp. 33–44.

[BOE01] Boehm, B., "The Spiral Model as a Tool for Evolutionary Software Acquisition," *CrossTalk,* May 2001, available at http://www.stsc.hill.af.mil/crosstalk/ 2001/05/boehm.html.

[BOO94] Booch, G., *Object-Oriented Analysis and Design,* 2nd ed., Benjamin Cummings, 1994.

[BRA94] Bradac, M., D. Perry, and L. Votta, "Prototyping a Process Monitoring Experiment," *IEEE Trans. Software Engineering,* vol. 20, no. 10, October 1994, pp. 774–784.

[BRO75] Brooks, F., *The Mythical Man-Month,* Addison-Wesley, 1975.

[BUT94] Butler, J., "Rapid Application Development in Action," *Managing System Development,* Applied Computer Research, vol. 14, no. 5, May 1994, pp. 6–8.

[DYE92] Dyer, M., *The Cleanroom Approach to Quality Software Development,* Wiley, 1992.

[ELR01] Elrad, T., R. Filman, and A. Bader (eds.), "Aspect-Oriented Programming," *Comm. ACM,* vol. 44, no. 10, October 2001, special issue.

[FOW99] Fowler, M., and K. Scott, *UML Distilled,* 2nd ed., Addison-Wesley, 1999.

[GIL88] Gilb, T., *Principles of Software Engineering Management,* Addison-Wesley, 1988.

[GRA03] Gradecki, J., and N. Lesiecki, *Mastering AspectJ: Aspect-Oriented Programming in Java,* Wiley, 2003.

[GRU02] Grundy, J., "Aspect-Oriented Component Engineering," 2002, http:// www.cs.auckland.ac.nz/~john-g/aspects.html.

[HAN95] Hanna, M., "Farewell to Waterfalls," *Software Magazine,* May 1995, pp. 38–46.

[HES96] Hesse, W., "Theory and Practice of the Software Process—A Field Study and its Implications for Project Management," *Software Process Technology, 5th European Workshop,* EWSPT 96, Springer LNCS 1149, 1996, pp. 241–256.

[HES01] Hesse, W., "Dinosaur Meets Archaeopteryx? Seven Theses on Rational's Unified Process (RUP)," *Proc. 8th Intl. Workshop on Evaluation of Modeling Methods in System Analysis and Design,* Ch. VII, Interlaken, 2001.

[JAC92] Jacobson, I., *Object-Oriented Software Engineering,* Addison-Wesley, 1992.

[JAC99] Jacobson, I., Booch, G., and J. Rumbaugh, *The Unified Software Development Process,* Addison-Wesley, 1999.

[JAC99] Jacobson, I., G. Booch, and J. Rumbaugh, *The Unified Software Development Process,* Addison-Wesley, 1999.

[KAU95] Kauffman, S., *At Home in the Universe,* Oxford, 1995.

[KER94] Kerr, J., and R. Hunter, *Inside RAD,* McGraw-Hill, 1994.

[KIS02] Kiselev, I., *Aspect-Oriented Programming with AspectJ,* Sams Publishers, 2002.

[MAR91] Martin, J., *Rapid Application Development,* Prentice-Hall, 1991.

[McDE93] McDermid, J., and P. Rook, "Software Development Process Models," in *Software Engineer's Reference Book,* CRC Press, 1993, pp. 15/26–15/28.

[MIL87] Mills, H. D., M. Dyer, and R. Linger, "Cleanroom Software Engineering," *IEEE Software,* September, 1987, pp. 19–25.

[NIE92] Nierstrasz, O., S. Gibbs, and D. Tsichritzis, "Component-Oriented Software Development," *CACM,* vol. 35, no. 9, September 1992, pp. 160–165.

[NOG00] Nogueira, J., C. Jones, and Luqi, "Surfing the Edge of Chaos: Applications to Software Engineering," Command and Control Research and Technology Symposium, Naval Post Graduate School, Monterey, CA, June 2000, download from http://www.dodccrp.org/2000CCRTS/cd/html/pdf_papers/Track_4/075.pdf.

[REE02] Reed, P., *Developing Applications with Java and UML,* Addison-Wesley, 2002.

[REI95] Reilly, J. P., "Does RAD Live Up to the Hype," *IEEE Software,* September 1995, pp. 24–26.

[ROO96] Roos, J., "The Poised Organization: Navigating Effectively on Knowledge Landscapes," 1996, available at http://www.imd.ch/fac/roos/paper_po.html.

[ROY70] Royce, W. W., "Managing the Development of Large Software Systems: Concepts and Techniques," *Proc. WESCON,* August 1970.

[RUM91] Rumbaugh, J., et al., *Object-Oriented Modeling and Design,* Prentice-Hall, 1991.

[STI01] Stiller, E., and C. LeBlanc, *Project-Based Software Engineering: An Object-Oriented Approach,* Addison-Wesley, 2001.

[WIR90] Wirfs-Brock, R., B. Wilkerson, and L. Weiner, *Designing Object-Oriented Software,* Prentice-Hall, 1990.

[YOU94] Yourdon, E., "Software Reuse," *Application Development Strategies,* vol. 6, no. 12, December, 1994, pp. 1–16.

[YOU95] Yourdon, E., "When Good Enough Is Best," *IEEE Software,* vol. 12, no. 3, May 1995, pp. 79–81.

Problems and Points to Ponder

3.1. Read [NOG00] and write a two- or three-page paper that discusses the impact of "chaos" on software engineering.

3.2. Provide three examples of software projects that would be amenable to the waterfall model. Be specific.

3.3. Provide three examples of software projects that would be amenable to the prototyping model. Be specific.

3.4. What process adaptations are required if the prototype will evolve into a deliverable system or product?

3.5. To achieve rapid development, the RAD model assumes the existence of one thing. What is it, and why is the assumption not always true?

3.6. Provide three examples of software projects that would be amenable to the incremental model. Be specific.

3.7. As you move outward along the spiral process flow, what can you say about the software that is being developed or maintained?

3.8. Is it possible to combine process models? If so, provide an example.

3.9. The concurrent process model defines a set of "states." Describe what these states represent in your own words, and then indicate how they come into play within the concurrent process model.

3.10. What are the advantages and disadvantages of developing software in which quality is "good enough"? That is, what happens when we emphasize development speed over product quality?

3.11. Provide three examples of software projects that would be amenable to the component-based model. Be specific.

3.12. It is possible to prove that a software component and even an entire program is correct. So why doesn't everyone do this?

3.13. Discuss the meaning of "cross-cutting concerns" in your own words. The literature of AOP is expanding rapidly. Do some research and write a brief paper on the current state-of-the-art.

3.14. Are the Unified Process and UML the same thing? Explain your answer.

3.15. What is the difference between a UP phase and a UP workflow?

Further Readings and Information Sources

Most software engineering textbooks consider prescriptive process models in some detail. Books by Sommerville (*Software Engineering,* sixth edition, Addison-Wesley, 2000), Pfleeger (*Software Engineering: Theory and Practice,* Prentice-Hall, 2001), and Schach (*Object-Oriented and Classical Software Engineering,* McGraw-Hill, 2001) consider conventional paradigms and discuss their strengths and weaknesses. Although not specifically dedicated to process, Brooks (*The Mythical Man-Month,* second edition, Addison-Wesley, 1995) presents age-old project wisdom that has everything to do with process. Firesmith and Henderson-Sellers (*The OPEN Process Framework: An Introduction,* Addison-Wesley, 2001) present a general template for creating "flexible, yet disciplined software processes" and discuss process attributes and objectives.

Sharpe and McDermott (*Workflow Modeling: Tools for Process Improvement and Application Development,* Artech House, 2001) present tools for modeling both software and business processes. Jacobson, Griss, and Jonsson (*Software Reuse,* Addison-Wesley, 1997) and McClure (*Software Reuse Techniques,* Prentice-Hall, 1997) present much useful information on component-based development. Heineman and Council (*Component-Based Software Engineering,* Addison-Wesley, 2001) describe the process required to implement component-based systems. Kenett and Baker (*Software Process Quality: Management and Control,* Marcel Dekker, 1999) consider how quality management and process design are intimately connected to one another.

Ambriola (*Software Process Technology,* Springer-Verlag, 2001), Derniame and his colleagues (*Software Process: Principles, Methodology, and Technology,* Springer-Verlag, 1999), and Gruhn and Hartmanis (*Software Process Technology,* Springer-Verlag, 1999) present edited conference proceedings that cover many research and theoretical issues that are relevant to the software process.

Jacobson, Booch, and Rumbaugh have written the seminal book on the Unified Process [JAC99]. However, books by Arlow and Neustadt [ARL02] and a three-volume series by Ambler and Constantine [AMB02] provide excellent complementary information. Krutchen (*The Rational Unified Process,* second edition, Addison-Wesley, 2000) has written a worthwhile introduction to the UP. Project management within the context of the UP is described in detail by Royce (*Software Project Management: A Unified Framework,* Addison-Wesley, 1998). The definitive description of the UP has been developed by the Rational Corporation and is available on-line at www.rational.com.

A wide variety of information sources on software engineering and the software process are available on the Internet. An up-to-date list of World Wide Web references that are relevant to the software process can be found at the SEPA Web site:
http://www.mhhe.com/pressman.

CHAPTER

Agile Development

Key Concepts

In 2001, Kent Beck and 16 other noted software developers, writers, and consultants [BEC01a] (referred to as the "Agile Alliance") signed the "Manifesto for Agile Software Development." It stated:

> We are uncovering better ways of developing software by doing it and helping others do it. Through this work we have come to value:
>
> *Individuals and interactions* over processes and tools
>
> *Working software* over comprehensive documentation
>
> *Customer collaboration* over contract negotiation
>
> *Responding to change* over following a plan
>
> That is, while there is value in the items on the right, we value the items on the left more.

A manifesto is normally associated with an emerging political movement—one that attacks the old guard and suggests revolutionary change (hopefully for the better). In some ways, that's exactly what agile development is all about.

Although the underlying ideas that guide agile development have been with us for many years, it has only been during the past decade that these ideas have crystallized into a "movement." In essence, agile[1] methods were developed in an effort to overcome perceived and actual weaknesses in conventional software engineering. Agile development can provide important benefits, but it is not applicable to all projects, products, people, and situations. It is also *not*

Quick Look

What is it? Agile software engineering combines a philosophy and a set of development guidelines. The philosophy encourages customer satisfaction and early incremental delivery of software; small, highly motivated project teams; informal methods; minimal software engineering work products; and overall development simplicity. The development guidelines stress delivery over analysis and design (although these activities are not discouraged), and active and continuous communication between developers and customers.

Who does it? Software engineers and other project stakeholders (managers, customers, end-users) work together on an agile team—a team that is self-organizing and in control of its own destiny. An agile team fosters communication and collaboration among all who serve on it.

Why is it important? The modern business environment that spawns computer-based systems and software products is fast-paced and

1 Agile methods are sometimes referred to as *light* or *lean* methods.

ever-changing. Agile software engineering represents a reasonable alternative to conventional software engineering for certain classes of software and certain types of software projects. It has been demonstrated to deliver successful systems quickly.

What are the steps? Agile development might best be termed "software engineering lite." The basic framework activities—customer communication, planning, modeling, construction, delivery and evaluation—remain. But they morph into a minimal task set that pushes the project team toward construction and delivery (some would argue that this is done at the expense of problem analysis and solution design).

What is the work product? Customers and software engineers who have adopted the agile philosophy have the same view—the only really important work product is an operational "software increment" that is delivered to the customer on the appropriate commitment date.

How do I ensure that I've done it right? If the agile team agrees that the process works and the team produces deliverable software increments that satisfy the customer, you've done it right.

antithetical to solid software engineering practice and can be applied as an overriding philosophy for all software work.

In the modern economy, it is often difficult or impossible to predict how a computer-based system (e.g., a Web-based application) will evolve as time passes. Market conditions change rapidly, end-user needs evolve, and new competitive threats emerge without warning. In many situations, we no longer are able to define requirements fully before the project begins. Software engineers must be agile enough to respond to a fluid business environment.

Does this mean that a recognition of these modern realities causes us to discard valuable software engineering principles, concepts, methods, and tools? Absolutely not! Like all engineering disciplines, software engineering continues to evolve. It can be adapted easily to meet the challenges posed by a demand for agility.

> "Agility: 1, everything else: 0."
>
> **Tom DeMarco**

In a thought-provoking book on agile software development, Alistair Cockburn [COC02a] argues that the prescriptive process models introduced in Chapter 3 have a major failing: *they forget the frailties of the people who build computer software.* Software engineers are not robots. They exhibit great variation in working styles and significant differences in skill level, creativity, orderliness, consistency, and spontaneity. Some communicate well in written form, others do not. Cockburn argues that process models can "deal with people's common weaknesses with [either] discipline or tolerance" [COC02a] and that most prescriptive process models choose discipline. He states: "Because consistency in action is a human weakness, high discipline methodologies are fragile" [COC02a].

If process models are to work, they must provide a realistic mechanism for encouraging the discipline that is necessary, or they must be characterized in a manner that shows "tolerance" for the people who do software engineering work. Invariably, tolerant practices are easier for software people to adopt and sustain, but (as Cockburn admits) they may be less productive. Like most things in life, trade-offs must be considered.

4.1 What Is Agility?

Just what is agility in the context of software engineering work? Ivar Jacobson [JAC02] provides a useful discussion:

> *Agility* has become today's buzzword when describing a modern software process. Everyone is agile. An agile team is a nimble team able to appropriately respond to changes. Change is what software development is very much about. Changes in the software being built, changes to the team members, changes because of new technology, changes of all kinds that may have an impact on the product they build or the project that creates the product. Support for changes should be built-in everything we do in software, something we embrace because it is the heart and soul of software. An agile team recognizes that software is developed by individuals working in teams and that the skills of these people, their ability to collaborate is at the core for the success of the project.

In Jacobson's view, the pervasiveness of change is the primary driver for agility. Software engineers must be quick on their feet if they are to accommodate the rapid changes that Jacobson describes.

> **Agility is dynamic, content specific, aggressively change embracing, and growth oriented.**
>
> **Steven Goldman et al.**

Don't make the mistake of assuming that agility gives you license to hack out solutions. A process is required, and discipline is essential.

But agility is more than an effective response to change. It also encompasses the philosophy espoused in the manifesto noted at the beginning of this chapter. It encourages team structures and attitudes that make communication (among team members, between technologists and business people, between software engineers and their managers) more facile. It emphasizes rapid delivery of operational software and de-emphasizes the importance of intermediate work products (not always a good thing); it adopts the customer as a part of the development team and works to eliminate the "us and them" attitude that continues to pervade many software projects; it recognizes that planning in an uncertain world has its limits and that a project plan must be flexible.

The Agile Alliance [AGI03] defines 12 principles for those who want to achieve agility:

1. Our highest priority is to satisfy the customer through early and continuous delivery of valuable software.
2. Welcome changing requirements, even late in development. Agile processes harness change for the customer's competitive advantage.
3. Deliver working software frequently, from a couple of weeks to a couple of months, with a preference to the shorter timescale.

4. Business people and developers must work together daily throughout the project.
5. Build projects around motivated individuals. Give them the environment and support they need, and trust them to get the job done.
6. The most efficient and effective method of conveying information to and within a development team is face–to–face conversation.
7. Working software is the primary measure of progress.
8. Agile processes promote sustainable development. The sponsors, developers, and users should be able to maintain a constant pace indefinitely.
9. Continuous attention to technical excellence and good design enhances agility.
10. Simplicity—the art of maximizing the amount of work not done—is essential.
11. The best architectures, requirements, and designs emerge from self–organizing teams.
12. At regular intervals, the team reflects on how to become more effective, then tunes and adjusts its behavior accordingly.

Agility can be applied to any software process. However, to accomplish this, it is essential that the process be designed in a way that allows the project team to adapt tasks and to streamline them, conduct planning in a way that understands the fluidity of an agile development approach, eliminate all but the most essential work products and keep them lean, and emphasize an incremental delivery strategy that gets working software to the customer as rapidly as feasible for the product type and operational environment.

4.2 What Is an Agile Process?

Any *agile software process* is characterized in a manner that addresses three key assumptions [FOW02] about the majority of software projects:

1. It is difficult to predict in advance which software requirements will persist and which will change. It is equally difficult to predict how customer priorities will change as a project proceeds.
2. For many types of software, design and construction are interleaved. That is, both activities should be performed in tandem so that design models are proven as they are created. It is difficult to predict how much design is necessary before construction is used to prove the design.
3. Analysis, design, construction, and testing are not as predictable (from a planning point of view) as we might like.

WebRef
A comprehensive collection of articles on the agile process can be found at **www.aanpo.org/articles/index.**

Given these three assumptions, an important question arises: How do we create a process that can manage unpredictability? The answer, as we have already noted, lies in process adaptability (to rapidly changing project and technical conditions). An agile process, therefore, must be *adaptable.*

But continual adaptation without forward progress accomplishes little. Therefore, an agile software process must adapt *incrementally.* To accomplish incremental adaptation, an agile team requires customer feedback (so that the appropriate adaptations can be made). An effective catalyst for customer feedback is an operational prototype or a portion of an operational system. Hence, an *incremental development strategy* should be instituted. *Software increments* (executable prototypes or a portion of an operational system) must be delivered in short time periods so that adaptation keeps pace with change (unpredictability). This iterative approach enables the customer to evaluate the software increment regularly, provide necessary feedback to the software team, and influence the process adaptations that are made to accommodate the feedback.

> "There is no substitute for rapid feedback, both on the development process and on the product itself."
> **Martin Fowler**

4.2.1 The Politics of Agile Development

There is considerable debate (sometimes strident) about the benefits and applicability of agile software development as opposed to more conventional software engineering processes. Jim Highsmith [HIG02a] (facetiously) states the extremes when he characterizes the feeling of the pro-agility camp ("agilists"). "Traditional methodologists are a bunch of stick-in-the-muds who'd rather produce flawless documentation than a working system that meets business needs." As a counterpoint, he states (again, facetiously) the position of the traditional software engineering camp: "Lightweight, er, 'agile' methodologists are a bunch of glorified hackers who are going to be in for a heck of a surprise when they try to scale up their toys into enterprise-wide software."

Like all software technology arguments, this methodology debate risks degenerating into a religious war. If warfare breaks out, rational thought disappears and beliefs rather than facts guide decision-making.

No one is against agility. The real question is: What is the best way to achieve it? As important, how do we build software that meets customers' needs today and exhibits the quality characteristics that will enable it to be extended and scaled to meet customers' needs over the long term?

You don't have to choose between agility and software engineering. Instead, define a software engineering approach that is agile.

There are no absolute answers to either of these questions. Even within the agile school itself, there are many proposed process models (Section 4.3), each with a subtly different approach to the agility problem. Within each model there is a set of "ideas" (agilists are loath to call them "work tasks") that represent a significant departure from conventional software engineering. And yet, many agile concepts are simply adaptations of good software engineering concepts. Bottom line: there is much that can be gained by considering the best of both schools and virtually nothing to be gained by denigrating either approach.

The interested reader should see [HIG01], [HIG02a], and [DEM02] for an entertaining summary of the important technical and political issues.

4.2.2 Human Factors

Proponents of agile software development take great pains to emphasize the importance of "people factors" in successful agile development. As Cockburn and Highsmith [COC01] state, "Agile development focuses on the talents and skills of individuals, molding the process to specific people and teams." The key point in this statement is that the *process molds to the needs of the people and team,* not the other way around.[2]

> "What counts as barely sufficient for one team is either overly sufficient or insufficient for another."
>
> **Alistair Cockburn**

If members of the software team are to drive the characteristics of the process that is applied to build software, a number of key traits must exist among the people on an agile team and the team itself:

? What key traits must exist among the people on an effective software team?

Competence. In an agile development (as well as conventional software engineering) context, "competence" encompasses innate talent, specific software related skills, and overall knowledge of the process that the team has chosen to apply. Skill and knowledge of process can and should be taught to all people who serve as agile team members.

Common focus. Although members of the agile team may perform different tasks and bring different skills to the project, all should be focused on one goal—to deliver a working software increment to the customer within the time promised. To achieve this goal, the team will also focus on continual adaptations (small and large) that will make the process fit the needs of the team.

Collaboration. Software engineering (regardless of process) is about assessing, analyzing, and using information that is communicated to the software team; creating information that will help the customer and others understand the work of the team; and building information (computer software and relevant databases) that provides business value for the customer. To accomplish these tasks, team members must collaborate—with one another, with the customer, and with business managers.

Decision-making ability. Any good software team (including agile teams) must be allowed the freedom to control its own destiny. This implies that the

---

2 Most successful software engineering organizations recognize this reality regardless of the process model they choose.

team is given autonomy—decision-making authority for both technical and project issues.

Fuzzy problem-solving ability. Software managers should recognize that the agile team will continually have to deal with ambiguity and will continually be buffeted by change. In some cases, the team must accept the fact that the problem they are solving today may not be the problem that needs to be solved tomorrow. However, lessons learned from any problem solving activity (including those that solve the wrong problem) may be of benefit to the team later in the project.

Mutual trust and respect. The agile team must become what DeMarco and Lister [DEM98] call a "jelled" team (see Chapter 21). A jelled team exhibits the trust and respect that are necessary to make them "so strongly knit that the whole is greater than the sum of the parts" [DEM98].

A self-organizing team is in control of the work it performs. The team makes its own commitments and defines plans to achieve them.

Self-organization. In the context of agile development, *self-organization* implies three things: (1) the agile team organizes itself for the work to be done; (2) the team organizes the process to best accommodate its local environment; (3) the team organizes the work schedule to best achieve delivery of the software increment. Self-organization has a number of technical benefits, but more importantly it serves to improve collaboration and boost team morale. In essence, the team serves as its own management. Ken Schwaber [SCH02] addresses these issues when he writes: "The team selects how much work it believes it can perform within the iteration, and the team commits to the work. Nothing demotivates a team as much as someone else making commitments for it. Nothing motivates a team as much as accepting the responsibility for fulfilling commitments that it made itself."

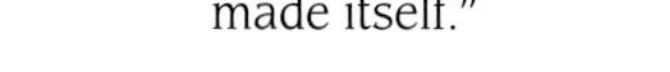

4.3 Agile Process Models

The history of software engineering is littered with dozens of obsolete process descriptions and methodologies, modeling methods and notations, tools, and technology. Each flared in notoriety and was then eclipsed by something new and (purportedly) better. With the introduction of a wide array of agile process models—each contending for acceptance within the software development community—the agile movement is following the same historical path.[3]

> "Our profession goes through methodologies like a 14-year-old goes through clothing."
>
> **Stephen Hawrysh and Jim Ruprecht**

3 This is not a bad thing. Before one or more models or methods are accepted as a de facto standard, all must contend for the hearts and minds of software engineers. The "winners" evolve into best practice while the "losers" either disappear or merge with the winning models.

In the sections that follow, we present an overview of a number of different *agile process models.* There are many similarities (in philosophy and practice) among these approaches. Our intent will be to emphasize those characteristics of each method that make it unique. It is important to note that *all* agile models conform (to a greater or lesser degree) to the *Manifesto for Agile Software Development* and the principles noted in Section 4.1.

4.3.1 Extreme Programming (XP)

Although early work on the ideas and methods associated with *Extreme Programming (XP)* occurred during the late 1980s, the seminal work on the subject, written by Kent Beck [BEC99] was published in 1999. Subsequent books by Jeffries et al [JEF01] on the technical details of XP, and additional work by Beck and Fowler [BEC01b] on XP planning, flesh out the details of the method.

WebRef
An excellent overview of "rules" for XP can be found at **www.extremeprogramming.org/rules.html.**

XP uses an object-oriented approach (Part 2 of this book) as its preferred development paradigm. XP encompasses a set of rules and practices that occur within the context of four framework activities: planning, design, coding, and testing. Figure 4.1 illustrates the XP process and notes some of the key ideas and tasks that are associated with each framework activity. Key XP activities are summarized in the paragraphs that follow.

Planning. The planning activity begins with the creation of a set of *stories* (also called *user stories*) that describe required features and functionality for software to be built. Each story (similar to use-cases described in Chapters 7 and 8) is written by the customer and is placed on an index card. The customer assigns a *value* (i.e., a

FIGURE 4.1
The Extreme Programming process

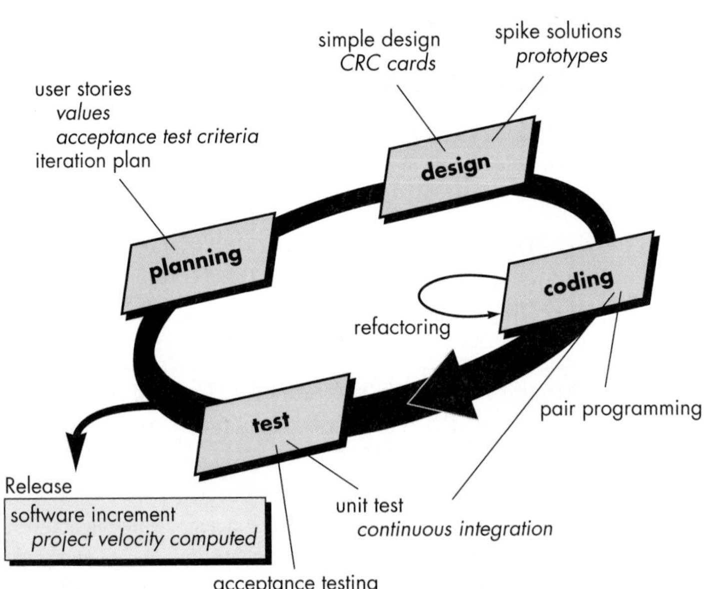

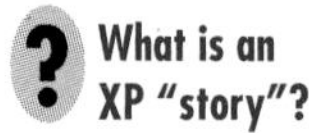
What is an XP "story"?

priority) to the story based on the overall business value of the feature or function.[4] Members of the XP team then assess each story and assign a *cost*—measured in development weeks—to it. If the story will require more than three development weeks, the customer is asked to split the story into smaller stories, and the assignment of value and cost occurs again. It is important to note that new stories can be written at any time.

Customers and the XP team work together to decide how to group stories into the next release (the next software increment) to be developed by the XP team. Once a basic *commitment* (agreement on stories to be included, delivery date, and other project matters) is made for a release, the XP team orders the stories that will be developed in one of three ways: (1) all stories will be implemented immediately (within a few weeks); (2) the stories with highest value will be moved up in the schedule and implemented first; or (3) the riskiest stories will be moved up in the schedule and implemented first.

WebRef
A worthwile XP "planning game" can be found at **c2.com/cgi/wiki?planningGame.**

After the first project release (also called a software increment) has been delivered, the XP team computes project velocity. Stated simply, *project velocity* is the number of customer stories implemented during the first release. Project velocity can then be used to (1) help estimate delivery dates and schedule for subsequent releases, and (2) determine whether an over-commitment has been made for all stories across the entire development project. If an over-commitment occurs, the content of releases is modified or end-delivery dates are changed.

As development work proceeds, the customer can add stories, change the value of an existing story, split stories, or eliminate them. The XP team then reconsiders all remaining releases and modifies its plans accordingly.

> "Extreme Programming is a discipline of software development based on values of simplicity, communication, feedback, and courage."
>
> **Ron Jeffries**

Design. XP design rigorously follows the KIS (keep it simple) principle. A simple design is always preferred over a more complex representation. In addition, the design provides implementation guidance for a story as it is written—nothing less, nothing more. The design of extra functionality (because the developer assumes it will be required later) is discouraged.[5]

XP encourages the use of CRC cards (Chapter 8) as an effective mechanism for thinking about the software in an object-oriented context. CRC (class-responsibility collaborator) cards identify and organize the object-oriented classes[6] that are relevant to the current software increment. The XP team conducts the design exercise using a

4 The value of a story may also depend on the presence of another story.

5 These design guidelines should be followed in every software engineering method, although there are times when sophisticated design notation and terminology may get in the way of simplicity.

6 Object-oriented classes are discussed in detail in Chapter 8 and throughout Part 2 of this book.

process similar to the one described in Chapter 8 (Section 8.7.4). The CRC cards are the only design work product produced as part of the XP process.

If a difficult design problem is encountered as part of the design of a story, XP recommends the immediate creation of an operational prototype of that portion of the design. Called a *spike solution,* the design prototype is implemented and evaluated. The intent is to lower risk when true implementation starts and to validate the original estimates for the story containing the design problem.

WebRef
Refactoring techniques and tools can be found at **www.refactoring.com.**

XP encourages *refactoring*—a construction technique that is also a design technique. Fowler [FOW00] describes refactoring in the following manner:

> Refactoring is the process of changing a software system in such a way that it does not alter the external behavior of the code yet improves the internal structure. It is a disciplined way to clean up code [and modify/simplify the internal design] that minimizes the chances of introducing bugs. In essence, when you refactor you are improving the design of the code after it has been written.

Because XP design uses virtually no notation and produces few, if any work products other than CRC cards and spike solutions, design is viewed as a transient artifact that can and should be continually modified as construction proceeds. The intent of refactoring is to control these modifications by suggesting small design changes that "can radically improve the design" [FOW00]. It should be noted, however, that effort required for refactoring can grow dramatically as the size of an application grows.

A central notion in XP is that design occurs both before *and after* coding commences. Refactoring means that design occurs continuously as the system is constructed. In fact, the construction activity itself will provide the XP team with guidance on how to improve the design.

WebRef
Useful information on XP can be obtained at **www.xprogramming.com.**

Coding. XP recommends that after stories are developed and preliminary design work is done, the team should not move to code, but rather develop a series of unit tests that will exercise each of the stories that is to be included in the current release (software increment).[7] Once the unit test has been created, the developer is better able to focus on what must be implemented to pass the unit test. Nothing extraneous is added (KIS). Once the code is complete, it can be unit tested immediately, thereby providing instantaneous feedback to the developers.

? What is pair programming?

A key concept during the coding activity (and one of the most talked about aspects of XP) is *pair programming.* XP recommends that two people work together at one computer workstation to create code for a story. This provides a mechanism for real-time problem solving (two heads are often better than one) and real-time quality assurance. It also keeps the developers focused on the problem at hand. In practice, each person takes on a slightly different role. For example, one person might think about the coding details of a particular portion of the design while the other ensures

7 This approach is analogous to knowing the exam questions before you begin to study. It makes studying much easier by focusing attention only on the questions that will be asked.

that coding standards (a required part of XP) are being followed and the code that is generated will "fit" into the broader design for the story.

As pair programmers complete their work, the code they develop is integrated with the work of others. In some cases this is performed on a daily basis by an integration team. In other cases, the pair programmers have integration responsibility. This "continuous integration" strategy helps to avoid compatibility and interfacing problems and provides a "smoke testing" environment (Chapter 13) that helps to uncover errors early.

Testing. We have already noted that the creation of a unit test[8] before coding commences is a key element of the XP approach. The unit tests that are created should be implemented using a framework that enables them to be automated (hence, they can be executed easily and repeatedly). This encourages a regression testing strategy (Chapter 13) whenever code is modified (which is often, given the XP refactoring philosophy).

As the individual unit tests are organized into a "universal testing suite" [WEL99], integration and validation testing of the system can occur on a daily basis. This provides the XP team with a continual indication of progress and also can raise warning flags early if things are going awry. Wells [WEL99] states: "Fixing small problems every few hours takes less time than fixing huge problems just before the deadline."

XP acceptance tests are derived from user stories.

XP *acceptance tests,* also called *customer tests,* are specified by the customer and focus on overall system features and functionality that are visible and reviewable by the customer. Acceptance tests are derived from user stories that have been implemented as part of a software release.

SAFEHOME

Considering Agile Software Development

The scene: Doug Miller's office.

The players: Doug Miller, software engineering manager; Jamie Lazar, software team member; Vinod Raman, software team member.

The conversation:

(A knock on the door)

Jamie: Doug, you got a minute?

Doug: Sure Jamie, what's up?

Jamie: We've been thinking about our process discussion yesterday . . . you know, what process we're going to choose for this new *SafeHome* project.

Doug: And?

Vinod: I was talking to a friend at another company, and he was telling me about Extreme Programming. It's an agile process model, heard of it?

Doug: Yeah, some good, some bad.

Jamie: Well, it sounds pretty good to us. Lets you develop software really fast, uses something called pair programming to do real-time quality checks . . . it's pretty cool, I think.

Doug: It does have a lot of really good ideas. I like the pair programming concept, for instance, and the idea that stakeholders should be part of the team.

8 Unit testing, discussed in detail in Chapter 13, focuses on an individual software component, exercising the component's interface, data structures, and functionality in an effort to uncover errors that are local to the component.

Jamie: Huh? You mean that marketing will work on the project team with us?

Doug (nodding): They're a stakeholder, aren't they?

Jamie: Jeez . . . they'll be requesting changes every five minutes.

Vinod: Not necessarily. My friend said that there are ways to "embrace" changes during an XP project.

Doug: So you guys think we should use XP?

Jamie: It's definitely worth considering.

Doug I agree. And even if we choose an incremental model as our approach, there's no reason why we can't incorporate much of what XP has to offer.

Vinod: Doug, before you said "some good, some bad." What was the "bad"?

Doug: The thing I don't like is the way XP downplays analysis and design . . . sort of says that writing code is where the action is.

(The team members look at one another and smile.)

Doug: So you agree with the XP approach?

Jamie (speaking for both): Writing code is what we do, Boss!

Doug (laughing): True, but I'd like to see you spend a little less time coding and then re-coding and a little more time analyzing what has to be done and designing a solution that works.

Vinod: Maybe we can have it both ways, agility with a little discipline.

Doug: I think we can, Vinod. In fact, I'm sure of it.

4.3.2 Adaptive Software Development (ASD)

Adaptive Software Development (ASD) has been proposed by Jim Highsmith [HIG00] as a technique for building complex software and systems. The philosophical underpinnings of ASD focus on human collaboration and team self-organization. Highsmith [HIG98] discusses this when he writes:

> Self-organization is a property of complex adaptive systems similar to a collective "aha," that moment of creative energy when the solution to some nagging problem emerges. Self-organization arises when individual, independent agents (cells in a body, species in an ecosystem, developers in a feature team) cooperate [collaborate] to create emergent outcomes. An emergent outcome is a property beyond the capability of any individual agent. For example, individual neurons in the brain do not possess consciousness, but collectively the property of consciousness emerges. We tend to view this phenomena of collective emergence as accidental, or at least unruly and undependable. The study of self-organization is proving that view to be wrong.

WebRef
Useful resources for ASD can be found at **www.adaptivesd.com.**

Highsmith argues that an agile, adaptive development approach based on collaboration is "as much a source of *order* in our complex interactions as discipline and engineering." He defines an ASD "life cycle" (Figure 4.2) that incorporates three phases: speculation, collaboration, and learning.

Speculation. During *speculation,* the project is initiated and *adaptive cycle planning* is conducted. Adaptive cycle planning uses project initiation information—the customer's mission statement, project constraints (e.g., delivery dates or user descrip-

FIGURE 4.2

Adaptive software development

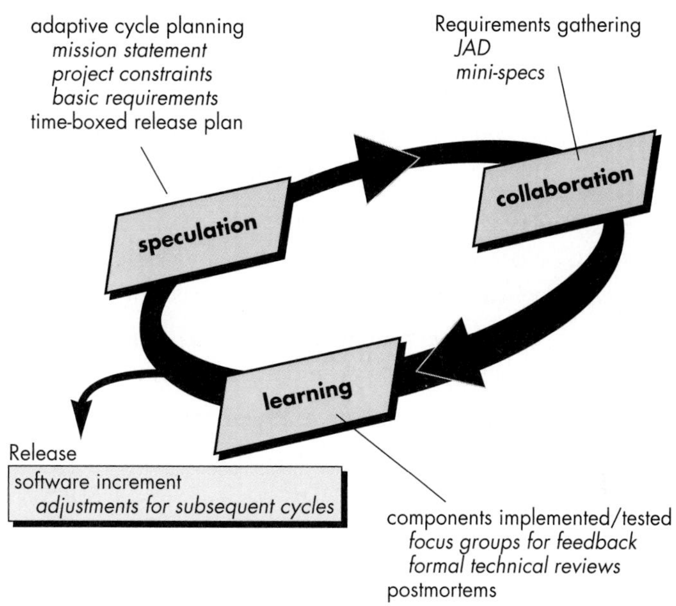

What are the characteristics of ASD adaptive cycles?

Effective collaboration with your customer will only occur if you jettison any "us and them" attitudes.

tions), and basic requirements—to define the set of release cycles (software increments) that will be required for the project.[9]

Collaboration. Motivated people work together in a way that multiplies their talent and creative output beyond their absolute numbers. This collaborative approach is a recurring theme in all agile methods. But collaboration is not easy. It is not simply communication, although communication is a part of it. It is not only a matter of teamwork, although a "jelled" team (Chapter 21) is essential for real collaboration to occur. It is not a rejection of individualism, because individual creativity plays an important role in collaborative thinking. It is, above all, a matter of trust. People working together must trust one another to (1) criticize without animosity; (2) assist without resentment; (3) work as hard or harder as they do; (4) have the skill set to contribute to the work at hand; and (5) communicate problems or concerns in a way that leads to effective action.

> "I like to listen. I have learned a great deal from listening carefully. Most people never listen."
>
> **Ernest Hemingway**

9 Note that the adaptive cycle plan can and probably will be adapted to changing project and business conditions.

Learning. As members of an ASD team begin to develop the components that are part of an adaptive cycle, the emphasis is on learning as much as it is on progress toward a completed cycle. In fact, Highsmith [HIG00] argues that software developers often overestimate their own understanding (of the technology, the process, and the project) and that learning will help them to improve their level of real understanding. ASD teams learn in three ways:

1. **Focus groups.** The customer and/or end-users provide feedback on software increments that are being delivered. This provides a direct indication of whether or not the product is satisfying business needs.
2. **Formal technical reviews.** ASD team members review the software components that are developed, improving quality and learning as they proceed.
3. **Postmortems.** The ASD team becomes introspective, addressing its own performance and process (with the intent of learning and then improving its approach).

It is important to note that the ASD philosophy has merit regardless of the process model that is used. ASD's overall emphasis on the dynamics of self-organizing teams, interpersonal collaboration, and individual and team learning yield software project teams that have a much higher likelihood of success.

4.3.3 Dynamic Systems Development Method (DSDM)

WebRef
Useful resources for DSDM can be found at **www.dsdm.org.**

The *Dynamic Systems Development Method* (DSDM) [STA97] is an agile software development approach that "provides a framework for building and maintaining systems which meet tight time constraints through the use of incremental prototyping in a controlled project environment" [CCS02]. Similar in some respects the RAD process discussed in Chapter 3, DSDM suggests a philosophy that is borrowed from a modified version of the Pareto principle. In this case, 80 percent of an application can be delivered in 20 percent of the time it would take to deliver the complete (100 percent) application.

Like XP and ASD, DSDM suggests an iterative software process. However, the DSDM approach to each iteration follows the 80 percent rule. That is, only enough work is required for each increment to facilitate movement to the next increment. The remaining detail can be completed later when more business requirements are known or changes have been requested and accommodated.

The DSDM Consortium (www.dsdm.org) is a worldwide group of member companies that collectively take on the role of "keeper" of the method. The consortium has defined an agile process model, called the *DSDM life cycle.* The DSDM life cycle defines three different iterative cycles, preceded by two additional life cycle activities:

WebRef
A useful overview of DSDM can be found at **www.cs3inc.com/DSDM.htm.**

Feasibility study—establishes the basic business requirements and constraints associated with the application to be built and then assesses whether the application is a viable candidate for the DSDM process.

Business study—establishes the functional and information requirements that will allow the application to provide business value; also, defines the basic application architecture and identifies the maintainability requirements for the application.

Functional model iteration—produces a set of incremental prototypes that demonstrate functionality for the customer (note: all DSDM prototypes are intended to evolve into the deliverable application). The intent during this iterative cycle is to gather additional requirements by eliciting feedback from users as they exercise the prototype.

Design and build iteration—revisits prototypes built during the functional model iteration to ensure that each has been engineered in a manner that will enable it to provide operational business value for end-users. In some cases, the functional model iteration and the design and build iteration occur concurrently.

Implementation—places the latest software increment (an "operationalized" prototype) into the operational environment. It should be noted that (1) the increment may not be 100 percent complete or (2) changes may be requested as the increment is put into place. In either case, DSDM development work continues by returning to the function model iteration activity.

DSDM can be combined with XP to provide a combination approach that defines a solid process model (the DSDM life cycle) with the nuts and bolts practices (XP) that are required to build software increments. In addition, the ASD concepts of collaboration and self-organizing teams can be adapted to a combined process model.

4.3.4 Scrum

Scrum (the name derived from an activity[10] that occurs during a rugby match) is an agile process model that was developed by Jeff Sutherland and his team in the early 1990s. In recent years, further development of the Scrum methods has been performed by Schwaber and Beedle [SCH01]. Scrum principles [ADM96] are consistent with the agile manifesto:

- Small working teams are organized to "maximize communication, minimize overhead, and maximize sharing of tacit, informal knowledge."
- The process must be adaptable to both technical and business changes "to ensure the best possible product is produced."
- The process yields frequent software increments "that can be inspected, adjusted, tested, documented, and built on."
- Development work and the people who perform it are partitioned "into clean, low coupling partitions, or packets."
- Constant testing and documentation is performed as the product is built.

10 A group of players forms around the ball and the teammates work together (sometimes violently!) to move the ball downfield.

- The Scrum process provides the "ability to declare a product 'done' whenever required (because the competition just shipped, because the company needs the cash, because the user/customer needs the functions, because that was when it was promised. . . ." [ADM96].

WebRef
Useful Scrum information and resources can be found at **www.controlchaos.com.**

Scrum principles are used to guide development activities within a process that incorporates the following framework activities: requirements, analysis, design, evolution, and delivery. Within each framework activity, work tasks occur within a process pattern (discussed in the following paragraph) called a *sprint*. The work conducted within a sprint (the number of sprints required for each framework activity will vary depending on product complexity and size) is adapted to the problem at hand and is defined and often modified in real-time by the Scrum team. The overall flow of the Scrum process is illustrated in Figure 4.3.

> "Scrum allows us to build softer software."
>
> **Mike Beetle et al.**

Scrum emphasizes the use of a set of "software process patterns" [NOY02] that have proven effective for projects with tight timelines, changing requirements, and business criticality. Each of these process patterns defines a set of development activities:

FIGURE 4.3
Scrum process flow

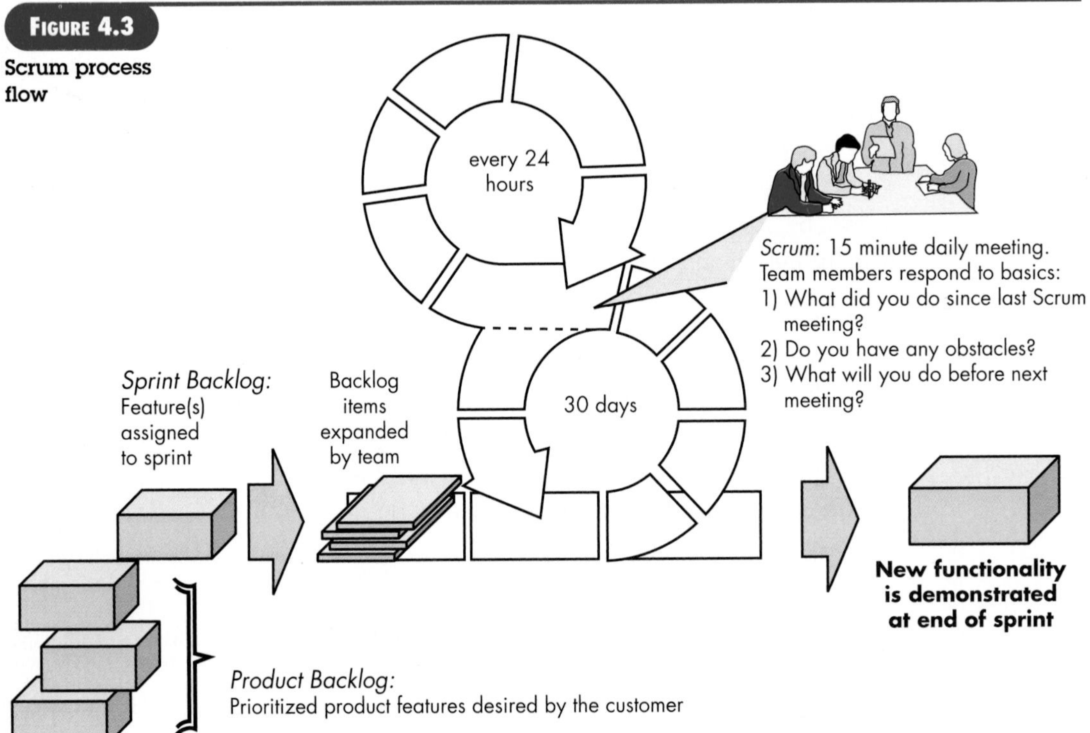
every 24 hours
30 days
Scrum: 15 minute daily meeting.
Team members respond to basics:
1) What did you do since last Scrum meeting?
2) Do you have any obstacles?
3) What will you do before next meeting?
Sprint Backlog:
Feature(s) assigned to sprint
Backlog items expanded by team
New functionality is demonstrated at end of sprint
Product Backlog:
Prioritized product features desired by the customer

Scrum incorporates a set of process patterns that emphasize project priorities, compartmentalized work units, communication, and frequent customer feedback.

Backlog—a prioritized list of project requirements or features that provide business value for the customer. Items can be added to the backlog at any time (this is how changes are introduced). The product manager assesses the backlog and updates priorities as required.

Sprints—consist of work units that are required to achieve a requirement defined in the backlog that must be fit into a predefined time-box (typically 30 days). During the sprint, the backlog items that the sprint work units address are frozen (i.e., changes are not introduced during the sprint). Hence, the sprint allows team members to work in a short-term, but stable environment.

Scrum meetings—are short (typically 15 minutes) meetings held daily by the Scrum team. Three key questions are asked and answered by all team members [NOY02]:

- What did you do since the last team meeting?
- What obstacles are you encountering?
- What do you plan to accomplish by the next team meeting?

A team leader, called a "Scrum master," leads the meeting and assesses the responses from each person. The Scrum meeting helps the team to uncover potential problems as early as possible. Also, these daily meetings lead to "knowledge socialization" [BEE99] and thereby promote a self-organizing team structure.

Demos—deliver the software increment to the customer so that functionality that has been implemented can be demonstrated and evaluated by the customer. It is important to note that the demo may not contain all planned functionality, but rather those functions that can be delivered within the time-box that was established.

Beedle and his colleagues [BEE99] present a comprehensive discussion of these patterns in which they state: "SCRUM assumes up-front the existence of chaos. . . ." The Scrum process patterns enable a software development team to work successfully in a world where the elimination of uncertainty is impossible.

4.3.5 Crystal

Alistair Cockburn [COC02a] and Jim Highsmith [HIG02b] created the *Crystal family of agile methods*[11] in order to achieve a software development approach that puts a premium on "maneuverability" during what Cockburn characterizes as "a resource-limited, cooperative game of invention and communication, with a primary goal of delivering useful, working software and a secondary goal of setting up for the next game" [COC02b].

To achieve maneuverability, Cockburn and Highsmith have defined a set of methodologies, each with core elements that are common to all, and roles, process

11 The name "crystal" is derived from the characteristics of geological crystals, each with its own color, shape, and hardness.

WebRef
A comprehensive discussion of Crystal can be found at **www.crystalmethodologies.org.**

patterns, work products, and practice that are unique to each. The Crystal family is actually a set of agile processes that have been proven effective for different types of projects. The intent is to allow agile teams to select the member of the crystal family that is most appropriate for their project and environment.

4.3.6 Feature Driven Development (FDD)

WebRef
A wide variety of articles and presentations on FDD can be found at **www.thecoadletter.com.**

Feature Driven Development (FDD) was originally conceived by Peter Coad and his colleagues [COA99] as a practical process model for object-oriented software engineering. Stephen Palmer and John Felsing [PAL02] have extended and enhanced Coad's work, describing an adaptive, agile process that can be applied to moderately sized and larger software projects.

In the context of FDD, a *feature* "is a client-valued function that can be implemented in two weeks or less" [COA99]. The emphasis on the definition of features provides the following benefits:

- Because features are small blocks of deliverable functionality, users can describe them more easily, understand how they relate to one another more readily, and better review them for ambiguity, error, or omissions.
- Features can be organized into a hierarchical business-related grouping.
- Since a feature is the FDD deliverable software increment, the team develops operational features every two weeks.
- Because features are small, their design and code representations are easier to inspect effectively.
- Project planning, scheduling, and tracking are driven by the feature hierarchy, rather than an arbitrarily adopted software engineering task set.

Coad and his colleagues [COA99] suggest the following template for defining a feature:

<action> the **<result> <by | for | of | to>** a(n) **<object>**

where an **<object>** is "a person, place, or thing (including roles, moments in time or intervals of time, or catalog-entry-like descriptions)." Examples of features for an e-commerce application might be:

Add the product to a shopping cart.

Display the technical-specifications of a product.

Store the shipping-information for a customer.

A feature set groups related features into business-related categories and is defined [COA99] as:

<action><-ing> a(n) **<object>**

For example: *Making a product sale* is a feature set that would encompass the features noted earlier and others.

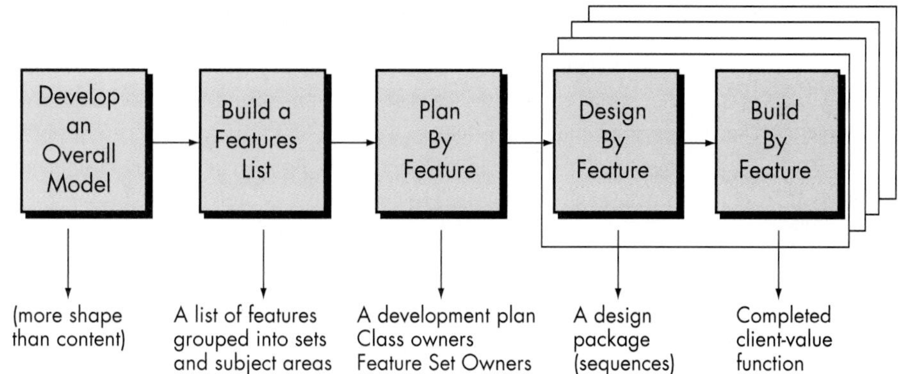

FIGURE 4.4 Feature Driven Development [COA99] (used with permission)

The FDD approach defines five "collaborating" [COA99] framework activities (in FDD these are called "processes") as shown in Figure 4.4.

FDD provides greater emphasis on project management guidelines and techniques than many other agile methods. As projects grow in size and complexity, ad hoc project management is often inadequate. It is essential for developers, their managers, and the customer to understand project status—what accomplishments have been made and problems have been encountered. If deadline pressure is significant, it is critical to determine if software increments (features) are properly scheduled. To accomplish this, FDD defines six milestones during the design and implementation of a feature: "design walkthrough, design, design inspection, code, code inspection, promote to build" [COA99].

4.3.7 Agile Modeling (AM)

> **WebRef**
> Comprehensive information on agile modeling can be found at **www.agilemodeling.com.**

There are many situations in which software engineers must build large, business-critical systems. The scope and complexity of such systems must be modeled so that (1) all constituencies can better understand what needs to be accomplished; (2) the problem can be partitioned effectively among the people who must solve it; and (3) quality can be assessed at every step as the system is being engineered and built.

Over the past 30 years, a wide variety of software engineering modeling methods and notation have been proposed for analysis and design (both architectural and component-level). These methods have significant merit, but they have proven difficult to apply and challenging to sustain (over many projects). Part of the problem is the "weight" of these modeling methods. By this we mean the volume of notation required, the degree of formalism suggested, the size of the models for large projects, and the difficulty in maintaining the model as changes occur. Yet analysis and design modeling have substantial benefit for large projects—if for no other reason than to make these projects intellectually manageable. Is there an agile approach to software engineering modeling that might provide an alternative?

At "The Official Agile Modeling Site," Scott Ambler [AMB02] describes *Agile Modeling* (AM) in the following manner:

> Agile Modeling (AM) is a practice-based methodology for effective modeling and documentation of software-based systems. Simply put, Agile Modeling is a collection of values, principles, and practices for modeling software that can be applied on a software development project in an effective and light-weight manner. Agile models are more effective than traditional models because they are just barely good, they don't have to be perfect.

In addition to the values that are consistent with the agile manifesto, Ambler suggests *courage* and *humility.* An agile team must have the courage to make decisions that may cause it to reject a design and refactor. It must have the humility to recognize that technologists do not have all the answers, that business experts and other stakeholders should be respected and embraced.

Although AM suggests a wide array of "core" and "supplementary" modeling principles, those that make AM unique are [AMB02]:

Model with a purpose. A developer who uses AM should have a specific goal (e.g., to communicate information to the customer or to help better understand some aspect of the software) in mind before creating the model. Once the goal for the model is identified, the type of notation to be used and level of detail required will be more obvious.

Use multiple models. There are many different models and notations that can be used to describe software. Only a small subset is essential for most projects. AM suggests that to provide needed insight, each model should present a different aspect of the system and only those models that provide value to their intended audience should be used.

"Traveling light" is an appropriate philosophy for all software engineering work. Build only those models that provide value—no more, no less.

Travel light. As software engineering work proceeds, keep only those models that will provide long-term value and jettison the rest. Every work product that is kept must be maintained as changes occur. This represents work that slows the team down. Ambler [AMB02] notes that "every time you decide to keep a model you trade-off agility for the convenience of having that information available to your team in an abstract manner (hence potentially enhancing communication within your team as well as with project stakeholders)."

Content is more important than representation. Modeling should impart information to its intended audience. A syntactically perfect model that imparts little useful content is not as valuable as a model with flawed notation that nevertheless provides valuable content for its audience.

Know the models and the tools you use to create them. Understand the strengths and weaknesses of each model and the tools that are used to create it.

Adapt locally. The modeling approach should be adapted to the needs of the agile team.

SOFTWARE TOOLS

Agile Development

Objective: The objective of agile development tools is to assist in one or more aspects of agile development with an emphasis on facilitating the rapid generation of operational software. These tools can also be used when prescriptive process models (Chapter 3) are applied.

Mechanics: Tool mechanics vary. In general, agile tool sets encompass automated support for project planning, use-case development and requirements gathering, rapid design, code generation, and testing.

Representative Tools:[12]

Note: Because agile development is a hot topic, most software tools vendors purport to sell tools that support the agile approach. The tools noted below have characteristics that make them particularly useful for agile projects.

Actif Extreme, developed by Microtool (www.microtool.com), provides agile process management support for various technical activities within the process.

Ideogramic UML, developed by Ideogramic (www.ideogramic.com), is a UML toolset specifically developed for use within an agile process.

Together Tool Set, distributed by Borland (www.borland.com or www.togethersoft.com), provides a tools suite that supports many technical activities within XP and other agile processes.

4.4 SUMMARY

An agile philosophy for software engineering stresses four key issues: the importance of self-organizing teams that have control over the work they perform; communication and collaboration between team members and between practitioners and their customers; a recognition that change represents an opportunity; and an emphasis on rapid delivery of software that satisfies the customer. Agile process models have been designed to address each of these issues.

Extreme Programming (XP) is the most widely used agile process. Organized as four framework activities—planning, design, coding, and testing—XP suggests a number of innovative and powerful techniques that allow an agile team to create frequent software releases delivering features and functionality that have been described and then prioritized by the customer.

Adaptive Software Development (ASD) stresses human collaboration and team self-organization. Organized as three framework activities—speculation, collaboration, and learning—ASD uses an iterative process that incorporates adaptive cycle planning, relatively rigorous requirements gathering methods, and an iterative development cycle that incorporates customer focus groups and formal technical reviews as real-time feedback mechanisms. The Dynamic Systems Development Method (DSDM) defines three different iterative cycles—functional model iteration, design and build iteration, and implementation—preceded by two additional life cycle activities—feasibility study and business study. DSDM advocates the use of time-

12 Tools noted here do not represent an endorsement, but rather a sampling of tools in this category. In most cases, tool names are trademarked by their respective developers.

box scheduling and suggests that only enough work is required for each software increment to facilitate movement to the next increment.

Scrum emphasizes the use of a set of software process patterns that have proven effective for projects with tight timelines, changing requirements, and business criticality. Each process pattern defines a set of development tasks and allows the Scrum team to construct a process that is adapted to the needs of the project.

Crystal is a family of agile process models that can be adopted to the specific characteristics of a project. Like other agile approaches, Crystal adopts an iterative strategy but adjusts the rigor of the process to accommodate projects of different sizes and complexities.

Feature Driven Development (FDD) is somewhat more "formal" than other agile methods, but still maintains agility by focusing the project team on the development of features—client-valued functions that can be implemented in two weeks or less. FDD provides greater emphasis on project and quality management than other agile approaches. Agile Modeling (AM) suggests that modeling is essential for all systems, but that the complexity, type, and size of the model must be tuned to the software to be built. By proposing a set of core and supplementary modeling principles, AM provides useful guidance for the practitioner during analysis and design tasks.

REFERENCES

[ADM96] Advanced Development Methods, Inc., "Origins of Scrum," 1996, http://www.controlchaos.com/.

[AGI03] The Agile Alliance Home Page, http://www.agilealliance.org/home.

[AMB02] Ambler, S., "What Is Agile Modeling (AM)?" 2002, http://www.agilemodeling.com/index.htm.

[BEC99] Beck, K., *Extreme Programming Explained: Embrace Change,* Addison-Wesley, 1999.

[BEC01a] Beck, K., et al., "Manifesto for Agile Software Development," http://www.agilemanifesto. org/.

[BEC01b] Beck, K., and M. Fowler, *Planning Extreme Programming,* Addison-Wesley, 2001.

[BEE99] Beedle, M., et al., "SCRUM: An extension pattern language for hyperproductive software development," included in: *Pattern Languages of Program Design 4,* Addison-Wesley Longman, Reading, MA, 1999. Download at http://jeffsutherland.com/scrum/scrum_plop.pdf.

[BUS00] Buschmann, F., et al., *Pattern-Oriented Software Architecture,* 2 volumes, Wiley, 1996, 2000.

[COA99] Coad, P., E. Lefebvre, and J. DeLuca, *Java Modeling in Color with UML,* Prentice-Hall, 1999.

[COC01] Cockburn, A., and J. Highsmith, "Agile Software Development: The People Factor," *IEEE Computer,* vol. 34, no. 11, November 2001, pp. 131–133.

[COC02a] Cockburn, A., *Agile Software Development,* Addison-Wesley, 2002.

[COC02b] Cockburn, A., "What Is Agile and What Does It Imply?" presented at the Agile Development Summit at Westminster College in Salt Lake City, March 2002, http://crystalmethodologies.org/.

[CCS02] CS3 Consulting Services, 2002, http://www.cs3inc.com/DSDM.htm.

[DEM98] DeMarco, T., and T. Lister, *Peopleware,* 2nd ed., Dorset House, 1998.

[DEM02] DeMarco, T., and B. Boehm, "The Agile Methods Fray," *IEEE Computer,* vol. 35, no. 6, June 2002, pp. 90–92.

[FOW00] Fowler, M., et al., *Refactoring: Improving the Design of Existing Code,* Addison-Wesley, 2000.

[FOW01] Fowler M., and J. Highsmith, "The Agile Manifesto," *Software Development Magazine,* August 2001, http://www.sdmagazine.com/documents/s=844/ sdm0108a/0108a.htm.

[FOW02] Fowler. M., "The New Methodology," June 2002, http://www.martinfowler.com/articles/newMethodology.html#N8B.

[HIG98] Highsmith, J., "Life—The Artificial and the Real," *Software Development,* 1998, at http://www.adaptivesd.com/articles/order.html.

[HIG00] Highsmith, J., *Adaptive Software Development: An Evolutionary Approach to Managing Complex Systems,* Dorset House Publishing, 1998.

[HIG01] Highsmith, J., ed., "The Great Methodologies Debate: Part 1," *Cutter IT Journal,* vol. 14, no. 12, December 2001.

[HIG02a] Highsmith, J., ed., "The Great Methodologies Debate: Part 2," *Cutter IT Journal,* vol. 15, no. 1, January 2002.

[HIG02b] Highsmith, J., *Agile Software Development Ecosystems,* Addison-Wesley, 2002.

[JAC02] Jacobson, I., "A Resounding 'Yes' to Agile Processes—But Also More," *Cutter IT Journal,* vol. 15, no. 1., January 2002, pp. 18–24.

[JEF01] Jeffries, R., et al., *Extreme Programming Installed,* Addison-Wesley, 2001.

[NOY02] Noyes, B., "Rugby, Anyone?" *Managing Development* (an on-line publication of Fawcette Technical Publications), June 2002, http://www.fawcette.com/resources/managingdev/methodologies/scrum/.

[PAL02] Palmer, S., and J. Felsing, *A Practical Guide to Feature Driven Development,* Prentice-Hall, 2002.

[SCH01] Schwaber, K., and M. Beedle, *Agile Software Development with SCRUM,* Prentice-Hall, 2001.

[SCH02] Schwaber, K., "Agile Processes and Self-Organization," Agile Alliance, 2002, http://www.aanpo.org/articles/index.

[STA97] Stapleton, J., *DSDM—Dynamic System Development Method: The Method in Practice,* Addison-Wesley, 1997.

[WEL99] Wells, D., "XP—Unit Tests," 1999, http://www.extremeprogramming.org/ rules/unittests.html.

Problems and Points to Ponder

4.1. Reread "The Manifesto for Agile Software Development" at the beginning of this chapter. Can you think of a situation in which one or more of the four "values" could get a software team into trouble?

4.2. Describe agility (for software projects) in your own words.

4.3. Why does an iterative process make it easier to manage change? Is every agile process discussed in this chapter iterative? Is it possible to complete a project in just one iteration and still be agile? Explain your answers.

4.4. Could each of the agile processes be described using the generic framework activities noted in Chapter 2? Build a table that maps the generic activities into the activities defined for each agile process.

4.5. Try to come up with one more "agility principle" that would help a software engineering team become even more maneuverable.

4.6. Select one agility principle noted in Section 4.1 and try to determine whether each of the process models presented in this chapter exhibits the principle.

4.7. Why do requirements change so much? After all, don't people know what they want?

4.8. Consider the seven traits noted in Section 4.2.2. Order the traits based on your perception of which is most important to which is least important.

4.9. Most agile process models recommend face-to-face communication. Yet today, members of a software team and their customers may be geographically separated from one another. Do you think this implies that geographical separation is something to avoid? Can you think of ways to overcome this problem?

4.10. Write an XP user story that describes the "favorite places" or "favorites" feature available on most Web browsers.

4.11. What is a spike solution in XP?

4.12. Describe the XP concepts of *refactoring* and *pair programming* in your own words.

4.13. Using the process pattern template presented in Chapter 2, develop a process patterns for any one of the Scrum patterns presented in Section 4.3.4.

4.14. Why is Crystal called a *family of agile methods*?

4.15. Using the FDD feature template described in Section 4.3.6, define a feature set for a Web browser. Now develop a set of features for the feature set.

4.16. Visit the Official Agile Modeling Site and make a complete list of all core and supplementary AM principles.

Further Readings and Information Sources

The overall philosophy and underlying principles of agile software development are considered in depth in books by Ambler (*Agile Modeling*, Wiley, 2002), Beck [BEC99], Cockburn [COC02], and Highsmith [HIG02b].

Books by Beck [BEC99], Jeffries and his colleagues (*Extreme Programming Installed,* Addison-Wesley, 2000), Succi and Marchesi (*Extreme Programming Examined,* Addison-Wesley, 2001), Newkirk and Martin (*Extreme Programming in Practice,* Addison-Wesley, 2001), and Auer and his colleagues (*Extreme Programming Applied: Play to Win,* Addison-Wesley, 2001) provide a nuts and bolts discussion of XP along with guidance on how best to apply it. McBreen (*Questioning Extreme Programming,* Addison-Wesley, 2003) takes a critical look at XP, defining when and where it is appropriate. An in-depth consideration of pair programming is presented by McBreen (*Pair Programming Illuminated,* Addison-Wesley, 2003).

Fowler and his colleagues (*Refactoring: Improving the Design of Existing Code,* Addison-Wesley, 1999) address the important XP concept of refactoring in considerable detail. McBreen (*Software Craftsmanship: The New Imperative,* Addison-Wesley, 2001) discusses software craftsmanship and argues for agile alternatives to traditional software engineering

ASD is addressed in depth by Highsmith [HIG00]. A worthwhile treatment of DSDM has been written by Stapleton (*DSDM: The Method in Practice,* Addison-Wesley, 1997). Palmer and Felsing [PAL02] present a detailed treatment of FDD. Carmichael and Haywood (*Better Software Faster,* Prentice-Hall, 2002) presents another useful treatment of FDD that includes a step-by-step journey through the mechanics of the process. Schwaber and his colleagues (*Agile Software Development with SCRUM,* Prentice-Hall, 2001) present a detailed treatment of Scrum.

Martin (*Agile Software Development,* Prentice-Hall, 2003) discusses agile principles, patterns, and practices with an emphasis on XP. Poppendieck and Poppendieck (*Lean Development: An Agile Toolkit for Software Development Managers,* Addison-Wesley, 2003) provide guidelines for managing and controlling agile projects. Highsmith (*Agile Software Development Ecosystems,* Addison-Wesley, 2002) presents a worthwhile survey of agile principles, processes, and practices.

A wide variety of information sources on agile software development are available on the Internet. An up-to-date list of World Wide Web references that are relevant to the agile process can be found at the SEPA Web site:

http://www.mhhe.com/ pressman.

PART

TWO

SOFTWARE ENGINEERING PRACTICE

In this part of *Software Engineering: A Practitioner's Approach* you'll learn about the principles, concepts, and methods that comprise software engineering practice. These questions are addressed in the chapters that follow:

- What concepts and principles guide software engineering practice?
- How does system engineering lead to effective software engineering?
- What is requirements engineering, and what are the underlying concepts that lead to good requirements analysis?
- How is the analysis model created, and what are its elements?
- What is design engineering, and what are the underlying concepts that lead to good design?
- What concepts, models, and methods are used to create architectural, interface, and component-level designs?
- What strategies are applicable to software testing?
- What methods are used to design effective test cases?
- What measures and metrics can be used to assess the quality of analysis and design models, source code, and test cases?

Once these questions are answered you'll be better prepared to apply software engineering practice.

CHAPTER

5 PRACTICE: A GENERIC VIEW

KEY CONCEPTS

In a book that explores the lives and thoughts of software engineers, Ellen Ullman [ULL97] depicts a slice of life as she relates the thoughts of practitioner under pressure:

> I have no idea what time it is. There are no windows in this office and no clock, only the blinking red LED display of a microwave, which flashes 12:00, 12:00, 12:00, 12:00. Joel and I have been programming for days. We have a bug, a stubborn demon of a bug. So the red pulse no-time feels right, like a read-out of our brains, which have somehow synchronized themselves at the same blink rate. . . .
>
> What are we working on? . . . The details escape me just now. We may be helping poor sick people or tuning a set of low-level routines to verify bits on a distributed database protocol—I don't care. I should care; in another part of my being—later, perhaps when we emerge from this room full of computers—I will care very much why and for whom and for what purpose I am writing software. But just now: no. I have passed through a membrane where the real world and its uses no longer matter. I am a software engineer. . . .

A dark image of software engineering practice to be sure, but upon reflection, many of the readers of this book will be able to relate to it.

QUICK LOOK

What is it? Practice is a broad array of concepts, principles, methods, and tools that you must consider as software is planned and developed. It represents the details—the technical considerations and how to's—that are below the surface of the software process: the things that you'll need to actually build high-quality computer software.

Who does it? The practice of software engineering is applied by software engineers and their managers.

Why is it important? The software process provides everyone involved in the creation of a computer-based system or product with a road map for getting to a destination successfully. Practice provides you with the detail you'll need to drive along the road. It tells you where the bridges, the roadblocks, and the forks are located. It helps you understand the concepts and principles that must be understood and followed to drive safely and rapidly. It instructs you on how to drive, where to slow down, and where to speed up. In the context of software engineering, practice is what you do day in and day out as software evolves from an idea to a reality.

What are the steps? Three elements of practice apply regardless of the process model that is chosen. They are: concepts, principles, and methods. A fourth element of practice—tools—supports the application of methods.

What is the work product? Practice encompasses the technical activities that produce all work products that are defined by the software process model that has been chosen.

How do I ensure that I've done it right? First, have a firm understanding of the concepts and principles that apply to the work (e.g., design) that you're doing at the moment. Then, be certain that you've chosen an appropriate method for the work; be sure that you understand how to apply the method and use automated tools when they're appropriate for the task, and be adamant about the need for techniques to ensure the quality of work products that are produced.

People who create computer software practice the art or craft or discipline[1] that is software engineering. But what is software engineering "practice"? In a generic sense, *practice* is a collection of concepts, principles, methods, and tools that a software engineer calls upon on a daily basis. Practice allows managers to manage software projects and software engineers to build computer programs. Practice populates a software process model with the necessary technical and management how-to's to get the job done. Practice transforms a haphazard unfocused approach into something that is more organized, more effective, and more likely to achieve success.

5.1 Software Engineering Practice

WebRef
A variety of thought-provoking quotes on the practice of software engineering can be found at **www.literateprogramming.com.**

In Chapter 2, we introduced a generic software process model composed of a set of activities that establish a framework for software engineering practice. Generic framework activities—communication, planning, modeling, construction, and deployment—and umbrella activities establish a skeleton architecture for software engineering work. All of the software process models presented in Chapters 3 and 4 can be mapped into this skeleton architecture. But how does the practice of *software engineering* fit in? In the sections that follow, we consider the generic concepts and principles that apply to framework activities.[2]

5.1.1 The Essence of Practice

You might argue that Polya's approach is simply common sense. True. But it's amazing how often common sense is uncommon in the software world.

In a classic book, *How to Solve It,* written before modern computers existed, George Polya [POL45] outlined the essence of problem solving, and consequently, the essence of software engineering practice:

1. *Understand the problem* (communication and analysis).
2. *Plan a solution* (modeling and software design).
3. *Carry out the plan* (code generation).
4. *Examine the result for accuracy* (testing and quality assurance).

1 Some writers argue for one of these terms to the exclusion of the others. In reality, software engineering is all three.

2 The reader is encouraged to revisit relevant sections within this chapter as specific software engineering methods and umbrella activities are discussed later in this book.

In the context of software engineering, these common sense steps lead to a series of essential questions [adapted from POL45]:

Understand the problem.

- *Who has a stake in the solution to the problem?* That is, who are the stakeholders?
- *What are the unknowns?* What data, functions, features, and behavior are required to properly solve the problem?
- *Can the problem be compartmentalized?* Is it possible to represent smaller problems that may be easier to understand?
- *Can the problem be represented graphically?* Can an analysis model be created?

Plan the solution.

- *Have you seen similar problems before?* Are there patterns that are recognizable in a potential solution? Is there existing software that implements the data, functions, features, and behavior that are required?
- *Has a similar problem been solved?* If so, are elements of the solution reusable?
- *Can subproblems be defined?* If so, are solutions readily apparent for the subproblems?
- *Can you represent a solution in a manner that leads to effective implementation?* Can a design model be created?

Carry out the plan.

- *Does the solution conform to the plan?* Is source code traceable to the design model?
- *Is each component part of the solution probably correct?* Has the design and code been reviewed, or better, have correctness proofs been applied to the algorithm?

Examine the result.

- *Is it possible to test each component part of the solution?* Has a reasonable testing strategy been implemented?
- *Does the solution produce results that conform to the data, functions, features, and behavior that are required?* Has the software been validated against all stakeholder requirements?

> "There is a grain of discovery in the solution of any problem."
>
> George Polya.

5.1.2 Core Principles

The dictionary defines the word *principle* as "an important underlying law or assumption required in a system of thought." Throughout this book we discuss principles at many different levels of abstraction. Some focus on software engineering as a whole, others consider a specific generic framework activity (e.g., customer communication), and still others focus on software engineering actions (e.g., architectural design) or technical tasks (e.g., write a usage scenario). Regardless of their level of focus, principles help us establish a mind set for solid software engineering practice. They are important for that reason.

David Hooker [HOO96] has proposed seven core principles that focus on software engineering practice as a whole. They are reproduced below:[3]

Before beginning a software project, be sure the software has a business purpose and that users perceive value in it.

The First Principle: *The Reason It All Exists*

A software system exists for one reason: *to provide value to its users.* All decisions should be made with this in mind. Before specifying a system requirement, before noting a piece of system functionality, before determining the hardware platforms or development processes, ask yourself questions such as: Does this add real value to the system? If the answer is no, don't do it. All other principles support this one.

The Second Principle: *KISS (Keep It Simple, Stupid!)*

Software design is not a haphazard process. There are many factors to consider in any design effort. *All design should be as simple as possible, but no simpler.* This facilitates having a more easily understood, and easily maintained system. This is not to say that features, even internal features, should be discarded in the name of simplicity. Indeed, the more elegant designs are usually the simple ones. Simple also does not mean "quick and dirty." In fact, it often takes a lot of thought and work over multiple iterations to simplify. The pay-off is software that is more maintainable and less error-prone.

> "There is a certain majesty in simplicity which is far above all the quaintness of wit."
> **Alexander Pope (1688–1744)**

The Third Principle: *Maintain the Vision*

A clear vision is essential to the success of a software project. Without one, a project almost unfailingly ends up being "of two [or more] minds" about itself. Without conceptual integrity, a system threatens to become a patchwork of incompatible designs, held together by the wrong kind of screws. . . .

Compromising the architectural vision of a software system weakens and will eventually break even a well-designed system. Having an empowered architect

---

3 Reproduced with permission of the author [HOO96]. Hooker defines patterns for these principles at: http://c2.com/cgi/wiki?SevenPrinciplesOfSoftwareDevelopment.

who can hold the vision and enforce compliance helps ensure a very successful software project.

KEY POINT

If software has value, it will change over its useful life. For that reason, software must be built to be maintainable.

The Fourth Principle: *What You Produce, Others Will Consume*

Seldom is an industrial-strength software system constructed and used in a vacuum. In some way or other, someone else will use, maintain, document, or otherwise depend on being able to understand your system. So, *always specify, design, and implement knowing someone else will have to understand what you are doing.* The audience for any product of software development is potentially large. Specify with an eye to the users. Design, keeping the implementers in mind. Code with concern for those who must maintain and extend the system. Someone may have to debug the code you write, and that makes them a user of your code. Making their job easier adds value to the system.

The Fifth Principle: *Be Open to the Future*

A system with a long lifetime has more value. In today's computing environments, where specifications change on a moment's notice and hardware platforms are obsolete after just a few months, software lifetimes are typically measured in months instead of years. However, true "industrial-strength" software systems must endure far longer. To do this successfully, these systems must be ready to adapt to these and other changes. Systems that do this successfully are those that have been designed this way from the start. *Never design yourself into a corner.* Always ask "what if," and prepare for all possible answers by creating systems that solve the general problem, not just the specific one.[4] This could very possibly lead to the reuse of an entire system.

The Sixth Principle: *Plan Ahead for Reuse*

Reuse saves time and effort.[5] Achieving a high level of reuse is arguably the hardest goal to accomplish in developing a software system. The reuse of code and designs has been proclaimed as a major benefit of using object-oriented technologies. However, the return on this investment is not automatic. To leverage the reuse possibilities that object-oriented [or conventional] programming provides requires forethought and planning. There are many techniques to realize reuse at every level of the system development process. Those at the detailed design and code level are well known and documented. New literature is addressing the reuse of design in the form of software patterns. However, this is just part of the battle.

---

4 Author's note: This advice can be dangerous if it is taken to extremes. Designing for the "general problem" sometimes requires performance compromises and can require more project effort.

5 Author's note: Although this is true for those who reuse the software on future projects, reuse can be expensive for those who must design and build reusable components. Studies indicate that designing and building reusable components can cost between 25 to 200 percent more than targeted software. In some cases, the cost differential cannot be justified.

Communicating opportunities for reuse to others in the organization is paramount. How can you reuse something that you don't know exists? *Planning ahead for reuse reduces the cost and increases the value of both the reusable components and the systems into which they are incorporated.*

The Seventh Principle: *Think!*

This last Principle is probably the most overlooked. *Placing clear, complete thought before action almost always produces better results.* When you think about something, you are more likely to do it right. You also gain knowledge about how to do it right again. If you do think about something and still do it wrong, it becomes valuable experience. A side effect of thinking is learning to recognize when you don't know something, at which point you can research the answer. When clear thought has gone into a system, value comes out. Applying the first six Principles requires intense thought, for which the potential rewards are enormous.

If every software engineer and every software team simply followed Hooker's seven principles, many of the difficulties we experience in building complex computer-based systems would be eliminated.

5.2 Communication Practices

Before customer requirements can be analyzed, modeled, or specified they must be gathered through a *communication* (also called *requirements elicitation*) activity. A customer has a problem that may be amenable to a computer-based solution. A developer responds to the customer's request for help. Communication has begun. But the road from communication to understanding is often full of potholes.

Effective communication (among technical peers, with the customer and other stakeholders, and with project managers) is among the most challenging activities that confront a software engineer. In this context, we discuss communication principles and concepts as they apply to customer communication. However, many of the principles apply equally to all forms of communication that occur within a software project.

Before communicating be sure you understand the point of view of the other party, know a bit about his or her needs, and then listen.

Principle #1: *Listen.* Try to focus on the speaker's words, rather than formulating your response to those words. Ask for clarification if something is unclear, but avoid constant interruptions. Never become contentious in your words or actions (e.g., rolling your eyes or shaking your head) as a person is talking.

Principle #2: *Prepare before you communicate.* Spend the time to understand the problem before you meet with others. If necessary, do some research to understand business domain jargon. If you have responsibility for conducting a meeting, prepare an agenda in advance of the meeting.

Principle #3: *Someone should facilitate the activity.* Every communication meeting should have a leader (facilitator) to keep the conversation moving in a productive direction; (2) to mediate any conflict that does occur; (3) to ensure than other principles are followed.

Principle #4: *Face-to-face communication is best.* But it usually works better when some other representation of the relevant information is present. For example, a participant may create a drawing or a "strawman" document that serves as a focus for discussion.

> "Plain questions and plain answers make the shortest road to most perplexities."
>
> **Mark Twain**

Principle #5: *Take notes and document decisions.* Things have a way of falling into the cracks. Someone participating in the communication should serve as a "recorder" and write down all important points and decisions.

Principle #6: *Strive for collaboration.* Collaboration and consensus occur when the collective knowledge of members of the team is combined to describe product or system functions or features. Each small collaboration serves to build trust among team members and creates a common goal for the team.

Principle #7: *Stay focused, modularize your discussion.* The more people involved in any communication, the more likely that discussion will bounce from one topic to the next. The facilitator should keep the conversation modular, leaving one topic only after it has been resolved (however, see Principle #9)

INFO

The Difference Between Customers and End-Users

Software engineers communicate with many different stakeholders, but customers and end-users have the most significant impact on the technical work that follows. In some cases the customer and the end-user are one in the same, but for many projects, the customer and the end-user are different people, working for different managers in different business organizations.

A *customer* is the person or group who: (1) originally requested the software to be built; (2) defines overall business objectives for the software; (3) provides basic product requirements; and (4) coordinates funding for the project. In a product or system business, the customer is often the marketing department. In an IT environment, the customer might be a business component or department.

An *end-user* is the person or group who: (1) will actually use the software that is built to achieve some business purpose, and (2) will define operational details of the software so the business purpose can be achieved.

Principle #8: *If something is unclear, draw a picture.* Verbal communication goes only so far. A sketch or drawing can often provide clarity when words fail to do the job.

Principle #9: *(a) Once you agree to something, move on; (b) If you can't agree to something, move on; (c) If a feature or function is unclear and can-*

? What happens if I can't come to an agreement with the customer on some project-related issue?

not be clarified at the moment, move on. Communication, like any software engineering activity, takes time. Rather than iterating endlessly, the people who participate should recognize that many topics require discussion (see Principle #2) and that "moving on" is sometimes the best way to achieve communication agility.

Principle #10: *Negotiation is not a contest or a game. It works best when both parties win.* There are many instances in which the software engineer and the customer must negotiate functions and features, priorities, and delivery dates. If the team has collaborated well, all parties have a common goal. Therefore, negotiation will demand compromise from all parties.

SAFEHOME

Communication Mistakes

The scene: Software engineering team workspace.

The players: Jamie Lazar, software team member; Vinod Raman, software team member; Ed Robbins software team member.

The conversation:

Ed: What have you heard about this *SafeHome* project?

Vinod: The kick-off meeting is scheduled for next week.

Jamie: I've already done a little bit of investigation, but it didn't go well."

Ed: What do you mean?

Jamie: Well, I gave Lisa Perez a call. She's the marketing honcho on this thing."

Vinod: And . . . ?

Jamie: I wanted her to tell me about *SafeHome* features and functions . . . that sort of thing. Instead, she began asking me questions about security systems, surveillance systems . . . I'm no expert.

Vinod: What does that tell you?

(Jamie shrugs.)

Vinod: That marketing will need us to act as consultants and that we'd better do some homework on this product area before our kick-off meeting. Doug said that he wanted us to "collaborate" with our customer, so we'd better learn how to do that.

Ed: Probably would have been better to stop by her office. Phone calls just don't work as well for this sort of thing.

Jamie: You're both right. We've got to get our act together or our early communications will be a struggle.

Vinod: I saw Doug reading a book on "requirements engineering." I'll bet that lists some principles of good communication. I'm going to borrow it from him.

Jamie: Good idea . . . then you can teach us.

Vinod (smiling): Yeah, right.

TASK SET

Generic Task Set for Communication

1. Identify primary customer and other stakeholders (Section 7.3.1).
2. Meet with primary customer to address "context free questions" (Section 7.3.4) that define:
   - Business need and business values.
   - End-users' characteristics/needs.
   - Required user-visible outputs.
   - Business constraints.

3. Develop a one-page written statement of project scope that is subject to revision (Sections 7.4.1 and 21.3.1).
4. Review statement of scope with stakeholders and amend as required.
5. Collaborate with customer/end-users to define:
   - Customer visible usage scenarios using standard format[6] (Section 7.5).
   - Resulting outputs and inputs.
   - Important software features, functions, and behavior.
   - Customer-defined business risks (Section 25.3).
6. Develop a brief written description (e.g., a set of lists) of scenarios, output/inputs, features/functions and risks.
7. Iterate with customer to refine scenarios, output/inputs, features/functions and risks.
8. Assign customer-defined priorities to each user scenario, feature, function, and behavior. (Section 7.4.2).
9. Review all information gathered during the communication activity with the customer and other stakeholders and amend as required.
10. Prepare for planning activity (Chapters 23 and 24).

5.3 Planning Practices

The communication activity helps a software team to define its overall goals and objectives (subject, of course, to change as time passes). However, understanding these goals and objectives is not the same as defining a plan for getting there. The *planning* activity encompasses a set of management and technical practices that enable the software team to define a road map as it travels toward its strategic goal and tactical objectives.

> "In preparing for battle I have always found that plans are useless, but planning is indispensable."
>
> **Dwight D. Eisenhower**

There are many different planning philosophies. Some people are "minimalists," arguing that change often obviates the need for a detailed plan. Others are "traditionalists," arguing that the plan provides an effective road map, and the more detail it has, the less likely the team will become lost. Still others are "agilists," arguing that a quick "planning game" may be necessary, but that the road map will emerge as "real work" on the software begins.

What to do? On many projects, overplanning is time consuming and fruitless (too many things change), but underplanning is a recipe for chaos. Like most things in life, planning should be conducted in moderation, enough to provide useful guidance for the team—no more, no less.

WebRef
An excellent repository of planning and project management information can be found at **www.4pm.com/repository.htm.**

Regardless of the rigor with which planning is conducted, the following principles always apply.

Principle #1: *Understand the scope of the project.* It's impossible to use a road map if you don't know where you're going. Scope provides the software team with a destination.

6 Formats for usage scenarios are discussed in Chapter 8.

Principle #2: *Involve the customer in the planning activity.* The customer defines priorities and establishes project constraints. To accommodate these realities, software engineers must often negotiate order of delivery, timelines, and other project related issues.

Principle #3: *Recognize that planning is iterative.* A project plan is never engraved in stone. As work begins, it is very likely that things will change. As a consequence, the plan must be adjusted to accommodate these changes. In addition, iterative, incremental process models dictate replanning (after the delivery of each software increment) based on feedback received from users.

Principle #4: *Estimate based on what you know.* The intent of estimation is to provide an indication of effort, cost, and task duration, based on the team's current understanding of the work to be done. If information is vague or unreliable, estimates will be equally unreliable.

Principle #5: *Consider risk as you define the plan.* If the team has defined risks that have high impact and high probability, contingency planning is necessary. In addition, the project plan (including the schedule) should be adjusted to accommodate the likelihood that one or more of these risks will occur.

Principle #6: *Be realistic.* People don't work 100 percent of every day. Noise always enters into any human communication. Omissions and ambiguity are facts of life. Change will occur. Even the best software engineers make mistakes. These and other realities should be considered as a project plan is established.

> "Success is more a function of consistent common sense than it is of genius."
>
> **An Wang**

The term *granularity* refers to the detail with which some element of planning is represented or conducted.

Principle #7: *Adjust granularity as you define the plan.* *Granularity* refers to the level of detail that is introduced as a project plan is developed. A "fine granularity" plan provides significant work task detail that is planned over relatively short time increments (so that tracking and control occur frequently). A "coarse granularity" plan provides broader work tasks that are planned over longer time periods. In general, granularity moves from fine to coarse as the project timeline moves away from the current date. Over the next few weeks or months, the project can be planned in significant detail. Activities that won't occur for many months do not require fine granularity (too much can change).

Principle #8: *Define how you intend to ensure quality.* The plan should identify how the software team intends to ensure quality. If formal technical reviews[7] are to be conducted, they should be scheduled. If pair programming (Chapter 4) is to be used during construction, it should be explicitly defined within the plan.

---

7 Formal technical reviews are discussed in Chapter 26.

Principle #9: *Describe how you intend to accommodate change.* Even the best planning can be obviated by uncontrolled change. The software team should identify how changes are to be accommodated as software engineering work proceeds. For example, can the customer request a change at any time? If a change is requested, is the team obliged to implement it immediately? How is the impact and cost of the change assessed?

Principle #10: *Track the plan frequently and make adjustments as required.* Software projects fall behind schedule one day at a time. Therefore, it makes sense to track progress on a daily basis, looking for problem areas and situations in which scheduled work does not conform to actual work conducted. When slippage is encountered, the plan is adjusted accordingly.

To be most effective, everyone on the software team should participate in the planning activity. Only then will team members "sign up" to the plan.

In an excellent paper on software process and projects, Barry Boehm [BOE96] states: "You need an organizing principle that scales down to provide simple [project] plans for simple projects." Boehm suggests an approach that addresses project objectives, milestones and schedules, responsibilities, management and technical approaches, and required resources. He calls it the *W^5HH principle*, after a series of questions that lead to a definition of key project characteristics and the resultant project plan:

? What questions must be asked and answered to develop a realistic project plan?

Why is the system being developed? All parties should assess the validity of business reasons for the software work. Stated in another way, does the business purpose justify the expenditure of people, time, and money?

What will be done? Identify the functionality to be built, and by implication, the tasks required to get the job done.

When will it be accomplished? Establish a workflow and timeline for key project tasks and identify the milestones required by the customer.

Who is responsible for a function? The role and responsibility of each member of the software team must be defined.

Where are they organizationally located? Not all roles and responsibilities reside within the software team itself. The customer, users, and other stakeholders also have responsibilities.

How will the job be done technically and managerially? Once product scope is established, a management and technical strategy for the project must be defined.

How much of each resource is needed? The answer to this question is derived by developing estimates (Chapter 23) based on answers to earlier questions.

The answers to Boehm's W^5HH questions are important regardless of the size or complexity of a software project. But how does the planning process begin?

> "We think that software developers are missing a vital truth: most organizations don't know what they do. They think they know, but they don't know."
>
> Tom DeMarco

TASK SET

Generic Task Set for Planning

1. Reevaluate project scope (Sections 7.4 and 21.3).
2. Assess risks (Section 25.4).
3. Develop and/or refine user scenarios (Sections 7.5 and 8.5).
4. Extract functions and features from the scenarios (Section 8.5).
5. Define technical functions and features that enable software infrastructure .
6. Group functions and features (scenarios) by customer priority
7. Create a coarse granularity project plan (Chapters 23 and 24).
   - Define the number of projected software increments.
   - Establish an overall project schedule (Chapter 24).
   - Establish projected delivery dates for each increment.
8. Create a fine granularity plan for the current iteration (Chapters 23 and 24).
   - Define work tasks for each function feature (Section 23.6).
   - Estimate effort for each work task (Section 23.6).
   - Assign responsibility for each work task (Section 23.4).
   - Define work products to be produced.
   - Identify quality assurance methods to be used (Chapter 26).
   - Describe methods for managing change (Chapter 27).
9. Track progress regularly (Section 24.5.2).
   - Note problem areas (e.g., schedule slippage).
   - Make adjustments as required.

5.4 Modeling Practice

We create models to gain a better understanding of the actual entity to be built. When the entity is a physical thing (e.g., a building, a plane, a machine), we can build a model that is identical in form and shape but smaller in scale. However, when the entity is software, our model must take a different form. It must be capable of representing the information that software transforms, the architecture and functions that enable the transformation to occur, the features that the users desires, and the behavior of the system as the transformation is taking place. Models must accomplish these objectives at different levels of abstraction—first depicting the software from the customer's viewpoint and later representing the software at a more technical level.

Analysis models represent customer requirements. Design models provide a concrete specification for the construction of the software.

In software engineering work, two classes of models are created: analysis models and design models. *Analysis models* represent the customer requirements by depicting the software in three different domains: the information domain, the functional domain, and the behavioral domain. *Design models* represent characteristics of the software that help practitioners to construct it effectively: the architecture (Chapter 10), the user interface (Chapter 12), and component-level detail (Chapter 11).

In the sections that follow we present basic principles and concepts that are relevant to analysis and design modeling. The technical methods and notation that allow software engineers to create analysis and design models are presented in later chapters.

> "The engineer's first problem in any design situation is to discover what the problem really is."
>
> **Author unknown**

5.4.1 Analysis Modeling Principles

Over the past three decades, a large number of analysis modeling methods have been developed. Investigators have identified analysis problems and their causes and have developed a variety of modeling notations and corresponding sets of heuristics to overcome them. Each analysis method has a unique point of view. However, all analysis methods are related by a set of operational principles:

Principle #1: *The information domain of a problem must be represented and understood.* The *information domain* encompasses the data that flow into the system (from end-users, other systems, or external devices), the data that flow out of the system (via the user interface, network interfaces, reports, graphics, and other means) and the data stores that collect and organize persistent data objects (i.e., data that are maintained permanently).

Analysis modeling focuses on three attributes of software: information to be processed, function to be delivered, and behavior to be exhibited.

Principle #2: *The functions that the software performs must be defined.* Software functions provide direct benefit to end-users and also provide internal support for those features that are user visible. Some functions transform data that flow into the system. In other cases, functions effect some level of control over internal software processing or external system elements. Functions can be described at many different levels of abstraction, ranging from a general statement of purpose to a detailed description of the processing elements that must be invoked.

Principle #3: *The behavior of the software (as a consequence of external events) must be represented.* The behavior of computer software is driven by its interaction with the external environment. Input provided by end-users, control data provided by an external system, or monitoring data collected over a network all cause the software to behave in a specific way.

Principle #4: *The models that depict information, function, and behavior must be partitioned in a manner that uncovers detail in a layered (or hierarchical) fashion.* Analysis modeling is the first step in software engineering problem solving. It allows the practitioner to better understand the problem and establishes a basis for the solution (design). Complex problems are difficult to solve in their entirety. For this reason, we use a divide and conquer strategy. A large, complex problem is divided into subproblems until each subproblem is relatively easy to understand. This concept is called *partitioning*, and it is a key strategy in analysis modeling.

Principle #5: *The analysis task should move from essential information toward implementation detail.* Analysis modeling begins by describing the problem from the end-user's perspective. The "essence" of the problem is described without any consideration of how a solution will be implemented. For example, a video game requires that the player "instruct" its protagonist on what direction to proceed as she moves into a dangerous maze. That is the essence of the problem. Implementation detail (normally described as part of the design model) indicates how the essence will be implemented. For the video game, voice input might be used. Alternatively, a keyboard command might be typed or a joystick (or mouse) might be pointed in a specific direction.

TASK SET

Generic Task Set for Analysis Modeling

1. Review business requirements, end-users' characteristics/needs, user-visible outputs, business constraints, and other technical requirements that were determined during the customer communication and planning activities.
2. Expand and refine user scenarios (Section 8.5).
   - Define all actors.
   - Represent how actors interact with the software.
   - Extract functions and features from the user scenarios.
   - Review the user scenarios for completeness and accuracy (Section 26.4).
3. Model the information domain (Section 8.3).
   - Represent all major information objects.
   - Define attributes for each information object.
   - Represent the relationships between information objects.
4. Model the functional domain (Section 8.6).
   - Show how functions modify data objects.
   - Refine functions to provide elaborative detail.
   - Write a processing narrative that describes each function and subfunction.
   - Review the functional models (Section 26.4).
5. Model the behavioral domain (Section 8.8).
   - Identify external events that cause behavioral changes within the system.
   - Identify states that represent each externally observable mode of behavior.
   - Depict how an event causes the system to move from one state to another.
   - Review the behavioral models (Section 26.4).
6. Analyze and model the user interface (Chapter 12).
   - Conduct task analysis.
   - Create screen image prototypes.
7. Review all models for completeness, consistency and omissions.

5.4.2 Design Modeling Principles

The software design model is the equivalent of an architect's plans for a house. It begins by representing the totality of the thing to be built (e.g., a three-dimensional rendering of the house) and slowly refines the thing to provide guidance for constructing each detail (e.g., the plumbing layout). Similarly, the design model that is created for software provides a variety of different views of the system.

> "See first that the design is wise and just: that ascertained, pursue it resolutely; do not for one repulse forego the purpose that you resolved to effect."
>
> **William Shakespeare**

There is no shortage of methods for deriving the various elements of a software design. Some methods are data-driven, allowing the data structure to dictate the program architecture and the resultant processing components. Others are pattern-driven, using information about the problem domain (the analysis model) to develop architectural styles and processing patterns. Still others are object-oriented, using problem domain objects as the driver for the creation of data structures and the methods that manipulate them. Yet all embrace a set of design principles that can be applied regardless of the method that is used:

Principle #1: *Design should be traceable to the analysis model.* The analysis model describes the information domain of the problem, user visible functions, system behavior, and a set of analysis classes that package business objects with the methods that service them. The design model translates this information into an architecture: a set of subsystems that implement major functions, and a set of component-level designs that are the realization of analysis classes. With the exception of design associated with the software infrastructure, the elements of the design model should be traceable to the analysis model.

WebRef
Insightful comments on the design process, along with a discussion of design aesthetics, can be found at **cs.wwc.edu/~aabyan/Design/.**

Principle #2: *Always consider the architecture of the system to be built.* Software architecture (Chapter 10) is the skeleton of the system to be built. It affects interfaces, data structures, program control flow and behavior, the manner in which testing can be conducted, the maintainability of the resultant system, and much more. For all of these reasons, design should start with architectural considerations. Only after the architecture has been established should component-level issues be considered.

Principle #3: *Design of data is as important as design of processing functions.* Data design is an essential element of architectural design. The manner in which data objects are realized within the design cannot be left to chance. A well-structured data design helps to simplify program flow, makes the design and implementation of software components easier, and makes overall processing more efficient.

Principle #4: *Interfaces (both internal and external) must be designed with care.* The manner in which data flows between the components of a system has much to do with processing efficiency, error propagation, and design simplicity. A well-designed interface makes integration easier and assists the tester in validating component functions.

Principle #5: *User interface design should be tuned to the needs of the end-user.* *However, in every case, it should stress ease of use.* The user interface is the visible manifestation of the software. No matter how sophisticated its internal functions, no matter how comprehensive its data structures, no matter how well-designed its architecture, a poor interface design often leads to the perception that the software is "bad."

Principle #6: *Component-level design should be functionally independent.* Functional independence is a measure of the "single-mindedness" of a software component. The functionality that is delivered by a component should be *cohesive*—that is, it should focus on one and only one function or subfunction.[8]

Principle #7: *Components should be loosely coupled to one another and to the external environment.* *Coupling* is achieved in many ways—via a component interface, by messaging, through global data. As the level of coupling increases, the likelihood or error propagation also increases and the overall maintainability of the software decreases. Therefore, component coupling should be kept as low as is reasonable.

Principle #8: *Design representations (models) should be easily understandable.* The purpose of design is to communicate information to practitioners who will generate code, to those who will test the software, and to others who may maintain the software in the future. If the design is difficult to understand, it will not serve as an effective communication medium.

Principle #9: *The design should be developed iteratively. With each iteration, the designer should strive for greater simplicity.* Like almost all creative activities, design occurs iteratively. The first iterations work to refine the design and correct errors, but later iterations should strive to make the design as simple as is possible.

When these design principles are properly applied, the software engineer creates a design that exhibits both external and internal quality factors. *External quality factors* are those properties of the software that can be readily observed by users (e.g., speed, reliability, correctness, usability). *Internal quality factors* are of importance to software engineers. They lead to a high-quality design from the technical perspective. To achieve internal quality factors, the designer must understand basic design concepts (Chapter 9).

INFO

Agile Modeling

In his book on agile modeling, Scott Ambler [AMB02] defines a set of principles[9] that are applicable when analysis and design are conducted within the context of the agile software development philosophy (Chapter 4):

Principle #1: The primary goal of the software team is to build software, not create models.

Principle #2: Travel light—don't create more models than you need.

Principle #3: Strive to produce the simplest model that will describe the problem or the software.

Principle #4: Build models in a way that makes them amenable to change.

Principle #5: Be able to state an explicit purpose for each model that is created.

---

8 Additional discussion of cohesion can be found in Chapter 9.

9 The principles noted in this section have been abbreviated and rephrased for the purposes of this book.

Principle #6: Adapt the models you develop to the system at hand.

Principle #7: Try to build useful models, but forget about building perfect models.

Principle #8: Don't become dogmatic about the syntax of the model. If it communicates content successfully, representation is secondary.

Principle #9: If your instincts tell you a model isn't right even though it seems okay on paper, you probably have reason to be concerned.

Principle #10: Get feedback as soon as you can.

Regardless of the process model that is chosen or the specific software engineering practices that are applied, every software team wants to be agile. Therefore, these principles can and should be applied regardless of the software process model that is chosen.

TASK SET

Generic Task Set for Design

1. Using the analysis model, select an architectural style (pattern) that is appropriate for the software (Chapter 10).
2. Partition the analysis model into design subsystems and allocate these subsystems within the architecture (Chapter 10).
   - Be certain that each subsystem is functionally cohesive.
   - Design subsystem interfaces.
   - Allocate analysis classes or functions to each subsystem.
   - Using the information domain model, design appropriate data structures.
3. Design the user interface (Chapter 12).
   - Review results of task analysis.
   - Specify action sequence based on user scenarios.
   - Create behavioral model of the interface.
   - Define interface objects, control mechanisms.
   - Review the interface design and revise as required (Section 26.4).
4. Conduct component-level design (Chapter 11).
   - Specify all algorithms at a relatively low level of abstraction.
   - Refine the interface of each component.
   - Define component level data structures.
   - Review the component level design (Section 26.4).
5. Develop a deployment model (Section 9.4.5).

5.5 Construction Practice

The *construction* activity encompasses a set of coding and testing tasks that lead to operational software that is ready for delivery to the customer or end-user. In modern software engineering work, coding may be: (1) the direct creation of programming language source code; (2) the automatic generation of source code using an intermediate design-like representation of the component to be built; (3) the automatic generation of executable code using a fourth generation programming language (e.g., Visual C++).

> "For much of my life, I have been a software voyeur, peeking furtively at other people's dirty code. Occasionally, I find a real jewel, a well-structured program written in a consistent style, free of kludges, developed so that each component is simple and organized, and designed so that the product is easy to change."
>
> **David Parnas**

The initial focus of testing is at the component level, often called *unit testing*. Other levels of testing include: (1) *integration testing* (conducted as the system is constructed); (2) *validation testing* that assesses whether requirements have been met for the complete system (or software increment); and (3) *acceptance testing* that is conducted by the customer in an effort to exercise all required features and functions.

A set of fundamental principles and concepts are applicable to coding and testing. They are considered in the sections that follow.

5.5.1 Coding Principles and Concepts

The principles and concepts that guide the coding task are closely aligned programming style, programming languages, and programming methods. However, there are a number of fundamental principles that can be stated:

Avoid developing an elegant program that solves the wrong problem. Pay particular attention to the first preparation principle.

Preparation principles: *Before you write one line of code, be sure you:*

1. Understand the problem you're trying to solve.
2. Understand basic design principles and concepts.
3. Pick a programming language that meets the needs of the software to be built and the environment in which it will operate.
4. Select a programming environment that provides tools that will make your work easier.
5. Create a set of unit tests that will be applied once the component you code is completed.

WebRef
A wide variety of links to coding standards can be found at **www.literateprogramming.com/fpstyle.html.**

Coding principles: *As you begin writing code, be sure you:*

1. Constrain your algorithms by following structured programming [BOH00] practice.
2. Select data structures that will meet the needs of the design.
3. Understand the software architecture and create interfaces that are consistent with it.
4. Keep conditional logic as simple as possible.
5. Create nested loops in a way that makes them easily testable.
6. Select meaningful variable names and follow other local coding standards.
7. Write code that is self-documenting.
8. Create a visual layout (e.g., indentation and blank lines) that aids understanding.

Validation principles: *After you've completed your first coding pass, be sure you:*

1. Conduct a code walkthrough when appropriate.

2. Perform unit tests and correct errors you've uncovered.
3. Refactor the code.

Books on coding and the principles that guide it include early works on programming style [KER78], practical software construction [MCC93], programming pearls [BEN99], the art of programming [KNU99], pragmatic programming issues [HUN99], and many, many others.

TASK SET

Generic Task Set for Construction

1. Build architectural infrastructure (Chapter 10).
   - Review the architectural design.
   - Code and test the components that enable architectural infrastructure.
   - Acquire reusable architectural patterns.
   - Test the infrastructure to ensure interface integrity.
2. Build a software component (Chapter 11).
   - Review the component-level design.
   - Create a set of unit tests for the component (Sections 13.3.1 and 14.7).
   - Code component data structures and interface.
   - Code internal algorithms and related processing functions.
   - Review code as it is written (Section 26.4).
   - Look for correctness.
   - Ensure that coding standards have been maintained.
   - Ensure that the code is self-documenting.
3. Unit test the component.
   - Conduct all unit tests.
   - Correct errors uncovered.
   - Reapply unit tests.
4. Integrate completed component into the architectural infrastructure.

5.5.2 Testing Principles

In a classic book on software *testing,* Glen Myers [MYE79] states a number of rules that can serve well as testing objectives:

? What are the objectives of software testing?

- Testing is a process of executing a program with the intent of finding an error.
- A good test case is one that has a high probability of finding an as-yet undiscovered error.
- A successful test is one that uncovers an as-yet-undiscovered error.

These objectives imply a dramatic change in viewpoint for some software developers. They move counter to the commonly held view that a successful test is one in which no errors are found. Our objective is to design tests that systematically uncover different classes of errors and to do so with a minimum amount of time and effort.

Davis [DAV95] suggests a set of testing principles[10] that have been adapted for use in this book:

10 Only a small subset of Davis's testing principles are noted here. For more information, see [DAV95].

Principle #1: ***All tests should be traceable to customer requirements.***[11] The objective of software testing is to uncover errors. It follows that the most severe defects (from the customer's point of view) are those that cause the program to fail to meet its requirements.

Principle #2: ***Tests should be planned long before testing begins.*** Test planning (Chapter 13) can begin as soon as the analysis model is complete. Detailed definition of test cases can begin as soon as the design model has been solidified. Therefore, all tests can be planned and designed before any code has been generated.

In a broader software design context, recall that we begin "in the large" by focusing on software architecture and end "in the small" focusing on components. For testing, we simply reverse the focus and test our way out.

Principle #3: ***The Pareto principle applies to software testing.*** Stated simply, the Pareto principle implies that 80 percent of all errors uncovered during testing will likely be traceable to 20 percent of all program components. The problem, of course, is to isolate these suspect components and to thoroughly test them.

Principle #4: ***Testing should begin "in the small" and progress toward testing "in the large."*** The first tests planned and executed generally focus on individual components. As testing progresses, focus shifts in an attempt to find errors in integrated clusters of components and ultimately in the entire system.

Principle #5: ***Exhaustive testing is not possible.*** The number of path permutations for even a moderately sized program is exceptionally large. For this reason, it is impossible to execute every combination of paths during testing. It is possible, however, to adequately cover program logic and to ensure that all conditions in the component-level design have been exercised (Chapter 14).

TASK SET

Generic Task Set for Testing

1. Design unit tests for each software component (Section 13.3.1).
   Review each unit test to ensure proper coverage.
   Conduct the unit test.
   Correct errors uncovered.
   Reapply unit tests.
2. Develop an integration strategy (Section 13.3.2).
   Establish order of and strategy to be used for integration.
   Define "builds" and the tests required to exercise them.
   Conduct smoke testing on a daily basis.
   Conduct regression tests as required.
3. Develop validation strategy (Section 13.5).
   Establish validation criteria.
   Define tests required to validate software.
4. Conduct integration and validation tests.
   Correct errors uncovered.
   Reapply tests as required.
5. Conduct high-order tests.
   Perform recovery testing (Section 13.6.1).
   Perform security testing (Section 13.6.2).
   Perform stress testing (Section 13.6.3).
   Perform performance testing (Section 13.6.4) .
6. Coordinate acceptance tests with customer (Section 13.5.3).

11 This principle refers to *functional* tests, i.e., tests that focus on requirements. *Structural* tests (tests that focus on architectural or logical detail) may not address specific requirements directly.

5.6 Deployment

As we noted in Chapter 2, the deployment activity encompasses three actions: delivery, support, and feedback. Because modern software process models are evolutionary in nature, deployment happens not once, but a number of times as software moves toward completion. Each delivery cycle provides the customer and end-users with an operational software increment that provides usable functions and features. Each support cycle provides documentation and human assistance for all functions and features introduced during all deployment cycles to date. Each feedback cycle provides the software team with important guidance that results in modifications to the functions, features, and approach taken for the next increment.

The delivery of a software increment represents an important milestone for any software project. A number of key principles should be followed as the team prepares to deliver an increment:

Be sure that your customer knows what to expect before a software increment is delivered. Otherwise, you can bet the customer will expect more than you deliver.

Principle #1: *Customer expectations for the software must be managed.* Too often, the customer expects more than the team has promised to deliver and disappointment occurs immediately. This results in feedback that is not productive and ruins team morale. In her book on managing expectations, Naomi Karten [KAR94] states: "The starting point for managing expectations is to become more conscientious about what you communicate and how." She suggests that a software engineer must be careful about sending the customer conflicting messages (e.g., promising more than you can reasonably deliver in the time frame provided or delivering more than you promise for one software increment and then less than promised for the next).

Principle #2: *A complete delivery package should be assembled and tested.* A CD-ROM or other media containing all executable software, support data files, support documents, and other relevant information must be assembled and thoroughly beta-tested with actual users. All installation scripts and other operational features should be thoroughly exercised in all possible computing configurations (i.e., hardware, operating systems, peripheral devices, networking arrangements).

Principle #3: *A support regime must be established before the software is delivered.* An end-user expects responsiveness and accurate information when a question or problem arises. If support is ad hoc, or worse, nonexistent, the customer will become dissatisfied immediately. Support should be planned, support material should be prepared, and appropriate record keeping mechanisms should be established so that the software team can conduct a categorical assessment of the kinds of support requested.

Principle #4: *Appropriate instructional materials must be provided to end-users.* The software team delivers more than the software itself. Appropriate training aids (if required) should be developed, trouble-shooting guidelines should be provided, and a "what's-different-about-this-software-increment" description should be published.[12]

Principle #5: *Buggy software should be fixed first, delivered later.* Under time pressure, some software organizations deliver low-quality increments with a warning to the customer that bugs "will be fixed in the next release." This is a mistake. There's a saying in the software business: "Customers will forget you delivered a high-quality product a few days late, but they will never forget the problems that a low-quality product caused them. The software reminds them every day."

The delivered software provides benefit for the end-user, but it also provides useful *feedback* for the software team. As the increment is put into use, the end-users should be encouraged to comment on features and functions, ease of use, reliability, and any other characteristics that are appropriate. Feedback should be collected and recorded by the software team and used to (1) make immediate modifications to the delivered increment (if required); (2) define changes to be incorporated into the next planned increment; (3) make necessary design modifications to accommodate changes; and (4) revise the plan (including delivery schedule) for the next increment to reflect the changes.

TASK SET

Generic Task Set for Deployment

1. Create delivery media.
   - Assemble and test all executable files.
   - Assemble and test all data files.
   - Create and test all user documentation.
   - Implement electronic (e.g., pdf) versions.
   - Implement hypertext "help" files.
   - Implement a troubleshooting guide.
   - Test delivery media with a small group of representative users.
2. Establish human support person or group.
   - Create documentation and/or computer support tools.
   - Establish contact mechanisms (e.g., Web site, phone, e-mail).
   - Establish problem-logging mechanisms.
   - Establish problem-reporting mechanisms.
   - Establish problem/error reporting database.
3. Establish user feedback mechanisms.
   - Define feedback process.
   - Define feedback forms (paper and electronic).
   - Establish feedback database.
   - Define feedback assessment process.
4. Disseminate delivery media to all users.
5. Conduct on-going support functions.
   - Provide installation and start-up assistance.
   - Provide continuing troubleshooting assistance.
6. Collect user feedback.
   - Log feedback.
   - Assess feedback.
   - Communicate with users on feedback.

12 During the communication activity, the software team should determine what types of help materials users want.

5.7 Summary

Software engineering practice encompasses concepts, principles, methods, and tools that software engineers apply throughout the software process. Every software engineering project is different, yet a set of generic principles and tasks apply to each process framework activity regardless of the project or the product.

A set of technical and management essentials are necessary if good software engineering practice is to be conducted. Technical essentials include the need to understand requirements and prototype areas of uncertainty, and the need to explicitly define software architecture and plan component integration. Management essentials include the need to define priorities and define a realistic schedule that reflects them, the need to actively manage risk, and the need to define appropriate project control measures for quality and change.

Customer communication principles focus on the need to reduce noise and improve bandwidth as the conversation between developer and customer progresses. Both parties must collaborate for the best communication to occur.

Planning principles all focus on guidelines for constructing the best map for the journey to a completed system or product. The plan may be designed solely for a single software increment, or it may be defined for the entire project. Regardless, it must address what will be done, who will do it, and when the work will be completed.

Modeling encompasses both analysis and design, describing representations of the software that progressively become more detailed. The intent of the models is to solidify understanding of the work to be done and to provide technical guidance to those who will implement the software.

Construction incorporates a coding and testing cycle in which source code for a component is generated and tested to uncover errors. Integration combines individual components and involves a series of tests that focus on overall function and local interfacing issues. Coding principles define generic actions that should occur before code is written, while it is being created, and after it has been completed. Although there are many testing principles, only one is dominant: testing is a process of executing a program with the intent of finding an error.

During evolutionary software development, deployment happens for each software increment that is presented to the customer. Key principles for delivery consider managing customer expectations and providing the customer with appropriate support information for the software. Support demands advance preparations. Feedback allows the customer to suggest changes that have business value and provide the developer with input for the next iterative software engineering cycle.

References

[AMB02] Ambler, S., and R. Jeffries, *Agile Modeling,* Wiley, 2002.

[BEN99] Bentley, J., *Programming Pearls,* 2nd ed., Addison-Wesley, 1999.

[BOE96] Boehm, B., "Anchoring the Software Process," *IEEE Software,* vol. 13, no. 4, July 1996, pp. 73–82.

[BOH00] Bohl, M., and M. Rynn, *Tools for Structured Design: An Introduction to Programming Logic,* 5th ed., Prentice-Hall, 2000.

[DAV95] Davis, A., *201 Principles of Software Development,* McGraw-Hill, 1995.

[FOW99] Fowler, M., et al., *Refactoring: Improving the Design of Existing Code,* Addison-Wesley, 1999.

[GAR95] Garlan, D., and M. Shaw, "An Introduction to Software Architecture," *Advances in Software Engineering and Knowledge Engineering,* vol. I (V. Ambriola and G. Tortora, eds.), World Scientific Publishing Company, 1995.

[HIG00] Highsmith, J., *Adaptive Software Development: An Evolutionary Approach to Managing Complex Systems,* Dorset House Publishing, 2000.

[HOO96] Hooker, D., "Seven Principles of Software Development," September 1996, available at http://c2.com/cgi/wikiSevenPrinciplesOfSoftwareDevelopment.

[HUN95] Hunt, D., A. Bailey, and B. Taylor, *The Art of Facilitation,* Perseus Book Group, 1995.

[HUN99] Hunt, A., D. Thomas, and W. Cunningham, *The Pragmatic Programmer,* Addison-Wesley, 1999.

[JUS99] Justice, T., et al., *The Facilitator's Fieldbook,* AMACOM, 1999.

[KAN93] Kaner, C., J. Falk, and H. Q. Nguyen, *Testing Computer Software,* 2nd ed., Van Nostrand-Reinhold, 1993.

[KAN96] Kaner, S., et al., *The Facilitator's Guide to Preparatory Decision Making,* New Society Publishing, 1996.

[KAR94] Karten, N., *Managing Expectations,* Dorset House, 1994.

[KER78] Kernighan, B., and P. Plauger, *The Elements of Programming Style,* 2nd ed., McGraw-Hill, 1978.

[KNU98] Knuth, D., *The Art of Computer Programming,* 3 volumes, Addison-Wesley, 1998.

[MCC93] McConnell, S., *Code Complete,* Microsoft Press, 1993.

[MCC97] McConnell, S., "Software's Ten Essentials," *IEEE Software,* vol. 14, no. 2, March/April, 1997, pp. 143–144.

[MYE78] Myers, G., *Composite Structured Design,* Van Nostrand, 1978.

[MYE79] Myers, G., *The Art of Software Testing,* Wiley, 1979.

[PAR72] Parnas, D. L., "On Criteria to Be Used in Decomposing Systems into Modules," *CACM,* vol. 14, no. 1, April 1972, pp. 221–227.

[POL45] Polya, G., *How to Solve It,* Princeton University Press, 1945.

[ROS75] Ross, D., J. Goodenough, and C. Irvine, "Software Engineering: Process, Principles and Goals," *IEEE Computer,* vol. 8, no. 5, May 1975.

[SHA95a] Shaw, M., and D. Garlan, "Formulations and Formalisms in Software Architecture," *Volume 1000—Lecture Notes in Computer Science,* Springer-Verlag, 1995.

[SHA95b] Shaw, M., et al., "Abstractions for Software Architecture and Tools to Support Them," *IEEE Trans. Software Engineering,* vol. SE-21, no. 4, April 1995, pp. 314–335.

[STE74] Stevens, W., G. Myers, and L. Constantine, "Structured Design," *IBM Systems Journal,* vol. 13, no. 2, 1974, pp. 115–139.

[TAY90] Taylor, D. A., *Object-Oriented Technology: A Manager's Guide,* Addison-Wesley, 1990.

[ULL97] Ullman, E., *Close to the Machine: Technophilia and its Discontents,* City Lights Books, 1997.

[WIR71] Wirth, N., "Program Development by Stepwise Refinement," *CACM,* vol. 14, no. 4, 1971, pp. 221–227.

[WOO95] Wood, J., and D. Silver, *Joint Application Design,* Wiley, 1995.

[ZAH90] Zahniser, R. A., "Building Software in Groups," *American Programmer,* vol. 3, nos. 7–8, July–August 1990.

Problems and Points to Ponder

5.1. Try to summarize David Hooker's "Seven Principles for Software Development" (Section 5.1) in a brief paragraph. Try to distill his guidance into just a few sentences without using his words.

5.2. Are there other technical "essentials" that might be recommended for software engineering? State each and explain why you've included it.

5.3. Are there other management "essentials" that might be recommended for software engineering? State each and explain why you've included it.

5.4. An important communication principle states "prepare before you communicate." How should this preparation manifest itself in the early work that you do? What work products might result as a consequence of early preparation?

5.5. Do some research of "facilitation" for the communication activity (use the references provided or others) and prepare a set of guidelines that focus solely on facilitation.

5.6. How does agile communication differ from tradition software engineering communication? How is it similar?

5.7. Why is it necessary to "move on"?

5.8. Do some research on "negotiation" for the communication activity, and prepare a set of guidelines that focus solely on negotiation.

5.9. Describe what *granularity* means in the context of a project schedule.

5.10. Why are models important in software engineering work? Are they always necessary? Are there qualifiers to your answer about necessity?

5.11. What three "domains" are considered during analysis modeling?

5.12. Try to add one additional principle to those stated for coding in Section 5.6.

5.13. What is a successful test?

5.14. Do you agree or disagree with the following statement: "Since we deliver multiple increments to the customer, why should we be concerned about quality in the early increments—we can fix problems in later iterations"? Explain your answer.

5.15. Why is feedback important to the software team?

Further Readings and Information Sources

Customer communication is a critically important activity in software engineering, yet few practitioner's spend any time reading about it. Books by Pardee (*To Satisfy and Delight Your Customer,* Dorset House, 1996) and Karten [KAR94] provide much insight into methods for effective customer interaction. Communication and planning concepts and principles are considered in many project management books. Useful project management offerings include: Hughs and Cotterell (*Software Project Management,* second edition, McGraw-Hill, 1999), Phillips (*The Software Project Manager's Handbook,* IEEE Computer Society Press, 1998), McConnell (*Software Project Survival Guide,* Microsoft Press, 1998), and Gilb (*Principles of Software Engineering Management,* Addison-Wesley, 1988).

Virtually every book on software engineering contains a useful discussion on concepts and principles for analysis, design and testing. Among the better offerings are books by Endres and his colleagues (*Handbook of Software and Systems Engineering,* Addison-Wesley, 2003), Sommerville (*Software Engineering,* sixth edition, Addison Wesley, 2000), Pfleeger (*Software Engineering: Theory and Practice,* Prentice-Hall, 2001) and Schach (*Object-Oriented and Classical*

Software Engineering, McGraw-Hill, 2001). An excellent collection of software engineering principles has been compiled by Davis [DAV95].

Modeling concepts and principles are considered in many books dedicated to requirements analysis and/or software design. Young (*Effective Requirements Practices,* Addison-Wesley, 2001) emphasizes a "joint team" of customers and developers who develop requirements collaboratively. Weigers (*Software Requirements,* Microsoft Press, 1999) presents many key requirements engineering and requirements management practices. Somerville and Kotonya (*Requirements Engineering: Processes and Techniques,* Wiley, 1998) discuss "elicitation" concepts and techniques and other requirements engineering principles.

Norman's (*The Design of Everyday Things,* Currency/Doubleday, 1990) is must reading for every software engineer who intends to do design work. Winograd and his colleagues (*Bringing Design to Software,* Addison-Wesley, 1996) have edited an excellent collection of essays that address practical issues for software design. Constantine and Lockwood (*Software for Use,* Addison-Wesley, 1999) present the concepts associated with "user-centered design." Tognazzini (*Tog on Software Design,* Addison-Wesley, 1995) presents a worthwhile philosophical discussion of the nature of design and the impact of decisions on quality and a team's ability to produce software that provides great value to its customer.

Hundreds of books address one or more elements of the construction activity. Kernighan and Plauger [KER78] have written a classic text on programming style, McConnell [MCC93] presents pragmatic guidelines for practical software construction, Bentley [BEN99] suggests a wide variety of programming pearls, Knuth [KNU98] has written a classic three-volume series on the art of programming, and Hunt [HUN99] suggests pragmatic programming guidelines. The testing literature has blossomed over the past decide. Myers [MYE79] remains a classic. Books by Whittaker (*How to Break Software,* Addison-Wesley, 2002), Kaner and his colleagues (*Lessons Learned in Software Testing,* Wiley, 2001), and Marick (*The Craft of Software Testing,* Prentice-Hall, 1997) each present important testing concepts and principles and much pragmatic guidance.

A wide variety of information sources on software engineering practice are available on the Internet. An up-to-date list of World Wide Web references that are relevant to software engineering practice can be found at the SEPA Web site:
http://www.mhhe.com/pressman.

CHAPTER

6 SYSTEM ENGINEERING

KEY CONCEPTS

Almost 500 years ago, Machiavelli said, "There is nothing more difficult to take in hand, more perilous to conduct or more uncertain in its success, than to take the lead in the introduction of a new order of things." During the past 50 years, computer-based systems have introduced a new order. Although technology has made great strides since Machiavelli spoke, his words continue to ring true.

Software engineering occurs as a consequence of a process called *system engineering*. Instead of concentrating solely on software, system engineering focuses on a variety of elements, analyzing, designing, and organizing those elements into a system that can be a product, a service, or a technology for the transformation of information or control.

The system engineering process takes on different forms depending on the application domain in which it is applied. *Business process engineering* is conducted when the context of the work focuses on a business enterprise. When a product (in this context, a product includes everything from a wireless telephone to an air traffic control system) is to be built, the process is called *product engineering*.

Both business process engineering and product engineering attempt to bring order to the development of computer-based systems. Although each is applied in a different application domain, both strive to put software into context. That is,

QUICK LOOK

What is it? Before software can be engineered, the "system" in which it resides must be understood. To accomplish this, the overall objective of the system must be determined; the role of hardware, software, people, database, procedures, and other system elements must be identified; and operational requirements must be elicited, analyzed, specified, modeled, validated, and managed. These activities are the foundation of system engineering.

Who does it? A system engineer works to understand system requirements by working with the customer, future users, and other stakeholders.

Why is it important? There's an old saying: "You can't see the forest for the trees." In this context, the "forest" is the system, and the trees are the technology elements (including software) that are required to realize the system. If you rush to build technology elements before you understand the system, you'll undoubtedly make mistakes that will disappoint your customer. Before you worry about the trees, understand the forest.

What are the steps? Objectives and more detailed operational requirements are identified by eliciting information from the customer; requirements are analyzed to assess their clarity, completeness, and consistency; a specification, often incorporating a system model, is created and then validated by both practitioners and customers. Finally, system requirements are managed to ensure that changes are properly controlled.

What is the work product? An effective representation of the system must be produced as a consequence of system engineering. This can be a prototype, a specification or even a symbolic model, but it must communicate the operational, functional, and behavioral characteristics of the system to be built and provide insight into the system architecture.

How do I ensure that I've done it right? Review all system engineering work products for clarity, completeness, and consistency. As important, expect changes to the system requirements and manage them using solid change management (Chapter 27) methods.

both business process engineering and product engineering[1] work to allocate a role for computer software and, at the same time, to establish the links that tie software to other elements of a computer-based system.

In this chapter, we focus on the management issues and the process-specific activities that enable a software organization to ensure that it does the right things at the right time in the right way.

6.1 Computer-Based Systems

The word *system* is possibly the most overused and abused term in the technical lexicon. We speak of political systems and educational systems, of avionics systems and manufacturing systems, of banking systems and subway systems. The word tells us little. We use the adjective describing *system* to understand the context in which the word is used. *Webster's Dictionary* defines system in the following way:

> 1. a set or arrangement of things so related as to form a unity or organic whole; 2. a set of facts, principles, rules, etc., classified and arranged in an orderly form so as to show a logical plan linking the various parts; 3. a method or plan of classification or arrangement; 4. an established way of doing something; method; procedure . . . .

Five additional definitions are provided in the dictionary, yet no precise synonym is suggested. *System* is a special word. Borrowing from Webster's definition, we define a *computer-based system* as

> A set or arrangement of elements that are organized to accomplish some predefined goal by processing information.

The goal may be to support some business function or to develop a product that can be sold to generate business revenue. To accomplish the goal, a computer-based system makes use of a variety of system elements:

Software. Computer programs, data structures, and related work products that serve to effect the logical method, procedure, or control that is required.

---

1 In reality, the term *system engineering* is often used in this context. However, for the purposes of this book system engineering is generic and is used to encompass both business process engineering and product engineering.

Don't be lured into taking a "software-centric" view. Begin by considering all elements of a system before you concentrate on software.

Hardware. Electronic devices that provide computing capability, the interconnectivity devices (e.g., network switches, telecommunications devices) that enable the flow of data, and electromechanical devices (e.g., sensors, motors, pumps) that provide external world function.

People. Users and operators of hardware and software.

Database. A large, organized collection of information that is accessed via software and persists over time.

Documentation. Descriptive information (e.g., models, specifications, hard-copy manuals, on-line help files, Web sites) that portrays the use and/or operation of the system.

Procedures. The steps that define the specific use of each system element or the procedural context in which the system resides.

These elements combine in a variety of ways to transform information. For example, a marketing department transforms raw sales data into a profile of the typical purchaser of a product; a robot transforms a command file containing specific instructions into a set of control signals that cause some specific physical action. Creating an information system to assist the marketing department and control software to support the robot both require system engineering.

> "Never trust a computer you can't throw out a window."
>
> **Steve Wozniak**

Complex systems are actually a hierarchy of macro elements that are themselves systems.

One complicating characteristic of computer-based systems is that the elements constituting one system may also represent one macro element of a still larger system. The *macro element* is a computer-based system that is one part of a larger computer-based system. As an example, we consider a *factory automation system* that is essentially a hierarchy of systems. At the lowest level of the hierarchy we have a numerical control machine, robots, and data entry devices. Each is a computer-based system in its own right. The elements of the numerical control machine include electronic and electromechanical hardware (e.g., processor and memory, motors, sensors), software (for communications and machine control), people (the machine operator), a database (the stored NC program), documentation, and procedures. A similar decomposition could be applied to the robot and data entry device. Each is a computer-based system.

At the next level in the hierarchy, a manufacturing cell is defined. The *manufacturing cell* is a computer-based system that may have elements of its own (e.g., computers, mechanical fixtures) and also integrates the macro elements that we have called numerical control machine, robot, and data entry device.

To summarize, the manufacturing cell and its macro elements each are composed of system elements with the generic labels: software, hardware, people, database, procedures, and documentation. In some cases, macro elements may share a generic element. For example, the robot and the NC machine both might be managed by a single operator (the people element). In other cases, generic elements are exclusive to one system.

The role of the system engineer is to define the elements for a specific computer-based system in the context of the overall hierarchy of systems (macro elements). In the sections that follow, we examine the tasks that constitute computer system engineering.

6.2 The System Engineering Hierarchy

WebRef
The International Council of System Engineering (INCOSE) provides many useful resources at **www.incose.org**

Regardless of its domain of focus, system engineering encompasses a collection of top-down and bottom-up methods to navigate the hierarchy illustrated in Figure 6.1. The system engineering process usually begins with a "world view." That is, the entire business or product domain is examined to ensure that the proper business or technology context can be established. The world view is refined to focus more fully on a specific domain of interest. Within a specific domain, the need for targeted system elements (e.g., data, software, hardware, people) is analyzed. Finally, the analysis, design, and construction of a targeted system element is initiated. At the top of the hierarchy, a very broad context is established and, at the bottom, detailed technical activities, performed by the relevant engineering discipline (e.g., hardware or software engineering), are conducted.[2]

KEY POINT
Good system engineering begins with a clear understanding of context—the world view—and then progressively narrows focus until technical detail is understood.

Stated in a slightly more formal manner, the *world view* (WV) is composed of a set of domains (D_i), which can each be a system or system of systems in its own right.

$$WV = \{D_1, D_2, D_3, \ldots, D_n\}$$

Each domain is composed of specific *elements* (E_j) each of which serves some role in accomplishing the objective and goals of the domain or component:

$$D_i = \{E_1, E_2, E_3, \ldots, E_m\}$$

Finally, each element is implemented by specifying the technical *components* (C_k) that achieve the necessary function for an element:

$$E_j = \{C_1, C_2, C_3, \ldots, C_k\}$$

In the software context, a component could be a computer program, a reusable program component, a module, a class or object, or even a programming language statement.

> **"Always design a thing by considering it in its next larger context—a chair in a room, a room in a house, a house in an environment, an environment in a city plan."**
>
> **Eliel Saarinen**

2 In some situations, however, system engineers must first consider individual system elements. Using this approach, subsystems are described bottom-up by first considering constituent detailed components of the subsystem.

FIGURE 6.1

The system engineering hierarchy

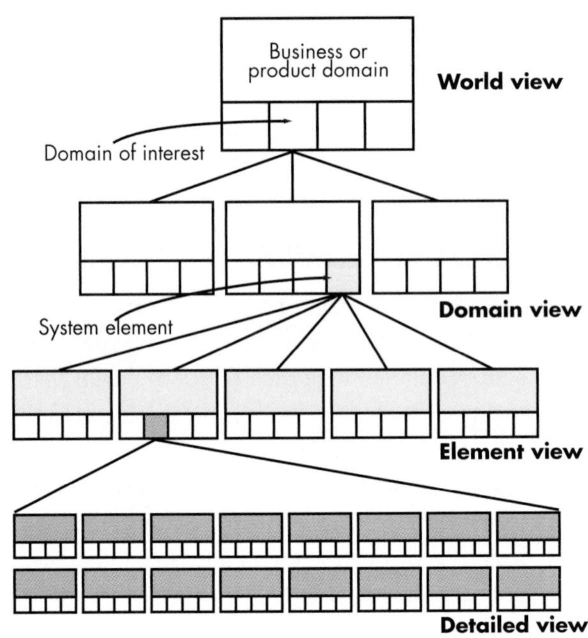

It is important to note that the system engineer narrows the focus of work as she moves downward in the hierarchy just described. However, the world view portrays a clear definition of overall functionality that will enable the engineer to understand the domain, and ultimately the system or product, in the proper context.

6.2.1 System Modeling

System modeling is an important element of the system engineering process. Whether the focus is on the world view or the detailed view, the engineer creates models that [MOT92]:

? What does a system engineering model accomplish?

- Define the processes that serve the needs of the view under consideration.
- Represent the behavior of the processes and the assumptions on which the behavior is based.
- Explicitly define both exogenous and endogenous input[3] to the model.
- Represent all linkages (including output) that will enable the engineer to better understand the view.

3 *Exogenous* inputs link one constituent of a given view with other constituents at the same level or other levels; *endogenous* input links individual components of a constituent at a particular view.

To construct a system model, the engineer should consider a number of restraining factors:

1. *Assumptions* that reduce the number of possible permutations and variations, thus enabling a model to reflect the problem in a reasonable manner. As an example, consider a three-dimensional rendering product used by the entertainment industry to create realistic animation. One domain of the product enables the representation of 3D human forms. Input to this domain encompasses the ability to specify movement from a live human actor, from video, or by the creation of graphical models. The system engineer makes certain assumptions about the range of allowable human movement (e.g., legs cannot be wrapped around the torso) so that the range of inputs and processing can be limited.

A system engineer considers the following factors when determining alternative solutions: assumptions, simplifications, limitations, constraints, and customer preferences.

2. *Simplifications* that enable the model to be created in a timely manner. To illustrate, consider an office products company that sells and services a broad range of copiers, scanners, and related equipment. The system engineer is modeling the needs of the service organization and is working to understand the flow of information that spawns a service order. Although a service order can be derived from many origins, the engineer categorizes only two sources: internal demand and external request. This enables a simplified partitioning of input that is required to generate the service order.
3. *Limitations* that help to bound the system. For example, an aircraft avionics system is being modeled for a next generation aircraft. Since the aircraft has a two-engine design, the monitoring domain for propulsion will be modeled to accommodate a maximum of two engines and associated redundant systems.
4. *Constraints* that will guide the manner in which the model is created and the approach taken when the model is implemented. For example, the technology infrastructure for the three-dimensional rendering system described previously uses dual G5-based processors. The computational complexity of problems must be constrained to fit within the processing bounds imposed by these processors.
5. *Preferences* that indicate the preferred architecture for all data, functions, and technology. The preferred solution sometimes comes into conflict with other restraining factors. Yet, customer satisfaction is often predicated on the degree to which the preferred approach is realized.

The resultant system model (at any view) may call for a completely automated solution, a semiautomated solution, or a nonautomated approach. In fact, it is often possible to characterize models of each type that serve as alternative solutions to the problem at hand. In essence, the system engineer simply modifies the relative influence of different system elements (people, hardware, software) to derive models of each type.

> "Simple things should be simple. Complex things should be possible."
>
> **Alan Kay**

If simulation capability is unavailable for a reactive system, project risk increases. Consider using an incremental process model that will enable you to deliver a working product in the first iteration and then use other iterations to tune performance.

6.2.2 System Simulation

Many computer-based systems interact with the real world in a reactive fashion. That is, real-world events are monitored by the hardware and software that form the computer-based system, and based on these events, the system imposes control on the machines, processes, and even people who cause the events to occur. Real-time and embedded systems often fall into the reactive systems category.

Many systems in the reactive category control machines and/or processes (e.g., commercial aircraft or petroleum refineries) that must operate with an extremely high degree of reliability. If the system fails, significant economic or human loss could occur. For this reason, system modeling and simulation tools are used to help eliminate surprises when reactive, computer-based systems are built. These tools are applied during the system engineering process, while the role of hardware and software, databases, and people is being specified. Modeling and simulation tools enable a system engineer to "test drive" a specification of the system.

SOFTWARE TOOLS

System Simulation Tools

Objective: System simulation tools provide the software engineer with the ability to predict the behavior of a real-time system prior to the time that it is built. In addition, these tools enable the software engineer to develop mock-ups of the real-time system, allowing the customer to gain insight into the function, operation, and response prior to actual implementation.

Mechanics: Tools in this category allow a team to define the elements of a computer-based system and then execute a variety of simulations to better understand the operating characteristics and overall performance of the system. Two broad categories of system simulation tools exist: (1) general purpose tools that can model virtually any computer-based system, and (2) special purpose tools that are designed to address a specific application domain (e.g., aircraft avionics systems, manufacturing systems, electronic-systems).

Representative Tools[4]

CSIM, developed by Lockheed Martin Advanced Technology Labs (www.atl.external.lmco.com), is a general purpose discrete-event simulator for block diagram-oriented systems.

Simics, developed by Virtutech (www.virtutech.com), is a system simulation platform that can model and analyze both hardware and software-based systems.

SLX, developed by Wolverine Software (www.wolverinesoftware.com), provides general purpose building blocks for modeling the performance of a wide variety of systems.

A useful set of links to a wide array of system simulation resources can be found at http://www.idsia.ch/~andrea/simtools.html.

4 Tools noted here do not represent an endorsement, but rather a sampling of tools in this category. In most cases, tool names are trademarked by their respective developers.

6.3 Business Process Engineering: An Overview

The goal of *business process engineering* (BPE) is to define architectures that will enable a business to use information effectively. When taking a world view of a company's information technology needs, there is little doubt that system engineering is required. Not only is the specification of the appropriate computing architecture required, but the software architecture that populates the organization's unique configuration of computing resources must be developed. Business process engineering is one approach for creating an overall plan for implementing the computing architecture [SPE93].

? What architectures are defined and developed as part of BPE?

Three different architectures must be analyzed and designed within the context of business objectives and goals:

- Data architecture
- Applications architecture
- Technology infrastructure

The *data architecture* provides a framework for the information needs of a business or business function. The individual building blocks of the architecture are the data objects that are used by the business. A data object contains a set of attributes that define some aspect, quality, characteristic, or descriptor of the data that are being described.

Once a set of data objects is defined, their relationships are identified. A *relationship* indicates how objects are connected to one another. As an example, consider the objects: **customer** and **productA.** The two objects can be connected by the relationship *purchases;* that is, a **customer** *purchases* **productA** or **productA** *is purchased by* **customer.** The data objects (there may be hundreds or even thousands for a major business activity) flow between business functions, are organized within a database, and are transformed to provide information that serves the needs of the business.

The *application architecture* encompasses those elements of a system that transform objects within the data architecture for some business purpose. In the context of this book, we consider the application architecture to be the system of programs (software) that performs this transformation. However, in a broader context, the application architecture might incorporate the role of people (who are information transformers and users) and business procedures that have not been automated.

As a software engineer, you may never get involved in ISP or BAA. However, if it's clear that these activities haven't been done, inform stakeholders that project risk is very high.

The *technology infrastructure* provides the foundation for the data and application architectures. The infrastructure encompasses the hardware and software that are used to support the applications and data. This includes computers, operating systems, networks, telecommunication links, storage technologies, and the architecture (e.g., client/server) that has been designed to implement these technologies.

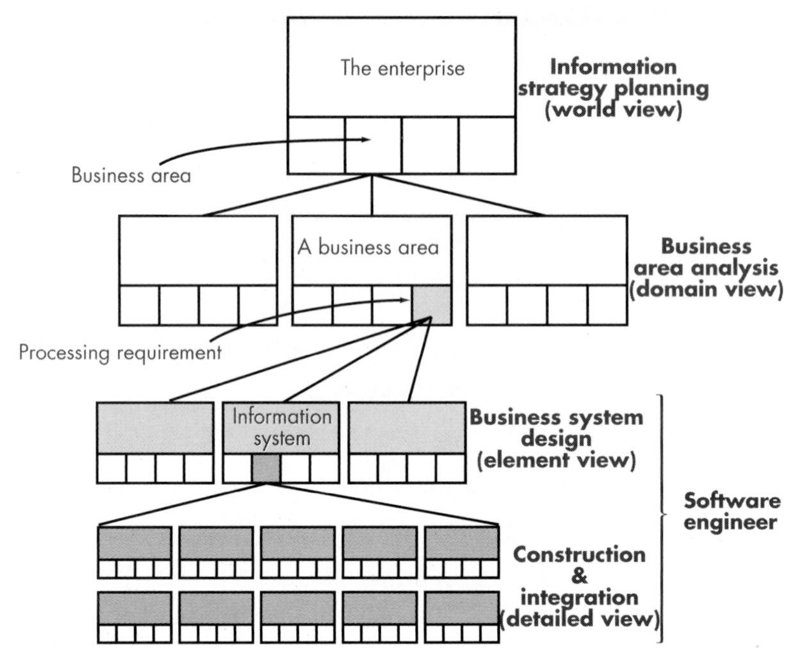

FIGURE 6.2
The business process engineering hierarchy [MAR90]

To model these system architectures, a hierarchy of business process engineering activities is defined and illustrated in Figure 6.2.

6.4 Product Engineering: An Overview

The goal of *product engineering* is to translate the customer's desire for a set of defined capabilities into a working product. To achieve this goal, product engineering—like business process engineering—must derive architecture and infrastructure. The architecture encompasses four distinct system components: software, hardware, data (and databases), and people. A support infrastructure is established and includes the technology required to tie the components together and the information (e.g., documents, CD-ROM, video) that is used to support the components.

The concurrent process model (Chapter 3) is often used in this context. Each engineering discipline works in parallel. Be certain that communication is encouraged as each discipline performs its work.

Referring to Figure 6.3, the world view is achieved through requirements engineering (Chapter 7). The overall requirements of the product are elicited from the customer. These requirements encompass information and control needs, product function and behavior, overall product performance, design and interfacing constraints, and other special needs. Once these requirements are known, the job of requirements engineering is to allocate function and behavior to each of the four components noted earlier.

Once allocation has occurred, system component engineering commences. System component engineering is actually a set of concurrent activities that address each of the system components separately: software engineering, hardware engineering, human engineering, and database engineering. Each of these engineering

FIGURE 6.3

The product engineering hierarchy

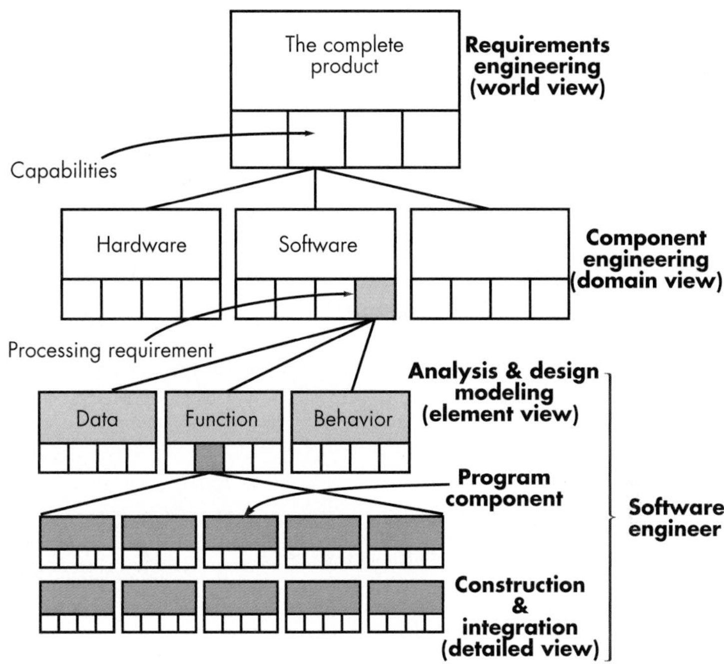

disciplines takes a domain-specific view, but it is important to note that the engineering disciplines must establish and maintain active communication with one another. Part of the role of requirements engineering is to establish the interfacing mechanisms that will enable this to happen.

The element view for product engineering is the engineering discipline itself applied to an allocated component. For software engineering, this means analysis and design modeling activities (covered in detail in later chapters) and construction and deployment activities that encompass code generation, testing, and support tasks. The analysis task models allocated requirements into representations of data, function, and behavior. Design maps the analysis model into data, architectural, interface, and software component-level designs.

SAFEHOME

Preliminary System Engineering

The scene: Software engineering team workspace after the *SafeHome* kickoff meeting has occurred.

The players: Jamie Lazar, software team member; Vinod Raman, software team member; Ed Robbins, software team member.

The conversation:

Ed: I think it went pretty well.

Vinod: Yeah . . . but all we did was look at the overall system—we've got plenty of requirements gathering work left to do for the software.

Jamie: That's why we have additional meetings scheduling for the next five days. By the way, I suggested that two of the "customers" move over here for the next few weeks. You know, live with us so we can really communicate, er, collaborate.

Vinod: How did that go?

Jamie: Well, they looked at me like I was crazy, but Doug [the software engineering manager] likes the idea—it's agile—so he's talking to them.

Ed: I was taking notes using my PDA during the meeting, and I came up with a list of basic functions.

Jamie: Cool, let's see.

Ed: I've already e-mailed both of you a copy. Take a look and we'll talk.

Vinod: How about after lunch?

(Jamie and Vinod received the following from Ed)
Preliminary notes of the structure/functionality of *SafeHome:*

- The system will make use of one or more PCs, various wall-mounted and/or handheld control panels, various sensors, and applicance/device controllers.
- All will communicate via wireless protocols (e.g., 802.11b) and will be designed for new-home construction and for application within existing homes.
- All hardware with the exception of our new wireless box will be off the shelf.

Basic software functionality that I could glean from our kick-off conversation.
Home security functions:

- Standard window/door/motion sensor monitoring for unauthorized access (break-ins).
- Monitoring for fire, smoke, and CO levels.
- Monitoring for water levels in basement (e.g., flood or broken water heater).
- Monitoring for outside movement.
- Change security setting via the Internet.

Home surveillance functions:

- Connect to one or more video cameras placed inside/outside house.
- Control pan/zoom for cameras.
- Define camera monitoring zones.
- Display camera views on PC.
- Access camera views via the Internet.
- Selectively record camera output digitally.
- Replay camera output.

Home management functions:

- Control lighting.
- Control appliances.
- Control HVAC.
- Control video/audio equipment throughout house.
- Ability to set house for "vacation/travel mode" with one button sets.
    - Set appliances/lighting/HVAC accordingly.
    - Set answering machine message.
    - Contacts vendors to stop paper, mail, etc.

Communication management functions:

- Answering machine functions.
    - List of callers via caller ID.
    - Messages, time-stamped.
    - Message text via voice recognition system.
- E-mail functions (all standard e-mail functions).
    - Standard e-mail display.
    - Voice read of e-mail via phone access.
- Personal phone book.
- Link to PDA.

Other functions:

As yet undefined.

All functions are accessible via the Internet with appropriate password protection.

6.5 System Modeling

Because a system can be represented at different levels of abstraction (e.g., the world view, the domain view, the element view), *system models* tend to be hierarchical or layered in nature. At the top of the hierarchy, a model of the complete system is presented (the world view). Major data objects, processing functions, and behaviors are represented without regard to the system component that will implement the elements of the world view model. As the hierarchy is refined or layered, component-level detail (in this case, representations of hardware, software, and so on) is modeled. Finally system models evolve into engineering models (which are further refined) that are specific to the appropriate engineering discipline.

6.5.1 Hatley-Pirbhai Modeling

Every computer-based system can be modeled as an information transform using an input-processing-output template. Hatley and Pirbhai [HAT87] have extended this view to include two additional system features—user interface processing and maintenance and self-test processing. Although these additional features are not present for every computer-based system, they are very common, and their specification makes any system model more robust.

The Hatley-Pirbhai model depicts input, processing, and output along with the user interface and maintenance/self-test.

Using a representation of input, processing, output, user interface processing, and self-test processing, a system engineer can create a model of system components that sets a foundation for later steps in each of the engineering disciplines.

To develop the system model, a system model template [HAT87] is used. The system engineer allocates system elements to each of five processing regions within the template: (1) user interface, (2) input, (3) system function and control, (4) output, and (5) maintenance and self-test.

Like nearly all modeling techniques used in system and software engineering, the system model template enables the analyst to create a hierarchy of detail. A *system context diagram* (SCD) resides at the top level of the hierarchy. The context diagram "establishes the information boundary between the system being implemented and the environment in which the system is to operate" [HAT87]. That is, the SCD defines all external producers of information used by the system, all external consumers of information created by the system, and all entities that communicate through the interface or perform maintenance and self-test.

To illustrate the use of the SCD, consider a conveyor line sorting system (CLSS) described with the following (somewhat nebulous) statement of objectives:

> CLSS must be developed such that boxes moving along a conveyor line will be identified and sorted into one of six bins at the end of the line. The boxes will pass by a sorting station where they will be identified. Based on an identification number printed on the side of the box and a bar code, the boxes will be shunted into the appropriate bins. Boxes pass in random order and are evenly spaced. The line is moving slowly.
>
> A desk-top computer located at the sorting station executes all CLSS software, interacts with the bar-code reader to read part numbers on each box, interacts with the conveyor line monitoring equipment to acquire conveyor line speed, stores all part numbers sorted, interacts with a sorting station operator to produce a variety of reports and diagnostics, sends control signals to the shunting hardware to sort the boxes, and communicates with a central factory automation system.

FIGURE 6.4

System context diagram for CLSS

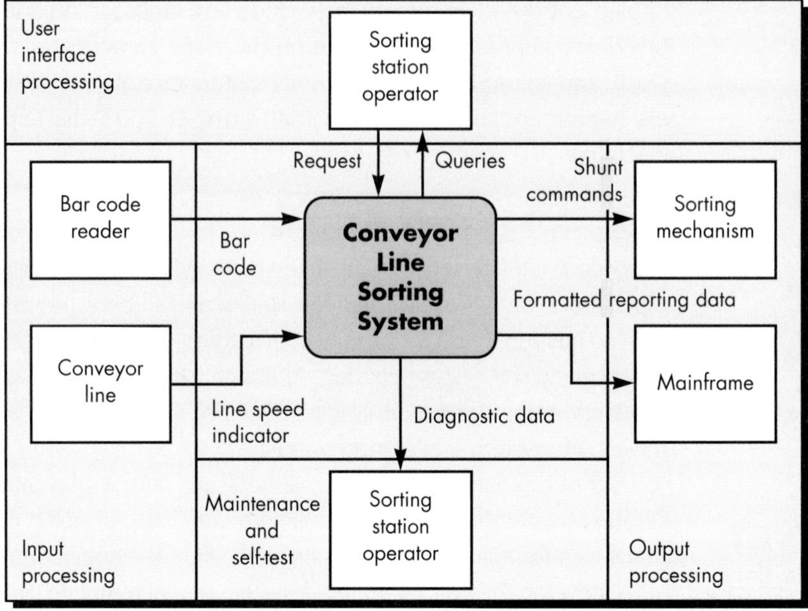

The SCD for CLSS is shown in Figure 6.4. The diagram is divided into five major segments. The top segment represents user interface processing, and the left and right segments depict input and output processing, respectively. The central segment contains process and control functions, and the bottom segment focuses on maintenance and self-test. Each box shown in the figure represents an *external entity*—that is, a producer or consumer of system information. For example, the bar-code reader produces information that is input to the CLSS system. The symbol for the entire system (or, at lower levels, major subsystems) is a rectangle with rounded corners. Hence, CLSS is represented in the processing and control region at the center of the SCD. The labeled arrows shown in the SCD represent information (data and control) as it moves from the external environment into the CLSS system. The external entity bar-code reader produces input information that is labeled bar code. In essence, the SCD places any system into the context of its external environment.

The system engineer refines the system context diagram by considering the shaded rectangle in Figure 6.4 in more detail. The major subsystems that enable the conveyor line sorting system to function within the context defined by the SCD are identified. The major subsystems are defined in a *system flow diagram* (SFD) that is derived from the SCD. Information flow across the regions of the SCD is used to guide the system engineer in developing the SFD—a more detailed "schematic" for CLSS. The system flow diagram shows major subsystems and important lines of informa-

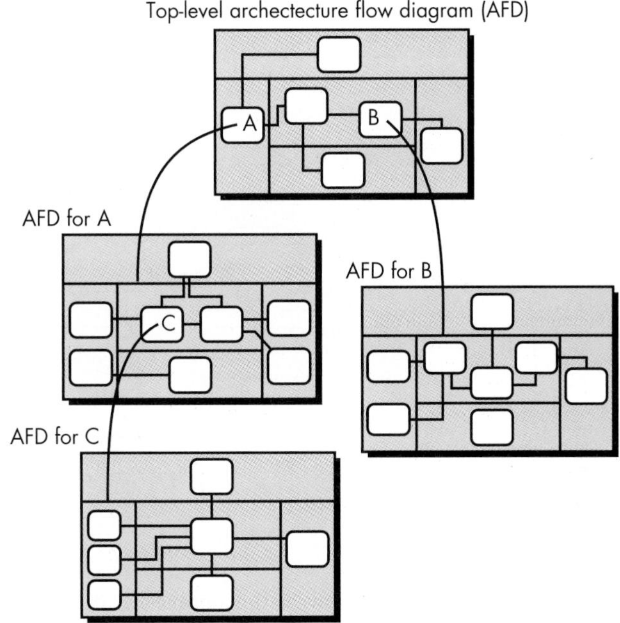

FIGURE 6.5
Building an SFD hierarchy

tion (data and control) flow. In addition, the system template partitions the subsystem processing into each of the five regions discussed earlier. At this stage, each of the subsystems can contain one or more system elements (e.g., hardware, software, people) as allocated by the system engineer.

The initial system flow diagram becomes the top node of a hierarchy of SFDs. Each rounded rectangle in the original SFD can be expanded into another architecture template dedicated solely to it. This process is illustrated schematically in Figure 6.5. Each of the SFDs for the system can be used as a starting point for subsequent engineering steps for the subsystem that has been described.

Subsystems and the information that flows between them can be specified (bounded) for subsequent engineering work. A narrative description of each subsystem and a definition of all data that flow between subsystems become important elements of the System Specification.

6.5.2 System Modeling with UML

UML provides a wide array of diagrams that can be used for analysis and design at both the system and the software level.[5] For the CLSS system, four important system elements

5 A more detailed discussion of UML diagrams is presented in Chapters 8 through 11. For a comprehensive discussion of UML, the interested reader should see [SCH02], [LAR01], or [BEN99].

FIGURE 6.6

Deployment diagram for CLSS hardware

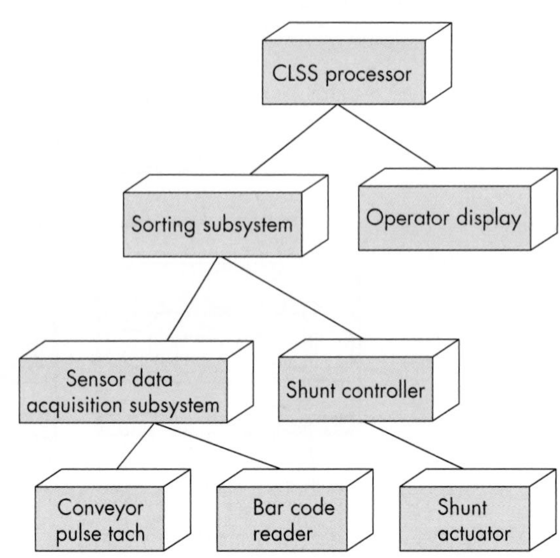

are modeled: (1) the hardware that enables CLSS; (2) the software that implements database access and sorting; (3) the operator who submits various requests to the system; and (4) the database that contains relevant bar code and destination information.

CLSS hardware can be modeled at the system level using a UML *deployment diagram* as illustrated in Figure 6.6. Each 3-D box depicts a hardware element that is part of the physical architecture of the system. In some cases, hardware elements will have to be designed and built as part of the project. In many cases, however, hardware elements can be acquired off-the-shelf. The challenge for the engineering team is to properly interface the hardware elements.

WebRef
A complete specification of the syntax and semantics of the UML (discussed in later chapters) can be found at **www.rational.com/uml/index.jsp.**

Software elements for CLSS can be depicted in a variety of ways using UML. Procedural aspects of CLSS software can be represented using an *activity diagram* (Figure 6.7). This UML notation is similar to the flowchart and is used to represent what happens as the system performs its functions. Rounded rectangles imply a specific system function; arrows imply flow through the system; the decision diamond represents a branching decision (each arrow emanating from the diamond is labeled); solid horizontal lines imply that parallel activities are occurring.

Another UML notation that can be used to model software is the *class diagram* (along with many class-related diagrams discussed later in this book). At the system engineering level, classes[6] are extracted from a statement of the problem. For

6 In earlier chapters we noted that a class represents a set of entities that is part of the system domain. These entities can be transformed or stored by the system or can serve as a producer or consumer of information produced by the system.

FIGURE 6.7

Activity diagram for CLSS

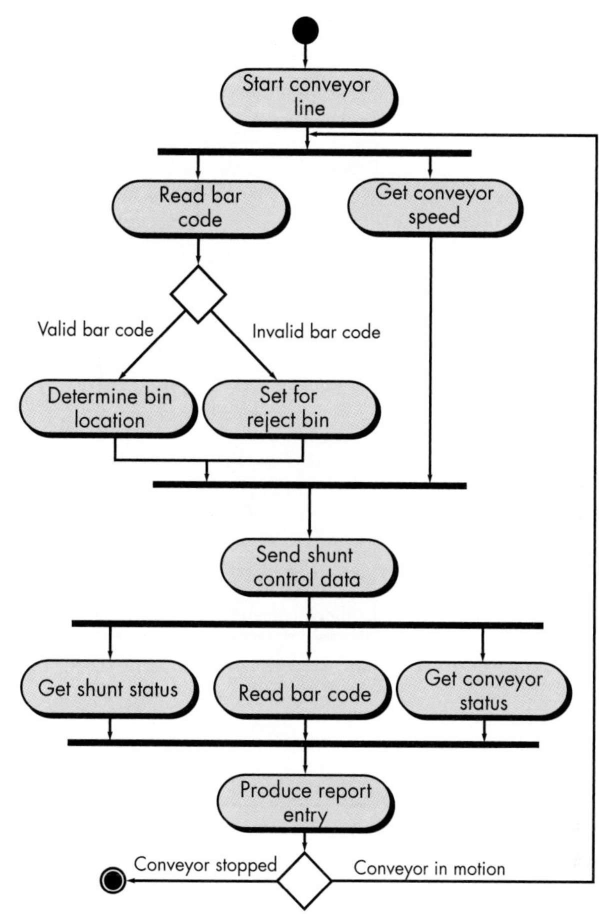

the CLSS, candidate classes might be: **Box, ConveyorLine, Bar-codeReader, ShuntController, OperatorRequest, Report, Product,** and others. Each class encapsulates a set of attributes that depict all necessary information about the class. A class description also contains a set of operations that are applied to the class in the context of the CLSS system. A UML class diagram for **Box** is shown in Figure 6.8.

The CLSS operator can be modeled with a UML use-case diagram as shown in Figure 6.9. The use-case diagram illustrates the manner in which an actor (in this case, the operator, represented by a stick figure) interacts with the system. Each labeled oval inside the box (which represents the CLSS system boundary) represents one use-case—a text scenario that describes an interaction with the system.

FIGURE 6.8

UML class diagram for Box class

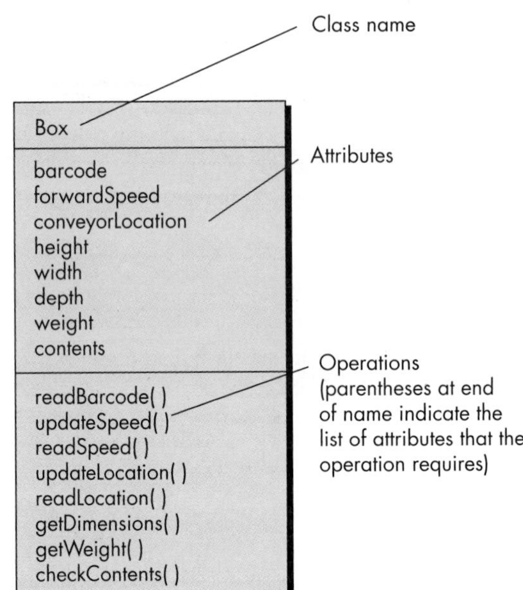

FIGURE 6.9

Use-case diagram for CLSS operator

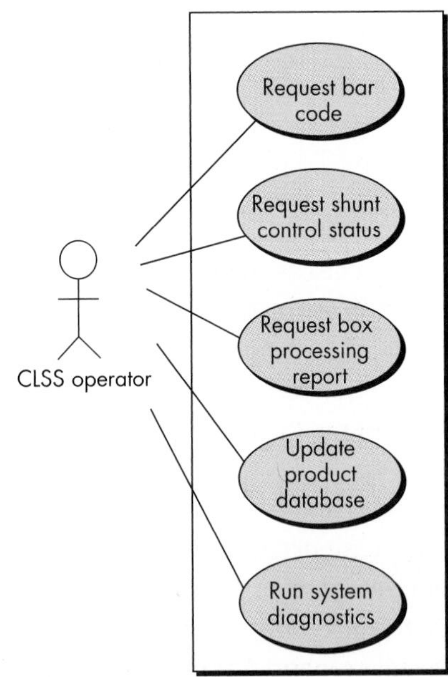

SOFTWARE TOOLS

System Modeling Tools

Objective: System modeling tools provide the software engineer with the ability to model all elements of a computer-based system using a notation that is specific to the tool.

Mechanics: Tool mechanics vary. In general, tools in this category enable a system engineer to model (1) the structure of all functional elements of the system; (2) the static and dynamic behavior of the system; and (3) the human-machine interface.

Representative Tools[7]

Describe, developed by Embarcadero Technologies (www.embarcadero.com), is a suite of UML-based modeling tools that can represent software or complete systems.

Rational XDE and Rose, developed by Rational Technologies (www.rational.com), provide a widely used, UML-based suite of modeling and development tools for computer-based systems.

Real-Time Studio, developed by Artisan Software (www.artisansw.com), is a suite of modeling and development tools that support real-time system development.

Telelogic Tau, developed by Telelogic (www.telelogic.com), is a UML-based tool suite that supports analysis and design modeling as well as links to software construction features.

6.6 Summary

A high-technology system encompasses a number of elements: software, hardware, people, database, documentation, and procedures. System engineering helps to translate a customer's needs into a model of a system that makes use of one or more of these elements.

System engineering begins by taking a "world view." A business domain or product is analyzed to establish all basic business requirements. Focus is then narrowed to a "domain view," where each of the system elements is analyzed individually. Each element is allocated to one or more engineering components, which are then addressed by the relevant engineering discipline.

Business process engineering is a system engineering approach that is used to define architectures that enable a business to use information effectively. The intent of business process engineering is to derive comprehensive data architecture, application architecture, and technology infrastructure that will meet the needs of the business strategy and the objectives and goals of each business area.

Product engineering is a system engineering approach that begins with system analysis. The system engineer identifies the customer's needs, determines economic and technical feasibility, and allocates function and performance to software, hardware, people, and databases—the key engineering components.

7 Tools noted here do not represent an endorsement, but rather a sampling of tools in this category. In most cases, tool names are trademarked by their respective developers.

References

[BEN99] Bennett, S., S. McRobb, and R. Farmer, *Object-Oriented Systems Analysis and Design Using UML,* McGraw-Hill, 1999.

[HAR93] Hares, J. S., *Information Engineering for the Advanced Practitioner,* Wiley, 1993, pp. 12–13.

[HAT87] Hatley, D. J., and I. A. Pirbhai, *Strategies for Real-Time System Specification,* Dorset House, 1987.

[LAR01] Larman, C., *Applying UML and Patterns: An Introduction to Object-Oriented Analysis and Design and the Unified Process,* 2nd ed., Prentice-Hall, 2001.

[MAR90] Martin, J., *Information Engineering: Book II—Planning and Analysis,* Prentice-Hall, 1990.

[MOT92] Motamarri, S., "Systems Modeling and Description," *Software Engineering Notes,* vol. 17, no. 2, April 1992, pp. 57–63.

[SCH02] Schmuller, J., *Teach Yourself UML in 24 Hours,* 2nd ed., Sams Publishing, 2002.

[SPE93] Spewak, S., *Enterprise Architecture Planning,* QED Publishing, 1993.

[THA97] Thayer, R. H., and M. Dorfman, *Software Requirements Engineering,* 2nd ed., IEEE Computer Society Press, 1997.

Problems and Points to Ponder

6.1. Find as many single-word synonyms for the word *system* as you can. Good luck!

6.2. Build a hierarchical "system of systems" for a system, product, or service with which you are familiar. Your hierarchy should extend down to simple system elements (hardware, software, etc.) along at least one branch of the "tree."

6.3. Select any large system or product with which you are familiar. Define the set of domains that describe the world view of the system or product. Describe the set of elements that make up one or two domains. For one element, identify the technical components that must be engineered.

6.4. Select any large system or product with which you are familiar. State the assumptions, simplifications, limitations, constraints, and preferences that would have to be made to build an effective (and realizable) system model.

6.5. Business process engineering strives to define *data* and *application architecture* as well as *technology infrastructure.* Describe what each of these terms means and provide an example.

6.6. A system engineer can come from one of three sources: the system developer, the customer, or some outside organization. Discuss the pros and cons that apply to each source. Describe an "ideal" system engineer.

6.7. Your instructor will distribute a high-level description of a computer-based system or product:

a. Develop a set of questions that you should ask as a system engineer.
b. Propose at least two different allocations for the system based on answers to your questions.
c. In class, compare your allocation to those of fellow students.

6.8. Develop a system context diagram for the computer-based system of your choice (or one assigned by your instructor).

6.9. Although information at this point is very sketchy, try to develop one UML deployment diagram, activity diagram, class diagram, and use-case diagram for the *SafeHome* product.

6.10. Research the literature and write a brief paper describing how modeling and simulation tools work. Alternate: Collect literature from two or more vendors that sell modeling and simulation tools and assess their similarities and differences.

6.11. Are there characteristics of a system that cannot be established during system engineering activities? Describe the characteristics, if any, and explain why a consideration of them must be delayed until later engineering steps.

6.12. Are there situations in which formal system specification can be abbreviated or eliminated entirely? Explain.

Further Readings and Information Sources

Books by Hatley and his colleagues (*Process for Systems Architecture and Requirements Engineering,* Dorset House, 2000), Buede (*The Engineering Design of Systems: Models and Methods,* Wiley, 1999), Weiss and his colleagues (*Software Product-Line Engineering,* Addison-Wesley, 1999), Blanchard and Fabrycky (*System Engineering and Analysis,* third edition, Prentice-Hall, 1998), Armstrong and Sage (*Introduction to Systems Engineering,* Wiley, 1997), and Martin (*Systems Engineering Guidebook,* CRC Press, 1996) present the system engineering process (with a distinct engineering emphasis) and provide worthwhile guidance. Blanchard (*System Engineering Management,* second edition, Wiley, 1997) and Lacy (*System Engineering Management,* McGraw-Hill, 1992) discuss system engineering management issues.

Chorafas (*Enterprise Architecture and New Generation Systems,* St. Lucie Press, 2001) presents information engineering and system architectures for "next generation" IT solutions including Internet-based systems. Wallnau and his colleagues (*Building Systems from Commercial Components,* Addison-Wesley, 2001) addresses component-based systems engineering issues for information systems and products. Lozinsky (*Enterprise-Wide Software Solutions: Integration Strategies and Practices,* Addison-Wesley, 1998) addresses the use of software packages as a solution that allows a company to migrate from legacy systems to modern business processes. A worthwhile discussion of risk and system engineering is presented by Bradley (*Elimination of Risk in Systems,* Tharsis Books, 2002).

Davis (*Business Process Modeling with Aris: A Practical Guide,* Springer-Verlag, 2001), Bustard and his colleagues (*System Models for Business Process Improvement,* Artech House, 2000), and Scheer (*Business Process Engineering: Reference Models for Industrial Enterprises,* Springer-Verlag, 1998) describe business process modeling methods for enterprise-wide information systems.

Davis and Yen (*The Information System Consultant's Handbook: Systems Analysis and Design,* CRC Press, 1998) present encyclopedic coverage of system analysis and design issues in the information systems domain. An excellent IEEE tutorial by Thayer and Dorfman [THA97] discusses the interrelationship between system and software-level requirements analysis issues.

Law and his colleagues (*Simulation Modeling and Analysis,* McGraw-Hill, 1999) discuss system simulation and modeling techniques for a wide variety of application domains.

For those readers actively involved in systems work or interested in a more sophisticated treatment of the topic, Gerald Weinberg's books (*An Introduction to General System Thinking,* Wiley-Interscience, 1976 and *On the Design of Stable Systems,* Wiley-Interscience, 1979) have become classics and provide an excellent discussion of "general systems thinking" that implicitly leads to a general approach to system analysis and design. More recent books by Weinberg (*General Principles of Systems Design,* Dorset House, 1988 and *Rethinking Systems Analysis and Design,* Dorset House, 1988) continue in the tradition of his earlier work.

A wide variety of information sources on system engineering and related subjects is available on the Internet. An up-to-date list of World Wide Web references that are relevant to system engineering, information engineering, business process engineering, and product engineering can be found at the SEPA Web site:
http://www.mhhe.com/pressman.

CHAPTER

7 REQUIREMENTS ENGINEERING

KEY CONCEPTS

Understanding the requirements of a problem is among the most difficult tasks that face a software engineer. When you first think about it, requirements engineering doesn't seem that hard. After all, doesn't the customer know what is required? Shouldn't the end-users have a good understanding of the features and functions that will provide benefit? Surprisingly, in many instances the answer to these questions is no. And even if customers and end-users are explicit in their needs, those needs will change throughout the project. Requirements engineering is hard.

In the forward to a book by Ralph Young [YOU01] on effective requirements practices, I wrote:

> It's your worst nightmare. A customer walks into your office, sits down, looks you straight in the eye, and says, "I know you think you understand what I said, but what you don't understand is what I said is not what I mean." Invariably, this happens late in the project, after deadline commitments have been made, reputations are on the line, and serious money is at stake.
>
> All of us who have worked in the systems and software business for more than a few years have lived this nightmare, and yet, few of us have learned to make it go away. We struggle when we try to elicit requirements from our customers. We have trouble understanding the information that we do acquire. We often record requirements in a

QUICK LOOK

What is it? Requirements engineering helps software engineers to better understand the problem they will work to solve. It encompasses the set of tasks that lead to an understanding of what the business impact of the software will be, what the customer wants, and how end-users will interact with the software.

Who does it? Software engineers (sometimes referred to as *system engineers* or *analysts* in the IT world) and other project stakeholders (managers, customers, end-users) all participate in requirements engineering.

Why is it important? Designing and building an elegant computer program that solves the wrong problem serves no one's needs. That's why it is important to understand what the customer wants before you begin to design and build a computer-based system.

What are the steps? Requirements engineering begins with inception—a task that defines the scope and nature of the problem to be solved. It moves onward to elicitation—a task that helps the customer to define what is required, and then elaboration—where basic requirements are refined and modified. As the customer defines the problem, negotiation occurs—what are the priorities, what is essential, when is it required? Finally, the problem is specified in some manner and then reviewed or validated to ensure that your understanding of the problem and the customers' understanding of the problem coincide.

What is the work product? The intent of the requirements engineering process is to provide all parties with a written understanding of the problem. This can be achieved though a number of work products: user scenarios, functions and features lists, analysis models, or a specification.

How do I ensure that I've done it right? Requirements engineering work products are reviewed with the customer and end-users to ensure that what you have learned is what they really meant. A word of warning: even after all parties agree, things will change, and they will continue to change throughout the project.

disorganized manner, and we spend far too little time verifying what we do record. We allow change to control us, rather than establishing mechanisms to control change. In short, we fail to establish a solid foundation for the system or software. Each of these problems is challenging. When they are combined, the outlook is daunting for even the most experienced managers and practitioners. But solutions do exist.

It would be dishonest to call requirements engineering the "solution" to the challenges noted above. But it does provide us with a solid approach for addressing these challenges.

7.1 A Bridge to Design and Construction

Designing and building computer software is challenging, creative, and just plain fun. In fact, building software is so compelling that many software developers want to jump right in before they have a clear understanding of what is needed. They argue that things will become clear as they build; that project stakeholders will be able to better understand need only after examining early iterations of the software; that things change so rapidly that requirements engineering is a waste of time; that the bottom line is producing a working program and that all else is secondary. What makes these arguments seductive is that they contain elements of truth.[1] But each is flawed, and all can lead to a failed software project.

> "The hardest single part of building a software system is deciding what to build. No part of the work so cripples the resulting system if done wrong. No other part is more difficult to rectify later."
>
> **Fred Brooks**

Requirements engineering, like all other software engineering activities, must be adapted to the needs of the process, the project, the product, and the people doing the work. From a software process perspective, requirements engineering (RE) is a software engineering action that begins during the communication activity and continues into the modeling activity.

In some cases, an abbreviated approach may be chosen. In others, every task defined for comprehensive requirements engineering must be performed rigorously.

1 This is particularly true for small projects (less than one month) and smaller, relatively simple software efforts. As software grows in size and complexity, these arguments begin to break down.

Overall, the software team must adapt its approach to RE. But adaptation does not mean abandonment. It is essential that the software team make a real effort to understand the requirements of a problem *before* the team attempts to solve the problem.

Requirements engineering establishes a solid base for design and construction. Without it, the resulting software has a high probability of not meeting customers' needs.

Requirements engineering builds a bridge to design and construction. But where does the bridge originate? One could argue that it begins at the feet of the project stakeholders (e.g., managers, customers, end-users), where business need is defined, user scenarios are described, functions and features are delineated, and project constraints are identified. Others might suggest that it begins with a broader system definition, where software is but one component (Chapter 6) of the larger system domain. But regardless of the starting point, the journey across the bridge takes us high above the project, allowing the software team to examine the context of the software work to be performed; the specific needs that design and construction must address; the priorities that guide the order in which work is to be completed; and the information, functions, and behaviors that will have a profound impact on the resultant design.

7.2 Requirements Engineering Tasks

Requirements engineering provides the appropriate mechanism for understanding what the customer wants, analyzing need, assessing feasibility, negotiating a reasonable solution, specifying the solution unambiguously, validating the specification, and managing the requirements as they are transformed into an operational system [THA97]. The requirements engineering process is accomplished through the execution of seven distinct functions: *inception, elicitation, elaboration, negotiation, specification, validation,* and *management.*

Expect to do a bit of design during requirements work and a bit of requirements work during design.

It is important to note that some of these requirements engineering functions occur in parallel and all are adapted to the needs of the project. All strive to define what the customer wants, and all serve to establish a solid foundation for the design and construction of what the customer gets.

7.2.1 Inception

How does a software project get started? Is there a single event that becomes the catalyst for a new computer-based system or product, or does the need evolve over time? There are no definitive answers to these questions.

> "The seeds of major software disasters are usually sown in the first three months of commencing the software project."
>
> **Capers Jones**

In some cases, a casual conversation is all that is needed to precipitate a major software engineering effort. But in general, most projects begin when a business need is identified or a potential new market or service is discovered. Stakeholders from the business community (e.g., business managers, marketing people, product managers) define a business case for the idea, try to identify the breadth and depth of the market, do a rough feasibility analysis, and identify a working description of the project's scope. All of this information is subject to change (a likely outcome), but it is sufficient to precipitate discussions with the software engineering organization.[2]

At project *inception,*[3] software engineers ask a set of context-free questions discussed in Section 7.3.4. The intent is to establish a basic understanding of the problem, the people who want a solution, the nature of the solution that is desired, and the effectiveness of preliminary communication and collaboration between the customer and the developer.

7.2.2 Elicitation

It certainly seems simple enough—ask the customer, the users, and others what the objectives for the system or product are, what is to be accomplished, how the system or product fits into the needs of the business, and finally, how the system or product is to be used on a day-to-day basis. But it isn't simple—it's very hard.

Christel and Kang [CRI92] identify a number of problems that help us understand why requirements *elicitation* is difficult:

? Why is it difficult to gain a clear understanding of what the customer wants?

- **Problems of scope.** The boundary of the system is ill-defined or the customers/users specify unnecessary technical detail that may confuse, rather than clarify, overall system objectives.
- **Problems of understanding.** The customers/users are not completely sure of what is needed, have a poor understanding of the capabilities and limitations of their computing environment, don't have a full understanding of the problem domain, have trouble communicating needs to the system engineer, omit information that is believed to be "obvious," specify requirements that conflict with the needs of other customers/users, or specify requirements that are ambiguous or untestable.
- **Problems of volatility.** The requirements change over time.

To help overcome these problems, requirements engineers must approach the requirements gathering activity in an organized manner.

7.2.3 Elaboration

The information obtained from the customer during inception and elicitation is expanded and refined during *elaboration.* This requirements engineering activity focuses on developing a refined technical model of software functions, features, and constraints.

---

2 If a computer-based system is to be developed, discussions begin with system engineering, an activity that defines the world-view and domain view (Chapter 6) for the system.

3 Readers of Chapter 3 will recall that the Unified Process defines a more comprehensive "inception phase" that encompasses the inception, elicitation, and elaboration tasks discussed in this chapter.

Elaboration is a good thing, but you have to know when to stop. The key is to describe the problem in a way that establishes a firm base for design. If you work beyond that point, you're doing design.

Elaboration is an analysis modeling action (Chapter 8) that is composed of a number of modeling and refinement tasks. Elaboration is driven by the creation and refinement of user scenarios that describe how the end-user (and other actors) will interact with the system. Each user scenario is parsed to extract analysis classes—business domain entities that are visible to the end-user. The attributes of each analysis class are defined and the *services*[4] that are required by each class are identified. The relationships and collaboration between classes are identified and a variety of supplementary UML diagrams are produced.

The end-result of elaboration is an analysis model that defines the informational, functional, and behavioral domain of the problem.

INFO

Analysis Modeling

Assume for a moment that you have been asked to specify all requirements for the construction of a gourmet kitchen. You know the dimensions of the room, the location of doors and windows, and the available wall space.

In order to fully specify what is to be built, you might list all cabinets and appliances (their manufacturer, model number, dimensions). You would then specify the countertops (laminate, granite, etc.), plumbing fixtures, flooring, and the like. These lists would provide a useful specification, but they do not provide a complete model of what you want. To complete the model, you might create a three-dimensional rendering that shows the position of the cabinets and appliances and their relationship to one another. From the model, it would be relatively easy to assess the efficiency of workflow (a requirement for all kitchens), and the aesthetic "look" of the room (a personal, but very important requirement).

We build analysis models for much the same reason that we would develop a blueprint or 3D rendering for the kitchen. It is important to evaluate the system's components in relationship to one another, to determine how requirements fit into this picture, and to assess the "aesthetics" of the system as it has been conceived.

7.2.4 Negotiation

It isn't unusual for customers and users to ask for more than can be achieved, given limited business resources. It is also relatively common for different customers or users to propose conflicting requirements, arguing that their version is "essential for our special needs."

There should be no winner and no loser in an effective negotiation. Both sides win because a "deal" that both can live with is solidified.

The requirements engineer must reconcile these conflicts through a process of *negotiation*. Customers, users, and other stakeholders are asked to rank requirements and then discuss conflicts in priority. Risks associated with each requirement are identified and analyzed (see Chapter 25 for details). Rough "guestimates" of development effort are made and used to assess the impact of each requirement on project cost and delivery time. Using an iterative approach, requirements are eliminated, combined, and/or modified so that each party achieves some measure of satisfaction.

---

4 The terms *operations* and *methods* are also used.

7.2.5 Specification

In the context of computer-based systems (and software), the term specification means different things to different people. A specification can be a written document, a set of graphical models, a formal mathematical model, a collection of usage scenarios, a prototype, or any combination of these.

The formality and format of a specification varies with the size and the complexity of the software to be built.

Some suggest that a "standard template" [SOM97] should be developed and used for a specification, arguing that this leads to requirements that are presented in a consistent and therefore more understandable manner. However, it is sometimes necessary to remain flexible when a specification is to be developed. For large systems, a written document, combining natural language descriptions and graphical models may be the best approach. However, usage scenarios may be all that are required for smaller products or systems that reside within well-understood technical environments.

The specification is the final work product produced by the requirements engineer. It serves as the foundation for subsequent software engineering activities. It describes the function and performance of a computer-based system and the constraints that will govern its development.

7.2.6 Validation

A key concern during requirements validation is consistency. Use the analysis model to ensure that requirements have been consistently stated.

The work products produced as a consequence of requirements engineering are assessed for quality during a *validation* step. Requirements validation examines the specification to ensure that all software requirements have been stated unambiguously; that inconsistencies, omissions, and errors have been detected and corrected; and that the work products conform to the standards established for the process, the project, and the product.

The primary requirements validation mechanism is the formal technical review (Chapter 26). The review team that validates requirements includes software engineers, customers, users, and other stakeholders who examine the specification looking for errors in content or interpretation, areas where clarification may be required, missing information, inconsistencies (a major problem when large products or systems are engineered), conflicting requirements, or unrealistic (unachievable) requirements.

INFO

Requirements Validation Checklist

It is often useful to examine each requirement against a set of checklist questions. Here is a small subset of those that might be asked:

- Are requirements stated clearly? Can they be misinterpreted?
- Is the source (e.g., a person, a regulation, a document) of the requirement identified? Has the final statement of the requirement been examined by or against the original source?
- Is the requirement bounded in quantitative terms?
- What other requirements relate to this requirement? Are they clearly noted via a cross-reference matrix or other mechanism?

- Does the requirement violate any system domain constraints?
- Is the requirement testable? If so, can we specify tests (sometimes called *validation criteria*) to exercise the requirement?
- Is the requirement traceable to any system model that has been created?
- Is the requirement traceable to overall system/product objectives?
- Is the specification structured in a way that leads to easy understanding, easy reference, and easy translation into more technical work products?
- Has an index for the specification been created?
- Have requirements associated with performance, behavior, and operational characteristics been clearly stated? What requirements appear to be implicit?

7.2.7 Requirements Management

WebRef
A variety of useful information on requirements management can be obtained at **www.jiludwig.com.**

In Chapter 6, we noted that requirements for computer-based systems change and that the desire to change requirements persists throughout the life of the system. *Requirements management* is a set of activities that help the project team identify, control, and track requirements and changes to requirements at any time as the project proceeds.[5] Many of these activities are identical to the software configuration management (SCM) techniques discussed in Chapter 27.

Requirements management begins with identification. Each requirement is assigned a unique identifier. Once requirements have been identified, traceability tables are developed. Shown schematically in Figure 7.1, each *traceability table* relates requirements to one or more aspects of the system or its environment. Among many possible traceability tables are the following:

Features traceability table. Shows how requirements relate to important customer observable system/product features.

FIGURE 7.1
Generic traceability table

Requirement \ Specific aspect of the system or its environment	A01	A02	A03	A04	A05				Aii
R01			✓		✓				
R02	✓		✓						
R03	✓			✓					✓
R04		✓			✓				
R05	✓	✓		✓					✓
Rnn	✓		✓						

5 Formal requirements management is initiated only for large projects that have hundreds of identifiable requirements. For small projects, this requirements engineering function is considerably less formal.

When a system is large and complex, determining the connections between requirements can be a daunting task. Use traceability tables to make the job a bit easier.

Source traceability table. Identifies the source of each requirement.

Dependency traceability table. Indicates how requirements are related to one another.

Subsystem traceability table. Categorizes requirements by the subsystem(s) that they govern.

Interface traceability table. Shows how requirements relate to both internal and external system interfaces.

In many cases, these traceability tables are maintained as part of a requirements database so that they can be quickly searched to understand how a change in one requirement will affect different aspects of the system to be built.

SOFTWARE TOOLS

Requirements Engineering

Objective: Requirements engineering tools assist in requirements gathering, requirements modeling, requirements management, and requirements validation.

Mechanics: Tool mechanics vary. In general, requirements engineering tools build a variety of graphical (e.g., UML) models that depict the informational, functional, and behavioral aspects of a system. These models form the basis for all other activities in the software process.

Representative Tools[6]

A reasonably comprehensive (and up-to-date) listing of requirements engineering tools has been prepared by The Atlantic Systems Guide, Inc. and can be found at http://www.systemsguild.com/GuildSite/Robs/retools.html. Requirements modeling tools are discussed in Chapter 8. Tools noted below focus on requirements management.

EasyRM, developed by Cybernetic Intelligence GmbH (www.easy-rm.com), builds a project-specific dictionary/glossary that contains detailed requirements descriptions and attributes.

OnYourMark Pro, developed by Omni-Vista (www.omni-vista.com), builds a requirements database, establishes relationships between requirements, and allows users to analyze the relationship between requirements and schedules/costs.

Rational RequisitePro, developed by Rational Software (www.rational.com), allow users to build a requirements database, represent relationships among requirements, and organize, prioritize, and trace requirements.

RTM, developed by Integrated Chipware (www.chipware.com), is a requirements description and traceability tool that also supports certain aspects of change control and test management.

It should be noted that many requirements management tasks can be performed using a simple spreadsheet or a small database system.

7.3 Initiating the Requirements Engineering Process

In an ideal setting, customers and software engineers work together on the same team.[7] In such cases, requirements engineering is simply a matter of conducting meaningful conversations with colleagues who are well-known members of the team. But reality is often quite different.

6 Tools noted here do not represent an endorsement, but rather a sampling of tools in this category. In most cases, tool names are trademarked by their respective developers.

7 This approach is recommended for all projects and is an integral part of the agile software development philosophy.

Customer(s) may be located in a different city or country, may have only a vague idea of what is required, may have conflicting opinions about the system to be built, may have limited technical knowledge, and limited time to interact with the requirements engineer. None of these things are desirable, but all are fairly common, and the software team is often forced to work within the constraints imposed by this situation.

In the sections that follow, we discuss the steps required to initiate requirements engineering—to get the project started in a way that will keep it moving forward toward a successful solution.

7.3.1 Identifying the Stakeholders

A stakeholder is anyone who has a direct interest in or benefits from the system that is to be developed.

Sommerville and Sawyer [SOM97] define a *stakeholder* as "anyone who benefits in a direct or indirect way from the system which is being developed." We have already identified the usual suspects: business operations managers, product managers, marketing people, internal and external customers, end-users, consultants, product engineers, software engineers, support and maintenance engineers, and others. Every stakeholder has a different view of the system, achieves different benefits when the system is successfully developed, and is open to different risks if the development effort should fail.

At inception, the requirements engineer should create of list of people who will contribute input as requirements are elicited (Section 7.4). The initial list will grow as stakeholders are contacted because every stakeholder will be asked: "Who else do you think I should talk to?"

7.3.2 Recognizing Multiple Viewpoints

Because many different stakeholders exist, the requirements of the system will be explored from many different points of view. For example, the marketing group is interested in functions and features that will excite the potential market, making the new system easy to sell. Business managers are interested in a feature set that can be built within budget and that will be ready to meet defined market windows. End-users may want features that are familiar to them and that are easy to learn and use. Software engineers may be concerned with functions that enable the infrastructure supporting more marketable functions and features. Support engineers may focus on the maintainability of the software.

> "Put three stakeholders in a room and ask them what kind of system they want. You're likely to get four or more different opinions."
>
> **Author unknown**

Each of these constituencies (and others) will contribute information to the requirements engineering process. As information from multiple viewpoints is collected, emerging requirements may be inconsistent or may conflict with one another. The job of the requirements engineer is to categorize all stakeholder information (including inconsistent and conflicting requirements) in a way that will allow decision makers to choose an internally consistent set of requirements for the system.

7.3.3 Working toward Collaboration

Throughout earlier chapters, we have noted that customers (and other stakeholders) should *collaborate* among themselves (avoiding petty turf battles) and with software engineering practitioners if a successful system is to result. But how is this collaboration accomplished?

The job of the requirements engineer is to identify areas of commonality (i.e., requirements on which all stakeholders agree) and areas of conflict or inconsistency (i.e., requirements that are desired by one stakeholder but conflict with the needs of another stakeholder). It is, of course, the latter category that presents a challenge.

INFO

Using "Priority Points"

One way of resolving conflicting requirements and at the same time better understanding the relative importance of all requirements is to use a "voting" scheme based on *priority points.* All stakeholders are provided with some number of priority points that can be "spent" on any number of requirements. A list of requirements is presented and each stakeholder indicates the relative importance of each (from his or her viewpoint) by spending one or more priority points on it. Points spent cannot be reused. Once a stakeholder's priority points are exhausted, no further action on requirements can be taken by that person. Overall points spent on each requirement by all stakeholders provide an indication of the overall importance of each requirement.

Collaboration does not necessarily mean that requirements are defined by committee. In many cases, stakeholders collaborate by providing their view of requirements, but a strong "project champion" (e.g., a business manager or a senior technologist) may make the final decision about which requirements make the cut.

7.3.4 Asking the First Questions

Earlier in this chapter, we noted that the questions asked at the inception of the project should be "context free" [GAU89]. The first set of context-free questions focuses on the customer and other stakeholders, overall goals, and benefits. For example, the requirements engineer might ask:

- Who is behind the request for this work?
- Who will use the solution?
- What will be the economic benefit of a successful solution?
- Is there another source for the solution that you need?

These questions help to identify all stakeholders who will have interest in the software to be built. In addition, the questions identify the measurable benefit of a successful implementation and possible alternatives to custom software development.

> "It is better to know some of the questions than all of the answers."
>
> **James Thurber**

The next set of questions enables the software team to gain a better understanding of the problem and allows the customer to voice his or her perceptions about a solution:

? What questions will help you gain a preliminary understanding of the problem?

- How would you characterize "good" output that would be generated by a successful solution?
- What problem(s) will this solution address?
- Can you show me (or describe) the business environment in which the solution will be used?
- Will special performance issues or constraints affect the way the solution is approached?

The final set of questions focuses on the effectiveness of the communication activity itself. Gause and Weinberg [GAU89] call these "meta-questions" and propose the following (abbreviated) list:

- Are you the right person to answer these questions? Are your answers "official"?
- Are my questions relevant to the problem that you have?
- Am I asking too many questions?
- Can anyone else provide additional information?
- Should I be asking you anything else?

> "He who asks a question is a fool for five minutes; he who does not ask a question is a fool forever."
>
> **Chinese proverb**

These questions (and others) will help to "break the ice" and initiate the communication that is essential to successful elicitation. But a question and answer meeting format is not an approach that has been overwhelmingly successful. In fact, the Q&A session should be used for the first encounter only and then replaced by a requirements elicitation format that combines elements of problem solving, negotiation, and specification. An approach of this type is presented in Section 7.4.

7.4 Eliciting Requirements

The question and answer format described in Section 7.3.4 is useful at inception, but it is not an approach that has been overwhelmingly successful for more detailed elicitation of requirements. In fact, the Q&A session should be used for the first encounter only and then replaced by a requirements elicitation format that combines elements of problem solving, elaboration, negotiation, and specification. An approach of this type is presented in the next section.

7.4.1 Collaborative Requirements Gathering

In order to encourage a collaborative, team-oriented approach to requirements gathering, a team of stakeholders and developers work together to identify the problem, propose elements of the solution, negotiate different approaches, and specify a preliminary set of solution requirements [ZAH90].[8]

Many different approaches to *collaborative requirements gathering* have been proposed. Each makes use of a slightly different scenario, but all apply some variation on the following basic guidelines:

? What are the basic guidelines for conducting a collaborative requirements gathering meeting?

- Meetings are conducted and attended by both software engineers and customers (along with other interested stakeholders).
- Rules for preparation and participation are established.
- An agenda is suggested that is formal enough to cover all important points but informal enough to encourage the free flow of ideas.
- A "facilitator" (can be a customer, a developer, or an outsider) controls the meeting.
- A "definition mechanism" (can be work sheets, flip charts, or wall stickers or an electronic bulletin board, chat room, or virtual forum) is used.
- The goal is to identify the problem, propose elements of the solution, negotiate different approaches, and specify a preliminary set of solution requirements in an atmosphere that is conducive to the accomplishment of the goal.

To better understand the flow of events as they occur, we present a brief scenario that outlines the sequence of events that lead up to the requirements gathering meeting, occur during the meeting, and follow the meeting.

> **"We spend a lot of time—the majority of project effort—not implementing or testing, but trying to decide what to build."**
>
> **Brian Lawrence**

During inception (Section 7.3) basic questions and answers establish the scope of the problem and the overall perception of a solution. Out of these initial meetings, the stakeholders write a one- or two-page "product request." A meeting place, time, and date are selected and a facilitator is chosen. Members of the software team and other stakeholder organizations are invited to attend. The product request is distributed to all attendees before the meeting date.

---

8 This approach is sometimes called *facilitated application specification techniques* (FAST).

WebRef

Joint Application Development (JAD) is a popular technique for requirements gathering. A good description can be found at **www.carolla.com/wp-jad.htm.**

While reviewing the product request in the days before the meeting, each attendee is asked to make a list of objects that are part of the environment that surrounds the system, other objects that are to be produced by the system, and objects that are used by the system to perform its functions. In addition, each attendee is asked to list services (processes or functions) that manipulate or interact with the objects. Finally, lists of constraints (e.g., cost, size, business rules) and performance criteria (e.g., speed, accuracy) are also developed. The attendees are informed that the lists are not expected to be exhaustive but are expected to reflect each person's perception of the system.

As an example,[9] consider an excerpt from a premeeting document written by a marketing person involved in the *SafeHome* project. This person writes the following narrative about the *home security function* that is to be part of *SafeHome:*

> Our research indicates that the market for home management systems is growing at a rate of 40 percent per year. The first *SafeHome* function we bring to market should be the home security function. Most people are familiar with "alarm systems" so this would be an easy sell.
>
> The home security function would protect against and/or recognize a variety of undesirable "situations" such as illegal entry, fire, flooding, carbon monoxide levels, and others. It'll use our wireless sensors to detect each situation, can be programmed by the homeowner, and will automatically telephone a monitoring agency when a situation is detected.

In reality, others would contribute to this narrative during the requirements gathering meeting, and considerably more information would be available. But even with additional information, ambiguity would be present, omissions would likely exist, and errors might occur. For now, the preceding "functional description" will suffice.

The requirements gathering team is composed of representatives from marketing, software and hardware engineering, and manufacturing. An outside facilitator is to be used.

If a system or product will serve many users, be absolutely certain that requirements are elicited from a representative cross-section of users. If only one user defines all requirements, acceptance risk is high.

Each person develops the lists described previously. Objects described for *SafeHome* might include the control panel, smoke detectors, window and door sensors, motion detectors, an alarm, an event (a sensor has been activated), a display, a PC, telephone numbers, a telephone call, and so on. The list of services might include *configuring* the system, *setting* the alarm, *monitoring* the sensors, *dialing* the phone, *programming* the control panel, and *reading* the display (note that services act on objects). In a similar fashion, each attendee will develop lists of constraints (e.g., the system must recognize when sensors are not operating, must be user-friendly, must interface directly to a standard phone line) and performance criteria (e.g., a sensor event should be recognized within one second; an event priority scheme should be implemented).

9 The *SafeHome* example (with extensions and variations) is used to illustrate important software engineering methods in many of the chapters that follow. As an exercise, it would be worthwhile to conduct your own requirements gathering meeting and develop a set of lists for it.

> "Facts do not cease to exist because they are ignored."
>
> **Aldous Huxley**

As the requirements gathering meeting begins, the first topic of discussion is the need and justification for the new product—everyone should agree that the product is justified. Once agreement has been established, each participant presents his lists for discussion. The lists can be pinned to the walls of the room using large sheets of paper, stuck to the walls using adhesive backed sheets, or written on a wall board. Alternatively, the lists may have been posted on an electronic bulletin board, at an internal Web site, or posed in a chat room environment for review prior to the meeting. Ideally, each listed entry should be capable of being manipulated separately so that lists can be combined, entries can be deleted, and additions can be made. At this stage, critique and debate are strictly prohibited.

ADVICE

Avoid the impulse to shoot down a customer's idea as "too costly" or "impractical." The idea here is to negotiate a list that is acceptable to all. To do this, you must keep an open mind.

After individual lists are presented in one topic area, a combined list is created by the group. The combined list eliminates redundant entries, adds any new ideas that come up during the discussion, but does not delete anything. After combined lists for all topic areas have been created, the facilitator coordinates discussion. The combined list is shortened, lengthened, or reworded to properly reflect the product/ system to be developed. The objective is to develop a consensus list in each topic area (objects, services, constraints, and performance). The lists are then set aside for later action.

Once the consensus lists have been completed, the team is divided into smaller subteams; each works to develop *mini-specifications* for one or more entries on each of the lists.[10] Each mini-specification is an elaboration of the word or phrase contained on a list. For example, the mini-specification for the *SafeHome* object **Control Panel** might be:

> The **Control Panel** is a wall-mounted unit that is approximately 9 × 5 inches in size. The control panel has wireless connectively to sensors and a PC. User interaction occurs through a keypad containing 12 keys. A 2 × 2 inch LCD display provides user feedback. Software provides interactive prompts, echo, and similar functions.

Each subteam then presents its mini-specs to all attendees for discussion. Additions, deletions, and further elaboration are made. In some cases, the development of mini-specs will uncover new objects, services, constraints, or performance requirements that will be added to the original lists. During all discussions, the team may raise an issue that cannot be resolved during the meeting. An *issues list* is maintained so that these ideas will be acted on later.

After the mini-specs are completed, each attendee makes a list of validation criteria for the product/system and presents her list to the team. A consensus list of

10 Rather than creating mini-specifications, many software teams elect to develop user scenarios called *use-cases*. These are considered in detail in Section 7.5.

validation criteria is then created. Finally, one or more participants (or outsiders) is assigned the task of writing a complete draft specification using all inputs from the meeting.

SAFEHOME

Conducting a Requirements Gathering Meeting

The scene: A meeting room. The first requirements gathering meeting is in progress.

The players: Jamie Lazar, software team member; Vinod Raman, software team member; Ed Robbins, software team member; Doug Miller, software engineering manager; three members of marketing; a product engineering representative; and a facilitator.

The conversation:

Facilitator (pointing at white board): So that's the current list of objects and services for the home security function.

Marketing person: That about covers it from our point of view.

Vinod: Didn't someone mention that they wanted all *SafeHome* functionality to be accessible via the Internet? That would include the home security function, no?

Marketing person: Yes, that's right . . . we'll have to add that functionality and the appropriate objects.

Facilitator: Does that also add some constraints?

Jamie: It does, both technical and legal.

Production rep: Meaning?

Jamie: We better make sure an outsider can't hack into the system, disarm it, and rob the place or worse. Heavy liability on our part.

Doug: Very true.

Marketing: But we still need Internet connectivity . . . just be sure to stop an outsider from getting in.

Ed: That's easier said than done and. . . .

Facilitator (interrupting): I don't want to debate this issue now. Let's note it as an action item and proceed. (Doug, serving as the recorder for the meeting, makes an appropriate note.)

Facilitator: I have a feeling there's still more to consider here.

(The group spends the next 45 minutes refining and expanding the details of the home security function.)

7.4.2 Quality Function Deployment

KEY POINT QFD defines requirements in a way that maximizes customer satisfaction.

Quality function deployment (QFD) is a technique that translates the needs of the customer into technical requirements for software. QFD "concentrates on maximizing customer satisfaction from the software engineering process [ZUL92]." To accomplish this, QFD emphasizes an understanding of what is valuable to the customer and then deploys these values throughout the engineering process. QFD identifies three types of requirements [ZUL92]:

Normal requirements. These requirements reflect objectives and goals stated for a product or system during meetings with the customer. If these requirements are present, the customer is satisfied. Examples of normal requirements might be requested types of graphical displays, specific system functions, and defined levels of performance.

Expected requirements. These requirements are implicit to the product or system and may be so fundamental that the customer does not explicitly state

Everyone wants to implement lots of exciting requirements, but be careful. That's how "requirements creep" sets in. On the other hand, exciting requirements lead to a breakthrough product!

them. Their absence will be a cause for significant dissatisfaction. Examples of expected requirements are ease of human/machine interaction, overall operational correctness and reliability, and ease of software installation.

Exciting requirements. These requirements reflect features that go beyond the customer's expectations and prove to be very satisfying when present. For example, word processing software is requested with standard features. The delivered product contains a number of page layout capabilities that are quite pleasing and unexpected.

In actuality, QFD spans the entire engineering process [PAR96]. However, many QFD concepts are applicable to the requirements elicitation activity. We present an overview of only these concepts (adapted for computer software) in the paragraphs that follow.

> **"Oft expectation fails, and most oft there where most it promises."**
>
> **William Shakespeare**

WebRef

Useful information on QFD can be obtained at **www.qfdi.org.**

In meetings with the customer, *function deployment* is used to determine the value of each function that is required for the system. *Information deployment* identifies both the data objects and events that the system must consume and produce. These are tied to the functions. Finally, *task deployment* examines the behavior of the system or product within the context of its environment. *Value analysis* is conducted to determine the relative priority of requirements determined during each of the three deployments.

QFD uses customer interviews and observation, surveys, and examination of historical data (e.g., problem reports) as raw data for the requirements gathering activity. These data are then translated into a table of requirements—called the *customer voice table*—that is reviewed with the customer. A variety of diagrams, matrices, and evaluation methods are then used to extract expected requirements and to attempt to derive exciting requirements [BOS91].

7.4.3 User Scenarios

As requirements are gathered, an overall vision of system functions and features begins to materialize. However, it is difficult to move into more technical software engineering activities until the software team understands how these functions and features will be used by different classes of end-users. To accomplish this, developers and users can create a set of scenarios that identify a thread of usage for the system to be constructed. The scenarios, often called *use-cases* [JAC92], provide a description of how the system will be used. Use-cases are discussed in greater detail in Section 7.5.

SAFEHOME

Developing a Preliminary User Scenario

The scene: A meeting room, continuing the first requirements gathering meeting.

The players: Jamie Lazar, software team member; Vinod Raman, software team member; Ed Robbins, software team member; Doug Miller, software engineering manager; three members of marketing; a product engineering representative; and a facilitator.

The conversation:

Facilitator: We've been talking about security for access to *SafeHome* functionality that will be accessible via the Internet. I'd like to try something.

Let's develop a user scenario for access to the home security function.

Jamie: How?

Facilitator: We can do it a couple of different ways, but for now, I'd like to keep things really informal. Tell us (he points at a marketing person) how you envision accessing the system.

Marketing person: Um. . . , well, this is the kind of thing I'd do if I was away from home and I had to let someone into the house, say a housekeeper or repair guy, who didn't have the security code.

Facilitator (smiling): That's the *reason* you'd do it . . . tell me *how* you'd actually do this.

Marketing person: Um . . . the first thing I'd need is a PC. I'd log on to a Web site we'd maintain for all users of *SafeHome*. I'd provide my user id and . . .

Vinod (interrupting): The Web page would have to be secure, encrypted, to guarantee that we're safe and. . . .

Facilitator (interrupting): That's good information, Vinod, but it's technical. Let's just focus on how the end-user will use this capability, OK?

Vinod: No problem.

Marketing person: So, as I was saying, I'd log on to a Web site and provide my user id and two levels of passwords.

Jamie: What if I forget my password?

Facilitator (interrupting): Good point, Jamie, but let's not address that now. We'll make a note of that and call it an "exception." I'm sure there'll be others.

Marketing person: After I enter the passwords, a screen representing all *SafeHome* functions will appear. I'd select the home security function. The system might request that I verify who I am, say by asking for my address or phone number or something. It would then display a picture of the security system control panel along with a list of functions that I can perform—arm the system, disarm the system, disarm one or more sensors. I suppose it might also allow me to reconfigure security zones and other things like that, but I'm not sure.

(As the marketing person continues talking, Doug takes copious notes. These form the basis for the first informal use-case scenario. Alternatively, the marketing person could have been asked to write the scenario, but this would be done outside the meeting.)

7.4.4 Elicitation Work Products

The work products produced as a consequence of requirements elicitation will vary depending on the size of the system or product to be built. For most systems, the work products include:

? **What information is produced as a consequence of requirements gathering?**

- A statement of need and feasibility.
- A bounded statement of scope for the system or product.
- A list of customers, users, and other stakeholders who participated in requirements elicitation.

- A description of the system's technical environment.
- A list of requirements (preferably organized by function) and the domain constraints that apply to each.
- A set of usage scenarios that provide insight into the use of the system or product under different operating conditions.
- Any prototypes developed to better define requirements.

Each of these work products is reviewed by all people who have participated in requirements elicitation.

7.5 Developing Use-Cases

In a book that discusses how to write effective use-cases, Alistair Cockburn [COC01] notes that "a use-case captures a contract . . . [that] describes the system's behavior under various conditions as the system responds to a request from one of its stakeholders." In essence, a *use-case* tells a stylized story about how an end-user (playing one of a number of possible roles) interacts with the system under a specific set of circumstances. The story may be narrative text, an outline of tasks or interactions, a template-based description, or a diagrammatic representation. Regardless of its form, a use-case depicts the software or system from the end-user's point of view.

Use-cases are defined from an actor's point of view. An actor is a role that people (users) or devices play as they interact with the software.

The first step in writing a use-case is to define the set of "actors" that will be involved in the story. *Actors* are the different people (or devices) that use the system or product within the context of the function and behavior that is to be described. Actors represent the roles that people (or devices) play as the system operates. Defined somewhat more formally, an actor is anything that communicates with the system or product and that is external to the system itself. Every actor has one or more goals when using the system.

It is important to note that an actor and an end-user are not necessarily the same thing. A typical user may play a number of different roles when using a system, whereas an actor represents a class of external entities (often, but not always, people) that play just one role in the context of the use-case. As an example, consider a machine operator (a user) who interacts with the control computer for a manufacturing cell that contains a number of robots and numerically controlled machines. After careful review of requirements, the software for the control computer requires four different modes (roles) for interaction: programming mode, test mode, monitoring mode, and troubleshooting mode. Therefore, four actors can be defined: programmer, tester, monitor, and troubleshooter. In some cases, the machine operator can play all of these roles. In others, different people may play the role of each actor.

WebRef

An excellent paper on use-cases can be downloaded from **www.rational.com/products/whitepapers/100622.jsp.**

Because requirements elicitation is an evolutionary activity, not all actors are identified during the first iteration. It is possible to identify primary actors [JAC92] during the first iteration and secondary actors as more is learned about the system. *Primary actors* interact to achieve required system function and derive the intended benefit from the system. They work directly and frequently with the software. *Secondary actors* support the system so that primary actors can do their work.

Once actors have been identified, use-cases can be developed. Jacobson [JAC92] suggests a number of questions[11] that should be answered by a use-case:

? What do I need to know in order to develop an effective use-case?

- Who is the primary actor(s), the secondary actor(s)?
- What are the actor's goals?
- What preconditions should exist before the story begins?
- What main tasks or functions are performed by the actor?
- What exceptions might be considered as the story is described?
- What variations in the actor's interaction are possible?
- What system information will the actor acquire, produce, or change?
- Will the actor have to inform the system about changes in the external environment?
- What information does the actor desire from the system?
- Does the actor wish to be informed about unexpected changes?

Recalling basic *SafeHome* requirements, we define three actors: the **homeowner** (a user), a **configuration manager** (likely the same person as **homeowner,** but playing a different role), **sensors** (devices attached to the system), and the **monitoring subsystem** (the central station that monitors the *SafeHome* home security function). For the purposes of this example, we consider only the **homeowner** actor. The homeowner interacts with the home security function in a number of different ways using either the alarm control panel or a PC:

- Enters a password to allow all other interactions.
- Inquires about the status of a security zone.
- Inquires about the status of a sensor.
- Presses the panic button in an emergency.
- Activates/deactivates the security system.

Considering the situation in which the homeowner uses the control panel, the basic use-case for system activation follows:[12]

11 Jacobson's questions have been extended to provide a more complete view of use-case content.

12 Note that this use-case differs from the situation in which the system is accessed via the Internet. In this case, interaction occurs via the control panel, not the GUI provided when a PC is used.

FIGURE 7.2

SafeHome control panel

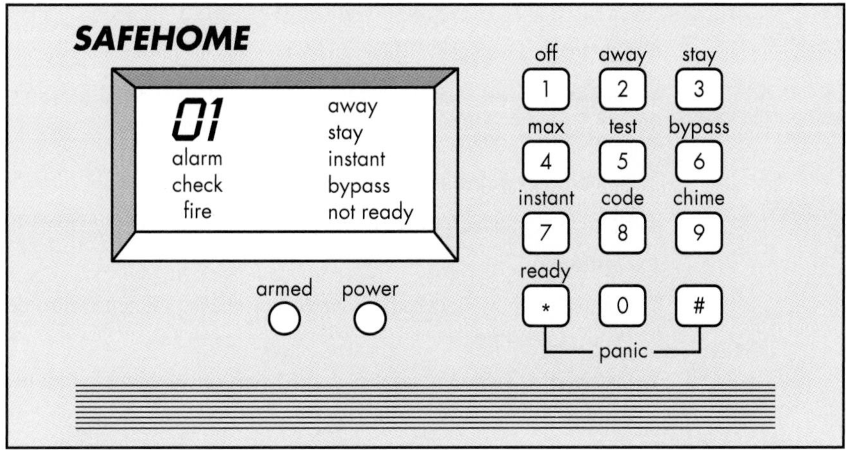

1. The homeowner observes the *SafeHome* control panel (Figure 7.2) to determine if the system is ready for input. If the system is not ready a *not ready* message is displayed on the LCD display, and the homeowner must physically close windows/doors so that the *not ready* message disappears. (A *not ready* message implies that a sensor is open; i.e., that a door or window is open.)
2. The homeowner uses the keypad to key in a four-digit password. The password is compared with the valid password stored in the system. If the password is incorrect, the control panel will beep once and reset itself for additional input. If the password is correct, the control panel awaits further action.
3. The homeowner selects and keys in *stay* or *away* (see Figure 7.2) to activate the system. Stay activates only perimeter sensors (inside motion detecting sensors are deactivated). Away activates all sensors.
4. When activation occurs, a red alarm light can be observed by the homeowner.

The basic use-case presents a high-level story that describes the interaction between the actor and the system.

ADVICE

Use-cases are often written informally. However, use the template shown here to ensure that you've addressed all key issues.

In many instances, use-case are further elaborated to provide considerably more detail about the interaction. For example, Cockburn [COC01]suggests the following template for detailed descriptions of use-cases:

Use-case: *InitiateMonitoring*

Primary actor: Homeowner.

Goal in context: To set the system to monitor sensors when the homeowner leaves the house or remains inside.

Preconditions: System has been programmed for a password and to recognize various sensors.

Trigger: The homeowner decides to "set" the system, i.e., to turn on the alarm functions.

Scenario:

1. Homeowner: observes control panel.
2. Homeowner: enters password.
3. Homeowner: selects "stay" or "away."
4. Homeowner: observes red alarm light to indicate that *SafeHome* has been armed.

Exceptions:

1. Control panel is *not ready:* homeowner checks all sensors to determine which are open; closes them.
2. Password is incorrect (control panel beeps once): homeowner reenters correct password.
3. Password not recognized: monitoring and response subsystem must be contacted to reprogram password.
4. *Stay* is selected: control panel beeps twice and a *stay* light is lit; perimeter sensors are activated.
5. *Away* is selected: control panel beeps three times and an *away* light is lit; all sensors are activated.

Priority: Essential, must be implemented.

When available: First increment.

Frequency of use: Many times per day.

Channel to actor: Via control panel interface.

Secondary actors: Support technician, sensors.

Channels to secondary actors:

Support technician: phone line.

Sensors: hardwired and wireless interfaces.

Open issues:

1. Should there be a way to activate the system without the use of a password or with an abbreviated password?
2. Should the control panel display additional text messages?
3. How much time does the homeowner have to enter the password from the time the first key is pressed?
4. Is there a way to deactivate the system before it actually activates?

Each use-case can be assessed by stakeholders, and the relative priority for each can be assigned.

Use-cases for other **homeowner** interactions would be developed in a similar manner. It is important to note that each use-case must be reviewed with care. If some element of the interaction is ambiguous, it is likely that a review of the use-case will uncover the problem.

SAFEHOME

Developing a High-Level Use-Case Diagram

The scene: A meeting room, continuing the requirements gathering meeting.

The players: Jamie Lazar, software team member; Vinod Raman, software team member; Ed Robbins, software team member; Doug Miller, software engineering manager; three members of marketing; a product engineering representative; and a facilitator.

The conversation:

Facilitator: We've spent a fair amount of time talking about *SafeHome* home security functionality. During the break I sketched a use-case diagram to summarize the important scenarios that are part of this function. Take a look.

(All attendees look at Figure 7.3.)

Jamie: I'm just beginning to learn UML notation. So the home security function is represented by the big box with the ovals inside it? And the ovals represent use-cases that we've written in text?

Facilitator: Yep. And the stick figures represent actors—the people or things that interact with the system as described by the use-case . . . oh, I use the labeled square to represent an actor that's not a person, in this case, sensors.

Doug: Is that legal in UML?

Facilitator: Legality isn't the issue. The point is to communicate information. I view the use of a human-like stick figure for representing a device to be misleading. So I've adapted things a bit. I don't think it creates a problem.

Vinod: Okay, so we have use-case narratives for each of the ovals. Do we need to develop the more detailed template-based narratives I've read about?

Facilitator: Probably, but that can wait until we've considered other *SafeHome* functions.

Marketing person: Wait, I've been looking at this diagram, and all of a sudden I realize we missed something.

Facilitator: Oh really. Tell me what we've missed.

(The meeting continues.)

FIGURE 7.3

Use-case diagram for *SafeHome* home security function

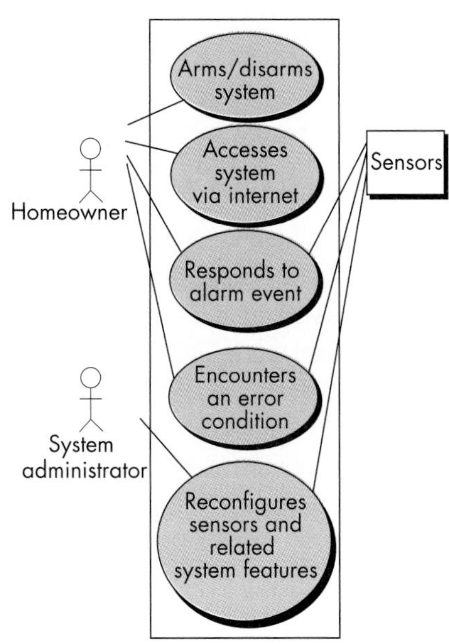

SOFTWARE TOOLS

Use-Case Development

Objective: Assist in the development of use-cases by providing automated templates and mechanisms for assessing clarity and consistency.

Mechanics: Tool mechanics vary. In general, use-case tools provide fill-in-the-blanks templates for creating effective use-cases. Most use-case functionality is embedded into a set of broader requirements engineering functions.

Representative Tools[13]

Clear Requirement Workbench, developed by LiveSpecs Software (www.livespecs.com), provides automated support for the creation and assessment of use-cases as well as a variety of other requirements engineering functions.

The vast majority of UML-based analysis modeling tools provide both text and graphical support for use-case development and modeling.

Objects by Design, a source for UML tools (www.objectsbydesign.com/tools/umltools_byCompany.html) provides comprehensive links to tools of this type.

A variety of use-case templates and a database to support them can be found at UseCases.org (www.usecases.org).

7.6 Building the Analysis Model

The intent of the analysis model is to provide a description of the required informational, functional, and behavioral domains for a computer-based system. The model changes dynamically as software engineers learn more about the system to be built, and stakeholders understand more about what they really require. For that reason, the analysis model is a snapshot of requirements at any given time. We expect it to change.

As the analysis model evolves, certain elements will become relatively stable, providing a solid foundation for the design tasks that follow. However, other elements of the model may be more volatile, indicating the customer does not yet fully understand requirements for the system.

The analysis model and the methods used to build it are presented in detail in Chapter 8. In the sections that follow, we present a brief overview.

7.6.1 Elements of the Analysis Model

There are many different ways to look at the requirements for a computer-based system. Some software people argue that it's best to select one mode of representation (e.g., the use-case) and apply it to the exclusion of all other modes. Other practitioners believe that it's worthwhile to use a number of different modes of representation to depict the analysis model. Different modes of representation force the software team to consider requirements from different viewpoints—an approach that has a higher probability of uncovering omissions, inconsistencies, and ambiguity.

The specific elements of the analysis model are dictated by the analysis modeling method (Chapter 8) that is to be used. However, a set of generic elements is common to most analysis models:

13 Tools noted here do not represent an endorsement, but rather a sampling of tools in this category. In most cases, tool names are trademarked by their respective developers.

It always a good idea to get stakeholders involved. One of the best ways to do this is to have each stakeholder write use-cases that describe how the software will be used.

Scenario-based elements. The system is described from the user's point of view using a scenario-based approach. For example, basic use-cases (Section 7.5) and their corresponding use-case diagrams (Figure 7.3) evolve into more elaborate template-based use-cases. Scenario-based elements of the analysis model are often the first part of the analysis model that is developed. As such, they serve as input for the creation of other modeling elements.

A somewhat different approach to scenario-based modeling depicts the activities or functions that have been defined as part of the requirement elicitation task. These functions exist within a processing context. That is, the sequence of activities (the terms *functions* or *operations* can also be used) that describe processing within a limited context are defined as part of the analysis model. Like most elements of the analysis model (and other software engineering models), activities (functions) can be represented at many different levels of abstraction. Models in this category can be defined iteratively. Each iteration provides additional processing detail. As an example, Figure 7.4 depicts a UML activity diagram for eliciting requirements.[14] Three levels of elaboration are shown.

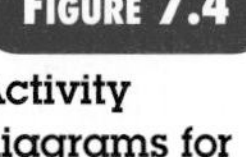

Activity diagrams for eliciting requirements

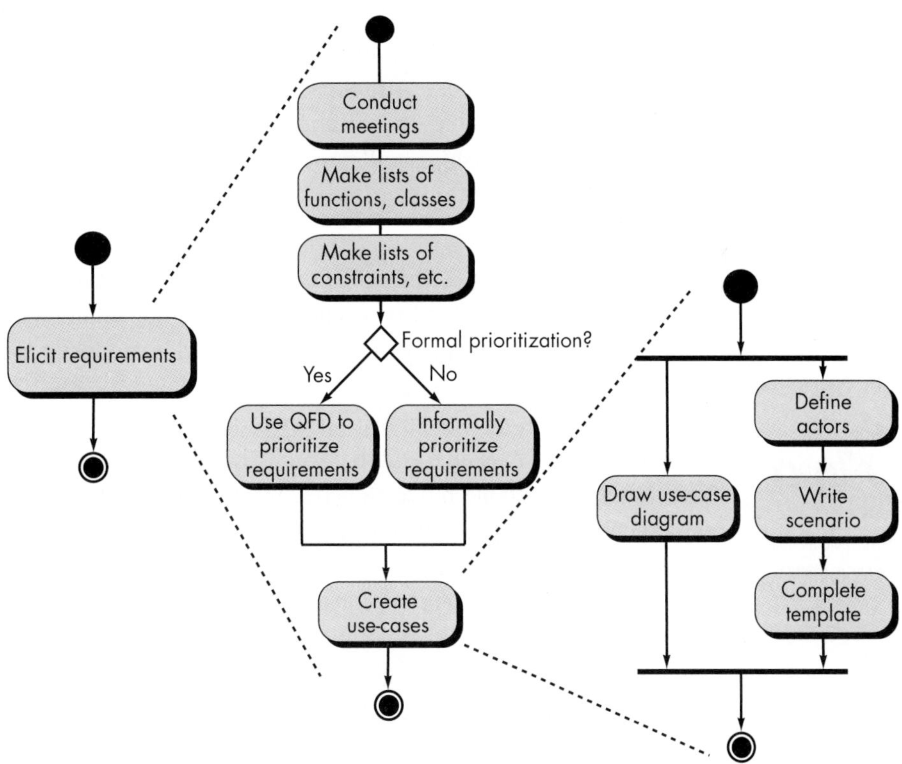

14 The activity diagram is quite similar to the flowchart—a graphical diagram for representing control-flow sequences and logic (Chapter 11).

FIGURE 7.5

Class diagram for Sensor

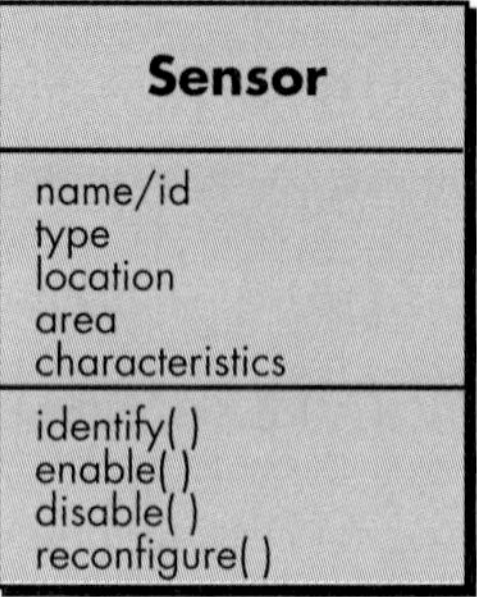

One way to isolate classes is to look for descriptive nouns in a use-case script. At least some of the nouns will be candidate classes. More on this in Chapter 8.

Class-based elements. Each usage scenario implies a set of "objects" that are manipulated as an actor interacts with the system. These objects are categorized into classes—a collection of things that have similar attributes and common behaviors. For example, a class diagram can be used to depict a **Sensor** class for the *SafeHome* security function (Figure 7.5). Note that the diagram lists the attributes of sensors (e.g., **name/id, type**) and the operations [e.g., *identify(), enable()*] that can be applied to modify these attributes. In addition to class diagrams, other analysis modeling elements depict the manner in which classes collaborate with one another and the relationships and interactions between classes. These are discussed in more detail in Chapter 8.

Behavioral elements. The behavior of a computer-based system can have a profound effect on the design that is chosen and the implementation approach that is applied. Therefore, the analysis model must provide modeling elements that depict behavior.

A state is an externally observable mode of behavior. External stimuli cause transitions between states.

The *state diagram* (Chapter 8) is one method for representing the behavior of a system by depicting its states and the events that cause the system to change state. A *state* is any observable mode of behavior. In addition, the state diagram indicates what actions (e.g., process activation) are taken as a consequence of a particular event.

To illustrate a state diagram, consider a *reading commands* state for an office photocopier. UML state diagram notation is shown in Figure 7.6. A rounded rectangle represents a state. The rectangle is divided into three areas: (1) the state name (e.g., Reading commands), (2) *state variables* that indicate how the state manifests itself to the outside world, and (3) *state activities* that indicate how the state is entered (**entry/**) and actions (**do:**) that are invoked while in the state.

FIGURE 7.6

UML state diagram notation

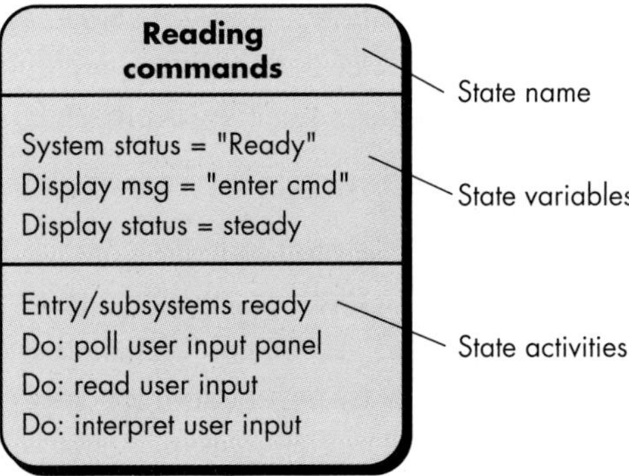

SAFEHOME

Preliminary Behavioral Modeling

The scene: A meeting room, continuing the requirements meeting.

The players: Jamie Lazar, software team member; Vinod Raman, software team member; Ed Robbins, software team member; Doug Miller, software engineering manager; three members of marketing; a product engineering representative; and a facilitator.

The conversation:

Facilitator: We've just about finished talking about *SafeHome* home security functionality. But before we do, I want to discuss the behavior of the function.

Marketing person: I don't understand what you mean by behavior.

Ed (laughing): That's when you give the product a "timeout" if it misbehaves.

Facilitator: Not exactly. Let me explain.
(The facilitator explains the basics of behavioral modeling to the requirements gathering team.)

Marketing person: This seems a little technical. I'm not sure I can help here.

Facilitator: Sure you can. What behavior do you observe from the user's point of view?

Marketing person: Uh. . . , well the system will be *monitoring* the sensors. It'll be *reading commands* from the homeowner. It'll be *displaying* its status.

Facilitator: See, you can do it.

Jamie: It'll also be *polling* the PC to determine if there is any input from it, for example Internet-based access or configuration information.

Vinod: Yeah, in fact, *configuring the system* is a state in its own right.

Doug: You guys are rolling. Let's give this a bit more thought . . . Is there a way to diagram this stuff?

Facilitator: There is, but let's postpone that until after the meeting.

Flow-oriented elements. Information is transformed as it flows through a computer-based system. The system accepts input in a variety of forms; applies functions to transform it; and produces output in a variety of forms. Input may be a control signal transmitted by a transducer, a series of numbers typed by a human operator, a packet of information transmitted on a network link, or a voluminous data file retrieved from secondary storage. The transform(s) may comprise a single logical comparison, a complex numerical algorithm, or a rule-inference approach of an expert system. Output may light a single LED or produce a 200-page report. In effect, we can create a flow model for any computer-based system, regardless of size and complexity. A more detailed discussion of flow modeling is presented in Chapter 8.

7.6.2 Analysis Patterns

Anyone who has done requirements engineering on more than a few software projects begins to notice that certain things reoccur across all projects within a specific application domain.[15] These can be called *analysis patterns* [FOW97] and represent something (e.g., a class, a function, a behavior) within the application domain that can be reused when modeling many applications.

Geyer-Schulz and Hahsler [GEY01] suggest two benefits that can be associated with the use of analysis patterns:

> First, analysis patterns speed up the development of abstract analysis models that capture the main requirements of the concrete problem by providing reusable analysis models with examples as well as a description of advantages and limitations. Second, analysis patterns facilitate the transformation of the analysis model into a design model by suggesting design patterns and reliable solutions for common problems.

WebRef
A useful patterns library and many other patterns resources can be obtained at **hillside.net/patterns.**

Analysis patterns are integrated into the analysis model by reference to the pattern name. They are also stored in a repository so that requirements engineers can use search facilities to find and reuse them.

Information about an analysis pattern is presented in a standard template that takes the form [GEY01]:[16]

? Is there a recommended template for describing patterns?

Pattern name: A descriptor that captures the essence of the pattern. The descriptor is used within the analysis model when reference is made to the pattern.

Intent: Describes what the pattern accomplishes or represents and/or what problem is addressed within the context of an application domain.

Motivation: A scenario that illustrates how the pattern can be used to address the problem.

Forces and context: A description of external issues (forces) that can affect how the pattern is used and also the external issues that will be resolved when the pattern is applied. External issues can encompass business-related subjects, external technical constraints, and people-related matters.

Solution: A description of how the pattern is applied to solve the problem with an emphasis on structural and behavioral issues.

Consequences: Addresses what happens when the pattern is applied and what trade-offs exist during its application.

---

15 In some cases, things reoccur regardless of the application domain. For example, the features and functions of user interfaces are common regardless of the application domain under consideration.

16 A variety of patterns templates have been proposed in the literature. Interested readers should see [FOW97], [BUS96], and [GAM95] among many sources.

Design: Discusses how the analysis pattern can be achieved through the use of known design patterns.

Known uses: Examples of uses within actual systems.

Related patterns: One or more analysis patterns that are related to the named pattern because the analysis pattern (1) is commonly used with the named pattern, (2) is structurally similar to the named pattern, (3) is a variation of the named pattern.

Examples of analysis patterns and further discussion of this topic are presented in Chapter 8.

INFO

Patterns

We see patterns in virtually everything we encounter in everyday life.

Consider action-adventure movies—more specifically action-adventure detective movies with comic overtones. We can define patterns for *Hero&Sidekick, CaptainWhoManagesHero, CriminalwithaHeart,* and many more.

For example, *CaptainWhoManagesHero* is invariably older, wears a tie (Hero doesn't), yells at *Hero&Sidekick* constantly, usually provides comic relief, or may be used in a more malevolent role to put bureaucratic or self-serving roadblocks in the way of *Hero&Sidekick.* A dramatic pattern is being established.

For a somewhat more technical example, consider a mobile phone. The following patterns are obvious: *MakeCall, LookUpNumber,* and *GetMessages* among many. Each of these patterns can be described once and then reused in software for any mobile phone.

7.7 Negotiating Requirements

In an ideal requirements engineering context, the inception, elicitation, and elaboration tasks determine customer requirements in sufficient detail to proceed to subsequent software engineering steps. Unfortunately, this rarely happens. In reality, the customer and the developer enter into a process of *negotiation,* where the customer may be asked to balance functionality, performance, and other product or system characteristics against cost and time to market. The intent of this negotiation is to develop a project plan that meets the needs of the customer while at the same time reflecting the real-world constraints (e.g., time, people, budget) that have been placed on the software team.

> **"A compromise is the art of dividing a cake in such a way that everyone believes he has the biggest piece."**
>
> **Ludwig Erhard**

The best negotiations strive for a "win-win" result.[17] That is, the customer wins by getting the system or product that satisfies the majority of the customer's needs, and the software team wins by working to realistic and achievable budgets and deadlines.

17 Dozens of books have been written on negotiating skills (e.g., [LEW00], [FAR97], [DON96]). It is one of the more important things that a young (or old) software engineer or manager can learn. Read one.

WebRef
A brief paper on negotiation for software requirements can be downloaded from **sunset.usc.edu/~aegyed/publications/Software_Requirements_Negotiation-Some_lessons_Learned.html.**

Boehm [BOE98] defines a set of negotiation activities at the beginning of each software process iteration. Rather than a single customer communication activity, the following activities are defined:

1. Identification of the system or subsystem's key stakeholders.
2. Determination of the stakeholders' "win conditions."
3. Negotiate of the stakeholders' win conditions to reconcile them into a set of win-win conditions for all concerned (including the software team).

Successful completion of these initial steps achieves a win-win result, which becomes the key criterion for proceeding to subsequent software engineering activities.

INFO

The Art of Negotiation

Learning how to negotiate effectively can serve you well throughout your personal and technical life. The following guidelines are well worth considering:

1. *Recognize that it's not a competition.* To be successful, both parties have to feel they've won or achieved something. Both will have to compromise.
2. *Map out a strategy.* Decide what you'd like to achieve; what the other party wants to achieve, and how you'll go about making both happen.
3. *Listen actively.* Don't work on formulating your response while the other party is talking. Listen. It's likely you'll gain knowledge that will help you to better negotiate your position.
4. *Focus on the other party's interests.* Don't take hard positions if you want to avoid conflict.
5. *Don't let it get personal.* Focus on the problem that needs to be solved.
6. *Be creative.* Don't be afraid to think out of the box if you're at an impasse.
7. *Be ready to commit.* Once an agreement has been reached, don't waffle: commit to it and move on.

SAFEHOME

The Start of a Negotiation

The scene: Lisa Perez's office, after the first requirements gathering meeting.

The players: Doug Miller, software engineering manager and Lisa Perez, marketing manager.

The conversation:

Lisa: So, I hear the first meeting went really well.

Doug: Actually, it did. You sent some good people to the meeting . . . they really contributed.

Lisa (smiling): Yeah, they actually told me they got into it, and it wasn't a propeller head activity.

Doug (laughing): I'll be sure to take off my techie beanie the next time I visit . . . Look, Lisa, I think we may have a problem with getting all of the functionality for the home security function out by the dates your management is talking about. It's early, I know, but I've already been doing a little back of the envelope planning and. . . .

Lisa: We've got to have it by that date, Doug. What functionality are you talking about?

Doug: I figure we can get full home security functionality out by the drop-dead date, but we'll have to delay Internet access till the second release.

Lisa: Doug, it's the Internet access that gives *SafeHome* "gee whiz" appeal. We're going to build our entire marketing campaign around it. We've gotta have it!

Doug: I understand your situation, I really do. The problem is that in order to give you Internet access, we'll need a fully secure Web site up and running. That takes time and people. We'll also have to build a lot of additional functionality into the first release . . . I don't think we can do it with the resources we've got.

Lisa (frowning): I see, but you've got to figure out a way to get it done. It's pivotal to home security functions and to other functions as well . . . the other functions can wait until the next releases . . . I'll agree to that.

Lisa and Doug appear to be at an impasse, and yet they must negotiate a solution to this problem. Can they both "win" here? Playing the role of a mediator, what would you suggest?

7.8 Validating Requirements

As each element of the analysis model is created, it is examined for consistency, omissions, and ambiguity. The requirements represented by the model are prioritized by the customer and grouped within requirements packages that will be implemented as software increments and delivered to the customer. A review of the analysis model addresses the following questions:

? When I review requirements, what questions should I ask?

- Is each requirement consistent with the overall objective for the system/product?
- Have all requirements been specified at the proper level of abstraction? That is, do some requirements provide a level of technical detail that is inappropriate at this stage?
- Is the requirement really necessary or does it represent an add-on feature that may not be essential to the objective of the system?
- Is each requirement bounded and unambiguous?
- Does each requirement have attribution? That is, is a source (generally, a specific individual) noted for each requirement?
- Do any requirements conflict with other requirements?
- Is each requirement achievable in the technical environment that will house the system or product?
- Is each requirement testable, once implemented?
- Does the requirements model properly reflect the information, function, and behavior of the system to be built?
- Has the requirements model been "partitioned" in a way that exposes progressively more detailed information about the system?
- Have requirements patterns been used to simplify the requirements model? Have all patterns been properly validated? Are all patterns consistent with customer requirements?

These and other questions should be asked and answered to ensure that the requirements model is an accurate reflection of the customer's needs and that it provides a solid foundation for design.

7.9 Summary

It is necessary to understand requirements before design and construction of a computer-based system can begin. To accomplish this, a set of requirements engineering tasks are conducted. Requirements engineering occurs during the customer communication and modeling activities that we have defined for the generic software process. Seven distinct requirements engineering functions—inception, elicitation, elaboration, negotiation, specification, validation, and management—are conducted by members of the software team.

At project inception, the developer and the customer (as well as other stakeholders) establish basic problem requirements, define overriding project constraints, and address major features and functions that must be present for the system to meet its objectives. This information is refined and expanded during elicitation—a requirements gathering activity that makes use of facilitated meetings, QFD, and the development of user scenarios.

Elaboration further expands requirements into an analysis model—a collection of scenario-based, activity-based, class-based, behavioral, and flow-oriented model elements. A variety of modeling notations may be used to create these elements. The model may reference analysis patterns—characteristics of the problem domain that have been seen to reoccur across different applications.

As requirements are identified and the analysis model is created, the software team and other project stakeholders negotiate the priority, availability, and relative cost of each requirement. The intent of this negotiation is to develop a realistic project plan. In addition, each requirement and the analysis model as a whole are validated against customer need to ensure that the right system is to be built.

References

[BOE98] Boehm, B., and A. Egyed, "Software Requirements Negotiation: Some Lessons Learned," *Proc. Intl. Conf. Software Engineering,* ACM/IEEE, 1998, pp. 503–506.

[BOS91] Bossert, J. L., *Quality Function Deployment: A Practitioner's Approach,* ASQC Press, 1991.

[BUS96] Buschmann, F., et al., *Pattern-Oriented Software Architecture: A System of Pattern,* Wiley, 1996.

[COC01] Cockburn, A., *Writing Effective Use-Cases,* Addison-Wesley, 2001.

[CRI92] Christel, M. G., and K. C. Kang, "Issues in Requirements Elicitation," Software Engineering Institute, CMU/SEI-92-TR-12 7, September 1992.

[DON96] Donaldson, M. C., and M. Donaldson, *Negotiating for Dummies,* IDG Books Worldwide, 1996.

[FAR97] Farber, D. C., *Common Sense Negotiation: The Art of Winning Gracefully,* Bay Press, 1997.

[FOW97] Fowler, M., *Analysis Patterns: Reusable Object Models,* Addison-Wesley, 1997.

[GAM95] Gamma, E., et al., *Design Patterns: Elements of Reusable Object-Oriented Software,* Addison-Wesley, 1995.

[GAU89] Gause, D. C,. and G. M. Weinberg, *Exploring Requirements: Quality Before Design,* Dorset House, 1989.

[GEY01] Geyer-Schulz, A., and M. Hahsler, *Software Engineering with Analysis Patterns,* Technical Report 01/2001, Institut für Informationsverarbeitung und-wirtschaft, Wirschaftsuniversität Wien, November 2001, downloaded from: http://wwwai.wu-wien.ac.at/~hahsler/research/virlib_working2001/virlib/.

[JAC92] Jacobson, I., *Object-Oriented Software Engineering,* Addison-Wesley, 1992.

[LEW00] Lewicki, R, D. Saunders, and J. Minton, *Essentials of Negotiation,* McGraw-Hill, 2000.

[PAR96] Pardee, W., *To Satisfy and Delight Your Customer,* Dorset House, 1996.

[SOM97] Somerville, I., and P. Sawyer, *Requirements Engineering,* Wiley, 1997.

[THA97] Thayer, R. H., and M. Dorfman, *Software Requirements Engineering,* 2nd ed., IEEE Computer Society Press, 1997.

[YOU01] Young, R., *Effective Requirements Practices,* Addison-Wesley, 2001.

[ZAH90] Zahniser, R. A., "Building Software in Groups," *American Programmer,* vol. 3, nos. 7–8, July–August 1990.

[ZUL92] Zultner, R., "Quality Function Deployment for Software: Satisfying Customers," *American Programmer,* February 1992, pp. 28–41.

PROBLEMS AND POINTS TO PONDER

7.1. Why is it that many software developers don't pay enough attention to requirements engineering? Are there ever circumstances where you can skip it?

7.2. What does "feasibility analysis" imply when it is discussed within the context of the inception function?

7.3. You have been given the responsibility to elicit requirements from a customer who tells you he is too busy to meet with you. What should you do?

7.4. Discuss some of the problems that occur when requirements must be elicited from three or four different customers.

7.5. Why do we say that the analysis model represents a snapshot of a system in time?

7.6. Let's assume that you've convinced the customer (you're a very good salesperson) to agree to every demand that you have as a developer. Does that make you a master negotiator? Why?

7.7. Develop at least three additional "context-free questions" that you might ask a stakeholder during inception.

7.8. Throughout this chapter we refer to the "customer." Describe the "customer" for information systems developers, for builders of computer-based products, for systems builders. Be careful here: there may be more to this problem than you first imagine!

7.9. Develop a facilitated requirements gathering "kit." The kit should include a set of guidelines for conducting a requirements gathering meeting and materials that can be used to facilitate the creation of lists and any other items that might help in defining requirements.

7.10. Your instructor will divide the class into groups of four or six students. Half of the group will play the role of the marketing department and half will take on the role of software engineering. Your job is to define requirements for the *SafeHome* security function described in this chapter. Conduct a requirements gathering meeting using the guidelines presented in this chapter.

7.11. Develop a complete use-case for one of the following activities:

a. Making a withdrawal at an ATM.
b. Using your charge card for a meal at a restaurant.
c. Buying a stock using an on-line brokerage account.
d. Searching for books (on a specific topic) using an on-line bookstore.
e. An activity specified by your instructor.

7.12. What do use-case "exceptions" represent?

7.13. Briefly discuss each of the elements of an analysis model. Indicate what each contributes to the model, how each is unique, and what general information is presented by each.

7.14. Describe an analysis pattern in your own words.

7.15. Using the template presented in Section 7.6.2, suggest one or more analysis patterns for an application suggested by your instructor.

7.16. What does "win-win" mean in the context of negotiation during the requirements engineering activity?

7.17. What do you think happens when requirements validation uncovers an error? Who is involved in correcting the error?

Further Readings and Information Sources

Because it is pivotal to the successful creation of any complex computer-based system, requirements engineering is discussed in a wide array of books. Hull and her colleagues (*Requirements Engineering,* Springer-Verlag, 2002), Bray (*An Introduction to Requirements Engineering,* Addison-Wesley, 2002), Arlow (*Requirements Engineering,* Addison-Wesley, 2001), Gilb (*Requirements Engineering,* Addison-Wesley, 2000), Graham (*Requirements Engineering and Rapid Development,* Addison-Wesley, 1999) and Sommerville and Kotonya (*Requirement Engineering: Processes and Techniques,* Wiley, 1998) are but a few of many books dedicated to the subject. Dan Berry (http://se. uwaterloo.ca/~dberry/bib.html) has published a wide variety of thought provoking papers on requirements engineering topics.

Lauesen (*Software Requirements: Styles and Techniques,* Addison-Wesley, 2002) presents a comprehensive survey of requirements analysis methods and notation. Weigers (*Software Requirements,* Microsoft Press, 1999) and Leffingwell and his colleagues (*Managing Software Requirements: A Unified Approach,* Addison-Wesley, 2000) present a useful collection of requirement best practices and suggest pragmatic guidelines for most aspects of the requirements engineering process.

Robertson and Robertson (*Mastering the Requirements Process,* Addison-Wesley, 1999) present a very detailed case study that helps to explain all aspects of the software requirements analysis and the analysis model. Kovitz (*Practical Software Requirements: A Manual of Content and Style,* Manning Publications, 1998) discusses a step-by-step approach to requirements analysis and a style guide for those who must develop requirements specifications. Jackson (*Software Requirements Analysis and Specification: A Lexicon of Practices, Principles and Prejudices,* Addison-Wesley, 1995) presents an intriguing look at the subject from A to Z (literally). Ploesch (*Assertions, Scenarios and Prototypes,* Springer-Verlag, 2003) discusses advanced techniques for developing software requirements.

Windle and Abreo (*Software Requirements Using the Unified Process,* Prentice-Hall, 2002) discuss requirements engineering within the context of the Unified Process and UML notation. Alexander and Steven (*Writing Better Requirements,* Addison-Wesley, 2002) present a brief set of guidelines for writing clear requirements, representing them as scenarios, and reviewing the end result.

Use-case modeling is often the driver for the creation of all other aspects of the analysis model. The subject is discussed at length by Bittner and Spence (*Use-Case Modeling,* Addison-Wesley, 2002), Cockburn [COC01], Armour and Miller (*Advanced Use-Case Modeling: Software Systems,* Addison-Wesley, 2000), Kulak and his colleagues (*Use Cases: Requirements in Context,* Addison-Wesley, 2000), and Schneider and Winters (*Applying Use Cases,* Addison-Wesley, 1998).

A wide variety of information sources on requirements engineering and analysis are available on the Internet. An up-to-date list of World Wide Web references that are relevant to requirements engineering and analysis can be found at the SEPA Web site:
http://www.mhhe.com/pressman.

ANALYSIS MODELING

KEY CONCEPTS

At a technical level, software engineering begins with a series of modeling tasks that lead to a specification of requirements and a comprehensive design representation for the software to be built. The *analysis model,* actually a set of models, is the first technical representation of a system.

In a seminal book on analysis modeling methods, Tom DeMarco [DEM79] describes the process in this way:

> Looking back over the recognized problems and failings of the analysis phase, I suggest that we need to make the following additions to our set of analysis phase goals:
>
> - The products of analysis must be highly maintainable. This applies particularly to the Target Document [software requirements specification].
> - Problems of size must be dealt with using an effective method of partitioning. The Victorian novel specification is out.
> - Graphics have to be used whenever possible.
> - We have to differentiate between logical [essential] and physical [implementation] considerations . . . .
>
> At the very least, we need . . .
>
> - Something to help us partition our requirements and document that partitioning before specification . . .
> - Some means of keeping track of and evaluating interfaces . . .
> - New tools to describe logic and policy, something better than narrative text.

Although DeMarco wrote about the attributes of analysis modeling more than a quarter of a century ago, his comments still apply to modern analysis modeling methods and notation.

QUICK LOOK

What is it? The written word is a wonderful vehicle for communication, but it is not necessarily the best way to represent the requirements for computer software. Analysis modeling uses a combination of text and diagrammatic forms to depict requirements for data, function, and behavior in a way that is relatively easy to understand, and more important, straightforward to review for correctness, completeness, and consistency.

Who does it? A software engineer (sometimes called an analyst) builds the model using requirements elicited from the customer.

Why is it important? To validate software requirements, you need to examine them from a number of different points of view. Analysis modeling represents requirements in multiple "dimensions," thereby increasing the probability that errors will be found, that inconsistency will surface, and that omissions will be uncovered.

What are the steps? Informational, functional, and behavioral requirements are modeled using a number of different diagrammatic formats. Scenario-based modeling represents the system from the user's point of view. Flow-oriented modeling provides an indication of how data objects are transformed by processing functions. Class-based modeling defines objects, attributes, and relationships. Behavioral modeling depicts the states of the system and its classes and the impact of events on these states. Once preliminary models are created, they are refined and analyzed to assess their clarity, completeness, and consistency. The final analysis model is then validated by all stakeholders.

What is the work product? A wide array of diagrammatic forms may be chosen for the analysis model. Each of these representations provides a view of one or more of the model elements.

How do I ensure that I've done it right? Analysis modeling work products must be reviewed for correctness, completeness, and consistency. They must reflect the needs of all stakeholders and establish a foundation from which design can be conducted.

8.1 Requirements Analysis

Requirements analysis results in the specification of software's operational characteristics; indicates software's interface with other system elements; and establishes constraints that software must meet. Requirements analysis allows the software engineer (sometimes called an *analyst* or *modeler* in this role) to elaborate on basic requirements established during earlier requirement engineering tasks and build models that depict user scenarios, functional activities, problem classes and their relationships, system and class behavior, and the flow of data as it is transformed.

KEY POINT
The analysis model and requirements specification provide a means for assessing quality once the software is built.

Requirements analysis provides the software designer with a representation of information, function, and behavior that can be translated to architectural, interface, and component-level designs. Finally, the analysis model and the requirements specification provide the developer and the customer with the means to assess quality once software is built.

Throughout analysis modeling, the software engineer's primary focus is on *what,* not *how.* What objects does the system manipulate, what functions must the system perform, what behaviors does the system exhibit, what interfaces are defined, and what constraints apply?[1]

In earlier chapters, we noted that complete specification of requirements may not be possible at this stage. The customer may be unsure of precisely what is required. The developer may be unsure that a specific approach will properly accomplish function and performance. These realities mitigate in favor of an iterative approach to re-

1 It should be noted that as customers become more technologically sophisticated, there is a trend toward specification of *how* as well as *what.* However, the primary focus should remain on *what.*

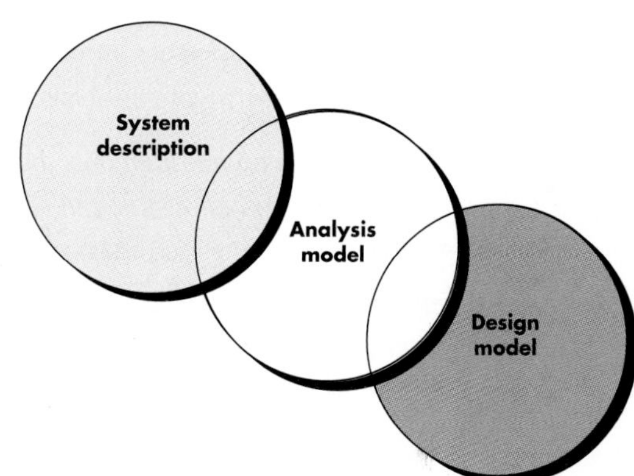

FIGURE 8.1 The analysis model as a bridge between the system description and the design model

quirements analysis and modeling. The analyst should model what is known and use that model as the basis for design of the software increment.[2]

8.1.1 Overall Objectives and Philosophy

The analysis model must achieve three primary objectives: (1) to describe what the customer requires, (2) to establish a basis for the creation of a software design, and (3) to define a set of requirements that can be validated once the software is built. The analysis model bridges the gap between a system-level description (Chapter 6) that describes overall system functionality as it is achieved by applying software, hardware, data, human, and other system elements and a software design (Chapter 9) that describes the software's application architecture, user interface, and component-level structure. This relationship is illustrated in Figure 8.1.

> "Problems worthy of attack prove their worth by hitting back."
>
> **Piet Hein**

It is important to note that some elements of the analysis model are present (at a higher level of abstraction) in the system description and that requirements engineering tasks actually begin as part of system engineering. In addition, all elements of the analysis model are directly traceable to parts of the design model. A clear division of design and analysis tasks between these two important modeling activities is not always possible. Some design invariably occurs as part of analysis, and some analysis will be conducted during design.

---

2 Alternatively, the software team may choose to create a prototype (Chapter 3) in an effort to better understand requirements for the system.

8.1.2 Analysis Rules of Thumb

Arlow and Neustadt [ARL02] suggest a number of worthwhile rules of thumb that should be followed when creating the analysis model:

- *The model should focus on requirements that are visible within the problem or business domain. The level of abstraction should be relatively high.* "Don't get bogged down in details" [ARL02] that try to explain how the system will work.
- *Each element of the analysis model should add to an overall understanding of software requirements and provide insight into the information domain, function, and behavior of the system.*
- *Delay consideration of infrastructure and other non-functional models until design.* For example, a database may be required, but the classes necessary to implement it, the functions required to access it, and the behavior that will be exhibited as it is used should be considered only after problem domain analysis has been completed.
- *Minimize coupling throughout the system.* It is important to represent relationships between classes and functions. However, if the level of "interconnectedness" is extremely high, efforts should be made to reduce it.
- *Be certain that the analysis model provides value to all stakeholders.* Each constituency has its own use for the model. For example, business stakeholders should use the model to validate requirements; designers should use the model as a basis for design; QA people should use the model to help plan acceptance tests.
- *Keep the model as simple as it can be.* Don't add additional diagrams when they provide no new information. Don't use complete notational forms, when a simple list will do.

8.1.3 Domain Analysis

WebRef
Many useful resources for domain analysis can be found at **www.iturls.com/English/SoftwareEngineering/SE_mod5.asp.**

In our discussion of requirements engineering (Chapter 7), we noted that analysis patterns often reoccur across many applications within a specific business domain. If these patterns are defined and categorized in a manner that allows a software engineer or analyst to recognize and reuse them, the creation of the analysis model is expedited. More important, the likelihood of applying reusable design patterns and executable software components grows dramatically. This improves time to market and reduces development costs.

But how are analysis patterns recognized in the first place? Who defines them, categorizes them, and readies them for use on subsequent projects? The answers to these questions lies in *domain analysis.* Firesmith [FIR93] describes domain analysis in the following way:

> Software domain analysis is the identification, analysis, and specification of common requirements from a specific application domain, typically for reuse on multiple projects

FIGURE 8.2 Input and output for domain analysis

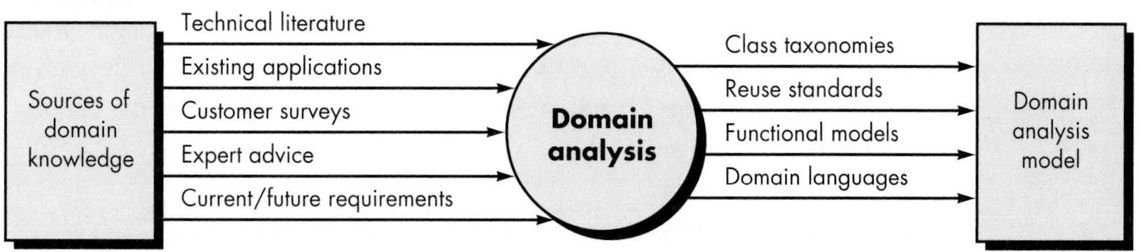

> within that application domain . . . [Object-oriented domain analysis is] the identification, analysis, and specification of common, reusable capabilities within a specific application domain, in terms of common objects, classes, subassemblies, and frameworks.

The "specific application domain" can range from avionics to banking, from multimedia video games to software embedded within medical devices. The goal of domain analysis is straightforward: to find or create those analysis classes and/or common functions and features that are broadly applicable, so that they may be reused.[3]

> **"The great art of learning is to understand but little at a time."**
>
> **John Locke**

WebRef
A worthwhile discussion of domain engineering and analysis can be found at **www.sei.cmu.edu/str/descriptions/deda.html.**

In a way, the role of a domain analyst is similar to the role of a master toolsmith in a heavy manufacturing environment. The job of the toolsmith is to design and build tools that may be used by many people doing similar but not necessarily the same jobs. The role of the domain analyst[4] is to discover and define reusable analysis patterns, analysis classes, and related information that may be used by many people working on similar but not necessarily the same applications.

Figure 8.2 [ARA89] illustrates key inputs and outputs for the domain analysis process. Sources of domain knowledge are surveyed in an attempt to identify objects that can be reused across the domain.

8.2 Analysis Modeling Approaches

One view of analysis modeling, called *structured analysis,* considers data and the processes that transform the data as separate entities. Data objects are modeled in a way that defines their attributes and relationships. Processes that manipulate data

3 A complementary view of domain analysis "involves modeling the domain so that software engineers and other stakeholders can better learn about it . . . not all domain classes necessarily result in the development of reusable classes" [LET03].

4 Do not make the assumption that because a domain analyst is at work, a software engineer need not understand the application domain. Every member of a software team should have some understanding of the domain in which the software is to be placed.

objects are modeled in a manner that shows how they transform data as data objects flow through the system.

A second approach to analysis modeling, called *object-oriented analysis,* focuses on the definition of classes and the manner in which they collaborate with one another to effect customer requirements. UML and the Unified Process (Chapter 3) are predominantly object-oriented.

> "[A]nalysis is frustrating, full of complex interpersonal relationships, indefinite, and difficult. In a word, it is fascinating. Once you're hooked, the old easy pleasures of system building are never again enough to satisfy you."
>
> **Tom DeMarco**

Although the analysis model that we propose in this book combines features of both approaches, software teams often choose one approach and exclude all representations from the other. The question is not which is best, but what combination of representations will provide stakeholders with the best model of software requirements and the most effective bridge to software design.

Analysis modeling leads to the derivation of each of the modeling elements shown in Figure 8.3. However, the specific content of each element (i.e., the diagrams that are used to construct the element and the model) may differ from project to project. As we have noted a number of times in this book, the software team must work to keep it simple. Only those modeling elements that add value to the model should be used.

> "Why should we build models? Why not just build the system itself? The answer is that we can construct models in such a way as to highlight, or emphasize, certain critical features of a system, while simultaneously de-emphasizing other aspects of the system."
>
> **Ed Yourdon**

FIGURE 8.3

Elements of the analysis model

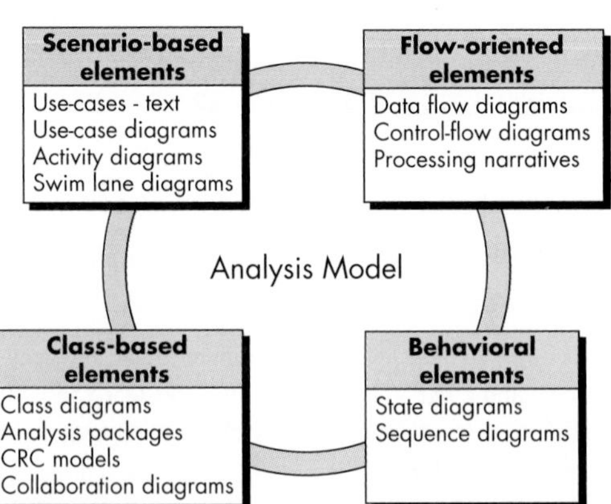

8.3 Data Modeling Concepts

WebRef
Useful information on data modeling can be found at **www.datamodel.org.**

Analysis modeling often begins with *data modeling.* The software engineer or analyst defines all data objects that are processed within the system, the relationships between the data objects, and other information that is pertinent to the relationships.

8.3.1 Data Objects

A *data object* is a representation of almost any composite information that must be understood by software. By *composite information,* we mean something that has a number of different properties or attributes. Therefore, "width" (a single value) would not be a valid data object, but **dimensions** (incorporating height, width, and depth) could be defined as an object.

? How does a data object manifest itself within the context of an application?

A data object can be an external entity (e.g., anything that produces or consumes information), a thing (e.g., a report or a display), an occurrence (e.g., a telephone call) or event (e.g., an alarm), a role (e.g., salesperson), an organizational unit (e.g., accounting department), a place (e.g., a warehouse), or a structure (e.g., a file). For example, a person or a car can be viewed as a data object in the sense that either can be defined in terms of a set of attributes. The data object description incorporates the data object and all of its attributes.

A data object is a representation of any composite information that is processed by software.

A data object encapsulates data only—there is no reference within a data object to operations that act on the data.[5] Therefore, the data object can be represented as a table as shown in Figure 8.4. The headings in the table reflect attributes of the object. In this case, a car is defined in terms of **make, model, ID number, body type, color** and **owner**. The body of the table represents specific instances of the data object. For example, a Chevy Corvette is an instance of the data object car.

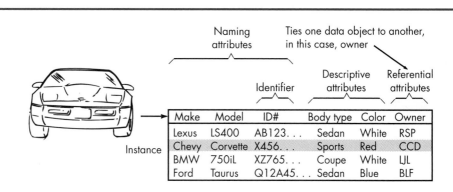

Figure 8.4
Tabular representation of data objects

Naming attributes
Ties one data object to another, in this case, owner
Identifier
Descriptive attributes
Referential attributes
Instance

Make	Model	ID#	Body type	Color	Owner
Lexus	LS400	AB123. . .	Sedan	White	RSP
Chevy	Corvette	X456. . .	Sports	Red	CCD
BMW	750iL	XZ765. . .	Coupe	White	LJL
Ford	Taurus	Q12A45. . .	Sedan	Blue	BLF

5 This distinction separates the data object from the class or object defined as part of the object-oriented approach.

KEY POINT Attributes name a data object, describe its characteristics, and, in some cases, make reference to another object.

8.3.2 Data Attributes

Data attributes define the properties of a data object and take on one of three different characteristics. They can be used to (1) name an instance of the data object, (2) describe the instance, or (3) make reference to another instance in another table. In addition, one or more of the attributes must be defined as an identifier—that is, the identifier attribute becomes a "key" when we want to find an instance of the data object. In some cases, values for the identifier(s) are unique, although this is not a requirement. Referring to the data object **car,** a reasonable identifier might be the ID number.

WebRef A concept called "normalization" is important to those who intend to do thorough data modeling. A useful introduction can be found at **www.datamodel.org.**

The set of attributes that is appropriate for a given data object is determined through an understanding of the problem context. The attributes for **car** might serve well for an application that would be used by a Department of Motor Vehicles, but these attributes would be useless for an automobile company that needs manufacturing control software. In the latter case, the attributes for car might also include **ID number, body type**, and **color**, but many additional attributes (e.g., **interior code, drive train type, trim package designator, transmission type**) would have to be added to make **car** a meaningful object in the manufacturing control context.

INFO

Data Objects and OO Classes—Are They the Same Thing?

A common question occurs when data objects are discussed: Is a data object the same thing as an object-oriented class? The answer is no.

A data object defines a composite data item; that is, it incorporates a collection of individual data items (attributes) and gives the collection of items a name (the name of the data object). An OO class encapsulates data attributes but also incorporates the operations that manipulate the data implied by those attributes. In addition, the definition of classes implies a comprehensive infrastructure that is part of the object-oriented software engineering approach. Classes communicate with one another via messages; they can be organized into hierarchies; they provide inheritance characteristics for objects that are an instance of a class.

KEY POINT Relationships indicate the manner in which data objects are connected to one another.

8.3.3 Relationships

Data objects are connected to one another in different ways. Consider the two data objects, **person** and **car.** These objects can be represented using the simple notation illustrated in Figure 8.5a. A connection is established between **person** and **car** because the two objects are related. But what are the relationships? To determine the answer, we must understand the role of people (owners, in this case) and cars within the context of the software to be built. We can define a set of object/relationship pairs that define the relevant relationships. For example,

- A person *owns* a car.
- A person *is insured to drive* a car.

FIGURE 8.5
Relationships between data objects

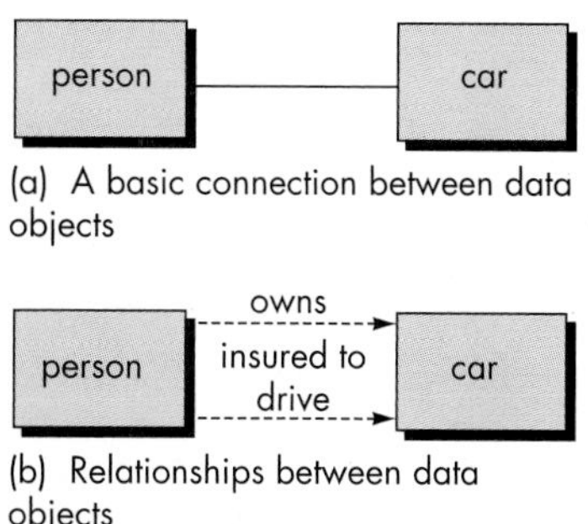

The relationships *owns* and *insured to drive* define the relevant connections between **person** and **car.** Figure 8.5b illustrates these object/relationship pairs graphically. The arrows noted in Figure 8.5b provide important information about the directionality of the relationship and often reduce ambiguity or misinterpretations.

8.3.4 Cardinality and Modality

The elements of data modeling—data objects, attributes, and relationships—provide the basis for understanding the information domain of a problem. However, additional information related to these basic elements must also be understood.

We have defined a set of objects and represented the object/relationship pairs that bind them. But a simple pair that states that **objectX** *relates* to **objectY** does not provide enough information for software engineering purposes. We must understand how many occurrences of **objectX** are related to how many occurrences of **objectY.** This leads to a data modeling concept called *cardinality.*

? How do I handle a situation in which one data object is related to many occurrences of another data object?

The data model must be capable of representing the number of occurrences of objects in a given relationship. Tillmann [TIL93] defines the cardinality of an object/relationship pair in the following manner: "Cardinality is the specification of the number of occurrences of one [object] that can be related to the number of occurrences of another [object]." For example, one object can relate to only one other object (a 1:1 relationship); one object can relate to many objects (a 1:N relationship); some number of occurrences of an object can relate to some other number of occurrences of another object (an M:N relationship).[6] Cardinality also defines "the maximum number of objects that can participate in a relationship" [TIL93]. It does not, however, provide an indication of whether or not a particular data object must participate in the relationship. To specify this information, the data model adds modality to the object/relationship pair.

6 For example, an uncle can have many nephews, and a nephew can have many uncles.

INFO

Entity-Relationship Diagrams

The object/relationship pair is the cornerstone of the data model. These pairs can be represented graphically using the entity/relationship diagram (ERD).[7] The ERD was originally proposed by Peter Chen [CHE77] for the design of relational database systems and has been extended by others. A set of primary components are identified for the ERD: data objects, attributes, relationships, and various type indicators. The primary purpose of the ERD is to represent data objects and their relationships.

Rudimentary ERD notation has already been introduced. Data objects are represented by a labeled rectangle. Relationships are indicated with a labeled line connecting objects. In some variations of the ERD, the connecting line contains a diamond that is labeled with the relationship. Connections between data objects and relationships are established using a variety of special symbols that indicate cardinality and modality.

For further information of data modeling and the entity relationship diagram, the interested reader should see [THA00].

The *modality* of a relationship is 0 if there is no explicit need for the relationship to occur or the relationship is optional. The modality is 1 if an occurrence of the relationship is mandatory.

> "For an information system to be useful, reliable, adaptable, and economic, it must be based first on sound data modeling, and only secondarily on process analysis . . . because the structure of data is inherently about truth, whereas process is about technique."
>
> **Duncan Dwelle**

SOFTWARE TOOLS

Data Modeling

Objective: Data modeling tools provide the software engineer with the ability to represent data objects, their characteristics and their relationships. Used primarily for large database applications and other information systems projects, data modeling tools provide an automated means for creating comprehensive entity-relation diagrams, data object dictionaries, and related models.

Mechanics: Tools in this category enable the user to describe data objects and their relationships. In some cases, the tools use ERD notation. In others, the tools model relations using some other mechanism. Tools in this category enable the creation of a database model by generating a database schema for common DBMSs.

Representative Tools[8]

AllFusion ERWin, developed by Computer Associates (www3.ca.com), assists in the design of data objects, proper structure, and key elements for databases.

ER/Studio, developed by Embarcadero Software (www.embarcadero.com), supports entity-relationship modeling.

Oracle Designer, developed by Oracle Systems (www.oracle.com), models business processes, data entities and relationships [that] are transformed into designs from which complete applications and databases are generated.

7 Although the ERD is still used in some database design applications, UML notation is now more commonly used for data design.

8 Tools noted here do not represent an endorsement, but rather a sampling of tools in this category. In most cases, tool names are trademarked by their respective developers.

MetaScope, developed by Madrone Systems (www.madronesystems.com), is a low cost data modeling tool that supports the graphical representation of data.

ModelSphere, developed by Magna Solutions GmbH (www.magnasolutions.com), supports a variety of relational modeling tools.

Visible Analyst, developed by Visible Systems (www.visible.com), supports a variety of analysis modeling functions including data modeling.

8.4 Object-Oriented Analysis

Any discussion of object-oriented analysis must begin by addressing the term *object-oriented.* What is an object-oriented viewpoint? Why is a method considered to be object-oriented? What is an object? As OO gained widespread adherents during the 1980s and 1990s, there were many different opinions (e.g., [BER93], [TAY90], [STR88], [BOO86]) about the correct answers to these questions. Today, a coherent view of OO has emerged.

The intent of object-oriented analysis (OOA) is to define all classes (and the relationships and behavior associated with them) that are relevant to the problem to be solved. To accomplish this, a number of tasks must occur:

1. Basic user requirements must be communicated between the customer and the software engineer (Chapter 7).
2. Classes must be identified (i.e., attributes and methods are defined).
3. A class hierarchy is defined.
4. Object-to-object relationships (object connections) should be represented.
5. Object behavior must be modeled.
6. Tasks 1 through 5 are reapplied iteratively until the model is complete.

Instead of examining a problem using a more conventional input-processing-output (information flow) model or a model derived exclusively from hierarchical information structures, OOA builds a class-oriented model that relies on an understanding of OO concepts.

Info

Object-Oriented Concepts

Object-oriented (OO) concepts have become well-established in the software engineering world. The following are abbreviated descriptions of important OO concepts that are often encountered during analysis modeling. Additional OO concepts, more closely aligned with software design, are presented in Chapter 10.

Attributes—a collection of data values that describe a class.

Class—encapsulates the data and procedural abstractions required to describe the content and behavior of some real world entity. Stated another way, a class is a generalized description (e.g., a template, pattern, or blueprint) that describes a collection of similar objects.

Objects—instances of a specific class. Objects inherit a class' attributes and operations.

Operations—also called *methods* and *services,* provide a representation of one of the behaviors of a class.

Subclass—a specialization of the superclass. A subclass can inherit both attributes and operations from a superclass.

Superclass—also called a *base class,* is a generalization of a set of classes that are related to it.

8.5 Scenario-Based Modeling

Although the success of a computer-based system or product is measured in many ways, user satisfaction resides at the top of the list. If software engineers understand how end-users (and other actors) want to interact with a system, the software team will be better able to properly characterize requirements and build meaningful analysis and design models. Hence, analysis modeling with UML begins with the creation of scenarios in the form of use-cases, activity diagrams, and swimlane diagrams.

8.5.1 Writing Use-Cases

A use-case captures the interactions that occur between producers and consumers of information and the system itself. In this section, we examine how use-cases are developed as part of the analysis modeling activity.[9]

The concept of a use-case (Chapter 7) is relatively easy to understand—describe a specific usage scenario in straightforward language from the point of view of a defined actor.[10] But how do we know (1) what to write about, (2) how much to write about it, (3) how detailed to make our description, and (4) how to organize the description? These are the questions that must be answered if use-cases are to provide value as an analysis modeling tool.

ADVICE

In some situations, use-cases become the dominant requirements engineering mechanism. However, this does not mean that you should discard the concepts and techniques discussed in Chapter 7.

> "[Use-cases] are simply an aid to defining what exists outside the system (actors) and what should be performed by the system (use-cases)."
>
> **Ivar Jacobson**

What to write about? The first two requirements engineering tasks[11]—inception and elicitation—provide us the information we need to begin writing use cases. Requirements gathering meetings, QFD, and other requirements engineering mecha-

9 Use-cases are a particularly important part of analysis modeling for user interfaces. Interface analysis is discussed in detail in Chapter 12.

10 An actor is not a specific person, but rather a role that a person (or a device) plays within a specific context. An actor "calls on the system to deliver one of its services" [COC01].

11 These requirements engineering tasks are discussed in detail in Chapter 7.

nisms are used to identify stakeholders, define the scope of the problem, specify overall operational goals, outline all known functional requirements, and describe the things (objects) that will be manipulated by the system.

To begin developing a set of use-cases, the functions or activities performed by a specific actor are listed. These may be obtained from a list of required system functions, through conversations with customers or end-users, or by an evaluation of activity diagrams (Section 8.5.2) developed as part of analysis modeling.

SAFEHOME

Developing Another Preliminary User Scenario

The scene: A meeting room, during the second requirements gathering meeting.

The players: Jamie Lazar, software team member; Ed Robbins, software team member; Doug Miller, software engineering manager; three members of marketing; a product engineering representative; and a facilitator.

The conversation:

Facilitator: It's time that we begin talking about the *SafeHome* surveillance function. Let's develop a user scenario for access to the home security function.

Jamie: Who plays the role of the actor on this?

Facilitator: I think Meredith (a marketing person) has been working on that functionality. Why don't you play the role.

Meredith: You want to do it the same way we did it last time, right?

Facilitator: Right . . . same way.

Meredith: Well, obviously the reason for surveillance is to allow the homeowner to check out the house while he or she is away, to record and play back video that is captured . . . that sort of thing.

Ed: Will the video be digital, and will it be stored on disk?

Facilitator: Good question, but let's postpone implementation issues for now. Meredith?

Meredith: Okay, so basically there are two parts to the surveillance function . . . the first configures the system including laying out a floor plan—we need tools to help the homeowner do this—and the second part is the actual surveillance function itself. Since the layout is part of the configuration activity, I'll focus on the surveillance function.

Facilitator (smiling): Took the words right out of my mouth.

Meredith: Um . . . I want to gain access to the surveillance function either via the PC or via the Internet. My feeling is that the Internet access would be more frequently used. Anyway, I want to be able to display camera views on a PC and control pan and zoom for a specific camera. I specify the camera by selecting it from the house floor plan. I want to selectively record camera output and replay camera output. I also want to be able to block access to one or more cameras with a specific password. And I want the option of seeing small windows that show views from all cameras and then be able to pick the one I want enlarged.

Jamie: Those are called thumbnail views.

Meredith: Okay, then I want thumbnail views from all the cameras. I also want the interface to the surveillance function to have the same look and feel as all other *SafeHome* interfaces. I want it to be intuitive, meaning I don't want to have to read a manual to use it.

Facilitator: Good job, now, let's go into this function in a bit more detail. . . .

The *SafeHome* home surveillance function (subsystem) discussed in the sidebar identifies the following functions (an abbreviated list) that are performed by the **homeowner** actor:

- Access camera surveillance via the Internet.

- Select camera to view.
- Request thumbnails from all cameras.
- Display camera views in a PC window.
- Control pan and zoom for a specific camera.
- Selectively record camera output.
- Replay camera output.

As further conversations with the stakeholder (who plays the role of a homeowner) progress, the requirements gathering team develops use-cases for each of the functions noted. In general, use-cases are written first in an informal narrative fashion. If more formality is required, the same use-case is rewritten using a structured format similar to the one proposed in Chapter 7 and reproduced later in this section as a sidebar.

To illustrate, consider the function "access camera surveillance—display camera views (ACS-DCV)." The stakeholder who takes on the role of the **homeowner** actor might write the following narrative:

Use-case: Access camera surveillance—display camera views (ACS-DCV)

Actor: homeowner

If I'm at a remote location, I can use any PC with appropriate browser software to log on to the SafeHome Products Web site. I enter my user ID and two levels of passwords and, once I'm validated, I have access to all functionality for my installed SafeHome system. To access a specific camera view, I select "surveillance" from the major function buttons displayed. I then select "pick a camera," and the floor plan of the house is displayed. I then select the camera that I'm interested in. Alternatively, I can look at thumbnail snapshots from all cameras simultaneously by selecting "all cameras" as my viewing choice. Once I choose a camera, I select "view," and a one-frame-per-second view appears in a viewing window that is identified by the camera ID. If I want to switch cameras, I select "pick a camera," and the original viewing window disappears, and the floor plan of the house is displayed again. I then select the camera that I'm interested in. A new viewing window appears.

A variation of a narrative use-case presents the interaction as an ordered sequence of user actions. Each action is represented as a declarative sentence. Revisiting the ACS-DCV function, we would write:

Use-case: Access camera surveillance—display camera views (ACS-DCV)

Actor: homeowner

1. The homeowner logs on to the *SafeHome Products* Web site.
2. The homeowner enters his or her user ID.
3. The homeowner enters two passwords (each at least eight characters in length).
4. The system displays all major function buttons.
5. The homeowner selects the "surveillance" from the major function buttons.

6. The homeowner selects "pick a camera."
7. The system displays the floor plan of the house.
8. The homeowner selects a camera icon from the floor plan.
9. The homeowner selects the "view" button.
10. The system displays a viewing window that is identified by the camera ID.
11. The system displays video output within the viewing window at one frame per second.

It is important to note that this sequential presentation does not consider any alternative interactions (the narrative is more free-flowing and did represent a few alternatives). Use-cases of this type are sometimes referred to as *primary scenarios* [SCH98].

> **"Use-cases can be used in many [software] processes. Our favorite is a process that is iterative and risk driven."**
>
> **Geri Schneider and Jason Winters**

Of course, a description of alternative interactions is essential to a complete understanding of the function that is being described. Therefore, each step in the primary scenario is evaluated by asking the following questions [SCH98]:

? How do I examine alternative courses of action when I develop a use-case?

- Can the actor take some other action at this point?
- Is it possible that the actor will encounter some error condition at this point? If so, what might it be?
- Is it possible that the actor will encounter some other behavior at this point (e.g., behavior that is invoked by some event outside the actor's control)? If so, what might it be?

Answers to these questions result in the creation of a set of secondary scenarios that are part of the original use-case but represent alternative behavior.

For example, consider steps 6 and 7 in the primary scenario presented earlier:

6. The homeowner selects "pick a camera."
7. The system displays the floor plan of the house.

Can the actor take some other action at this point? The answer is yes. Referring to the free-flow narrative, the actor may choose to view thumbnail snapshots of all cameras simultaneously. Hence, one secondary scenario might be: "View thumbnail snapshots for all cameras."

Is it possible that the actor will encounter some error condition at this point? Any number of error conditions can occur as a computer-based system operates. In this context, we consider only error conditions that are likely as a direct result of the action described in step 6 or step 7. Again the answer to the question is yes. A floor plan with camera icons may have never been configured. Hence, selecting "pick a camera" results in an error condition: "No floor plan configured for this house."[12] This error condition becomes a secondary scenario.

Is it possible that the actor will encounter some other behavior at this point? Again the answer to the question is yes. As steps 6 and 7 occur, the system may encounter an alarm condition. This would result in the system displaying a special alarm notification (type, location, system action) and providing the actor with a number of options relevant to the nature of the alarm. Because this secondary scenario can occur for virtually all interactions, it will not become part of the **ACS-DCV** use-case. Rather, a separate use-case—"Alarm condition encountered"—would be developed and referenced from other use-cases as required.

Referring to the formal use-case template shown in the sidebar, the secondary scenarios are represented as exceptions to the basic sequence described for **ACS-DCV.**

SAFEHOME

Use-Case Template for Surveillance

Use-case: Access camera surveillance—display camera views (ACS-DCV).

Primary actor: Homeowner.

Goal in context: To view output of camera placed throughout the house from any remote location via the Internet.

Preconditions: System must be fully configured; appropriate user ID and passwords must be obtained.

Trigger: The homeowner decides to take a look inside the house while away.

Scenario:

1. The homeowner logs onto the *SafeHome Products* Web site.
2. The homeowner enters his or her user ID.
3. The homeowner enters two passwords (each at least eight characters in length).
4. The system displays all major function buttons.
5. The homeowner selects "surveillance" from the major function buttons.
6. The homeowner selects "pick a camera."
7. The system displays the floor plan of the house.
8. The homeowner selects a camera icon from the floor plan.
9. The homeowner selects the "view" button.
10. The system displays a viewing window that is identified by the camera ID.
11. The system displays video output within the viewing window at one frame per second.

Exceptions:

1. ID or passwords are incorrect or not recognized—see use-case: "validate ID and passwords."
2. Surveillance function not configured for this system—system displays appropriate error message; see use-case: "configure surveillance function."
3. Homeowner selects "view thumbnail snapshots for all cameras"—see use-case: "view thumbnail snapshots for all cameras."
4. A floor plan is not available or has not been configured—display appropriate error message and see use-case: "configure floor plan."
5. An alarm condition is encountered—see use-case: "alarm condition encountered."

Priority: Moderate priority, to be implemented after basic functions.

When available: Third increment.

Frequency of use: Infrequent.

---

12 In this case, another actor, the **system administrator,** would have to configure the floor plan, install and initialize (e.g., assign an equipment ID) all cameras, and test to be certain that each is accessible via the system and through the floor plan.

Channel to actor: Via PC-based browser and Internet connection to *SafeHome* Web site.

Secondary actors: System administrator, cameras.

Channels to secondary actors:

1. System administrator: PC-based system
2. Cameras: wireless connectivity

Open issues:

1. What mechanisms protect unauthorized use of this capability by employees of the company?
2. Is security sufficient? Hacking into this feature would represent a major invasion of privacy.
3. Will system response via the Internet be acceptable given the bandwidth required for camera views?
4. Will we develop a capability to provide video at a higher frames-per-second rate when high bandwidth connections are available?

WebRef

When are you finished writing use-cases? For a worthwhile discussion of this topic, see **ootips.org/use-cases-done.htmlootips.org/use-cases-done.html.**

In many cases, there is no need to create a graphical representation of a usage scenario. However, diagrammatic representation can facilitate understanding, particularly when the scenario is complex. As we noted in Chapter 7, UML does provide use-case diagramming capability. Figure 8.6 depicts a preliminary use-case diagram for the *SafeHome* product. Each use-case is represented by an oval. Only the use-case, **ACS-DCV** has been discussed in detail in this section.

8.5.2 Developing an Activity Diagram

The UML activity diagram (discussed briefly in Chapters 6 and 7) supplements the use-case by providing a graphical representation of the flow of interaction within a specific scenario. Similar to the flowchart, an activity diagram uses rounded rectangles to imply a specific system function, arrows to represent flow through the system, decision diamonds to depict a branching decision (each arrow emanating from the diamond is labeled), and solid horizontal lines to indicate that parallel activities are

FIGURE 8.6

Preliminary use-case diagram for the *SafeHome* system

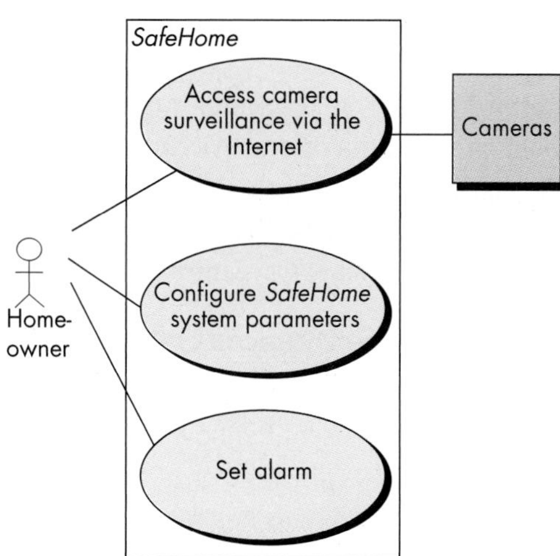

FIGURE 8.7

Activity diagram for Access camera surveillance—display camera views function

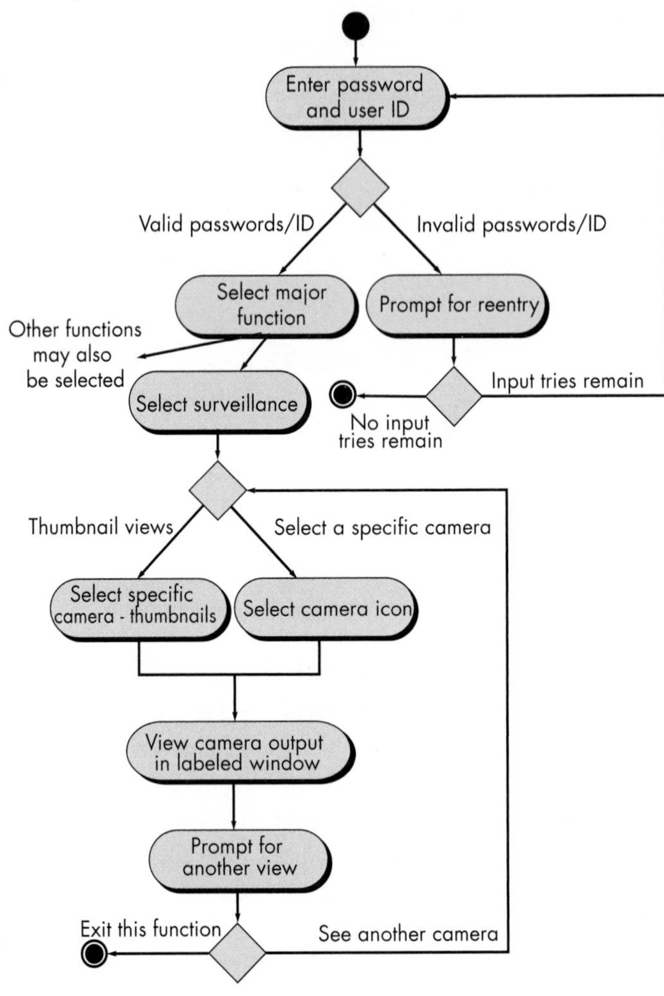

A UML activity diagram represents the actions and decisions that occur as some function is performed.

occurring. An activity diagram for the **ACS-DCV** function is shown in Figure 8.7. It should be noted that the activity diagram adds additional detail not directly mentioned (but implied) by the use-case. For example, a user may only attempt to enter **userID** and **password** a limited number of times. This is represented by a decision diamond below *prompt for* reentry.

8.5.3 Swimlane Diagrams

The UML *swimlane diagram* is a useful variation of the activity diagram and allows the modeler to represent the flow of activities described by the use-case and at the same time indicate which actor (if there are multiple actors involved in a specific function) or analysis class has responsibility for the action described by an activity

FIGURE 8.8 Swimlane diagram for Access camera surveillance—display camera views function

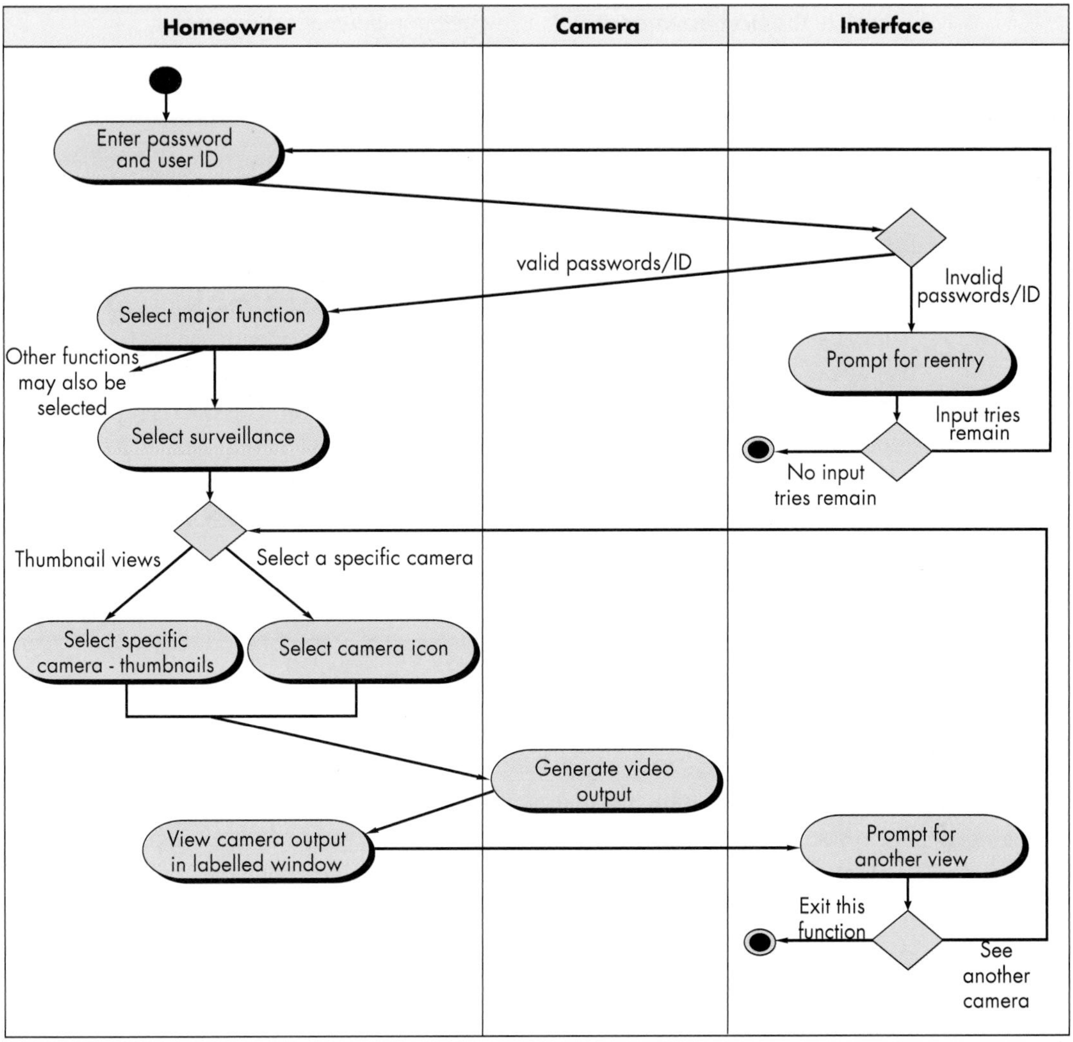

A UML swimlane diagram represents the flow of actions and decisions and indicates which actors perform each.

rectangle. Responsibilities are represented as parallel segments that divide the diagram vertically, like the lanes in a swimming pool.

Three analysis classes—**Homeowner, Interface,** and **Camera**—have direct or indirect responsibilities in the context of the activity diagram represented in Figure 8.7. Referring to Figure 8.8, the activity diagram is rearranged so that activities associated with a particular analysis class fall inside the swimlane for that class. For example, the **Interface** class represents the user interface as seen by the homeowner. The activity diagram notes two prompts that are the responsibility of the interface—*prompt for* *reentry* and *prompt for another view.* These prompts and the decisions associated with them fall within the **Interface** swimlane. However, arrows lead from that swimlane back to the **Homeowner** swimlane, where homeowner actions occur.

8.6 Flow-Oriented Modeling

Data flow-oriented modeling continues to be one of the most widely used analysis notations today.[13] Although the *data flow diagram* (DFD) and related diagrams and information are not a formal part of UML, they can be used to complement UML diagrams and provide additional insight into system requirements and flow.

The DFD takes an input-process-output view of a system. That is, data objects flow into the software, are transformed by processing elements, and resultant data objects flow out of the software. Data objects are represented by labeled arrows and transformations are represented by circles (also called *bubbles*). The DFD is presented in a hierarchical fashion. That is, the first data flow model (sometimes called a *level 0 DFD* or *context diagram*) represents the system as a whole. Subsequent data flow diagrams refine the context diagram, providing increasing detail with each subsequent level.

> "The purpose of data flow diagrams is to provide a semantic bridge between users and systems developers."
>
> **Kenneth Kozar**

Some will suggest that the DFD is "old school" and has no place in modern practice. That's a view that excludes a potentially useful mode of representation at the analysis level. If it can help, use the DFD.

8.6.1 Creating a Data Flow Model

The data flow diagram enables the software engineer to develop models of the information domain and functional domain at the same time. As the DFD is refined into greater levels of detail, the analyst performs an implicit functional decomposition of the system. At the same time, the DFD refinement results in a corresponding refinement of data as it moves through the processes that embody the application.

A few simple guidelines can aid immeasurably during derivation of a data flow diagram: (1) the level 0 data flow diagram should depict the software/system as a single bubble; (2) primary input and output should be carefully noted; (3) refinement should begin by isolating candidate processes, data objects, and data stores to be represented at the next level; (4) all arrows and bubbles should be labeled with meaningful names; (5) information flow continuity must be maintained from level to level;[14] and (6) one bubble at a time should be refined. There is a natural tendency to overcomplicate the data flow diagram. This occurs when the analyst attempts to show too much detail too early or represents procedural aspects of the software in lieu of information flow.

---

13 Data flow modeling is a core modeling activity in *structured analysis.*

14 That is, the data objects that flow into the system or any transformation at one level must be the same data objects (or their constituent parts) that flow into the transformation at a more refined level.

FIGURE 8.9

Context-level DFD for the *SafeHome* security function

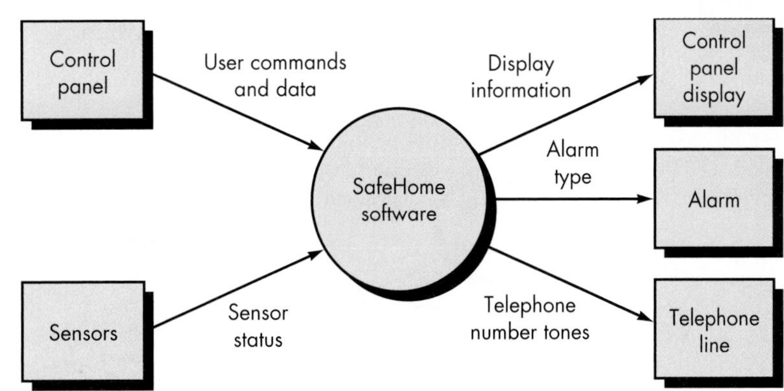

To illustrate the use of the DFD and related notation, we again consider the *SafeHome* security function. A context-level DFD for the security function is shown in Figure 8.9. The primary external entities (boxes) produce information for use by the system and consume information generated by the system. The labeled arrows represent data objects or data object hierarchies. For example, **user commands and data** encompasses all configuration commands, all activation/deactivation commands, all miscellaneous interactions, and all data that are entered to qualify or expand a command.

Information flow continuity must be maintained as each DFD level is refined. This means that input and output at one level must be the same as input and output at a refined level.

The level 0 DFD is now expanded into a level 1 data flow model. But how do we proceed? A simple, yet effective approach is to perform a "grammatical parse" [ABB83] on the narrative that describes the context level bubble. That is, we isolate all nouns (and noun phrases) and verbs (and verb phrases) in a *SafeHome processing narrative*[15] derived during the first requirements gathering meeting. To illustrate, consider the following processing narrative text with the first occurrence of all nouns underlined and the first occurrence of all verbs italicized.[16]

> The <u>SafeHome security function</u> *enables* the <u>homeowner</u> to *configure* the <u>security system</u> when it is *installed, monitors* all <u>sensors</u> *connected* to the security system, and *interacts* with the homeowner through the <u>Internet,</u> a <u>PC,</u> or a <u>control panel.</u>
>
> During <u>installation,</u> the SafeHome PC is used to *program* and *configure* the <u>system.</u> Each sensor is assigned a <u>number</u> and <u>type,</u> a <u>master password</u> is programmed for *arming* and *disarming* the system, and <u>telephone number(s)</u> are *input* for *dialing* when a <u>sensor event</u> occurs.

15 A processing narrative is similar to the use-case in style but somewhat different in purpose. The processing narrative provides an overall description of the function to be developed. It is not a scenario written from one actor's point of view.

16 It should be noted that nouns or verbs that are synonyms or have no direct bearing on the modeling process are omitted. It should also be noted that a similar grammatical parse will be used when we consider class-based modeling in Section 8.7.

FIGURE 8.10

Level 1 DFD for *SafeHome* security function

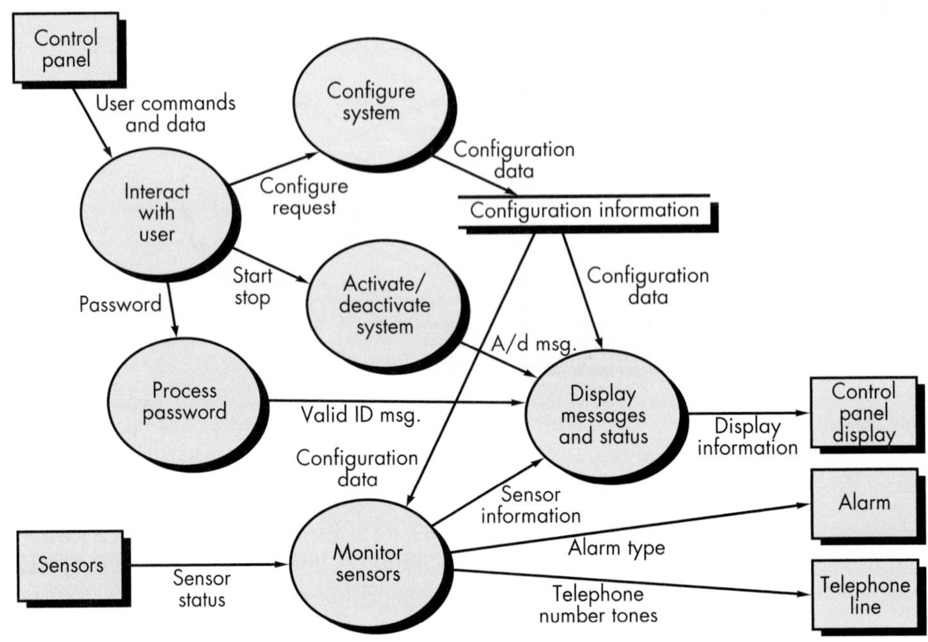

The grammatical parse is not foolproof, but it can provide you with an excellent jump start, if you're struggling to define data objects and the transforms that operate on them.

When a sensor event is *recognized,* the software *invokes* an audible alarm attached to the system. After a delay time that is specified by the homeowner during system configuration activities, the software dials a telephone number of a monitoring service, *provides* information about the location, *reporting* the nature of the event that has been detected. The telephone number will be *redialed* every 20 seconds until a telephone connection is *obtained.*

The homeowner *receives* security information via a control panel, the PC, or a browser, collectively called an interface. The interface *displays* prompting messages and system status information on the control panel, the PC, or the browser window. Homeowner interaction takes the following form. . . .

Be certain that the processing narrative you intend to parse is written at the same level of abstraction throughout.

Referring to the grammatical parse, a pattern begins to emerge. Verbs are *SafeHome* processes; that is, they may ultimately be represented as bubbles in a subsequent DFD. Nouns are either external entities (boxes), data or control objects (arrows), or data stores (double lines). Note further that nouns and verbs can be associated with one another. For example, each sensor is assigned a number and type, therefore **number** and **type** are attributes of the data object **sensor**. Therefore, by performing a grammatical parse on the processing narrative for a bubble at any DFD level, we can generate much useful information about how to proceed with the refinement to the next level. Using this information, a level 1 DFD is shown in Figure 8.10. The context level process shown in Figure 8.9 has been expanded into six processes derived from an ex-

FIGURE 8.11

Level 2 DFD that refines the monitor sensors process

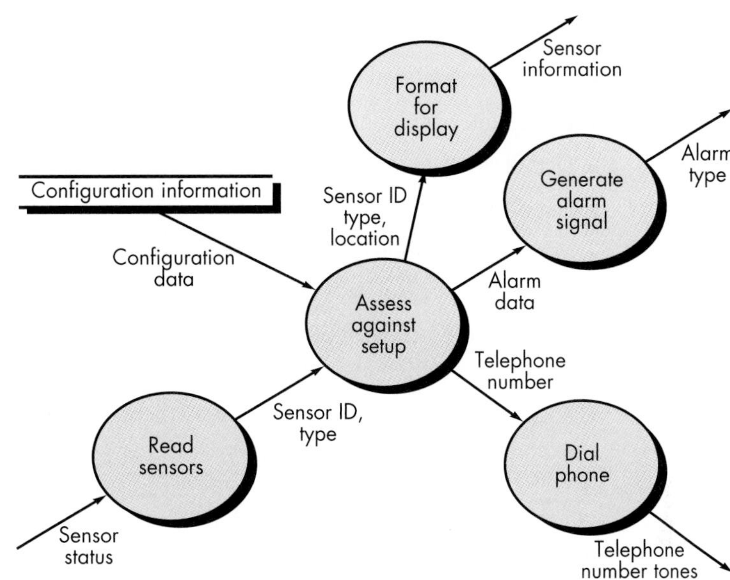

amination of the grammatical parse. Similarly, the information flow between processes at level 1 has been derived from the parse. In addition, information flow continuity is maintained between levels 0 and 1.

The processes represented at DFD level 1 can be further refined into lower levels. For example, the process *monitor sensors* can be refined into a level 2 DFD as shown in Figure 8.11. Note once again that information flow continuity has been maintained between levels.

The refinement of DFDs continues until each bubble performs a simple function. That is, until the process represented by the bubble performs a function that would be easily implemented as a program component. In Chapter 9, we discuss a concept, called *cohesion,* that can be used to assess the simplicity of a given function. For now, we strive to refine DFDs until each bubble is "single-minded."

8.6.2 Creating a Control Flow Model

For many types of applications, the data model and the data flow diagram are all that is necessary to obtain meaningful insight into software requirements. As we have already noted, however, a large class of applications are "driven" by events rather than data, produce control information rather than reports or displays, and process information with heavy concern for time and performance. Such applications require the use of *control flow modeling* in addition to data flow modeling.

We have already noted that an event or control item is implemented as a Boolean value (e.g., true or false, on or off, 1 or 0) or a discrete list of conditions (empty, jammed, full). To select potential candidate events, the following guidelines are suggested:

How do I select potential events for a control flow diagram, state diagram, or CSPEC?

- List all sensors that are "read" by the software.
- List all interrupt conditions.
- List all "switches" that are actuated by an operator.
- List all data conditions.
- Recalling the noun/verb parse that was applied to the processing narrative, review all "control items" as possible for control flow inputs/outputs.
- Describe the behavior of a system by identifying its states; identify how each state is reached; and define the transitions between states.
- Focus on possible omissions—a very common error in specifying control; for example, ask: "Is there any other way I can get to this state or exit from it?"

8.6.3 The Control Specification

The *control specification* (CSPEC) represents the behavior of the system (at the level from which it has been referenced) in two different ways.[17] The CSPEC contains a state diagram that is a sequential specification of behavior. It can also contain a program activation table—a combinatorial specification of behavior.

Figure 8.12 depicts a preliminary state diagram[18] for the level 1 control flow model for *SafeHome*. The diagram indicates how the system responds to events as it traverses the four states defined at this level. By reviewing the state diagram, a software engineer can determine the behavior of the system and, more importantly, can ascertain whether there are "holes" in the specified behavior.

For example, the state diagram (Figure 8.12) indicates that the transitions from the *Idle* state can occur if the system is reset, activated, or powered off. If the system is activated (i.e., alarm system is turned on), a transition to the *MonitoringSystemStatus* state occurs, display messages are changed as shown, and the process **monitorAndControlSystem** is invoked. Two transitions occur out of the *MonitoringSystemStatus* state—(1) when the system is deactivated a transition occurs back to the *Idle* state; (2) when a sensor is triggered a transition to the *ActingOnAlarm* state occurs. All transitions and the content of all states are considered during the review.

The CSPEC describes the behavior of the system, but it gives us no information about the inner working of the processes that are activated as a result of this behavior. The modeling notation that provides this information is discussed in Section 8.6.4.

---

17 Additional behavioral modeling notation is presented later in this chapter.

18 The state diagram notation used here conforms to UML notation. A "state transition diagram" is available in structured analysis, but the UML format is superior in information content and representation.

FIGURE 8.12 State diagram for *SafeHome* security function

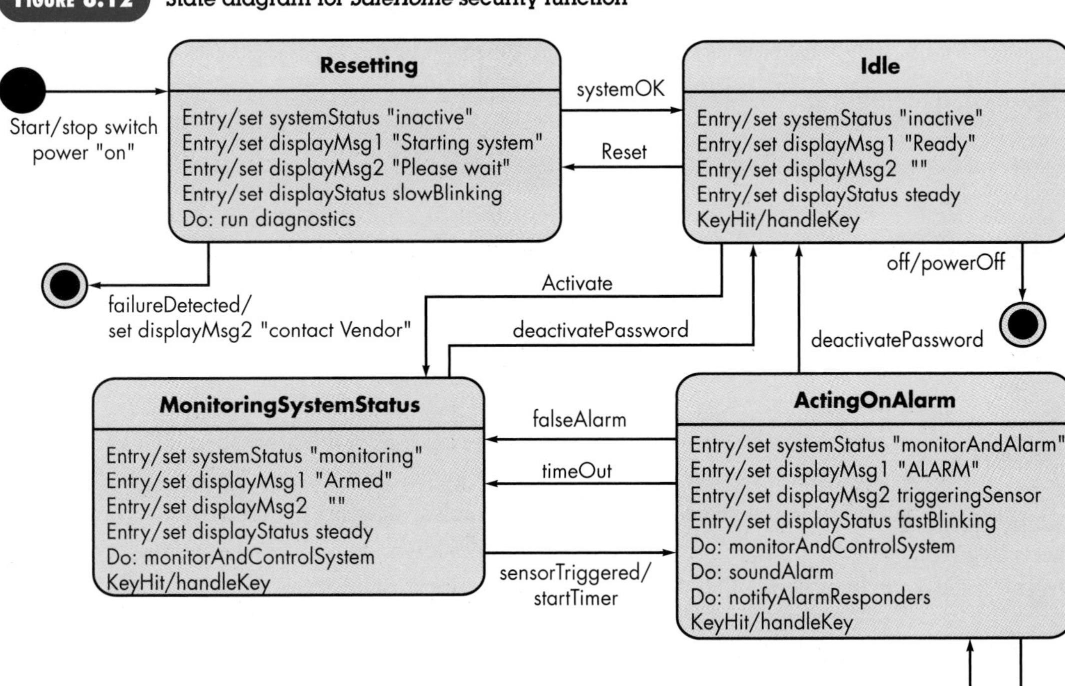

SAFEHOME

Data Flow Modeling

The scene: Jamie's cubicle, after the last requirements gathering meeting has concluded.

The players: Jamie, Vinod, and Ed—all members of the *SafeHome* software engineering team.

The conversation:

(Jamie has sketched out the models shown in Figures 8.9 through 8.12 and is showing them to Ed and Vinod.)

Jamie: I took a software engineering course in college, and they taught us this stuff. The prof said it's a bit old fashioned, but you know what? It helps me to clarify things.

Ed: That's cool. But I don't see any classes or objects here.

Jamie: No . . . this is just a flow model with a little behavioral stuff thrown in.

Vinod: So these DFDs represent an I-P-O view of the software, right?

Ed: I-P-O?

Vinod: Input-process-output. The DFDs are actually pretty intuitive . . . if you look at 'em for a moment, they show how data objects flow through the system and get transformed as they go.

Ed: Looks like we could convert every bubble into an executable component . . . at least at the lowest level of the DFD.

Jamie: That's the cool part, you can. In fact there's a way to translate the DFDs into a design architecture.

Ed: Really?

Jamie: Yeah, but first we've got to develop a complete analysis model, and this isn't it.

Vinod: Well, it's a first step, but we're going to have to address class-based elements and also behavior aspects, although this state diagram does some of that.

Ed: We've got a lot of work to do and not much time to do it.

(Doug—the software engineering manager—walks into the cubical.)

Doug: So the next few days will be spent developing the analysis model, huh?

Jamie (looking proud): We've already begun.

Doug: Good, we've got a lot of work to do and not much time to do it.

(The three software engineers look at one another and smile.)

8.6.4 The Process Specification

The PSPEC is a "mini-specification" for each transform at the lowest refined level of a DFD.

The *process specification* (PSPEC) is used to describe all flow model processes that appear at the final level of refinement. The content of the process specification can include narrative text, a program design language (PDL) description[19] of the process algorithm, mathematical equations, tables, diagrams, or charts. By providing a PSPEC to accompany each bubble in the flow model, the software engineer creates a "mini-spec" that can serve as a guide for design of the software component that will implement the process.

To illustrate the use of the PSPEC, consider the *process password* transform represented in the flow model for *SafeHome* (Figure 8.10). The PSPEC for this function might take the form:

> **PSPEC: process password (at control panel).** The *process password* transform performs password validation at the control panel for the *SafeHome* security function. *Process password* receives a four-digit password from the *interact with user* function. The password is first compared to the master password stored within the system. If the master password matches, [valid id message = true] is passed to the *message and status display* function. If the master password does not match, the four digits are compared to a table of secondary passwords (these may be assigned to house guests and/or workers who require entry to the home when the owner is not present). If the password matches an entry within the table, [valid id message = true] is passed to the *message and status display function.* If there is no match, [valid id message = false] is passed to the message and status display function.

If additional algorithmic detail is desired at this stage, a program design language representation may also be included as part of the PSPEC. However, many believe that the PDL version should be postponed until component design commences.

19 Program design language (PDL) mixes programming language syntax with narrative text to provide procedural design detail. PDL is discussed in Chapter 11.

SOFTWARE TOOLS

Structured Analysis

Objective: Structured analysis tools allow a software engineer to create data models, flow models, and behavioral models in a manner that enables consistency and continuity checking and easy editing and extension. Models created using these tools provide the software engineer with insight into the analysis representation and help to eliminate errors before they propagate into design, or worse, into implementation itself.

Mechanics: Tools in this category use a "data dictionary" as the central database for the description of all data objects. Once entries in the dictionary are defined, entity-relationship diagrams can be created and object hierarchies can be developed. Data flow diagramming features allow easy creation of this graphical model and also provide features for the creation of PSPECs and CSPECs. Analysis tools also enable the software engineer to create behavioral models using the state diagram as the operative notation.

Representative Tools[20]

AxiomSys, developed by STG, Inc. (www.stgcase.com), provides a complete structure analysis tools suite including Hatley-Pirbhai extensions for the modeling of real-time systems.

MacA&D, WinA&D developed by Excel Software (www.excelsoftware.com), provides a set of simple and inexpensive analysis and design tools for Macs and Windows machines.

MetaCASE Workbench, developed by MetaCase Consulting (www.metacase.com), is a metatool used to define an analysis or design method (including structured analysis): its concepts, rules, notations, and generators.

System Architect, developed by Popkin Software (www.popkin.com), provides a broad range of analysis and design tools including tools for data modeling and structured analysis.

8.7 CLASS-BASED MODELING

How do we go about developing the class-based elements of an analysis model—classes and objects, attributes, operations, packages, CRC models, and collaboration diagrams? The sections that follow present a series of informal guidelines that will assist in their identification and representation.

8.7.1 Identifying Analysis Classes

If you look around a room, there is a set of physical objects that can be easily identified, classified, and defined (in terms of attributes and operations). But when you "look around" the problem space of a software application, classes (and objects) may be more difficult to comprehend.

> "The really hard problem is discovering what are the right objects [classes] in the first place."
>
> **Carl Argila**

We can begin to identify classes by examining the problem statement or (using the terminology applied earlier in this chapter) by performing a "grammatical parse" on

20 Tools noted here do not represent an endorsement, but rather a sampling of tools in this category. In most cases, tool names are trademarked by their respective developers.

the use-cases or processing narratives developed for the system to be built. Classes are determined by underlining each noun or noun clause and entering it into a simple table. Synonyms should be noted. If the class is required to implement a solution, then it is part of the solution space; otherwise, if a class is necessary only to describe a solution, it is part of the problem space. What should we look for once all of the nouns have been isolated? *Analysis classes* manifest themselves in one of the following ways:

? How do analysis classes manifest themselves as elements of the solution space?

- *External entities* (e.g., other systems, devices, people) that produce or consume information to be used by a computer-based system.
- *Things* (e.g., reports, displays, letters, signals) that are part of the information domain for the problem.
- *Occurrences or events* (e.g., a property transfer or the completion of a series of robot movements) that occur within the context of system operation.
- *Roles* (e.g., manager, engineer, salesperson) played by people who interact with the system.
- *Organizational units* (e.g., division, group, team) that are relevant to an application.
- *Places* (e.g., manufacturing floor or loading dock) that establish the context of the problem and the overall function of the system.
- *Structures* (e.g., sensors, four-wheeled vehicles, or computers) that define a class of objects or related classes of objects.

This categorization is but one of many that have been proposed in the literature.[21] For example, Budd [BUD96] suggests a taxonomy of classes that includes producers (sources) and consumers (sinks) of data, data managers, view or observer classes, and helper classes.

It is also important to note what classes or objects are not. In general, a class should never have an "imperative procedural name" [CAS89]. For example, if the developers of software for a medical imaging system defined an object with the name **InvertImage** or even **ImageInversion,** they would be making a subtle mistake. The **Image** obtained from the software could, of course, be a class (it is a thing that is part of the information domain). Inversion of the image is an operation that is applied to the class. It is likely that *inversion()* would be defined as an operation for the class **Image,** but it would not be defined as a separate class to connote "image inversion." As Cashman [CAS89] states: "the intent of object-orientation is to encapsulate, but still keep separate, data and operations on the data."

To illustrate how analysis classes might be defined during the early stages of modeling, we return to the *SafeHome* security function. In Section 8.6.1, we performed a

21 Another important categorization—defining entity, boundary, and controller classes—is discussed in Section 8.7.4.

"grammatical parse" on a processing narrative[22] for the security function. Extracting the nouns, we can propose a number of potential classes:

Potential class	**General classification**
homeowner	role or external entity
sensor	external entity
control panel	external entity
installation	occurrence
system (alias security system)	thing
number, type	not objects, attributes of sensor
master password	thing
telephone number	thing
sensor event	occurrence
audible alarm	external entity
monitoring service	organizational unit or external entity

The list would be continued until all nouns in the processing narrative have been considered. Note that we call each entry in the list a potential object. We must consider each further before a final decision is made.

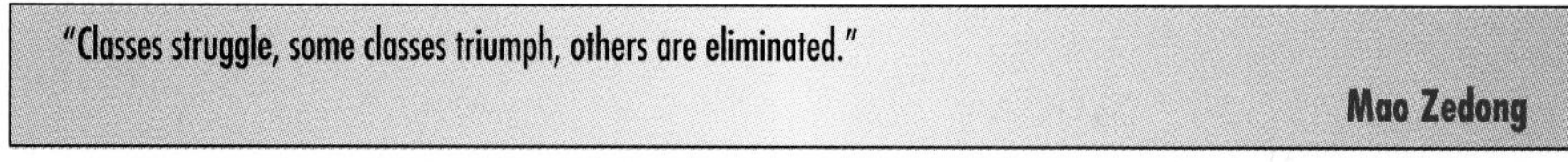

"Classes struggle, some classes triumph, others are eliminated."

Mao Zedong

? How do I determine whether a potential class should, in fact, become an analysis class?

Coad and Yourdon [COA91] suggest six selection characteristics that should be used as an analyst considers each potential class for inclusion in the analysis model:

1. *Retained information.* The potential class will be useful during analysis only if information about it must be remembered so that the system can function.
2. *Needed services.* The potential class must have a set of identifiable operations that can change the value of its attributes in some way.
3. *Multiple attributes.* During requirement analysis, the focus should be on "major" information; a class with a single attribute may, in fact, be useful during design, but is probably better represented as an attribute of another class during the analysis activity.
4. *Common attributes.* A set of attributes can be defined for the potential class, and these attributes apply to all instances of the class.

22 It is important to note that this technique should also be used for every use-case developed as part of the requirements gathering (elicitation) activity. That is, use-cases can be grammatically parsed to extract potential analysis classes.

5. *Common operations.* A set of operations can be defined for the potential class, and these operations apply to all instances of the class.
6. *Essential requirements.* External entities that appear in the problem space and produce or consume information essential to the operation of any solution for the system will almost always be defined as classes in the requirements model.

To be considered a legitimate class for inclusion in the requirements model, a potential class should satisfy all (or almost all) of these characteristics. The decision for inclusion of potential classes in the analysis model is somewhat subjective, and later evaluation may cause a class to be discarded or reinstated. However, the first step of class-based modeling is the definition of classes, and decisions (even subjective ones) must be made. With this in mind, we apply the selection characteristics to the list of potential *SafeHome* classes:

Potential class	Characteristic number that applies
homeowner	rejected: 1, 2 fail even though 6 applies
sensor	accepted: all apply
control panel	accepted: all apply
installation	rejected
system (alias security function)	accepted: all apply
number, type	rejected: 3 fails, attributes of sensor
master password	rejected: 3 fails
telephone number	rejected: 3 fails
sensor event	accepted: all apply
audible alarm	accepted: 2, 3, 4, 5, 6 apply
monitoring service	rejected: 1, 2 fail even though 6 applies

It should be noted that (1) the preceding list is not all-inclusive—additional classes would have to be added to complete the model; (2) some of the rejected potential classes will become attributes for those classes that were accepted (e.g., **number** and **type** are attributes of **Sensor,** and **master password** and **telephone number** may become attributes of **System**); (3) different statements of the problem might cause different "accept or reject" decisions to be made (e.g., if each homeowner had an individual password or was identified by voice print, the **Homeowner** class would satisfy characteristics 1 and 2 and would have been accepted).

Attributes are the set of data objects that fully define the class within the context of the problem.

8.7.2 Specifying Attributes

Attributes describe a class that has been selected for inclusion in the analysis model. In essence, it is the attributes that define the class—that clarify what is meant by the class in the context of the problem space.

To develop a meaningful set of attributes for an analysis class, a software engineer can again study a use-case and select those "things" that reasonably "belong" to the class. In addition, the following question should be answered for each class: What data items (composite and/or elementary) fully define this class in the context of the problem at hand?

To illustrate, we consider the **System** class defined for *SafeHome.* We have noted that the homeowner can configure the security function to reflect sensor information, alarm response information, activation/deactivation information, identification information, and so forth. We can represent these composite data items in the following manner:

identification information = system ID + verification phone number + system status

alarm response information = delay time + telephone number

activation/deactivation information = master password + number of allowable tries + temporary password

Some of the data items to the right of the equal sign could be further refined to an elementary level, but for our purposes, they constitute a reasonable list of attributes for the **System** class (shaded portion of Figure 8.13).

Sensors are part of the overall *SafeHome* system, and yet they are not listed as data items or as attributes in Figure 8.13. **Sensor** has already been defined as a class, and multiple **Sensor** objects will be associated with the **System** class. In general, we avoid defining an item as an attribute if more than one of the items is to be associated with the class.

8.7.3 Defining Operations

Operations define the behavior of an object. Although many different types of operations exist, they can generally be divided into three broad categories: (1) operations

FIGURE 8.13

Class diagram for the system class

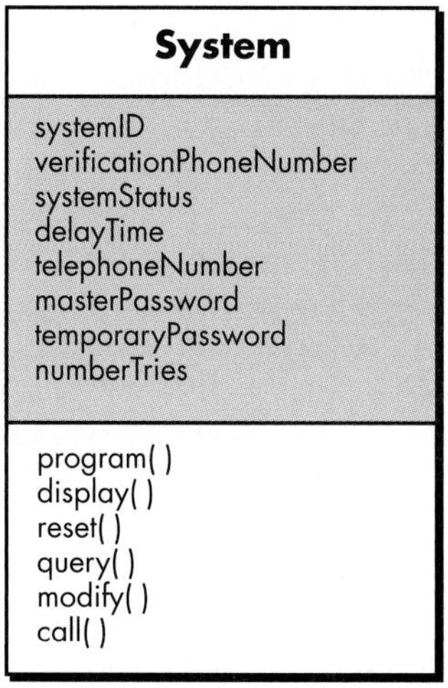

System
systemID verificationPhoneNumber systemStatus delayTime telephoneNumber masterPassword temporaryPassword numberTries
program( ) display( ) reset( ) query( ) modify( ) call( )

When you define operations for an analysis class, focus on problem-oriented behavior rather than behaviors required for implementation.

that manipulate data in some way (e.g., adding, deleting, reformatting, selecting), (2) operations that perform a computation, (3) operations that inquire about the state of an object, and (4) operations that monitor an object for the occurrence of a controlling event. These functions are accomplished by operating on attributes and/or associations (Section 8.7.5). Therefore, an operation must have "knowledge" of the nature of the class' attributes and associations.

As a first iteration at deriving a set of operations for an analysis class, the analyst can again study a processing narrative (or use-case) and select those operations that reasonably belong to the class. To accomplish this, the grammatical parse is again studied and verbs are isolated. Some of these verbs will be legitimate operations and can be easily connected to a specific class. For example, from the *SafeHome* processing narrative presented earlier in this chapter, we see that "sensor is assigned a number and type" or "a master password is programmed for arming and disarming the system." These phrases indicate a number of things:

- That an *assign()* operation is relevant for the **Sensor** class.
- That a *program()* operation is encapsulated by the **System** class.
- That *arm()* and *disarm()* are operations that apply to **System** class.

Upon further investigation, it is likely that the operation *program()* will be divided into a number of more specific suboperations required to configure the system. For example, *program()* implies specifying phone numbers, configuring system characteristics (e.g., creating the sensor table, entering alarm characteristics), and entering password(s). But for now, we specify *program()* as a single operation.

SAFEHOME

Class Models

The scene: Ed's cubicle, as analysis modeling begins.

The players: Jamie, Vinod, and Ed—all members of the *SafeHome* software engineering team.

The conversation:

(Ed has been working to extract classes from the use-case template for **Access camera surveillance—display camera views"** [presented in an earlier sidebar in this chapter] and is presenting the classes he has extracted to his colleagues.)

Ed: So when the homeowner wants to pick a camera, he or she has to pick it from a floor plan. I've defined a **FloorPlan** class. Here's the diagram.

(They look at Figure 8.14.)

Jamie: So **FloorPlan** is a class that is put together with walls that are composed of wall segments, doors and windows, and also cameras; that's what those labeled lines mean, right?

Ed: Yeah, they're called "associations." One class is associated with another according to the associations I've shown. [Associations are discussed in Section 8.7.5.]

Vinod: So the actual floor plan is made up of walls and contains cameras and sensors that are placed within those walls. How does the floor plan know where to put those objects?

Ed: It doesn't, but the other classes do. See the attributes under, say, **WallSegment,** which is used to build a wall. The wall segment has start and stop coordinates and the *draw* () operation does the rest.

Jamie: And the same goes for windows and doors. Looks like camera has a few extra attributes.

Ed: Yeah, I need them to provide pan and zoom info.

Vinod: I have a question. Why does the camera have an ID but the others don't?

Ed: We'll need to identify each camera for display purposes.

Jamie: Makes sense to me, but I do have a few more questions.

(Jamie asks questions which result in minor modifications.)

Vinod: Do you have CRC cards for each of the classes? If so, we ought to role play through them, just make sure nothing has been omitted.

Ed:" I'm not quite sure how to do them.

Vinod: It's not hard, and they really pay off. I'll show you.

FIGURE 8.14 Class diagram for FloorPlan (see sidebar discussion)

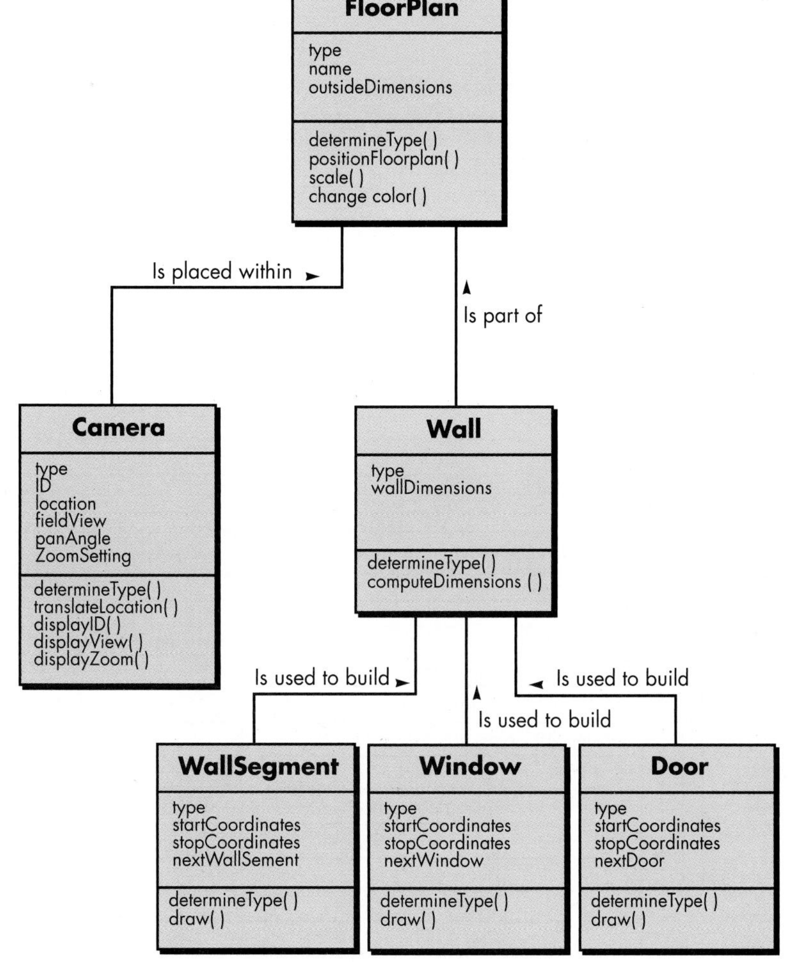

8.7.4 Class-Responsibility-Collaborator (CRC) Modeling

Class-responsibility-collaborator (CRC) modeling [WIR90] provides a simple means for identifying and organizing the classes that are relevant to system or product requirements. Ambler [AMB95] describes CRC modeling in the following way:

> A CRC model is really a collection of standard index cards that represent classes. The cards are divided into three sections. Along the top of the card you write the name of the class. In the body of the card you list the class responsibilities on the left and the collaborators on the right.

In reality, the CRC model may make use of actual or virtual index cards. The intent is to develop an organized representation of classes. *Responsibilities* are the attributes and operations that are relevant for the class. Stated simply, a responsibility is "anything the class knows or does" [AMB95]. *Collaborators* are those classes that are required to provide a class with the information needed to complete a responsibility. In general, a collaboration implies either a request for information or a request for some action.

> "One purpose of CRC cards is to fail early, to fail often, and to fail inexpensively. It is a lot cheaper to tear up a bunch of cards than it would be to reorganize a large amount of source code."
>
> **C. Horstmann**

A simple CRC index card for the **FloorPlan** class is illustrated in Figure 8.15. The list of responsibilities shown on the CRC card is preliminary and subject to additions or modification. The classes **Wall** and **Camera** are noted next to the responsibility that will require their collaboration.

FIGURE 8.15

A CRC model index card

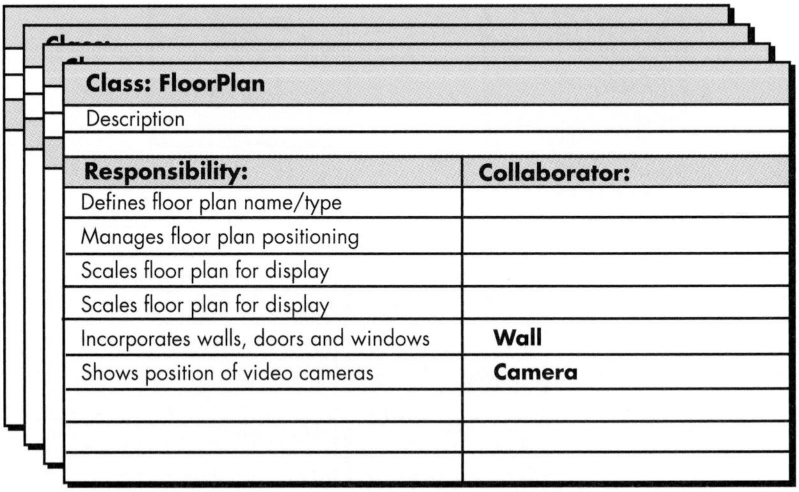

Class: FloorPlan

Description

Responsibility:	**Collaborator:**
Defines floor plan name/type	
Manages floor plan positioning	
Scales floor plan for display	
Scales floor plan for display	
Incorporates walls, doors and windows	**Wall**
Shows position of video cameras	**Camera**

Classes. Basic guidelines for identifying classes and objects have been presented earlier in this chapter. The taxonomy of class types presented in Section 8.7.1 can be extended by considering the following categories:

WebRef
An excellent discussion of these class types can be found at **www.theumlcafe.com/a0079.htm.**

- *Entity classes,* also called *model* or *business* classes, are extracted directly from the statement of the problem (e.g., **FloorPlan** and **Sensor**). These classes typically represent things that are to be stored in a database and persist throughout the duration of the application (unless they are specifically deleted).
- *Boundary classes* are used to create the interface (e.g., interactive screen or printed reports) that the user sees and interacts with as the software is used. Entity classes contain information that is important to users, but they do not display themselves. Boundary classes are designed with the responsibility of managing the way entity objects are represented to users. For example, a boundary class called **CameraWindow** would have the responsibility of displaying surveillance camera output for the *SafeHome* system.
- *Controller classes* manage a "unit of work" [UML03] from start to finish. That is, controller classes can be designed to manage (1) the creation or update of entity objects; (2) the instantiation of boundary objects as they obtain information from entity objects; (3) complex communication between sets of objects; and (4) validation of data communicated between objects or between the user and the application. In general, controller classes are not considered until design has begun.

> "Objects can be classified scientifically into three major categories: those that don't work, those that break down, and those that get lost."
>
> **Russell Baker**

Responsibilities. Basic guidelines for identifying responsibilities (attributes and operations) have been presented in Sections 8.7.2 and 8.7.3. Wirfs-Brock and her colleagues [WIR90] suggest five guidelines for allocating responsibilities to classes:

? What guidelines can be applied for allocating responsibilities to classes?

1. **System intelligence should be distributed across classes to best address the needs of the problem.** Every application encompasses a certain degree of intelligence, that is, what the system knows and what it can do. This intelligence can be distributed across classes in a number of different ways. "Dumb" classes (those that have few responsibilities) can be modeled to act as servants to a few "smart" classes (those having many responsibilities). Although this approach makes the flow of control in a system straightforward, it has a few disadvantages: (a) it concentrates all intelligence within a few classes, making changes more difficult, and (b) it tends to require more classes, hence more development effort.

If system intelligence is more evenly distributed across the classes in an application, each object knows about and does only a few things (that are generally well-focused), and the cohesiveness of the system is improved. This enhances the maintainability of the software and reduces the impact of side effects due to change.

To determine whether system intelligence is properly distributed, the responsibilities noted on each CRC model index card should be evaluated to determine if any class has an extraordinarily long list of responsibilities. This indicates a concentration of intelligence.[23] In addition, the responsibilities for each class should exhibit the same level of abstraction.

2. **Each responsibility should be stated as generally as possible.** This guideline implies that general responsibilities (both attributes and operations) should reside high in the class hierarchy (because they are generic, they will apply to all subclasses).
3. **Information and the behavior related to it should reside within the same class.** This achieves the OO principle called *encapsulation.* Data and the processes that manipulate the data should be packaged as a cohesive unit.
4. **Information about one thing should be localized with a single class, not distributed across multiple classes.** A single class should take on the responsibility for storing and manipulating a specific type of information. This responsibility should not, in general, be shared across a number of classes. If information is distributed, software becomes more difficult to maintain and more challenging to test.
5. **Responsibilities should be shared among related classes, when appropriate.** There are many cases in which a variety of related objects must all exhibit the same behavior at the same time. As an example, consider a video game that must display the following classes: **Player, PlayerBody, PlayerArms, PlayerLegs, PlayerHead.** Each of these classes has its own attributes (e.g., **position, orientation, color, speed**) and all must be updated and displayed as the user manipulates a joystick. The responsibilities *update()* and *display()* must therefore be shared by each of the objects noted. **Player** knows when something has changed and *update()* is required. It collaborates with the other objects to achieve a new position or orientation, but each object controls its own display.

Collaborations. Classes fulfill their responsibilities in one of two ways: (1) a class can use its own operations to manipulate its own attributes, thereby fulfilling a particular responsibility, or (2) a class can collaborate with other classes.

---

23 In such cases, it may be necessary to split the class into multiple classes or complete subsystems in order to distribute intelligence more effectively.

Wirfs-Brock and her colleagues [WIR90] define *collaborations* in the following way:

> Collaborations represent requests from a client to a server in fulfillment of a client responsibility. A collaboration is the embodiment of the contract between the client and the server. . . .We say that an object collaborates with another object if, to fulfill a responsibility, it needs to send the other object any messages. A single collaboration flows in one direction—representing a request from the client to the server. From the client's point of view, each of its collaborations are associated with a particular responsibility implemented by the server.

Collaborations identify relationships between classes. When a set of classes all collaborate to achieve some requirement, they can be organized into a subsystem (a design issue).

If a class cannot fulfill all of its obligations itself, then a collaboration is required.

Collaborations are identified by determining whether a class can fulfill each responsibility itself. If it cannot, then it needs to interact with another class. Hence, a collaboration.

As an example, consider the *SafeHome* security function. As part of the activation procedure, the **ControlPanel** object must determine whether any sensors are open. A responsibility named *determine-sensor-status()* is defined. If sensors are open, **ControlPanel** must set a **status** attribute to "not ready." Sensor information can be acquired from each **Sensor** object. Therefore, the responsibility *determine-sensor-status()* can be fulfilled only if **ControlPanel** works in collaboration with **Sensor.**

To help in the identification of collaborators, the analyst can examine three different generic relationships between classes [WIR90]: (1) the *is-part-of* relationship, (2) the *has-knowledge-of* relationship, and (3) the *depends-upon* relationship. Each of the three generic relationships is considered briefly in the paragraphs that follow.

All classes that are part of an aggregate class are connected to the aggregate class via an *is-part-of* relationship. Consider the classes defined for the video game noted earlier, the class **PlayerBody** *is-part-of* **Player,** as are **PlayerArms, PlayerLegs,** and **PlayerHead.** In UML, these relationships are represented as the aggregation shown in Figure 8.16.

When one class must acquire information from another class, the *has-knowledge-of* relationship is established. The *determine-sensor-status()* responsibility noted earlier is an example of a *has-knowledge-of* relationship.

The *depends-upon* relationship implies that two classes have a dependency that is not achieved by *has-knowledge-of* or *is-part-of.* For example, **PlayerHead** must always be connected to **PlayerBody** (unless the video game is particularly violent), yet each object could exist without direct knowledge of the other. An attribute of the **PlayerHead** object called **center-position** is determined from the center position of **PlayerBody.** This information is obtained via a third object, **Player,** that acquires it from **PlayerBody.** Hence, **PlayerHead** *depends-upon* **PlayerBody.**

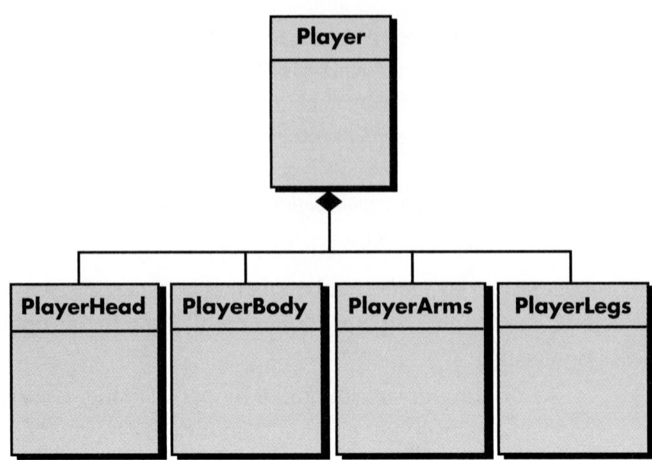

FIGURE 8.16 A composite aggregate class

In all cases, the collaborator class name is recorded on the CRC model index card next to the responsibility that has spawned the collaboration. Therefore, the index card contains a list of responsibilities and the corresponding collaborations that enable the responsibilities to be fulfilled (Figure 8.15).

When a complete CRC model has been developed, representatives from the customer and software engineering organizations can review the model using the following approach [AMB95]:

1. All participants in the review (of the CRC model) are given a subset of the CRC model index cards. Cards that collaborate should be separated (i.e., no reviewer should have two cards that collaborate).
2. All use-case scenarios (and corresponding use-case diagrams) should be organized into categories.
3. The review leader reads the use-case deliberately. As the review leader comes to a named class, she passes a token to the person holding the corresponding class index card. For example, a use-case for *SafeHome* contains the following narrative:

   The homeowner observes the *SafeHome* control panel to determine if the system is ready for input. If the system is not ready, the homeowner must physically close windows/doors so that the ready indicator is present. [A not-ready indicator implies that a sensor is open, i.e., that a door or window is open.]

   When the review leader comes to "control panel," in the use-case narrative, the token is passed to the person holding the **ControlPanel** index card. The phrase "implies that a sensor is open" requires that the index card contain a responsibility that will validate this implication (the responsibility *determine-sensor-status()* accomplishes this). Next to the responsibility on the index card is the collaborator **Sensor.** The token is then passed to the **Sensor** class.

4. When the token is passed, the holder of the class card is asked to describe the responsibilities noted on the card. The group determines whether one (or more) of the responsibilities satisfies the use-case requirement.
5. If the responsibilities and collaborations noted on the index cards cannot accommodate the use-case, modifications are made to the cards. This may include the definition of new classes (and corresponding CRC index cards) or the specification of new or revised responsibilities or collaborations on existing cards.

This modus operandi continues until the use-case is finished. When all use-cases have been reviewed, analysis modeling continues.

SAFEHOME

CRC models

The scene: Ed's cubicle, as analysis modeling continues.

The players: Vinod, and Ed—members of the *SafeHome* software engineering team.

The conversation:

(Vinod has decided to show Ed how to develop CRC cards by showing him an example.)

Vinod: While you've been working on surveillance and Jamie has been tied up with security, I've been working on the home management function.

Ed: What's the status of that? Marketing kept changing its mind.

Vinod: Here's the first cut use-case for the whole function . . . we've refined it a bit, but it should give you an overall view.

Use-case: *SafeHome* home management function.

Narrative: We want to use the home management interface on a PC or an Internet connection to control electronic devices that have wireless interface controllers. The system should allow me to turn specific lights on and off, to control appliances that are connected to a wireless interface, to set my heating and air conditioning system to temperatures that I define. To do this, I want to select the devices from a floor plan of the house. Each device must be identified on the floor plan. As an optional feature, I want to control all audio-visual devices—audio, television, DVD, digital recorders, and so forth.

With a single selection, I want to be able to set the entire house for various situations. One is *home,* another is *away,* a third is *overnight travel,* and a fourth is *extended travel.* All of these situations will have settings that will be applied to all devices. In the *overnight travel* and *extended travel* states, the system should turn lights on and off at random intervals (to make it look like someone is home) and control the heating and air conditioning system. I should be able to override these settings via the Internet with appropriate password protection.

Ed: The hardware guys have got all the wireless interfacing figured out?

Vinod (smiling): They're working on it, say it's no biggy. Anyway, I extracted a bunch of classes for home management, and we can use one as an example. Let's use the **HomeManagementInterface** class.

Ed: Okay . . . so the responsibilities are . . . the attributes and operations for the class, and the collaborations are the classes that the responsibilities point to.

Vinod: I thought you didn't understand CRC.

Ed: Maybe a little, but go ahead.

Vinod: So here's my class definition for **HomeManagementInterface.**

Attributes:

optionsPanel—provides info on buttons that enable user to select functionality

situationPanel—provides info on buttons that enable user to select situation

FloorPlan—same as surveillance object but this one displays devices

deviceIcons—info on icons representing lights, appliances, HVAC, etc.

devicePanels—simulation of appliance or device control panel; allows control

Operations:

displayControl(), selectControl(), displaySituation(), selectSituation(), accessFloorplan(), selectDeviceIcon(), displayDevicePanel(), accessDevicePanel(), ...

Class: HomeManagementInterface

Responsibility	**Collaborator**
displayControl	**OptionsPanel** (class)
selectControl	**OptionsPanel** (class)
displaySituation	**SituationPanel** (class)
selectSituation	**SituationPanel** (class)
accessFloorplan	**FloorPlan** (class) . . .

•

•

•

Ed: So when the operation *accessFloorplan()* is invoked, it collaborates with the **FloorPlan** object just like the one we developed for surveillance. Wait, I have a description of it here. (They look at Figure 8.14.)

Vinod: Exactly. And if we wanted to review the entire class model, we could start with this index card, then go to the collaborator's index card, and from there to one of the collaborator's collaborators, and so on.

Ed: Good way to find omissions or errors.

Vinod: Yep.

An association defines a relationship between classes. Multiplicity defines how many of one class are related to how many of another class.

8.7.5 Associations and Dependencies

In many instances, two analysis classes are related to one another in some fashion, much like two data objects may be related to one another (Section 8.3.3). In UML these relationships are called *associations.* Referring back to Figure 8.14, the **FloorPlan** class is defined by identifying a set of associations between **FloorPlan** and two other classes, **Camera** and **Wall.** The class **Wall** is associated with three classes that allow a wall to be constructed, **WallSegment, Window,** and **Door.**

In some cases, an association may be further defined by indicating *multiplicity* (the term *cardinality* was used earlier in this chapter). Referring to Figure 8.14, a **Wall** object is constructed from one or more **WallSegment** objects. In addition, the **Wall** object may contain 0 or more **Window** objects and 0 or more **Door** objects. These multiplicity constraints are illustrated in Figure 8.17, where "one or more" is represented using 1 . . *, and "0 or more" by 0 . . * . In UML, the asterisk indicates an unlimited upper bound on the range.[24]

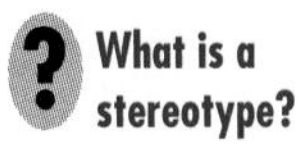

What is a stereotype?

In many instances, a client-server relationship exists between two analysis classes. In such cases, a client-class depends on the server-class in some way and a *dependency relationship* is established. Dependencies are defined by a stereotype. A *stereotype* is an "extensibility mechanism" [ARL02] within UML that allows a software

24 Other multiplicity relations—one to one, one to many, many to many, one to a specified range with lower and upper limits, and others—may be indicated as part of an association.

FIGURE 8.17

Multiplicity

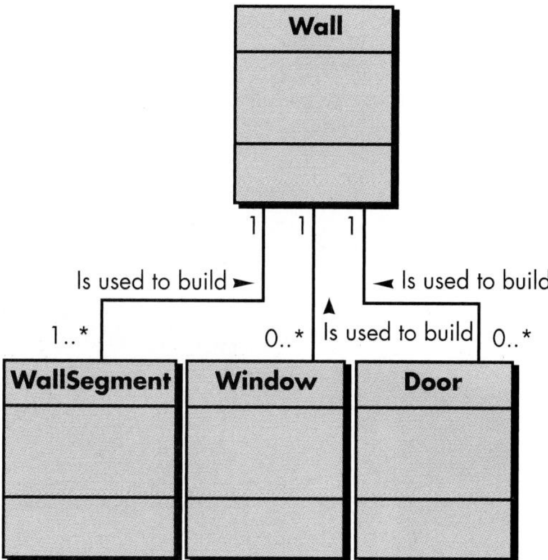

FIGURE 8.18

Dependencies

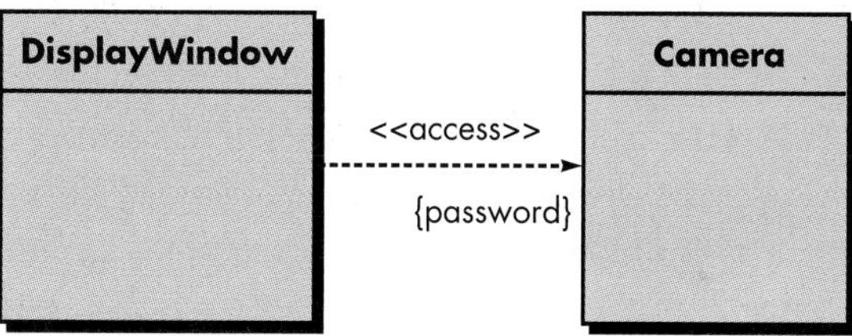

engineer to define a special modeling element whose semantics are custom-defined. In UML stereotypes are represented in double angle brackets (e.g., «stereotype»).

As an illustration of a simple dependency within the *SafeHome* surveillance system, a **Camera** object (in this case, the server-class) provides a video image to a **DisplayWindow** object (in this case, the client-class). The relationship between these two objects is not a simple association, yet a dependency association does exist. In a use-case written for surveillance (not shown), the modeler learns that a special password must be provided in order to view specific camera locations. One way to achieve this is to have **Camera** request a password and then grant permission to the **DisplayWindow** to produce the video display. This can be represented as shown in Figure 8.18 where «access» implies that the use of the camera output is controlled by a special password.

8.7.6 Analysis Packages

An important part of analysis modeling is categorization. That is, various elements of the analysis model (e.g., use-cases, analysis classes) are categorized in a manner

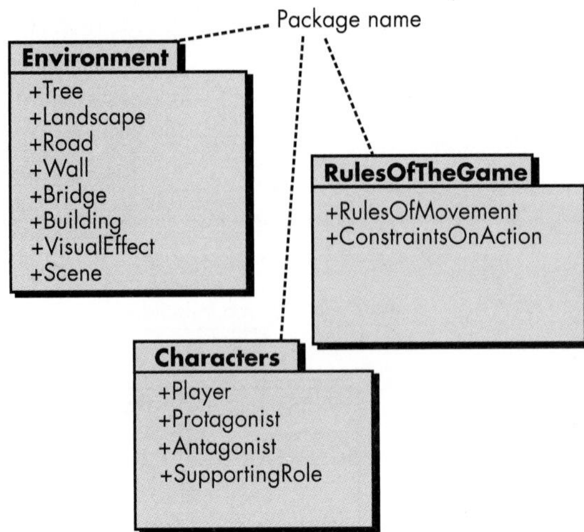

FIGURE 8.19
Packages

that packages them as a grouping—called an *analysis package*—that is given a representative name.

A package is used to assemble a collection of related classes.

To illustrate the use of analysis packages, consider the video game that we introduced earlier. As the analysis model for the video game is developed, a large number of classes are derived. Some focus on the game environment—the visual scenes that the user sees as the game is played. Classes such as **Tree, Landscape, Road, Wall, Bridge, Building, VisualEffect,** might fall within this category. Others focus on the characters within the game, describing their physical features, actions, and constraints. Classes such as **Player** (described earlier), **Protagonist, Antagonist, SupportingRoles,** might be defined. Still others describe the rules of the game—how a player navigates through the environment. Classes such as **Rules OfMovement** and **ConstraintsOnAction** are candidates here. Many other categories might exist. These classes can be represented as analysis packages as shown in Figure 8.19.

The plus sign preceding the analysis class name in each package indicates that the classes have public visibility and are therefore accessible from other packages. Although they are not shown in the figure, other symbols can precede an element within a package. A minus sign indicates that an element is hidden from all other packages and a # symbol indicates that an element is accessible only to classes contained within a given package.

8.8 CREATING A BEHAVIORAL MODEL

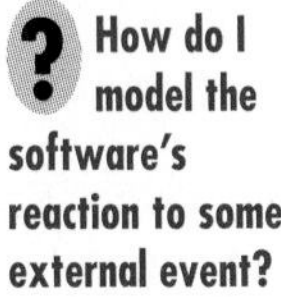

How do I model the software's reaction to some external event?

Class diagrams, CRC index cards, and other class-oriented models discussed in Section 8.7 represent static elements of the analysis model. It is now time to make a transition to the dynamic behavior of the system or product. To accomplish this, we must represent the behavior of the system as a function of specific events and time.

The *behavioral model* indicates how software will respond to external events or stimuli. To create the model, the analyst must perform the following steps:

Use-cases are parsed to define events. To accomplish this, the use-case is examined for points of information exchange.

1. Evaluate all use-cases to fully understand the sequence of interaction within the system.
2. Identify events that drive the interaction sequence and understand how these events relate to specific classes.
3. Create a sequence for each use-case.
4. Build a state diagram for the system.
5. Review the behavioral model to verify accuracy and consistency.

Each of these steps is discussed in the sections that follow.

8.8.1 Identifying Events with the Use-Case

As we noted in Section 8.5, the use-case represents a sequence of activities that involves actors and the system. In general, an event occurs whenever the system and an actor exchange information. Recalling our earlier discussion of behavioral modeling in Section 8.6.3, it is important to note that an event is not the information that has been exchanged, but rather the *fact* that information has been exchanged.

A use-case is examined for points of information exchange. To illustrate, we reconsider the use-case for a small portion of the *SafeHome* security function.

> The homeowner uses the keypad to key in a four-digit password. The password is compared with the valid password stored in the system. If the password is incorrect, the control panel will beep once and reset itself for additional input. If the password is correct, the control panel awaits further action.

The underlined portions of the use-case scenario indicate events. An actor should be identified for each event; the information that is exchanged should be noted; and any conditions or constraints should be listed.

As an example of a typical event, consider the underlined use-case phrase "homeowner uses the keypad to key in a four-digit password." In the context of the analysis model, the object, **Homeowner,**[25] transmits an event to the object **ControlPanel.** The event might be called *password entered.* The information transferred is the four digits that constitute the password, but this is not an essential part of the behavioral model. It is important to note that some events have an explicit impact on the flow of control of the use-case, while others have no direct impact on the flow of control. For example, the event *password entered* does not explicitly change the flow of control of the use-case, but the results of the event *compare password* (derived from the interaction "password is compared with the valid password

25 In this example, we assume that each user (homeowner) that interacts with *SafeHome* has an identifying password and is therefore a legitimate object.

stored in the system") will have an explicit impact on the information and control flow of the *SafeHome* software.

Once all events have been identified, they are allocated to the objects involved. Objects can be responsible for generating events (e.g., **Homeowner** generates the *password entered* event) or recognizing events that have occurred elsewhere (e.g., **ControlPanel** recognizes the binary result of the *compare password* event).

8.8.2 State Representations

In the context of behavioral modeling, two different characterizations of states must be considered: (1) the state of each class as the system performs its function and (2) the state of the system as observed from the outside as the system performs its function.[26]

KEY POINT

The system has states that represent specific externally observable behavior; a class has states that represent its behavior as the system performs its functions.

The state of a class takes on both passive and active characteristics [CHA93]. A *passive state* is simply the current status of all of an object's attributes. For example, the passive state of the class **Player** (in the video game application discussed earlier) would include the current **position** and **orientation** attributes of **Player** as well as other features of **Player** that are relevant to the game (e.g., an attribute that indicates **magic wishes remaining**). The *active state* of an object indicates the current status of the object as it undergoes a continuing transformation or processing. The class **Player** might have the following active states: *moving, at rest, injured, being cured, trapped, lost,* and so forth. An event (sometimes called a *trigger*) must occur to force an object to make a transition from one active state to another.

Two different behavioral representations are discussed in the paragraphs that follow. The first indicates how an individual class changes state based on external events, and the second shows the behavior of the software as a function of time.

State diagrams for analysis classes. One component of a behavioral model is a UML state diagram that represents active states for each class and the events (triggers) that cause changes between these active states. Figure 8.20 illustrates a state diagram for the **ControlPanel** class in the *SafeHome* security function.

Each arrow shown in Figure 8.20 represents a transition from one active state of a class to another. The labels shown for each arrow represent the event that triggers the transition. Although the active state model provides useful insight into the "life history" of a class, it is possible to specify additional information to provide more depth in understanding the behavior of a class. In addition to specifying the event that causes the transition to occur, the analyst can specify a guard and an action [CHA93]. A *guard* is a Boolean condition that must be satisfied in order for the

---

26 The state diagrams presented in Section 8.6.3 depict the state of the system. Our discussion in this section will focus on the state of each class within the analysis model.

FIGURE 8.20

State diagram for the Control-Panel class

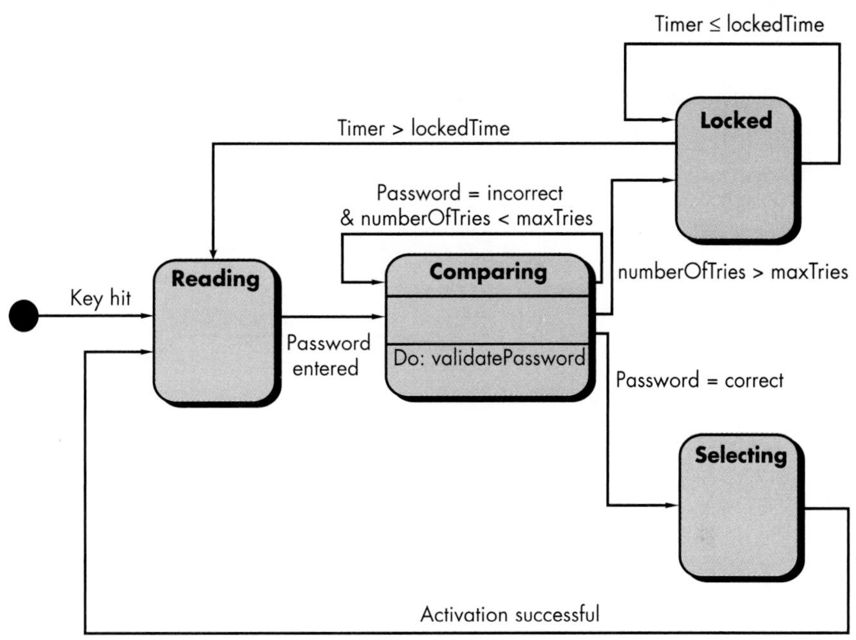

transition to occur. For example, the guard for the transition from the "reading" state to the "comparing state" in Figure 8.20 can be determined by examining the use-case:

if (password input = 4 digits) then compare to stored password

In general, the guard for a transition usually depends upon the value of one or more attributes of an object. In other words, the guard depends on the passive state of the object.

Unlike a state diagram that represents behavior without noting the classes involved, a sequence diagram represents behavior by describing how classes move from state to state.

An *action* occurs concurrently with the state transition or as a consequence of it and generally involves one or more operations (responsibilities) of the object. For example, the action connected to the *password entered* event (Figure 8.20) is an operation named *validatePassword()* that accesses a **password** object and performs a digit-by-digit comparison to validate the entered password.

Sequence diagrams. The second type of behavioral representation, called a *sequence diagram* in UML, indicates how events cause transitions from object to object. Once events have been identified by examining a use-case, the modeler creates a sequence diagram—a representation of how events cause flow from one object to

FIGURE 8.21 Sequence diagram (partial) for the *SafeHome* security function

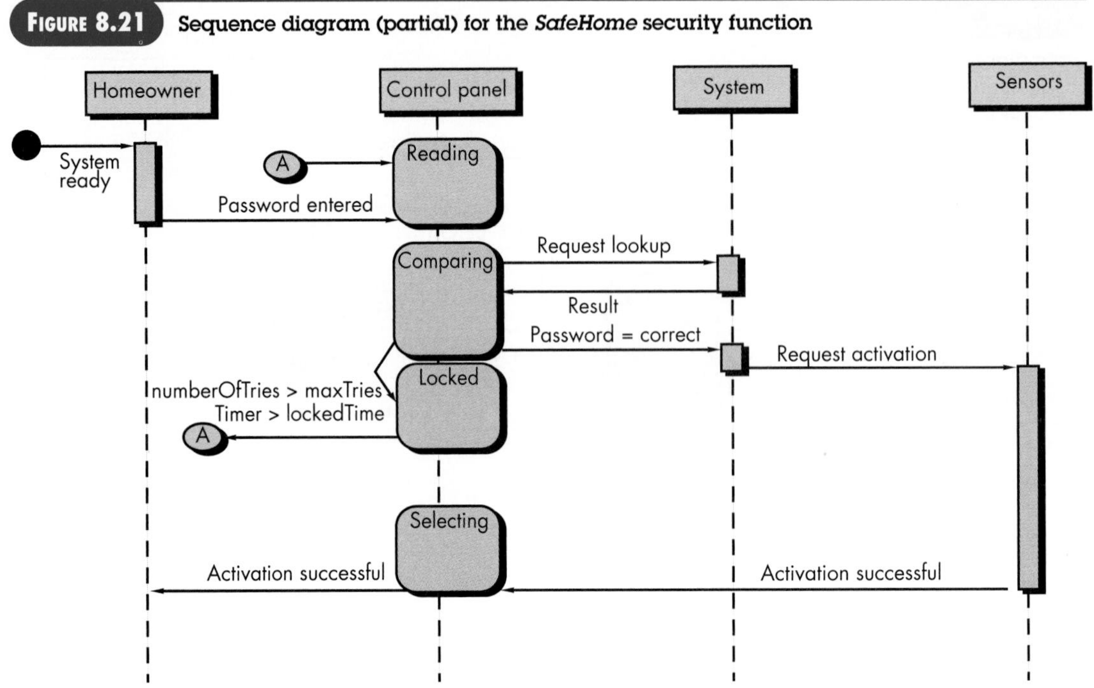

another as a function of time. In essence, the sequence diagram is a shorthand version of the use-case. It represents key classes and the events that cause behavior to flow from class to class.

Figure 8.21 illustrates a partial sequence diagram for the *SafeHome* security function. Each of the arrows represents an event (derived from a use-case) and indicates how the event channels behavior between *SafeHome* objects. Time is measured vertically (downward), and the narrow vertical rectangles represent time spent in processing an activity. States may be shown along a vertical timeline.

The first event, *system ready,* is derived from the external environment and channels behavior to a **Homeowner** object. The homeowner enters a password. A *request lookup* event is passed to **System** which looks up the password in a simple database and returns a *result* (*found* or *not found*) to **ControlPanel** (now in the *comparing* state). A valid password results in a *password=correct* event to **System** which activates sensors with a *request activation* event. Ultimately, control is passed back to the homeowner with the *activation successful* event.

Once a complete sequence diagram has been developed, all of the events that cause transitions between system objects can be collated into a set of input events and output events (from an object). This information is useful in the creation of an effective design for the system to be built.

SOFTWARE TOOLS

Generalized Analysis Modeling in UML

Objective: Analysis modeling tools provide the capability to develop scenario-based models, class-based models, and behavioral models using UML notation.

Mechanics: Tools in this category support the full range of UML diagrams required to build an analysis model (these tools also support design modeling). In addition to diagramming, tools in this category (1) perform consistency and correctness checks for all UML diagrams; (2) provide links for design and code generation; (3) build a database that enables the management and assessment of large UML models required for complex systems.

Representative Tools[27]

The following tools support a full range of UML diagrams required for analysis modeling:

ArgoUML, an open source tool (argouml.tigris.org).

Control Center, developed by TogetherSoft (www.togethersoft.com).

Enterprise Architect, developed by Sparx Systems (www.sparxsystems.com.au).

Object Technology Workbench (OTW), developed by OTW Software (www.otwsoftware.com).

PowerDesigner, developed by Sybase (www.sybase.com).

Rational Rose, developed by Rational Corporation (www.rational.com).

System Architect, developed by Popkin Software (www.popkin.com).

UML Studio, developed by Pragsoft Corporation (www.pragsoft.com).

Visio, developed by Microsoft (www.microsoft.com).

Visual UML, developed by Visal Object Modelers (www.visualuml.com).

8.9 Summary

The objective of analysis modeling is to create a variety of representations that depict software requirements for information, function, and behavior. To accomplish this, two different (but potentially complementary) modeling philosophies can be applied: structured analysis and object-oriented analysis. Structured analysis views software as an information transformer. It assists the software engineer in identifying data objects, their relationships, and the manner in which those data objects are transformed as they flow through software processing functions. Object-oriented analysis examines a problem domain defined as a set of use-cases in an effort to extract classes that define the problem. Each class has a set of attributes and operations. Classes are related to one another in a variety of different ways and are modeled using UML diagrams. The analysis model is composed of four modeling elements: scenario-based models, flow models, class-based models, and behavioral models.

Scenario-based models depict software requirements from the user's point of view. The use-case—a narrative or template-driven description of an interaction between an actor and the software—is the primary modeling element. Derived during requirement elicitation, the use-case defines the key steps for a specific function or interaction. The

27 Tools noted here do not represent an endorsement, but rather a sampling of tools in this category. In most cases, tool names are trademarked by their respective developers.

degree of use-case formality and detail varies, but the end result provides necessary input to all other analysis modeling activities. Scenarios can also be described using an activity diagram—a flowchart-like graphical representation that depicts the processing flow within a specific scenario. Swimlane diagrams illustrate how the processing flow is allocated to various actors or classes.

Flow models focus on the flow of data objects as they are transformed by processing functions. Derived from structured analysis, flow models use the data flow diagram, a modeling notation that depicts how input is transformed into output as data objects move through a system. Each software function that transforms data is described by a process specification or narrative. In addition to data flow, this modeling element also depicts control flow—a representation that illustrates how events affect the behavior of a system.

Class-based modeling uses information derived from scenario-based and flow-oriented modeling elements to identify analysis classes. A grammatical parse may be used to extract candidate classes, attributes, and operations from text-based narratives. Criteria for the definition of a class are defined. The class-responsibility-collaborator index card can be used to define relationships between classes. In addition, a variety of UML modeling notation can be applied to define hierarchies, relationships, associations, aggregations, and dependencies among classes. Analysis packages are used to categorize and group classes in a manner that makes them more manageable for large systems.

The first three analysis modeling elements provide a static view of the software. Behavioral modeling depicts dynamic behavior. The behavioral model uses input from scenario-based, flow-oriented, and class-based elements to represent the states of analysis classes and the system as a whole. To accomplish this, states are identified, the events that cause a class (or the system) to make a transition from one state to another are defined, and the actions that occur as transition is accomplished are also identified. State diagrams and sequence diagrams are the UML notation used for behavioral modeling.

References

[ABB83] Abbott, R., "Program Design by Informal English Descriptions," *CACM,* vol. 26, no. 11, November 1983, pp. 892–894.

[AMB95] Ambler, S., "Using Use-Cases," *Software Development,* July 1995, pp. 53–61.

[ARA89] Arango, G., and R. Prieto-Diaz, "Domain Analysis: Concepts and Research Directions," *Domain Analysis: Acquisition of Reusable Information for Software Construction,* (Arango, G. and R. Prieto-Diaz, eds.), IEEE Computer Society Press, 1989.

[ARL02] Arlow, J., and I. Neustadt, *UML and the Unified Process,* Addison-Wesley, 2002.

[BER93] Berard, E. V., *Essays on Object-Oriented Software Engineering,* Addison-Wesley, 1993.

[BOO86] Booch, G., "Object-Oriented Development," *IEEE Trans. Software Engineering,* vol. SE-12, no. 2, February 1986, pp. 211ff.

[BUD96] Budd, T., *An Introduction to Object-Oriented Programming,* 2nd ed., Addison-Wesley, 1996.

[CAS89] Cashman, M., "Object-Oriented Domain Analysis," *ACM Software Engineering Notes,* vol. 14, no. 6, October 1989, p. 67.

[CHA93] de Champeaux, D., D. Lea, and P. Faure, *Object-Oriented System Development,* Addison-Wesley, 1993.

[CHE77] Chen, P., *The Entity-Relationship Approach to Logical Database Design,* QED Information Systems, 1977.

[COA91] Coad, P., and E. Yourdon, *Object-Oriented Analysis,* 2nd ed., Prentice-Hall, 1991.

[COC01] Cockburn, A., *Writing Effective Use Cases,* Addison-Wesley, 2001.

[DAV93] Davis, A., *Software Requirements: Objects, Functions and States,* Prentice-Hall, 1993.

[DEM79] DeMarco, T., *Structured Analysis and System Specification,* Prentice-Hall, 1979.

[FIR93] Firesmith, D. G., *Object-Oriented Requirements Analysis and Logical Design,* Wiley, 1993.

[LET03] Lethbridge, T., personal communication on domain analysis, May, 2003.

[OMG03] Object Management Group, OMG Unified Modeling Language Specification, version 1.5, March 2003, available from http://www.rational.com/uml/ resources/documentation/.

[SCH02] Schmuller, J., *Teach Yourself UML in 24 Hours,* 2nd ed., SAMS Publishing, 2002.

[SCH98] Schneider, G., and J. Winters, *Applying Use Cases,* Addison-Wesley, 1998.

[STR88] Stroustrup, B., "What Is Object-Oriented Programming?" IEEE Software, vol. 5, no. 3, May 1988, pp. 10–20.

[TAY90] Taylor, D. A., *Object-Oriented Technology: A Manager's Guide,* Addison-Wesley, 1990.

[THA00] Thalheim, B., *Entity Relationship Modeling,* Springer-Verlag, 2000.

[TIL93] Tillmann, G., *A Practical Guide to Logical Data Modeling,* McGraw-Hill, 1993.

[UML03] The UML Café, "Customers Don't Print Themselves," available at http://www.theumlcafe.com/a0079.htm, May, 2003.

[WIR90] Wirfs-Brock, R., B. Wilkerson, and L. Weiner, *Designing Object-Oriented Software,* Prentice-Hall, 1990.

Problems and Points to Ponder

8.1. Is it possible to begin coding immediately after an analysis model has been created? Explain your answer and then argue the counterpoint.

8.2. An analysis rule of thumb is that the model "should focus on requirements that are visible within the problem or business domain." What types of requirements are *not* visible in these domains? Provide a few examples.

8.3. What is the purpose of domain analysis? How is it related to the concept of requirements patterns?

8.4. In a few sentences, try to describe the primary differences between structured analysis and object-oriented analysis.

8.5. Is it possible to develop an effective analysis model without developing all four elements shown in Figure 8.3? Explain.

8.6. You have been asked to build one of the following systems:

a. A network-based course registration system for your university.
b. A Web-based order-processing system for a computer store.
c. A simple invoicing system for a small business.
d. Software that replaces a Rolodex and is built into a wireless phone.
e. An automated cookbook that is built into an electric range or microwave.

Select the system that is of interest to you and describe data objects, relationships, and attributes.

8.7. Draw a context-level model (level 0 DFD) for one of the five systems that are listed in Problem 8.6. Write a context-level processing narrative for the system.

8.8. Using the context-level DFD developed in Problem 8.7, develop level 1 and level 2 data flow diagrams. Use a "grammatical parse" on the context-level processing narrative to get yourself started. Remember to specify all information flow by labeling all arrows between bubbles. Use meaningful names for each transform.

8.9. Develop CSPECs and PSPECs for the system you selected in Problem 8.6. Try to make your model as complete as possible.

8.10. The department of public works for a large city has decided to develop a Web-based pothole tracking and repair system (PHTRS). A description follows:

> Citizens can log onto a Web site and report the location and severity of potholes. As potholes are reported they are logged within a "public works department repair system" and are assigned an identifying number, stored by street address, size (on a scale of 1 to 10), location (middle, curb, etc.), district (determined from street address), and repair priority (determined from the size of the pothole). Work order data are associated with each pothole and include pothole location and size, repair crew identifying number, number of people on a crew, equipment assigned, hours applied to repair, hole status (work in progress, repaired, temporary repair, not repaired), amount of filler material used, and cost of repair (computed from hours applied, number of people, material, and equipment used). Finally, a damage file is created to hold information about reported damage due to the pothole and includes the citizen's name, address, phone number, type of damage, dollar amount of damage. PHTRS is a Web-based system; all queries are to be made interactively.

Using structured analysis notation, develop an analysis model for PHTRS.

8.11. Describe the object-oriented terms *encapsulation* and *inheritance.*

8.12. Write a template-based use-case for the *SafeHome* home management system described informally in the sidebar following Section 8.7.4.

8.13. Draw a UML use-case diagram for the PHTRS system introduced in Problem 8.10. You'll have to make a number of assumptions about the manner in which a user interacts with this system.

8.14. Develop a class model for the PHTRS system introduced in Problem 8.10.

8.15. Develop a complete set of CRC model index cards for the PHTRS system introduced in Problem 8.10.

8.16. Conduct a review of the CRC index cards with your colleagues. How many additional classes, responsibilities, and collaborators were added as a consequence of the review?

8.17. Describe the difference between an association and a dependency for an analysis class.

8.18. What is an analysis package, and how might it be used?

8.19. How does a state diagram for analysis classes differ from the state diagrams presented for the complete system?

Further Readings and Information Sources

Dozens of books have been published on structured analysis. Most cover the subject adequately, but only a few do a truly excellent job. DeMarco and Plauger (*Structured Analysis and System Specification,* Pearson, 1985) is a classic that remains a good introduction to the basic notation. Books by Kendall and Kendall (*Systems Analysis and Design,* fifth edition, Prentice-Hall, 2002) and Hoffer et al. (*Modern Systems Analysis and Design,* Addison-Wesley, third edition., 2001) are worthwhile references. Yourdon's book (*Modern Structured Analysis,* Yourdon-Press, 1989) on the subject remains among the most comprehensive coverage published to date.

Allen (*Data Modeling for Everyone,* Wrox Press, 2002), Simpson and Witt (*Data Modeling Essentials,* second edition, Coriolis Group, 2000) Reingruber and Gregory (*Data Modeling Handbook,* Wiley, 1995) present detailed tutorials for creating industry-quality data models. An interesting book by Hay (*Data Modeling Patterns,* Dorset House, 1995) presents typical data model patterns that are encountered in many different businesses. A detailed treatment of behavioral modeling can be found in Kowal (*Behavior Models: Specifying User's Expectations,* Prentice-Hall, 1992).

Use-cases form the foundation of object-oriented analysis. Books by Bittner and Spence (*Use Case Modeling,* Addison-Wesley, 2002), Cockburn [COC01], Armour and Miller (*Advanced Use-Case Modeling: Software Systems,* Addison-Wesley, 2000), and Rosenberg and Scott (*Use-Case Driven Object Modeling with UML: A Practical Approach,* Addison-Wesley, 1999) provide worthwhile guidance in the creation and use of this important requirements elicitation and representation mechanism.

Worthwhile discussions of UML have been written by Arlow and Neustadt [ARL02], Schmuller [SCH02], Fowler and Scott (*UML Distilled,* second edition, Addison-Wesley, 1999), Booch and his colleagues (*The UML User Guide,* Addison-Wesley, 1998), and Rumbaugh and his colleagues (*The Unified Modeling Language Reference Manual,* Addison-Wesley, 1998).

The underlying analysis and design methods that support the Unified Process are discussed by Larman (*Applying UML and Patterns: An Introduction to Object-Oriented Analysis and Design and the Unified Process,* second edition, Prentice-Hall, 2001), Dennis and his colleagues (*System Analysis and Design: An Object-Oriented Approach with UML,* Wiley, 2001), and Rosenberg and Scott (*Use-Case Driven Object Modeling with UML,* Addison-Wesley, 1999). Balcer and Mellor (*Executable UML: A Foundation for Model Driven Architecture,* Addison-Wesley, 2002) discuss the overall semantics of UML, the models that can be created, and a way to consider UML as an executable language. Starr (*Executable UML: How to Build Class Models,* Prentice-Hall, 2001) provides useful guidelines and detailed suggestions for creating effective analysis and design classes.

A wide variety of information sources on analysis modeling are available on the Internet. An up-to-date list of World Wide Web references that are relevant to analysis modeling can be found at the SEPA Web site:
http://www.mhhe.com/pressman.

CHAPTER

9 DESIGN ENGINEERING

KEY CONCEPTS

Design engineering encompasses the set of principles, concepts, and practices that lead to the development of a high-quality system or product. Design principles (discussed in Chapter 5) establish an overriding philosophy that guides the designer in the work that is performed. Design concepts must be understood before the mechanics of design practice are applied, and design practice itself leads to the creation of various representations of the software that serve as a guide for the construction activity that follows.

Design engineering is not a commonly used phrase in the software engineering context. And yet, it should be. Design is a core engineering activity. In the early 1990s Mitch Kapor, the creator of Lotus 1-2-3, presented a "software design manifesto" in *Dr. Dobbs Journal.* He said:

> What is design? It's where you stand with a foot in two worlds—the world of technology and the world of people and human purposes—and you try to bring the two together. . .
>
> The Roman architecture critic Vitruvius advanced the notion that well-designed buildings were those which exhibited firmness, commodity, and delight. The same might be said of good software. *Firmness:* A program should not have any bugs that inhibit its function. *Commodity:* A program should be suitable for the purposes for which it was intended. *Delight:* The experience of using the program should be a pleasurable one. Here we have the beginnings of a theory of design for software.

QUICK LOOK

What is it? Design is what virtually every engineer wants to do. It is the place where creativity rules—where customer requirements, business needs, and technical considerations all come together in the formulation of a product or system. Design creates a representation or model of the software, but unlike the analysis model (that focuses on describing required data, function, and behavior), the design model provides detail about software data structures, architecture, interfaces, and components that are necessary to implement the system.

Who does it? Software engineers conduct each of the design tasks.

Why is it important? Design allows a software engineer to model the system or product that is to be built. This model can be assessed for quality and improved before code is generated, tests are conducted, and end-users become involved in large numbers. Design is the place where software quality is established.

What are the steps? Design depicts the software in a number of different ways. First, the architecture of the system or product must be represented. Then, the interfaces that connect the software to end-users, to other systems and devices, and to its own constituent components are modeled. Finally, the software components that are used to construct the system are designed. Each of these views represents a different design action, but all must conform to a set of basic design concepts that guide all software design work.

What is the work product? A design model that encompasses architectural, interface, component-level, and deployment representations is the primary work product that is produced during software design.

How do I ensure that I've done it right? The design model is assessed by the software team in an effort to determine whether it contains errors, inconsistencies, or omissions; whether better alternatives exist; and whether the model can be implemented within the constraints, schedule, and cost that have been established.

The goal of design engineering is to produce a model or representation that exhibits firmness, commodity, and delight. To accomplish this, a designer must practice diversification and then convergence. Belady [BEL81] states that "diversification is the acquisition of a repertoire of alternatives, the raw material of design: components, component solutions, and knowledge, all contained in catalogs, textbooks, and the mind." Once this diverse set of information is assembled, the designer must pick and choose elements from the repertoire that meet the requirements defined by requirements engineering (Chapter 7) and the analysis model (Chapter 8). As this occurs, alternatives are considered and rejected, and the design engineer converges on "one particular configuration of components, and thus the creation of the final product" [BEL81].

Diversification and convergence demand intuition and judgment. These qualities are based on experience in building similar entities, a set of principles and/or heuristics that guide the way in which the model evolves, a set of criteria that enables quality to be judged, and a process of iteration that ultimately leads to a final design representation.

Design engineering for computer software changes continually as new methods, better analysis, and broader understanding evolve. Even today, most software design methodologies lack the depth, flexibility, and quantitative nature that are normally associated with more classical engineering design disciplines. However, methods for software design do exist, criteria for design quality are available, and design notation can be applied. In this chapter, we explore the fundamental concepts and principles that are applicable to all software design, the elements of the design model, and the impact of patterns on the design process. In Chapters 10, 11, and 12 we examine a variety of software design methods as they are applied to architectural, interface, and component-level design.

9.1 Design within the Context of Software Engineering

Software design sits at the technical kernel of software engineering and is applied regardless of the software process model that is used. Beginning once software requirements have been analyzed and modeled, software design is the last software engineering action within the modeling activity and sets the stage for construction (code generation and testing).

> "The most common miracle of software engineering is the transition from analysis to design and design to code."
>
> **Richard Due**

Design engineering should always begin with a consideration of data—the foundation for all other elements of the design. After the foundation is laid, the architecture must be derived. Only then, should you perform other design tasks.

Each of the elements of the analysis model (Chapter 8) provides information that is necessary to create the four design models required for a complete specification of design. The flow of information during software design is illustrated in Figure 9.1. The analysis model, manifested by scenario-based, class-based, flow-oriented and behavioral elements, feed the design task. Using design notation and design methods discussed in later chapters, design produces a data/class design, an architectural design, an interface design, and a component design.

The data/class design transforms analysis-class models (Chapter 8) into design class realizations and the requisite data structures required to implement the software. The classes and relationships defined by CRC index cards and the detailed data content depicted by class attributes and other notation provide the basis for the data design activity. Part of class design may occur in conjunction with the design of software architecture. More detailed class design occurs as each software component is designed.

The architectural design defines the relationship between major structural elements of the software, the architectural styles and design patterns that can be used to achieve the requirements defined for the system, and the constraints that affect

FIGURE 9.1 Translating the analysis model into the design model

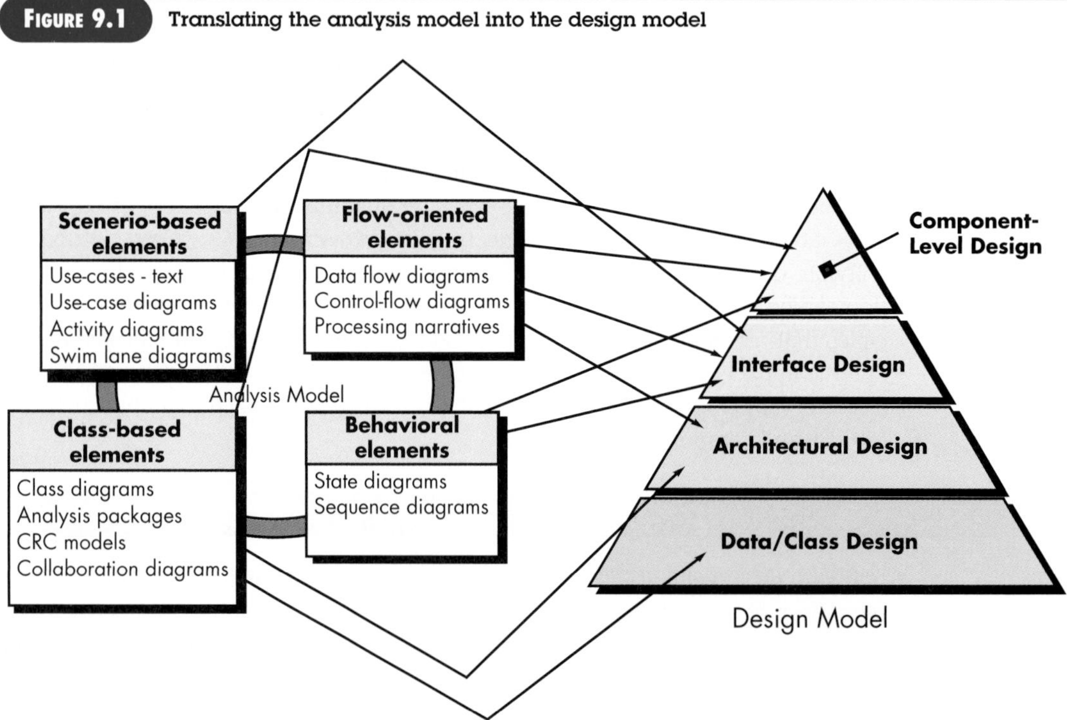

the way in which architectural can be implemented [SHA96]. The architectural design representation—the framework of a computer-based system—can be derived from the system specification, the analysis model, and the interaction of subsystems defined within the analysis model.

The interface design describes how the software communicates with systems that interoperate with it, and with humans who use it. An interface implies a flow of information (e.g., data and/or control) and a specific type of behavior. Therefore, usage scenarios and behavioral models provide much of the information required for interface design.

The component-level design transforms structural elements of the software architecture into a procedural description of software components. Information obtained from the class-based models, flow models, and behavioral models serve as the basis for component design.

> **"There are two ways of constructing a software design. One way is to make it so simple that there are obviously no deficiencies, and the other way is to make it so complicated that there are obviously no deficiencies. The first method is far more difficult."**
>
> **C.A.R. Hoare**

During design we make decisions that will ultimately affect the success of software construction and, as important, the ease with which software can be maintained. But why is design so important?

The importance of software design can be stated with a single word—*quality*. Design is the place where quality is fostered in software engineering. Design provides us with representations of software that can be assessed for quality. Design is the only way that we can accurately translate a customer's requirements into a finished software product or system. Software design serves as the foundation for all the software engineering and software support activities that follow. Without design, we risk building an unstable system—one that will fail when small changes are made; one that may be difficult to test; one whose quality cannot be assessed until late in the software process, when time is short and many dollars have already been spent.

9.2 Design Process and Design Quality

Software design is an iterative process through which requirements are translated into a "blueprint" for constructing the software. Initially, the blueprint depicts a holistic view of software. That is, the design is represented at a high level of abstraction—a level that can be directly traced to the specific system objective and more detailed data, functional, and behavioral requirements. As design iterations occur, subsequent refinement leads to design representations at much lower levels of abstraction. These can still be traced to requirements, but the connection is more subtle.

Throughout the design process, the quality of the evolving design is assessed with a series of formal technical reviews or design walkthroughs discussed in Chapter 26. McGlaughlin [MCG91] suggests three characteristics that serve as a guide for the evaluation of a good design:

- The design must implement all of the explicit requirements contained in the analysis model, and it must accommodate all of the implicit requirements desired by the customer.
- The design must be a readable, understandable guide for those who generate code and for those who test and subsequently support the software.
- The design should provide a complete picture of the software, addressing the data, functional, and behavioral domains from an implementation perspective.

Each of these characteristics is actually a goal of the design process. But how is each of these goals achieved?

> "[W]riting a clever piece of code that works is one thing; designing something that can support a long-lasting business is quite another."
>
> **C. Ferguson**

Quality guidelines. In order to evaluate the quality of a design representation, we must establish technical criteria for good design. Later in this chapter, we discuss design concepts that also serve as software quality criteria. For the time being, we present the following guidelines:

? What are the characteristics of a good design?

1. A design should exhibit an architecture that (a) has been created using recognizable architectural styles or patterns, (b) is composed of components that exhibit good design characteristics (these are discussed later in this chapter), and (c) can be implemented in an evolutionary fashion,[1] thereby facilitating implementation and testing.
2. A design should be modular; that is, the software should be logically partitioned into elements or subsystems.
3. A design should contain distinct representations of data, architecture, interfaces, and components.
4. A design should lead to data structures that are appropriate for the classes to be implemented and are drawn from recognizable data patterns.
5. A design should lead to components that exhibit independent functional characteristics.
6. A design should lead to interfaces that reduce the complexity of connections between components and with the external environment.

---

1 For smaller systems, design can sometimes be developed linearly.

7. A design should be derived using a repeatable method that is driven by information obtained during software requirements analysis.
8. A design should be represented using a notation that effectively communicates its meaning.

These design guidelines are not achieved by chance. Design engineering encourages good design through the application of fundamental design principles, systematic methodology, and thorough review.

INFO

Assessing Design Quality—The Formal Technical Review

Design is important because it allows a software team to assess the quality[2] of the software before it is implemented—at a time when errors, omissions, or inconsistencies are easy and inexpensive to correct. But how do we assess quality during design? The software can't be tested because there is no executable software to test. What to do?

During design, quality is assessed by conducting a series of formal technical reviews (FTRs). FTRs are discussed in detail in Chapter 26,[3] but it's worth providing a summary of the technique at this point. An FTR is a meeting conducted by members of the software team. Usually two, three, or four people participate depending on the scope of the design information to be reviewed. Each person plays a role: the *review leader* plans the meeting, sets an agenda, and then runs the meeting; the *recorder* takes notes so that nothing is missed; the *producer* is the person whose work product (e.g., the design of a software component) is being reviewed. Prior to the meeting, each person on the review team is given a copy of the design work product and is asked to read it, looking for errors, omissions, or ambiguity. When the meeting commences, the intent is to note all problems with the work product so that they can be corrected before implementation begins. The FTR typically lasts between 90 minutes and two hours. At the conclusion of the FTR, the review team determines whether further actions are required on the part of the producer before the design work product can be approved as part of the final design model.

> "Quality isn't something you lay on top of subjects and objects like tinsel on a Christmas tree."
>
> **Robert Pirsig**

Quality attributes. Hewlett-Packard [GRA87] developed a set of software quality attributes that has been given the acronym FURPS—functionality, usability, reliability, performance, and supportability. The FURPS quality attributes represent a target for all software design:

- *Functionality* is assessed by evaluating the feature set and capabilities of the program, the generality of the functions that are delivered, and the security of the overall system.

---

2 The quality factors discussed in Chapter 15 can assist the review team as it assesses quality.

3 You might consider reviewing Section 26.4 at this time. FTRs are a critical part of the design process and are an important mechanism for achieving design quality.

Software designers tend to focus on the problem to be solved. Just don't forget that the FURPS attributes are always part of the problem. They must be considered.

- *Usability* is assessed by considering human factors (Chapter 12), overall aesthetics, consistency, and documentation.
- *Reliability* is evaluated by measuring the frequency and severity of failure, the accuracy of output results, the mean-time-to-failure (MTTF), the ability to recover from failure, and the predictability of the program.
- *Performance* is measured by processing speed, response time, resource consumption, throughput, and efficiency.
- *Supportability* combines the ability to extend the program (extensibility), adaptability, serviceability—these three attributes represent a more common term, *maintainability*—in addition, testability, compatibility, configurability (the ability to organize and control elements of the software configuration, (Chapter 27), the ease with which a system can be installed, and the ease with which problems can be localized.

Not every software quality attribute is weighted equally as the software design is developed. One application may stress functionality with a special emphasis on security. Another may demand performance with particular emphasis on processing speed. A third might focus on reliability. Regardless of the weighting, it is important to note that these quality attributes must be considered as design commences, *not* after the design is complete and construction has begun.

TASK SET

Generic Task Set for Design

1. Examine the information domain model and design appropriate data structures for data objects and their attributes.
2. Using the analysis model, select an architectural style (pattern) that is appropriate for the software.
3. Partition the analysis model into design subsystems and allocate these subsystems within the architecture.
   Be certain that each subsystem is functionally cohesive.
   Design subsystem interfaces.
   Allocate analysis classes or functions to each subsystem.
4. Create a set of design classes or components.
   Translate each analysis class description into a design class.
   Check each design class against design criteria; consider inheritance issues.
   Define methods and messages associated with each design class.
   Evaluate and select design patterns for a design class or a subsystem.
   Review design classes and revise as required.
5. Design any interface required with external systems or devices.
6. Design the user interface.
   Review results of task analysis.
   Specify action sequence based on user scenarios.
   Create behavioral model of the interface.
   Define interface objects, control mechanisms.
   Review the interface design and revise as required.
7. Conduct component-level design.
   Specify all algorithms at a relatively low level of abstraction.
   Refine the interface of each component.
   Define component-level data structures.
   Review each component and correct all errors uncovered.
8. Develop a deployment model.

9.3 Design Concepts

A set of fundamental software design concepts has evolved over the history of software engineering. Although the degree of interest in each concept has varied over the years, each has stood the test of time. Each provides the software designer with a foundation from which more sophisticated design methods can be applied.

M. A. Jackson [JAC75] once said: "The beginning of wisdom for a [software engineer] is to recognize the difference between getting a program to work, and getting it right." Fundamental software design concepts provide the necessary framework for "getting it right."

9.3.1 Abstraction

When we consider a modular solution to any problem, many *levels of abstraction* can be posed. At the highest level of abstraction, a solution is stated in broad terms using the language of the problem environment. At lower levels of abstraction, a more detailed description of the solution is provided.

> "Abstraction is one of the fundamental ways that we as humans cope with complexity."
>
> **Grady Booch**

As a designer, work hard to derive both procedural and data abstractions that serve the problem at hand. If they can serve an entire domain of problems, that's even better.

As we move through different levels of abstraction, we work to create procedural and data abstractions. A *procedural abstraction* refers to a sequence of instructions that have a specific and limited function. The name of procedural abstraction implies these functions, but specific details are suppressed. An example of a procedural abstraction would be the word *open* for a door. *Open* implies a long sequence of procedural steps (e.g., walk to the door, reach out and grasp knob, turn knob and pull door, step away from moving door, etc.).[4]

A *data abstraction* is a named collection of data that describes a data object. In the context of the procedural abstraction *open,* we can define a data abstraction called **door.** Like any data object, the data abstraction for **door** would encompass a set of attributes that describe the door (e.g., **door type, swing direction, opening mechanism, weight, dimensions**). It follows that the procedural abstraction *open* would make use of information contained in the attributes of the data abstraction **door.**

9.3.2 Architecture

Software architecture alludes to "the overall structure of the software and the ways in which that structure provides conceptual integrity for a system" [SHA95a]. In its simplest form, architecture is the structure or organization of program components

---

4 It should be noted, however, that one set of operations can be replaced with another, as long as the function implied by the procedural abstraction remains the same. Therefore, the steps required to implement *open* would change dramatically if the door were automatic and attached to a sensor.

(modules), the manner in which these components interact, and the structure of data that are used by the components. In a broader sense, however, components can be generalized to represent major system elements and their interactions.

> "A software architecture is the development work product that gives the highest return on investment with respect to quality, schedule, and cost."
>
> **Len Bass et al.**

WebRef

An in depth discussion of software architecture can be found at **www.sei.cmu.edu/ata/ata_init.html.**

One goal of software design is to derive an architectural rendering of a system. This rendering serves as a framework from which more detailed design activities are conducted. A set of architectural patterns enable a software engineer to reuse design-level concepts.

Don't just let architecture happen. If you do, you'll spend the rest of the project trying to force fit the design. Design architecture explicitly.

The architectural design can be represented using one or more of a number of different models [GAR95]. *Structural models* represent architecture as an organized collection of program components. *Framework models* increase the level of design abstraction by attempting to identify repeatable architectural design frameworks that are encountered in similar types of applications. *Dynamic models* address the behavioral aspects of the program architecture, indicating how the structure or system configuration may change as a function of external events. *Process models* focus on the design of the business or technical process that the system must accommodate. Finally, *functional models* can be used to represent the functional hierarchy of a system. Architectural design is discussed in Chapter 10.

9.3.3 Patterns

Brad Appleton defines a *design pattern* in the following manner: "A pattern is a named nugget of insight which conveys the essence of a proven solution to a recurring problem within a certain context amidst competing concerns" [APP98]. Stated in another way, a design pattern describes a design structure that solves a particular design problem within a specific context and amid "forces" that may have an impact on the manner in which the pattern is applied and used.

> "Each pattern describes a problem which occurs over and over again in our environment, and then describes the core of the solution to that problem, in such a way that you can use this solution a million times over, without ever doing it the same way twice."
>
> **Christopher Alexander**

The intent of each design pattern is to provide a description that enables a designer to determine (1) whether the pattern is applicable to the current work, (2) whether the pattern can be reused (hence, saving design time), and (3) whether the pattern can serve as a guide for developing a similar, but functionally or structurally different pattern. Design patterns are discussed in more detail in Section 9.5.

9.3.4 Modularity

Software architecture and design patterns embody *modularity;* that is, software is divided into separately named and addressable components, sometimes called *modules,* that are integrated to satisfy problem requirements.

It has been stated that "modularity is the single attribute of software that allows a program to be intellectually manageable" [MYE78]. Monolithic software (i.e., a large program composed of a single module) cannot be easily grasped by a software engineer. The number of control paths, span of reference, number of variables, and overall complexity would make understanding close to impossible. To illustrate this point, consider the following argument based on observations of human problem solving.

Consider two problems, p_1 and p_2. If the perceived complexity of p_1 is greater than the perceived complexity of p_2, it follows that the effort required to solve p_1 is greater than the effort required to solve p_2. As a general case, this result is intuitively obvious. It does take more time to solve a difficult problem.

It also follows that the perceived complexity of two problems when they are combined is often greater than the sum of the perceived complexity when each is taken separately. This leads to a "divide and conquer" strategy—it's easier to solve a complex problem when you break it into manageable pieces. This has important implications with regard to modularity and software. It is, in fact, an argument for modularity.

Don't overmodularize. The simplicity of each small module will be overshadowed by the complexity of integration.

It is possible to conclude that, if we subdivide software indefinitely, the effort required to develop it will become negligibly small! Unfortunately, other forces come into play, causing this conclusion to be (sadly) invalid. Referring to Figure 9.2, the effort (cost) to develop an individual software module does decrease as the total number of modules increases. Given the same set of requirements, more modules means smaller individual size. However, as the number of modules grows, the effort (cost) associated with integrating the modules also grows. These

FIGURE 9.2

Modularity and software cost

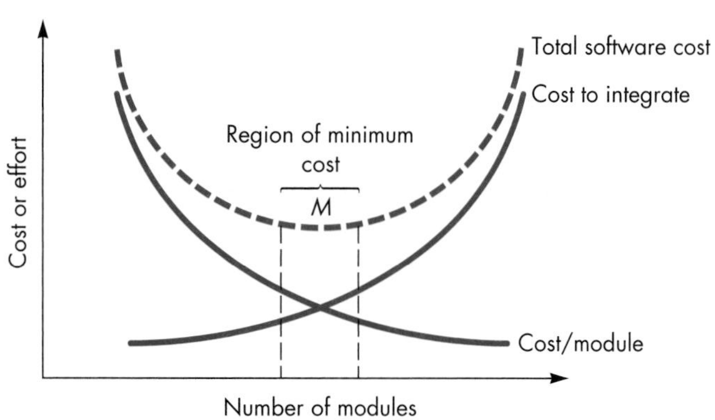

characteristics lead to a total cost or effort curve shown in the figure. There is a number, *M*, of modules that would result in minimum development cost, but we do not have the necessary sophistication to predict *M* with assurance.

The curves shown in Figure 9.2 do provide useful guidance when modularity is considered. We should modularize, but care should be taken to stay in the vicinity of *M*. Undermodularity or overmodularity should be avoided. But how do we know the vicinity of *M*? How modular should we make software? The answers to these questions require an understanding of other design concepts considered later in this chapter.

We modularize a design (and the resulting program) so that development can be more easily planned; software increments can be defined and delivered; changes can be more easily accommodated; testing and debugging can be conducted more efficiently, and long-term maintenance can be conducted without serious side effects.

9.3.5 Information Hiding

The concept of modularity leads every software designer to a fundamental question: How do we decompose a software solution to obtain the best set of modules? The principle of *information hiding* [PAR72] suggests that modules be "characterized by design decisions that (each) hides from all others." In other words, modules should be specified and designed so that information (algorithms and data) contained within a module is inaccessible to other modules that have no need for such information.

The intent of information hiding is to hide the details of data structures and procedural processing behind a module interface. Knowledge of the details need not be known by users of the module.

Hiding implies that effective modularity can be achieved by defining a set of independent modules that communicate with one another only that information necessary to achieve software function. Abstraction helps to define the procedural (or informational) entities that make up the software. Hiding defines and enforces access constraints to both procedural detail within a module and any local data structure used by the module [ROS75].

The use of information hiding as a design criterion for modular systems provides the greatest benefits when modifications are required during testing and later, during software maintenance. Because most data and procedure are hidden from other parts of the software, inadvertent errors introduced during modification are less likely to propagate to other locations within the software.

9.3.6 Functional Independence

The concept of *functional independence* is a direct outgrowth of modularity and the concepts of abstraction and information hiding. In landmark papers on software design Wirth [WIR71] and Parnas [PAR72] allude to refinement techniques that enhance module independence. Later work by Stevens, Myers, and Constantine [STE74] solidified the concept.

Functional independence is achieved by developing modules with "single-minded" function and an "aversion" to excessive interaction with other modules. Stated another way, we want to design software so that each module addresses a specific subfunction of requirements and has a simple interface when viewed from other parts of the program structure. It is fair to ask why independence is important.

Software with effective modularity, that is, independent modules, is easier to develop because function may be compartmentalized and interfaces are simplified (consider the ramifications when development is conducted by a team). Independent modules are easier to maintain (and test) because secondary effects caused by design or code modification are limited, error propagation is reduced, and reusable modules are possible. To summarize, functional independence is a key to good design, and design is the key to software quality.

Cohesion is a qualitative indication of the degree to which a module focuses on just one thing.

Independence is assessed using two qualitative criteria: cohesion and coupling. *Cohesion* is an indication of the relative functional strength of a module. *Coupling* is an indication of the relative interdependence among modules.

Cohesion is a natural extension of the information hiding concept described in Section 9.3.5. A cohesive module performs a single task, requiring little interaction with other components in other parts of a program. Stated simply, a cohesive module should (ideally) do just one thing.

Coupling is a qualitative indication of the degree to which a module is connected to other modules and to the outside world.

Coupling is an indication of interconnection among modules in a software structure. Coupling depends on the interface complexity between modules, the point at which entry or reference is made to a module, and what data pass across the interface. In software design, we strive for lowest possible coupling. Simple connectivity among modules results in software that is easier to understand and less prone to a "ripple effect" [STE74], caused when errors occur at one location and propagate throughout a system.

9.3.7 Refinement

Stepwise *refinement* is a top-down design strategy originally proposed by Niklaus Wirth [WIR71]. A program is developed by successively refining levels of procedural detail. A hierarchy is developed by decomposing a macroscopic statement of function (a procedural abstraction) in a stepwise fashion until programming language statements are reached.

There is a tendency to move immediately to full detail, skipping refinement steps. This leads to errors and omissions and makes the design much more difficult to review. Perform stepwise refinement.

Refinement is actually a process of *elaboration*. We begin with a statement of function (or description of data) that is defined at a high level of abstraction. That is, the statement describes function or information conceptually but provides no information about the internal workings of the function or the internal structure of the data. Refinement causes the designer to elaborate on the original statement, providing more and more detail as each successive refinement (elaboration) occurs.

Abstraction and refinement are complementary concepts. Abstraction enables a designer to specify procedure and data and yet suppress low-level details. Refinement helps the designer to reveal low-level details as design progresses. Both concepts aid the designer in creating a complete design model as the design evolves.

> "I have not failed. I've just found 10,000 ways that won't work."
>
> Thomas Edison

9.3.8 Refactoring

WebRef
Excellent resources for refactoring can be found at **www.refactoring.com.**

An important design activity suggested for many agile methods (Chapter 4), *refactoring* is a reorganization technique that simplifies the design (or code) of a component without changing its function or behavior. Fowler [FOW99] defines refactoring in the following manner: "Refactoring is the process of changing a software system in such a way that it does not alter the external behavior of the code [design] yet improves its internal structure."

When software is refactored, the existing design is examined for redundancy, unused design elements, inefficient or unnecessary algorithms, poorly constructed or inappropriate data structures, or any other design failure that can be corrected to yield a better design. For example, a first design iteration might yield a component that exhibits low cohesion (i.e., it performs three functions that have only limited relationship to one another). The designer may decide that the component should be refactored into three separate components, each exhibiting high cohesion. The result will be software that is easier to integrate, easier to test, and easier to maintain.

SAFEHOME

Design Concepts

The scene: Vinod's cubicle, as design modeling begins.

The players: Vinod, Jamie, and Ed—members of the *SafeHome* software engineering team . Also, Shakira, a new member of the team.

The conversation:

(All four team members have just returned from a morning seminar, entitled "Applying Basic Design Concepts," offered by a local computer science professor.)

Vinod: Did you get anything out of the seminar?

Ed: Knew most of the stuff, but it's not a bad idea to hear it again, I suppose.

Jamie: When I was an undergrad CS major, I never really understood why information hiding was as important as they say it is.

Vinod: Because . . . bottom line . . . it's a technique for reducing error propagation in a program. Actually, functional independence also accomplishes the same thing.

Shakira: I wasn't a CS grad, so a lot of the stuff the instructor mentioned is new to me. I can generate good code and fast. I don't see why this stuff is so important.

Jamie: I've seen your work, Shak, and you know what, you do a lot of this stuff naturally . . . that's why your designs and code work.

Shakira (smiling): Well, I always do try to partition the code, keep it focused on one thing, keep interfaces simple and constrained, reuse code whenever I can . . . that sort of thing.

Ed: Modularity, functional independence, hiding, patterns . . . see.

Jamie: I still remember the very first programming course I took . . . they taught us to refine the code iteratively.

Vinod: Same thing can be applied to design, you know.

Ed: The only concept I hadn't heard of before was "refactoring."

Shakira: That's used in Extreme Programming, I think she said.

Ed: Yep. It's not a whole lot different than refinement, only you do it after the design or code is completed. Kind of an optimization pass through the software, if you ask me.

Jamie: Let's get back to *SafeHome* design. I think we should put these concepts on our review checklist as we develop the design model for *SafeHome*.

Vinod: I agree. But as important, let's all commit to think about them as we develop the design.

9.3.9 Design Classes

In Chapter 8, we noted that the analysis model defines a complete set of analysis classes. Each of these classes describes some element of the problem domain, focusing on aspects of the problem that are user or customer visible. The level of abstraction of an analysis class is relatively high.

As the design model evolves, the software team must define a set of *design classes* that (1) refine the analysis classes by providing design detail that will enable the classes to be implemented, and (2) create a new set of design classes that implement a software infrastructure to support the business solution. Five different types of design classes, each representing a different layer of the design architecture are suggested [AMB01]:

? What types of classes does the designer create?

- *User interface classes* define all abstractions that are necessary for human-computer interaction (HCI). In many cases, HCI occurs within the context of a *metaphor* (e.g., a checkbook, an order form, a fax machine) and the design classes for the interface may be visual representations of the elements of the metaphor.
- *Business domain classes* are often refinements of the analysis classes defined earlier. The classes identify the attributes and services (methods) that are required to implement some element of the business domain.
- *Process classes* implement lower-level business abstractions required to fully manage the business domain classes.
- *Persistent classes* represent data stores (e.g., a database) that will persist beyond the execution of the software.
- *System classes* implement software management and control functions that enable the system to operate and communicate within its computing environment and with the outside world.

As the design model evolves, the software team must develop a complete set of attributes and operations for each design class. The level of abstraction is reduced as each analysis class is transformed into a design representation. That is, analysis classes represent objects (and associated services that are applied to them) using the jargon of the business domain. Design classes present significantly more technical detail as a guide for implementation.

Arlow and Neustadt [ARL02] suggest that each design class be reviewed to ensure that it is "well-formed." They define four characteristics of a well-formed design class:

What is a "well-formed" design class?

Complete and sufficient. A design class should be the complete encapsulation of all attributes and methods that can reasonably be expected (based on a knowledgeable interpretation of the class name) to exist for the class. For example, the class **Scene** defined for video editing software is complete only if it contains all attributes and methods that can reasonably be associated with the creation of a video scene. Sufficiency ensures that the design class contains only those methods that are sufficient to achieve the intent of the class, no more and no less.

Primitiveness. Methods associated with a design class should be focused on accomplishing one service for the class. Once the service has been implemented with a method, the class should not provide another way to accomplish the same thing. For example, the class **VideoClip** of the video editing software might have attributes **start-point** and **end-point** to indicate the start and end points of the clip (note that the raw video loaded into the system may be longer than the clip that is used). The methods, *setStartPoint()* and *setEndPoint()* provide the only means for establishing start and end points for the clip.

High cohesion. A cohesive design class has a small, focused set of responsibilities and single-mindedly applies attributes and methods to implement those responsibilities. For example, the class **VideoClip** of the video editing software might contain a set of methods for editing the video clip. As long as each method focuses solely on attributes associated with the video clip, cohesion is maintained.

Low coupling. Within the design model, it is necessary for design classes to collaborate with one another. However, collaboration should be kept to an acceptable minimum. If a design model is highly coupled (all design classes collaborate with all other design classes) the system is difficult to implement, to test, and to maintain over time. In general, design classes within a subsystem should have only limited knowledge of classes in other subsystems. This restriction, called the *Law of Demeter* [LIE03], suggests that a method should only send messages to methods in neighboring classes.[5]

5 A less formal way of stating the Law of Demeter is "Each unit should only talk to its friends; don't talk to strangers."

SafeHome

Refining an Analysis Class into a Design Class

The scene: Ed's cubicle, as design modeling continues.

The players: Vinod and Ed—members of the *SafeHome* software engineering team.

The conversation:

(Ed is working on the **FloorPlan** class [see sidebar discussion in Section 8.7.4 and Figure 8.14] and has refined it for the design model.)

Ed: So you remember the **FloorPlan** class, right? It's used as part of the surveillance and home management functions.

Vinod (nodding): Yeah, I seem to recall that we used it as part of our CRC discussions for home management.

Ed: We did. Anyway, I'm refining it for design. Want to show how we'll actually implement the **FloorPlan** class. My idea is to implement it as a set of linked lists [a specific data structure]. So . . . I had to refine the analysis class **FloorPlan** (Figure 8.14) and, actually, sort of simplify it.

Vinod: The analysis class showed only things in the problem domain, well, actually on the computer screen, that were visible to the end-user, right?

Ed: Yep, but for the **FloorPlan** design class, I've got to add some things that are implementation specific. I needed to show that **FloorPlan** is an aggregation of segments—hence the **Segment** class—and that the **Segment** class is composed of lists for wall segments, windows, doors, and so on. The class **Camera** collaborates with **FloorPlan,** and obviously, there can be many cameras in the floor plan.

Vinod: Phew, let's see a picture of this new **FloorPlan** design class.

(Ed shows Vinod the drawing shown in Figure 9.3.)

Vinod: Okay, I see what you're trying to do. This allows you to modify the floor plan easily because new items can be added or deleted to the list—the aggregation—without any problems.

Ed (nodding): Yeah, I think it'll work.

Vinod: So do I.

Figure 9.3

Design class for FloorPlan and composite aggregation for the class (see sidebar discussion)

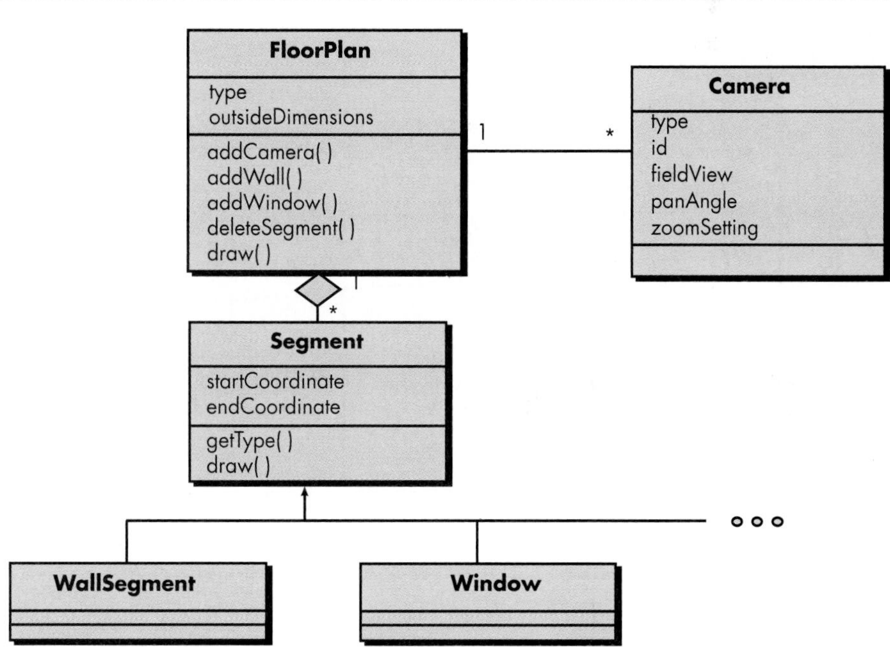

9.4 The Design Model

The *design model* can be viewed in two different dimensions as illustrated in Figure 9.4. The *process* dimension indicates the evolution of the design model as design tasks are executed as part of the software process. The *abstraction* dimension represents the level of detail as each element of the analysis model is transformed into a design equivalent and then refined iteratively. Referring to the figure, the dashed line indicates the boundary between the analysis and design models. In some cases, a clear distinction between the analysis and design models is possible. In other cases, the analysis model slowly blends into the design and a clear distinction is less obvious.

KEY POINT
The design model has four major elements: data, architecture, components, and interface.

The elements of the design model use many of the same UML diagrams that were used in the analysis model. The difference is that these diagrams are refined and elaborated as part of design; more implementation-specific detail is provided, and architectural structure and style, components that reside within the architecture, and interfaces between the components and with the outside world are all emphasized.

> **"Questions about whether design is necessary or affordable are quite beside the point: design is inevitable. The alternative to good design is bad design, not no design at all."**
>
> **Douglas Martin**

FIGURE 9.4 Dimensions of the design model

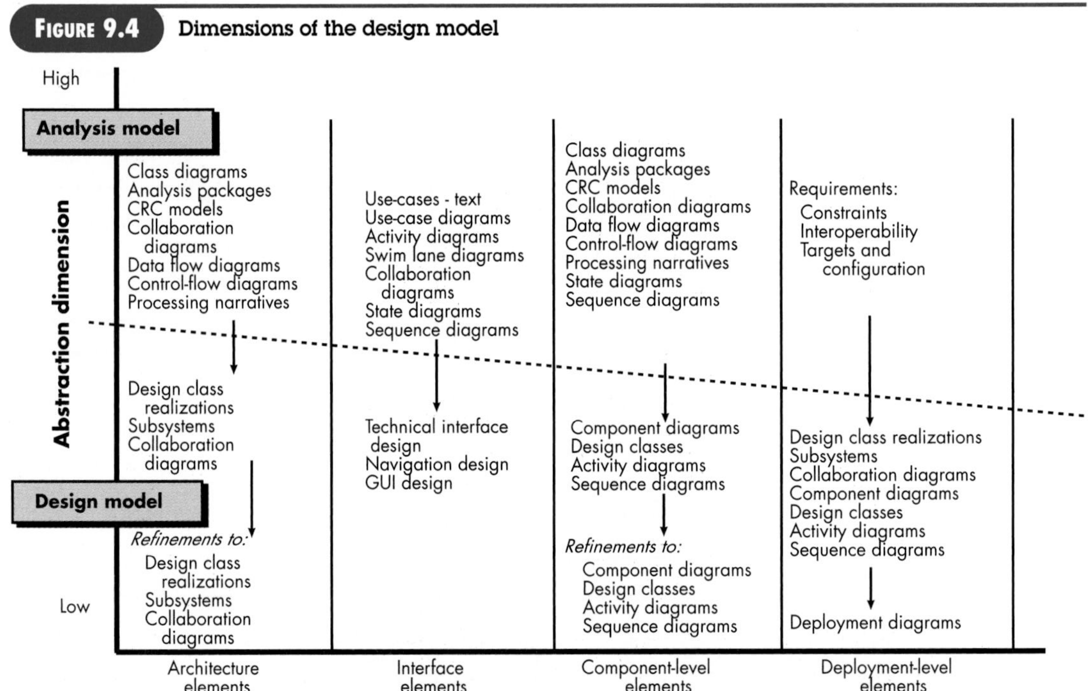

It is important to mention however, that model elements noted along the horizontal axis are not always developed in a sequential fashion. In most cases preliminary architectural design sets the stage and is followed by interface design and component-level design, which often occur in parallel. The deployment model is usually delayed until the design has been fully developed.

9.4.1 Data Design Elements

Like other software engineering activities, *data design* (sometimes referred to as *data architecting*) creates a model of data and/or information that is represented at a high level of abstraction (the customer/user's view of data). This data model is then refined into progressively more implementation-specific representations that can be processed by the computer-based system. In many software applications, the architecture of the data will have a profound influence on the architecture of the software that must process it.

At the architectural (application) level, data design focuses on files or data bases; at the component level, data design considers the data structures that are required to implement local data objects.

The structure of data has always been an important part of software design. At the program component level, the design of data structures and the associated algorithms required to manipulate them is essential to the creation of high-quality applications. At the application level, the translation of a data model (derived as part of requirements engineering) into a database is pivotal to achieving the business objectives of a system. At the business level, the collection of information stored in disparate databases and reorganized into a "data warehouse" enables data mining or knowledge discovery that can have an impact on the success of the business itself. In every case, data design plays an important role. Data design is discussed in more detail in Chapter 10.

9.4.2 Architectural Design Elements

The architectural model is derived from the application domain, the analysis model, and available styles and patterns.

The *architectural design* for software is the equivalent to the floor plan of a house. The floor plan depicts the overall layout of the rooms, their size, shape, and relationship to one another, and the doors and windows that allow movement into and out of the rooms. The floor plan gives us an overall view of the house. Architectural design elements give us an overall view of the software.

> "You can use an eraser on the drafting table or a sledge hammer on the construction site."
>
> **Frank Lloyd Wright**

The architectural model [SHA96] is derived from three sources: (1) information about the application domain for the software to be built; (2) specific analysis model elements such as data flow diagrams or analysis classes, their relationships and collaborations for the problem at hand, and (3) the availability of architectural patterns (Section 9.5) and styles (Chapter 10).

9.4.3 Interface Design Elements

The *interface design* for software is the equivalent to a set of detailed drawings (and specifications) for the doors, windows, and external utilities of a house. These drawings depict the size and shape of doors and windows, the manner in which they operate, the way in which utilities connections (e.g., water, electrical, gas, telephone) come into the house and are distributed among the rooms depicted in the floor plan. They tell us where the door bell is located, whether an intercom is to be used to announce a visitor's presence and how a security system is to be installed. In essence, the detailed drawings (and specifications) for the doors, windows, and external utilities tell us how things and information flow into and out of the house and within the rooms that are part of the floor plan. The interface design elements for software tell how information flows into and out of the system and how it is communicated among the components defined as part of the architecture.

> **"The public is more familiar with bad design than good design. It is, in effect, conditioned to prefer bad design, because that is what it lives with. The new becomes threatening, the old reassuring."**
>
> **Paul Rand**

There are three parts to the interface design element: the user interface; interfaces to systems external to the application, and interfaces to components within the application.

There are three important elements of interface design: (1) the user interface (UI); (2) external interfaces to other systems, devices, networks, or other producers or consumers of information; and (3) internal interfaces between various design components. These interface design elements allow the software to communicate externally and enable internal communication and collaboration among the components that populate the software architecture.

UI design is a major software engineering action and is considered in detail in Chapter 12. The design of a UI incorporates aesthetic elements (e.g., layout, color, graphics, interaction mechanisms), ergonomic elements (e.g., information layout and placement, metaphors, UI navigation), and technical elements (e.g., UI patterns, reusable components). In general, the UI is a unique subsystem within the overall application architecture.

The design of external interfaces requires definitive information about the entity to which information is sent or received. In every case, this information should be collected during requirements engineering (Chapter 7) and verified once the interface design commences.[6] The design of external interfaces should incorporate error checking and (when necessary) appropriate security features.

The design of internal interfaces is closely aligned with component-level design (Chapter 11). Design realizations of analysis classes represent all operations and the messaging schemes required to enable communication and collaboration between operations in various classes. Each message must be designed to accom-

6 It is not uncommon for interface characteristics to change with time. Therefore, a designer should ensure that the specification for the interface is kept up-to-date.

FIGURE 9.5

UML interface representation for Control-Panel

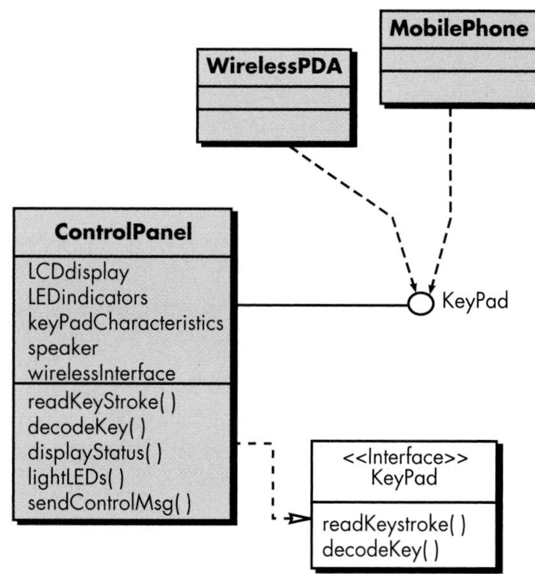

modate the requisite information transfer and the specific functional requirements of the operation that has been requested.

WebRef
Extremely valuable information on UI design can be found at **www.useit.com.**

In some cases, an interface is modeled in much the same way as a class. UML defines an *interface* in the following manner [OMG01]: "An interface is a specifier for the externally-visible [public] operations of a class, component, or other classifier (including subsystems) without specification of internal structure." Stated more simply, an interface is a set of operations that describes some part of the behavior of a class and provides access to those operations.

For example, the *SafeHome* security function makes use of a control panel that allows a homeowner to control certain aspects of the security function. In an advanced version of the system, control panel functions may be implemented via a wireless PDA or a mobile phone.

The **ControlPanel** class (Figure 9.5) provides the behavior associated with a keypad, and, therefore, it must implement operations *readKeyStroke()* and *decodeKey()*. If these operations are to be provided to other classes (in this case, **WirelessPDA** and **MobilePhone**), it is useful to define an interface as shown in the figure. The interface, named **KeyPad,** is shown as an <<interface>> stereotype or as a small, labeled circle connected to the class with a line. The interface is defined with no attributes and the set of operations that are necessary to achieve the behavior of a keypad.

> "A common mistake that people make when trying to design something completely foolproof was to underestimate the ingenuity of complete fools."
>
> **Douglas Adams**

The dashed line with an open triangle at its end (Figure 9.5) indicates that the **ControlPanel** class provides **KeyPad** operations as part of its behavior. In UML, this is characterized as a *realization*. That is, part of the behavior of **ControlPanel** will be implemented by realizing **KeyPad** operations. These operations will be provided to other classes that access the interface.

9.4.4 Component-Level Design Elements

The component-level design for software is equivalent to a set of detailed drawings (and specifications) for each room in a house. These drawings depict wiring and plumbing within each room, the location of electrical receptacles and switches, faucets, sinks, showers, tubs, drains, cabinets, and closets. They also describe the flooring to be used, the moldings to be applied, and every other detail associated with a room. The component-level design for software fully describes the internal detail of each software component. To accomplish this, the component-level design defines data structures for all local data objects and algorithmic detail for all processing that occurs within a component and an interface that allows access to all component operations (behaviors).

> "The details are not the details. They make the design."
>
> **Charles Eames**

Within the context of object-oriented software engineering, a component is represented in UML diagrammatic form as shown in Figure 9.6. In this figure, a component named **SensorManagement** (part of the *SafeHome* security function) is represented. A dashed arrow connects the component to a class named **Sensor** that is assigned to it. The **SensorManagement** component performs all functions associated with *SafeHome* sensors including monitoring and configuring them. Further discussion of component diagrams is presented in Chapter 11.

The design details of a component can be modeled at many different levels of abstraction. An activity diagram can be used to represent processing logic. Detailed procedural flow for a component can be represented using either pseudocode (a programming language-like representation described in Chapter 11) or some diagrammatic form (e.g., an activity diagram or flowchart).

FIGURE 9.6

UML component diagram for SensorManagement

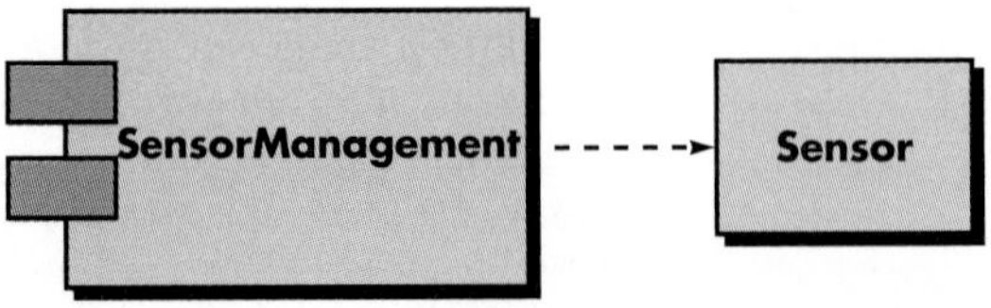

9.4.5 Deployment-Level Design Elements

Deployment-level design elements indicate how software functionality and subsystems will be allocated within the physical computing environment that will support the software. For example, the elements of the *SafeHome* product are configured to operate within three primary computing environments—a home-based PC, the *SafeHome* control panel, and a server housed at CPI Corp. (providing Internet-based access to the system).

Deployment diagrams begin in descriptor form, where the deployment environment is described in general terms. Later, instance form is used, and elements of the configuration are explicitly described.

During design, a UML deployment diagram is developed and then refined as shown in Figure 9.7. In the figure, three computing environments are shown (in actuality, there would be more including sensors, cameras, and others). The subsystems (functionality) housed within each computing element are indicated. For example, the personal computer houses subsystems that implement security, surveillance, home management and communications features. In addition, an external access subsystem has been designed to manage all attempts to access the *SafeHome* system from an external source. Each subsystem would be elaborated to indicate the components that it implements.

The diagram shown in Figure 9.7 is in *descriptor form.* This means that the deployment diagram shows the computing environment but does not explicitly indicate configuration details. For example, the "personal computer" is not further identified. It could be a "Wintel" PC or a Macintosh, a Sun workstation or a Linux-box. These

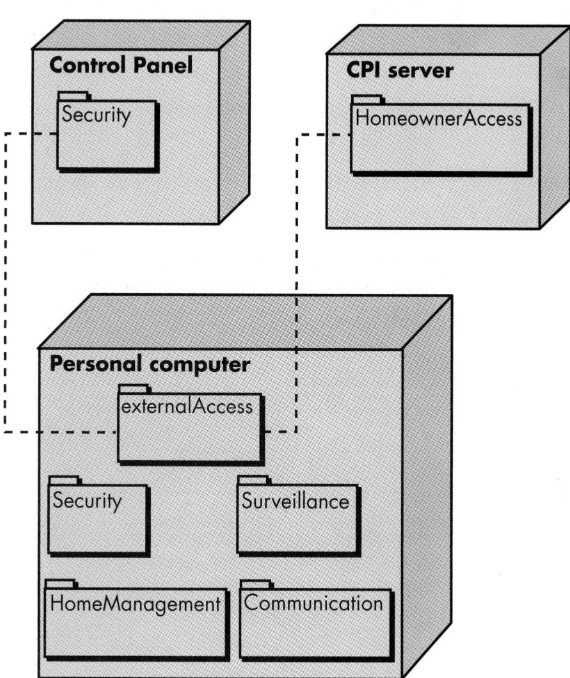

FIGURE 9.7

UML deployment diagram for *SafeHome*

details are provided when the deployment diagram is revisited in *instance form* during latter stages of design or as construction begins. Each instance of the deployment (a specific, named hardware configuration) is identified.

> "Every now and then go away, have a little relaxation, for when you come back to your work your judgment will be surer. Go some distance away because then the work appears smaller and more of it can be taken in at a glance and a lack of harmony and proportion is more readily seen."
>
> **Leonardo DaVinci**

9.5 Pattern-Based Software Design

WebRef
If you need to find a design (or other) patterns, visit **www.patterndepot.com/pages/.**

The best designers in any field have an uncanny ability to see patterns that characterize a problem and corresponding patterns that can be combined to create a solution. Throughout the design process, a software engineer should look for every opportunity to reuse existing design patterns (when they meet the needs of the design) rather than creating new ones.

9.5.1 Describing a Design Pattern

Mature engineering disciplines make use of thousands of design patterns. For example, a mechanical engineer uses a two-step, keyed shaft as a design pattern. Inherent in the pattern are attributes (the diameters of the shaft, the dimensions of the keyway, etc.) and operations (e.g., shaft rotation, shaft connection). An electrical engineer uses an integrated circuit (an extremely complex design pattern) to solve a specific element of a new problem. Design patterns may be described using the template [MAI03] shown in the sidebar.

INFO

Design Pattern Template

Pattern name—describes the essence of the pattern in a short but expressive name.
Intent—describes the pattern and what it does.
Also-known-as—lists any synonyms for the pattern.
Motivation—provides an example of the problem.
Applicability—notes specific design situations in which the pattern is applicable.
Structure—describes the classes that are required to implement the pattern.
Participants—describes the responsibilities of the classes that are required to implement the pattern.
Collaborations—describes how the participants collaborate to carry out their responsibilities.
Consequences—describes the "design forces" that affect the pattern and the potential trade-offs that must be considered when the pattern is implemented.
Related patterns—cross-references related design patterns.

A description of the design pattern may also consider a set of design forces. *Design forces* describe nonfunctional requirements (e.g., ease of maintainability, portability) associated the software for which the pattern is to be applied. In addition forces define the constraints that may restrict the manner in which the design is to

Design forces are those characteristics of the problem and attributes of the solution that constrain the way in which the design can be developed.

be implemented. In essence, design forces describe the environment and conditions that must exist to make the design pattern applicable. The pattern characteristics (classes, responsibilities, and collaborations) indicate the attributes of the design that may be adjusted to enable the pattern to accommodate a variety of problems [GAM95]. These attributes represent characteristics of the design that can be searched (e.g., via a database) so that an appropriate pattern can be found. Finally, guidance associated with the use of a design pattern provides an indication of the ramifications of design decisions.

> "Patterns are half-baked—meaning you always have to finish them yourself and adapt them to your own environment."
>
> **Martin Fowler**

The names of design patterns should be chosen with care. One of the key technical problems in software reuse is the inability to find existing reusable patterns when hundreds or thousands of candidate patterns exist. The search for the "right" pattern is aided immeasurably by a meaningful pattern name.

9.5.2 Using Patterns in Design

Design patterns can be used throughout software design. Once the analysis model (Chapter 8) has been developed, the designer can examine a detailed representation of the problem to be solved and the constraints that are imposed by the problem. The problem description is examined at various levels of abstraction to determine if it is amenable to one or more of the following types of design patterns:

? What types of design patterns are available for the software engineer?

Architectural patterns. These patterns define the overall structure of the software, indicate the relationships among subsystems and software components, and define the rules for specifying relationships among the elements (classes, packages, components, subsystems) of the architecture.

Design patterns. These patterns address a specific element of the design such as an aggregation of components to solve some design problem, relationships among components, or the mechanisms for effecting component-to-component communication.

Idioms. Sometimes called *coding patterns,* these language-specific patterns generally implement an algorithmic element of a component, a specific interface protocol, or a mechanism for communication among components.

Each of these pattern types differs in the level of abstraction with which it is represented and the degree to which it provides direct guidance for the construction activity (in this case, coding) of the software process.

9.5.3 Frameworks

In some cases it may be necessary to provide an implementation-specific skeletal infrastructure, called a *framework,* for design work. That is, the designer may select a

A framework is a code skeleton that can be fleshed out with specific classes or functionality that have been designed to address the problem at hand.

"*reusable mini-architecture* that provides the generic structure and behavior for a family of software abstractions, along with a context . . . which specifies their collaboration and use within a given domain" [APP98].

A framework is not an architectural pattern, but rather a skeleton with a collection of "plug points" (also called *hooks* and *slots*) that enable it to be adapted to a specific problem domain. The plug points enable a designer to integrate problem specific classes or functionality within the skeleton. In an object-oriented context, a framework is a collection of cooperating classes.

In essence, the designer of a framework will argue that one reusable mini-architecture is applicable to all software to be developed within a limited domain of application. To be most effective, frameworks are applied with no changes. Additional design elements may be added, but only via the plug points that allow the designer to flesh out the framework skeleton.

9.6 Summary

Design engineering commences as the first iteration of requirements engineering comes to a conclusion. The intent of software design is to apply a set of principles, concepts, and practices that lead to the development of a high-quality system or product. The goal of design is to create a model of software that will implement all customer requirements correctly and bring delight to those who use it. Design engineers must sift through many design alternatives and converge on a solution that best suits the needs of project stakeholders.

The design process moves from a "big picture" view of software to a more narrow view that defines the detail required to implement a system. The process begins by focusing on architecture. Subsystems are defined; communication mechanisms among subsystems are established; components are identified; and a detailed description of each component is developed. In addition, external, internal, and user interfaces are designed.

Design concepts have evolved over the first half-century of software engineering work. They describe attributes of computer software that should be present regardless of the software engineering process that is chosen, the design methods that are applied, or the programming languages that are used.

The design model encompasses four different elements. As each of these elements is developed, a more complete view of the design evolves. The architectural element uses information derived from the application domain, the analysis model, and available catalogs for patterns and styles to derive a complete structural representation of the software, its subsystems and components. Interface design elements model external and internal interfaces and the user interface. Component-level elements define each of the modules (components) that populate the architecture. Finally, deployment-level design elements allocate the architecture, its components, and the interfaces to the physical configuration that will house the software.

Pattern-based design is a technique that reuses design elements that have proven successful in the past. Each architectural pattern, design pattern, or idiom is cataloged, thoroughly documented, and carefully considered as it is assessed for inclusion in a specific application. Frameworks, an extension of patterns, provide an architectural skeleton for the design of complete subsystems within a specific application domain.

References

[AMB01] Ambler, S., *The Object Primer,* Cambridge Univ. Press, 2nd ed., 2001.

[APP98] Appleton, B., "Patterns and Software: Essential Concepts and Terminology," downloadable at http://www.enteract.com/~bradapp/docs/patterns-intro.html.

[ARL02] Arlow, J., and I. Neustadt, *UML and the Unified Process,* Addison-Wesley, 2002.

[BEL81] Belady, L., Foreword to *Software Design: Methods and Techniques* (L.J. Peters, author), Yourdon Press, 1981.

[FOW00] Fowler, M., et al., *Refactoring: Improving the Design of Existing Code,* Addison-Wesley, 2000.

[GAM95] Gamma, E., et al., *Design Patterns,* Addison-Wesley, 1995.

[GAR95] Garlan, D., and M. Shaw, "An Introduction to Software Architecture," *Advances in Software Engineering and Knowledge Engineering,* vol. I (V. Ambriola and G. Tortora, eds.), World Scientific Publishing Company, 1995.

[GRA87] Grady, R. B., and D. L. Caswell, *Software Metrics: Establishing a Company-Wide Program,* Prentice-Hall, 1987.

[JAC75] Jackson, M. A., *Principles of Program Design,* Academic Press, 1975.

[LIE03] Lieberherr, K., "Demeter: Aspect-Oriented Programming," May 2003, available at: http://www.ccs.neu.edu/home/lieber/LoD.html.

[MAI03] Maioriello, J., "What Are Design Patterns and Do I Need Them?," developer.com, 2003, available at http://www.developer.com/design/article.php/ 1474561.

[MCG91] McGlaughlin, R., "Some Notes on Program Design," *Software Engineering Notes,* vol. 16, no. 4, October 1991, pp. 53–54.

[MYE78] Myers, G., *Composite Structured Design,* Van Nostrand,1978.

[OMG01] Object Management Group, *OMG Unified Modeling Language Specification,* version 1.4, September 2001.

[PAR72] Parnas, D. L., "On Criteria to be used in Decomposing Systems into Modules," *CACM,* vol. 14, no. 1, April 1972, pp. 221–227.

[ROS75] Ross, D., J. Goodenough, and C. Irvine, "Software Engineering: Process, Principles and Goals," *IEEE Computer,* vol. 8, no. 5, May 1975.

[SCH02] Schmuller, J., *Teach Yourself UML,* SAMS Publishing, 2002.

[SHA96] Shaw, M., and D. Garlan, *Software Architecture,* Prentice-Hall, 1996.

[STA02] "Metaphor," *The Stanford HCI Learning Space,* 2002, http://hci.stanford.edu/ hcils/ concepts/metaphor.html.

[STE74] Stevens, W., G. Myers, and L. Constantine, "Structured Design," *IBM Systems Journal,* vol. 13, no. 2, 1974, pp. 115–139.

[WIR71] Wirth, N., "Program Development by Stepwise Refinement," *CACM,* vol. 14, no. 4, 1971, pp. 221–227.

Problems and Points to Ponder

9.1. Do you design software when you "write" a program? What makes software design different from coding?

9.2. If a software design is not a program (and it isn't), then what is it?

9.3. How do we assess the quality of a software design?

9.4. Examine the task set presented for design. Where is quality assessed within the task set? How is this accomplished?

9.5. Provide examples of three data abstractions and the procedural abstractions that can be used to manipulate them.

9.6. Describe software architecture in your own words.

9.7. Suggest a design pattern that you encounter in a category of everyday things (e.g., consumer electronics, automobiles, appliances). Fully document the pattern using the template provided in Section 9.5.

9.8. Is there a case when complex problems require less effort to solve? How might such a case affect the argument for modularity?

9.9. When should a modular design be implemented as monolithic software? How can this be accomplished? Is performance the only justification for implementation of monolithic software?

9.10. Discuss the relationship between the concept of information hiding as an attribute of effective modularity and the concept of module independence.

9.11. How are the concepts of coupling and software portability related? Provide examples to support your discussion.

9.12. Apply a "stepwise refinement approach" to develop three different levels of procedural abstraction for one or more of the following programs: (a) Develop a check writer that, given a numeric dollar amount, will print the amount in words normally required on a check; (b) Iteratively solve for the roots of a transcendental equation; (c) Develop a simple task scheduling algorithm for an operating system.

9.13. Do a bit of research on Extreme Programming and write a brief paper on the use of refactoring for that agile software development process.

9.14. Visit a design patterns repository (on the Web) and spend a few minutes browsing through the patterns. Pick one and present it to your class.

Further Readings and Information Sources

Donald Norman has written two books (*The Design of Everyday Things,* Doubleday, 1990, and *The Psychology of Everyday Things,* HarperCollins, 1988) that have become classics in the design literature and "must" reading for anyone who designs anything that humans use. Adams (*Conceptual Blockbusting,* third edition, Addison-Wesley, 1986) has written a book that is essential reading for designers who want to broaden their way of thinking. Finally, a classic text by Polya (*How to Solve It,* Princeton University Press, second edition, 1988) provides a generic problem-solving process that can help software designers when they are faced with complex problems.

Following in the same tradition, Winograd et al. (*Bringing Design to Software,* Addison-Wesley, 1996) discusses software designs that work, those that don't, and why. A fascinating book edited by Wixon and Ramsey (*Field Methods Casebook for Software Design,* Wiley, 1996) suggests field research methods (much like those used by anthropologists) to understand how end-users do the work they do and then provides guidance for designing software that meets their needs. Beyer and Holtzblatt (*Contextual Design: A Customer-Centered Approach to Systems Designs,* Academic Press, 1997) offer another view of software design that integrates the customer/user into every aspect of the software design process.

McConnell (*Code Complete,* Microsoft Press, 1993) presents an excellent discussion of the practical aspects of designing high-quality computer software. Robertson (*Simple Program Design,* third edition, Boyd and Fraser Publishing, 1999) offers an introductory discussion of software design that is useful for those beginning their study of the subject. Fowler and his colleagues (*Refactoring: Improving the Design of Existing Code,* Addison-Wesley, 1999) discuss techniques for the incremental optimization of software designs.

Over the past decade, many books on pattern-based design have been written for software engineers. Gamma and his colleagues [GAM95] have written the seminal book on the subject. Other books by Douglass (*Real-Time Design Patterns,* Addison-Wesley, 2002), Metsker (*Design Patterns Java Workbook,* Addison-Wesley, 2002), Juric et al. (*J2EE Design Patterns Applied,* Wrox Press, 2002), Marinescu and Roman (*EJB Design Patterns,* Wiley, 2002), and Shalloway and Trott (*Design Patterns Explained,* Addison-Wesley, 2001) discuss design patterns in specific application and language environments. In addition, classic books by the architect Christopher Alexander (*Notes on the Synthesis of Form,* Harvard University Press, 1964 and *A Pattern Language: Towns, Buildings, Construction,* Oxford University Press, 1977) are must reading for a software designer who intends to fully understand design patterns.

A wide variety of information sources on design engineering are available on the Internet. An up-to-date list of World Wide Web references that are relevant to software design and design engineering can be found at the SEPA Web site:
http://www.mhhe.com/pressman.

CHAPTER

10 ARCHITECTURAL DESIGN

KEY CONCEPTS

Design has been described as a multistep process in which representations of data and program structure, interface characteristics, and procedural detail are synthesized from information requirements. This description is extended by Freeman [FRE80]:

> [D]esign is an activity concerned with making major decisions, often of a structural nature. It shares with programming a concern for abstracting information representation and processing sequences, but the level of detail is quite different at the extremes. Design builds coherent, well-planned representations of programs that concentrate on the interrelationships of parts at the higher level and the logical operations involved at the lower levels. . . .

As we have noted in Chapter 9, design is information driven. Software design methods are derived from consideration of each of the three domains of the analysis model. The informational, functional, and behavioral domains serve as a guide for the creation of the software design.

Methods required to create "coherent, well planned representations" of the data and architectural layers of the design model are presented in this chapter. The objective is to provide a systematic approach for the derivation of the architectural design—the preliminary blueprint from which software is constructed.

QUICK LOOK

What is it? Architectural design represents the structure of data and program components that are required to build a computer-based system. It considers the architectural style that the system will take, the structure and properties of the components that constitute the system, and the interrelationships that occur among all architectural components of a system.

Who does it? Although a software engineer can design both data and architecture, the job is often allocated to specialists when large, complex systems are to be built. A database or data warehouse designer creates the data architecture for a system. The "system architect" selects an appropriate architectural style for the requirements derived during system engineering and software requirements analysis.

Why is it important? You wouldn't attempt to build a house without a blueprint, would you? You also wouldn't begin drawing blueprints by sketching the plumbing layout for the house. You'd need to look at the big picture—the house itself—before you worry about details. That's what architectural design does—it provides you with the big picture and ensures that you've got it right.

What are the steps? Architectural design begins with data design and then proceeds to the derivation of one or more representations of the architectural structure of the system. Alternative architectural styles or patterns are analyzed to derive the structure that is best suited to customer requirements and quality attributes. Once an alternative has been selected, the architecture is elaborated using an architectural design method.

What is the work product? An architecture model encompassing data architecture and program structure is created during architectural design. In addition, component properties and relationships (interactions) are described.

How do I ensure that I've done it right? At each stage, software design work products are reviewed for clarity, correctness, completeness, and consistency with requirements and with one another.

10.1 Software Architecture

In their landmark book on the subject, Shaw and Garlan [SHA96] discuss software architecture in the following manner:

> Ever since the first program was divided into modules, software systems have had architectures, and programmers have been responsible for the interactions among the modules and the global properties of the assemblage. Historically, architectures have been implicit—accidents of implementation, or legacy systems of the past. Good software developers have often adopted one or several architectural patterns as strategies for system organization, but they use these patterns informally and have no means to make them explicit in the resulting system.

Today, effective software architecture and its explicit representation and design have become dominant themes in software engineering.

> "The architecture of a system is a comprehensive framework that describes its form and structure—its components and how they fit together."
>
> **Jerrold Grochow**

10.1.1 What Is Architecture?

When we discuss the architecture of a building, many different attributes come to mind. At the most simplistic level, we consider the overall shape of the physical structure. But in reality, architecture is much more. It is the manner in which the various components of the building are integrated to form a cohesive whole. It is the way in which the building fits into its environment and meshes with other buildings in its vicinity. It is the degree to which the building meets its stated purpose and satisfies the needs of its owner. It is the aesthetic feel of the structure—the visual impact of the building—and the way textures, colors, and materials are combined to create the external facade and the internal "living environment." It is small details—the design of lighting fixtures, the type of flooring, the placement of wall hangings, the list is almost endless. And finally, it is art.

Software architecture must model the structure of a system and the manner in which data and procedural components collaborate with one another.

But what about *software architecture?* Bass, Clements, and Kazman [BAS03] define this elusive term in the following way:

> The software architecture of a program or computing system is the structure or structures of the system, which comprise software components, the externally visible properties of those components, and the relationships among them.

The architecture is not the operational software. Rather, it is a representation that enables a software engineer to (1) analyze the effectiveness of the design in meeting its stated requirements, (2) consider architectural alternatives at a stage when making design changes is still relatively easy, and (3) reduce the risks associated with the construction of the software.

> "Marry your architecture in haste, repent at your leisure."
>
> **Barry Boehm**

WebRef
Useful pointers to many software architecture sites can be obtained at **www2.umassd.edu/SECenter/SAResources.html.**

This definition emphasizes the role of "software components" in any architectural representation. In the context of architectural design, a software component can be something as simple as a program module or an object-oriented class, but it can also be extended to include databases and "middleware" that enable the configuration of a network of clients and servers.

In this book the design of software architecture considers two levels of the design pyramid (Figure 9.1)—*data design* and *architectural design.* In the context of the preceding discussion, data design enables us to represent the data component of the architecture in conventional systems and class definitions (encapsulating attributes and operations) in object-oriented systems. Architectural design focuses on the representation of the structure of software components, their properties, and interactions.

10.1.2 Why Is Architecture Important?

In a book dedicated to software architecture, Bass and his colleagues [BAS03] identify three key reasons that software architecture is important:

The architectural model provides a Gestalt view of the system, allowing the software engineer to examine it as a whole.

- Representations of software architecture are an enabler for communication between all parties (stakeholders) interested in the development of a computer-based system.
- The architecture highlights early design decisions that will have a profound impact on all software engineering work that follows and, as important, on the ultimate success of the system as an operational entity.
- Architecture "constitutes a relatively small, intellectually graspable model of how the system is structured and how its components work together" [BAS03].

The architectural design model and the architectural patterns contained within it are transferable. That is, architecture styles and patterns (Section 10.3.1) can be applied to the design of other systems and represent a set of abstractions that enable software engineers to describe architecture in predictable ways.

10.2 Data Design

The *data design* action translates data objects defined as part of the analysis model (Chapter 8) into data structures at the software component level and, when necessary, a database architecture at the application level. In some situations, a database must be designed and built specifically for a new system. In others, however, one or more existing databases are used.

10.2.1 Data Design at the Architectural Level

Today, businesses large and small are awash in data. It is not unusual for even a moderately sized business to have dozens of databases serving many applications encompassing hundreds of gigabytes of data. The challenge is to extract useful information from this data environment, particularly when the information desired is cross-functional (e.g., information that can be obtained only if specific marketing data are cross-correlated with product engineering data).

> **"Data quality is the difference between a data warehouse and a data garbage dump."**
>
> **Jarrett Rosenberg**

WebRef
Information of data warehouse technologies can be obtained at **www.dataware house.com.**

To solve this challenge, the business IT community has developed *data mining* techniques, also called *knowledge discovery in databases* (KDD), that navigate through existing databases in an attempt to extract appropriate business-level information. However, the existence of multiple databases, their different structures, the degree of detail contained with the databases, and many other factors make data mining difficult within an existing database environment. An alternative solution, called a *data warehouse,* adds an additional layer to the data architecture.

A data warehouse is a separate data environment that is not directly integrated with day-to-day applications but encompasses all data used by a business [MAT96]. In a sense, a data warehouse is a large, independent database that has access to the data that are stored in databases that serve the set of applications required by a business.

A detailed discussion of the design of data structures, databases, and the data warehouse is best left to books dedicated to these subjects (e.g., [DAT00], [PRE98], [KIM98]). The interested reader should see the *Further Readings and Information Sources* section of this chapter for additional references.

SOFTWARE TOOLS

Data Mining/Warehousing

Objective: Data mining tools assist in the identification of significant relationships among attributes that describe a specific data object or set of data objects. Tools for data warehousing assist in the design of data models for a data warehouse.

Mechanics: Tool mechanics vary. In general, mining tools accept large data sets as input and allow the user to query the data in an effort to better understand relationships among various data items. Warehousing tools that are used for design provide entity relationship or other modeling capabilities.

Representative Tools[1]

Data Mining:

Business Objects, developed by Business Objects, SA (www.business objects.com), is a data design tool set hat supports "data integration, query, reporting, analysis, and analytics."

SPSS, developed by SPSS, Inc. (www.spss.com), provides a wide array of statistical functions to allow the analysis of large data sets.

Data Warehousing:

Industry Warehouse Studio, developed by Sybase (www.sybase.com), provides a packaged data warehouse infrastructure that "jumpstarts" data warehouse design.

IFW Business Intelligence Suite, developed by Modelware (www.modelwarepl.com), is a set of models, software tools, and database designs that "provide a fast path to data warehouse and datamart design and implementation."

A comprehensive list of data mining/warehousing tools and resources can be found at the Data Warehousing Information Center (www.dwinfocenter.org).

10.2.2 Data Design at the Component Level

Data design at the component level focuses on the representation of data structures that are directly accessed by one or more software components. Wasserman [WAS80] has proposed a set of principles that may be used to specify and design such data structures. In actuality, the design of data begins during the creation of the analysis model. Recalling that requirements analysis and design often overlap, we consider the following set of principles (adapted from [WAS80]) for data specification:

What principles are applicable to data design?

1. *The systematic analysis principles applied to function and behavior should also be applied to data.* Representations of data flow and content should also be developed and reviewed, data objects should be identified, alternative data organizations should be considered, and the impact of data modeling on software design should be evaluated.
2. *All data structures and the operations to be performed on each should be identified.* The design of an efficient data structure must take the operations to be performed on the data structure into account. The attributes and operations encapsulated within a class satisfy this principle.
3. *A mechanism for defining the content of each data object should be established and used to define both data and the operations applied to it.* Class diagrams

1 Tools noted here do not represent an endorsement, but rather a sampling of tools in this category. In most cases, tool names are trademarked by their respective developers.

(Chapter 8) define the data items (attributes) contained within a class and the processing (operations) that are applied to these data items.

4. *Low-level data design decisions should be deferred until late in the design process.* A process of stepwise refinement may be used for the design of data. That is, overall data organization may be defined during requirements analysis, refined during data design work, and specified in detail during component-level design.
5. *The representation of a data structure should be known only to those modules that must make direct use of the data contained within the structure.* The concept of information hiding and the related concept of coupling (Chapter 9) provide important insight into the quality of a software design.
6. *A library of useful data structures and the operations that may be applied to them should be developed.* A class library achieves this.
7. *A software design and programming language should support the specification and realization of abstract data types.* The implementation of a sophisticated data structure can be made exceedingly difficult if no means for direct specification of the structure exists in the programming language chosen for implementation.

These principles form a basis for a component-level data design approach that can be integrated into both the analysis and design activities.

10.3 Architectural Styles and Patterns

When a builder uses the phrase "center hall colonial" to describe a house, most people familiar with houses in the United States will be able to conjure a general image of what the house will look like and what the floor plan is likely to be. The builder has used an *architectural style* as a descriptive mechanism to differentiate the house from other styles (e.g., A-frame, raised ranch, Cape Cod). But more importantly, the architectural style is also a template for construction. Further details of the house must be defined, its final dimensions must be specified, customized features may be added, building materials are to be determined, but the style—a "center hall colonial"—guides the builder in his work.

> **"There is at the back of every artist's mind, a pattern or type of architecture."**
>
> **G. K. Chesterton**

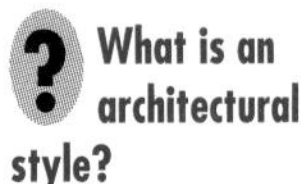
What is an architectural style?

The software that is built for computer-based systems also exhibits one of many architectural styles. Each style describes a system category that encompasses (1) a set of components (e.g., a database, computational modules) that perform a function required by a system; (2) a set of connectors that enable "communication, coordination, and cooperation" among components; (3) constraints that define how components can be integrated to form the system; and (4) semantic models that enable a designer to understand the overall properties of a system by analyzing the known properties of its constituent parts [BAS03].

WebRef
Attribute-based architectural styles (ABAS) can be used as building blocks for software architectures. Information can be obtained at **www.sei.cmu.edu/ata/abas.html.**

An architectural style is a transformation that is imposed on the design of an entire system. The intent is to establish a structure for all components of the system. In the case where an existing architecture is to be reengineered (Chapter 31), the imposition of an architectural style will result in fundamental changes to the structure of the software including a reassignment of the functionality of components [BOS00].

An *architectural pattern,* like an architectural style, imposes a transformation on the design of an architecture. However, a pattern differs from a style in a number of fundamental ways: (1) the scope of a pattern is less broad, focusing on one aspect of the architecture rather than the architecture in its entirety; (2) a pattern imposes a rule on the architecture, describing how the software will handle some aspect of its functionality at the infrastructure level (e.g., concurrency) [BOS00]; (3) architectural patterns tend to address specific behavioral issues within the context of the architectural, e.g., how a real-time application handles synchronization or interrupts. Patterns can be used in conjunction with an architectural style to establish the shape the overall structure of a system. In the section that follows, we consider commonly used architectural styles and patterns for software.

10.3.1 A Brief Taxonomy of Architectural Styles

Although millions of computer-based systems have been created over the past 50 years, the vast majority can be categorized (see [SHA96], [BUS96], [BAS03]) into one of a relatively small number of architectural styles:

Data-centered architecture. A data store (e.g., a file or database) resides at the center of this architecture and is accessed frequently by other components that update, add, delete, or otherwise modify data within the store. Figure 10.1 illustrates a typical data-centered style. Client software accesses a central repository. In some cases the data repository is passive. That is, client software accesses the data independent of any changes to the data or the actions of other client software. A variation on this approach transforms the repository into a "blackboard" that sends notifications to client software when data of interest to the client changes.

A data-centered architecture promotes *integrability* [BAS03]. That is, existing components can be changed and new client components added to the architecture without concern about other clients (because the client components operate independently). In addition, data can be passed among clients using the blackboard mechanism (i.e., the blackboard component serves to coordinate the transfer of information between clients). Client components independently execute processes.

Data-flow architecture. This architecture is applied when input data are to be transformed through a series of computational or manipulative components into

FIGURE 10.1

Data-centered architecture

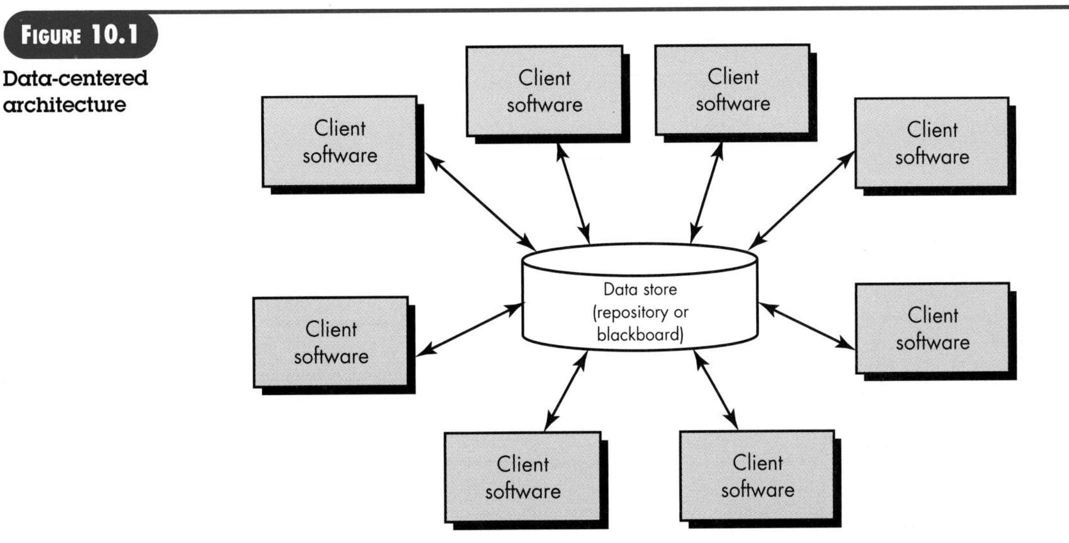

FIGURE 10.2

Data-flow architecture

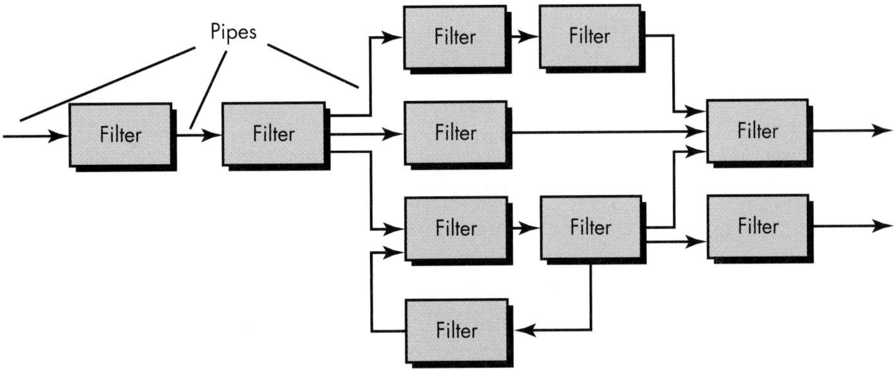

Pipes and filters

output data. A pipe and filter structure (Figure 10.2) has a set of components, called *filters,* connected by *pipes* that transmit data from one component to the next. Each filter works independently of those components upstream and downstream, is designed to expect data input of a certain form, and produces data output (to the next filter) of a specified form. However, the filter does not require knowledge of the workings of its neighboring filters.

> "The use of patterns and styles of design is pervasive in engineering disciplines."
>
> **Mary Shaw and David Garlan**

FIGURE 10.3 Main program/subprogram architecture

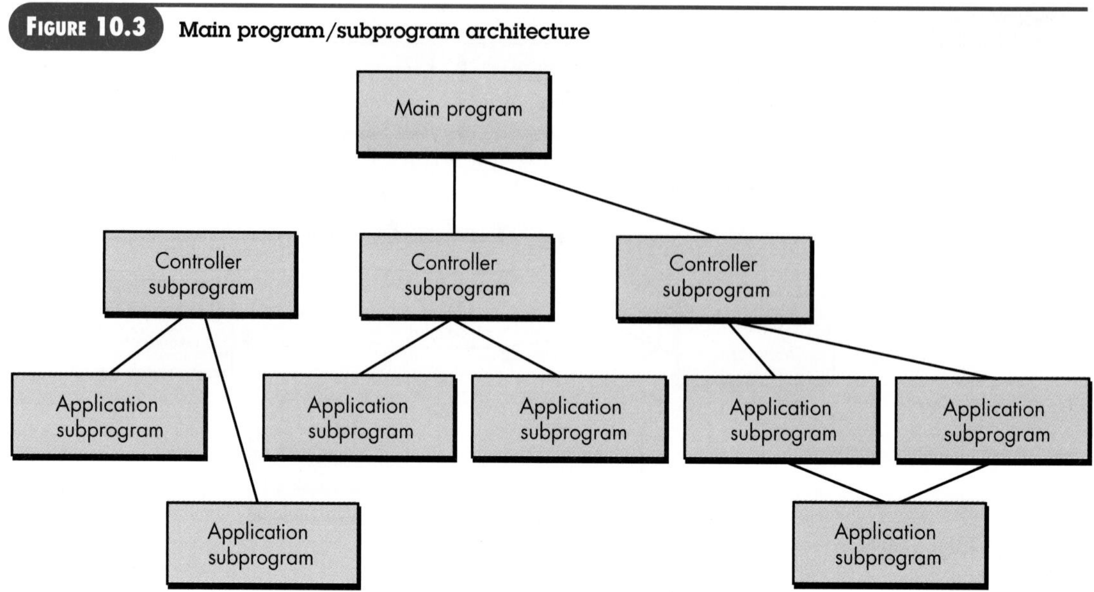

If the data flow degenerates into a single line of transforms, it is termed *batch sequential.* This structure accepts a batch of data and then applies a series of sequential components (filters) to transform it.

Call and return architecture. This architectural style enables a software designer (system architect) to achieve a program structure that is relatively easy to modify and scale. Two substyles [BAS03] exist within this category:

- *Main program/subprogram architecture.* This classic program structure decomposes function into a control hierarchy where a "main" program invokes a number of program components, which in turn may invoke still other components. Figure 10.3 illustrates an architecture of this type.
- *Remote procedure call architecture.* The components of a main program/subprogram architecture are distributed across multiple computers on a network.

Object-oriented architecture. The components of a system encapsulate data and the operations that must be applied to manipulate the data. Communication and coordination between components is accomplished via message passing.

Layered architecture. The basic structure of a layered architecture is illustrated in Figure 10.4. A number of different layers are defined, each accomplishing operations that progressively become closer to the machine instruction set. At the outer layer, components service user interface operations. At the inner layer, components perform operating system interfacing. Intermediate layers provide utility services and application software functions.

FIGURE 10.4

Layered architecture

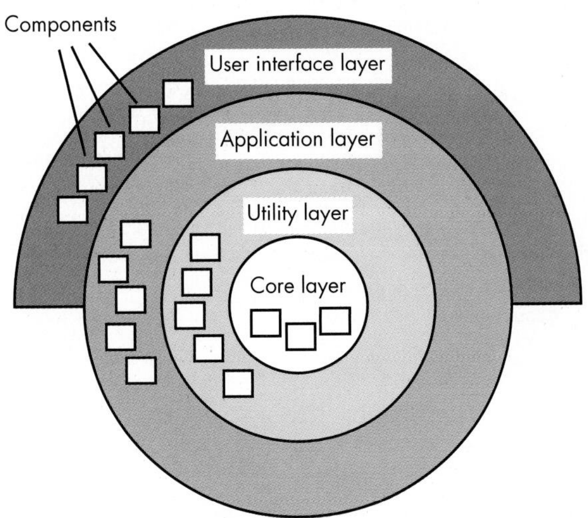

These architectural styles are only a small subset of those available to the software designer.[2] Once requirements engineering uncovers the characteristics and constraints of the system to be built, the architectural style or combination of styles that best fits those characteristics and constraints can be chosen. In many cases, more than one style might be appropriate, and alternatives might be designed and evaluated. For example, a layered style (appropriate for most systems) can be combined with a data-centered architecture in many database applications.

SAFEHOME

Choosing an Architectural Style

The scene: Jamie's cubicle, as design modeling continues.

The players: Jamie and Ed—members of the *SafeHome* software engineering team.

The conversation:

Ed (frowning): We've been modeling the security function using UML . . . you know classes, relationships, that sort of stuff. So I guess the object-oriented architecture[3] is the right way to go.

Jamie: But. . . ?

Ed: But . . . I have trouble visualizing what an object-oriented architecture is. I get the call and return architecture, sort of a conventional process hierarchy, but OO . . I don't know. It seems sort of amorphous.

---

2 See [BOS00], [HOF00], [BAS03], [SHA97], [BUS96], and [SHA96] for a detailed discussion of architectural styles and patterns.

3 It can be argued that the *SafeHome* architecture should be considered at a higher level than the architecture noted. *SafeHome* has a variety of subsystems—home monitoring functionality, the company's monitoring site, and the subsystem running in the owner's PC. Within subsystems, concurrent processes (e.g. those monitoring sensors) and event handling are prevalent. Some architectural decisions at this level are made during system or product engineering (Chapter 6), but architectural design within software engineering may very well have to consider these issues.

Jamie (smiling): Amorphous, huh?

Ed: Yeah . . . what I mean is I can't visualize a real structure, just design classes floating in space.

Jamie: Well, that's not true. There are class hierarchies . . . think of the hierarchy (aggregation) we did for the **FloorPlan** object [Figure 9.3]. An OO architecture is a combination of that structure and the interconnections—you know, collaborations—between the classes. We can show it by fully describing the attributes and operations, the messaging that goes on, and the structure of the classes.

Ed: I'm going to spend an hour mapping out a call and return architecture, then I'll go back and consider an OO architecture.

Jamie: Doug'll have no problem with that. He said that we should consider architectural alternatives. By the way, there's absolutely no reason why both of these architectures couldn't be used in combination with one another.

Ed: Good. I'm on it.

10.3.2 Architectural Patterns

If a house builder decides to construct a center-hall colonial, there is a single architectural style that can be applied. The details of the style (e.g., number of fireplaces, façade of the house, placement of doors and windows) can vary considerably, but once the decision on the overall architecture of the house is made, the style is imposed on the design.[4]

Architectural patterns are a bit different.[5] For example, every house (and every architectural style for houses) employs a *kitchen* pattern. The *kitchen* pattern defines the need for placement of basic kitchen appliances, the need for a sink, the need for cabinets, and possibly, rules for placement of these things relative to workflow in the room. In addition, the pattern might specify the need for counter tops, lighting, wall switches, a central island, flooring, and so on. Obviously, there is more than a single design for a kitchen, but every design can be conceived within the context of the "solution" suggested by the *kitchen* pattern.

A software architecture may have a number of architectural patterns that address issues such as concurrency, persistence, and distribution.

As we have already noted, architectural patterns for software define a specific approach for handling some behavioral characteristic of the system. Bosch [BOS00] defines a number of architectural pattern domains. Representative examples are provided in the paragraphs that follow.

Concurrency. Many applications must handle multiple tasks in a manner that simulates parallelism (i.e., this occurs whenever multiple "parallel" tasks or components are managed by a single processor). There are a number of different ways in which an

4 This implies that there will be a central foyer and hallway, that rooms will be placed to the left and right of the foyer, that the house will have two (or more) stories, that the bedrooms of the house will be upstairs, and so on. These "rules" are imposed once the decision is made to use the *center-hall colonial* style.

5 It is important to note that there is not universal agreement on this terminology. Some people (e.g., [BUS96]) use the terms *styles* and *patterns* synonymously, while others make the subtle distinction suggested in this section.

application can handle concurrency, and each can be presented by a different architectural pattern. For example, one approach is to use an *operating system process management* pattern that provides built-in OS features that allow components to execute concurrently. The pattern also incorporates OS functionality that manages communication between processes, scheduling, and other capabilities required to achieve concurrency. Another approach might be to define a task scheduler at the application level. A *task scheduler* pattern contains a set of active objects that each contains a *tick()* operation [BOS00]. The scheduler periodically invokes *tick()* for each object, which then performs the functions it must perform before returning control back to the scheduler, which then invokes the *tick()* operation for the next concurrent object.

Persistence. Data persists if it survives past the execution of the process that created it. Persistent data are stored in a database or file and may be read or modified by other processes at a later time. In object-oriented environments, the idea of a persistent object extends the persistence concept a bit further. The values of all of the object's attributes, the general state of the object, and other supplementary information are stored for future retrieval and use. In general, two architectural patterns are used to achieve persistence—a *database management system* pattern that applies the storage and retrieval capability of a DBMS to the application architecture or an *application level persistence* pattern that builds persistence features into the application architecture (e.g., word processing software that manages its own document structure).

Distribution. The distribution problem addresses the manner in which systems or components within systems communicate with one another in a distributed environment. There are two elements to this problem: (1) the way in which entities connect to one another, and (2) the nature of the communication that occurs. The most common architectural pattern established to address the distribution problem is the *broker* pattern. A broker acts as a "middle-man" between the client component and a server component. The client sends a message to the broker (containing all appropriate information for the communication to be effected), and the broker completes the connection. CORBA (Chapter 30) is an example of a broker architecture.

Before any one of the architectural patterns noted in the preceding paragraphs can be chosen, it must be assessed for its appropriateness for the application and the overall architectural style, as well as its maintainability, reliability, security, and performance.

10.3.3 Organization and Refinement

Because the design process often leaves a software engineer with a number of architectural alternatives, it is important to establish a set of design criteria that can be used to assess an architectural design. The following questions [BAS03] provide insight into the architectural style that has been derived.

? How do I assess an architectural style that has been derived?

Control. How is control managed within the architecture? Does a distinct control hierarchy exist, and if so, what is the role of components within this control hierarchy? How do components transfer control within the system? How is control shared among components? What is the control topology (i.e., the geometric form that the control takes)? Is control synchronized or do components operate asynchronously?

Data. How are data communicated between components? Is the flow of data continuous, or are data objects passed to the system sporadically? What is the mode of data transfer (i.e., are data passed from one component to another or are data available globally to be shared among system components)? Do data components (e.g., a blackboard or repository) exist, and if so, what is their role? How do functional components interact with data components? Are data components passive or active (i.e., does the data component actively interact with other components in the system)? How do data and control interact within the system?

These questions provide the designer with an early assessment of design quality and lay the foundation for more detailed analysis of the architecture.

10.4 Architectural Design

As architectural design begins, the software to be developed must be put into context—that is, the design should define the external entities (other systems, devices, people) that the software interacts with and the nature of the interaction. This information can generally be acquired from the analysis model and all other information gathered during requirements engineering. Once context is modeled and all external software interfaces have been described, the designer specifies the structure of the system by defining and refining software components that implement the architecture. This process continues iteratively until a complete architectural structure has been derived.

> "A doctor can bury his mistakes, but an architect can only advise his client to plant vines."
>
> **Frank Lloyd Wright**

10.4.1 Representing the System in Context

Architectural context represents how the software interacts with entities external to its boundaries.

In Chapter 6, we noted that a system engineer must model context. A system context diagram (Figure 6.4) accomplishes this requirement by representing the flow of information into and out of the system, the user interface, and relevant support processing. At the architectural design level, a software architect uses an architectural context diagram (ACD) to model the manner in which software interacts with entities external to its boundaries. The generic structure of the architectural context diagram is illustrated in Figure 10.5.

Referring to the figure, systems that interoperate with the *target system* (the system for which an architectural design is to be developed) are represented as:

FIGURE 10.5

Architectural context diagram (adapted from [BOS00])

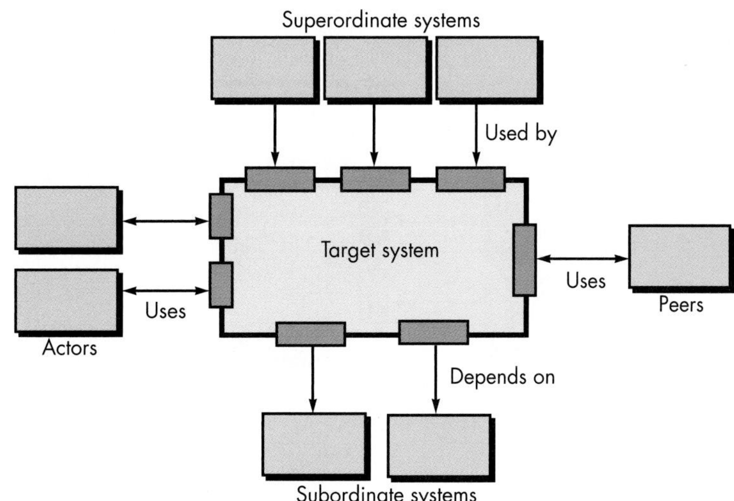

How do systems interoperate with one another?

- *Superordinate systems*—those systems that use the target system as part of some higher level processing scheme.
- *Subordinate systems*—those systems that are used by the target system and provide data or processing that are necessary to complete target system functionality.
- *Peer-level systems*—those systems that interact on a peer-to-peer basis (i.e., information is either produced or consumed by the peers and the target system).
- *Actors*—those entities (people, devices) that interact with the target system by producing or consuming information that is necessary for requisite processing.

Each of these external entities communicates with the target system through an interface (the small shaded rectangles).

To illustrate the use of the ACD we again consider the home security function of the *SafeHome* product. The overall *SafeHome* product controller and the Internet-based system are both superordinate to the security function and are shown above the function in Figure 10.6. The surveillance function is a *peer system* and uses (is used by) the home security function in later versions of the product. The homeowner and control panels are actors that are both producers and consumers of information used/produced by the security software. Finally, sensors are used by the security software and are shown as subordinate to it.

As part of the architectural design, the details of each interface shown in Figure 10.6 would have to be specified. All data that flow into and out of the target system must be identified at this stage.

FIGURE 10.6 **Architectural context diagram for the *SafeHome* security function**

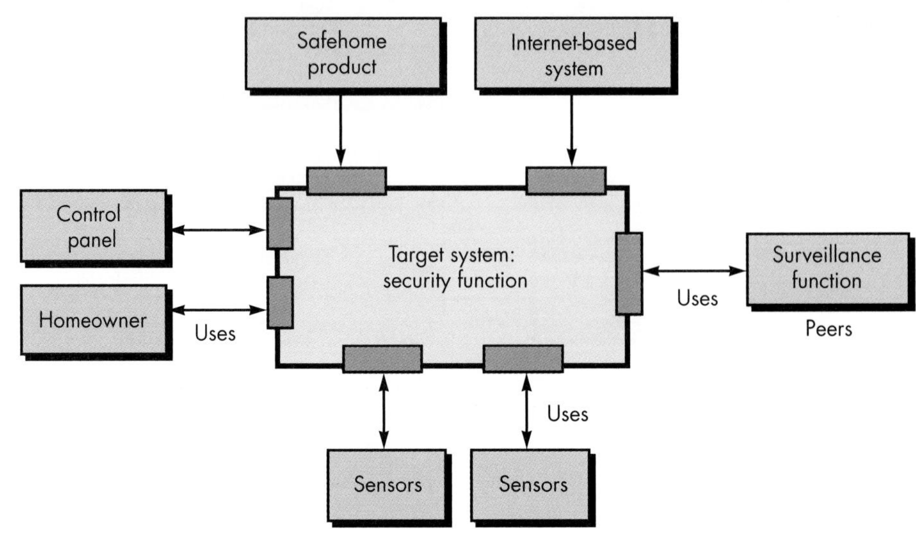

10.4.2 Defining Archetypes

KEY POINT Archetypes are the abstract building blocks of an architectural design.

An *archetype* is a class or pattern that represents a core abstraction that is critical to the design of an architecture for the target system. In general, a relatively small set of archetypes is required to design even relatively complex systems. The target system architecture is composed of these archetypes, which represent stable elements of the architecture but may be instantiated in many different ways based on the behavior of the system.

In many cases, archetypes can be derived by examining the analysis classes defined as part of the analysis model. Continuing our discussion of the *SafeHome* home security function, we might define the following archetypes:

- **Node.** Represents a cohesive collection of input and output elements of the home security function. For example a node might be comprised of (1) various sensors, and (2) a variety of alarm (output) indicators.
- **Detector.** An abstraction that encompasses all sensing equipment that feeds information into the target system.
- **Indicator.** An abstraction that represents all mechanisms (e.g., alarm siren, flashing lights, bell) for indicating that an alarm condition is occurring.
- **Controller.** An abstraction that depicts the mechanism that allows the arming or disarming of a node. If controllers reside on a network, they have the ability to communicate with one another.

Each of these archetypes is depicted using UML notation as shown in Figure 10.7.

FIGURE 10.7

UML relationships for *SafeHome* security function archetypes (adapted from [BOS00])

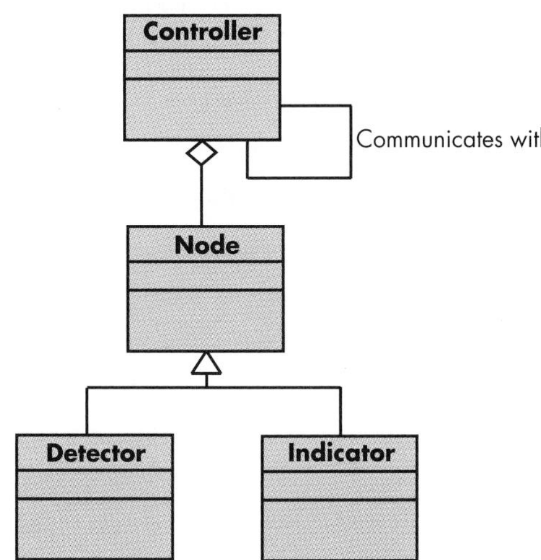

Recall that the archetypes form the basis for the architecture but are abstractions that must be further refined as architectural design proceeds. For example, **Detector** might be refined into a class hierarchy of sensors.

10.4.3 Refining the Architecture into Components

Components of the software architecture are derived from three sources—the application domain, the infrastructure domain, and the interface domain. Because analysis modeling does not address infrastructure, allocate sufficient design time to consider it carefully.

As the software architecture is refined into components, the structure of the system begins to emerge. But how are these components chosen? In order to answer this question, the architectural designer begins with the classes that were described as part of the analysis model.[6] These analysis classes represent entities within the application (business) domain that must be addressed within the software architecture. Hence, the application domain is one source for the derivation and refinement of components. Another source is the infrastructure domain. The architecture must accommodate many infrastructure components that enable application components but have no business connection to the application domain. For example, memory management components, communication components, database components, and task management components are often integrated into the software architecture.

The interfaces depicted in the architecture context diagram (Section 10.4.1) imply one or more specialized components that process the data that flow across the interface. In some cases (e.g. a graphical user interface), a complete subsystem architecture with many components must be designed.

6 If a conventional (non-object-oriented) approach is chosen, components can be derived from the data flow model. We discuss this approach in Section 10.6.

> "The structure of a software system provides the ecology in which code is born, matures, and dies. A well-designed habitat allows for the successful evolution of all the components needed in a software system."
>
> **R. Pattis**

Continuing the *SafeHome* home security function example, we might define the set of top-level components that address the following functionality:

- *External communication management*—coordinates communication of the security function with external entities, for example, Internet-based systems, external alarm notification.
- *Control panel processing*—manages all control panel functionality.
- *Detector management*—coordinates access to all detectors attached to the system.
- *Alarm processing*—verifies and acts on all alarm conditions.

Each of these top-level components would have to be elaborated iteratively and then positioned within the overall *SafeHome* architecture. Design classes (with appropriate attributes and operations) would be defined for each. It is important to note, however, that the design details of all attributes and operations would not be specified until component-level design (Chapter 11).

The overall architectural structure (represented as a UML component diagram) is illustrated in Figure 10.8. Transactions are acquired by *External communication management* as they move in from components that process the *SafeHome GUI* and the *Internet interface*. This information is managed by a *SafeHome executive* component that

FIGURE 10.8 **Overall architectural structure for *SafeHome* with top-level components**

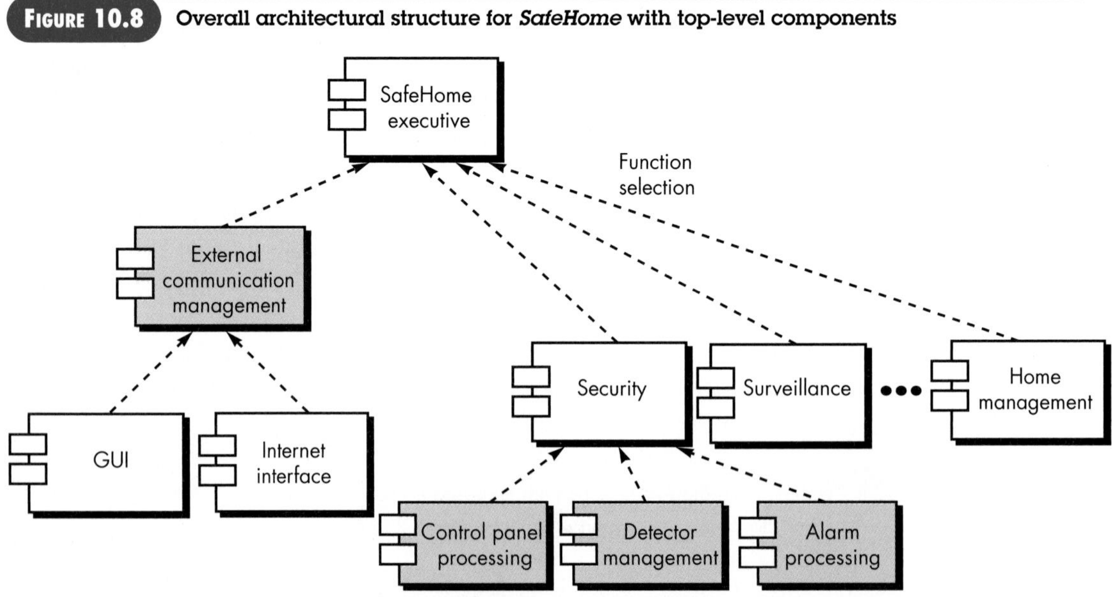

selects the appropriate product function (in this case, security). The *control panel processing* component interacts with the homeowner to arm/disarm the security function. The *detector management* component polls sensors to detect an alarm condition, and the *alarm processing* component produces output when an alarm is detected.

10.4.4 Describing Instantiations of the System

The architectural design that has been modeled to this point is still relatively high level. The context of the system has been represented; archetypes that indicate the important abstractions within the problem domain have been defined; the overall structure of the system is apparent; and the major software components have been identified. However, further refinement (recall that all design is iterative) is still necessary.

To accomplish this, an actual *instantiation* of the architecture is developed. By this we mean that the architecture is applied to a specific problem with the intent of demonstrating that the structure and components are appropriate.

Figure 10.9 illustrates an instantiation of the *SafeHome* architecture for the security system. Components shown in Figure 10.8 are refined further to show additional detail. For example, the *detector management* component interacts with a *scheduler*

FIGURE 10.9 An instantiation of the security function with component elaboration

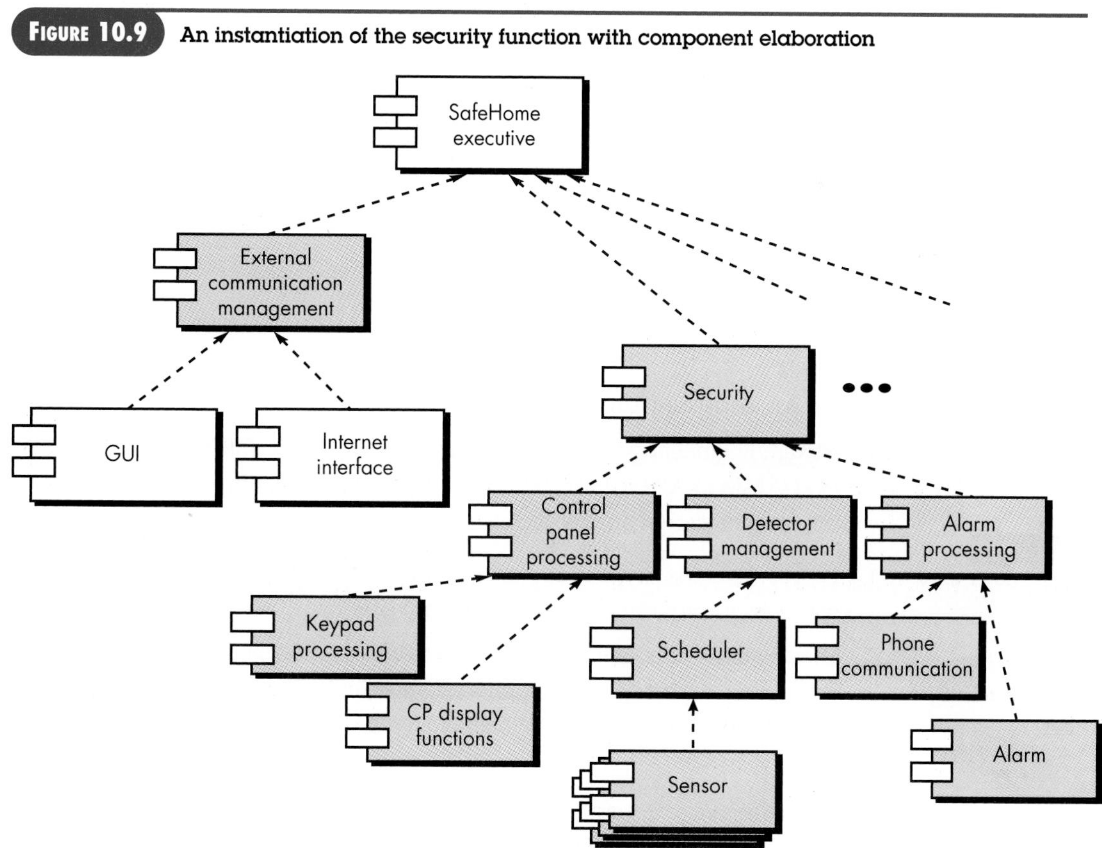

infrastructure component that implements "concurrent" polling of each *sensor* object used by the security system. Similar elaboration is performed for each of the components represented in Figure 10.8.

SOFTWARE TOOLS

Architectural Design

Objective: Architectural design tools model the overall software structure by representing component interfaces, dependencies and relationships, and interactions.

Mechanics: Tool mechanics vary. In most cases, architectural design capability is part of the functionality provided by automated tools for analysis and design modeling.

Representative Tools[7]

Adalon, developed by Synthis Corp. (www.synthis.com), is a specialized design tool for the design and construction of specific Web-based component architectures.

ObjectiF, developed by microTOOL GmbH (www.microtool.com), is a UML-based design tool that leads to architectures (e.g., Coldfusion, J2EE, Fusebox) amenable to component-based software engineering (Chapter 30).

Rational Rose, developed by Rational (www.rational.com), is a UML-based design tool that supports all aspects of architectural design.

10.5 ASSESSING ALTERNATIVE ARCHITECTURAL DESIGNS

At its best, design results in a number of architectural alternatives that are each assessed to determine which is the most appropriate for the problem to be solved. In the sections that follow, we consider the assessment of alternative architectural designs.

> "Maybe it's in the basement. Let me go upstairs and check."
>
> **M. C. Escher**

10.5.1 An Architecture Trade-Off Analysis Method

The Software Engineering Institute (SEI) has developed an *architecture trade-off analysis method* (ATAM) [KAZ98] that establishes an iterative evaluation process for software architectures. The design analysis activities that follow are performed iteratively:

WebRef
In-depth information on ATAM can be obtained at **www.sei.cmu.edu/ata/ata_method.html.**

1. *Collect scenarios.* A set of use-cases (Chapters 7 and 8) is developed to represent the system from the user's point of view.
2. *Elicit requirements, constraints, and environment description.* This information is required as part of requirements engineering and is used to be certain that all stakeholder concerns have been addressed.

7 Tools noted here do not represent an endorsement, but rather a sampling of tools in this category. In most cases, tool names are trademarked by their respective developers.

3. *Describe the architectural styles/patterns that have been chosen to address the scenarios and requirements.*
4. *Evaluate quality attributes by considering each attribute in isolation.* Quality attributes for architectural design assessment include reliability, performance, security, maintainability, flexibility, testability, portability, reusability, and interoperability.
5. *Identify the sensitivity of quality attributes to various architectural attributes for a specific architectural style.* This can be accomplished by making small changes in the architecture and determining how sensitive a quality attribute, say performance, is to the change. Any attributes that are significantly affected by variation in the architecture are termed *sensitivity points.*
6. *Critique candidate architectures (developed in step 3) using the sensitivity analysis conducted in step 5.* The SEI describes this approach in the following manner [KAZ98]:

> Once the architectural sensitivity points have been determined, finding trade-off points is simply the identification of architectural elements to which multiple attributes are sensitive. For example, the performance of a client-server architecture might be highly sensitive to the number of servers (performance increases, within some range, by increasing the number of servers). . . . The number of servers, then, is a trade-off point with respect to this architecture.

These six steps represent the first ATAM iteration. Based on the results of steps 5 and 6, some architecture alternatives may be eliminated, one or more of the remaining architectures may be modified and represented in more detail, and then the ATAM steps are reapplied.[8]

SAFEHOME

Architecture Assessment

The scene: Doug Miller's office as architectural design modeling proceeds.

The players: Vinod, Jamie, Shakira, and Ed—members of the *SafeHome* software engineering team. Also, Doug Miller, manager of the software engineering group.

The conversation:

Doug: I know you guys are deriving a couple of different architectures for the *SafeHome* product, and that's a good thing. I guess my question is, how are we going to choose the one that's best?

Ed: I'm working on a call and return style, and then either Jamie or I are going to derive an OO architecture.

Doug: Okay, and how do we choose?

Shakira: I took a course in design in my senior year, and I remember that there are a number of ways to do it.

8 The *Software Architecture Analysis Method* (SAAM) is an alternative to ATAM and is well-worth examining by those readers interested in architectural analysis. A paper on SAAM can be downloaded from: http://www.sei.cmu.edu/publications/articles/saam-metho-propert-sas.html.

Vinod: There are, but they're a bit academic. Look, I think we can do our assessment and choose the right one using use-cases and scenarios.

Doug: Isn't that the same thing?

Vinod: Not when you're talking about architectural assessment. We already have a complete set of use-cases. So we apply each to both architectures and see how the system reacts—how components and connectors work in the use-case context.

Ed: That's a good idea. Makes sure we didn't leave anything out.

Vinod: True, but it also tells us whether the architectural design is convoluted, whether the system has to twist itself into a pretzel to get the job done.

Jamie: Scenarios aren't just another name for use-cases?

Vinod: No, in this case a scenario implies something different.

Doug: You're talking about a quality scenario or a change scenario, right?

Vinod: Yes. What we do is go back to the stakeholders and ask them how *SafeHome* is likely to change over the next, say, three years. You know, new versions, features, that sort of thing. We build a set of change scenarios. We also develop a set of quality scenarios that define the attributes we'd like to see in the software architecture.

Jamie: And we apply them to the alternatives.

Vinod: Exactly. The style that handles the use-cases and scenarios best is the one we choose.

10.5.2 Architectural Complexity

A useful technique for assessing the overall complexity of a proposed architecture is to consider dependencies between components within the architecture. These dependencies are driven by information/control flow within the system. Zhao [ZHA98] suggests three types of dependencies:

> *Sharing dependencies* represent dependence relationships among consumers who use the same resource or producers who produce for the same consumers. For example, for two components *u* and *v*, if *u* and *v* refer to the same global data, then there exists a shared dependence relationship between *u* and *v*.
>
> *Flow dependencies* represent dependence relationships between producers and consumers of resources. For example, for two components *u* and *v*, if *u* must complete before control flows into *v* (prerequisite), or if *u* communicates with *v* by parameters, then there exists a flow dependence relationship between *u* and *v*.
>
> *Constrained dependencies* represent constraints on the relative flow of control among a set of activities. For example, for two components *u* and *v*, if *u* and *v* cannot execute at the same time (mutual exclusion), then there exists a constrained dependence relationship between *u* and *v*.

The sharing and flow dependencies noted by Zhao are similar to the concept of coupling discussed in Chapter 9. Coupling is an important design concept that is applicable at the architectural level and at the component level. Simple metrics for evaluating coupling are discussed in Chapter 15.

10.5.3 Architectural Description Languages

The architect of a house has a set of standardized tools and notation that allow the design to be represented in an unambiguous, understandable fashion. Although the software architect can draw on UML notation, other diagrammatic forms, and a few related tools, there is a need for a more formal approach to the specification of an architectural design.

Architectural description language (ADL) provides a semantics and syntax for describing a software architecture. Hofmann and his colleagues [HOF01] suggest that an ADL should provide the designer with the ability to decompose architectural components, compose individual components into larger architectural blocks, and represent interfaces (connection mechanisms) between components. Once descriptive, language-based techniques for architectural design have been established, it is more likely that effective assessment methods for architectures will be established as the design evolves.

SOFTWARE TOOLS

Architectural Description Languages

The following summary of a number of important ADLs was prepared by Rickard Land [LAN02] and is reprinted with the author's permission. It should be noted that the first five ADLs listed have been developed for research purposes and are not commercial products.

Rapide (poset.stanford.edu/rapide/) [LUC95] builds on the notion of partial ordered sets.

UniCon (www.cs.cmu.edu/~UniCon) [SHA96] defines software architectures in terms of abstractions that designers find useful.

Aesop (www.cs.cmu.edu/~able/aesop/) [GAR94] addresses the problem of style reuse.

Wright (www.cs.cmu.edu/~able/wright/) [ALL97] formalizes architectural styles using predicates, thus allowing for static checks to determine the consistency and completeness of an architecture.

Acme (www.cs.cmu.edu/~acme/) [GAR00] is a second-generation ADL.

UML (www.uml.org/) includes many of the artifacts needed for architectural descriptions, but is not as complete as other ADLs.

10.6 Mapping Data Flow into a Software Architecture

The styles discussed in Section 10.3.1 represent radically different architectures, so it should come as no surprise that a comprehensive mapping that accomplishes the transition from the analysis model to a variety of architectural styles does not exist. In fact, there is no practical mapping for some architectural styles. The designer must approach the translation of requirements to design for these styles by using the techniques discussed in Section 10.4.

To illustrate one approach to architectural mapping, we consider a mapping technique for the *call and return* architecture—an extremely common structure for many types of systems. This mapping technique enables a designer to derive reasonably complex call and return architectures from data flow diagrams within the analysis model. The technique, sometimes called *structured design,* is presented in books by Myers [MYE78] and Yourdon and Constantine [YOU79].

Structured design is often characterized as a data flow-oriented design method because it provides a convenient transition from a data flow diagram (Chapter 8) to software architecture. The type of information flow is the driver for the mapping approach.

10.6.1 Transform Flow

Information must enter and exit software in an "external world" form. For example, data typed on a keyboard, tones on a telephone line, and video images in a multimedia application are all forms of external world information. Such externalized data must be converted into an internal form for processing. Information enters the system along paths that transform external data into an internal form. These paths are identified as *incoming flow.* At the kernel of the software, a transition occurs. Incoming data are passed through a *transform center* and begin to move along paths that now lead "out" of the software. Data moving along these paths are called *outgoing flow.* The overall flow of data occurs in a sequential manner and follows one, or only a few, "straight line" paths.[9] When a segment of a data flow diagram exhibits these characteristics, *transform* flow is present.

10.6.2 Transaction Flow

Information flow is often characterized by a single data item, called a *transaction,* that triggers other data flow along one of many paths. When a DFD takes the form shown in Figure 10.10, transaction flow is present.

Transaction flow is characterized by data moving along an incoming path that converts external world information into a transaction. The transaction is evalu-

FIGURE 10.10

Transaction flow

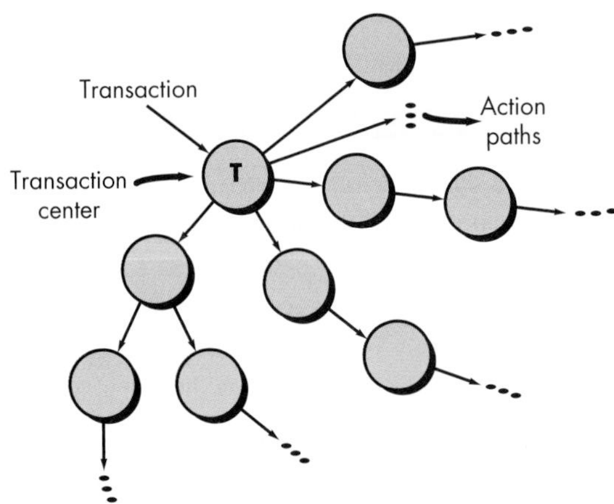

9 An obvious mapping for this type of information flow is the data flow architecture described in Section 10.3.1. There are many cases, however, where the data flow architecture may not be the best choice for a complex system. Examples include systems that will undergo substantial change over time or systems in which the processing associated with the data flow is not necessarily sequential.

ated and, based on its value, flow along one of many *action paths* is initiated. The hub of information flow from which many action paths emanate is called a *transaction center*.

It should be noted that, within a DFD for a large system, both transform and transaction flow may be present. For example, in a transaction-oriented flow, information flow along an action path may have transform flow characteristics.

10.6.3 Transform Mapping

Transform mapping is a set of design steps that allows a DFD with transform flow characteristics to be mapped into a specific architectural style. To illustrate this approach, we again consider the *SafeHome* security function.[10] One element of the analysis model is a set of data flow diagrams that describe information flow within the security function. To map these data flow diagrams into an architecture, the following design steps are initiated:

Step 1. Review the fundamental system model. The fundamental system model or context diagram depicts the security function as a single transformation, representing the external producers and consumers of data that flow into and out of the function. Figure 10.11 depicts a level 0 model, and Figure 10.12 depicts refined data flow for the security function.

If the DFD is refined further at this time, strive to derive bubbles that exhibit high cohesion.

Step 2. Review and refine data flow diagrams for the software. Information obtained from the analysis models is refined to produce greater detail. For example, the level 2 DFD for *monitor sensors* (Figure 10.13) is examined, and a level 3 data flow

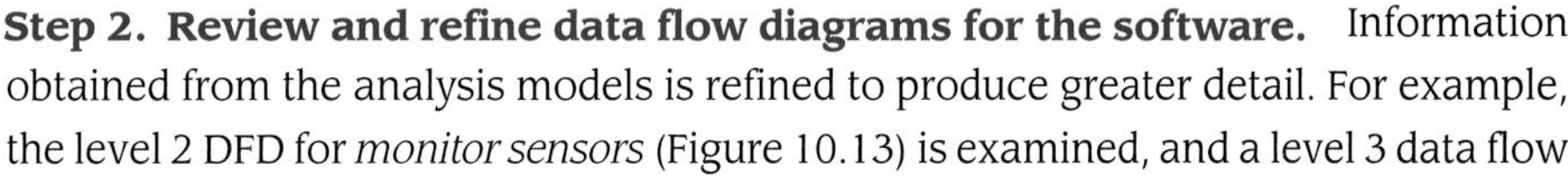

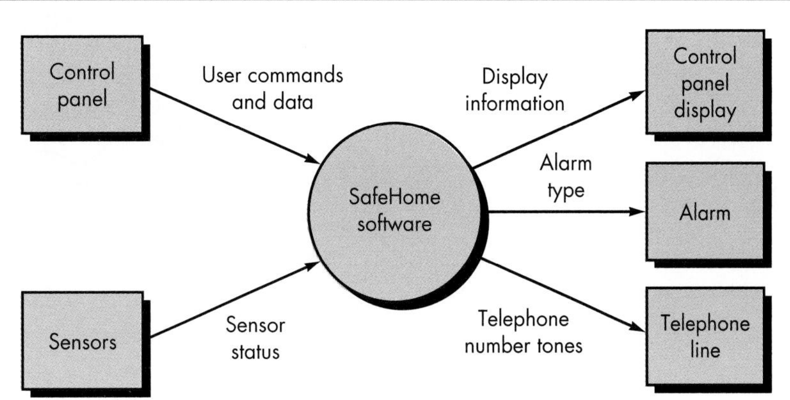

FIGURE 10.11 **Context level DFD for the *SafeHome* security function**

10 We consider only the portion of the *SafeHome* security function that uses the control panel. Other features, discussed earlier in this book and this chapter, will not be considered here.

FIGURE 10.12

Level 1 DFD for the *SafeHome* security function

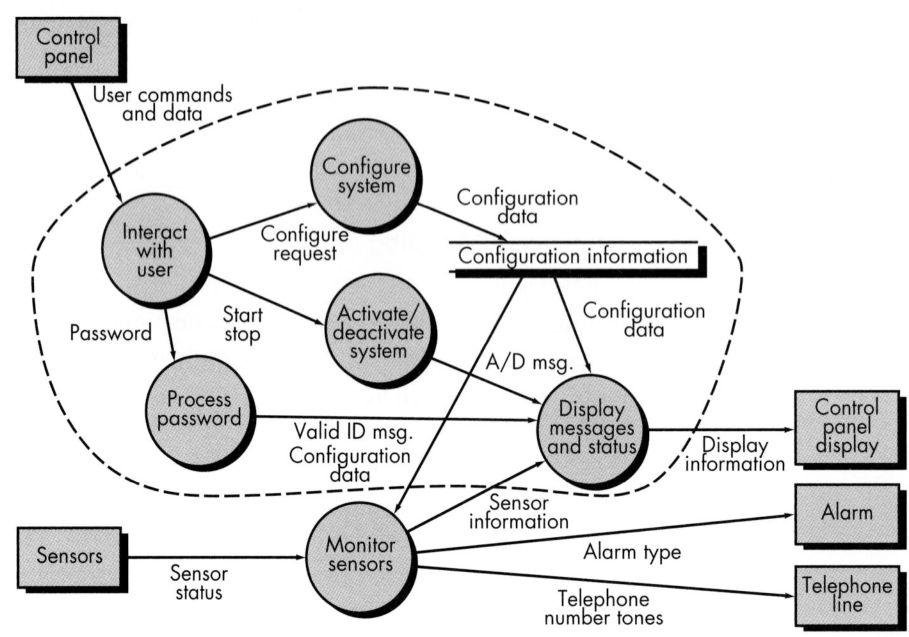

FIGURE 10.13

Level 2 DFD that refines the *monitor sensors* transform

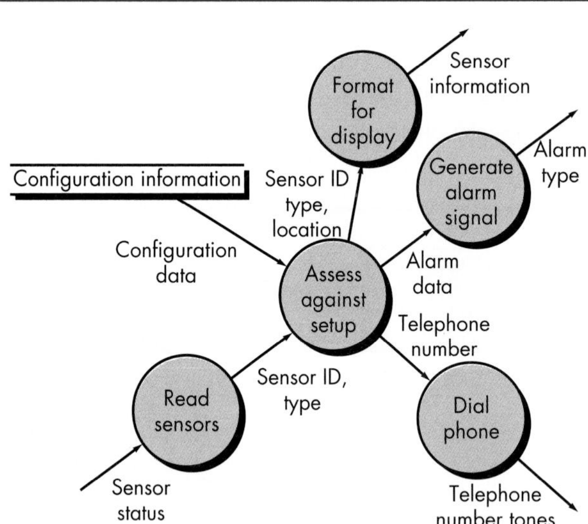

diagram is derived as shown in Figure 10.14. At level 3, each transform in the data flow diagram exhibits relatively high cohesion (Chapter 9). That is, the process implied by a transform performs a single, distinct function that can be implemented as a component in the *SafeHome* software. Therefore, the DFD in Figure 10.14 contains sufficient detail for a "first cut" at the design of architecture for the *monitor sensors* subsystem, and we proceed without further refinement.

FIGURE 10.14 Level 3 DFD for *monitor sensors* with flow boundaries

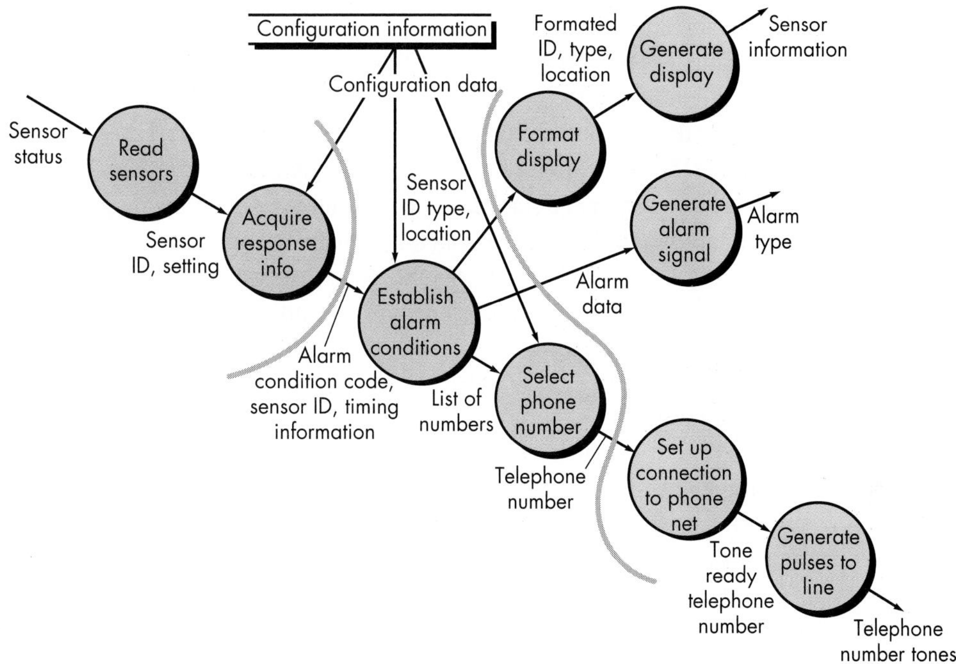

You will often encounter both types of data flow within the same flow-oriented model. The flows are partitioned and program structure is derived using the appropriate mapping.

Step 3. Determine whether the DFD has transform or transaction flow characteristics. In general, information flow within a system can always be represented as transform. However, when an obvious transaction characteristic (Figure 10.10) is encountered, a different design mapping is recommended. In this step, the designer selects global (software-wide) flow characteristics based on the prevailing nature of the DFD. In addition, local regions of transform or transaction flow are isolated. These *subflows* can be used to refine program architecture derived from a global characteristic described previously. For now, we focus our attention only on the *monitor sensors* subsystem data flow depicted in Figure 10.14.

Evaluating the DFD (Figure 10.14), we see data entering the software along one incoming path and exiting along three outgoing paths. No distinct transaction center is implied (although the transform establishes alarm conditions that could be perceived as such). Therefore, an overall transform characteristic will be assumed for information flow.

Vary the location of flow boundaries in an effort to explore alternative program structures. This takes very little time and provides important insight.

Step 4. Isolate the transform center by specifying incoming and outgoing flow boundaries. In the preceding section incoming flow was described as a path that converts information from external to internal form; outgoing flow converts from internal to external form. Incoming and outgoing flow boundaries are open to interpretation. That is, different designers may select slightly different points in the flow as boundary locations. In fact, alternative design solutions can be derived by varying the placement of flow boundaries. Although care should be taken when boundaries are selected, a variance of one bubble along a flow path will generally have little impact on the final program structure.

Flow boundaries for the example are illustrated as shaded curves running vertically through the flow in Figure 10.14. The transforms (bubbles) that constitute the transform center lie within the two shaded boundaries that run from top to bottom in the figure. An argument can be made to readjust a boundary (e.g., an incoming flow boundary separating *read sensors* and *acquire response info* could be proposed). The emphasis in this design step should be on selecting reasonable boundaries, rather than lengthy iteration on placement of boundaries.

ADVICE

Don't become dogmatic at this stage. It may be necessary to establish two or more controllers for input processing or computation, based on the complexity of the system to be built. If common sense dictates this approach, do it!

Step 5. Perform "first-level factoring." The program architecture derived using this mapping results in a top-down distribution of control. *Factoring* results in a program structure in which top-level components perform decision-making and low-level components perform most input, computation, and output work. Middle-level components perform some control and do moderate amounts of work.

When transform flow is encountered, a DFD is mapped to a specific structure (a call and return architecture) that provides control for incoming, transform, and outgoing information processing. This first-level factoring for the *monitor sensors* subsystem is illustrated in Figure 10.15. A main controller (called *monitor sensors*

FIGURE 10.15

First-level factoring for *monitor sensors*

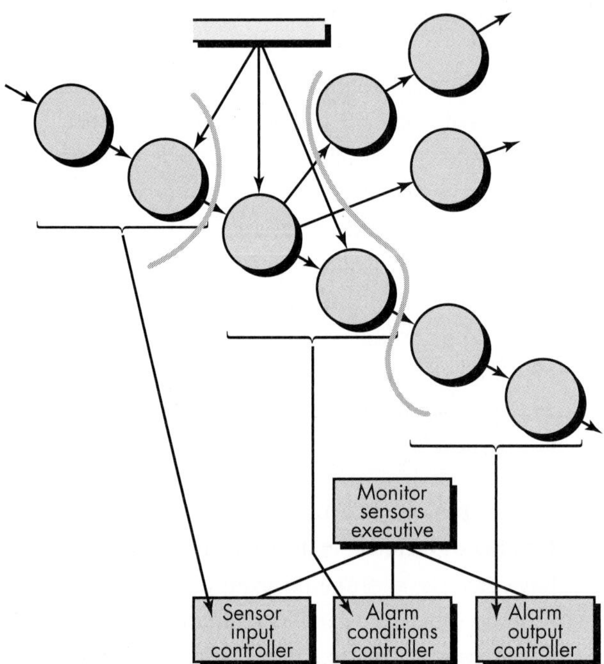

executive) resides at the top of the program structure and coordinates the following subordinate control functions:

- An incoming information processing controller, called *sensor input controller,* coordinates receipt of all incoming data.
- A transform flow controller, called *alarm conditions controller,* supervises all operations on data in internalized form (e.g., a module that invokes various data transformation procedures).
- An outgoing information processing controller, called *alarm output controller,* coordinates production of output information.

Although a three-pronged structure is implied by Figure 10.15, complex flows in large systems may dictate two or more control modules for each of the generic control functions described previously. The number of modules at the first level should be limited to the minimum that can accomplish control functions and still maintain good functional independence characteristics.

Keep "worker" modules low in the program structure. This will lead to an architecture that is easier to maintain.

Step 6. Perform "second-level factoring." Second-level factoring is accomplished by mapping individual transforms (bubbles) of a DFD into appropriate modules within the architecture. Beginning at the transform center boundary and moving outward along incoming and then outgoing paths, transforms are mapped into subordinate levels of the software structure. The general approach to second-level factoring is illustrated in Figure 10.16

Although Figure 10.16 illustrates a one-to-one mapping between DFD transforms and software modules, different mappings frequently occur. Two or even three bubbles can be combined and represented as one component, or a single bubble may be expanded to two or more components. Practical considerations and measures of design quality dictate the outcome of second-level factoring. Review and refinement may lead to changes in this structure, but it can serve as a "first-iteration" design.

Eliminate redundant control modules. That is, if a control module does nothing except control one other module, its control function should be imploded to a higher level module.

Second-level factoring for incoming flow follows in the same manner. Factoring is again accomplished by moving outward from the transform center boundary on the incoming flow side. The transform center of *monitor sensors* subsystem software is mapped somewhat differently. Each of the data conversion or calculation transforms of the transform portion of the DFD is mapped into a module subordinate to the transform controller. A completed first-iteration architecture is shown in Figure 10.17.

The components mapped in the preceding manner and shown in Figure 10.17 represent an initial design of software architecture. Although components are named in a way that implies function, a brief processing narrative (adapted from the PSPEC created during analysis modeling) should be written for each.

Focus on the functional independence of the modules you've derived. High cohesion and low coupling should be your goal.

Step 7. Refine the first-iteration architecture using design heuristics for improved software quality. A first-iteration architecture can always be refined by applying concepts of functional independence (Chapter 9). Components are exploded or imploded to produce sensible factoring, good cohesion, minimal coupling,

FIGURE 10.16

Second-level factoring for *monitor sensors*

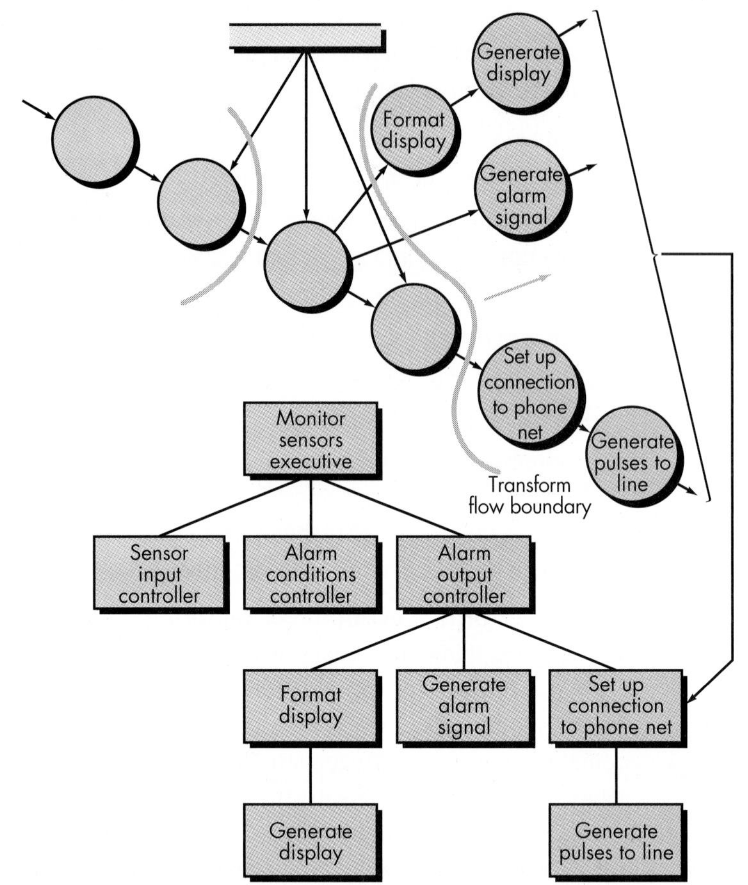

FIGURE 10.17 First iteration structure for *monitor sensors*

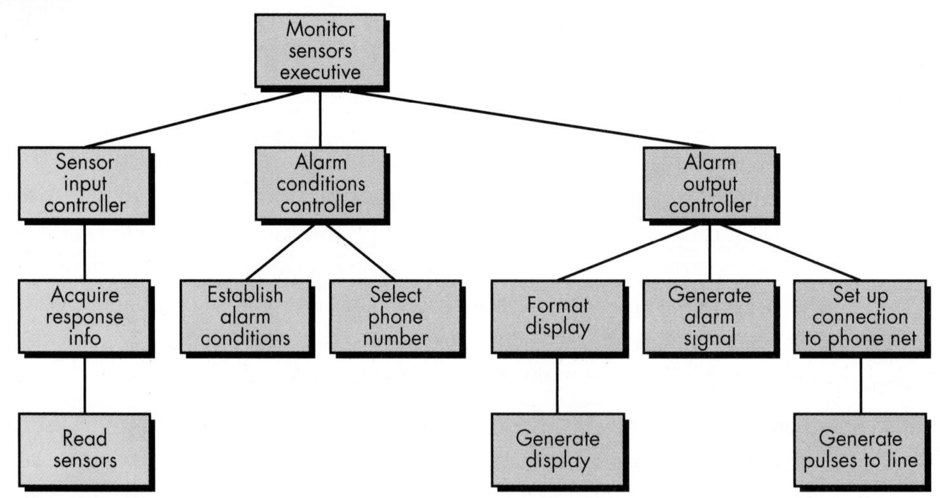

and most importantly, a structure that can be implemented without difficulty, tested without confusion, and maintained without grief.

Refinements are dictated by the analysis and assessment methods described briefly in Section 10.5, as well as practical considerations and common sense. There are times, for example, when the controller for incoming data flow is totally unnecessary, when some input processing is required in a component that is subordinate to the transform controller, when high coupling due to global data cannot be avoided, or when optimal structural characteristics cannot be achieved. Software requirements coupled with human judgment is the final arbiter.

The objective of the preceding seven steps is to develop an architectural representation of software. That is, once structure is defined, we can evaluate and refine software architecture by viewing it as a whole. Modifications made at this time require little additional work, yet can have a profound impact on software quality.

The reader should pause for a moment and consider the difference between the design approach described and the process of "writing programs." If code is the only representation of software, the developer will have great difficulty evaluating or refining at a global or holistic level and will, in fact, have difficulty "seeing the forest for the trees."

SAFEHOME

Refining a First-Cut Architecture

The scene: Jamie's cubicle, as design modeling continues.

The players: Jamie and Ed—members of the *SafeHome* software engineering team.

The conversation:

(Ed has just completed a first-cut design of the *monitor sensors* subsystem. He stops in to ask Jamie her opinion.)

Ed: So here's the architecture that I derived.

(Ed shows Jamie Figure 10.17, which she studies for a few moments.)

Jamie: That's cool, but I think we can do a few things to make it simpler . . . and better.

Ed: Such as?

Jamie: Well, why did you use the *sensor input controller* component?

Ed: Because you need a controller for the mapping.

Jamie: Not really. The controller doesn't do much, since we're managing a single flow path for incoming data. We can eliminate the controller with no ill effects.

Ed: I can live with that, I'll make the change and . . .

Jamie (smiling): Hold up! We can also implode the components *establish alarm conditions* and *select phone number*. The transform controller you show isn't really necessary, and the small decrease in cohesion is tolerable.

Ed: Simplification, huh?

Jamie: Yep. And while we're making refinements, it would be a good idea to implode the components *format display* and *generate display*. Display formatting for the control panel is simple. We can define a new module called *produce display*.

Ed (sketching): So this is what you think we should do?

(He shows Jamie Figure 10.18.)

Jamie: It's a start.

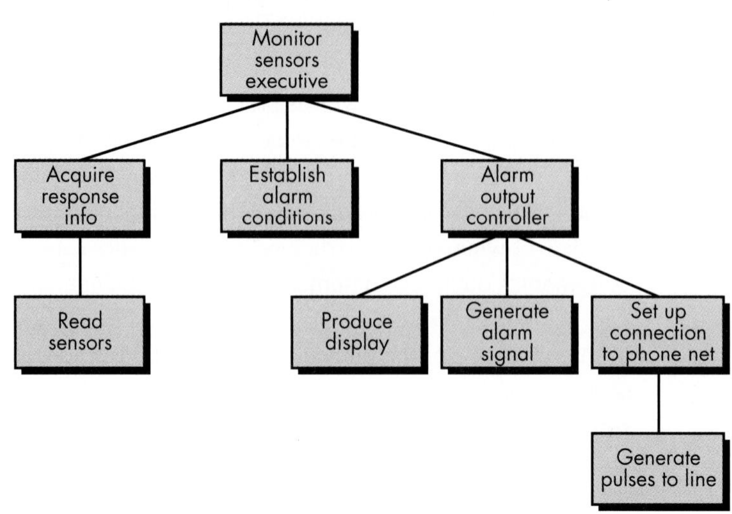

FIGURE 10.18 Refined program structure for *monitor sensors*

10.6.4 Transaction Mapping

In many software applications, a single data item triggers one of a number of information flows that effect a function implied by the triggering data item. The data item, called a *transaction,* and its corresponding flow characteristics are discussed in Section 10.6.2. In this section we consider design steps used to map transaction flow into a software architecture.

Transaction mapping will be illustrated by considering the user interaction subsystem of the *SafeHome* security function. Level 1 data flow for this subsystem is shown as part of Figure 10.12. Refining the flow, a level 2 data flow diagram is developed and shown in Figure 10.19. The data object **user commands** flows into the system and results in additional information flow along one of three action paths. A single data item, **command type,** causes the data flow to fan outward from a hub. Therefore, the overall data flow characteristic is transaction-oriented.

It should be noted that information flow along two of the three action paths accommodates additional incoming flow (e.g., **system parameters and data** are input on the "configure" action path). Each action path flows into a single transform, *display messages and status.*

The design steps for transaction mapping are similar and in some cases identical to steps for transform mapping (Section 10.6.3). A major difference lies in the mapping of DFD to software structure.

Step 1. Review the fundamental system model.

Step 2. Review and refine data flow diagrams for the software.

FIGURE 10.19 Level 2 DFD for user interaction subsystem

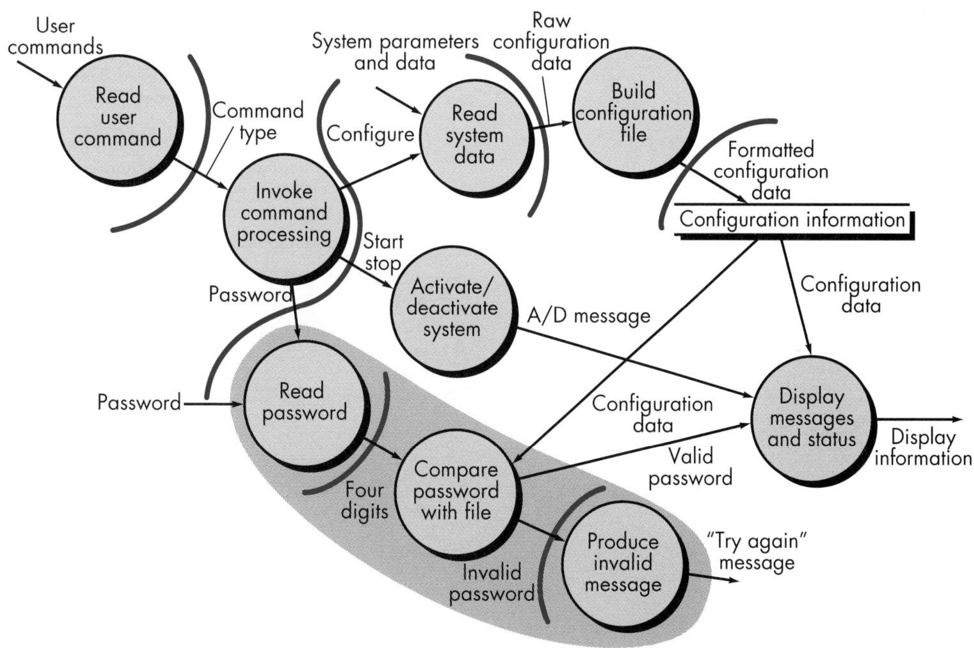

Step 3. Determine whether the DFD has transform or transaction flow characteristics.

Steps 1, 2, and 3 are identical to corresponding steps in transform mapping. The DFD shown in Figure 10.19 has a classic transaction flow characteristic. However, flow along two of the action paths emanating from the *invoke command processing* bubble appears to have transform flow characteristics. Therefore, flow boundaries must be established for both flow types.

Step 4. Identify the transaction center and the flow characteristics along each of the action paths. The location of the transaction center can be immediately discerned from the DFD. The transaction center lies at the origin of a number of actions paths that flow radially from it. For the flow shown in Figure 10.19, the *invoke command processing* bubble is the transaction center.

First-level factoring results in the derivation of a control hierarchy for the software. Second-level factoring distributes "worker" modules under the appropriate controller.

The incoming path (i.e., the flow path along which a transaction is received) and all action paths must also be isolated. Each action path must be evaluated for its individual flow characteristic. For example, the "password" path (shown enclosed by a shaded area in Figure 10.19) has transform characteristics. Incoming, transform, and outgoing flow are indicated with boundaries.

Step 5. Map the DFD in a program structure amenable to transaction processing. Transaction flow is mapped into an architecture that contains an incoming branch and a dispatch branch. The structure of the incoming branch is

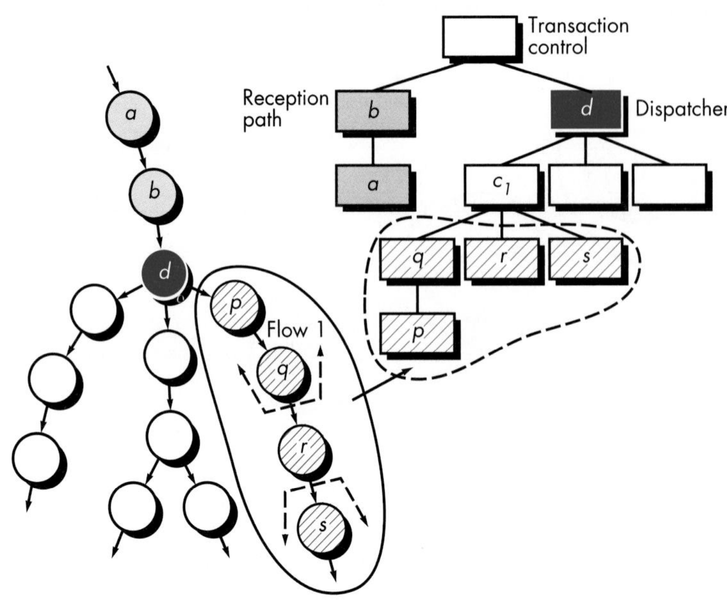

FIGURE 10.20 Transaction mapping

developed in much the same way as transform mapping. Starting at the transaction center, bubbles along the incoming path are mapped into modules. The structure of the dispatch branch contains a dispatcher module that controls all subordinate action modules. Each action flow path of the DFD is mapped to a structure that corresponds to its specific flow characteristics. This process is illustrated schematically in Figure 10.20.

Considering the user interaction subsystem data flow, first-level factoring for step 5 is shown in Figure 10.21. The bubbles *read user command* and *activate/deactivate system* map directly into the architecture without the need for intermediate control modules. The transaction center, *invoke command processing,* maps directly into a dispatcher module of the same name. Controllers for system configuration and password processing are created as illustrated in Figure 10.21.

Step 6. Factor and refine the transaction structure and the structure of each action path. Each action path of the data flow diagram has its own information flow characteristics. We have already noted that transform or transaction flow may be encountered. The action path-related "substructure" is developed using the design steps discussed in this and the preceding section.

As an example, consider the password processing information flow shown (inside shaded area) in Figure 10.19. The flow exhibits classic transform characteristics. A **password** is input (incoming flow) and transmitted to a transform center where it is compared against stored passwords. An alarm and warning message (outgoing flow) are produced (if a match is not obtained). The "configure" path is drawn simi-

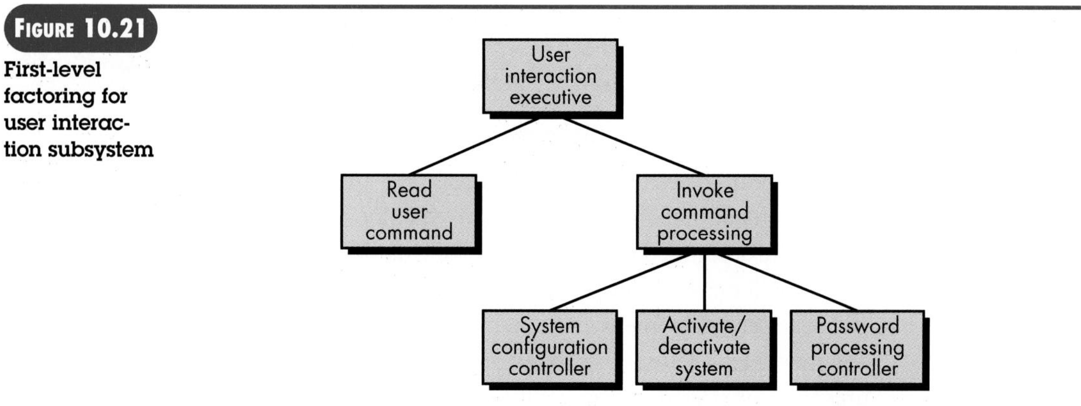

FIGURE 10.21 First-level factoring for user interaction subsystem

FIGURE 10.22 First iteration architecture for user interaction subsystem

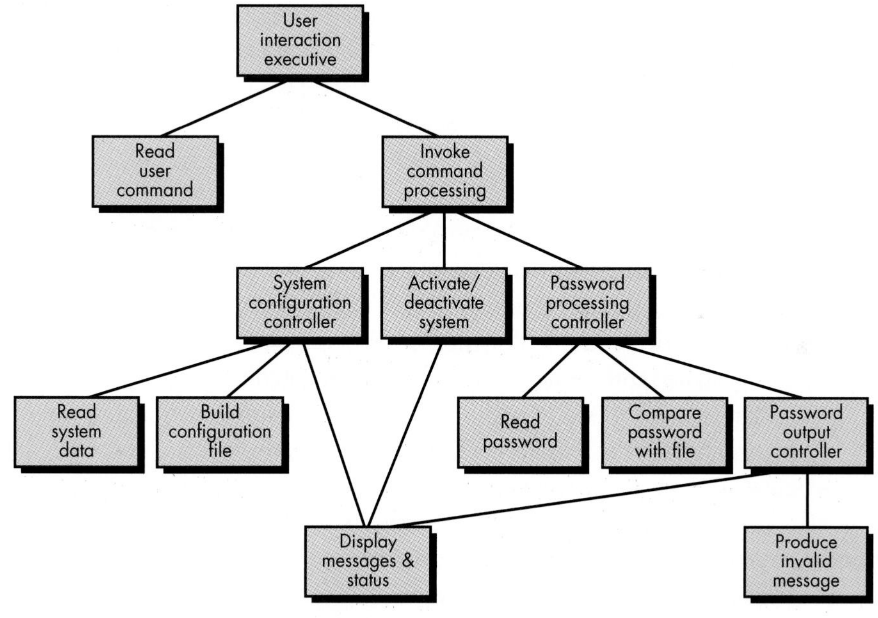

larly using the transform mapping. The resultant software architecture is shown in Figure 10.22.

Step 7. Refine the first-iteration architecture using design heuristics for improved software quality. This step for transaction mapping is identical to the corresponding step for transform mapping. In both design approaches, criteria such as module independence, practicality (efficacy of implementation and test), and maintainability must be carefully considered as structural modifications are proposed.

> "Make it as simple as possible. But no simpler."
>
> **Albert Einstein**

10.6.5 Refining the Architectural Design

Any discussion of design refinement should be prefaced with the following comment: Remember that an "optimal design" that doesn't work has questionable merit. The software designer should be concerned with developing a representation of software that will meet all functional and performance requirements and merit acceptance based on design measures and heuristics.

Refinement of software architecture during early stages of design is to be encouraged. As we discussed earlier in this chapter, alternative architectural styles may be derived, refined, and evaluated for the "best" approach. This approach to optimization is one of the true benefits derived by developing a representation of software architecture.

It is important to note that structural simplicity often reflects both elegance and efficiency. Design refinement should strive for the smallest number of components that is consistent with effective modularity and the least complex data structure that adequately serves information requirements.

10.7 Summary

Software architecture provides a holistic view of the system to be built. It depicts the structure and organization of software components, their properties, and the connections between them. Software components include program modules and the various data representations that are manipulated by the program. Therefore, data design is an integral part of the derivation of the software architecture. Architecture highlights early design decisions and provides a mechanism for considering the benefits of alternative system structures.

Data design translates the data objects defined in the analysis model into data structures that reside within the software. The attributes that describe the object, the relationships between data objects and their use within the program all influence the choice of data structures. At a higher level of abstraction, data design may lead to the definition of an architecture for a database or a data warehouse.

A number of different architectural styles and patterns are available to the software engineer. Each style describes a system category that (1) encompasses a set of components that perform a function required by a system, (2) a set of connectors that enable communication, coordination and cooperation among components, (3) constraints that define how components can be integrated to form the system, and (4) semantic models that enable a designer to understand the overall properties of a system.

In a general sense, architectural design is accomplished using four distinct steps. First, the system must be represented in context. That is, the designer should define the external entities that the software interacts with and the nature of the interaction. Once context has been specified, the designer should identify a set of top-level abstractions, called archetypes, that represent pivotal elements of the system's behavior or function. After abstractions have been defined, the design begins to move closer to the implementation domain. Components are identified and represented within the context of an architecture that supports them. Finally, specific instantiations of the architecture are developed to "prove" the design in a real world context.

As a simple example of architectural design, the mapping method presented in this chapter uses data flow characteristics to derive a commonly used architectural style. A data flow diagram is mapped into program structure using one of two mapping approaches—transform mapping or transaction mapping. Once an architecture has been derived, it is elaborated and then analyzed against quality criteria.

REFERENCES

[AHO83] Aho, A. V., J. Hopcroft, and J. Ullmann, *Data Structures and Algorithms,* Addison-Wesley, 1983.

[ALL97] Allen R., "A Formal Approach to Software Architecture," Ph.D. Thesis, Carnegie Mellon University, Technical Report Number: CMU-CS-97-144 1997.

[BAR00] Barroca, L. and P. Hall (eds.), *Software Architecture: Advances and Applications,* Springer-Verlag, 2000.

[BAS03] Bass, L., P. Clements, and R. Kazman, *Software Architecture in Practice,* 2nd ed. Addison-Wesley, 2003.

[BOS00] Bosch, J., *Design & Use of Software Architectures,* Addison-Wesley, 2000.

[BUS96] Buschmann, F., *Pattern-Oriented Software Architecture,* Wiley, 1996.

[DAT00] Date, C. J., *An Introduction to Database Systems,* 7th ed., Addison-Wesley, 2000.

[DIK00] Dikel, D., D. Kane, and J. Wilson, *Software Architecture: Organizational Principles and Patterns,* Prentice-Hall, 2000.

[FRE80] Freeman, P., "The Context of Design," in *Software Design Techniques,* 3rd ed. (P. Freeman and A. Wasserman, eds.), IEEE Computer Society Press, 1980, pp. 2–4.

[GAR94] Garlan D., R. Allen, and J. Ockerbloom, "Exploiting Style in Architectural Design Environments," in *Proceedings of SIGSOFT '94 Symposium on the Foundations of Software Engineering,* 1994.

[GAR00] Garlan D., R. T. Monroe, and D. Wile, "Acme: Architectural Description of Component-Based Systems," in *Foundations of Component-Based Systems,* G. T. Leavens and M. Sitarman, eds. Cambridge University Press, 2000.

[HOF00] Hofmeister, C., R. Nord, and D. Soni, *Applied Software Architecture,* Addison-Wesley, 2000.

[HOF01] Hofmann, C., et al., "Approaches to Software Architecture," downloadable from: http://citeseer.nj.nec.com/84015.html.

[KAZ98] Kazman, R., et al., *The Architectural Tradeoff Analysis Method,* Software Engineering Institute, CMU/SEI-98-TR-008, July 1998.

[KIM98] Kimball, R., L. Reeves, M. Ross, and W. Thornthwaite, *The Data Warehouse Lifecycle Toolkit: Expert Methods for Designing, Developing, and Deploying Data Warehouses,* Wiley, 1998.

[LAN02] Land R., A Brief Survey of Software Architecture, Technical Report, Dept. of Computer Engineering, Mälardalen University, Sweden, February, 2002.

[LUC95] Luckham D. C., et al., "Specification and Analysis of System Architecture Using Rapide," *IEEE Transactions on Software Engineering,* issue "Special Issue on Software Architecture," 1995.

[MAT96] Mattison, R., *Data Warehousing: Strategies, Technologies and Techniques,* McGraw-Hill, 1996.

[MYE78] Myers, G., *Composite Structured Design,* Van Nostrand, 1978.

[PRE98] Preiss, B. R., *Data Structures and Algorithms: With Object-Oriented Design Patterns in C++*, Wiley, 1998.

[SHA96] Shaw, M., and D. Garlan, *Software Architecture,* Prentice-Hall, 1996.

[SHA97] Shaw, M., and P. Clements, "A Field Guide to Boxology: Preliminary Classification of Architectural Styles for Software Systems," *Proc. COMPSAC,* Washington, DC, August 1997.

[WAS80] Wasserman, A., "Principles of Systematic Data Design and Implementation," in *Software Design Techniques* (P. Freeman and A. Wasserman, eds.), 3rd ed., IEEE Computer Society Press, 1980, pp. 287–293.

[YOU79] Yourdon, E., and L. Constantine, *Structured Design,* Prentice-Hall, 1979.

[ZHA98] Zhao, J., "On Assessing the Complexity of Software Architectures," *Proc. Intl. Software Architecture Workshop,* ACM, Orlando, FL, 1998, pp. 163–167.

Problems and Points to Ponder

10.1. Using the architecture of a house or building as a metaphor, draw comparisons with software architecture. How are the disciplines of classical architecture and software architecture similar? How do they differ?

10.2. Write a three- to five-page paper that presents guidelines for selecting data structures based on the nature of the problem. Begin by delineating the classical data structures encountered in software work and then describe criteria for selecting from these for particular types of problems.

10.3. Explain the difference between a database that services one or more conventional business applications and a data warehouse.

10.4. Present two or three examples of applications for each of the architectural styles noted in Section 10.3.1.

10.5. Some of the architectural styles noted in Section 10.3.1 are hierarchical in nature and others are not. Make a list of each type. How would the architectural styles that are not hierarchical be implemented?

10.6. The terms *architectural style, architectural pattern,* and *framework* are often encountered in discussions of software architecture. Do some research (use the Web) and describe how each of these terms differs from its counterparts.

10.7. Select an application with which you are familiar. Answer each of the questions posed for control and data in Section 10.3.3.

10.8. Research the ATAM (use the SEI Web site) and present a detailed discussion of the six steps presented in Section 10.5.1.

10.9. Some designers contend that all data flow may be treated as transform-oriented. Discuss how this contention will affect the software architecture that is derived when a transaction-oriented flow is treated as transform. Use an example flow to illustrate important points.

10.10. If you haven't done so, complete Problem 8.10. Use the design methods described in this chapter to develop a software architecture for the PHTRS.

10.11. Using a data flow diagram and a processing narrative, describe a computer-based system that has distinct transform flow characteristics. Define flow boundaries and map the DFD into a software architecture using the technique described in Section 10.6.3.

10.12. Using a data flow diagram and a processing narrative, describe a computer-based system that has distinct transaction flow characteristics. Define flow boundaries and map the DFD into a software structure using the technique described in Section 10.6.4.

Further Readings and Information Sources

The literature on software architecture has exploded over the past decade. Books by Fowler (*Patterns of Enterprise Application Architecture,* Addison-Wesley, 2003), Clements and his colleagues (*Documenting Software Architecture: View and Beyond,* Addison-Wesley, 2002), Schmidt and his colleagues (*Pattern-Oriented Software Architectures,* two volumes, Wiley, 2000), Bosch [BOS00], Dikel and his colleagues [DIK00], Hofmeister and his colleagues [HOF00], Bass, Clements, and Kazman [BAS03], Shaw and Garlan [SHA96], and Buschmann et al. [BUS96] provide in-depth treatment of the subject. Earlier work by Garlan (*An Introduction to Software Architecture,* Software Engineering Institute, CMU/SEI-94-TR-021, 1994) provides an excellent introduction. Clements and Northrop (*Software Product Lines: Practices and Patterns,* Addison-Wesley, 2001)) address the design of architectures that support software product lines. Clements and his colleagues (*Evaluating Software Architectures,* Addison-Wesley, 2002) consider the issues associated with the assessment of architectural alternatives and the selection of the best architecture for a given problem domain.

Implementation-specific books on architecture address architectural design within a specific development environment or technology. Wallnau and his colleagues (*Building Systems from Commercial Components,* Addison-Wesley, 2001) present methods for constructing component-based architectures. Pritchard (*COM and CORBA Side-by-Side,* Addison-Wesley, 1999), Mowbray (CORBA Design Patterns, Wiley, 1997) and Mark et al. (*Object Management Architecture Guide,* Wiley, 1996) provide detailed design guidelines for the CORBA distributed application support framework. Shanley (*Protected Mode Software Architecture,* Addison-Wesley, 1996) provides architectural design guidance for anyone designing PC-based real-time operating systems, multi-task operating systems, or device drivers.

Current software architecture research is documented yearly in the *Proceedings of the International Workshop on Software Architecture,* sponsored by the ACM and other computing organizations, and the *Proceedings of the International Conference on Software Engineering.* Barroca and Hall [BAR00] present a useful survey of recent research.

Data modeling is a prerequisite to good data design. Books by Teory (*Database Modeling and Design,* Academic Press, 1998); Schmidt (*Data Modeling for Information Professionals,* Prentice-Hall, 1998); Bobak (*Data Modeling and Design for Today's Architectures,* Artech House, 1997); Silverston, Graziano, and Inmon (*The Data Model Resource Book,* Wiley, 1997); Date [DAT00], and Reingruber and Gregory (*The Data Modeling Handbook: A Best-Practice Approach to Building Quality Data Models,* Wiley, 1994) contain detailed presentations of data modeling notation, heuristics, and database design approaches. The design of data warehouses has become increasingly important in recent years. Books by Humphreys, Hawkins, and Dy (*Data Warehousing: Architecture and Implementation,* Prentice-Hall, 1999); Kimball et al. [KIM98]; and Inmon [INM95] cover the topic in considerable detail.

General treatment of software design with discussion of architectural and data design issues can be found in most books dedicated to software engineering. More rigorous treatments of the subject can be found in Feijs (*A Formalization of Design Methods,* Prentice-Hall, 1993), Witt et al. (*Software Architecture and Design Principles,* Thomson Publishing, 1994), and Budgen (*Software Design,* Addison-Wesley, 1994).

Complete presentations of data flow-oriented design may be found in Myers [MYE78], Yourdon and Constantine [YOU79], and Page-Jones (*The Practical Guide to Structured Systems Design,* 2nd ed., Prentice-Hall, 1988). These books are dedicated to design alone and provide comprehensive tutorials in the data flow approach.

A wide variety of information sources on architectural design are available on the Internet. An up-to-date list of World Wide Web references that are relevant to architectural design can be found at the SEPA Web site:
http://www.mhhe.com/pressman.

CHAPTER

Component-Level Design

Key Concepts

Component-level design occurs after the first iteration of architectural design has been completed. At this stage, the overall data and program structure of the software has been established. The intent is to translate the design model into operational software. But the level of abstraction of the existing design model is relatively high, and the abstraction level of the operational program is low. The translation can be challenging, opening the door to the introduction of subtle errors that are difficult to find and correct in later stages of the software process. In a famous lecture, Edsgar Dijkstra, a major contributor to our understanding of software design, stated [DIJ72]:

> Software seems to be different from many other products, where as a rule higher quality implies a higher price. Those who want really reliable software will discover that they must find a means of avoiding the majority of bugs to start with, and as a result, the programming process will become cheaper . . . effective programmers . . . should not waste their time debugging—they should not introduce bugs to start with.

Although these words were spoken many years ago, they remain true today. When the design model is translated into source code, we must follow a set of design principles that not only perform the translation but also do not "introduce bugs to start with."

It is possible to represent the component-level design using a programming language. In essence, the program is created using the architectural design model as a guide. An alternative approach is to represent the component-level design

Quick Look

What is it? A complete set of software components is defined during architectural design. But the internal data structures and processing details of each component are not represented at a level of abstraction that is close to code. Component-level design defines the data structures, algorithms, interface characteristics, and communication mechanisms allocated to each software component.

Who does it? A software engineer performs component-level design.

Why is it important? You have to be able to determine whether the software will work before you build it. The component-level design represents the software in a way that allows you to review the details of the design for correctness and consistency with earlier design representations (i.e., the data, architectural, and interface designs). It provides a means for assessing whether data structures, interfaces, and algorithms will work.

What are the steps? Design representations of data, architecture, and interfaces form the foundation for component-level design. The class definition or processing narrative for each component is translated into a detailed design that makes use of diagrammatic or text-based forms that specify internal data structures, local interface detail, and processing logic. Design notation encompasses UML diagrams and supplementary representations. Procedural design is specified using a set of structured programming constructs.

What is the work product? The design for each component, represented in graphical, tabular, or text-based notation, is the primary work product produced during component-level design.

How do I ensure that I've done it right? A design walkthrough or inspection is conducted. The design is examined to determine whether data structures, interfaces, processing sequences, and logical conditions are correct and will produce the appropriate data or control transformation allocated to the component during earlier design steps.

using some intermediate (e.g., graphical, tabular, or text-based) representation that can be translated easily into source code. Regardless of the mechanism that is used to represent the component-level design, the data structures, interfaces, and algorithms defined should conform to a variety of well-established design guidelines that help us to avoid errors as the procedural design evolves. In this chapter, we examine these design guidelines and the methods available for achieving them.

11.1 What Is a Component?

Stated in a general fashion, a *component* is a modular building block for computer software. More formally, the *OMG Unified Modeling Language Specification* [OMG01] defines a component as "a modular, deployable, and replaceable part of a system that encapsulates implementation and exposes a set of interfaces."

As we discussed in Chapter 10, components populate the software architecture, and, as a consequence, play a role in achieving the objectives and requirements of the system to be built. Because components reside within the software architecture, they must communicate and collaborate with other components and with entities (e.g., other systems, devices, people) that exist outside the boundaries of the software.

> "The details are not the details. They make the design."
>
> **Charles Eames**

The true meaning of the term "component" will differ depending on the point of view of the software engineer who uses it. In the sections that follow, we examine three important views of what a component is and how it is used as design modeling proceeds.

11.1.1 An Object-Oriented View

From an OO viewpoint, a component is a set of collaborating classes.

In the context of object-oriented software engineering, a component contains a set of collaborating classes.[1] Each class within a component has been fully elaborated to include all attributes and operations that are relevant to its implementation. As part of the design elaboration, all interfaces (messages) that enable the classes to communicate and collaborate with other design classes must also be defined. To accomplish this, the designer begins with the analysis model and elaborates analysis classes (for components that relate to the problem domain) and infrastructure classes (for components that provide support services for the problem domain).

To illustrate this process of design elaboration, consider software to be built for a sophisticated print shop. The overall intent of the software is to collect the customer's requirements at the front counter, cost a print job, and then pass the job on to an automated production facility. During requirements engineering, an analysis class called **PrintJob** was derived. The attributes and operations defined during analysis are noted at the top left of Figure 11.1. During architectural design, **PrintJob** is defined as a component within the software architecture and is represented using the shorthand UML notation shown in the middle right of the figure. Note that **PrintJob** has two interfaces, *computeJob,* that provides job costing capability, and *initiateJob,* that passes the job along to the production facility. These are represented using the "lollipop" symbols shown to the left of the component box.

Recall that analysis modeling and design modeling are both iterative actions. Elaborating the original analysis class may require additional analysis steps, which are then followed with design modeling steps to represent the elaborated design class (the details of the component).

Component-level design begins at this point. The details of the component **PrintJob** must be elaborated to provide sufficient information to guide implementation. The original analysis class is elaborated to flesh out all attributes and operations required to implement the class as the component **PrintJob.** Referring to the lower right portion of Figure 11.1, the elaborated design class **PrintJob** contains more detailed attribute information as well as an expanded description of operations required to implement the component. The interfaces *computeJob* and *initiateJob* imply communication and collaboration with other components (not shown here). For example, the operation *computePageCost()* (part of the *computeJob* interface) might collaborate with a **PricingTable** component that contains job pricing information. The *checkPriority()* operation (part of the *initiateJob* interface) might collaborate with a **JobQueue** component to determine the types and priorities of jobs currently awaiting production.

This elaboration activity is applied to every component defined as part of the architectural design. Once it is completed, further elaboration is applied to each attribute, operation, and interface. The data structures appropriate for each attribute must be specified. In addition, the algorithmic detail required to implement the processing logic associated with each operation is designed. This procedural design activity is discussed later in this chapter. Finally, the mechanisms required to implement the interface are designed. For OO software, this may encompass the description of all messaging that is required to effect communication between objects within the system.

1 In some cases, a component may contain a single class.

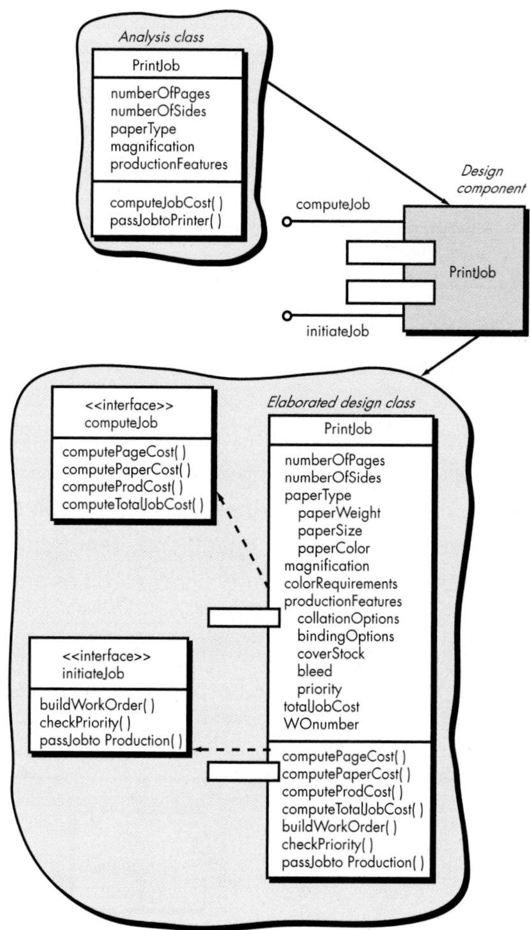

FIGURE 11.1
Elaboration of a design component

11.1.2 The Conventional View

In the context of conventional software engineering, a component is a functional element of a program that incorporates processing logic, the internal data structures that are required to implement the processing logic, and an interface that enables the component to be invoked and data to be passed to it. A conventional component, also called a *module,* resides within the software architecture and serves one of three important roles as: (1) a *control component* that coordinates the invocation of all other problem domain components, (2) a *problem domain component* that implements a complete or partial function that is required by the customer, or (3) an *infrastructure component* that is responsible for functions that support the processing required in the problem domain.

Like object-oriented components, conventional software components are derived from the analysis model. In this case, however, the data flow-oriented element of the analysis model serves as the basis for the derivation. Each transform (bubble) represented at the lowest levels of the data flow diagram (Chapter 8) is mapped (Section 10.6) into a module hierarchy. Control components (modules) reside near the top of the hierarchy (architecture), and problem domain components tend to reside toward the bottom of the hierarchy. To achieve effective modularity, design concepts like functional independence (Chapter 9) are applied as components are elaborated.

> "A complex system that works is invariably found to have evolved from a simple system that worked."
>
> **John Gall**

To illustrate this process of design elaboration for conventional components, we again consider software to be built for a sophisticated photocopying center. A set of data flow diagrams would be derived during analysis modeling. We'll assume that these are mapped (Section 10.6) into an architecture shown in Figure 11.2. Each box represents a software component. Note that the shaded boxes are equivalent in function to the operations defined for the **PrintJob** class discussed in Section 11.1.1. In this case, however, each operation is represented as a separate module that is invoked as shown in the figure. Other modules are used to control processing and are therefore control components.

During component-level design, each module in Figure 11.2 is elaborated. The module interface is defined explicitly. That is, each data or control object that flows

FIGURE 11.2

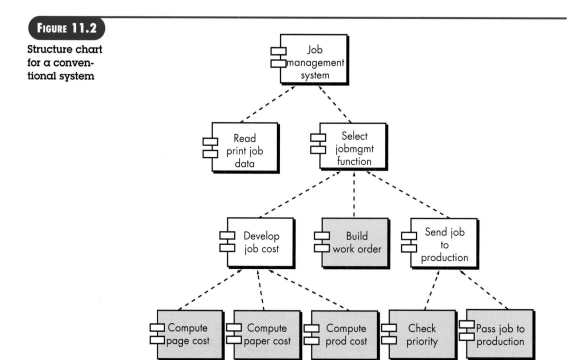

Structure chart for a conventional system

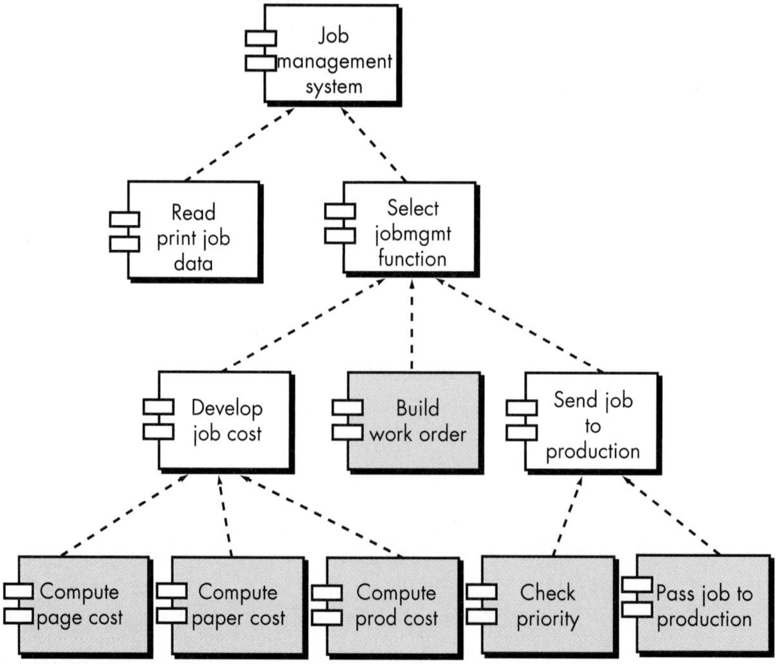

across the interface is represented. The data structures that are used internal to the module are defined. The algorithm that allows the module to accomplish its intended function is designed using the stepwise refinement approach discussed in Chapter 9. The behavior of the module is sometimes represented using a state diagram.

As the design for each software component is elaborated, the focus shifts to the design of specific data structures and procedural design to manipulate the data structures. However, don't forget the architecture that must house the components or the global data structures that may serve many components.

To illustrate this process, consider the module *ComputePageCost.* The intent of this module is to compute the printing cost per page based on specifications provided by the customer. Data required to perform this function are: **number of pages in the document, total number of documents to be produced, one- or two-side printing, color requirements, size requirements.** These data are passed to *ComputePageCost* via the module's interface. *ComputePageCost* uses these data to determine a page cost that is based on the size and complexity of the job—a function of all data passed to the module via the interface. Page cost is inversely proportional to the size of the job and directly proportional to the complexity of the job.

Figure 11.3 represents the component-level design using a modified UML notation. The *ComputePageCost* module accesses data by invoking the modules *getJob-Data,* which allows all relevant data to be passed to the component, and a database

FIGURE 11.3 Component-level design for *ComputePageCost*

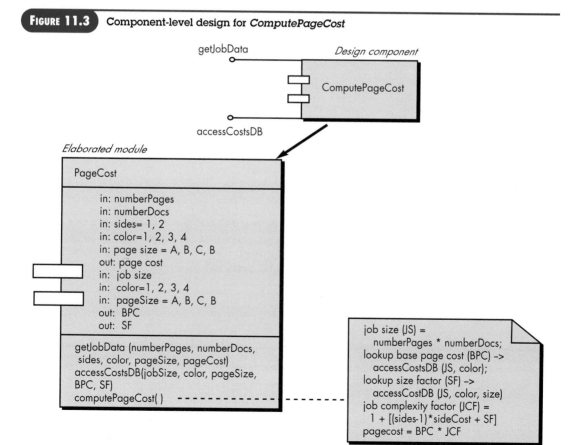

interface, *accessCostsDB,* which enables the module to access a database that contains all printing costs. As design continues, the *ComputePageCost* module is elaborated to provide algorithm and interface detail (Figure 11.3). Algorithm detail can be represented using the pseudocode text shown in the figure or with a UML activity diagram. The interfaces are represented as a collection of input and output data objects or items. Design elaboration continues until sufficient detail is provided to guide construction of the component.

11.1.3 A Process-Related View

The object-oriented and conventional views of component-level design presented in the preceding sections assume that the component is being designed from scratch. That is, the designer must create a new component based on specifications derived from the analysis model. There is, of course, another approach.

Over the past decade, the software engineering community has emphasized the need to build systems that make use of existing software components. In essence, a catalog of proven design or code-level components is made available to the software engineer as design work proceeds. As the software architecture is developed, components or design patterns are chosen from the catalog and used to populate the architecture. Because these components have been created with reusability in mind, a complete description of their interface, the function(s) they perform, and the communication and collaboration they require are all available to the designer. Component-based software engineering is discussed in considerable detail in Chapter 30.

SOFTWARE TOOLS

Middleware and Component-Based Software Engineering

One of the key elements that leads to the success or failure of CBSE is the availability of middleware. *Middleware* is a collection of infrastructure components that enable problem domain components to communicate with one another across a network or within a complex system. Three competing standards are available to software engineers who want to use component-based software engineering as their software process:

OMG CORBA (http://www.corba.org/).
Microsoft COM (http://www.microsoft.com/com/tech/complus.asp).
Sun JavaBeans (http://java.sun.com/products/ejb/).

The Web sites noted present a wide array of tutorials, white papers, tools, and general resources on these important middleware standards. Further information on CBSE can be found in Chapter 30.

11.2 Designing Class-Based Components

As we have already noted, component-level design draws on information developed as part of the analysis model (Chapter 8) and represented as part of the architectural model (Chapter 10). When an object-oriented software engineering approach is chosen, component-level design focuses on the elaboration of analysis classes (problem domain specific classes), and the definition and refinement of infrastructure classes.

The detailed description of the attributes, operations, and interfaces used by these classes is the design detail required as a precursor to the construction activity.

11.2.1 Basic Design Principles

Four basic design principles are applicable to component-level design and have been widely adopted when object-oriented software engineering is applied. The underlying motivation for the application of these principles is to create designs that are more amenable to change and to reduce the propagation of side effects when changes do occur. These principles can be used to guide the designer as each software component is developed.

The Open-Closed Principle (OCP). *"A module [component] should be open for extension but closed for modification"* [MAR00]. This statement seems to be a contradiction, but it represents one of the most important characteristics of a good component-level design. Stated simply, the designer should specify the component in a way that allows it to be extended (within the functional domain that it addresses) without the need to make internal (code or logic-level) modifications to the component itself. To accomplish this, the designer creates abstractions that serve as a buffer between the functionality that is likely to be extended and the design class itself.

For example, assume that the *SafeHome* security function makes use of a **Detector** class that must check the status of each type of security sensor. It is likely that as time passes, the number and types of security sensors will grow. If internal processing logic is implemented as a sequence of if-then-else constructs, each addressing a different sensor type, the addition of a new sensor type will require additional internal processing logic (still another if-then-else). This is a violation of OCP.

One way to accomplish OCP for the **Detector** class is illustrated in Figure 11.4. The *sensor* interface presents a consistent view of sensors to the **Detector** component. If a new type of sensor is added no change is required for the **Detector** class (component). The OCP is preserved.

FIGURE 11.4
Following the OCP

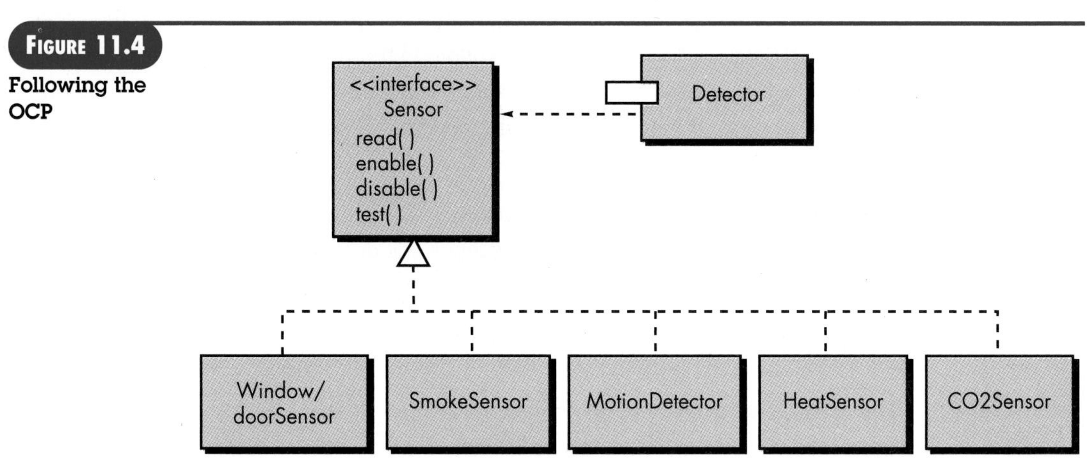

SAFEHOME

The OCP in Action

The scene: Vinod's cubicle.

The players: Vinod and Shakira—members of the *SafeHome* software engineering team.

The conversation:

Vinod: I just got a call from Doug [the team manager]. He says marketing wants to add a new sensor.

Shakira (smirking): Not again, jeez!

Vinod: Yeah . . . and you're not going to believe what these guys have come up with.

Shakira: Amaze me.

Vinod (laughing): They call it a doggie angst sensor.

Shakira: Say what?

Vinod: It's for people who leave their pets home in apartments or condos or houses that are close to one another. The dog starts to bark. The neighbor gets angry and complains. With this sensor, if the dog barks for more than, say, a minute, the sensor sets a special alarm mode that calls the owner on his or her cell phone.

Shakira: You're kidding me, right?

Vinod: Nope. Doug wants to know how much time it's going to take to add it to the security function.

Shakira (thinking a moment): Not much . . . look. [She shows Vinod Figure 11.4] We've isolated the actual sensor classes behind the **sensor** interface. As long as we have specs for the doggie sensor, adding it should be a piece of cake. Only thing I'll have to do is create an appropriate component . . . uh, class, for it. No change to the **Detector** component at all.

Vinod: So I'll tell Doug it's no big deal.

Shakira: Knowing Doug, he'll keep us focused and not deliver the doggie thing until the next release.

Vinod: That's not a bad thing, but can you implement now if he wants you to?

Shakira: Yeah, the way we designed the interface lets me do it with no hassle.

Vinod (thinking a moment): Have you ever heard of the "Open-Closed Principle"?

Shakira (shrugging): Never heard of it.

Vinod (smiling): Not a problem.

The Liskov Substitution Principle (LSP). *"Subclasses should be substitutable for their base classes"* [MAR00]. This design principle, originally proposed by Barbara Liskov [LIS88] suggests that a component that uses a base class should continue to function properly if a class derived from the base class is passed to the component instead. LSP demands that any class derived from a base class must honor any implied contract between the base class and the components that use it. In the context of this discussion, a "contract" is a *precondition* that must be true before the component uses a base class and a *post-condition* that should be true after the component uses a base class. When a designer creates *derived* classes, they must also conform to the pre- and post-conditions.

ADVICE

If you dispense with design and hack out code, just remember that code is the ultimate "concretion." You're violating DIP.

Dependency Inversion Principle (DIP). *"Depend on abstractions. Do not depend on concretions"* [MAR00]. As we have seen in the discussion of the OCP, abstractions are the place where a design can be extended without great complication. The more a component depends on other concrete components (rather than on abstractions such as an interface), the more difficult it will be to extend.

The Interface Segregation Principle (ISP). *"Many client-specific interfaces are better than one general purpose interface"*[MAR00]. There are many instances in which multiple client components use the operations provided by a server class. ISP suggests that the designer should create a specialized interface to serve each major category of clients. Only those operations that are relevant to a particular category of clients should be specified in the interface for that client. If multiple clients require the same operations, they should be specified in each of the specialized interfaces.

As an example, consider the **FloorPlan** class that is used for the *SafeHome* security and surveillance functions. For the security functions, **FloorPlan** is used only during configuration activities and uses the operations *placeDevice(), showDevice(), groupDevice(),* and *removeDevice()* to place, show, group, and remove sensors from the floor plan. The *SafeHome* surveillance function uses the four operations noted for security, but also requires special operations to manage cameras: *showFOV()* and *showDeviceID().* Hence, ISP suggests that client components from the two *SafeHome* functions have specialized interfaces defined for them. The interface for security would encompass only the operations *placeDevice(), showDevice(), groupDevice(),* and *removeDevice().* The interface for surveillance would incorporate the operations *placeDevice(), showDevice(), groupDevice(),* and *removeDevice(), showFOV(),* and *showDeviceID().*

Although component-level design principles provide useful guidance, components themselves do not exist in a vacuum. In many cases, individual components or classes are organized into subsystems or packages. It is reasonable to ask how this packaging activity should occur. Exactly how should components be organized as the design proceeds? Martin [MAR00] suggests additional packaging principles that are applicable to component-level design:

Designing components for reuse requires more than good technical design. It also requires effective configuration control mechanisms (Chapter 27).

The Release Reuse Equivalency Principle (REP). *"The granule of reuse is the granule of release"* [MAR00]. When classes or components are designed for reuse, there is an implicit contract that is established between the developer of the reusable entity and the people who will use it. The developer commits to establish a release control system that supports and maintains older versions of the entity while the users slowly upgrade to the most current version. Rather than addressing each class individually, it is often advisable to group reusable classes into packages that can be managed and controlled as newer versions evolve.

The Common Closure Principle (CCP). *"Classes that change together belong together"* [MAR00]. Classes should be packaged cohesively. That is, when classes are packaged as part of a design, they should address the same functional or behavioral area. When some characteristic of that area must change, it is likely that only those classes within the package will require modification. This leads to more effective change control and release management.

The Common Reuse Principle (CRP). *"Classes that aren't reused together should not be grouped together"* [MAR00]. When one or more classes with a package changes, the release number of the package changes. All other classes or packages that rely on the package that has been changed must now update to the most recent release of the package and be tested to ensure that the new release operates without incident. If classes are not grouped cohesively, it is possible that a class with no relationship to other classes within a package is changed. This will precipitate unnecessary integration and testing. For this reason, only classes that are reused together should be included within a package.

11.2.2 Component-Level Design Guidelines

In addition to the principles discussed in Section 11.2.1, a set of pragmatic design guidelines can be applied as component-level design proceeds. These guidelines apply to components, their interfaces, and the dependencies and inheritance characteristics that have an impact on the resultant design. Ambler [AMB02] suggests the following guidelines:

? What should we consider when we name components?

Components. Naming conventions should be established for components that are specified as part of the architectural model and then refined and elaborated as part of the component-level model. Architectural component names should be drawn from the problem domain and should have meaning to all stakeholders who view the architectural model. For example, the class name **FloorPlan** is meaningful to everyone reading it regardless of technical background. On the other-hand, infrastructure components or elaborated component-level classes should be named to reflect implementation-specific meaning. If a linked list is to be managed as part of the **FloorPlan** implementation, the operation *manageList()* is appropriate, even if a nontechnical person might misinterpret it.[2]

It is also worthwhile to use stereotypes to help identify the nature of components at the detailed design level. For example, **<<infrastructure>>** might be used to identify an infrastructure component; **<<database>>** could be used to identify a database that services one or more design classes or the entire system; **<<table>>** could be used to identify a table within a database.

Interfaces. Interfaces provide important information about communication and collaboration (as well as helping us to achieve the OCP). However, unfettered representation of interfaces tends to complicate component diagrams. Ambler [AMB02] recommends that (1) lollipop representation of an interface should be used in lieu of the more formal UML box and dashed arrow approach, when diagrams grow complex; (2) for consistency, interfaces should flow from the left-hand side of the component box; (3) only those interfaces that are relevant to the component under consideration should be shown, even if other interfaces are available. These recommendations are intended to simplify the visual nature of UML component diagrams.

Dependencies and inheritance. For improved readability, it is a good idea to model dependencies from left to right and inheritance from bottom (derived classes)

---

2 It is unlikely that someone from marketing or the customer organization (a nontechnical type) would examine detailed design information.

FIGURE 11.5
Layer cohesion

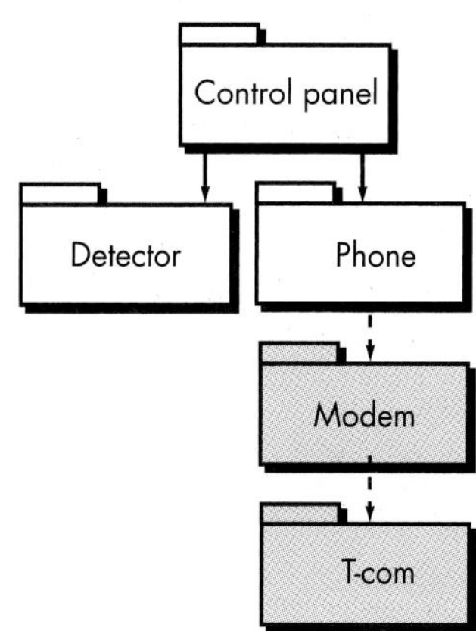

to top (base classes). In addition, component interdependencies should be represented via interfaces, rather than by representation of a component-to-component dependency. Following the philosophy of the OCP, this will help to make the system more maintainable.

11.2.3 Cohesion

In Chapter 9, we described cohesion as the "single-mindedness" of a component. Within the context of component-level design for object-oriented systems, *cohesion* implies that a component or class encapsulates only attributes and operations that are closely related to one another and to the class or component itself. Lethbridge and Laganiére [LET01] define a number of different types of cohesion (listed in order of the level of the cohesion[3]):

Functional. Exhibited primarily by operations, this level of cohesion occurs when a module performs one and only one computation and then returns a result.

ADVICE

Although an understanding of the various levels of cohesion is instructive, it is more important to be aware of the general concept as you design components. Keep cohesion as high as is possible.

Layer. Exhibited by packages, components, and classes, this type of cohesion occurs when a higher layer accesses the services of a lower layer, but lower layers do not access higher layers. Consider for example, the *SafeHome* security function requirement to make an outgoing phone call if an alarm is sensed. It might be possible to define a set of layered packages as shown in Figure 11.5. The shaded packages contain infrastructure components. Access is from the control panel package downward.

Communicational. All operations that access the same data are defined within one class. In general, such classes focus solely on the data in question, accessing and storing it.

3 In general, the higher the level of cohesion, the easier the component is to implement, test, and maintain.

Classes and components that exhibit functional, layer, and communicational cohesion are relatively easy to implement, test, and maintain. The designer should strive to achieve these levels of cohesion. However, there are many instances when the following lower levels of cohesion are encountered:

Sequential. Components or operations are grouped in a manner that allows the first to provide input to the next and so on. The intent is to implement a sequence of operations.

Procedural. Components or operations are grouped in a manner that allows one to be invoked immediately after the preceding one was invoked, even when there is no data passed between them.

Temporal. Operations that are performed to reflect a specific behavior or state, e.g., an operation performed at start-up or all operations performed when an error is detected.

Utility. Components, classes, or operations that exist within the same category but are otherwise unrelated are grouped together. For example, a class called **Statistics** exhibits utility cohesion if it contains all attributes and operations required to compute six simple statistical measures.

These levels of cohesion are less desirable and should be avoided when design alternatives exist. It is important to note, however, that pragmatic design and implementation issues sometimes force a designer to opt for lower levels of cohesion.

SAFEHOME

Cohesion in Action

The scene: Jamie's cubicle.

The players: Jamie and Ed—members of the *SafeHome* software engineering team who are working on the surveillance function.

The conversation:

Ed: I have a first-cut design of the camera component.

Jamie: Wanna do a quick review?

Ed: I guess . . . but really, I'd like your input on something.

(Jamie gestures for him to continue.)

Ed: We originally defined five operations for **camera.** Look . . . [shows Jamie the list]

determineType() tells me the type of camera.

translateLocation() allows me to move the camera around the floor plan.

displayID() gets the camera ID and displays it near the camera icon.

displayView() shows me the field of view of the camera graphically.

displayZoom() shows me the magnification of the camera graphically.

Ed: I've designed each separately, and they're pretty simple operations. So I thought it might be a good idea to combine all of the display operations into just one that's called *displayCamera()*—it'll show the ID, the view, and the zoom. Whaddaya think?

Jamie (grimacing): Not sure that's such a good idea.

Ed (frowning): Why? All of these little ops can cause headaches.

Jamie: The problem with combining them is we lose cohesion. You know, the *displayCamera()* op won't be single-minded.

Ed (mildly exasperated): So what? The whole thing will be less than 100 source lines, max. It'll be easier to implement, I think.

Jamie: And what if marketing decides to change the way that we represent the view field?

Ed: I'll just jump into the *displayCamera()* op and make the mod.

Jamie: What about side effects?

Ed: Whaddaya mean?

Jamie: Well, say you make the change but inadvertently create a problem with the ID display.

Ed: I wouldn't be that sloppy.

Jamie: Maybe not, but what if some support person two years from now has to make the mod. He might not understand the op as well as you do and, who knows, he might be sloppy.

Ed: So you're against it?

Jamie: You're the designer . . . it's your decision . . . just be sure you understand the consequences of low cohesion.

Ed (thinking a moment): Maybe we'll go with separate display ops.

Jamie: Good decision.

11.2.4 Coupling

In earlier discussions of analysis and design, we noted that communication and collaboration are essential elements of any object-oriented system. There is, however, a darker side to this important (and necessary) characteristic. As the amount of communication and collaboration increases (i.e., as the degree of "connectedness" between classes grows), the complexity of the system also increases. And as complexity rises, the difficulty of implementing, testing, and maintaining software also increases.

Coupling is a qualitative measure of the degree to which classes are connected to one another. As classes (and components) become more interdependent, coupling increases. An important objective in component-level design is to keep coupling as low as is possible.

Class coupling can manifest itself in a variety of ways. Lethbridge and Laganiére [LET01] define the following coupling categories:

As the design for each software component is elaborated, the focus shifts to the design of specific data structures and procedural designs to manipulate the data structures. However, don't forget the architecture that must house the components or the global data structures that may serve many components.

Content coupling. Occurs when one component "surreptitiously modifies data that is internal to another component" [LET01]. This violates information hiding—a basic design concept.

Common coupling. Occurs when a number of components all make use of a global variable. Although this is sometimes necessary (e.g., for establishing default values that are applicable throughout an application), common coupling can lead to uncontrolled error propagation and unforeseen side effects when changes are made.

Control coupling. Occurs when *operation A()* invokes *operation B()* and passes a control flag to *B*. The control flag then "directs" logical flow within *B*. The problem with this form of coupling is that an unrelated change in *B* can result in the necessity to change the meaning of the control flag that *A* passes. If this is overlooked, an error will result.

Stamp coupling. Occurs when **ClassB** is declared as a type for an argument of an operation of **ClassA.** Because **ClassB** is now a part of the definition of **ClassA,** modifying the system becomes more complex.

Data coupling. Occurs when operations pass long strings of data arguments. The "bandwidth" of communication between classes and components grows and the complexity of the interface increases. Testing and maintenance are more difficult.

Routine call coupling. Occurs when one operation invokes another. This level of coupling is common and is often quite necessary. However, it does increase the connectedness of a system.

Type use coupling. Occurs when component **A** uses a data type defined in component **B** (e.g., this occurs whenever "a class declares an instance variable or a local variable as having another class for its type" [LET01]). If the type definition changes, every component that uses the definition must also change.

Inclusion or import coupling. Occurs when component **A** imports or includes a package or the content of component **B.**

External coupling. Occurs when a component communicates or collaborates with infrastructure components (e.g., operating system functions, database capability, telecommunication functions). Although this type of coupling is necessary, it should be limited to a small number of components or classes within a system.

Software must communicate internally and externally. Therefore, coupling is a fact of life. However, the designer should work to reduce coupling whenever possible and understand the ramifications of high coupling when it cannot be avoided.

SafeHome

Coupling in Action

The scene: Shakira's cubicle.

The players: Vinod and Shakira—members of the *SafeHome* software engineering team who are working on the security function.

The conversation:

Shakira: I had what I thought was a great idea . . . then I thought about it a little, and it seemed like a not-so-great idea. I finally rejected it, but I just thought I'd run it by you.

Vinod: Sure, what's the idea?

Shakira: Well, each of the sensors recognizes an alarm condition of some kind, right?

Vinod (smiling): That's why we call them sensors, Shakira.

Shakira (exasperated): Sarcasm, Vinod. You've got to work on your interpersonal skills.

Vinod: You were saying?

Shakira: Okay, anyway, I figured . . . why not create an operation within each sensor object called *makeCall()* that would collaborate directly with the **OutgoingCall** component, well, with an interface to the **OutgoingCall** component.

Vinod (pensive): You mean rather than having that collaboration occur out of a component like **ControlPanel** or something?

Shakira: Yeah . . . but then I said to myself, that means that every sensor object will be connected to the **OutgoingCall** component, and that means that it's indirectly coupled to the outside world and . . . well, I just thought it made things complicated.

Vinod: I agree. In this case, it's a better idea to let the sensor interface pass info to the **ControlPanel** and let it initiate the outgoing call. Besides, different sensors might result in different phone numbers. You don't want the sensor to store that information because if it changes . . .

Shakira: It just didn't feel right.

Vinod: Design heuristics for coupling tell us it's not right.

Shakira: Whatever. . . .

11.3 Conducting Component-Level Design

Earlier in this chapter we noted that component-level design is elaborative in nature. The designer must transform information from the analysis and architectural models into a design representation that provides sufficient detail to guide the construction (coding and testing) activity. The following steps represent a typical task set for component-level design, when it is applied for an object-oriented system.

Step 1. Identify all design classes that correspond to the problem domain. Using the analysis and architectural models, each analysis class and architectural component is elaborated as described in Section 11.1.1.

If you're working in a non-OO environment, the first three steps focus on refinement of data objects and processing functions (transforms) identified as part of the analysis model.

Step 2. Identify all design classes that correspond to the infrastructure domain. These classes are not described in the analysis model and are often missing from the architecture model, but they must be described at this point. As we have noted earlier, classes and components in this category include GUI components, operating system components, object and data management components, and others.

Step 3. Elaborate all design classes that are not acquired as reusable components. Elaboration requires that all interfaces, attributes, and operations necessary to implement the class be described in detail. Design heuristics (e.g., component cohesion and coupling) must be considered as this task is conducted.

Step 3a. Specify message details when classes or components collaborate. The analysis model makes use of a collaboration diagram to show how analysis classes collaborate with one another. As component-level design proceeds, it is sometimes useful to show the details of these collaborations by specifying the structure of messages that are passed between objects within a system. Although this design activity is optional, it can be used as a precursor to the specification of interfaces that show how components within the system communicate and collaborate.

Figure 11.6 illustrates a simple collaboration diagram for the printing system discussed earlier. Three objects, **ProductionJob, WorkOrder,** and **JobQueue,** collaborate to prepare a print job for submission to the production stream. Messages are passed between objects as illustrated by the arrows in the figure. During analysis modeling the messages are specified as shown in the figure. However, as design

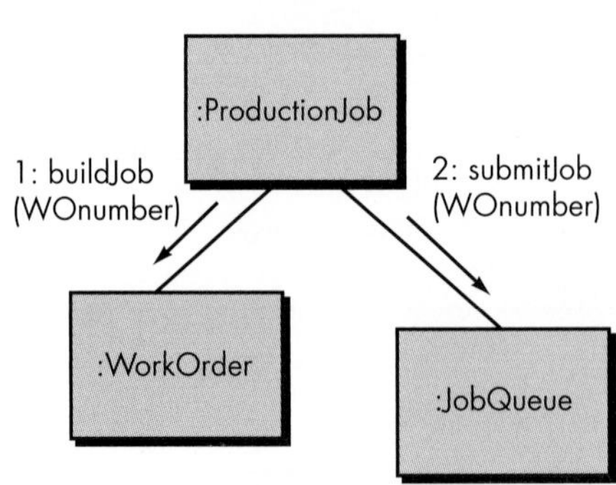

FIGURE 11.6
Collaboration diagram with messaging

proceeds, each message is elaborated by expanding its syntax in the following manner [BEN02]:

> **[guard condition] sequence expression (return value) :=**
> **message name (argument list)**

where a **[guard condition]** is written in Object Constraint Language (OCL)[4] and specifies any set of conditions that must be met before the message can be sent; **sequence expression** is an integer value (or other ordering indicator, e.g., 3.1.2) that indicates the sequential order in which a message is sent; **(return value)** is the name of the information that is returned by the operation invoked by the message; **message name** identifies the operation that is to be invoked, and **(argument list)** is the list of attributes that are passed to the operation.

Step 3b. Identify appropriate interfaces for each component. Within the context of component-level design, a UML interface is "a group of externally visible (i.e., public) operations. The interface contains no internal structure, it has no attributes, no associations. . . ." [BEB02]. Stated more formally, an interface is the equivalent of an abstract class that provides a controlled connection between design classes. The elaboration of interfaces is illustrated in Figure 11.1. In essence, operations defined for the design class are categorized into one or more abstract classes. Every operation within the abstract class (the interface) should be cohesive; that is, it should exhibit processing that focuses on one limited function or subfunction.

Referring to Figure 11.1, it can be argued that the interface *initiateJob* does not exhibit sufficient cohesion. In actuality, it performs three different subfunctions: building a work order, checking job priority, and passing a job to production. The interface design should be refactored. One approach might be to reexamine the design classes and define a new class **WorkOrder** that would take care of all activities associated with the assembly of a work order. The operation *buildWorkOrder()* becomes a part

4 OCL is discussed briefly in Section 11.4 and in Chapter 28.

FIGURE 11.7 Refactoring interfaces and class definitions for PrintJob

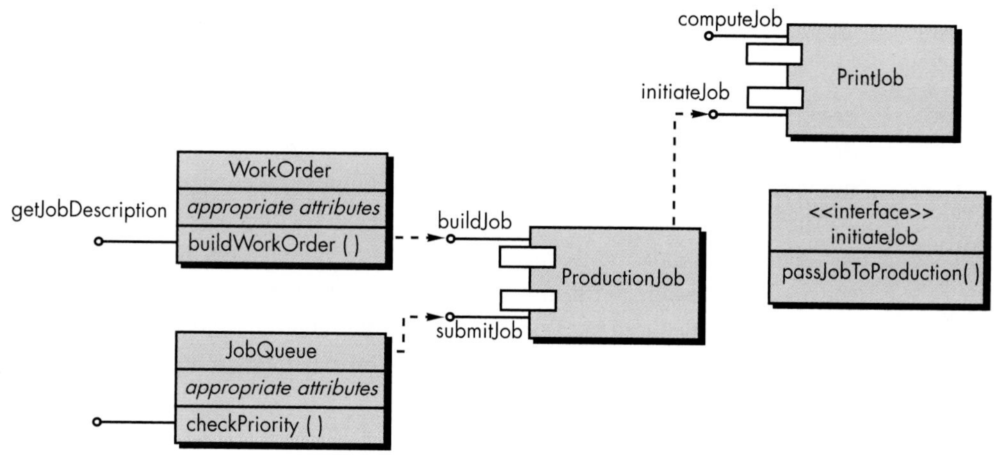

of that class. Similarly, we might define a class **JobQueue** that would incorporate the operation *checkPriority().* A class **ProductionJob** would encompass all information associated with a production job to be passed to the production facility. The interface *initiateJob* would then take the form shown in Figure 11.7. The interface *initiateJob* is now cohesive, focusing on one function. The interfaces associated with **ProductionJob, WorkOrder,** and **JobQueue** are similarly single-minded.

Step 3c. Elaborate attributes and define data types and data structures required to implement them. In general, data structures and types used to describe attributes are defined within the context of the programming language that is to be used for implementation. UML defines an attribute's data type using the following syntax:

name : type-expression = initial-value {property string}

where **name** is the attribute name and **type expression** is the data type; **initial value** is the value that the attribute takes when an object is created; and **property-string** defines a property or characteristic of the attribute.

During the first component-level design iteration, attributes are normally described by name. Referring once again to Figure 11.1, the attribute list for **PrintJob** lists only the names of the attributes. However, as design elaboration proceeds, each attribute is defined using the UML attribute format noted. For example, **paperType-weight** is defined in the following manner:

paperType-weight: string = "A" { contains 1 of 4 values - A, B, C, or D}

which defines **paperType-weight** as a string variable initialized to the value A that can take on one of four values from the set {A,B,C,D}.

If an attribute appears repeatedly across a number of design classes, and it has a relatively complex structure, it is best to create a separate class to accommodate the attribute.

Step 3d. Describe processing flow within each operation in detail. This may be accomplished using a programming language-based pseudocode (Section 11.5.5) or with a UML activity diagram. Each software component is elaborated through a number of iterations that apply the stepwise refinement concept (Chapter 9).

The first iteration defines each operation as part of the design class. In every case, the operation should be characterized in a way that ensures high cohesion; that is, the operation should perform a single targeted function or subfunction. The next iteration does little more than expand the operation name. For example, the operation *computePaperCost()* noted in Figure 11.1 can be expanded in the following manner:

```
computePaperCost (weight, size, color): numeric
```

This indicates that *computePaperCost()* requires the attributes **weight, size** and **color** as input and returns a value that is numeric (actually a dollar value) as output.

> "If I had more time, I would have written a shorter letter."
>
> **Blaise Pascal**

Use stepwise elaboration as you refine the component design. Always ask, "Is there a way this can be simplified and yet still accomplish the same result?"

If the algorithm required to implement *computePaperCost()* is simple and widely understood, no further design elaboration may be necessary. The software engineer who does the coding will provide the detail necessary to implement the operation. However, if the algorithm is more complex or arcane, further design elaboration is required at this stage. Figure 11.8 depicts a UML activity diagram for *computePaperCost().* When activity diagrams are used for component-level design specification, they are generally represented at a level of abstraction that is somewhat higher than source code. An alternative approach—the use of pseudocode for design specification—is discussed later in this chapter.

Step 4. Describe persistent data sources (databases and files) and identify the classes required to manage them. Databases and files normally transcend the design description of an individual component. In most cases, these persistent data stores are initially specified as part of architectural design. However, as design elaboration proceeds, it is often useful to provide additional detail about the structure and organization of these persistent data sources.

Step 5. Develop and elaborate behavioral representations for a class or component. UML state diagrams were used as part of the analysis model to represent the externally observable behavior of the system and the more localized behavior of individual analysis classes. During component-level design, it is sometimes necessary to model the behavior of a design class.

FIGURE 11.8 **UML activity diagram for *computePaperCost()***

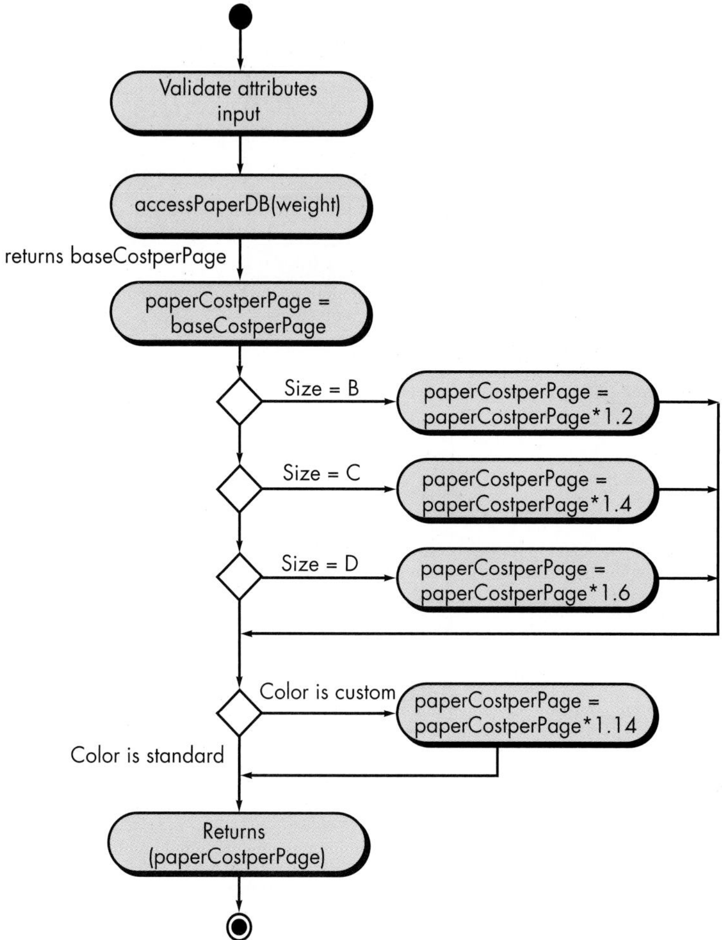

The dynamic behavior of an object (an instantiation of a design class as the program executes) is affected by events that are external to it and the current state (mode of behavior) of the object. To understand the dynamic behavior of an object, the designer must examine all use-cases that are relevant to the design class throughout its life. These use-cases provide information that helps the designer to delineate the events that affect the object and the states in which the object resides as time passes and events occur. The transitions between states (driven by events) is represented using a UML statechart [BEN02] as illustrated in Figure 11.9.

The transition from one state (represented by a rectangle with rounded corners) to another occurs as a consequence of an event that takes the form:

Event-name (parameter-list) [guard-condition] / action expression

FIGURE 11.9 Statechart fragment for the PrintJob class

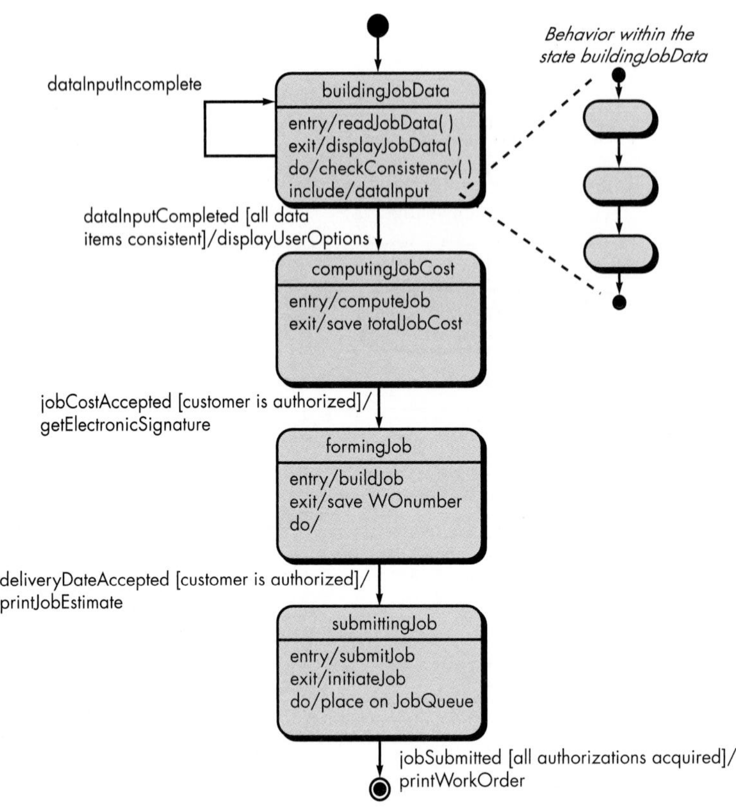

where **event-name** identifies the event; **parameter-list** incorporates data that are associated with the event; **guard-condition** is written in Object Constraint Language (OCL) and specifies a condition that must be met before the event can occur, and **action expression** defines an action that occurs as the transition takes place.

Referring to Figure 11.9, each state may define *entry/* and *exit/* actions that occur as transitions into and out of the state occur. In most cases, these actions correspond to operations that are relevant to the class that is being modeled. The *do/* indicator provides a mechanism for indicating activities that occur while in the state and the *include/* indicator provides a means for elaborating the behavior by embedding more statechart detail within the definition of a state.

It is important to note that the behavioral model often contains information that is not immediately obvious in other design models. For example, careful examination of the statechart in Figure 11.9 indicates that the dynamic behavior of the **PrintJob** class is contingent upon two customer approvals as costs and schedule data for the print job are derived. Without approvals (the guard condition ensures that the customer is authorized to approve) the print job cannot be submitted because there is no way to reach the *submittingJob* state.

Step 6. Elaborate deployment diagrams to provide additional implementation detail. Deployment diagrams (Chapter 9) are used as part of architectural design and are represented in descriptor form. In this form, major system functions (often represented as subsystems) are represented within the context of the computing environment that will house them.

During component-level design, deployment diagrams can be elaborated to represent the location of key packages of components. However, components generally are not represented individually within a component diagram. The reason for this is to avoid diagrammatic complexity. In some cases, deployment diagrams are elaborated into instance form at this time. This means that the specific hardware and operating system environment(s) that will be used is (are) specified and the location of component packages within this environment is indicated.

Step 7. Factor every component-level design representation and always consider alternatives. Throughout this book, we have emphasized that design is an iterative process. The first component-level model you create will not be as complete, consistent, or accurate as the *n*th iteration you apply to the model. It is essential to refactor as design work is conducted.

In addition, a designer should not suffer from tunnel vision. There are always alternative design solutions, and the best designers consider all (or most) of them before settling on the final design model. Develop alternatives and consider each carefully, using the design principles and concepts presented in Chapters 5 and 9 and in this chapter.

11.4 Object Constraint Language

The wide variety of diagrams available as part of UML provide a designer with a rich set of representational forms for the design model. However, graphical representations are often not enough. The designer needs a mechanism for explicitly and formally representing information that constrains some element of the design model. It is possible, of course, to describe constraints in a natural language such as English, but this approach invariably leads to inconsistency and ambiguity. For this reason, a more formal language—one that draws on set theory and formal specification languages (Chapter 28) but has the somewhat less mathematical syntax of a programming language—seems appropriate.

OCL provides a formal grammar and syntax for describing component-level design elements.

The *Object Constraint Language* (OCL) complements UML by allowing a software engineer to use a formal grammar and syntax to construct unambiguous statements about various design model elements (e.g., classes and objects, events, messages, interfaces). The simplest OCL language statements are constructed in four parts: (1) a *context* that defines the limited situation in which the statement is valid; (2) a *property* that represents some characteristics of the context (e.g., if the context is a class, a property might be an attribute); (3) an *operation* (e.g., arithmetic, set-oriented) that manipulates or qualifies a property; and (4) *keywords* (e.g., **if, then, else, and, or, not, implies**) that are used to specify conditional expressions.

As a simple example of an OCL expression, consider the guard condition placed on the *jobCostAccepted* event that causes a transition between the states **computingJobCost** and **formingJob** within the statechart diagram for the **PrintJob** class (Figure 11.9). In the diagram, the guard condition is expressed in natural language and implies that authorization can only occur if the customer is authorized to approve the cost of the job. In OCL, the expression may take the form:

```
customer
   self.authorizationAuthority = 'yes'
```

where a Boolean attribute, **authorizationAuthority,** of the class (actually a specific instance of the class) named **Customer** must be set to **yes** for the guard condition to be satisfied.

WebRef
The complete OCL specification can be downloaded from **www.omg.org.**

As the design model is created, there are often instances (e.g., Section 11.2.1) in which pre- or post-conditions must be satisfied prior to completion of some action specified by the design. OCL provides a powerful tool for specifying pre- and post conditions in a formal manner. As an example, consider an extension to the print shop system (discussed throughout this chapter) in which the customer provides an upper cost bound for the print job and a "drop-dead" delivery date at the same time as other print job characteristics are specified. If cost and delivery estimates exceed these bounds, the job is not submitted and the customer must be notified. In OCL, a set of pre- and post-conditions may be specified in the following manner:

```
context PrintJob::validate(upperCostBound : Integer, custDeliveryReq :
  Integer)
   pre: upperCostBound > 0
      and custDeliveryReq > 0
      and self.jobAuthorization = 'no'
   post: if self.totalJobCost <= upperCostBound
         and self.deliveryDate <= custDeliveryReq
      then
         self.jobAuthorization = 'yes'
      endif
```

This OCL statement defines an *invariant*—conditions that must exist prior to (**pre**) and after (**post**) some behavior. Initially, a precondition establishes that bounding cost and delivery date must be specified by the customer, and authorization must be set to "no." After costs and delivery are determined, the post-condition is applied. It should also be noted that the expression: **self.jobAuthorization = 'yes'** is not assigning the value "yes," but is declaring that the **jobAuthorization** must have been set to "yes" by the time the operation finishes.

A complete description of OCL is beyond the scope of this book.[5] Interested readers should see [WAR98] and [OMG01] for additional detail.

SOFTWARE TOOLS

UML/OCL

Objective: A wide variety of UML tools are available to assist the designer at all levels of design. Some of these tools provide OCL support.

Mechanics: Tools in this category enable a designer to create all UML diagrams that are necessary to build a complete design model. More importantly, many tools provide solid syntax and semantic checking, and version and change control management (Chapter 27). When OCL capability is provided, tools enable the designer to create OCL expressions and, in some cases, "compile" them for various types of evaluation and analysis.

Representative Tools[6]

ArgoUML, distributed at Tigress.org (http://argouml.tigris.org/), supports the complete UML and OCL and includes a variety of design assist tools that go beyond the generation of UML diagrams and OCL expressions.

Dresden OCL toolkit, developed by Frank Finger at the Dresden University of Technology (http://dresden-ocl.sourceforge.net/), is a toolkit based on an OCL compiler encompassing several modules which parse, type check, and normalize OCL constraints.

OCL parser, developed by IBM (http://www-3.ibm.com/software/ad/library/standards/ocl-download.html), is written in Java and is available for free to the object-oriented community to encourage the use of OCL with UML modelers.

11.5 DESIGNING CONVENTIONAL COMPONENTS

The foundations of component-level design for conventional software components[7] were formed in the early 1960s and were solidified with the work of Edsgar Dijkstra and his colleagues ([BOH66], [DIJ65], [DIJ76]). In the late 1960s, Dijkstra and others proposed the use of a set of constrained logical constructs from which any program could be formed. The constructs emphasized "maintenance of functional domain." That is, each construct had a predictable logical structure, was entered at the top and exited at the bottom, enabling a reader to follow procedural flow more easily.

---

5 However, further discussion of OCL (presented in the context of formal methods) is presented in Chapter 28.

6 Tools noted here do not represent an endorsement, but rather a sampling of tools in this category. In most cases, tool names are trademarked by their respective developers.

7 A conventional software component implements an element of processing that addresses a function or subfunction in the problem domain or some capability in the infrastructure domain. Often called *modules, procedures,* or *subroutines,* conventional components do not encapsulate data in the way that OO components do.

Structured programming is a design technique that constrains logic flow to three constructs: sequence, condition, and repetition.

The constructs are sequence, condition, and repetition. *Sequence* implements processing steps that are essential in the specification of any algorithm. *Condition* provides the facility for selected processing based on some logical occurrence, and *repetition* allows for looping. These three constructs are fundamental to *structured programming*—an important component-level design technique.

The structured constructs were proposed to limit the procedural design of software to a small number of predictable operations. Complexity metrics (Chapter 15) indicate that the use of the structured constructs reduces program complexity and thereby enhances readability, testability, and maintainability. The use of a limited number of logical constructs also contributes to a human understanding process that psychologists call *chunking.* To understand this process, consider the way in which you are reading this page. You do not read individual letters but rather recognize patterns or chunks of letters that form words or phrases. The structured constructs are logical chunks that allow a reader to recognize procedural elements of a module, rather than reading the design or code line by line. Understanding is enhanced when readily recognizable logical patterns are encountered.

11.5.1 Graphical Design Notation

We have discussed the UML activity diagram earlier in this chapter and in Chapters 7 and 8. The activity diagram allows a designer to represent sequence, condition, and repetition—all elements of structured programming—and is the descendent of an earlier pictorial design representation (still used widely) called a *flowchart.*

A flowchart, like an activity diagram, is quite simple pictorially. A box is used to indicate a processing step. A diamond represents a logical condition, and arrows show the flow of control. Figure 11.10 illustrates three structured constructs. The

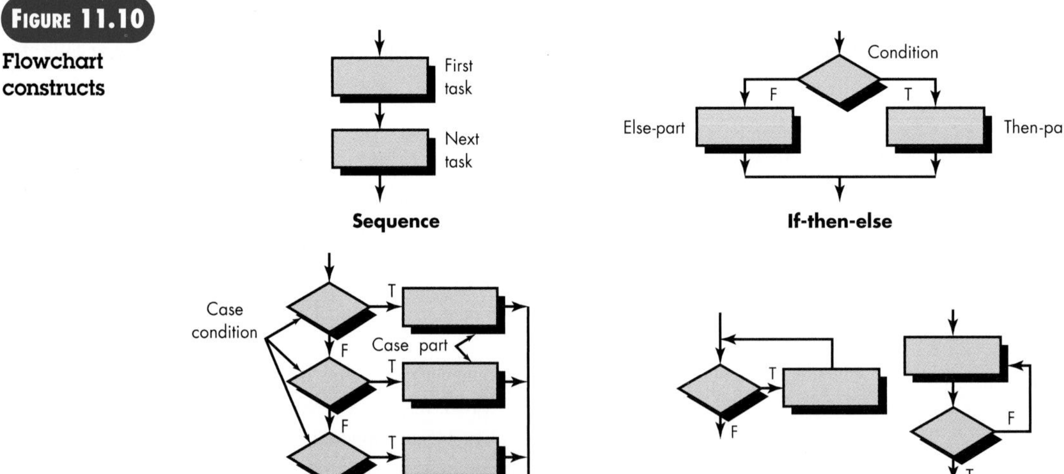

FIGURE 11.10
Flowchart constructs

sequence is represented as two processing boxes connected by a line (arrow) of control. *Condition,* also called *if-then-else,* is depicted as a decision diamond that if true, causes *then-part* processing to occur, and if false, invokes *else-part* processing. *Repetition* is represented using two slightly different forms. The *do while* tests a condition and executes a loop task repetitively as long as the condition holds true. A *repeat until* executes the loop task first, then tests a condition and repeats the task until the condition fails. The *selection* (or *select-case*) construct shown in the figure is actually an extension of the *if-then-else.* A parameter is tested by successive decisions until a true condition occurs and a *case part* processing path is executed.

Structured programming constructs should make it easier to understand the design. If using them without "violation" introduces unnecessary complexity, it is okay to violate.

In general, the dogmatic use of only the structured constructs can introduce inefficiency when an escape from a set of nested loops or nested conditions is required. More importantly, additional complication of all logical tests along the path of escape can cloud software control flow, increase the possibility of error, and have a negative impact on readability and maintainability. What can we do?

The designer is left with two options: (1) The procedural representation is redesigned so that the "escape branch" is not required at a nested location in the flow of control or (2) the structured constructs are violated in a controlled manner; that is, a constrained branch out of the nested flow is designed. Option 1 is obviously the ideal approach, but option 2 can be accommodated without violating of the spirit of structured programming.

11.5.2 Tabular Design Notation

Use a decision table when a complex set of conditions and actions are encountered within a component.

In many software applications, a module may be required to evaluate a complex combination of conditions and select appropriate actions based on these conditions. *Decision tables* [HUR83] provide a notation that translates actions and conditions (described in a processing narrative) into a tabular form. The table is difficult to misinterpret and may even be used as a machine readable input to a table driven algorithm.

A decision table is divided into four quadrants. The upper left-hand quadrant contains a list of all conditions. The lower left-hand quadrant contains a list of all actions that are possible based on combinations of conditions. The right-hand quadrants form a matrix that indicates condition combinations and the corresponding actions that will occur for a specific combination. Therefore, each column of the matrix may be interpreted as a *processing rule.* The following steps are applied to develop a decision table:

? How do I build a decision table?

1. List all actions that can be associated with a specific procedure (or module).
2. List all conditions (or decisions made) during execution of the procedure.
3. Associate specific sets of conditions with specific actions, eliminating impossible combinations of conditions; alternatively, develop every possible permutation of conditions.
4. Define rules by indicating what action(s) occurs for a set of conditions.

FIGURE 11.11

Resultant decision table

	Rules					
Conditions	1	2	3	4	5	6
Regular customer	T	T				
Silver customer			T	T		
Gold customer					T	T
Special discount	F	T	F	T	F	T
Actions						
No discount	✓					
Apply 8 percent discount			✓	✓		
Apply 15 percent discount					✓	✓
Apply additional *x* percent discount		✓		✓		✓

To illustrate the use of a decision table, consider the following excerpt from an informal use-case that has just been proposed for the print shop system:

> Three types of customers are defined: a regular customer, a silver customer, and a gold customer (these types are assigned by the amount of business the customer does with the print shop over a 12-month period). A regular customer receives normal print rates and delivery. A silver customer gets an 8 percent discount on all quotes and is placed ahead of all regular customers in the job queue. A gold customer gets a 15 percent reduction in quoted prices and is placed ahead of both regular and silver customers in the job queue. A special discount of *x* percent in addition to other discounts can be applied to any customer's quote at the discretion of management.

Figure 11.11 illustrates a decision table representation of the preceding informal use-case. Each of the six rules indicates one of six viable conditions. As a general rule, the decision table can be used effectively to supplement other procedural design notation.

11.5.3 Program Design Language

Program design language (PDL), also called *structured English* or *pseudocode,* is "a pidgin language in that it uses the vocabulary of one language (i.e., English) and the overall syntax of another (i.e., a structured programming language)" [CAI75]. In this chapter, PDL is used as a generic reference for a design language.

At first glance PDL may look like a programming language. The difference between PDL and a real programming language lies in the use of narrative text (e.g., English) embedded directly within PDL statements. Given the use of narrative text embedded directly into a syntactical structure, PDL cannot be compiled. However, tools can translate PDL into a programming language "skeleton" and/or a graphical representation (e.g., a flowchart) of design. These tools also produce nesting maps, a design operation index, cross-reference tables, and a variety of other information.

It's a good idea to use your programming language as the basis for PDL. You can then generate a code skeleton mixed with narrative text as you develop the design.

A program design language may be a simple transposition of a language such as Ada, C, or Java. Basic PDL syntax should include constructs for component definition, interface description, data declaration, block structuring, condition constructs, repetition constructs, and I/O constructs. It should be noted that PDL can be extended to include keywords for multitasking and/or concurrent processing, interrupt handling, interprocess synchronization, and many other features. The application design for which PDL is to be used should dictate the final form for the design language. The format and semantics for some of these PDL constructs are presented in the example that follows.

To illustrate the use of PDL, we consider a procedural design for the *SafeHome* security function discussed in earlier chapters. The system monitors alarms for fire, smoke, burglar, water, and temperature (e.g., furnace breaks while homeowner is away during winter), produces an alarm bell, and calls a monitoring service, generating a voice-synthesized message. In the PDL that follows, we illustrate some of the important constructs noted in earlier sections.

Recall that PDL is *not* a programming language. The designer can adapt as required without worry of syntax errors. However, the design for the monitoring software would have to be reviewed (do you see any problems?) and further refined before code could be written. The following PDL[8] provides an elaboration of the procedural design for an early version of an alarm management component.

```
component alarmManagement;
The intent of this component is to manage control panel switches and input from sensors by
type and to act on any alarm condition that is encountered.
    set default values for systemStatus (returned value), all data items
    initialize all system ports and reset all hardware
    check controlPanelSwitches (cps)
        if cps = "test" then invoke alarm set to "on"
        if cps = "alarmOff" then invoke alarm set to "off"
        •
        •
        •
        default for cps = none
    reset all signalValues and switches
    do for all sensors
        invoke checkSensor procedure returning signalValue
        if signalValue > bound [alarmType]
            then phone.message = message [alarmType]
                set alarmBell to "on" for alarmTimeSeconds
```

8 The level of detail represented by the PDL is defined locally. Some people prefer a more natural language-oriented description while others prefer something that is close to code.

```
                set system status = "alarmCondition"
                parbegin
                    invoke alarm procedure with "on", alarmTimeSeconds;
                    invoke phone procedure set to alarmType, phoneNumber
                parend
            else skip
        endif
    enddofor
end alarmManagement
```

Note that the designer for the alarm management component has used the construct **parbegin . . . parend** that specifies a parallel block. All tasks specified within the **parbegin** block are executed in parallel. In this case, implementation details are not considered.

SOFTWARE TOOLS

Program Design Language

Objective: Although the vast majority of software engineers who use PDL or pseudocode develop a version that is adapted from the programming language that they intend to use for implementation, a number of PDL tools do exist.

Mechanics: In some cases, the tools reverse engineer existing source code (a sad reality in a world where some programs have absolutely no documentation at all). Others allow a designer to create PDL with an automated assist.

Representative Tools[9]

PDL/81, developed by Caine, Farber, and Gordon (http://www.cfg.com/pdl81/lpd.html), supports the creation of designs using a defined version of PDL.

DocGen, distributed by Software Improvement Group (http://www.software-improvers.com/DocGen.htm), is a reverse engineering tool that generates PDL-like documentation from Ada and C code.

PowerPDL, developed by Iconix (http://www.iconixsw.com/SpecSheets/PowerPDL.html), allows a designer to create PDL based designs and then translates pseudocode into the forms that can generate other design representations.

11.5.4 Comparison of Design Notation

Design notation should lead to a procedural representation that is easy to understand and review. In addition, the notation should enhance "code to" ability so that code does, in fact, become a natural by-product of design. Finally, the design representation must be easily maintainable so that design always represents the program correctly.

A natural question that arises in any discussion of design notation is: What notation is really the best, given the attributes noted above? Any answer to this question is subjective and open to debate. However, it appears that program design language offers the best combination of characteristics. PDL may be embedded directly into source listings, improving documentation and making design maintenance less dif-

9 Tools noted here do not represent an endorsement, but rather a sampling of tools in this category. In most cases, tool names are trademarked by their respective developers.

ficult. Editing can be accomplished with any text editor or word-processing system, automatic processors already exist, and the potential for "automatic code generation" is good.

However, it does not follow that other design notation is necessarily inferior to PDL or is "not good" in specific attributes. The pictorial nature of activity diagrams and flowcharts provides a perspective on control flow that many designers prefer. The precise tabular content of decision tables is an excellent tool for table-driven applications. And many other design representations (e.g., Petri nets), not presented in this book, offer their own unique benefits. In the final analysis, the choice of a design tool may be more closely related to human factors than to technical attributes.

11.6 Summary

The component-level design action encompasses a sequence of tasks that slowly reduces the level of abstraction with which software is represented. Component-level design ultimately depicts the software at a level of abstraction that is close to code.

Two different views of component-level design may be taken, depending on the nature of the software to be developed. The object-oriented view focuses on the elaboration of design classes that come from both the problem and infrastructure domain. The conventional view refines three different types of components or modules: control modules, problem domain modules, and infrastructure modules. In both cases, basic design principles and concepts that lead to high-quality software are applied. When considered from a process viewpoint, component-level design draws on reusable software components and design patterns that are pivotal elements of component-based software engineering.

Object-oriented component-level design is class-based. A number of important principles and concepts guide the designer as classes are elaborated. Principles such as the Open-Closed Principle and the Dependency Inversion Principle, and concepts such as coupling and cohesion guide the software engineer in building testable, implementable, and maintainable software components. To conduct component-level design in this context, classes are elaborated by specifying messaging details, identifying appropriate interfaces, elaborating attributes and defining data structures to implement them, describing processing flow within each operation, and representing behavior at a class or component level. In every case, design iteration (refactoring) is an essential activity.

Conventional component-level design requires the represention of data structures, interfaces, and algorithms for a program module in sufficient detail to guide in the generation of programming language source code. To accomplish this, the designer uses one of a number of design notations that represent component-level detail in either graphical, tabular, or text-based formats.

Structured programming is a procedural design philosophy that constrains the number and type of logical constructs used to represent algorithmic detail. The intent of structured programming is to assist the designer in defining algorithms that are less complex and therefore easier to read, test, and maintain.

References

[AMB02] Ambler, S., "UML Component Diagramming Guidelines," available at http://www.modelingstyle.info/, 2002.

[BEN02] Bennett, S., S. McRobb, and R. Farmer, *Object-Oriented Analysis and Design,* 2nd ed., McGraw-Hill, 2002.

[BOH66] Bohm, C., and G. Jacopini, "Flow Diagrams, Turing Machines and Languages with Only Two Formation Rules," *CACM,* vol. 9, no. 5, May 1966, pp. 366–371.

[CAI75] Caine, S. and K. Gordon, "PDL—A Tool for Software Design," in *Proc. National Computer Conference,* AFIPS Press, 1975, pp. 271–276.

[DIJ65] Dijkstra, E., "Programming Considered as a Human Activity," in *Proc. 1965 IFIP Congress,* North-Holland Publishing Co., 1965.

[DIJ72] Dijkstra, E., "The Humble Programmer," 1972 ACM Turing Award Lecture, *CACM,* vol. 15, no. 10, October, 1972, pp. 859–866.

[DIJ76] Dijkstra, E., "Structured Programming," in *Software Engineering, Concepts and Techniques,* (J. Buxton et al., eds.), Van Nostrand-Reinhold, 1976.

[HUR83] Hurley, R. B., *Decision Tables in Software Engineering,* Van Nostrand-Reinhold, 1983.

[LET01] Lethbridge, T., and R. Laganiere, *Object-Oriented Software Engineering: Practical Software Development Using UML and Java,* McGraw-Hill, 2001.

[LIS88] Liskov, B., "Data Abstraction and Hierarchy," *SIGPLAN Notices,* vol. 23, no. 5, May 1988.

[MAR00] Martin, R., "Design Principles and Design Patterns," downloaded from http://www.objectmentor.com, 2000.

[OMG01] *OMG Unified Modeling Specification,* Object Management Group, version 1.4, September, 2001.

[WAR98] Warmer, J., and A. Klepp, *Object Constraint Language: Precise Modeling with UML,* Addison-Wesley, 1998.

Problems and Points to Ponder

11.1. The term *component* is sometimes a difficult one to define. First provide a generic definition, and then provide more explicit definitions for OO and conventional software. Finally, pick three programming languages with which you are familiar and illustrate how each defines a component.

11.2. Why are control components necessary in conventional software and generally not required in object-oriented software?

11.3. Describe the OCP in your own words. Why is it important to create abstractions that serve as an interface between components?

11.4. Describe the DIP in your own words. What might happen if a designer depends too heavily on concretions?

11.5. Select three components that you have developed recently and assess the types of cohesion that each exhibits. If you had to define the primary benefit of high cohesion, what would it be?

11.6. Select three components that you have developed recently and assess the types of coupling that each exhibits. If you had to define the primary benefit of low coupling, what would it be?

11.7. Is it reasonable to say that problem domain components should never exhibit external coupling? If you agree, what types of components would exhibit external coupling?

11.8. Do some research and develop a list of typical categories for infrastructure components.

11.9. What is a guard-condition, and when is it used?

11.10. What is the role of interfaces in a class-based component-level design?

11.11. The terms *public* and *private attributes* are often used in component-level design work. What do you think each means and what design concepts do they try to enforce?

11.12. What is a persistent data source?

11.13. Develop (1) an elaborated design class; (2) interface descriptions; (3) an activity diagram for one of the operations within the class; (4) a detailed statechart diagram for one of the *SafeHome* classes that we have discussed in earlier chapters.

11.14. Are stepwise refinement and factoring the same thing? If not, how do they differ?

11.15. Do a bit of research and describe three or four OCL constructs or operators that have not been discussed in Section 11.4.

11.16. Select a small portion of an existing program (approximately 50–75 source lines). Isolate the structured programming constructs by drawing boxes around them in the source code. Does the program excerpt have constructs that violate the structured programming philosophy? If so, redesign the code to make it conform to structured programming constructs. If not, what do you notice about the boxes that you've drawn?

Further Readings and Information Sources

Design principles, concepts, guidelines, and techniques for object-oriented design classes and components are discussed in many books on object-oriented software engineering and OO analysis and design. Among the many sources of information are Bennett and his colleagues [BEN02], Larman (*Applying UML and Patterns,* Prentice-Hall, 2001), Lethridge and Laganiere [LET01], and Nicola and her colleagues (*Streamlined Object Modeling: Patterns, Rules and Implementation,* Prentice-Hall, 2001), Schach (*Object-Oriented and Classical Software Engineering,* fifth edition, McGraw-Hill, 2001), Dennis and his colleagues (Systems Analysis and Design: An Object-Oriented Approach with UML, Wiley, 2001), Graham (*Object-Oriented Methods: Principles and Practice,* Addison-Wesley, 2000), Richter (*Designing Flexible Object-Oriented Systems with UML,* Macmillan, 1999), Stevens and Pooley (*Using UML: Software Engineering with Objects and Components,* revised edition, Addison-Wesley, 1999), and Riel (*Object-Oriented Design Heuristics,* Addison-Wesley, 1996).

The design by contract concept is a useful design paradigm. Books by Mitchell and McKim (*Design by Contract by Example,* Addison-Wesley, 2001) and Jezequel and his colleagues (*Design Patterns and Contracts,* Addison-Wesley, 1999) cover this topic in some detail. Metsker (*Design Patterns Java Workbook,* Addison-Wesley, 2002) and Shalloway and Trott (*Design Patterns Explained: A New Perspective on Object-Oriented Design,* Addison-Wesley, 2001) consider the impact of patterns on the design of software components. Design iteration is essential for the creation of high-quality designs. Fowler (*Refactoring: Improving the Design of Existing Code,* Addison-Wesley, 1999) provides useful guidance that can be applied as a design evolves.

The work of Linger, Mills, and Witt (*Structured Programming—Theory and Practice,* Addison-Wesley, 1979) remains a definitive treatment of the subject. The text contains a good PDL as well as detailed discussions of the ramifications of structured programming. Other books that focus on procedural design issues for traditional systems include those by Robertson (*Simple Program Design,* third edition, Course Technology, 2000), Farrell (*A Guide to Programming Logic and Design,* Course Technology, 1999), Bentley (*Programming Pearls,* second edition, Addison-Wesley, 1999), and Dahl (*Structured Programming,* Academic Press, 1997).

Relatively few recent books have been dedicated solely to component-level design. In general, programming language books address procedural design in some detail but always in the context of the language that is introduced by the book. Hundreds of titles are available.

A wide variety of information sources on component-level design are available on the Internet. An up-to-date list of World Wide Web references that are relevant to component-level design can be found at the SEPA Web site:
http://www.mhhe.com/pressman.

CHAPTER

12 User Interface Design

Key Concepts

The blueprint for a house (its architectural design) is not complete without a representation of doors, windows, and utility connections for water, electricity, and telephone (not to mention cable TV). The "doors, windows, and utility connections" for computer software make up the interface design of a system.

Interface design focuses on three areas of concern: (1) the design of interfaces between software components, (2) the design of interfaces between the software and other nonhuman producers and consumers of information (i.e., other external entities), and (3) the design of the interface between a human (i.e., the user) and the computer. In this chapter we focus exclusively on the third interface design category—*user interface design.*

In the preface to his classic book on user interface design, Ben Shneiderman [SHN90] states:

> Frustration and anxiety are part of daily life for many users of computerized information systems. They struggle to learn command language or menu selection systems that are supposed to help them do their job. Some people encounter such serious cases of computer shock, terminal terror, or network neurosis that they avoid using computerized systems.

The problems to which Shneiderman alludes are real. It is true that graphical user interfaces, windows, icons, and mouse picks have eliminated many of the most

Quick Look

What is it? User interface design creates an effective communication medium between a human and a computer. Following a set of interface design principles, design identifies interface objects and actions and then creates a screen layout that forms the basis for a user interface prototype.

Who does it? A software engineer designs the user interface by applying an iterative process that draws on widely accepted design principles.

Why is it important? If software is difficult to use, if it forces you into mistakes, or if it frustrates your efforts to accomplish your goals, you won't like it, regardless of the computational power it exhibits or the functionality it offers. The interface has to be right because it molds a user's perception of the software.

What are the steps? User interface design begins with the identification of user, task, and environmental requirements. Once user tasks have been identified, user scenarios are created and analyzed to define a set of interface objects and actions. These form the basis for the creation of screen layouts that depict graphical design and placement of icons, definition of descriptive screen text, specification and titling for windows, and specification of major and minor menu items. Tools are used to prototype and ultimately implement the design model, and the result is evaluated for quality.

What is the work product? User scenarios are created, and screen layouts are generated. An interface prototype is developed and modified in an iterative fashion.

How do I ensure that I've done it right? The prototype is "test driven" by the users and feedback from the test drive is used for the next iterative modification of the prototype.

horrific interface problems. But even in a "Windows world," we all have encountered user interfaces that are difficult to learn, hard to use, confusing, counterintuitive, unforgiving, and in many cases, totally frustrating. Yet, someone spent time and energy building each of these interfaces, and it is not likely that the builder created these problems purposely.

User interface design has as much to do with the study of people as it does with technology issues. Who is the user? How does the user learn to interact with a new computer-based system? How does the user interpret information produced by the system? What will the user expect of the system? These are only a few of the many questions that must be asked and answered as part of user interface design.

12.1 The Golden Rules

In his book on interface design, Theo Mandel [MAN97] coins three "golden rules":

1. Place the user in control.
2. Reduce the user's memory load.
3. Make the interface consistent.

These golden rules actually form the basis for a set of user interface design principles that guide this important software design action.

12.1.1 Place the User in Control

During a requirements-gathering session for a major new information system, a key user was asked about the attributes of the windows-oriented graphical interface. "What I really would like," said the user solemnly, "is a system that reads my mind. It knows what I want to do before I need to do it and makes it very easy for me to get it done. That's all, just that."

My first reaction was to shake my head and smile, but I paused for a moment. There was absolutely nothing wrong with the user's request. She wanted a system that reacted to her needs and helped her get things done. She wanted to control the computer, not have the computer control her.

Most interface constraints and restrictions that are imposed by a designer are intended to simplify the mode of interaction. But for whom? In many cases, the designer might introduce constraints and limitations to simplify the implementation of the interface. The result may be an interface that is easy to build, but frustrating to use.

Mandel [MAN97] defines a number of design principles that allow the user to maintain control:

Define interaction modes in a way that does not force a user into unnecessary or undesired actions. An interaction mode is the current state of the interface. For example, if *spell check* is selected in a word-processor menu, the software moves to a spell-checking mode. There is no reason to force the user to remain in spell-checking mode if the user desires to make a small text edit along the way. The user should be able to enter and exit the mode with little or no effort.

Provide for flexible interaction. Because different users have different interaction preferences, choices should be provided. For example, software might allow a user to interact via keyboard commands, mouse movement, a digitizer pen, or voice recognition commands. But every action is not amenable to every interaction mechanism. Consider, for example, the difficulty of using keyboard commands (or voice input) to draw a complex shape.

Allow user interaction to be interruptible and undoable. Even when involved in a sequence of actions, the user should be able to interrupt the sequence to do something else (without losing the work that had been done). The user should also be able to "undo" any action.

Streamline interaction as skill levels advance and allow the interaction to be customized. Users often find that they perform the same sequence of interactions repeatedly. It is worthwhile to design a "macro" mechanism that enables an advanced user to customize the interface to facilitate interaction.

Hide technical internals from the casual user. The user interface should move the user into the virtual world of the application. The user should not be aware of the operating system, file management functions, or other arcane computing technology. In essence, the interface should never require that the user interact at a level that is "inside" the machine (e.g., a user should never be required to type operating system commands from within application software).

Design for direct interaction with objects that appear on the screen. The user feels a sense of control when able to manipulate the objects that are necessary to perform a task in a manner similar to what would occur if the object were a physical thing. For example, an application interface that allows a user to "stretch" an object (scale it in size) is an implementation of direct manipulation.

> "I have always wished that my computer would be as easy to use as my telephone. My wish has come true. I no longer know how to use my telephone."
>
> **Bjarne Stronstrup (originator of C++)**

12.1.2 Reduce the User's Memory Load

The more a user has to remember, the more error-prone interaction with the system will be. It is for this reason that a well-designed user interface does not tax the user's memory. Whenever possible, the system should "remember" pertinent information and assist the user with an interaction scenario that assists recall. Mandel [MAN97] defines design principles that enable an interface to reduce the user's memory load:

Reduce demand on short-term memory. When users are involved in complex tasks, the demand on short-term memory can be significant. The interface should be designed to reduce the requirement to remember past actions and results. This can be accomplished by providing visual cues that enable a user to recognize past actions, rather than having to recall them.

Establish meaningful defaults. The initial set of defaults should make sense for the average user, but a user should be able to specify individual preferences. However, a "reset" option should be available, enabling the redefinition of original default values.

Define shortcuts that are intuitive. When mnemonics are used to accomplish a system function (e.g., alt-P to invoke the print function), the mnemonic should be tied to the action in a way that is easy to remember (e.g., first letter of the task to be invoked).

The visual layout of the interface should be based on a real world metaphor. For example, a bill payment system should use a check book and check register metaphor to guide the user through the bill paying process. This enables the user to rely on well-understood visual cues, rather than memorizing an arcane interaction sequence.

Disclose information in a progressive fashion. The interface should be organized hierarchically. That is, information about a task, an object, or some behavior should be presented first at a high level of abstraction. More detail should be presented after the user indicates interest with a mouse pick. An example, common to many word-processing applications, is the underlining function. The function itself is one of a number of functions under a *text style* menu. However, every underlining capability is not listed. The user must pick underlining, and then all underlining options (e.g., single underline, double underline, dashed underline) are presented.

SAFEHOME

Violating a UI "Golden Rule"

The scene: Vinod's cubicle, as user interface design begins.

The players: Vinod and Jamie, members of the *SafeHome* software engineering team.

The conversation:

Jamie: I've been thinking about the surveillance function interface.

Vinod (smiling): Thinking is good.

Jamie: I think maybe we can simplify matters some.

Vinod: Meaning?

Jamie: Well, what if we eliminate the floor plan entirely? It's flashy, but it's going to take serious development effort. Instead we just ask the user to specify the camera he wants to see and then display the video in a video window.

Vinod: How does the homeowner remember how many cameras are set up and where they are?

Jamie (mildly irritated): He's the homeowner, he should know.

Vinod: But what if he doesn't?

Jamie: He should.

Vinod: That's not the point . . . what if he forgets?

Jamie: Uh, we could provide a list of operational cameras and their locations.

Vinod: That's possible, but why should he have to ask for a list?

Jamie: Okay, we provide the list whether he asks or not.

Vinod: Better. At least he doesn't have to remember stuff that we can give him.

Jamie (thinking for a moment): But you like the floor plan, don't you?

Vinod: Uh huh.

Jamie: Which one will marketing like, do you think?

Vinod: You're kidding, right?

Jamie: No.

Vinod: Duh . . . the one with the flash . . . they love sexy product features . . . they're not interested in which is easier to build.

Jamie (sighing): Okay, maybe I'll prototype both.

Vinod: Good idea . . . then we let the customer decide.

12.1.3 Make the Interface Consistent

The interface should present and acquire information in a consistent fashion. This implies that (1) all visual information is organized according to a design standard that is maintained throughout all screen displays, (2) input mechanisms are constrained to a limited set that is used consistently throughout the application, and (3) mechanisms for navigating from task to task are consistently defined and implemented. Mandel [MAN97] defines a set of design principles that help make the interface consistent:

> "Things that look different should act different. Things that look the same should act the same."
>
> **Larry Marine**

Allow the user to put the current task into a meaningful context. Many interfaces implement complex layers of interactions with dozens of screen images. It is important to provide indicators (e.g., window titles, graphical icons, consistent color coding) that enable the user to know the context of the work at hand. In addition, the user should be able to determine where he has come from and what alternatives exist for a transition to a new task.

Maintain consistency across a family of applications. A set of applications (or products) should all implement the same design rules so that consistency is maintained for all interaction.

If past interactive models have created user expectations, do not make changes unless there is a compelling reason to do so. Once a particular interactive sequence has become a de facto standard (e.g., the use of alt-S to save a file), the user expects this in every application she encounters. A change (e.g., using alt-S to invoke scaling) will cause confusion.

The interface design principles discussed in this and the preceding sections provide basic guidance for a software engineer. In the sections that follow, we examine the interface design process itself.

INFO

Usability

In an insightful paper on usability, Larry Constantine [CON95] asks a question that has significant bearing on the subject: "What do users want, anyway?" He answers this way: "What users really want are good tools. All software systems, from operating systems and languages to data entry and decision support applications, are just tools. End users want from the tools we engineer for them much the same as we expect from the tools we use. They want systems that are easy to learn and that help them do their work. They want software that doesn't slow them down, that doesn't trick or confuse them, that does make it easier to make mistakes or harder to finish the job."

Constantine argues that usability is not derived from aesthetics, state-of-the-art interaction mechanisms, or built-in interface intelligence. Rather, it occurs when the architecture of the interface fits the needs of the people who will be using it.

A formal definition of usability is somewhat illusive. Donahue and his colleagues [DON99] define it in the following manner: "Usability is a measure of how well a computer system . . . facilitates learning; helps learners remember what they've learned; reduces the likelihood of errors; enables them to be efficient, and makes them satisfied with the system."

The only way to determine whether "usability" exists within a system you are building is to conduct usability assessment or testing. Watch users interact with the system and answer the following questions [CON95]:

- Is the system usable without continual help or instruction?
- Do the rules of interaction help a knowledgeable user to work efficiently?
- Do interaction mechanisms become more flexible as users become more knowledgeable?
- Has the system been tuned to the physical and social environment in which it will be used?
- Is the user aware of the state of the system? Does the user know where she is at all times?
- Is the interface structured in a logical and consistent manner?
- Are interaction mechanisms, icons, and procedures consistent across the interface?
- Does the interaction anticipate errors and help the user correct them?
- Is the interface tolerant of errors that are made?
- Is the interaction simple?

If each of these questions is answered yes, it is likely that usability has been achieved.

Among the many measurable benefits derived from a usable system are [DON99] increased sales and customer satisfaction, competitive advantage, better reviews in the media, better word of mouth, reduced support costs, improved end-user productivity, reduced training costs, reduced documentation costs, reduced likelihood of litigation from unhappy customers.

12.2 User Interface Analysis and Design

The overall process for analyzing and designing a user interface begins with the creation of different models of system function (as perceived from the outside). The human- and computer-oriented tasks that are required to achieve system function

WebRef

An excellent source of UI design information can be found at **www.useit.com.**

are then delineated; design issues that apply to all interface designs are considered; tools are used to prototype and ultimately implement the design model; and the result is evaluated by end-users for quality.

12.2.1 Interface Analysis and Design Models

Four different models come into play when a user interface is to be analyzed and designed. A human engineer (or the software engineer) establishes a *user model,* the software engineer creates a *design model,* the end-user develops a mental image that is often called the user's *mental model* or the *system perception,* and the implementers of the system create a *implementation model.* Unfortunately, each of these models may differ significantly. The role of interface designer is to reconcile these differences and derive a consistent representation of the interface.

> **"If there's a 'trick' to it, the UI is broken."**
>
> **Douglas Anderson**

The user model establishes the profile of end-users of the system. To build an effective user interface, "all design should begin with an understanding of the intended users, including profiles of their age, sex, physical abilities, education, cultural or ethnic background, motivation, goals and personality" [SHN90]. In addition, users can be categorized as

Even a novice user wants short-cuts; even knowledgeable, frequent users sometimes need guidance. Give them what they need.

Novices. No syntactic knowledge[1] of the system and little semantic knowledge[2] of the application or computer usage in general.

Knowledgeable, intermittent users. Reasonable semantic knowledge of the application but relatively low recall of syntactic information necessary to use the interface.

Knowledgeable, frequent users. Good semantic and syntactic knowledge that often leads to the "power-user syndrome," that is, individuals who look for shortcuts and abbreviated modes of interaction.

A design model of the entire system incorporates data, architectural, interface, and procedural representations of the software. The requirements specification may establish certain constraints that help define the user of the system, but the interface design is often only incidental to the design model.[3]

The user's *mental model* (system perception) is the image of the system that end-users carry in their heads. For example, if the user of a particular page layout system

---

1 In this context, *syntactic knowledge* refers to the mechanics of interaction that is required to use the interface effectively.

2 *Semantic knowledge* refers to the underlying sense of the application—an understanding of the functions that are performed, the meaning of input and output, and the goals and objectives of the system.

3 This is not the way things should be. In many cases, user interface design is as important as architectural and component-level design.

The user's mental model shapes how the user perceives the interface and whether the UI meets the user's needs.

were asked to describe its operation, the system perception would guide the response. The accuracy of the description will depend upon the user's profile (e.g., novices would provide a sketchy response at best) and overall familiarity with software in the application domain. A user who understands page layout fully but has worked with the specific system only once might actually be able to provide a more complete description of its function than the novice who has spent weeks trying to learn the system.

> "[P]ay attention to what users do, not what they say."
>
> **Jakob Nielsen**

The implementation model combines the outward manifestation of the computer-based system (the look and feel of the interface), coupled with all supporting information (books, manuals, videotapes, help files) that describe system syntax and semantics. When the implementation model and the user's mental model are coincident, users generally feel comfortable with the software and use it effectively. To accomplish this "melding" of the models, the design model must have been developed to accommodate the information contained in the user model, and the implementation model must accurately reflect syntactic and semantic information about the interface.

The models described in this section are "abstractions of what the user is doing or thinks he is doing or what somebody else thinks he ought to be doing when he uses an interactive system" [MON84]. In essence, these models enable the interface designer to satisfy a key element of the most important principle of user interface design: *Know the user, know the tasks.*

12.2.2 The Process

The analysis and design process for user interfaces is iterative and can be represented using a spiral model similar to the one discussed in Chapter 3. Referring to Figure 12.1, the user interface analysis and design process encompasses four distinct framework activities [MAN97]:

1. User, task, and environment analysis and modeling.
2. Interface design.
3. Interface construction (implementation).
4. Interface validation.

The spiral shown in Figure 12.1 implies that each of these tasks will occur more than once, with each pass around the spiral representing additional elaboration of requirements and the resultant design. In most cases, the construction activity involves prototyping—the only practical way to validate what has been designed.

Interface analysis focuses on the profile of the users who will interact with the system. Skill level, business understanding, and general receptiveness to the new system

FIGURE 12.1 The user interface design process

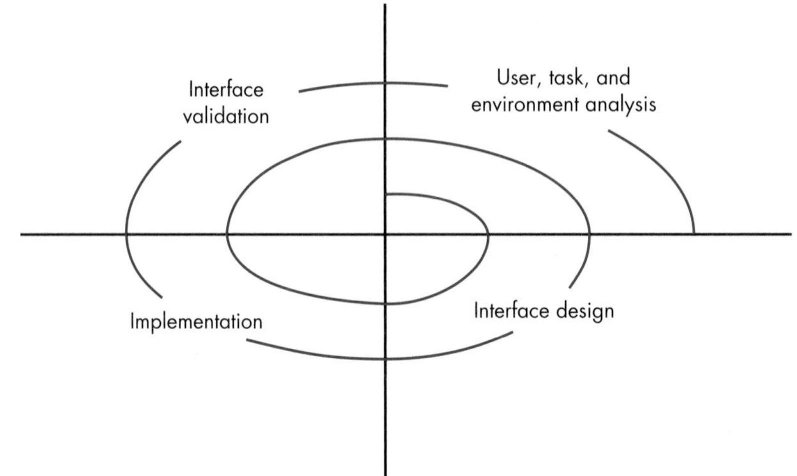

are recorded; and different user categories are defined. For each user category, requirements are elicited. In essence, the software engineer attempts to understand the system perception (Section 12.2.1) for each class of users.

> *"It's better to design the user experience than rectify it."*
>
> **Jon Meads**

Once general requirements have been defined, a more detailed task analysis is conducted. Those tasks that the user performs to accomplish the goals of the system are identified, described, and elaborated (over a number of iterative passes through the spiral). Task analysis is discussed in more detail in Section 12.3.

The analysis of the user environment focuses on the physical work environment. Among the questions to be asked are:

? What do we need to know about the environment as we begin UI design?

- Where will the interface be located physically?
- Will the user be sitting, standing, or performing other tasks unrelated to the interface?
- Does the interface hardware accommodate space, light, or noise constraints?
- Are there special human factors considerations driven by environmental factors?

The information gathered as part of the analysis activity is used to create an analysis model for the interface. Using this model as a basis, the design activity commences.

The goal of interface design is to define a set of interface objects and actions (and their screen representations) that enable a user to perform all defined tasks in a manner that meets every usability goal defined for the system. Interface design is discussed in more detail in Section 12.4.

The construction activity normally begins with the creation of a prototype that enables usage scenarios to be evaluated. As the iterative design process continues, user interface development tools (see sidebar in Section 12.4) may be used to complete the construction of the interface.

Validation focuses on (1) the ability of the interface to implement every user task correctly, to accommodate all task variations, and to achieve all general user requirements; (2) the degree to which the interface is easy to use and easy to learn; and (3) the users' acceptance of the interface as a useful tool in their work.

As we have already noted, the activities described in this section occur iteratively. Therefore, there is no need to attempt to specify every detail (for the analysis or design model) on the first pass. Subsequent passes through the process elaborate task detail, design information, and the operational features of the interface.

12.3 Interface Analysis[4]

A key tenet of all software engineering process models is this: *you better understand the problem before you attempt to design a solution.* In the case of user interface design, understanding the problem means understanding (1) the people (end-users) who will interact with the system through the interface; (2) the tasks that end-users must perform to do their work, (3) the content that is presented as part of the interface, and (4) the environment in which these tasks will be conducted. In the sections that follow, we examine each of these elements of interface analysis with the intent of establishing a solid foundation for the design tasks that follow.

12.3.1 User Analysis

Earlier we noted that each user has a mental image or system perception of the software that may be different from the mental image developed by other users. In addition, the user's mental image may be vastly different from the software engineer's design model. The only way that a designer can get the mental image and the design model to converge is to work to understand the users themselves as well as how these people will use the system. Information from a broad array of sources can be used to accomplish this:

How do we learn what the user wants from the UI?

User Interviews. The most direct approach, interviews involve representatives from the software team who meet with end-users to better understand their needs,

4 It is reasonable to argue that this section could be placed in Chapter 8, since requirements analysis issues are discussed there. It has been positioned here because interface analysis and design are intimately connected to one another, and the boundary between the two is often fuzzy.

motivations, work culture, and a myriad of other issues. This can be accomplished in one-on-one meetings or through focus groups.

ADVICE

Above all, spend time talking to actual users, but be careful. One strong opinion doesn't necessarily mean that the majority of users will agree.

Sales input. Sales people meet with customers and users on a regular basis and can gather information that will help the software team to categorize users and better understand their requirements.

Marketing input. Market analysis can be invaluable in the definition of market segments while providing an understanding of how each segment might use the software in subtly different ways.

Support input. Support staff talk with users on a daily basis, making them the most likely source of information on what works and what doesn't, what users like and what they dislike, what features generate questions, and what features are easy to use.

The following set of questions (adapted from [HAC98]) will help the interface designer better understand the users of a system:

How do we learn about the demographics and characteristics of end-users?

- Are users trained professionals, technicians, clerical or manufacturing workers?
- What level of formal education does the average user have?
- Are the users capable of learning from written materials or have they expressed a desire for classroom training?
- Are users expert typists or keyboard phobic?
- What is the age range of the user community?
- Will the users be represented predominately by one gender?
- How are users compensated for the work they perform?
- Do users work normal office hours, or do they work until the job is done?
- Is the software to be an integral part of the work users do, or will it be used only occasionally?
- What is the primary spoken language among users?
- What are the consequences if a user makes a mistake using the system?
- Are users experts in the subject matter that is addressed by the system?
- Do users want to know about the technology that sits behind the interface?

The answers to these and similar questions will allow the designer to understand who the end-users are, what is likely to motivate and please them, how they can be grouped into different user classes or profiles, what their mental models of the system are, and how the user interface must be characterized to meet their needs.

12.3.2 Task Analysis and Modeling

The user's goal is to accomplish one or more tasks via the UI. To accomplish this, the UI must provide mechanisms that allow the user to achieve her goal.

The goal of task analysis is to answer the following questions:

- What work will the user perform in specific circumstances?
- What tasks and subtasks will be performed as the user does the work?
- What specific problem domain objects will the user manipulate as work is performed?
- What is the sequence of work tasks—the workflow?
- What is the hierarchy of tasks?

To answer these questions, the software engineer must draw upon analysis techniques discussed in Chapters 7 and 8, but in this instance, these techniques are applied to the user interface.

Use-cases. In earlier chapters we noted that the use-case describes the manner in which an actor (in the context of user interface design, an actor is always a person) interacts with a system. When used as part of task analysis, the use-case is developed to show how an end-user performs some specific work-related task. In most instances, the use-case is written in an informal style (a simple paragraph) in the first-person. For example, assume that a small software company wants to build a computer-aided design system explicitly for interior designers. To get a better understanding of how they do their work, actual interior designers are asked to describe specific design functions. When asked "How do you decide where to put furniture in a room?" an interior designer writes the following informal use-case:

> I begin by sketching the floor plan of the room, the dimensions and the location of windows and doors. I'm very concerned about light as it enters the room, about the view out of the windows (if it's beautiful, I want to draw attention to it), about the running length of unobstructed walls, about the flow of movement through the room. I then look at the list of furniture my customer and I have chosen—tables, chairs, sofa, cabinets, the list of accents—lamps, rugs, paintings, sculpture, plants, smaller pieces, and my notes on any desires my customer has for placement. I then draw each item from my lists using a template that is scaled to the floor plan. I label each item and use pencil because I always move things. I consider a number of alternative placements and decide on the one I like best. Then, I draw a rendering (a 3-D picture) of the room to give my customer a feel for what it'll look like.

This use-case provides a basic description of one important work task for the computer-aided design system. From it, the software engineer can extract tasks, objects, and the overall flow of the interaction. In addition, additional features of the system that would please the interior designer can also be conceived. For example, a digital photo could be taken looking out each window in a room. When the room is rendered, the actual outside view could be represented through the each window.

SAFEHOME

Use-Cases for UI Design

The scene: Vinod's cubicle, as user interface design continues.

The players: Vinod and Jamie, members of the *SafeHome* software engineering team.

The conversation:

Jamie: I pinned down our marketing contact and had her write a use-case for the surveillance interface.

Vinod: From who's point of view?

Jamie: The home owner's, who else is there?

Vinod: There's also the system administrator role. Even if it's the homeowner playing the role, it's a different point of view. The "administrator" sets the system up, configures stuff, lays out the floor plan, places the cameras . . .

Jamie: All I had marketing do was play the role of a homeowner who wants to see video.

Vinod: That's okay. It's one of the major behaviors of the surveillance function interface. But we're going to have to examine the system administration behavior as well.

Jamie (irritated): You're right.

(Jamie leaves to find the marketing person. She returns a few hours later.)

Jamie: I was lucky. I found our marketing contact and we worked through the administrator use-case together. Basically, we're going to define "administration" as one function that's applicable to all other *SafeHome* functions. Here's what we came up with.

(Jamie shows the informal use-case to Vinod.)

Informal use-case: I want to be able to set or edit the system layout at any time. When I set up the system, I select an administration function. It asks me whether I want to do a new set-up, or whether I want to edit an existing set-up. If I select a new set-up, the system displays a drawing screen that will enable me to draw the floor plan onto a grid. There will be icons for walls, windows, and doors so that drawing is easy. I just stretch the icons to their appropriate lengths. The system will display the lengths in feet or meters (I can select the measurement system). I can select from a library of sensors and cameras and place them on the floor plan. I get to label each, or the system will do automatic labeling. I can establish settings for sensors and cameras from appropriate menus. If I select edit, I can move sensors or cameras, add new ones or delete existing ones, edit the floor plan, and edit the setting for cameras and sensors. In every case, I expect the system to do consistency checking and to help me avoid mistakes.

Vinod (after reading the scenario): Okay, there are probably some useful design patterns or reusable components for GUIs for drawing programs. I'll betcha 50 bucks we can implement some or most of the administrator interface using them.

Jamie: Agreed. I'll check it out.

Task elaboration. In Chapter 9, we discussed stepwise elaboration (also called *functional decomposition* or *stepwise refinement*) as a mechanism for refining the processing tasks that are required for software to accomplish some desired function. Task analysis for interface design uses an elaborative approach to assist in understanding the human activities the user interface must accommodate.

Task analysis can be applied in two ways. As we have already noted, an interactive, computer-based system is often used to replace a manual or semi-automated activity. To understand the tasks that must be performed to accomplish the goal of the activity, a human engineer[5] must understand the tasks that humans currently

5 In many cases, the tasks described in this section are performed by a software engineer. Ideally, this person has had some training in human engineering and user interface design.

Task elaboration is quite useful, but it can also be dangerous. Just because you have elaborated a task, do not assume that there isn't another way to do it, and that the other way will be tried when the UI is implemented.

perform (when using a manual approach) and then map these into a similar (but not necessarily identical) set of tasks that are implemented in the context of the user interface. Alternatively, the human engineer can study an existing specification for a computer-based solution and derive a set of user tasks that will accommodate the user model, the design model, and the system perception.

Regardless of the overall approach to task analysis, a human engineer must first define and classify tasks. We have already noted that one approach is stepwise elaboration. For example, assume that a small software company wants to build a computer-aided design system explicitly for interior designers. By observing an interior designer at work, the engineer notices that interior design comprises a number of major activities: furniture layout (note the use-case discussed earlier), fabric and material selection, wall and window coverings selection, presentation (to the customer), costing, and shopping. Each of these major tasks can be elaborated into subtasks. For example, using information contained in the use-case, furniture layout can be refined into the following tasks: (1) draw a floor plan based on room dimensions; (2) place windows and doors at appropriate locations; (3a) use furniture templates to draw scaled furniture outlines on floor plan; (3b) use accent templates to draw scaled accents on floor plan. (4) move furniture outlines and accent outlines to get best placement; (5) label all furniture and accent outlines; (6) draw dimensions to show location; (7) draw perspective rendering view for customer. A similar approach could be used for each of the other major tasks.

Subtasks 1–7 can each be refined further. Subtasks 1–6 will be performed by manipulating information and performing actions within the user interface. On the other hand, subtask 7 can be performed automatically in software and will result in little direct user interaction.[6] The design model of the interface should accommodate each of these tasks in a way that is consistent with the user model (the profile of a "typical" interior designer) and system perception (what the interior designer expects from an automated system).

Although object-elaboration is useful, it should not be used as a standalone approach. The user's voice must be considered during task analysis.

Object elaboration. Rather than focusing on the tasks that a user must perform, the software engineer examines the use-case and other information obtained from the user and extracts the physical objects that are used by the interior designer. These objects can be categorized into classes. Attributes of each class are defined, and an evaluation of the actions applied to each object provide the designer with a list of operations. For example, the furniture template might translate into a class called **Furniture** with attributes that might include **size, shape, location** and others. The interior designer would *select* the object from the **Furniture** class, *move* it to a position on the floor plan (another object in this context), *draw* the furniture outline, and so forth. The tasks *select, move,* and *draw* are operations. The user interface analysis

6 However, this may not be the case. The interior designer might want to specify the perspective to be drawn, the scaling, the use of color and other information. The use-case related to drawing perspective renderings would provide the information we need to address this task.

model would not provide a literal implementation for each of these operations. However, as the design is elaborated, the details of each operation are defined.

Workflow analysis. When a number of different users, each playing different roles, makes use of a user interface, it is sometimes necessary to go beyond task analysis and object elaboration and apply *workflow analysis.* This technique allows a software engineer to understand how a work process is completed when several people (and roles) are involved. Consider a company that intends to fully automate the process of prescribing and delivering prescription drugs. The entire process[7] will revolve around a Web-based application that is accessible by physicians (or their assistants), pharmacists, and patients. Workflow can be represented effectively with a UML swimlane diagram (a variation on the activity diagram).

We consider only a small part of the work process: the situation that occurs when a patient asks for a refill. Figure 12.2 presents a swimlane diagram that indicates the tasks and decisions for each of the three roles noted above. This information may have been elicited via interview or from use-cases written by each actor. Regardless, the flow of events (shown in the figure) enable the interface designer to recognize three key interface characteristics:

1. Each user implements different tasks via the interface; therefore, the look and feel of the interface designed for the patient will be different from the one defined for pharmacists or physicians.
2. The interface design for pharmacists and physicians must accommodate access to and display of information from secondary information sources (e.g., access to inventory for the pharmacist and access to information about alternative medications for the physician).
3. Many of the activities noted in the swimlane diagram can be further elaborated using task analysis and/or object elaboration (e.g., *fills prescription* could imply a mail-order delivery, a visit to a pharmacy, or a visit to a special drug distribution center).

Hierarchical representation. As the interface is analyzed, a process of elaboration occurs. Once workflow has been established, a task hierarchy can be defined for each user type. The hierarchy is derived by a stepwise elaboration of each task identified for the user. For example, consider the user task *requests that a prescription be refilled.* The following task hierarchy is developed:

Request that a prescription be refilled

- *Provide identifying information*
  - *Specify name*

7 This example has been adapted from [HAC98].

FIGURE 12.2 Swimlane diagram for prescription refill function

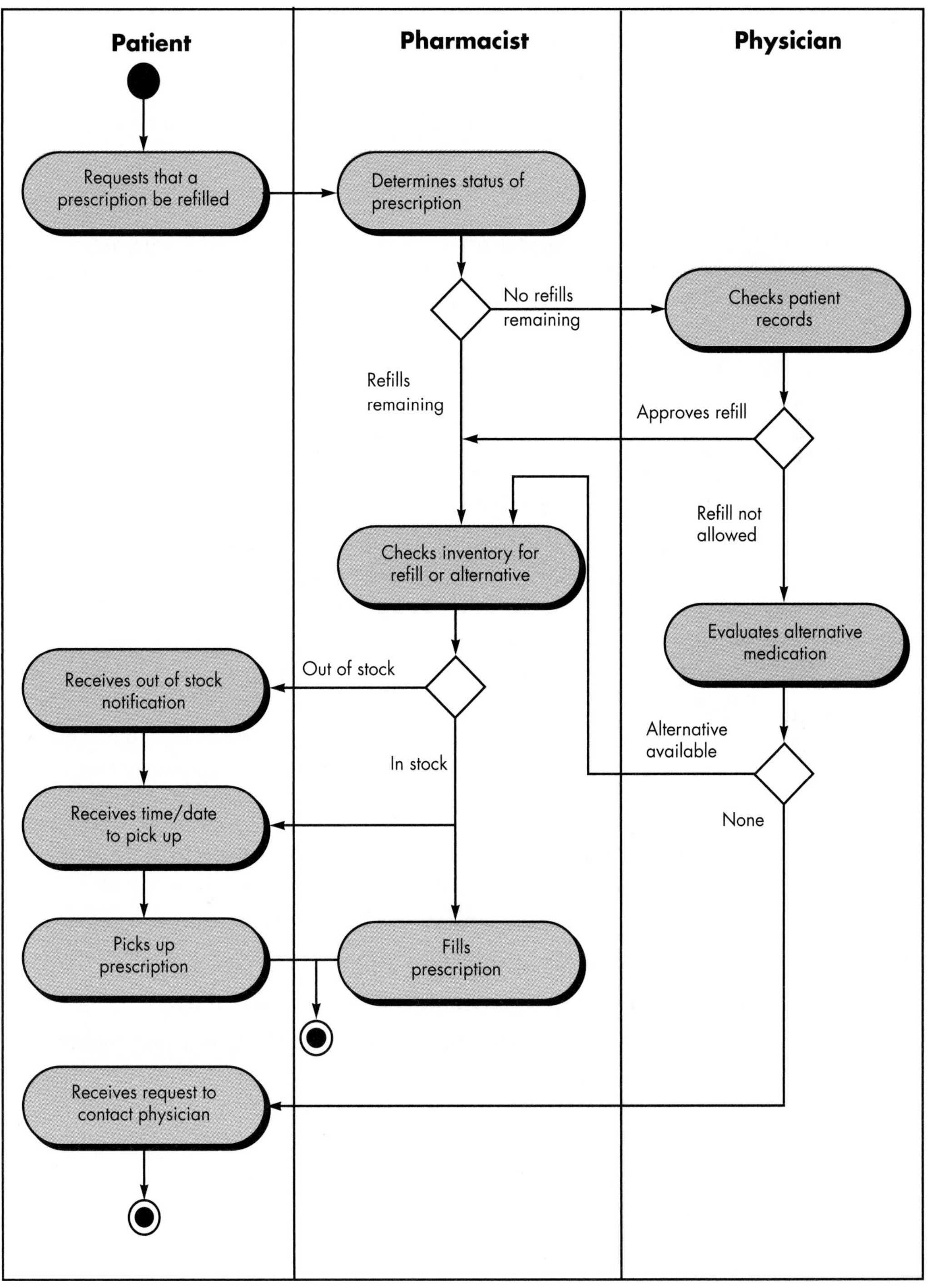

- *Specify userid*
- *Specify PIN and password*
- *Specify prescription number*
- *Specify date refill is required*

To complete the *request that a prescription be refilled* tasks, three subtasks are defined. One of these subtasks, *provide identifying information,* is further elaborated in three additional sub-subtasks.

> "It is a far better to adapt the technology to the user than to force the user to adapt to the technology."
> **Larry Marine**

12.3.3 Analysis of Display Content

The user tasks identified in the preceding section lead to the presentation of a variety of different types of content. For modern applications, display content can range from character-based reports (e.g., a spreadsheet), graphical displays (e.g., a histogram, a 3-D model, a picture of a person), or specialized information (e.g., audio or video files). The analysis modeling techniques discussed in Chapter 8 identify the output data objects that are produced by an application. These data objects may be (1) generated by components (unrelated to the interface) in other parts of the application; (2) acquired from data stored in a database that is accessible from the application; or (3) transmitted from systems external to the application in question.

During this interface analysis step, the format and aesthetics of the content (as it is displayed by the interface) are considered. Among the questions that are asked and answered are:

? How do we determine the format and aesthetics of content displayed as part of the UI?

- Are different types of data assigned to consistent geographic locations on the screen (e.g., photos always appear in the upper right hand corner)?
- Can the user customize the screen location for content?
- Is proper on-screen identification assigned to all content?
- How is a large report partitioned for ease of understanding?
- Will mechanisms be available for moving directly to summary information for large collections of data.
- Will graphical output be scaled to fit within the bounds of the display device that is used?
- How will color be used to enhance understanding?
- How will error messages and warnings be presented to the user?

As each of these (and other) questions are answered, the requirements for content presentation are established.

12.3.4 Analysis of the Work Environment

Hackos and Redish [HAC98] discuss the importance of work environment analysis when they state:

> People do not perform their work in isolation. They are influenced by the activity around them, the physical characteristics of the workplace, the type of equipment they are using, and the work relationships they have with other people. If the products you design do not fit into the environment, they may be difficult or frustrating to use.

In some applications the user interface for a computer-based system is placed in a "user-friendly location" (e.g., proper lighting, good display height, easy keyboard access), but in others (e.g., a factory floor or an airplane cockpit) lighting may be suboptimal, noise may be a factor, a keyboard or mouse may not be an option, display placement may be less than ideal. The interface designer may be constrained by factors that mitigate against ease of use.

In addition to physical environmental factors, the work place culture also comes into play. Will system interaction be measured in some manner (e.g., time per transaction or accuracy of a transaction)? Will two or more people have to share information before an input can be provided? How will support be provided to users of the system? These and many related questions should be answered before the interface design commences.

12.4 Interface Design Steps

Once interface analysis has been completed, all tasks (or objects and actions) required by the end-user have been identified in detail, and the interface design activity commences. Interface design, like all software engineering design, is an iterative process. Each user interface design step occurs a number of times, each elaborating and refining information developed in the preceding step.

Although many different user interface design models (e.g., [NOR86], [NIE00]) have been proposed, all suggest some combination of the following steps:

1. Using information developed during interface analysis (Section 12.3), define interface objects and actions (operations).
2. Define events (user actions) that will cause the state of the user interface to change. Model this behavior.
3. Depict each interface state as it will actually look to the end-user.
4. Indicate how the user interprets the state of the system from information provided through the interface.

In some cases, the interface designer may begin with sketches of each interface state (i.e., what the user interface looks like under various circumstances) and then work backward to define objects, actions, and other important design information. Regardless of the sequence of design tasks, the designer must (1) always follow the golden rules discussed in Section 12.1, (2) model how the interface will be implemented, and (3) consider the environment (e.g., display technology, operating system, development tools) that will be used.

> "Interactive design [is] a seamless blend of graphic arts, technology, and psychology."
>
> **Brad Wieners**

12.4.1 Applying Interface Design Steps

An important step in interface design is the definition of interface objects and the actions that are applied to them. To accomplish this, use-cases are parsed in much the same way as described in Chapter 8. That is, a description of a use-case is written. Nouns (objects) and verbs (actions) are isolated to create a list of objects and actions.

Once the objects and actions have been defined and elaborated iteratively, they are categorized by type. Target, source, and application objects are identified. A *source object* (e.g., a report icon) is dragged and dropped onto a *target object* (e.g., a printer icon). The implication of this action is to create a hard-copy report. An *application object* represents application-specific data that are not directly manipulated as part of screen interaction. For example, a mailing list is used to store names for a mailing. The list itself might be sorted, merged, or purged (menu-based actions), but it is not dragged and dropped via user interaction.

When the designer is satisfied that all important objects and actions have been defined (for one design iteration), screen layout is performed. Like other interface design activities, *screen layout* is an interactive process in which graphical design and placement of icons, definition of descriptive screen text, specification and titling for windows, and definition of major and minor menu items is conducted. If a real world metaphor is appropriate for the application, it is specified at this time, and the layout is organized in a manner that complements the metaphor.

To provide a brief illustration of the design steps noted previously, we consider a user scenario for the *SafeHome* system (discussed in earlier chapters). A preliminary use-case (written by the homeowner) for the interface follows:

> **Preliminary use-case:** I want to gain access to my *SafeHome* system from any remote location via the Internet. Using browser software operating on my notebook computer (while I'm at work or traveling), I can determine the status of the alarm system; arm or disarm the system; reconfigure security zones; and view different rooms within the house via preinstalled video cameras.
>
> To access *SafeHome* from a remote location, I provide an identifier and a password. These define levels of access (e.g., all users may not be able to reconfigure the system) and provide security. Once validated, I can check the status of the system and change status by arming or disarming *SafeHome*. I can reconfigure the system by displaying a floor plan of the house, viewing each of the security sensors, displaying each currently configured zone, and modifying zones as required. I can view the interior of the house via strategically placed video cameras. I can pan and zoom each camera to provide different views of the interior.

Based on this use-case, the following homeowner tasks, objects, and data items are identified:

- *accesses* the *SafeHome* system
- *enters* an **ID** and **password** to allow remote access
- *checks* **system status**
- *arms* or *disarms SafeHome* system
- *displays* **floor plan** and **sensor locations**
- *displays* **zones** on floor plan
- *changes* **zones** on floor plan
- *displays* **video camera locations** on **floor plan**
- *selects* **video camera** for viewing
- *views* **video images**
- *pans* or *zooms* the **video camera**

Objects (boldface) and actions (italics) are extracted from this list of homeowner tasks. The majority of objects noted are application objects. However, **video camera location** (a source object) is dragged and dropped onto **video camera** (a target object) to create a **video image** (a window that contains the video display).

ADVICE

Although automated tools can be useful in developing layout prototypes, sometimes a pencil and paper are all that are needed.

A preliminary sketch of the screen layout for video monitoring is created (Figure 12.3).[8] To invoke the video image, a video camera location icon, *C,* located in the floor plan displayed in the monitoring window, is selected. In this case, a camera location in the living room, LR, is then dragged and dropped onto the video camera icon in the upper left-hand portion of the screen. The video image window appears, displaying streaming video from the camera located in the living room (LR). The zoom and pan control slides are used to control the magnification and direction of the video image. To select a view from another camera, the user simply drags and drops a different camera location icon into the camera icon in the upper left-hand corner of the screen.

The layout sketch shown would have to be supplemented with an expansion of each menu item within the menu bar, indicating what actions are available for the video monitoring mode (state). A complete set of sketches for each homeowner task noted in the user scenario would be created during the interface design.

WebRef

A wide variety of UI design patterns have been proposed. For pointers to a variety of pattern sites, visit **www.hicpatterns.org.**

12.4.2 User Interface Design Patterns

Sophisticated graphical user interfaces have become so common that a wide variety of user interface design patterns has emerged. As we noted earlier in this book, a

8 Note that this differs somewhat from the implementation of these features in earlier chapters. This might be considered a first draft design and represents one alternative that might be considered.

FIGURE 12.3

Preliminary screen layout

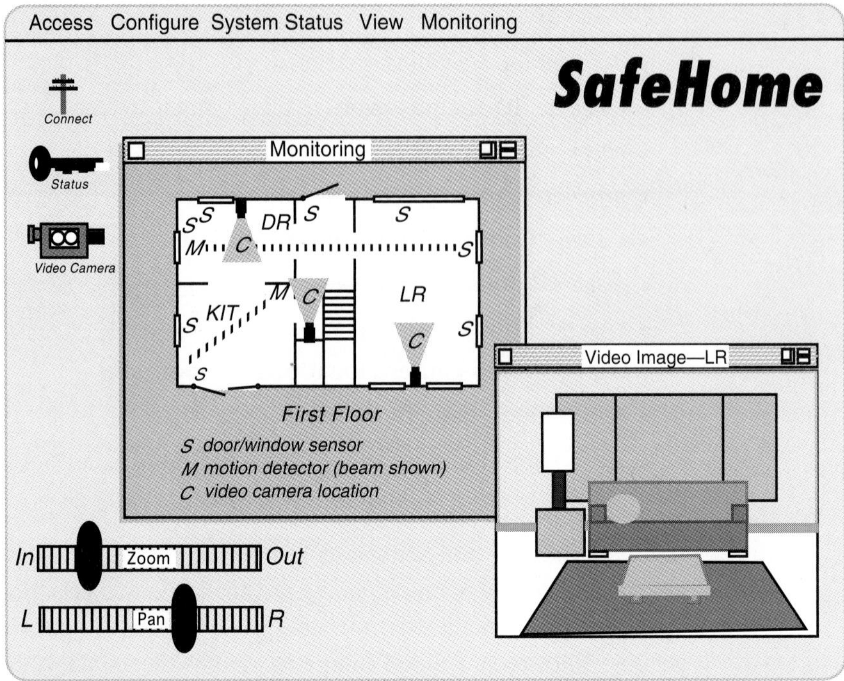

design pattern is an abstraction that prescribes a design solution to a specific, well-bounded design problem. Each of the example patterns (and all patterns within each category) presented in the sidebar would also have a complete component-level design, including design classes, attributes, operations, and interfaces.

INFO

User Interface Patterns

Hundreds of UI patterns have been proposed over the past decade. Tidwell [TID02] and vanWelie [WEL01] provide taxonomies[9] of user interface design patterns that can be organized into 10 categories. Example patterns within each of these categories are presented in this sidebar.

Whole UI. Provides design guidance for top-level structure and navigation.

Pattern: *top-level navigation*

Brief description: Provides a top-level menu, often coupled with a logo or identifying graphic, that enables direct navigation to any of the system's major functions.

Page layout. Addresses the general organization of pages (for Web sites) or distinct screen displays (for interactive applications).

Pattern: *card stack*

Brief description: Provides the appearance of a stack of tabbed cards, each selectable with a mouse click and each representing specific subfunctions or content categories.

9 Full patterns descriptions (along with dozens of other patterns) can be found at [TID02] and [WEL01].

Forms and input. Considers a variety of design techniques for completing form-level input.
Pattern: *fill-in-the-blanks*
Brief description: Allow alphanumeric data to be entered in a "text box."

Tables. Provide design guidance for creating and manipulating tabular data of all kinds.
Pattern: *sortable table*
Brief description: Displays a long list of records that can be sorted by selecting a toggle mechanism for any column label.

Direct data manipulation. Addresses data editing, modification, and transformation.
Pattern: *bread crumbs*
Brief description: Provides a full navigation path when the user is working with a complex hierarchy of pages or display screens.

Navigation. Assists the user in navigating through hierarchical menus, Web pages, and interactive display screens.
Pattern: *edit-in-place*
Brief description: Provides simple text editing capability for certain types of content in the location that it is displayed.

Searching. Enables content-specific searches through information maintained within a Web site or contained by persistent data stores that are accessible via an interactive application.
Pattern: *simple search*
Brief description: Provides the ability to search a Web site or persistent data source for a simple data item described by an alphanumeric string.

Page elements. Implement specific elements of a Web page or display screen.
Pattern: *wizard*
Brief description: Takes the user through a complex task one step at a time, providing guidance for the completion of the task through a series of simple window displays.

E-commerce. Specific to Web sites, these patterns implement recurring elements of e-commerce applications.
Pattern: *shopping cart*
Brief description: Provides a list of items selected for purchase.

Miscellaneous. Patterns that do not easily fit into one of the preceding categories. In some cases, these patterns are domain dependent or occur only for specific classes of users.
Pattern: *progress indicator*
Brief description: Provides an indication of progress when an operation is under way.

A comprehensive discussion of user interface patterns is beyond the scope of this book. The interested reader should see [DUY02], [BOR01], [WEL01], and [TID02] for further information.

12.4.3 Design Issues

As the design of a user interface evolves, four common design issues almost always surface: system response time, user help facilities, error information handling, and command labeling. Unfortunately, many designers do not address these issues until relatively late in the design process (sometimes the first inkling of a problem doesn't occur until an operational prototype is available). Unnecessary iteration, project delays, and customer frustration often result. It is far better to establish each as a design issue to be considered at the beginning of software design, when changes are easy and costs are low.

> "A common mistake that people make when trying to design something completely foolproof is to underestimate the ingenuity of complete fools."
>
> **Douglas Adams**

Response time. System response time is the primary complaint for many interactive applications. In general, system response time is measured from the point at which the user performs some control action (e.g., hits the return key or clicks a mouse) until the software responds with the desired output or action.

System response time has two important characteristics: length and variability. If system response is too long, user frustration and stress is the inevitable result. *Variability* refers to the deviation from average response time, and, in many ways, it is the most important response time characteristic. Low variability enables the user to establish an interaction rhythm, even if response time is relatively long. For example, a 1-second response to a command will often be preferable to a response that varies from 0.1 to 2.5 seconds. When variability is significant, the user is always off balance, always wondering whether something "different" has occurred behind the scenes.

Help facilities. Almost every user of an interactive, computer-based system requires help now and then. In some cases, a simple question addressed to a knowledgeable colleague can do the trick. In others, detailed research in a multivolume set of "user manuals" may be the only option. In most cases, however, modern software provides on-line help facilities that enable a user to get a question answered or resolve a problem without leaving the interface.

A number of design issues [RUB88] must be addressed when a help facility is considered:

- Will help be available for all system functions and at all times during system interaction? Options include help for only a subset of all functions and actions or help for all functions.
- How will the user request help? Options include a help menu, a special function key, or a HELP command.
- How will help be represented? Options include a separate window, a reference to a printed document (less than ideal), or a one- or two-line suggestion produced in a fixed screen location.
- How will the user return to normal interaction? Options include a return button displayed on the screen, a function key, or control sequence.
- How will help information be structured? Options include a "flat" structure in which all information is accessed through a keyword, a layered hierarchy of information that provides increasing detail as the user proceeds into the structure, or the use of hypertext.

Error handling. Error messages and warnings are "bad news" delivered to users of interactive systems when something has gone awry. At their worst, error messages and warnings impart useless or misleading information and serve only to increase user frustration. There are few computer users who have not encountered an error of the form: *"Application XXX has been forced to quit because an error of type 1023 has been encountered."* Somewhere, an explanation for error 1023 must exist; otherwise, why would the designers have added the identification? Yet, the error message provides no real indication of what went wrong or where to look to get additional information. An error message presented in this manner does nothing to assuage user anxiety or to help correct the problem.

> **"The interface from hell—'to correct this error and continue, enter any 11-digit prime number . . .' "**
>
> **Author unknown**

In general, every error message or warning produced by an interactive system should have the following characteristics:

? What characteristics should a "good" error message have?

- The message should describe the problem in language the user can understand.
- The message should provide constructive advice for recovering from the error.
- The message should indicate any negative consequences of the error (e.g., potentially corrupted data files) so that the user can check to ensure that they have not occurred (or correct them if they have).
- The message should be accompanied by an audible or visual cue. That is, a beep might be generated to accompany the display of the message, or the message might flash momentarily or be displayed in a color that is easily recognizable as the "error color."
- The message should be nonjudgmental. That is, the wording should never place blame on the user.

Because no one really likes bad news, few users will like an error message no matter how well designed. But an effective error message philosophy can do much to improve the quality of an interactive system and will significantly reduce user frustration when problems do occur.

Menu and command labeling. The typed command was once the most common mode of interaction between users and system software and was commonly used for applications of every type. Today, the use of window-oriented, point and pick interfaces has reduced reliance on typed commands, but many power-users continue to prefer a command-oriented mode of interaction. A number of design issues arise when typed commands or menu labels are provided as a mode of interaction:

- Will every menu option have a corresponding command?
- What form will commands take? Options include a control sequence (e.g., alt-P), function keys, or a typed word.
- How difficult will it be to learn and remember the commands? What can be done if a command is forgotten?

- Can commands be customized or abbreviated by the user?
- Are menu labels self-explanatory within the context of the interface?
- Are submenus consistent with the function implied by a master menu item?

As we noted earlier in this chapter, conventions for command usage should be established across all applications. It is confusing and often error-prone for a user to type alt-D when a graphics object is to be duplicated in one application and alt-D when a graphics object is to be deleted in another. The potential for error is obvious.

WebRef
Guidelines for developing accessible software can be found at **www-3.ibm.com/able/guidelines/software/accesssoftware.html.**

Application accessibility. As computing applications become ubiquitous, software engineers must ensure that interface design encompasses mechanisms that enable easy access for those with special needs. *Accessibility* for users (and software engineers) who may be physically challenged is an imperative for moral, legal, and business reasons. A variety of accessibility guidelines (e.g., [W3C03])—many designed for Web applications but often applicable to all types of software—provide detailed suggestions for designing interfaces that achieve varying levels of accessibility. Others (e.g., [APP03], [MIC03]) provide specific guidelines for "assistive technology" that addresses the needs of those with visual, hearing, mobility, speech, and learning impairments.

Internationalization. Software engineers and their managers invariably underestimate the effort and skills required to create user interfaces that accommodate the needs of different locales and languages. Too often, interfaces are designed for one locale and language and then jury-rigged to work in other countries. The challenge for interface designers is to create "globalized" software. That is, user interfaces should be designed to accommodate a generic core of functionality that can be delivered to all who use the software. Localization features enable the interface to be customized for a specific market.

A variety of internationalization guidelines (e.g., [IBM03]) are available to software engineers. These guidelines address broad design issues (e.g., screen layouts may differ in various markets) and discrete implementation issues (e.g., different alphabets may create specialized labeling and spacing requirements). The *Unicode* standard [UNI03] has been developed to address the daunting challenge of managing dozens of natural languages with hundred of characters and symbols.

SOFTWARE TOOLS

User Interface Development

Objective: These tools enable a software engineer to create a sophisticated GUI with relatively little custom software development. The tools provide access to reusable components and make the creation of an interface a matter of selecting from predefined capabilities that are assembled using the tool.

Mechanics: Modern user interfaces are constructed with a set of reusable components that are coupled with some custom components developed to provide specialized features. Most user interface development tools enable a software engineer to create an interface using "drag and drop" capability. That is, the developer selects from many predefined capabilities (e.g., forms builders, interaction mechanisms, command processing capability) and places these capabilities within the content of the interface to be created.

Representative Tools[10]

Macromedia Authorware, developed by macromedia Inc. www.macromedia.com/software/), has been designed for the creation of e-learning interfaces and environments. Makes use of sophisticated construction capabilities.

Motif Common Desktop Environment, developed by The Open Group www.osf.org/tech/desktop/ cde/), is an integrated graphical user interface for open systems desktop computing. It delivers a single, standard graphical interface for the management of data, files, and applications.

PowerDesigner/PowerBuilder, developed by Sybase www.sybase.com/products/internetappdevttools), is a comprehensive set of CASE tools that include many capabilities for designing and building GUIs.

12.5 Design Evaluation

Once an operational user interface prototype has been created, it must be evaluated to determine whether it meets the needs of the user. Evaluation can span a formality spectrum that ranges from an informal "test drive," in which a user provides impromptu feedback to a formally designed study that uses statistical methods for the evaluation of questionnaires completed by a population of end-users.

The user interface evaluation cycle takes the form shown in Figure 12.4. After the design model has been completed, a first-level prototype is created. The prototype is

Figure 12.4

The interface design evaluation cycle

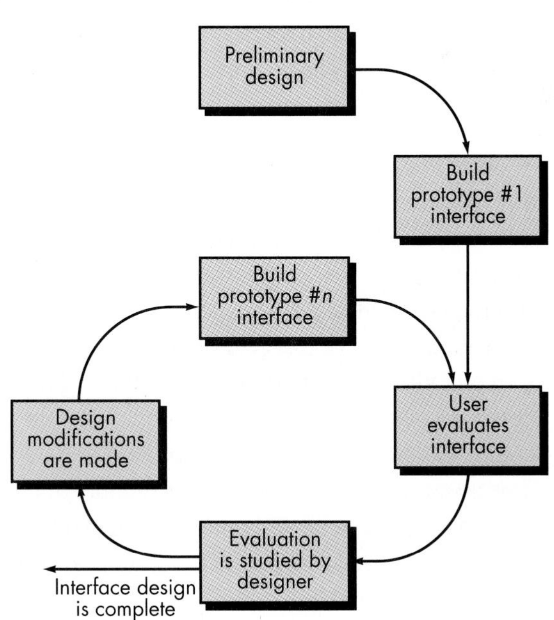

10 Tools noted here do not represent an endorsement, but rather a sampling of tools in this category. In most cases, tool names are trademarked by their respective developers.

evaluated by the user,[11] who provides the designer with direct comments about the efficacy of the interface. In addition, if formal evaluation techniques are used (e.g., questionnaires, rating sheets), the designer may extract information from these data (e.g., 80 percent of all users did not like the mechanism for saving data files). Design modifications are made based on user input, and the next level prototype is created. The evaluation cycle continues until no further modifications to the interface design are necessary.

The prototyping approach is effective, but is it possible to evaluate the quality of a user interface before a prototype is built? If potential problems can be uncovered and corrected early, the number of loops through the evaluation cycle will be reduced and development time will shorten. If a design model of the interface has been created, a number of evaluation criteria [MOR81] can be applied during early design reviews:

1. The length and complexity of the written specification of the system and its interface provide an indication of the amount of learning required by users of the system.
2. The number of user tasks specified and the average number of actions per task provide an indication of interaction time and the overall efficiency of the system.
3. The number of actions, tasks, and system states indicated by the design model imply the memory load on users of the system.
4. Interface style, help facilities, and error handling protocol provide a general indication of the complexity of the interface and the degree to which it will be accepted by the user.

Once the first prototype is built, the designer can collect a variety of qualitative and quantitative data that will assist in evaluating the interface. To collect qualitative data, questionnaires can be distributed to users of the prototype. Questions can be (1) simple yes/no response, (2) numeric response, (3) scaled (subjective) response, (4) Likert scales (e.g., strongly agree, somewhat agree), (5) percentage (subjective) response, or (6) open-ended.

If quantitative data are desired, a form of time study analysis can be conducted. Users are observed during interaction, and data—such as number of tasks correctly completed over a standard time period, frequency of actions, sequence of actions, time spent "looking" at the display, number and types of errors, error recovery time, time spent using help, and number of help references per standard time period—are collected and used as a guide for interface modification.

---

11 It is important to note that experts in ergonomics and interface design may also conduct reviews of the interface. These reviews are called *heuristic evaluations* or *cognitive walkthroughs.*

A complete discussion of user interface evaluation methods is best left to books dedicated to the subject. For further information, see [LEA88], [MAN97], and [HAC98].

12.6 Summary

The user interface is arguably the most important element of a computer-based system or product. If the interface is poorly designed, the user's ability to tap the computational power of an application may be severely hindered. In fact, a weak interface may cause an otherwise well-designed and solidly implemented application to fail.

Three important principles guide the design of effective user interfaces: (1) place the user in control, (2) reduce the user's memory load, and (3) make the interface consistent. To achieve an interface that abides by these principles, an organized design process must be conducted.

The development of a user interface begins with a series of analysis tasks. These include user identification, task, and environmental analysis/modeling. User analysis defines the profiles of various end-users and applies information gathered from a variety of business and technical sources. Task analysis defines user tasks and actions using either an elaborative or object-oriented approach, applying use-cases, task and object elaboration, workflow analysis, and hierarchical task representations to fully understand the human-computer interaction. Environmental analysis identifies the physical and social structures in which the interface must operate.

Once tasks have been identified, user scenarios are created and analyzed to define a set of interface objects and actions. This provides a basis for the creation of screen layout that depicts graphical design and placement of icons, definition of descriptive screen text, specification and titling for windows, and specification of major and minor menu items. Design issues such as response time, command and action structure, error handling, and help facilities are considered as the design model is refined. A variety of implementation tools are used to build a prototype for evaluation by the user.

References

[APP03] Apple Computer, *People with Special Needs,* 2003, available at http://www.apple.com/disability/.

[BOR01] Borchers, J., *A Pattern Approach to Interaction Design,* Wiley, 2001.

[CON95] Constantine, L., "What DO Users Want? Engineering Usability in Software," *Windows Tech Journal,* December, 1995, available from http://www.forUse.com.

[DON99] Donahue, G., S. Weinschenck, and J. Nowicki, "Usability Is Good Business," Compuware Corp., July, 1999, available from http://www.compuware.com.

[DUY02] vanDuyne, D., J. Landay, and J. Hong, *The Design of Sites,* Addison-Wesley, 2002.

[HAC98] Hackos, J., and J. Redish, *User and Task Analysis for Interface Design,* Wiley, 1998.

[IBM03] IBM, *Overview of Software Globalization,* 2003, available at http://oss.software.ibm.com/icu/userguide/i18n.html.

[LEA88] Lea, M., "Evaluating User Interface Designs," *User Interface Design for Computer Systems,* Halstead Press (Wiley), 1988.

[MAN97] Mandel, T., *The Elements of User Interface Design,* Wiley, 1997.

[MIC03] *Microsoft Accessibility Technology for Everyone,* 2003, available at http://www.microsoft.com/enable/.

[MON84] Monk, A., (ed.), *Fundamentals of Human-Computer Interaction,* Academic Press, 1984.

[MOR81] Moran, T. P., "The Command Language Grammar: A Representation for the User Interface of Interactive Computer Systems," *Intl. Journal of Man-Machine Studies,* vol. 15, pp. 3–50.

[NIE00] Nielsen, J., *Designing Web Usability,* New Riders Publishing, 2000.

[NOR86] Norman, D. A., "Cognitive Engineering," in *User Centered Systems Design,* Lawrence Earlbaum Associates, 1986.

[RUB88] Rubin, T., *User Interface Design for Computer Systems,* Halstead Press (Wiley), 1988.

[SHN90] Shneiderman, B., *Designing the User Interface,* 3rd ed., Addison-Wesley, 1990.

[TID99] Tidwell, J., "Common Ground: A Pattern Language for HCI Design," available at http://www.mit.edu/~jtidwell/interaction_patterns.html, May 1999.

[TID02] Tidwell, J., "IU Patterns and Techniques," available at http://time-tripper.com/uipatterns/index.html, May 2002.

[UNI03] Unicode, Inc., *The Unicode Home Page,* 2003, available at http://www.unicode.org/.

[W3C03] World Wide Web Consortium, *Web Content Accessibility Guidelines,* 2003, available at http://www.w3.org/TR/2003/WD-WCAG20-20030624/.

[WEL01] vanWelie, M., "Interaction Design Patterns," available at http://www.welie. com/patterns/, 2001.

Problems and Points to Ponder

12.1. Describe the best and worst interfaces that you have ever worked with and critique them relative to the concepts introduced in this chapter.

12.2. Develop two additional design principles that "place the user in control."

12.3. Develop two additional design principles that "reduce the user's memory load."

12.4. Develop two additional design principles that "make the interface consistent."

12.5. You have been asked to develop a Web-based home banking system. Develop a user model, design model, mental model, and an implementation model.

12.6. Perform a detailed task analysis for the system in Problem 12.5. Use either an elaborative or object-oriented approach.

12.7. Add at least five additional questions to the list developed for content analysis in Section 12.3.3.

12.8. Continuing Problem 12.6, define interface objects and actions for the application. Identify each object type.

12.9. Develop a set of screen layouts with a definition of major and minor menu items for the system in Problem 12.5.

12.10. Develop a set of screen layouts with a definition of major and minor menu items for the *SafeHome* system. You may elect to take a different approach than the one shown for the screen layout in Figure 12.3.

12.11. Describe your approach to user help facilities for the task analysis you have performed as part of Problem 12.5.

12.12. Provide a few examples that illustrate why response time variability can be an issue.

12.13. Develop an approach that would automatically integrate error messages and a user help facility. That is, the system would automatically recognize the error type and provide a help window with suggestions for correcting it. Perform a reasonably complete software design that considers appropriate data structures and algorithms.

12.14. Develop an interface evaluation questionnaire that contains 20 generic questions that would apply to most interfaces. Have 10 classmates complete the questionnaire for an interactive system that you all use. Summarize the results and report them to your class.

Further Readings and Information Sources

Although his book is not specifically about human/computer interfaces, much of what Donald Norman (*The Design of Everyday Things,* reissue edition, Currency/Doubleday, 1990) has to say about the psychology of effective design applies to the user interface. It is recommended reading for anyone who is serious about doing high-quality interface design.

Graphical user interfaces are ubiquitous in the modern world of computing. Whether it is used for an ATM, a mobile phone, a PDA, a Web site, or a business application, the user interface provides a window into the software. It is for this reason that books addressed to interface design abound. Galitz (*The Essential Guide to User Interface Design,* Wiley, 2002), Cooper (*About Face 2.0: The Essentials of User Interface Design,* IDG Books, 2003), Beyer and Holtzblatt (*Contextual Design: A Customer Centered Approach to Systems Design,* Morgan-Kaufmann, 2002), Raskin (*The Humane Interface,* Addison-Wesley, 2000), Constantine and Lockwood (*Software for Use,* ACM Press, 1999), Mayhew (*The Usability Engineering Lifecycle,* Morgan-Kaufmann, 1999) all discuss usability, user interface concepts, principles, and design techniques and contain many useful examples.

Johnson (*GUI Bloopers: Don'ts and Do's for Software Developers and Web Designers,* Morgan-Kaufmann, 2000) provides useful guidance for those that learn more effectively by examining counter-examples. An enjoyable book by Cooper (*The Inmates Are Running the Asylum,* Sams Publishing, 1999) discusses why high-tech products drive us crazy and how to design ones that don't.

Task analysis and modeling are pivotal interface design activities. Hackos and Redish [HAC98] have written a book dedicated to these subjects and provide a detailed method for approaching task analysis. Wood (*User Interface Design: Bridging the Gap from User Requirements to Design,* CRC Press, 1997) considers the analysis activity for interfaces and the transition to design tasks.

The evaluation activity focuses on usability. Books by Rubin (*Handbook of Usability Testing: How to Plan, Design, and Conduct Effective Tests,* Wiley, 1994) and Nielsen (*Usability Inspection Methods,* Wiley, 1994) address the topic in considerable detail.

In a unique book that may be of considerable interest to product designers, Murphy (*Front Panel: Designing Software for Embedded User Interfaces,* R&D Books, 1998) provides detailed guidance for the design of interfaces for embedded systems and addresses safety hazards inherent in controls, handling heavy machinery, and interfaces for medical or transport systems. Interface design for embedded products is also discussed by Garrett (*Advanced Instrumentation and Computer I/O Design: Real-Time System Computer Interface Engineering,* IEEE, 1994).

A wide variety of information sources on user interface design are available on the Internet. An up-to-date list of World Wide Web references that are relevant to user interface design can be found at the SEPA Web site:
http://www.mhhe.com/pressman.

CHAPTER

13 SOFTWARE TESTING STRATEGIES

A strategy for software testing integrates software test case design methods into a well-planned series of steps that result in the successful construction of software. The strategy provides a road map that describes the steps to be conducted as part of testing, when these steps are planned and then undertaken, and how much effort, time, and resources will be required. Therefore, any testing strategy must incorporate test planning, test case design, test execution, and resultant data collection and evaluation.

A software testing strategy should be flexible enough to promote a customized testing approach. At the same time, it must be rigid enough to promote reasonable planning and management tracking as the project progresses. Shooman [SHO83] discusses these issues:

> In many ways, testing is an individualistic process, and the number of different types of tests varies as much as the different development approaches. For many years, our only defense against programming errors was careful design and the native intelligence of the programmer. We are now in an era in which modern design techniques [and formal technical reviews] are helping us to reduce the number of initial errors that are inherent in the code. Similarly, different test methods are beginning to cluster themselves into several distinct approaches and philosophies.

These "approaches and philosophies" are what we shall call *strategy.* In Chapter 14, the technology of software testing is presented. In this chapter, we focus our attention on the strategy for software testing.

QUICK LOOK

What is it? Software is tested to uncover errors that were made inadvertently as it was designed and constructed. But how do you conduct the tests? Should you develop a formal plan for your tests? Should you test the entire program as a whole or run tests only on a small part of it? Should you rerun tests you've already conducted as you add new components to a large system? When should you involve the customer? These and many other questions are answered when you develop a software testing strategy.

Who does it? A strategy for software testing is developed by the project manager, software engineers, and testing specialists.

Why is it important? Testing often accounts for more project effort than any other software engineering activity. If it is conducted haphazardly, time is wasted, unnecessary effort is expended, and even worse, errors sneak through undetected. It would therefore seem reasonable to establish a systematic strategy for testing software.

What are the steps? Testing begins "in the small" and progresses "to the large." By this we mean that early testing focuses on a single component or a small group of related components and applies tests to uncover errors in the data and processing logic that have been encapsulated by the component(s). After components are tested they must be integrated until the complete system is constructed. At this point, a series of high-order tests are executed to uncover errors in meeting customer requirements. As errors are uncovered, they must be diagnosed and corrected using a process that is called debugging.

What is the work product? A *Test Specification* documents the software team's approach to testing by defining a plan that describes an overall strategy and a procedure that defines specific testing steps and the tests that will be conducted.

How do I ensure that I've done it right? By reviewing the *Test Specification* prior to testing, you can assess the completeness of test cases and testing tasks. An effective test plan and procedure will lead to the orderly construction of the software and the discovery of errors at each stage in the construction process.

13.1 A Strategic Approach to Software Testing

Testing is a set of activities that can be planned in advance and conducted systematically. For this reason a template for software testing—a set of steps into which we can place specific test case design techniques and testing methods—should be defined for the software process.

A number of software testing strategies have been proposed in the literature. All provide the software developer with a template for testing and all have the following generic characteristics:

WebRef
Useful resources for software testing can be found at **www.mtsu.edu/~storm/.**

- To perform effective testing, a software team should conduct effective formal technical reviews (Chapter 26). By doing this, many errors will be eliminated before testing commences.
- Testing begins at the component level and works "outward" toward the integration of the entire computer-based system.
- Different testing techniques are appropriate at different points in time.
- Testing is conducted by the developer of the software and (for large projects) an independent test group.
- Testing and debugging are different activities, but debugging must be accommodated in any testing strategy.

A strategy for software testing must accommodate low-level tests that are necessary to verify that a small source code segment has been correctly implemented as well as high-level tests that validate major system functions against customer requirements. A strategy must provide guidance for the practitioner and a set of milestones for the manager. Because the steps of the test strategy occur at a time when deadline pressure begins to rise, progress must be measurable and problems must surface as early as possible.

13.1.1 Verification and Validation

Software testing is one element of a broader topic that is often referred to as verification and validation (V&V). *Verification* refers to the set of activities that ensure that software correctly implements a specific function. *Validation* refers to a different set of activities that ensure that the software that has been built is traceable to customer requirements.[1] Boehm [BOE81] states this another way:

Verification: Are we building the product right?

Validation: Are we building the right product?

The definition of V&V encompasses many of the activities that are encompassed by software quality assurance (SQA) and discussed in detail in Chapter 26.

Verification and validation encompasses a wide array of SQA activities that include formal technical reviews, quality and configuration audits, performance monitoring, simulation, feasibility study, documentation review, database review, algorithm analysis, development testing, usability testing, qualification testing, and installation testing [WAL89]. Although testing plays an extremely important role in V&V, many other activities are also necessary.

> **"Testing is the unavoidable part of any responsible effort to develop a software system."**
>
> **William Howden**

Don't get sloppy and view testing as a "safety net" that will catch all errors that occurred because of weak software engineering practices. It won't. Stress quality and error detection throughout the software process.

Testing does provide the last bastion from which quality can be assessed and, more pragmatically, errors can be uncovered. But testing should not be viewed as a safety net. As they say, "You can't test in quality. If it's not there before you begin testing, it won't be there when you're finished testing." Quality is incorporated into software throughout the process of software engineering. Proper application of methods and tools, effective formal technical reviews, and solid management and measurement all lead to quality that is confirmed during testing.

Miller [MIL77] relates software testing to quality assurance by stating that "the underlying motivation of program testing is to affirm software quality with methods that can be economically and effectively applied to both large-scale and small-scale systems."

13.1.2 Organizing for Software Testing

For every software project, there is an inherent conflict of interest that occurs as testing begins. The people who have built the software are now asked to test the

---

1 It should be noted that there is a strong divergence of opinion about what types of testing constitute "validation." Some people believe that *all* testing is verification and that validation is conducted when requirements are reviewed and approved, and later, by the user when the system is operational. Other people view unit and integration testing (Sections 13.3.1 and 13.3.2) as verification and higher-order testing (discussed later in this chapter) as validation.

software. This seems harmless in itself; after all, who knows the program better than its developers? Unfortunately, these same developers have a vested interest in demonstrating that the program is error free, that it works according to customer requirements, and that it will be completed on schedule and within budget. Each of these interests mitigate against thorough testing.

> **"Optimism is the occupational hazard of programming; testing is the treatment."**
>
> **Kent Beck**

From a psychological point of view, software analysis and design (along with coding) are constructive tasks. The software engineer analyzes, models, and then creates a computer program and its documentation. Like any builder, the software engineer is proud of the edifice that has been built and looks askance at anyone who attempts to tear it down. When testing commences, there is a subtle, yet definite, attempt to "break" the thing that the software engineer has built. From the point of view of the builder, testing can be considered to be (psychologically) destructive. So the builder treads lightly, designing and executing tests that will demonstrate that the program works, rather than uncovering errors. Unfortunately, errors will be present. And, if the software engineer doesn't find them, the customer will!

An independent test group does not have the "conflict of interest" that builders of the software might experience.

There are often a number of misconceptions that can be erroneously inferred from the preceding discussion: (1) that the developer of software should do no testing at all, (2) that the software should be "tossed over the wall" to strangers who will test it mercilessly, (3) that testers get involved with the project only when the testing steps are about to begin. Each of these statements is incorrect.

The software developer is always responsible for testing the individual units (components) of the program, ensuring that each performs the function or exhibits the behavior for which it was designed. In many cases, the developer also conducts integration testing—a testing step that leads to the construction (and test) of the complete software architecture. Only after the software architecture is complete does an independent test group become involved.

If an ITG does not exist within your organization, you'll have to take its point of view. When you test, try to break the software.

The role of an *independent test group* (ITG) is to remove the inherent problems associated with letting the builder test the thing that has been built. Independent testing removes the conflict of interest that may otherwise be present. After all, ITG personnel are paid to find errors.

However, the software engineer doesn't turn the program over to ITG and walk away. The developer and the ITG work closely throughout a software project to ensure that thorough tests will be conducted. While testing is conducted, the developer must be available to correct errors that are uncovered.

> **"The first mistake that people make is thinking that the testing team is responsible for assuring quality."**
>
> **Brian Marick**

The ITG is part of the software development project team in the sense that it becomes involved during analysis and design and stays involved (planning and specifying test procedures) throughout a large project. However, in many cases the ITG reports to the software quality assurance organization, thereby achieving a degree of independence that might not be possible if it were a part of the software engineering organization.

13.1.3 A Software Testing Strategy for Conventional Software Architectures

The software process may be viewed as the spiral illustrated in Figure 13.1. Initially, system engineering defines the role of software and leads to software requirements analysis, where the information domain, function, behavior, performance, constraints, and validation criteria for software are established. Moving inward along the spiral, we come to design and finally to coding. To develop computer software, we spiral inward along streamlines that decrease the level of abstraction on each turn.

? What is the overall strategy for software testing?

A strategy for software testing may also be viewed in the context of the spiral (Figure 13.1). *Unit testing* begins at the vortex of the spiral and concentrates on each unit (i.e., component) of the software as implemented in source code. Testing progresses by moving outward along the spiral to *integration testing,* where the focus is on design and the construction of the software architecture. Taking another turn outward on the spiral, we encounter *validation testing,* where requirements established as part of software requirements analysis are validated against the software that has been constructed. Finally, we arrive at *system testing,* where the software and other system elements are tested as a whole. To test computer software, we spiral out along streamlines that broaden the scope of testing with each turn.

WebRef
Useful resources for software testers can be found at **www.SQAtester.com.**

Considering the process from a procedural point of view, testing within the context of software engineering is actually a series of four steps that are implemented sequentially. The steps are shown in Figure 13.2. Initially, tests focus on each component individually, ensuring that it functions properly as a unit. Hence, the name

FIGURE 13.1
Testing strategy

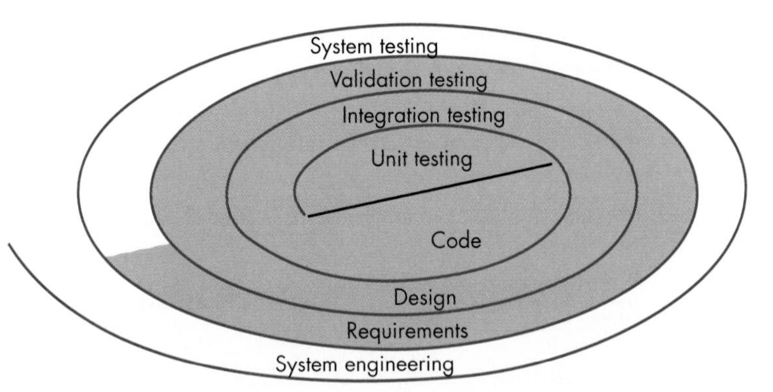

FIGURE 13.2

Software testing steps

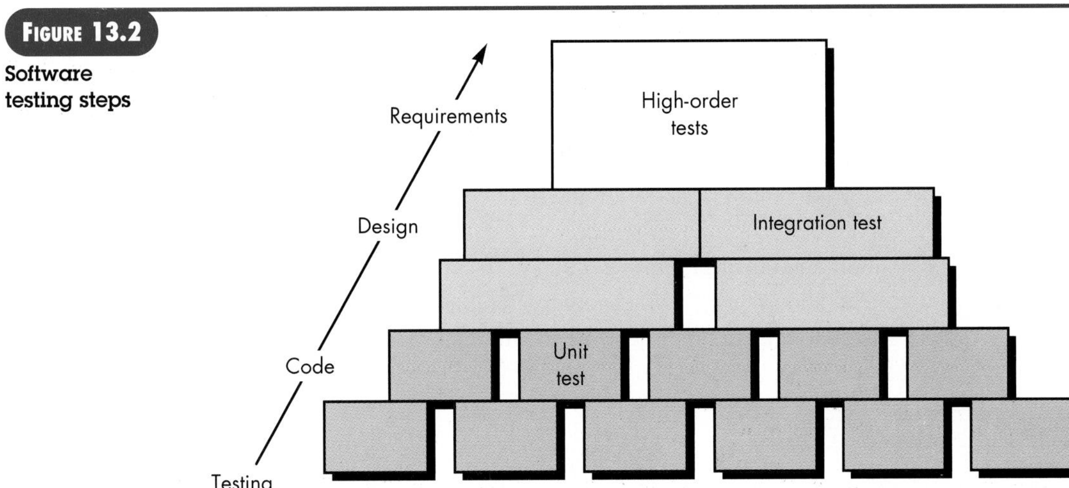

unit testing. Unit testing makes heavy use of testing techniques that exercise specific paths in a component's control structure to ensure complete coverage and maximum error detection. Next, components must be assembled or integrated to form the complete software package. Integration testing addresses the issues associated with the dual problems of verification and program construction. Test case design techniques that focus on inputs and outputs are more prevalent during integration, although techniques that exercise specific program paths may be used to ensure coverage of major control paths. After the software has been integrated (constructed), a set of high-order tests are conducted. Validation criteria (established during requirements analysis) must be evaluated. Validation testing provides final assurance that software meets all functional, behavioral, and performance requirements.

The last high-order testing step falls outside the boundary of software engineering and into the broader context of computer system engineering. Software, once validated, must be combined with other system elements (e.g., hardware, people, databases). System testing verifies that all elements mesh properly and that overall system function/performance is achieved.

13.1.4 A Software Testing Strategy for Object-Oriented Architectures

The testing of object-oriented systems presents a different set of challenges for the software engineer. The definition of testing must be broadened to include error discovery techniques (e.g., formal technical reviews) that are applied to analysis and design models. The completeness and consistency of object-oriented representations must be assessed as they are built. Unit testing loses some of its meaning, and integration strategies change significantly. In summary, both testing strategies and testing tactics (Chapter 14) must account for the unique characteristics of object-oriented software.

Like conventional testing, OO testing begins "in the small." However, in most cases, the smallest element tested is a class or package of collaborating classes.

The overall strategy for object-oriented software is identical in philosophy to the one applied for conventional architectures, but differs in approach. We begin with "testing in the small" and work outward toward "testing in the large." However, our focus when "testing in the small" changes from an individual module (the conventional view) to a class that encompasses attributes and operations and implies communication and collaboration. As classes are integrated into an object-oriented architecture, a series of regression tests are run to uncover errors due to communication and collaboration between classes (components) and side effects caused by the addition of new classes (components). Finally, the system as a whole is tested to ensure that errors in requirements are uncovered.

SAFEHOME

Preparing for Testing

The scene: Doug Miller's office, as component-level design continues and construction of certain components begins.

The players: Doug Miller, software engineering manager; Vinod, Jamie, Ed, and Shakira—members of the *SafeHome* software engineering team.

The conversation:

Doug: It seems to me that we haven't spent enough time talking about testing.

Vinod: True, but we've all been just a little busy. And besides, we have been thinking about it . . . in fact, more than thinking.

Doug (smiling): I know . . . we're all overloaded, but we've still got to think down the line.

Shakira: I like the idea of designing unit tests before I begin coding any of my components, so that's what I've been trying to do. I have a pretty big file of tests to run once code for my components is complete.

Doug: That's an Extreme Programming [an agile software development process, see Chapter 4] concept, no?

Ed: It is. Even though we're not using Extreme Programming per se, we decided that it would be a good idea to design unit tests before we build the component—the design gives us all of the information we need.

Jamie: I've been doing the same thing.

Vinod: And I've taken on the role of the integrator, so every time one of the guys passes a component to me, I'll integrate it and run a series of regression tests on the partially integrated program. I've been working to design a set of appropriate tests for each function in the system.

Doug (to Vinod): How often will you run the tests?

Vinod: Every day . . . until the system is integrated . . . well, I mean until the software increment we plan to deliver is integrated.

Doug: You guys are way ahead of me!

Vinod (laughing): Anticipation is everything in the software biz, Boss.

13.1.5 Criteria for Completion of Testing

A classic question arises every time software testing is discussed: When are we done testing—how do we know that we've tested enough? Sadly, there is no definitive answer to this question, but there are a few pragmatic responses and early attempts at empirical guidance.

? When are we finished testing?

One response to the question is: You're never done testing; the burden simply shifts from you (the software engineer) to your customer. Every time the customer/user executes a computer program, the program is being tested. This sobering fact underlines the importance of other software quality assurance activities.

Another response (somewhat cynical but nonetheless accurate) is: You're done testing when you run out of time or you run out of money.

Although few practitioners would argue with these responses, a software engineer needs more rigorous criteria for determining when sufficient testing has been conducted. Musa and Ackerman [MUS89] suggest a response that is based on statistical criteria: "No, we cannot be absolutely certain that the software will never fail, but relative to a theoretically sound and experimentally validated statistical model, we have done sufficient testing to say with 95 percent confidence that the probability of 1000 CPU hours of failure-free operation in a probabilistically defined environment is at least 0.995." Using statistical modeling and software reliability theory, models of software failures (uncovered during testing) as a function of execution time can be developed (e.g., see [MUS89], [SIN99] or [IEE01]).

By collecting metrics during software testing and making use of existing software reliability models, it is possible to develop meaningful guidelines for answering the question: When are we done testing? There is little debate that further work remains to be done before quantitative rules for testing can be established, but the empirical approaches that currently exist are considerably better than raw intuition.

13.2 Strategic Issues

Later in this chapter, we explore a systematic strategy for software testing. But even the best strategy will fail if a series of overriding issues are not addressed. Tom Gilb [GIL95] argues that the following issues must be addressed if a successful software testing strategy is to be implemented:

? What guidelines lead to a successful software testing strategy?

Specify product requirements in a quantifiable manner long before testing commences. Although the overriding objective of testing is to find errors, a good testing strategy also assesses other quality characteristics such as portability, maintainability, and usability (Chapter 15). These should be specified in a way that is measurable so that testing results are unambiguous.

State testing objectives explicitly. The specific objectives of testing should be stated in measurable terms. For example, test effectiveness, test coverage, mean time to failure, the cost to find and fix defects, remaining defect density or frequency of occurrence, and test work-hours per regression test all should be stated within the test plan [GIL95].

Understand the users of the software and develop a profile for each user category. Use-cases that describe the interaction scenario for each class of user can reduce overall testing effort by focusing testing on actual use of the product.

Develop a testing plan that emphasizes "rapid cycle testing." Gilb [GIL95] recommends that a software engineering team "learn to test in rapid cycles (2 percent of project effort) of customer-useful, at least field 'trialable,' increments of functionality and/or quality improvement." The feedback generated from these rapid cycle tests can be used to control quality levels and the corresponding test strategies.

Build "robust" software that is designed to test itself. Software should be designed in a manner that uses antibugging (Section 13.3.1) techniques. That is, software should be capable of diagnosing certain classes of errors. In addition, the design should accommodate automated testing and regression testing.

WebRef
An excellent list of testing resources can be found at **www.io.com/~wazmo/qa/.**

Use effective formal technical reviews as a filter prior to testing. Formal technical reviews (Chapter 26) can be as effective as testing in uncovering errors. For this reason, reviews can reduce the amount of testing effort that is required to produce high-quality software.

Conduct formal technical reviews to assess the test strategy and test cases themselves. Formal technical reviews can uncover inconsistencies, omissions, and outright errors in the testing approach. This saves time and also improves product quality.

Develop a continuous improvement approach for the testing process. The test strategy should be measured. The metrics collected during testing should be used as part of a statistical process control approach for software testing.

> **"Testing only to end user requirements is like inspecting a building based on the work done by the interior designer at the expense of the foundations, girders, and plumbing."**
>
> **Boris Beizer**

13.3 Test Strategies for Conventional Software

There are many strategies that can be used to test software. At one extreme, a software team could wait until the system is fully constructed and then conduct tests on the overall system in hopes of finding errors. This approach, although appealing, simply does not work. It will result in buggy software that disappoints the customer and end-user. At the other extreme, a software engineer could conduct tests on a daily basis, whenever any part of the system is constructed. This approach, although less appealing to many, can be very effective. Unfortunately, most software developers hesitate to use it. What to do?

A testing strategy that is chosen by most software teams falls between the two extremes. It takes an incremental view of testing, beginning with the testing of individual program units, moving to tests designed to facilitate the integration of the units, and culminating with tests that exercise the constructed system. Each of these classes of tests is described in the sections that follow.

13.3.1 Unit Testing

Unit testing focuses verification effort on the smallest unit of software design—the software component or module. Using the component-level design description as a guide, important control paths are tested to uncover errors within the boundary of the module. The relative complexity of tests and the errors those tests uncover is limited by the constrained scope established for unit testing. The unit test focuses on the internal processing logic and data structures within the boundaries of a component. This type of testing can be conducted in parallel for multiple components.

Unit Test Considerations. The tests that occur as part of unit tests are illustrated schematically in Figure 13.3. The module interface is tested to ensure that information properly flows into and out of the program unit under test. Local data structures are examined to ensure that data stored temporarily maintains its integrity during all steps in an algorithm's execution. All independent paths (basis paths) through the control structure are exercised to ensure that all statements in a module have been executed at least once. Boundary conditions are tested to ensure that the module operates properly at boundaries established to limit or restrict processing. And finally, all error handling paths are tested.

Tests of data flow across a module interface are required before any other test is initiated. If data do not enter and exit properly, all other tests are moot. In addition, local data structures should be exercised and the local impact on global data should be ascertained (if possible) during unit testing.

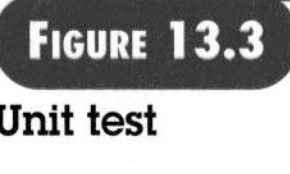

What errors are commonly found during unit testing?

Selective testing of execution paths is an essential task during the unit test. Test cases should be designed to uncover errors due to erroneous computations, incorrect comparisons, or improper control flow. Among the more common errors in computation are (1) misunderstood or incorrect arithmetic precedence, (2) mixed mode operations, (3) incorrect initialization, (4) precision inaccuracy, and (5) incorrect symbolic representation of an expression. Comparison and control flow are closely coupled to one another (i.e., change of flow frequently occurs after a com-

FIGURE 13.3

Unit test

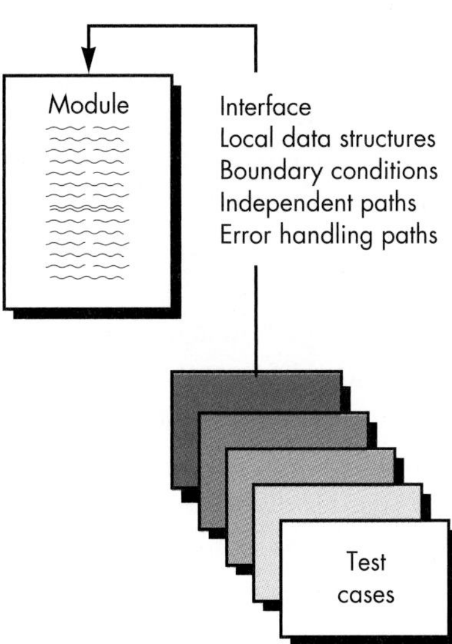

parison). Test cases should uncover errors such as (1) comparison of different data types, (2) incorrect logical operators or precedence, (3) expectation of equality when precision error makes equality unlikely, (4) incorrect comparison of variables, (5) improper or nonexistent loop termination, (6) failure to exit when divergent iteration is encountered, and (7) improperly modified loop variables.

WebRef

Useful information on a wide variety of articles and resources for "agile testing" can be found at **testing.com/agile/.**

Boundary testing is one of the most important unit testing tasks. Software often fails at its boundaries. That is, errors often occur when the *n*th element of an *n*-dimensional array is processed, when the *i*th repetition of a loop with *i* passes is invoked, when the maximum or minimum allowable value is encountered. Test cases that exercise data structure, control flow, and data values just below, at, and just above maxima and minima are very likely to uncover errors.

Good design dictates that error conditions be anticipated and error-handling paths set up to reroute or cleanly terminate processing when an error does occur. Yourdon [YOU75] calls this approach *antibugging.* Unfortunately, there is a tendency to incorporate error handling into software and then never test it. A true story may serve to illustrate:

Be sure that you design tests to execute every error-handling path. If you don't, the path may fail when it is invoked, exacerbating an already dicey situation.

> A computer-aided design system was developed under contract. In one transaction processing module, a practical joker placed the following error handling message after a series of conditional tests that invoked various control flow branches: ERROR! THERE IS NO WAY YOU CAN GET HERE. This "error message" was uncovered by a customer during user training!

Among the potential errors that should be tested when error handling is evaluated are: (1) error description is unintelligible; (2) error noted does not correspond to error encountered; (3) error condition causes operating system intervention prior to error handling; (4) exception-condition processing is incorrect, or (5) error description does not provide enough information to assist in the location of the cause of the error.

Unit test procedures. Unit testing is normally considered as an adjunct to the coding step. The design of unit tests can be performed before coding begins (a preferred agile approach) or after source code has been generated. A review of design information provides guidance for establishing test cases that are likely to uncover errors in each of the categories discussed earlier. Each test case should be coupled with a set of expected results.

There are some situations in which you will not have the resources to do comprehensive unit testing. Select critical modules and those with high cyclomatic complexity, and unit test only those.

Because a component is not a stand-alone program, driver and/or stub software must be developed for each unit test. The unit test environment is illustrated in Figure 13.4. In most applications a *driver* is nothing more than a "main program" that accepts test case data, passes such data to the component (to be tested), and prints relevant results. *Stubs* serve to replace modules that are subordinate to (called by) the component to be tested. A stub or "dummy subprogram" uses the subordinate module's interface, may do minimal data manipulation, provides verification of entry, and returns control to the module undergoing testing.

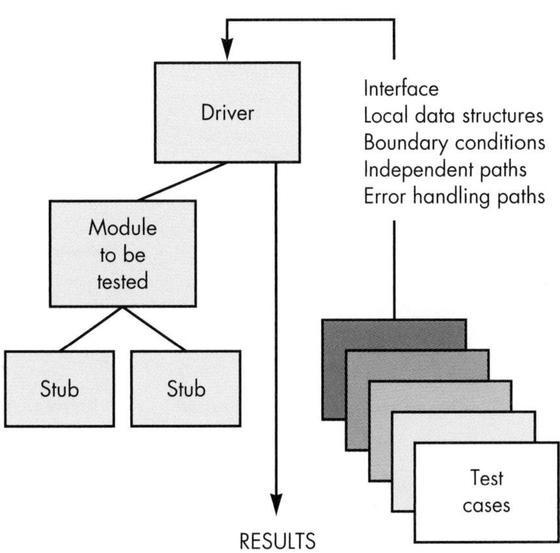

FIGURE 13.4
Unit test environment

Drivers and stubs represent overhead. That is, both are software that must be written (formal design is not commonly applied) but that is not delivered with the final software product. If drivers and stubs are kept simple, actual overhead is relatively low. Unfortunately, many components cannot be adequately unit tested with "simple" overhead software. In such cases, complete testing can be postponed until the integration test step (where drivers or stubs are also used).

Unit testing is simplified when a component with high cohesion is designed. When only one function is addressed by a component, the number of test cases is reduced and errors can be more easily predicted and uncovered.

13.3.2 Integration Testing

A neophyte in the software world might ask a seemingly legitimate question once all modules have been unit tested: "If they all work individually, why do you doubt that they'll work when we put them together?" The problem, of course, is "putting them together"—interfacing. Data can be lost across an interface; one module can have an inadvertent, adverse affect on another; subfunctions, when combined, may not produce the desired major function; individually acceptable imprecision may be magnified to unacceptable levels; global data structures can present problems. Sadly, the list goes on and on.

Integration testing is a systematic technique for constructing the software architecture while at the same time conducting tests to uncover errors associated with interfacing. The objective is to take unit tested components and build a program structure that has been dictated by design.

FIGURE 13.5

Top-down integration

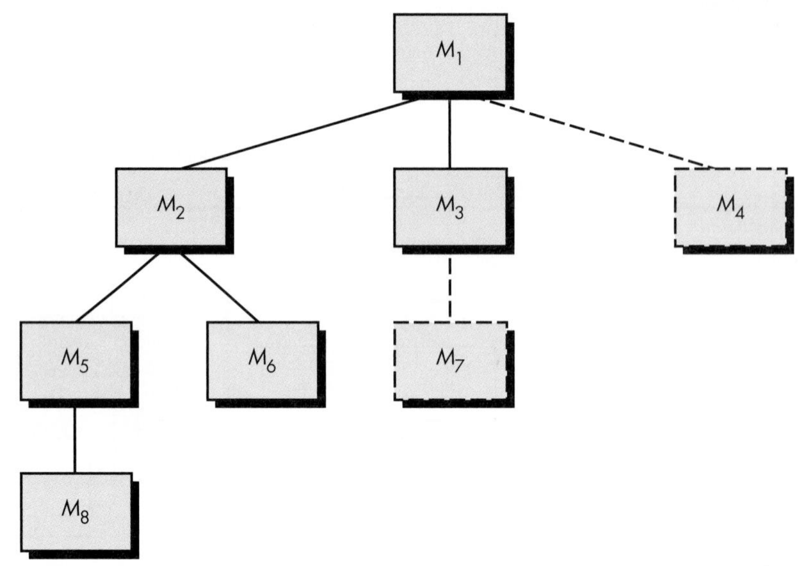

Taking the "big bang" approach to integration is a lazy strategy that is doomed to failure. Integrate incrementally, testing as you go.

There is often a tendency to attempt nonincremental integration that is, to construct the program using a "big bang" approach. All components are combined in advance. The entire program is tested as a whole. And chaos usually results! A set of errors is encountered. Correction is difficult because isolation of causes is complicated by the vast expanse of the entire program. Once these errors are corrected, new ones appear and the process continues in a seemingly endless loop.

Incremental integration is the antithesis of the big bang approach. The program is constructed and tested in small increments, where errors are easier to isolate and correct; interfaces are more likely to be tested completely; and a systematic test approach may be applied. In the paragraphs that follow, a number of different incremental integration strategies are discussed.

ADVICE

When you develop a project schedule, you'll have to consider the manner in which integration will occur so that components will be available when needed.

Top-down integration. *Top-down integration testing* is an incremental approach to construction of the software architecture. Modules are integrated by moving downward through the control hierarchy, beginning with the main control module (main program). Modules subordinate (and ultimately subordinate) to the main control module are incorporated into the structure in either a depth-first or breadth-first manner.

Referring to Figure 13.5, *depth-first integration* integrates all components on a major control path of the program structure. Selection of a major path is somewhat arbitrary and depends on application-specific characteristics. For example, selecting the left-hand path, components M_1, M_2, M_5 would be integrated first. Next, M_8 or (if necessary for proper functioning of M_2) M_6 would be integrated. Then, the central and right-hand control paths are built. *Breadth-first integration* incorporates all components directly subordinate at each level, moving across the structure horizontally. From the figure, components M_2, M_3, and M_4 would be integrated first. The next control level, M_5, M_6, and so on, follows. The integration process is performed in a series of five steps:

? What are the steps for top-down integration?

1. The main control module is used as a test driver, and stubs are substituted for all components directly subordinate to the main control module.
2. Depending on the integration approach selected (i.e., depth or breadth first), subordinate stubs are replaced one at a time with actual components.
3. Tests are conducted as each component is integrated.
4. On completion of each set of tests, another stub is replaced with the real component.
5. Regression testing (discussed later in this section) may be conducted to ensure that new errors have not been introduced.

The process continues from step 2 until the entire program structure is built.

The top-down integration strategy verifies major control or decision points early in the test process. In a well-factored program structure, decision making occurs at upper levels in the hierarchy and is therefore encountered first. If major control problems do exist, early recognition is essential. If depth-first integration is selected, a complete function of the software may be implemented and demonstrated. For example, consider a classic transaction structure (Chapter 10) in which a complex series of interactive inputs is requested, acquired, and validated via an incoming path. The incoming path may be integrated in a top-down manner. All input processing (for subsequent transaction dispatching) may be demonstrated before other elements of the structure have been integrated. Early demonstration of functional capability is a confidence builder for both the developer and the customer.

? What problems may be encountered when top-down integration is chosen?

Top-down strategy sounds relatively uncomplicated, but, in practice, logistical problems can arise. The most common of these problems occurs when processing at low levels in the hierarchy is required to adequately test upper levels. Stubs replace low-level modules at the beginning of top-down testing; therefore, no significant data can flow upward in the program structure. The tester is left with three choices: (1) delay many tests until stubs are replaced with actual modules, (2) develop stubs that perform limited functions that simulate the actual module, or (3) integrate the software from the bottom of the hierarchy upward.

The first approach (delay tests until stubs are replaced by actual modules) causes us to lose some control over correspondence between specific tests and incorporation of specific modules. This can lead to difficulty in determining the cause of errors and tends to violate the highly constrained nature of the top-down approach. The second approach is workable but can lead to significant overhead, as stubs become more and more complex. The third approach, called *bottom-up testing,* is discussed in the next section.

Bottom-up integration. *Bottom-up integration testing,* as its name implies, begins construction and testing with atomic modules (i.e., components at the lowest levels in the program structure). Because components are integrated from the bottom up, processing required for components subordinate to a given level is always available and the need for stubs is eliminated. A bottom-up integration strategy may be implemented with the following steps:

? What are the steps for bottom-up integration?

1. Low-level components are combined into *clusters* (sometimes called *builds*) that perform a specific software subfunction.
2. A driver (a control program for testing) is written to coordinate test case input and output.
3. The cluster is tested.
4. Drivers are removed and clusters are combined moving upward in the program structure.

Bottom-up integration eliminates the need for complex stubs.

Integration follows the pattern illustrated in Figure 13.6. Components are combined to form clusters 1, 2, and 3. Each of the clusters is tested using a driver (shown as a dashed block). Components in clusters 1 and 2 are subordinate to M_a. Drivers D_1 and D_2 are removed and the clusters are interfaced directly to M_a. Similarly, driver D_3 for cluster 3 is removed prior to integration with module M_b. Both M_a and M_b will ultimately be integrated with component M_c, and so forth.

FIGURE 13.6

Bottom-up integration

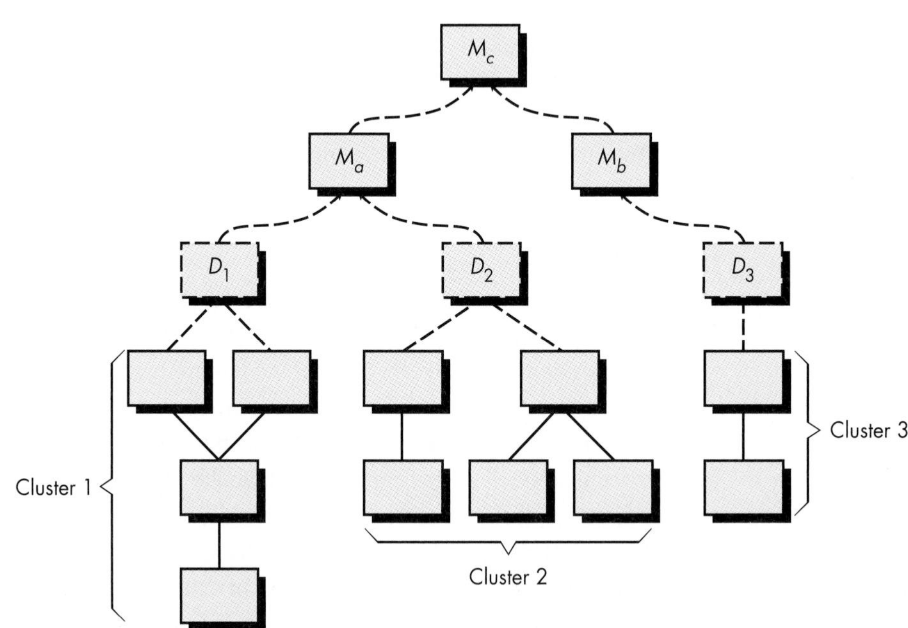

As integration moves upward, the need for separate test drivers lessens. In fact, if the top two levels of program structure are integrated top down, the number of drivers can be reduced substantially and integration of clusters is greatly simplified.

Regression testing is an important strategy for reducing "side effects." Run regression tests every time a major change is made to the software (including the integration of new components).

Regression testing. Each time a new module is added as part of integration testing, the software changes. New data flow paths are established, new I/O may occur, and new control logic is invoked. These changes may cause problems with functions that previously worked flawlessly. In the context of an integration test strategy, *regression testing* is the re-execution of some subset of tests that have already been conducted to ensure that changes have not propagated unintended side effects.

In a broader context, successful tests (of any kind) result in the discovery of errors, and errors must be corrected. Whenever software is corrected, some aspect of the software configuration (the program, its documentation, or the data that support it) is changed. Regression testing is the activity that helps to ensure that changes (due to testing or for other reasons) do not introduce unintended behavior or additional errors.

Regression testing may be conducted manually, by re-executing a subset of all test cases or using automated capture/playback tools. *Capture/playback tools* enable the software engineer to capture test cases and results for subsequent playback and comparison. The regression test suite (the subset of tests to be executed) contains three different classes of test cases:

- A representative sample of tests that will exercise all software functions.
- Additional tests that focus on software functions that are likely to be affected by the change.
- Tests that focus on the software components that have been changed.

As integration testing proceeds, the number of regression tests can grow quite large. Therefore, the regression test suite should be designed to include only those tests that address one or more classes of errors in each of the major program functions. It is impractical and inefficient to re-execute every test for every program function once a change has occurred.

Smoke testing might be characterized as a rolling integration strategy. The software is rebuilt (with new components added) and smoke tested every day.

Smoke testing. *Smoke testing* is an integration testing approach that is commonly used when software products are being developed. It is designed as a pacing mechanism for time-critical projects, allowing the software team to assess its project on a frequent basis. In essence, the smoke testing approach encompasses the following activities:

1. Software components that have been translated into code are integrated into a "build." A build includes all data files, libraries, reusable modules, and engineered components that are required to implement one or more product functions.
2. A series of tests is designed to expose errors that will keep the build from properly performing its function. The intent should be to uncover "show

stopper" errors that have the highest likelihood of throwing the software project behind schedule.

3. The build is integrated with other builds and the entire product (in its current form) is smoke tested *daily.* The integration approach may be top down or bottom up.

The daily frequency of testing the entire product may surprise some readers. However, frequent tests give both managers and practitioners a realistic assessment of integration testing progress. McConnell [MCO96] describes the smoke test in the following manner:

> The smoke test should exercise the entire system from end to end. It does not have to be exhaustive, but it should be capable of exposing major problems. The smoke test should be thorough enough that if the build passes, you can assume that it is stable enough to be tested more thoroughly.

Smoke testing provides a number of benefits when it is applied on complex, time-critical software engineering projects:

- *Integration risk is minimized.* Because smoke tests are conducted daily, incompatibilities and other show-stopper errors are uncovered early, thereby reducing the likelihood of serious schedule impact when errors are uncovered.
- *The quality of the end-product is improved.* Because the approach is construction (integration) oriented, smoke testing is likely to uncover both functional errors and architectural and component-level design errors. If these errors are corrected early, better product quality will result.
- *Error diagnosis and correction are simplified.* Like all integration testing approaches, errors uncovered during smoke testing are likely to be associated with "new software increments"—that is, the software that has just been added to the build(s) is a probable cause of a newly discovered error.
- *Progress is easier to assess.* With each passing day, more of the software has been integrated and more has been demonstrated to work. This improves team morale and gives managers a good indication that progress is being made.

> **"Treat the daily build as the heartbeat of the project. If there's no heartbeat, the project is dead."**
>
> **Jim McCarthy**

Strategic options. There has been much discussion (e.g., [BEI84]) of the relative advantages and disadvantages of top-down versus bottom-up integration testing. In general, the advantages of one strategy tend to result in disadvantages for the other strategy. The major disadvantage of the top-down approach is the need for stubs and

WebRef
Pointers to commentary on testing strategies can be found at **www.qalinks.com.**

the attendant testing difficulties that can be associated with them. Problems associated with stubs may be offset by the advantage of testing major control functions early. The major disadvantage of bottom-up integration is that "the program as an entity does not exist until the last module is added" [MYE79]. This drawback is tempered by easier test case design and a lack of stubs.

Selection of an integration strategy depends upon software characteristics and, sometimes, project schedule. In general, a combined approach (sometimes called *sandwich testing*) that uses top-down tests for upper levels of the program structure, coupled with bottom-up tests for subordinate levels may be the best compromise.

? What is a "critical module" and why should we identify it?

As integration testing is conducted, the tester should identify critical modules. A *critical module* has one or more of the following characteristics: (1) addresses several software requirements, (2) has a high level of control (resides relatively high in the program structure), (3) is complex or error prone, or (4) has definite performance requirements. Critical modules should be tested as early as possible. In addition, regression tests should focus on critical module functions.

Integration test documentation. An overall plan for integration of the software and a description of specific tests are documented in a *Test Specification.* This document contains a test plan, a test procedure, is a work product of the software process, and becomes part of the software configuration.

The test plan describes the overall strategy for integration. Testing is divided into phases and builds that address specific functional and behavioral characteristics of the software. For example, integration testing for a CAD system might be divided into the following test phases:

- User interaction (command selection, drawing creation, display representation, error processing and representation).
- Data manipulation and analysis (symbol creation, dimensioning, rotation, computation of physical properties).
- Display processing and generation (two-dimensional displays, three-dimensional displays, graphs and charts).
- Database management (access, update, integrity, performance).

Each of these phases and subphases (denoted in parentheses) delineates a broad functional category within the software and can generally be related to a specific domain within the software architecture. Therefore, program builds (groups of modules) are created to correspond to each phase. The following criteria and corresponding tests are applied for all test phases:

Interface integrity. Internal and external interfaces are tested as each module (or cluster) is incorporated into the structure.

Functional validity. Tests designed to uncover functional errors are conducted.

Information content. Tests designed to uncover errors associated with local or global data structures are conducted.

Performance. Tests designed to verify performance bounds established during software design are conducted.

A schedule for integration, the development of overhead software, and related topics is also discussed as part of the test plan. Start and end dates for each phase are established and "availability windows" for unit tested modules are defined. A brief description of overhead software (stubs and drivers) concentrates on characteristics that might require special effort. Finally, test environment and resources are described. Unusual hardware configurations, exotic simulators, and special test tools or techniques are a few of many topics that may also be discussed.

The detailed testing procedure that is required to accomplish the test plan is described next. The order of integration and corresponding tests at each integration step are described. A listing of all test cases (annotated for subsequent reference) and expected results is also included.

A history of actual test results, problems, or peculiarities is recorded in a *Test Report* that can be appended to the *Test Specification,* if desired. Information contained in this section can be vital during software maintenance. Appropriate references and appendixes are also presented.

Like all other elements of a software configuration, the test specification format may be tailored to the local needs of a software engineering organization. It is important to note, however, that an integration strategy (contained in a test plan) and testing details (described in a test procedure) are essential ingredients and must appear.

> **"The best tester isn't the one who finds the most bugs . . . the best tester is the one who gets the most bugs fixed."**
>
> **Cem Kaner et al.**

13.4 Test Strategies for Object-Oriented Software

The objective of testing, stated simply, is to find the greatest possible number of errors with a manageable amount of effort applied over a realistic time span. Although this fundamental objective remains unchanged for object-oriented software, the nature of object-oriented software changes both testing strategy and testing tactics (Chapter 14).

13.4.1 Unit Testing in the OO Context

When object-oriented software is considered, the concept of the unit changes. Encapsulation drives the definition of classes. This means that each class and each instance of a class (object) packages attributes (data) and the operations (functions) that manipulate these data. An encapsulated class is usually the focus of unit testing. However, operations within the class are the smallest testable units. Because a class can contain a number of different operations and a particular operation may exist as part of a number of different classes, the tactics applied to unit testing must change.

Class testing for OO software is analogous to module testing for conventional software. It is not advisable to test operations in isolation.

We can no longer test a single operation in isolation (the conventional view of unit testing) but rather as part of a class. To illustrate, consider a class hierarchy in which an operation *X* is defined for the superclass and is inherited by a number of subclasses. Each subclass uses operation *X*, but it is applied within the context of the private attributes and operations that have been defined for the subclass. Because the context in which operation *X* is used varies in subtle ways, it is necessary to test operation *X* in the context of each of the subclasses. This means that testing operation *X* in a standalone fashion (the conventional unit testing approach) is usually ineffective in the object-oriented context.

Class testing for OO software is the equivalent of unit testing for conventional software. Unlike unit testing of conventional software, which tends to focus on the algorithmic detail of a module and the data that flow across the module interface, class testing for OO software is driven by the operations encapsulated by the class and the state behavior of the class.

13.4.2 Integration Testing in the OO Context

Because object-oriented software does not have an obvious hierarchical control structure, traditional top-down and bottom-up integration strategies (Section 13.3.2) have little meaning. In addition, integrating operations one at a time into a class (the conventional incremental integration approach) is often impossible because of the "direct and indirect interactions of the components that make up the class" [BER93].

An important strategy for integration testing of OO software is thread-based testing. Threads are sets of classes that respond to an input or event. Use-based tests focus on classes that do not collaborate heavily with other classes.

There are two different strategies for integration testing of OO systems [BIN94]. The first, *thread-based testing,* integrates the set of classes required to respond to one input or event for the system. Each thread is integrated and tested individually. Regression testing is applied to ensure that no side effects occur. The second integration approach, *use-based testing,* begins the construction of the system by testing those classes (called *independent classes*) that use very few (if any) *server* classes. After the independent classes are tested, the next layer of classes, called *dependent classes,* which use the independent classes, are tested. This sequence of testing layers of dependent classes continues until the entire system is constructed.

The use of drivers and stubs also changes when integration testing of OO systems is conducted. Drivers can be used to test operations at the lowest level and for the testing of whole groups of classes. A driver can also be used to replace the user interface so that tests of system functionality can be conducted prior to implementation of the interface. Stubs can be used in situations in which collaboration between classes is required but one or more of the collaborating classes has not yet been fully implemented.

Cluster testing is one step in the integration testing of OO software. Here, a cluster of collaborating classes (determined by examining the CRC and object-relationship model) is exercised by designing test cases that attempt to uncover errors in the collaborations.

13.5 Validation Testing

Like all other testing steps, validation tries to uncover errors, but the focus is at the requirements level— on things that will be immediately apparent to the end-user.

Validation testing begins at the culmination of integration testing, when individual components have been exercised, the software is completely assembled as a package, and interfacing errors have been uncovered and corrected. At the validation or system level, the distinction between conventional and object-oriented software disappears. Testing focuses on user-visible actions and user-recognizable output from the system.

Validation can be defined in many ways, but a simple (albeit harsh) definition is that validation succeeds when software functions in a manner that can be reasonably expected by the customer. At this point a battle-hardened software developer might protest: "Who or what is the arbiter of reasonable expectations?"

Reasonable expectations are defined in the *Software Requirements Specification*— a document that describes all user-visible attributes of the software. The specification contains a section called *Validation Criteria.* Information contained in that section forms the basis for a validation testing approach.

13.5.1 Validation Test Criteria

Software validation is achieved through a series of tests that demonstrate conformity with requirements. A test plan outlines the classes of tests to be conducted, and a test procedure defines specific test cases. Both the plan and procedure are designed to ensure that all functional requirements are satisfied, all behavioral characteristics are achieved, all performance requirements are attained, documentation is correct, and usability and other requirements are met (e.g., transportability, compatibility, error recovery, maintainability).

After each validation test case has been conducted, one of two possible conditions exist: (1) The function or performance characteristic conforms to specification and is accepted, or (2) a deviation from specification is uncovered and a deficiency list is created. Deviation or error discovered at this stage in a project can rarely be corrected prior to scheduled delivery. It is often necessary to negotiate with the customer to establish a method for resolving deficiencies.

13.5.2 Configuration Review

An important element of the validation process is a *configuration review.* The intent of the review is to ensure that all elements of the software configuration have been properly developed, are cataloged, and have the necessary detail to bolster the support phase of the software life cycle. The configuration review, sometimes called an *audit,* is discussed in more detail in Chapter 27.

13.5.3 Alpha and Beta Testing

It is virtually impossible for a software developer to foresee how the customer will really use a program. Instructions for use may be misinterpreted; strange combinations of data may be regularly used; output that seemed clear to the tester may be unintelligible to a user in the field.

When custom software is built for one customer, a series of acceptance tests are conducted to enable the customer to validate all requirements. Conducted by the end-user rather than software engineers, an acceptance test can range from an informal "test drive" to a planned and systematically executed series of tests. In fact, acceptance testing can be conducted over a period of weeks or months, thereby uncovering cumulative errors that might degrade the system over time.

> **"Given enough eyeballs, all bugs are shallow (e.g., given a large enough beta-tester and co-developer base, almost every problem will be characterized quickly and the fix obvious to someone)."**
>
> **E. Raymond**

If software is developed as a product to be used by many customers, it is impractical to perform formal acceptance tests with each one. Most software product builders use a process called *alpha* and *beta testing* to uncover errors that only the end-user seems able to find.

The *alpha test* is conducted at the developer's site by end-users. The software is used in a natural setting with the developer "looking over the shoulder" of typical users and recording errors and usage problems. Alpha tests are conducted in a controlled environment.

The *beta test* is conducted at end-user sites. Unlike alpha testing, the developer is generally not present. Therefore, the beta test is a "live" application of the software in an environment that cannot be controlled by the developer. The end-user records all problems (real or imagined) that are encountered during beta testing and reports these to the developer at regular intervals. As a result of problems reported during beta tests, software engineers make modifications and then prepare for release of the software product to the entire customer base.

SAFEHOME

Preparing for Validation

The scene: Doug Miller's office, as component-level design continues and construction of certain components begins.

The players: Doug Miller, software engineering manager, Vinod, Jamie, Ed, and Shakira—members of the *SafeHome* software engineering team.

The conversation:

Doug: The first increment will be ready for validation in what . . . about three weeks?

Vinod: That's about right. Integration is going well. We're smoke testing daily, finding some bugs but nothing we can't handle. So far, so good.

Doug: Talk to me about validation.

Shakira: Well, we'll use all of the use-cases as the basis for our test design. I haven't started yet, but I'll be developing tests for all of the use-cases that I've been responsible for.

Ed. Same here.

Jamie: Me too, but we've got to get our act together for acceptance testing and also for alpha and beta testing, no?

Doug: Yes, In fact I've been thinking that we could bring in an outside contractor to help us with validation. I have the money in the budget . . . and it would give us a new point of view.

Vinod: I think we've got it under control.

Doug: I'm sure you do, but an ITG gives us an independent look at the software.

Jamie: We're tight on time here, Doug. I, for one, don't have the time to baby-sit anybody you bring in to do the job.

Doug: I know, I know. But if an ITG works from requirements and use-cases, not too much baby sitting will be required.

Vinod: I still think we've got it under control.

Doug: I hear you, Vinod, but I'm going to overrule on this one. Let's plan to meet with the ITG rep later this week. Get 'em started and see what they come up with.

Vinod: Okay, maybe it'll lighten the load a bit.

13.6 System Testing

At the beginning of this book, we stressed the fact that software is only one element of a larger computer-based system. Ultimately, software is incorporated with other system elements (e.g., hardware, people, information), and a series of system integration and validation tests are conducted. These tests fall outside the scope of the software process and are not conducted solely by software engineers. However, steps taken during software design and testing can greatly improve the probability of successful software integration in the larger system.

> **"Like death and taxes, testing is both unpleasant and inevitable."**
>
> **Ed Yourdon**

A classic system testing problem is "finger-pointing." This occurs when an error is uncovered, and each system element developer blames the other for the problem. Rather than indulging in such nonsense, the software engineer should anticipate potential interfacing problems and (1) design error-handling paths that test all information coming from other elements of the system, (2) conduct a series of tests that simulate bad data or other potential errors at the software interface, (3) record the results of tests to use as "evidence" if finger-pointing does occur, and (4) participate in planning and design of system tests to ensure that software is adequately tested.

System testing is actually a series of different tests whose primary purpose is to fully exercise the computer-based system. Although each test has a different purpose, all work to verify that system elements have been properly integrated and perform allocated functions. In the sections that follow, we discuss the types of system tests [BEI84] that are worthwhile for software-based systems.

13.6.1 Recovery Testing

Many computer-based systems must recover from faults and resume processing within a prespecified time. In some cases, a system must be *fault tolerant;* that is, processing faults must not cause overall system function to cease. In other cases, a system failure must be corrected within a specified period of time or severe economic damage will occur.

Recovery testing is a system test that forces the software to fail in a variety of ways and verifies that recovery is properly performed. If recovery is automatic (performed by the system itself), reinitialization, checkpointing mechanisms, data recovery, and restart are evaluated for correctness. If recovery requires human intervention, the *mean-time-to-repair* (MTTR) is evaluated to determine whether it is within acceptable limits.

13.6.2 Security Testing

Any computer-based system that manages sensitive information or causes actions that can improperly harm (or benefit) individuals is a target for improper or illegal penetration. Penetration spans a broad range of activities: hackers who attempt to penetrate systems for sport; disgruntled employees who attempt to penetrate for revenge; dishonest individuals who attempt to penetrate for illicit personal gain.

Security testing verifies that protection mechanisms built into a system will, in fact, protect it from improper penetration. To quote Beizer [BEI84]: "The system's security must, of course, be tested for invulnerability from frontal attack—but must also be tested for invulnerability from flank or rear attack."

During security testing, the tester plays the role(s) of the individual who desires to penetrate the system. Anything goes! The tester may attempt to acquire passwords through external clerical means; may attack the system with custom software designed to break down any defenses that have been constructed; may overwhelm the system, thereby denying service to others; may purposely cause system errors, hoping to penetrate during recovery; may browse through insecure data, hoping to find the key to system entry.

Given enough time and resources, good security testing will ultimately penetrate a system. The role of the system designer is to make penetration cost more than the value of the information that will be obtained.

13.6.3 Stress Testing

Software testing steps discussed earlier in this chapter result in thorough evaluation of normal program functions and performance. Stress tests are designed to confront programs with abnormal situations. In essence, the tester who performs stress testing asks: "How high can we crank this up before it fails?"

Stress testing executes a system in a manner that demands resources in abnormal quantity, frequency, or volume. For example, (1) special tests may be designed that generate ten interrupts per second, when one or two is the average rate, (2) input data rates may be increased by an order of magnitude to determine how input functions will respond, (3) test cases that require maximum memory or other resources are executed, (4) test cases that may cause memory management problems are designed, (5) test cases that may cause excessive hunting for disk-resident data are created. Essentially, the tester attempts to overwhelm the program.

> **"If you're trying to find true system bugs and you haven't subjected your software to a real stress test, then it is high time you started."**
>
> **Boris Beizer**

A variation of stress testing is a technique called *sensitivity testing*. In some situations (the most common occur in mathematical algorithms), a very small range of data contained within the bounds of valid data for a program may cause extreme and even erroneous processing or profound performance degradation. Sensitivity testing attempts to uncover data combinations within valid input classes that may cause instability or improper processing.

13.6.4 Performance Testing

For real-time and embedded systems, software that provides required function but does not conform to performance requirements is unacceptable. *Performance testing* is designed to test the run-time performance of software within the context of an integrated system. Performance testing occurs throughout all steps in the testing process. Even at the unit level, the performance of an individual module may be assessed as tests are conducted. However, it is not until all system elements are fully integrated that the true performance of a system can be ascertained.

Performance tests are often coupled with stress testing and usually require both hardware and software instrumentation. That is, it is often necessary to measure resource utilization (e.g., processor cycles) in an exacting fashion. External instrumentation can monitor execution intervals, log events (e.g., interrupts) as they occur, and sample machine states on a regular basis. By instrumenting a system, the tester can uncover situations that lead to degradation and possible system failure.

SOFTWARE TOOLS

Test Planning and Management

Objective: These tools assist the software team in planning the testing strategy that is chosen and managing the testing process as it is conducted.

Mechanics: Tools in this category address test planning, test storage, management and control, requirements traceability, integration, error tracking, and report generation. Project managers use them to supplement project scheduling tools. Testers use these tools to plan testing activities and to control the flow of information as the testing process proceeds.

Representative Tools[2]

OTF (Object Testing Framework), developed by MCG Software, Inc. (www.mcgsoft.com), provides a framework for managing suites of tests for Smalltalk objects.

QADirector, developed by Compuware Corp. (www.compuware.com/qacenter), provides a single point of control for managing all phases of the testing process.

TestWorks, developed by Software Research, Inc. (www.soft.com/Products/index.html), contains a fully integrated suite of testing tools including tools for test management and reporting.

13.7 The Art of Debugging

Software testing is an action that can be systematically planned and specified. Test case design can be conducted, a strategy can be defined, and results can be evaluated against prescribed expectations.

Debugging occurs as a consequence of successful testing. That is, when a test case uncovers an error, debugging is an action that results in the removal of the error. Although debugging can and should be an orderly process, it is still very much an art. A software engineer, evaluating the results of a test, is often confronted with a "symptomatic" indication of a software problem. That is, the external manifestation of the error and the internal cause of the error may have no obvious relationship to one another. The poorly understood mental process that connects a symptom to a cause is debugging.

> "As soon as we started programming, we found to our surprise that it wasn't as easy to get programs right as we had thought. Debugging had to be discovered. I can remember the exact instant when I realized that a large part of my life from then on was going to be spent in finding mistakes in my own programs."
>
> **Maurice Wilkes, discovers debugging, 1949**

13.7.1 The Debugging Process

Debugging is not testing but always occurs as a consequence of testing.[3] Referring to Figure 13.7, the debugging process begins with the execution of a test case. Results are assessed and a lack of correspondence between expected and actual performance is encountered. In many cases, the noncorresponding data are a symptom of an underlying cause as yet hidden. Debugging attempts to match symptom with cause, thereby leading to error correction.

Debugging will always have one of two outcomes: (1) the cause will be found and corrected, or (2) the cause will not be found. In the latter case, the person perform-

2 Tools noted here do not represent an endorsement, but rather a sampling of tools in this category. In most cases, tool names are trademarked by their respective developers.

3 In making the statement, we take the broadest possible view of testing. Not only does the developer test software prior to release, but the customer/user tests software every time it is used!

FIGURE 13.7

The debugging process

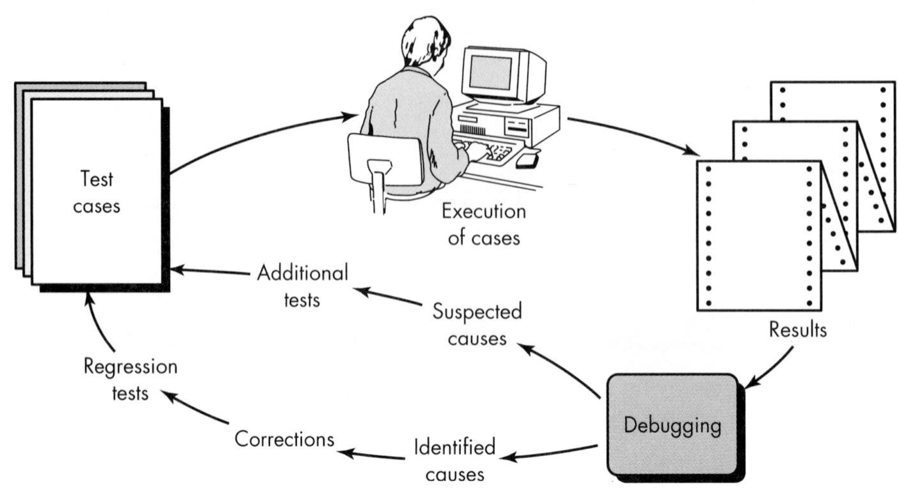

ing debugging may suspect a cause, design one or more test cases to help validate that suspicion, and work toward error correction in an iterative fashion.

Why is debugging so difficult? In all likelihood, human psychology (see the next section) has more to do with an answer than software technology. However, a few characteristics of bugs provide some clues:

? Why is debugging so difficult?

1. The symptom and the cause may be geographically remote. That is, the symptom may appear in one part of a program, while the cause may actually be located at a site that is far removed. Highly coupled components (Chapter 11) exacerbate this situation.
2. The symptom may disappear (temporarily) when another error is corrected.
3. The symptom may actually be caused by nonerrors (e.g., round-off inaccuracies).
4. The symptom may be caused by human error that is not easily traced.
5. The symptom may be a result of timing problems, rather than processing problems.
6. It may be difficult to accurately reproduce input conditions (e.g., a real-time application in which input ordering is indeterminate).
7. The symptom may be intermittent. This is particularly common in embedded systems that couple hardware and software inextricably.
8. The symptom may be due to causes that are distributed across a number of tasks running on different processors [CHE90].

During debugging, we encounter errors that range from mildly annoying (e.g., an incorrect output format) to catastrophic (e.g., the system fails, causing serious economic or physical damage). As the consequences of an error increase, the amount of pressure to find the cause also increases. Often, pressure forces a software developer to fix one error while at the same time introducing two more.

> "Everyone knows that debugging is twice as hard as writing a program in the first place. So if you are as clever as you can be when you write it, how will you ever debug it?"
>
> **Brian Kernighan**

13.7.2 Psychological Considerations

Unfortunately, there appears to be some evidence that debugging prowess is an innate human trait. Some people are good at it, and others aren't. Although experimental evidence on debugging is open to many interpretations, large variances in debugging ability have been reported for programmers with the same education and experience.

Commenting on the human aspects of debugging, Shneiderman [SHN80] states:

> Debugging is one of the more frustrating parts of programming. It has elements of problem solving or brain teasers, coupled with the annoying recognition that you have made a mistake. Heightened anxiety and the unwillingness to accept the possibility of errors increases the task difficulty. Fortunately, there is a great sigh of relief and a lessening of tension when the bug is ultimately . . . corrected.

Although it may be difficult to "learn" debugging, a number of approaches to the problem can be proposed. We examine these in the next section.

SAFEHOME

Debugging

The scene: Ed's cubical as coding and unit testing is conducted.

The players: Ed and Shakira—members of the *SafeHome* software engineering team.

The conversation:

Shakira (looking in through the entrance to the cubical): Hey . . . where were you at lunch time?

Ed: Right here . . . working.

Shakira: You look miserable . . . what's the matter?

Ed (sighing audibly): I've been working on this <bleep> bug since I discovered it at 9:30 this morning, and it's what, 2:45? I'm clueless.

Shakira: I thought we all agreed to spend no more than one hour debugging stuff on our own, then we'd get help, right?

Ed: Yeah, but . . .

Shakira (walking into the cubical): So what's the problem?

Ed: It's complicated. And besides, I've been looking at this for, what, 5 hours? You're not going to find it.

Shakira: Indulge me . . . what's the problem?

(Ed explains the problem to Shakira who looks at it for about 30 seconds without speaking.)

Shakira (a smile gathering on her face): Uh, right there, the variable named *setAlarmCondition*. Shouldn't it be set to "false" before the loop gets started?

(Ed stares at the screen in disbelief, bends forward, and begins to bang his head gently against the monitor. Shakira, smiling broadly now, stands and walks out.)

13.7.3 Debugging Strategies

Regardless of the approach that is taken, debugging has one overriding objective: to find and correct the cause of a software error. The objective is realized by a combination of systematic evaluation, intuition, and luck. Bradley [BRA85] describes the debugging approach in this way:

> Debugging is a straightforward application of the scientific method that has been developed over 2,500 years. The basis of debugging is to locate the problem's source [the cause] by binary partitioning, through working hypotheses that predict new values to be examined.
>
> Take a simple non-software example: A lamp in my house does not work. If nothing in the house works, the cause must be in the main circuit breaker or outside. I look around to see whether the neighborhood is blacked out. I plug the suspect lamp into a working socket and a working appliance into the suspect circuit. So goes the alternation of hypothesis and test.

In general, three debugging strategies have been proposed [MYE79]: (1) brute force, (2) backtracking, and (3) cause elimination. Each of these strategies can be conducted manually, but modern debugging tools can make the process much more effective.

> "The first step in fixing a broken program is getting it to fail repeatably (on the simplest example possible)."
>
> T. Duff

Set a time limit, say, one hour, on the time you spend trying to debug a problem on your own. After that, get help!

Debugging tactics. The *brute force* category of debugging is probably the most common and least efficient method for isolating the cause of a software error. We apply brute force debugging methods when all else fails. Using a "let the computer find the error" philosophy, memory dumps are taken, run-time traces are invoked, and the program is loaded with output statements. We hope that somewhere in the morass of information that is produced we will find a clue that can lead us to the cause of an error. Although the mass of information produced may ultimately lead to success, it more frequently leads to wasted effort and time. Thought must be expended first!

Backtracking is a fairly common debugging approach that can be used successfully in small programs. Beginning at the site where a symptom has been uncovered, the source code is traced backward (manually) until the site of the cause is found. Unfortunately, as the number of source lines increases, the number of potential backward paths may become unmanageably large.

The third approach to debugging—*cause elimination*—is manifested by induction or deduction and introduces the concept of *binary partitioning*. Data related to the error occurrence are organized to isolate potential causes. A "cause hypothesis" is devised, and the aforementioned data are used to prove or disprove the hypothesis. Alternatively, a list of all possible causes is developed, and tests are conducted to eliminate each. If initial tests indicate that a particular cause hypothesis shows promise, data are refined in an attempt to isolate the bug.

Automated debugging. Each of these debugging approaches can be supplemented with debugging tools that provide semi-automated support for the software engineer as debugging strategies are attempted. Hailpern and Santhanam [HAI02] summarize the state of these tools when they note, ". . . many new approaches have been proposed and many commercial debugging environments are available. Integrated development environments (IDEs) provide a way to capture some of the language-specific predetermined errors (e.g., missing end-of-statement characters, undefined variables, and so on) without requiring compilation." One area that has caught the imagination of the industry is the visualization of the necessary underlying programming constructs as a means to analyze a program [BAE97]. A wide variety of debugging compilers, dynamic debugging aids ("tracers"), automatic test case generators, and cross-reference mapping tools are available. However, tools are not a substitute for careful evaluation based on a complete design model and clear source code.

SOFTWARE TOOLS

Debugging

Objective: These tools provide automated assistance for those who must debug software problems. The intent is to provide insight that may be difficult to obtain if approaching the debugging process manually.

Mechanics: Most debugging tools are programming language and environment specific. Debugging features assist in the diagnosis of errors that are found.

Representative Tools[4]

Jprobe ThreadAnalyzer, developed by Sitraka (www.sitraka.com), helps in the evaluation of thread problems—deadlocks, stalls, and race conditions that can pose serious hazards to application performance in Java apps.

C++Test, developed by Parasoft (www.parasoft.com), is a unit testing tool that supports a full range of tests on C and C++ code.

CodeMedic, developed by NewPlanet Software (www.newplanetsoftware.com/medic/), provides a graphical interface for the standard UNIX debugger, *gdb,* and implements its most important features. *gdb* currently supports C/C++, Java, PalmOS, various embedded systems, assembly language, FORTRAN, and Modula-2.

BugCollector Pro, developed by Nesbitt Software Corp. (www.nesbitt.com/), implements a multiuser database that assists a software team in keeping track of reported bugs and other maintenance requests and managing debugging workflow.

GNATS, a freeware application (www.gnu.org/software/gnats/), is a set of tools for tracking bug reports.

The people factor. Any discussion of debugging approaches and tools is incomplete without mention of a powerful ally—other people! A fresh viewpoint, unclouded by hours of frustration, can do wonders.[5] A final maxim for debugging might be: When all else fails, get help!

---

4 Tools noted here do not represent an endorsement, but rather a sampling of tools in this category. In most cases, tool names are trademarked by their respective developers.

5 The concept of pair programming (recommended as part of the Extreme Programming process model discussed in Chapter 4) provides a mechanism for "debugging" as the software is designed and coded.

13.7.4 Correcting the Error

Once a bug has been found, it must be corrected. But, as we have already noted, the correction of a bug can introduce other errors and therefore do more harm than good. Van Vleck [VAN89] suggests three simple questions that every software engineer should ask before making the "correction" that removes the cause of a bug:

? When I correct an error, what questions should I ask myself?

1. *Is the cause of the bug reproduced in another part of the program?* In many situations, a program error is caused by an erroneous pattern of logic that may be reproduced elsewhere. Explicit consideration of the logical pattern may result in the discovery of other errors.
2. *What "next bug" might be introduced by the fix that I'm about to make?* Before the correction is made, the source code (or, better, the design) should be evaluated to assess coupling of logic and data structures. If the correction is to be made in a highly coupled section of the program, special care must be taken when any change is made.
3. *What could we have done to prevent this bug in the first place?* This question is the first step toward establishing a statistical software quality assurance approach (Chapter 26). If we correct the process as well as the product, the bug will be removed from the current program and may be eliminated from all future programs.

13.8 Summary

Software testing accounts for the largest percentage of technical effort in the software process. Yet we are only beginning to understand the subtleties of systematic test planning, execution, and control.

The objective of software testing is to uncover errors. To fulfill this objective, a series of test steps—unit, integration, validation, and system tests—are planned and executed. Unit and integration tests concentrate on functional verification of a component and incorporation of components into the software architecture. Validation testing demonstrates traceability to software requirements, and system testing validates software once it has been incorporated into a larger system.

Each test step is accomplished through a series of systematic test techniques that assist in the design of test cases. With each testing step, the level of abstraction with which software is considered is broadened.

Unlike testing (a systematic, planned activity), debugging must be viewed as an art. Beginning with a symptomatic indication of a problem, the debugging activity must track down the cause of an error. Of the many resources available during debugging, the most valuable is the counsel of other members of the software engineering staff.

The requirement for higher-quality software demands a more systematic approach to testing. To quote Dunn and Ullman [DUN82],

> What is required is an overall strategy, spanning the strategic test space, quite as deliberate in its methodology as was the systematic development on which analysis, design and code were based.

In this chapter, we have examined the strategic test space, considering the steps that have the highest likelihood of meeting the overriding test objective: to find and remove errors in an orderly and effective manner.

References

[BAE97] Baecker, R., C. DiGiano, and A. Marcus, "Software Visualization for Debugging," *Communications of the ACM,* vol. 40 ,no. 4, April 1997, pp. 44–54, and other papers in the same issue.

[BEI84] Beizer, B., *Software System Testing and Quality Assurance,* Van Nostrand-Reinhold, 1984.

[BER93] Berard, E., *Essays on Object-Oriented Software Engineering,* vol. 1, Addison-Wesley, 1993.

[BIN94] Binder, R., "Testing Object-Oriented Systems: A Status Report," *American Programmer,* vol. 7, no. 4, April 1994, pp. 23–28.

[BOE81] Boehm, B., *Software Engineering Economics,* Prentice-Hall, 1981, p. 37.

[BRA85] Bradley, J. H., "The Science and Art of Debugging," *Computerworld,* August 19, 1985, pp. 35–38.

[CHE90] Cheung, W. H., J. P. Black, and E. Manning, "A Framework for Distributed Debugging," *IEEE Software,* January 1990, pp. 106–115.

[DUN82] Dunn, R., and R. Ullman, *Quality Assurance for Computer Software,* McGraw-Hill, 1982, p. 158.

[GIL95] Gilb, T., "What We Fail to Do in Our Current Testing Culture," *Testing Techniques Newsletter,* (on-line edition, ttn@soft.com), Software Research, January 1995.

[HAI02] Hailpern, B., and P. Santhanam, "Software Debugging, Testing and Verification," IBM Systems Journal, vol. 41, no. 1, 2002, available at http://www.research.ibm.com/journal/sj/411/hailpern.html

[IEE01] *Software Reliability Engineering, 12th International Symposium,* IEEE, 2001.

[MCO96] McConnell, S., "Best Practices: Daily Build and Smoke Test," *IEEE Software,* vol. 13, no. 4, July 1996, pp. 143–144.

[MIL77] Miller, E., "The Philosophy of Testing," in *Program Testing Techniques,* IEEE Computer Society Press, 1977, pp. 1–3.

[MUS89] Musa, J. D., and A. F. Ackerman, "Quantifying Software Validation: When to Stop Testing?" *IEEE Software,* May 1989, pp. 19–27.

[MYE79] Myers, G., *The Art of Software Testing,* Wiley, 1979.

[SHO83] Shooman, M. L., *Software Engineering,* McGraw-Hill, 1983.

[SHN80] Shneiderman, B., *Software Psychology,* Winthrop Publishers, 1980, p. 28.

[SIN99] Singpurwalla, N., and S. Wilson, *Statistical Methods in Software Engineering: Reliability and Risk,* Springer-Verlag, 1999.

[VAN89] Van Vleck, T., "Three Questions About Each Bug You Find," *ACM Software Engineering Notes,* vol. 14, no. 5, July 1989, pp. 62–63.

[WAL89] Wallace, D. R., and R. U. Fujii, "Software Verification and Validation: An Overview," *IEEE Software,* May 1989, pp. 10–17.

[YOU75] Yourdon, E., *Techniques of Program Structure and Design,* Prentice-Hall, 1975.

Problems and Points to Ponder

13.1. Using your own words, describe the difference between verification and validation. Do both make use of test case design methods and testing strategies?

13.2. List some problems that might be associated with the creation of an independent test group. Are an ITG and an SQA group made up of the same people?

13.3. Is it always possible to develop a strategy for testing software that uses the sequence of testing steps described in Section 13.1.3? What possible complications might arise for embedded systems?

13.4. Why is a highly coupled module difficult to unit test?

13.5. The concept of "antibugging" (Section 13.3.1) is an extremely effective way to provide built-in debugging assistance when an error is uncovered:

a. Develop a set of guidelines for antibugging.
b. Discuss advantages of using the technique.
c. Discuss disadvantages of using the technique.

13.6. How can project scheduling affect integration testing?

13.7. Is unit testing possible or even desirable in all circumstances? Provide examples to justify your answer.

13.8. Who should perform the validation test—the software developer or the software user? Justify your answer.

13.9. Develop a complete test strategy for the *SafeHome* system discussed throughout this book. Document it in a *Test Specification.*

13.10. As a class project, develop a *Debugging Guide* for your installation. The guide should provide language and system-oriented hints that have been learned through the school of hard knocks! Begin with an outline of topics that will be reviewed by the class and your instructor. Publish the guide for others in your local environment.

Further Readings and Information Sources

Virtually every book on software testing discusses strategies along with methods for test case design. Craig and Kaskiel (*Systematic Software Testing,* Artech House, 2002), Tamres (*Introducing Software Testing,* Addison-Wesley, 2002), Whittaker (*How to Break Software,* Addison-Wesley, 2002), Jorgensen (*Software Testing: A Craftman's Approach,* CRC Press, 2002), Splaine and his colleagues (*The Web Testing Handbook,* Software Quality Engineering Publishing, 2001), Patton (*Software Testing,* Sams Publishing, 2000), Kaner and his colleagues (*Testing Computer Software,* second edition, Wiley, 1999) all discuss testing principles, concepts, strategies and methods. Books by Black (*Managing the Testing Process,* Microsoft Press, 1999) and Perry (*Surviving the Top Ten Challenges of Software Testing: A People-Oriented Approach,* Dorset House, 1997) also address software testing strategies.

For those readers with interest in agile software development methods, Crispin and House (*Testing Extreme Programming,* Addison-Wesley, 2002) and Beck (*Test Driven Development: By Example,* Addison-Wesley, 2002) present testing strategies and tactics for Extreme Programming. Kamer and his colleagues (*Lessons Learned in Software Testing,* Wiley, 2001) present a collection of over 300 pragmatic "lessons" (guidelines) that every software tester should learn. Watkins (*Testing IT: An Off-the Shelf Testing Process,* Cambridge University Press, 2001) establishes an effective testing framework for all types of developed and acquired software.

Lewis (*Software Testing and Continuous Quality Improvement,* CRC Press, 2000) and Koomen and his colleagues (*Test Process Improvement,* Addison-Wesley, 1999) discuss strategies for continuously improving the testing process.

Sykes and McGregor (*Practical Guide to Testing Object-Oriented Software,* Addison-Wesley, 2001), Bashir and Goel (*Testing Object-Oriented Software,* Springer-Verlag, 2000), Binder (*Testing Object-Oriented Systems,* Addison-Wesley, 1999), Kung and his colleagues (*Testing Object-Oriented Software,* IEEE Computer Society Press, 1998), and Marick (*The Craft of Software Testing,* Prentice-Hall, 1997) present strategies and methods for testing OO systems.

Guidelines for debugging are contained in a books by Agans (*Debugging: The Nine Indispensable Rules for Finding Even the Most Elusive Hardware and Software Problems,* AMACON,

2002), Tells and Hsieh (*The Science of Debugging,* The Coreolis Group, 2001), Robbins (*Debugging Applications,* Microsoft Press, 2000), and Dunn (*Software Defect Removal,* McGraw-Hill, 1984). Rosenberg (*How Debuggers Work,* Wiley, 1996) addresses the technology for debugging tools. Younessi (*Object-Oriented Defect Management of Software,* Prentice-Hall, 2002) presents techniques for managing defects that are encountered in object-oriented systems. Beizer [BEI84] presents an interesting "taxonomy of bugs" that can lead to effective methods for test planning. Ball (*Debugging Embedded Microprocessor Systems,* Newnes Publishing, 1998) addresses the special nature of debugging for embedded microprocessor software.

A wide variety of information sources on software testing strategies are available on the Internet. An up-to-date list of World Wide Web references that are relevant to software testing strategies can be found at the SEPA Web site:
http://www.mhhe.com/pressman.

CHAPTER

14 SOFTWARE TESTING TECHNIQUES

KEY CONCEPTS

Testing presents an interesting anomaly for the software engineers, who by their nature are constructive people. Testing requires that the developer discard preconceived notions of the "correctness" of software just developed and then work hard to design test cases to "break" the software. Beizer [BEI90] describes this situation effectively when he states:

> There's a myth that if we were really good at programming, there would be no bugs to catch. If only we could really concentrate, if only everyone used structured programming, top-down design, decision tables, if programs were written in SQUISH, if we had the right silver bullets, then there would be no bugs. So goes the myth. There are bugs, the myth says, because we are bad at what we do; and if we are bad at it, we should feel guilty about it. Therefore, testing and test case design is an admission of failure, which instills a goodly dose of guilt. And the tedium of testing is just punishment for our errors. Punishment for what? For being human? Guilt for what? For failing to achieve inhuman perfection? For not distinguishing between what another programmer thinks and what he says? For failing to be telepathic? For not solving human communications problems that have been kicked around . . . for forty centuries?

Should testing instill guilt? Is testing really destructive? The answer to these questions is No!

In this chapter, we discuss techniques for software test case design. Test case design focuses on a set of techniques for the creation of test cases that meet overall testing objectives and the testing strategies discussed in Chapter 13.

QUICK LOOK

What is it? Once source code has been generated, software must be tested to uncover (and correct) as many errors as possible before delivery to your customer. Your goal is to design a series of test cases that have a high likelihood of finding errors—but how? That's where software testing techniques enter the picture. These techniques provide systematic guidance for designing tests that (1) exercise the internal logic and interfaces of every software component, and (2) exercise the input and output domains of the program to uncover errors in program function, behavior, and performance.

Who does it? During early stages of testing, a software engineer performs all tests. However, as the testing progresses, testing specialists may become involved.

Why is it important? Reviews and other SQA activities can and do uncover errors, but they are not sufficient. Every time the program is executed, the customer tests it! Therefore, you have to execute the program before it gets to the customer with the specific intent of finding and removing all errors. In order to find the highest possible number of errors, tests must be conducted systematically and test cases must be designed using disciplined techniques.

What are the steps? For conventional applications, software is tested from two different perspectives: (1) internal program logic is exercised using "white box" test case design techniques. Software requirements are exercised using "black box" test case design techniques. For object-oriented applications, "testing" begins prior to the existence of source code, but once code has been generated, a series of tests are designed to exercise operations with a class and examine whether errors exist as one class collaborates with others. As classes are integrated to form a subsystem, use-based testing, along with fault-based approaches, is applied to fully exercise collaborating classes. Finally, use-cases assist in the design of tests to uncover errors at the software validation level. In every case, the intent is to find the maximum number of errors with the minimum amount of effort and time.

What is the work product? A set of test cases designed to exercise both internal logic, interfaces, component collaborations, and external requirements is designed and documented, expected results are defined, and actual results are recorded.

How do I ensure that I've done it right? When you begin testing, change your point of view. Try hard to "break" the software! Design test cases in a disciplined fashion and review the test cases you do create for thoroughness. In addition, you can evaluate test coverage and track error detection activities.

14.1 Software Testing Fundamentals

Fundamental testing goals and principles were discussed in Chapter 5. Recall that the goal of testing is to find errors and that a good test is one that has a high probability of finding an error. Therefore, a software engineer should design and implement a computer-based system or a product with "testability" in mind. At the same time, the tests themselves must exhibit a set of characteristics that achieve the goal of finding the most errors with a minimum of effort.

> "Every program does something right; it just may not be the thing we want it to do."
>
> **Author unknown**

Testability. James Bach[1] provides the following definition for testability: "*Software testability* is simply how easily [a computer program] can be tested." The following characteristics lead to testable software.

? What are the characteristics of testability?

Operability. "The better it works, the more efficiently it can be tested." If a system is designed and implemented with quality in mind, relatively few bugs will block the execution of tests, allowing testing to progress without fits and starts.

1 The paragraphs that follow are used with permission of James Bach (copyright 1994) and have been adapted from material that originally appeared in a posting in the newsgroup comp.software-eng.

Observability. "What you see is what you test." Inputs provided as part of testing produce distinct outputs. System states and variables are visible or queriable during execution. Incorrect output is easily identified. Internal errors are automatically detected and reported. Source code is accessible.

Controllability. "The better we can control the software, the more the testing can be automated and optimized." Software and hardware states and variables can be controlled directly by the test engineer. Tests can be conveniently specified, automated, and reproduced.

Decomposability. "By controlling the scope of testing, we can more quickly isolate problems and perform smarter retesting." The software system is built from independent modules that can be tested independently.

Simplicity. "The less there is to test, the more quickly we can test it." The program should exhibit *functional simplicity* (e.g., the feature set is the minimum necessary to meet requirements), *structural simplicity* (e.g., architecture is modularized to limit the propagation of faults), and *code simplicity* (e.g., a coding standard is adopted for ease of inspection and maintenance).

Stability. "The fewer the changes, the fewer the disruptions to testing." Changes to the software are infrequent, controlled when they do occur, and do not invalidate existing tests. The software recovers well from failures.

Understandability. "The more information we have, the smarter we will test." The architectural design and the dependencies between internal, external, and shared components are well understood. Technical documentation is instantly accessible, well organized, specific and detailed, and accurate. Changes to the design are communicated to testers.

The attributes suggested by Bach can be used by a software engineer to develop a software configuration (i.e., programs, data, and documents) that is amenable to testing.

> **"Errors are more common, more pervasive, and more troublesome in software than with other technologies."**
> **David Parnas**

Test characteristics. And what about the tests themselves? Kaner, Falk, and Nguyen [KAN93] suggest the following attributes of a "good" test:

? What is a "good" test?

1. *A good test has a high probability of finding an error.* To achieve this goal, the tester must understand the software and attempt to develop a mental picture of how the software might fail. Ideally, the classes of failure are probed. For example, one class of potential failure in a GUI (graphical user interface) is a failure to recognize proper mouse position. A set of tests would be designed to exercise the mouse in an attempt to demonstrate an error in mouse position recognition.

2. *A good test is not redundant.* Testing time and resources are limited. There is no point in conducting a test that has the same purpose as another test. Every test should have a different purpose (even if it is subtly different).
3. *A good test should be "best of breed"* [KAN93]. In a group of tests that have a similar intent, time and resource limitations may mitigate toward the execution of only a subset of these tests. In such cases, the test that has the highest likelihood of uncovering a whole class of errors should be used.
4. *A good test should be neither too simple nor too complex.* Although it is sometimes possible to combine a series of tests into one test case, the possible side effects associated with this approach may mask errors. In general, each test should be executed separately.

SAFEHOME

Designing Unique Tests

The scene: Vinod's cubical.

The players: Vinod and Ed—members of the *SafeHome* software engineering team.

The conversation:

Vinod: So these are the test cases you intend to run for the *passwordValidation* operation.

Ed: Yeah, they should cover pretty much all possibilities for the kinds of passwords a user might enter.

Vinod: So let's see . . . you note that the correct password will be 8080, right?

Ed: Uh huh.

Vinod: And you specify passwords 1234 and 6789 to test for errors in recognizing invalid passwords?

Ed: Right, and I also test passwords that are close to the correct password, see . . . 8081 and 8180.

Vinod: Those are okay, but I don't see much point in running both the 1234 and 6789 inputs. They're redundant . . . test the same thing, don't they?

Ed: Well, they're different values.

Vinod: That's true, but if 1234 doesn't uncover an error . . . in other words . . . the *passwordValidation* operation notes that it's an invalid password, it is not likely that 6789 will show us anything new.

Ed: I see what you mean.

Vinod: I'm not trying to be picky here . . . it's just that we have limited time to do testing, so it's a good idea to run tests that have a high likelihood of finding new errors.

Ed: Not a problem . . . I'll give this a bit more thought.

14.2 Black-Box and White-Box Testing

Any engineered product (and most other things) can be tested in one of two ways: (1) Knowing the specified function that a product has been designed to perform, tests can be conducted that demonstrate each function is fully operational while at the same time searching for errors in each function; (2) knowing the internal workings of a product, tests can be conducted to ensure that "all gears mesh"; that is, internal operations are performed according to specifications, and all internal components have been adequately exercised. The first test approach is called black-box testing and the second, white-box testing.[2]

Black-box testing alludes to tests that are conducted at the software interface. A black-box test examines some fundamental aspect of a system with little regard for the internal logical structure of the software. *White-box testing* of software is predicated on close examination of procedural detail. Logical paths through the software and collaborations between components are tested by providing test cases that exercise specific sets of conditions and/or loops.

> "There is only one rule in designing test cases: cover all features, but do not make too many test cases."
>
> **Tsuneo Yamaura**

White-box tests can be designed only after component-level design (or source code) exists. The logical details of the program must be available.

At first glance it would seem that very thorough white-box testing would lead to 100 percent correct programs. All we need to do is identify all logical paths, develop test cases to exercise them, and evaluate results, that is, generate test cases to exercise program logic exhaustively. Unfortunately, exhaustive testing presents certain logistical problems (see the sidebar discussion). White-box testing should not, however, be dismissed as impractical. A limited number of important logical paths can be selected and exercised. Important data structures can be probed for validity.

INFO

Exhaustive Testing

Consider the 100-line program in the language C. After some basic data declaration, the program contains two nested loops that execute from 1 to 20 times each, depending on conditions specified at input. Inside the interior loop, four if-then-else constructs are required. There are approximately 10^{14} possible paths that may be executed in this program!

To put this number into perspective, we assume that a magic test processor ("magic" because no such processor exists) has been developed for exhaustive testing. The processor can develop a test case, execute it, and evaluate the results in one millisecond. Working 24 hours a day, 365 days a year, the processor would work for 3170 years to test the program. This would, undeniably, cause havoc in most development schedules.

Therefore, it is reasonable to assert that exhaustive testing is impossible for large software systems.

14.3 White-Box Testing

White-box testing, sometimes called *glass-box testing,* is a test case design philosophy that uses the control structure described as part of component-level design to derive test cases. Using white-box testing methods, the software engineer can derive test cases that (1) guarantee that all independent paths within a module have been ex-

2 The terms *functional testing* and *structural testing* are sometimes used in place of black-box and white-box testing, respectively.

ercised at least once, (2) exercise all logical decisions on their true and false sides, (3) execute all loops at their boundaries and within their operational bounds, and (4) exercise internal data structures to ensure their validity.

> "Bugs lurk in corners and congregate at boundaries."
>
> **Boris Beizer**

14.4 Basis Path Testing

Basis path testing is a white-box testing technique first proposed by Tom McCabe [MCC76]. The basis path method enables the test case designer to derive a logical complexity measure of a procedural design and use this measure as a guide for defining a basis set of execution paths. Test cases derived to exercise the basis set are guaranteed to execute every statement in the program at least one time during testing.

14.4.1 Flow Graph Notation

A flow graph should be drawn only when the logical structure of a component is complex. The flow graph allows you to trace program paths more readily.

Before the basis path method can be introduced, a simple notation for the representation of control flow, called a *flow graph* (or *program graph*) must be introduced.[3] The flow graph depicts logical control flow using the notation illustrated in Figure 14.1. Each structured construct (Chapter 11) has a corresponding flow graph symbol.

To illustrate the use of a flow graph, we consider the procedural design representation in Figure 14.2a. Here, a flowchart is used to depict program control structure. Figure 14.2b maps the flowchart into a corresponding flow graph (assuming that no compound conditions are contained in the decision diamonds of the flowchart). Referring to Figure 14.2b, each circle, called a *flow graph node,* represents one or more procedural statements. A sequence of process boxes and a decision diamond can map into a single node. The arrows on the flow graph, called *edges* or *links,* represent

FIGURE 14.1

Flow graph notation

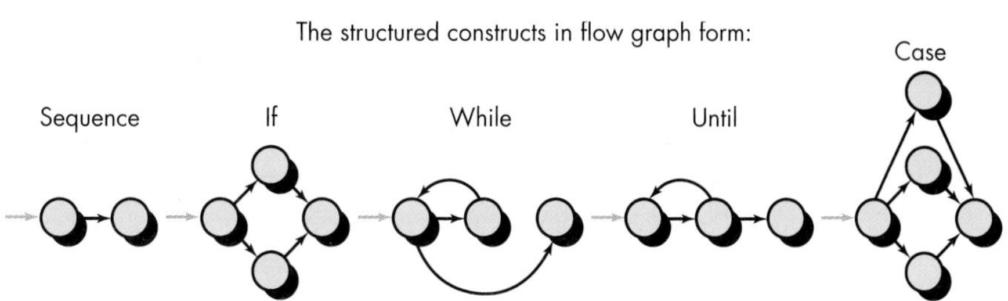

The structured constructs in flow graph form:
Sequence
If
While
Until
Case
Where each circle represents one or more nonbranching PDL or source code statements

3 In actuality, the basis path method can be conducted without the use of flow graphs. However, they serve as a useful notation for understanding control flow and illustrating the approach.

FIGURE 14.2 (a) Flowchart and (b) flow graph

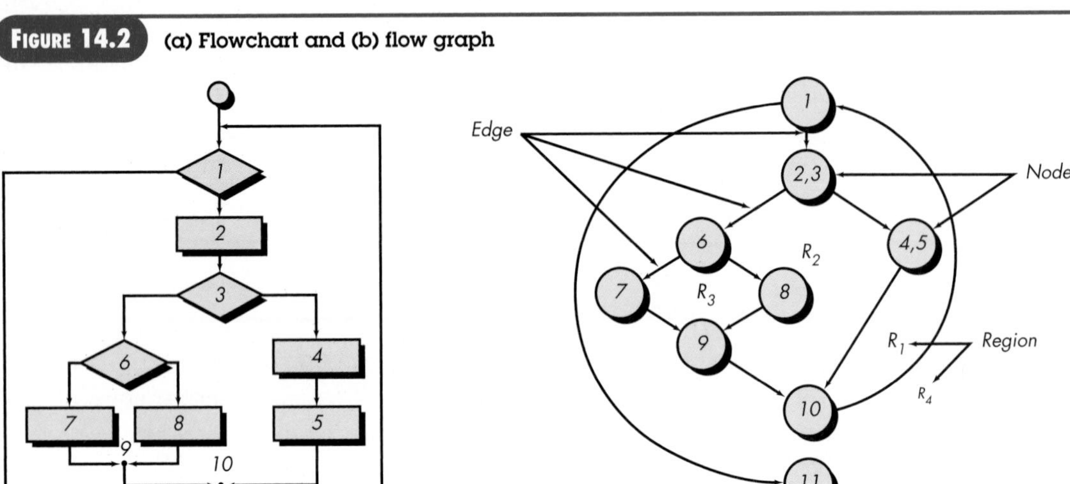

flow of control and are analogous to flowchart arrows. An edge must terminate at a node, even if the node does not represent any procedural statements (e.g., see the flow graph symbol for the if-then-else construct in Figure 14.1). Areas bounded by edges and nodes are called *regions.* When counting regions, we include the area outside the graph as a region.[4]

When compound conditions are encountered in a procedural design, the generation of a flow graph becomes slightly more complicated. A compound condition occurs when one or more Boolean operators (logical OR, AND, NAND, NOR) is present in a conditional statement. Referring to Figure 14.3, the PDL segment translates into the flow graph shown. Note that a separate node is created for each of the conditions *a* and *b* in the statement IF *a* OR *b.* Each node that contains a condition is called a *predicate node* and is characterized by two or more edges emanating from it.

14.4.2 Independent Program Paths

An *independent path* is any path through the program that introduces at least one new set of processing statements or a new condition. When stated in terms of a flow graph, an independent path must move along at least one edge that has not been traversed before the path is defined. For example, a set of independent paths for the flow graph illustrated in Figure 14.2b is:

path 1: 1-11

path 2: 1-2-3-4-5-10-1-11

4 A more detailed discussion of graphs and their uses is presented in Section 14.6.1.

FIGURE 14.3
Compound logic

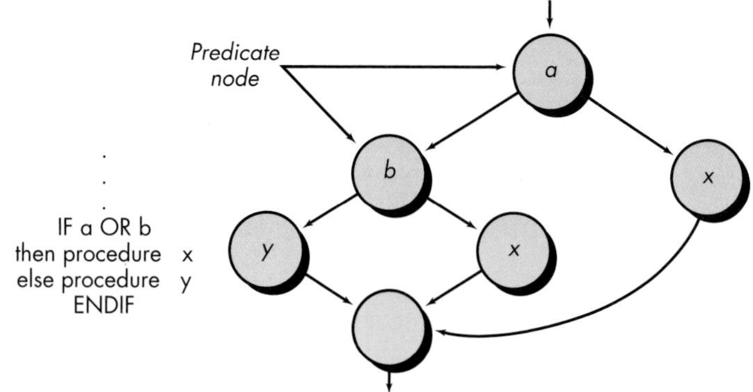

path 3: 1-2-3-6-8-9-10-1-11

path 4: 1-2-3-6-7-9-10-1-11

Note that each new path introduces a new edge. The path

1-2-3-4-5-10-1-2-3-6-8-9-10-1-11

is not considered to be an independent path because it is simply a combination of already specified paths and does not traverse any new edges.

Cyclomatic complexity is a useful metric for predicting those modules that are likely to be error prone. Use it for test planning as well as test case design.

Paths 1, 2, 3, and 4 constitute a *basis set* for the flow graph in Figure 14.2b. That is, if tests can be designed to force execution of these paths (a basis set), every statement in the program will have been guaranteed to be executed at least one time, and every condition will have been executed on its true and false sides. It should be noted that the basis set is not unique. In fact, a number of different basis sets can be derived for a given procedural design.

How do we know how many paths to look for? The computation of cyclomatic complexity provides the answer. *Cyclomatic complexity* is a software metric that provides a quantitative measure of the logical complexity of a program. When used in the context of the basis path testing method, the value computed for cyclomatic complexity defines the number of independent paths in the basis set of a program and provides us with an upper bound for the number of tests that must be conducted to ensure that all statements have been executed at least once.

Cyclomatic complexity has a foundation in graph theory and is computed in one of three ways:

? How do I compute cyclomatic complexity?

1. The number of regions corresponds to the cyclomatic complexity.
2. Cyclomatic complexity, $V(G)$, for a flow graph, G, is defined as

   $V(G) = E - N + 2$

   where E is the number of flow graph edges, and N is the number of flow graph nodes.

Cyclomatic complexity provides the upper bound on the number of test cases that will be required to guarantee that every statement in the program has been executed at least one time.

3. Cyclomatic complexity, $V(G)$, for a flow graph, G, is also defined as

   $V(G) = P + 1$

   where P is the number of predicate nodes contained in the flow graph G.

Referring once more to the flow graph in Figure 14.2b, the cyclomatic complexity can be computed using each of the algorithms just noted:

1. The flow graph has four regions.
2. $V(G) = 11$ edges $- 9$ nodes $+ 2 = 4$.
3. $V(G) = 3$ predicate nodes $+ 1 = 4$.

More important, the value for $V(G)$ provides us with an upper bound for the number of independent paths that form the basis set and, by implication, an upper bound on the number of tests that must be designed and executed to guarantee coverage of all program statements.

SAFEHOME

Using Cyclomatic Complexity

The scene: Shakira's cubicle.

The players: Vinod and Shakira—members of the *SafeHome* software engineering team who are working on test planning for the security function.

The conversation:

Shakira: Look . . . I know that we should unit test all the components for the security function, but there are a lot of 'em and if you consider the number of operations that have to be exercised, I don't know . . . maybe we should forget white-box testing, integrate everything, and start running black-box tests.

Vinod: You figure we don't have enough time to do component tests, exercise the operations, and then integrate?

Shakira: The deadline for the first increment is getting closer than I'd like . . . yeah, I'm concerned.

Vinod: Why don't you at least run white-box tests on the operations that are likely to be the most error prone?

Shakira (exasperated): And exactly how do I know which are likely to be the most error prone?

Vinod: *V* of *G*.

Shakira: Huh?

Vinod: Cyclomatic complexity—*V* of *G*. Just compute *V*(*G*) for each of the operations within each of the components and see which have the highest values for *V*(*G*). They're the ones that are most likely to be error prone.

Shakira: And how do I compute *V* of *G*?

Vinod: It's really easy. Here's a book that describes how to do it.

Shakira (leafing through the pages): Okay, it doesn't look hard. I'll give it a try. The ops with the highest *V*(*G*) will be the candidates for white-box tests.

Vinod: Just remember that there are no guarantees. A component with a low *V*(*G*) can still be error prone.

Shakira: Alright. But at least this'll help me to narrow down the number of components that have to undergo white-box testing.

14.4.3 Deriving Test Cases

The basis path testing method can be applied to a procedural design or to source code. In this section, we present basis path testing as a series of steps. The procedure *average,* depicted in PDL in Figure 14.4, will be used as an example to illustrate

FIGURE 14.4

PDL with nodes identified

```
PROCEDURE average;

   *  This procedure computes the average of 100 or fewer
      numbers that lie between bounding values; it also computes the
      sum and the total number valid.

   INTERFACE RETURNS average, total.input, total.valid;
   INTERFACE ACCEPTS value, minimum, maximum;

   TYPE value[1:100] IS SCALAR ARRAY;
   TYPE average, total.input, total.valid;
      minimum, maximum, sum IS SCALAR;
   TYPE i IS INTEGER;
1  { i = 1;
   { total.input = total.valid = 0;    2
   { sum = 0;
   { DO WHILE value[i] <> -999 AND total.input < 100   3
   4  increment total.input by 1;
      IF value[i] > = minimum AND value[i] < = maximum   6
5 →     { THEN increment total.valid by 1;
   7    {          sum = s sum + value[i]
        { ELSE skip
8  { ENDIF
   { increment i by 1;
9  ENDDO
   IF total.valid > 0   10
   11 THEN average = sum / total.valid;
12 →  ELSE average = -999;
13 ENDIF
END average
```

each step in the test case design method. Note that *average,* although an extremely simple algorithm, contains compound conditions and loops. The following steps can be applied to derive the basis set:

1. **Using the design or code as a foundation, draw a corresponding flow graph.** A flow graph is created using the symbols and construction rules presented in Section 14.4.1. Referring to the PDL for *average* in Figure 14.4, a flow graph is created by numbering those PDL statements that will be mapped into corresponding flow graph nodes. The corresponding flow graph is in Figure 14.5.

2. **Determine the cyclomatic complexity of the resultant flow graph.** The cyclomatic complexity, $V(G)$, is determined by applying the algorithms described in Section 14.4.2. It should be noted that $V(G)$ can be determined without developing a flow graph by counting all conditional statements in the PDL (for the procedure *average,* compound conditions count as two) and adding 1. Referring to Figure 14.5,

   $V(G) = 6$ regions
   $V(G) = 17$ edges $- 13$ nodes $+ 2 = 6$
   $V(G) = 5$ predicate nodes $+ 1 = 6$

> "To err is human, to find a bug is divine."
>
> **Robert Dunn**

Figure 14.5

Flow graph for the procedure *average*

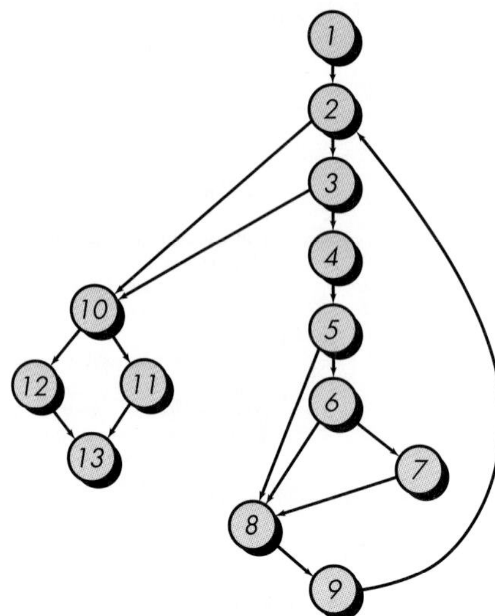

3. **Determine a basis set of linearly independent paths.** The value of *V*(*G*) provides the number of linearly independent paths through the program control structure. In the case of procedure average, we expect to specify six paths:

   path 1: 1-2-10-11-13

   path 2: 1-2-10-12-13

   path 3: 1-2-3-10-11-13

   path 4: 1-2-3-4-5-8-9-2-. . .

   path 5: 1-2-3-4-5-6-8-9-2-. . .

   path 6: 1-2-3-4-5-6-7-8-9-2-. . .

   The ellipsis (. . .) following paths 4, 5, and 6 indicates that any path through the remainder of the control structure is acceptable. It is often worthwhile to identify predicate nodes as an aid in the derivation of test cases. In this case, nodes 2, 3, 5, 6, and 10 are predicate nodes.

4. **Prepare test cases that will force execution of each path in the basis set.** Data should be chosen so that conditions at the predicate nodes are appropriately set as each path is tested. Each test case is executed and compared to expected results. Once all test cases have been completed, the tester can be sure that all statements in the program have been executed at least once.

It is important to note that some independent paths (e.g., path 1 in our example) cannot be tested in stand-alone fashion. That is, the combination of data required to traverse the path cannot be achieved in the normal flow of the program. In such cases, these paths are tested as part of another path test.

FIGURE 14.6
Graph matrix

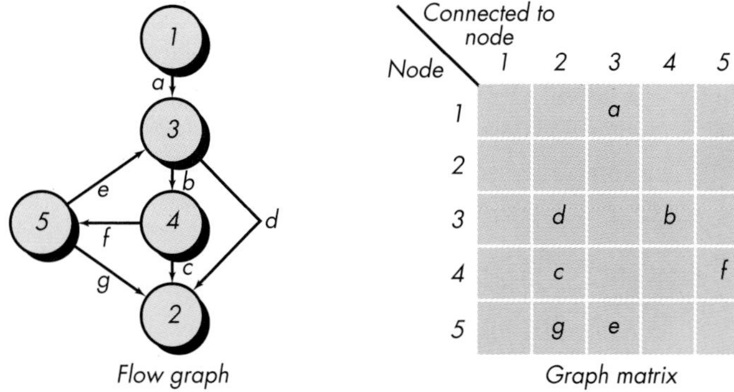

14.4.4 Graph Matrices

The procedure for deriving the flow graph and even determining a set of basis paths is amenable to mechanization. To develop a software tool that assists in basis path testing, a data structure, called a *graph matrix,* can be quite useful.

A graph matrix is a square matrix whose size (i.e., number of rows and columns) is equal to the number of nodes on the flow graph. Each row and column corresponds to an identified node, and matrix entries correspond to connections (an edge) between nodes. A simple example of a flow graph and its corresponding graph matrix [BEI90] is shown in Figure 14.6.

Referring to the figure, each node on the flow graph is identified by numbers, while each edge is identified by letters. A letter entry is made in the matrix to correspond to a connection between two nodes. For example, node 3 is connected to node 4 by edge b.

? What is a graph matrix, and how do we extend it for use in testing?

To this point, the graph matrix is nothing more than a tabular representation of a flow graph. However, by adding a *link weight* to each matrix entry, the graph matrix can become a powerful tool for evaluating program control structure during testing. The link weight provides additional information about control flow. In its simplest form, the link weight is 1 (a connection exists) or 0 (a connection does not exist). But link weights can be assigned other, more interesting properties:

- The probability that a link (edge) will be executed.
- The processing time expended during traversal of a link.
- The memory required during traversal of a link.
- The resources required during traversal of a link.

Beizer [BEI90] provides a thorough treatment of additional mathematical algorithms that can be applied to graph matrices. Using these techniques, the analysis required to design test cases can be partially or fully automated.

> "Paying more attention to running tests than to designing them is a classic mistake."
>
> **Brian Marick**

14.5 Control Structure Testing

The basis path testing technique described in Section 14.4 is one of a number of techniques for control structure testing. Although basis path testing is simple and effective, it is not sufficient in itself. In this section, variations on control structure testing are discussed briefly. These broaden testing coverage and improve quality of white-box testing.

14.5.1 Condition Testing

Errors are much more common in the neighborhood of logical conditions than they are in the locus of sequential processing statements.

Condition testing [TAI89] is a test case design method that exercises the logical conditions contained in a program module. *A simple condition* is a Boolean variable or a relational expression, possibly preceded with one NOT (¬) operator. A relational expression takes the form

E_1 <relational-operator> E_2

where E_1 and E_2 are arithmetic expressions and <relational-operator> is one of the following: $<$, $\leq$, $=$, $\neq$ (nonequality), $>$, or $\geq$. A *compound condition* is composed of two or more simple conditions, Boolean operators, and parentheses. We assume that Boolean operators allowed in a compound condition include OR (|), AND (&) and NOT (¬). A condition without relational expressions is referred to as a Boolean expression. Therefore, the possible types of elements in a condition include a Boolean operator, a Boolean variable, a pair of parentheses (surrounding a simple or compound Boolean condition), a relational operator, or an arithmetic expression.

If a condition is incorrect, then at least one component of the condition is incorrect. Therefore, types of errors in a condition include Boolean operator errors (incorrect/missing/extra Boolean operators), Boolean variable errors, Boolean parenthesis errors, relational operator errors, and arithmetic expression errors. The condition testing method focuses on testing each condition in the program to ensure that it does not contain errors.

14.5.2 Data Flow Testing

The *data flow testing* method selects test paths of a program according to the locations of definitions and uses of variables in the program.To illustrate the data flow testing approach, assume that each statement in a program is assigned a unique statement number and that each function does not modify its parameters or global variables. For a statement with S as its statement number,

$$\text{DEF}(S) = \{X \mid \text{statement } S \text{ contains a definition of } X\}$$
$$\text{USE}(S) = \{X \mid \text{statement } S \text{ contains a use of } X\}$$

If statement S is an *if* or *loop* statement, its DEF set is empty and its USE set is based on the condition of statement S. The definition of variable X at statement S is said to be live at statement S' if there exists a path from statement S to statement S' that contains no other definition of X.

A *definition-use (DU) chain* of variable X is of the form [X, S, S'], where S and S' are statement numbers, X is in DEF(S) and USE(S'), and the definition of X in statement S is live at statement S'.

ADVICE

It is unrealistic to assume that data flow testing will be used extensively when testing a large system. However, it can be used in a targeted fashion for areas of software that are suspect.

One simple data flow testing strategy is to require that every DU chain be covered at least once. We refer to this strategy as the *DU testing strategy*. It has been shown that DU testing does not guarantee the coverage of all branches of a program. However, a branch is not guaranteed to be covered by DU testing only in rare situations such as if-then-else constructs in which the *then part* has no definition of any variable and the *else part* does not exist. In this situation, the else branch of the *if* statement is not necessarily covered by DU testing. A number of data flow testing strategies have been studied and compared (e.g., [FRA88], [NTA88], [FRA93]). The interested reader is urged to consider these other references.

> "Good testers are masters at noticing 'something funny' and acting on it."
>
> **Brian Marick**

14.5.3 Loop Testing

Loops are the cornerstone for the vast majority of all algorithms implemented in software. And yet, we often pay them little heed while conducting software tests.

Loop testing is a white-box testing technique that focuses exclusively on the validity of loop constructs. Four different classes of loops [BEI90] can be defined: simple loops, concatenated loops, nested loops, and unstructured loops (Figure 14.7).

FIGURE 14.7

Classes of loops

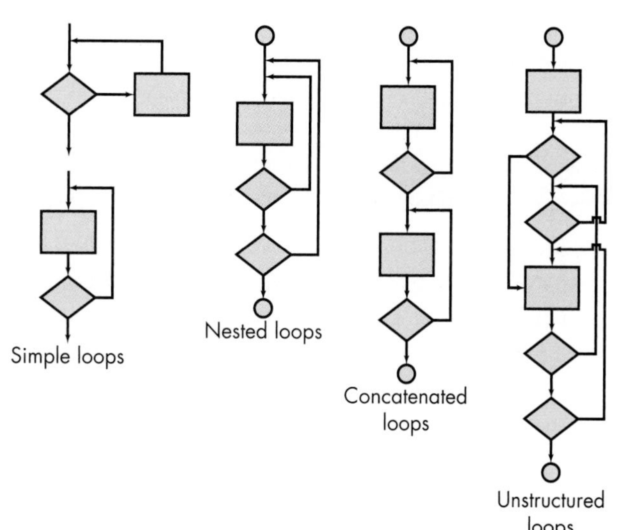

Simple loops. The following set of tests can be applied to simple loops, where n is the maximum number of allowable passes through the loop.

1. Skip the loop entirely.
2. Only one pass through the loop.
3. Two passes through the loop.
4. m passes through the loop where $m < n$.
5. $n - 1, n, n + 1$ passes through the loop.

Nested loops. If we were to extend the test approach for simple loops to nested loops, the number of possible tests would grow geometrically as the level of nesting increased. This would result in an impractical number of tests. Beizer [BEI90] suggests an approach that will help to reduce the number of tests:

1. Start at the innermost loop. Set all other loops to minimum values.
2. Conduct simple loop tests for the innermost loop while holding the outer loops at their minimum iteration parameter (e.g., loop counter) values. Add other tests for out-of-range or excluded values.
3. Work outward, conducting tests for the next loop, but keeping all other outer loops at minimum values and other nested loops to "typical" values.
4. Continue until all loops have been tested.

Concatenated loops. Concatenated loops can be tested using the approach defined for simple loops, if each of the loops is independent of the other. However, if two loops are concatenated and the loop counter for loop 1 is used as the initial value for loop 2, then the loops are not independent. When the loops are not independent, the approach applied to nested loops is recommended.

You can't test unstructured loops effectively. Redesign them.

Unstructured loops. Whenever possible, this class of loops should be redesigned to reflect the use of the structured programming constructs (Chapter 11).

14.6 Black-Box Testing

Black-box testing, also called *behavioral testing,* focuses on the functional requirements of the software. That is, black-box testing enables the software engineer to derive sets of input conditions that will fully exercise all functional requirements for a program. Black-box testing is not an alternative to white-box techniques. Rather, it is a complementary approach that is likely to uncover a different class of errors than white-box methods.

Black-box testing attempts to find errors in the following categories: (1) incorrect or missing functions, (2) interface errors, (3) errors in data structures or external data base access, (4) behavior or performance errors, and (5) initialization and termination errors.

Unlike white-box testing, which is performed early in the testing process, black-box testing tends to be applied during later stages of testing (see Chapter 13). Because black-box testing purposely disregards control structure, attention is focused on the information domain. Tests are designed to answer the following questions:

? What questions do black-box tests answer?

- How is functional validity tested?
- How are system behavior and performance tested?
- What classes of input will make good test cases?
- Is the system particularly sensitive to certain input values?
- How are the boundaries of a data class isolated?
- What data rates and data volume can the system tolerate?
- What effect will specific combinations of data have on system operation?

By applying black-box techniques, we derive a set of test cases that satisfy the following criteria [MYE79]: (1) test cases that reduce, by a count that is greater than one, the number of additional test cases that must be designed to achieve reasonable testing, and (2) test cases that tell us something about the presence or absence of classes of errors, rather than an error associated only with the specific test at hand.

14.6.1 Graph-Based Testing Methods

A graph represents the relationships between data objects and program objects, enabling us to derive test cases that search for errors associated with these relationships.

The first step in black-box testing is to understand the objects[5] that are modeled in software and the relationships that connect these objects. Once this has been accomplished, the next step is to define a series of tests that verify "all objects have the expected relationship to one another" [BEI95]. Stated in another way, software testing begins by creating a graph of important objects and their relationships and then devising a series of tests that will cover the graph so that each object and relationship is exercised and errors are uncovered.

To accomplish these steps, the software engineer begins by creating a *graph*—a collection of *nodes* that represent objects; *links* that represent the relationships between objects; *node weights* that describe the properties of a node (e.g., a specific data value or state behavior); and *link weights* that describe some characteristic of a link.

The symbolic representation of a graph is shown in Figure 14.8a. Nodes are represented as circles connected by links that take a number of different forms. A *directed link* (represented by an arrow) indicates that a relationship moves in only one direction. A *bidirectional link,* also called a *symmetric link,* implies that the relationship applies in both directions. *Parallel links* are used when a number of different relationships are established between graph nodes.

---

5 In this context, we consider the term "objects" in the broadest possible context. It encompasses data objects, traditional components (modules), and object-oriented elements of computer software.

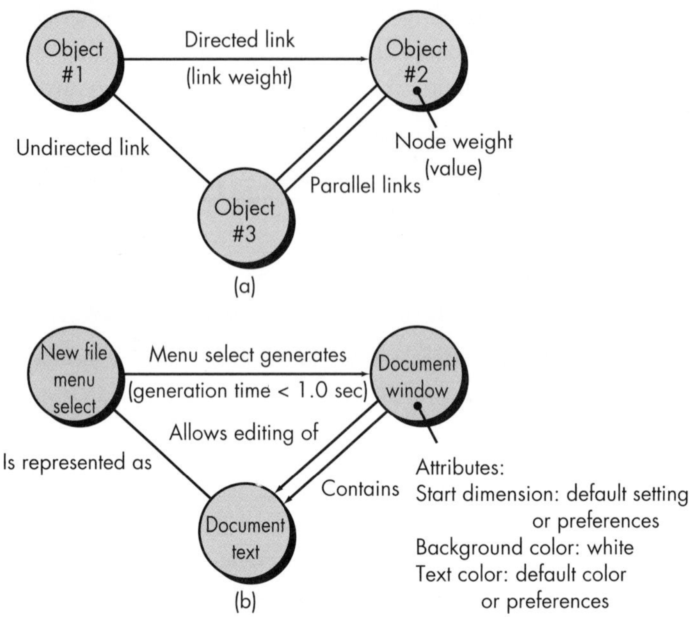

FIGURE 14.8 (a) Graph notation, (b) simple example

As a simple example, consider a portion of a graph for a word-processing application (Figure 14.8b) where

Object #1 = **newFile** (menu selection)

Object #2 = **documentWindow**

Object #3 = **documentText**

Referring to the figure, a menu select on **newFile** generates a document window. The node weight of **documentWindow** provides a list of the window attributes that are to be expected when the window is generated. The link weight indicates that the window must be generated in less than 1.0 second. An undirected link establishes a symmetric relationship between the **newFile** menu selection and **documentText,** and parallel links indicate relationships between **documentWindow** and **documentText.** In reality, a far more detailed graph would have to be generated as a precursor to test case design. The software engineer then derives test cases by traversing the graph and covering each of the relationships shown. These test cases are designed in an attempt to find errors in any of the relationships.

Beizer [BEI95] describes a number of behavioral testing methods that can make use of graphs:

Transaction flow modeling. The nodes represent steps in some transaction (e.g., the steps required to make an airline reservation using an on-line service), and the links represent the logical connection between steps. The data flow diagram (Chapter 8) can be used to assist in creating graphs of this type.

Finite state modeling. The nodes represent different user observable states of the software (e.g., each of the "screens" that appear as an order entry clerk takes a phone order), and the links represent the transitions that occur to move from state to state. The state diagram (Chapter 8) can be used to assist in creating graphs of this type.

Data flow modeling. The nodes are data objects, and the links are the transformations that occur to translate one data object into another. For example, the node **FICA tax withheld** (**FTW**) is computed from **gross wages** (**GW**) using the relationship, **FTW = 0.62 × GW.**

Timing modeling. The nodes are program objects, and the links are the sequential connections between those objects. Link weights are used to specify the required execution times as the program executes.

A detailed discussion of each of these graph-based testing methods is beyond the scope of this book. The interested reader should see [BEI95] for comprehensive coverage.

14.6.2 Equivalence Partitioning

Equivalence partitioning is a black-box testing method that divides the input domain of a program into classes of data from which test cases can be derived. An ideal test case single-handedly uncovers a class of errors (e.g., incorrect processing of all character data) that might otherwise require many cases to be executed before the general error is observed. Equivalence partitioning strives to define a test case that uncovers classes of errors, thereby reducing the total number of test cases that must be developed.

Input classes are known relatively early in the software process. For this reason, begin thinking about equivalence partitioning as the design is created.

Test case design for equivalence partitioning is based on an evaluation of equivalence classes for an input condition. Using concepts introduced in the preceding section, if a set of objects can be linked by relationships that are symmetric, transitive, and reflexive, an equivalence class is present [BEI95]. An *equivalence class* represents a set of valid or invalid states for input conditions. Typically, an input condition is either a specific numeric value, a range of values, a set of related values, or a Boolean condition. Equivalence classes may be defined according to the following guidelines:

? How do I define equivalence classes for testing?

1. If an input condition specifies a range, one valid and two invalid equivalence classes are defined.
2. If an input condition requires a specific value, one valid and two invalid equivalence classes are defined.
3. If an input condition specifies a member of a set, one valid and one invalid equivalence class are defined.
4. If an input condition is Boolean, one valid and one invalid class are defined.

By applying these guidelines for the derivation of equivalence classes, test cases for each input domain data object can be developed and executed. Test cases are selected so that the largest number of attributes of an equivalence class are exercised at once.

14.6.3 Boundary Value Analysis

A greater number of errors occurs at the boundaries of the input domain rather than in the "center." It is for this reason that *boundary value analysis* (BVA) has been developed as a testing technique. BVA leads to a selection of test cases that exercise bounding values.

BVA extends equivalence partitioning by focusing on data at the "edges" of an equivalence class.

Boundary value analysis is a test case design technique that complements equivalence partitioning. Rather than selecting any element of an equivalence class, BVA leads to the selection of test cases at the "edges" of the class. Rather than focusing solely on input conditions, BVA derives test cases from the output domain as well [MYE79].

Guidelines for BVA are similar in many respects to those provided for equivalence partitioning:

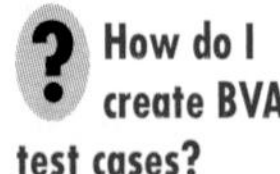
How do I create BVA test cases?

1. If an input condition specifies a range bounded by values *a* and *b,* test cases should be designed with values *a* and *b* as well as just above and just below *a* and *b*.
2. If an input condition specifies a number of values, test cases should be developed that exercise the minimum and maximum numbers. Values just above and below minimum and maximum are also tested.
3. Apply guidelines 1 and 2 to output conditions. For example, assume that a temperature vs. pressure table is required as output from an engineering analysis program. Test cases should be designed to create an output report that produces the maximum (and minimum) allowable number of table entries.
4. If internal program data structures have prescribed boundaries (e.g., an array has a defined limit of 100 entries), be certain to design a test case to exercise the data structure at its boundary.

Most software engineers intuitively perform BVA to some degree. By applying these guidelines, boundary testing will be more complete, thereby having a higher likelihood for error detection.

> "The Ariane 5 rocket blew up on lift-off due solely to a software defect (a bug) involving the conversion of a 64-bit floating point value into a 16-bit integer. The rocket and its four satellites were *uninsured* and worth $500 million. A comprehensive system test would have found the bug but was vetoed for budgetary reasons."
>
> **A news report**

14.6.4 Orthogonal Array Testing

There are many applications in which the input domain is relatively limited. That is, the number of input parameters is small and the values that each of the parameters may take are clearly bounded. When these numbers are very small (e.g., three input parameters taking on three discrete values each), it is possible to consider every input permutation and exhaustively test processing of the input domain. However, as the number of input values grows and the number of discrete values for each data item increases, exhaustive testing becomes impractical or impossible.

Orthogonal array testing can be applied to problems in which the input domain is relatively small but too large to accommodate exhaustive testing. The orthogonal array testing method is particularly useful in finding errors associated with *region faults*—an error category associated with faulty logic within a software component.

Orthogonal array testing enables you to design test cases that provide maximum test coverage with a reasonable number of test cases.

To illustrate the difference between orthogonal array testing and more conventional "one input item at a time" approaches, consider a system that has three input items, *X, Y,* and *Z.* Each of these input items has three discrete values associated with it. There are $3^3 = 27$ possible test cases. Phadke [PHA97] suggests a geometric view of the possible test cases associated with *X, Y,* and *Z* illustrated in Figure 14.9. Referring to the figure, one input item at a time may be varied in sequence along each input axis. This results in relatively limited coverage of the input domain (represented by the left-hand cube in the figure).

When orthogonal array testing occurs, an *L9 orthogonal array* of test cases is created. The L9 orthogonal array has a "balancing property [PHA97]." That is, test cases (represented by blue dots in the figure) are "dispersed uniformly throughout the test domain," as illustrated in the right-hand cube in Figure 14.9. Test coverage across the input domain is more complete.

FIGURE 14.9

A geometric view of test cases [PHA97]

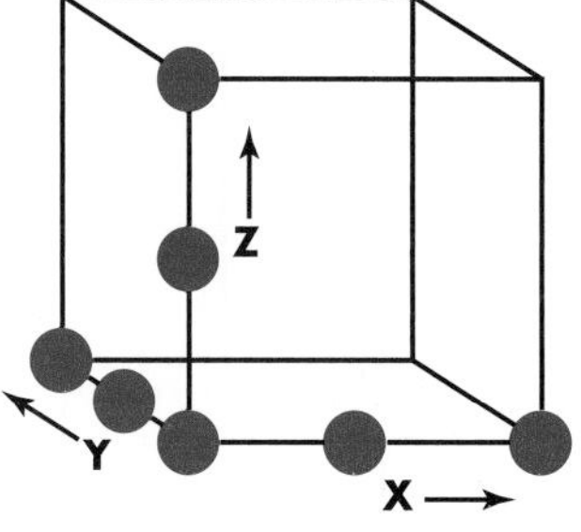

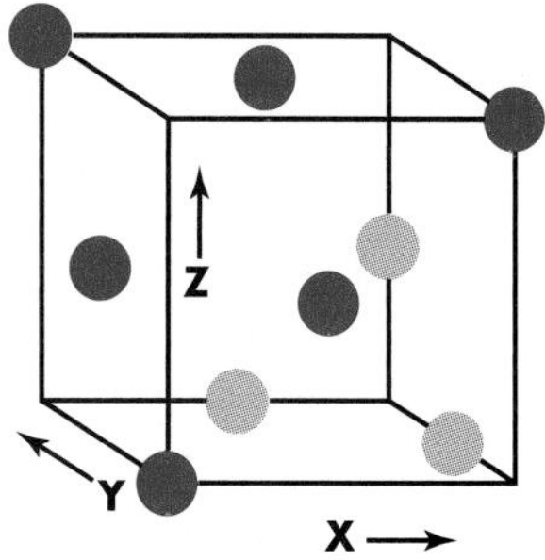

To illustrate the use of the L9 orthogonal array, consider the *send* function for a fax application. Four parameters, P1, P2, P3, and P4, are passed to the *send* function. Each takes on three discrete values. For example, P1 takes on values:

P1 = 1, send it now
P1 = 2, send it one hour later
P1 = 3, send it after midnight

P2, P3, and P4 would also take on values of 1, 2, and 3, signifying other send functions.

If a "one input item at a time" testing strategy were chosen, the following sequence of tests (P1, P2, P3, P4) would be specified: (1, 1, 1, 1), (2, 1, 1, 1), (3, 1, 1, 1), (1, 2, 1, 1), (1, 3, 1, 1), (1, 1, 2, 1), (1, 1, 3, 1), (1, 1, 1, 2), and (1, 1, 1, 3). Phadke [PHA97] assesses these test cases by stating:

> Such test cases are useful only when one is certain that these test parameters do not interact. They can detect logic faults where a single parameter value makes the software malfunction. These faults are called *single mode faults.* This method cannot detect logic faults that cause malfunction when two or more parameters simultaneously take certain values; that is, it cannot detect any interactions. Thus its ability to detect faults is limited.

Given the relatively small number of input parameters and discrete values, exhaustive testing is possible. The number of tests required is $3^4 = 81$, large, but manageable. All faults associated with data item permutation would be found, but the effort required is relatively high.

The orthogonal array testing approach enables us to provide good test coverage with far fewer test cases than the exhaustive strategy. An L9 orthogonal array for the fax *send* function is illustrated in Figure 14.10.

FIGURE 14.10

An L9 orthogonal array

Test case	Test parameters			
	P_1	P_2	P_3	P_4
1	1	1	1	1
2	1	2	2	2
3	1	3	3	3
4	2	1	2	3
5	2	2	3	1
6	2	3	1	2
7	3	1	3	2
8	3	2	1	3
9	3	3	2	1

Phadke [PHA97] assesses the result of tests using the L9 orthogonal array in the following manner:

> **Detect and isolate all single mode faults.** A single mode fault is a consistent problem with any level of any single parameter. For example, if all test cases of factor P1 = 1 cause an error condition, it is a single mode failure. In this example, tests 1, 2, and 3 [Figure 14.10] will show errors. By analyzing the information about which tests show errors, one can identify which parameter values cause the fault. In this example, by noting that tests 1, 2, and 3 cause an error, one can isolate [logical processing associated with "send it now" (P1 = 1)] as the source of the error. Such an isolation of fault is important to fix the fault.
>
> **Detect all double mode faults.** If there exists a consistent problem when specific levels of two parameters occur together, it is called a *double mode fault.* Indeed, a double mode fault is an indication of pairwise incompatibility or harmful interactions between two test parameters.
>
> **Multimode faults.** Orthogonal arrays [of the type shown] can assure the detection of only single and double mode faults. However, many multimode faults are also detected by these tests.

A detailed discussion of orthogonal array testing can be found in [PHA89].

SOFTWARE TOOLS

Test Case Design

Objective: To assist the software team in developing a complete set of test cases for both black-box and white-box testing.

Mechanics: These tools fall into two broad categories: static testing and dynamic testing. Three different types of static testing tools are used in the industry: code-based testing tools, specialized testing languages, and requirements-based testing tools. Code-based testing tools accept source code as input and perform a number of analyses that result in the generation of test cases. Specialized testing languages (e.g., ATLAS) enable a software engineer to write detailed test specifications that describe each test case and the logistics for its execution. Requirements-based testing tools isolate specific user requirements and suggest test cases (or classes of tests) that will exercise the requirements. Dynamic testing tools interact with an executing program, checking path coverage, testing assertions about the value of specific variables, and otherwise instrumenting the execution flow of the program.

Representative Tools[6]

McCabe Test, developed by McCabe & Associates (www.mccabe.com), implements a variety of path testing techniques derived from an assessment of cyclomatic complexity and other software metrics.

Panorama, developed by International Software Automation, Inc. (www.softwareautomation.com), encompasses a complete set of tools for object-oriented software development including tools that assist test case design and test planning.

TestWorks, developed by Software Research, Inc. (www.soft.com/Products), is a complete set of automated testing tools that assists in the design of test cases for software developed in C/C++ and Java and provides support for regression testing.

T-Vec Test Generation System, developed by T-VEC Technologies (www.t-vec.com), is a tool set that supports unit, integration, and validation testing by assisting in the design of test cases using information contained in an OO requirements specification.

6 Tools noted here do not represent an endorsement, but rather a sampling of tools in this category. In most cases, tool names are trademarked by their respective developers.

14.7 Object-Oriented Testing Methods

The architecture of object-oriented software results in a series of layered subsystems that encapsulate collaborating classes. Each of these system elements (subsystems and classes) perform functions that help to achieve system requirements. It is necessary to test an OO system at a variety of different levels to uncover errors that may occur as classes collaborate with one another and subsystems communicate across architectural layers.

Object-oriented testing is strategically similar to the testing of conventional systems, but it is tactically different. Because OO analysis and design models are similar in structure and content to the resultant OO program, "testing" can begin with the review of these models. Once code has been generated, actual OO testing begins "in the small" with a series of tests designed to exercise class operations and examine whether errors exist as one class collaborates with other classes. As classes are integrated to form a subsystem, use-based testing, along with fault-based approaches, is applied to fully exercise collaborating classes. Finally, use-cases are used to uncover errors at the software validation level.

Conventional test case design is driven by an input-process-output view of software or the algorithmic detail of individual modules. Object-oriented testing focuses on designing appropriate sequences of operations to exercise the states of a class.

14.7.1 The Test Case Design Implications of OO Concepts

WebRef
An excellent collection of papers and resources on OO testing can be found at **www.rbsc.com.**

As a class evolves through the analysis and design models, it becomes a target for test case design. Because attributes and operations are encapsulated, testing operations outside of the class is generally unproductive. Although encapsulation is an essential design concept for OO, it can create a minor obstacle when testing. As Binder [BIN94] notes, "Testing requires reporting on the concrete and abstract state of an object." Yet, encapsulation can make this information somewhat difficult to obtain. Unless built-in operations are provided to report the values for class attributes, a snapshot of the state of an object may be difficult to acquire.

Inheritance also leads to additional challenges for the test case designer. We have already noted that each new context of usage requires retesting, even though reuse has been achieved. In addition, multiple inheritance[7] complicates testing further by increasing the number of contexts for which testing is required [BIN94]. If subclasses instantiated from a superclass are used within the same problem domain, it is likely that the set of test cases derived for the superclass can be used when testing the subclass. However, if the subclass is used in an entirely different context, the superclass test cases will have little applicability and a new set of tests must be designed.

7 An OO concept that should be used with extreme care.

14.7.2 Applicability of Conventional Test Case Design Methods

The white-box testing methods described in earlier sections can be applied to the operations defined for a class. Basis path, loop testing, or data flow techniques can help to ensure that every statement in an operation has been tested. However, the concise structure of many class operations causes some to argue that the effort applied to white-box testing might be better redirected to tests at a class level.

Black-box testing methods are as appropriate for OO systems as they are for systems developed using conventional software engineering methods. As we noted earlier in this chapter, use-cases can provide useful input in the design of black-box and state-based tests [AMB95].

14.7.3 Fault-Based Testing[8]

The strategy for fault-based testing is to hypothesize a set of plausible faults and then derive tests to prove each hypothesis.

The objective of *fault-based testing* within an OO system is to design tests that have a high likelihood of uncovering plausible faults. Because the product or system must conform to customer requirements, the preliminary planning required to perform fault-based testing begins with the analysis model. The tester looks for plausible faults (i.e., aspects of the implementation of the system that may result in defects). To determine whether these faults exist, test cases are designed to exercise the design or code.

Of course, the effectiveness of these techniques depends on how testers perceive a plausible fault. If real faults in an OO system are perceived to be implausible, then this approach is really no better than any random testing technique. However, if the analysis and design models can provide insight into what is likely to go wrong, then fault-based testing can find significant numbers of errors with relatively low expenditures of effort.

? What types of faults are encountered in operation calls and message connections?

Integration testing (when applied in an OO context) looks for plausible faults in operation calls or message connections. Three types of faults are encountered in this context: unexpected result, wrong operation/message used, incorrect invocation. To determine plausible faults as functions (operations) are invoked, the behavior of the operation must be examined.

Integration testing applies to attributes as well as to operations. The "behaviors" of an object are defined by the values that its attributes are assigned. Testing should exercise the attributes to determine whether proper values occur for distinct types of object behavior.

It is important to note that integration testing attempts to find errors in the client object, not the server. Stated in conventional terms, the focus of integration testing is

8 Sections 14.7.3 through 14.7.6 have been adapted from an article by Brian Marick posted on the Internet newsgroup **comp.testing.** This adaptation is included with the permission of the author. For further information on these topics, see [MAR94]. It should be noted that the techniques discussed in Sections 14.7.3 through 14.7.6 are also applicable for conventional software.

to determine whether errors exist in the calling code, not the called code. The operation call is used as a clue, a way to find test requirements that exercise the calling code.

> "If you want and expect a program to work, you will more likely see a working program—you will miss failures."
> **Cem Kaner et al.**

14.7.4 Test Cases and Class Hierarchy

Inheritance does not obviate the need for thorough testing of all derived classes. In fact, it can actually complicate the testing process. Consider the following situation. A class **Base** contains operations *inherited()* and *redefined()*. A class **Derived** redefines *redefined()* to serve in a local context. There is little doubt the **Derived::redefined()** has to be tested because it represents a new design and new code. But does **Derived::inherited()** have to be retested?

Even though a base class has been thoroughly tested, you will still have to test all classes derived from it.

If **Derived::inherited()** calls *redefined()* and the behavior of *redefined()* has changed, **Derived::inherited()** may mishandle the new behavior. Therefore, it needs new tests even though the design and code have not changed. It is important to note, however, that only a subset of all tests for **Derived::inherited()** may have to be conducted. If part of the design and code for *inherited()* does not depend on *redefined()* (i.e., that does not call it, nor any code that indirectly calls it), that code need not be retested in the derived class.

Base::redefined() and **Derived::redefined()** are two different operations with different specifications and implementations. Each would have a set of test requirements derived from the specification and implementation. Those test requirements probe for plausible faults: integration faults, condition faults, boundary faults, and so forth. But the operations are likely to be similar. Their sets of test requirements will overlap. The better the OO design, the greater is the overlap. New tests need to be derived only for those **Derived::redefined()** requirements that are not satisfied by the **Base::redefined()** tests.

To summarize, the **Base::redefined()** tests are applied to objects of class **Derived.** Test inputs may be appropriate for both base and derived classes, but the expected results may differ in the derived class.

14.7.5 Scenario-Based Testing

KEY POINT

Scenario-based testing will uncover errors that occur when any actor interacts with the software.

Fault-based testing misses two main types of errors: (1) incorrect specifications and (2) interactions among subsystems. When errors associated with incorrect specifications occur, the product doesn't do what the customer wants. It might do the wrong thing, or it might omit important functionality. But in either circumstance, quality (conformance to requirements) suffers. Errors associated with subsystem interactions occur when the behavior of one subsystem creates circumstances (e.g., events, data flow) that cause another subsystem to fail.

Scenario-based testing concentrates on what the user does, not what the product does. This means capturing the tasks (via use-cases) that the user has to perform, then applying them and their variants as tests.

Scenarios uncover interaction errors. But to accomplish this, test cases must be more complex and more realistic than fault-based tests. Scenario-based testing tends to exercise multiple subsystems in a single test (users do not limit themselves to the use of one subsystem at a time).

As an example, consider the design of scenario-based tests for a text editor by reviewing the informal use-cases that follow:

Use-Case: *Fix the Final Draft*

Background: It's not unusual to print the "final" draft, read it, and discover some annoying errors that weren't obvious from the on-screen image. This use-case describes the sequence of events that occurs when this happens.

1. Print the entire document.
2. Move around in the document, changing certain pages.
3. As each page is changed, it's printed.
4. Sometimes a series of pages is printed.

This scenario describes two things: a test and specific user needs. The user needs are obvious: (1) a method for printing single pages and (2) a method for printing a range of pages. As far as testing goes, there is a need to test editing after printing (as well as the reverse). The tester hopes to discover that the printing function causes errors in the editing function; that is, that the two software functions are not properly independent.

Although scenario-based testing has merit, you will get a higher return on time invested by reviewing use-cases when they are developed as part of the analysis model.

Use-Case: *Print a New Copy*

Background: Someone asks the user for a fresh copy of the document. It must be printed.

1. Open the document.
2. Print it.
3. Close the document.

Again, the testing approach is relatively obvious, except that this document didn't appear out of nowhere. It was created in an earlier task. Does that task affect this one?

In many modern editors, documents remember how they were last printed. By default, they print the same way the next time. After the *Fix the Final Draft* scenario, just selecting "Print" in the menu and clicking the Print button in the dialog box will cause the last corrected page to print again. So, according to the editor, the correct scenario should look like this:

Use-Case: *Print a New Copy*

1. Open the document.
2. Select "Print" in the menu.
3. Check if you're printing a page range; if so, click to print the entire document.
4. Click on the Print button.
5. Close the document.

But this scenario indicates a potential specification error. The editor does not do what the user reasonably expects it to do. Customers will often overlook the check noted in step 3 above. They will then be annoyed when they trot off to the printer and find one page when they wanted 100. Annoyed customers signal specification bugs.

A test case designer might miss this dependency in test design, but it is likely that the problem would surface during testing. The tester would then have to contend with the probable response, "That's the way it's supposed to work!"

14.7.6 Testing Surface Structure and Deep Structure

Surface structure refers to the externally observable structure of an OO program. That is, the structure that is immediately obvious to an end-user. Rather than performing functions, the users of many OO systems may be given objects to manipulate in some way. But whatever the interface, tests are still based on user tasks. Capturing these tasks involves understanding, watching, and talking with representative users (and as many nonrepresentative users as are worth considering).

Testing surface structure is analogous to black-box testing. Deep structure testing is similar to white-box testing.

There will surely be some difference in detail. For example, in a conventional system with a command-oriented interface, the user might use the list of all commands as a testing checklist. If no test scenarios exist to exercise a command, testing has likely overlooked some user tasks (or the interface has useless commands). In an object-based interface, the tester might use the list of all objects as a testing checklist.

The best tests are derived when the designer looks at the system in a new or unconventional way. For example, if the system or product has a command-based interface, more thorough tests will be derived if the test case designer pretends that operations are independent of objects. Ask questions like, "Might the user want to use this operation—which applies only to the **Scanner** object—while working with the printer?" Whatever the interface style, test case design that exercises the surface structure should use both objects and operations as clues leading to overlooked tasks.

Deep structure refers to the internal technical details of an OO program. That is, the structure that is understood by examining the design and/or code. Deep structure testing is designed to exercise dependencies, behaviors, and communication mechanisms that have been established as part of the design model (Chapters 9 through 12) for OO software.

The analysis and design models are used as the basis for deep structure testing. For example, the UML collaboration diagram or the deployment model depicts collaborations between objects and subsystems that may not be externally visible. The test case designer then asks: Have we captured (as a test) some task that exercises the collaboration noted on the collaboration diagram? If not, why not?

> "Be not ashamed of mistakes and thus make them crimes."
>
> **Confucius**

14.8 Testing Methods Applicable at the Class Level

In Chapter 13, we noted that software testing begins "in the small" and slowly progresses toward testing "in the large." Testing in the small focuses on a single class and the methods that are encapsulated by the class. Random testing and partitioning are methods that can be used to exercise a class during OO testing [KIR94].

14.8.1 Random Testing for OO Classes

The number of possible permutations for random testing can grow quite large. A strategy similar to orthogonal array testing can be used to improve testing efficiency.

To provide brief illustrations of these methods, consider a banking application in which an **Account** class has the following operations: *open(), setup(), deposit(), withdraw(), balance(), summarize(), creditLimit(),* and *close()* [KIR94]. Each of these operations may be applied for **Account,** but certain constraints (e.g., the account must be opened before other operations can be applied and closed after all operations are completed) are implied by the nature of the problem. Even with these constraints, there are many permutations of the operations. The minimum behavioral life history of an instance of **Account** includes the following operations:

open • setup • deposit • withdraw • close

This represents the minimum test sequence for **Account.** However, a wide variety of other behaviors may occur within this sequence:

open • setup • deposit • [deposit | withdraw | balance | summarize | creditLimit]^n • withdraw • close

A variety of different operation sequences can be generated randomly. For example:

Test case r_1: **open • setup • deposit • deposit • balance • summarize • withdraw • close**

Test case r_2: **open • setup • deposit • withdraw • deposit • balance • creditLimit • withdraw • close**

These and other random order tests are conducted to exercise different class instance life histories.

SAFEHOME

Class Testing

The scene: Shakira's cubicle.

The players: Jamie and Shakira—members of the *SafeHome* software engineering team who are working on test case design for the security function.

The conversation:

Shakira: I've developed some tests for the **Detector** class [Figure 11.4]—you know, the one that allows access to all of the **Sensor** objects for the security function. You familiar with it?

Jamie (laughing): Sure, it's the one that allowed you to add the "doggie angst" sensor.

Shakira: The one and only. Anyway, it has an interface with four ops: *read(), enable(), disable(),* and *test().* Before a sensor can be read, it must be enabled. Once it's enabled, it can be read and tested. It can be disabled at any time, except if an alarm condition is being processed. So I defined a simple test sequence that will exercise its behavioral life history.

(Shows Jamie the following sequence.)

#1: enable•test•read•disable

Jamie: That'll work, but you've got to do more testing than that!

Shakira: I know, I know. Here are some other sequences I've come up with.

(She shows Jamie the following sequences.)

#2: enable•test•[read]^n•test•disable

#3: [read]^n

#4: enable•disable•[test | read]

Jamie: So let me see if I understand the intent of these. #1 goes through a normal life history, sort of a conventional usage. #2 repeats the read operation *n* times, and that's a likely scenario. #3 tries to read the sensor before it's been enabled . . . that should produce an error message of some kind, right? #4 enables and disables the sensor and then tries to read it. Isn't that the same as test #3?

Shakira: Actually no. In #4, the sensor has been enabled. What #4 really tests is whether the disable op works as it should. A read() or test() after disable() should generate the error message. If it doesn't, then we have an error in the disable op.

Jamie: Cool. Just remember that the four tests have to be applied for every sensor type since all the ops may be subtly different depending on the type of sensor.

Shakira: Not to worry. That's the plan.

14.8.2 Partition Testing at the Class Level

Partition testing reduces the number of test cases required to exercise the class in much the same manner as equivalence partitioning (Section 14.6.2) for conventional software. Input and output are categorized and test cases are designed to exercise each category. But how are the partitioning categories derived?

? What testing options are available at the class level?

State-based partitioning categorizes class operations based on their ability to change the state of the class. Again considering the **Account** class, state operations include *deposit()* and *withdraw(),* whereas nonstate operations include *balance(), summarize(),* and *creditLimit().* Tests are designed in a way that exercises operations that change state and those that do not change state separately. Therefore,

Test case p_1: **open•setup•deposit•deposit•withdraw•withdraw•close**

Test case p_2: **open•setup•deposit•summarize•creditLimit•withdraw•close**

Test case p_1 changes state, while test case p_2 exercises operations that do not change state (other than those in the minimum test sequence).

Attribute-based partitioning categorizes class operations based on the attributes that they use. For the **Account** class, the attributes **balance** and **creditLimit** can be used to define partitions. Operations are divided into three partitions: (1) operations that use **creditLimit,** (2) operations that modify **creditLimit,** and (3) operations that do not use or modify **creditLimit.** Test sequences are then designed for each partition.

Category-based partitioning categorizes class operations based on the generic function that each performs. For example, operations in the **Account** class can be categorized as initialization operations—*open()*, *setup()*, computational operations—*deposit()*, *withdraw()*, queries—*balance()*, *summarize()*, *creditLimit()*) and termination operations—*close()*.

14.9 InterClass Test Case Design

Test case design becomes more complicated as integration of the object-oriented system begins. It is at this stage that testing of collaborations between classes must begin. To illustrate "interclass test case generation" [KIR94], we expand the banking example introduced in Section 14.8 to include the classes and collaborations noted in Figure 14.11. The direction of the arrows in the figure indicates the direction of messages, and the labeling indicates the operations that are invoked as a consequence of the collaborations implied by the messages.

Like the testing of individual classes, class collaboration testing can be accomplished by applying random and partitioning methods, as well as scenario-based testing and behavioral testing.

14.9.1 Multiple Class Testing

Kirani and Tsai [KIR94] suggest the following sequence of steps to generate multiple class random test cases:

1. For each client class, use the list of class operations to generate a series of random test sequences. The operations will send messages to other server classes.
2. For each message that is generated, determine the collaborator class and the corresponding operation in the server object.

FIGURE 14.11

Class collaboration diagram for banking application (adapted from [KIR94])

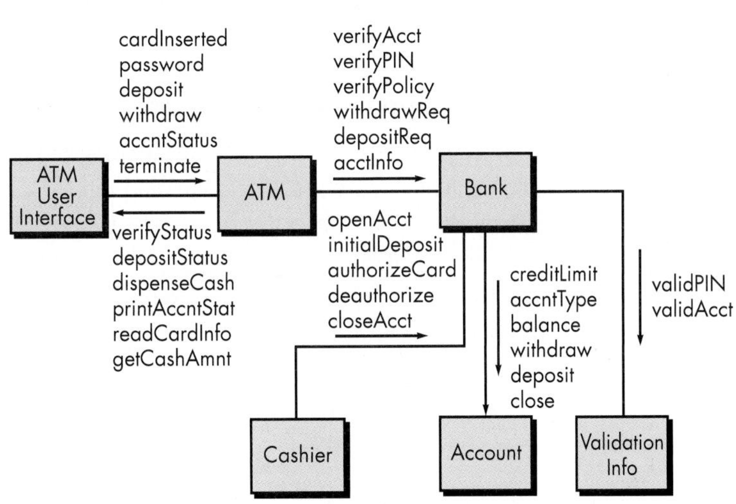

3. For each operation in the server object (that has been invoked by messages sent from the client object), determine the messages that it transmits.
4. For each of the messages, determine the next level of operations that are invoked and incorporate these into the test sequence.

To illustrate [KIR94], consider a sequence of operations for the **Bank** class relative to an **ATM** class (Figure 14.11):

verifyAcct•verifyPIN•[[verifyPolicy•withdrawReq]|depositReq|acctInfoREQ]^n

A random test case for the **Bank** class might be

Test case r_3 = **verifyAcct•verifyPIN•depositReq**

In order to consider the collaborators involved in this test, the messages associated with each of the operations noted in test case r_3 is considered. **Bank** must collaborate with **ValidationInfo** to execute *verifyAcct()* and *verifyPIN().* Bank must collaborate with **Account** to execute *depositReq().* Hence, a new test case that exercises these collaborations is

Test case r_4 = **verifyAcctBank[validAcctValidationInfo]•verifyPINBank•[validPinValidationInfo]•depositReq•[depositaccount]**

The approach for multiple class partition testing is similar to the approach used for partition testing of individual classes. A single class is partitioned as discussed in Section 14.8.2. However, the test sequence is expanded to include those operations that are invoked via messages to collaborating classes. An alternative approach partitions tests based on the interfaces to a particular class. Referring to Figure 14.11, the **Bank** class receives messages from the **ATM** and **Cashier** classes. The methods within **Bank** can therefore be tested by partitioning them into those that serve **ATM** and those that serve **Cashier.** State-based partitioning (Section 14.8.2) can be used to refine the partitions further.

14.9.2 Tests Derived from Behavior Models

In Chapter 8, we discussed the use of the state diagram as a model that represents the dynamic behavior of a class. The state diagram for a class can be used to help derive a sequence of tests that will exercise the dynamic behavior of the class (and those classes that collaborate with it). Figure 14.12 [KIR94] illustrates a state diagram for the **Account** class discussed earlier. Referring to the figure, initial transitions move through the *empty acct* and *setup acct* states. The majority of all behavior for instances of the class occurs while in the *working acct* state. A final withdrawal and account closure cause the **Account** class to make transitions to the *nonworking acct* and *dead acct* states, respectively.

FIGURE 14.12

State diagram for the Account class (adapted from [KIR94])

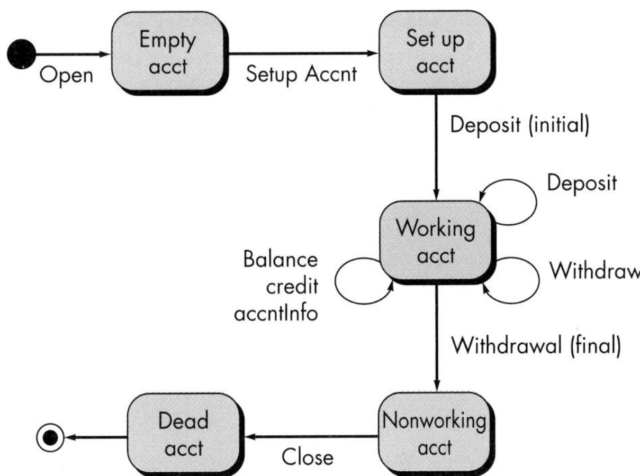

The tests to be designed should achieve all state coverage [KIR94]. That is, the operation sequences should cause the **Account** class to make a transition through all allowable states:

Test case s_1: **open•setupAccnt•deposit (initial)•withdraw (final)•close**

It should be noted that this sequence is identical to the minimum test sequence discussed in Section 14.9.1. Adding additional test sequences to the minimum sequence,

Test case s_2: **open•setupAccnt•deposit(initial)•deposit•balance•credit•withdraw (final)•close**

Test case s_3: **open•setupAccnt•deposit(initial)•deposit•withdraw•accntInfo•withdraw (final)•close**

Still more test cases could be derived to ensure that all behaviors for the class have been adequately exercised. In situations in which the class behavior results in a collaboration with one or more classes, multiple state diagrams are used to track the behavioral flow of the system.

The state model can be traversed in a "breadth-first" [MGR94] manner. In this context, breadth first implies that a test case exercises a single transition. When a new transition is to be tested only previously tested transitions are used.

Consider a **CreditCard** object that is part of the banking system. The initial state of **CreditCard** is *undefined* (i.e., no credit card number has been provided). Upon reading the credit card during a sale, the object takes on a *defined* state; that is, the attributes **card number** and **expiration date,** along with bank-specific identifiers are defined. The credit card is *submitted* when it is sent for authorization, and it is *approved* when authorization is received. The transition of **CreditCard** from one state to another can be tested by deriving test cases that cause the transition to occur. A breadth-first approach to this type of testing would not exercise *submitted* before it exercised *undefined* and *defined.* If it did, it would make use of transitions that had not been previously tested and would therefore violate the breadth-first criterion.

14.10 Testing for Specialized Environments, Architectures, and Applications

The testing methods discussed in preceding sections are generally applicable across all environments, architectures, and applications, but unique guidelines and approaches to testing are sometimes warranted. In this section we consider testing guidelines for specialized environments, architectures, and applications that are commonly encountered by software engineers.

14.10.1 Testing GUIs

A testing strategy similar to random or partition testing (Section 14.8) can be used to design UI tests.

Graphical user interfaces (GUIs) present interesting challenges for software engineers. Because of reusable components provided as part of GUI development environments, the creation of the user interface has become less time consuming and more precise (Chapter 12). But, at the same time, the complexity of GUIs has grown, leading to more difficulty in the design and execution of test cases.

Because many modern GUIs have the same look and feel, a series of standard tests can be derived. Finite state modeling graphs may be used to derive a series of tests that address specific data and program objects relevant to the GUI.

Due to the large number of permutations associated with GUI operations, testing should be approached using automated tools. A wide array of GUI testing tools has appeared on the market over the past few years. For further discussion, see Chapter 12.

14.10.2 Testing of Client/Server Architectures

WebRef
Useful client/server testing information and resources can be found at **www.csst-technologies.com.**

Client/server architectures represent a significant challenge for software testers. The distributed nature of client/server environments, the performance issues associated with transaction processing, the potential presence of a number of different hardware platforms, the complexities of network communication, the need to service multiple clients from a centralized (or in some cases, distributed) database, and the coordination requirements imposed on the server all combine to make testing of client/server software architectures considerably more difficult than standalone applications. In fact, recent industry studies indicate a significant increase in testing time and cost when client/server environments are developed.

> "The topic of testing is one area in which a good deal of commonality exists between traditional system and client/server systems."
>
> **Kelley Bourne**

In general, the testing of client/server software occurs at three different levels: (1) individual client applications are tested in a "disconnected" mode; the operation of the server and the underlying network are not considered; (2) the client software and associated server applications are tested in concert, but network operations are not explicitly exercised; (3) the complete client/server architecture, including network operation and performance, is tested.

Although many different types of tests are conducted at each of these levels of detail, the following testing approaches are commonly encountered for client/server applications:

? What types of tests are conducted for client/server systems?

- **Application function tests.** The functionality of client applications is tested using the methods discussed earlier in this chapter. In essence, the application is tested in standalone fashion.
- **Server tests.** The coordination and data management functions of the server are tested. Server performance (overall response time and data throughput) is also considered.
- **Database tests.** The accuracy and integrity of data stored by the server is tested. Transactions posted by client applications are examined to ensure that data are properly stored, updated, and retrieved. Archiving is also tested.
- **Transaction tests.** A series of tests are created to ensure that each class of transactions is processed according to requirements. Tests focus on the correctness of processing and also on performance issues (e.g., transaction processing times and transaction volume).
- **Network communication tests.** These tests verify that communication among the nodes of the network occurs correctly and that message passing, transactions, and related network traffic occur without error. Network security tests may also be conducted as part of these tests.

To accomplish these testing approaches, Musa [MUS93] recommends the development of *operational profiles* derived from client/server usage scenarios.[9] An operational profile indicates how different types of users interoperate with the client/server system. That is, the profiles provide a "pattern of usage" that can be applied when tests are designed and executed.

14.10.3 Testing Documentation and Help Facilities

The term *software testing* conjures images of large numbers of test cases prepared to exercise computer programs and the data that they manipulate. Recalling the definition of software presented in the first chapter of this book, it is important to note

9 It should be noted that operational profiles can be used in testing for all types of system architectures, not just client/server.

that testing must also extend to the third element of the software configuration—documentation.

Errors in documentation can be as devastating to the acceptance of the program as errors in data or source code. Nothing is more frustrating than following a user guide or an on-line help facility exactly and getting results or behaviors that do not coincide with those predicted by the documentation. It is for this reason that documentation testing should be a meaningful part of every software test plan.

Documentation testing can be approached in two phases. The first phase, review and inspection (Chapter 26), examines the document for editorial clarity. The second phase, live test, uses the documentation in conjunction with the use of the actual program.

INFO

Documentation Testing

The following questions should be answered during documentation and/or help facility testing:

- Does the documentation accurately describe how to accomplish each mode of use?
- Is the description of each interaction sequence accurate?
- Are examples accurate?
- Are terminology, menu descriptions, and system responses consistent with the actual program?
- Is it relatively easy to locate guidance within the documentation?
- Can troubleshooting be accomplished easily with the documentation?
- Are the document table of contents and index accurate and complete?
- Is the design of the document (layout, typefaces, indentation, graphics) conducive to understanding and quick assimilation of information?
- Are all software error messages displayed for the user described in more detail in the document? Are actions to be taken as a consequence of an error message clearly delineated?
- If hypertext links are used, are they accurate and complete?
- If hypertext is used, is the navigation design appropriate for the information required?

The only viable way to answer these questions is to have an independent third party (e.g., selected users) test the documentation in the context of program usage. All discrepancies are noted and areas of document ambiguity or weakness are defined for potential rewrite.

14.10.4 Testing for Real-Time Systems

The time-dependent, asynchronous nature of many real-time applications adds a new and potentially difficult element to the testing mix—time. Not only does the test case designer have to consider conventional test cases but also event handling (i.e., interrupt processing), the timing of the data, and the parallelism of the tasks (processes) that handle the data. In many situations, test data provided when a real-time system is in one state will result in proper processing, while the same data provided when the system is in a different state may lead to error.

For example, the real-time software that controls a new photocopier accepts operator interrupts (i.e., the machine operator hits control keys such as RESET or DARKEN) with no error when the machine is making copies (in the *copying* state). If these same operator interrupts are input when the machine is in the *jammed* state, a display of the diagnostic code (indicating the location of the jam) will be lost (an error).

In addition, the intimate relationship that exists between real-time software and its hardware environment can also cause testing problems. Software tests must consider the impact of hardware faults on software processing. Such faults can be extremely difficult to simulate realistically.

? What is an effective strategy for testing a real-time system?

Comprehensive test case design methods for real-time systems continue to evolve. However, a four-step strategy can be proposed:

- **Task testing.** The first step in the testing of real-time software is to test each task independently. That is, conventional tests are designed and executed for each task. Each task is executed independently during these tests. Task testing uncovers errors in logic and function, but not timing or behavior.
- **Behavioral testing.** Using system models created with automated tools, it is possible to simulate the behavior of a real-time system and examine its behavior as a consequence of external events. These analysis activities can serve as the basis for the design of test cases that are conducted when the real-time software has been built.
- **Intertask testing.** Once errors in individual tasks and in system behavior have been isolated, testing shifts to time-related errors. Asynchronous tasks that are known to communicate with one another are tested with different data rates and processing load to determine if intertask synchronization errors will occur. In addition, tasks that communicate via a message queue or data store are tested to uncover errors in the sizing of these data storage areas.
- **System testing.** Software and hardware are integrated and a full range of system tests (Chapter 13) are conducted in an attempt to uncover errors at the software/hardware interface. Most real-time systems process interrupts. Therefore, testing the handling of these Boolean events is essential. Using the state diagram and the control specification (Chapter 8), the tester develops a list of all possible interrupts and the processing that occurs as a consequence of the interrupts. Tests are then designed to assess the following system characteristics:

  —Are interrupt priorities properly assigned and properly handled?

  —Is processing for each interrupt handled correctly?

  —Does the performance (e.g., processing time) of each interrupt-handling procedure conform to requirements?

  —Does a high volume of interrupts arriving at critical times create problems in function or performance?

In addition, global data areas that are used to transfer information as part of interrupt processing should be tested to assess the potential for the generation of side effects.

14.11 Testing Patterns

WebRef
Pointers to over 70 testing patterns can be found at **www.rbsc.com.**

In earlier chapters, we have discussed the use of patterns as a mechanism for describing software building blocks or software engineering situations. These building blocks or situations are encountered repeatedly as different applications are built or different projects are conducted. Like their counterparts in analysis and design, *testing patterns* describe often-encountered building blocks or situations that software testers may be able to reuse as they approach the testing of some new or revised system.

Not only do testing patterns provide software engineers with useful guidance as testing activities commence, they also provide three additional benefits described by Marick [MAR02]:

KEY POINT
Testing patterns can help a software team communicate more effectively about testing and better understand the forces that lead to a specific testing approach.

1. They provide a vocabulary for problem-solvers. "Hey, you know, we should use a Null Object."
2. They focus attention on the forces behind a problem. That allows [test case] designers to better understand when and why a solution applies.
3. They encourage iterative thinking. Each solution creates a new context in which new problems can be solved.

Although these benefits are "soft," they should not be overlooked. Much of software testing, even during the past decade, has been an ad hoc activity. If testing patterns can help a software team communicate about testing more effectively, understand the motivating forces that lead to a specific approach to testing, and approach the design of test cases as an evolutionary activity, they have accomplished much.

Testing patterns are described in much the same way as analysis and design patterns (Chapters 7 and 9). Dozens of testing patterns have been proposed in the literature (e.g., [BIN99], [MAR02]). The following three testing patterns (presented in abstract form only) provide representative examples:

WebRef
Patterns that describe testing organization, efficiency, strategy, and problem resolution can be found at **www.agcs.com/supportv2/techpapers/patterns/papers/systestp.htm.**

Pattern name: **pair testing**

Abstract: A process-oriented pattern, **pair testing** describes a technique that is analogous to pair programming (Chapter 4) in which two testers work together to design and execute a series of tests that can be applied to unit, integration, or validation testing activities.

Pattern name: **separate test interface**

Abstract: There is a need to test every class in an object-oriented system, including "internal classes" (i.e., classes that do not expose any interface outside of the component that used them). The **separate test interface** pattern describes how to create "a test interface that can be used to describe specific tests on classes that are visible only internally to a component" [LAN01].

Pattern name: **scenario testing**

Abstract: Once unit and integration tests have been conducted, there is a need to determine whether the software will perform in a manner that satisfies users. The **scenario testing** pattern describes a technique for exercising the software from the user's point of view. A failure at this level indicates that the software has failed to meet a user visible requirement [KAN01].

A comprehensive discussion of testing patterns is beyond the scope of this book. The interested reader should see [BIN99] and [MAR02] for further information on this important topic.

14.12 Summary

The primary objective for test case design is to derive a set of tests that have the highest likelihood of uncovering errors in software. To accomplish this objective, two different categories of test case design techniques—applicable to conventional and object-oriented systems—are used: white-box testing and black-box testing.

White-box tests focus on the program control structure. Test cases are derived to ensure that all statements in the program have been executed at least once during testing and that all logical conditions have been exercised. Basis path testing, a white-box technique, makes use of program graphs (or graph matrices) to derive a set of linearly independent tests that will ensure coverage. Condition and data flow testing further exercise program logic, and loop testing complements other white-box techniques by providing a procedure for exercising loops of varying degrees of complexity.

Black-box tests are designed to validate functional requirements without regard to the internal workings of a program. Black-box testing techniques focus on the information domain of the software, deriving test cases by partitioning the input and output domain of a program in a manner that provides thorough test coverage. Equivalence partitioning divides the input domain into classes of data that are likely to exercise specific software function. Boundary value analysis probes the program's ability to handle data at the limits of acceptability. Orthogonal array testing provides an efficient, systematic method for testing systems with small numbers of input parameters.

Although the overall objective of object-oriented testing—to find the maximum number of errors with a minimum amount of effort—is identical to the objective of conventional software testing, the strategy and tactics for OO testing differ somewhat. The view of testing broadens to include the review of both the analysis and design model. In addition, the focus of testing moves away from the procedural component (the module) and toward the class. The design of tests for a class uses a variety of methods: fault-based testing, random testing, and partition testing. Each of these methods exercises the operations encapsulated by the class. Test sequences are designed to ensure that relevant operations are exercised. The state of the class, represented by the values of its attributes, is examined to determine if errors exist.

Integration testing can be accomplished using a use-based strategy. Use-based testing constructs the system in layers, beginning with those classes that do not use server classes. Integration test case design methods can also use random and partition tests. In addition, scenario-based testing and tests derived from behavioral models can be used to test a class and its collaborators. A test sequence tracks the flow of operations across class collaborations.

Specialized testing methods encompass a broad array of software capabilities and application areas. Testing for graphical user interfaces, client/server architectures, documentation and help facilities, and real-time systems each require specialized guidelines and techniques.

Experienced software developers often say, "Testing never ends, it just gets transferred from you [the software engineer] to your customer. Every time your customer uses the program, a test is being conducted." By applying test case design, the software engineer can achieve more complete testing and thereby uncover and correct the highest number of errors before the "customer's tests" begin.

References

[AMB95] Ambler, S., "Using Use Cases," *Software Development,* July 1995, pp. 53–61.

[BEI90] Beizer, B., *Software Testing Techniques,* 2nd ed., Van Nostrand-Reinhold, 1990.

[BEI95] Beizer, B., *Black-Box Testing,* Wiley, 1995.

[BIN94] Binder, R. V., "Testing Object-Oriented Systems: A Status Report," *American Programmer,* vol. 7, no. 4, April 1994, pp. 23–28.

[BIN99] Binder, R., *Testing Object-Oriented Systems: Models, Patterns, and Tools,* Addison-Wesley, 1999.

[DEU79] Deutsch, M., "Verification and Validation," in *Software Engineering* (R. Jensen and C. Tonies, eds.), Prentice-Hall, 1979, pp. 329–408.

[FRA88] Frankl, P. G., and E. J. Weyuker, "An Applicable Family of Data Flow Testing Criteria," *IEEE Trans. Software Engineering,* vol. SE-14, no. 10, October 1988, pp. 1483–1498.

[FRA93] Frankl, P. G., and S. Weiss, "An Experimental Comparison of the Effectiveness of Branch Testing and Data Flow," *IEEE Trans. Software Engineering,* vol. SE-19, no. 8, August 1993, pp. 770–787.

[KAN93] Kaner, C., J. Falk, and H. Q. Nguyen, *Testing Computer Software,* 2nd ed., Van Nostrand-Reinhold, 1993.

[KAN01] Kaner, C., "Pattern: Scenario Testing," (draft), 2001, available at http://www.testing.com/test-patterns/patterns/pattern-scenario-testing-kaner.html.

[KIR94] Kirani, S., and W. T. Tsai, "Specification and Verification of Object-Oriented Programs," Technical Report TR 94-64, Computer Science Department, University of Minnesota, December 1994.

[LAN01] Lange, M., "It's Testing Time! Patterns for Testing Software, June, 2001, downloadable from http://www.testing.com/test-patterns/patterns/index.html.

[LIN94] Lindland, O. I., et al., "Understanding Quality in Conceptual Modeling," *IEEE Software,* vol. 11, no 4, July 1994, pp. 42–49.

[MAR94] Marick, B., *The Craft of Software Testing,* Prentice-Hall, 1994.

[MAR02] Marick, B., "Software Testing Patterns," 2002, http://www.testing.com/test-patterns/index.html.

[MCC76] McCabe, T., "A Software Complexity Measure," *IEEE Trans. Software Engineering,* vol. SE-2, December 1976, pp. 308–320.

[MGR94] McGregor, J. D., and T. D. Korson, "Integrated Object-Oriented Testing and Development Processes," *CACM,* vol. 37, no. 9, September 1994, pp. 59–77.

[MUS93] Musa, J., "Operational Profiles in Software Reliability Engineering," *IEEE Software,* March 1993, pp. 14–32.

[MYE79] Myers, G., *The Art of Software Testing,* Wiley, 1979.

[NTA88] Ntafos, S. C., "A Comparison of Some Structural Testing Strategies," *IEEE Trans. Software Engineering,* vol. SE-14, no. 6, June 1988, pp. 868–874.

[PHA89] Phadke, M. S., *Quality Engineering Using Robust Design,* Prentice-Hall, 1989.

[PHA97] Phadke, M. S., "Planning Efficient Software Tests," *Crosstalk,* vol. 10, no. 10, October 1997, pp. 11–15.

[TAI89] Tai, K. C., "What to Do Beyond Branch Testing," *ACM Software Engineering Notes,* vol. 14, no. 2, April 1989, pp. 58–61.

Problems and Points to Ponder

14.1. Myers [MYE79] uses the following program as a self-assessment of one's ability to specify adequate testing: A program reads three integer values. The three values are interpreted as representing the lengths of the sides of a triangle. The program prints a message that states whether the triangle is scalene, isosceles, or equilateral. Develop a set of test cases that you feel will adequately test this program.

14.2. Design and implement the program (with error handling where appropriate) specified in Problem 14.1. Derive a flow graph for the program and apply basis path testing to develop test cases that will guarantee that all statements in the program have been tested. Execute the cases and show your results.

14.3. Can you think of any additional testing characteristics that are not discussed in Section 14.1?

14.4. Select a software component that you have designed and implemented recently. Design a set of test cases that will ensure that all statements have been executed using basis path testing.

14.5. Specify, design, and implement a software tool that will compute the cyclomatic complexity for the programming language of your choice. Use the graph matrix as the operative data structure in your design.

14.6. Read Beizer [BEI95] and determine how the program you have developed in Problem 14.5 can be extended to accommodate various link weights. Extend your tool to process execution probabilities or link processing times.

14.7. Design an automated tool that will recognize loops and categorize them as indicated in Section 14.5.3.

14.8. Extend the tool described in Problem 14.7 to generate test cases for each loop category, once encountered. It will be necessary to perform this function interactively with the tester.

14.9. Give at least three examples in which black-box testing might give the impression that "everything's OK," while white-box tests might uncover an error. Give at least three examples in which white-box testing might give the impression that "everything's OK," while black-box tests might uncover an error.

14.10. Will exhaustive testing (even if it is possible for very small programs) guarantee that the program is 100 percent correct?

14.11. In your own words, describe why the class is the smallest reasonable unit for testing within an OO system.

14.12. Why do we have to retest subclasses that are instantiated from an existing class, if the existing class has already been thoroughly tested? Can we use the test cases designed for the existing class?

14.13. Apply random testing and partitioning to three classes defined in the design for the *Safe-Home* system. Produce test cases that indicate the operation sequences that will be invoked.

14.14. Apply multiple class testing and tests derived from the behavioral model to the *Safe-Home* design.

14.15. Test a user manual (or help facility) for an application that you use frequently. Find at least one error in the documentation.

Further Readings and Information Sources

Among dozens of books that present test case design methods are Craig and Kaskiel (*Systematic Software Testing,* Artech House, 2002), Tamres (*Introducing Software Testing,* Addison-Wesley, 2002), Whittaker (*How to Break Software,* Addison-Wesley, 2002), Jorgensen (*Software Testing: A Craftman's Approach,* CRC Press, 2002), Splaine and his colleagues (*The Web Testing Handbook,* Software Quality Engineering Publishing, 2001), Patton (*Software Testing,* Sams Publishing, 2000), Kaner and his colleagues (*Testing Computer Software,* second edition, Wiley, 1999).In addition, Hutcheson (*Software Testing Methods and Metrics: The Most Important Tests,* McGraw-Hill, 1997) and Marick (*The Craft of Software Testing: Subsystem Testing Including Object-Based and Object-Oriented Testing,* Prentice-Hall, 1995) present treatments of testing methods and strategies.

Myers [MYE79] remains a classic text, covering black-box techniques in considerable detail. Beizer [BEI90] provides comprehensive coverage of white-box techniques, introducing a level of mathematical rigor that has often been missing in other treatments of testing. His later book [BEI95] presents a concise treatment of important methods. Perry (*Effective Methods for Software Testing,* Wiley-QED, 1995) and Friedman and Voas (*Software Assessment: Reliability, Safety, Testability,* Wiley, 1995) present good introductions to testing strategies and tactics. Mosley (*The Handbook of MIS Application Software Testing,* Prentice-Hall, 1993) discusses testing issues for large information systems, and Marks (*Testing Very Big Systems,* McGraw-Hill, 1992) discusses the special issues that must be considered when testing major programming systems.

Sykes and McGregor (*Practical Guide for Testing Object-Oriented Software,* Addison-Wesley, 2001), Bashir and Goel (*Testing Object-Oriented Software,* Springer-Verlag, 2000), Binder (*Testing Object-Oriented Systems,* Addison-Wesley, 1999), Kung and his colleagues (*Testing Object-Oriented Software,* IEEE Computer Society Press, 1998), Marick (*The Craft of Software Testing,* Prentice-Hall, 1997) and Siegel and Muller (*Object-Oriented Software Testing: A Hierarchical Approach,* Wiley, 1996) present strategies and methods for testing OO systems.

Software testing is a resource-intensive activity. It is for this reason that many organizations automate parts of the testing process. Books by Dustin, Rashka, and Poston (*Automated Software Testing: Introduction, Management, and Performance,* Addison-Wesley, 1999), Graham and her colleagues (*Software Test Automation*, Addison-Wesley, 1999), and Poston (*Automating Specification-Based Software Testing,* IEEE Computer Society, 1996) discuss tools, strategies, and methods for automated testing.

A number of books consider testing methods and strategies in specialized application areas. Gardiner (*Testing Safety-Related Software: A Practical Handbook,* Springer-Verlag, 1999) has edited a book that addresses testing of safety-critical systems. Mosley (*Client/Server Software Testing on the Desk Top and the Web,* Prentice-Hall, 1999) discusses the test process for clients, servers, and network components. Rubin (*Handbook of Usability Testing,* Wiley, 1994) has written a useful guide for those who must exercise human interfaces.

Binder [BIN99] describes almost 70 testing patterns that cover testing of methods, classes/clusters, subsystems, reusable components, frameworks, and systems as well as test automation and specialized database testing. A list of these patterns can be found at www.rbsc.com/pages/TestPatternList.htm.

A wide variety of information sources on test case design methods are available on the Internet. An up-to-date list of World Wide Web references that are relevant to testing techniques can be found at the SEPA Web site:
http://www.mhhe.com/pressman.

CHAPTER 15 PRODUCT METRICS FOR SOFTWARE

A key element of any engineering process is measurement. We use measures to better understand the attributes of the models that we create and to assess the quality of the engineered products or systems that we build. But unlike other engineering disciplines, software engineering is not grounded in the basic quantitative laws of physics. Direct measures, such as voltage, mass, velocity, or temperature, are uncommon in the software world. Because software measures and metrics are often indirect, they are open to debate. Fenton [FEN91] addresses this issue when he states:

> Measurement is the process by which numbers or symbols are assigned to the attributes of entities in the real world in such a way as to define them according to clearly defined rules . . . In the physical sciences, medicine, economics, and more recently the social sciences, we are now able to measure attributes that we previously thought to be unmeasurable . . . Of course, such measurements are not as refined as many measurements in the physical sciences . . ., but they exist [and important decisions are made based on them]. We feel that the obligation to attempt to "measure the unmeasurable" in order to improve our understanding of particular entities is as powerful in software engineering as in any discipline.

But some members of the software community continue to argue that software is "unmeasurable" or that attempts at measurement should be postponed until we better understand software and the attributes that should be used to describe it. That is a mistake.

QUICK LOOK

What is it? By its nature, engineering is a quantitative discipline. Engineers use numbers to help them design and assess the product to be built. Until recently, software engineers had little quantitative guidance in their work—but that's changing. Product metrics help software engineers gain insight into the design and construction of the software they build. Unlike process and project metrics that apply to the project (or process) as a whole, product metrics focus on specific attributes of software engineering work products and are collected as technical tasks (analysis, design, coding, and testing) are being conducted.

Who does it? Software engineers use product metrics to help them build higher-quality software.

Why is it important? There will always be a qualitative element to the creation of computer software. The problem is that qualitative assessment may not be enough. A software engineer needs objective criteria to help guide the design of data, architecture, interfaces, and components. The tester needs quantitative guidance that will help in the selection of test cases and their targets. Product metrics provide a basis from which analysis, design, coding, and testing can be conducted more objectively and assessed more quantitatively.

What are the steps? The first step in the measurement process is to derive the software measures and metrics that are appropriate for the representation of software that is being considered. Next, data required to derive the formulated metrics are collected. Once computed, appropriate metrics are analyzed based on preestablished guidelines and past data. The results of the analysis are interpreted to gain insight into the quality of the software, and the results of the interpretation lead to modification of analysis and design models, source code, or test cases. In some instances, it may also lead to modification of the software process itself.

What is the work product? Product metrics that are computed from data collected from the analysis and design models, source code, and test cases.

How do I ensure that I've done it right? You should establish the objectives of measurement before data collection begins, defining each product metric in an unambiguous manner. Define only a few metrics and then use them to gain insight into the quality of a software engineering work product.

Although product metrics for computer software are often not absolute, they provide us with a systematic way to assess quality based on a set of clearly defined rules. They also provide the software engineer with on-the-spot, rather than after-the-fact insight. This enables the engineer to discover and correct potential problems before they become catastrophic defects.

In this chapter, we consider measures that can be used to assess the quality of the product as it is being engineered. These measures of internal product attributes provide the software engineer with a real-time indication of the efficacy of the analysis, design, and code models; the effectiveness of test cases; and the overall quality of the software to be built.

15.1 Software Quality

Even the most jaded software developers will agree that high-quality software is an important goal. But how do we define quality? In the most general sense, software quality is *conformance to explicitly stated functional and performance requirements, explicitly documented development standards, and implicit characteristics that are expected of all professionally developed software.*

There is little question that the preceding definition could be modified or extended and debated endlessly. For the purposes of this book, the definition serves to emphasize three important points:

1. Software requirements are the foundation from which quality is measured. Lack of conformance to requirements is lack of quality.[1]

1 It is important to note that quality extends to the technical characteristics of analysis and design models and the source code realization of those models. Models that exhibit high quality (in the technical sense) will lead to software that exhibits high quality from the customer's point of view.

2. Specified standards define a set of development criteria that guide the manner in which software is engineered. If the criteria are not followed, lack of quality will almost surely result.
3. There is a set of implicit requirements that often goes unmentioned (e.g., the desire for ease of use). If software conforms to its explicit requirements but fails to meet implicit requirements, software quality is suspect.

Software quality is a complex mix of factors that will vary across different applications and the customers who request them. In the sections that follow, software quality factors are identified and the human activities required to achieve them are described.

15.1.1 McCall's Quality Factors

The factors that affect software quality can be categorized in two broad groups: (1) factors that can be directly measured (e.g., defects uncovered during testing) and (2) factors that can be measured only indirectly (e.g., usability or maintainability). In each case measurement should occur. We must compare the software (programs, data, documents) to some datum and arrive at an indication of quality.

It's interesting to note that McCall's quality factors are as valid today as they were in the 1970s. Therefore, it's reasonable to assert that the factors that affect software quality do not change with time.

McCall, Richards, and Walters [MCC77] propose a useful categorization of factors that affect software quality. These software quality factors, shown in Figure 15.1, focus on three important aspects of a software product: its operational characteristics, its ability to undergo change, and its adaptability to new environments.

Referring to the factors noted in Figure 15.1, McCall and his colleagues provide the following descriptions:

Correctness. The extent to which a program satisfies its specification and fulfills the customer's mission objectives.

Reliability. The extent to which a program can be expected to perform its intended function with required precision. [It should be noted that other, more complete definitions of reliability have been proposed (see Chapter 26).]

FIGURE 15.1

McCall's software quality factors

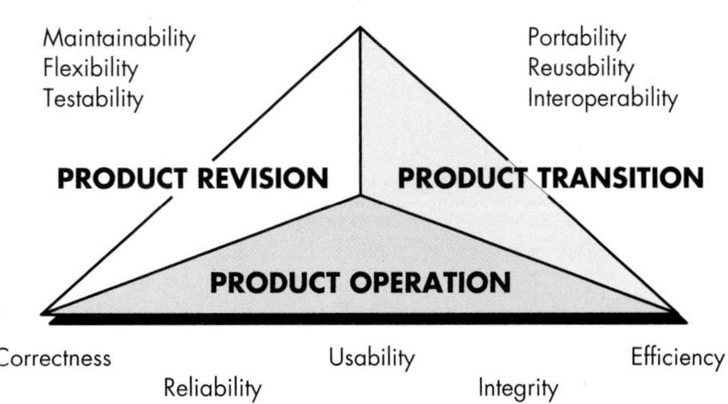

Efficiency. The amount of computing resources and code required by a program to perform its function.

Integrity. The extent to which access to software or data by unauthorized persons can be controlled.

Usability. The effort required to learn, operate, prepare input for, and interpret output of a program.

Maintainability. The effort required to locate and fix an error in a program. [This is a very limited definition.]

Flexibility. The effort required to modify an operational program.

Testability. The effort required to test a program to ensure that it performs its intended function.

Portability. The effort required to transfer the program from one hardware and/or software system environment to another.

Reusability. The extent to which a program [or parts of a program] can be reused in other applications—related to the packaging and scope of the functions that the program performs.

Interoperability. The effort required to couple one system to another.

> "A product's quality is a function of how much it changes the world for the better."
>
> **Tom DeMarco**

Build your own checklist using these factors. First assign each a relative importance for your project. Then, grade your work products to assess the quality of the software you're building.

It is difficult, and in some cases impossible, to develop direct measures[2] of these quality factors. In fact, many of the metrics defined by McCall et al. can be measured only subjectively. The metrics may be in the form of a checklist that is used to "grade" specific attributes of the software [CAV78].

15.1.2 ISO 9126 Quality Factors

The ISO 9126 standard was developed in an attempt to identify quality attributes for computer software. The standard identifies six key quality attributes:

Functionality. The degree to which the software satisfies stated needs as indicated by the following sub-attributes: *suitability, accuracy, interoperability, compliance,* and *security.*

Reliability. The amount of time that the software is available for use as indicated by the following sub-attributes: *maturity, fault tolerance, recoverability.*

Usability. The degree to which the software is easy to use as indicated by the following sub-attributes: *understandability, learnability, operability.*

---

2 A *direct measure* implies that there is a single countable value that provides a direct indication of the attribute being examined. For example, the "size" of a program can be measured directly by counting the number of lines of code.

Efficiency. The degree to which the software makes optimal use of system resources as indicated by the following sub-attributes: *time behavior, resource behavior.*

Maintainability. The ease with which repair may be made to the software as indicated by the following sub-attributes: *analyzability, changeability, stability, testability.*

Portability. The ease with which the software can be transposed from one environment to another as indicated by the following sub-attributes: *adaptability, installability, conformance, replaceability.*

Like other software quality factors discussed in Chapter 9 and Section 15.1.1, the ISO 9126 factors do not necessarily lend themselves to direct measurement. However, they do provide a worthwhile basis for indirect measures and an excellent checklist for assessing the quality of a system.

> **"Any activity becomes creative when the doer cares about doing it right, or better."**
>
> **John Updike**

15.1.3 The Transition to a Quantitative View

In the preceding sections, a set of qualitative factors for the "measurement" of software quality was discussed. We strive to develop precise measures for software quality and are sometimes frustrated by the subjective nature of the activity. Cavano and McCall [CAV78] discuss this situation:

> The determination of quality is a key factor in every day events—wine tasting contests, sporting events [e.g., gymnastics], talent contests, etc. In these situations, quality is judged in the most fundamental and direct manner: side by side comparison of objects under identical conditions and with predetermined concepts. The wine may be judged according to clarity, color, bouquet, taste, etc. However, this type of judgment is very subjective; to have any value at all, it must be made by an expert.
>
> Subjectivity and specialization also apply to determining software quality. To help solve this problem, a more precise definition of software quality is needed as well as a way to derive quantitative measurements of software quality for objective analysis . . .

In the sections that follow, we examine a set of software metrics that can be applied to the quantitative assessment of software quality. In all cases, the metrics represent indirect measures; that is, we never really measure quality but rather some manifestation of quality. The complicating factor is the precise relationship between the variable that is measured and the quality of software.

> **"Just as temperature measurement began with an index finger . . . and grew to sophisticated scales, tools and techniques, so too is software measurement maturing."**
>
> **Shari Pfleeger**

15.2 A Framework for Product Metrics

As we noted in the introduction to this chapter, measurement assigns numbers or symbols to attributes of entities in the real word. To accomplish this, a measurement model encompassing a consistent set of rules is required. Although the theory of measurement (e.g., [KYB84]) and its application to computer software (e.g., [DEM81], [BRI96], [ZUS97]) are topics that are beyond the scope of this book, it is worthwhile to establish a fundamental framework and a set of basic principles for the measurement of product metrics for software.

15.2.1 Measures, Metrics, and Indicators

Although the terms *measure, measurement,* and *metrics* are often used interchangeably, it is important to note the subtle differences between them. Because *measure* can be used either as a noun or a verb, definitions of the term can become confusing. Within the software engineering context, a *measure* provides a quantitative indication of the extent, amount, dimension, capacity, or size of some attribute of a product or process. *Measurement* is the act of determining a measure. The *IEEE Standard Glossary* [IEE93] defines *metric* as "a quantitative measure of the degree to which a system, component, or process possesses a given attribute."

When a single data point has been collected (e.g., the number of errors uncovered within a single software component), a measure has been established. Measurement occurs as the result of the collection of one or more data points (e.g., a number of component reviews and unit tests are investigated to collect measures of the number of errors for each). A software metric relates the individual measures in some way (e..g, the average number of errors found per review or the average number of errors found per unit test).

A software engineer collects measures and develops metrics so that indicators will be obtained. An *indicator* is a metric or combination of metrics that provides insight into the software process, a software project, or the product itself. An indicator provides insight that enables the project manager or software engineers to adjust the process, the project, or the product to make things better.

> "A science is as mature as its measurement tools."
>
> **Louis Pasteur**

15.2.2 The Challenge of Product Metrics

Over the past three decades, many researchers have attempted to develop a single metric that provides a comprehensive measure of software complexity. Fenton [FEN94] characterizes this research as a search for "the impossible holy grail." Although dozens of complexity measures have been proposed [ZUS90], each takes a somewhat different view of what complexity is and what attributes of a system lead to complexity. By analogy, consider a metric for evaluating an attractive car. Some observers might emphasize body design, others might consider mechanical characteristics, still others might tout cost, or performance, or fuel economy, or the ability to recycle when the car is junked. Since any one of these characteristics may be at odds with others, it is difficult to derive a single value for "attractiveness." The same problem occurs with computer software.

WebRef
Voluminous information on product metrics has been compiled by Horst Zuse at **irb.cs.tuberlin.de/~zuse/.**

Yet there is a need to measure and control software complexity. And if a single value of this quality metric is difficult to derive, it should be possible to develop measures of different internal program attributes (e.g., effective modularity, functional independence, and other attributes discussed in Chapters 9 through 12). These measures and the metrics derived from them can be used as independent indicators of the quality of analysis and design models. But here again, problems arise. Fenton [FEN94] notes this when he states: "The danger of attempting to find measures which characterize so many different attributes is that inevitably the measures have to satisfy conflicting aims. This is counter to the representational theory of measurement." Although Fenton's statement is correct, many people argue that product measurement conducted during the early stages of the software process provides software engineers with a consistent and objective mechanism for assessing quality.

It is fair to ask, however, just how valid product metrics are. That is, how closely aligned are product metrics to the long-term reliability and quality of a computer-based system? Fenton [FEN91] addresses this question in the following way:

> In spite of the intuitive connections between the internal structure of software products [product metrics] and its external product and process attributes, there have actually been very few scientific attempts to establish specific relationships. There are a number of reasons why this is so; the most commonly cited is the impracticality of conducting relevant experiments.

Each of the "challenges" noted here is a cause for caution, but it is no reason to dismiss product metrics.[3] Measurement is essential if quality is to be achieved.

15.2.3 Measurement Principles

Before we introduce a series of product metrics that (1) assist in the evaluation of analysis and design models, (2) provide an indication of the complexity of procedural designs and source code, and (3) facilitate the design of more effective testing, it is important to understand basic measurement principles. Roche [ROC94] suggests a measurement process that can be characterized by five activities:

? What are the steps of an effective measurement process?

- *Formulation.* The derivation of software measures and metrics appropriate for the representation of the software that is being considered.

3 Although criticism of specific metrics is common in the literature, many critiques focus on esoteric issues and miss the primary objective of metrics in the real world: to help the software engineer establish a systematic and objective way to gain insight into his or her work and to improve product quality as a result.

- *Collection.* The mechanism used to accumulate data required to derive the formulated metrics.
- *Analysis.* The computation of metrics and the application of mathematical tools.
- *Interpretation.* The evaluation of metrics in an effort to gain insight into the quality of the representation.
- *Feedback.* Recommendations derived from the interpretation of product metrics transmitted to the software team.

Software metrics will be useful only if they are characterized effectively and validated so that their worth is proven. The following principles [LET03] are representative of many that can be proposed for metrics characterization and validation:

In reality, many product metrics in use today do not conform to these principles as well as they should. But that doesn't mean that they have no value—just be careful when you use them, understanding that they are intended to provide insight, not hard scientific verification.

- *A metric should have desirable mathematical properties.* That is, the metric's value should be in a meaningful range (e.g., zero to one, where zero truly means absence, one indicates the maximum value, and 0.5 represents the "half-way point"). Also, a metric that purports to be on a rational scale should not be composed of components that are only measured on an ordinal scale.
- *When a metric represents a software characteristic that increases when positive traits occur or decreases when undesirable traits are encountered, the value of the metric should increase or decrease in the same manner.*
- *Each metric should be validated empirically in a wide variety of contexts before being published or used to make decisions.* A metric should measure the factor of interest, independently of other factors. It should "scale up" to large systems and work in a variety of programming languages and system domains.

Although formulation, characterization, and validation are critical, collection and analysis are the activities that drive the measurement process. Roche [ROC94] suggests the following guidelines for these activities: (1) whenever possible, data collection and analysis should be automated; (2) valid statistical techniques should be applied to establish relationships between internal product attributes and external quality characteristics (e.g., whether the level of architectural complexity is correlated with the number of defects reported in production use); and (3) interpretative guidelines and recommendations should be established for each metric.

15.2.4 Goal-Oriented Software Measurement

WebRef
A useful discussion of GQM can be found at **www.thedacs.com/GoldPractices/practices/gqma.html.**

The *Goal/Question/Metric* (GQM) paradigm was developed by Basili and Weiss [BAS84] as a technique for identifying meaningful metrics for any part of the software process. GQM emphasizes the need to (1) establish an explicit measurement *goal* that is specific to the process activity or product characteristic that is to be assessed; (2) define a set of *questions* that must be answered in order to achieve the goal, and (3) identify well-formulated *metrics* that help to answer these questions.

A *goal definition template* [BAS94] can be used to define each measurement goal. The template takes the form:

> **Analyze** {the name of activity or attribute to be measured} **for the purpose of** {the overall objective of the analysis[4]} **with respect to** {the aspect of the activity or attribute that is considered} **from the viewpoint of** {the people who have an interest in the measurement} **in the context of** {the environment in which the measurement takes place}.

As an example, consider a goal definition template for *SafeHome:*

> **Analyze** the *SafeHome* software architecture **for the purpose of** evaluating architectural components **with respect to** the ability to make *SafeHome* more extensible **from the viewpoint of** the software engineers performing the work **in the context of** product enhancement over the next three years.

With a measurement goal explicitly defined, a set of questions is developed. Answers to these questions help the software team (or other stakeholders) to determine whether the measurement goal has been achieved. Among the questions that might be asked are:

Q_1: Are architectural components characterized in a manner that compartmentalizes function and related data?

Q_2: Is the complexity of each component within bounds that will facilitate modification and extension?

Each of these questions should be answered quantitatively, using one or more measures and metrics. For example, a metric that provides an indication of the cohesion (Chapter 9) of an architectural component might be useful in answering Q_1. Cyclomatic complexity and metrics discussed in Section 15.4.1 or 15.4.2 might provide insight for Q_2.

In actuality, there may be a number of measurement goals with related questions and metrics. In every case, the metrics that are chosen (or derived) should conform to the measurement principles discussed in Section 15.2.3 and the measurement attributes discussed in Section 15.2.5. For further information of GQM, the interested reader should see [SHE98] or [SOL99].

15.2.5 The Attributes of Effective Software Metrics

Hundreds of metrics have been proposed for computer software, but not all provide practical support to the software engineer. Some demand measurement that is too complex, others are so esoteric that few real world professionals have any hope of understanding them, and others violate the basic intuitive notions of what high-quality software really is.

---

4 van Solingen and Berghout [SOL99] suggest that the objective is almost always "understanding, controlling, or improving" the process activity or product attribute.

Ejiogu [EJI91] defines a set of attributes that should be encompassed by effective software metrics. The derived metric and the measures that lead to it should be:

? How should we assess the quality of a proposed software metric?

ADVICE

Experience indicates that a product metric will be used only if it is intuitive and easy to compute. If dozens of "counts" have to be made, and complex computations are required, it is unlikely that the metric will be widely adopted.

- *Simple and computable.* It should be relatively easy to learn how to derive the metric, and its computation should not demand inordinate effort or time.
- *Empirically and intuitively persuasive.* The metric should satisfy the engineer's intuitive notions about the product attribute under consideration.
- *Consistent and objective.* The metric should always yield results that are unambiguous.
- *Consistent in the use of units and dimensions.* The mathematical computation of the metric should use measures that do not lead to bizarre combinations of units.
- *Programming language independent.* Metrics should be based on the analysis model, the design model, or the structure of the program itself.
- *An effective mechanism for high-quality feedback.* That is, the metric should lead to a higher-quality end product.

Although most software metrics satisfy these attributes, some commonly used metrics may fail to satisfy one or two of them. An example is the function point (discussed in Section 15.3.1)—a measure of the "functionality" delivery by the software. It can be argued[5] that the *consistent and objective* attribute fails because an independent third party may not be able to derive the same function point value as a colleague using the same information about the software. Should we therefore reject the FP measure? The answer is: Of course not! FP provides useful insight and therefore provides distinct value, even if it fails to satisfy one attribute perfectly.

15.2.6 The Product Metrics Landscape

Although a wide variety of metrics taxonomies have been proposed, the following outline addresses the most important metrics areas:

Metrics for the analysis model. These metrics address various aspects of the analysis model and include:

Functionality delivered—provides an indirect measure of the functionality that is packaged within the software.

System size—measures of the overall size of the system defined in terms of information available as part of the analysis model.

Specification quality—provides an indication of the specificity and completeness of a requirements specification.

---

5 An equally vigorous counter-argument can be made. Such is the nature of software metrics.

Metrics for the design model. These metrics quantify design attributes in a manner that allows a software engineer to assess design quality. Metrics include:

Architectural metrics—provide an indication of the quality of the architectural design.

Component-level metrics—measure the complexity of software components and other characteristics that have a bearing on quality.

Interface design metrics—focus primarily on usability.

Specialized OO design metrics—measure characteristics of classes and their communication and collaboration characteristics.

Metrics for source code. These metrics measure the source code and can be used to assess its complexity, maintainability, and testability, among other characteristics:

Halstead metrics—controversial but nonetheless fascinating, these metrics provide unique measures of a computer program.

Complexity metrics—measure the logical complexity of source code (can also be considered to be component-level design metrics).

Length metrics—provide an indication of the size of the software.

Metrics for testing. These metrics assist in the design of effective test cases and evaluate the efficacy of testing:

Statement and branch coverage metrics—lead to the design of test cases that provide program coverage.

Defect-related metrics—focus on bugs found, rather than on the tests themselves.

Testing effectiveness—provide a real-time indication of the effectiveness of tests that have been conducted.

In-process metrics—process related metrics that can be determined as testing is conducted.

In many cases, metrics for one model may be used in later software engineering activities. For example, design metrics may be used to estimate the effort required to generate source code. In addition, design metrics may be used in test planning and test case design.

SAFEHOME

Debating Product Metrics

The scene: Vinod's cubicle.

The players: Vinod, Jamie and Ed—members of the *SafeHome* software engineering team, who are continuing work on component-level design and test case design.

The conversation:

Vinod: Doug [Doug Miller, software engineering manager] told me that we should all use product metrics, but he was kind of vague. He also said that he wouldn't push the matter . . . using them was up to us.

Jamie: That's good, 'cause there's no way I have time to start measuring stuff. We're fighting to maintain the schedule as it is.

Ed: I agree with Jamie. We're up against it, here . . . no time.

Vinod: Yeah, I know, but there's probably some merit to using them.

Jamie: I'm not arguing that, Vinod. It's a time thing . . . and I for one don't have any to spare.

Vinod: But what if measuring saves you time?

Ed: Wrong, it takes time and like Jamie said . . .

Vinod: No, wait . . . what if it saves us time?

Jamie: How?

Vinod: Rework . . . that's how. If a metric we use helps us avoid one major or even moderate problem, and that saves us from having to rework a part of the system, we save time. No?

Ed: It's possible, I suppose, but can you guarantee that some product metric will help us find a problem?

Vinod: Can you guarantee that it won't?

Jamie: So what are you proposing?

Vinod: I think we should select a few design metrics, probably class-oriented, and use them as part of our review process for every component we develop.

Ed: I'm not real familiar with class-oriented metrics.

Vinod: I'll spend some time checking them out and make a recommendation . . . okay with you guys?

(Ed and Jamie nod without much enthusiasm.)

15.3 Metrics for the Analysis Model

Although relatively few analysis and specification metrics have appeared in the literature, it is possible to adapt metrics that are often used for project estimation and apply them in this context. These metrics examine the analysis model with the intent of predicting the "size" of the resultant system. Size is sometimes (but not always) an indicator of design complexity and is almost always an indicator of increased coding, integration, and testing effort.

15.3.1 Function-Based Metrics

WebRef
Much useful information about function points can be obtained at **www.ifpug.org** and **www.functionpoints.com.**

The *function point metric* (FP), first proposed by Albrecht [ALB79], can be used effectively as a means for measuring the functionality delivered by a system.[6] Using historical data, the FP can then be used to (1) estimate the cost or effort required to design, code, and test the software; (2) predict the number of errors that will be encountered during testing, and (3) forecast the number of components and/or the number of projected source lines in the implemented system.

Function points are derived using an empirical relationship based on countable (direct) measures of software's information domain and assessments of software complexity. Information domain values are defined in the following manner:[7]

6 Since Albrecht's original work, hundreds of books, papers, and articles have been written on FP. A worthwhile bibliography can be found at [IFP03].

7 In actuality, the definition of information domain values and the manner in which they are counted are a bit more complex. The interested reader should see [IFP01] for more details.

Number of external inputs (EIs). Each *external input* originates from a user or is transmitted from another application and provides distinct application-oriented data or control information. Inputs are often used to update *internal logical files* (ILFs). Inputs should be distinguished from inquiries, which are counted separately.

Number of external outputs (EOs). Each *external output* is derived within the application and provides information to the user. In this context external output refers to reports, screens, error messages, and so on. Individual data items within a report are not counted separately.

Number of external inquiries (EQs). An *external inquiry* is defined as an on-line input that results in the generation of some immediate software response in the form of an on-line output (often retrieved from an ILF).

Number of internal logical files (ILFs). Each *internal logical file* is a logical grouping of data that resides within the application's boundary and is maintained via external inputs.

Number of external interface files (EIFs). Each *external interface file* is a logical grouping of data that resides external to the application but provides data that may be of use to the application.

Once these data have been collected, the table in Figure 15.2 is completed and a complexity value is associated with each count. Organizations that use function point methods develop criteria for determining whether a particular entry is simple, average, or complex. Nonetheless, the determination of complexity is somewhat subjective.

To compute function points (FP), the following relationship is used:

$$FP = \text{count total} \times [0.65 + 0.01 \times \Sigma (F_i)] \qquad (15\text{-}1)$$

where count total is the sum of all FP entries obtained from Figure 15.2.

The F_i (i = 1 to 14) are *value adjustment factors* (VAF) based on responses to the following questions [LON02]:

1. Does the system require reliable backup and recovery?

FIGURE 15.2

Computing function points

Information Domain Value	Count		Weighting factor Simple	Average	Complex		
External Inputs (EIs)		×	3	4	6	=	
External Outputs (EOs)		×	4	5	7	=	
External Inquiries (EQs)		×	3	4	6	=	
Internal Logical Files (ILFs)		×	7	10	15	=	
External Interface Files (EIFs)		×	5	7	10	=	
Count total						→	

Value adjustment factors are used to provide an indication of problem complexity.

2. Are specialized data communications required to transfer information to or from the application?
3. Are there distributed processing functions?
4. Is performance critical?
5. Will the system run in an existing, heavily utilized operational environment?
6. Does the system require on-line data entry?
7. Does the on-line data entry require the input transaction to be built over multiple screens or operations?
8. Are the ILFs updated on-line?
9. Are the inputs, outputs, files, or inquiries complex?
10. Is the internal processing complex?
11. Is the code designed to be reusable?
12. Are conversion and installation included in the design?
13. Is the system designed for multiple installations in different organizations?
14. Is the application designed to facilitate change and for ease of use by the user?

Each of these questions is answered using a scale that ranges from 0 (not important or applicable) to 5 (absolutely essential). The constant values in Equation (15-1) and the weighting factors that are applied to information domain counts are determined empirically.

WebRef
An on-line FP calculator can be found at **irb.cs.unimagdeburg.de/sw-eng/us/java/fp/.**

To illustrate the use of the FP metric in this context, we consider a simple analysis model representation, illustrated in Figure 15.3. Referring to the figure, a data flow diagram (Chapter 8) for a function within the *SafeHome* software is represented. The function manages user interaction, accepting a user password to activate or deactivate the system, and allows inquiries on the status of security zones and various security sensors. The function displays a series of prompting messages and sends appropriate control signals to various components of the security system.

FIGURE 15.3

A data flow model for *SafeHome* software

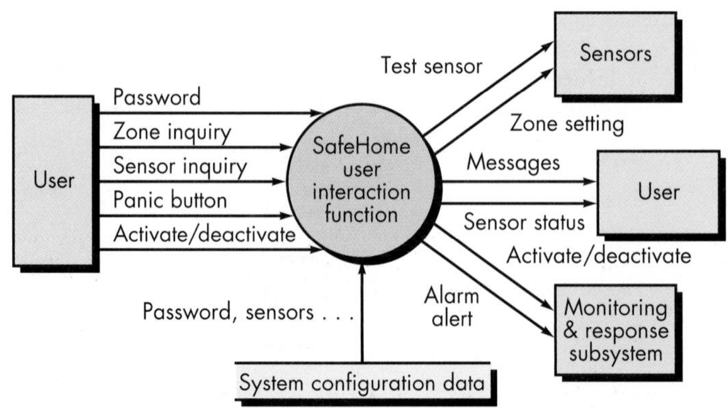

The data flow diagram is evaluated to determine a set of key information domain measures required for computation of the function point metric. Three external inputs—**password, panic button,** and **activate/deactivate**—are shown in the figure along with two external inquires—**zone inquiry** and **sensor inquiry.** One ILF **(system configuration file)** is shown. Two external outputs **(messages** and **sensor status)** and four EIFs **(test sensor, zone setting, activate/deactivate,** and **alarm alert)** are also present. These data, along with the appropriate complexity, are shown in Figure 15.4.

The count total shown in Figure 15.4 must be adjusted using Equation (15-1):

$$\text{FP} = \text{count total} \times [0.65 + 0.01 \times \Sigma\ (F_i)]$$

where count total is the sum of all FP entries obtained from Figure 15.4 and F_i ($i = 1$ to 14) are value adjustment factors. For the purposes of this example, we assume that $\Sigma\ (F_i)$ is 46 (a moderately complex product). Therefore,

$$\text{FP} = 50 \times [0.65 + (0.01 \times 46)] = 56$$

Based on the projected FP value derived from the analysis model, the project team can estimate the overall implemented size of the *SafeHome* user interaction function. Assume that past data indicates that one FP translates into 60 lines of code (an object-oriented language is to be used) and that 12 FPs are produced for each person-month of effort. These historical data provide the project manager with important planning information that is based on the analysis model rather than preliminary estimates. Assume further that past projects have found an average of three errors per function point during analysis and design reviews and four errors per function point during unit and integration testing. These data can help software engineers assess the completeness of their review and testing activities.

Uemura and his colleagues [UEM99] suggest that function points can also be computed from UML class and sequence diagrams (Chapters 8 and 10). The interested reader should see [UEM99] for details.

FIGURE 15.4

Computing function points

Information Domain Value	Count		Weighting factor Simple	Average	Complex		
External Inputs (EIs)	3	×	(3)	4	6	=	9
External Outputs (EOs)	2	×	(4)	5	7	=	8
External Inquiries (EQs)	2	×	(3)	4	6	=	6
Internal Logical Files (ILFs)	1	×	(7)	10	15	=	7
External Interface Files (EIFs)	4	×	(5)	7	10	=	20
Count total						→	50

> "Rather than just musing on what 'new metric' might apply . . . we should also be asking ourselves the more basic question, 'What will we do with metrics?' "
>
> **Michael Mah and Larry Putnam**

15.3.2 Metrics for Specification Quality

Davis and his colleagues [DAV93] propose a list of characteristics that can be used to assess the quality of the analysis model and the corresponding requirements specification: *specificity* (lack of ambiguity), *completeness, correctness, understandability, verifiability, internal and external consistency, achievability, concision, traceability, modifiability, precision,* and *reusability.* In addition, the authors [DAV93] note that high-quality specifications are electronically stored, executable or at least interpretable, annotated by relative importance, stable, versioned, organized, cross-referenced, and specified at the right level of detail.

By measuring characteristics of the specification, it is possible to gain quantitative insight into specificity and completeness.

Although many of these characteristics appear to be qualitative in nature, Davis et al. [DAV93] suggest that each can be represented using one or more metrics. For example, we assume that there are n_r requirements in a specification, such that

$$n_r = n_f + n_{nf}$$

where n_f is the number of functional requirements and n_{nf} is the number of nonfunctional (e.g., performance) requirements.

To determine the *specificity* (lack of ambiguity) of requirements, Davis et al. suggest a metric that is based on the consistency of the reviewers' interpretation of each requirement:

$$Q_1 = n_{ui}/n_r$$

where n_{ui} is the number of requirements for which all reviewers had identical interpretations. The closer the value of Q to 1, the lower is the ambiguity of the specification.

The *completeness* of functional requirements can be determined by computing the ratio

$$Q_2 = n_u/[n_i \times n_s]$$

where n_u is the number of unique function requirements, n_i is the number of inputs (stimuli) defined or implied by the specification, and n_s is the number of states specified. The Q_2 ratio measures the percentage of necessary functions that have been specified for a system. However, it does not address nonfunctional requirements. To incorporate these into an overall metric for completeness, we must consider the degree to which requirements have been validated:

$$Q_3 = n_c/[n_c + n_{nv}]$$

where n_c is the number of requirements that have been validated as correct and n_{nv} is the number of requirements that have not yet been validated.

> "Measure what is measurable, and what is not measurable, make measurable."
>
> **Galileo**

15.4 Metrics for the Design Model

It is inconceivable that the design of a new aircraft, a new computer chip, or a new office building would be conducted without defining design measures, determining metrics for various aspects of design quality, and using them to guide the manner in which the design evolves. And yet, the design of complex software-based systems often proceeds with virtually no measurement. The irony of this is that design metrics for software are available, but the vast majority of software engineers continue to be unaware of their existence.

Design metrics for computer software, like all other software metrics, are not perfect. Debate continues over their efficacy and the manner in which they should be applied. Many experts argue that further experimentation is required before design measures can be used. And yet, design without measurement is an unacceptable alternative.

15.4.1 Architectural Design Metrics

Architectural design metrics focus on characteristics of the program architecture (Chapter 10) with an emphasis on the architectural structure and the effectiveness of modules or components within the architecture. These metrics are "black box" in the sense that they do not require any knowledge of the inner workings of a particular software component.

Card and Glass [CAR90] define three software design complexity measures: structural complexity, data complexity, and system complexity.

For hierarchical architectures (e.g., call and return architectures), *structural complexity* of a module *i* is defined in the following manner:

$$S(i) = f^2_{\text{out}}(i) \qquad (15\text{-}2)$$

where $f_{\text{out}}(i)$ is the fan-out[8] of module *i*.

KEY POINT
Metrics can provide insight into structural data and system complexity associated with architectural design.

Data complexity provides an indication of the complexity in the internal interface for a module *i* and is defined as

$$D(i) = v(i)/[f_{\text{out}}(i) + 1] \qquad (15\text{-}3)$$

where $v(i)$ is the number of input and output variables that are passed to and from module *i*.

8 *Fan-out* is defined as the number of modules immediately subordinate to the module *i*, that is, the number of modules that are directly invoked by module *i*. *Fan-in* is defined as the number of modules that directly invoke module *i*.

Finally, *system complexity* is defined as the sum of structural and data complexity, specified as

$$C(i) = S(i) + D(i) \quad (15\text{-}4)$$

As each of these complexity values increases, the overall architectural complexity of the system also increases. This leads to a greater likelihood that integration and testing effort will also increase.

Fenton [FEN91] suggests a number of simple morphology (i.e., shape) metrics that enable different program architectures to be compared using a set of straightforward dimensions. Referring to the call-and-return architecture in Figure 15.5, the following metrics can be defined:

$$\text{size} = n + a$$

where n is the number of nodes and a is the number of arcs. For the architecture shown in Figure 15.5,

size = 17 + 18 = 35
depth = 4, the longest path from the root (top) node to a leaf node.
width = 6, maximum number of nodes at any one level of the architecture.
arc-to-node ratio, $r = a/n$,

which measures the connectivity density of the architecture and may provide a simple indication of the coupling of the architecture. For the architecture shown in Figure 15.5, $r = 18/17 = 1.06$.

The U.S. Air Force Systems Command [USA87] has developed a number of software quality indicators that are based on measurable design characteristics of a computer program. Using concepts similar to those proposed in IEEE Std. 982.1-1988 [IEE94], the Air Force uses information obtained from data and architectural design

FIGURE 15.5

Morphology metrics

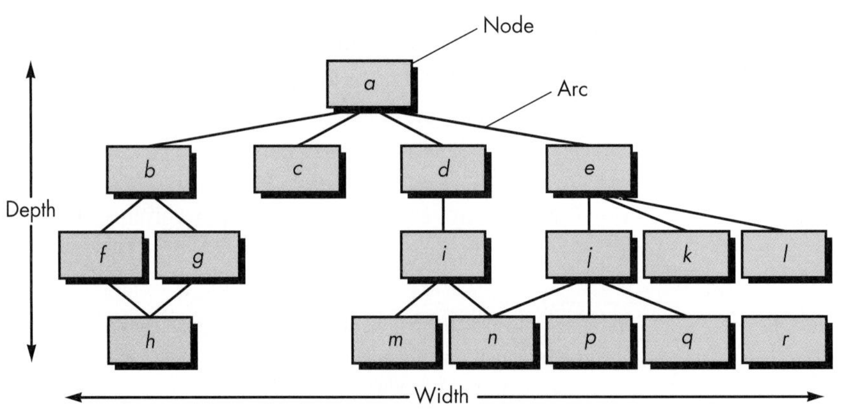

to derive a design structure quality index (DSQI) that ranges from 0 to 1. The following values must be ascertained to compute the DSQI [CHA89]:

S_1 = the total number of modules defined in the program architecture

S_2 = the number of modules whose correct function depends on the source of data input or that produce data to be used elsewhere (in general, control modules, among others, would not be counted as part of S_2)

S_3 = the number of modules whose correct function depends on prior processing

S_4 = the number of database items (includes data objects and all attributes that define objects)

S_5 = the total number of unique database items

S_6 = the number of database segments (different records or individual objects)

S_7 = the number of modules with a single entry and exit (exception processing is not considered to be a multiple exit)

Once values S_1 through S_7 are determined for a computer program, the following intermediate values can be computed:

Program structure: D_1, where D_1 is defined as follows: If the architectural design was developed using a distinct method (e.g., data flow-oriented design or object-oriented design), then $D_1 = 1$, otherwise $D_1 = 0$.

Module independence: $D_2 = 1 - (S_2/S_1)$

Modules not dependent on prior processing: $D_3 = 1 - (S_3/S_1)$

Database size: $D_4 = 1 - (S_5/S_4)$

Database compartmentalization: $D_5 = 1 - (S_6/S_4)$

Module entrance/exit characteristic: $D_6 = 1 - (S_7/S_1)$

With these intermediate values determined, the DSQI is computed in the following manner:

$$\text{DSQI} = \Sigma\, w_i D_i \qquad (15\text{-}5)$$

where $i = 1$ to 6, w_i is the relative weighting of the importance of each of the intermediate values, and $\Sigma\, w_i = 1$ (if all D_i are weighted equally, then $w_i = 0.167$).

The value of DSQI for past designs can be determined and compared to a design that is currently under development. If the DSQI is significantly lower than average, further design work and review are indicated. Similarly, if major changes are to be made to an existing design, the effect of those changes on DSQI can be calculated.

> "Measurement can be seen as a detour. This detour is necessary because humans mostly are not able to make clear and objective decisions [without quantitative support]."
>
> **Horst Zuse**

15.4.2 Metrics for Object-Oriented Design

There is much about object-oriented design that is subjective—an experienced designer "knows" how to characterize an OO system so that it will effectively implement customer requirements. But, as an OO design model grows in size and complexity, a more objective view of the characteristics of the design can benefit both the experienced designer (who gains additional insight) and the novice (who obtains an indication of quality that would otherwise be unavailable).

In a detailed treatment of software metrics for OO systems, Whitmire [WHI97] describes nine distinct and measurable characteristics of an OO design:

? What characteristics can be measured when we assess an OO design?

Size. Size is defined in terms of four views: population, volume, length, and functionality. *Population* is measured by taking a static count of OO entities such as classes or operations. *Volume* measures are identical to population measures but are collected dynamically—at a given instant of time. *Length* is a measure of a chain of interconnected design elements (e.g., the depth of an inheritance tree is a measure of length). *Functionality* metrics provide an indirect indication of the value delivered to the customer by an OO application.

Complexity. Like size, there are many differing views of software complexity [ZUS97]. Whitmire views complexity in terms of structural characteristics by examining how classes of an OO design are interrelated to one another.

Coupling. The physical connections between elements of the OO design (e.g., the number of collaborations between classes or the number of messages passed between objects) represent coupling within an OO system.

Sufficiency. Whitmire defines sufficiency as "the degree to which an abstraction possesses the features required of it, or the degree to which a design component possesses features in its abstraction, from the point of view of the current application." Stated another way, we ask: What properties does this abstraction (class) need to possess to be useful to me? [WHI97]. In essence, a design component (e.g., a class) is sufficient if it fully reflects all properties of the application domain object that it is modeling—that is, that the abstraction (class) possesses the features required of it.

> "Many of the decisions for which I had to rely on folklore and myth can now be made using quantitative data."
>
> **Scott Whitmire**

Completeness. The only difference between completeness and sufficiency is "the feature set against which we compare the abstraction or design component" [WHI97]. Sufficiency compares the abstraction from the point of view of the current application. Completeness considers multiple points of view, asking the question: What properties are required to fully represent the problem domain object? Because the criterion for completeness considers different points of view, it indirectly implies the degree to which the abstraction or design component can be reused.

Cohesion. Like its counterpart in conventional software, an OO component should be designed in a manner that has all operations working together to achieve a single, well-defined purpose. The cohesiveness of a class is determined by examining the degree to which "the set of properties it possesses is part of the problem or design domain" [WHI97].

Primitiveness. A characteristic that is similar to simplicity, primitiveness (applied to both operations and classes) is the degree to which an operation is atomic—that is, the operation cannot be constructed out of a sequence of other operations contained within a class. A class that exhibits a high degree of primitiveness encapsulates only primitive operations.

Similarity. The degree to which two or more classes are similar in terms of their structure, function, behavior, or purpose is indicated by this measure.

Volatility. As we have seen earlier in this book, design changes can occur when requirements are modified or when modifications occur in other parts of an application, resulting in mandatory adaptation of the design component in question. Volatility of an OO design component measures the likelihood that a change will occur.

In reality, product metrics for OO systems can be applied not only to the design model, but also the analysis model. In the sections that follow, we explore metrics that provide an indication of quality at the OO class level and the operation level.

15.4.3 Class-Oriented Metrics—The CK Metrics Suite

The class is the fundamental unit of an OO system. Therefore, measures and metrics for an individual class, the class hierarchy, and class collaborations will be invaluable to a software engineer who must assess design quality. In earlier chapters, we saw that the class encapsulates operations (processing) and attributes (data). The class is often the "parent" for subclasses (sometimes called *children*) that inherit its attributes and operations. The class often collaborates with other classes. Each of these characteristics can be used as the basis for measurement.[9]

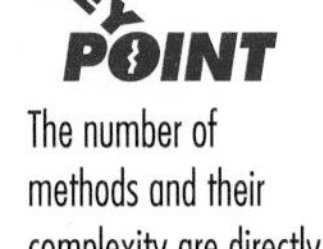

The number of methods and their complexity are directly correlated to the effort required to test a class.

One of the most widely referenced sets of OO software metrics has been proposed by Chidamber and Kemerer [CHI94]. Often referred to as the *CK metrics suite,* the authors have proposed six class-based design metrics for OO systems.[10]

Weighted methods per class (WMC). Assume that n methods of complexity c_1, $c_2, \ldots, c_n$ are defined for a class **C.** The specific complexity metric that is chosen (e.g.,

9 It should be noted that the validity of some of the metrics discussed in this chapter is currently debated in the technical literature. Those who champion measurement theory demand a degree of formalism that some OO metrics do not provide. However, it is reasonable to state that the metrics noted provide useful insight for the software engineer.

10 Chidamber and Kemerer use the term *methods* rather than *operations.* Their usage of the term is reflected in this section.

cyclomatic complexity) should be normalized so that nominal complexity for a method takes on a value of 1.0.

$$WMC = \Sigma c_i$$

for $i = 1$ to n. The number of methods and their complexity are reasonable indicators of the amount of effort required to implement and test a class. In addition, the larger the number of methods, the more complex is the inheritance tree (all subclasses inherit the methods of their parents). Finally, as the number of methods grows for a given class, it is likely to become more and more application specific, thereby limiting potential reuse. For all of these reasons, WMC should be kept as low as is reasonable.

Although it would seem relatively straightforward to develop a count for the number of methods in a class, the problem is actually more complex than it seems. A consistent counting approach for methods should be developed. [CHU95]

Inheritance is an extremely powerful feature that can get you into trouble, if you use it without care. Use DIT and other metrics to give yourself a reading on the complexity of class hierarchies.

Depth of the inheritance tree (DIT). This metric is "the maximum length from the node to the root of the tree" [CHI94]. Referring to Figure 15.6, the value of DIT for the class-hierarchy shown is 4. As DIT grows, it is likely that lower-level classes will inherit many methods. This leads to potential difficulties when attempting to predict the behavior of a class. A deep class hierarchy (DIT is large) also leads to greater design complexity. On the positive side, large DIT values imply that many methods may be reused.

Number of children (NOC). The subclasses that are immediately subordinate to a class in the class hierarchy are termed its *children.* Referring to Figure 15.6, class $\mathbf{C_2}$ has three children—subclasses $\mathbf{C_{21}}$, $\mathbf{C_{22}}$, and $\mathbf{C_{23}}$. As the number of children grows, reuse increases but also, as NOC increases, the abstraction represented by

FIGURE 15.6
A class hierarchy

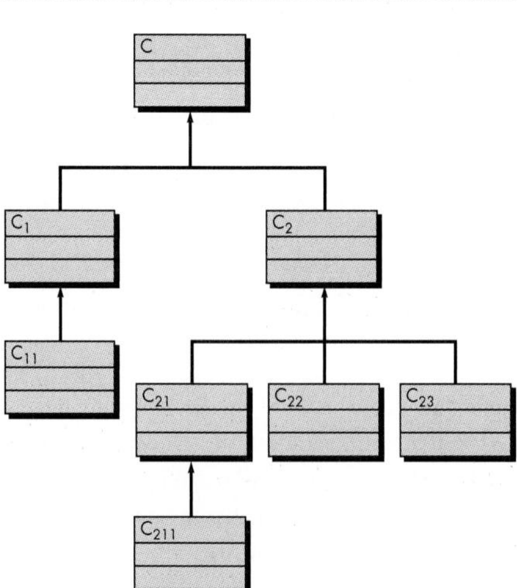

the parent class can be diluted if some of the children are not appropriate members of the parent class. As NOC increases, the amount of testing (required to exercise each child in its operational context) will also increase.

Coupling between object classes (CBO). The CRC model (Chapter 8) may be used to determine the value for CBO. In essence, CBO is the number of collaborations listed for a class on its CRC index card.[11] As CBO increases, it is likely that the reusability of a class will decrease. High values of CBO also complicate modifications and the testing that ensues when modifications are made. In general, the CBO values for each class should be kept as low as is reasonable. This is consistent with the general guideline to reduce coupling in conventional software.

The concepts of coupling and cohesion apply to both conventional and OO software. Keep class coupling low and class and operation cohesion high.

Response for a class (RFC). The response set of a class is "a set of methods that can potentially be executed in response to a message received by an object of that class" [CHI94]. RFC is the number of methods in the response set. As RFC increases, the effort required for testing also increases because the test sequence (Chapter 14) grows. It also follows that, as RFC increases, the overall design complexity of the class increases.

Lack of cohesion in methods (LCOM). Each method within a class, **C**, accesses one or more attributes (also called *instance variables*). LCOM is the number of methods that access one or more of the same attributes.[12] If no methods access the same attributes, then LCOM = 0. To illustrate the case where LCOM ≠ 0, consider a class with six methods. Four of the methods have one or more attributes in common (i.e., they access common attributes). Therefore, LCOM = 4. If LCOM is high, methods may be coupled to one another via attributes. This increases the complexity of the class design. Although there are cases in which a high value for LCOM is justifiable, it is desirable to keep cohesion high; that is, keep LCOM low.[13]

SAFEHOME

Applying CK Metrics

The scene: Vinod's cubicle.

The players: Vinod, Jamie, Shakira, and Ed—members of the *SafeHome* software engineering team, who are continuing work on component-level design and test case design.

The conversation:

Vinod: Did you guys get a chance to read the description of the CK metrics suite I sent you on Wednesday and make those measurements?

---

11 If CRC index cards are developed manually, completeness and consistency must be assessed before CBO can be determined reliably.

12 The formal definition is a bit more complex. See [CHI94] for details.

13 The LCOM metric provides useful insight in some situations, but it can be misleading in others. For example, keeping coupling encapsulated within a class increases the cohesion of the system as a whole. Therefore, in at least one important sense, higher LCOM actually suggests that a class may have higher cohesion, not lower.

Shakira: Wasn't too complicated. I went back to my UML class and sequence diagrams, like you suggested, and got rough counts for DIT, RFC, and LCOM. I couldn't find the CRC model, so I didn't count CBO.

Jamie (smiling): You couldn't find the CRC model because I had it.

Shakira: That's what I love about this team, superb communication.

Vinod: I did my counts . . . did you guys develop numbers for the CK metrics?

(Jamie and Ed nod in the affirmative.)

Jamie: Since I had the CRC cards, I took a look at CBO, and it looked pretty uniform across most of the classes. There was one exception, which I noted.

Ed: There are a few classes where RFC is pretty high, compared with the averages . . . maybe we should take a look at simplifying them.

Jamie: Maybe yes, maybe no. I'm still concerned about time, and I don't want to fix stuff that isn't really broken.

Vinod: I agree with that. Maybe we should look for classes that have bad numbers in at least two or more of the CK metrics. Kind of two strikes and you're modified.

Shakira (looking over Ed's list of classes with high RFC): Look, see this class? It's got a high LCOM as well as a high RFC. Two strikes?

Vinod: Yeah I think so . . . it'll be difficult to implement because of complexity and difficult to test for the same reason. Probably worth designing two separate classes to achieve the same behavior.

Jamie: You think modifying it'll save us time?

Vinod: Over the long haul, yes.

15.4.4 Class-Oriented Metrics—The MOOD Metrics Suite

Harrison, Counsell, and Nithi [HAR98] propose a set of metrics for object-oriented design that provide quantitative indicators for OO design characteristics. A small sampling of MOOD metrics follows:

Method inheritance factor (MIF). The degree to which the class architecture of an OO system makes use of inheritance for both methods (operations) and attributes is defined as

$$\text{MIF} = \Sigma\, M_i(C_i)/\Sigma\, M_a(C_i)$$

where the summation occurs over $i = 1$ to T_c. T_c is defined as the total number of classes in the architecture; C_i is a class within the architecture; and

$$M_a(C_i) = M_d(C_i) + M_i(C_i)$$

where

$M_a(C_i)$ = the number of methods that can be invoked in association with C_i.
$M_d(C_i)$ = the number of methods declared in the class C_i.
$M_i(C_i)$ = the number of methods inherited (and not overridden) in C_i.

The value of MIF (the attribute inheritance factor, AIF, is defined in an analogous manner) provides an indication of the impact of inheritance on the OO software.

> "Analyzing OO software in order to evaluate its quality is becoming increasingly important as the [OO] paradigm continues to increase in popularity."
>
> **Rachel Harrison et al.**

Coupling factor (CF). Earlier in this chapter we noted that coupling is an indication of the connections between elements of the OO design. The MOOD metrics suite defines coupling in the following way:

$$CF = \Sigma_i \Sigma_j \, is\_client\,(C_i, C_j)/(T_c^2 - T_c)$$

where the summations occur over $i = 1$ to T_C and $j = 1$ to T_C. The function

is_client = 1, if and only if a relationship exists between the client class, C_c, and the server class, C_s, and $C_c \neq C_s$
= 0, otherwise

Although many factors affect software complexity, understandability, and maintainability, it is reasonable to conclude that, as the value for CF increases, the complexity of the OO software will also increase, and understandability, maintainability, and the potential for reuse may suffer as a result.

Harrison and her colleagues [HAR98] present a detailed analysis of MIF and CF, along with other metrics and examine their validity for use in the assessment of design quality.

15.4.5 OO Metrics Proposed by Lorenz and Kidd

In their book on OO metrics, Lorenz and Kidd [LOR94] divide class-based metrics into four broad categories that each have a bearing on component-level design: size, inheritance, internals, and externals. Size-oriented metrics for an OO design class focus on counts of attributes and operations for an individual class and average values for the OO system as a whole. Inheritance-based metrics focus on the manner in which operations are reused through the class hierarchy. Metrics for class internals look at cohesion and code-oriented issues, and external metrics examine coupling and reuse. A sampling of metrics proposed by Lorenz and Kidd follows:

During review of the analysis model, CRC index cards will provide a reasonable indication of expected values for CS. If you encounter a class with a large number of responsibilities, consider partitioning it.

Class size (CS). The overall size of a class can be determined with the following measures:

- The total number of operations (both inherited and private instance operations) that are encapsulated within the class.
- The number of attributes (both inherited and private instance attributes) that are encapsulated by the class.

The WMC metric proposed by Chidamber and Kemerer (Section 15.4.3) is also a weighted measure of class size. As we noted earlier, large values for CS indicate that a class may have too much responsibility. This will reduce the reusability of the class and complicate implementation and testing. In general, inherited or public operations and attributes should be weighted more heavily in determining class size [LOR94]. Private operations and attributes enable specialization and are more localized in the design. Averages for the number of class attributes and operations may also be computed. The lower the average values for CS, the more likely that classes within the system can be reused widely.

Number of operations added by a subclass (NOA). Subclasses are specialized by adding operations and attributes. As the value for NOA increases, the subclass drifts away from the abstraction implied by the superclass. In general, as the depth of the class hierarchy increases (DIT becomes large), the value for NOA at lower levels in the hierarchy should go down.

15.4.6 Component-Level Design Metrics

Component-level design metrics for conventional software components focus on internal characteristics of a software component and include measures of the "three Cs"—module cohesion, coupling, and complexity. These measures can help a software engineer to judge the quality of a component-level design.

The metrics presented in this section are "glass box" in the sense that they require knowledge of the inner working of the module under consideration. Component-level design metrics may be applied once a procedural design has been developed. Alternatively, they may be delayed until source code is available.

Cohesion metrics. Bieman and Ott [BIE94] define a collection of metrics that provide an indication of the cohesiveness (Chapter 9) of a module. The metrics are defined in terms of five concepts and measures:

It is possible to compute measures of the functional independence—coupling and cohesion—of a component and to use these to assess the quality of a design.

Data slice. Stated simply, a data slice is a backward walk through a module that looks for data values that affect the state of the module when the walk began. It should be noted that both program slices (which focus on statements and conditions) and data slices can be defined.

Data tokens. The variables defined for a module can be defined as data tokens for the module.

Glue tokens. This set of data tokens lies on one or more data slice.

Superglue tokens. These data tokens are common to every data slice in a module.

Stickiness. The relative stickiness of a glue token is directly proportional to the number of data slices that it binds.

Bieman and Ott develop metrics for *strong functional cohesion* (SFC), *weak functional cohesion* (WFC), and *adhesiveness* (the relative degree to which glue tokens bind data slices together). These metrics can be interpreted in the following manner [BIE94]:

All of these cohesion metrics range in value between 0 and 1. They have a value of 0 when a procedure has more than one output and exhibits none of the cohesion attribute indicated by a particular metric. A procedure with no superglue tokens, no tokens that are common to all data slices, has zero strong functional cohesion—there are no data tokens that contribute to all outputs. A procedure with no glue tokens, that is no tokens common to more than one data slice (in procedures with more than one data slice), exhibits zero weak functional cohesion and zero adhesiveness—there are no data tokens that contribute to more than one output.

Strong functional cohesion and adhesiveness are encountered when the Bieman and Ott metrics take on a maximum value of 1.

Coupling metrics. Module coupling provides an indication of the "connectedness" of a module to other modules, global data, and the outside environment. In Chapter 9, coupling was discussed in qualitative terms.

Dhama [DHA95] has proposed a metric for module coupling that encompasses data and control flow coupling, global coupling, and environmental coupling. The measures required to compute module coupling are defined in terms of each of the three coupling types noted previously. For data and control flow coupling,

d_i = number of input data parameters
c_i = number of input control parameters
d_o = number of output data parameters
c_o = number of output control parameters

For global coupling,

g_d = number of global variables used as data
g_c = number of global variables used as control

For environmental coupling,

w = number of modules called (fan-out)
r = number of modules calling the module under consideration (fan-in)

Using these measures, a module coupling indicator, m_c, is defined in the following way:

$$m_c = k/M$$

where k is a proportionality constant and

$$\text{M} = d_i + (a \times c_i) + d_o + (b \times c_o) + g_d + (c \times g_c) + w + r \tag{15-6}$$

Values for k, a, b, and c must be derived empirically.

As the value of m_c increases, the overall module coupling decreases. In order to have the coupling metric move upward as the degree of coupling increases, a revised coupling metric may be defined as

$$\text{C} = 1 - m_c$$

where the degree of coupling increases as the measures in Equation (15-6) increase.

Complexity metrics. A variety of software metrics can be computed to determine the complexity of program control flow. Many of these are based on the flow graph. As we discussed in Chapter 14, a graph is a representation composed of nodes and links (also called edges). When the links (edges) are directed, the flow graph is a directed graph.

McCabe and Watson [MCC94] identify a number of important uses for complexity metrics:

> Complexity metrics can be used to predict critical information about reliability and maintainability of software systems from automatic analysis of source code [or procedural design information]. Complexity metrics also provide feedback during the software project to help control the [design activity]. During testing and maintenance, they provide detailed information about software modules to help pinpoint areas of potential instability.

Cyclomatic complexity is only one of a large number of complexity metrics.

The most widely used (and debated) complexity metric for computer software is cyclomatic complexity, originally developed by Thomas McCabe [MCC76], [MCC89] and discussed in detail in Chapter 14.

Zuse ([ZUS90], [ZUS97]) presents an encyclopedic discussion of no fewer than 18 different categories of software complexity metrics. The author presents the basic definitions for metrics in each category (e.g., there are a number of variations on the cyclomatic complexity metric) and then analyzes and critiques each. Zuse's work is the most comprehensive published to date.

15.4.7 Operation-Oriented Metrics

Because the class is the dominant unit in OO systems, fewer metrics have been proposed for operations that reside within a class. Churcher and Shepperd [CHU95] discuss this when they state: "Results of recent studies indicate that methods tend to be small, both in terms of number of statements and in logical complexity [WIL93], suggesting that the connectivity structure of a system may be more important than the content of individual modules." However, some insights can be gained by examining average characteristics for methods (operations). Three simple metrics, proposed by Lorenz and Kidd [LOR94], are appropriate:

Average operation size (OS_{avg}). Although lines of code could be used as an indicator for operation size, the LOC measure suffers from a set of problems discussed in Chapter 22. For this reason, the number of messages sent by the operation provides an alternative for operation size. As the number of messages sent by a single operation increases, it is likely that responsibilities have not been well-allocated within a class.

Operation complexity (OC). The complexity of an operation can be computed using any of the complexity metrics proposed for conventional software [ZUS90]. Because operations should be limited to a specific responsibility, the designer should strive to keep OC as low as possible.

Average number of parameters per operation (NP_{avg}). The larger the number of operation parameters, the more complex the collaboration between objects. In general, NP_{avg} should be kept as low as possible.

15.4.8 User Interface Design Metrics

Although there is significant literature on the design of human/computer interfaces (Chapter 12), relatively little information has been published on metrics that would provide insight into the quality and usability of the interface.

Sears [SEA93] suggests that *layout appropriateness* (LA) is a worthwhile design metric for human/computer interfaces. A typical GUI uses layout entities—graphic icons, text, menus, windows, and the like—to assist the user in completing tasks. To accomplish a given task using a GUI, the user must move from one layout entity to the next. The absolute and relative position of each layout entity, the frequency with which it is used, and the "cost" of the transition from one layout entity to the next all contribute to the appropriateness of the interface.

> "You can learn at least one principal of user interface design by loading a dishwasher. If you crowd a lot in there, nothing gets very clean."
>
> **Author unknown**

Interface design metrics are fine, but above all else, be absolutely sure that your end-users like the interface and are comfortable with the interactions required.

Kokol and his colleagues [KOK95] define a cohesion metric for UI screens that measures the relative connection of on-screen content to other on-screen content. If data (or other content) presented on a screen belongs to a single major data object (as defined within the analysis model), UI cohesion for that screen is high. If many different types of data or content are presented and these data are related to different data objects, UI cohesion is low. The authors provide empirical models for cohesion [KOK95].

In addition, direct measures of UI interaction can focus on the measurement of time required to achieve a specific scenario or operation, time required to recover from an error condition, counts of specific operations or tasks required to achieve a use-case, the number of data or content objects presented on a screen, text density and size, and many others. However, these direct measures must be organized to create meaningful UI metrics that will lead to improved UI quality and/or improved usability.

It is important to note that the selection of a GUI design can be guided with metrics such as LA or UI screen cohesion, but the final arbiter should be user input based on GUI prototypes. Nielsen and Levy [NIE94] report that "one has a reasonably large chance of success if one chooses between interface [designs] based solely on users' opinions. Users' average task performance and their subjective satisfaction with a GUI are highly correlated."

15.5 Metrics for Source Code

Halstead's theory of "software science" [HAL77] proposed the first analytical "laws" for computer software.[14] Halstead assigned quantitative laws to the development of computer software, using a set of primitive measures that may be derived after code is generated or estimated once design is complete. The measures are:

n_1 = the number of distinct operators that appear in a program.
n_2 = the number of distinct operands that appear in a program.
N_1 = the total number of operator occurrences.
N_2 = the total number of operand occurrences.

Operators include all flow of control constructs, conditionals, and math operations. Operands encompass all program variables and constants.

Halstead uses these primitive measures to develop expressions for the overall program length, potential minimum volume for an algorithm, the actual volume (number of bits required to specify a program), the program level (a measure of software complexity), the language level (a constant for a given language), and other features such as development effort, development time, and even the projected number of faults in the software.

Halstead shows that length N can be estimated

$$N = n_1 \log_2 n_1 + n_2 \log_2 n_2$$

and program volume may be defined

$$V = N \log_2 (n_1 + n_2)$$

It should be noted that V will vary with programming language and represents the volume of information (in bits) required to specify a program.

> "The human brain follows a more rigid set of rules [for developing algorithms] than it has been aware of."
> **Maurice Halstead**

Theoretically, a minimum volume must exist for a particular algorithm. Halstead defines a volume ratio L as the ratio of volume of the most compact form of a program to the volume of the actual program. In actuality, L must always be less than 1. In terms of primitive measures, the volume ratio may be expressed as

$$L = 2/n_1 \times n_2/N_2$$

Halstead's work is amenable to experimental verification, and a large body of research has been conducted to investigate software science. For further information, see [ZUS90], [FEN91], and [ZUS97].

---

14 It should be noted that Halstead's "laws" have generated substantial controversy, and many believe that the underlying theory has flaws. However, experimental verification for selected programming languages has been performed (e.g. [FEL89]).

15.6 Metrics for Testing

Although much has been written on software metrics for testing (e.g., [HET93]), the majority of metrics proposed focus on the process of testing, not the technical characteristics of the tests themselves. In general, testers must rely on analysis, design, and code metrics to guide them in the design and execution of test cases.

Function-based metrics (Section 15.3.1) can be used as a predictor for overall testing effort. Various project-level characteristics (e.g., testing effort and time, errors uncovered, number of test cases produced) for past projects can be collected and correlated with the number of function points produced by a project team. The team can then project "expected values" of these characteristics for the current project.

KEY POINT

Testing metrics fall into two broad categories: (1) metrics that attempt to predict the likely number of tests required at various testing levels, and (2) metrics that focus on test coverage for a given component.

Architectural design metrics provide information on the ease or difficulty associated with integration testing (Chapter 13) and the need for specialized testing software (e.g., stubs and drivers). Cyclomatic complexity (a component-level design metric) lies at the core of basis path testing, a test case design method presented in Chapter 14. In addition, cyclomatic complexity can be used to target modules as candidates for extensive unit testing. Modules with high cyclomatic complexity are more likely to be error prone than modules whose cyclomatic complexity is lower. For this reason, the tester should expend above average effort to uncover errors in such modules before they are integrated in a system.

15.6.1 Halstead Metrics Applied to Testing

Testing effort can also be estimated using metrics derived from Halstead measures (Section 15.5). Using the definitions for program volume, V, and program level, PL, Halstead effort, e, can be computed as

$$PL = 1/[(n_1/2) \times (N_2/n_2)] \qquad (15\text{-}7a)$$

$$e = V/PL \qquad (15\text{-}7b)$$

The percentage of overall testing effort to be allocated to a module k can be estimated using the following relationship:

$$\text{percentage of testing effort } (k) = e(k)/\Sigma e(i) \qquad (15\text{-}8)$$

where $e(k)$ is computed for module k using Equations (15-7) and the summation in the denominator of Equation (15-8) is the sum of Halstead effort across all modules of the system.

15.6.2 Metrics for Object-Oriented Testing

The OO design metrics noted in Section 15.4 provide an indication of design quality. They also provide a general indication of the amount of testing effort required to exercise an OO system.

Binder [BIN94] suggests a broad array of design metrics that have a direct influence on the "testability" of an OO system. The metrics consider aspects of encapsulation and inheritance. A sampling follows:

OO testing can be quite complex. Metrics can assist you in targeting testing resources at threads, scenarios, and packages of classes that are "suspect" based on measured characteristics. Use them.

Lack of cohesion in methods (LCOM).[15] The higher the value of LCOM, the more states must be tested to ensure that methods do not generate side effects.

Percent public and protected (PAP). This metric indicates the percentage of class attributes that are public or protected. High values for PAP increase the likelihood of side effects among classes because public and protected attributes lead to high potential for coupling (Chapter 9).[16] Tests must be designed to ensure that such side effects are uncovered.

Public access to data members (PAD). This metric indicates the number of classes (or methods) that can access another class's attributes, a violation of encapsulation. High values for PAD lead to the potential for side effects among classes. Tests must be designed to ensure that such side effects are uncovered.

Number of root classes (NOR). This metric is a count of the distinct class hierarchies that are described in the design model. Test suites for each root class and the corresponding class hierarchy must be developed. As NOR increases, testing effort also increases.

Fan-in (FIN). When used in the OO context, fan-in for the inheritance hierarchy is an indication of multiple inheritance. FIN > 1 indicates that a class inherits its attributes and operations from more than one root class. FIN > 1 should be avoided when possible.

Number of children (NOC) and depth of the inheritance tree (DIT).[17] As we discussed in Chapter 14, superclass methods will have to be retested for each subclass.

15.7 Metrics for Maintenance

All of the software metrics introduced in this chapter can be used for the development of new software and the maintenance of existing software. However, metrics designed explicitly for maintenance activities have been proposed.

IEEE Std. 982.1-1988 [IEE94] suggests a *software maturity index* (SMI) that provides an indication of the stability of a software product (based on changes that occur for each release of the product). The following information is determined:

---

15 See Section 15.4.3 for a description of LCOM.

16 Some people promote designs in which none of the attributes are public or private; that is, PAP = 0. This implies that all attributes must be accessed in other classes via methods.

17 See Section 15.4.3 for a description of NOC and DIT.

M_T = the number of modules in the current release
F_c = the number of modules in the current release that have been changed
F_a = the number of modules in the current release that have been added
F_d = the number of modules from the preceding release that were deleted in the current release

The software maturity index is computed in the following manner:

$$\text{SMI} = [M_T - (F_a + F_c + F_d)]/M_T$$

As SMI approaches 1.0, the product begins to stabilize. SMI may also be used as a metric for planning software maintenance activities. The mean time to produce a release of a software product can be correlated with SMI, and empirical models for maintenance effort can be developed.

SOFTWARE TOOLS

Product Metrics

Objective: To assist software engineers in developing meaningful metrics that assess the work products produced during analysis and design modeling, source code generation, and testing.

Mechanics: Tools in this category span a broad array of metrics and are implemented either as standalone applications or (more commonly) as functionality that exists within tools for analysis and design, coding or testing. In most cases, the metrics tool analyzes a representation of the software (e.g., a UML model or source code) and develops one or more metrics as a result.

Representative Tools[18]

Krakatau Metrics, developed by Power Software (www.powersoftware.com/products), computes complexity, Halstead, and related metrics for C/C++ and Java.

Metrics4C, developed by +1 Software Engineering (www.plus-one.com/Metrics4C_fact_sheet.html), computes a variety of architectural, design, and code-oriented metrics as well as project-oriented metrics.

Rational Rose, developed by Rational Corporation (www.rational.com), is a comprehensive tool set for UML modeling that incorporates a number of metrics analysis features.

RSM, developed by M-Squared Technologies (msquaredtechnologies.com/m2rsm/index.html), computes a wide variety of code-oriented metrics for C, C++ and Java.

Understand, developed by Scientific Toolworks, Inc. (www.scitools.com), calculates code-oriented metrics for a variety of programming languages.

15.8 SUMMARY

Software metrics provide a quantitative way to assess the quality of internal product attributes, thereby enabling a software engineer to assess quality before the product is built. Metrics provide the insight necessary to create effective analysis and design models, solid code, and thorough tests.

18 Tools noted here do not represent an endorsement, but rather a sampling of tools in this category. In most cases, tool names are trademarked by their respective developers.

To be useful in a real world context, a software metric must be simple and computable, persuasive, consistent, and objective. It should be programming language independent and provide effective feedback to the software engineer.

Metrics for the analysis model focus on function, data, and behavior—the three components of the analysis model. Metrics for design consider architecture, component-level design, and interface design issues. Architectural design metrics consider the structural aspects of the design model. Component-level design metrics provide an indication of module quality by establishing indirect measures for cohesion, coupling, and complexity. User interface design metrics provide an indication of the ease with which a GUI can be used.

Metrics for OO systems focus on measurement that can be applied to the class and design characteristics—localization, encapsulation, information hiding, inheritance, and object abstraction techniques—that make the class unique.

Halstead provides an intriguing set of metrics at the source code level. Using the number of operators and operands present in the code, a variety of metrics are developed to assess program quality.

Few product metrics have been proposed for direct use in software testing and maintenance. However, many other product metrics can be used to guide the testing process and as a mechanism for assessing the maintainability of a computer program. A wide variety of OO metrics have been proposed to assess the testability of an OO system.

REFERENCES

[ALB79] Albrecht, A. J., "Measuring Application Development Productivity," *Proc. IBM Application Development Symposium,* Monterey, CA, October 1979, pp. 83–92.

[ALB83] Albrecht, A. J., and J. E. Gaffney, "Software Function, Source Lines of Code and Development Effort Prediction: A Software Science Validation," *IEEE Trans. Software Engineering,* November 1983, pp. 639–648.

[BAS84] Basili, V. R., and D. M. Weiss, "A Methodology for Collecting Valid Software Engineering Data," *IEEE Trans. Software Engineering,* vol. SE-10, 1984, pp. 728–738.

[BER95] Berard, E., "Metrics for Object-Oriented Software Engineering," an Internet posting on comp.software-eng, January 28, 1995.

[BIE94] Bieman, J. M., and L. M. Ott, "Measuring Functional Cohesion," *IEEE Trans. Software Engineering,* vol. SE-20, no. 8, August 1994, pp. 308–320.

[BIN94] Binder, R. V., "Object-Oriented Software Testing," *CACM,* vol. 37, no. 9, September 1994, p. 29.

[BRI96] Briand, L. C., S. Morasca, and V. R. Basili, "Property-Based Software Engineering Measurement," *IEEE Trans. Software Engineering,* vol. SE-22, no. 1, January 1996, pp. 68–85.

[CAR90] Card, D. N., and R. L. Glass, *Measuring Software Design Quality,* Prentice-Hall, 1990.

[CAV78] Cavano, J. P., and J. A. McCall, "A Framework for the Measurement of Software Quality," *Proc. ACM Software Quality Assurance Workshop,* November 1978, pp. 133–139.

[CHA89] Charette, R. N., *Software Engineering Risk Analysis and Management,* McGraw-Hill/Intertext, 1989.

[CHI94] Chidamber, S. R., and C. F. Kemerer, "A Metrics Suite for Object-Oriented Design," *IEEE Trans. Software Engineering,* vol. SE-20, no. 6, June 1994, pp. 476–493.

[CHI98] Chidamber, S. R., D. P. Darcy, and C. F. Kemerer, "Management Use of Metrics for Object-Oriented Software: An Exploratory Analysis," *IEEE Trans. Software Engineering,* vol. SE-24, no. 8, August 1998, pp. 629–639.

[CHU95] Churcher, N. I., and M. J. Shepperd, "Towards a Conceptual Framework for Object-Oriented Metrics," *ACM Software Engineering Notes,* vol. 20, no. 2, April 1995, pp. 69–76.

[CUR80] Curtis, W., "Management and Experimentation in Software Engineering," *Proc. IEEE,* vol. 68, no. 9, September 1980.

[DAV93] Davis, A., et al., "Identifying and Measuring Quality in a Software Requirements Specification," *Proc. First Intl. Software Metrics Symposium,* IEEE, Baltimore, MD, May 1993, pp. 141–152.

[DEM81] DeMillo, R. A., and R. J. Lipton, "Software Project Forecasting," in *Software Metrics* (A. J. Perlis, F. G. Sayward, and M. Shaw, eds.), MIT Press, 1981, pp. 77–89.

[DEM82] DeMarco, T., Controlling Software Projects, Yourdon Press, 1982.

[DHA95] Dhama, H., "Quantitative Models of Cohesion and Coupling in Software," *Journal of Systems and Software,* vol. 29, no. 4, April 1995.

[EJI91] Ejiogu, L., *Software Engineering with Formal Metrics,* QED Publishing, 1991.

[FEL89] Felican, L., and G. Zalateu, "Validating Halstead's Theory for Pascal Programs," *IEEE Trans. Software Engineering,* vol. SE-15, no. 2, December 1989, pp. 1630–1632.

[FEN91] Fenton, N., *Software Metrics,* Chapman and Hall, 1991.

[FEN94] Fenton, N., "Software Measurement: A Necessary Scientific Basis," *IEEE Trans. Software Engineering,* vol. SE-20, no. 3, March 1994, pp. 199–206.

[GRA87] Grady, R. B., and D. L. Caswell, *Software Metrics: Establishing a Company-Wide Program,* Prentice-Hall, 1987.

[HAL77] Halstead, M., *Elements of Software Science,* North-Holland, 1977.

[HAR98] Harrison, R., S. J. Counsell, and R. V. Nithi, "An Evaluation of the MOOD Set of Object-Oriented Software Metrics," *IEEE Trans. Software Engineering,* vol. SE-24, no. 6, June 1998, pp. 491–496.

[HET93] Hetzel, B., *Making Software Measurement Work,* QED Publishing, 1993.

[IEE93] *IEEE Standard Glossary of Software Engineering Terminology,* IEEE, 1993.

[IEE94] *Software Engineering Standards,* 1994 edition, IEEE, 1994.

[IFP01] *Function Point Counting Practices Manual,* Release 4.1.1, International Function Point Users Group, 2001, available from http://www.ifpug.org/publications/ manual.htm.

[IFP03] Function Point Bibliography/Reference Library, International Function Point Users Group, 2003, available from http://www.ifpug.org/about/bibliography. htm

[KOK95] Kokol, P., I. Rozman, and V. Venuti, "User Interface Metrics," *ACM SIGPLAN Notices*, vol. 30, no. 4, April 1995, can be downloaded from: http://portal.acm.org/.

[KYB84] Kyburg, H. E., *Theory and Measurement,* Cambridge University Press, 1984.

[LET03] Lethbridge, T., private communication of software metrics, June, 2003.

[LON02] Longstreet, D., "Fundamental of Function Point Analysis," Longstreet Consulting, Inc, 2002, available at http://www.ifpug.com/fpafund.htm.

[LOR94] Lorenz, M., and J. Kidd, *Object-Oriented Software Metrics,* Prentice-Hall, 1994.

[MCC76] McCabe, T. J., "A Software Complexity Measure," *IEEE Trans. Software Engineering,* vol. SE-2, December 1976, pp. 308–320.

[MCC77] McCall, J., P. Richards, and G. Walters, "Factors in Software Quality," three volumes, NTIS AD-A049-014, 015, 055, November 1977.

[MCC89] McCabe, T. J., and C. W. Butler, "Design Complexity Measurement and Testing," *CACM,* vol. 32, no. 12, December 1989, pp. 1415–1425.

[MCC94] McCabe, T. J., and A. H. Watson, "Software Complexity," *Crosstalk,* vol. 7, no. 12, December 1994, pp. 5–9.

[NIE94] Nielsen, J., and J. Levy, "Measuring Usability: Preference vs. Performance," *CACM,* vol. 37, no. 4, April 1994, pp. 65–75.

[ROC94] Roche, J. M., "Software Metrics and Measurement Principles," *Software Engineering Notes,* ACM, vol. 19, no. 1, January 1994, pp. 76–85.

[SEA93] Sears, A., "Layout Appropriateness: A Metric for Evaluating User Interface Widget Layout, *IEEE Trans. Software Engineering,* vol. SE-19, no. 7, July 1993, pp. 707–719.

[SHE98] Sheppard, M., *Goal, Question, Metric,* 1998, available at http://dec. bournemouth.ac.uk/ESERG/mshepperd/SEMGQM.html.

[SOL99] van Solingen, R., and E. Berghout, *The Goal/Question/Metric Method,* McGraw-Hill, 1999.

[UEM99] Uemura, T., S. Kusumoto, and K. Inoue, "A Function Point Measurement Tool for UML Design Specifications," *Proc. of Sixth International Symposium on Software Metrics,* IEEE, November 1999, pp. 62–69.

[USA87] *Management Quality Insight,* AFCSP 800-14 (U.S. Air Force), January 20, 1987.

[WHI97] Whitmire, S., *Object-Oriented Design Measurement,* Wiley, 1997.

[WIL93] Wilde, N., and R. Huitt, "Maintaining Object-Oriented Software," *IEEE Software,* January 1993, pp. 75–80.

[ZUS90] Zuse, H., *Software Complexity: Measures and Methods,* DeGruyter, 1990.

[ZUS97] Zuse, H., *A Framework of Software Measurement,* DeGruyter, 1997.

Problems and Points to Ponder

15.1. Measurement theory is an advanced topic that has a strong bearing on software metrics. Using [ZUS97], [FEN91], [ZUS90], [KYB84] or some other source, write a brief paper that outlines the main tenets of measurement theory. Individual project: Develop a presentation on the subject and present it to your class.

15.2. McCall's quality factors were developed during the 1970s. Almost every aspect of computing has changed dramatically since the time that they were developed, and yet, McCall's factors continue to apply to modern software. Can you draw any conclusions based on this fact?

15.3. Why is it that a single, all-encompassing metric cannot be developed for program complexity or program quality?

15.4. Try to come up with a measure or metric from everyday life that violates the attributes of effective software metrics defined in Section 15.2.5.

15.5. A system has 12 external inputs, 24 external outputs, fields 30 different external queries, manages 4 internal logical files, and interfaces with 6 different legacy systems (6 EIFs). All of these data are of average complexity, and the overall system is relatively simple. Compute FP for the system.

15.6. Software for System *X* has 24 individual functional requirements and 14 nonfunctional requirements. What is the specificity of the requirements? The completeness?

15.7. A major information system has 1140 modules. There are 96 modules that perform control and coordination functions and 490 modules whose function depends on prior processing. The system processes approximately 220 data objects that each have an average of three attributes. There are 140 unique data base items and 90 different database segments. Finally, 600 modules have single entry and exit points. Compute the DSQI for this system.

15.8. A class, **X**, has 12 operations. Cyclomatic complexity has been computed for all operations in the OO system, and the average value of module complexity is 4. For class **X**, the complexity for operations 1 to 12 is 5, 4, 3, 3, 6, 8, 2, 2, 5, 5, 4, 4, respectively. Compute the weighted methods per class.

15.9. Develop a software tool that will compute cyclomatic complexity for a programming language module. You may choose the language.

15.10. Develop a small software tool that will perform a Halstead analysis on programming language source code of your choosing.

15.11. A legacy system has 940 modules. The latest release required that 90 of these modules be changed. In addition, 40 new modules were added and 12 old modules were removed. Compute the software maturity index for the system.

FURTHER READINGS AND INFORMATION SOURCES

There is a surprisingly large number of books that are dedicated to software metrics, although the majority focus on process and project metrics to the exclusion of product metrics. Kan (*Metrics and Models in Software Quality Engineering,* Addison-Wesley, second edition, 2002), Fenton and Pfleeger (*Software Metrics: A Rigourous and Practical Approach,* Brooks-Cole Publishing, 1998), and Zuse [ZUS97] have written thorough treatments of product metrics.

Books by Card and Glass [CAR90], Zuse [ZUS90], Fenton [FEN91], Ejiogu [EJI91], Moeller and Paulish (*Software Metrics,* Chapman and Hall, 1993), and Hetzel [HET93] all address product metrics in some detail. Oman and Pfleeger (*Applying Software Metrics,* IEEE Computer Society Press, 1997) have edited an anthology of important papers on software metrics. In addition, the following books are worth examining:

Conte, S. D., H. E. Dunsmore, and V. Y. Shen, *Software Engineering Metrics and Models,* Benjamin-Cummings, 1984.

Grady, R. B., *Practical Software Metrics for Project Management and Process Improvement,* Prentice-Hall, 1992.

Sheppard, M., *Software Engineering Metrics,* McGraw-Hill, 1992.

The theory of software measurement is presented by Denvir, Herman, and Whitty in an edited collection of papers (*Proceedings of the International BCS-FACS Workshop: Formal Aspects of Measurement,* Springer-Verlag, 1992). Shepperd (*Foundations of Software Measurement,* Prentice-Hall, 1996) also addresses measurement theory in some detail. Current research is presented in the *Proceedings of the Symposium on Software Metrics* (IEEE, published annually).

A comprehensive summary of dozens of useful software metrics is presented in [IEE94]. In general, a discussion of each metric has been distilled to the essential "primitives" (measures) required to compute the metric and the appropriate relationships to effect the computation. An appendix provides discussion and many references.

Whitmire [WHI97] presents the most comprehensive and mathematically sophisticated treatment of OO metrics published to date. Lorenz and Kidd [LOR94] and Hendersen-Sellers (*Object-Oriented Metrics: Measures of Complexity,* Prentice-Hall, 1996) offer the only other books dedicated to OO metrics. Hutcheson (*Software Testing Fundamentals: Methods and Metrics,* Wiley, 2003) presents useful guidance in the application and use of metrics for software testing.

A wide variety of information sources on software metrics are available on the Internet. An up-to-date list of World Wide Web references that are relevant to software metrics can be found at the SEPA Web site:

http://www.mhhe.com/pressman.

PART Three

APPLYING WEB ENGINEERING

In this part of *Software Engineering: A Practitioner's Approach* you'll learn about the principles, concepts, and methods that are used to create high-quality Web applications. These questions are addressed in the chapters that follow:

- Are Web applications (WebApps) different from other types of software?
- What is Web engineering, and what elements of software engineering practice can it adopt?
- What are the elements of a Web engineering process?
- How does one formulate and plan a Web engineering project?
- How are requirements for WebApps analyzed and modeled?
- What concepts and principles guide a practitioner in the design of WebApps?
- How does one conduct architecture, interface, and navigation design for WebApps?
- What construction techniques can be applied to implement the design model?
- What testing concepts, principles, and methods are applicable to Web engineering?

Once these questions are answered you'll be better prepared to engineer high-quality Web applications.

CHAPTER

16 Web Engineering

The World Wide Web and the Internet that empowers it are arguably the most important developments in the history of computing. These technologies have drawn us all (with billions more who will eventually follow) into the information age. They have become integral to daily life in the first decade of the twenty-first century.

For those of us who can remember a world without the Web, the chaotic growth of the technology harkens back to another era—the early days of software. It was a time of little discipline, but enormous enthusiasm and creativity. It was a time when programmers often hacked together systems—some good, some bad. The prevailing attitude seemed to be "Get it done fast, and get it into the field; we'll clean it up (and better understand what we really need to build) as we go." Sound familiar?

In a virtual round table published in *IEEE Software* [PRE98], I staked out my position with regard to Web engineering:

> It seems to me that just about any important product or system is worth engineering. Before you start building it, you'd better understand the problem, design a workable solution, implement it in a solid way, and test it thoroughly. You should probably also control changes to it as you work and have some mechanism for ensuring the end result's quality. Many Web developers don't argue with this; they just think their world is really different and that conventional software engineering approaches simply don't apply.

Quick Look

What is it? Web-based systems and applications (WebApps) deliver a complex array of content and functionality to a broad population of end-users. Web engineering (WebE) is the process that is used to create high-quality WebApps. WebE is not a perfect clone of software engineering, but it borrows many of software engineering's fundamental concepts and principles. In addition, the WebE process emphasizes similar technical and management activities. There are subtle differences in the way these activities are conducted, but the overriding philosophy dictates a disciplined approach to the development of a computer-based system.

Who does it? Web engineers and nontechnical content developers create the WebApp.

Why is it important? As WebApps become increasingly integrated in business strategies for small and large companies (e.g., e-commerce), the need to build reliable, usable, and adaptable systems grows in importance. That's why a disciplined approach to WebApp development is necessary.

What are the steps? Like any engineering discipline, WebE applies a generic approach that is tempered with specialized strategies, tactics, and methods. The WebE process begins with a formulation of the problem to be solved by the WebApp. The WebE project is planned, and the requirements and design of the WebApp are modeled. The system is constructed using specialized technologies and tools associated with the Web. It is then delivered to end-users and evaluated using both technical and business criteria. Because WebApps evolve continuously, mechanisms for configuration control, quality assurance, and on-going support must be established.

What is the work product? A variety of WebE work products are produced. The final output is the operational WebApp.

How do I ensure that I've done it right? It's sometimes hard to be sure until end-users exercise the WebApp. However, SQA practices can be applied to assess the quality of WebE models, overall system content and function, usability, performance, and security.

This leads us to a pivotal question: *Can software engineering principles, concepts, and methods be applied to Web development?* Many of them can, but their application may require a somewhat different spin.

But what if an undisciplined approach to Web development persists? In the absence of a disciplined process for developing Web-based systems, there is increasing concern that we may face serious problems in their successful development, deployment, and maintenance. In essence, the application infrastructure that we are creating today may lead to a "tangled Web" as we move further into this new century. This phrase connotes a morass of poorly developed Web-based applications that have too high a probability of failure. Worse, as Web-based systems grow more complex, a failure in one can and will propagate broad-based problems across many. When this happens, confidence in the entire Internet may be shaken. Worse, it may lead to unnecessary and ill-conceived government regulation, leading to irreparable harm to these unique technologies.

To avoid a tangled Web and achieve greater success in development and application of large-scale, complex Web-based systems, there is a pressing need for disciplined approaches and new methods and tools for development, deployment, and evaluation of Web-based systems and applications. Such approaches and techniques must take into account the special features of the new medium, the operational environments and scenarios, and the multiplicity of user profiles which pose additional challenges to Web-based application development.

Web engineering (WebE) applies "sound scientific, engineering, and management principles and disciplined and systematic approaches to the successful development, deployment and maintenance of high-quality Web-based systems and applications." [MUR99]

16.1 Attributes of Web-Based Systems and Applications

In the early days of the World Wide Web (circa 1990 to 1995), "Web sites" consisted of little more than a set of linked hypertext files that presented information using text and limited graphics. As time passed, HTML was augmented by development tools (e.g., XML, Java) that enabled Web engineers to provide computing capability along with information. Web-based systems and applications[1] (we will refer to these collectively as *WebApps*) were born. Today, WebApps have evolved into sophisticated computing tools that not only provide standalone function to the end-user, but also have been integrated with corporate databases and business applications.

> "By the time we see any sort of stabilization, the Web will have turned into something completely different."
> **Louis Monier**

There is little debate that WebApps *are* different than the many other categories of computer software discussed in Chapter 1. Powell summarizes the primary differences when he states that Web-based systems "involve a mixture between print publishing and software development, between marketing and computing, between internal communications and external relations, and between art and technology." [POW98] The following attributes are encountered in the vast majority of WebApps.

ADVICE

It can be argued that a traditional application within any of the software domains discussed in Chapter 1 can exhibit this list of attributes. However, WebApps almost always do.

Network intensiveness. A WebApp resides on a network and must serve the needs of a diverse community of clients. A WebApp may reside on the Internet (thereby enabling open worldwide communication). Alternatively, an application may be placed on an Intranet (implementing communication across an organization) or an Extranet (inter-network communication).

Concurrency. A large number of users may access the WebApp at one time. In many cases, the patterns of usage among end-users will vary greatly.

Unpredictable load. The number of users of the WebApp may vary by orders of magnitude from day to day. 100 users may show up on Monday; 10,000 may use the system on Thursday.

Performance. If a WebApp user must wait too long (for access, for server-side processing, for client-side formatting and display), he or she may decide to go elsewhere.

Availability. Although expectation of 100 percent availability is unreasonable, users of popular WebApps often demand access on a "24/7/365" basis. Users in Australia or Asia might demand access during times when traditional domestic software applications in North America might be taken off-line for maintenance.

Data driven. The primary function of many WebApps is to use hypermedia to present text, graphics, audio, and video content to the end-user. In addition, WebApps are commonly used to access information that exists on databases that were

1 In the context of this chapter, the term "Web application" (WebApp) encompasses everything from a simple Web page that might help a consumer compute an automobile lease payment to a comprehensive Web site that provides complete travel services for business people and vacationers. Included within this category are complete Web sites, specialized functionality within Web sites, and information processing applications that reside on the Internet or on an Intranet or ExtraNet.

not originally an integral part of the Web-based environment (e.g., e-commerce or financial applications).

Content sensitive. The quality and aesthetic nature of content remains an important determinant of the quality of a WebApp.

Continuous evolution. Unlike conventional application software that evolves over a series of planned, chronologically spaced releases, Web applications evolve continuously. It is not unusual for some WebApps (specifically, their content) to be updated on a minute-by-minute schedule or for content to be independently computed for each request. Some argue that the continuous evolution of WebApps makes the work performed on them analogous to gardening. Lowe [LOW99] discusses this when he writes:

> Engineering is about adopting a consistent and scientific approach, tempered by a specific practical context, to development and commissioning of systems or applications. Web site development is often much more about creating an infrastructure (laying out the garden) and then "tending" the information which grows and blooms within this garden. Over time the garden (i.e., Web site) will continue to evolve, change, and grow. A good initial architecture should allow this growth to occur in a controlled and consistent manner. . . .

Continual care and feeding allows a Web site to grow (in robustness and importance). But unlike a garden, Web applications must serve (and adapt to) the needs of more than the gardener.

Immediacy. Although *immediacy*—the compelling need to get software to market quickly—is a characteristic of many application domains, WebApps often exhibit a time to market that can be a matter of a few days or weeks.[2] Web engineers must use methods for planning, analysis, design, implementation, and testing that have been adapted to the compressed time schedules required for WebApp development.

Security. Because WebApps are available via network access, it is difficult, if not impossible, to limit the population of end-users who may access the application. In order to protect sensitive content and provide secure modes of data transmission, strong security measures must be implemented throughout the infrastructure that supports a WebApp and within the application itself.

Aesthetics. An undeniable part of the appeal of a WebApp is its look and feel. When an application has been designed to market or sell products or ideas, aesthetics may have as much to do with success as technical design.

These general attributes apply to all WebApps, but with different degrees of influence.

2 With modern tools, sophisticated Web pages can be produced in only a few hours.

But what about the WebApps themselves? What problems do they address? The following application categories are most commonly encountered in WebE work [DAR99]:

? What categories of WebApps are encountered in WebE work?

- *Informational*—read-only content is provided with simple navigation and links.
- *Download*—a user downloads information from the appropriate server.
- *Customizable*—the user customizes content to specific needs.
- *Interaction*—communication among a community of users occurs via chatroom, bulletin boards, or instant messaging.
- *User input*—forms-based input is the primary mechanism for communicating need.
- *Transaction-oriented*—the user makes a request (e.g., places an order) that is fulfilled by the WebApp.
- *Service-oriented*—the application provides a service to the user, e.g., assists the user in determining a mortgage payment.
- *Portal*—the application channels the user to other Web content or services outside the domain of the portal application.
- *Database access*—the user queries a large database and extracts information.
- *Data warehousing*—the user queries a collection of large databases and extracts information.

The attributes noted earlier in this section and the application categories noted above represent important facts of life for Web engineers. The key is living within the constraints imposed by these attributes and still producing a successful WebApp.

16.2 WebApp Engineering Layers

The development of Web-based systems and applications incorporates specialized process models, software engineering methods adapted to the characteristics of WebApp development, and a set of important enabling technologies. Process, methods, and technologies (tools) provide a layered approach to WebE that is conceptually identical to the software engineering layers described in Figure 2.1.

> "Web Engineering deals with disciplined and systematic approaches to development, deployment, and maintenance of Web-based systems and applications."
>
> **Yogesh Deshpande**

16.2.1 Process

WebE process models (discussed in detail in Section 16.3) embrace the agile development philosophy (Chapter 4). Agile development emphasizes a lean development

The WebE process is often agile and is almost always incremental. Note, however, that the agile model may not be chosen for major Web engineering projects.

approach that incorporates rapid development cycles. Aoyama [AOY98] describes the motivation for the agile approach in the following manner:

> The Internet changed software development's top priority from *what* to *when.* Reduced time-to-market has become the competitive edge that leading companies strive for. Thus, reducing the development cycle is now one of software engineering's most important missions.

Even when rapid cycle times dominate development thinking, it is important to recognize that the problem must still be analyzed, a design should be developed, implementation should proceed in an incremental fashion, and an organized testing approach must be initiated. However, these framework activities must be defined within a process that (1) embraces change, (2) encourages the creativity and independence of development staff and strong interaction with WebApp stakeholders, (3) builds systems using small development teams, and (4) emphasizes evolutionary or incremental development using short development cycles [MCD01].

16.2.2 Methods

The WebE methods landscape encompasses a set of technical tasks that enable a Web engineer to understand, characterize, and then build a high-quality WebApp. WebE methods (discussed in detail in Chapters 18 through 20) can be categorized in the following manner:

It's important to note that many WebE methods have been adopted directly from their software engineering counterparts. Others are in their formative stages. Some of these will survive; others will be discarded as better approaches are suggested.

Communication methods—define the approach used to facilitate communication between Web engineers and all other WebApp stakeholders (e.g., end-users, business clients, problem domain experts, content designers, team leaders, project managers). Communication techniques are particularly important during requirements gathering and whenever a WebApp increment is to be evaluated.

Requirements analysis methods—provide a basis for understanding the content to be delivered by a WebApp, the function to be provided for the end-user, and the modes of interaction that each class of user will require as navigation through the WebApp occurs.

Design methods—encompass a series of design techniques that address WebApp content, application and information architecture, interface design, and navigation structure.

Testing methods—incorporate formal technical reviews of both the content and design model and a wide array of testing techniques that address component-level and architectural issues, navigation testing, usability testing, security testing, and configuration testing.

It is important to note that although WebE methods adopt many of the same underlying concepts and principles as the software engineering methods described in Part 2 of this book, the mechanics of analysis, design, and testing must be adapted to accommodate the special characteristics of WebApps.

In addition to the technical methods that have just been outlined, a series of umbrella activities (with associated methods) are essential for successful Web engineering. These include project management techniques (e.g., estimation, scheduling, risk analysis), software configuration management techniques, and review techniques.

16.2.3 Tools and Technology

WebRef
Excellent resources for WebE technology can be found at **webdeveloper.com** and **www.eborcom.com/webmaker.**

A vast array of tools and technology has evolved over the past decade as WebApps have become more sophisticated and pervasive. These technologies encompass a wide array of content description and modeling languages (e.g., HTML, VRML, XML), programming languages (e.g., Java) component-based development resources (e.g., CORBA, COM, ActiveX, .NET), browsers, multimedia tools, site authoring tools, database connectivity tools, security tools, servers and server utilities, and site management and analysis tools.

A comprehensive discussion of tools and technology for Web engineering is beyond the scope of this book. The interested reader should visit one or more of the following Web sites: *Web Developer's Virtual Encyclopedia* (www.wdlv.com), *WebDeveloper* (www.webdeveloper.com), *Developer Shed* (www.devshed.com), *Webknowhow.net* (www.webknowhow.net), or *WebReference* (www.webreference.com).

16.3 The Web Engineering Process

The attributes of Web-based systems and applications have a profound influence on the WebE process that is chosen. In Chapter 3 we noted that a software engineer chooses a process model based on the attributes of the software that is to be developed. The same holds true for a Web engineer.

If immediacy and continuous evolution are primary attributes of a WebApp, a Web engineering team might choose an agile process model (Chapter 4) that produces WebApp releases in rapid-fire sequence. On the other hand, if a WebApp is to be developed over a longer time period (e.g., a major e-commerce application), an incremental process model (Chapter 3) might be chosen.

> "Web development is an adolescent . . . Like most adolescents, it wants to be accepted as an adult as it tries to pull away from its parents. If it is going to reach its full potential, it must take a few lessons from the more seasoned world of software development."
>
> **Doug Wallace et al.**

The network intensive nature of applications in this domain suggests a population of users that is diverse (thereby making special demands on requirements elicitation and modeling) and an application architecture that can be highly specialized (thereby making demands on design). Because WebApps are often content-driven with an emphasis on aesthetics, it is likely that parallel development activities will be scheduled within the WebE process and involve a team of both technical and non-technical people (e.g., copywriters, graphic designers).

16.3.1 Defining the Framework

Any one of the agile process models (e.g., Extreme Programming, Adaptive Software Development, SCRUM) presented in Chapter 4 can be applied successfully as a WebE process. The process framework that is presented here is an amalgam of the principles and ideas discussed in Chapter 4.

To be effective, any engineering process must be adaptable. That is, the organization of the project team, the modes of communication among team members, the engineering activities and tasks to be performed, the information that is collected and created, and the methods used to produce a high-quality product must all be adapted to the people doing the work, the project timeline and constraints, and the problem to be solved. Before we define a process framework for WebE, we must recognize that:

The WebE process model is predicated on three points: incremental delivery, continuous change, and short timelines.

1. *WebApps are often delivered incrementally.* That is, framework activities will occur repeatedly as each increment is engineered and delivered.
2. *Changes will occur frequently.* These changes may occur as a result of the evaluation of a delivered increment or as a consequence of changing business conditions.
3. *Timelines are short.* This mitigates against the creation and review of voluminous engineering documentation, but it does not preclude the simple reality that critical analysis, design, and testing must be recorded in some manner.

In addition, the principles defined as part of the "Manifesto for Agile Software Development" (Chapter 4) should be applied. However, the principles are not the Ten Commandments. It is sometimes reasonable to adopt the spirit of these principles without necessarily abiding by the letter of the manifesto.

With these issues in mind, we discuss the WebE process within the generic process framework presented in Chapter 2.

The generic process model (introduced in Chapter 2) is applicable to Web engineering.

Customer communication. Within the WebE process, customer communication is characterized by two major tasks: business analysis and formulation. *Business analysis* defines the business/organizational context for the WebApp. In addition, stakeholders are identified, potential changes in business environment or requirements are predicted, and integration between the WebApp and other business applications, databases, and functions is defined. *Formulation* is a requirements gathering activity involving all stakeholders. The intent is to describe the problem that the WebApp is to solve (along with basic requirements for the WebApp) using the best information available. In addition, an attempt is made to identify areas of uncertainty and where potential changes will occur.

Planning. The project plan for the WebApp increment is created. The plan consists of a task definition and a timeline schedule for the time period (usually measured in weeks) projected for the development of the WebApp increment.

Modeling. Conventional software engineering analysis and design tasks are adapted to WebApp development, merged, and then melded into the WebE modeling activity (Chapters 18 and 19). The intent is to develop "rapid" analysis and design models that define requirements and at the same time represent a WebApp that will satisfy them.

Construction. WebE tools and technology are applied to construct the WebApp that has been modeled. Once the WebApp increment has been constructed, a series of rapid tests are conducted to ensure that errors in design (i.e., content, architecture, interface, navigation) are uncovered. Additional testing addresses other WebApp characteristics.

Deployment. The WebApp is configured for its operational environment, delivered to end-users, and then an evaluation period commences. Evaluation feedback is presented to the WebE team, and the increment is modified as required.

These five WebE framework activities are applied using an incremental process flow as shown in Figure 16.1.

FIGURE 16.1

The WebE process

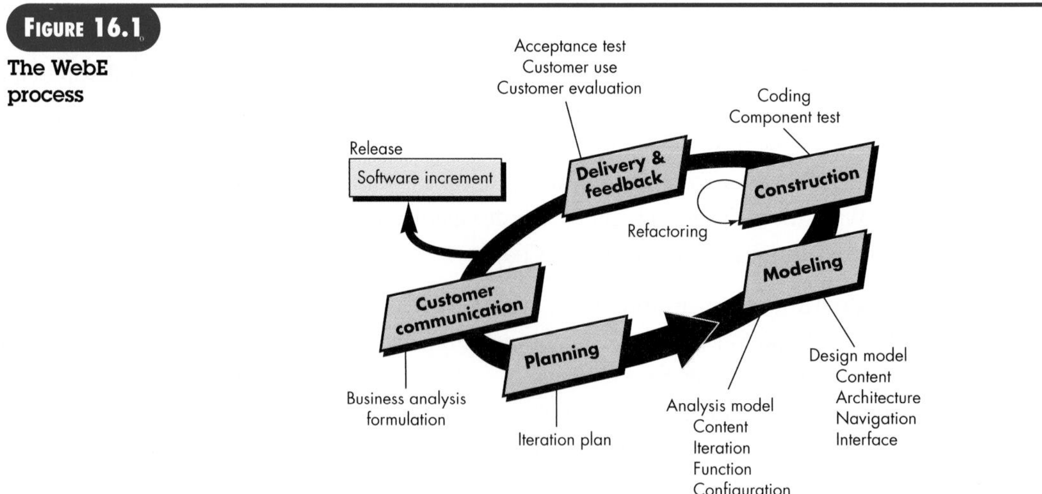

INFO

Web Engineering—Basic Questions

The engineering of any product involves subtleties that are not immediately obvious to those without substantial experience. The characteristics of WebApps force Web engineers to answer a variety of questions that should be addressed during early framework activities. Strategic questions related to business needs and product objectives are addressed during formulation. Requirements questions related to features and functions must be considered during analysis modeling. Broad-based design questions related to WebApp architecture, interface characteristics, and navigational issues are considered as the design model evolves. Finally, a set of human issues, related to the manner in which a user actually interacts with the WebApp, are addressed on a continual basis.

Susan Weinshenk [WEI02] suggests a set of questions that must be considered as analysis and design progress. A small (adapted) subset are noted here:

- How important is a Web-site home page? Should it contain useful information or a simple listing of links that lead a user to more detail at lower levels?
- What is the most effective page layout (e.g., menu on top, on the right or left?), and does it vary depending upon the type of WebApp being developed?
- Which media options have the most impact? Are graphics more effective than text? Is video (or audio) an effective option? When should various media options be chosen?
- How much work can we expect a user to do when he or she is looking for information? How many clicks are people willing to make?
- How important are navigational aids when WebApps are complex?
- How complex can forms input be before it becomes irritating for the user? How can forms input be expedited?
- How important are search capabilities? What percentage of users browse, and what percent use specific searches? How important is it to structure each page in a manner that assumes a link from some outside source?
- Will the WebApp be designed in a manner that makes it accessible to those who have physical or other disabilities?

There are no absolute answers to questions such as these, and yet, they must be addressed as WebE proceeds. We'll consider potential answers in Chapters 17 through 20.

16.3.2 Refining the Framework

We have already noted that the WebE process model must be adaptable. That is, a definition of the engineering tasks required to refine each framework activity is left to the discretion of the Web engineering team. In some cases, a framework activity is conducted informally. In others, a series of distinct tasks will be defined and conducted by team members. In every case, the team has responsibility for producing a high-quality WebApp increment within the time period allocated.

It is important to emphasize that tasks associated with WebE framework activities may be modified, eliminated, or extended based on the characteristics of the problem, the product, the project, and the people on the Web engineering team.

> "There are those of us who believe that the best practices for software development are practical and deserve implementation. And then there are those of us who believe that best practices are interesting in an academic sort of way, but are not for the real world, thank you very much."
>
> **Warren Keuffel**

16.4 Web Engineering Best Practices

Will every WebApp developer use the WebE process framework and task set defined in Section 16.3? Probably not. Web engineering teams are sometimes under enormous time pressure and will try to take short-cuts (even if these are ill-advised and result in *more* development effort, not less). But a set of fundamental best practices—adopted from the software engineering practices discussed throughout Part 2 of this book—should be applied if industry-quality WebApps are to be built.

Be sure that the business need for a WebApp has been clearly enunciated by someone. If it hasn't, your WebE project is at risk.

1. *Take the time to understand business needs and product objectives, even if the details of the WebApp are vague.* Many WebApp developers erroneously believe that vague requirements (which are quite common) relieve them from the need to be sure that the system they are about to engineer has a legitimate business purpose. The end result is (too often) good technical work that results in the wrong system built for the wrong reasons for the wrong audience. If stakeholders cannot enunciate a business need for the WebApp, proceed with extreme caution. If stakeholders struggle to identify a set of clear objectives for the product (WebApp), do not proceed until they can.
2. *Describe how users will interact with the WebApp using a scenario-based approach.* Stakeholders must be convinced to develop use-cases (discussed throughout Part 2 of this book) to reflect how various actors will interact with the WebApp. These scenarios can then be used (1) for project planning and tracking, (2) to guide analysis and design modeling, and (3) as important input for the design of tests.
3. *Develop a project plan, even if it is very brief.* Base the plan on a predefined process framework that is acceptable to all stakeholders. Because project timelines are very short, schedule granularity should be fine; i.e., in many instances, the project should be scheduled and tracked on a daily basis.
4. *Spend some time modeling what it is that you're going to build.* Generally, comprehensive analysis and design models are not developed during Web engineering. However, UML class and sequence diagrams along with other selected UML notation (e.g., state diagrams) may provide invaluable insight.
5. *Review the models for consistency and quality.* Formal technical reviews (Chapter 26) should be conducted throughout a WebE project. The time spent on reviews pays important dividends because it often eliminates rework and results in a WebApp that exhibits high quality—thereby increasing customer satisfaction.
6. *Use tools and technology that enable you to construct the system with as many reusable components as possible.* A wide array of WebApp tools are available for virtually every aspect of WebApp construction. Many of these tools enable

a Web engineer to build significant portions of the application using reusable components.

7. *Don't rely on early users to debug the WebApp—design comprehensive tests and execute them before releasing the system.* Users of a WebApp will often give it one chance. If it fails to perform, they move elsewhere—never to return. It is for this reason that "test first, then deploy" should be an overriding philosophy, even if deadlines must be stretched.

INFO

Quality Criteria/Guidelines for WebApps

WebE strives to produce high-quality WebApps. But what is "quality" in this context, and what guidelines are available for achieving it? In his paper on Web-site quality assurance, Quibeldey-Cirkel [QUI01] suggests a comprehensive set of on-line resources that address these issues:

W3C: Style Guide for Online Hypertext
www.w3.org/Provider/Style

The Sevloid Guide to Web Design
www.sev.com.au/webzone/design/guide.asp

Web Pages That Suck
www.webpagesthatsuck.com/index.html

Resources on Web Style
www.westegg.com/unmaintained/badpages

Gartner's Web Evaluation Tool
www.gartner.com/ebusiness/website-ings

IBM Corp: Web Guidelines
www-3.ibm.com/ibm/easy/eou_ext.nsf/Publish/572

World Wide Web Usability
ijhcs.open.ac.uk

Interface Hall of Shame
www.iarchitect.com/mshame.htm

Art and the Zen of Web Sites
www.tlc-systems.com/webtips.shtml

Designing for the Web: Empirical Studies
www.microsoft.com/usability/webconf.htm

Nielsen's useit.com
www.useit.com

Quality of Experience
www.qualityofexperience.org

Creating Killer Web Sites
www.killersites.com/core.html

All Things at Web
www.pantos.org/atw

SUN's New Web Design
www.sun.com/980113/sunonnet

Tognazzini, Bruce: Homepage
www.asktog.com

Webmonkey
hotwired.lycos.com/webmonkey/design/?tw=design

World's Best WebSites
www.worldbestwebsites.com

Yale University: Yale Web-Style Guide
info.med.yale.edu/caim/manual

16.5 Summary

The impact of Web-based systems and applications is arguably the single most significant event in the history of computing. As WebApps grow in importance, a disciplined WebE approach—adapted from software engineering principles, concepts, process, and methods—has begun to evolve.

WebApps are different from other categories of computer software. They are network intensive, content driven, and continuously evolving. The immediacy that drives their development, the overriding need for security in their operation, and the demand for aesthetic as well as functional content delivery are additional differentiating factors. Like other types of software, WebApps can be assessed using a variety of quality criteria that include usability, functionality, reliability, efficiency, maintainability, security, availability, scalability, and time to market.

WebE can be described in three layers—process, methods, and tools/technology. The WebE process adopts the agile development philosophy that emphasizes a "lean" engineering approach that leads to the incremental delivery of the system to be built. The generic process framework—communication, planning, modeling, construction, and deployment—is applicable to WebE. These framework activities are refined into a set of WebE tasks that are adapted to the needs of each project. A set of umbrella activities similar to those applied during software engineering work—SQA, SCM, project management—apply to all WebE projects.

References

[AOY98] Aoyama, M., "Web-Based Agile Software Development, *IEEE Computer,* November/December, 1998, pp. 56–65.

[DAR99] Dart, S., "Containing the Web Crisis Using Configuration Management," *Proc. First ICSE Workshop on Web Engineering,* ACM, Los Angeles, May 1999. (*The Proceedings of the First ICSE Workshop on Web Engineering* are published on-line at http://fistserv.macarthur.uws.edu.au/san/icse99-WebE/ICSE99-WebE-Proc/ default.htm).

[FOW01] Fowler M., and J. Highsmith, "The Agile Manifesto," *Software Development Magazine,* August 2001, http://www.sdmagazine.com/documents/s=844/ sdm0108a/0108a.htm.

[MCD01] McDonald, A., and R. Welland, *Agile Web Engineering (AWE) Process,* Department of Computer Science, University of Glascow, Technical Report TR-2001-98, 2001, downloadable from http://www.dcs.gla.ac.uk/~andrew/TR-2001-98.pdf.

[MUR99] Murugesan, S., *WebE Home Page,* http://fistserv.macarthur.uws.edu.au/ san/WebEHome, July, 1999.

[NOR99] Norton, K., "Applying Cross Functional Evolutionary Methodologies to Web Development," *Proc. First ICSE Workshop on Web Engineering,* ACM, Los Angeles, May 1999.

[POW98] Powell, T. A., *Web Site Engineering,* Prentice-Hall, 1998.

[PRE98] Pressman, R. S. (moderator), "Can Internet-Based Applications Be Engineered?" *IEEE Software,* September 1998, pp. 104–110.

[QUI01] Quibeldey-Cirkel, K., "Checklist for Web Site Quality Assurance," *Quality Week Europe,* 2001, downloadable from www.fbi.fh-darmstadt.de/~quibeldey/ Projekte/QWE2001/ Paper_Quibeldey_Cirkel.pdf.

[WEI02] Weinschenk, S., "Psychology and the Web: Designing for People," 2002, http://www.weinschenk.com/learn/facts.asp.

Problems and Points to Ponder

16.1. Are there other generic attributes that differentiate WebApps from more conventional software applications? Try to name two or three.

16.2. How do you judge the "quality" of a Web site? Make a prioritized list of 10 quality attributes that you believe are most important.

16.3. Do a bit of research and write a two to three page paper that summarizes one of the technologies noted in Section 16.2.3.

16.4. Using an actual Web site as an example, illustrate the different manifestations of WebApp "content."

16.5. Review the software engineering processes described in Chapter 3 and 4. Is/are there another process(es)—other than the agile process model—that might be applicable to Web engineering? If yes, indicate which process(es) and why.

16.6. Review the discussion of the "Manifesto for Agile Software Development" presented in Chapter 4. Which of the 12 principles would work well for a two-year project (involving dozens of people) that will build a major e-commerce system for an automobile company? Which of the 12 principles would work well for a two-month project that will build an informational site for a small real estate firm?

16.7. Make a list of "risks" that would be likely during the development of a new e-commerce application that is designed to sell mobile phones and service directly over the Web.

Further Readings and Information Sources

Hundreds of books that discuss one or more Web engineering topics have been published in recent years, although relatively few address all aspects of WebE. Sarukkai (*Foundations of Web Technology,* Kluwar Academic Publishers, 2002) presents a worthwhile compilation of the technologies that are required for WebE. Murugusan and Deshpande (*Web Engineering: Managing Diversity and Complexity of Web Development,* Springer-Verlag, 2001) have edited a collection of useful papers on WebE. Proceedings of international conferences on Web Engineering and Web Information Systems Engineering are published yearly by the IEEE Computer Society Press.

Flor (*Web Business Engineering,* Addison-Wesley, 2000) discusses business analysis and related concerns that enable the Web engineer to better understand customer needs. Bean (*Engineering Global E-Commerce Sites,* Morgan Kaufmann, 2003) presents guidelines for the development of global WebApps. Lowe and Hall (*Hypermedia and the Web: An Engineering Approach,* Wiley, 1999) and Powell [POW98] provide reasonably complete coverage. Umar (*Application Re-engineering: Building Web-Based Applications and Dealing with Legacy Systems,* Prentice-Hall, 1997) addresses one of the most difficult issues in WebE—the re-engineering of legacy systems to make them compatible with Web-based systems. IEEE Std. 2001-1999 defines basic WebE practices.

A wide variety of information sources on Web engineering is available on the Internet. An up-to-date list of World-Wide Web references that are relevant to Web Engineering can be found at the SEPA Web site:
http://www.mhhe.com/pressman.

CHAPTER

17 FORMULATION AND PLANNING FOR WEB ENGINEERING

KEY CONCEPTS

During the roaring 1990s, the Internet boom generated more hubris than any other event in the history of computers. WebApp developers at hundreds of young dot.com companies argued that a new paradigm for software development had arisen, that old rules no longer applied, that time-to-market trumped all other concerns. They laughed at the notion that careful formulation and planning should occur before construction commenced. And who could argue? Money was everywhere, 24-year olds became multimillionaires (on paper, at least)—maybe things really had changed. And then the bottom fell out.

It became painfully apparent as the twenty-first century began that a "build it and they will come" philosophy just doesn't work, that problem formulation is essential to ensure that a WebApp is really needed, and that planning is worth the effort, even when development schedules are tight. Constantine and Lockwood [CON02] note this situation when they write:

> Despite breathless declarations that the Web represents a new paradigm defined by new rules, professional developers are realizing that lessons learned in the pre-Internet days of software development still apply. Web pages are user interfaces, HTML programming is programming, and browser-deployed applications are software systems that can benefit from basic software engineering principles.

Among the most fundamental principles of software engineering is: *Understand the problem before you begin to solve it, and be sure that the solution you conceive is one that people really want.* That's the basis of formulation, the first major activity in Web engineering. Another fundamental software engineering principle is: *Plan the work before you begin performing it.* That's the philosophy that underlies project planning.

QUICK LOOK

What is it? Getting started is always difficult. On one hand, there is a tendency to procrastinate, to wait until every *t* is crossed and every *i* is dotted before work begins. On the other hand, there is a desire to jump right in, to begin building even before you really know what needs to be done. Both approaches are inappropriate, and that's why the first two Web engineering framework activities emphasize formulation and planning. Formulation assesses the underlying need for the WebApp, the overall features and functions that users desire, and the scope of the development effort. Planning addresses the things that must be defined to establish a work flow and a schedule, and to track work as the project proceeds.

Who does it? Web engineers, their managers, and nontechnical stakeholders all participate in formulation and planning.

Why is it important? It's hard to travel to a place you've never visited without directions or a map. You may arrive eventually (or you may not), but the journey is sure to be frustrating and unnecessarily long. Formulation and planning provide a map for a Web engineering team.

What are the steps? Formulation begins with customer (stakeholder) communication that addresses the reasons for the WebApp—what is the business need; which end-users are targeted; what features and functions are desired; what existing systems and databases are to be accessed; is the concept feasible; how will success be measured? Planning establishes a work plan, develops estimates to assess the feasibility of desired delivery dates, considers risk, defines a schedule, and establishes mechanisms for tracking and control.

What is the work product? Because Web engineering work often adopts an agile philosophy, work products for formulation and planning are usually lean—but they do exist, and they should be recorded in written form. Information gathered during formulation is recorded in a written document that serves as the basis for planning and analysis modeling. The project plan lays out the project schedule and presents any other information that is necessary to communicate to members of the Web engineering team and outsiders.

How do I ensure that I've done it right? Develop enough detail to establish a solid roadmap, but not so much that you become bogged down. Formulation and planning information should be reviewed with stakeholders to ensure that inconsistencies and omissions are identified early.

17.1 Formulating Web-Based Systems

Formulation of Web-based systems and applications represents a sequence of Web engineering actions that begins with the identification of business needs, moves into a description of WebApp objectives, defines major features and functions, and performs requirements gathering that leads to the development of an analysis model. Formulation allows stakeholders and the Web engineering team to establish a common set of goals and objectives for the construction of the WebApp. It also identifies the scope of the development effort and provides a means for determining a successful outcome. Analysis—a technical activity that is a continuation of formulation—identifies the data, functional, and behavioral requirements for the WebApp.

Formulation focuses on the "big picture"—on business needs and objectives and related information.

Before we consider formulation in more detail, it is reasonable to ask where formulation stops and requirements analysis begins. There is no easy answer to this question. Formulation focuses on the "big picture"—on business needs and objectives and related information. However, it is virtually impossible to maintain this level of abstraction. Stakeholders and Web engineers want to define required content, discuss specific functionality, enumerate specific features, and identify the manner in which end-users will interact with the WebApp. Is this formulation or requirements gathering? The answer is both.

17.1.1 Formulation Questions

Powell [POW98] suggests a set of questions that should be asked and answered at the beginning of the formulation step:

- What is the main motivation (business need) for the WebApp?

- What are the objectives that the WebApp must fulfill?
- Who will use the WebApp?

The answer to each of these simple questions should be stated as succinctly as possible. For example, assume that the manufacturer of *SafeHome*[1] has decided to establish an e-commerce Web site to sell its products directly to consumers. A statement describing the motivation for the WebApp might be:

> SafeHomeAssured.com will allow consumers to configure and purchase all components required to install a home/business management system.

ADVICE

As you begin formulating the problem, try to describe the WebApp you intend to build in a single sentence. If you can't, you don't understand the overall goals of the work.

It is important to note that detail is not provided in this statement. The objective here is to bound the overall intent of the WebApp and to place it within a legitimate business context.

After discussion with various stakeholders, an answer to the second question is stated:

> SafeHomeAssured.com will allow us to sell directly to consumers, thereby eliminating middleman costs and improving our profit margins. It will also allow us to increase sales by a projected 25 percent over current annual sales and will allow us to penetrate geographic regions where we currently do not have sales outlets.

Finally, the company defines the demographic for the WebApp: "Projected users of SafeHomeAssured.com are homeowners and owners of small businesses."

The answers stated above imply specific goals for the SafeHomeAssured.com Web site. In general, two categories of goals [GNA99] are identified:

- *Informational goals*—indicate an intention to provide specific content and/or information for the end-user.
- *Applicative goals*—indicate the ability to perform some task within the WebApp.

In the context of the SafeHomeAssured.com WebApp, one informational goal might be:

> The site will provide users with a detailed product specification, including technical descriptions, installation instructions, pricing information.

Examination of the answers to the questions posed above might lead to the statement of an applicative goal:

> SafeHomeAssured.com will query the user about the facility (i.e., house, office/retail space) that is to be protected and make customized recommendations about the product and configuration to be used.

Once all informational and applicative goals have been identified, a user profile is developed. The user profile captures "relevant features related to potential users

1 The *SafeHome* product has been used as an example throughout Parts 1 and 2 of this book.

including their background, knowledge, preferences and even more" [GNA99]. In the case of SafeHomeAssured.com, a user profile would identify the characteristics of a typical purchaser of security systems (this information would be supplied by the marketing department).

> **"If you're hacking [WebApps], your philosophy is probably 'ready, fire, aim.' If you're serious about making 'em work, it ought to be 'ready, aim, fire.' "**
>
> **Author unknown**

Once goals and user profiles have been developed, the formulation activity focuses on a statement of scope for the WebApp. In many cases, the goals already developed are integrated into the statement of scope. In addition, however, it is useful to indicate the degree of integration to be expected of the WebApp. That is, it is often necessary to integrate existing information systems (e.g., an existing database application) with a Web-based front end. Connectivity issues are considered at this stage.

17.1.2 Requirements Gathering for WebApps

Methods for requirements gathering have been discussed in Chapter 7. Although the requirements gathering activity for Web engineering may be abbreviated, the overall requirements gathering objectives proposed for software engineering remain unchanged. Adapted for WebApps, these objectives become:

- Identify content requirements.
- Identify functional requirements.
- Define interaction scenarios for different classes of users.

The following requirements gathering steps are conducted to achieve these objectives:

? What requirements gathering steps are used for WebApps?

1. Ask stakeholders to define user categories and develop descriptions for each category.
2. Communicate with stakeholders to define basic WebApp requirements.
3. Analyze information gathered and use information to follow-up with stakeholders.
4. Define use-cases (Chapter 8) that describe interaction scenarios for each user class.

Understanding the user's background, motivation, and objectives is critical in all software engineering work. If you build a WebApp without knowing these things, your work is at risk.

Defining user categories. It can be argued that WebApp complexity is directly proportional to the number of user categories for the system. To define a user category a set of fundamental questions must be addressed:

- *What is the user's overall objective when using the WebApp?* For example, a user of the SafeHomeAssured.com e-commerce site might be interested in gathering information about home management products. Another user might want to do a price comparison. A third user wants to purchase the

SafeHome product. Each represents a different user class or category; each will have different needs and will navigate through the WebApp differently. A fourth user already owns *SafeHome* and is looking for technical support or wants to purchase additional sensors or accessories.

- *What is the user's background and sophistication relative to the content and functionality of the WebApp?* If a user has a technical background and significant sophistication, elementary content or functionality will provide little benefit. Alternatively, a neophyte demands elementary content and functionality and would be confused if it were missing.
- *How will the user arrive at the WebApp?* Will arrival occur through a link from another Web site (likely to content or functionality within the WebApp), or will arrival occur in a more controlled manner?
- *What generic WebApp characteristics does the user like/dislike?* Different types of users may have distinct and predictable likes and dislikes. It's worth attempting to determine whether they do or not. In many situations, the answer to this question can be ascertained by asking for their favorite and least favorite WebApps.

Using the answers to these questions, the smallest reasonable set of user classes should be defined. As requirements gathering proceeds, each defined user class must be polled for input.

SAFEHOME

Requirements Gathering for WebApps

The scene: Doug Miller's office.

The players: Doug Miller, manager of the software engineering group; Vinod Raman, a member of the *SafeHome* software engineering team; and later, three marketing people.

The conversation:

Doug: Management has decided that we're going to build an e-commerce site to sell *SafeHome*.

Vinod: Whoa, Doug! We have no time to do that . . . we're swamped with product software work.

Doug: I know, I know . . . we're going to outsource the development to a company that specializes in constructing e-commerce sites. They tell us that they'll get it up and running in under one month . . . lots of reusable components.

Vinod: Hmmm. Okay . . . then why am I here?

Doug: To expedite things—they want us to take a pass at requirements gathering for the site. I'd like you to meet with the various stakeholders to gather some insight into basic requirements.

Vinod (exasperated): Doug . . . you're not hearing me . . . we're maxed out timewise and this . . . .

Doug (interrupting): Just give it one day of your time, Vinod. Meet with the marketing types and get them to spec the basic content, function, you know, the usual drill.

Vinod (resigned): Okay, I'll give 'em a call and schedule something for tomorrow, but you're not making my life any easier.

Doug (smiling): That's why you get the big bucks.

Vinod: Right.

(Vinod meets with three marketing people the following day.)

Vinod: You were telling me about the user's objectives and background.

Marketing person #1: Like I said, we want the user to be able to customize the entire *SafeHome* system, you know, pick sensors, control panels, features and functions, then get a "bill of materials" automatically generated, get pricing, and then purchase the system via the Web site.

Marketing person #2: We assume that the user is a homeowner—not technical—so we need to guide him or her through the process step by step.

Marketing person #3: I'm not technical, but I'm worried about the specialty stuff that we need to do in addition to the basic e-commerce stuff.

Vinod (addressing #3): Meaning?

Marketing person #3: The hard part is going to be guiding the user through the "customizing process" in a way that is simple and complete. The actual e-commerce stuff is pretty straightforward.

Marketing person #1: We've got to provide an 800 number for people who don't want to do the customization themselves.

Marketing person #3: I agree.

Vinod: Okay, we're going to have to talk about exactly how you'd like to do the product customization as a presales activity, but let's hold on that for a moment. I have a few other fundamental questions.

Vinod (looking at Marketing person #2): You said that you wanted to guide the users through the process. Any special approach?

Marketing person #2: I'd like to see a step-by-step process, with fill-in-the-blanks responses to basic requirements questions, pull down menus, that sort of thing. Each step is a window, and each window's data is validated before moving to the next step.

Vinod: Have you checked that out with representative users?

Marketing person #2: No, but I will.

Vinod: One more thing . . . how does a user find our site?

Marketing person #1: We're working on an ad campaign that will paste www.SafeHomeAssured.com in magazine ads, targeted direct mail, context-sensitive ads that appear in search engines, and maybe even some TV and radio spots.

Vinod: What I mean is . . . they'll always enter through the home page.

Marketing person #3: That's what we'd like.

Vinod: Okay, now we've got to get to work. Let's explore the details of how you want to customize systems on-line.

Communicating with stakeholders and end-users. Most WebApps have a broad population of end-users. Although the creation of user categories or classes makes an evaluation of user requirements more manageable, it is not advisable to use information gathered from just one or two people as the basis for formulation or analysis. More people (and more opinions/points of view) must be considered.

Communication can be accomplished using one or more of the following mechanisms [FUC02a]:

? What communication mechanisms can be used in WebE work?

- *Traditional focus groups*—a trained moderator meets with a small (usually fewer than 10 people) group of representative end-users (or internal stakeholders playing the role of end-users). The intent is to discuss the WebApp to be developed, and, out of the discussion, to better understand requirements for the system.
- *Electronic focus groups*—a moderated electronic discussion conducted with a group of representative end-users and stakeholders. The number of people who participate can be larger. Because all users can participate at the same

time, more information can be collected in a shorter time period. Since all discussion is text-based, a contemporaneous record is automatic.

- *Iterative surveys*—a series of brief surveys, addressed to representative users and requesting answers to specific questions about the WebApp are conducted via a Web site or e-mail. Responses are analyzed and used to fine-tune the next survey.
- *Exploratory surveys*—a Web-based survey that is tied to one or more WebApps that have users who are similar to the ones that will use the WebApp to be developed. Users link to the survey and respond to a series of questions (usually receiving some reward for participation).
- *Scenario-building*—selected users are asked to create informal use-cases that describe specific interactions with the WebApp.

An evaluation of content objects and operations can be delayed until analysis modeling begins. At this point it's more important to collect information, not evaluate it.

Analyzing information gathered. As information is gathered, it is categorized by user class and transaction type, and then assessed for relevance. The objective is to develop lists of content objects, operations that are applied to content objects within a specific user transaction, functions (e.g., informational, computational, logical, and help-oriented) that the WebApp provides for end-users, and other nonfunctional requirements that are noted during the communication activities.

Fuccella and Pizzolato [FUC02b] suggest a simple (low-tech) method for understanding how content and functionality should be organized. A stack of "cards" is created for content objects, operations applied to content objects, WebApp functions, and other nonfunctional requirements. The cards are shuffled into random order and then distributed to representatives from each user category. The users are asked to arrange the cards into groupings that reflect how they would like content and functionality to be organized within the WebApp. Users are then asked to describe each grouping and the reasons why it is important to them. Once each user performs this exercise, the Web engineering team looks for common groupings among different user classes and other groupings that are unique to a specific user class.

The WebE team develops a list of labels that would be used to point to information within each of the groupings derived using the card stacks. Different representative users are then given the card stacks and asked to allocate content and functionality to each of the labels. The intent here is to determine when the labels (links within the actual WebApp) properly imply access to content and functions that the users expect to find behind the label. This step is applied iteratively until consensus is achieved.

> "If you cannot describe what you are doing as a process, you don't know what you're doing."
>
> **W. E. Deming**

Use-cases have been discussed in detail in Part 2 of this book. Although many advocate the development of lengthy use-cases, even an informal narrative provides some benefit. Convince users to write use-cases.

Developing use-cases. Use-cases[2] describe how a specific user category (called an *actor*) will interact with the WebApp to accomplish a specific action. The action may be as simple as acquiring defined content, or as complex as conducting detailed user-guided analysis of selected records maintained in an on-line database. The use-case describes the interaction from the user's point of view.

Although developing and analyzing them takes time, use-cases (1) help the developer to understand how users perceive their interaction with the WebApp; (2) provide the detail necessary to create an effective analysis model; (3) help compartmentalize WebE work; and (4) provide important guidance for those who must test the WebApp.

TASK SET

Customer Communication (Analysis/Formulation)

1. *Identify business stakeholders.* Exactly who is the "customer" for the WebApp? What business people can serve as experts and representative end-users? Who will serve as an active member of the team?
2. *Formulate the business context.* How does the WebApp fit into a broader business strategy?
3. *Define key business goals and objectives for the WebApp.* How is the success of the WebApp to be measured in both qualitative and quantitative terms?
4. *Define informational and applicative goals.* What classes of content are to be provided to end-users? What functions/tasks are to be accomplished when using the WebApp?
5. *Identify the problem.* What specific problem does the WebApp solve?
6. *Gather requirements.* What user tasks will be accomplished using the WebApp? What content is to be developed? What interaction metaphor will be used? What computational functions will be provided by the WebApp? How will the WebApp be configured for network utilization? What navigation scheme is desired?

For small projects, a simple "requirements database" may be maintained (using a spreadsheet) in lieu of UML models. This allows all members of a WebE team to trace requirements to the content and function delivered and to better control the inevitable stream of changes that will occur.

17.1.3 The Bridge to Analysis Modeling

As we have noted earlier in this chapter, the activities that lead a Web engineering team from formulation to analysis modeling represent a continuum. In essence, the level of abstraction considered during the early stages of formulation is business strategic. However, as formulation proceeds, tactical details are discussed and specific WebApp requirements are addressed. Ultimately, these requirements are modeled (using use-cases and UML notation).

The concepts and principles discussed for software requirements analysis (Chapters 7 and 8) apply without revision for the Web engineering analysis activity. During analysis, scope defined during the formulation activity is elaborated to create a complete analysis model for the WebApp. Four different types of analysis are conducted during WebE: content analysis, interaction analysis, function analysis and configuration analysis. Each of these analysis tasks and the modeling techniques associated with them is discussed in Chapter 18.

---

2 Techniques for developing use-cases have been presented in detail in Chapters 7 and 8.

> "By failing to prepare, you are preparing to fail."
>
> **Benjamin Franklin**

17.2 Planning for Web Engineering Projects

Given the immediacy of WebApps, it is reasonable to ask: Do we really need to spend time planning and managing a WebApp effort? Shouldn't we just let a WebApp evolve naturally, with little or no explicit management? More than a few Web developers would opt for little or no management, but that doesn't make them right!

WebRef
Tools that assist an e-project manager can be found at **www.eproject.com.**

Figure 17.1 presents a table adapted from Kulik and Samuelsen [KUL00] that indicates how "e-projects" (their term for WebApp projects) compare to traditional software projects. Referring to the figure, traditional software projects and major e-projects have substantial similarities. Since project management is indicated for traditional projects, it would seem reasonable to argue that it would also be indicated for major e-projects. Small e-projects do have special characteristics that make them different from traditional projects. However, even in the case of small e-projects, planning must occur, risks must be considered, a schedule must be established, and controls must be defined so that confusion, frustration, and failure are avoided.

FIGURE 17.1 Differences between traditional projects and e-projects [adapted from KUL00]

	Traditional projects	Small e-Projects	Major e-Projects
Requirements gathering	Rigorous	Limited	Rigorous
Technical specifications	Robust: models, spec	Descriptive overview	Robust: UML models, spec
Project duration	Measured in months or years	Measured in days, weeks or months	Measured in months or years
Testing and QA	Focused on achieving quality targets	Focused on risk control	SQA as described in Chapter 26
Risk management	Explicit	Inherent	Explicit
Half-life of deliverables	18 months or longer	3 to 6 months or shorter	6 to 12 months or shorter
Release process	Rigorous	Expedited	Rigorous
Post-release customer feedback	Requires proactive effort	Automatically obtained from user interaction	Obtained both automatically and via solicited feedback

17.3 The Web Engineering Team

A successful Web engineering team melds a wide variety of talents who must work as a team in a high-pressure project environment. Timelines are short, changes are relentless, and the technology keeps shifting. Creating a team that jells (see Chapter 21) is no simple matter.

> "In today's net-centric and Web-enabled world, one now needs to know a lot about a lot."
>
> **Scott Tilley and Shihoug Huang**

17.3.1 The Players

The creation of a successful Web application demands a broad array of skills. Tilley and Huang [TIL99] address this issue when they state: "There are so many different aspects to [Web] application software that there is a (re)emergence of the renaissance person, one who is comfortable operating in several disciplines. . . ." While the authors are absolutely correct, "renaissance" people are in relatively short supply, and given the demands associated with major WebApp development projects, the diverse skill set required might be better distributed over a Web engineering team.

Web engineering teams can be organized in much the same way as traditional software teams (Chapter 21). However, the players and their roles are often quite different. Among the many skills that must be distributed across WebE team members are component-based software engineering, networking, architectural and navigational design, Internet standards/languages, human interface design, graphic design, content layout, and WebApp testing.

The following roles[3] should be distributed among the members of the WebE team:

? What roles do people play on a WebE team?

Content developers/providers. Because WebApps are inherently content-driven, one role on the WebE team must focus on the generation and/or collection of content. Recalling that content spans a broad array of data objects, content developers/providers may come from diverse (nonsoftware) backgrounds.

Web publisher. The diverse content generated by content developers/providers must be organized for inclusion within the WebApp. In addition, someone must act as liaison between technical staff who engineer the WebApp and nontechnical content developers/providers. This role is filled by the *Web publisher*, who must understand both content and WebApp technology.

Web engineer. A Web engineer becomes involved in a wide range of activities during the development of a WebApp including requirements elicitation, analysis

3 These roles have been adapted from Hansen and his colleagues [HAN99].

modeling, architectural, navigational and interface design, WebApp implementation, and testing. The Web engineer should also have a solid understanding of component technologies, client/server architectures, HTML/XML, and database technologies and a working knowledge of multimedia concepts, hardware/software platforms, network security, and Web-site support issues.

Business domain experts. A business domain expert should be able to answer all questions related to the business goals, objectives and requirements associated with the WebApp.

Support specialist. This role is assigned to the person (people) who have responsibility for continuing WebApp support. Because WebApps continuously evolve, the support specialist is responsible for corrections, adaptations, and enhancements to the site, including updates to content, implementation of new procedures and forms, and changes to the navigation pattern.

Administrator. Often called the "Web Master," this person has responsibility for the day-to-day operation of the WebApp including: development and implementation of policies for the operation of the WebApp, establishment of support and feedback procedures, implementation of security and access rights, measurement and analysis of Web-site traffic, coordination of change control procedures (Chapter 27), and coordination with support specialists. The administrator may also be involved in the technical activities performed by Web engineers and support specialists.

17.3.2 Building the Team

In Chapter 21, guidelines for building successful software engineering teams are discussed in some detail. But do these guidelines apply in the pressure-packed world of WebApp projects? The answer is yes.

ADVICE

These characteristics are typical of collaborative, self-organizing teams that have adopted an agile philosophy (Chapter 4). The better your team, the better the software product you produce.

In his best selling book on a computer industry long past, Tracy Kidder [KID00] tells the story of a computer company's heroic attempt to build a computer to meet the challenge of a new product built by a larger competitor.[4] The story is a metaphor for teamwork, leadership, and the grinding stress that all technologists encounter when critical projects don't go as smoothly as planned.

A summary of Kidder's book hardly does it justice, but these key points [PIC01] have particular relevance when an organization builds a Web engineering team:

A set of team guidelines should be established. These encompass what is expected of each person, how problems are to be dealt with, and what mechanisms exist for improving the effectiveness of the team as the project proceeds.

4 Kidder's *The Soul of a New Machine,* originally published in 1981, is highly recommended reading for anyone who intends to make computing a career and everyone who already has!

Strong leadership is a must. The team leader must lead by example and by contact. She must exhibit a level of enthusiasm that gets other team members to "sign up" psychologically to the work that confronts them.

Respect for individual talents is critical. Not everyone is good at everything. The best teams make use of individual strengths. The best team leaders allow individuals the freedom to run with a good idea.

Every member of the team should commit. The main protagonist in Kidder's book calls this "signing up."

It's easy to get started, but it's very hard to sustain momentum. The best teams never let an "insurmountable" problem stop them. Team members develop a "good enough" solution and proceed, hoping that the momentum of forward progress may lead to an even better solution in the long term.

17.4 Project Management Issues for Web Engineering

Once formulation has occurred and basic WebApp requirements have been identified, a business must choose from one of two Web engineering options: (1) the WebApp is *outsourced*—Web engineering is performed by a third party vendor who has the expertise, talent, and resources that may be lacking within the business, or (2) the WebApp is developed *in-house* using Web engineers that are employed by the business. A third alternative, doing some Web engineering work in-house and outsourcing other work is also an option.

> **"As Thomas Hobbs observed in the 17th century, life under mob rule is solitary, poor, nasty, brutish, and short. Life on a poorly run software project is solitary, poor, nasty, brutish, and hardly ever short enough."**
>
> **Steve McConnell**

The work to be performed remains the same regardless of whether a WebApp is outsourced, developed in-house, or distributed between an outside vendor and in-house staff. But the communication requirements, the distribution of technical activities, the degree of interaction among stakeholders and developers, and a myriad of other critically important issues do change.

Figure 17.2 illustrates the organizational difference between outsourcing and in-house development for WebApps. In-house development (Figure 17.2a) integrates (the dashed circle implies integration) all members of the Web engineering team directly. Communication occurs using normal organizational pathways. For outsourcing (Figure 17.2b), it is both impractical and inadvisable to have each in-house constituency (e.g., content developers, stakeholders, internal Web engineers) communicate directly with the outsourcing vendor without some vendor liaison to coordinate and control communication. In the sections that follow, we examine planning for outsourcing and in-house development in more detail.

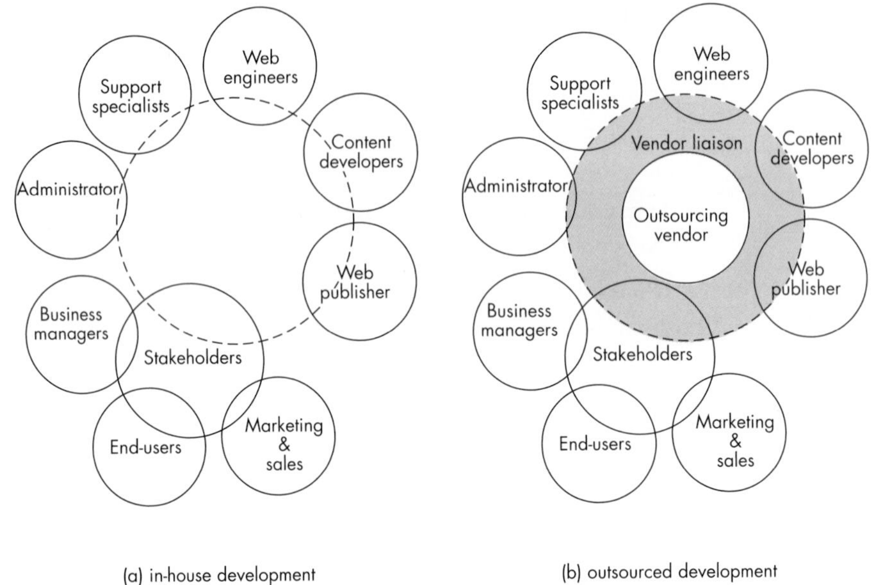

FIGURE 17.2 The organizational difference between outsourcing and in-house development

Do not assume that because you've outsourced a WebApp, your responsibilities are minimal. In fact, it's likely that more oversight and management, not less, will be required.

17.4.1 WebApp Planning—Outsourcing

A substantial percentage of WebApps are outsourced to vendors who (purportedly) specialize in the development of Web-based systems and applications.[5] In such cases, a business (the customer) asks for a fixed price quote for WebApp development from two or more vendors, evaluates competing quotes, and then selects a vendor to do the work. But what does the contracting organization look for? How is the competence of a WebApp vendor determined? How does one know whether a price quote is reasonable? What degree of planning, scheduling, and risk assessment can be expected as an organization (and its outsourcing contractor) embarks on a major WebApp development effort?

> "Many Fortune 500 enterprises have discovered the software as a service model [outsourcing] and are employing similar models internally or externally."
>
> **Nick Evans**

These questions are not always easy to answer, but a few guidelines are worth considering.

5 Although reliable industry data are difficult to find, it is safe to say that this percentage is considerably higher than the one encountered in conventional software work. Additional discussion of outsourcing may be found in Chapter 23.

Initiate the project. If outsourcing is the strategy to be chosen for WebApp development, an organization must perform a number of tasks before searching for an outsourcing vendor to do the work:

1. *Many of the analysis tasks discussed in Section 17.1.3 (and Chapter 18) should be performed internally.* The audience for the WebApp is identified; internal stakeholders who may have interest in the WebApp are listed; the overall goals for the WebApp are defined and reviewed; the information/services to be delivered by the WebApp are specified; competing Web sites are noted; and qualitative and quantitative "measures" of a successful WebApp are identified. This information should be documented in a product specification that is provided to the outsourcing vendor.
2. *A rough design for the WebApp should be developed internally.* Obviously, an expert Web developer will create a complete design, but time and cost can be saved if the general look and feel of the WebApp is identified for the outsourcing vendor (this can always be modified during preliminary stages of the project). The design should include an indication of the type and volume of content to be presented by the WebApp and the types of interactive processing (e.g., forms, order entry) to be performed. This information should be added to the product specification.

ADVICE

Some people argue that "rough design" is unnecessary. Look at it as a "first offer" that the outsourcing vendor can modify and improve upon. At least you're communicating your ideas about what the end-result should look like.

3. *A rough project schedule, including not only final delivery dates, but also milestone dates should be developed.* Milestones should be attached to deliverable versions (increments) of the WebApp as it evolves.
4. *A list of responsibilities for the internal organization and the outsourcing vendor is created.* In essence, this task addresses what information, contacts, and other resources are required of both organizations.
5. *The degree of oversight and interaction by the contracting organization with the vendor should be identified.* This should include the naming of a vendor liaison and the identification of the liaison's responsibilities and authority, the definition of quality review points as development proceeds, and the vendor's responsibilities with respect to interorganizational communication.

All of the information developed during these steps should be organized into a request for quote that is transmitted to candidate vendors.[6]

? What guidelines should we use when considering various outsourcing vendors?

Select candidate outsourcing vendors. In recent years, thousands of "Web design" companies have emerged to help businesses establish a Web presence and/or engage in e-commerce. Many have become adept at the WebE process, but many others are little more than hackers. In order to select candidate Web developers, the

6 If WebApp development work is to be conducted by an internal group, nothing changes! The project is initiated in the same manner.

contractor must perform due diligence: (1) interview past clients to determine the Web vendor's professionalism, ability to meet schedule and cost commitments, and ability to communicate effectively; (2) determine the name of the vendor's chief Web engineer(s) for successful past projects (and later, be certain that this person is contractually obligated to be involved in your project); and (3) carefully examine samples of the vendor's work that are similar in look and feel (and business area) to the WebApp that is to be contracted. Even before a request for quote is offered, a face-to-face meeting may provide substantial insight into the "fit" between contractor and vendor.

> "You pay peanuts, you get monkeys."
>
> **George Peppard playing Col. John "Hannibal" Smith on *The A-Team* (a 1980s TV show)**

Assess the validity of price quotes and the reliability of estimates. Because relatively little historical data exist and the scope of WebApps is notoriously fluid, estimation is inherently risky. For this reason, some vendors will embed substantial safety margins into the cost quoted for a project. This is both understandable and appropriate. The question is *not* have we gotten the best bang for our buck. Rather, the questions should be:

- Does the quoted cost of the WebApp provide a direct or indirect return-on-investment that justifies the project?
- Does the vendor that has provided the quote exhibit the professionalism and experience we require?

If the answers to these questions are yes, the price quote is fair.

Understand the degree of project management you can expect/perform. The formality associated with project management tasks (performed by both the vendor and the contracting organization) is directly proportional to the size, cost, and complexity of the WebApp. For large, complex projects, a detailed project schedule that defines work tasks, SQA checkpoints, engineering work products, customer review points, and major milestones should be developed. The vendor and contractor should assess risk jointly and develop plans for mitigating, monitoring, and managing those risks that are deemed important. Mechanisms for quality assurance and change control should be explicitly defined in writing. Methods for effective communication between the contractor and the vendor should be established.

Assess the development schedule. Because WebApp development schedules span a relatively short period of time (often less than one or two months per delivered increment), the development schedule should have a fine granularity. That is, work tasks and minor milestones should be scheduled on a daily timeline. This fine granularity allows both the contracting organization and the vendor to recognize schedule slippage before it threatens the final completion date.

To manage scope, the work to be performed within an increment is frozen. Changes are delayed until the next WebApp increment.

Manage scope. Because it is highly likely that scope will change as a WebApp project moves forward, the WebE process model is adaptable and incremental. This allows the vendor's development team to "freeze" scope for one increment so that an operational WebApp release can be created. The next increment may address scope changes suggested by a review of the preceding increment, but once the second increment commences, scope is again "frozen" temporarily. This approach enables the WebApp team to work without having to accommodate a continual stream of changes, but still recognizes the continuous evolution characteristic of most WebApps.

The guidelines suggested above are not intended to be a foolproof cookbook for the production of low-cost, on-time WebApps. However, they will help both the contracting organization and the vendor initiate work smoothly with a minimum of misunderstandings.

SAFEHOME

Outsourcing Preliminaries

The scene: Doug Miller's office.

The players: Doug Miller (manager of the *SafeHome* software engineering team) and Sharon Woods—an employee of e-CommerceSystems, the outsourcing vendor for the *SafeHome* e-commerce Web site and manager of the Web engineering team that will be doing the work.

The conversation:

Doug: Good to finally meet with you, Sharon. We've certainly got some work to do over the next month or so.

Sharon (smiling): We do, but you guys seem to have your act together. Vinod has already given us a draft specification for the site and has also defined most of the important content objects and site functionality.

Doug: Good. What else do you need?

Sharon: The e-commerce functionality is easy. The thing that worries me is the front end . . . the work required to have the user customize the product pre-purchase.

Doug: Vinod gave you the basic procedure, didn't he?

Sharon: He did, but I'd like to validate it with some real users. We'll also need to contact your content developers to get proper descriptions for each sensor, pictures, pricing, interface/interconnection info, that sort of thing.

Doug: Did Vinod have time to do a rough storyboard of the customization process for you?

Sharon: He's working on it as we speak. Said he had to put out a fire on the product side. He knows it's critical . . . said he'd e-mail it to me tomorrow morning.

Doug: Okay . . . look, I'd like to stay in the loop on this project. Can we establish some ground rules for oversight on our end. I don't want to get in your way, but. . . .

Sharon: Not a problem, we like to keep our clients involved.

Doug: I'll serve as liaison for this project. All communication will come through me or someone like Vinod that I appoint. Since we're on a tight schedule, I'd like to establish a schedule that has one-day granularity and talk or e-mail with you everyday about accomplishments, problems, etc. I know it's a lot, but that's what I think is appropriate.

Sharon: That's okay.

Doug (picking up a few pages of paper from his desktop and handing them to Sharon): I've written up a rough schedule with milestone dates . . . what do you think?

Sharon (after studying the schedule): Hmmm. I'm not sure this'll work for us. Let me work up an alternative and e-mail it to you later today.

Doug: Sure.

17.4.2 WebApp Planning—In-House Web Engineering

As WebApps become more pervasive and business strategic, many companies have opted to control development in-house. Not surprisingly, in-house WebE is managed somewhat differently that an outsourcing effort.

> "What do you do when you need to have a Web site done yesterday?"
>
> **James Lewin**

The management of small and moderately-sized (i.e., less than 3–5 months in duration) WebE projects requires an agile approach that deemphasizes project management but does *not* eliminate the need to plan. Basic project management principles (Chapter 21) still apply, but the overall approach is leaner and less formal. However, as the size of the WebApp project grows, Web engineering project management becomes more and more like software engineering project management (Part 4 of this book). The steps that follow are recommended for small and moderately-sized WebE projects:

It's important to recognize that the steps discussed in this section can be performed quickly. In no case, should WebE planning for projects of this size take more than 5 percent of overall project effort.

Understand scope, the dimensions of change, and project constraints. No project—regardless of how tight the time constraints—can begin until the project team understands what must be built. Requirements gathering and customer communication are essential precursors to effective WebApp planning.

Define an incremental project strategy. We have already noted that WebApps evolve over time. If evolution is uncontrolled and chaotic, the likelihood of a successful outcome is small. However, if the team establishes a project strategy that defines WebApp increments (releases) that provide useful content and functionality for end-users, engineering effort can be more effectively focused.

Perform risk analysis. A detailed discussion of risk analysis for traditional software engineering projects is presented in Chapter 25.[7] All risk management tasks are performed for WebE projects, but the approach to them is abbreviated.

Schedule risk and technology risk dominate the concern of most Web engineering teams. Among the many risk-related questions that the team must ask and answer are: Can planned WebApp increments be delivered within the timeframe defined? Will these increments provide on-going value for end-users while additional increments are being engineered? How will requests for change impact delivery schedules? Does the team understand the required Web engineering methods, technologies, and tools? Is the available technology appropriate for the job? Will likely changes require the introduction of new technology?

---

7 Those readers who are unfamiliar with basic risk management terminology and practices are urged to examine Chapter 25 at this time.

Develop a quick estimate. The focus of estimation for most Web engineering projects is on macroscopic, rather than microscopic, issues. The WebE team assesses whether planned WebApp increments can be developed with available resources according to the defined schedule constraints. This is accomplished by considering each increment's content and function as a whole. "Microscopic" functional or work breakdowns of the increment, followed by the computation of multi-data point estimates (see Chapter 23) are normally not conducted.

Select a task set (process description). Using a process framework (Chapter 16), select a set of Web engineering tasks that is appropriate for the characteristics of the problem, the product, the project, and the people on the Web engineering team. Recognize that the task set may be adapted to fit each development increment.

Establish a schedule. A WebE project schedule has relatively fine granularity for tasks to be performed in the short-term and then much more coarse granularity during later time periods (when additional increments are to be delivered). That is, Web engineering tasks are distributed along the project timeline for the increment to be developed. Task distribution for subsequent WebApp increments is delayed until delivery of the scheduled increment.

Regardless of project size, it's important to establish project milestones so that progress can be assessed.

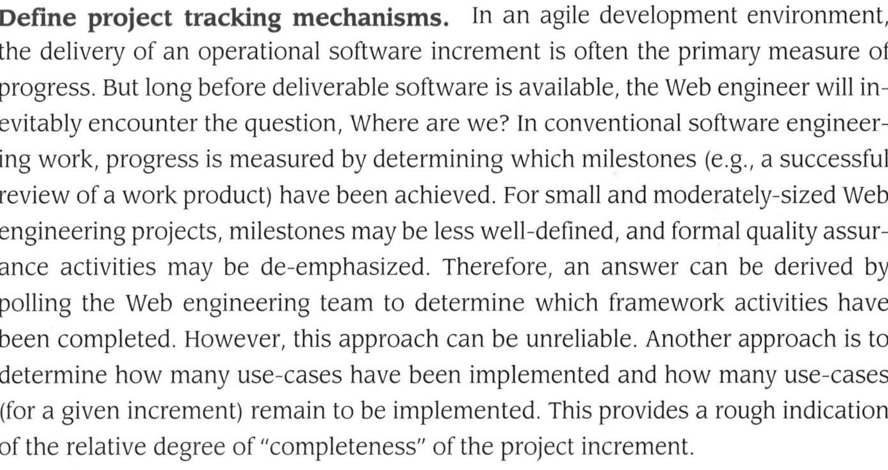

Define project tracking mechanisms. In an agile development environment, the delivery of an operational software increment is often the primary measure of progress. But long before deliverable software is available, the Web engineer will inevitably encounter the question, Where are we? In conventional software engineering work, progress is measured by determining which milestones (e.g., a successful review of a work product) have been achieved. For small and moderately-sized Web engineering projects, milestones may be less well-defined, and formal quality assurance activities may be de-emphasized. Therefore, an answer can be derived by polling the Web engineering team to determine which framework activities have been completed. However, this approach can be unreliable. Another approach is to determine how many use-cases have been implemented and how many use-cases (for a given increment) remain to be implemented. This provides a rough indication of the relative degree of "completeness" of the project increment.

> "Progress is made by correcting the mistakes resulting from the making of progress."
>
> **Claude Gibb**

Establish a change management approach. Change management is facilitated by the incremental development strategy that has been recommended for WebApps. Because the development time for an increment is short, it is often possible to delay the introduction of a change until the next increment, thereby reducing the delaying effects associated with changes that must be implemented "on the fly." A discussion of configuration and content management for WebApps is presented in Chapter 27.

SOFTWARE TOOLS

WebE Project Management

Objective: To assist a Web engineering team in planning, managing, controlling, and tracking Web engineering projects.

Mechanics: Project management tools enable a WebE team to establish a set of work tasks, assign effort and specific responsibility for each task, establish task dependencies, define a schedule, and track and control project activities. Many tools in this category are Web-based.

Representative Tools[8]

Business Engine, developed by Business Engine (www.businessengine.com), is a suite of Web-based tools that provide full project management facilities for WebE and conventional software projects.

Iteamwork, developed by iTeamwork.com (www.iteamwork.com), "is a free, on-line, Web-based team project management application that you use with your web browser."

OurProject, developed by Our Project (www.ourproject.com), is a suite of project management tools that are applicable to WebE and conventional software projects.

Proj-Net, developed by Rational Concepts, Inc. (www.rationalconcepts.com), implements a "virtual project office (VPO) for collaboration and communication."

StartWright (www.startwright.com/project1.htm) has developed one of the Web's most comprehensive resources for both WebE and conventional software project management tools and information.

It should be noted that many conventional project management tools (Part 4 of this book) can also be used effectively for WebE projects.

17.5 METRICS FOR WEB ENGINEERING AND WEBAPPS

Web engineers develop complex systems, and like other technologists who perform this task, they should use metrics to improve the Web engineering process and product. In Chapter 15, we discussed the strategic and tactical uses for software metrics in a software engineering context. These uses also apply to Web engineering.

To summarize, software metrics provide a basis for improving the software process, increasing the accuracy of project estimates, enhancing project tracking, and improving software quality. Web engineering metrics could, if properly characterized, achieve all these benefits and also improve usability, WebApp performance, and user satisfaction.

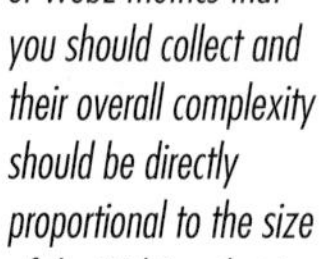

In general, the number of WebE metrics that you should collect and their overall complexity should be directly proportional to the size of the WebApp that is to be built.

In the context of Web engineering, metrics have three primary goals: (1) to provide an indication of the quality of the WebApp from a technical point of view, (2) to provide a basis for effort estimation, and (3) to provide an indication of the success of the WebApp from a business point of view.

In this section, we summarize a set of common effort and complexity metrics[9] for WebApps. These may be used to develop a historical database for effort estimation. In addition, complexity metrics may ultimately lead to an ability to quantitatively assess one or more of the technical attributes of WebApps discussed in Chapter 16.

---

8 Tools noted here do not represent an endorsement, but rather a sampling of tools in this category. In most cases, tool names are trademarked by their respective developers.

9 It is important to note that WebE metrics are still in their infancy.

17.5.1 Metrics for Web Engineering Effort

Web engineers expend human effort performing a variety of work tasks as a WebApp evolves. Mendes and her colleagues [MEN01] suggest a number of possible effort measures for WebApps. Some or all of these could be recorded by a Web engineering team and later used to build a historical database for estimation (Chapter 23).

Application Authoring and Design Tasks

Suggested measure	Description
structuring effort	time to structure WebApp and/or derive architecture
interlinking effort	time to interlink pages to build the WebApp's structure
interface planning	time taken to plan WebApp's interface
interface building	time taken to implement WebApp's interface
link-testing effort	time taken to test all links in WebApp
media-testing effort	time taken to test all media in WebApp
total effort	structuring effort + interlinking effort + interface planning + interface building + link-testing effort + media-testing effort

Page Authoring

Suggested measure	Description
text effort	time taken to author or reuse text in page
page-linking effort	time taken to author links in page
page-structuring effort	time taken to structure page
total page effort	text effort + page-linking effort + page-structuring effort

Media Authoring

Suggested measure	Description
media effort	time taken to author or reuse media files
media-digitizing effort	time taken to digitize media
total media effort	media effort + media-digitizing effort

Program Authoring

Suggested measure	Description
programming effort	time taken to author HTML, Java, or related language implementations
reuse effort	time to reuse/modify existing programming

17.5.2 Metrics for Assessing Business Value

WebRef
An excellent reference on many subjects related to Internet business is **www.internet.com.**

It's interesting to note that business people have considerably outpaced Web engineers in developing, collecting, and using metrics for WebApps (e.g. [STE02], [NOB01]). By understanding the demographics of end-users and their usage patterns, a company or organization can develop immediate input for more meaningful WebApp content, more effective sales and marketing efforts, and better profitability for the business.

The mechanisms required to collect business value data are often implemented by the Web engineering team, but evaluation of the data and actions that result are performed by other constituencies. For example, assume that the number of page views can be determined for each unique visitor. Based on metrics collected, visitors arriving from search engine *X* average nine page views while visitors from portal *Y* have only two page views. These averages can be used by the marketing department to allocate banner advertising budgets (advertising at search engine *X* provides greater exposure, based on metrics collected, than advertising at portal *Y*).

A complete discussion of the collection and use of business value metrics (including the on-going debate about personal privacy) is beyond the scope of this book. The interested reader should examine [INA02], [EIS02], [PAT02] or [RIG01].

SOFTWARE TOOLS

Web Metrics

Objective: To assess the manner in which a WebApp is being used, the categories of users, and the usability of the WebApp.

Mechanics: The vast majority of Web metrics tools capture usage information once the WebApp goes on-line. These tools provide a broad array of data that can be used to assess which elements of the WebApp are most used, how they are used, and who uses them.

Representative Tools[10]

Clicktracks, developed by clicktracks.com (www.clicktracks.com), is a log file analysis tool that displays Web site visitor behavior directly on pages of the Web site.

Marketforce, developed by Coremetrics (www.Coremetrics.com), is representative of many tools that collect data that can be used to assess the success of e-commerce WebApps.

Web Metrics Testbed, developed by NIST (zing.ncsl.nist.gov/WebTools/), is a suite of Web-based tools that assess the usability of a WebApp.

WebTrends, developed by netIQ (www.NetIQ.com), collects a broad range of usage data for WebApps of all types.

17.6 "Worst Practices" for WebApp Projects

Sometimes the best way to learn how to do something correctly is to examine how not to do it! Over the past decade, more than a few WebApps have failed because (1) a disregard for project and change management principles (however informal) resulted

10 Tools noted here do not represent an endorsement, but rather a sampling of tools in this category. In most cases, tool names are trademarked by their respective developers.

in a Web engineering team that "bounced off the walls"; (2) an ad hoc approach to WebApp development failed to yield a workable system; (3) a cavalier approach to requirements gathering and analysis failed to yield a system that met user needs; (4) an incompetent approach to design failed to yield development of a WebApp that was usable, functional, extensible (maintainable), and testable; (5) an unfocused approach to testing failed to yield a system that worked prior to its introduction.

With these realities in mind, it might be worthwhile to consider a set of Web engineering "worst practices," adapted from an article by Tom Bragg [BRA00]. If your e-project exhibits any of them, immediate remedial action is necessary.

Worst practice #1: *We have a great idea, so let's begin building the WebApp—now.* Don't bother considering whether the WebApp is business justified, whether users will really want to use it, whether you understand the business requirements. Time is short, we have to start.

Reality: Take a few hours/days and make a business case for the WebApp. Be sure that the idea is endorsed by those who will fund it and those who will use it.

Worst practice #2: *Stuff will change constantly, so there's no point in trying to understand WebApp requirements.* Never write anything down (wastes time). Rely solely on word of mouth.

Reality: It is true that WebApp requirements evolve as Web engineering activities proceed. It's also fast and simple to convey information verbally. However, a cavalier approach to requirements gathering and analysis is a catalyst for even more (unnecessary) change.

Worst practice #3: *Developers whose dominant experience has been in traditional software development can develop WebApps immediately. No new training is required.* After all, software is software, isn't it?

Reality: WebApps are different. A broad array of methods, technologies, and tools must be expertly applied. Training and experience with them is essential.[11]

Worst practice #4: *Be bureaucratic.* Insist on leaden process models, time sheets, lots of unnecessary "progress" meetings, and project leaders who have never managed a WebApp project.

Reality: Encourage an agile process that emphasizes the competence and creativity of an experienced Web engineering team. Then get out of the way and let them do the work. If project-related data must be collected (for legal reasons or for the computation of metrics), data entry/collection should be as simple and unobtrusive as possible.

Worst practice #5: *Testing? Why bother?* We'll give it to a few end-users and let them tell us what works and what doesn't.

---

11 Many large WebE projects require integration with conventional applications and databases. In such instances, individuals with only conventional experience can and should be involved.

Reality: Over time, end-users do perform thorough "tests," but they are so upset by unreliability and poor performance that they leave (never to return) long before problems are corrected.

In the chapters that follow, we consider Web engineering methods that will help you avoid these mistakes.

17.7 Summary

Formulation is a customer communication activity that defines the problem that a WebApp is to solve. Business need, project goals and objectives, end-user categories, major functions and features, and the degree of interoperability with other applications are all identified. As more detailed and technical information is acquired, formulation becomes requirements analysis.

The WebE team is composed of a group of technical and nontechnical members who are organized in a manner that gives them considerable autonomy and flexibility. Project management is required during Web engineering, but project management tasks are abbreviated and considerably less formal than those applied for conventional software engineering projects. Many WebApp projects are outsourced, but there is a growing trend toward in-house WebApp development. Project management for each approach differs in both strategy and tactics.

Web engineering metrics are in their infancy but have the potential to provide an indication of the WebApp quality, provide a basis for effort estimation, and provide an indication of the success of the WebApp from a business point of view.

References

[BRA00] Bragg, T., "Worst Practices for e-Business Projects: We Have Met the Enemy and He Is Us!" *Cutter IT Journal,* vol. 13, no. 4, April 2000, pp. 35–39.

[CON02] Constantine, L., and L. Lockwood, "User-Centered Engineering for Web Applications," *IEEE Software,* vol. 19, no. 2, March/April 2002, pp. 42–50.

[EIS02] Eisenberg, B., "How to Interpret Web Metrics," *ClickZ Today,* March 2002, available at http://www.clickz.com/sales/traffic/article.php/992351.

[FUC02a] Fuccella, J., J. Pizzolato, and J. Franks, "Finding Out What Users Want from your Web Site," IBM developerWorks, 2002, http://www-106.ibm.com/developerworks/library/moderator-guide/requirements.html.

[FUC02b] Fuccella, J., and J. Pizzolato, "Giving People What They Want: How to Involve Users in Site Design," IBM developerWorks, 2002, http://www-106.ibm.com/developerworks/library/design-by-feedback/expectations.html.

[GNA99] Gnado, C., and F. Larcher, "A User-Centered Methodology for Complex and Customizable Web Applications Engineering," *Proc. First ICSE Workshop in Web Engineering,* ACM, Los Angeles, May 1999.

[HAN99] Hansen, S., Y. Deshpande, and S. Murugesan, "A Skills Hierarchy for Web Information System Development," *Proc. First ICSE Workshop on Web Engineering,* ACM, Los Angeles, May 1999.

[INA02] Inan, H., and M. Kean, *Measuring the Success of Your Web Site,* Longman Publishing, 2002.

[KID00] Kidder, T., *The Soul of a New Machine,* Back Bay Books (reprint edition), 2000.

[KUL00] Kulik, P., and R. Samuelsen, "e-Project Management for a New e-Reality," Project Management Institute, December, 2000, http://www.seeprojects.com/e-Projects/ e-projects.html.

[LOW98] Lowe, D., and W. Hall, eds., *Hypertext and the Web—An Engineering Approach,* Wiley, 1998.

[MEN01] Mendes, E., N. Mosley, and S. Counsell, "Estimating Design and Authoring Effort," *IEEE Multimedia,* January–March 2001, pp. 50–57.

[NOB01] Nobles, R., and K. Grady, *Web Site Analysis and Reporting,* Premier Press, 2001.

[PAT02] Patton, S., "Web Metrics That Matter," *CIO,* November 15, 2002. available at http://www.computerworld.com/developmenttopics/websitemgmt/story/0,10801,76002,00.html.

[PIC01] Pickering, C., "Building an Effective E-Project Team," *E-Project Management Advisory Service,* Cutter Consortium, vol. 2, no. 1, 2001, http://www.cutter.com/ consortium.

[POW98] Powell, T.A., *Web Site Engineering,* Prentice-Hall, 1998.

[RIG01] Riggins, F., and S. Mitra, "A Framework for Developing E-Business Metrics through Functionality Interaction, January 2001, download from http:// digitalenterprise.org/metrics/metrics.html.

[STE02] Sterne, J., *Web Metrics: Proven Methods for Measuring Web Site Success,* Wiley, 2002.

[TIL99] Tilley, S., and S. Huang, "On the Emergence of the Renaissance Software Engineer," *Proc. 1st ICSE Workshop on Web Engineering,* ACM, Los Angeles, May 1999.

Problems and Points to Ponder

17.1. How does formulation differ from requirements gathering? How does formulation differ from requirements analysis and analysis modeling?

17.2. Three fundamental formulation questions are posed in Section 17.1.1. Are there any other questions that you think might be asked at this point? If so what are they, and why would you ask them?

17.3. In the context of requirements gathering, what is a "user category"? Give examples of three user categories for an on-line book seller.

17.4. Considering the *SafeHome* e-commerce site discussed in this chapter, what user communication mechanism would you use to elicit system requirements, and why?

17.5. In your own words, discuss how information gathered during customer communication is "analyzed" and what the output from this activity is.

17.6. What benefits can be derived from requiring the development of use-cases as part of the requirements gathering activity?

17.7. Review the table presented in Figure 17.1. Add three more rows that will further distinguish traditional projects from e-projects.

17.8. Describe the role of the Web publisher in your own words.

17.9. Review the characteristics of agile development teams discussed in Chapter 4. Do you feel that an agile team organization is appropriate for WebE? Would you make any changes to the organization for WebApp development?

17.10. Describe five risks associated with outsourcing WebApp development.

17.11. Describe five risks associated with in-house WebApp development.

17.12. Consider the metrics for Web engineering effort discussed in Section 17.5.1. Try to develop five or more additional metrics for one or more categories.

17.13. The ease of navigation through a Web site is an important indicator of WebApp quality. Develop two or three metrics that could be used to indicate the ease of navigation.

17.14. Using one of the references noted in Section 17.5.2, discuss how business value metrics can be used to assist in pragmatic business decision making.

Further Readings and Information Sources

Methods for WebApp formulation and requirements gathering can be adapted from discussions of similar methods for conventional application software. Further readings recommended in Chapters 7 and 8 contain much useful information for the Web engineer.

Flor (*Web Business Engineering,* Addison-Wesley, 2000) discusses business analysis and related concerns that enable the Web engineer to better understand customer needs. WebApp usability is a concept that underlies much of the information defined as part of formulation and requirements gathering. Krug and Black (*Don't Make Me Think: A Common Sense Approach to Web Usability,* Que Publishing, 2000) contains many guidelines and examples that can help the Web engineer translate user requirements into an effective WebApp.

Project management for WebE projects draws from many of the same principles and concepts that are applied for conventional software projects. However, agility is a watchword. Wallace (*Extreme Programming for Web Projects,* Addison-Wesley, 2003) describes how agile development can be used for WebE and contains useful discussions of project management issues. Shelford and Remillard (*Real Web Project Management,* Addison-Wesley, 2003), O'Connell (*How to Run Successful Projects in Web Time,* Artech House, 2000), Freidlein (*Web Project Management,* Morgan Kaufman, 2000), and Gilbert (*90 Days to Launch: Internet Projects on Time and on Budget,* Wiley, 2000) discuss a wide array of project management issues for WebE. Whitehead (*Leading a Software Development Team,* Addison-Wesley, 2001) presents many useful guidelines that can be adapted for Web engineering teams.

Techniques for using Web metrics in business decision making are presented in books by Sterne [STE02], Inan [INA02], Nobles [NOB01] and Menasce and Almeida (*Capacity Planning for Web Services: Metrics, Models and Methods,* Prentice-Hall, 2001). "Worst practices" are considered by Ferry and Ferry (*77 Sure-Fire Ways to Kill a Software Project,* iUniverse.com, 2000).

A wide variety of information sources on formulation and planning for Web engineering is available on the Internet. An up-to-date list of World Wide Web references that are relevant to formulation and planning can be found at the SEPA Web site:
http://www.mhhe.com/pressman.

CHAPTER

18

ANALYSIS MODELING FOR WEB APPLICATIONS

KEY CONCEPTS

At first glance, there is an apparent contradiction when we consider analysis modeling within the context of Web engineering. After all, we have noted (Chapter 16) that WebApps have an immediacy and a volatility that mitigate against detailed modeling at either the analysis or the design level. And if we do any modeling at all, the agile philosophy (an appropriate process model for many Web engineering projects) suggests that analysis modeling is downplayed in favor of limited design modeling. Franklin [FRA02] notes this situation when he writes:

> Web sites are typically complex and highly dynamic. They require short development phases in order to get the product up and running quickly. Frequently, developers go straight to the coding phase without really understanding what they are trying to build or how they want to build it. Server-side coding is often done *ad hoc,* database tables are added as needed, and the architecture evolves in a sometimes unintentional manner. But some modeling and disciplined software engineering can make the software development process much smoother and ensure that the Web system is more maintainable in the future.

Is it possible to have it both ways? Can we do "some modeling and disciplined software engineering" and still work effectively in a world where immediacy and volatility reign? The answer is a qualified yes.

QUICK LOOK

What is it? The analysis of a potential Web application focuses on three important questions: (1) what information or content is to be presented or manipulated; (2) what functions are to be performed for the end-user; and (3) what behaviors will the WebApp exhibit as it presents content and performs functions? The answers to these questions are represented as part of an analysis model that encompasses a variety of UML representations.

Who does it? Web engineers, nontechnical content developers, and stakeholders participate in the creation of the analysis model.

Why is it important? Throughout this book we have emphasized the need to understand the problem before you begin to solve it. Analysis modeling is important not because it enables a Web engineering team to develop a concrete model of WebApp requirements (things change too frequently for this to be a realistic expectation), but rather, analysis modeling enables a Web engineer to define fundamental aspects of the problem—things that are unlikely to change (in the near term). When fundamental content, function, and behavior are understood, design and construction are facilitated.

What are the steps? Analysis modeling focuses on four fundamental aspects of the problem—content, interaction, function, and configuration. Content analysis identifies content classes and collaborations. Interaction analysis describes basic elements of user interaction, navigation, and the system behaviors that occur as a consequence. Function analysis defines the WebApp functions that are performed for the user and the sequence of processing that occurs as a consequence. Configuration analysis identifies the operational environment(s) in which the WebApp resides.

What is the work product? The analysis model is comprised of a set of UML diagrams and text that describe content, interaction, function, and configuration.

How do I ensure that I've done it right? Analysis modeling work products must be reviewed for correctness, completeness, and consistency.

A Web engineering team should embrace analysis modeling when most or all of the following conditions are met:

- The WebApp to be built is large and/or complex.
- The number of stakeholders is large.
- The number of Web engineers and other contributors is large.
- The goals and objectives (determined during formulation) for the WebApp will effect the business' bottom line.
- The success of the WebApp will have a strong bearing on the success of the business.

If these conditions are not present, it is possible to de-emphasize analysis modeling, using information obtained during formulation and requirements gathering (Chapter 17) as the basis for creating a design model for the WebApp. In such circumstances, limited analysis modeling may occur, but it will be rolled into design.

18.1 Requirements Analysis for WebApps

Requirements analysis for WebApps encompasses three major tasks: formulation, requirements gathering,[1] and analysis modeling. During formulation, the basic motivation (goals) and objectives for the WebApp are identified, and the categories of users are defined. As requirements gathering begins, communication between the Web engineering team and WebApp stakeholders (e.g., customers, end-users) intensifies. Content and functional requirements are listed and interaction scenarios (use-cases) written from the end-user's point-of-view are developed. The intent is to establish a basic understanding of why the WebApp is to be built, who will use it, and what problem(s) it will solve for its users.

> "The engineering principles of planning before designing and designing before building have withstood every prior technology transition; they'll survive this transition as well."
>
> **Watts Humphrey**

1 Formulation and requirements gathering are discussed in detail in Chapter 17.

18.1.1 The User Hierarchy

The categories of end-users who will interact with the WebApp are identified as part of the formulation and requirements gathering tasks. In most cases, user categories are relatively limited and a UML representation of them is unnecessary. However, when the number of user categories grows, it is sometimes advisable to develop a *user hierarchy* as shown in Figure 18.1. The figure depicts users for the SafeHome-Assured.com e-commerce site discussed in Chapters 16 and 17.

It's a good idea to build a user hierarchy. It provides you with a snapshot of the user population and a cross-check to help ensure that the needs of every user have been addressed.

The user categories (often called *actors*) shown in Figure 18.1 provide an indication of the functionality to be provided by the WebApp and indicate a need for use-cases to be developed for each end-user (actor) noted in the hierarchy. Referring to the figure, the **SafeHomeAssured.com user** at the top of the hierarchy represents the most general user class (category) and is refined in levels below. A **guest** is a user who visits the site but does not register. Such users are often searching for general information, comparison shopping, or otherwise interested in "free" content or functionality. A **registered user** takes the time to provide contact information (along with other demographic data requested by forms input). Subcategories for **registered user** include:

- **new customer**—a registered user who wants to customize and then purchase *SafeHome* components (and hence, must interact with the WebApp e-commerce functionality);
- **existing customer**—a user who already owns *SafeHome* components and is using the WebApp to (1) purchase additional components; (2) to acquire tech support information; or (3) contact customer support.

FIGURE 18.1

User hierarchy for SafeHome-Assured.com

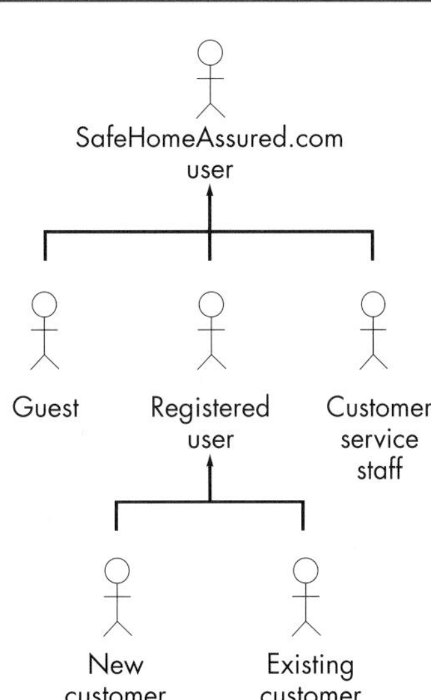

Members of **customer service staff** are special users who can also interact with SafeHomeAssured.com content and functionality as they assist customers who have contacted *SafeHome* customer support.

18.1.2 Developing Use-Cases

Franklin [FRA01] refers to use-cases as "bundles of functionality." This description captures the essence of this important analysis modeling technique.[2] Use-cases are developed for each user category described in the user hierarchy. In the context of Web engineering, the use-case itself is relatively informal—a narrative paragraph that describes a specific interaction between a user and the WebApp.[3]

Figure 18.2 represents a UML use-case diagram for the **new customer** user category (Figure 18.1). Each oval in the diagram represents a use-case that describes a specific interaction between **new customer** and the WebApp. For example, the first interaction is described by the *log-in to SafeHomeAssured.com* use-case. No more than a single paragraph would be required to describe this common interaction.

Major WebApp functionality (and the use-cases that are relevant for it) are noted inside the dashed boxes in Figure 18.2. These are referred to a "packages" in

FIGURE 18.2

Use-case diagram for new-customer

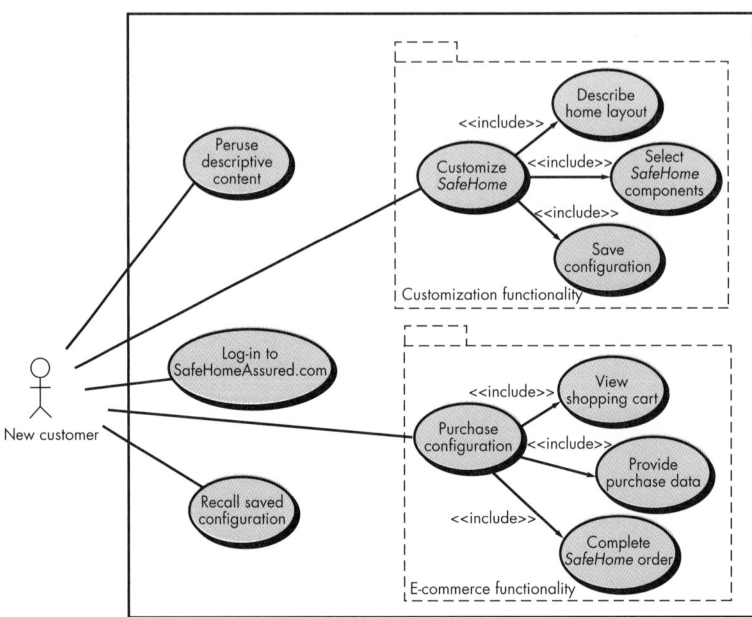

2 Techniques for developing use-cases have been discussed in detail earlier in this book (see Chapters 7 and 8).

3 Although it is possible to develop more formal use-case descriptions, the need for WebE agility often precludes this approach.

UML and represent specific functionality. Two packages are noted: *customization* and *e-commerce*.

As an example, we consider the *customization* package of use-cases. A new customer must describe the home environment into which *SafeHome* will be installed. To accomplish this, the use-cases *describe home layout, select SafeHome hardware,* and *save configuration* are initiated by **new customer.** Consider these preliminary use-cases written from the point of view of a **new customer:**

As the size of a WebApp grows and analysis modeling becomes more rigorous, the preliminary use-cases presented here would have to be expanded to conform more closely to the format suggested in Section 8.5 of Chapter 8.

Use-case: *describe home layout*

The WebApp will ask some general questions about the environment in which I plan to install *SafeHome*—the number of rooms, size of rooms, type of room, the number of floors, the number of exterior doors and windows. The WebApp will enable me to build a rough floor plan by putting together outline shapes of the rooms for each floor. I'll be able to give the floor plan a name and save it for future reference (see use-case: *save configuration*).

Use-case: *select SafeHome components*

The WebApp will then recommend product components (e.g., control panels, sensors, cameras) and other features (e.g., PC-based functionality implemented in software) for each room and exterior entrance. If I request alternatives, the WebApp will provide them, if they exist. I will be able to get descriptive and pricing information for each product component. The WebApp will create and display a bill-of-materials as I select various components. I'll be able to give the bill-of-materials a name and save it for future reference (see use-case: *save configuration*).

Use-case: *save configuration*

The WebApp will allow me to save customization data so that I can return to it later. I can save the house layout and the *SafeHome* bill-of materials I choose for the layout. To accomplish this, I provide a unique identifier for the house layout and the bill-of-materials. I also provide a special configuration password that must be validated before I can gain access to the saved information.

Although considerably more detail could be provided for each of these use-cases, the informal text description provides useful insight. Similar descriptions would be developed for each oval in Figure 18.2.

SAFEHOME

Refining Use-Cases for WebApps

The scene: Doug Miller's office.

The players: Doug Miller (manager of the *SafeHome* software engineering group), Sharon Woods, manager of the outsourcing vendor's Web engineering team for the *SafeHome* e-commerce Web site, and Sam Chen, manager of the SafeHomeAssured.com customer support organization.

The conversation:

Doug: Glad to hear things are progressing well, Sharon. Analysis modeling is almost complete?

Sharon (smiling): We're making progress. The only set of use-cases left to develop from the user hierarchy [Figure 18.1] is the *customer service staff* category.

Doug (looking at Sam): And you have those now, Sam?

Sam: I do. I've e-mailed them to you, Sharon, and cc'd you, Doug. Here's the hardcopy version. (He hands sheets of paper to Doug and Sharon.)

Sam: The way we look at it, we want to use the SafeHomeAssured.com Web site as a support tool when customers phone in an order. Our phone reps will complete all necessary forms, etc. and process the order for the customer.

Doug: Why not just refer the customer to the Web site?

Sam (smiling): You techies think that everyone is comfortable with the Web. They're not! Plenty of people still like the telephone, so we have to give them that option. But we don't want to build a separate order processing system when most of the pieces are already in place on the Web.

Sharon: Makes sense.

(All parties read the use-cases [an example follows]):

Use-case: *describe home layout* [note that this differs from the use-case of the same name for *new customer* category]

I will ask the customer (via the phone) to describe each room of the house and will enter room dimensions and other characteristics on one big form designed specifically for customer support personnel. Once the house data are entered I can save the data under the customer's name or phone number.

Sharon: Sam, you've been kind of terse in your preliminary use-case desriptions. I think we're going to need to flesh them out a bit.

Doug (nodding): I agree.

Sam (frowning): How so?

Sharon: Well . . . you mention "one big form designed specifically for customer support personnel." We're going to need more detail.

Sam: What I meant was that we don't need to walk our reps through the process like you do for an on-line customer. One big form should do the trick.

Sharon: Let's sketch out what the form should look like.

The parties work to provide sufficient detail to allow Sharon's team to make effective use of the use-case.

18.1.3 Refining the Use-Case Model

As use-case diagrams are created for each user category, a top-level view of externally observable WebApp requirements is developed. Use-cases are organized into functional packages, and each package is assessed [CON00] to ensure that it is:

? How do we assess packages of use-cases that have been grouped by user function?

- *Comprehensible*—all stakeholders understand the purpose of the package.
- *Cohesive*—the package addresses functions that are closely related to one another.
- *Loosely coupled*—functions or classes within the package collaborate with one another, but collaboration outside the package is kept to a minimum.
- *Hierarchically shallow*—deep functional hierarchies are difficult to navigate and hard for end-users to understand; therefore, the number of levels within a use-case hierarchy should be minimized whenever possible.

Because requirements analysis and modeling are iterative activities, it is likely that new use-cases will be added to packages that have been defined, that existing use-cases will be refined, and that specific use-cases might be reallocated to different packages.

18.2 The Analysis Model for WebApps

A WebApp *analysis model* is driven by information contained within the use-cases that have been developed for the application. Use-case descriptions are parsed to identify potential analysis classes and the operations and attributes associated with each class. Content to be presented by the WebApp is identified, and functions to be performed are extracted from the use-case descriptions. Finally, implementation-specific requirements should be developed so that the environment and infrastructure that support the WebApp can be built.

Four analysis activities—each contributing to the creation of a complete analysis model are:

? What types of analysis activity occur during modeling of a WebApp?

- *Content analysis* identifies the full spectrum of content to be provided by the WebApp. Content includes text, graphics and images, and video and audio data.
- *Interaction analysis* describes the manner in which the user interacts with the WebApp.
- *Functional analysis* defines the operations that will be applied to WebApp content and describes other processing functions that are independent of content but necessary to the end-user.
- *Configuration analysis* describes the environment and infrastructure in which the WebApp resides.

The information collected during these four analysis tasks should be reviewed, modified as required, and then organized into a model that can be passed to WebApp designers.

The model itself contains structural and dynamic elements. *Structural elements* identify the analysis classes and content objects that are required to create a WebApp that meets stakeholders needs. The *dynamic elements* of the analysis model describe how the structural elements interact with one another and with end-users.

> "Successful [WebApps] allow customers to meet their needs better, faster, or cheaper themselves, rather than working through [a company's] employee end-users."
>
> **Mark McDonald**

18.3 The Content Model

The *content model* contains structural elements that provide an important view of content requirements for a WebApp. These structural elements encompass content objects (e.g., text, graphical images, photographs, video images, audio) that are presented as part of the WebApp. In addition, the content model includes all analysis classes—user-visible entities that are created or manipulated as a user interacts with the WebApp. An analysis class encompasses attributes that describe it, operations that effect behavior required of the class, and collaborations that allow the class to communicate with other classes.

Like other elements of the analysis model, the content model is derived from a careful examination of use-cases developed for the WebApp. Use-cases are parsed to extract content objects and analysis classes.

18.3.1 Defining Content Objects

KEY POINT
A content object is any item of cohesive information that is to be presented to an end-user. Typically, content objects are extracted from use-cases.

Web applications present pre-existing information—called *content*—to an end-user. The type and form of content spans a broad spectrum of sophistication and complexity. Content may be developed prior to the implementation of the WebApp, while the WebApp is being built, or long after the WebApp is operational. In every case, it is incorporated via navigational reference into the overall WebApp structure. A *content object* might be a textual description of a product, an article describing a news event, an action photograph taken at a sporting event, an animated representation of a corporate logo, a short video of a speech, or an audio overlay for a collection of Powerpoint slides.

Content objects are extracted from use-cases by examining the scenario description for direct and indirect references to content. For example, in the use-case *select SafeHome components,* we encounter the sentence:

> I will be able to get descriptive and pricing information for each product component.

Although there is no direct reference to content, it is implied. The Web engineer would meet with the author of the use-case and gain a more detailed understanding of what "descriptive and pricing information" means. In this case, the author of the use-case might indicate that "descriptive information" includes (1) a one paragraph general description of the component; (2) a photograph of the component; (3) a multiparagraph technical description of the component; (4) a schematic diagram of the component showing how it fits into a typical *SafeHome* system, and (5) a thumbnail video that shows how to install the component in a typical household setting.

It is important to note that each of these content objects must be developed (often by content developers who are *not* Web engineers) or acquired for integration into the WebApp architecture (discussed in Chapter 19).

> "The Web—so much content, so little time."
>
> **Author unknown**

18.3.2 Content Relationships and Hierarchy

KEY POINT
A *data tree* represents a hierarchy of content objects.

In many instances, a simple list of content objects, coupled with a brief description of each object, is sufficient to define the requirements for content that must be designed and implemented. However, in some cases, the content model may contain

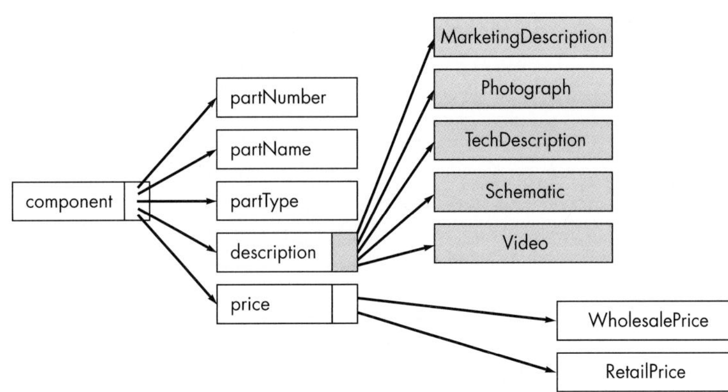

FIGURE 18.3 Data tree for a *SafeHome* component

entity relationship diagrams (Chapter 8) or *data trees* [SRI01] that depict the relationships among content objects and/or the hierarchy of content maintained by a WebApp.

Consider the data tree created for a *SafeHome* component shown in Figure 18.3. The tree represents a hierarchy of information that is used to describe the component (later we will see that a *SafeHome* component is actually an analysis class for this application). Simple or composite data items (one or more data values) are represented as unshaded rectangles. Content objects are represented as shaded rectangles. In the figure, **description** is defined by five content objects (the shaded rectangles). In some cases, one or more of these objects would be further refined as the data tree expands.

18.3.3 Analysis Classes[4] for WebApps

As we have already noted, analysis classes are derived by examining each use-case. For example, consider the preliminary use-case: *select SafeHome components* presented in Section 18.1.2.

Use-case: *select SafeHome components*

The WebApp will then recommend product components (e.g., control panels, sensors, cameras) and other features (e.g., PC-based functionality implemented in software) for each room and exterior entrance. If I request alternatives, the WebApp will provide them, if they exist. I will be able to get descriptive and pricing information for each product component. The WebApp will create and display a bill-of-materials as I select various components. I'll be able to give the bill-of-materials a name and save it for future reference (see use-case: *save configuration*).

A quick grammatical parse of the use-case identifies two candidate classes (underlined): **ProductComponent** and **BillOfMaterials.** A first-cut description of each class is shown in Figure 18.4.

4 A detailed discussion of the mechanics for identifying and representing analysis classes has been presented in Chapter 8. If you have not already done so, review Chapter 8 at this time.

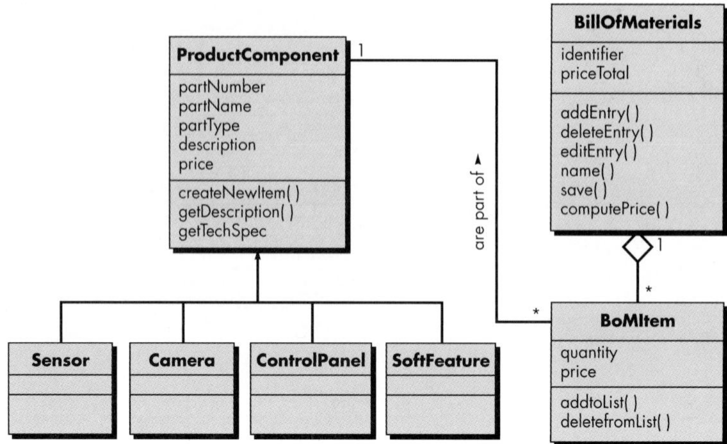

FIGURE 18.4 **Analysis classes for use-case: *select SafeHome components***

The **ProductComponent** class encompasses all *SafeHome* components that may be purchased to customize the product for a particular installation. It is a generalized representation of **Sensor, Camera, ControlPanel,** and **SoftFeature.** Each **ProductComponent** object contains information corresponding to the data tree shown in Figure 18.3 for the class. Some of these class attributes are single or composite data items and others are content objects (see Figure 18.3). Operations relevant to the class are also shown.

The **BillOfMaterials** class encompasses a list of components that **new customer** has selected. **BillOfMaterials** is actually an aggregation of **BoMItem** (many instances of **BoMItem** comprise one **BillOfMaterials**)—a class that builds a list composed of each component to be purchased and specific attributes about the component as shown in Figure 18.4.

Each use-case identified for SafeHomeAssured.com is parsed for analysis objects. Class models similar to the one described in this section are developed for each use-case.

18.4 The Interaction Model

The vast majority of WebApps enable a "conversation" between an end-user and application functionality, content, and behavior. This *interaction model* is composed of four elements: (1) use-cases, (2) sequence diagrams, (3) state diagrams,[5] and (4) a user interface prototype. In addition to these representations, the interaction is also represented within the context of the navigation model (Section 18.7).

5 Each of these is an important UML notation and has been described in Chapter 8.

FIGURE 18.5

Sequence diagram for use-case: *select SafeHome components*

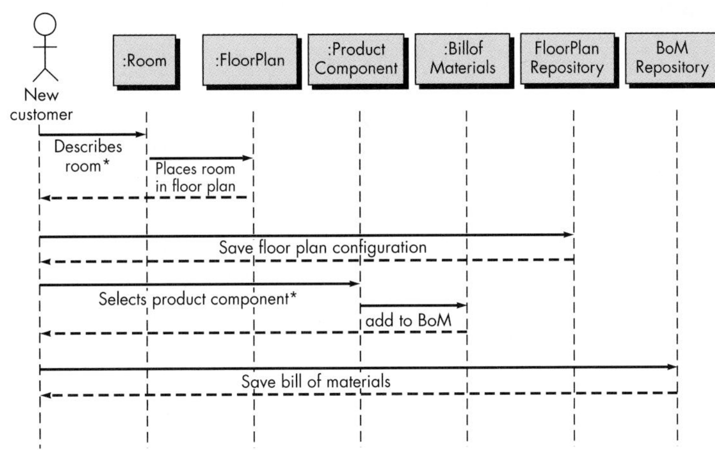

The techniques associated with task analysis (Chapter 12) can be used to help define modes of user interaction.

Use-cases. Use-cases are the dominant element of the interaction model for WebApps. It is not uncommon to describe 100 or more use-cases when large, complex WebApps are analyzed, designed, and constructed. However, a relatively small percentage of these use-cases describe the major interactions between end-user categories (actors) and the system. Other use-cases refine the interactions, providing the analysis detail necessary to guide design and construction.

Sequence diagrams. UML sequence diagrams provide a shorthand representation of the manner in which user actions (the dynamic elements of a system defined by use-cases) collaborate with analysis classes (the structural elements of a system defined by class diagrams). Since analysis classes are extracted from use-case descriptions, there is a need to ensure that traceability exists between the classes that have been defined and the use-cases that describe system interaction.

In earlier chapters we noted that sequence diagrams provide a link between the actions described in the use-case and the analysis classes (structural entities). Conallen [CON00] notes this when he writes: "The merging of dynamic and structural elements of the [analysis] model is the key link in the traceability of the model and should be taken very seriously."

In some cases, excerpts from the actual text of the use-case can be reproduced in the left hand column (below the user) so that direct traceability can be represented.

A sequence diagram for the *select SafeHome components* use-case is shown in Figure 18.5. The vertical axis of the diagram depicts actions that are defined within the use-case. The horizontal axis identifies the analysis classes that are used as the use-case proceeds. For example, a new customer must first describe each room within the house (the asterisk following "describe room" indicates that the action is iterative). To accomplish this, the new customer answers questions about the room's size, doors, and windows, and so forth. Once a room is defined, it is placed in a floor plan for the house. The new customer then describes the next room or proceeds to the next action (which is to save the floor plan configuration). The movement across and down the sequence diagram ties each analysis class to use-case actions. If a use-case action

FIGURE 18.6 Partial state diagram for new customer interaction

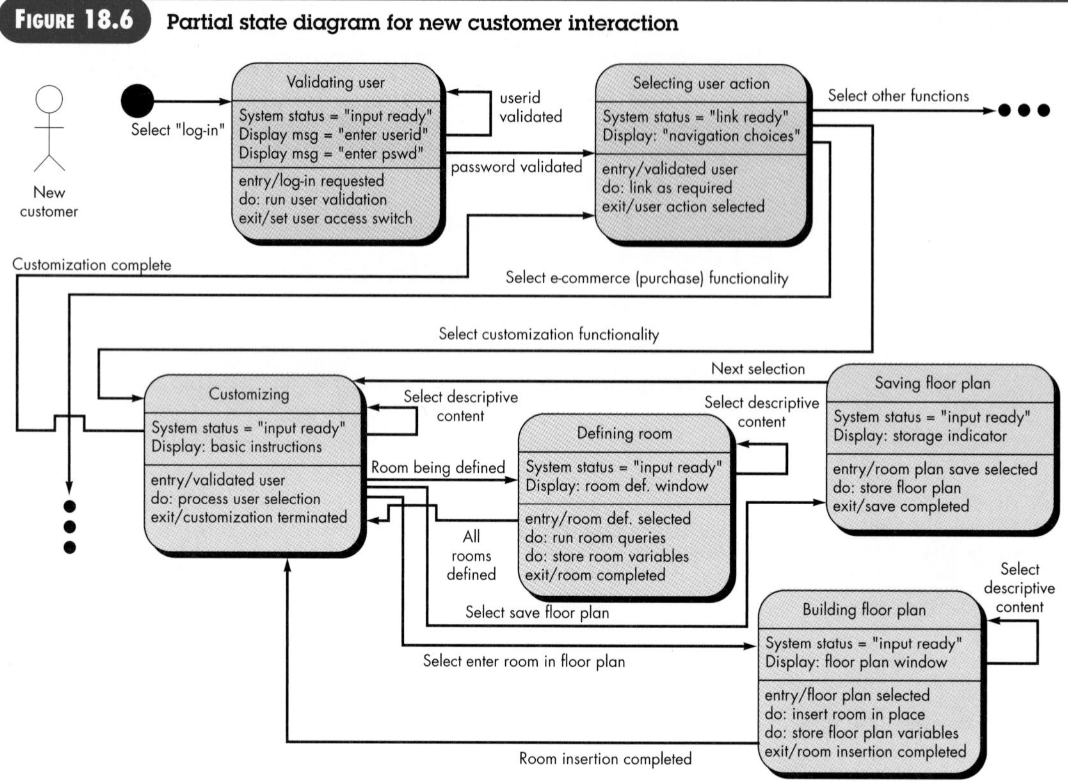

is missing from the diagram, the Web engineer must re-evaluate the description of analysis classes to determine if one or more classes is missing. Sequence diagrams can be created for each use-case once analysis classes are defined for the use-case.

State diagrams. The UML state diagram (Chapter 8) provides another representation of the dynamic behavior of the WebApp as an interaction occurs. Like most modeling representations used in Web engineering (or software engineering), the state diagram can be represented at different levels of abstraction. Figure 18.6 depicts a partial, top-level (high level of abstraction) state diagram for the interaction between a new customer and the SafeHomeAssured.com WebApp.

In the state diagram shown, six externally observable states are identified: *validating user, selecting user action, customizing, defining room, building floor plan,* and *saving floor plan.* The state diagram indicates the events that are required to move the new customer from one state to another, the information that is displayed as a state is entered, the processing that occurs within a state, and the exit condition that causes a transition from one state to another.

Because use-cases, sequence diagrams, and state diagrams all present related information, it is reasonable to ask why all three are necessary. In some cases, they are not. Use-cases may be sufficient in some situations. However, use-cases provide a rather one-dimensional view of the interaction. Sequence diagrams present a second dimension that is more procedural (dynamic) in nature. State diagrams provide a third dimension that is more behavioral and contains information about potential navigation pathways that is not provided by use-cases or the sequence diagram. When all three dimensions are used, omissions or inconsistencies that might escape discovery in one dimension become obvious when a second (or third) dimension is examined. It is for this reason that large complex WebApps can benefit from an interaction model that encompasses all three representations.

User interface prototype. The layout of the user interface, the content it presents, the interaction mechanisms it implements, and the overall aesthetic of the user-WebApp connections have much to do with user satisfaction and the overall acceptance of the WebApp. Although it can be argued that the creation of a user interface prototype is a design activity, it is a good idea to perform it during the creation of the analysis model. The sooner that a physical representation of a user interface can be reviewed, the higher the likelihood that end-users will get what they want. User interface analysis and design are discussed in detail in Chapter 12.

ADVICE

Some Web engineers prefer a pencil and paper storyboard of major WebApp pages (screens). Although such storyboards can be developed very quickly, the navigation flow is less obvious than with an operational prototype.

Because WebApp development tools are plentiful, relatively inexpensive, and functionally powerful, it is best to create the interface prototype using such tools. The prototype should implement the major navigational links and represent the overall screen layout in much the same way that it will be constructed.

18.5 The Functional Model

The *functional model* addresses two processing elements of the WebApp, each representing a different level of procedural abstraction: (1) user observable functionality that is delivered by the WebApp to end-users, and (2) the operations contained within analysis classes that implement behaviors associated with the class.

User-observable functionality encompasses any processing functions that are initiated directly by the user. For example, a financial Web site might implement a variety of financial functions (e.g., a college tuition savings calculator or a retirement savings calculator). These functions may actually be implemented using operations within analysis classes, but from the point of view of the end-user, the function (more correctly, the data provided by the function) is the visible outcome.

At a lower level of procedural abstraction, the analysis model describes the processing to be performed by analysis class operations. These operations manipulate class attributes and are involved as classes collaborate with one another to accomplish some required behavior.

Regardless of the level of procedural abstraction, the UML activity diagram can be used to represent processing details. Figure 18.7 depicts an activity diagram for the

FIGURE 18.7

Activity diagram for *computePrice()* operation

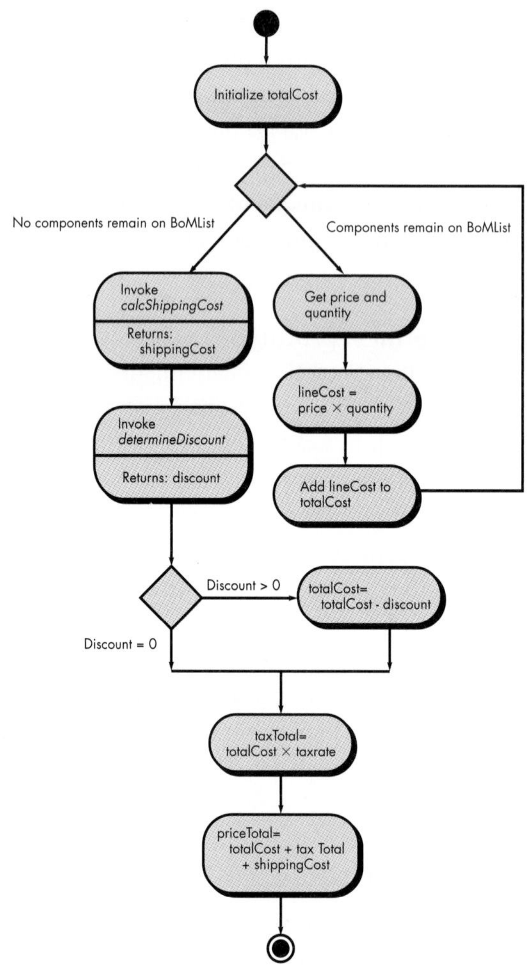

As an alternative, you can also write a simple processing narrative or program design language representation (Chapter 11). However, many people prefer a graphical representation.

computePrice() operation that is part of the **BillOfMaterials** analysis class.[6] As we noted in Chapter 8, the activity diagram is similar to the flowchart, illustrating the processing flow and logical decisions with the flow. It should be noted that two additional operations are invoked within the procedural flow: *calcShippingCost(),* which calculates the cost of shipping depending upon the shipping method chosen by the customer, and *determineDiscount(),* which determines any special discounts for the *SafeHome* components that were selected for purchase. The construction details indicating how these operations are invoked and the interface details for each operation are not considered until WebApp design commences.

6 A review of the **BillOfMaterials** analysis class might determine that in the interest of cohesion, the *computePrice()* operation might best be placed within an **Invoice** class. This suggestion has merit. However, it remains within the **BillOfMaterials** analysis class for the purposes of this example.

18.6 The Configuration Model

WebApps must be designed and implemented in a manner that accommodates a variety of environments on both the server-side and the client-side.[7] The WebApp can reside on a server that provides access via the Internet, an Intranet, or an Extranet. Server hardware and operating system environment must be specified. In addition, interoperability considerations on the server-side should be considered. If the WebApp must access a large database or interoperate with corporate applications that exist on the server side, appropriate interfaces, communication protocols, and related collaborative information must be specified.

Although it's very important to consider all configurations that are likely to be used, remember that a WebApp must be engineered to serve its end-users, not the idiosyncrasies of a particular browser.

Client-side software provides the infrastructure that enables access to the WebApp from the user's location. In general, browser software is used to deliver the WebApp content and functionality that is downloaded from the server. Although standards do exist, each browser has its own peculiarities. For this reason, the WebApp must be thoroughly tested within every browser configuration that is specified as part of the *configuration model.*

In some cases, the configuration model is nothing more than a list of server-side and client-side attributes. However, for more complex WebApps, a variety of configuration complexities (e.g., distributing load among multiple servers, caching architectures, remote databases, multiple servers serving various objects on the same Web page) may have an impact on analysis and design. The UML deployment diagram (Chapter 10) can be used in situations in which complex configuration architectures must be considered.

18.7 Relationship-Navigation Analysis

The elements of the analysis model described in the preceding sections identify content and functional elements along with the manner in which they are used to implement user interaction. As analysis evolves into design, these elements become part of the WebApp architecture. In the context of Web applications, each architectural element has the potential to be linked to all other architectural elements. But as the number of links increases, navigational complexity throughout the WebApp also increases. The question, then, is how to establish the appropriate links between content objects and among the functions that provide user-required capabilities.

> **"[Navigation] is not only the action of jumping from page to page, but the idea of moving through an information space."**
>
> **A. Reina and J. Torres**

---

7 The *server-side* hosts the WebApp and all related system features that enable multiple users to gain access to the WebApp via a network. The *client-side* provides a software environment (e.g., browsers) that enable end-users to interact with the WebApp on the user's desktop.

Relationship-navigation analysis (RNA) provides a series of analysis steps that strive to identify relationships among the elements uncovered as part of the creation of the analysis model.[8] Yoo and Bieber [YOO00] describe RNA in the following manner:

> RNA provides systems analysts with a systematic technique for determining the relationship structure of an application, helping them to discover all potentially useful relationships in application domains. These later may be implemented as links. RNA also helps determine appropriate navigational structures on top of these links. RNA enhances system developers' understanding of application domains by broadening and deepening their conceptual model of the domain. Developers can then enhance their implementation by including additional links, metainformation, and navigation.

The RNA approach is organized into five steps:

- *Stakeholder analysis*—identifies the various user categories (as described in Section 18.1) and establishes an appropriate stakeholder hierarchy.
- *Element analysis*—identifies the content objects and functional elements that are of interest to end-users (as described in Sections 18.3 and 18.5).
- *Relationship analysis*—describes the relationships that exist among the WebApp elements.
- *Navigation analysis*—examines how users might access individual elements or groups of elements.
- *Evaluation analysis*—considers pragmatic issues (e.g., cost/benefit) associated with implementing the relationships defined earlier.

The first two steps in the RNA approach have been discussed earlier in this chapter. In the sections that follow, we consider methods for establishing the relationships that exist among content objects and functions.

18.7.1 Relationship Analysis—Key Questions

Yoo and Bieder [YOO00] suggest a list of questions that a Web engineer or systems analyst should ask about each element (content object or function) that has been identified within the analysis model. The following list, adapted for WebApps, is representative [YOO00]:

? How do we assess analysis model elements to understand the relationships between them?

- Is the element a member of a broader category of elements?
- What attributes or parameters have been identified for the element?
- Does descriptive information about the element already exist? If so, where is it?
- Does the element appear in different locations within the WebApp? If so, where?
- Is the element composed of other smaller elements? If so, what are they?

8 It should be noted that RNA can be applied to any information system and was originally developed for hypermedia systems in general. It can, however, be adapted nicely for Web engineering.

- Is the element a member of a larger collection of elements? If so, what is it and what is its structure?
- Is the element described by an analysis class?
- Are other elements similar to the element being considered? If so, is it possible that they could be combined into one element?
- Is the element used in a specific ordering of other elements? Does its appearance depend on other elements?
- Does another element always follow the appearance of the element being considered?
- What pre- and post-conditions must be met for the element to be used?
- Do specific user categories use the element? Do different user categories use the element differently? If so, how?
- Can the element be associated with a specific formulation goal or objective? With a specific WebApp requirement?
- Does this element always appear at the same time as other elements appear? If so, what are the other elements?
- Does this element always appear in the same place (e.g., same location of the screen or page) as other elements? If so, what are the other elements?

The answers to these and other questions help the Web engineer to position the element in question within the WebApp and to establish relationships among elements.

It is possible to develop a relationship taxonomy and to categorize each relationship identified as a result of the questions noted. The interested reader should refer to [YOO00] for more detail.

18.7.2 Navigation Analysis

Once relationships have been developed among elements defined within the analysis model, the Web engineer must consider the requirements that dictate how each user category will navigate from one element (e.g., content object) to another. The mechanics of navigation are defined as part of design. At this stage, developers should consider overall navigation requirements. The following questions should be asked and answered:

? What questions should be asked to better understand navigation requirements?

- Should certain elements be easier to reach (require fewer navigation steps) than others? What is the priority for presentation?
- Should certain elements be emphasized to force users to navigate in their direction?
- How should navigation errors be handled?
- Should navigation to related groups of elements be given priority over navigation to a specific element?

- Should navigation be accomplished via links, via search-based access, or by some other means?
- Should certain elements be presented to users based on the context of previous navigation actions?
- Should a navigation log be maintained for users?
- Should a full navigation map or menu (as opposed to a single "back" link or directed pointer) be available at every point in a user's interaction?
- Should navigation design be driven by the most commonly expected user behaviors or by the perceived importance of the defined WebApp elements?
- Can a user "store" his previous navigation through the WebApp to expedite future usage?
- For which user category should optimal navigation be designed?
- How should links external to the WebApp be handled? Overlaying the existing browser window? As a new browser window? As a separate frame?

As you analyze navigational requirements, remember that the user must always know where she is and where she can go. To do this, the user needs a "map."

These and many other questions should be asked and answered as part of navigation analysis.

The Web engineering team and its stakeholders must also determine overall requirements for navigation. For example, will a "site map" be provided to give users an overview of the entire WebApp structure? Can a user take a "guided tour" that will highlight the most important elements (content objects and functions) that are available? Will a user be able to access content objects or functions based on defined attributes of those elements (e.g., a user might want to access all photographs of a specific building or all functions that allow computation of weight).

18.8 Summary

Formulation, requirements gathering, and analysis modeling are performed as part of requirements analysis for WebApps. The intent of these activities is to (1) describe the basic motivation (goals) and objectives for the WebApp; (2) define the categories of users; (3) note the content and functional requirements for the WebApp; and (4) establish a basic understanding of why the WebApp is to be built, who will use it, and what problem(s) it will solve for its users.

Use-cases are the catalyst for all requirements analysis and modeling activities. Use-cases can be organized into functional packages, and each package is assessed to ensure that it is comprehensible, cohesive, loosely coupled, and hierarchically shallow.

Four analysis activities contribute to the creation of a complete analysis model: content analysis identifies the full spectrum of content to be provided by the WebApp; interaction analysis describes the manner in which the user interacts with the WebApp; functional analysis defines the operations that will be applied to WebApp content and describes other processing functions that are independent of content but necessary to the end-user, and configuration analysis describes the environment and infrastructure in which the WebApp resides.

The content model describes the spectrum of content objects that are to be incorporated into a WebApp. These content objects must be developed or acquired for integration into the WebApp architecture. A data tree can be used to represent a content object hierarchy. Analysis classes (derived from use-cases) provide another means for representing key objects that the WebApp will manipulate.

The interaction model is constructed with use-cases, UML sequence diagrams, and UML state diagrams to describe the "conversation" between the user and the WebApp. In addition, an interface prototype may be constructed to assist in developing layout and navigation requirements.

The functional model describes user-observable functions and class operations using the UML activity diagram. The configuration model describes the environment that the WebApp will require on both the server-side and the client-side of the system.

Relationship-navigation analysis identifies relationships among the content and functional elements defined in the analysis model and establishes requirements for defining appropriate navigation links throughout the system. A series of questions help to establish relationships and identify characteristics that will have an influence on navigation design.

References

[CON00] Conallen, J., *Building Web Applications with UML,* Addison-Wesley, 2000.

[FRA01] Franklin, S., "Planning Your Web Site with UML," *webReview,* available at http://www.webreview.com/2001/05_18/developers/index01.shtml.

[SRI01] Sridhar, M., and N. Mandyam, "Effective Use of Data Models in Building Web Applications," 2001, available at http://www2002.org/CDROM/alternate/698/.

[YOO99] Yoo, J., and M. Bieber, "A Systematic Relationship Analysis for Modeling Information Domains," 1999, download from http://citeseer.nj.nec.com/ 312025. html.

[YOO00] Yoo, J., and M. Bieber, "Toward a Relationship Navigation Analysis," *Proc. 33rd Hawaii Conf. On System Sciences,* vol. 6., IEEE, January 2000, download from www.cs.njit.edu/~bieber/pub/hicss00/INWEB02.pdf.

Problems and Points to Ponder

18.1. Using the vast array of resources on agile software development available on the Web, do a bit of research and make an argument against analysis modeling for WebApps. Do you believe that your argument applies in all cases?

18.2. If you were forced to do "analysis modeling lite"—that is, minimal analysis modeling—what representations, diagrams, and information would you define during this Web engineering activity?

18.3. Using a diagram similar to the one shown in Figure 18.1, establish a user hierarchy for (a) a financial services Web site or (b) a book-seller Web site.

18.4. What does a use-case package represent?

18.5. Use-cases or use-case packages are assessed to ensure that they are *comprehensible, cohesive, loosely coupled, and hierarchically shallow.* Describe what these terms mean in your own words.

Select a WebApp that you visit regularly from one of the following categories: (a) news or sports, (b) entertainment, (c) e-commerce, (d) gaming, (e) computer-related, (f) a WebApp recommended by your instructor. Perform the activities noted in Problems 18.6 through 18.12:

18.6. Develop one or more use-cases that describe specific user behavior for the WebApp.

18.7. Represent a partial content hierarchy and define at least three analysis classes for the WebApp.

18.8. Develop a UML sequence diagram and a UML state diagram that describes a specific interaction within the WebApp.

18.9. Consider the existing WebApp interface. Prototype a change to the interface that you believe will improve it.

18.10. Select a user observable function provided by the WebApp and model it using a UML activity diagram.

18.11. Select a content object or function that is part of the WebApp architecture and answer the relationship-navigation questions listed in Section 18.7.1.

18.12. Considering the existing WebApp, answer the relationship-navigation questions listed in Section 18.7.2.

Further Readings and Information Sources

Many books dedicated to analysis modeling for conventional software—with particular emphasis on use-cases and UML notation—contain much useful information that can be readily adapted by Web engineers. Use-cases form the foundation of analysis modeling for WebApps. Books by Kulak and his colleagues (*Use Cases: Requirements in Context,* second edition, Addison-Wesley, 2004), Bittner and Spence (*Use Case Modeling,* Addison-Wesley, 2002), Cockburn (*Writing Effective Use Cases,* Addison-Wesley, 2001), Armour and Miller (*Advanced Use-Case Modeling: Software Systems,* Addison-Wesley, 2000), Rosenberg and Scott (*Use Case Driven Object Modeling with UML: A Practical Approach,* Addison-Wesley, 1999), and Schneider, Winters, and Jacobson (*Applying Use Cases: A Practical Guide,* Addison-Wesley, 1998) provide worthwhile guidance in the creation and use of this important requirements representation mechanism. Worthwhile discussions of UML have been written by Arlow and Neustadt (*UML and the Unified Process,* Addison-Wesley, 2002), Schmuller (*Teach Yourself UML,* Sams Publishing, 2002), Booch and his colleagues (*The UML User Guide,* Addison-Wesley, 1998), and Rumbaugh and his colleagues (*The Unified Modeling Language Reference Manual,* Addison-Wesley, 1998).

Books dedicated to Web site design often contain one or two chapters that discuss analysis issues (although these are often cursory discussions). The following books contain one or more aspects of analysis within the context of Web engineering: Van Duyne and his colleagues (*The Design of Sites,* Addison-Wesley, 2002), Rosenfeld and Morville (*Information Architecture for the World Wide Web,* O'Reilly & Associates, 2002), Wodtke (*Information Architecture,* New Riders Publishing, 2002), Garrett (*The Elements of User Experience: User Centered Design for the Web,* New Riders Publishing, 2002), Niederst (*Web Design in a Nutshell,* O'Reilly & Associates, 2001), Lowe and Hall (*Hypertext and the Web: An Engineering Approach,* Wiley, 1999), and Powell (*Web Site Engineering,* Prentice-Hall, 1998) provide reasonably complete coverage. Norris, West, and Watson (*Media Engineering: A Guide to Developing Information Products,* Wiley, 1997), Navarro and Khan (*Effective Web Design: Master the Essentials,* Sybex, 1998), and Fleming and Koman (*Web Navigation: Designing the User Experience,* O'Reilly & Associates, 1998) provide additional guidance for analysis and design.

A wide variety of information sources on analysis modeling for Web engineering is available on the Internet. An up-to-date list of World Wide Web references can be found under "software engineering resources" at the SEPA Web site:
http://www.mhhe.com/pressman.

CHAPTER

19 DESIGN MODELING FOR WEB APPLICATIONS

KEY CONCEPTS

In his authoritative book on Web design, Jakob Nielsen [NIE00] states: "There are essentially two basic approaches to design: the artistic ideal of expressing yourself and the engineering ideal of solving a problem for a customer." During the first decade of Web development, the artistic idea was the approach that many developers chose. Design occurred in an ad hoc manner and was usually conducted as HTML was generated. Design evolved out of an artistic vision that itself evolved as WebApp construction occurred.

Even today, the most "extreme" proponents of agile software development (Chapter 4) use Web applications as poster children for "limited design." They argue that WebApp immediacy and volatility mitigate against formal design, that design evolves as an application is built (coded), and that relatively little time should be spent on creating a detailed design model. This argument has merit, but only for relatively simple WebApps. When content and function are complex; when the size of the WebApp encompasses hundreds of content objects, functions, and analysis classes; when the success of the WebApp will have a direct impact on the success of the business, design cannot and should not be taken lightly.

This reality leads us to Nielsen's second approach—"the engineering ideal of solving a problem for a customer." Web engineering adopts this philosophy, and a more rigorous approach to WebApp design enables developers to achieve it.

QUICK LOOK

What is it? Design for WebApps encompasses technical and nontechnical activities. The look and feel of content is developed as part of graphic design; the aesthetic layout of the user interface is created as part of interface design; and the technical structure of the WebApp is modeled as part of architectural and navigational design. In every instance, a design model should be created before construction begins, but a good Web engineer recognizes that the design will evolve as more is learned about stakeholder requirements as the WebApp is built.

Who does it? Web engineers, graphic designers, content developers, and other stakeholders all participate in the creation of a design model for Web engineering.

Why is it important? Design allows a Web engineer to create a model that can be assessed for quality and improved before content and code are generated, tests are conducted, and end-users become involved in large numbers. Design is the place where WebApp quality is established.

What are the steps? WebApp design encompasses six major steps that are driven by information obtained during analysis modeling.

Content design uses information contained within the analysis model as a basis for establishing the design of content objects and their relationships. Aesthetic design (also called graphic design) establishes the look and feel that the end-user sees. Architectural design focuses on the overall hypermedia structure of all content objects and functions. Interface design establishes the overall layout and interaction mechanisms that define the user interface. Navigation design defines how the end-user navigates through the hypermedia structure, and component design represents the detailed internal structure of functional elements of the WebApp.

What is the work product? A design model that encompasses content, aesthetics, architecture, interface, navigation, and component-level design issues is the primary work product of Web engineering design.

How do I ensure that I've done it right? Each element of the design model is reviewed by the Web engineering team (and selected stakeholders) in an effort to uncover errors, inconsistencies, or omissions. In addition, alternative solutions are considered, and the degree to which the current design model will lead to an effective implementation is also assessed.

19.1 Design Issues for Web Engineering

When design is applied within the context of Web engineering, both generic and specific issues must be considered. From a generic viewpoint, design results in a model that guides the construction of the WebApp. The design model, regardless of its form, should contain enough information to reflect how stakeholder requirements (defined in an analysis model) are to be translated into content and executable code. But design must also be specific. It must address key attributes of a WebApp in a manner that enables a Web engineer to build and test effectively.

19.1.1 Design and WebApp Quality

In earlier chapters, we noted that design is the engineering activity that leads to a high-quality product. This leads us to a recurring question that is encountered in all engineering disciplines: What is quality? In this section we examine the answer within the context of Web engineering.

Every person who has surfed the Web or used a corporate Intranet has an opinion about what makes a "good" WebApp. Individual viewpoints vary widely. Some users enjoy flashy graphics, others want simple text. Some demand copious information, others desire an abbreviated presentation. Some like sophisticated analytical tools or database access, others like to keep it simple. In fact, the user's perception of "goodness" (and the resultant acceptance or rejection of the WebApp as a consequence) might be more important that any technical discussion of WebApp quality.

But how is WebApp quality perceived? What attributes must be exhibited to achieve goodness in the eyes of end-users and at the same time exhibit the technical characteristics of quality that will enable a Web engineer to correct, adapt, enhance, and support the application over the long term?

In reality, all of the general characteristics of software quality discussed in Chapters 9, 15, and 26 apply to WebApps. However, the most relevant of these characteristics—usability, functionality, reliability, efficiency, and maintainability—provide a useful basis for assessing the quality of Web-based systems.

> "If products are designed to better fit the natural tendencies of human behavior, then people will be more satisfied, more fulfilled, and more productive."
>
> **Susan Weinschenk**

Olsina and his colleagues [OLS99] have prepared a "quality requirement tree" that identifies a set of technical attributes—usability, functionality, reliability, efficiency, and maintainability—that lead to high-quality WebApps.[1] Figure 19.1 summarizes their work. The criteria noted in the figure are of particular interest to Web engineers who must design, build, and maintain WebApps over the long term.

Offutt [OFF02] extends the five major quality attributes noted in Figure 19.1 by adding the following attributes:

? **What are the major attributes of quality for WebApps?**

Security. WebApps have become heavily integrated with critical corporate and government databases. E-commerce applications extract and then store sensitive customer information. For these and many other reasons, WebApp security is paramount in many situations. The key measure of security is the ability of the WebApp and its server environment to rebuff unauthorized access and/or thwart an outright

FIGURE 19.1

Quality requirements tree [OLS99]

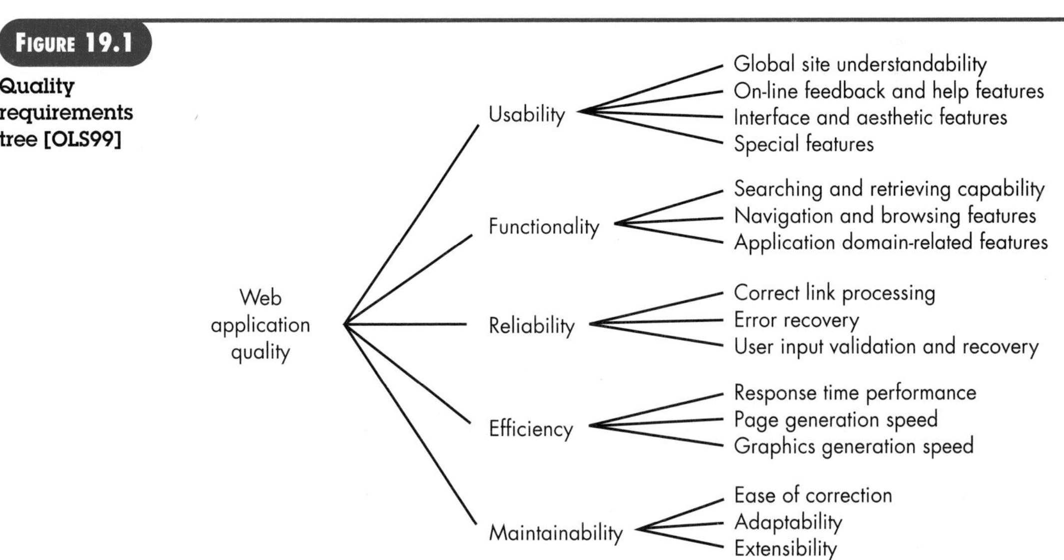

1 These quality attributes are quite similar to those presented in Chapters 9, 15, and 26. The implication: quality characteristics are universal for all software.

malevolent attack. A detailed discussion of WebApp security is beyond the scope of this book. The interested reader should see [MCC01], [NOR02], or [KAL03].

Availability. Even the best WebApp will not meet users' needs if it is unavailable. In a technical sense, availability is the measure of the percentage of time that a WebApp is available for use. The typical end-user expects WebApps to be available 24/7/365. Anything less is deemed unacceptable.[2] But "up-time" is not the only indicator of availability. Offutt [OFF02] suggests that "using features available on only one browser or one platform" makes the WebApp unavailable to those with a different browser/platform configuration. The user will invariably go elsewhere.

Scalability. Can the WebApp and its server environment be scaled to handle 100, 1000, 10,000, or 100,000 users? Will the WebApp and the systems with which it is interfaced handle significant variation in volume or will responsiveness drop dramatically (or cease altogether)? It is not enough to build a WebApp that is successful. It is equally important to build a WebApp that can accommodate the burden of success (significantly more end-users) and become even more successful.

Time-to-market. Although time to market is not a true quality attribute in the technical sense, it is a measure of quality from a business point of view. The first WebApp in the market often captures a disproportionate number of end-users.

INFO

WebApp Design Quality Checklist

The following checklist, adapted from information presented at Webreference.com, provides a set of questions that will help both Web engineers and end-users assess overall WebApp quality:

- Can content and/or function and/or navigation options be tailored to the user's preferences?
- Can content and/or functionality be customized to the bandwidth over which the user communicates.
- Have graphics and other nontext media been used appropriately? Are graphics file sizes optimized for display efficiency?
- Are tables organized and sized in a manner that makes them understandable and displayed efficiently?
- Is HTML optimized to eliminate inefficiencies?
- Is the overall page design easy to read and navigate?
- Do all pointers (links) provide links to information that is of interest to users?
- Is it likely that most links have persistence on the Web?
- Is the WebApp instrumented with site management utilities that include tools for usage tracking, link testing, local searching, and security?

Billions of Web pages are available for those in search of information on the World Wide Web. Even well-targeted Web searches result in an avalanche of content. With so many sources of information to choose from, how does the user assess the quality (e.g., veracity, accuracy, completeness, timeliness) of the content that is presented within a WebApp? Tillman [TIL00] suggests a useful set of criteria for assessing the quality of content:

2 This expectation is, of course, unrealistic. Major WebApps must schedule "downtime" for fixes and upgrades.

What should we consider when assessing content quality?

- Can the scope and depth of content be easily determined to ensure that it meets the user's needs?
- Can the background and authority of the content's authors be easily identified?
- Is it possible to determine the currency of the content, the last update, and what was updated?
- Is the content and its location stable (i.e., will it remain at the referenced URL)?

In addition these content-related questions, the following might be added:

- Is content credible?
- Is content unique? That is, does the WebApp provide some unique benefit to those who use it?
- Is content valuable to the targeted user community?
- Is content well-organized? Indexed? Easily accessible?

The checklists noted in this section represent only a small sampling of the issues that should be addressed as the design of a WebApp evolves. An important goal of Web engineering is to develop systems in which affirmative answers are provided to all quality-related questions.

> "Just because you can, doesn't mean you should."
>
> **Jean Kaiser**

19.1.2 Design Goals

In her regular column on Web design, Jean Kaiser [KAI02] suggests the following design goals that are applicable to virtually every WebApp regardless of application domain, size, or complexity:

Simplicity. Although it may seem old-fashioned, the aphorism "all things in moderation" applies to WebApps. There is a tendency among some designers to provide the end-user with "too much"—exhaustive content, extreme visuals, intrusive animation, enormous Web pages, the list is long. Better to strive for moderation and simplicity.

Consistency. This design goal applies to virtually every element of the design model. Content should be constructed consistently (e.g., text formatting and font styles should be the same across all text documents; graphic art should have a consistent look, color scheme, and style). Graphic design (aesthetics) should present a consistent look across all parts of the WebApp. Architectural design should establish templates that lead to a consistent hypermedia structure. Interface design should define consistent modes of interaction, navigation, and content display. Navigation mechanisms should be used consistently across all WebApp elements.

Identity. The aesthetic, interface, and navigational design of a WebApp must be consistent with the application domain for which it is to be built. A Web site for a hip-hop group will undoubted have a different look and feel than a WebApp designed for a financial services company. The WebApp architecture will be entirely different, interfaces will be constructed to accommodate different categories of users, navigation will be organized to accomplish different objectives. A Web engineer (and other design contributors) should work to establish an identity for the WebApp through the design.

Robustness. Based on the identity that has been established, a WebApp often makes an implicit "promise" to a user. The user expects robust content and functions that are relevant to the user's needs. If these elements are missing or insufficient, it is likely that the WebApp will fail.

Navigability. We have already noted that navigation should be simple and consistent. It should also be designed in a manner that is intuitive and predictable. That is, the user should understand how to move about the WebApp without having to search for navigation links or instructions.

Visual appeal. Of all software categories, Web applications are unquestionably the most visual, the most dynamic, and the most unapologetically aesthetic. Beauty (visual appeal) is undoubtedly in the eye of the beholder, but many design characteristics (e.g., the look and feel of content, interface layout, color coordination, the balance of text, graphics and other media, navigation mechanisms) do contribute to visual appeal.

Compatibility. A WebApp will be used in a variety of environments (e.g., different hardware, Internet connection types, operating systems, browsers) and must be designed to be compatible with each.

> **"To some, Web design focuses on visual look and feel ... To others, Web design is about structuring information and navigation through the document space. Others might even consider Web design to be about the technology used to build interactive Web applications. In reality, design includes all of these things and maybe more."**
>
> **Thomas Powell**

19.2 The WebE Design Pyramid

What is design in the context of Web engineering? This simple question is more difficult to answer than one might believe. Design leads to a model that contains the appropriate mix of aesthetics, content, and technology. The mix will vary depending upon the nature of the WebApp, and as a consequence the design activities that are emphasized will also vary.

WebE encompasses six different types of design. Each contributes to the overall quality of the WebApp.

Figure 19.2 depicts a design pyramid for Web engineering. Each level of the pyramid represents one of the following design activities:

- *Interface design*—describes the structure and organization of the user interface. Includes a representation of screen layout, a definition of the modes of interaction, and a description of navigation mechanisms.

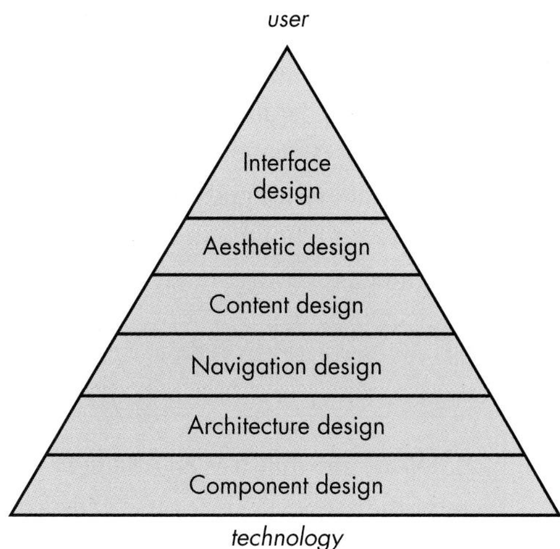

FIGURE 19.2 The WebE design pyramid

- *Aesthetic design*—also called *graphic design,* describes the "look and feel" of the WebApp. Includes color schemes, geometric layout, text size, font and placement, the use of graphics, and related aesthetic decisions.
- *Content design*—defines the layout, structure, and outline for all content that is presented as part of the WebApp. Establishes the relationships between content objects.
- *Navigation design*—represents the navigational flow between content objects and for all WebApp functions.
- *Architecture design*—identifies the overall hypermedia structure for the WebApp.
- *Component design*—develops the detailed processing logic required to implement functional components.

Each of these design activities are considered in more detail in the sections that follow.

19.3 WebApp Interface Design[3]

Every user interface—whether it is designed for a WebApp, a traditional software application, a consumer product, or an industrial device—should exhibit the following characteristics: easy to use, easy to learn, easy to navigate, intuitive, consistent, efficient, error-free, and functional. It should provide the end-user with a satisfying

3 Most, if not all, of the guidelines presented in Chapter 12 apply equally to the design of WebApp interfaces. If you have not already done so, read Chapter 12 at this time.

and rewarding experience. Interface design concepts, principles, and methods provide the Web engineer with the tools required to achieve this list of attributes.

In Chapter 12, we noted that interface design begins not with a consideration of technology, but with a careful examination of the end-user. During analysis modeling for Web engineering (Chapter 18), a user hierarchy is developed. Each user category may have subtly different needs, may want to interact with the WebApp in different ways, and may require unique functionality and content. This information is derived during requirements analysis, but it is revisited as the first step in interface design.

> "If a site is perfectly usable but it lacks an elegant and appropriate design style, it will fail."
>
> **Curt Cloninger**

If it is likely that users may enter your WebApp at various locations and levels in the content hierarchy, be sure to design every page with navigation features that will lead the user to other points of interest.

Dix [DIX99] argues that a Web engineer must design an interface so that it answers three primary questions for the end-user:

Where am I? The interface should (1) provide an indication of the WebApp that has been accessed[4] and (2) inform the user of her location in the content hierarchy.

What can I do now? The interface should always help the user understand his current options—what functions are available, what links are live, what content is relevant.

Where have I been; where am I going? The interface must facilitate navigation. Hence, it must provide a "map" (implemented in a way that is easy to understand) of where the user has been and what paths may be taken to move elsewhere within the WebApp.

An effective WebApp interface must provide answers for each of these questions as the end-user navigates through content and functionality.

19.3.1 Interface Design Principles and Guidelines

Bruce Tognozzi [TOG01] defines a set of fundamental characteristics that all interfaces should exhibit and, in doing so, establishes a philosophy that should be followed by every WebApp interface designer:

A good WebApp interface is understandable and forgiving, providing the user with a sense of control.

> Effective interfaces are visually apparent and forgiving, instilling in their users a sense of control. Users quickly see the breadth of their options, grasp how to achieve their goals, and do their work.
>
> Effective interfaces do not concern the user with the inner workings of the system. Work is carefully and continuously saved, with full option for the user to undo any activity at any time.
>
> Effective applications and services perform a maximum of work, while requiring a minimum of information from users.

4 Each of us has bookmarked a Web-site page, only to revisit later and have no indication of the Web site or the context for the page (as well as no way to move to another location within the site).

In order to design interfaces that exhibit these characteristics, Tognozzi [TOG01] identifies a set of overriding design principles:[5]

Anticipation—A WebApp should be designed so that it anticipates the user's next move. For example, consider a customer support WebApp developed by a manufacturer of computer printers. A user has requested a content object that presents information about a printer driver for a newly released operating system. The designer of the WebApp should anticipate that the user might request a download of the driver and should provide navigation facilities that allow this to happen without requiring the user to search for this capability.

A WebApp interface should be designed to conform to the set of principles noted here.

Communication—The interface should communicate the status of any activity initiated by the user. Communication can be obvious (e.g., a text message) or subtle (e.g., a sheet of paper moving through a printer to indicate that printing is underway). The interface should also communicate user status (e.g., the user's identification) and location within the WebApp content hierarchy.

Consistency—The use of navigation controls, menus, icons, and aesthetics (e.g., color, shape, layout) should be consistent throughout the WebApp. For example, if underlined blue text implies a navigation link, content should never incorporate blue underlined text that does not imply a link. Every feature of the interface should respond in a manner that is consistent with user expectations.[6]

Controlled autonomy—The interface should facilitate user movement throughout the WebApp, but it should do so in a manner that enforces navigation conventions that have been established for the application. For example, navigation to secure portions of the WebApp should be controlled by userID and password, and there should be no navigation mechanism that enables a user to circumvent these controls.

Efficiency—The design of the WebApp and its interface should optimize the user's work efficiency, not the efficiency of the Web engineer who designs and builds it or the client-server environment that executes it. Tognozzi [TOG01] discusses this when he writes: "This simple truth is why it is so important for everyone involved in a software project to appreciate the importance of making user productivity goal one and to understand the vital difference between building an efficient system and empowering an efficient user."

Flexibility—The interface should be flexible enough to enable some users to accomplish tasks directly and others to explore the WebApp in a somewhat random fashion. In every case, it should enable the user to understand where he is and provide the user with functionality that can undo mistakes and retrace poorly chosen navigation paths.

---

5 Tognozzi's original principles have been adapted and extended for use in this book. See [TOG01] for further discussion of these principles.

6 Tognozzi [TOG01] notes that the only way to be sure that user expectations are properly understood is through comprehensive user testing (Chapter 20).

Focus—The WebApp interface (and the content it presents) should stay focused on the user task(s) at hand. In all hypermedia there is a tendency to route the user to loosely related content. Why? Because it's very easy to do! The problem is that the user can rapidly become lost in many layers of supporting information and lose site of the original content that she wanted in the first place.

Fitt's Law—"The time to acquire a target is a function of the distance to and size of the target" [TOG01]. Based on a study conducted in the 1950s [FIT54], Fitt's Law "is an effective method of modeling rapid, aimed movements, where one appendage (like a hand) starts at rest at a specific start position, and moves to rest within a target area" [ZHA02]. If a sequence of selections or standardized inputs (with many different options within the sequence) is defined by a user task, the first selection (e.g., mouse pick) should be physically close to the next selection. For example, consider a WebApp home page interface at an e-commerce site that sells consumer electronics.

Each user option implies a set of follow-on user choices or actions. For example, a "buy a product" option requires that the user enter a product category followed by the product name. The product category (e.g., audio equipment, televisions, DVD players) appears as a pull-down menu as soon as "buy a product" is picked. Therefore, the next choice is immediately obvious (it is nearby), and the time to acquire it is negligible. If, on the other hand, the choice appeared on a menu that was located on the other side of the screen, the time for the user to acquire it (and then make the choice) would be far too long.

WebRef

A search on the Web will uncover many available libraries, e.g., Java API packages, interfaces, and classes at **java.sun.com** or COM, DCOM, and Type Libraries at **msdn.Microsoft.com.**

Human interface objects—A vast library of reusable human interface objects has been developed for WebApps. Use them. Any interface object that can be "seen, heard, touched or otherwise perceived" [TOG01] by an end-user can be acquired from any one of a number of object libraries.

Latency reduction—Rather than making the user wait for some internal operation to complete (e.g., downloading a complex graphical image), the WebApp should use multitasking in a way that lets the user proceed with work as if the operation has been completed. In addition to reducing latency, delays must be acknowledged so that the user understands what is happening. This includes (1) providing audio feedback (e.g., a click or bell tone) when a selection does not result in an immediate action by the WebApp; (2) displaying an animated clock or progress bar to indicate that processing is under way; (3) provide some entertainment (e.g., an animation or text presentation) while lengthy processing occurs.

> "The best journey is the one with the fewest steps. Shorten the distance between the user and their goal."
>
> **Author unknown**

Learnability—A WebApp interface should be designed to minimize learning time, and once learned, to minimize relearning required when the WebApp is revisited. In general the interface should emphasize a simple, intuitive design that organizes content and functionality into categories that are obvious to the user.

Metaphors—An interface that uses an interaction metaphor is easier to learn and easier to use, as long as the metaphor is appropriate for the application and the user. A metaphor should call on images and concepts from the user's experience, but it does not need to be an exact reproduction of a real world experience. For example, an e-commerce site that implements automated bill paying for a financial institution uses a checkbook metaphor (not surprisingly) to assist the user in specifying and scheduling bill payments. However, when a user "writes" a check, he need not enter the complete payee name but can pick from a list of payees or have the system select based on the first few typed letters. The metaphor remains intact, but the user gets an assist from the WebApp.

Metaphors are an excellent idea because they mirror real world experience. Just be sure that the metaphor you choose is well known among end-users.

Maintain work product integrity. A work product (e.g., a form completed by the user, a user specified list) must be automatically saved so that it will not be lost if an error occurs. Each of us has experienced the frustration associated with completing a lengthy WebApp form only to have the content lost because of an error (made by us, by the WebApp, or in transmission from client to server). To avoid this, a WebApp should be designed to auto-save all user specified data.

Readability—All information presented through the interface should be readable by young and old. The interface designer should emphasize readable type styles, font sizes, and color background choices that enhance contrast.

Track state—When appropriate, the state of the user interaction should be tracked and stored so that a user can log-off and return later to pick up where she left off. In general, cookies can be designed to store state information. However, cookies are a controversial technology, and other design solutions may be more palatable for some users.

Visible navigation—A well-designed WebApp interface provides "the illusion that users are in the same place, with the work brought to them" [TOG01]. When this approach is used, navigation is not a user concern. Rather, the user retrieves content objects and selects functions that are displayed and executed through the interface.

SAFEHOME

Interface Design Review

The scene: Doug Miller's office.

The players: Doug Miller (manager of the *SafeHome* software engineering group) and Vinod Raman, a member of the *SafeHome* product software engineering team.

The conversation:

Doug: Vinod, have you and the team had a chance to review the SafeHomeAssured.com e-commerce interface prototype?

Vinod: Yeah . . . we all went through it from a technical point of view, and I have a bunch of notes. I e-mailed 'em to Sharon [manager of the Web engineering team for the outsourcing vendor for the *SafeHome* e-commerce Web site] yesterday.

Doug: You and Sharon can get together and discuss the small stuff . . . give me a summary of the important issues.

Vinod: Overall, they've done a good job, nothing ground breaking, but it's a typical e-commerce interface, decent aesthetics, reasonable layout. They've hit all the important functions. . . .

Doug (smiling ruefully): But?

Vinod: Well, there are a few things. . . .

Doug: Such as . . . ?

Vinod (showing Doug a sequence of storyboards for the interface prototype): Here's the major functions menu that's displayed on the home page:

Learn about *SafeHome*
Describe your home
Get *SafeHome* component recommendations
Purchase a *SafeHome* system
Get technical support

The problem isn't with these functions, they're all okay, but the level of abstraction isn't right.

Doug: They're all major functions, aren't they?

Vinod: They are, but here's the thing . . . you can purchase a system by inputting a list of components . . . no real need to describe the house, if you don't want to. I'd suggest only four menu options on the home page:

Learn about *SafeHome*
Specify the *SafeHome* system you need
Purchase a *SafeHome* system
Get technical support

When you select **specify the *SafeHome* system you need,** you'll then have the following options:

Select *SafeHome* components
Get *SafeHome* component recommendations

If you're a knowledgeable user, you'll select components from a set of categorized pull-down menus for sensors, cameras, control panels, etc. If you need help, you'll ask for a recommendation and that will require that you describe your house. I think it's a bit more logical.

Doug: I agree. Have you talked with Sharon about this?

Vinod: No, I want to discuss this with marketing first, and then I'll give her a call.

Nielsen and Wagner [NIE96] suggest a few pragmatic interface design guidelines (based on their redesign of a major WebApp) that provide a nice complement to the principles suggested earlier in this section:

- Reading speed on a computer monitor is approximately 25 percent slower than reading speed for hardcopy. Therefore, do not force the user to read voluminous amounts of text, particularly when the text explains the operation of the WebApp or assists in navigation.
- Avoid "under construction" signs—they raise expectations and cause an unnecessary link that is sure to disappoint.
- Users prefer not to scroll. Important information should be placed within the dimensions of a typical browser window.
- Navigation menus and head bars should be designed consistently and should be available on all pages that are available to the user. The design should not rely on browser functions to assist in navigation.
- Aesthetics should never supersede functionality. For example, a simple button might be a better navigation option than an aesthetically pleasing, but vague image or icon whose intent is unclear.

- Navigation options should be obvious, even to the casual user. The user shouldn't have to search the screen to determine how to link to other content or services.

A well-designed interface improves the user's perception of the content or services provided by the site. It need not necessarily be flashy, but it should always be well-structured and ergonomically sound.

> "People have very little patience for poorly designed WWW sites."
>
> **Jakob Nielsen and Annette Wagner**

19.3.2 Interface Control Mechanisms

The objectives of a WebApp interface are to (1) establish a consistent window into the content and functionality provided by the interface, (2) guide the user through a series of interactions with the WebApp, and (3) organize the navigation options and content available to the user. To achieve a consistent interface, the designer must first use aesthetic design (Section 19.4) to establish a coherent "look" for the interface. This encompasses many characteristics, but must emphasize the layout and form of navigation mechanisms. To guide user interaction, the interface designer may draw on an appropriate metaphor[7] that enables the user to gain an intuitive understanding of the interface. To implement navigation options, the designer selects from one of a number of interaction mechanisms:

? What interaction mechanisms are available to WebApp designers?

- *Navigation menus*—keyword menus (organized vertically or horizontally) that list key content and or functionality. These menus may be implemented so that the user can choose from a hierarchy of subtopics that is displayed when the primary menu option is selected.
- *Graphic icons*—button, switches, and similar graphical images that enable the user to select some property or specify a decision.
- *Graphic images*—some graphical representation that is selectable by the user and implements a link to a content object or WebApp functionality.

It is important to note that one or more of these control mechanisms should be provided at every level of the content hierarchy.

19.3.3 Interface Design Workflow

Although an in-depth discussion of interface design for WebApps is best left to textbooks that are dedicated to the subject (e.g., [GAL02], [RAS00], or [NIE00]), a brief overview of the key design tasks is worthwhile. In Chapter 12, we noted that user interface design begins with the identification of user, task, and environmental

---

7 In this context, a *metaphor* is a representation (drawn for the user's real word experience) that can be modeled within the context of the interface. A simple example might be a slider switch that is used to control the auditory volume of an .mpg file.

FIGURE 19.3

Mapping user objectives into interface actions

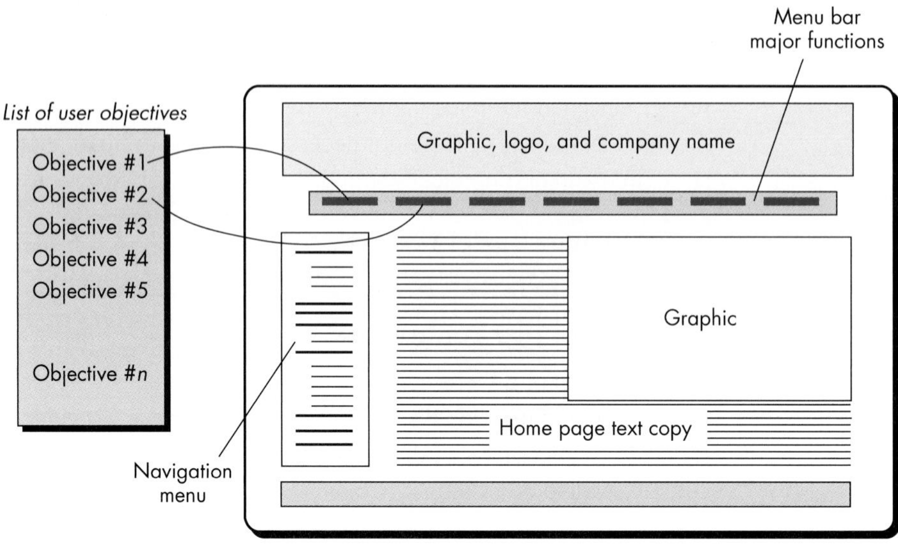

requirements. Once user tasks have been identified, user scenarios (use-cases) are created and analyzed to define a set of interface objects and actions. This work is represented as part of the WebApp analysis model discussed in Chapter 18.

The following tasks represent a rudimentary work flow for WebApp interface design:

1. **Review information contained in the analysis model and refine as required.**
2. **Develop a rough sketch of the WebApp interface layout.** An interface prototype (including the layout) may have been developed as part of the analysis modeling activity. If the layout already exists, it should be reviewed and refined as required. If the interface layout has not been developed, the Web engineering team should work with stakeholders to develop it at this time. A schematic first-cut layout sketch is shown in Figure 19.3.
3. **Map user objectives into specific interface actions.** For the vast majority of WebApps, the user will have a relatively small (typically between four and seven) set of primary objectives. These should be mapped into specific interface actions as shown in Figure 19.3.
4. **Define a set of user tasks that are associated with each action.** Each interface action (e.g., "buy a product") is associated with a set of user tasks. These tasks have been identified during analysis modeling. During design, they must be mapped into specific interactions that encompass navigation issues, content objects, and WebApp functions.
5. **Storyboard screen images for each interface action.** As each action is considered, a sequence of storyboard images (screen images) should be cre-

ated to depict how the interface responds to user interaction. Content objects should be identified (even if they have not yet been designed and developed), WebApp functionality should be shown, and navigation links should be indicated.

6. **Refine interface layout and storyboards using input from aesthetic design.** Rough layout and storyboarding is completed by Web engineers, but the aesthetic look and feel for a major commercial site is often developed by artistic, rather than technical, professionals.
7. **Identify user interface objects that are required to implement the interface.** This task may require a search through an existing object library to find those reusable objects (classes) that are appropriate for the WebApp interface. In addition, any custom classes are specified at this time.
8. **Develop a procedural representation of the user's interaction with the interface.** This optional task uses UML sequence diagrams and/or activity diagrams (discussed in Chapter 18) to depict the flow of activities (and decisions) that occur as the user interacts with the WebApp.
9. **Develop a behavioral representation of the interface.** This optional task makes use of UML state diagrams (discussed in Chapter 18) to represent state transitions and the events that cause them. Control mechanisms (i.e., the objects and actions available to the user to alter a WebApp state) are defined.
10. **Describe the interface layout for each state.** Using design information developed in Tasks 2 and 5, associate a specific layout or screen image with each WebApp state described in Task 9.
11. **Refine and review the interface design model.** Review of the interface should focus on usability (Chapter 12).

It is important to note that the final task set chosen by a Web engineering team must be adapted to the special requirements of the application that is to be built.

19.4 Aesthetic Design

Not every Web engineer (or software engineer) has artistic (aesthetic) talent. If you fall into this category, hire an experienced graphic designer for aesthetic design work.

Aesthetic design, also called *graphic design,* is an artistic endeavor that complements the technical aspects of Web engineering. Without it, a WebApp may be functional, but unappealing. With it, a WebApp draws its users into a world that embraces them on a visceral, as well as an intellectual, level.

But what is aesthetic? There is an old saying, "beauty exists in the eye of the beholder." This is particularly appropriate when aesthetic design for WebApps is considered. To perform effective aesthetic design, we again return to the user hierarchy developed as part of the analysis model (Chapter 18) and ask, who are the WebApp's users and what "look" do they desire?

> "We find that people quickly evaluate a site by visual design alone."
>
> **Stanford Guidelines for Web Credibility**

19.4.1 Layout Issues

Every Web page has a limited amount of "real estate" that can be used to support nonfunctional aesthetics, navigation features, information content, and user-directed functionality. The "development" of this real estate is planned during aesthetic design.

Like all aesthetic issues, there are no absolute rules when screen layout is designed. However, a number of general layout guidelines are worth considering:

Don't be afraid of white space. It is inadvisable to pack every square inch of a Web page with information. The resulting clutter makes it difficult for the user to identify needed information or features and creates visual chaos that is not pleasing to the eye.

Emphasize content. After all, that's the reason the user is there. Nielsen [NIE00] suggests that the typical Web page should be 80 percent content with the remaining real estate dedicated to navigation and other features.

Organize layout elements from top-left to bottom-right. The vast majority of users will scan a Web page in much the same way as they scan the page of a book—top-left to bottom-right.[8] If layout elements have specific priorities, high-priority elements should be placed in the upper-left portion of the page real estate.

Group navigation, content, and function geographically within the page. Humans look for patterns in virtually all things. If there are no discernable patterns within a Web page, user frustration is likely to increase (due to unnecessary searching for needed information).

Don't extend your real estate with the scrolling bar. Although scrolling is often necessary, most studies indicate that users would prefer not to scroll. It is better to reduce page content or to present necessary content on multiple pages.

Consider resolution and browser window size when designing layout. Rather than defining fixed sizes within a layout, the design should specify all layout items as a percentage of available space [NIE00].

19.4.2 Graphic Design Issues

Graphic design considers every aspect of the look and feel of a WebApp. The graphic design process begins with layout (Section 19.4.1) and proceeds into a consideration of global color schemes, typefaces, sizes, and styles, the use of supplementary media (e.g., audio, video, animation), and all other aesthetic elements of an application. The interested reader can obtain design tips and guidelines from many Web sites that

8 There are exceptions that are cultural and language-based, but this rule does hold for most users.

are dedicated to the subject (e.g., www.graphic-design.com, www.grantasticdesigns.com, www.wpdfd.com) or from one or more print resources (e.g., [BAG01], [CLO01], or [HEI02]).

INFO

Well-Designed Web Sites

Sometimes, the best way to understand good WebApp design is to look at a few examples. In his article, "The Top Twenty Web Design Tips," Marcelle Toor (http://www.graphic-design.com/Web/feature/tips.html) suggests the following Web sites as examples of good graphic design:

www.primo.com—a design firm headed by Primo Angeli.
www.workbook.com—this site showcases work by illustrators and designers.
www.pbs.org/riverofsong—a television series for public TV and radio about American music.
www.RKDINC.com—a design firm with an on-line portfolio and good design tips.
www.commarts.com/career/index.html—*Communication Arts* magazine, a trade periodical for graphic designers. A good source for other well-designed sites.
www.btdnyc.com—a design firm headed by Beth Toudreau.

19.5 Content Design

Content design focuses on two different design issues, each addressed by individuals with different skill sets. Content design develops a design representation for content objects and represents the mechanisms required to instantiate their relationships to one another. This design activity is conducted by Web engineers.

In addition, content design is concerned with the representation of information within a specific content object—a design activity that is conducted by copywriters, graphic designers, and others who generate the content to be used within a WebApp.

> "Good designers can create normalcy out of chaos; they can clearly communicate ideas through the organizing and manipulating of words and pictures."
>
> **Jeffery Veen**

19.5.1 Content Objects

The relationship between content objects defined as part of the WebApp analysis model (e.g., Figure 18.3) and design objects representing content is analogous to the relationship between analysis classes and design components described in Chapter 11. In the context of Web engineering, a *content object* is more closely aligned with a data object for conventional software. A content object has attributes that include content specific information (normally defined during WebApp analysis modeling) and implementation specific attributes that are specified as part of design.

As an example, consider the analysis class developed for the *SafeHome* e-commerce system named **ProductComponent** that was developed in Chapter 18 and represented as shown in Figure 19.4. In Chapter 18, we noted an attribute **description**

FIGURE 19.4

Design representation of content objects

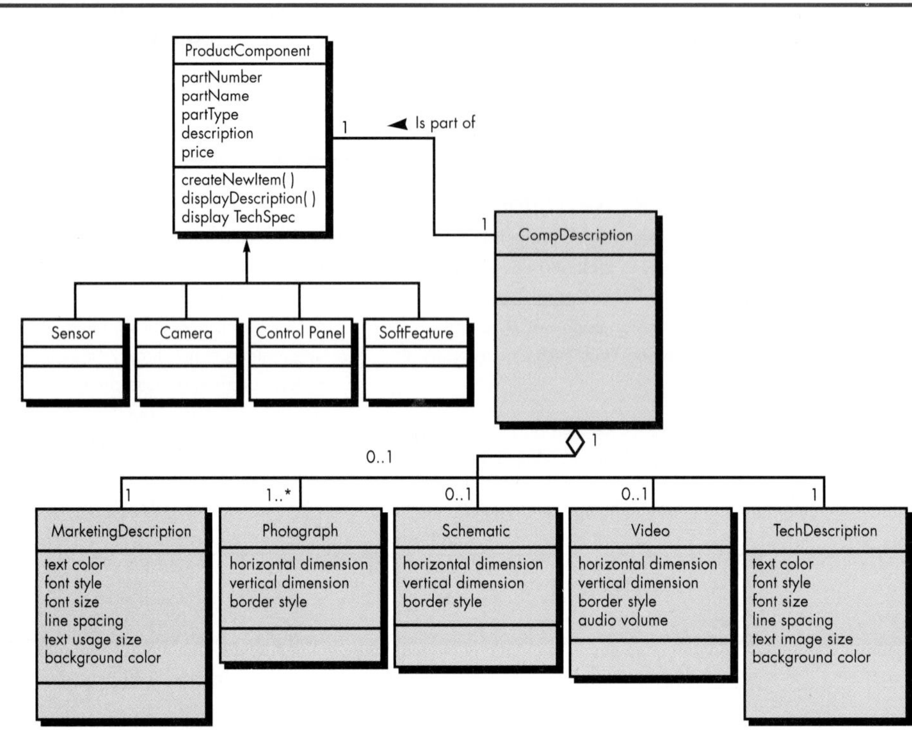

that is represented here as a design class named **CompDescription** composed of five content objects: **MarketingDescription, Photograph, TechDescription, Schematic,** and **Video** shown as shaded objects noted in the figure. Information contained within the content object is noted as attributes. For example, **Photograph** (a .jpg image) has the attributes **horizontal dimension, vertical dimension,** and **border style.**

UML association and an aggregation[9] may be used to represent relationships between content objects. For example, the UML association shown in Figure 19.4 indicates that one **CompDescription** is used for each instance of the **ProductComponent** class. **CompDescription** is composed of the five content objects shown. However, the multiplicity notation shown indicates that **Schematic** and **Video** are optional (0 occurrences are possible), one **MarketingDescription** and **TechDescription** is required, and one or more instances of **Photograph** is used.

19.5.2 Content Design Issues

Once all content objects are modeled, the information that each object is to deliver must be authored and then formatted to best meet the customer's needs. Content authoring is the job of specialists who design the content object by providing an outline of information to be delivered and an indication of the types of generic content

9 Both of these representations are discussed in Chapter 8.

Users tend to tolerate vertical scrolling more readily than horizontal scrolling. Avoid wide page formats.

objects (e.g., descriptive text, graphic images, photographs) that will be used to deliver the information. Aesthetic design (Section 19.4) may also be applied to represent the proper look and feel for the content.

As content objects are designed, they are "chunked" [POW00] to form WebApp pages. The number of content objects incorporated into a single page is a function of user needs, constraints imposed by download speed of the Internet connections, and restrictions imposed by the amount of scrolling that the user will tolerate.

19.6 Architecture Design

Architecture design is tied to the goals established for a WebApp, the content to be presented, the users who will visit, and the navigation philosophy that has been established. The architectural designer must identify content architecture and WebApp architecture. *Content architecture*[10] focuses on the manner in which content objects (or composite objects such as Web pages) are structured for presentation and navigation. *WebApp architecture* addresses the manner in which the application is structured to manage user interaction, handle internal processing tasks, effect navigation, and present content.

> "[T]he architectural structure of a well designed site is not always apparent to the user—nor should it be."
>
> **Thomas Powell**

In most cases, architecture design is conducted in parallel with interface, aesthetic, and content design. Because the WebApp architecture may have a strong influence on navigation, the decisions made during this design activity will influence work conducted during navigation design.

19.6.1 Content Architecture

The design of *content architecture* focuses on the definition of the overall hypermedia structure of the WebApp. The design can choose from four different content structures [POW00]:

Linear structures (Figure 19.5) are encountered when a predictable sequence of interactions (with some variation or diversion) is common. A classic example might be a tutorial presentation in which pages of information along with related graphics, short videos, or audio are presented only after prerequisite information has been presented. The sequence of content presentation is predefined and generally linear. Another example might be a product order entry sequence in which specific information must be specified in a specific order. In such cases, the structures shown in Figure 19.5 are appropriate. As content and processing become more complex, the purely linear flow shown on the left of the figure gives way to

10 The term *information architecture* is also used to connote structures that lead to better organization, labeling, navigation, and searching of content objects.

FIGURE 19.5

Linear structures

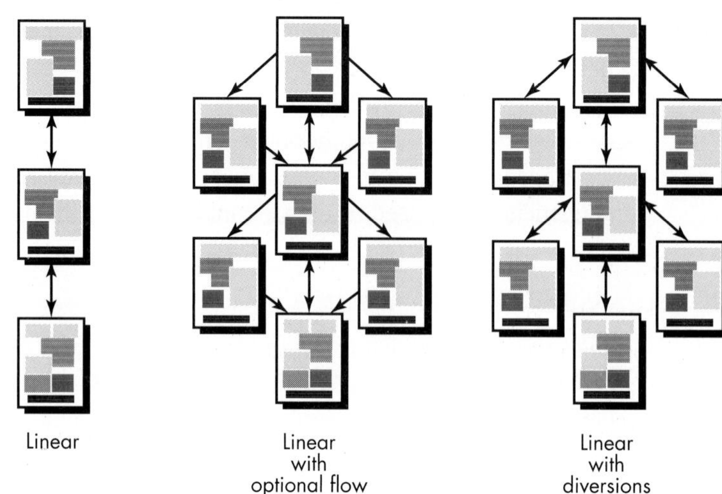

FIGURE 19.6

Grid structure

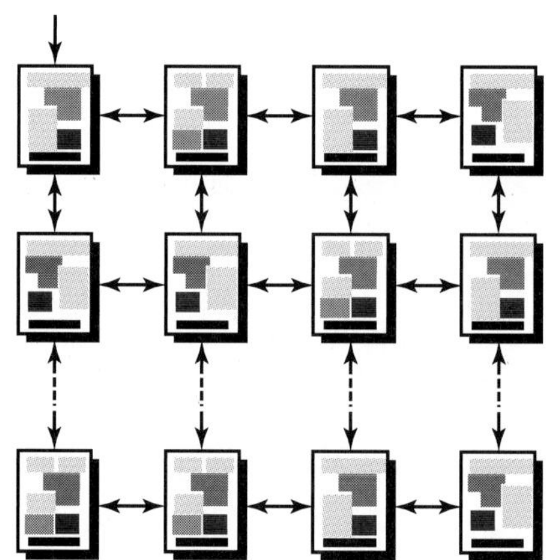

more sophisticated linear structures in which alternative content may be invoked or a diversion to acquire complementary content (structure shown on the right side of Figure 19.5) occurs.

Grid structures (Figure 19.6) are an architectural option that can be applied when WebApp content can be organized categorically in two (or more) dimensions. For example, consider a situation in which an e-commerce site sells golf clubs. The horizontal dimension of the grid represents the type of club to be sold (e.g., woods, irons, wedges, putters). The vertical dimension represents the offerings provided by various golf club manufacturers. Hence, a user might navigate the grid horizontally to find the putters column and then vertically to examine the offerings provided by those manufacturers that sell putters. This WebApp architecture is useful only when highly regular content is encountered [POW00].

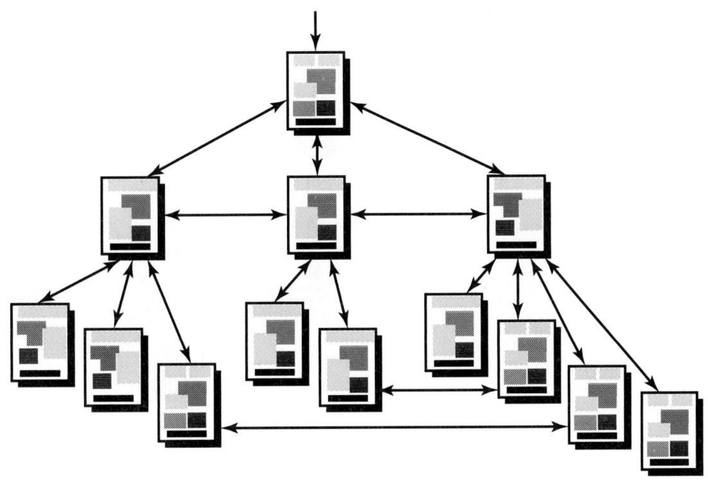

FIGURE 19.7
Hierarchical structure

Hierarchical structures (Figure 19.7) are undoubtedly the most common WebApp architecture. Unlike the partitioned software hierarchies discussed in Chapter 10 that encourage flow of control only along vertical branches of the hierarchy, a WebApp hierarchical structure can be designed in a manner that enables (via hypertext branching) flow of control horizontally, across vertical branches of the structure. Hence, content presented on the far left-hand branch of the hierarchy can have hypertext links that lead to content that exists in the middle or right-hand branch of the structure. It should be noted, however, that although such branching allows rapid navigation across WebApp content, it can lead to confusion on the part of the user.

A *networked* or *"pure web" structure* (Figure 19.8) is similar in may ways to the architecture that evolves for object-oriented systems. Architectural components (in this case Web pages) are designed so that they may pass control (via hypertext links) to virtually every other component in the system. This approach allows considerable navigation flexibility, but at the same time can be confusing to a user.

The architectural structures discussed in the preceding paragraphs can be combined to form *composite structures.* The overall architecture of a WebApp may be hierarchical, but part of the structure may exhibit linear characteristics, while another part of the architecture may be networked. The goal for the architectural designer is to match the WebApp structure to the content to be presented and the processing to be conducted.

19.6.2 WebApp Architecture

WebApp architecture describes an infrastructure that enables a Web-based system or application to achieve its business objectives. Jacyntho and his colleagues [JAC02] describe the basic characteristics of this infrastructure in the following manner:

> Applications should be built using layers in which different concerns are taken into account; in particular, application data should be separated from the page's contents

FIGURE 19.8

Network structure

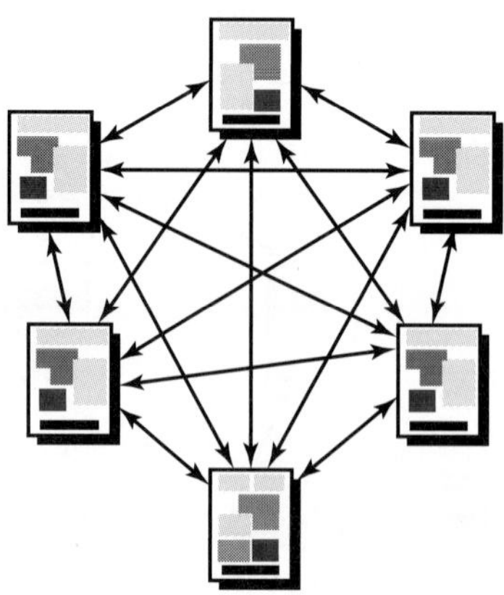

(navigation nodes) and these contents, in turn, should be clearly separated from the interface look-and-feel (pages).

The authors suggest a three-layer design architecture that decouples interface from navigation and from application behavior, and argue that keeping interface, application, and navigation separate simplifies implementation and enhances reuse.

The MVC architecture decouples the user interface from WebApp functionality and information content.

The *Model-View-Controller* (MVC) architecture [KRA88][11] is one of a number of suggested WebApp infrastructure models that decouples the user interface from the WebApp functionality and informational content. The *model* (sometimes referred to as the "model object") contains all application specific content and processing logic, including all content objects, access to external data/information sources, and all processing functionality that are application specific. The *view* contains all interface specific functions and enables the presentation of content and processing logic, including all content objects, access to external data/information sources, and all processing functionality required by the end-user. The *controller* manages access to the *model* and the *view* and coordinates the flow of data between them. In a WebApp, "view is updated by the controller with data from the model based on user input" [WMT02]. A schematic representation of the MVC architecture is shown in Figure 19.9.

Referring to the figure, user requests or data are handled by the controller. The controller also selects the view object that is applicable based on the user request. Once the type of request is determined, a behavior request is transmitted to the model, which implements the functionality or retrieves the content required to accommodate the request. The model object can access data stored in a corporate database, as part of a local data store or as a collection of independent files. The data developed by the model must be formatted and organized by the appropriate view

11 It should be noted that MVC is actually an architectural design pattern developed for the Smalltalk environment (see http://www.cetus-links.org/oo_smalltalk.html) and can be used for any interactive application.

FIGURE 19.9 The MVC architecture (adapted from [JAC02])

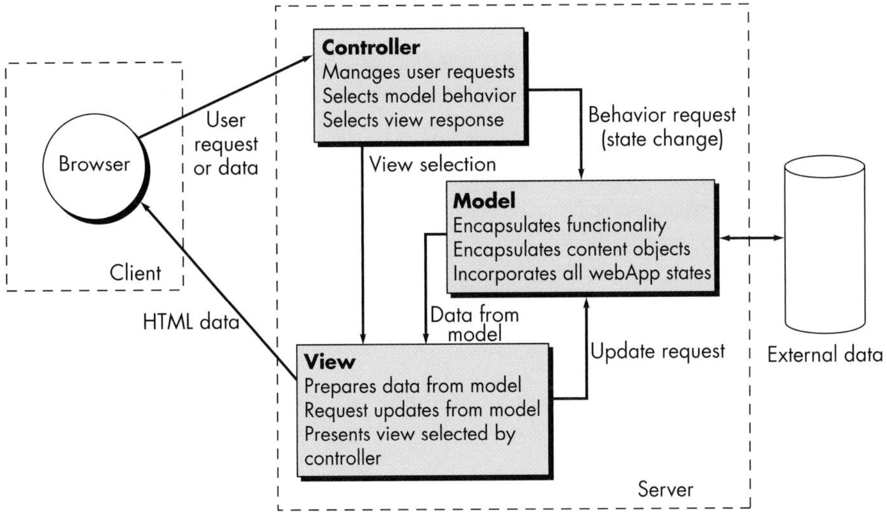

object and then transmitted from the application server back to the client-based browser for display on the customer's machine.

In many cases, WebApp architecture is defined within the context of the development environment in which the application is to be implemented (e.g., ASP.net, JWAA, or J2EE). The interested reader should see [FOW03] for further discussion of modern development environments and their role in the design of Web application architectures.

19.7 Navigation Design

Once the WebApp architecture has been established and the components (pages, scripts, applets, and other processing functions) of the architecture have been identified, the designer must define navigation pathways that enable users to access WebApp content and functions. To accomplish this, the designer should (1) identify the semantics of navigation for different users of the site, and (2) define the mechanics (syntax) of achieving the navigation.

> **"Just wait, Gretel, until the moon rises, and then we shall see the crumbs of bread which I have strewn about, they will show us our way home again."**
>
> **from Hansel and Gretel**

19.7.1 Navigation Semantics

Like many Web engineering activities, navigation design begins with a consideration of the user hierarchy and related use-cases (Chapter 18) developed for each category of user (actor). Each actor may use the WebApp somewhat differently and therefore have different navigation requirements. In addition, the use-cases developed for each actor will define a set of classes that encompass one or more content objects or WebApp functions. As each user interacts with the WebApp, she encounters a series of *navigation semantic units* (NSUs)—"a set of information and related navigation structures that collaborate in the fulfillment of a subset of related user requirements" [CAC02].

Gnaho and Larcher [GNA99] describe the NSU in the following way:

> The structure of a NSU is composed of a set of navigational sub-structures that we call *ways of navigating* (WoN). A WoN represents the best navigation way or path for users with certain profiles to achieve their desired goal or sub-goal. Therefore, the concept of WoN is associated to the concept of User Profile.
>
> The structure of a WoN is made out of a set of relevant *navigational nodes* (NN) connected by *navigational links,* including sometimes other NSUs. That means that NSUs may themselves be aggregated to form a higher-level NSU, or may be nested to any depth.

To illustrate the development of an NSU, consider the use-case, *select SafeHome components,* described in Section 18.1.2 and reproduced here:

> **Use-case:** *select SafeHome components*
>
> The WebApp will recommend product components (e.g., control panels, sensors, cameras) and other features (e.g., PC-based functionality implemented in software) for each room and exterior entrance. If I request alternatives, the WebApp will provide them, if they exist. I will be able to get descriptive and pricing information for each product component. The WebApp will create and display a bill-of-materials as I select various components. I'll be able to give the bill-of-materials a name and save it for future reference (see use-case: *save configuration*).

A NSU describes the navigation requirements for each use-case. In essence, the NSU shows how an actor moves between content objects or WebApp functions.

The underlined items in the use-case description represent classes and content objects that will be incorporated into one or more NSUs that will enable a new customer to perform the scenario described in the *select SafeHome components* use-case.

Figure 19.10 depicts a partial semantic analysis of the navigation implied by the *select SafeHome component* use-case. Using the terminology introduced earlier, the figure also represents a way of navigating (WoN) for the SafeHomeAssured.com WebApp. Important problem domain classes are shown along with selected content objects (in this case the package of content objects named **CompDescription,** an attribute of the **ProductComponent** class). These items are navigation nodes. Each of the arrows represents a navigation link[12] and is labeled with the use-initiated action that causes the link to occur.

The WebApp designer creates a NSU for each use-case associated with each user role [GNA99]. For example, a **new customer** (Figure 18.1) may have three different use-cases, all resulting in access to different information and WebApp functions. A NSU is created for each goal.

During the initial stages of navigation design, the WebApp content architecture is assessed to determine one or more WoN for each use-case. As noted above, a WoN

12 These are sometimes referred to as *navigation semantic links* (NSL) [CAC02].

FIGURE 19.10 Creating a NSU

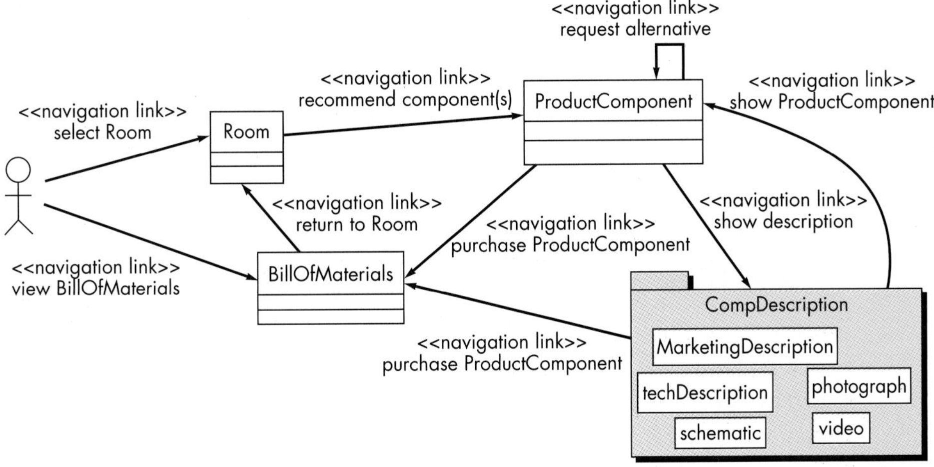

identifies navigation nodes (e.g., content) and the links that enable navigation between them. The WoN are then organized into NSUs.

> "The problem of Web site navigation is conceptual, technical, spatial, philosophical and logistic. Consequently, solutions tend to call for complex improvisational combinations of art, science, and organizational psychology."
>
> **Tim Horgan**

19.7.2 Navigation Syntax

As design proceeds, the mechanics of navigation are defined. Among many possible options are:

ADVICE *In most situations, choose either horizontal or vertical navigation mechanisms, but not both.*

- *Individual navigation link*—text-based links, icons, buttons and switches, and graphical metaphors.
- *Horizontal navigation bar*—lists major content or functional categories in a bar containing appropriate links. In general, between four and seven categories are listed.
- *Vertical navigation column*— (1) lists major content or functional categories, or (2) lists virtually all major content objects within the WebApp. If the second option is chosen, such navigation columns can "expand" to present content objects as part of a hierarchy.
- *Tabs*—a metaphor that is nothing more than a variation of the navigation bar or column, representing content or functional categories as tab sheets that are selected when a link is required.
- *Site maps*—provide an all-inclusive table of contents for navigation to all content objects and functionality contained within the WebApp.

The site map should be accessible from every page. The map itself should be organized so that the structure of WebApp information is readily apparent.

In addition to choosing the mechanics of navigation, the designer should also establish appropriate navigation conventions and aids. For example, icons and graphical links should look "clickable" by beveling the edges to give the image a three-dimensional look. Audio or visual feedback should be designed to provide the user with an indication that a navigation option has been chosen. For text-based navigation, color should be used to indicate navigation links and to provide an indication of links already traveled. These are but a few of dozens of design conventions that make navigation user-friendly.

19.8 Component Level Design

Modern Web applications deliver increasingly sophisticated processing functions that (1) perform localized processing to generate content and navigation capability in a dynamic fashion; (2) provide computation or data processing capability that are appropriate for the WebApp's business domain; (3) provide sophisticated database query and access; (4) establish data interfaces with external corporate systems. To achieve these (and many other) capabilities, the Web engineer must design and construct program components that are identical in form to software components for conventional software.

In Chapter 11, we consider component-level design in some detail. The design methods discussed in Chapter 11 apply to WebApp components with little, if any, modification. The implementation environment, programming languages, and reusable patterns, frameworks, and software may vary somewhat, but the overall design approach remains the same.

19.9 Hypermedia Design Patterns

Design patterns that are used in Web engineering encompass two major classes: (1) generic design patterns that are applicable to all types of software (e.g., [BUS96] and [GAM95]) and (2) *hypermedia design patterns* that are specific to WebApps. Generic design patterns have been discussed in Chapter 9. A number of hypermedia patterns catalogs and repositories can be accessed via the Internet.[13]

> **"Each pattern is a three-part rule which expresses a relationship between a certain context, a problem, and a solution."**
> **Christopher Alexander**

As we noted earlier in this book, design patterns are a generic approach for solving some small design problem that can be adapted to a much wider variety of specific problems. In the context of Web-based systems German and Cowan [GER00] suggest the following patterns categories:

13 See the sidebar at the end of this section.

Architectural patterns. These patterns assist in the design of content and WebApp architecture. Sections 19.6.1 and 19.6.2 present architectural patterns for content and WebApp architecture. In addition, many related architectural patterns are available (e.g., *Java Blueprints* at java.sun.com/blueprints/) for Web engineers who must design WebApps in a variety of business domains.

Component construction patterns. These patterns recommend methods for combining WebApp components (e.g., content objects, functions) into composite components. When data processing functionality is required within a WebApp, the architectural and component-level design patterns proposed by [BUS96], [GAM95], and others are applicable.

Navigation patterns. These patterns assist in the design of NSUs, navigation links, and the overall navigation flow of the WebApp.

Presentation patterns. These patterns assist in the presentation of content as it is presented to the user via the interface. Patterns in this category address how to organize user interface control functions for better usability; how to show the relationship between an interface action and the content objects it affects; how to establish effective content hierarchies; and many others.

Behavior/user interaction patterns. These patterns assist in the design of user-machine interaction. Patterns in this category address how the interface informs the user of the consequences of a specific action; how a user expands content based on usage context and user desires; how to best describe the destination that is implied by a link; how to inform the user about the status of an on-going interaction and others.

Sources of information on hypermedia design patterns have expanded dramatically in recent years. Interested readers should see [GAR97], [PER99], and [GER00].

SOFTWARE TOOLS

Hypermedia Design Patterns Repositories

The IAWiki Web site (http://iawiki.net/WebsitePatterns) is a collaborative discussion space for information architects that contains many useful resources. Among them are links to a number of useful hypermedia patterns catalogs and repositories. Hundreds of design patterns are represented:

Hypermedia Design Patterns Repository
http://www.designpattern.lu.unisi.ch/

InteractionPatterns by Tom Erickson
http://www.pliant.org/personal/Tom_Erickson/InteractionPatterns.html

Web Design Patterns by Martijn vanWelie
http://www.welie.com/patterns/

Improving Web Information Systems with Navigational Patterns
http://www8.org/w8-papers/5b-hypertext-media/improving/improving.html

An HTML 2.0 Pattern Language
http://www.anamorph.com/docs/patterns/default.html

Common Ground
http://www.mit.edu/~jtidwell/interaction_patterns.html

Patterns for Personal Web Sites
http://www.rdrop.com/~half/Creations/Writings/Web.patterns/index.html

Indexing Pattern Language
http://www.cs.brown.edu/~rms/InformationStructures/Indexing/Overview.html

19.10 Object-Oriented Hypermedia Design Method (OOHDM)

A number of design methods for Web applications have been proposed over the past decade. To date, no single method has achieved dominance. In this section we present a brief overview of one of the most widely discussed WebApp design methods—OOHDM.[14]

Object-Oriented Hypermedia Design Method (OOHDM) was originally proposed by Daniel Schwabe and his colleagues [SCH95, SCH98]. OOHDM is composed of four different design activities: conceptual design, navigational design, abstract interface design, and implementation. A summary of these design activities is shown in Figure 19.11 and discussed briefly in the sections that follow.

19.10.1 Conceptual Design for OOHDM

OOHDM *conceptual design* creates a representation of the subsystems, classes, and relationships that define the application domain for the WebApp. UML may be used[15] to create appropriate class diagrams, aggregations and composite class representa-

Figure 19.11 Summary of the OOHDM method (adapted from [SCH95])

	Conceptual design	Navigational design	Abstract interface design	Implementation
Work products	Classes, sub-systems, relationships, attributes	Nodes links, access structures, navigational contexts, navigational transformations	Abstract interface objects, responses to external events, transformations	executable WebApp
Design mechanisms	Classification, composition, aggregation, generalization specialization	Mapping between conceptual and navigation objects	Mapping between navigation and perceptible objects	Resource provided by target environment
Design concerns	Modeling semantics of the application domain	Takes into account user profile and task. Emphasis on cognitive aspects.	Modeling perceptible objects, implementing chosen metaphors. Describe interface for navigational objects	Correctness; Application performance; completeness

14 A comprehensive comparison of 10 hypermedia design methods has been developed by Koch [KOC99].

15 OOHDM does not prescribe a specific notation; however, the use of UML is common when this method is applied.

tions, collaboration diagrams, and other information that describes the application domain (see Part 2 of this book for more detail).

As a simple example of OOHDM conceptual design, we again consider the SafeHomeAssured.com e-commerce application. A partial "conceptual schema" for SafeHomeAssured.com is shown in Figure 19.12. The class diagrams, aggregations, and related information developed as part of WebApp analysis are reused during conceptual design to represent relationships between classes.

19.10.2 Navigational Design for OOHDM

Navigational design identifies a set of "objects" that are derived from the classes defined in conceptual design. A series of "navigational classes" or "nodes" are defined to encapsulate these objects. UML may be used to create appropriate use-cases, state charts, and sequence diagrams—all representations that assist the designer in better understanding navigational requirements. In addition, design patterns for navigation design may be used as the design is developed. OOHDM uses a predefined set of navigation classes—nodes, links, anchors, and access structures [SCH98]. Access structures are more elaborate and include mechanisms such as a WebApp index, a site map, or a guided tour.

FIGURE 19.12 Partial conceptual schema for SafeHomeAssured.com

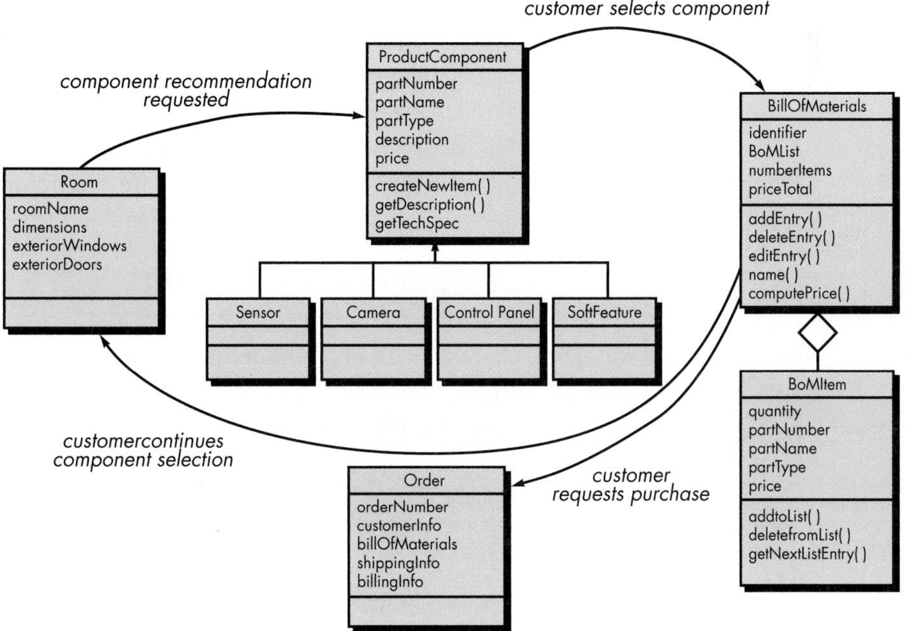

Once navigation classes are defined, OOHDM "structures the navigation space by grouping navigation objects into sets called contexts" [SCH98]. Schwabe describes a *context* in the following manner:

> Each context definition includes, besides which elements are included in it, the specification of its internal navigation structure, an entry point, access restrictions in terms of user classes and operations, and an associated access structure.

A context template (analogous to CRC cards discussed in Chapter 8) is developed and may be used to track the navigation requirements of each category of user through the various contexts defined in OOHDM. Doing this, specific navigation paths (what we called WoN in Section 19.7.1) emerge.

19.10.3 Abstract Interface Design and Implementation

The *abstract interface design* activity specifies the interface objects that the user sees as WebApp interaction occurs. A formal model of interface objects, called an *abstract data view* (ADV), is used to represent the relationship between interface objects and navigation objects, and the behavioral characteristics of interface objects.

The ADV model defines a "static layout" [SCH98] that represents the interface metaphor and includes a representation of navigation objects within the interface and the specification of the interface objects (e.g., menus, buttons, icons) that assist in navigation and interaction. In addition, the ADV model contains a behavioral component (similar to the UML state diagram) that indicates how external events "trigger navigation and which interface transformations occur when the user interacts with the application" [SCH01]. For a detailed discussion of the ADV, the interested reader should see [SCH98] and [SCH01].

The OOHDM *implementation* activity represents a design iteration that is specific to the environment in which the WebApp will operate. Classes, navigation, and the interface are each characterized in a manner that can be constructed for the client/server environment, operating systems, support software, programming languages, and other environmental characteristics that are relevant to the problem.

19.11 Design Metrics for WebApps

Design metrics should be characterized in a manner that provides Web engineers with a real-time indication quality. In essence, a useful set of measures and metrics provides quantitative answers to the following questions:

- Does the user interface promote usability?
- Are the aesthetics of the WebApp appropriate for the application domain and pleasing to the user?
- Is the content designed in a manner that imparts the most information with the least effort?

- Is navigation efficient and straightforward?
- Has the WebApp architecture been designed to accommodate the special goals and objectives of WebApp users, the structure of content and functionality, and the flow of navigation required to use the system effectively?
- Are components designed in a manner that reduces procedural complexity and enhances correctness, reliability, and performance?

Today, each of these questions can be addressed qualitatively,[16] but a validated suite of metrics that would provide quantitative answers does not yet exist.

Metrics for WebApp design are in their infancy, and few have been validated widely. The interested reader should see [IVO01] and [MEN01] for a sampling of proposed WebApp design metrics.

SOFTWARE TOOLS

Technical Metrics for WebApps

Objective: To assist Web engineers in developing meaningful WebApp metrics that provide insight into the overall quality of an application.

Mechanics: Tool mechanics vary.

Representative Tools[17]

Netmechanic Tools, developed by Netmechanic (www.netmechanic.com), is a collection of tools that help to improve Web-site performance, focusing on implementation-specific issues.

NIST Web Metrics Testbed, developed by The National Institute of Standards and Technology (zing.ncsl.nist.gov/WebTools/), encompasses the following collection of useful tools that are available for download:

Web Static Analyzer Tool (WebSAT)—checks web page HTML against typical usability guidelines.

Web Category Analysis Tool (WebCAT)—lets the usability engineer construct and conduct a Web category analysis.

Web Variable Instrumenter Program (WebVIP)—instruments a Web site to capture a log of user interaction.

Framework for Logging Usability Data (FLUD)—implements a file formatter and parser for representation of user interaction logs.

VisVIP Tool—produces a 3D visualization of user navigation paths through a Web site.

TreeDec—adds navigation aids to the pages of a Web site.

19.12 SUMMARY

The quality of a WebApp—defined in terms of usability, functionality, reliability, efficiency, maintainability, security, scalability, and time-to-market—is introduced during design. To achieve these quality attributes, a good WebApp design should exhibit simplicity, consistency, identity, robustness, navigability, and visual appeal.

Interface design describes the structure and organization of the user interface. It includes a representation of screen layout, a definition of the modes of interaction, and a description of navigation mechanisms.

16 See Chapter 16 (Section 16.4) and Section 19.1.1 for a qualitative discussion of WebApp quality.

17 Tools noted here do not represent an endorsement, but rather a sampling of tools in this category.

Aesthetic design, also called graphic design, describes the "look and feel" of the WebApp and includes color schemes, geometric layout, text size, font and placement, the use of graphics, and related aesthetic decisions. A set of graphic design guidelines provides the basis for a design approach.

Content design defines the layout, structure, and outline for all content that is presented as part of the WebApp and establishes the relationships between content objects. Content design begins with the representation of content objects, their associations, and relationships. A set of browsing primitives establishes the basis for navigation design.

Architecture design identifies the overall hypermedia structure for the WebApp and encompasses both content architecture and WebApp architecture. Architectural styles for content include linear, grid, hierarchical, and network structures. WebApp architecture describes an infrastructure that enables a Web-based system or application to achieve its business objectives.

Navigation design represents the navigational flow between content objects and for all WebApp functions. Navigation is defined by describing a set of navigation semantic units. Each unit is composed of ways of navigation and navigational links and nodes. Navigation syntax mechanisms are used for effecting the navigation described as part of the semantics.

Component design develops the detailed processing logic required to implement WebApp functional components. Design techniques described in Chapter 11 apply to the engineering of WebApp components.

Patterns for WebApp design encompass generic design patterns that apply to all types of software and hypermedia patterns that are especially relevant for WebApps. Architecture, navigation, component, presentation, and behavior/user design patterns have been proposed.

The Object-Oriented Hypermedia Design Method (OOHDM) is one of a number of methods proposed for WebApp design. OOHDM suggests a design process that includes conceptual design, navigational design, abstract interface design, and implementation.

Design metrics for Web engineering are in their infancy and have yet to be fully validated. However, a variety of measures and metrics have been proposed to address each of the design activities discussed within this chapter.

References

[AME96] Amento, B., et al., "Fitt's Law," *CS 5724: Models and Theories of Human-Computer Interactions,* Virginia Tech, 1996, available at http://ei.cs.vt.edu/ ~cs5724/g1/.

[BAG01] Baggerman, L., and S. Bowman, *Web Design That Works,* Rockport Publishers, 2001.

[BUS96] Buschmann, F., et al., *Pattern-Oriented Software Architecture,* Wiley, 1996.

[CAC02] Cachero, C., et al., "Conceptual Navigation Analysis: a Device and Platform Independent Navigation Specification," *Proc. 2nd Intl. Workshop on Web-Oriented Technology,* June 2002, download from www.dsic.upv.es/~west/iwwost02/papers/cachero.pdf.

[CLO01] Cloninger, C., *Fresh Styles for Web Designers,* New Riders Publishing, 2001.

[DIX99] Dix, A., "Design of User Interfaces for the Web," *Proc. Of User Interfaces to Data Systems Conference, September 1999, download from http://www.comp.lancs. ac.uk/computing/users/dixa/topics/webarch/.*

[FIT54] Fitts, P., "The Information Capacity of the Human Motor System in Controlling the Amplitude of Movement, Journal of Experimental Psychology, vol. 47, 1954, pp. 381–391.

[FOW03] Fowler, M., et al., *Patterns of Enterprise Application Architecture,* Addison-Wesley, 2003.

[GAL02] Galitz, W., *The Essential Guide to User Interface Design,* Wiley, 2002.

[GAM95] Gamma, E. et al., *Design Patterns,* Addison-Wesley, 1995.

[GAR97] Garrido, A., G. Rossi, and D. Schwabe, "Patterns Systems for Hypermedia," 1997, download at www.inf.puc-rio.br/~schwabe/papers/PloP97.pdf.

[GER00] German, D., and D. Cowan, "Toward a Unified Catalog of Hypermedia Design Patterns," *Proc. 33rd Hawaii Intl. Conf. on System Sciences,* IEEE, vol. 6, Maui, Hawaii, June 2000, download from www.turingmachine.org/~dmg/research/papers/dmg_hicss2000.pdf.

[GNA99] Gnaho, C., and F. Larcher, "A User-Centered Methodology for Complex and Customizable Web Engineering," *Proc. 1st ICSE Workshop on Web Engineering,* ACM, Los Angeles, May 1999.

[HEI02] Heinicke, E., *Layout: Fast Solutions for Hands-On Design,* Rockport Publishers, 2002.

[IVO01] Ivory, M., R. Sinha, and M. Hearst, "Empirically Validated Web Page Design Metrics, ACM SIGCHI '01, Seattle, WA, April 2001, available at http://www.rashmisinha.com/articles/WebTangoCHI01.html.

[JAC02] Jacyntho, D., D. Schwabe, and G. Rossi, "An Architecture for Structuring Complex Web Applications," 2002, available at http://www2002.org/CDROM/alternate/478/.

[KAI02] Kaiser, J., "Elements of Effective Web Design," About, Inc., 2002, available at http://webdesign.about.com/library/weekly/aa091998.htm.

[KAL03] Kalman, S., *Web Security Field Guide,* Cisco Press, 2003.

[KOC99] Koch, N., "A Comparative Study of Methods for Hypermedia Development, Technical Report 9905, Ludwig-Maximilians Universitat, Munich, Germany, 1999, download from http://www.dsic.upv.es/~west2001/iwwost01/files/contributions/NoraKoch/hypdev.pdf.

[KRA88] Krasner, G., and S. Pope, "A Cookbook for Using the Model-View Controller User Interface Paradigm in Smalltalk-80," *Journal of Object-Oriented Programming,* vol. 1, no. 3, August/September 1988, pp. 26–49.

[LOW98] Lowe, D., and W. Hall, eds., *Hypertext and the Web—An Engineering Approach,* John Wiley & Sons, 1998.

[MCC01] McClure, S., J. Scambray, and G. Kurtz, *Hacking Exposed,* McGraw-Hill/Osborne, 2001.

[MEN01] Mendes, E., N. Mosley, and S. Counsell, "Estimating Design and Authoring Effort" *IEEE Multimedia,* January–March 2001, pp. 50–57.

[MIL00] Miller, E., "The Website Quality Challenge," Software Research, Inc., 2000, http://www.soft.com/eValid/Technology/White.Papers/website.quality.challenge.html.

[NIE96] Nielsen, J., and A. Wagner, "User Interface Design for the WWW," *Proc. CHI '96 Conf. On Human Factors in Computing Systems,* ACM Press, 1996, pp. 330–331.

[NIE00] Nielsen, J., *Designing Web Usability,* New Riders Publishing, 2000.

[NOR02] Northcutt, S., and J. Novak, *Network Intrusion Detection,* New Riders Publishing, 2002.

[OFF02] Offutt, J., "Quality Attributes of Web Software Applications," *IEEE Software,* March/April, 2002, pp. 25–32.

[OLS98] Olsina, L., "Building a Web-Based Information System Applying the Hypermedia Flexible Process Modeling Strategy," Proc. *1st Intl. Workshop on Hypermedia Development*, 1998.

[OLS99] Olsina, L. et al., "Specifying Quality Characteristics and Attributes for Web Sites," *Proc. 1st ICSE Workshop on Web Engineering,* ACM, Los Angeles, May 1999.

[PER99] Perzel, K., and D. Kane, "Usability Patterns for Applications on the World Wide Web," 1999, download at http://jerry.cs.uiuc.edu/~plop/plop99/proceedings/Kane/perzel_kane.pdf.

[POW00] Powell, T., *Web Design,* McGraw-Hill/Osborne, 2000.

[RAS00] Raskin, J., *The Humane Interface*, Addison-Wesley, 2000.

[RHO98] Rho, Y., and T. Gedeon, "Surface Structures in Browsing the Web," *Proc. Australasian Computer Human Interaction Conference,* IEEE, December, 1998.

[SCH95] Schwabe, D., and G. Rossi, "The Object-Oriented Hypermedia Design Model," *CACM,* vol. 38, no. 8, August 1995, pp. 45–46.

[SCH98] Schwabe, D., and G. Rossi, Developing Hypermedia Applications Using OOHDM, *Proc. Workshop on Hypermedia Development Process, Methods and Models, Hypertext '98,* 1998, download from http://citeseer.nj.nec.com/schwabe 98developing.html.

[SCH01] Schwabe, D., G. Rossi, and S. Barbosa, "Systematic Hypermedia Application Design Using OOHDM, 2001, available at http://www-di.inf.puc-rio.br/~schwabe/HT96WWW/ section1.html.

[TIL00] Tillman, H. N, "Evaluating Quality On the Net," Babson College, May 30, 2000, available at http://www.hopetillman.com/findqual.html#2.

[TOG01] Tognozzi, B., "First Principles," *askTOG,* 2001, available at http://www.asktog.com/ basics/firstPrinciples.html.

[WMT02] Web Mapping Testbed Tutorial, 2002, available at http://www.webmapping.org/ vcgdocuments/vcgTutorial/.

[ZHA02] Zhao, H., "Fitt's Law: Modeling Movement Time in HCl," *Theories in Computer Human Interaction,* University of Maryland, October 2002, available at http://www.cs.umd.edu/ class/fall2002/cmsc838s/tichi/fitts.html.

Problems and Points to Ponder

19.1. Why is the "artistic ideal" an insufficient design philosophy when modern WebApps are built? Is there ever a case in which the artistic ideal is the philosophy to follow?

19.2. In this chapter we discuss a broad array of quality attributes for WebApps. Select the three that you believe are most important and make an argument that explains why each should be emphasized in Web engineering design work.

19.3. Add at least five additional questions to the WebApp Design—Quality Checklist presented in a sidebar in Section 19.1.1.

19.4. Review Tognozzi's interface design principles discussed in Section 19.3.1. Consider each principle for an operational WebApp with which you are familiar. Grade the WebApp (use A, B, C, D, or F grades) relative to the degree to which it has achieved the principle. Explain the reason for each grade.

19.5. Design a prototype interface for the SafeHomeAssured.com WebApp. Try to be innovative, but at the same time, be certain the interface conforms to the principles for good interface design.

19.6. Have you encountered interface control mechanisms that are different from those noted in Section 19.3.2? If so, describe them briefly.

19.7. You are a WebApp designer for a distance learning company. You intend to implement an Internet-based "learning engine" that will enable you to deliver course content to students. The learning engine provides the basic infrastructure for delivering learning content on any subject (content designers will prepare appropriate content). Develop a prototype interface design for the learning engine.

19.8. What is the most aesthetically pleasing Web site you have ever visited and why?

19.9. Consider the content object **order**, generated once a user of SafeHomeAssured.com has completed the selection of all components and is ready to finalize his purchase. Develop a UML description for **order** along with all appropriate design representations.

19.10. What is the difference between content architecture and WebApp architecture?

19.11. Reconsidering the "learning engine" described in Problem 19.7, select a content architecture that would be appropriate for the WebApp. Discuss why you made the choice.

19.12. Use UML to develop three or four design representations for content objects that would be encountered as the "learning engine" described in Problem 19.7 is designed.

19.13. Do a bit of additional research on the MVC architecture and decide whether it would be an appropriate WebApp architecture for the "learning engine" discussed in Problem 19.7.

19.14. What is the difference between navigation syntax and navigation semantics?

19.15. Define two or three NSUs for the SafeHomeAssured.com WebApp. Describe each in some detail.

19.16. Do some research and present two or three complete hypermedia design patterns to your class.

Further Readings and Information Sources

Although hundreds of books have been written on "Web design," very few discuss any meaningful technical methods for doing design work. At best, a variety of useful guidelines for WebApp design are presented, worthwhile examples of Web pages and Java programming are shown, and the technical details important for implementing modern WebApps are discussed. Among the many offerings in this category, Powell's encyclopedic discussion [POW00] is worth considering. In addition, books by Galitz [GAL02], Heinicke [HEI02], Schmitt (*Designing CSS Web Pages,* New Riders Publishing, 2002), Donnelly (*Designing Easy-to-Use Websites,* Addison-Wesley, 2001), and Nielsen [NIE00] provide much useful guidance.

The agile view of design (and other topics) for WebApps is presented by Wallace and his colleagues (*Extreme Programming for Web Projects,* Addison-Wesley, 2003). Conallen (*Building Web Applications with UML,* second edition, Addison-Wesley, 2002) and Rosenberg and Scott (*Applying Use-Case Driven Object Modeling with UML,* Addison-Wesley, 2001) present detailed examples of WebApps modeled using UML.

Van Duyne and his colleagues (*The Design of Sites: Patterns, Principles and Processes,* Addison-Wesley, 2002) have written an excellent book that covers most important aspects of the Web engineering design process. Design process models and design patterns are covered in detail. Wodtke (*Information Architecture,* New Riders Publishing, 2003), Rosenfeld and Morville (*Information Architecture for the World Wide Web,* O'Reilly & Associates, 2002), and Reiss (*Practical Information Architecture,* Addison-Wesley, 2000) address content architecture and other topics.

Design techniques are also mentioned in books written about specific development environments. Interested readers should examine books on J2EE, Java, ASP.NET, CSS, XML, Perl, and a variety of WebApp creation applications (*Dreamweaver, HomePage, Frontpage, GoLive, MacroMedia Flash,* etc.) for useful design tidbits.

A wide variety of information sources on design for Web engineering is available on the Internet. An up-to-date list of World Wide Web references can be found at the SEPA Web site: **http://www.mhhe.com/pressman.**

CHAPTER

20 TESTING WEB APPLICATIONS

KEY CONCEPTS

There is an urgency that always pervades the Web engineering process. As formulation, planning, analysis, design, and construction are conducted, stakeholders—concerned about competition from other WebApps, coerced by customer demands, and worried that they'll miss a market window—press to get the WebApp on-line. As a consequence, technical activities that often occur late in the Web engineering process, such as WebApp testing, are sometimes given short shrift. This can be a catastrophic mistake. To avoid it, the Web engineering team must ensure that each WebE work product exhibits high quality. Wallace and his colleagues [WAL03] note this when they state:

> Testing shouldn't wait until the project is finished. Start testing before you write one line of code. Test constantly and effectively, and you will develop a much more durable Web site.

Since analysis and design models cannot be tested in the classical sense, the Web engineering team should conduct formal technical reviews (Chapter 26) as well as executable tests. The intent is to uncover and correct errors before the WebApp is made available to its end-users.

QUICK LOOK

What is it? WebApp testing is a collection of related activities with a single goal: to uncover errors in WebApp content, function, usability, navigability, performance, capacity, and security. To accomplish this, a testing strategy that encompasses both reviews and executable testing is applied throughout the Web engineering process.

Who does it? Web engineers and other project stakeholders (managers, customers, end-users) all participate in WebApp testing.

Why is it important? If end-users encounter errors that shake their faith in the WebApp, they will go elsewhere for the content and function they need, and the WebApp will fail. For this reason, Web engineers must work to eliminate as many errors as possible before the WebApp goes on-line.

What are the steps? The WebApp testing process begins by focusing on user-visible aspects of the WebApp and proceeds to tests that exercise technology and infrastructure. Seven testing steps are performed: content, interface, navigation, component, configuration, performance, and security testing.

What is the work product? In some instances a WebApp test plan is produced. In every instance, a suite of test cases is developed for every testing step and an archive of test results is maintained for future use.

How do I ensure that I've done it right? Although you can never be sure that you've performed every test that is needed, you can be certain that testing has uncovered errors (and that those errors have been corrected). In addition, if you've established a test plan, you can check to ensure that all planned tests have been conducted.

20.1 Testing Concepts for WebApps

In Chapter 13, we noted that testing is the process of exercising software with the intent of finding (and ultimately correcting) errors. This fundamental philosophy does not change for WebApps. In fact, because Web-based systems and applications reside on a network and interoperate with many different operating systems, browsers (or other interface devices such as PDAs or mobile phones), hardware platforms, communications protocols, and "backroom" applications, the search for errors represents a significant challenge for Web engineers.

To understand the objectives of testing within a Web engineering context, we must consider the many dimensions of WebApp quality.[1] In the context of this discussion, we consider quality dimensions that are particularly relevant in any discussion of testing for Web engineering work. We also consider the nature of the errors that are encountered as a consequence of testing, and the testing strategy that is applied to uncover these errors.

20.1.1 Dimensions of Quality

Quality is incorporated into a Web application as a consequence of good design. It is evaluated by applying a series of technical reviews that assess various elements of the design model and by applying a testing process that is discussed throughout this chapter. Both reviews and testing examine one or more of the following quality dimensions [MIL00]:

? How do we assess quality within the context of a WebApp and its environment?

- *Content* is evaluated at both a syntactic and semantic level. At the syntactic level, spelling, punctuation, and grammar are assessed for text-based documents. At a semantic level, correctness (of information presented), consistency (across the entire content object and related objects), and lack of ambiguity are all assessed.
- *Function* is tested to uncover errors that indicate lack of conformance to customer requirements. Each WebApp function is assessed for correctness, instability, and general conformance to appropriate implementation standards (e.g., Java or XML language standards).

1 WebApp quality has also been considered in Chapter 19.

- *Structure* is assessed to ensure that it properly delivers WebApp content and function, that it is extensible, and that it can be supported as new content or functionality is added.
- *Usability* is tested to ensure that each category of user is supported by the interface; can learn and apply all required navigation syntax and semantics.
- *Navigability* is tested to ensure that all navigation syntax and semantics are exercised to uncover any navigation errors (e.g., dead links, improper links, erroneous links).
- *Performance* is tested under a variety of operating conditions, configurations, and loading to ensure that the system is responsive to user interaction and handles extreme loading without unacceptable operational degradation.
- *Compatibility* is tested by executing the WebApp in a variety of different host configurations on both the client and server sides. The intent is to find errors that are specific to a unique host configuration.
- *Interoperability* is tested to ensure that the WebApp properly interfaces with other applications and/or databases.
- *Security* is tested by assessing potential vulnerabilities and attempting to exploit each. Any successful penetration attempt is deemed a security failure.

A strategy and tactics for WebApp testing has been developed to exercise each of these quality dimensions and is discussed later in this chapter.

> **"Innovation is a bittersweet deal for software testers. Just when it seems that we know how to test a particular technology, a new one [WebApps] comes along and all bets are off."**
>
> **James Bach**

20.1.2 Errors within a WebApp Environment

We have already noted that the primary intent of testing in any software context is to uncover errors (and correct them). Errors encountered as a consequence of successful WebApp testing have a number of unique characteristics [NGU00]:

? What makes errors encountered during WebApp execution somewhat different from those encountered for conventional software?

1. Because many types of WebApp tests uncover problems that are first evidenced on the client side (i.e., via an interface implemented on a specific browser or a PDA or a mobile phone), the Web engineer sees a symptom of the error, not the error itself.
2. Because a WebApp is implemented in a number of different configurations and within different environments, it may be difficult or impossible to reproduce an error outside the environment in which the error was originally encountered.

3. Although some errors are the result of incorrect design or improper HTML (or other programming language) coding, many errors can be traced to the WebApp configuration.
4. Because WebApps reside within a client/server architecture, errors can be difficult to trace across three architectural layers: the client, the server, or the network itself.
5. Some errors are due to the *static operating environment* (i.e., the specific configuration in which testing is conducted), while others are attributable to the dynamic operating environment (i.e., instantaneous resource loading or time-related errors).

These five error attributes suggest that environment plays an important role in the diagnosis of all errors uncovered during the Web engineering process. In some situations (e.g., content testing), the site of the error is obvious, but in many other types of WebApp testing (e.g., navigation testing, performance testing, security testing) the underlying cause of the error may be considerably more difficult to determine.

20.1.3 Testing Strategy

The strategy for WebApp testing adopts the basic principles for all software testing (Chapter 13) and applies a strategy and tactics that have been recommended for object-oriented systems (Chapter 14). The following steps summarize the approach:

The overall strategy for WebApp testing can be summarized in the 10 steps noted here.

1. The content model for the WebApp is reviewed to uncover errors.
2. The interface model is reviewed to ensure that all use-cases can be accommodated.
3. The design model for the WebApp is reviewed to uncover navigation errors.
4. The user interface is tested to uncover errors in presentation and/or navigation mechanics.
5. Selected functional components are unit tested.
6. Navigation throughout the architecture is tested.
7. The WebApp is implemented in a variety of different environmental configurations and is tested for compatibility with each configuration.
8. Security tests are conducted in an attempt to exploit vulnerabilities in the WebApp or within its environment.
9. Performance tests are conducted.
10. The WebApp is tested by a controlled and monitored population of end-users; the results of their interaction with the system are evaluated for content and navigation errors, usability concerns, compatibility concerns, and WebApp reliability and performance.

WebRef

Excellent articles on WebApp testing can be found at **www.stickyminds.com/testing.asp.**

Because many WebApps evolve continuously, WebApp testing is an on-going activity conducted by Web support staff who use regression tests derived from the tests developed when the WebApp was first engineered.

20.1.4 Test Planning

The use of the word *planning* (in any context) is anathema to some Web developers. As we noted in earlier chapters, these developers just start—hoping that a killer WebApp will emerge. A Web engineer recognizes that planning establishes a roadmap for all work that follows. It's worth the effort.

In their book on WebApp testing, Splaine and Jaskiel [SPL01] state:

> Except for the simplest of Web sites, it quickly becomes apparent that some sort of test planning is needed. All too often, the initial number of bugs found from ad hoc testing is large enough that not all of them are fixed the first time they're detected. This puts an additional burden on people who test Web sites and applications. Not only must they conjure up imaginative new tests, but they must also remember how previous tests were executed in order to reliably re-test the Web site/application, and ensure that known bugs have been removed and that no new bugs have been introduced.

The test plan identifies a testing task set, the work products to be developed, and the way in which results are to be evaluated, recorded, and reused.

The question for every Web engineer is: How do we "conjure up imaginative new tests," and what should those tests focus on? The answers to these questions are contained within a test plan.

A WebApp test plan identifies (1) a task set[2] to be applied as testing commences, (2) the work products to be produced as each testing task is executed, and (3) the manner in which the results of testing are evaluated, recorded, and reused when regression testing is conducted. In some cases, the test plan is integrated with the project plan. In others, the test plan is a separate document.

20.2 The Testing Process—An Overview

The testing process for Web engineering begins with tests that exercise content and interface functionality that is immediately visible to end-users. As testing proceeds, aspects of the design architecture and navigation are exercised. The user may or may not be cognizant of these WebApp elements. Finally, the focus shifts to tests that exercise technological capabilities that are not always apparent to end-users—WebApp infrastructure and installation/implementation issues.

> "In general, the software testing techniques [Chapters 13 and 14] that are applied to other applications are the same as those applied to Web-based applications . . . The difference between the two types of testing is that the technology variables in the Web environment multiply."
>
> **Hung Nguyen**

2 Task sets are discussed in Chapter 2. A related term—*work flow*—has also been used in this book to describe a series of tasks required to accomplish a software engineering activity.

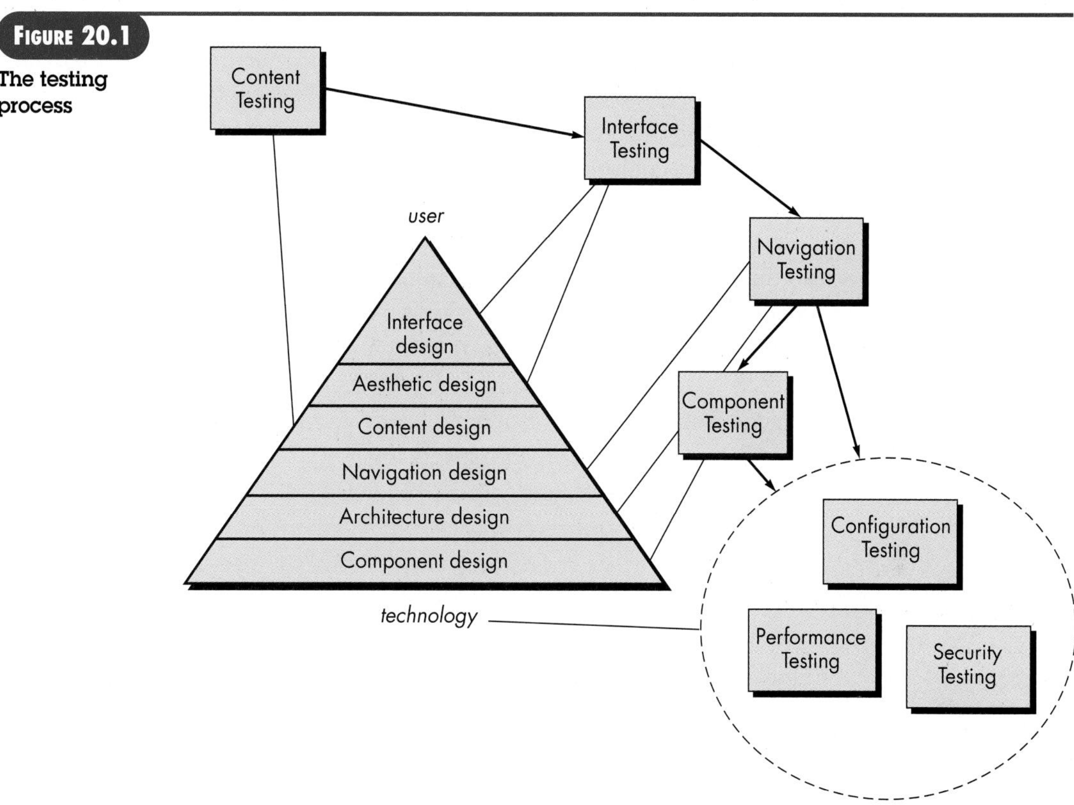

FIGURE 20.1 The testing process

Figure 20.1 juxtaposes the WebApp testing process with the design pyramid discussed in Chapter 19. Note that as the testing flow proceeds from left to right and top to bottom, user visible elements of the WebApp design (top elements of the pyramid) are tested first, followed by infrastructure design elements.

Content testing (and reviews) attempts to uncover errors in content. This testing activity is similar in many respects to copy-editing for a written document. In fact, a large Web site might enlist the services of a professional copy editor to uncover typographical errors, grammatical mistakes, errors in content consistency, errors in graphical representations, and cross referencing errors. In addition to examining static content for errors, this testing step also considers dynamic content derived from data maintained as part of a database system that has been integrated with the WebApp.

Interface testing exercises interaction mechanisms and validates aesthetic aspects of the user interface. The intent is to uncover errors that result from poorly implemented interaction mechanisms or omissions, inconsistencies or ambiguities that have been introduced into the interface inadvertently.

Navigation testing applies use-cases, derived as part of the analysis activity, in the design of test cases that exercise each usage scenario against the navigation design.

Navigation mechanisms (e.g., menu bars) implemented within the interface layout are tested against use-cases and NSUs (Chapter 19) to ensure that any errors that impede completion of a use-case are identified and corrected.

Component testing exercises content and functional units within the WebApp. When WebApps are considered, the concept of the unit (introduced in Chapter 13) changes. The "unit" of choice within the content architecture (Chapter 19) is the Web page. Each Web page encapsulates content, navigation links, and processing elements (forms, scripts, applets). A "unit" within the WebApp architecture may be a defined functional component that provides service directly to an end-user or an infrastructure component that enables the WebApp to perform all of its capabilities. Each functional component is tested in much the same way as an individual module is tested in conventional software. In most cases, tests are black-box oriented. However, if processing is complex, white-box tests may also be used.[3] In addition to functional testing, database capabilities are also exercised.

The strategy for integration testing depends upon the WebApp architecture that has been chosen during design.

As the WebApp architecture is constructed, navigation and component testing are used as *integration tests.* The strategy for integration testing depends on the content and WebApp architecture that has been chosen (Chapter 19). If the content architecture has been designed with a linear, grid, or simple hierarchical structure, it is possible to integrate Web pages in much the same way as we integrate modules for conventional software. However, if a mixed hierarchy or network (Web) architecture is used, integration testing is similar to the approach used for OO systems. Thread-based testing (Chapter 14) can be used to integrate the set of Web pages (a NSU may be used to define the appropriate set) required to respond to a user event. Each thread is integrated and tested individually. Regression testing is applied to ensure that no side effects occur. Cluster testing integrates a set of collaborating pages (determined by examining the use-cases and NSU). Test cases are derived to uncover errors in the collaborations.

Each element of the WebApp architecture is unit tested to the extent possible. For example, in a MVC architecture (Chapter 19) the *model*, *view* and *controller* components are each tested individually. Upon integration, the flow of control and data across each of these elements is assessed in detail.

Configuration testing attempts to uncover errors that are specific to a particular client or server environment. A cross-reference matrix that defines all probable operating systems, browsers,[4] hardware platforms, and communications protocols is created. Tests are then conducted to uncover errors associated with each possible configuration.

---

3 Black-box and white-box testing techniques are discussed in Chapter 14.

4 Browsers are notorious for implementing their own subtly different "standard" interpretations of HTML and Javascript.

Security testing incorporates a series of tests designed to exploit vulnerabilities in the WebApp and its environment. The intent is to demonstrate that a security breach is possible.

Performance testing encompasses a series of tests that are designed to assess (1) how WebApp response time and reliability are affected by increased user traffic, (2) which WebApp components are responsible for performance degradation and what usage characteristics cause degradation to occur, and (3) how performance degradation impacts overall WebApp objectives and requirements.

TASK SET

WebApp Testing

1. Review stakeholder requirements.
   Identify key user goals and objectives.
   Review use-cases for each user category.
2. Establish priorities to ensure that each user goal and objective will be adequately tested.
3. Define WebApp testing strategy by describing the types of tests (Section 20.2) that will be conducted.
4. Develop a test plan.
   Define a test schedule and assign responsibilities for each test.
   Specify automated tools for testing.
   Define acceptance criteria for each class of test.
   Specify defect tracking mechanisms.
   Define problem reporting mechanisms.
5. Perform "unit" tests.
   Review content for syntax and semantics errors.
   Review content for proper clearances and permissions.
   Test interface mechanisms for correct operation.
   Test each component (e.g., script) to ensure proper function.
6. Perform "integration" tests.
   Test interface semantics against use-cases.
   Conduct navigation tests.
7. Perform configuration tests.
   Assess client-side configuration compatibility.
   Assess server-side configurations.
8. Conduct performance tests.
9. Conduct security tests.

20.3 CONTENT TESTING

Although formal technical reviews are not a part of testing, content review should be performed to ensure that content has quality.

Errors in WebApp content can be as trivial as minor typographical errors or as significant as incorrect information, improper organization, or violation of intellectual property laws. *Content testing* attempts to uncover these and many other problems before the user encounters them.

Content testing combines both reviews and the generation of executable test cases. Review is applied to uncover semantic errors in content (discussed in Section 20.3.1). Executable testing is used to uncover content errors that can be traced to dynamically derived content driven by data acquired from one or more databases.

20.3.1 Content Testing Objectives

Content testing has three important objectives: (1) to uncover syntactic errors (e.g., typos, grammar mistakes) in text-based documents, graphical representations, and

Content testing objectives are (1) to uncover syntactic errors in content, (2) to uncover semantic errors, (3) to find structural errors.

other media, (2) to uncover semantic errors (i.e., errors in the accuracy or completeness of information) in any content object presented as navigation occurs, and (3) to find errors in the organization or structure of content that is presented to the end-user.

To accomplish the first objective, automated spelling and grammar checkers may be used. However, many syntactic errors evade detection by such tools and must be discovered by a human reviewer (tester). As we noted in the preceding section, copy editing is the single best approach for finding syntactic errors.

? What questions should be asked and answered to uncover semantic errors in content?

Semantic testing focuses on the information presented within each content object. The reviewer (tester) must answer the following questions:

- Is the information factually accurate?
- Is the information concise and to the point?
- Is the layout of the content object easy for the user to understand?
- Can information embedded within a content object be found easily?
- Have proper references been provided for all information derived from other sources?
- Is the information presented consistent internally and consistent with information presented in other content objects?
- Is the content offensive, misleading, or does it open the door to litigation?
- Does the content infringe on existing copyrights or trademarks?
- Does the content contain internal links that supplement existing content? Are the links correct?
- Does the aesthetic style of the content conflict with the aesthetic style of the interface?

Obtaining answers to each of these questions for a large WebApp (containing hundreds of content objects) can be a daunting task. However, failure to uncover semantic errors will shake the user's faith in the WebApp and can lead to failure of the Web-based application.

Content objects exist within an architecture that has a specific style (Chapter 19). During content testing, the structure and organization of the content architecture is tested to ensure that required content is presented to the end-user in the proper order and relationships. For example, the SafeHomeAssured.com WebApp[5] presents a variety of information about sensors that are used as part of security and surveillance products. Content objects provide descriptive information, technical specifications, a photographic representation and related information. Tests of the SafeHomeAssured.com content architecture strive to uncover errors in the presentation of this information (e.g., a description of Sensor *X* is presented with a photo of Sensor *Y*).

5 The SafeHomeAssured.com WebApp has been used as an example throughout Part 3 of this book.

20.3.2 Database Testing

Modern Web applications do much more than present static content objects. In many application domains, WebApps interface with sophisticated database management systems and build dynamic content objects that are created in real-time using the data acquired from a database.

For example, a financial services WebApp can produce complex text-based, tabular, and graphical information about a specific equity (e.g., a stock or mutual fund). The composite content object that presents this information is created dynamically after the user has made a request for information about a specific equity. To accomplish this, the following steps are required: (1) a large equities database is queried, (2) relevant data are extracted from the database, (3) the extracted data must be organized as a content object, and (4) this content object (representing customized information requested by an end-user) is transmitted to the client environment for display. Errors can and do occur as a consequence of each of these steps. The objective of database testing is to uncover these errors.

Database testing for WebApps is complicated by a variety of factors:

? What issues complicate database testing for WebApps?

1. *The original client-side request for information is rarely presented in the form (e.g., structured query language, SQL) that can be input to a database management system (DBMS).* Therefore, tests should be designed to uncover errors made in translating the user's request into a form that can be processed by these DBMS.
2. *The database may be remote to the server that houses the WebApp.* Therefore, tests that uncover errors in communication between the WebApp and the remote database should be developed.[6]
3. *Raw data acquired from the database must be transmitted to the WebApp server and properly formatted for subsequent transmittal to the client.* Therefore, tests that demonstrate the validity of the raw data received by the WebApp server should be developed, and additional tests that demonstrate the validity of the transformations applied to the raw data to create valid content objects must also be created.
4. *The dynamic content object(s) must be transmitted to the client in a form that can be displayed to the end-user.* Therefore, a series of tests should be designed to (a) uncover errors in the content object format, and (b) test compatibility with different client environment configurations.

Considering these four factors, test case design methods should be applied for each of the "layers of interaction" [NGU01] noted in Figure 20.2. Testing should ensure that (1) valid information is passed between the client and server from the interface layer;

6 These tests can become complex when distributed databases are encountered or when access to a data warehouse (Chapter 10) is required.

FIGURE 20.2

Layers of interaction

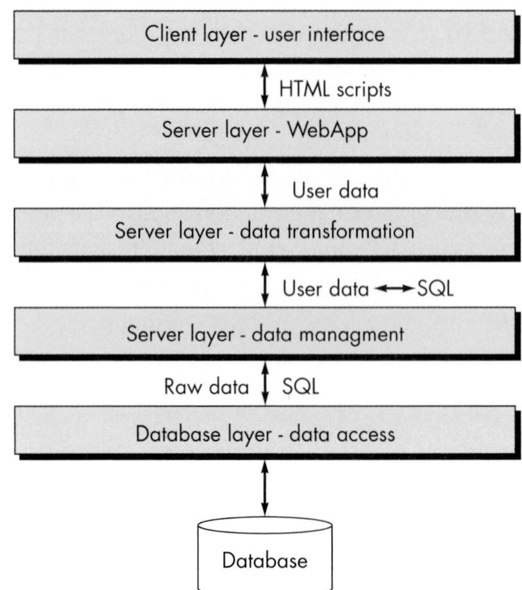

(2) the WebApp processes scripts correctly and properly extracts or formats user data; (3) user data are passed correctly to a server side data transformation function that formats appropriate queries (e.g., SQL); (4) queries are passed to a data management layer[7] that communicates with database access routines (potentially located on another machine).

Data transformation, data management, and database access layers shown in Figure 20.2 are often constructed with reusable components that have been validated separately and as a package. If this is the case, WebApp testing focuses on the design of test cases to exercise the interactions between the client layer and the first two server layers (WebApp and data transformation) shown in the figure.

The user interface layer is tested to ensure that HTML scripts are properly constructed for each user query and properly transmitted to the server side. The WebApp layer on the server side is tested to ensure that user data are properly extracted from HTML scripts and properly transmitted to the data transformation layer on the server side.

The data transformation functions are tested to ensure that correct SQL is created and passed to appropriate data management components.

A detailed discussion of the underlying technology that must be understood to adequately design these database tests is beyond the scope of this book. The interested reader should see [SCE02], [NGU01], and [BRO01].

7 The data management layer typically incorporates an SQL call-level interface (SQL-CLI) such as Microsoft OLE/ADO or Java Database Connectivity (JDBC).

> "As e-customers (whether business or consumer), we are unlikely to have confidence in a Web site that suffers frequent downtime, hangs in the middle of a transaction, or has a poor sense of usability. Testing, therefore, has a crucial role in the overall development process."
>
> Wing Lam

20.4 User Interface Testing

Verification and validation of a WebApp user interface occurs at three distinct points in the Web engineering process. During formulation and requirements analysis (Chapters 17 and 18), the interface model is reviewed to ensure that it conforms to customer requirements and to other elements of the analysis model. During design (Chapter 19), the interface design model is reviewed to ensure that generic quality criteria established for all user interfaces have been achieved and that application-specific interface design issues have been properly addressed. During testing, the focus shifts to the execution of application-specific aspects of user interaction as they are manifested by interface syntax and semantics. In addition, testing provides a final assessment of usability.

20.4.1 Interface Testing Strategy

The overall strategy for interface testing is to (1) uncover errors related to specific interface mechanisms (e.g., errors in the proper execution of a menu link or the way data are entered in a form) and (2) uncover errors in the way the interface implements the semantics of navigation, WebApp functionality, or content display. To accomplish this strategy, a number of objectives must be achieved:

With the exception of WebApp-oriented specifics, the interface strategy noted here is applicable to all types of client/server software.

- *Interface features are tested to ensure that design rules, aesthetics, and related visual content are available for the user without error.* Features include type fonts, the use of color, frames, images, borders, tables, and related elements that are generated as WebApp execution proceeds.
- *Individual interface mechanisms are tested in a manner that is analogous to unit testing.* For example, tests are designed to exercise all forms, client-side scripting, dynamic HTML, CGI scripts, streaming content, and application specific interface mechanisms (e.g., a shopping cart for an e-commerce application). In many cases, testing can focus exclusively on one of these mechanisms (the "unit") to the exclusion of other interface features and functions.
- *Each interface mechanism is tested within the context of a use-case or NSU (Chapter 19) for a specific user category.* This testing approach is analogous to integration testing (Chapter 13) in that tests are conducted as interface mechanisms are integrated to allow a use-case or NSU to be executed.
- *The complete interface is tested against selected use-cases and NSUs to uncover errors in the semantics of the interface.* This testing approach is analogous to

validation testing (Chapter 13) because the purpose is to demonstrate conformance to specific use-case or NSU semantics. It is at this stage that a series of usability tests are conducted.

- *The interface is tested within a variety of environments (e.g., browsers) to ensure that it will be compatible.* In actuality, this series of tests can also be considered to be part of configuration testing.

20.4.2 Testing Interface Mechanisms

When a user interacts with a WebApp, the interaction occurs through one or more interface mechanisms. In the paragraphs that follow, we present a brief overview of testing considerations for each interface mechanism [SPL01].

External link testing should occur throughout the life of the WebApp. Part of a support strategy should be regularly scheduled link tests.

Links. Each navigation link is tested to ensure that the proper content object or function is reached.[8] The Web engineer builds a list of all links associated with the interface layout (e.g., menu bars, index items) and then executes each individually. In addition, links within each content object must be exercised to uncover bad URLs or links to improper content objects or functions. Finally, links to external WebApps should be tested for accuracy and also evaluated to determine the risk that they will become invalid over time.

Forms. At a macroscopic level, tests are performed to ensure that (1) labels correctly identify fields within the form and that mandatory fields are identified visually for the user; (2) the server receives all information contained within the form and that no data are lost in the transmission between client and server; (3) appropriate defaults are used when the user does not select from a pull-down menu or set of buttons; (4) browser functions (e.g., the "back" arrow) do not corrupt data entered in a form; and (5) scripts that perform error checking on data entered work properly and provide meaningful error messages.

At a more targeted level, tests should ensure that (1) form fields have proper width and data types; (2) the form establishes appropriate safeguards that preclude the user from entering text strings longer than some predefined maximum; (3) all appropriate options for pull-down menus are specified and ordered in a way that is meaningful to the end-user; (4) browser "auto-fill" features do not lead to data input errors; and (5) the tab key (or some other key) initiates proper movement between form fields.

ADVICE

Client-side scripting tests and tests associated with dynamic HTML should be repeated whenever a new version of a popular browser is released.

Client-side scripting. Black-box tests are conducted to uncover any errors in processing as the script (e.g., Javascript) is executed. These tests are often coupled with forms testing, because script input is often derived from data provided as part of forms processing. A compatibility test should be conducted to ensure that the scripting language that has been chosen will work properly in the environmental configuration(s) that supports the WebApp. In addition to testing the script itself, Splaine

8 These tests can be performed as part of either interface or navigation testing.

and Jaskiel [SPL01] suggest that "you should ensure that your company's [WebApp] standards state the preferred language and version of scripting language to be used for client-side (and server-side) scripting."

Dynamic HTML. Each Web page that contains dynamic HTML is executed to ensure that the dynamic display is correct. In addition, a compatibility test should be conducted to ensure that the dynamic HTML works properly in the environmental configuration(s) that supports the WebApp.

Pop-up windows.[9] A series of tests ensure that (1) the pop-up is properly sized and positioned; (2) the pop-up does not cover the original WebApp window; (3) the aesthetic design of the pop-up is consistent with the aesthetic design of the interface; and (4) scroll bars and other control mechanisms appended to the pop-up work, are properly located, and function as required.

CGI scripts. Black-box tests are conducted with an emphasis on data integrity (as data are passed to the CGI script) and script processing once validated data have been received. In addition, performance testing can be conducted to ensure that the server-side configuration can accommodate the processing demands of multiple invocations of CGI scripts [SPL01].

Streaming content. Tests should demonstrate that streaming data are up-to-date, properly displayed, and can be suspended without error and restarted without difficulty.

Cookies. Both server-side and client-side testing are required. On the server side, tests should ensure that a cookie is properly constructed (contains correct data) and properly transmitted to the client side when specific content or functionality is requested. In addition, the proper persistence of the cookie is tested to ensure that its expiration date is correct. On the client side, tests determine whether the WebApp properly attaches existing cookies to a specific request (sent to the server).

Application specific interface mechanisms. Tests conform to a checklist of functionality and features that are defined by the interface mechanism. For example, Splaine and Jaskiel [SPL01] suggest the following checklist for shopping cart functionality defined for an e-commerce application:

- Boundary test (Chapter 14) the minimum and maximum number of items that can be placed in the shopping cart.
- Test a "check out" request for an empty shopping cart.
- Test proper deletion of an item from the shopping cart.
- Test to determine whether a purchase empties the cart of its contents.

---

9 Pop-ups have become pervasive and are a major irritant to many users. They should be used judiciously or not at all.

- Test to determine the persistence of shopping cart contents (this should be specified as part of customer requirements).
- Test to determine whether the WebApp can recall shopping cart contents at some future date (assuming that no purchase was made) if the user requests that contents be saved.

20.4.3 Testing Interface Semantics

Once each interface mechanism has been "unit" tested, the focus of interface testing changes to a consideration of interface semantics. Interface semantics testing "evaluates how well the design takes care of users, offers clear direction, delivers feedback, and maintains consistency of language and approach" [NGU01].

A thorough review of the interface design model can provide partial answers to the questions implied by the preceding paragraph. However, each use-case scenario (for each user category) should be tested once the WebApp has been implemented. In essence, a use-case becomes the input for the design of a testing sequence. The intent of the testing sequence is to uncover errors that will preclude a user from achieving the objective associated with the use-case.

As each use-case is tested, the Web engineering team maintains a checklist to ensure that every menu item has been exercised at least one time and that every embedded link within a content object has been used. In addition, the test sequence should include improper menu selection and link usage. The intent is to determine whether the WebApp provides effective error handling and recovery.

20.4.4 Usability Tests

WebRef
A worthwhile guide to usability testing can be found at **www.ahref.com/guides/design/199806/0615jef.html.**

Usability testing is similar to interface semantics testing (Section 20.4.3) in the sense that it also evaluates the degree to which users can interact effectively with the WebApp and the degree to which the WebApp guides users' actions, provides meaningful feedback, and enforces a consistent interaction approach. Rather than focusing intently on the semantics of some interactive objective, usability reviews and tests are designed to determine the degree to which the WebApp interface makes the user's life easy.[10]

Usability tests may be designed by a Web engineering team, but the tests themselves are conducted by end-users. The following sequence of steps is applied [SPL01]:

1. Define a set of usability testing categories and identify goals for each.
2. Design tests that will enable each goal to be evaluated.

10 The term "user-friendliness" has been used in this context. The problem, of course, is that one user's perception of a "friendly" interface may be radically different from another's.

3. Select participants who will conduct the tests.
4. Instrument participants' interaction with the WebApp while testing is conducted.
5. Develop a mechanism for assessing the usability of the WebApp.

Usability testing can occur at a variety of different levels of abstraction: (1) the usability of a specific interface mechanism (e.g., a form) can be assessed; (2) the usability of a complete Web page (encompassing interface mechanisms, data objects, and related functions) can be evaluated; or (3) the usability of the complete WebApp can be considered.

The first step in usability testing is to identify a set of usability categories and establish testing objectives for each category. The following test categories and objectives (written in the form of a question) illustrate this approach:[11]

? What characteristics of usability become the focus of testing, and what specific objectives are addressed?

Interactivity—Are interaction mechanisms (e.g., pull-down menus, buttons, pointers) easy to understand and use?

Layout—Are navigation mechanisms, content, and functions placed in a manner that allows the user to find them quickly?

Readability—Is text well-written and understandable?[12] Are graphic representations easy to understand?

Aesthetics—Do layout, color, typeface, and related characteristics lead to ease of use? Do users "feel comfortable" with the look and feel of the WebApp?

Display characteristics—Does the WebApp make optimal use of screen size and resolution?

Time sensitivity—Can important features, functions, and content be used or acquired in a timely manner?

Personalization—Does the WebApp tailor itself to the specific needs of different user categories or individual users?

Accessibility—Is the WebApp accessible to people who have disabilities?

Within each of these categories, a series of tests is designed. In some cases, the "test" may be a visual review of a Web page. In other cases interface semantics tests may be executed again, but in this instance usability concerns are paramount.

As an example, we consider usability assessment for interaction and interface mechanisms. Constantine and Lockwood [CON03] suggest that the following list of interface features should be reviewed and tested for usability: animation, buttons, color, control, dialogue, fields, forms, frames, graphics, labels, links, menus,

11 For additional usability questions, see the "usability" sidebar in Chapter 12.

12 The FOG Readability Index and others may be used to provide a quantitative assessment of readbility. See http://developer.gnome.org/documents/usability/usability-readability.html for more details.

FIGURE 20.3

Qualitative assessment of usability

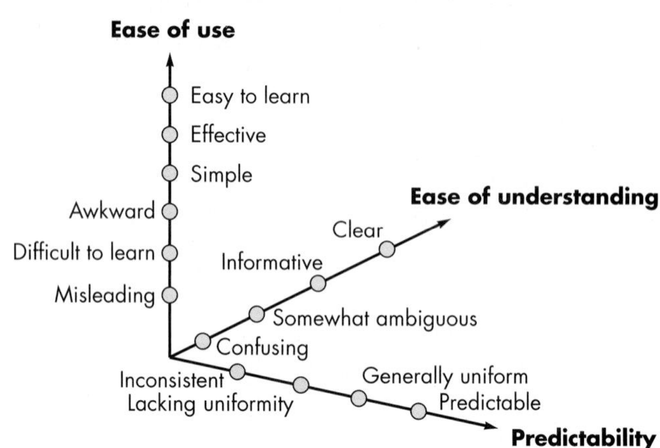

messages, navigation, pages, selectors, text, and tool bars. As each feature is assessed, it is graded on a qualitative scale by the users who are doing the testing. Figure 20.3 depicts a possible set of assessment "grades" that can be selected by users. These grades are applied to each feature individually, to a complete Web page, or to the WebApp as a whole.

20.4.5 Compatibility Tests

WebApps execute within a variety of client-side environments. The objective of compatibility testing is to uncover errors associated with a specific environment (e.g., browser).

WebApps must operate within environments that differ from one another. Different computers, display devices, operating systems, browsers, and network connection speeds can have a significant influence on WebApp operation. Each computing configuration can result in differences in client-side processing speeds, display resolution, and connection speeds. Operating system vagaries may cause WebApp processing issues. Different browsers sometimes produce slightly different results, regardless of the degree of HTML standardization within the WebApp. Required plug-ins may or may not be readily available for a particular configuration.

In some cases, small compatibility issues present no significant problems, but in others, serious errors can be encountered. For example, download speeds may become unacceptable, lack of a required plug-in may make content unavailable, browser differences can change page layout dramatically, font styles may be altered and become illegible, or forms may be improperly organized. *Compatibility testing* strives to uncover these problems before the WebApp goes on-line.

The first step in compatibility testing is to define a set of "commonly encountered" client-side computing configurations and their variants. In essence, a tree structure is created, identifying each computing platform, typical display devices, the operating systems supported on the platform, the browsers available, likely Internet connection speeds, and similar information. Next, the Web engineering team derives a series of compatibility validation tests, derived from existing interface tests, navigation tests, performance tests, and security tests. The intent of these tests is to uncover errors or execution problems that can be traced to configuration differences.

SAFEHOME

WebApp Testing

The scene: Doug Miller's office.

The players: Doug Miller (manager of the *SafeHome* software engineering group) and Vinod Raman, a member of the product software engineering team.

The conversation:

Doug: What do you think of the SafeHomeAssured.com e-commerce WebApp V0.0?

Vinod: The outsourcing vendor's done a good job. Sharon [development manager for the vendor] tells me they're testing as we speak.

Doug: I'd like you and the rest of the team to do a little informal testing on the e-commerce site.

Vinod (grimacing): I thought we were going to hire a third-party testing company to validate the WebApp. We're still killing ourselves trying to get the product software out the door.

Doug: We're going to hire a testing vendor for performance and security testing, and our outsourcing vendor is already testing. Just thought another point of view would be helpful, and besides, we'd like to keep costs in line, so . . .

Vinod (sighs): What are you looking for?

Doug: I want to be sure that the interface and all navigation are solid.

Vinod: I suppose we can start with the use-cases for each of the major interface functions:

Learn about *SafeHome*
Specify the *SafeHome* system you need
Purchase a *SafeHome* system
Get technical support

Doug: Good. But take the navigation paths all the way to their conclusion.

Vinod (looking through a notebook of use-cases): Yeah, when you select **Specify the *SafeHome* system you need,** that'll take you to:

Select *SafeHome* components
Get *SafeHome* component recommendations

We can exercise the semantics of each path.

Doug: While you're there, check out the content that appears at each navigation node.

Vinod: Of course . . . and the functional elements as well. Who's testing usability?

Doug: Oh . . . the testing vendor will coordinate usability testing. We've hired a market research firm to line up 20 typical users for the usability study, but if you guys uncover any usability issues . . .

Vinod: I know, pass them along.

Doug: Thanks, Vinod.

20.5 COMPONENT-LEVEL TESTING

Component-level testing, also called *function testing,* focuses on a set of tests that attempt to uncover errors in WebApp functions. Each WebApp function is a software module (implemented in one of a variety of programming or scripting languages) and can be tested using black-box (and, in some cases, white-box) techniques discussed in Chapter 14.

Component-level test cases are often driven by forms-level input. Once forms data are defined, the user selects a button or other control mechanism to initiate execution. The following test case design methods (Chapter 14) are typical:

- *Equivalence partitioning*—The input domain of the function is divided into input categories or classes from which test cases are derived. The input form is assessed to determine what classes of data are relevant for the function. Test cases for each class of input are derived and executed while other classes of input are held constant. For example, an e-commerce application may implement a function that computes shipping charges. Among a variety of shipping information provided via a form is the user's postal code. Test cases are designed in an attempt to uncover errors in postal code processing by specifying postal code values that might uncover different classes of errors (e.g., an incomplete postal code, a correct postal code, a nonexistent postal code, an erroneous postal code format).
- *Boundary value analysis*—Forms data are tested at their boundaries. For example, the shipping calculation function noted previously requests the maximum number of days required for product delivery. A minimum of 2 days and a maximum of 14 are noted on the form. However, boundary value tests might input values of 0, 1, 2, 13, 14, and 15 to determine how the function reacts to data at and outside the boundaries of valid input.[13]
- *Path testing*—If the logical complexity of the function is high,[14] path testing (a white-box test case design method) can be used to ensure that every independent path in the program has been exercised.

In addition to these test case design methods, a technique called *forced error testing* [NGU01] is used to derive test cases that purposely drive the WebApp component into an error condition. The purpose is to uncover errors that occur during error-handling (e.g., incorrect or nonexistent error messages, WebApp failure as a consequence of the error, erroneous output driven by erroneous input, side-effects that are related to component processing).

Each component-level test case specifies all input values and the expected output to be provided by the component. The actual output produced as a consequence of the test is recorded for future reference during support and maintenance.

In many situations, the correct execution of a WebApp function is tied to proper interfacing with a database that may be external to the WebApp. Therefore, database testing becomes an integral part of the component-testing regime. Hower [HOW97] discusses this when he writes:

> Database-driven Web sites can involve a complex interaction among Web browsers, operating systems, plug-in applications, communications protocols, Web servers, databases, [scripting language] programs . . . , security enhancements, and firewalls. Such

13 In this case, a better input design might eliminate potential errors. The maximum number of days could be selected from a pull-down menu, precluding the user from specifying out-of-bounds input.

14 Logical complexity can be determined by computing cyclomatic complexity of the algorithm. See Chapter 14 for additional details.

WebRef

A variety of testing resources can be found at **www.pantos.org/atw/xref.html.**

complexity makes it impossible to test every possible dependency and everything that could go wrong with a site. The typical Web site development project will also be on an aggressive schedule, so the best testing approach will employ risk analysis to determine where to focus testing efforts. Risk analysis should include consideration of how closely the test environment will match the real production environment. . . . Other typical considerations in risk analysis include:

- Which functionality in the Web site is most critical to its purpose?
- Which areas of the site require the heaviest database interaction?
- Which aspects of the site's CGI, applets, ActiveX components, and so on are most complex?
- What types of problems would cause the most complaints or the worst publicity?
- What areas of the site will be the most popular?
- What aspects of the site have the highest security risks?

Each of the risk-related issues discussed by Hower should be considered when designing test cases for WebApp components and related database functions.

20.6 Navigation Testing

A user travels through a WebApp in much the same way as a visitor walks through a store or museum. There are many pathways that can be taken, many stops that can be made, many things to learn and look at, activities to initiate, and decisions to make. As we have already discussed, this navigation process is predictable in the sense that every visitor has a set of objectives when he arrives. At the same time, the navigation process can be unpredictable because the visitor, influenced by something he sees or learns, may choose a path or initiate an action that is not typical for the original objective. The job of navigation testing is (1) to ensure that the mechanisms that allow the WebApp user to travel through the WebApp are all functional and (2) to validate that each navigation semantic unit (NSU) can be achieved by the appropriate user category.

> "We're not lost. We're locationally challenged."
>
> **John M. Ford**

20.6.1 Testing Navigation Syntax

The first phase of navigation testing actually begins during interface testing. Navigation mechanisms are tested to ensure that each performs its intended function. Splaine and Jaskiel [SPL01] suggest that each of the following navigation mechanisms should be tested:

- *Navigation links*—internal links within the WebApp, external links to other WebApps, and anchors within a specific Web page should be tested to ensure that proper content or functionality is reached when the link is chosen.

- *Redirects*—these links come into play when a user requests a nonexistent URL or selects a link whose destination has been removed or whose name has changed. A message is displayed for the user, and navigation is redirected to another page (e.g., the home page). Redirects should be tested by requesting incorrect internal links or external URLs and assessing how the WebApp handles these requests.
- *Bookmarks*—although bookmarks are a browser function, the WebApp should be tested to ensure that a meaningful page title can be extracted as the bookmark is created.
- *Frames and framesets*—each frame contains the content of a specific Web page; a frameset contains multiple frames and enables the display of multiple Web pages at the same time. Because it is possible to nest frames and framesets within one another, these navigation and display mechanisms should be tested for correct content, proper layout and sizing, download performance, and browser compatibility.
- *Site maps*—entries should be tested to ensure that the link takes the user to the proper content or functionality.
- *Internal search engines*—complex WebApps often contain hundreds or even thousands of content objects. An internal search engine allows the user to perform a keyword search within the WebApp to find needed content. Search engine testing validates the accuracy and completeness of the search, the error-handling properties of the search engine, and advanced search features (e.g., the use of Boolean operators in the search field).

Some of the tests noted can be performed by automated tools (e.g., link checking) while others are designed and executed manually. The intent throughout is to ensure that errors in navigation mechanics are found before the WebApp goes on-line.

20.6.2 Testing Navigation Semantics

In Chapter 19 we defined a navigation semantic unit (NSU) as "a set of information and related navigation structures that collaborate in the fulfillment of a subset of related user requirements" [CAC02]. Each NSU is defined by a set of navigation paths (called "ways of navigating") that connect navigation nodes (e.g., Web pages, content objects, or functionality). Taken as a whole, each NSU allows a user to achieve specific requirements defined by one or more use-cases for a user category. Navigation testing exercises each NSU to ensure that these requirements can be achieved.

? What questions must be asked and answered as each NSU is tested?

As each NSU is tested, the Web engineering team must answer the following questions:

- Is the NSU achieved in its entirety without error?

- Is every navigation node (defined for a NSU) reachable within the context of the navigation paths defined for the NSU?
- If the NSU can be achieved using more than one navigation path, has every relevant path been tested?
- If guidance is provided by the user interface to assist in navigation, are directions correct and understandable as navigation proceeds?
- Is there a mechanism (other than the browser "back" arrow) for returning to the preceding navigation node and to the beginning of the navigation path?
- Do mechanisms for navigation within a large navigation node (i.e., a long Web page) work properly?
- If a function is to be executed at a node and the user chooses not to provide input, can the remainder of the NSU be completed?
- If a function is executed at a node and an error in function processing occurs, can the NSU be completed?
- Is there a way to discontinue the navigation before all nodes have been reached, but then return to where the navigation was discontinued and proceed from there?
- Is every node reachable from the site map? Are node names meaningful to end-users?
- If a node within a NSU is reached from some external source, is it possible to process to the next node on the navigation path? Is it possible to return to the previous node on the navigation path?
- Does the user understand his location within the content architecture as the NSU is executed?

If NSUs have not been created as part of Web engineering analysis or design, you can apply use-cases for the design of navigation test cases. The same set of questions are asked and answered.

Navigation testing, like interface and usability testing, should be conducted by as many different constituencies as possible. Early stages of testing are conducted by Web engineers, but later stages should be conducted by other project stakeholders, an independent testing team, and ultimately, by nontechnical users. The intent is to exercise WebApp navigation thoroughly.

20.7 Configuration Testing

Configuration variability and instability are important factors that make Web engineering a challenge. Hardware, operating system(s), browsers, storage capacity, network communication speeds, and a variety of other client-side factors are difficult to predict for each user. In addition, the configuration for a given user can change (e.g., OS updates, new ISP and connection speeds) on a regular basis. The result can be a client-side environment that is prone to errors that are both subtle and significant. One user's impression of the WebApp and the manner in which he interacts with it can differ significantly from another user's experience, if both users are not working within the same client-side configuration.

The job of *configuration testing* is not to exercise every possible client-side configuration. Rather, it is to test a set of probable client-side and server-side configurations to ensure that the user experience will be the same on all of them and to isolate errors that may be specific to a particular configuration.

20.7.1 Server-Side Issues

On the server side, configuration test cases are designed to verify that the projected server configuration (i.e., WebApp server, database server, operating system(s), firewall software, concurrent applications) can support the WebApp without error. In essence, the WebApp is installed within the server-side environment and tested with the intent of finding configuration-related errors.

As server-side configuration tests are designed, the Web engineer should consider each component of the server configuration. Among the questions that need to be asked and answered during server-side configuration testing are:

? What questions must be asked and answered as server-side configuration testing is conducted?

- Is the WebApp fully compatible with the server OS?
- Are system files, directories, and related system data created correctly when the WebApp is operational?
- Do system security measures (e.g., firewalls or encryption) allow the WebApp to execute and service users without interference or performance degradation?
- Has the WebApp been tested with the distributed server configuration[15] (if one exists) that has been chosen?
- Is the WebApp properly integrated with database software? Is the WebApp sensitive to different versions of database software?
- Do server-side WebApp scripts execute properly?
- Have system administrator errors been examined for their affect on WebApp operations?
- If proxy servers are used, have differences in their configuration been addressed with on-site testing?

20.7.2 Client-Side Issues

On the client side, configuration tests focus more heavily on WebApp compatibility with configurations that contain one or more permutation of the following components [NGU01]:

15 For example, a separate application server and database server may be used. Communication between the two machines occurs across a network connection.

- *Hardware*—CPU, memory, storage, and printing devices.
- *Operating systems*—Linux, Macintosh OS, Microsoft Windows, a mobile-based OS.
- *Browser software*—Internet Explorer, Mozilla/Netscape, Opera, Safari, and others.
- *User interface components*—Active X, Java applets, and others.
- *Plug-ins*—QuickTime, RealPlayer, and many others.
- *Connectivity*—cable, DSL, regular modem, T1.

In addition to these components, other variables include networking software, the vagaries of the ISP, and applications running concurrently.

To design client-side configuration tests, the Web engineering team must reduce the number of configuration variables to a manageable number.[16] To accomplish this, each user category is assessed to determine the likely configurations to be encountered within the category. In addition, industry market share data may be used to predict the most likely combinations of components. The WebApp is then tested within these environments.

20.8 Security Testing

WebApp security is a complex subject that must be fully understood before effective security testing can be accomplished.[17] WebApps and the client-side and server-side environments in which they are housed represent an attractive target for external hackers, disgruntled employees, dishonest competitors, and anyone else who wishes to steal sensitive information, maliciously modify content, degrade performance, disable functionality, or embarrass a person, organization, or business.

> **"The Internet is a risky place to conduct business or store assets. Hackers, crackers, snoops, spoofers, . . . thieves, vandals, virus launchers, and rogue program purveyors run loose."**
>
> **Dorothy and Peter Denning**

Security tests are designed to probe vulnerabilities of the client-side environment, the network communications that occur as data are passed from client to server and back again, and the server-side environment. Each of these domains can be attacked, and it is the job of the security tester to uncover weaknesses that can be exploited by those with the intent to do so.

---

16 Running tests on every possible combination of configuration components is far too time consuming.

17 Books by Trivedi [TRE03], McClure and his colleagues [MCC03], and Garfinkel and Spafford [GAR02] provide useful information about the subject.

If the WebApp is business critical, maintains sensitive data, or is a likely target of hackers, it's a good idea to outsource security testing to a vendor who specializes in it.

On the client-side, vulnerabilities can often be traced to pre-existing bugs in browsers, e-mail programs, or communication software. Nguyen [NGU01] describes a typical security hole:

> One of the commonly mentioned bugs is Buffer Overflow, which allows malicious code to be executed on the client machine. For example, entering a URL into a browser that is much longer than the buffer size allocated for the URL will cause a memory overwrite (buffer overflow) error if the browser does not have error detection code to validate the length of the input URL. A seasoned hacker can cleverly exploit this bug by writing a long URL with code to be executed that can cause the browser to crash or alter security settings (from high to low), or, at worst, to corrupt user data.

Another potential vulnerability on the client-side is unauthorized access to cookies placed within the browser. Web sites created with malicious intent can acquire information contained within legitimate cookies and use this information in ways that jeopardize the user's privacy, or worse, set the stage for identity theft.

Data communicated between the client and server are vulnerable to *spoofing*. Spoofing occurs when one end of the communication pathway is subverted by an entity with malicious intent. For example, a user can be spoofed by a malicious Web site that acts as if it is the legitimate WebApp server (identical look and feel). The intent is to steal passwords, proprietary information, or credit data.

On the server-side, vulnerabilities include denial-of-service attacks and malicious scripts that can be passed along to the client side or used to disable server operations. In addition, server-side databases can be accessed without authorization (data theft).

To protect against these (and many other) vulnerabilities, one or more of the following security elements is implemented [NGU01]:

Security tests should be designed to exercise firewalls, authentication, encryption, and authorization.

- *Firewalls*—a filtering mechanism that is a combination of hardware and software that examines each incoming packet of information to ensure that it is coming from a legitimate source, blocking any data that are suspect.
- *Authentication*—a verification mechanism that validates the identity of all clients and servers, allowing communication to occur only when both sides are verified.
- *Encryption*—an encoding mechanism that protects sensitive data by modifying it in a way that makes it impossible to read by those with malicious intent. Encryption is strengthened by using *digital certificates* that allow the client to verify the destination to which the data are transmitted.
- *Authorization*—a filtering mechanism that allows access to the client or server environment only by those individuals with appropriate authorization codes (e.g., userID and password)

The intent of security testing is to expose holes in these security elements that can be exploited by those with malicious intent. The actual design of security tests requires in-depth knowledge of the inner workings of each security element and a comprehensive understanding of a full range of networking technologies. In many cases, security testing is outsourced to firms that specialize in these technologies.

20.9 Performance Testing

Nothing is more frustrating than a WebApp that takes minutes to load content when competitive sites download similar content in seconds. Nothing is more aggravating than trying to log-in to a WebApp and receiving a "server-busy" message, with the suggestion that you try again later. Nothing is more disconcerting than a WebApp that responds instantly in some situations, and then seems to go into an infinite wait-state in other situations. All of these occurrences happen on the Web every day, and all of them are performance-related.

Performance testing is used to uncover performance problems that can result from lack of server-side resources, inappropriate network bandwidth, inadequate database capabilities, faulty or weak operating system capabilities, poorly designed WebApp functionality, and other hardware or software issues that can lead to degraded client-server performance. The intent is twofold: (1) to understand how the system responds to *loading* (i.e., number of users, number of transactions, or overall data volume), and (2) to collect metrics that will lead to design modifications to improve performance.

20.9.1 Performance Testing Objectives

Performance tests are designed to simulate real-world loading situations. As the number of simultaneous WebApp users grows, or the number of on-line transactions increases, or the amount of data (downloaded or uploaded) increases, performance testing will help answer the following questions:

Some aspects of WebApp performance, at least as it is perceived by the end-user, are difficult to test, including network loading, the vagaries of network interfacing hardware, and similar issues.

- Does the server response time degrade to a point where it is noticeable and unacceptable?
- At what point (in terms of users, transactions, or data loading) does performance become unacceptable?
- What system components are responsible for performance degradation?
- What is the average response time for users under a variety of loading conditions?
- Does performance degradation have an impact on system security?
- Is WebApp reliability or accuracy affected as the load on the system grows?
- What happens when loads that are greater than maximum server capacity are applied?

To develop answers to these questions, two different performance tests are conducted:

- *Load testing*—real world loading is tested at a variety of load levels and in a variety of combinations.
- *Stress testing*—loading is increased to the breaking point to determine how much capacity the WebApp environment can handle.

Each of these testing strategies is considered in the sections that follow.

20.9.2 Load Testing

The intent of *load testing* is to determine how the WebApp and its server-side environment will respond to various loading conditions. As testing proceeds, permutations to the following variables define a set of test conditions:

N, the number of concurrent users
T, the number of on-line transactions per user per unit time
D, the data load processed by the server per transaction

If a WebApp uses multiple servers to provide significant capacity, load testing must be performed in a multiserver environment.

In every case, these variables are defined within normal operating bounds of the system. As each test condition is run, one or more of the following measures are collected: average user response, average time to download a standardized unit of data, or average time to process a transaction. The Web engineering team examines these measures to determine whether a precipitous decrease in performance can be traced to a specific combination of *N*, *T*, and *D*.

Load testing can also be used to assess recommended connection speeds for users of the WebApp. Overall throughput, *P*, is computed in the following manner:

$$P = N \times T \times D$$

As an example, consider a popular sports news site. At a given moment, 20,000 concurrent users submit a request (a transaction, *T*) once every two minutes on average. Each transaction requires the WebApp to download a new article that averages 3 K bytes in length. Therefore, throughput can be calculated as:

$$P = [20{,}000 \times 0.5 \times 3 \text{ Kb}]/60 = 500 \text{ Kbytes/sec}$$
$$= 4 \text{ megabits per second}$$

The network connection for the server would therefore have to support this data rate and should be tested to ensure that it does.

The intent of stress testing is to better understand how a system fails as it is stressed beyond its operational limits.

20.9.3 Stress Testing

Stress testing (Chapter 13) is a continuation of load testing, but in this instance the variables, *N*, *T*, and *D* are forced to meet and then exceed operational limits. The intent of these tests is to answer each of the following questions:

- Does the system degrade "gently" or does the server shut down as capacity is exceeded?

- Does server software generate "server not available" messages? More generally, are users aware that they cannot reach the server?
- Does the server queue requests for resources and empty the queue once capacity demands diminish?
- Are transactions lost as capacity is exceeded?
- Is data integrity affected as capacity is exceeded?
- What values of *N, T,* and *D* force the server environment to fail? How does failure manifest itself? Are automated notifications sent to technical support staff at the server site?
- If the system does fail, how long will it take to come back on-line?
- Are certain WebApp functions (e.g., compute intensive functionality, data streaming capabilities) discontinued as capacity reaches the 80 or 90 percent level?

A variation of stress testing is sometimes referred to as *spike/bounce testing* [SPL01]. In this testing regime, load is spiked to capacity, then lowered quickly to normal operating conditions, and then spiked again. By bouncing system loading a tester can determine how well the server can marshall resources to meet very high demand and then release them when normal conditions reappear (so that they are ready for the next spike).

SOFTWARE TOOLS

Tools Taxonomy for WebApp Testing

In his paper on the testing of e-commerce systems, Lam [LAM01] presents a useful taxonomy of automated tools that have direct applicability for testing in a Web engineering context. We have appended representative tools in each category.[18]

Configuration and content management tools manage version and change control of WebApp content objects and functional components.

Representative tool(s):
Comprehensive list at www.daveeaton.com/scm/CMTools.html

Database performance tools measure database performance, such as the time to perform selected database queries. These tools facilitate database optimization.

Representative tool(s): BMC Software (www.bmc.com)

Debuggers are typical programming tools that find and resolve software defects in the code. They are part of most modern application development environments.

Representative tool(s):
Accelerated Technology (www.acceleratedtechnology.com)
IBM *VisualAge Environment* (www.ibm.com)
JDebugTool (www.debugtools.com)

Defect management systems record defects and track their status and resolution. Some include reporting tools to provide management information on defect spread and defect resolution rates.

Representative tool(s):
EXCEL *Quickbugs* (www.excelsoftware.com)

18 Tools noted here do not represent an endorsement, but rather a sampling of tools in this category. In addition, tool names are registered trademarks of the companies noted.

McCabe *TRUETrack* (www.mccabe.com)
Rational *ClearQuest* (www.rational.com)

Network monitoring tools watch the level of network traffic. They are useful for identifying network bottlenecks and testing the link between front- and back-end systems.
Representative tool(s):
Comprehensive list at www.slac.stanford.edu/xorg/nmtf/nmtf-tools.html

Regression testing tools store test cases and test data and can reapply the test cases after successive software changes.
Representative tool(s):
Compuware *QARun* (www.compuware.com/products/qacenter/qarun)
Rational *VisualTest* (www.rational.com)
Seque Software (www.seque.com)

Site monitoring tools monitor a site's performance, often from a user perspective. Use them to compile statistics such as end-to-end response time and throughput, and to periodically check a site's availability.
Representative tool(s):
Keynote Systems (www.keynote. com)

Stress tools help developers explore system behavior under high levels of operational usage and find a system's breakpoints.
Representative tool(s):
Mercury Interactive (www.merc-int.com)
Scapa Technologies (www.scapatech.com)

System resource monitors are part of most OS server and Web server software; they monitor resources such as disk space, CPU usage, and memory.
Representative tool(s):
Successful Hosting.com (www.successfulhosting.com)
Quest *Software Foglight* (www.quest.com)

Test data generation tools assist users in generating test data.
Representative tool(s):
Comprehensive list at www.softwareqatest.com/qatweb1.html

Test result comparators help compare the results of one set of testing to that of another set. Use them to check that code changes have not introduced adverse changes in system behavior.
Representative tool(s):
Useful list at www.aptest.com/resources.html

Transaction monitors measure the performance of high-volume transaction processing systems.
Representative tool(s):
QuotiumPro (www.quotium.com)
Software Research *eValid* (www.soft.com/eValid/index.html)

Web-site security tools help detect potential security problems. You can often set up security probing and monitoring tools to run on a scheduled basis.
Representative tool(s):
Comprehensive list at www.timberlinetechnologies.com/products/www.html)

20.10 Summary

The goal of WebApp testing is to exercise each of the many dimensions of WebApp quality with the intent of finding errors or uncovering issues that may lead to quality failures. Testing focuses on content, function, structure, usability, navigability, performance, compatibility, interoperability, capacity, and security. Testing also incorporates reviews that occur as the WebApp is designed.

The WebApp testing strategy exercises each quality dimension by initially examining "units" of content, functionality, or navigation. Once individual units have been validated, the focus shifts to tests that exercise the WebApp as a whole. To accomplish this, many tests are derived from the users' perspectives and are driven by information contained in use-cases. A Web engineering test plan is developed and identifies testing steps, work products (e.g., test cases), and mechanisms for the evaluation of test results. The testing process encompasses seven different types of testing.

Content testing (and reviews) focus on various categories of content. The intent is to uncover both semantic or syntactic errors that affect the accuracy of content or the manner in which it is presented to the end-user. Interface testing exercises the interaction mechanisms that enable a user to communicate with the WebApp and validates aesthetic aspects of the interface. The intent is to uncover errors that result from poorly implemented interaction mechanisms, or omissions, inconsistencies, or ambiguities in interface semantics.

Navigation testing applies use-cases, derived as part of the analysis activity, in the design of test cases that exercise each usage scenario against the navigation design. Navigation mechanisms are tested to ensure that any errors impeding completion of a use-case are identified and corrected. Component testing exercises content and functional units within the WebApp. Each Web page encapsulates content, navigation links, and processing elements that form a "unit" within the WebApp architecture. These units must be tested.

Configuration testing attempts to uncover errors and/or compatibility problems that are specific to a particular client or server environment. Tests are then conducted to uncover errors associated with each possible configuration. Security testing incorporates a series of tests designed to exploit vulnerabilities in the WebApp and its environment. The intent is to find security holes. Performance testing encompasses a series of tests that are designed to assess WebApp response time and reliability as demands on server-side resource capacity increase.

References

[BRO01] Brown, B., *Oracle9i Web Development,* McGraw-Hill, 2nd ed., 2001.

[CAC02] Cachero, C., et al., "Conceptual Navigation Analysis: A Device and Platform Independent Navigation Specification," *Proc. 2nd Intl. Workshop on Web-Oriented Technology,* June 2002, download from www.dsic.upv.es/~west/iwwost02/papers/cachero.pdf.

[CON03] Constantine, L., and L. Lockwood, *Software for Use,* Addison-Wesley, 1999; see also http://www.foruse.com/.

[GAR02] Garfinkel, S., and G. Spafford, *Web Security, Privacy and Commerce,* O'Reilly & Associates, 2002.

[HOW97] Hower, Rick, "Beyond Broken Links," *Internet Systems,* 1997 available at http://www.dbmsmag.com/9707i03.html.

[LAM01] Lam, W., "Testing E-Commerce Systems: A Practical Guide," *IEEE IT Pro,* March/April 2001, pp. 19–28.

[MCC03] McClure, S., S. Shah, and S. Shah, *Web Hacking: Attacks and Defense,* Addison-Wesley, 2003.

[MIL00] Miller, E., "WebSite Testing," 2000, available at http://www.soft.com/ eValid/Technology/White.Papers/website.testing.html.

[NGU00] Nguyen, H., "Testing Web-Based Applications," *Software Testing and Quality Engineering,* May/June, 2000, available at http://www.stqemagazine.com.

[NGU01] Nguyen, H., *Testing Applications on the Web,* Wiley, 2001.
[SCE02] Sceppa, D., *Microsoft ADO.NET,* Microsoft Press, 2002.
[SPL01] Splaine, S., and S. Jaskiel, *The Web Testing Handbook,* STQE Publishing, 2001.
[TRE03] Trivedi, R., *Professional Web Services Security,* Wrox Press, 2003.
[WAL03] Wallace, D., I. Raggett, and J. Aufgang, *Extreme Programming for Web Projects,* Addison-Wesley, 2003.

Problems and Points to Ponder

20.1. Are there any situations in which WebApp testing should be totally disregarded?

20.2. In your own words, discuss the objectives of testing in a Web engineering context.

20.3. Compatibility is an important quality dimension. What must be tested to ensure that compatibility exists for a WebApp?

20.4. Which errors tend to be more serious—client-side errors or server-side errors? Why?

20.5. What elements of the WebApp can be "unit tested"? What types of tests must be conducted only after the WebApp elements are integrated?

20.6. Is it always necessary to develop a formal written test plan? Explain.

20.7. Is it fair to say that the overall WebApp testing strategy begins with user-visible elements and moves toward technology elements? Are there exceptions to this strategy?

20.8. Is content testing *really* testing in a conventional sense? Explain.

20.9. Describe the steps associated with database testing for a WebApp. Is database testing predominantly a client-side or server-side activity?

20.10. What is the difference between testing that is associated with interface mechanisms and testing that addresses interface semantics?

20.11. Assume that you are developing an on-line pharmacy (CornerPharmacy.com) that caters to senior citizens. The pharmacy provides typical functions, but also maintains a database for each customer so that it can provide drug information and warn of potential drug interactions. Discuss any special usability tests for this WebApp.

20.12. Assume that you have implemented a drug interaction checking function for CornerPharmacy.com (Problem 20.11). Discuss the types of component-level tests that would have to be conducted to ensure that this function works properly. [Note: a database would have to be used to implement this function.]

20.13. What is the difference between testing for navigation syntax and for navigation semantics?

20.14. Is it possible to test every configuration that a WebApp is likely to encounter on the server-side? On the client-side? If it is not, how does a Web engineer select a meaningful set of configuration tests?

20.15. What is the objective of security testing? Who performs this testing activity?

20.16. CornerPharmacy.com (Problem 20.11) has become wildly successful and the number of users has increased dramatically in the first two months of operation. Draw a graph that depicts probable response time as a function of number of users for a fixed set of server-side resources. Label the graph to indicate points of interest on the "response curve."

20.17. In response to its success CornerPharmacy.com (Problem 20.11) has implemented a special server solely to handle prescription refills. On average, 1000 concurrent users submit a refill request once every two minutes. The WebApp downloads a 500 byte block of data in response. What is the approximate required throughput for this server in megabits per second?

20.18. What is the difference between load testing and stress testing?

Further Readings and Information Sources

The literature for WebApp testing is still evolving. Books by Ash (*The Web Testing Companion,* Wiley, 2003), Dustin and his colleagues (*Quality Web Systems,* Addison-Wesley, 2002), Nguyen [NGU01], and Splaine and Jaskiel [SPL01] are among the most complete treatments of the subject published to date. Mosley (*Client-Server Software Testing on the Desktop and the Web,* Prentice-Hall, 1999) addresses both client-side and server-side testing issues.

Useful information on WebApp testing strategies and methods, as well as a worthwhile discussion of automated testing tools is presented by Stottlemeyer (*Automated Web Testing Toolkit,* Wiley, 2001). Graham and her colleagues (*Software Test Automation,* Addison-Wesley, 1999) present additional material on automated tools.

Nguyen and his colleagues (*Testing Applications for the Web,* second edition, Wiley, 2003) have developed a major update to [NGU01] and provide unique guidance for testing mobile applications. Although Microsoft (*Performance Testing Microsoft .NET Web Applications,* Microsoft Press, 2002) focuses predominantly on its .NET environment, its comments on performance testing can be useful to anyone interested in the subject.

Splaine (*Testing Web Security,* Wiley, 2002), Klevinsky and his colleagues (*Hack I.T.: Security through Penetration Testing,* Addison-Wesley, 2002), Chirillo (*Hack Attacks Revealed,* second edition, Wiley, 2003), and Skoudis (*Counter Hack,* Prentice-Hall, 2001) provide much useful information for those who must design security tests.

A wide variety of information sources on testing for Web engineering is available on the Internet. An up-to-date list of World Wide Web references can be found at the SEPA Web site: **http://www.mhhe.com/pressman.**

PART

Four

MANAGING SOFTWARE PROJECTS

In this part of *Software Engineering: A Practitioner's Approach,* we consider the management techniques required to plan, organize, monitor, and control software projects. In the chapters that follow, we address the following questions:

- How must people, process, and problems be managed during a software project?
- How can software metrics be used to manage a software project and the software process?
- How do we estimate effort, cost, and project duration?
- What techniques can be used to formally assess the risks that can impact project success?
- How does a software project manager select a set of software engineering work tasks?
- How is a project schedule created?
- What is quality management?
- Why are formal technical reviews so important?
- How is change managed during the development of computer software and after delivery to the customer?

Once these questions are answered, you'll be better prepared to manage software projects in a way that will lead to timely delivery of a high-quality product.

CHAPTER

21 PROJECT MANAGEMENT CONCEPTS

KEY CONCEPTS

In the preface to his book on software project management, Meiler Page-Jones [PAG85] makes a statement that can be echoed by many software engineering consultants:

> I've visited dozens of commercial shops, both good and bad, and I've observed scores of data processing managers, again, both good and bad. Too often, I've watched in horror as these managers futilely struggled through nightmarish projects, squirmed under impossible deadlines, or delivered systems that outraged their users and went on to devour huge chunks of maintenance time.

What Page-Jones describes are symptoms that result from an array of management and technical problems. However, if a post mortem were to be conducted for every project, it is very likely that a consistent theme would be encountered: project management was weak.

In this chapter and the six that follow, we consider the key concepts that lead to effective software project management. This chapter considers basic software project management concepts and principles. Chapter 22 presents process and project metrics, the basis for effective management decision making. The techniques that are used to estimate cost, define a realistic schedule, and establish an effective project plan are discussed in Chapters 23 and 24. The management activities that lead to effective risk monitoring, mitigation, and management are presented in Chapter 25. Finally, Chapters 26 and 27 consider techniques for ensuring quality as a project is conducted and managing changes throughout the life of an application.

QUICK LOOK

What is it? Although many of us (in our darker moments) take Dilbert's view of "management," it remains a very necessary activity when computer-based systems and products are built. Project management involves the planning, monitoring, and control of the people, process, and events that occur as software evolves from a preliminary concept to an operational implementation.

Who does it? Everyone "manages" to some extent, but the scope of management activities varies among people involved in a software project. A software engineer manages her day-to-day activities, planning, monitoring, and controlling technical tasks. Project managers plan, monitor, and control the work of a team of software engineers. Senior managers coordinate the interface between the business and software professionals.

Why is it important? Building computer software is a complex undertaking, particularly if it involves many people working over a relatively long time. That's why software projects need to be managed.

What are the steps? Understand the four P's—people, product, process, and project. People must be organized to perform software work effectively. Communication with the customer and other stakeholders must occur so that product scope and requirements are understood. A process must be selected that is appropriate for the people and the product. The project must be planned by estimating effort and calendar time to accomplish work tasks: defining work products, establishing quality checkpoints, and identifying mechanisms to monitor and control work defined by the plan.

What is the work product? A project plan is produced as management activities commence. The plan defines the process and tasks to be conducted, the people who will do the work, and the mechanisms for assessing risks, controlling change, and evaluating quality.

How do I ensure that I've done it right? You're never completely sure that the project plan is right until you've delivered a high-quality product on time and within budget. However, a project manager does it right when he encourages software people to work together as an effective team, focusing their attention on customer needs and product quality.

21.1 The Management Spectrum

Effective software project management focuses on the four P's: people, product, process, and project. The order is not arbitrary. The manager who forgets that software engineering work is an intensely human endeavor will never have success in project management. A manager who fails to encourage comprehensive stakeholder communication early in the evolution of a project risks building an elegant solution for the wrong problem. The manager who pays little attention to the process runs the risk of inserting competent technical methods and tools into a vacuum. The manager who embarks without a solid project plan jeopardizes the success of the product.

21.1.1 The People

The cultivation of motivated, highly skilled software people has been discussed since the 1960s (e.g., [COU80], [WIT94], [DEM98]). In fact, the "people factor" is so important that the Software Engineering Institute has developed a people management capability maturity model (PM-CMM), "to enhance the readiness of software organizations to undertake increasingly complex applications by helping to attract, grow, motivate, deploy, and retain the talent needed to improve their software development capability" [CUR94].

The people management maturity model defines the following key practice areas for software people: recruiting, selection, performance management, training, compensation, career development, organization and work design, and team/culture development. Organizations that achieve high levels of maturity in the people management area have a higher likelihood of implementing effective software engineering practices.

The PM-CMM is a companion to the Software Capability Maturity Model Integration (Chapter 2) that guides organizations in the creation of a mature software process. Issues associated with people management and structure for software projects are considered later in this chapter.

21.1.2 The Product

ADVICE

In this context, the term product *is used to encompass any software that is built at the request of others. It includes not only shrink-wrapped software products, but also computer-based systems, embedded software, WebApps, and problem-solving software (e.g., programs for engineering/scientific problem solving).*

Before a project can be planned, product objectives and scope should be established, alternative solutions should be considered, and technical and management constraints should be identified. Without this information, it is impossible to define reasonable (and accurate) estimates of the cost, an effective assessment of risk, a realistic breakdown of project tasks, or a manageable project schedule that provides a meaningful indication of progress.

The software developer and customer must meet to define product objectives and scope. In many cases, this activity begins as part of the system engineering or business process engineering (Chapter 6) and continues as the first step in software requirements engineering (Chapter 7). Objectives identify the overall goals for the product (from the customer's point of view) without considering how these goals will be achieved. Scope identifies the primary data, functions, and behaviors that characterize the product, and more importantly, attempts to bound these characteristics in a quantitative manner.

Once the product objectives and scope are understood, alternative solutions are considered. Although relatively little detail is discussed, the alternatives enable managers and practitioners to select a "best" approach, given the constraints imposed by delivery deadlines, budgetary restrictions, personnel availability, technical interfaces, and myriad other factors.

21.1.3 The Process

Those who adhere to the agile process philosophy (Chapter 4) argue that their process is leaner than others. That may be true, but they still have a process, and agile software engineering still requires discipline.

A software process (Chapters 2, 3, and 4) provides the framework from which a comprehensive plan for software development can be established. A small number of framework activities are applicable to all software projects, regardless of their size or complexity. A number of different task sets—tasks, milestones, work products, and quality assurance points—enable the framework activities to be adapted to the characteristics of the software project and the requirements of the project team. Finally, umbrella activities—such as software quality assurance, software configuration management, and measurement—overlay the process model. Umbrella activities are independent of any one framework activity and occur throughout the process.

21.1.4 The Project

We conduct planned and controlled software projects for one primary reason—it is the only known way to manage complexity. And yet, we still struggle. In 1998, industry data indicated that 26 percent of software projects failed outright and 46 percent experienced cost and schedule overruns [REE99]. Although the success rate for software projects has improved somewhat, our project failure rate remains higher than it should be.[1]

1 Given these statistics, it's reasonable to ask how the impact of computers continues to grow exponentially. Part of the answer, I think, is that a substantial number of these "failed" projects are ill-conceived in the first place. Customers lose interest quickly (because what they've requested wasn't really as important as they first thought), and the projects are cancelled.

> "A project is like a road trip. Some projects are simple and routine, like driving to the store in broad daylight. But most projects worth doing are more like driving a truck off-road, in the mountains, at night."
>
> **Cem Kaner, James Bach, and Bret Pettichord**

To avoid project failure, a software project manager and the software engineers who build the product must heed a set of common warning signs, understand the critical success factors that lead to good project management, and develop a commonsense approach for planning, monitoring, and controlling the project. Each of these issues is discussed in Section 21.5 and in the chapters that follow.

21.2 People

In a study published by the IEEE [CUR88], the engineering vice presidents of three major technology companies were asked the most important contributor to a successful software project. They answered in the following way:

> VP 1: I guess if you had to pick one thing out that is most important in our environment, I'd say it's not the tools that we use, it's the people.
>
> VP 2: The most important ingredient that was successful on this project was having smart people . . . very little else matters in my opinion . . . The most important thing you do for a project is selecting the staff . . . The success of the software development organization is very, very much associated with the ability to recruit good people.
>
> VP 3: The only rule I have in management is to ensure I have good people—real good people—and that I grow good people—and that I provide an environment in which good people can produce.

Indeed, this is a compelling testimonial on the importance of people in the software engineering process. And yet, all of us, from senior engineering vice presidents to the lowliest practitioner, often take people for granted. Managers argue (as the preceding group had) that people are primary, but their actions sometimes belie their words. In this section we examine the stakeholders who participate in the software process and the manner in which they are organized to perform effective software engineering.

21.2.1 The Stakeholders

The software process (and every software project) is populated by stakeholders who can be categorized into one of five constituencies:

1. *Senior managers* who define business issues that often have significant influence on the project.
2. *Project (technical) managers* who must plan, motivate, organize, and control the practitioners who do software work.
3. *Practitioners* who deliver the technical skills that are necessary to engineer a product or application.

4. *Customers* who specify the requirements for the software to be engineered and other stakeholders who have a peripheral interest in the outcome.
5. *End-users* who interact with the software once it is released for production use.

Every software project is populated by people who fall within this taxonomy.[2] To be effective, the project team must be organized in a way that maximizes each person's skills and abilities. And that's the job of the team leader.

21.2.2 Team Leaders

Project management is a people-intensive activity, and for this reason, competent practitioners often make poor team leaders. They simply don't have the right mix of people skills. And yet, as Edgemon states: "Unfortunately and all too frequently it seems, individuals just fall into a project manager role and become accidental project managers"[EDG95].

In an excellent book of technical leadership, Jerry Weinberg [WEI86] suggests a MOI model of leadership:

What do we look for when choosing someone to lead a software project?

Motivation. The ability to encourage (by "push or pull") technical people to produce to their best ability.

Organization. The ability to mold existing processes (or invent new ones) that will enable the initial concept to be translated into a final product.

Ideas or innovation. The ability to encourage people to create and feel creative even when they must work within bounds established for a particular software product or application.

Weinberg suggests that successful project leaders apply a problem solving management style. That is, a software project manager should concentrate on understanding the problem to be solved, managing the flow of ideas, and at the same time, letting everyone on the team know (by words and, far more important, by actions) that quality counts and that it will not be compromised.

> "In simplest terms, a leader is one who knows where he wants to go, and gets up, and goes."
>
> **John Erskine**

Another view [EDG95] of the characteristics that define an effective project manager emphasizes four key traits:

Problem solving. An effective software project manager can diagnose the technical and organizational issues that are most relevant, systematically structure a solution or properly motivate other practitioners to develop the solution, apply

---

2 When Web applications are developed (Part 3 of this book), other nontechnical people may be involved in content creation.

lessons learned from past projects to new situations, and remain flexible enough to change direction if initial attempts at problem solution are fruitless.

Managerial identity. A good project manager must take charge of the project. She must have the confidence to assume control when necessary and the assurance to allow good technical people to follow their instincts.

Achievement. To optimize the productivity of a project team, a manager must reward initiative and accomplishment and demonstrate through his own actions that controlled risk taking will not be punished.

Influence and team building. An effective project manager must be able to "read" people; she must be able to understand verbal and nonverbal signals and react to the needs of the people sending these signals. The manager must remain under control in high-stress situations.

21.2.3 The Software Team

There are almost as many human organizational structures for software development as there are organizations that develop software. For better or worse, organizational structure cannot be easily modified. Concern with the practical and political consequences of organizational change are not within the software project manager's scope of responsibility. However, the organization of the people directly involved in a software project is within the project manager's purview.

> "Not every group is a team, and not every team is effective."
>
> **Glenn Parker**

The "best" team structure depends on the management style of your organization, the number of people who will populate the team and their skill levels, and the overall problem difficulty. Mantei [MAN81] describes seven project factors that should be considered when planning the structure of software engineering teams:

? **What factors should be considered when the structure of a software team is chosen?**

- The difficulty of the problem to be solved.
- The "size" of the resultant program(s) in lines of code or function points (Chapter 22).
- The time that the team will stay together (team lifetime).
- The degree to which the problem can be modularized.
- The required quality and reliability of the system to be built.
- The rigidity of the delivery date.
- The degree of sociability (communication) required for the project.

> "If you want to be incrementally better: Be competitive. If you want to be exponentially better: Be cooperative."
>
> **Author unknown**

Constantine [CON93] suggests four "organizational paradigms" for software engineering teams:

? What options do we have when defining the structure of a software team?

1. A *closed paradigm* structures a team along a traditional hierarchy of authority. Such teams can work well when producing software that is quite similar to past efforts, but they will be less likely to be innovative when working within the closed paradigm.
2. A *random paradigm* structures a team loosely and depends on individual initiative of the team members. When innovation or technological breakthrough is required, teams following the random paradigm will excel. But such teams may struggle when "orderly performance" is required.
3. An *open paradigm* attempts to structure a team in a manner that achieves some of the controls associated with the closed paradigm but also much of the innovation that occurs when using the random paradigm. Work is performed collaboratively. Heavy communication and consensus-based decision making are the trademarks of open paradigm teams. Open paradigm team structures are well suited to the solution of complex problems but may not perform as efficiently as other teams.
4. A *synchronous paradigm* relies on the natural compartmentalization of a problem and organizes team members to work on pieces of the problem with little active communication among themselves.

> **"Working with people is difficult, but not impossible."**
>
> **Peter Drucker**

As an historical footnote, one of the earliest software team organizations was a closed paradigm structure originally called the *chief programmer team.* This structure was first proposed by Harlan Mills and described by Baker [BAK72]. The nucleus of the team is composed of a *senior engineer* (the chief programmer), who plans, coordinates, and reviews all technical activities of the team; *technical staff* (normally two to five people), who conduct analysis and development activities; and a *backup engineer,* who supports the senior engineer in his or her activities and can replace the senior engineer with minimum loss in project continuity.

The chief programmer may be served by one or more *specialists* (e.g., telecommunications expert, database designer), *support staff* (e.g., technical writers, clerical personnel), and a *software librarian.*

As a counterpoint to the chief programmer team structure, Constantine's random paradigm [CON93] suggests a software team with creative independence whose approach to work might best be termed *innovative anarchy.* Although the free-spirited approach to software work has appeal, channeling creative energy into a high-performance team must be a central goal of a software engineering organization. To achieve a high-performance team:

- Team members must have trust in one another.
- The distribution of skills must be appropriate to the problem.
- Mavericks may have to be excluded from the team, if team cohesiveness is to be maintained.

Regardless of team organization, the objective for every project manager is to help create a team that exhibits cohesiveness. In their book, *Peopleware,* DeMarco and Lister [DEM98] discuss this issue:

? What is a "jelled" team?

> We tend to use the word *team* fairly loosely in the business world, calling any group of people assigned to work together a "team." But many of these groups just don't seem like teams. They don't have a common definition of success or any identifiable team spirit. What is missing is a phenomenon that we call *jell.*
>
> A jelled team is a group of people so strongly knit that the whole is greater than the sum of the parts . . .
>
> Once a team begins to jell, the probability of success goes way up. The team can become unstoppable, a juggernaut for success . . . They don't need to be managed in the traditional way, and they certainly don't need to be motivated. They've got momentum.

DeMarco and Lister contend that members of jelled teams are significantly more productive and more motivated than average. They share a common goal, a common culture, and in many cases, a "sense of eliteness" that makes them unique.

? Why do teams fail to jell?

But not all teams jell. In fact, many teams suffer from what Jackman [JAC98] calls "team toxicity." She defines five factors that "foster a potentially toxic team environment": (1) a frenzied work atmosphere, (2) high frustration that causes friction among team members, (3) a "fragmented or poorly coordinated" software process, (4) an unclear definition of roles on the software team, and (5) "continuous and repeated exposure to failure."

To avoid a frenzied work environment, the project manager should be certain that the team has access to all information required to do the job and that major goals and objectives, once defined, should not be modified unless absolutely necessary. A software team can avoid frustration (and stress) if it is given as much responsibility for decision making as possible. An inappropriate process (e.g., unnecessary or burdensome work tasks or poorly chosen work products) can be avoided by understanding the product to be built and the people doing the work, and by allowing the team to select its own process model. The team itself should establish mechanisms for accountability (formal technical reviews and pair programming are excellent ways to accomplish this) and define a series of corrective approaches when a member of the team fails to perform. And finally, the key to avoiding an atmosphere of failure is to establish team-based techniques for feedback and problem solving.

> **"Do or do not. There is no try."**
>
> **Yoda from *Star Wars***

In addition to the five toxins described by Jackman, a software team often struggles with the differing human traits of its members. Some team members are extroverts; others are introverted. Some people gather information intuitively, distilling broad concepts from disparate facts. Others process information linearly, collecting and organizing minute details from the data provided. Some team members are comfortable making decisions only when a logical, orderly argument is presented. Others are intuitive, willing to make a decision based on "feel." Some practitioners want a detailed schedule populated by organized tasks that enable them to achieve closure for some element of a project. Others prefer a more spontaneous environment in which open issues are okay. Some work hard to get things done long before a milestone date, thereby avoiding stress as the date approaches, while others are energized by the rush to make a last minute deadline. A detailed discussion of the psychology of these traits and the ways in which a skilled team leader can help people with opposing traits to work together is beyond the scope of this book.[3] However, it is important to note that recognition of human differences is the first step toward creating teams that jell.

21.2.4 Agile Teams

In recent years, agile software development (Chapter 4) has been proposed as an antidote to many of the problems that have plagued software project work. To review, the agile philosophy encourages customer satisfaction and early incremental delivery of software; small highly motivated project teams; informal methods; minimal software engineering work products, and overall development simplicity.

The small, highly motivated project team, also called an *agile team,* adopts many of the characteristics of successful software project teams discussed in the preceding section and avoids many of the toxins that create problems. However, the agile philosophy stresses individual (team member) competency coupled with group collaboration as critical success factors for the team. Cockburn and Highsmith [COC01] note this when they write:

> If the people on the project are good enough, they can use almost any process and accomplish their assignment. If they are not good enough, no process will repair their inadequacy—"people trump process" is one way to say this. However, lack of user and executive support can kill a project—"politics trump people." Inadequate support can keep even good people from accomplishing the job . . .

To make effective use of the competencies of each team member and to foster effective collaboration through a software project, agile teams are *self-organizing.* A self-organizing team does not necessarily maintain a single team structure but in-

---

3 An excellent introduction to these issues as they relate to software project teams can be found in [FER98].

stead uses elements of Constantine's random, open, and synchronous paradigms discussed in Section 21.2.3.

> "Collective ownership is nothing more than an instantiation of the idea that products should be attributable to the [agile] team, not individuals who make up the team."
>
> **Jim Highsmith**

An agile team is a self-organizing team that has autonomy to plan and make technical decisions.

Many agile process models (e.g., Scrum) give the agile team significant autonomy to make the project management and technical decisions required to get the job done. Planning is kept to a minimum, and the team is allowed to select its own approach (e.g., process, methods, tools), constrained only by business requirements and organizational standards. As the project proceeds, the team self-organizes to focus individual competency in a way that is most beneficial to the project at a given point in time. To accomplish this, an agile team might conduct brief daily team meetings to coordinate and synchronize the work that must be accomplished for that day.

Based on information obtained during these meetings, the team adapts its approach in a way that accomplishes an increment of work. As each day passes, continual self-organization and collaboration move the team toward a completed software increment.

21.2.5 Coordination and Communication Issues

There are many reasons that software projects get into trouble. The scale of many development efforts is large, leading to complexity, confusion, and significant difficulties in coordinating team members. Uncertainty is common, resulting in a continuing stream of changes that ratchets the project team. Interoperability has become a key characteristic of many systems. New software must communicate with existing software and conform to predefined constraints imposed by the system or product.

These characteristics of modern software—scale, uncertainty, and interoperability—are facts of life. To deal with them effectively, a software engineering team must establish effective methods for coordinating the people who do the work. To accomplish this, mechanisms for formal and informal communication among team members and between multiple teams must be established. Formal communication is accomplished through "writing, structured meetings, and other relatively noninteractive and impersonal communication channels" [KRA95]. Informal communication is more personal. Members of a software team share ideas on an ad hoc basis, ask for help as problems arise, and interact with one another on a daily basis.

SafeHome

Team Structure

The scene: Doug Miller's office prior to the initiation of the *SafeHome* software project.

The players: Doug Miller (manager of the *SafeHome* software engineering team) and Vinod Raman, Jamie Lazar, and other members of the product software engineering team.

The conversation:

Doug: Have you guys had a chance to look over the preliminary info on *SafeHome* that marketing's prepared?

Vinod (nodding and looking at his teammates): Yes. But we have a bunch of questions.

Doug: Let's hold on that for a moment. I'd like to talk about how we're going to structure the team, who's responsible for what. . . .

Jamie: I'm really into the agile philosophy, Doug. I think we should be a self-organizing team.

Vinod: I agree. Given the tight time line and some of the uncertainty, and that fact that we're all really competent [laughs], that seems like the right way to go.

Doug: That's okay with me, but you guys know the drill.

Jamie (smiling and talking as if she were reciting something): We make tactical decisions, about who does what and when, but it's our responsibility to get product out the door on time.

Vinod: And with quality.

Doug: Exactly. But remember there are constraints. Marketing defines the software increments to be produced—in consultation with us, of course.

Jamie: And?

Doug: And, we're going to use UML as our modeling approach.

Vinod: But keep extraneous documentation to an absolute minimum.

Doug: Who is the liaison with me?

Jamie: We decided that Vinod will be the tech lead—he's got the most experience, so Vinod is your liaison, but feel free to talk to any of us.

Doug (laughing): Don't worry, I will.

21.3 The Product

A software project manager is confronted with a dilemma at the very beginning of a software engineering project. Quantitative estimates and an organized plan are required, but solid information is unavailable. A detailed analysis of software requirements would provide necessary information for estimates, but analysis often takes weeks or months to complete. Worse, requirements may be fluid, changing regularly as the project proceeds. Yet, a plan is needed "now!"

Therefore, we must examine the product and the problem it is intended to solve at the very beginning of the project. At a minimum, the scope of the product must be established and bounded.

21.3.1 Software Scope

The first software project management activity is the determination of *software scope.* Scope is defined by answering the following questions:

Context. How does the software to be built fit into a larger system, product, or business context, and what constraints are imposed as a result of the context?

If you can't bound a characteristic of the software you intend to build, list the characteristic as a project risk (Chapter 25).

Information objectives. What customer-visible data objects (Chapter 8) are produced as output from the software? What data objects are required for input?

Function and performance. What functions does the software perform to transform input data into output? Are there any special performance characteristics to be addressed?

Software project scope must be unambiguous and understandable at the management and technical levels. A statement of software scope must be bounded. That is, quantitative data (e.g., number of simultaneous users, size of mailing list, maximum allowable response time) are stated explicitly; constraints and/or limitations (e.g., product cost restricts memory size) are noted, and mitigating factors (e.g., desired algorithms are well understood and available in C++) are described.

21.3.2 Problem Decomposition

Problem decomposition, sometimes called *partitioning* or *problem elaboration,* is an activity that sits at the core of software requirements analysis (Chapters 7 and 8). During the scoping activity no attempt is made to fully decompose the problem. Rather, decomposition is applied in two major areas: (1) the functionality that must be delivered and (2) the process that will be used to deliver it.

To develop a reasonable project plan, you must decompose the problem. This can be accomplished using a list of functions, or with use-cases, or for agile work, user stories.

Human beings tend to apply a divide-and-conquer strategy when they are confronted with a complex problem. Stated simply, a complex problem is partitioned into smaller problems that are more manageable. This is the strategy that applies as project planning begins. Software functions, described in the statement of scope, are evaluated and refined to provide more detail prior to the beginning of estimation (Chapter 23). Because both cost and schedule estimates are functionally oriented, some degree of decomposition is often useful.

As an example, consider a project that will build a new word-processing product. Among the unique features of the product are continuous voice as well as keyboard input, extremely sophisticated "automatic copy edit" features, page layout capability, automatic indexing and table of contents, and others. The project manager must first establish a statement of scope that bounds these features (as well as other more mundane functions such as editing, file management, document production, and the like). For example, will continuous voice input require that the product be "trained" by the user? Specifically, what capabilities will the copy edit feature provide? Just how sophisticated will the page layout capability be?

As the statement of scope evolves, a first level of partitioning naturally occurs. The project team learns that the marketing department has talked with potential customers and found that the following functions should be part of automatic copy editing: (1) spell checking, (2) sentence grammar checking, (3) reference checking for large documents (e.g., Is a reference to a bibliography entry found in the list of entries in the bibliography?), and (4) section and chapter reference validation for large documents. Each of these features represents a subfunction to be implemented in software. Each can be further refined if the decomposition will make planning easier.

21.4 The Process

The framework activities (Chapter 2) that characterize the software process are applicable to all software projects. The problem is to select the process model that is appropriate for the software to be engineered by a project team.

The project manager must decide which process model is most appropriate for (1) the customers who have requested the product and the people who will do the work, (2) the characteristics of the product itself, and (3) the project environment in which the software team works. When a process model has been selected, the team then defines a preliminary project plan based on the set of process framework activities. Once the preliminary plan is established, process decomposition begins. That is, a complete plan, reflecting the work tasks required to populate the framework activities, must be created. We explore these activities briefly in the sections that follow and present a more detailed view in Chapter 24.

ADVICE

An automated project scheduling tool can be used to create a "task network" (Chapter 24). The network is loaded with estimated resource requirements, start/end dates, and other pertinent data. This resource loaded network can then be used for project tracking and control.

21.4.1 Melding the Product and the Process

Project planning begins with the melding of the product and the process. Each function to be engineered by the software team must pass through the set of framework activities that have been defined for a software organization. Assume that the organization has adopted the following set of framework activities (Chapter 2): communications, planning, modeling, construction, and deployment.

The team members who work on a product function will apply each of the framework activities to it. In essence, a matrix similar to the one shown in Figure 21.1 is created. Each major product function (the figure notes functions for the word-

FIGURE 21.1

Melding the problem and the process

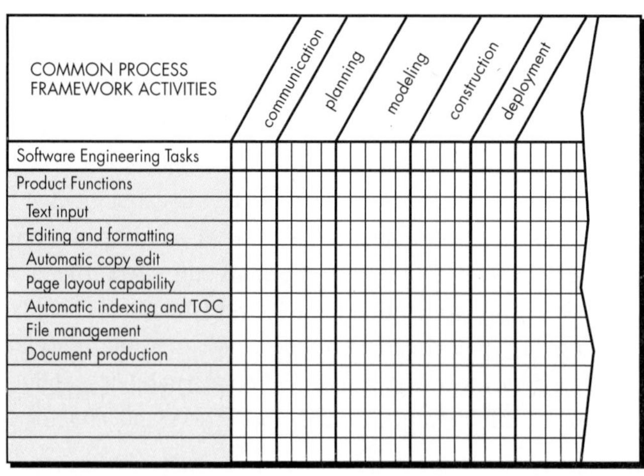

The process framework establishes a skeleton for project planning. It is adapted by allocating a task set that is appropriate to the project.

processing software discussed earlier) is listed in the left-hand column. Framework activities are listed in the top row. Software engineering work tasks (for each framework activity) would be entered in the following row.[4] The job of the project manager (and other team members) is to estimate resource requirements for each matrix cell, start and end dates for the tasks associated with each cell, and work products to be produced as a consequence of each task. These activities are considered in Chapter 24.

21.4.2 Process Decomposition

A software team should have a significant degree of flexibility in choosing the software process model that is best for the project and the software engineering tasks that populate the process model once it is chosen. A relatively small project that is similar to past efforts might be best accomplished using the linear sequential approach. If very tight time constraints are imposed and the problem can be heavily compartmentalized, the RAD model is probably the right option. If the deadline is so tight that full functionality cannot reasonably be delivered, an incremental strategy might be best. Similarly, projects with other characteristics (e.g., uncertain requirements, breakthrough technology, difficult customers, significant reuse potential) will lead to the selection of other process models.[5]

Once the process model has been chosen, the process framework is adapted to it. In every case, the generic framework discussed earlier—communication, planning, modeling, construction, and deployment—can be used. It will work for linear models, for iterative and incremental models, for evolutionary models, and even for concurrent or component assembly models. The process framework is invariant and serves as the basis for all software work performed by a software organization.

But actual work tasks do vary. Process decomposition commences when the project manager asks, "How do we accomplish this framework activity?" For example, a small, relatively simple project might require the following work tasks for the communication activity:

1. Develop list of clarification issues.
2. Meet with customer to address clarification issues.
3. Jointly develop a statement of scope.
4. Review the statement of scope with all concerned.
5. Modify the statement of scope as required.

These events might occur over a period of less than 48 hours. They represent a process decomposition that is appropriate for the small, relatively simple project.

4 It should be noted that work tasks must be adapted to the specific needs of the project.

5 Recall that project characteristics also have a strong bearing on the structure of the software team (Section 21.2.3).

Now, we consider a more complex project, which has a broader scope and more significant business impact. Such a project might require the following work tasks for the communication activity:

1. Review the customer request.
2. Plan and schedule a formal, facilitated meeting with the customer.
3. Conduct research to specify the proposed solution and existing approaches.
4. Prepare a "working document" and an agenda for the formal meeting.
5. Conduct the meeting.
6. Jointly develop mini-specs that reflect data, function, and behavioral features of the software. Alternatively, develop use-cases that describe the software from the user's point of view.
7. Review each mini-spec or use-case for correctness, consistency, and lack of ambiguity.
8. Assemble the mini-specs into a scoping document.
9. Review the scoping document or collection of use-cases with all concerned.
10. Modify the scoping document or use-cases as required.

Both projects perform the framework activity that we call "communication," but the first project team performed half as many software engineering work tasks as the second.

21.5 The Project

To manage a successful software project, we must understand what can go wrong (so that problems can be avoided). In an excellent paper on software projects, John Reel [REE99] defines 10 signs that indicate that an information systems project is in jeopardy:

What are the signs that a software project is in jeopardy?

1. Software people don't understand their customer's needs.
2. The product scope is poorly defined.
3. Changes are managed poorly.
4. The chosen technology changes.
5. Business needs change [or are ill-defined].
6. Deadlines are unrealistic.
7. Users are resistant.
8. Sponsorship is lost [or was never properly obtained].
9. The project team lacks people with appropriate skills.
10. Managers [and practitioners] avoid best practices and lessons learned.

Jaded industry professionals often refer (half-facetiously) to the 90–90 rule when discussing particularly difficult software projects: The first 90 percent of a system absorbs 90 percent of the allotted effort and time. The last 10 percent takes the other 90 percent of the allotted effort and time [ZAH94]. The seeds that lead to the 90–90 rule are contained in the signs noted in the preceding list.

> **"We don't have time to stop for gas, we're already late."**
>
> **M. Cleron**

But enough negativity! How does a manager act to avoid the problems just noted? Reel [REE99] suggests a five-part common-sense approach to software projects:

1. *Start on the right foot.* This is accomplished by working hard (very hard) to understand the problem that is to be solved and then setting realistic objectives and expectations for everyone who will be involved in the project. It is reinforced by building the right team (Section 21.2.3) and giving the team the autonomy, authority, and technology needed to do the job.
2. *Maintain momentum.* Many projects get off to a good start and then slowly disintegrate. To maintain momentum, the project manager must provide incentives to keep turnover of personnel to an absolute minimum, the team should emphasize quality in every task it performs, and senior management should do everything possible to stay out of the team's way.[6]
3. *Track progress.* For a software project, progress is tracked as work products (e.g., models, source code, sets of test cases) are produced and approved (using formal technical reviews) as part of a quality assurance activity. In addition, software process and project measures (Chapter 22) can be collected and used to assess progress against averages developed for the software development organization.
4. *Make smart decisions.* In essence, the decisions of the project manager and the software team should be to "keep it simple." Whenever possible, decide to use commercial off-the-shelf software or existing software components, decide to avoid custom interfaces when standard approaches are available, decide to identify and then avoid obvious risks, and decide to allocate more time than you think is needed to complex or risky tasks (you'll need every minute).
5. *Conduct a postmortem analysis.* Establish a consistent mechanism for extracting lessons learned for each project. Evaluate the planned and actual schedules, collect and analyze software project metrics, get feedback from team members and customers, and record findings in written form.

---

6 The implication of this statement is that bureaucracy is reduced to a minimum, extraneous meetings are eliminated, and dogmatic adherence to process and project rules is eliminated. The team should be self-organizing and autonomous.

21.6 The W^5HH Principle

In an excellent paper on software process and projects, Barry Boehm [BOE96] states: "you need an organizing principle that scales down to provide simple [project] plans for simple projects." Boehm suggests an approach that addresses project objectives, milestones and schedules, responsibilities, management and technical approaches, and required resources. He calls it the W^5HH principle, after a series of questions that lead to a definition of key project characteristics and the resultant project plan:

? How do we define key project characteristics?

Why is the system being developed? The answer to this question enables all parties to assess the validity of business reasons for the software work. Stated in another way, does the business purpose justify the expenditure of people, time, and money?

What will be done? The answer to this question establishes the task set that will be required for the project.

When will it be done? The answer to this question helps the team to establish a project schedule by identifying when project tasks are to be conducted and when milestones are to be reached.

Who is responsible for a function? Earlier in this chapter, we noted that the role and responsibility of each member of the software team must be defined. The answer to this question helps accomplish this.

Where are they organizationally located? Not all roles and responsibilities reside within the software team itself. The customer, users, and other stakeholders also have responsibilities.

How will the job be done technically and managerially? Once product scope is established, a management and technical strategy for the project must be defined.

How much of each resource is needed? The answer to this question is derived by developing estimates (Chapter 23) based on answers to earlier questions.

Boehm's W^5HH principle is applicable regardless of the size or complexity of a software project. The questions noted provide an excellent planning outline for the project manager and the software team.

21.7 Critical Practices

The Airlie Council[7] has developed a list of "critical software practices for performance-based management." These practices are "consistently used by, and considered critical by, highly successful software projects and organizations whose 'bottom line' performance is consistently much better than industry averages" [AIR99].

7 The Airlie Council is a team of software engineering experts chartered by the U.S. Department of Defense to help develop guidelines for best practices in software project management and software engineering.

Critical practices[8] include: metrics-based project management (Chapter 22), empirical cost and schedule estimation (Chapters 23 and 24), earned value tracking (Chapter 24), formal risk management (Chapter 25), defect tracking against quality targets (Chapter 26), and people-aware management (Section 21.2). Each of these critical practices is addressed throughout Part 4 of this book.

SOFTWARE TOOLS

Software Tools for Project Managers

The "tools" listed here are generic and apply to a broad range of activities performed by project managers. Specific project management tools (e.g., scheduling tools, estimating tools, risk analysis tools) are considered in later chapters).

Representative Tools[9]

The Software Program Manager's Network (www.spmn.com) has developed a simple tool called *Project Control Panel* which provides project managers with a direct indication of project status. The tool has "gauges" much like a dashboard and is implemented with Microsoft Excel. It is available for download at http://www.spmn.com/products_software.html.

Ganthead.com has developed a set of useful *checklists for project managers* that can be downloaded from http://www.gantthead.com/.

Ittoolkit.com (www.ittoolkit.com) provides "a collection of planning guides, process templates and smart worksheets" available on CD-ROM.

21.8 SUMMARY

Software project management is an umbrella activity within software engineering. It begins before any technical activity is initiated and continues throughout the definition, development, and support of computer software.

Four P's have a substantial influence on software project management—people, product, process, and project. People must be organized into effective teams, motivated to do high-quality software work, and coordinated to achieve effective communication. The product requirements must be communicated from customer to developer, partitioned (decomposed) into their constituent parts, and positioned for work by the software team. The process must be adapted to the people and the problem. A common process framework is selected, an appropriate software engineering paradigm is applied, and a set of work tasks is chosen to get the job done. Finally, the project must be organized in a manner that enables the software team to succeed.

The pivotal element in all software projects is people. Software engineers can be organized in a number of different team structures that range from traditional control hierarchies to "open paradigm" teams. A variety of coordination and communication techniques can be applied to support the work of the team. In general,

8 Only those critical practices associated with "project integrity" are noted here.

9 Tools noted here do not represent an endorsement, but rather a sampling of tools in this category. In most cases, tool names are trademarked by their respective developers.

formal reviews and informal person-to-person communication have the most value for practitioners.

The project management activity encompasses measurement and metrics, estimation and scheduling, risk analysis, tracking, and control. Each of these topics is considered in the chapters that follow.

References

[AIR99] Airlie Council, "Performance Based Management: The Program Manager's Guide Based on the 16-Point Plan and Related Metrics," Draft Report, March 8, 1999.

[BAK72] Baker, F. T., "Chief Programmer Team Management of Production Programming," *IBM Systems Journal,* vol. 11, no. 1, 1972, pp. 56–73.

[BOE96] Boehm, B., "Anchoring the Software Process," *IEEE Software,* vol. 13, no. 4, July 1996, pp. 73–82.

[COC01] Cockburn, A., and J. Highsmith, "Agile Software Development: The People Factor," *IEEE Computer,* vol. 34, no. 11, November 2001, pp. 131–133.

[CON93] Constantine, L., "Work Organization: Paradigms for Project Management and Organization," *CACM,* vol. 36, no. 10, October 1993, pp. 34–43.

[COU80] Cougar, J., and R. Zawacki, *Managing and Motivating Computer Personnel,* Wiley, 1980.

[CUR88] Curtis, B., et al., "A Field Study of the Software Design Process for Large Systems," *IEEE Trans. Software Engineering,* vol. SE-31, no. 11, November 1988, pp. 1268–1287.

[CUR94] Curtis, B., et al., *People Management Capability Maturity Model,* Software Engineering Institute, 1994.

[DEM98] DeMarco, T., and T. Lister, *Peopleware,* 2nd ed., Dorset House, 1998.

[EDG95] Edgemon, J., "Right Stuff: How to Recognize It When Selecting a Project Manager," *Application Development Trends,* vol. 2, no. 5, May 1995, pp. 37–42.

[FER98] Ferdinandi, P. L., "Facilitating Communication," *IEEE Software,* September 1998, pp. 92–96.

[JAC98] Jackman, M., "Homeopathic Remedies for Team Toxicity," *IEEE Software,* July 1998, pp. 43–45.

[KRA95] Kraul, R., and L. Streeter, "Coordination in Software Development," *CACM,* vol. 38, no. 3, March 1995, pp. 69–81.

[MAN81] Mantei, M., "The Effect of Programming Team Structures on Programming Tasks," *CACM,* vol. 24, no. 3, March 1981, pp. 106–113.

[PAG85] Page-Jones, M., *Practical Project Management,* Dorset House, 1985, p. vii.

[REE99] Reel, J. S., "Critical Success Factors in Software Projects," *IEEE Software,* May, 1999, pp. 18–23.

[WEI86] Weinberg, G., *On Becoming a Technical Leader,* Dorset House, 1986.

[WIT94] Whitaker, K., *Managing Software Maniacs,* Wiley, 1994.

[ZAH94] Zahniser, R., "Timeboxing for Top Team Performance," *Software Development,* March 1994, pp. 35–38.

Problems and Points to Ponder

21.1. Based on information contained in this chapter and your own experience, develop "10 commandments" for empowering software engineers. That is, make a list of 10 guidelines that will lead to software people who work to their full potential.

21.2. The Software Engineering Institute's people management capability maturity model (PM-CMM) takes an organized look at "key practice areas" that cultivate good software people. Your instructor will assign you one KPA for analysis and summary.

21.3. Describe three real-life situations in which the customer and the end-user are the same. Describe three situations in which they are different.

21.4. The decisions made by senior management can have a significant impact on the effectiveness of a software engineering team. Provide five examples to illustrate that this is true.

21.5. Review a copy of Weinberg's book [WEI86] and write a two- or three-page summary of the issues that should be considered in applying the MOI model.

21.6. You have been appointed a project manager within an information systems organization. Your job is to build an application that is quite similar to others your team has built, although this one is larger and more complex. Requirements have been thoroughly documented by the customer. What team structure would you choose and why? What software process model(s) would you choose and why?

21.7. You have been appointed a project manager for a small software products company. Your job is to build a breakthrough product that combines virtual reality hardware with state-of-the-art software. Because competition for the home entertainment market is intense, there is significant pressure to get the job done. What team structure would you choose and why? What software process model(s) would you choose and why?

21.8. You have been appointed a project manager for a major software products company. Your job is to manage the development of the next generation version of its widely used word-processing software. Because new revenue must be generated, tight deadlines have been established and announced. What team structure would you choose and why? What software process model(s) would you choose and why?

21.9. You have been appointed a software project manager for a company that services the genetic engineering world. Your job is to manage the development of a new software product that will accelerate the pace of gene typing. The work is R&D oriented, but the goal is to produce a product within the next year. What team structure would you choose and why? What software process model(s) would you choose and why?

21.10. You have been asked to develop a small application that analyzes each course offered by a university and reports the average grade obtained in the course (for a given term). Write a statement of scope that bounds this problem.

21.11. Do a first level functional decomposition of the page layout function discussed briefly in Section 21.3.2.

Further Readings and Information Sources

The Project Management Institute (*Guide to the Project Management Body of Knowledge,* PMI, 2001) covers all important aspects of project management. Murch (*Project Management: Best Practices for IT Professionals,* Prentice-Hall, 2000) teaches basic skills and provides detailed guidance for all phases of an IT project. Lewis (*Project Managers Desk Reference,* McGraw-Hill, 1999) presents a 16-step process for planning, monitoring, and controlling any type of project. McConnell (*Professional Software Development,* Addison-Wesley, 2004) offers pragmatic advice for achieving "shorter schedules, higher quality products, and more successful projects."

An excellent four-volume series written by Weinberg (*Quality Software Management,* Dorset House, 1992, 1993, 1994, 1996) introduces basic systems thinking and management concepts; explains how to use measurements effectively; and addresses "congruent action," the ability to establish "fit" between the manager's needs, the needs of technical staff, and the needs of the business. It will provide both new and experienced managers with useful information. Futrell and his colleagues (*Quality Software Project Management,* Prentice-Hall, 2002) present a voluminous treatment of project management.

Phillips (*IT Project Management: On Track from Start to Finish,* McGraw-Hill/Osborne, 2002), Charvat (*Project Management Nation,* Wiley, 2002), Schwalbe (*Information Technology Project Management,* second edition, Course Technology, 2001) and Holtsnider and Jaffe (*IT Manager's Handbook,* Morgan Kaufmann Publishers, 2000) are representative of the many books that have been written on software project management. Brown and his colleagues (*AntiPatterns in Project Management,* Wiley, 2000) discuss what not to do during the management of a software project.

Brooks (*The Mythical Man-Month,* Anniversary Edition, Addison-Wesley, 1995) has updated his classic book to provide new insight into software project and management issues. McConnell (*Software Project Survival Guide,* Microsoft Press, 1997) presents excellent pragmatic guidance for those who must manage software projects. Purba and Shah (*How to Manage a Successful Software Project,* second edition, Wiley, 2000) present a number of case studies that indicate why some projects succeed and others fail. Bennatan (*On Time Within Budget,* third edition, Wiley, 2000) presents useful tips and guidelines for software project managers.

It can be argued that the most important aspect of software project management is people management. Cockburn (*Agile Software Development,* Addison-Wesley, 2002) presents one of the best discussions of software people written to date. DeMarco and Lister [DEM98] have written the definitive book on software people and software projects. In addition, the following books on this subject have been published in recent years and are worth examining:

Beaudouin-Lafon, M., *Computer Supported Cooperative Work,* Wiley-Liss, 1999.

Carmel, E., *Global Software Teams: Collaborating Across Borders and Time Zones,* Prentice Hall, 1999.

Constantine, L., *Peopleware Papers: Notes on the Human Side of Software,* Prentice-Hall, 2001.

Humphrey, W. S., *Managing Technical People: Innovation, Teamwork, and the Software Process,* Addison-Wesley, 1997.

Humphrey, W. S., *Introduction to the Team Software Process,* Addison-Wesley, 1999.

Jones, P. H., *Handbook of Team Design: A Practitioner's Guide to Team Systems Development,* McGraw-Hill, 1997.

Karolak, D. S., *Global Software Development: Managing Virtual Teams and Environments,* IEEE Computer Society, 1998.

Ensworth (*The Accidental Project Manager,* Wiley, 2001) provides much useful guidance to those who must survive "the transition from techie to project manager." Another excellent book by Weinberg [WEI86] is must reading for every project manager and every team leader. It will give you insight and guidance that will enable you to do your job more effectively.

Even though they do not relate specifically to the software world and sometimes suffer from over-simplification and broad generalization, best-selling "management" books by Bossidy (*Execution: The Discipline of Getting Things Done,* Crown Publishing, 2002), Drucker (*Management Challenges for the 21st Century,* Harper Business, 1999), Buckingham and Coffman (*First, Break All the Rules: What the World's Greatest Managers Do Differently,* Simon and Schuster, 1999) and Christensen (*The Innovator's Dilemma,* Harvard Business School Press, 1997) emphasize "new rules" defined by a rapidly changing economy. Older titles such as *Who Moved My Cheese?, The One-Minute Manager,* and *In Search of Excellence* continue to provide valuable insights that can help you to manage people and projects more effectively.

A wide variety of information sources on software project management is available on the Internet. An up-to-date list of World Wide Web references can be found at the SEPA Web site: **http://www.mhhe.com/pressman.**

CHAPTER

22 PROCESS AND PROJECT METRICS

KEY CONCEPTS

Measurement enables us to gain insight into the process and the project by providing a mechanism for objective evaluation. Lord Kelvin once said:

> When you can measure what you are speaking about and express it in numbers, you know something about it; but when you cannot measure, when you cannot express it in numbers, your knowledge is of a meager and unsatisfactory kind: it may be the beginning of knowledge, but you have scarcely, in your thoughts, advanced to the stage of a science.

The software engineering community has taken Lord Kelvin's words to heart. But not without frustration and more than a little controversy!

Measurement can be applied to the software process with the intent of improving it on a continuous basis. Measurement can be used throughout a software project to assist in estimation, quality control, productivity assessment, and project control. Finally, measurement can be used by software engineers to help assess the quality of work products and to assist in tactical decision-making as a project proceeds (Chapter 15).

In their guidebook on software measurement, Park, Goethert, and Florac [PAR96] note the reasons that we measure: (1) to *characterize* in an effort to gain an understanding "of processes, products, resources, and environments, and to establish baselines for comparisons with future assessments"; (2) to *evaluate* "to determine status with respect to plans"; (3) to *predict* by "gaining understandings

QUICK LOOK

What is it? Software process and project metrics are quantitative measures that enable software engineers to gain insight into the efficacy of the software process and the projects that are conducted using the process as a framework. Basic quality and productivity data are collected. These data are then analyzed, compared against past averages, and assessed to determine whether quality and productivity improvements have occurred. Metrics are also used to pinpoint problem areas so that remedies can be developed and the software process can be improved.

Who does it? Software metrics are analyzed and assessed by software managers. Measures are often collected by software engineers.

Why is it important? If you don't measure, judgment can be based only on subjective evaluation. With measurement, trends (either good or bad) can be spotted, better estimates can be made, and true improvement can be accomplished over time.

What are the steps? Begin by defining a limited set of process and project measures that are easy to collect. These measures are often normalized using either size- or function-oriented metrics. The result is analyzed and compared to past averages for similar projects performed within the organization. Trends are assessed and conclusions are generated.

What is the work product? A set of software metrics that provides insight into the process and an understanding of the project.

How do I ensure that I've done it right? By applying a consistent, yet simple measurement scheme that is never used to assess, reward, or punish individual performance.

of relationships among processes and products and building models of these relationships"; and (4) to *improve* by "identify[ing] roadblocks, root causes, inefficiencies, and other opportunities for improving product quality and process performance."

Measurement is a management tool. If conducted properly, it provides a project manager with insight. And as a result, it assists the project manager and the software team in making decisions that will lead to a successful project.

22.1 Metrics in the Process and Project Domains

Process metrics have long-term impact. Their intent is to improve the process itself. Project metrics often contribute to the development of process metrics.

Process metrics are collected across all projects and over long periods of time. Their intent is to provide a set of process indicators that lead to long-term software process improvement. *Project metrics* enable a software project manager to (1) assess the status of an ongoing project, (2) track potential risks, (3) uncover problem areas before they go "critical," (4) adjust work flow or tasks, and (5) evaluate the project team's ability to control quality of software work products.

Measures that are collected by a project team and converted into metrics for use during a project can also be transmitted to those with responsibility for software process improvement. For this reason, many of the same metrics are used in both the process and project domain.

22.1.1 Process Metrics and Software Process Improvement

The only rational way to improve any process is to measure specific attributes of the process, develop a set of meaningful metrics based on these attributes, and then use the metrics to provide indicators that will lead to a strategy for improvement. But before we discuss software metrics and their impact on software process improvement, it is important to note that process is only one of a number of "controllable factors in improving software quality and organizational performance" [PAU94].

Referring to Figure 22.1, process sits at the center of a triangle connecting three factors that have a profound influence on software quality and organizational performance. The skill and motivation of people has been shown [BOE81] to be the single most influential factor in quality and performance. The complexity of the product can have a substantial impact on quality and team performance. The technology (i.e., the software engineering methods and tools) that populates the process also has an impact.

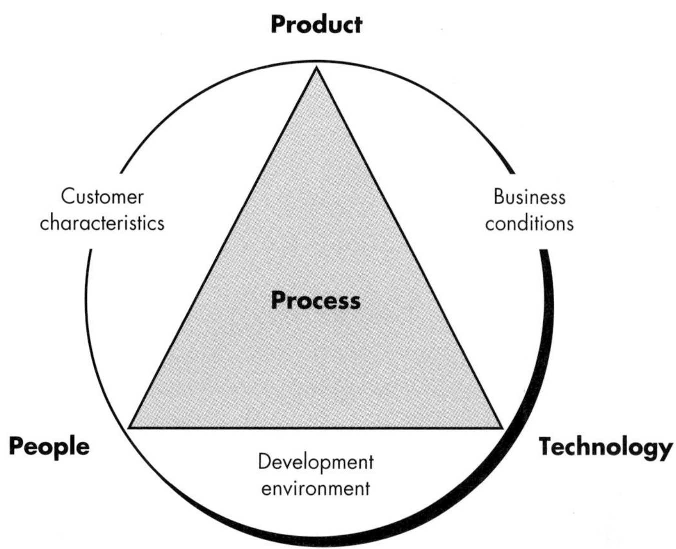

FIGURE 22.1 Determinants for software quality and organizational effectiveness (adapted from [PAU94])

In addition, the process triangle exists within a circle of environmental conditions that include the development environment (e.g., CASE tools), business conditions (e.g., deadlines, business rules), and customer characteristics (e.g., ease of communication and collaboration).

KEY POINT: The skill and motivation of the software people doing the work are the most important factors that influence software quality.

We measure the efficacy of a software process indirectly. That is, we derive a set of metrics based on the outcomes that can be derived from the process. Outcomes include measures of errors uncovered before release of the software, defects delivered to and reported by end-users, work products delivered (productivity), human effort expended, calendar time expended, schedule conformance, and other measures. We also derive process metrics by measuring the characteristics of specific software engineering tasks. For example, we might measure the effort and time spent performing the generic software engineering activities described in Chapter 2.

> "Software metrics let you know when to laugh and when to cry."
>
> Tom Gilb

? What is the difference between private and public uses for software metrics?

Grady [GRA92] argues that there are "private and public" uses for different types of process data. Because it is natural that individual software engineers might be sensitive to the use of metrics collected on an individual basis, these data should be private to the individual and serve as an indicator for the individual only. Examples of *private metrics* include defect rates by individual, defect rates by software component, and errors found during development.

The "private process data" philosophy conforms well with the personal software process approach (Chapter 2) proposed by Humphrey [HUM95]. Humphrey recognizes that software process improvement can and should begin at the individual level. Private process data can serve as an important driver as the individual software engineer works to improve.

Some process metrics are private to the software project team but public to all team members. Examples include defects reported for major software functions (that have been developed by a number of practitioners), errors found during formal technical reviews, and lines of code or function points per component or function.[1] These data are reviewed by the team to uncover indicators that can improve team performance.

Public metrics generally assimilate information that originally was private to individuals and teams. Project level defect rates (absolutely not attributed to an individual), effort, calendar times, and related data are collected and evaluated in an attempt to uncover indicators that can improve organizational process performance.

Software process metrics can provide significant benefit as an organization works to improve its overall level of process maturity. However, like all metrics, these can be misused, creating more problems than they solve. Grady [GRA92] suggests a "software metrics etiquette" that is appropriate for both managers and practitioners as they institute a process metrics program:

? What guidelines should be applied when we collect software metrics?

- Use common sense and organizational sensitivity when interpreting metrics data.
- Provide regular feedback to the individuals and teams who collect measures and metrics.
- Don't use metrics to appraise individuals.
- Work with practitioners and teams to set clear goals and metrics that will be used to achieve them.
- Never use metrics to threaten individuals or teams.
- Metrics data that indicate a problem area should not be considered "negative." These data are merely an indicator for process improvement.
- Don't obsess on a single metric to the exclusion of other important metrics.

As an organization becomes more comfortable with the collection and use of process metrics, the derivation of simple indicators gives way to a more rigorous approach called *statistical software process improvement* (SSPI). In essence, SSPI uses software failure analysis to collect information about all errors and defects[2] encountered as an application, system, or product is developed and used.

---

1 Lines of code and function point metrics are discussed in Sections 22.2.1 and 22.2.2.

2 In this book, an *error* is defined as some flaw in a software engineering work product that is uncovered before the software is delivered to the end-user. A *defect* is a flaw that is uncovered *after* delivery to the end-user. It should be noted that others do not make this distinction. Further discussion is presented in Chapter 26.

22.1.2 Project Metrics

Unlike software process metrics that are used for strategic purposes, software project metrics are tactical. That is, project metrics and the indicators derived from them are used by a project manager and a software team to adapt project workflow and technical activities.

The first application of project metrics on most software projects occurs during estimation. Metrics collected from past projects are used as a basis from which effort and time estimates are made for current software work. As a project proceeds, measures of effort and calendar time expended are compared to original estimates (and the project schedule). The project manager uses these data to monitor and control progress.

As technical work commences, other project metrics begin to have significance. Production rates represented in terms of models created, review hours, function points, and delivered source lines are measured. In addition, errors uncovered during each software engineering task are tracked. As the software evolves from requirements into design, technical metrics (Chapter 15) are collected to assess design quality and to provide indicators that will influence the approach taken to code generation and testing.

? How should we use metrics during the project itself?

The intent of project metrics is twofold. First, these metrics are used to minimize the development schedule by making the adjustments necessary to avoid delays and mitigate potential problems and risks. Second, project metrics are used to assess product quality on an ongoing basis and, when necessary, modify the technical approach to improve quality.

As quality improves, defects are minimized, and as the defect count goes down, the amount of rework required during the project is also reduced. This leads to a reduction in overall project cost.

SAFEHOME

Establishing a Metrics Approach

The scene: Doug Miller's office as the *SafeHome* software project is about to begin.

The players: Doug Miller (manager of the *SafeHome* software engineering team) and Vinod Raman and Jamie Lazar, members of the product software engineering team.

The conversation:

Doug: Before we start work on this project, I'd like you guys to define and collect a set of simple metrics. To start, you'll have to define your goals.

Vinod (frowning): We've never done that before, and . . .

Jamie (interrupting): And based on the timeline management has been talking about, we'll never have the time. What good are metrics anyway?

Doug (raising his hand to stop the onslaught): Slow down and take a breath, guys. The fact that we've never done it before is all the more reason to start now, and the metrics work I'm talking about shouldn't take much time at all . . . in fact, it just might save us time.

Vinod: How?

Doug: Look, we're going to be doing a lot more in-house software engineering as our products get more intelligent, become Web enabled, all that . . . and we need to understand the process we use to build software . . . and improve it so we can build software better. The only way to do that is to measure.

Jamie: But we're under time pressure, Doug. I'm not in favor of more paper pushing . . . we need the time to do our work, not collect data.

Doug (calmly): Jamie, an engineer's work involves collecting data, evaluating it, and using the results to improve the product and the process. Am I wrong?

Jamie: No, but . . .

Doug: What if we hold the number of measures we collect to no more than five or six and focus on quality?

Vinod: No one can argue against high quality . . .

Jamie: True . . . but, I don't know, I still think this isn't necessary.

Doug: I'm going to ask you to humor me on this one. How much do you guys know about software metrics?

Jamie (looking at Vinod): Not much.

Doug: Here are some Web refs . . . spend a few hours getting up to speed.

Jamie (smiling): I thought you said this wouldn't take any time.

Doug: Time you spend learning is never wasted . . . go do it and then we'll establish some goals, ask a few questions, and define the metrics we need to collect.

22.2 Software Measurement

In Chapter 15, we noted that software measurement can be categorized in two ways: (1) *direct measures* of the software process (e.g., cost and effort applied) and product (e.g., lines of code (LOC) produced, execution speed, and defects reported over some set period of time), and (2) *indirect measures* of the product that include functionality, quality, complexity, efficiency, reliability, maintainability, and many other "–abilities" discussed in Chapter 15.

> **"Not everything that can be counted counts, and not everything that counts can be counted."**
>
> **Albert Einstein**

Project metrics can be consolidated to create process metrics that are public to the software organization as a whole. But how does an organization combine metrics that come from different individuals or projects?

Because many factors affect software work, don't use metrics to compare individuals or teams.

To illustrate, we consider a simple example. Individuals on two different project teams record and categorize all errors that they find during the software process. Individual measures are then combined to develop team measures. Team A found 342 errors during the software process prior to release. Team B found 184 errors. All other things being equal, which team is more effective in uncovering errors throughout the process? Because we do not know the size or complexity of the projects, we cannot answer this question. However, if the measures are normalized, it is possible to create software metrics that enable comparison to broader organizational averages. Both size- and function-oriented metrics are normalized in this manner.

22.2.1 Size-Oriented Metrics

Size-oriented software metrics are derived by normalizing quality and/or productivity measures by considering the *size* of the software that has been produced. If a software organization maintains simple records, a table of size-oriented measures, such as the one shown in Figure 22.2, can be created. The table lists each software development project that has been completed over the past few years and corresponding measures for that project. Referring to the table entry (Figure 22.2) for project alpha: 12,100 lines of code were developed with 24 person-months of effort at a cost of $168,000. It should be noted that the effort and cost recorded in the table represent all software engineering activities (analysis, design, code, and test), not just coding. Further information for project alpha indicates that 365 pages of documentation were developed, 134 errors were recorded before the software was released, and 29 defects were encountered after release to the customer within the first year of operation. Three people worked on the development of software for project alpha.

To develop metrics that can be assimilated with similar metrics from other projects, we choose *lines of code* as our normalization value. From the rudimentary data contained in the table, a set of simple size-oriented metrics can be developed for each project: errors per KLOC (thousand lines of code), defects per KLOC, $ per KLOC, pages of documentation per KLOC. In addition, other interesting metrics can be computed: errors per person-month, KLOC per person-month, $ per page of documentation.

Size-oriented metrics are widely used, but debate about their validity and applicability continues.

Size-oriented metrics are not universally accepted as the best way to measure the software process [JON86]. Most of the controversy swirls around the use of lines of code as a key measure. Proponents of the LOC measure claim that LOC is an "artifact" of all software development projects that can be easily counted, that many existing software estimation models use LOC or KLOC as a key input, and that a large body of literature and data predicated on LOC already exists. On the other hand,

FIGURE 22.2

Size-oriented metrics

Project	LOC	Effort	$(000)	Pp. doc.	Errors	Defects	People
alpha	12,100	24	168	365	134	29	3
beta	27,200	62	440	1224	321	86	5
gamma	20,200	43	314	1050	256	64	6
•	•	•	•	•	•		
•	•	•	•	•	•		
•	•	•	•	•	•		

opponents argue that LOC measures are programming language dependent, that when productivity is considered, they penalize well-designed but shorter programs, that they cannot easily accommodate nonprocedural languages, and that their use in estimation requires a level of detail that may be difficult to achieve (i.e., the planner must estimate the LOC to be produced long before analysis and design have been completed).

22.2.2 Function-Oriented Metrics

Function-oriented software metrics use a measure of the functionality delivered by the application as a normalization value. The most widely used function-oriented metric is the *function point* (FP). Computation of the function point is based on characteristics of the software's information domain and complexity. The mechanics of FP computation has been discussed in Chapter 15.[3]

The function point, like the LOC measure, is controversial. Proponents claim that FP is programming language independent, making it ideal for applications using conventional and nonprocedural languages, and that it is based on data that are more likely to be known early in the evolution of a project, making FP more attractive as an estimation approach. Opponents claim that the method requires some "sleight of hand" in that computation is based on subjective rather than objective data, that counts of the information domain (and other dimensions) can be difficult to collect after the fact, and that FP has no direct physical meaning—it's just a number.

22.2.3 Reconciling LOC and FP Metrics

The relationship between lines of code and function points depends upon the programming language that is used to implement the software and the quality of the design. A number of studies have attempted to relate FP and LOC measures. To quote Albrecht and Gaffney [ALB83]:

> The thesis of this work is that the amount of function to be provided by the application (program) can be estimated from the itemization of the major components[4] of data to be used or provided by it. Furthermore, this estimate of function should be correlated to both the amount of LOC to be developed and the development effort needed.

The following table[5] [QSM02] provides rough estimates of the average number of lines of code required to build one function point in various programming languages:

---

3 See Section 15.3.1 for a detailed discussion of FP computation.

4 It is important to note that "the itemization of major components" can be interpreted in a variety of ways. Software engineers who work in an object-oriented development environment use the number of classes or objects as the dominant size metric. A maintenance organization might view project size in terms of the number of engineering change orders (Chapter 27). An information systems organization might view the number of business processes affected by an application.

5 Used with permission of Quantitative Software Management (www.qsm.com), copyright 2002.

Programming Language	**LOC per Function point**			
	Avg.	**Median**	**Low**	**High**
Access	35	38	15	47
Ada	154	—	104	205
APS	86	83	20	184
ASP 69	62	—	32	127
Assembler	337	315	91	694
C	162	109	33	704
C++	66	53	29	178
Clipper	38	39	27	70
COBOL	77	77	14	400
Cool:Gen/IEF	38	31	10	180
Culprit	51	—	—	—
DBase IV	52	—	—	—
Easytrieve+	33	34	25	41
Excel47	46	—	31	63
Focus	43	42	32	56
FORTRAN	—	—	—	—
FoxPro	32	35	25	35
Ideal	66	52	34	203
IEF/Cool:Gen	38	31	10	180
Informix	42	31	24	57
Java	63	53	77	—
JavaScript	58	63	42	75
JCL	91	123	26	150
JSP	59	—	—	—
Lotus Notes	21	22	15	25
Mantis	71	27	22	250
Mapper	118	81	16	245
Natural	60	52	22	141
Oracle	30	35	4	217
PeopleSoft	33	32	30	40
Perl	60	—	—	—
PL/1	78	67	22	263
Powerbuilder	32	31	11	105
REXX	67	—	—	—
RPG II/III	61	49	24	155
SAS	40	41	33	49
Smalltalk	26	19	10	55
SQL	40	37	7	110
VBScript36	34	27	50	—
Visual Basic	47	42	16	158

A review of these data indicates that one LOC of C++ provides approximately 2.4 times the "functionality" (on average) as one LOC of C. Furthermore, one LOC of a Smalltalk provides at least four times the functionality of a LOC for a conventional programming language such as Ada, COBOL, or C. Using the information contained in the table, it is possible to "backfire" [JON98] existing software to estimate the number of function points, once the total number of programming language statements are known.

Function points and LOC-based metrics have been found to be relatively accurate predictors of software development effort and cost. However, to use LOC and FP for estimation (Chapter 23), a historical baseline of information must be established.

Within the context of process and project metrics, we are concerned primarily with productivity and quality—measures of software development "output" as a function of effort and time applied and measures of the "fitness for use" of the work products that are produced. For process improvement and project planning purposes, our interest is historical. What was software development productivity on past projects? What was the quality of the software that was produced? How can past productivity and quality data be extrapolated to the present? How can it help us improve the process and plan new projects more accurately?

22.2.4 Object-Oriented Metrics

Conventional software project metrics (LOC or FP) can be used to estimate object-oriented software projects. However, these metrics do not provide enough granularity for the schedule and effort adjustments that are required as we iterate through an evolutionary or incremental process. Lorenz and Kidd [LOR94] suggest the following set of metrics for OO projects:

It is not uncommon for multiple scenario scripts to mention the same functionality or data objects. Therefore, be careful when using script counts.

Number of scenario scripts. A scenario script (analogous to use-cases discussed throughout Parts 2 and 3 of this book) is a detailed sequence of steps that describes the interaction between the user and the application. The number of scenario scripts is directly correlated to the size of the application and to the number of test cases that must be developed to exercise the system once it is constructed.

Number of key classes. *Key classes* are the "highly independent components" [LOR94] that are defined early in object-oriented analysis (Chapter 8).[6] Because key classes are central to the problem domain, the number of such classes is an indication of the amount of effort required to develop the software and also an indication of the potential amount of reuse to be applied during system development.

Classes can vary in size and complexity. Therefore, it's worth considering classifying class counts by size and complexity.

Number of support classes. *Support classes* are required to implement the system but are not immediately related to the problem domain. Examples might be UI classes, database access and manipulation classes, and computation classes. In addition, support classes can be developed for each of the key classes. The number of support classes is an indication of the amount of effort required to develop the software and an indication of the potential amount of reuse to be applied during system development.

Average number of support classes per key class. In general, key classes are known early in the project. Support classes are defined throughout. If the average number of support classes per key class were known for a given problem domain, estimating (based on total number of classes) would be much simplified. Lorenz and

---

6 Key classes were referred to as *analysis classes* in Part 2 of this book.

Kidd suggest that applications with a GUI have between two and three times the number of support classes as key classes. Non-GUI applications have between one and two times the number of support classes as key classes.

Number of subsystems. A *subsystem* is an aggregation of classes that support a function that is visible to the end-user of a system. Once subsystems are identified, it is easier to lay out a reasonable schedule in which work on subsystems is partitioned among project staff.

To be used effectively in an object-oriented software engineering environment, metrics similar to those noted above must be collected along with project measures such as effort expended, errors and defects uncovered, and models or documentation pages produced. As the database grows (after a number of projects have been completed), relationships between object-oriented measures and project measures will provide metrics that can aid in project estimation.

22.2.5 Use-Case Oriented Metrics

It would seem reasonable to apply the use-case[7] as a normalization measure similar to LOC or FP. Like FP, the use-case is defined early in the software process, allowing it to be used for estimation before significant modeling and construction activities are initiated. Use-cases describe (indirectly, at least) user-visible functions and features that are basic requirements for a system. The use-case is independent of programming language. In addition, the number of use-cases is directly proportional to the size of the application in LOC and to the number of test cases that will have to be designed to fully exercise the application.

Because use-cases can be created at vastly different levels of abstraction, there is no standard size for a use-case. Without a standard measure of what a use-case is, its application as a normalization measure (e.g., effort expended per use-case) is suspect. Although a number of researchers (e.g., [SMI99]), have attempted to derive use-case metrics, much work remains to be done.

22.2.6 Web Engineering Project Metrics

The objective of all Web engineering projects (Part 3 of this book) is to build a Web application (WebApp) that delivers a combination of content and functionality to the end-user. Measures and metrics used for traditional software engineering projects are difficult to translate directly to WebApps. Yet, a Web engineering organization should develop a database that allows it to assess its internal productivity and quality over a number of projects. Among the measures that can be collected are:

Number of static Web pages. Web pages with static content (i.e., the end-user has no control over the content displayed on the page) are the most common of all WebApp features. These pages represent low relative complexity and generally

7 Use-cases are discussed throughout Parts 2 and 3 of this book.

require less effort to construct than dynamic pages. This measure provides an indication of the overall size of the application and the effort required to develop it.

Number of dynamic Web pages. Web pages with dynamic content (i.e., end-user actions result in customized content displayed on the page) are essential in all e-commerce applications, search engines, financial applications, and many other WebApp categories. These pages represent higher relative complexity and require more effort to construct than static pages. This measure provides an indication of the overall size of the application and the effort required to develop it.

Number of internal page links. Internal page links are pointers that provide a hyperlink to some other Web page within the WebApp. This measure provides an indication of the degree of architectural coupling within the WebApp. As the number of page links increases, the effort expended on navigational design and construction also increases.

Number of persistent data objects. One or more persistent data objects (e.g., a database or data file) may be accessed by a WebApp. As the number of persistent data objects grows, the complexity of the WebApp also grows, and effort to implement it increases proportionally.

Number of external systems interfaced. WebApps must often interface with "backroom" business applications. As the requirement for interfacing grows, system complexity and development effort also increase.

Number of static content objects. Static content objects encompass static text-based, graphical, video, animation, and audio information that are incorporated within the WebApp. Multiple content objects may appear on a single Web page.

Number of dynamic content objects. Dynamic content objects are generated based on end-user actions and encompass internally generated text-based, graphical, video, animation, and audio information that are incorporated within the WebApp. Multiple content objects may appear on a single Web page.

Number of executable functions. An executable function (e.g., a script or applet) provides some computational service to the end-user. As the number of executable functions increases, modeling and construction effort also increase.

Each of the measures noted above can be determined at a relatively early stage of the Web engineering process.

For example, we can define a metric that reflects the degree of end-user customization that is required for the WebApp and correlate it to the effort expended on the WebE project and/or the errors uncovered as reviews and testing are conducted. To accomplish this, we define

N_{sp} = number of static Web pages
N_{dp} = number of dynamic Web pages

Then,

$$\text{Customization index, } C = N_{dp}/(N_{dp} + N_{sp})$$

The value of C ranges from 0 to 1. As C grows larger the level of WebApp customization becomes a significant technical issue.

Similar Web application metrics can be computed and correlated with project measures such as effort expended, errors and defects uncovered, and models or documentation pages produced. As the database grows (after a number of projects have been completed), relationships between the WebApp measures and project measures will provide indicators that can aid in project estimation.

SOFTWARE TOOLS

Project and Process Metrics

Objective: To assist in the definition, collection, evaluation, and reporting of software measures and metrics.

Mechanics: Each tool varies in its application, but all provide mechanisms for collecting and evaluating data that lead to the computation of software metrics.

Representative Tools[8]

Function Point WORKBENCH, developed by Charismatek (www.charismatek.com.au), offers a wide array of FP-oriented metrics.

MetricCenter, developed by Distributive Software (www.distributive.com), supports automated data collection, analysis, chart formatting, report generation, and other measurement tasks.

PSM Insight, developed by Practical Software and Systems Measurement (www.psmsc.com), assists in the creation and subsequent analysis of a project measurement database.

SLIM tool set, developed by QSM (www.qsm.com), provides a comprehensive set of metrics and estimation tools.

SPR tool set, developed by Software Productivity Research (www.spr.com), offers a comprehensive collection of FP-oriented tools.

TychoMetrics, developed by Predicate Logic, Inc. (www.predicate.com), is a tool suite for management metrics collection and reporting.

22.3 METRICS FOR SOFTWARE QUALITY

The overriding goal of software engineering is to produce a high-quality system, application, or product within a timeframe that satisfies a market need. To achieve this goal, software engineers must apply effective methods coupled with modern tools within the context of a mature software process. In addition, a good software engineer (and good software engineering managers) must measure if high quality is to be realized.

Private metrics collected by individual software engineers are assimilated to provide project-level results. Although many quality measures can be collected, the

8 Tools noted here do not represent an endorsement, but rather a sampling of tools in this category. In most cases, tool names are trademarked by their respective developers.

primary thrust at the project level is to measure errors and defects. Metrics derived from these measures provide an indication of the effectiveness of individual and group software quality assurance and control activities.

Metrics such as work product (e.g., requirements or design) errors per function point, errors uncovered per review hour, and errors uncovered per testing hour provide insight into the efficacy of each of the activities implied by the metric. Error data can also be used to compute the *defect removal efficiency* (DRE) for each process framework activity. DRE is discussed in Section 22.3.2.

22.3.1 Measuring Quality

Although there are many measures of software quality,[9] correctness, maintainability, integrity, and usability provide useful indicators for the project team. Gilb [GIL88] suggests definitions and measures for each.

WebRef
An excellent source of information on software quality and related topics (including metrics) can be found at **www.qualityworld.com**

Correctness. A program must operate correctly or it provides little value to its users. Correctness is the degree to which the software performs its required function. The most common measure for correctness is defects per KLOC, where a defect is defined as a verified lack of conformance to requirements. When considering the overall quality of a software product, defects are those problems reported by a user of the program after the program has been released for general use. For quality assessment purposes, defects are counted over a standard period of time, typically one year.

Maintainability. Software maintenance accounts for more effort than any other software engineering activity. Maintainability is the ease with which a program can be corrected if an error is encountered, adapted if its environment changes, or enhanced if the customer desires a change in requirements. There is no way to measure maintainability directly; therefore, we must use indirect measures. A simple time-oriented metric is *mean-time-to-change* (MTTC), the time it takes to analyze the change request, design an appropriate modification, implement the change, test it, and distribute the change to all users. On average, programs that are maintainable will have a lower MTTC (for equivalent types of changes) than programs that are not maintainable.

Integrity. Software integrity has become increasingly important in the age of cyber-terrorists and hackers. This attribute measures a system's ability to withstand attacks (both accidental and intentional) to its security. Attacks can be made on all three components of software: programs, data, and documents.

To measure integrity, two additional attributes must be defined: threat and security. *Threat* is the probability (which can be estimated or derived from empirical evidence) that an attack of a specific type will occur within a given time. *Security* is the probability (which can be estimated or derived from empirical evidence) that

9 A detailed discussion of the factors that influence software quality and the metrics that can be used to assess software quality has been presented in Chapter 15.

the attack of a specific type will be repelled. The integrity of a system can then be defined as:

$$\text{integrity} = \Sigma\ [1 - (\text{threat} \times (1 - \text{security}))]$$

For example, if threat (the probability that an attack will occur) is 0.25 and security (the likelihood of repelling an attack) is 0.95, the integrity of the system is 0.99 (very high). If, on the other hand, the threat probability is 0.50 and the likelihood of repelling an attack is only 0.25, the integrity of the system is 0.63 (unacceptably low).

Usability. If a program is not easy to use, it is often doomed to failure, even if the functions that it performs are valuable. Usability is an attempt to quantify ease-of-use and can be measured in terms of characteristics presented in Chapter 12.

The four factors just described are only a sampling of those that have been proposed as measures for software quality. Chapter 15 considers this topic in additional detail.

22.3.2 Defect Removal Efficiency

A quality metric that provides benefits at both the project and process level is *defect removal efficiency* (DRE). In essence, DRE is a measure of the filtering ability of quality assurance and control activities as they are applied throughout all process framework activities.

When considered for a project as a whole, DRE is defined in the following manner:

$$\text{DRE} = E / (E + D)$$

where E is the number of errors found before delivery of the software to the end-user, and D is the number of defects found after delivery.

If DRE is low as you move through analysis and design, spend some time improving the way you conduct formal technical reviews.

The ideal value for DRE is 1. That is, no defects are found in the software. Realistically, D will be greater than 0, but the value of DRE can still approach 1. As E increases (for a given value of D), the overall value of DRE begins to approach 1. In fact, as E increases, it is likely that the final value of D will decrease (errors are filtered out before they become defects). If used as a metric that provides an indicator of the filtering ability of quality control and assurance activities, DRE encourages a software project team to institute techniques for finding as many errors as possible before delivery.

DRE can also be used within the project to assess a team's ability to find errors before they are passed to the next framework activity or software engineering task. For example, the requirements analysis task produces an analysis model that can be reviewed to find and correct errors. Those errors that are not found during the review of the analysis model are passed on to design (where they may or may not be found). When used in this context, we redefine DRE as

$$\text{DRE}_i = E_i / (E_i + E_{i+1})$$

where E_i is the number of errors found during software engineering activity i and E_{i+1} is the number of errors found during software engineering activity $i + 1$ that are traceable to errors that were not discovered in software engineering activity i.

A quality objective for a software team (or an individual software engineer) is to achieve DRE_i that approaches 1. That is, errors should be filtered out before they are passed on to the next activity.

SAFEHOME

Establishing a Metrics Approach

The scene: Doug Miller's office two days after initial meeting on software metrics.

The players: Doug Miller (manager of the *SafeHome* software engineering team) and Vinod Raman and Jamie Lazar, members of the product software engineering team.

The conversation:

Doug: You both had a chance to learn a little about process and project metrics?

Vinod and Jamie: [Both nod]

Doug: It's always a good idea to establish goals when you adopt any metrics. What are yours?

Vinod: Our metrics should focus on quality. In fact, our overall goal is to keep the number of errors we pass on from one software engineering activity to the next to an absolute minimum.

Doug: And be very sure you keep the number of defects released with the product to as close to zero as possible.

Vinod (nodding): Of course.

Jamie: I like DRE as a metric, and I think we can use it for the entire project. Also, we can use it as we move from one framework activity to the next. It'll encourage us to find errors at each step.

Vinod: I'd also like to collect the number of hours we spend on reviews.

Jamie: And the overall effort we spend on each software engineering task.

Doug: You can compute a review-to-development ratio . . . might be interesting.

Jamie: I'd like to track some use-case data as well. Like the amount of effort required to develop a use-case, the amount of effort required to build software to implement a use-case, and . . .

Doug (smiling): I thought we were going to keep this simple.

Vinod: We should, but once you get into this metrics stuff, there's a lot of interesting things to look at.

Doug: I agree, but let's walk before we run, and stick to our goal. Limit data to be collected to five or six items, and we're ready to go.

22.4 Integrating Metrics within the Software Process

The majority of software developers still do not measure, and sadly, most have little desire to begin. As we noted earlier in this chapter, the problem is cultural. Attempting to collect measures where none had been collected in the past often precipitates resistance. "Why do we need to do this?" asks a harried project manager. "I don't see the point," complains an overworked practitioner.

In this section, we consider some arguments for software metrics and present an approach for instituting a metrics collection program within a software engineering organization. But before we begin, some words of wisdom are suggested by Grady and Caswell [GRA87]:

> Some of the things we describe here will sound quite easy. Realistically, though, establishing a successful company-wide software metrics program is hard work. When we say

> that you must wait at least three years before broad organizational trends are available, you get some idea of the scope of such an effort.

The caveat suggested by the authors is well worth heeding, but the benefits of measurement are so compelling that the hard work is worth it.

22.4.1 Arguments for Software Metrics

Why is it so important to measure the process of software engineering and the product (software) that it produces? The answer is relatively obvious. If we do not measure, there is no real way of determining whether we are improving. And if we are not improving, we are lost.

By requesting and evaluating productivity and quality measures, a software team (and their management) can establish meaningful goals for improvement of the software process. In Chapter 1 we noted that software is a strategic business issue for many companies. If the process through which it is developed can be improved, a direct impact on the bottom line can result. But to establish goals for improvement, the current status of software development must be understood. Hence, measurement is used to establish a process baseline from which improvements can be assessed.

> **"We manage things by the numbers in many aspects of our lives . . . These numbers give us insight and help steer our actions."**
>
> **Michael Mah and Larry Putnam**

The day-to-day rigors of software project work leave little time for strategic thinking. Software project managers are concerned with more mundane (but equally important) issues: developing meaningful project estimates, producing higher-quality systems, getting product out the door on time. By using measurement to establish a project baseline, each of these issues becomes more manageable. We have already noted that the baseline serves as a basis for estimation. Additionally, the collection of quality metrics enables an organization to "tune" its software process to remove the "vital few" causes of defects that have the greatest impact on software development.[10]

22.4.2 Establishing a Baseline

? What is a metrics baseline, and what benefit does it provide to a software engineer?

By establishing a metrics baseline, benefits can be obtained at the process, project, and product (technical) levels. Yet the information that is collected need not be fundamentally different. The same metrics can serve many masters. The metrics baseline consists of data collected from past software development projects and can be as simple as the table presented in Figure 22.2 or as complex as a comprehensive database containing dozens of project measures and the metrics derived from them.

---

10 These ideas have been formalized into an approach called *statistical software quality assurance* and are discussed in detail in Chapter 26.

FIGURE 22.3

Software metrics collection process

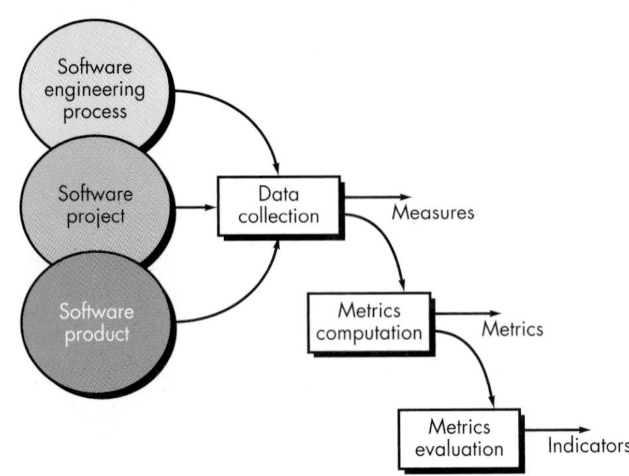

To be an effective aid in process improvement and/or cost and effort estimation, baseline data must have the following attributes: (1) data must be reasonably accurate—"guestimates" about past projects are to be avoided; (2) data should be collected for as many projects as possible; (3) measures must be consistent, for example, a line of code must be interpreted consistently across all projects for which data are collected; (4) applications should be similar to work that is to be estimated—it makes little sense to use a baseline for batch information systems work to estimate a real-time, embedded application.

22.4.3 Metrics Collection, Computation, and Evaluation

Baseline metrics data should be collected from a large representative sampling of past software projects.

The process for establishing a metrics baseline is illustrated in Figure 22.3. Ideally, data needed to establish a baseline has been collected in an on-going manner. Sadly, this is rarely the case. Therefore, data collection requires a historical investigation of past projects to reconstruct required data. Once measures have been collected (unquestionably the most difficult step), metrics computation is possible. Depending on the breadth of measures collected, metrics can span a broad range of application-oriented metrics (e.g., LOC, FP, object-oriented, WebApp) as well as other quality- and project-oriented metrics. Finally, metrics should be evaluated and applied during estimation, technical work, project control, and process improvement. Metrics evaluation focuses on the underlying reasons for the results obtained and produces a set of indicators that guide the project or process.

22.5 METRICS FOR SMALL ORGANIZATIONS

The vast majority of software development organizations have fewer than 20 software people. It is unreasonable, and in most cases unrealistic, to expect that such organizations will develop comprehensive software metrics programs. However, it

If you're just starting to collect metrics data, remember to keep it simple. If you bury yourself with data, your metrics effort will fail.

is reasonable to suggest that software organizations of all sizes measure and then use the resultant metrics to help improve their local software process and the quality and timeliness of the products they produce.

A common-sense approach to the implementation of any software process related activity is: keep it simple, customize to meet local needs, and be sure it adds value. In the paragraphs that follow, we examine how these guidelines relate to metrics for small shops.[11]

? How should we derive a set of "simple" software metrics?

"Keep it simple" is a guideline that works reasonably well in many activities. But how do we derive a "simple" set of software metrics that still provides value, and how can we be sure that these simple metrics will meet the needs of a particular software organization? We begin by focusing not on measurement but rather on results. The software group is polled to define a single objective that requires improvement. For example, "reduce the time to evaluate and implement change requests." A small organization might select the following set of easily collected measures:

- Time (hours or days) elapsed from the time a request is made until evaluation is complete, t_{queue}.
- Effort (person-hours) to perform the evaluation, W_{eval}.
- Time (hours or days) elapsed from completion of evaluation to assignment of change order to personnel, t_{eval}.
- Effort (person-hours) required to make the change, W_{change}.
- Time required (hours or days) to make the change, t_{change}.
- Errors uncovered during work to make the change, E_{change}.
- Defects uncovered after change is released to the customer base, D_{change}.

Once these measures have been collected for a number of change requests, it is possible to compute the average total elapsed time from change request to implementation of the change and the percentage of elapsed time absorbed by initial queuing, evaluation and change assignment, and change implementation. Similarly, the percentage of effort required for evaluation and implementation can be determined. These metrics can be assessed in the context of quality data, E_{change} and D_{change}. The percentages provide insight into where the change request process slows down and may lead to process improvement steps to reduce t_{queue}, W_{eval}, t_{eval}, W_{change}, and/or E_{change}. In addition, the defect removal efficiency can be computed as

$$\text{DRE} = E_{change}/(E_{change} + D_{change})$$

DRE can be compared to elapsed time and total effort to determine the impact of quality assurance activities on the time and effort required to make a change.

11 This discussion is equally relevant to software teams that have adopted an agile software development process (Chapter 4)

22.6 Establishing a Software Metrics Program

The Software Engineering Institute has developed a comprehensive guidebook [PAR96] for establishing a "goal-driven" software metrics program. The guidebook suggests the following steps:

WebRef
A Guidebook for Goal Driven Software Measurement can be downloaded from: **www.sei.cmu.edu.**

1. Identify your business goals.
2. Identify what you want to know or learn.
3. Identify your subgoals.
4. Identify the entities and attributes related to your subgoals.
5. Formalize your measurement goals.
6. Identify quantifiable questions and the related indicators that you will use to help you achieve your measurement goals.
7. Identify the data elements that you will collect to construct the indicators that help answer your questions.
8. Define the measures to be used, and make these definitions operational.
9. Identify the actions that you will take to implement the measures.
10. Prepare a plan for implementing the measures.

A detailed discussion of these steps is best left to the SEI's guidebook. However, a brief overview of key points is worthwhile.

The software metrics you choose should be driven by the business and technical goals you wish to accomplish.

Because software supports business functions, differentiates computer-based systems or products, or acts as a product in itself, goals defined for the business can almost always be traced downward to specific goals at the software engineering level. For example, consider a company that makes advanced home security systems which have substantial software content. Working as a team, software engineering and business managers can develop a list of prioritized business goals:

1. Improve our customers' satisfaction with our products.
2. Make our products easier to use.
3. Reduce the time it takes us to get a new product to market.
4. Make support for our products easier.
5. Improve our overall profitability.

The software organization examines each business goal and asks: What activities do we manage or execute, and what do we want to improve within these activities? To answer these questions the SEI recommends the creation of an "entity-question list" in which all things (entities) within the software process that are managed or influenced by the software organization are noted. Examples of entities include development resources, work products, source code, test cases, change requests, software engineering tasks, and schedules. For each entity listed, software people develop a set of questions that assess quantitative characteristics of the entity (e.g., size, cost, time to develop). The questions derived as a consequence of the creation of an entity-question list lead to the derivation of a set of subgoals that relate directly to the entities created and the activities performed as part of the software process.

Consider the fourth goal: "Make support for our products easier." The following list of questions might be derived for this goal [PAR96]:

- Do customer change requests contain the information we require to adequately evaluate the change and then implement it in a timely manner?
- How large is the change request backlog?
- Is our response time for fixing bugs acceptable, based on customer need?
- Is our change control process (Chapter 27) followed?
- Are high-priority changes implemented in a timely manner?

Based on these questions, the software organization can derive the following subgoal: *Improve the performance of the change management process.* The software process entities and attributes that are relevant to the subgoal are identified, and measurement goals associated with them are delineated.

The SEI [PAR96] provides detailed guidance for steps 6 through 10 of its goal-driven measurement approach. In essence, a process of stepwise refinement is applied in which goals are refined into questions that are further refined into entities and attributes that are then refined into metrics.

INFO

Establishing a Metrics Program

The Software Productivity Center (www.spc.ca) suggests an eight-step approach for establishing a metrics program within a software organization that can be used as an alternative to the SEI approach described in Section 22.6. Their approach is summarized in this sidebar.

1. Understand the existing software process.
   Framework activities (Chapter 2) are identified.
   Input information for each activity is described.
   Tasks associated with each activity are defined.
   Quality assurance functions are noted.
   Work products that are produced are listed.
2. Define the goals to be achieved by establishing a metrics program.
   Examples: improve accuracy of estimation, improve product quality.
3. Identify metrics required to achieve goals.
   Questions to be answered are defined; e.g., how many errors found in one framework activity can be traced to the preceding framework activity?
   Create measures and metrics to be collected and computed.
4. Identify the measures and metrics to be collected and computed.
5. Establish a measurement collection process by answering these questions:
   What is the source of the measurements?
   Can tools be used to collect the data?
   Who is responsible for collecting the data?
   When are data collected and recorded?
   How are data stored?
   What validation mechanisms are used to ensure that the data are correct?
6. Acquire appropriate tools to assist in collection and assessment.

7. Establish a metrics database.
   - The relative sophistication of the database is established.
   - Use of related tools (e.g., a SCM repository, Chapter 27) is explored.
   - Existing database products are evaluated.
8. Define appropriate feedback mechanisms.
   - Who requires on-going metrics information?
   - How is the information to be delivered?
   - What is the format of the information?

A considerably more detailed description of these eight steps can be downloaded from: http://www.spc.ca/resources/metrics/.

22.7 Summary

Measurement enables managers and practitioners to improve the software process; assist in the planning, tracking, and control of a software project; and assess the quality of the product (software) that is produced. Measures of specific attributes of the process, project, and product are used to compute software metrics. These metrics can be analyzed to provide indicators that guide management and technical actions.

Process metrics enable an organization to take a strategic view by providing insight into the effectiveness of a software process. Project metrics are tactical. They enable a project manager to adapt project workflow and a technical approach in a real-time manner.

Both size- and function-oriented metrics are used throughout the industry. Size-oriented metrics use the line of code as a normalizing factor for other measures such as person-months or defects. The function point is derived from measures of the information domain and a subjective assessment of problem complexity. In addition, object-oriented metrics and Web application metrics can be used.

Software quality metrics, like productivity metrics, focus on the process, the project, and the product. By developing and analyzing a metrics baseline for quality, an organization can correct those areas of the software process that are the cause of software defects.

Measurement results in cultural change. Data collection, metrics computation, and metrics analysis are the three steps that must be implemented to begin a metrics program. In general, a goal-driven approach helps an organization focus on the right metrics for its business. By creating a metrics baseline—a database containing process and product measurements—software engineers and their managers can gain better insight into the work that they do and the product that they produce.

References

[ALB83] Albrecht, A. J., and J. E. Gaffney, "Software Function, Source Lines of Code and Development Effort Prediction: A Software Science Validation," *IEEE Trans. Software Engineering,* November 1983, pp. 639–648.

[BOE81] Boehm, B., *Software Engineering Economics,* Prentice-Hall, 1981.

[GRA87] Grady, R. B., and D. L. Caswell, *Software Metrics: Establishing a Company-Wide Program,* Prentice-Hall, 1987.

[GRA92] Grady, R. G., *Practical Software Metrics for Project Management and Process Improvement,* Prentice-Hall, 1992.

[GIL88] Gilb, T., *Principles of Software Project Management,* Addison-Wesley, 1988.

[HET93] Hetzel, W., *Making Software Measurement Work,* QED Publishing Group, 1993.

[HUM95] Humphrey, W., *A Discipline for Software Engineering,* Addison-Wesley, 1995.

[IEE93] *IEEE Software Engineering Standards,* Standard 610.12-1990, pp. 47–48.

[JON86] Jones, C., *Programming Productivity,* McGraw-Hill, 1986.

[JON91] Jones, C., *Applied Software Measurement,* McGraw-Hill, 1991.

[JON98] Jones, C., *Estimating Software Costs,* McGraw-Hill, 1998.

[LOR94] Lorenz, M., and J. Kidd, *Object-Oriented Software Metrics,* Prentice-Hall, 1994.

[PAR96] Park, R. E., W. B. Goethert, and W. A. Florac, *Goal Driven Software Measurement—A Guidebook,* CMU/SEI-96-BH-002, Software Engineering Institute, Carnegie Mellon University, August 1996.

[PAU94] Paulish, D., and A. Carleton, "Case Studies of Software Process Improvement Measurement," *Computer,* vol. 27, no. 9, September 1994, pp. 50–57.

[QSM02] "QSM Function Point Language Gearing Factors," Version 2.0, Quantitative Software Management, 2002, http://www.qsm.com/FPGearing.html.

[RAG95] Ragland, B., "Measure, Metric or Indicator: What's the Difference?" *Crosstalk,* vol. 8, no. 3, March 1995, p. 29–30.

[SMI99] Smith, J., "The Estimation of Effort Based on Use-Cases," a white paper by Rational Corporation, 1999, downloaded from http://www.rational.com/products/rup/whitepapers.jsp.

Problems and Points to Ponder

22.1. Describe the difference between process and project metrics in your own words.

22.2. Why should some software metrics be kept "private"? Provide examples of three metrics that should be private. Provide examples of three metrics that should be public.

22.3. What is an indirect measure, and why are such measures common in software metrics work?

22.4. Grady suggests an etiquette for software metrics. Can you add three more rules to those noted in Section 22.1.1?

22.5. Team A found 342 errors during the software engineering process prior to release. Team B found 184 errors. What additional measures would have to be made for projects A and B to determine which of the teams eliminated errors more efficiently? What metrics would you propose to help in making the determination? What historical data might be useful?

22.6. Present an argument against lines of code as a measure for software productivity. Will your case hold up when dozens or hundreds of projects are considered?

22.7. Compute the function point value for a project with the following information domain characteristics:

Number of external inputs: 32
Number of external outputs: 60
Number of external inquiries: 24
Number of internal logical files: 8
Number of external interface files: 2

Assume that all complexity adjustment values are average. Use the algorithm noted in Chapter 15.

22.8. Using the table presented in Section 22.2.3, make an argument against the use of assembler language based on the functionality delivered per statement of code. Again referring to the table, discuss why C++ would present a better alternative than C.

22.9. The software used to control a photocopier requires 32,000 of C and 4200 lines of Smalltalk. Estimate the number of function points for the software inside the copier.

22.10. A Web engineering team has built a e-commerce WebApp that contains 145 individual pages. Of these pages, 65 are dynamic; i.e., they are internally generated based on end-user input. What is the customization index for this application?

22.11. A WebApp and its support environment has not been fully fortified against attack. Web engineers estimate that the likelihood of repelling an attack is only 30 percent. The system does not contain sensitive or controversial information, so the threat probability is 25 percent. What is the integrity of the WebApp?

22.12. At the conclusion of a project that used the Unified Process (Chapter 3), it has been determined that 30 errors were found during the elaboration phase and 12 errors were found during construction phase that were traceable to errors that were not discovered in the elaboration phase. What is the DRE for these two phases?

22.13. A software increment is delivered to end-users by a software team. The users uncover 8 defects during the first month of use. Prior to delivery, the software team found 242 errors during formal technical reviews and all testing tasks. What is the overall DRE for the project?

Further Readings and Information Sources

Software process improvement (SPI) has received a significant amount of attention over the past two decades. Since measurement and software metrics are key to successfully improving the software process, many books on SPI also discuss metrics. Worthwhile sources of information on process metrics include:

Burr, A., and M. Owen, *Statistical Methods for Software Quality,* International Thomson Publishing, 1996.

El Emam, K., and N. Madhavji (eds.), *Elements of Software Process Assessment and Improvement,* IEEE Computer Society, 1999.

Florac, W. A., and A. D. Carleton, *Measuring the Software Process: Statistical Process Control for Software Process Improvement,* Addison-Wesley, 1999.

Garmus, D., and D. Herron, *Measuring the Software Process: A Practical Guide to Functional Measurements,* Prentice-Hall, 1996.

Humphrey, W., *Introduction to the Team Software Process,* Addison-Wesley/Longman, 2000.

Kan, S. H., *Metrics and Models in Software Quality Engineering,* Addison-Wesley, 1995.

McGarry and his colleagues (*Practical Software Measurement,* Addison-Wesley, 2001) present in-depth advice for assessing the software process. A worthwhile collection of papers has been edited by Haug and his colleagues (*Software Process Improvement: Metrics, Measurement, and Process Modeling,* Springer-Verlag, 2001). Florac and Carlton (*Measuring the Software Process,* Addison-Wesley, 1999) and Fenton and Pfleeger (*Software Metrics: A Rigorous and Practical Approach,* Revised, Brooks/Cole Publishers, 1998) discuss how software metrics can be used to provide the indicators necessary to improve the software process.

Putnam and Myers (*Five Core Metrics,* Dorset House, 2003) draw on a database of more the 6000 software projects to demonstrate how five core metrics—time, effort, size, reliability, and process productivity—can be used to control software projects. Maxwell (*Applied Statistics for Software Managers,* Prentice-Hall, 2003) presents techniques for analyzing software project data. Munson (*Software Engineering Measurement,* Auerbach, 2003) discusses a broad array of software engineering measurement issues. Jones (*Software Assessments, Benchmarks and Best Practices,* Addison-Wesley, 2000) describes both quantitative measurement and qualitative factors that help an organization assess its software process and practices. Garmus and Herron (*Function Point Analysis: Measurement Practices for Successful Software Projects,* Addison-Wesley, 2000) discuss process metrics with an emphasis on function point analysis.

Lorenze and Kidd [LOR94] and DeChampeax (*Object-Oriented Development Process and Metrics,* Prentice-Hall, 1996) consider the OO process and describe a set of metrics for assessing it. Whitmire (*Object-Oriented Design Measurement,* Wiley, 1997) and Henderson-Sellers (*Object-Oriented Metrics: Measures of Complexity,* Prentice-Hall, 1995) focus on technical metrics for OO work, but also consider measures and metrics that can be used at the process and product level.

Relatively little has been published on metrics for Web engineering work. However, Stern (*Web Metrics: Proven Methods for Measuring Web Site Success,* Wiley, 2002), Inan and Kean (*Measuring the Success of Your Website,* Longman, 2002), and Nobles and Grady (*Web Site Analysis and Reporting,* Premier Press, 2001) address Web metrics from a business and marketing perspective.

The latest research in the metrics area is summarized by the IEEE (*Symposium on Software Metrics,* published yearly). A wide variety of information sources on the process and project metrics is available on the Internet. An up-to-date list of World Wide Web references can be found at the SEPA Web site:
http://www.mhhe.com/pressman.

CHAPTER

23 ESTIMATION FOR SOFTWARE PROJECTS

KEY CONCEPTS

Software project management begins with a set of activities that are collectively called *project planning.* Before the project can begin, the project manager and the software team must estimate the work to be done, the resources that will be required, and the time that will elapse from start to finish. Once these activities are accomplished, the software team must establish a project schedule that defines software engineering tasks and milestones, identifies who is responsible for conducting each task, and specifies the inter-task dependencies that may have a strong bearing on progress.

In an excellent guide to "software project survival," Steve McConnell [MCC98] presents a real-world view of project planning:

> Many technical workers would rather do technical work than spend time planning. Many technical managers do not have sufficient training in technical management to feel confident that their planning will improve a project's outcome. Since neither party wants to do planning, it often doesn't get done.
>
> But failure to plan is one of the most critical mistakes a project can make . . . effective planning is needed to resolve problems upstream [early in the project] at low cost, rather than downstream [late in the project] at high cost. The average project spends *80 percent* of its time on rework—fixing mistakes that were made earlier in the project.

McConnell argues that every project can find the time to plan (and to adapt the plan throughout the project) simply by taking a small percentage of the time that would have been spent on rework that occurs because planning was not conducted.

QUICK LOOK

What is it? A real need for software has been established; stakeholders are on-board; software engineers are ready to start; and the project is about to begin. But how do you proceed? Software project planning encompasses five major activities—estimation, scheduling, risk analysis, quality management planning, and change management planning. In the context of this chapter, we consider only estimation—your attempt to determine how much money, effort, resources, and time it will take to build a specific software-based system or product.

Who does it? Software project managers—using information solicited from stakeholders and software engineers and software metrics data collected from past projects.

Why is it important? Would you build a house without knowing how much you were about to spend, the tasks you needed to perform, and the timeline for the work to be conducted? Of course not, and since most computer-based systems and products cost considerably more to build than a large house, it would seem reasonable to develop an estimate before you start creating the software.

What are the steps? Estimation begins with a description of the scope of the product. The problem is then decomposed into a set of smaller problems, and each of these is estimated using historical data and experience as guides. Problem complexity and risk are considered before a final estimate is made.

What is the work product? A simple table delineating the tasks to be performed, the functions to be implemented, and the cost, effort, and time involved for each is generated.

How do I ensure that I've done it right? That's hard, because you won't really know until the project has been completed. However, if you have experience and follow a systematic approach, generate estimates using solid historical data, create estimation data points using at least two different methods, establish a realistic schedule, and continually adapt it as the project moves forward, you can feel confident that you've given it your best shot.

23.1 Observations on Estimation

Planning requires technical managers and members of the software team to make an initial commitment, even though it's likely that this "commitment" will be proven wrong. Whenever estimates are made, we look into the future and accept some degree of uncertainty as a matter of course. To quote Frederick Brooks [BRO75]:

> [O]ur techniques of estimating are poorly developed. More seriously, they reflect an unvoiced assumption that is quite untrue, i.e., that all will go well . . . Because we are uncertain of our estimates, software managers often lack the courteous stubbornness to make people wait for a good product.

Although estimating is as much art as it is science, this important activity need not be conducted in a haphazard manner. Useful techniques for time and effort estimation do exist. Process and project metrics can provide historical perspective and powerful input for the generation of quantitative estimates. Past experience (of all people involved) can aid immeasurably as estimates are developed and reviewed. Because estimation lays a foundation for all other project planning activities, and project planning provides the road map for successful software engineering, we would be ill-advised to embark without it.

> **"Good estimating approaches and solid historical data offer the best hope that reality will win out over impossible demands."**
>
> **Capers Jones**

Estimation of resources, cost, and schedule for a software engineering effort requires experience, access to good historical information (metrics), and the courage to commit to quantitative predictions when qualitative information is all that exists. Estimation carries inherent risk[1], and this risk leads to uncertainty.

---

1 Systematic techniques for risk analysis are presented in Chapter 25.

The availability of historical information has a strong influence on estimation risk. By looking back, we can emulate things that worked and improve areas where problems arose. When comprehensive software metrics (Chapter 22) are available for past projects, estimates can be made with greater assurance, schedules can be established to avoid past difficulties, and overall risk is reduced.

> "It is the mark of an instructed mind to rest satisfied with the degree of precision that the nature of the subject admits, and not to seek exactness when only an approximation of the truth is possible."
>
> **Aristotle**

Estimation risk is measured by the degree of uncertainty in the quantitative estimates established for resources, cost, and schedule. If project scope is poorly understood or project requirements are subject to change, uncertainty and estimation risk become dangerously high. The planner, and more importantly, the customer should recognize that variability in software requirements means instability in cost and schedule.

However, a project manager should not become obsessive about estimation. Modern software engineering approaches (e.g., incremental process models) take an iterative view of development. In such approaches, it is possible—although not always politically acceptable—to revisit the estimate (as more information is known) and revise it when the customer makes changes to requirements.

23.2 The Project Planning Process

The more you know, the better you estimate. Therefore, update your estimates as the project progresses.

The objective of software project planning is to provide a framework that enables the manager to make reasonable estimates of resources, cost, and schedule. In addition, estimates should attempt to define best-case and worst-case scenarios so that project outcomes can be bounded. Although there is an inherent degree of uncertainty, the software team embarks on a plan that has been established as a consequence of planning tasks. Therefore, the plan must be adapted and updated as the project proceeds. In the following sections, each of the activities associated with software project planning is discussed.

Task Set

Task Set for Project Planning

1. Establish project scope
2. Determine feasibility
3. Analyze risks (Chapter 25)
4. Define required resources
   a. Determine human resources required
   b. Define reusable software resources
   c. Identify environmental resources
5. Estimate cost and effort
   a. Decompose the problem
   b. Develop two or more estimates using size, function points, process tasks, or use-cases
   c. Reconcile the estimates
6. Develop a project schedule (Chapter 24)
   a. Establish a meaningful task set
   b. Define a task network
   c. Use scheduling tools to develop a timeline chart
   d. Define schedule tracking mechanisms

23.3 Software Scope and Feasibility

Although there are many reasons for uncertainty, incomplete information about problem requirements dominates.

Software scope describes the functions and features that are to be delivered to end-users, the data that are input and output, the "content" that is presented to users as a consequence of using the software, and the performance, constraints, interfaces, and reliability that *bound* the system. Scope is defined using one of two techniques:

1. A narrative description of software scope is developed after communication with all stakeholders.
2. A set of use-cases[2] is developed by end-users.

Functions described in the statement of scope (or within the use-cases) are evaluated and in some cases refined to provide more detail prior to the beginning of estimation. Because both cost and schedule estimates are functionally oriented, some degree of decomposition is often useful. Performance considerations encompass processing and response time requirements. Constraints identify limits placed on the software by external hardware, available memory, or other existing systems.

ADVICE

Project feasibility is important, but a consideration of business need is even more important. It does no good to build a high-tech system or product that no one wants.

Once scope has been identified (with the concurrence of the customer), it is reasonable to ask: Can we build software to meet this scope? Is the project feasible? All too often, software engineers rush past these questions (or are pushed past them by impatient managers or customers), only to become mired in a project that is doomed from the onset. Putnam and Myers [PUT97a] address this issue when they write:

> [N]ot everything imaginable is feasible, not even in software, evanescent as it may appear to outsiders. On the contrary, software feasibility has four solid dimensions: *Technology*—Is a project technically feasible? Is it within the state of the art? Can defects be reduced to a level matching the application's needs? *Finance*—Is it financially feasible? Can development be completed at a cost the software organization, its client, or the market can afford? *Time*—Will the project's time-to-market beat the competition? *Resources*—Does the organization have the resources needed to succeed?

Putnam and Myers correctly suggest that scoping is not enough. Once scope is understood, the software team and others must work to determine if it can be done within the dimensions just noted. This is a crucial, although often overlooked, part of the estimation process.

23.4 Resources

The second planning task is estimation of the resources required to accomplish the software development effort. Figure 23.1 depicts the three major categories of software engineering resources—people, reusable software components, and the development environment (hardware and software tools). Each resource is specified with

2 Use-cases have been discussed in detail throughout Parts 2 and 3 of this book. A use-case is a scenario-based description of the user's interaction with the software from the user's point of view.

FIGURE 23.1

Project resources

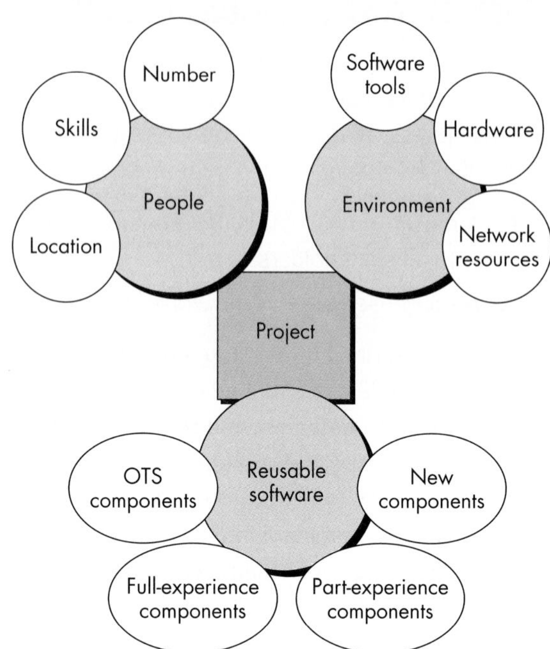

four characteristics: description of the resource; a statement of availability; time when the resource will be required; duration of time that resource will be applied. The last two characteristics can be viewed as a *time window.* Availability of the resource for a specified window must be established at the earliest practical time.

23.4.1 Human Resources

The planner begins by evaluating software scope and selecting the skills required to complete development. Both organizational position (e.g., manager, senior software engineer) and specialty (e.g., telecommunications, database, client/server) are specified. For relatively small projects (a few person-months), a single individual may perform all software engineering tasks, consulting with specialists as required. For larger projects, the software team may be geographically dispersed across a number of different locations. Hence, the location of each human resource is specified.

The number of people required for a software project can be determined only after an estimate of development effort (e.g., person-months) is made. Techniques for estimating effort are discussed later in this chapter.

23.4.2 Reusable Software Resources

Component-based software engineering (Chapter 30) emphasizes reusability—that is, the creation and reuse of software building blocks [HOO91]. Such building blocks, often called *components,* must be cataloged for easy reference, standardized for easy application, and validated for easy integration.

Bennatan [BEN92] suggests four software resource categories that should be considered as planning proceeds:

Never forget that integrating a variety of reusable components can be a significant challenge. The integration problem often resurfaces as various components are upgraded.

Off-the-shelf components. Existing software can be acquired from a third party or has been developed internally for a past project. COTS (commercial off-the-shelf) components are purchased from a third party, are ready for use on the current project, and have been fully validated.

Full-experience components. Existing specifications, designs, code, or test data developed for past projects are similar to the software to be built for the current project. Members of the current software team have had full experience in the application area represented by these components. Therefore, modifications required for full-experience components will be relatively low-risk.

Partial-experience components. Existing specifications, designs, code, or test data developed for past projects are related to the software to be built for the current project but will require substantial modification. Members of the current software team have only limited experience in the application area represented by these components. Therefore, modifications required for partial-experience components have a fair degree of risk.

New components. Software components must be built by the software team specifically for the needs of the current project.

Ironically, reusable software components are often neglected during planning, only to become a paramount concern during the development phase of the software process. It is better to specify software resource requirements early. In this way technical evaluation of the alternatives can be conducted and timely acquisition can occur.

23.4.3 Environmental Resources

The environment that supports a software project, often called the *software engineering environment* (SEE), incorporates hardware and software. Hardware provides a platform that supports the tools (software) required to produce the work products that are an outcome of good software engineering practice.[3] Because most software organizations have multiple constituencies that require access to the SEE, a project planner must prescribe the time window required for hardware and software and verify that these resources will be available.

When a computer-based system (incorporating specialized hardware and software) is to be engineered, the software team may require access to hardware elements being developed by other engineering teams. For example, software for a numerical control (NC) used on a class of machine tools may require a specific machine tool (e.g., an

---

3 Other hardware—the target environment—is the computer(s) on which the software will execute when it has been released to the end-user.

NC lathe) as part of the validation test step; a software project for advanced page-layout may need a high-quality printer at some point during development. Each hardware element must be specified by the software project planner.

23.5 Software Project Estimation

Software is the most expensive element of virtually all computer-based systems. For complex, custom systems, a large cost estimation error can make the difference between profit and loss. Cost overrun can be disastrous for the developer.

> "In an age of outsourcing and increased competition, the ability to estimate more accurately . . . has emerged as a critical success factor for many IT groups."
>
> **Rob Thomsett**

Although software engineering effort is a dominant element of project cost, it's important to remember that other costs (e.g., development environment and tools, travel, training, office space, hardware) must also be considered.

Software cost and effort estimation will never be an exact science.[4] Too many variables—human, technical, environmental, political—can affect the ultimate cost of software and effort applied to develop it. However, software project estimation can be transformed from a black art to a series of systematic steps that provide estimates with acceptable risk. To achieve reliable cost and effort estimates, a number of options arise:

1. Delay estimation until late in the project (obviously, we can achieve 100 percent accurate estimates after the project is complete!).
2. Base estimates on similar projects that have already been completed.
3. Use relatively simple decomposition techniques to generate project cost and effort estimates.
4. Use one or more empirical models for software cost and effort estimation.

Unfortunately, the first option, however attractive, is not practical. Cost estimates must be provided "up front." However, we should recognize that the longer we wait, the more we know, and the more we know, the less likely we are to make serious errors in our estimates.

The second option can work reasonably well, if the current project is quite similar to past efforts and other project influences (e.g., the software team, the customer, business conditions, the SEE, deadlines) are roughly equivalent. Unfortunately, past experience has not always been a good indicator of future results.

The remaining options are viable approaches to software project estimation. Ideally, the techniques noted for each option should be applied in tandem; each used as a cross-check for the other. Decomposition techniques take a "divide and conquer" approach to software project estimation. By decomposing a project into major func-

4 Bennatan [BEN03] reports that 40 percent of software developers continue to struggle with estimation and that software size and development time are very difficult to estimate accurately.

tions and related software engineering activities, cost and effort estimation can be performed in a stepwise fashion. Empirical estimation models can be used to complement decomposition techniques and offer a potentially valuable estimation approach in their own right. These models are discussed in Section 23.7.

Each of the viable software cost estimation options is only as good as the historical data used to seed the estimate. If no historical data exist, costing rests on a very shaky foundation. In Chapter 22, we examined the characteristics of some of the software metrics that provide the basis for historical estimation data.

23.6 Decomposition Techniques

Software project estimation is a form of problem solving, and in most cases, the problem to be solved (i.e., developing a cost and effort estimate for a software project) is too complex to be considered in one piece. For this reason, we decompose the problem, recharacterizing it as a set of smaller (and hopefully, more manageable) problems.

In Chapter 21, the decomposition approach was discussed from two different points of view: decomposition of the problem and decomposition of the process. Estimation uses one or both forms of partitioning. But before an estimate can be made, the project planner must understand the scope of the software to be built and generate an estimate of its "size."

23.6.1 Software Sizing

The "size" of software to be built can be estimated using a direct measure, LOC, or an indirect measure, FP.

The accuracy of a software project estimate is predicated on a number of things: (1) the degree to which the planner has properly estimated the size of the product to be built; (2) the ability to translate the size estimate into human effort, calendar time, and dollars (a function of the availability of reliable software metrics from past projects); (3) the degree to which the project plan reflects the abilities of the software team; and (4) the stability of product requirements and the environment that supports the software engineering effort.

In this section, we consider the *software sizing* problem. Because a project estimate is only as good as the estimate of the size of the work to be accomplished, sizing represents the project planner's first major challenge. In the context of project planning, *size* refers to a quantifiable outcome of the software project. If a direct approach is taken, size can be measured in lines of code (LOC). If an indirect approach is chosen, size is represented as function points (FP).

Putnam and Myers [PUT92] suggest four different approaches to the sizing problem:

? How do we size the software that we're planning to build?

- *"Fuzzy logic" sizing.* To apply this approach, the planner must identify the type of application, establish its magnitude on a qualitative scale, and then refine the magnitude within the original range.
- *Function point sizing.* The planner develops estimates of the information domain characteristics discussed in Chapter 15.

- *Standard component sizing.* Software is composed of a number of different "standard components" that are generic to a particular application area. For example, the standard components for an information system are subsystems, modules, screens, reports, interactive programs, batch programs, files, LOC, and object-level instructions. The project planner estimates the number of occurrences of each standard component and then uses historical project data to determine the delivered size per standard component.
- *Change sizing.* This approach is used when a project encompasses the use of existing software that must be modified in some way as part of a project. The planner estimates the number and type (e.g., reuse, adding code, changing code, deleting code) of modifications that must be accomplished.

Putnam and Myers suggest that the results of each of these sizing approaches be combined statistically to create a *three-point* or *expected-value* estimate. This is accomplished by developing optimistic (low), most likely, and pessimistic (high) values for size and combining them using Equation (23-1) described in the next section.

23.6.2 Problem-Based Estimation

In Chapter 22, lines of code and function points were described as measures from which productivity metrics can be computed. LOC and FP data are used in two ways during software project estimation: (1) as an estimation variable to "size" each element of the software and (2) as baseline metrics collected from past projects and used in conjunction with estimation variables to develop cost and effort projections.

? What do LOC- and FP-based estimation have in common?

LOC and FP estimation are distinct estimation techniques. Yet both have a number of characteristics in common. The project planner begins with a bounded statement of software scope and from this statement attempts to decompose software into problem functions that can each be estimated individually. LOC or FP (the estimation variable) is then estimated for each function. Alternatively, the planner may choose another component for sizing such as classes or objects, changes, or business processes affected.

When collecting productivity metrics for projects, be sure to establish a taxonomy of project types. This will enable you to compute domain-specific averages, making estimation more accurate.

Baseline productivity metrics (e.g., LOC/pm or FP/pm[5]) are then applied to the appropriate estimation variable, and cost or effort for the function is derived. Function estimates are combined to produce an overall estimate for the entire project.

It is important to note, however, that there is often substantial scatter in productivity metrics for an organization, making the use of a single baseline productivity metric suspect. In general, LOC/pm or FP/pm averages should be computed by project domain. That is, projects should be grouped by team size, application area, complexity, and other relevant parameters. Local domain averages should then be computed. When a new project is estimated, it should first be allocated to a domain,

5 The acronym *pm* means person-month of effort.

and then the appropriate domain average for productivity should be used in generating the estimate.

The LOC and FP estimation techniques differ in the level of detail required for decomposition and the target of the partitioning. When LOC is used as the estimation variable, decomposition is absolutely essential and is often taken to considerable levels of detail. The greater the degree of partitioning, the more likely reasonably accurate estimates of LOC can be developed.

For FP estimates, decomposition focuses on information domain characteristics.

For FP estimates, decomposition works differently. Rather than focusing on function, each of the five information domain characteristics as well as the 14 complexity adjustment values discussed in Chapter 15 are estimated. The resultant estimates can then be used to derive a FP value that can be tied to past data and used to generate an estimate.

Regardless of the estimation variable that is used, the project planner begins by estimating a range of values for each function or information domain value. Using historical data or (when all else fails) intuition, the planner estimates an optimistic, most likely, and pessimistic size value for each function or count for each information domain value. An implicit indication of the degree of uncertainty is provided when a range of values is specified.

? How do we compute the "expected value" for software size?

A three-point or expected-value can then be computed. The *expected-value* for the estimation variable (size), S, can be computed as a weighted average of the optimistic (s_{opt}), most likely (s_m), and pessimistic (s_{pess}) estimates. For example,

$$S = (s_{opt} + 4s_m + s_{pess})/6 \tag{23–1}$$

gives heaviest credence to the "most likely" estimate and follows a beta probability distribution. We assume that there is a very small probability the actual size result will fall outside the optimistic or pessimistic values.

Once the expected value for the estimation variable has been determined, historical LOC or FP productivity data are applied. Are the estimates correct? The only reasonable answer to this question is: We can't be sure. Any estimation technique, no matter how sophisticated, must be cross-checked with another approach. Even then, common sense and experience must prevail.

23.6.3 An Example of LOC-Based Estimation

As an example of LOC and FP problem-based estimation techniques, let us consider a software package to be developed for a computer-aided design application for mechanical components. The software is to execute on an engineering workstation and must interface with various peripherals including a mouse, digitizer, high-resolution color display, and laser printer. A preliminary statement of software scope can be developed:

> The mechanical CAD software will accept two- and three-dimensional geometric data from an engineer. The engineer will interact and control the CAD system through a user interface that will exhibit characteristics of good human/machine interface design. All

Many modern applications reside on a network or are part of a client/server architecture. Therefore, be sure that your estimates include the effort required to develop "infrastructure" software.

> geometric data and other supporting information will be maintained in a CAD database. Design analysis modules will be developed to produce the required output, which will be displayed on a variety of graphics devices. The software will be designed to control and interact with peripheral devices that include a mouse, digitizer, laser printer, and plotter.

This statement of scope is preliminary—it is not bounded. Every sentence would have to be expanded to provide concrete detail and quantitative bounding. For example, before estimation can begin, the planner must determine what "characteristics of good human/machine interface design" means or what the size and sophistication of the "CAD database" are to be.

For our purposes, we assume that further refinement has occurred and that the major software functions listed in Figure 23.2 are identified. Following the decomposition technique for LOC, an estimation table, shown in Figure 23.2, is developed. A range of LOC estimates is developed for each function. For example, the range of LOC estimates for the 3D geometric analysis function is optimistic—4600 LOC, most likely—6900 LOC, and pessimistic—8600 LOC. Applying Equation (23-1), the expected value for the 3D geometric analysis function is 6800 LOC. Other estimates are derived in a similar fashion. By summing vertically in the estimated LOC column, an estimate of 33,200 lines of code is established for the CAD system.

ADVICE

Do not succumb to the temptation to use this result as your project estimate. You should derive another result using a different approach.

A review of historical data indicates that the organizational average productivity for systems of this type is 620 LOC/pm. Based on a burdened labor rate of $8,000 per month, the cost per line of code is approximately $13. Based on the LOC estimate and the historical productivity data, the total estimated project cost is $431,000 and the estimated effort is 54 person-months.[6]

FIGURE 23.2

Estimation table for the LOC methods

Function	Estimated LOC
User interface and control facilities (UICF)	2,300
Two-dimensional geometric analysis (2DGA)	5,300
Three-dimensional geometric analysis (3DGA)	6,800
Database management (DBM)	3,350
Computer graphics display facilities (CGDF)	4,950
Peripheral control function (PCF)	2,100
Design analysis modules (DAM)	8,400
Estimated lines of code	*33,200*

6 Estimates are rounded to the nearest $1,000 and person month. Further precision is unnecessary and unrealistic, given the limitation of estimation accuracy.

SAFEHOME

Estimating

The scene: Doug Miller's office as project planning begins.

The players: Doug Miller (manager of the *SafeHome* software engineering team) and Vinod Raman, Jamie Lazar, and other members of the product software engineering team.

The conversation:

Doug: We need to develop an effort estimate for the project, and then we've got to define a micro-schedule for the first increment and a macro schedule for the remaining increments.

Vinod (nodding): Okay, but we haven't defined any increments yet.

Doug: True, but that's why we need to estimate.

Jamie (frowning): You want to know how long it's going to take us?

Doug: Here's what I need. First, we need to functionally decompose the *SafeHome* software . . . at a high level . . . then we've got to estimate the number of lines of code that each function will take . . . then. . . .

Jamie: Whoa! How are we supposed to do that?

Vinod: I've done it on past projects. You use use-cases, determine the functionality required to implement each, guesstimate the LOC count for each piece of the function. The best approach is to have everyone do it independently and then compare results.

Doug: Or you can do a functional decomposition for the entire project.

Jamie: But that'll take forever, and we've got to get started.

Vinod: No . . . it can be done in a few hours . . . this morning, in fact.

Doug: I agree . . . we can't expect exactitude, just a ball-park idea of what the size of *SafeHome* will be.

Jamie: I think we should just estimate effort . . . that's all.

Doug: We'll do that too. Then use both estimates as a cross check.

Vinod: Let's go do it. . . .

23.6.4 An Example of FP-Based Estimation

Decomposition for FP-based estimation focuses on information domain values rather than software functions. Referring to the table presented in Figure 23.3, the project planner estimates external inputs, external outputs, external inquiries, internal logical files, and external interface files for the CAD software. FP are computed using the technique discussed in Chapter 15. For the purposes of this estimate, the

FIGURE 23.3

Estimating information domain values

Information domain value	Opt.	Likely	Pess.	Est. count	Weight	FP count
Number of external inputs	20	24	30	24	4	97
Number of external outputs	12	15	22	16	5	78
Number of external inquiries	16	22	28	22	5	88
Number of internal logical files	4	4	5	4	10	42
Number of external interface files	2	2	3	2	7	15
Count total						*320*

complexity weighting factor is assumed to be average. Figure 23.3 presents the results of this estimate.

Each of the complexity weighting factors is estimated and the value adjustment factor is computed as described in Chapter 15:

Factor	Value
1. Backup and recovery	4
2. Data communications	2
3. Distributed processing	0
4. Performance critical	4
5. Existing operating environment	3
6. On-line data entry	4
7. Input transaction over multiple screens	5
8. ILFs updated online	3
9. Information domain values complex	5
10. Internal processing complex	5
11. Code designed for reuse	4
12. Conversion/installation in design	3
13. Multiple installations	5
14. Application designed for change	5
Value adjustment factor	**1.17**

Finally, the estimated number of FP is derived:

$$FP_{\text{estimated}} = \text{count-total} \times [0.65 + 0.01 \times \Sigma\ (F_i)]$$
$$FP_{\text{estimated}} = 375$$

The organizational average productivity for systems of this type is 6.5 FP/pm. Based on a burdened labor rate of $8,000 per month, the cost per FP is approximately $1,230. Based on the FP estimate and the historical productivity data, the total estimated project cost is $461,000 and the estimated effort is 58 person-months.

If time permits, use finer granularity when specifying tasks in Figure 23.4. For example, break analysis into its major tasks and estimate each separately.

23.6.5 Process-Based Estimation

The most common technique for estimating a project is to base the estimate on the process that will be used. That is, the process is decomposed into a relatively small set of tasks and the effort required to accomplish each task is estimated.

Like problem-based techniques, process-based estimation begins with a delineation of software functions obtained from the project scope. A series of framework activities must be performed for each function. Functions and related framework activities[7] may be represented as part of a table similar to the one presented in Figure 23.4.

7 The framework activities chosen for this project differ somewhat from the generic activities discussed in Chapter 2. They are customer communication (CC), planning, risk analysis, engineering, and construction/release.

FIGURE 23.4

Process-based estimation table

Activity →	CC	Planning	Risk analysis	Engineering		Construction release		CE	Totals
Task →				Analysis	Design	Code	Test		
Function									
↓									
UICF				0.50	2.50	0.40	5.00	n/a	8.40
2DGA				0.75	4.00	0.60	2.00	n/a	7.35
3DGA				0.50	4.00	1.00	3.00	n/a	8.50
CGDF				0.50	3.00	1.00	1.50	n/a	6.00
DBM				0.50	3.00	0.75	1.50	n/a	5.75
PCF				0.25	2.00	0.50	1.50	n/a	4.25
DAM				0.50	2.00	0.50	2.00	n/a	5.00
Totals	0.25	0.25	0.25	3.50	20.50	4.50	16.50		46.00
% effort	1%	1%	1%	8%	45%	10%	36%		

CC = customer communication CE = customer evaluation

Once problem functions and process activities are melded, the planner estimates the effort (e.g., person-months) that will be required to accomplish each software process activity for each software function. These data constitute the central matrix of the table in Figure 23.4. Average labor rates (i.e., cost/unit effort) are then applied to the effort estimated for each process activity. It is very likely the labor rate will vary for each task. Senior staff are heavily involved in early framework activities and are generally more expensive than junior staff involved in construction and release.

Costs and effort for each function and framework activity are computed as the last step. If process-based estimation is performed independently of LOC or FP estimation, we now have two or three estimates for cost and effort that may be compared and reconciled. If both sets of estimates show reasonable agreement, there is good reason to believe that the estimates are reliable. If, on the other hand, the results of these decomposition techniques show little agreement, further investigation and analysis must be conducted.

> **"It's best to understand the background of an estimate before you use it."**
>
> **Barry Boehm and Richard Fairley**

23.6.6 An Example of Process-Based Estimation

To illustrate the use of process-based estimation, we again consider the CAD software introduced in Section 23.6.3. The system configuration and all software functions remain unchanged and are indicated by project scope.

Referring to the completed process-based table shown in Figure 23.4, estimates of effort (in person-months) for each software engineering activity are provided for each CAD software function (abbreviated for brevity). The engineering and construction release activities are subdivided into the major software engineering tasks shown. Gross estimates of effort are provided for customer communication, planning, and risk analysis. These are noted in the total row at the bottom of the table. Horizontal and vertical totals provide an indication of estimated effort required for analysis, design, code, and test. It should be noted that 53 percent of all effort is expended on front-end engineering tasks (requirements analysis and design), indicating the relative importance of this work.

Based on an average burdened labor rate of $8,000 per month, the total estimated project cost is $368,000, and the estimated effort is 46 person-months. If desired, labor rates could be associated with each framework activity or software engineering task and computed separately.

23.6.7 Estimation with Use-Cases

As we have noted throughout Parts 2 and 3 of this book, use-cases provide a software team with insight into software scope and requirements. However, developing an estimation approach with use-cases is problematic for the following reasons [SMI99]:

? Why is it difficult to develop an estimation technique using use-cases?

- Use-cases are described using many different formats and styles—there is no standard form.
- Use-cases represent an external view (the user's view) of the software and are often written at different levels of abstraction.
- Use-cases do not address the complexity of the functions and features that are described.
- Use-cases do not describe complex behavior (e.g., interactions) that involves many functions and features.

Unlike a LOC or a function point, one person's "use-case" may require months of effort while another person's use-case may be implemented in a day or two.

Although a number of investigators have considered use-cases as an estimation input, no proven estimation method has emerged to date. Smith [SMI99] suggests that use-cases can be used for estimation, but only if they are considered within the context of the "structural hierarchy" that the use-cases describe.

Smith argues that any level of this structural hierarchy can be described by no more than 10 use-cases. Each of these use-cases would encompass no more than 30 distinct scenarios. Obviously, use-cases that describe a large system are written at a much higher level of abstraction (and represent considerably more development effort) than use-cases that are written to describe a single subsystem. Therefore, before use-cases can be used for estimation, the level within the structural hierarchy is established, the average length (in pages) of each use-case is determined, the type of software (e.g., real-time, business, engineering/scientific, embedded) is defined, and a rough architecture for the system is considered. Once these characteristics are established, empirical data may be used to establish the estimated number of LOC or

FP per use case (for each level of the hierarchy). Historical data are then used to compute the effort required to develop the system.

To illustrate how this computation might be made, consider the following relationship:[8]

$$\text{LOC estimate} = N \times \text{LOC}_{avg} + [(S_a/S_h - 1) + (P_a/P_h - 1)] \times \text{LOC}_{adjust} \quad (23\text{-}2)$$

where

N = actual number of use-cases
LOC_{avg} = historical average LOC per use-case for this type of subsystem
LOC_{adjust} = represents an adjustment based on n percent of LOC_{avg} where n is defined locally and represents the difference between this project and "average" projects
S_a = actual scenarios per use-case
S_h = average scenarios per use-case for this type of subsystem
P_a = actual pages per use-case
P_h = average pages per use-case for this type of subsystem

Expression (23-2) is used to develop a rough estimate of the number of LOC based on the actual number of use-cases adjusted by the number of scenarios and the page length of the use-cases. The adjustment represents up to n percent of the historical average LOC per use case.

23.6.8 An Example of Use-Case Based Estimation

The CAD software introduced in Section 23.6.3 is composed of three subsystem groups:

- User interface subsystem (includes UICF).
- Engineering subsystem group (includes the 2DGA subsystem, 3DGA subsystem, and DAM subsystem).
- Infrastructure subsystem group (includes CGDF subsystem and PCF subsystem).

Six use-cases describe the user interface subsystem. Each use case is described by no more than 10 scenarios and has an average length of six pages. The engineering subsystem group is described by 10 use-cases (these are considered to be at a higher level of the structural hierarchy). Each of these use-cases has no more than 20 scenarios associated with it and has an average length of eight pages. Finally, the infrastructure subsystem group is described by five use-cases with an average of only six scenarios and an average length of five pages.

8 It is important to note that Expression (23-2) is used for illustrative purposes only. Like all estimation models, it must be validated locally before it can be used with confidence.

FIGURE 23.5

Use-case estimation

	use-cases	scenarios	pages	scenarios	pages	LOC	LOC estimate
User interface subsystem	6	10	6	12	5	560	3,366
Engineering subsystem group	10	20	8	16	8	3100	31,233
Infrastructure subsystem group	5	6	5	10	6	1650	7,970
Total LOC estimate							42,568

Using the relationship noted in Expression (23-2) with $n = 30$ percent, the table shown in Figure 23.5 is developed. Considering the first row of the table, historical data indicate that UI software requires an average of 800 LOC per use-case when the use-case has no more than 12 scenarios and is described in less than five pages. These data conform reasonably well for the CAD system. Hence the LOC estimate for the user interface subsystem is computed using Expression (23-2). Using the same approach, estimates are made for both the engineering and infrastructure subsystem groups. Figure 23.5 summarizes the estimates and indicates that the overall size of the CAD software is estimated at 42,500 LOC.

Using 620 LOC/pm as the average productivity for systems of this type and a burdened labor rate of $8,000 per month, the cost per line of code is approximately $13. Based on the use-case estimate and the historical productivity data, the total estimated project cost is $552,000 and the estimated effort is 68 person-months.

23.6.9 Reconciling Estimates

The estimation techniques discussed in the preceding sections result in multiple estimates which must be reconciled to produce a single estimate of effort, project duration, or cost. To illustrate this reconciliation procedure, we again consider the CAD software introduced in Section 23.6.3.

> "Complicated methods might not yield a more accurate estimate, particularly when developers can incorporate their own intuition into the estimate."
>
> **Philip Johnson et al.**

Total estimated effort for the CAD software range from a low of 46 person-months (derived using a process-based estimation approach) to a high of 68 person-months (derived with use-case estimation). The average estimate (using all four approaches) is 56 person-months. The variation from the average estimate is approximately 18 percent on the low side and 21 percent on the high side.

What happens when agreement between estimates is poor? The answer to this question requires a reevaluation of information used to make the estimates. Widely divergent estimates can often be traced to one of two causes:

1. The scope of the project is not adequately understood or has been misinterpreted by the planner.

2. Productivity data used for problem-based estimation techniques is inappropriate for the application, obsolete (in that it no longer accurately reflects the software engineering organization), or has been misapplied.

The planner must determine the cause of divergence and then reconcile the estimates.

INFO

Automated Estimation Techniques for Software Projects

Automated estimation tools allow the planner to estimate cost and effort and to perform "what-if" analyses for important project variables such as delivery date or staffing. Although many automated estimation tools exist (see sidebar later in this chapter), all exhibit the same general characteristics, and all perform the following six generic functions [JON96]:

1. *Sizing of project deliverables.* The "size" of one or more software work products is estimated. Work products include the external representation of software (e.g., screens, reports), the software itself (e.g., KLOC), functionality delivered (e.g., function points), and descriptive information (e.g. documents).
2. *Selecting project activities.* The appropriate process framework is selected, and the software engineering task set is specified.
3. *Predicting staffing levels.* The number of people who will be available to do the work is specified. Because the relationship between people available and work (predicted effort) is highly nonlinear, this is an important input.
4. *Predicting software effort.* Estimation tools use one or more models (Section 23.7) that relate the size of the project deliverables to the effort required to produce them.
5. *Predicting software cost.* Given the results of step 4, costs can be computed by allocating labor rates to the project activities noted in step 2.
6. *Predicting software schedules.* When effort, staffing level, and project activities are known, a draft schedule can be produced by allocating labor across software engineering activities based on recommended models for effort distribution discussed later in Chapter 24.

When different estimation tools are applied to the same project data, a relatively large variation in estimated results can be encountered. More important, predicted values sometimes are significantly different than actual values. This reinforces the notion that the output of estimation tools should be used as one "data point" from which estimates are derived—not as the only source for an estimate.

23.7 EMPIRICAL ESTIMATION MODELS

An estimation model reflects the population of projects from which it has been derived. Therefore, the model is domain sensitive.

An estimation model for computer software uses empirically derived formulas to predict effort as a function of LOC or FP.[9] Values for LOC or FP are estimated using the approach described in Sections 23.6.3 and 23.6.4. But instead of using the tables described in those sections, the resultant values for LOC or FP are plugged into the estimation model.

The empirical data that support most estimation models are derived from a limited sample of projects. For this reason, no estimation model is appropriate for all classes of software and in all development environments. Therefore, the results obtained from such models must be used judiciously.

9 An empirical model using use-cases as the independent variable is suggested in Section 23.6.7. However, relatively few have appeared in the literature to date.

An estimation model should be calibrated to reflect local conditions. The model should be tested by applying data collected from completed projects, plugging the data into the model, and then comparing actual to predicted results. If agreement is poor, the model must be tuned and retested before it can be used.

23.7.1 The Structure of Estimation Models

A typical estimation model is derived using regression analysis on data collected from past software projects. The overall structure of such models takes the form [MAT94]

$$E = A + B \times (e_v)^C \tag{23-3}$$

where A, B, and C are empirically derived constants, E is effort in person-months, and e_v is the estimation variable (either LOC or FP). In addition to the relationship noted in Equation (23-3), the majority of estimation models have some form of project adjustment component that enables E to be adjusted by other project characteristics (e.g., problem complexity, staff experience, development environment). Among the many LOC-oriented estimation models proposed in the literature are

None of these models should be used without careful calibration to your environment.

$E = 5.2 \times (\text{KLOC})^{0.91}$	Walston-Felix model
$E = 5.5 + 0.73 \times (\text{KLOC})^{1.16}$	Bailey-Basili model
$E = 3.2 \times (\text{KLOC})^{1.05}$	Boehm simple model
$E = 5.288 \times (\text{KLOC})^{1.047}$	Doty model for KLOC > 9

FP-oriented models have also been proposed. These include

$E = -91.4 + 0.355\ \text{FP}$	Albrecht and Gaffney model
$E = -37 + 0.96\ \text{FP}$	Kemerer model
$E = -12.88 + 0.405\ \text{FP}$	small project regression model

A quick examination of these models indicates that each will yield a different result for the same values of LOC or FP. The implication is clear. Estimation models must be calibrated for local needs!

WebRef

Detailed information on COCOMO II, including downloadable software, can be obtained at **sunset.usc.edu/research/COCOMOII/cocomo_main.html.**

23.7.2 The COCOMO II Model

In his classic book on "software engineering economics," Barry Boehm [BOE81] introduced a hierarchy of software estimation models bearing the name COCOMO, for *COnstructive COst MOdel.* The original COCOMO model became one of the most widely used and discussed software cost estimation models in the industry. It has evolved into a more comprehensive estimation model, called COCOMO II [BOE96, BOE00]. Like its predecessor, COCOMO II is actually a hierarchy of estimation models that address the following areas:

- *Application composition model.* Used during the early stages of software engineering, when prototyping of user interfaces, consideration of software and system interaction, assessment of performance, and evaluation of technology maturity are paramount.

- *Early design stage model.* Used once requirements have been stabilized and basic software architecture has been established.
- *Post-architecture stage model.* Used during the construction of the software.

Like all estimation models for software, the COCOMO II models require sizing information. Three different sizing options are available as part of the model hierarchy: object points, function points, and lines of source code.

The COCOMO II application composition model uses object points —an indirect software measure that is computed using counts of the number of (1) screens (at the user interface), (2) reports, and (3) components likely to be required to build the application. Each object instance (e.g., a screen or report) is classified into one of three complexity levels (i.e., simple, medium, or difficult) using criteria suggested by Boehm [BOE96]. In essence, complexity is a function of the number and source of the client and server data tables that are required to generate the screen or report and the number of views or sections presented as part of the screen or report.

? What is an object point?

Once complexity is determined, the number of screens, reports, and components are weighted according to the table illustrated in Figure 23.6. The object point count is then determined by multiplying the original number of object instances by the weighting factor in the figure and summing to obtain a total object point count. When component-based development or general software reuse is to be applied, the percent of reuse (%reuse) is estimated and the object point count is adjusted:

$$\text{NOP} = (\text{object points}) \times [(100 - \%\text{reuse})/100]$$

where NOP is defined as new object points.

To derive an estimate of effort based on the computed NOP value, a "productivity rate" must be derived. Figure 23.7 presents the productivity rate

$$\text{PROD} = \text{NOP/person-month}$$

for different levels of developer experience and development environment maturity. Once the productivity rate has been determined, an estimate of project effort can be derived as

$$\text{estimated effort} = \text{NOP/PROD}$$

FIGURE 23.6

Complexity weighting for object types [BOE96]

Object type	Complexity weight		
	Simple	Medium	Difficult
Screen	1	2	3
Report	2	5	8
3GL component			10

FIGURE 23.7 Productivity rate for object points [BOE96]

Developer's experience/capability	Very low	Low	Nominal	High	Very high
Environment maturity/capability	Very low	Low	Nominal	High	Very high
PROD	4	7	13	25	50

In more advanced COCOMO II models,[10] a variety of scale factors, cost drivers, and adjustment procedures are required. The interested reader should see [BOE00] or visit the COCOMO II Web site.

23.7.3 The Software Equation

WebRef
Information on software cost estimation tools that have evolved from the software equation can be found at **www.qsm.com.**

The software equation [PUT92] is a multivariable model that assumes a specific distribution of effort over the life of a software development project. The model has been derived from productivity data collected for over 4000 contemporary software projects. Based on these data, an estimation model of the form

$$E = [\text{LOC} \times B^{0.333}/P]^3 \times (1/t^4) \quad (23\text{-}4)$$

where

E = effort in person-months or person-years
t = project duration in months or years
B = "special skills factor"[11]
P = "productivity parameter" that reflects: overall process maturity and management practices, the extent to which good software engineering practices are used, the level of programming languages used, the state of the software environment, the skills and experience of the software team, and the complexity of the application.

Typical values might be $P = 2000$ for development of real-time embedded software; $P = 10{,}000$ for telecommunication and systems software; $P = 28{,}000$ for business systems applications. The productivity parameter can be derived for local conditions using historical data collected from past development efforts.

It is important to note that the software equation has two independent parameters: (1) an estimate of size (in LOC) and (2) an indication of project duration in calendar months or years.

10 As noted earlier, these models use FP and KLOC counts for the size variable.

11 B increases slowly as "the need for integration, testing, quality assurance, documentation, and management skills grows" [PUT92]. For small programs (KLOC = 5 to 15), $B = 0.16$. For programs greater than 70 KLOC, $B = 0.39$.

To simplify the estimation process and use a more common form for their estimation model, Putnam and Myers [PUT92] suggest a set of equations derived from the software equation. Minimum development time is defined as

$$t_{min} = 8.14\ (LOC/P)^{0.43} \text{ in months for } t_{min} > 6 \text{ months} \qquad (23\text{-}5a)$$
$$E = 180\ Bt^3 \text{ in person-months for } E \geq 20 \text{ person-months} \qquad (23\text{-}5b)$$

Note that t in Equation (23-5b) is represented in years.

Using Equations (23-5) with P = 12,000 (the recommended value for scientific software) for the CAD software discussed earlier in this chapter,

$$t_{min} = 8.14\ (33200/12000)^{0.43}$$
$$t_{min} = 12.6 \text{ calendar months}$$
$$E = 180 \times 0.28 \times (1.05)^3$$
$$E = 58 \text{ person-months}$$

The results of the software equation correspond favorably with the estimates developed in Section 23.6. Like the COCOMO model noted in the preceding section, the software equation has evolved over the past decade. Further discussion of an extended version of this estimation approach can be found in [PUT97b].

23.8 Estimation for Object-Oriented Projects

It is worthwhile to supplement conventional software cost estimation methods with an approach that has been designed explicitly for OO software. Lorenz and Kidd [LOR94] suggest the following approach:

1. Develop estimates using effort decomposition, FP analysis, and any other method that is applicable for conventional applications.
2. Using object-oriented analysis modeling (Chapter 8), develop use-cases and determine a count. Recognize that the number of use-cases may change as the project progresses.
3. From the analysis model, determine the number of key classes (called *analysis classes* in Chapter 8).
4. Categorize the type of interface for the application, and develop a multiplier for support classes:

Interface type	**Multiplier**
No GUI	2.0
Text-based user interface	2.25
GUI	2.5
Complex GUI	3.0

Multiply the number of key classes (step 3) by the multiplier to obtain an estimate for the number of support classes.

5. Multiply the total number of classes (key + support) by the average number of work-units per class. Lorenz and Kidd suggest 15 to 20 person-days per class.
6. Cross-check the class-based estimate by multiplying the average number of work-units per use-case.

23.9 Specialized Estimation Techniques

The estimation techniques discussed in Sections 23.6, 23.7 and 23.8 can be used for any software project. However, when a software team encounters an extremely short project duration (weeks rather than months) that is likely to have a continuing stream of changes, project planning in general and estimation in particular should be abbreviated.[12] In the sections that follow, we examine two specialized estimation techniques.

23.9.1 Estimation for Agile Development

Because the requirements for an agile project (Chapter 4) are defined as a set of user scenarios (e.g., "stories" in Extreme Programming) it is possible to develop an estimation approach that is informal, yet reasonably disciplined and meaningful within the context of project planning for each software increment.

Estimation for agile projects uses a decomposition approach that encompasses the following steps:

? How are estimates developed when an agile process is applied?

1. Each user scenario (the equivalent of a mini-use-case created at the very start of a project by end-users or other stakeholders) is considered separately for estimation purposes.
2. The scenario is decomposed into the set of functions and the software engineering tasks that will be required to develop them.

In the context of estimation for agile projects, "volume" is an estimate of the overall size of a user scenario in LOC or FP.

3a. Each task is estimated separately. Note: estimation can be based on historical data, an empirical model, or "experience."

3b. Alternatively, the "volume" (size) of the scenario can be estimated in LOC, FP, or some other volume-oriented measure (e.g., object points).

4a. Estimates for each task are summed to create an estimate for the scenario.

12 "Abbreviated" does *not* mean eliminated. Even short duration projects must be planned, and estimation is the foundation of solid planning.

4b. Alternatively, the volume estimate for the scenario is translated into effort using historical data.

5. The effort estimates for all scenarios that are to be implemented for a given software increment are summed to develop the effort estimate for the increment.

Because the project duration required for the development of a software increment is quite short (typically 3–6 weeks), this estimation approach serves two purposes: (1) to ensure that the number of scenarios to be included in the increment conforms to the available resources, and (2) to establish a basis for allocating effort as the increment is developed.

23.9.2 Estimation for Web Engineering Projects

As we noted in Chapter 16, Web engineering projects often adopt the agile process model. A modified function point measure, coupled with the steps outlined in Section 23.9.1, can be used to develop an estimate for the WebApp.

Roetzheim [ROE00] suggests the following information domain values when adapting function points (Chapters 15 and 22) for WebApp estimation:

- *Inputs* are each input screen or form (for example, CGI or Java), each maintenance screen, and if you use a tab notebook metaphor anywhere, each tab.
- *Outputs* are each static Web page, each dynamic Web page script (for example, ASP, ISAPI, or other DHTML script), and each report (whether Web based or administrative in nature).
- *Tables* are each logical table in the database plus, if you are using XML to store data in a file, each XML object (or collection of XML attributes).
- *Interfaces* retain their definition as logical files (for example, unique record formats) into our out-of-the-system boundaries.
- *Queries* are each externally published or use a message-oriented interface. A typical example is DCOM or COM external references.

Function points (computed using the information domain values noted) are a reasonable indicator of volume for a WebApp.

Mendes and her colleagues [MEN01] suggest that the volume of a WebApp is best determined by collecting measures (called "predictor variables") associated with the application (e.g., page count, media count, function count), its Web page characteristics (e.g., page complexity, linking complexity, graphic complexity), media characteristics (e.g., media duration), and functional characteristics (e.g., code length, reused code length). These measures can be used to develop empirical estimation models for total project effort, page authoring effort, media authoring effort, and scripting effort. However, further work remains to be done before such models can be used with confidence.

Effort and Cost Estimation

Objective: The objective of effort and cost estimation tools is to provide a project team with estimates of effort required, project duration, and cost in a manner that addresses the specific characteristics of the project at hand and the environment in which the project is to be built.

Mechanics: In general, cost estimation tools make use of a historical database derived from local projects, data collected across the industry, and an empirical model (e.g., COCOMO II) that is used to derive effort, duration and cost estimates. Characteristics of the project and the development environment are input, and the tool provides a range of estimation outputs.

Representative Tools[13]

Costar, developed by Softstar Systems (www.softstarsystems.com), uses the COCOMO II model to develop software estimates.

Cost Xpert, developed by Cost Xpert Group, Inc. (www.costxpert.com), integrates multiple estimation models and a historical project database.

Estimate Professional, developed by the Software Productivity Centre, Inc. (www.spc.com), is based on COCOMO II and the SLIM Model.

Knowledge Plan, developed by Software Productivity Research (www.spr.com), uses function point input as the primary driver for a complete estimation package.

Price S, developed by Price Systems (www.pricesystems.com), is one of the oldest and most widely used estimating tools for large-scale software development projects.

SEER/SEM, developed by Galorath Inc., (www.galorath.com), provides comprehensive estimation capability, sensitivity analysis, risk assessment, and other features.

SLIM-Estimate, developed by QSM (www.qsm.com), draws on comprehensive "industry knowledge bases" to provide a "sanity check" for estimates derived using local data.

23.10 The Make/Buy Decision

In many software application areas, it is often more cost effective to acquire rather than develop computer software. Software engineering managers are faced with a make/buy decision that can be further complicated by a number of acquisition options: (1) software may be purchased (or licensed) off the shelf, (2) "full-experience" or "partial-experience" software components (see Section 23.4.2) may be acquired and then modified and integrated to meet specific needs, or (3) software may be custom built by an outside contractor to meet the purchaser's specifications.

The steps involved in the acquisition of software are defined by the criticality of the software to be purchased and the end cost. In the final analysis, the make/buy decision is made based on the following conditions: (1) Will the software product be available sooner than internally developed software? (2) Will the cost of acquisition plus the cost of customization be less than the cost of developing the software internally? (3) Will the cost of outside support (e.g., a maintenance contract) be less than the cost of internal support? These conditions apply for each of the acquisition options.

---

13 Tools noted here do not represent an endorsement, but rather a sampling of tools in this category. In most cases, tool names are trademarked by their respective developers.

23.10.1 Creating a Decision Tree

Is there a systematic way to sort through the options associated with the make/buy decision?

The steps just described can be augmented using statistical techniques such as *decision tree analysis* [BOE89]. For example, Figure 23.8 depicts a decision tree for a software-based system, *X*. In this case, the software engineering organization can (1) build system *X* from scratch, (2) reuse existing "partial-experience" components to construct the system, (3) buy an available software product and modify it to meet local needs, or (4) contract the software development to an outside vendor.

If the system is to be built from scratch, there is a 70 percent probability that the job will be difficult. Using the estimation techniques discussed earlier in this chapter, the project planner projects that a difficult development effort will cost \$450,000. A "simple" development effort is estimated to cost \$380,000. The *expected value* for cost, computed along any branch of the decision tree, is

$$\text{expected cost} = \Sigma\ (\text{path probability})_i \times (\text{estimated path cost})_i$$

where *i* is the decision tree path. For the build path,

$$\text{expected cost}_{\text{build}} = 0.30\ (\$380\text{K}) + 0.70\ (\$450\text{K}) = \$429\text{K}$$

Following other paths of the decision tree, the projected costs for reuse, purchase and contract, under a variety of circumstances, are also shown. The expected costs for these paths are

$$\text{expected cost}_{\text{reuse}} = 0.40\ (\$275\text{K}) + 0.60\ [0.20\ (\$310\text{K}) + 0.80\ (\$490\text{K})] = \$382\text{K}$$
$$\text{expected cost}_{\text{buy}} = 0.70\ (\$210\text{K}) + 0.30\ (\$400\text{K})] = \$267\text{K}$$
$$\text{expected cost}_{\text{contract}} = 0.60\ (\$350\text{K}) + 0.40\ (\$500\text{K})] = \$410\text{K}$$

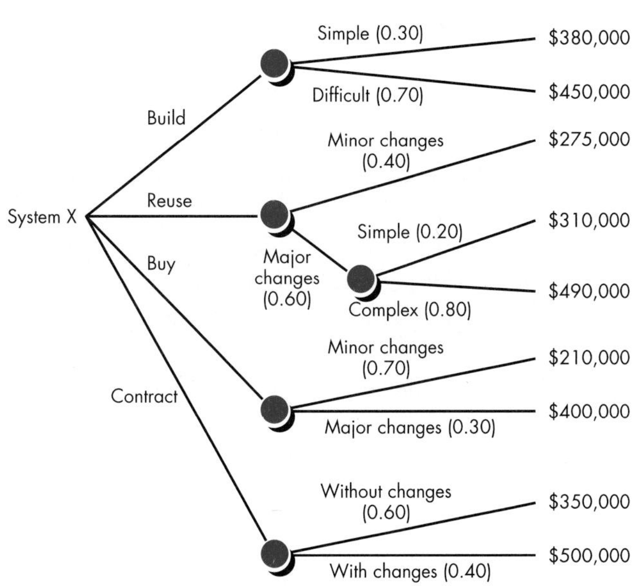

FIGURE 23.8 A decision tree to support the make/buy decision

Based on the probability and projected costs that have been noted in Figure 23.8, the lowest expected cost is the "buy" option.

It is important to note, however, that many criteria—not just cost—must be considered during the decision-making process. Availability, experience of the developer/vendor/contractor, conformance to requirements, local "politics," and the likelihood of change are but a few of the criteria that may affect the ultimate decision to build, reuse, buy, or contract.

23.10.2 Outsourcing

Sooner or later, every company that develops computer software asks a fundamental question: Is there a way that we can get the software and systems we need at a lower price? The answer to this question is not a simple one, and the emotional discussions that occur in response to the question always lead to a single word: *outsourcing.*

In concept, outsourcing is extremely simple. Software engineering activities are contracted to a third party who does the work at lower cost and, hopefully, higher quality. Software work conducted within a company is reduced to a contract management activity.[14]

> **"As a rule outsourcing requires even more skillful management than in-house development."**
>
> **Steve McConnell**

The decision to outsource can be either strategic or tactical. At the strategic level, business managers consider whether a significant portion of all software work can be contracted to others. At the tactical level, a project manager determines whether part or all of a project can be best accomplished by subcontracting the software work.

Regardless of the breadth of focus, the outsourcing decision is often a financial one. A detailed discussion of the financial analysis for outsourcing is beyond the scope of this book and is best left to others (e.g., [MIN95]). However, a brief review of the pros and cons of the decision is worthwhile.

On the positive side, cost savings can usually be achieved by reducing the number of software people and the facilities (e.g., computers, infrastructure) that support them. On the negative side, a company loses some control over the software that it needs. Since software is a technology that differentiates its systems, services, and products, a company runs the risk of putting the fate of its competitiveness into the hands of a third party.

14 Outsourcing can be viewed more generally as any activity that leads to the acquisition of software or software components from a source outside the software engineering organization.

SAFEHOME

Outsourcing

The scene: Meeting room at CPI Corporation.

The players: Mal Golden, senior manager, product development; Lee Warren, engineering manager; Joe Camalleri, executive VP, business development; Doug Miller, project manager, software engineering.

The conversation:

Joe: We're considering outsourcing the *SafeHome* software engineering portion of the product.

Doug (shocked): When did this happen?

Lee: We got a quote from an offshore developer. It comes in at 30 percent below what your group seems to believe it will cost. Here. [Hands the quote to Doug who reads it.]

Mal: As you know, Doug, we're trying to keep costs down, and 30 percent is 30 percent. Besides, these people come highly recommended.

Doug (taking a breath and trying to remain calm): You guys caught me by surprise here, but before you make a final decision, a few comments?

Joe (nodding): Sure, go ahead.

Doug: We haven't worked with this outsourcing company before, right?

Mal: Right, but. . . .

Doug: And they note that any changes to spec will be billed at an additional rate, right?

Joe (frowning): True, but we expect that things will be reasonably stable.

Doug: A bad assumption, Joe.

Joe: Well, ...

Doug: It's likely that we'll release new versions of this product over the next few years. And it's reasonable to assume that software will provide many of the new features, right?

[All nod.]

Doug: Have we ever coordinated an international project before?

Lee (looking concerned): No, but I'm told. . . .

Doug (trying to suppress his anger): So what you're telling me is: (1) we're about to work with an unknown vendor, (2) the costs to do this are not as low as they seem, (3) we're de facto committing to work with them over many product releases, no matter what they do on the first one, and (4) we're going to learn on-the-job relative to an international project.

[All remain silent.]

Doug: Guys . . . I think this is a mistake, and I'd like you to take a day to reconsider. We'll have far more control if we do the work in house. We have the expertise, and I can guarantee that it won't cost us much more . . . the risk will be lower, and I know you're all risk averse, as I am.

Joe (frowning): You've made a few good points, but you have a vested interest in keeping this project in-house.

Doug: That's true, but it doesn't change the facts.

Joe (with a sigh): Okay, let's table this for a day or two, give it some more thought, and meet again for a final decision. Doug, can I speak with you privately?

Doug: Sure . . . I really do want to be sure we do the right thing.

23.11 SUMMARY

The software project planner must estimate three things before a project begins: how long it will take, how much effort will be required, and how many people will be involved. In addition, the planner must predict the resources (hardware and software) that will be required and the risk involved.

The statement of scope helps the planner develop estimates using one or more techniques that fall into two broad categories: decomposition and empirical modeling.

Decomposition techniques require a delineation of major software functions, followed by estimates of either (1) the number of LOC, (2) selected values within the information domain, (3) the number of use-cases, (4) the number of person-months required to implement each function, or (5) the number of person-months required for each software engineering activity. Empirical techniques use empirically derived expressions for effort and time to predict these project quantities. Automated tools can be used to implement a specific empirical model.

Accurate project estimates generally use at least two of the three techniques just noted. By comparing and reconciling estimates derived using different techniques, the planner is more likely to derive an accurate estimate. Software project estimation can never be an exact science, but a combination of good historical data and systematic techniques can improve estimation accuracy.

References

[BEN92] Bennatan, E. M., *Software Project Management: A Practitioner's Approach,* McGraw-Hill, 1992.

[BEN03] Bennatan, E. M., ""So What Is the State of Software Estimation?" *The Cutter Edge* (an online newsletter), February 11, 2003, available from http:// www.cutter.com.

[BOE81] Boehm, B., *Software Engineering Economics*, Prentice-Hall, 1981.

[BOE89] Boehm, B., *Risk Management*, IEEE Computer Society Press, 1989.

[BOE96] Boehm, B., "Anchoring the Software Process," IEEE *Software*, vol. 13, no. 4, July 1996, pp. 73–82.

[BOE00] Boehm, B., et al., *Software Cost Estimation in COCOMO II*, Prentice-Hall, 2000.

[BRO75] Brooks, F., *The Mythical Man-Month*, Addison-Wesley, 1975.

[GAU89] Gause, D. C., and G. M. Weinberg, *Exploring Requirements: Quality Before Design,* Dorset House, 1989.

[HOO91] Hooper, J., and R. O. Chester, *Software Reuse: Guidelines and Methods,* Plenum Press, 1991.

[JON96] Jones, C., "How Software Estimation Tools Work," *American Programmer,* vol. 9, no. 7, July 1996, pp. 19–27.

[LOR94] Lorenz, M., and J. Kidd, *Object-Oriented Software Metrics,* Prentice-Hall, 1994.

[MAT94] Matson, J., B. Barrett, and J. Mellichamp, "Software Development Cost Estimation Using Function Points," *IEEE Trans. Software Engineering,* vol. SE-20, no. 4, April 1994, pp. 275–287.

[MCC98] McConnell, S., *Software Project Survival Guide*, Microsoft Press, 1998.

[MEN01] Mendes, E., N. Mosley, and S. Counsell, "Web Metrics—Estimating Design and Authoring Effort," *IEEE Multimedia,* January–March 2001, pp. 50–57.

[MIN95] Minoli, D., *Analyzing Outsourcing,* McGraw-Hill, 1995.

[PHI98] Phillips, D., *The Software Project Manager's Handbook,* IEEE Computer Society Press, 1998.

[PUT78] Putnam, L., "A General Empirical Solution to the Macro Software Sizing and Estimation Problem," *IEEE Trans. Software Engineering,* Vol SE-4, No. 4, July 1978, pp. 345–361.

[PUT92] Putnam, L., and W. Myers, *Measures for Excellence,* Yourdon Press, 1992.

[PUT97a] Putnam, L., and W. Myers, "How Solved Is the Cost Estimation Problem?" *IEEE Software,* November 1997, pp. 105–107.

[PUT97b] Putnam, L., and W. Myers, *Industrial Strength Software: Effective Management Using Measurement,* IEEE Computer Society Press, 1997.

[ROE00] Roetzheim, W., "Estimating Internet Development," *Software Development,* August 2000, available at http://www.sdmagazine.com/documents/s=741/ sdm0008d/0008d.htm.

[SMI99] Smith, J., "The Estimation of Effort Based on Use Cases," Rational Software Corp., 1999, download from http://www.rational.com/media/whitepapers/ finalTP171.PDF.

Problems and Points to Ponder

23.1. Assume that you are the project manager for a company that builds software for household robots. You have been contracted to build the software for a robot that mows the lawn for a homeowner. Write a statement of scope that describes the software. Be sure your statement of scope is bounded. If you're unfamiliar with robots, do a bit of research before you begin writing. Also, state your assumptions about the hardware that will be required. Alternate: Replace the lawn mowing robot with another robotics problem that is of interest to you.

23.2. Software project complexity influences estimation accuracy. Develop a list of software characteristics (e.g., concurrent operation, graphical output) that affect the complexity of a project. Prioritize the list.

23.3. Performance is an important consideration during planning. Discuss how performance can be interpreted differently depending upon the software application area.

23.4. Do a functional decomposition of the robot software you described in Problem 23.1. Estimate the size of each function in LOC. Assuming that your organization produces 450 LOC/pm with a burdened labor rate of $7,000 per person-month, estimate the effort and cost required to build the software using the LOC-based estimation technique described in this chapter.

23.5. Use the COCOMO II model to estimate the effort required to build software for a simple ATM that produces 12 screens, 10 reports, and will require approximately 80 software components. Assume average complexity and average developer/environment maturity. Use the application composition model with object points.

23.6. Use the software equation to estimate the lawn mowing robot software from Problem 23.1. Assume that Equations (23-5) are applicable and that P = 8000.

23.7. Compare the effort estimates derived in Problems 23.4 and 23.6. What is the standard deviation, and how does it affect your degree of certainty about the estimate?

23.8. Using the results obtained in Problem 23.7, determine whether it's reasonable to expect that the software can be built within the next six months and how many people would have to be used to get the job done.

23.9. Develop a spreadsheet model that implements one or more of the estimation techniques described in this chapter. Alternatively, acquire one or more on-line models for software project estimation from Web-based sources.

23.10. For a project team, develop a software tool that implements each of the estimation techniques developed in this chapter.

23.11. It seems odd that cost and schedule estimates are developed during software project planning—before detailed software requirements analysis or design has been conducted. Why do you think this is done? Are there circumstances when it should not be done?

23.12. Recompute the expected values noted for the decision tree in Figure 23.8 assuming that every branch has a 50–50 probability. Would this change your final decision?

Further Readings and Information Sources

Most software project management books contain discussions of project estimation. The Project Management Institute (*PMBOK Guide,* PMI, 2001), Wysoki and his colleagues (*Effective Project Management,* Wiley, 2000), Lewis (*Project Planning Scheduling and Control,* third edition, McGraw-Hill, 2000), Bennatan (*On Time, Within Budget: Software Project Management Practices and Techniques,* third edition, Wiley, 2000), and Phillips [PHI98] provide useful estimation guidelines.

Jones (*Estimating Software Costs,* McGraw-Hill, 1998) has written one of the most comprehensive treatments of the subject published to date. His book contains models and data that are applicable to software estimating in every application domain. Coombs (*IT Project Estimation,* Cambridge University Press, 2002), Roetzheim and Beasley (*Software Project Cost and Schedule Estimating: Best Practices,* Prentice-Hall, 1997), and Wellman (*Software Costing,* Prentice-Hall, 1992) present many useful models and suggest step-by-step guidelines for generating the best possible estimates.

Putnam and Myer's detailed treatment of software cost estimating ([PUT92] and [PUT97b]) and Boehm's books on software engineering economics ([BOE81] and COCOMO II [BOE00]) describe empirical estimation models. These books provide detailed analysis of data derived from hundreds of software projects. An excellent book by DeMarco (*Controlling Software Projects,* Yourdon Press, 1982) provides valuable insight into the management, measurement, and estimation of software projects. Lorenz and Kidd (*Object-Oriented Software Metrics,* Prentice-Hall, 1994) and Cockburn (*Surviving Object-Oriented Projects,* Addison-Wesley, 1998) consider estimation for object-oriented systems.

A wide variety of information sources on software estimation is available on the Internet. An up-to-date list of World Wide Web references can be found at the SEPA Web site: **http://www.mhhe.com/pressman.**

CHAPTER 24

Software Project Scheduling

Key Concepts

In the late 1960s, a bright-eyed young engineer was chosen to "write" a computer program for an automated manufacturing application. The reason for his selection was simple. He was the only person in his technical group who had attended a computer programming seminar. He knew the ins and outs of assembly language and FORTRAN but nothing about software engineering and even less about project scheduling and tracking.

His boss gave him the appropriate manuals and a verbal description of what had to be done. He was informed that the project must be completed in two months.

He read the manuals, considered his approach, and began writing code. After two weeks, the boss called him into his office and asked how things were going.

"Really great," said the young engineer with youthful enthusiasm, "This was much simpler than I thought. I'm probably close to 75 percent finished."

The boss smiled and encouraged the young engineer to keep up the good work. They planned to meet again in a week's time.

A week later the boss called the engineer into his office and asked, "Where are we?"

"Everything's going well," said the youngster, "but I've run into a few small snags. I'll get them ironed out and be back on track soon."

"How does the deadline look?" the boss asked.

Quick Look

What is it? You selected an appropriate process model; you identified the software engineering tasks that have to be performed; you estimated the amount of work and the number of people; you know the deadline; you even considered the risks. Now it's time to connect the dots. That is, you have to create a network of software engineering tasks that will enable you to get the job done on time. Once the network is created, you have to assign responsibility for each task, make sure it gets done, and adapt the network as risks become reality. In a nutshell, that's software project scheduling and tracking.

Who does it? At the project level, software project managers using information solicited from software engineers. At an individual level, software engineers themselves.

Why is it important? To build a complex system, many software engineering tasks occur in parallel, and the result of work performed during one task may have a profound effect on work conducted in another task. These interdependencies are very difficult to understand without a schedule. It's also virtually impossible to assess progress on a moderate or large software project without a detailed schedule.

What are the steps? The software engineering tasks dictated by the software process model are refined for the functionality to be built. Effort and duration are allocated to each task, and a task network (also called an "activity network") is created in a manner that enables the software team to meet the delivery deadline established.

What is the work product? The project schedule and related information are produced.

How do I ensure that I've done it right? Proper scheduling requires that (1) all tasks appear in the network, (2) effort and timing are intelligently allocated to each task, (3) interdependencies between tasks are properly indicated, (4) resources are allocated for the work to be done, and (5) closely spaced milestones are provided so that progress can be tracked.

"No problem," said the engineer. "I'm close to 90 percent complete."

If you've been working in the software world for more than a few years, you can finish the story. It'll come as no surprise that the young engineer[1] stayed 90 percent complete for the entire project duration and finished (with the help of others) only one month late.

This story has been repeated tens of thousands of times by software developers during the past four decades. The big question is why?

24.1 Basic Concepts

Although there are many reasons why software is delivered late, most can be traced to one or more of the following root causes:

- An unrealistic deadline established by someone outside the software engineering group and forced on managers and practitioners within the group.
- Changing customer requirements that are not reflected in schedule changes.
- An honest underestimate of the amount of effort and/or the number of resources that will be required to do the job.
- Predictable and/or unpredictable risks that were not considered when the project commenced.
- Technical difficulties that could not have been foreseen in advance.
- Human difficulties that could not have been foreseen in advance.
- Miscommunication among project staff that results in delays.
- A failure by project management to recognize that the project is falling behind schedule and a lack of action to correct the problem.

> "Excessive or irrational schedules are probably the single most destructive influence in all of software."
>
> **Capers Jones**

Aggressive (read "unrealistic") deadlines are a fact of life in the software business. Sometimes such deadlines are demanded for reasons that are legitimate, from the point of view of the person who sets the deadline. But common sense says that legitimacy must also be perceived by the people doing the work.

1 In case you were wondering, this story is autobiographical.

Napoleon once said: "Any commander-in-chief who undertakes to carry out a plan which he considers defective is at fault; he must put forth his reasons, insist on the plan being changed, and finally tender his resignation rather than be the instrument of his army's downfall." These are strong words that many software project managers should ponder.

The estimation activities discussed in Chapter 23 and the scheduling techniques described in this chapter are often implemented under the constraint of a defined deadline. If best estimates indicate that the deadline is unrealistic, a competent project manager should "protect his or her team from undue [schedule] pressure . . . [and] reflect the pressure back to its originators" [PAG85].

To illustrate, assume that a software engineering team has been asked to build a real-time controller for a medical diagnostic instrument that is to be introduced to the market in nine months. After careful estimation and risk analysis (Chapter 25), the software project manager comes to the conclusion that the software, as requested, will require 14 calendar months to create with available staff. How does the project manager proceed?

> **"I love deadlines. I like the whooshing sound they make as they fly by."**
>
> **Douglas Adams**

It is unrealistic to march into the customer's office (in this case the likely customer is marketing/sales) and demand that the delivery date be changed. External market pressures have dictated the date, and the product must be released. It is equally foolhardy to refuse to undertake the work (from a career standpoint). So, what to do? The following steps are recommended in this situation:

? What should we do when management demands that we make a deadline that is impossible?

1. Perform a detailed estimate using historical data from past projects. Determine the estimated effort and duration for the project.
2. Using an incremental process model (Chapter 3), develop a software engineering strategy that will deliver critical functionality by the imposed deadline, but delay other functionality until later. Document the plan.
3. Meet with the customer and (using the detailed estimate), explain why the imposed deadline is unrealistic. Be certain to note that all estimates are based on performance on past projects. Also be certain to indicate the percent improvement that would be required to achieve the deadline as it currently exists.[2] The following comment is appropriate:

   "I think we may have a problem with the delivery date for the XYZ controller software. I've given each of you an abbreviated breakdown of production rates

2 If the required improvement is 10 to 25 percent, it may actually be possible to get the job done. But, more likely, the required improvement in team performance will be greater than 50 percent. This is an unrealistic expectation.

for past projects and an estimate that we've done a number of different ways. You'll note that I've assumed a 20 percent improvement in past production rates, but we still get a delivery date that's 14 calendar months rather than 9 months away."

4. Offer the incremental development strategy as an alternative:

   "We have a few options, and I'd like you to make a decision based on them. First, we can increase the budget and bring on additional resources so that we'll have a shot at getting this job done in nine months. But understand that this will increase risk of poor quality due to the tight timeline.[3] Second, we can remove a number of the software functions and capabilities that you're requesting. This will make the preliminary version of the product somewhat less functional, but we can announce all functionality and then deliver over the 14 month period. Third, we can dispense with reality and wish the project complete in nine months. We'll wind up with nothing that can be delivered to a customer. The third option, I hope you'll agree, is unacceptable. Past history and our best estimates say that it is unrealistic and a recipe for disaster."

There will be some grumbling, but if solid estimates based on good historical data are presented, it's likely that negotiated versions of option 1 or 2 will be chosen. The unrealistic deadline evaporates.

24.2 Project Scheduling

Fred Brooks, the well-known author of *The Mythical Man-Month* [BRO95], was once asked how software projects fall behind schedule. His response was as simple as it was profound: "One day at a time."

The reality of a technical project (whether it involves building a hydroelectric plant or developing an operating system) is that hundreds of small tasks must occur to accomplish a larger goal. Some of these tasks lie outside the mainstream and may be completed without worry about impact on project completion date. Other tasks lie on the "critical path." If these "critical" tasks fall behind schedule, the completion date of the entire project is put into jeopardy.

ADVICE

The tasks required to achieve a project manager's objective should not be performed manually. There are many excellent scheduling tools. Use them.

The project manager's objective is to define all project tasks, build a network that depicts their interdependencies, identify the tasks that are critical within the network, and then track their progress to ensure that delay is recognized "one day at a time." To accomplish this, the manager must have a schedule that has been defined at a degree of resolution that allows progress to be monitored and the project to be controlled.

3 You might also add that increasing the number of people does not reduce calendar time proportionally.

Software project scheduling is an activity that distributes estimated effort across the planned project duration by allocating the effort to specific software engineering tasks. It is important to note, however, that the schedule evolves over time. During early stages of project planning, a macroscopic schedule is developed. This type of schedule identifies all major process framework activities and the product functions to which they are applied. As the project gets under way, each entry on the macroscopic schedule is refined into a detailed schedule. Here, specific software tasks (required to accomplish an activity) are identified and scheduled.

> **"Overly optimistic scheduling doesn't result in shorter actual schedules, it results in longer ones."**
>
> **Steve McConnell**

Scheduling for software engineering projects can be viewed from two rather different perspectives. In the first, an end-date for release of a computer-based system has already (and irrevocably) been established. The software organization is constrained to distribute effort within the prescribed time frame. The second view of software scheduling assumes that rough chronological bounds have been discussed but that the end-date is set by the software engineering organization. Effort is distributed to make best use of resources and an end-date is defined after careful analysis of the software. Unfortunately, the first situation is encountered far more frequently than the second.

24.2.1 Basic Principles

Like all other areas of software engineering, a number of basic principles guide software project scheduling:

Compartmentalization. The project must be compartmentalized into a number of manageable activities, actions, and tasks. To accomplish compartmentalization, both the product and the process are decomposed.

When you develop a schedule, compartmentalize the work, note task interdependencies, allocate effort and time to each task, define responsibilities, outcomes, and milestones.

Interdependency. The interdependency of each compartmentalized activity, action, or task must be determined. Some tasks must occur in sequence while others can occur in parallel. Some actions or activities cannot commence until the work product produced by another is available. Other actions or activities can occur independently.

Time allocation. Each task to be scheduled must be allocated some number of work units (e.g., person-days of effort). In addition, each task must be assigned a start date and a completion date that are a function of the interdependencies and whether work will be conducted on a full-time or part-time basis.

Effort validation. Every project has a defined number of people on the software team. As time allocation occurs, the project manager must ensure that no more than the allocated number of people have been scheduled at any given time. For example, consider a project that has three assigned software engineers (e.g., three person-days are available per day of assigned effort[4]). On a given day, seven concurrent tasks must be accomplished. Each task requires 0.50 person days of effort. More effort has been allocated than there are people to do the work.

Defined responsibilities. Every task that is scheduled should be assigned to a specific team member.

Defined outcomes. Every task that is scheduled should have a defined outcome. For software projects, the outcome is normally a work product (e.g., the design of a module) or a part of a work product. Work products are often combined in deliverables.

Defined milestones. Every task or group of tasks should be associated with a project milestone. A milestone is accomplished when one or more work products has been reviewed for quality (Chapter 26) and has been approved.

Each of these principles is applied as the project schedule evolves.

24.2.2 The Relationship Between People and Effort

In a small software development project a single person can analyze requirements, perform design, generate code, and conduct tests. As the size of a project increases, more people must become involved. (We can rarely afford the luxury of approaching a 10 person-year effort with one person working for 10 years!)

ADVICE

If you must add people to a late project, be sure that you've assigned them work that is highly compartmentalized.

There is a common myth that is still believed by many managers who are responsible for software development effort: "If we fall behind schedule, we can always add more programmers and catch up later in the project." Unfortunately, adding people late in a project often has a disruptive effect on the project, causing schedules to slip even further. The people who are added must learn the system, and the people who teach them are the same people who were doing the work. During teaching, no work is done, and the project falls further behind.

In addition to the time it takes to learn the system, more people increase the number of communication paths and the complexity of communication throughout a project. Although communication is absolutely essential to successful software development, every new communication path requires additional effort and therefore additional time.

Over the years, empirical data and theoretical analysis have demonstrated that project schedules are elastic. That is, it is possible to compress a desired project completion date (by adding additional resources) to some extent. It is also possible to extend a completion date (by reducing the number of resources).

The *Putnam-Norden-Rayleigh (PNR) Curve*[5] provides an indication of the relationship between effort applied and delivery time for a software project. A version of the curve,

---

4 In reality, less than three person-days of effort are available because of unrelated meetings, sickness, vacation, and a variety of other reasons. For our purposes, however, we assume 100 percent availability.

5 Original research can be found in [NOR70] and [PUT78].

FIGURE 24.1 The relationship between effort and delivery time

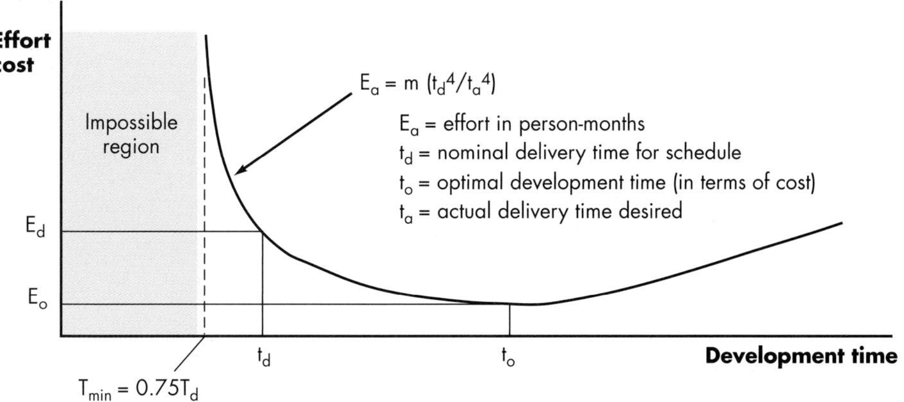

representing project effort as a function of delivery time, is shown in Figure 24.1. The curve indicates a minimum value, t_o, that indicates the least cost time for delivery (i.e., the delivery time that will result in the least effort expended). As we move left of t_o (i.e., as we try to accelerate delivery), the curve rises nonlinearly.

If delivery can be delayed, the PNR curve indicates that project costs can be reduced substantially.

As an example, we assume that a project team has estimated a level of effort, E_a, will be required to achieve a nominal delivery time, t_d, that is optimal in terms of schedule and available resources. Although it is possible to accelerate delivery, the curve rises very sharply to the left of t_d. In fact, the PNR curve indicates that the project delivery time cannot be compressed much beyond 0.75 t_d. If we attempt further compression, the project moves into "the impossible region" and risk of failure becomes very high. The PNR curve also indicates that the lowest cost delivery option, $t_o = 2\ t_d$. The implication here is that delaying project delivery can reduce costs significantly. Of course, this must be weighed against the business cost associated with the delay.

The software equation [PUT92] introduced in Chapter 23 is derived from the PNR curve and demonstrates the highly nonlinear relationship between chronological time to complete a project and human effort applied to the project. The number of delivered lines of code (source statements), *L*, is related to effort and development time by the equation:

As the project deadline becomes tighter and tighter, you reach a point at which the work cannot be completed on schedule, regardless of the number of people doing the work. Face reality and define a new delivery date.

$$L = P \times E^{1/3}t^{4/3}$$

where *E* is development effort in person-months, *P* is a productivity parameter that reflects a variety of factors that lead to high-quality software engineering work (typical values for *P* range between 2000 and 12,000), and *t* is the project duration in calendar months.

Rearranging this software equation, we can arrive at an expression for development effort *E*:

$$E = L^3/(P^3t^4) \qquad (24\text{-}1)$$

where E is the effort expended (in person-years) over the entire life cycle for software development and maintenance, and t is the development time in years. The equation for development effort can be related to development cost by the inclusion of a burdened labor rate factor ($/person-year).

This leads to some interesting results. Consider a complex, real-time software project estimated at 33,000 LOC, 12 person-years of effort. If eight people are assigned to the project team, the project can be completed in approximately 1.3 years. If, however, we extend the end-date to 1.75 years, the highly nonlinear nature of the model described in Equation (24-1) yields:

$$E = L^3/(P^3t^4) \sim 3.8 \text{ person-years.}$$

This implies that, by extending the end-date six months, we can reduce the number of people from eight to four! The validity of such results is open to debate, but the implication is clear: benefit can be gained by using fewer people over a somewhat longer time span to accomplish the same objective.

24.2.3 Effort Distribution

? How should effort be distributed across the software process workflow?

Each of the software project estimation techniques discussed in Chapter 23 leads to estimates of work units (e.g., person-months) required to complete software development. A recommended distribution of effort across the software process is often referred to as the *40–20–40 rule.* Forty percent of all effort is allocated to front-end analysis and design. A similar percentage is applied to back-end testing. You can correctly infer that coding (20 percent of effort) is deemphasized.

This effort distribution should be used as a guideline only.[6] The characteristics of each project must dictate the distribution of effort. Work expended on project planning rarely accounts for more than 2–3 percent of effort, unless the plan commits an organization to large expenditures with high risk. Requirements analysis may comprise 10–25 percent of project effort. Effort expended on analysis or prototyping should increase in direct proportion with project size and complexity. A range of 20 to 25 percent of effort is normally applied to software design. Time expended for design review and subsequent iteration must also be considered.

Because of the effort applied to software design, code should follow with relatively little difficulty. A range of 15–20 percent of overall effort can be achieved. Testing and subsequent debugging can account for 30–40 percent of software development effort. The criticality of the software often dictates the amount of testing that is required. If software is human rated (i.e., software failure can result in loss of life), even higher percentages are typical.

6 Today, the 40-20-40 rule is under attack. Some believe that more than 40 percent of overall effort should be expended during analysis and design. On the other hand, some proponents of agile development (Chapter 4) argue that less time should be expended "up front" and that a team should move quickly to construction.

24.3 Defining a Task Set for the Software Project

A number of different process models were described in Part 1 of this book. Regardless of whether a software team chooses a linear sequential model, an incremental model, an evolutionary model, or some permutation, the process model is populated by a set of tasks that enables a software team to define, develop, and ultimately support computer software.

No single task set is appropriate for all projects. The set of tasks that would be appropriate for a large, complex system would likely be perceived as overkill for a small, relatively simple software product. Therefore, an effective software process should define a collection of task sets, each designed to meet the needs of different types of projects.

As we noted in Chapter 2, a task set is a collection of software engineering work tasks, milestones, and work products that must be accomplished to complete a particular project. The task set should provide enough discipline to achieve high software quality. But, at the same time, it must not burden the project team with unnecessary work.

To develop a project schedule, a task set must be distributed on the project time line. The task set will vary depending upon the project type and the degree of rigor with which the software team decides to do its work. Although it is difficult to develop a comprehensive taxonomy of software project types, most software organizations encounter the following projects:

1. *Concept development projects* that are initiated to explore some new business concept or application of some new technology.
2. *New application development* projects that are undertaken as a consequence of a specific customer request.
3. *Application enhancement* projects that occur when existing software undergoes major modifications to function, performance, or interfaces that are observable by the end-user.
4. *Application maintenance projects* that correct, adapt, or extend existing software in ways that may not be immediately obvious to the end-user.
5. *Reengineering projects* that are undertaken with the intent of rebuilding an existing (legacy) system in whole or in part.

> **WebRef**
> An adaptable process model (APM) has been developed to assist in defining task sets for various software projects. A complete description of the APM can be found at **www.rspa.com/apm.**

Even within a single project type, many factors influence the task set to be chosen. These include [PRE99]: size of the project, number of potential users, mission criticality, application longevity, stability of requirements, ease of customer/developer communication, maturity of applicable technology, performance constraints, embedded and nonembedded characteristics, project staff, and reengineering factors. When taken in combination, these factors provide an indication of the *degree of rigor* with which the software process should be applied.

24.3.1 A Task Set Example

Each of the project types described may be approached using a process model that is linear sequential, iterative (e.g., the prototyping or incremental models), or evolutionary (e.g., the spiral model). In some cases, one project type flows smoothly into the next. For example, concept development projects that succeed often evolve into new application development projects. As a new application development project ends, an application enhancement project sometimes begins. This progression is both natural and predictable and will occur regardless of the process model that is adopted by an organization. Therefore, the major software engineering tasks described in the sections that follows are applicable to all process model flows. As an example, we consider the software engineering tasks for a concept development project.

Concept development projects are initiated when the potential for some new technology must be explored. There is no certainty that the technology will be applicable, but a customer (e.g., marketing) believes that potential benefit exists. Concept development projects are approached by applying the following major tasks:

1.1 **Concept scoping** determines the overall scope of the project.

1.2 **Preliminary concept planning** establishes the organization's ability to undertake the work implied by the project scope.

1.3 **Technology risk assessment** evaluates the risk associated with the technology to be implemented as part of project scope.

1.4 **Proof of concept** demonstrates the viability of a new technology in the software context.

1.5 **Concept implementation** implements the concept representation in a manner that can be reviewed by a customer and is used for "marketing" purposes when a concept must be sold to other customers or management.

1.6 **Customer reaction** to the concept solicits feedback on a new technology concept and targets specific customer applications.

A quick scan of these tasks should yield few surprises. In fact, the software engineering flow for concept development projects (and for all other types of projects as well) is little more than common sense.

24.3.2 Refinement of Major Tasks

The major tasks described in the preceding section may be used to define a macroscopic schedule for a project. However, the macroscopic schedule must be refined to create a detailed project schedule. Refinement begins by taking each major task and decomposing it into a set of subtasks (with related work products and milestones).

As an example of task decomposition, consider Task 1.1, Concept Scoping. Task refinement can be accomplished using an outline format, but in this book, a process design language approach is used to illustrate the flow of the concept scoping activity:

Task definition: Task 1.1 Concept Scoping

1.1.1 Identify need, benefits and potential customers;

1.1.2 Define desired output/control and input events that drive the application;

Begin Task 1.1.2

1.1.2.1 FTR: Review written description of need[7]

1.1.2.2 Derive a list of customer visible outputs/inputs

1.1.2.3 FTR: Review outputs/inputs with customer and revise as required;

endtask Task 1.1.2

1.1.3 Define the functionality/behavior for each major function;

Begin Task 1.1.3

1.1.3.1 FTR: Review output and input data objects derived in task 1.1.2;

1.1.3.2 Derive a model of functions/behaviors;

1.1.3.3 FTR: Review functions/behaviors with customer and revise as required;

endtask Task 1.1.3

1.1.4 Isolate those elements of the technology to be implemented in software;

1.1.5 Research availability of existing software;

1.1.6 Define technical feasibility;

1.1.7 Make quick estimate of size;

1.1.8 Create a Scope Definition;

endTask definition: Task 1.1

The tasks and subtasks noted in the process design language refinement form the basis for a detailed schedule for the concept scoping activity.

24.4 Defining a Task Network

The task network is a useful mechanism for depicting intertask dependencies and determining the critical path.

Individual tasks and subtasks have interdependencies based on their sequence. In addition, when more than one person is involved in a software engineering project, it is likely that development activities and tasks will be performed in parallel. When this occurs, concurrent tasks must be coordinated so that they will be complete when later tasks require their work product(s).

A *task network,* also called an *activity network,* is a graphic representation of the task flow for a project. It is sometimes used as the mechanism through which task sequence and dependencies are input to an automated project scheduling tool. In its simplest form (used when creating a macroscopic schedule), the task network depicts major software engineering tasks. Figure 24.2 shows a schematic task network for a concept development project.

The concurrent nature of software engineering activities leads to a number of important scheduling requirements. Because parallel tasks occur asynchronously, the planner must determine intertask dependencies to ensure continuous progress

7 FTR indicates that a formal technical review (Chapter 26) is to be conducted.

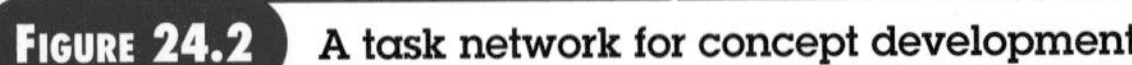

FIGURE 24.2 A task network for concept development

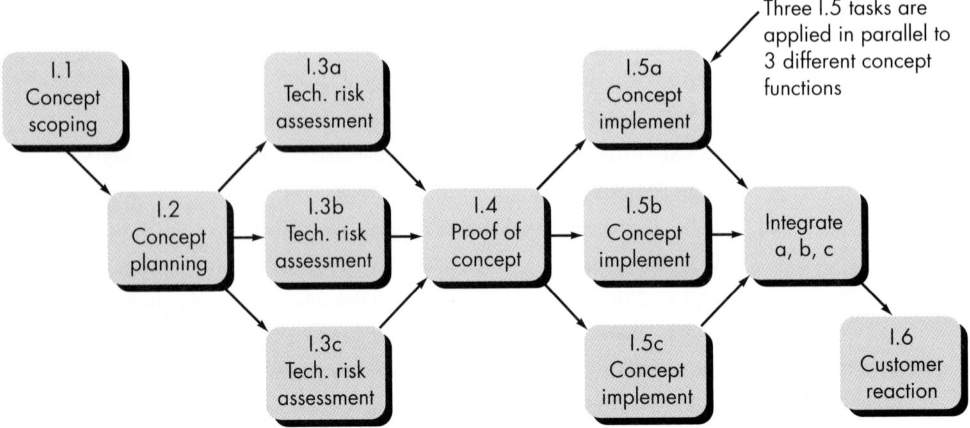

toward completion. In addition, the project manager should be aware of those tasks that lie on the *critical path.* That is, tasks that must be completed on schedule if the project as a whole is to be completed on schedule. These issues are discussed in more detail later in this chapter.

It is important to note that the task network shown in Figure 24.2 is macroscopic. In a detailed task network (a precursor to a detailed schedule), each activity shown in the figure would be expanded. For example, Task 1.1 would be expanded to show all tasks detailed in the refinement of Tasks 1.1 shown in Section 24.3.2.

24.5 SCHEDULING

Scheduling of a software project does not differ greatly from scheduling of any multitask engineering effort. Therefore, generalized project scheduling tools and techniques can be applied with little modification for software projects.

Program evaluation and review technique (PERT) and the *critical path method* (CPM) are two project scheduling methods that can be applied to software development. Both techniques are driven by information already developed in earlier project planning activities:

- Estimates of effort.
- A decomposition of the product function.
- The selection of the appropriate process model and task set.
- Decomposition of tasks.

Interdependencies among tasks may be defined using a task network. Tasks, sometimes called the project *work breakdown structure* (WBS), are defined for the product as a whole or for individual functions.

> *"All we have to decide is what to do with the time that is given to us."*
> **Gandalf in *The Lord of the Rings: Fellowship of the Ring***

Both PERT and CPM provide quantitative tools that allow the software planner to (1) determine the critical path—the chain of tasks that determines the duration of the project; (2) establish "most likely" time estimates for individual tasks by applying statistical models; and (3) calculate "boundary times" that define a time "window" for a particular task.

SOFTWARE TOOLS

Project Scheduling

Objective: The objective of project scheduling tools is to enable a project manager to define work tasks, establish their dependencies, assign human resources to tasks, and develop a variety of graphs, charts, and tables that aid in tracking and control of the software project.

Mechanics: In general, project scheduling tools require the specification of a work breakdown structure or the generation of a task network. Once the task breakdown (an outline) or network is defined, start and end dates, human resources, hard deadlines, and other data are attached to each task. The tool then generates a variety of timeline charts and other tables that enable a manager to assess the task flow of a project. These data can be updated continually as the project is conducted.

Representative Tools[8]

AMS Realtime, developed by Advanced Management Systems (www.amsusa.com), provides scheduling capabilities for projects of all sizes and types.

Microsoft Project, developed by Microsoft (www.microsoft.com), is the most widely used PC-based project scheduling tool.

Viewpoint, developed by Artemis Internation Solutions Corp. (www.atemispm.com), supports all aspects of project planning including scheduling.

A comprehensive list of project management software vendors and products can be found at www.infogoal.com/pmc/pmcswr.htm.

24.5.1 Timeline Charts

When creating a software project schedule, the planner begins with a set of tasks (the work breakdown structure). If automated tools are used, the work breakdown is input as a task network or task outline. Effort, duration, and start date are then input for each task. In addition, tasks may be assigned to specific individuals.

A timeline chart enables you to determine what tasks will be conducted at a given point in time.

As a consequence of this input, a *timeline chart,* also called a *Gantt chart,* is generated. A timeline chart can be developed for the entire project. Alternatively, separate charts can be developed for each project function or for each individual working on the project.

Figure 24.3 illustrates the format of a timeline chart. It depicts a part of a software project schedule that emphasizes the concept scoping task for a word-processing (WP) software product. All project tasks (for concept scoping) are listed in

8 Tools noted here do not represent an endorsement, but rather a sampling of tools in this category. In most cases, tool names are trademarked by their respective developers.

FIGURE 24.3 An example timeline chart

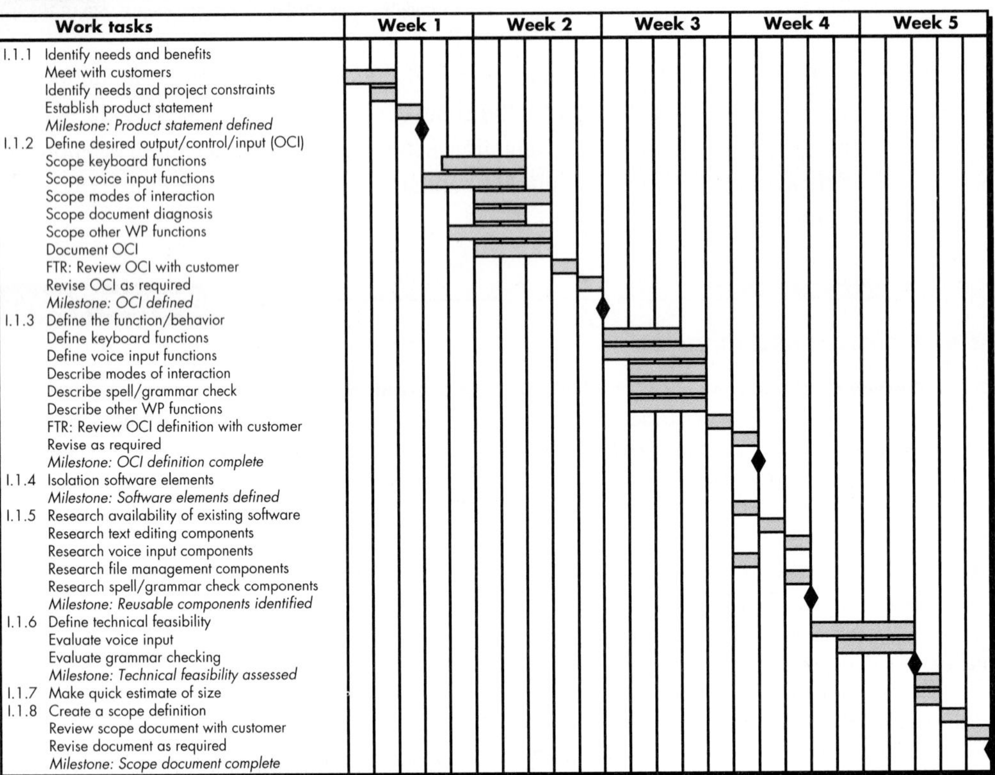

the left-hand column. The horizontal bars indicate the duration of each task. When multiple bars occur at the same time on the calendar, task concurrency is implied. The diamonds indicate milestones.

Once the information necessary for the generation of a timeline chart has been input, the majority of software project scheduling tools produce *project tables*—a tabular listing of all project tasks, their planned and actual start- and end-dates, and a variety of related information (Figure 24.4). Used in conjunction with the timeline chart, project tables enable the project manager to track progress.

24.5.2 Tracking the Schedule

The project schedule provides a road map for a software project manager. If it has been properly developed, the project schedule defines the tasks and milestones that must be tracked and controlled as the project proceeds. Tracking can be accomplished in a number of different ways:

- Conducting periodic project status meetings in which each team member reports progress and problems.

FIGURE 24.4 An example resource table

Work tasks	Planned start	Actual start	Planned complete	Actual complete	Assigned person	Effort allocated	Notes
I.1.1 Identify needs and benefits							Scoping will require more effort/time
Meet with customers	wk1, d1	wk1, d1	wk1, d2	wk1, d2	BLS	2 p-d	
Identify needs and project constraints	wk1, d2	wk1, d2	wk1, d2	wk1, d2	JPP	1 p-d	
Establish product statement	wk1, d3	wk1, d3	wk1, d3	wk1, d3	BLS/JPP	1 p-d	
Milestone: Product statement defined	wk1, d3	wk1, d3	wk1, d3	wk1, d3			
I.1.2 Define desired output/control/input (OCI)							
Scope keyboard functions	wk1, d4	wk1, d4	wk2, d2		BLS	1.5 p-d	
Scope voice input functions	wk1, d3	wk1, d3	wk2, d2		JPP	2 p-d	
Scope modes of interaction	wk2, d1		wk2, d3		MLL	1 p-d	
Scope document diagnostics	wk2, d1		wk2, d2		BLS	1.5 p-d	
Scope other WP functions	wk1, d4	wk1, d4	wk2, d3		JPP	2 p-d	
Document OCI	wk2, d1		wk2, d3		MLL	3 p-d	
FTR: Review OCI with customer	wk2, d3		wk2, d3		all	3 p-d	
Revise OCI as required	wk2, d4		wk2, d4		all	3 p-d	
Milestone: OCI defined	wk2, d5		wk2, d5				
I.1.3 Define the function/behavior							

- Evaluating the results of all reviews conducted throughout the software engineering process.
- Determining whether formal project milestones (the diamonds shown in Figure 24.3) have been accomplished by the scheduled date.
- Comparing actual start-date to planned start-date for each project task listed in the resource table (Figure 24.4).
- Meeting informally with practitioners to obtain their subjective assessment of progress to date and problems on the horizon.
- Using earned value analysis (Section 24.6) to assess progress quantitatively.

In reality, all of these tracking techniques are used by experienced project managers.

> "The basic rule of software status reporting can be summarized in a single phrase: No surprises."
>
> Capers Jones

The best indication of progress is the completion and successful review of a defined software work product.

Control is employed by a software project manager to administer project resources, cope with problems, and direct project staff. If things are going well (i.e., the project is on schedule and within budget, reviews indicate that real progress is being made, and milestones are being reached), control is light. But when problems occur, the project manager must exercise control to reconcile them as quickly as possible. After a problem has been diagnosed, additional resources may be focused on the problem area: staff may be redeployed or the project schedule can be redefined.

When faced with severe deadline pressure, experienced project managers sometimes use a project scheduling and control technique called *time-boxing* [ZAH95]. The time-boxing strategy recognizes that the complete product may not be deliverable by the predefined deadline. Therefore, an incremental software paradigm (Chapter 3) is chosen and a schedule is derived for each incremental delivery.

The tasks associated with each increment are then time-boxed. This means that the schedule for each task is adjusted by working backward from the delivery date for the increment. A "box" is put around each task. When a task hits the boundary of its time box (plus or minus 10 percent), work stops and the next task begins.

The initial reaction to the time-boxing approach is often negative: If the work isn't finished, how can we proceed? The answer lies in the way work is accomplished. By the time the time-box boundary is encountered, it is likely that 90 percent of the task has been completed.[9] The remaining 10 percent, although important, can (1) be delayed until the next increment or (2) be completed later if required. Rather than becoming "stuck" on a task, the project proceeds toward the delivery date.

24.5.3 Tracking Progress for an OO Project

Although an iterative model is the best framework for an OO project, task parallelism makes project tracking difficult. The project manager can have difficulty establishing meaningful milestones for an OO project because a number of different things are happening at once. In general, the following major milestones can be considered "completed" when the criteria noted have been met.

Technical milestone: OO analysis completed

- All classes and the class hierarchy have been defined and reviewed.
- Class attributes and operations associated with a class have been defined and reviewed.
- Class relationships (Chapter 8) have been established and reviewed.
- A behavioral model (Chapter 8) has been created and reviewed.
- Reusable classes have been noted.

Technical milestone: OO design completed

- The set of subsystems (Chapter 9) has been defined and reviewed.
- Classes are allocated to subsystems and reviewed.
- Task allocation has been established and reviewed.
- Responsibilities and collaborations (Chapters 8 and 9) have been identified.

---

9 A cynic might recall the saying: The first 90 percent of the system takes 90 percent of the time; the remaining 10 percent of the system takes 90 percent of the time.

- Design classes have been created and reviewed.
- The communication model has been created and reviewed.

Technical milestone: OO programming completed

- Each new class has been implemented in code from the design model.
- Extracted classes (from a reuse library) have been implemented.
- Prototype or increment has been built.

Technical milestone: OO testing

Debugging and testing occur in concert with one another. The status of debugging is often assessed by considering the type and number of "open" errors (bugs).

- The correctness and completeness of OO analysis and design models has been reviewed.
- A class-responsibility-collaboration network (Chapter 8) has been developed and reviewed.
- Test cases are designed, and class-level tests (Chapter 14) have been conducted for each class.
- Test cases are designed, and cluster testing (Chapter 14) is completed and the classes are integrated.
- System level tests have been completed.

Recalling that the OO process model is iterative, each of these milestones may be revisited as different increments are delivered to the customer.

SAFEHOME

Tracking the Schedule

The scene: Doug Miller's office, prior to the initiation of the *SafeHome* software project.

The players: Doug Miller (manager of the *SafeHome* software engineering team) and Vinod Raman, Jamie Lazar, and other members of the product software engineering team.

The conversation:

Doug (glancing at a Powerpoint slide): The schedule for the first *SafeHome* increment seems reasonable, but we're going to have trouble tracking progress.

Vinod (a concerned look on his face): Why? We have tasks scheduled on a daily basis, plenty of work products, and we've been sure that we're not over-allocating resources.

Doug: All good, but how do we know when the analysis model for the first increment is complete?

Jamie: Things are iterative, so that's difficult.

Doug: I understand that, but . . . well, for instance, take *analysis classes defined*. You indicated that as a milestone.

Vinod: We have.

Doug: Who makes that determination?

Jamie (aggravated): They're done when they're done.

Doug: That's not good enough, Jamie. We have to schedule FTRs [formal technical reviews, Chapter 26], and you haven't done that. The successful completion of a review on the analysis model, for instance, is a reasonable milestone. Understand?

Jamie (frowning): Okay, back to the drawing board.

Doug: It shouldn't take more than an hour to make the corrections . . . everyone else can get started now.

24.6 Earned Value Analysis

Earned value provides a quantitative indication of progress.

In Section 24.5, we discussed a number of qualitative approaches to project tracking. Each provides the project manager with an indication of progress, but an assessment of the information provided is somewhat subjective. It is reasonable to ask whether there is a quantitative technique for assessing progress as the software team moves through the work tasks allocated to the project schedule. In fact, a technique for performing quantitative analysis of progress does exist. It is called *earned value analysis* (EVA). Humphrey [HUM95] discusses earned value in the following manner:

> The earned value system provides a common value scale for every [software project] task, regardless of the type of work being performed. The total hours to do the whole project are estimated, and every task is given an earned value based on its estimated percentage of the total.

Stated even more simply, earned value is a measure of progress. It enables us to assess the "percent of completeness" of a project using quantitative analysis rather than rely on a gut feeling. In fact, Fleming and Koppleman [FLE98] argue that earned value analysis "provides accurate and reliable readings of performance from as early as 15 percent into the project."

To determine the earned value, the following steps are performed:

? How do I compute earned value and use it to assess progress?

1. The *budgeted cost of work scheduled* (BCWS) is determined for each work task represented in the schedule. During estimation, the work (in person-hours or person-days) of each software engineering task is planned. Hence, $BCWS_i$ is the effort planned for work task *i*. To determine progress at a given point along the project schedule, the value of BCWS is the sum of the $BCWS_i$ values for all work tasks that should have been completed by that point in time on the project schedule.
2. The BCWS values for all work tasks are summed to derive the *budget at completion,* BAC. Hence,

   $BAC = \Sigma\ (BCWS_k)$ for all tasks k

3. Next, the value for *budgeted cost of work performed* (BCWP) is computed. The value for BCWP is the sum of the BCWS values for all work tasks that have actually been completed by a point in time on the project schedule.

Wilkens [WIL99] notes that "the distinction between the BCWS and the BCWP is that the former represents the budget of the activities that were planned to be completed and the latter represents the budget of the activities that actually were completed." Given values for BCWS, BAC, and BCWP, important progress indicators can be computed:

Schedule performance index, SPI = BCWP/BCWS

Schedule variance, SV = BCWP − BCWS

WebRef
A wide array of earned value analysis resources can be found at **www.acq.osd.mil/pm/.**

SPI is an indication of the efficiency with which the project is utilizing scheduled resources. An SPI value close to 1.0 indicates efficient execution of the project schedule. SV is simply an absolute indication of variance from the planned schedule.

Percent scheduled for completion = BCWS/BAC

provides an indication of the percentage of work that should have been completed by time *t*.

Percent complete = BCWP/BAC

provides a quantitative indication of the percent of completeness of the project at a given point in time, *t*.

It is also possible to compute the *actual cost of work performed,* ACWP. The value for ACWP is the sum of the effort actually expended on work tasks that have been completed by a point in time on the project schedule. It is then possible to compute

Cost performance index, CPI = BCWP/ACWP
Cost variance, CV = BCWP − ACWP

A CPI value close to 1.0 provides a strong indication that the project is within its defined budget. CV is an absolute indication of cost savings (against planned costs) or shortfall at a particular stage of a project.

Like over-the-horizon radar, earned value analysis illuminates scheduling difficulties before they might otherwise be apparent. This enables the software project manager to take corrective action before a project crisis develops.

24.7 Summary

Scheduling is the culmination of a planning activity that is a primary component of software project management. When combined with estimation methods and risk analysis, scheduling establishes a road map for the project manager.

Scheduling begins with process decomposition. The characteristics of the project are used to adapt an appropriate task set for the work to be done. A task network depicts each engineering task, its dependency on other tasks, and its projected duration. The task network is used to compute the critical path, a timeline chart and a variety of project information. Using the schedule as a guide, the project manager can track and control each step in the software process.

References

[BRO95] Brooks, M., *The Mythical Man-Month,* anniversary edition, Addison-Wesley, 1995.

[FLE98] Fleming, Q. W., and J. M. Koppelman, "Earned Value Project Management," *Crosstalk,* vol. 11, no. 7, July 1998, p. 19.

[HUM95] Humphrey, W., *A Discipline for Software Engineering,* Addison-Wesley, 1995.

[NOR70] Norden, P., "Useful Tools for Project Management," in *Management of Production,* M. K. Starr, ed., Penguin Books, 1970.

[PAG85] Page-Jones, M., *Practical Project Management,* Dorset House, 1985, pp. 90–91.

[PRE99] Pressman, R. S., *Adaptable Process Model,* R. S. Pressman & Associates, 1999.

[PUT78] Putnam, L., "A General Empirical Solution to the Macro Software Sizing and Estimation Problem," *IEEE Trans. Software Engineering,* vol SE-4, no. 4, July 1978, pp. 345–361.

[PUT92] Putnam, L., and W. Myers, *Measures for Excellence,* Yourdon Press, 1992.

[WIL99] Wilkens, T. T., "Earned Value, Clear and Simple," Primavera Systems, April 1, 1999, p. 2.

[ZAH95] Zahniser, R., "Time-boxing for Top Team Performance," *Software Development,* March 1995, pp. 34–38.

Problems and Points to Ponder

24.1. "Unreasonable" deadlines are a fact of life in the software business. How should you proceed if you're faced with one?

24.2. What is the difference between a macroscopic schedule and a detailed schedule. Is it possible to manage a project if only a macroscopic schedule is developed? Why?

24.3. Is there ever a case where a software project milestone is not tied to a review? If so, provide one or more examples.

24.4. "Communication overhead" can occur when multiple people work on a software project. The time spent communicating with others reduces individual productivity (LOC/person-month), and the result is less productivity for the team. Illustrate (quantitatively) how engineers who are well-versed in good software engineering practices and use formal technical reviews can increase the production rate of a team (when compared to the sum of individual production rates). Hint: You can assume that reviews reduce rework and that rework can account for 20–40 percent of a person's time.

24.5. Although adding people to a late software project can make it later, there are circumstances in which this is not true. Describe them.

24.6. The relationship between people and time is highly nonlinear. Using Putnam's software equation (described in Section 24.2.2), develop a table that relates number of people to project duration for a software project requiring 50,000 LOC and 15 person-years of effort (the productivity parameter is 5000). Assume that the software must be delivered in 24 months plus or minus 12 months.

24.7. Assume that you have been contracted by a university to develop an on-line course registration system (OLCRS). First, act as the customer (if you're a student, that should be easy!) and specify the characteristics of a good system. (Alternatively, your instructor will provide you with a set of preliminary requirements for the system.) Using the estimation methods discussed in Chapter 23, develop an effort and duration estimate for OLCRS. Suggest how you would:

a. Define parallel work activities during the OLCRS project.
b. Distribute effort throughout the project.
c. Establish milestones for the project.

24.8. Select an appropriate task set for the OLCRS project.

24.9. Define a task network for OLCRS, or alternatively, for another software project that interests you. Be sure to show tasks and milestones and to attach effort and duration estimates to each task. If possible, use an automated scheduling tool to perform this work.

24.10. If an automated scheduling tool is available, determine the critical path for the network defined in Problem 24.9.

24.11. Using a scheduling tool (if available) or paper and pencil (if necessary), develop a timeline chart for the OLCRS project.

24.12. Assume you are a software project manager and that you've been asked to compute earned value statistics for a small software project. The project has 56 planned work tasks that are estimated to require 582 person-days to complete. At the time that you've been asked to do the earned value analysis, 12 tasks have been completed. However the project schedule indicates that 15 tasks should have been completed. The following scheduling data (in person-days) are available:

Task	Planned Effort	Actual Effort
1	12.0	12.5
2	15.0	11.0
3	13.0	17.0
4	8.0	9.5
5	9.5	9.0
6	18.0	19.0
7	10.0	10.0
8	4.0	4.5
9	12.0	10.0
10	6.0	6.5
11	5.0	4.0
12	14.0	14.5
13	16.0	—
14	6.0	—
15	8.0	—

Compute the SPI, schedule variance, percent scheduled for completion, percent complete, CPI, and cost variance for the project.

Further Readings and Information Sources

Virtually every book written on software project management contains a discussion of scheduling. The Project Management Institute (*PMBOK Guide,* PMI, 2001), Wysoki and his colleagues (*Effective Project Management,* Wiley, 2000), Lewis (*Project Planning Scheduling and Control,* third edition, McGraw-Hill, 2000), Bennatan (*On Time, Within Budget: Software Project Management Practices and Techniques,* third edition, Wiley, 2000), McConnell (*Software Project Survival Guide,* Microsoft Press, 1998), and Roetzheim and Beasley (*Software Project Cost and Schedule Estimating: Best Practices,* Prentice-Hall, 1997) contain worthwhile discussions of the subject. Boddie (Crunch Mode, Prentice-Hall, 1987) has written a book for all managers who "have 90 days to do a six-month project."

McConnell (*Rapid Development,* Microsoft Press, 1996) presents an excellent discussion of the issues that lead to overly optimistic software project scheduling and what you can do about it. O'Connell (*How to Run Successful Projects II: The Silver Bullet,* Prentice-Hall, 1997) presents a step-by-step approach to project management that will help you develop a realistic schedule for your projects.

Webb and Wake (*Using Earned Value: A Project Manager's Guide,* Ashgate Publishing, 2003) and Fleming and Koppelman (*Earned Value Project Management,* Project Management Institute Publications, 1996) discuss the use of earned value techniques for project planning, tracking, and control in considerable detail.

A wide variety of information sources on software project scheduling is available on the Internet. An up-to-date list of World Wide Web references can be found at the SEPA Web site: **http://www.mhhe.com/pressman.**

CHAPTER

25 RISK MANAGEMENT

KEY CONCEPTS

In his book on risk analysis and management, Robert Charette [CHA89] presents a conceptual definition of risk:

> First, risk concerns future happenings. Today and yesterday are beyond active concern, as we are already reaping what was previously sowed by our past actions. The question is, can we, therefore, by changing our actions today, create an opportunity for a different and hopefully better situation for ourselves tomorrow. This means, second, that risk involves change, such as in changes of mind, opinion, actions, or places ... [Third,] risk involves choice, and the uncertainty that choice itself entails. Thus paradoxically, risk, like death and taxes, is one of the few certainties of life.

When risk is considered in the context of software engineering, Charette's three conceptual underpinnings are always in evidence. The future is our concern—what risks might cause the software project to go awry? Change is our concern—how will changes in customer requirements, development technologies, target environments, and all other entities connected to the project affect timeliness and overall success? Last, we must grapple with choices—what methods and tools should we use, how many people should be involved, how much emphasis on quality is "enough"?

Peter Drucker [DRU75] once said, "While it is futile to try to eliminate risk, and questionable to try to minimize it, it is essential that the risks taken be the right risks." Before we can identify the "right risks" to be taken during a software project, it is important to identify all risks that are obvious to both managers and practitioners.

QUICK LOOK

What is it? Risk analysis and management are a series of steps that help a software team to understand and manage uncertainty. Many problems can plague a software project. A risk is a potential problem—it might happen, it might not. But, regardless of the outcome, it's a really good idea to identify it, assess its probability of occurrence, estimate its impact, and establish a contingency plan should the problem actually occur.

Who does it? Everyone involved in the software process—managers, software engineers, and stakeholders—participate in risk analysis and management.

Why is it important? Think about the Boy Scout motto: Be prepared. Software is a difficult undertaking. Lots of things can go wrong, and frankly, many often do. It's for this reason that being prepared—understanding the risks and taking proactive measures to avoid or manage them—is a key element of good software project management.

What are the steps? Recognizing what can go wrong is the first step, called "risk identification." Next, each risk is analyzed to determine the likelihood that it will occur and the damage that it will do if it does occur. Once this information is established, risks are ranked, by probability and impact. Finally, a plan is developed to manage those risks with high probability and high impact.

What is the work product? A risk mitigation, monitoring, and management (RMMM) plan or a set of risk information sheets is produced.

How do I ensure that I've done it right? The risks that are analyzed and managed should be derived from thorough study of the people, the product, the process, and the project. The RMMM plan should be revisited as the project proceeds to ensure that risks are kept up to date. Contingency plans for risk management should be realistic.

25.1 Reactive vs. Proactive Risk Strategies

Reactive risk strategies have been laughingly called the "Indiana Jones school of risk management" [THO92]. In the 1980s-era movies that carried his name, Indiana Jones, when faced with overwhelming difficulty, would invariably say, "Don't worry, I'll think of something!" Never worrying about problems until they happened, Indy would react in some heroic way.

> "If you don't actively attack the risks, they will actively attack you."
>
> **Tom Gilb**

Sadly, the average software project manager is not Indiana Jones, and the members of the software project team are not his trusty sidekicks. Yet, the majority of software teams rely solely on reactive risk strategies. At best, a reactive strategy monitors the project for likely risks. Resources are set aside to deal with them, should they become actual problems. More commonly, the software team does nothing about risks until something goes wrong. Then, the team flies into action in an attempt to correct the problem rapidly. This is often called a *fire-fighting mode.* When this fails, "crisis management" [CHA92] takes over and the project is in real jeopardy.

A considerably more intelligent strategy for risk management is to be proactive. A proactive strategy begins long before technical work is initiated. Potential risks are identified, their probability and impact are assessed, and they are ranked by importance. Then, the software team establishes a plan for managing risk. The primary objective is to avoid risk, but because not all risks can be avoided, the team works to develop a contingency plan that will enable it to respond in a controlled and effective manner. Throughout the remainder of this chapter, we discuss a proactive strategy for risk management.

25.2 Software Risks

Although there has been considerable debate about the proper definition for software risk, there is general agreement that risk always involves two characteristics [HIG95]:

- *Uncertainty*—the risk may or may not happen; that is, there are no 100% probable risks.[1]
- *Loss*—if the risk becomes a reality, unwanted consequences or losses will occur.

When risks are analyzed, it is important to quantify the level of uncertainty and the degree of loss associated with each risk. To accomplish this, different categories of risks are considered.

? What types of risks are we likely to encounter as software is built?

Project risks threaten the project plan. That is, if project risks become real, it is likely that project schedule will slip and that costs will increase. Project risks identify potential budgetary, schedule, personnel (staffing and organization), resource, stakeholder, and requirements problems and their impact on a software project. In Chapter 23, project complexity, size, and the degree of structural uncertainty were also defined as project (and estimation) risk factors.

Technical risks threaten the quality and timeliness of the software to be produced. If a technical risk becomes a reality, implementation may become difficult or impossible. Technical risks identify potential design, implementation, interface, verification, and maintenance problems. In addition, specification ambiguity, technical uncertainty, technical obsolescence, and "leading-edge" technology are also risk factors. Technical risks occur because the problem is harder to solve than we thought it would be.

Business risks threaten the viability of the software to be built. Business risks often jeopardize the project or the product. Candidates for the top five business risks are (1) building an excellent product or system that no one really wants (market risk), (2) building a product that no longer fits into the overall business strategy for the company (strategic risk), (3) building a product that the sales force doesn't understand how to sell (sales risk), (4) losing the support of senior management due to a change in focus or a change in people (management risk), and (5) losing budgetary or personnel commitment (budget risk).

It is extremely important to note that simple risk categorization won't always work. Some risks are simply unpredictable in advance.

Another general categorization of risks has been proposed by Charette [CHA89]. *Known risks* are those that can be uncovered after careful evaluation of the project plan, the business and technical environment in which the project is being developed, and other reliable information sources (e.g., unrealistic delivery date, lack of documented requirements or software scope, poor development environment). *Pre-*

---

1 A risk that is 100 percent probable is a constraint on the software project.

dictable risks are extrapolated from past project experience (e.g., staff turnover, poor communication with the customer, dilution of staff effort as ongoing maintenance requests are serviced). *Unpredictable risks* are the joker in the deck. They can and do occur, but they are extremely difficult to identify in advance.

INFO

Seven Principles of Risk Management

The Software Engineering Institute (SEI) (www.sei.cmu.edu) identifies seven principles that "provide a framework to accomplish effective risk management." They are:

Maintain a global perspective—view software risks within the context of system in which it is a component and the business problem that it is intended to solve.

Take a forward-looking view—think about the risks that may arise in the future (e.g., due to changes in the software); establish contingency plans so that future events are manageable.

Encourage open communication—if someone states a potential risk, don't discount it. If a risk is proposed in an informal manner, consider it. Encourage all stakeholders and users to suggest risks at any time.

Integrate—a consideration of risk must be integrated into the software process.

Emphasize a continuous process—the team must be vigilant throughout the software process, modifying identified risks as more information is known and adding new ones as better insight is achieved.

Develop a shared product vision—if all stakeholders share the same vision of the software, it is likely that better risk identification and assessment will occur.

Encourage teamwork—the talents, skills and knowledge of all stakeholders should be pooled when risk management activities are conducted.

25.3 Risk Identification

Risk identification is a systematic attempt to specify threats to the project plan (estimates, schedule, resource loading, etc.). By identifying known and predictable risks, the project manager takes a first step toward avoiding them when possible and controlling them when necessary.

There are two distinct types of risks for each of the categories that have been presented in Section 25.2: generic risks and product-specific risks. *Generic risks* are a potential threat to every software project. *Product-specific risks* can be identified only by those with a clear understanding of the technology, the people, and the environment that is specific to the software that is to be built. To identify product-specific risks, the project plan and the software statement of scope are examined, and an answer to the following question is developed: "What special characteristics of this product may threaten our project plan?"

> "Projects with no real risks are losers. They are almost always devoid of benefit; that's why they weren't done years ago."
>
> **Tom DeMarco and Tim Lister**

Although generic risks are important to consider, it's the product-specific risks that cause the most headaches. Be certain to spend the time to identify as many product-specific risks as possible.

One method for identifying risks is to create a risk item checklist. The checklist can be used for risk identification and focuses on some subset of known and predictable risks in the following generic subcategories:

- *Product size*—risks associated with the overall size of the software to be built or modified.
- *Business impact*—risks associated with constraints imposed by management or the marketplace.
- *Customer characteristics*—risks associated with the sophistication of the customer and the developer's ability to communicate with the customer in a timely manner.
- *Process definition*—risks associated with the degree to which the software process has been defined and is followed by the development organization.
- *Development environment*—risks associated with the availability and quality of the tools to be used to build the product.
- *Technology to be built*—risks associated with the complexity of the system to be built and the "newness" of the technology that is packaged by the system.
- *Staff size and experience*—risks associated with the overall technical and project experience of the software engineers who will do the work.

The risk item checklist can be organized in different ways. Questions relevant to each of the topics can be answered for each software project. The answers to these questions allow the planner to estimate the impact of risk. A different risk item checklist format simply lists characteristics that are relevant to each generic subcategory. Finally, a set of "risk components and drivers" [AFC88] are listed along with their probability of occurrence. Drivers for performance, support, cost, and schedule are discussed in answer to later questions.

A number of comprehensive checklists for software project risk have been proposed in the literature (e.g., [SEI93], [KAR96]). These provide useful insight into generic risks for software projects and should be used whenever risk analysis and management are instituted. However, a relatively short list of questions [KEI98] can be used to provide a preliminary indication of whether a project is "at risk."

25.3.1 Assessing Overall Project Risk

The following questions have been derived from risk data obtained by surveying experienced software project managers in different parts of the world [KEI98]. The questions are ordered by their relative importance to the success of a project.

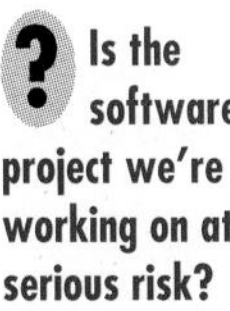

Is the software project we're working on at serious risk?

1. Have top software and customer managers formally committed to support the project?
2. Are end-users enthusiastically committed to the project and the system/product to be built?

3. Are requirements fully understood by the software engineering team and its customers?
4. Have customers been involved fully in the definition of requirements?
5. Do end-users have realistic expectations?
6. Is project scope stable?
7. Does the software engineering team have the right mix of skills?
8. Are project requirements stable?
9. Does the project team have experience with the technology to be implemented?
10. Is the number of people on the project team adequate to do the job?
11. Do all customer/user constituencies agree on the importance of the project and on the requirements for the system/product to be built?

WebRef
Risk radar is a database and tools that help managers identify, rank, and communicate project risks. It can be found at **www.spmn.com.**

> "Risk management is project management for adults."
>
> **Tim Lister**

If any one of these questions is answered negatively, mitigation, monitoring, and management steps should be instituted without fail. The degree to which the project is at risk is directly proportional to the number of negative responses to these questions.

25.3.2 Risk Components and Drivers

The U.S. Air Force [AFC88] has written a pamphlet that contains excellent guidelines for software risk identification and abatement. The Air Force approach requires that the project manager identify the risk drivers that affect software risk components—performance, cost, support, and schedule. In the context of this discussion, the risk components are defined in the following manner:

- *Performance risk*—the degree of uncertainty that the product will meet its requirements and be fit for its intended use.
- *Cost risk*—the degree of uncertainty that the project budget will be maintained.
- *Support risk*—the degree of uncertainty that the resultant software will be easy to correct, adapt, and enhance.
- *Schedule risk*—the degree of uncertainty that the project schedule will be maintained and that the product will be delivered on time.

The impact of each risk driver on the risk component is divided into one of four impact categories—negligible, marginal, critical, or catastrophic. Referring to Figure 25.1 [BOE89], a characterization of the potential consequences of errors (rows labeled 1) or a failure to achieve a desired outcome (rows labeled 2) are described. The impact category is chosen based on the characterization that best fits the description in the table.

FIGURE 25.1

Impact assessment [BOE89]

Category \ Components		Performance	Support	Cost	Schedule
Catastrophic	1	Failure to meet the requirement would result in mission failure		Failure results in increased costs and schedule delays with expected values in excess of $500K	
	2	Significant degradation to nonachievement of technical performance	Nonresponsive or unsupportable software	Significant financial shortages, budget overrun likely	Unachievable IOC
Critical	1	Failure to meet the requirement would degrade system performance to a point where mission success is questionable		Failure results in operational delays and/or increased costs with expected value of $100K to $500K	
	2	Some reduction in technical performance	Minor delays in software modifications	Some shortage of financial resources, possible overruns	Possible slippage in IOC
Marginal	1	Failure to meet the requirement would result in degradation of secondary mission		Costs, impacts, and/or recoverable schedule slips with expected value of $1K to $100K	
	2	Minimal to small reduction in technical performance	Responsive software support	Sufficient financial resources	Realistic, achievable schedule
Negligible	1	Failure to meet the requirement would create inconvenience or nonoperational impact		Error results in minor cost and/or schedule impact with expected value of less than $1K	
	2	No reduction in technical performance	Easily supportable software	Possible budget underrun	Early achievable IOC

Note: (1) The potential consequence of undetected software errors or faults.
(2) The potential consequence if the desired outcome is not achieved.

25.4 Risk Projection

Risk projection, also called *risk estimation,* attempts to rate each risk in two ways—(1) the likelihood or probability that the risk is real and (2) the consequences of the problems associated with the risk, should it occur. The project planner, along with other managers and technical staff, performs four risk projection steps:

1. Establish a scale that reflects the perceived likelihood of a risk.
2. Delineate the consequences of the risk.
3. Estimate the impact of the risk on the project and the product.
4. Note the overall accuracy of the risk projection so that there will be no misunderstandings.

The intent of these steps is to consider risks in a manner that leads to prioritization. No software team has the resources to address every possible risk with the same de-

FIGURE 25.2

Sample risk table prior to sorting

Risks	Category	Probability	Impact	RMMM
Size estimate may be significantly low	PS	60%	2	
Larger number of users than planned	PS	30%	3	
Less reuse than planned	PS	70%	2	
End-users resist system	BU	40%	3	
Delivery deadline will be tightened	BU	50%	2	
Funding will be lost	CU	40%	1	
Customer will change requirements	PS	80%	2	
Technology will not meet expectations	TE	30%	1	
Lack of training on tools	DE	80%	3	
Staff inexperienced	ST	30%	2	
Staff turnover will be high	ST	60%	2	
• • •				

Impact values:
1—catastrophic
2—critical
3—marginal
4—negligible

gree of rigor. By prioritizing risks, the team can allocate resources where they will have the most impact.

25.4.1 Developing a Risk Table

A risk table provides a project manager with a simple technique for risk projection.[2] A sample risk table is illustrated in Figure 25.2.

Think hard about the software you're about to build and ask, yourself, what can go wrong? Create your own list and ask other members of the team to do the same.

A project team begins by listing all risks (no matter how remote) in the first column of the table. This can be accomplished with the help of the risk item checklists referenced in Section 25.3. Each risk is categorized in the second column (e.g., PS implies a project size risk, BU implies a business risk). The probability of occurrence of each risk is entered in the next column of the table. The probability value for each risk can be estimated by team members individually. Individual team members are polled in round-robin fashion until their assessment of risk probability begins to converge.

Next, the impact of each risk is assessed. Each risk component is assessed using the characterization presented in Figure 25.1, and an impact category is determined. The categories for each of the four risk components—performance, support, cost, and schedule—are averaged[3] to determine an overall impact value.

---

2 The risk table can be implemented as a spreadsheet model. This enables easy manipulation and sorting of the entries.

3 A weighted average can be used if one risk component has more significance for a project.

A risk table is sorted by probability and impact to rank risks.

Once the first four columns of the risk table have been completed, the table is sorted by probability and by impact. High-probability, high-impact risks percolate to the top of the table, and low-probability risks drop to the bottom. This accomplishes first-order risk prioritization.

The project manager studies the resultant sorted table and defines a cutoff line. The *cutoff line* (drawn horizontally at some point in the table) implies that only risks that lie above the line will be given further attention. Risks that fall below the line are reevaluated to accomplish second-order prioritization. Referring to Figure 25.3, risk impact and probability have a distinct influence on management concern. A risk factor that has a high impact but a very low probability of occurrence should not absorb a significant amount of management time. However, high-impact risks with moderate to high probability and low-impact risks with high probability should be carried forward into the risk analysis steps that follow.

All risks that lie above the cutoff line must be managed. The column labeled RMMM contains a pointer into a *Risk Mitigation, Monitoring, and Management Plan* or alternatively, a collection of *risk information sheets* developed for all risks that lie above the cutoff. The RMMM plan and risk information sheets are discussed in Sections 25.5 and 25.6.

> "[Today,] no one has the luxury of getting to know a task so well that it holds no surprises, and surprises mean risk."
> **Stephen Grey**

Risk probability can be determined by making individual estimates and then developing a single consensus value. Although that approach is workable, more so-

FIGURE 25.3

Risk and management concern

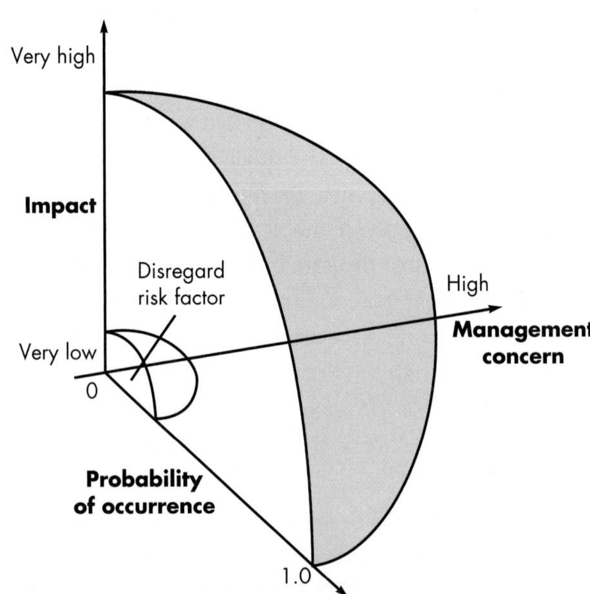

phisticated techniques for determining risk probability have been developed [AFC88]. Risk drivers can be assessed on a qualitative probability scale that has the following values: impossible, improbable, probable, and frequent. Mathematical probability can then be associated with each qualitative value (e.g., a probability of 0.7 to 0.95 implies a highly probable risk).

25.4.2 Assessing Risk Impact

Three factors affect the consequences that are likely if a risk does occur: its nature, scope, and timing. The nature of the risk indicates the problems that are likely if it occurs. For example, a poorly defined external interface to customer hardware (a technical risk) will preclude early design and testing and will likely lead to system integration problems late in a project. The scope of a risk combines the severity (just how serious is it?) with its overall distribution (how much of the project will be affected, or how many customers are harmed?). Finally, the timing of a risk considers when and for how long the impact will be felt. In most cases, a project manager might want the "bad news" to occur as soon as possible, but in some cases, the longer the delay, the better.

Returning once more to the risk analysis approach proposed by the U.S. Air Force [AFC88], the following steps are recommended to determine the overall consequences of a risk:

? How do we assess the consequences of a risk?

1. Determine the average probability of occurrence value for each risk component.
2. Using Figure 25.1, determine the impact for each component based on the criteria shown.
3. Complete the risk table and analyze the results as described in the preceding sections.

The overall *risk exposure,* RE, is determined using the following relationship [HAL98]:

$$\text{RE} = P \times C$$

where P is the probability of occurrence for a risk, and C is the cost to the project should the risk occur.

For example, assume that the software team defines a project risk in the following manner:

Risk identification. Only 70 percent of the software components scheduled for reuse will, in fact, be integrated into the application. The remaining functionality will have to be custom developed.

Risk probability. 80 percent (likely).

Risk impact. 60 reusable software components were planned. If only 70 percent can be used, 18 components would have to be developed from scratch (in addition to other custom software that has been scheduled for development). Since the average component is 100 LOC and local data indicate that the software engineering cost for each LOC is $14.00, the overall cost (impact) to develop the components would be $18 \times 100 \times 14 = \$25,200$.

Risk exposure. RE $= 0.80 \times 25,200 \sim \$20,200$.

Compare RE for all risks to the cost estimate for the project. If RE is greater than 50 percent of the project cost, the viability of the project must be reevaluated.

Risk exposure can be computed for each risk in the risk table, once an estimate of the cost of the risk is made. The total risk exposure for all risks (above the cutoff line in the risk table) can provide a means for adjusting the final cost estimate for a project. It can also be used to predict the probable increase in staff resources required at various points during the project schedule.

The risk projection and analysis techniques described in Sections 25.4.1 and 25.4.2 are applied iteratively as the software project proceeds. The project team should revisit the risk table at regular intervals, reevaluating each risk to determine when new circumstances cause its probability and impact to change. As a consequence of this activity, it may be necessary to add new risks to the table, remove some risks that are no longer relevant, and change the relative positions of others.

SAFEHOME

Risk Analysis

The scene: Doug Miller's office, prior to the initiation of the *SafeHome* software project.

The players: Doug Miller (manager of the *SafeHome* software engineering team) and Vinod Raman, Jamie Lazar, and other members of the product software engineering team.

The conversation:

Doug: I'd like to spend some time brainstorming risks for the *SafeHome* project.

Jamie: As in what can go wrong?

Doug: Yep. Here are a few categories where things can go wrong. [He shows everyone the categories noted in the introduction to Section 25.3.]

Vinod: Umm . . . do you want us to just call them out, or . . .

Doug: No here's what I thought we'd do. Everyone make a list of risks . . . right now . . .

(Ten minutes pass; everyone is writing.)

Doug: Okay, stop.

Jamie: But I'm not done!

Doug: That's okay. We'll revisit the list again. Now, for each item on your list, assign a percent likelihood that the risk will occur. Then, assign an impact to the project on a scale of 1 (minor) to 5 (catastrophic).

Vinod: So if I think that the risk is a coin flip, I specify a 50 percent likelihood, and if I think it'll have a moderate project impact, I specify a 3, right?

Doug: Exactly.

(Five minutes pass; everyone is writing.)

Doug: Okay, stop. Now we'll make a group list on the white board. I'll do the writing, we'll call out one entry from your list in round robin format.

(Fifteen minutes pass; the list is created.)

Jamie (pointing at the board and laughing): Vinod, that risk (pointing toward an entry on the board) is ridiculous. There's a higher likelihood that we'll all get hit by lightning. We should remove it.

Doug: No, let's leave it for now. We consider all risks, no matter how weird. Later we'll winnow the list.

Jamie: But we already have over 40 risks . . . how on earth can we manage them all?

Doug: We can't. That's why we'll define a cut-off after we sort these guys. I'll do that off-line, and we'll meet again tomorrow. For now, get back to work . . . and in your spare time, think about any risks that we've missed.

25.5 Risk Refinement

During early stages of project planning, a risk may be stated quite generally. As time passes and more is learned about the project and the risk, it may be possible to refine the risk into a set of more detailed risks, each somewhat easier to mitigate, monitor, and manage.

? What's a good way to describe a risk?

One way to do this is to represent the risk in *condition-transition-consequence* (CTC) format [GLU94]. That is, the risk is stated in the following form:

> Given that <condition> then there is concern that (possibly) <consequence>.

Using the CTC format for the reuse risk noted in Section 25.4.2, we can write:

> Given that all reusable software components must conform to specific design standards and that some do not conform, then there is concern that (possibly) only 70 percent of the planned reusable modules may actually be integrated into the as-built system, resulting in the need to custom engineer the remaining 30 percent of components.

This general condition can be refined in the following manner:

Subcondition 1. Certain reusable components were developed by a third party with no knowledge of internal design standards.

Subcondition 2. The design standard for component interfaces has not been solidified and may not conform to certain existing reusable components.

Subcondition 3. Certain reusable components have been implemented in a language that is not supported on the target environment.

The consequences associated with these refined subconditions remain the same (i.e., 30 percent of software components must be custom engineered), but the refinement helps to isolate the underlying risks and might lead to easier analysis and response.

25.6 Risk Mitigation, Monitoring, and Management

All of the risk analysis activities presented to this point have a single goal—to assist the project team in developing a strategy for dealing with risk. An effective strategy must consider three issues:

- Risk avoidance.
- Risk monitoring.
- Risk management and contingency planning.

If a software team adopts a proactive approach to risk, avoidance is always the best strategy. This is achieved by developing a plan for risk mitigation. For example, assume that high staff turnover is noted as a project risk, r_1. Based on past history and management intuition, the likelihood, l_1, of high turnover is estimated to be 0.70 (70 percent, rather high) and the impact, x_1, is projected as critical. That is, high turnover will have a critical impact on project cost and schedule.

> "If I take so many precautions, it is because I leave nothing to chance."
>
> **Napoleon**

To mitigate this risk, project management must develop a strategy for reducing turnover. Among the possible steps to be taken are:

? What can we do to mitigate a risk?

- Meet with current staff to determine causes for turnover (e.g., poor working conditions, low pay, competitive job market).
- Mitigate those causes that are under our control before the project starts.
- Once the project commences, assume turnover will occur and develop techniques to ensure continuity when people leave.
- Organize project teams so that information about each development activity is widely dispersed.
- Define documentation standards and establish mechanisms to ensure that documents are developed in a timely manner.
- Conduct peer reviews of all work (so that more than one person is "up to speed").
- Assign a backup staff member for every critical technologist.

As the project proceeds, risk monitoring activities commence. The project manager monitors factors that may provide an indication of whether the risk is becoming more or less likely. In the case of high staff turnover, the following factors can be monitored:

- General attitude of team members based on project pressures.
- The degree to which the team has jelled.
- Interpersonal relationships among team members.
- Potential problems with compensation and benefits.
- The availability of jobs within the company and outside it.

In addition to monitoring these factors, a project manager should monitor the effectiveness of risk mitigation steps. For example, a risk mitigation step noted earlier called for the definition of documentation standards and mechanisms to be sure that documents are developed in a timely manner. This is one mechanism for ensuring continuity, should a critical individual leave the project. The project manager should monitor documents carefully to ensure that each can stand on its own and that each imparts information that would be necessary if a newcomer were forced to join the software team somewhere in the middle of the project.

Risk management and contingency planning assumes that mitigation efforts have failed and that the risk has become a reality. Continuing the example, the project is well underway, and a number of people announce that they will be leaving. If the mitigation strategy has been followed, backup is available, information is documented, and knowledge has been dispersed across the team. In addition, the project manager may temporarily refocus resources (and readjust the project schedule) to those functions that are fully staffed, enabling newcomers who must be added to the team to "get up to speed." Those individuals who are leaving are asked to stop all work and spend their last weeks in "knowledge transfer mode." This might include video-based knowledge capture, the development of "commentary documents," and/or meeting with other team members who will remain on the project.

If RE for a specific risk is less than the cost of risk mitigation, don't try to mitigate the risk but continue to monitor it.

It is important to note that risk mitigation, monitoring, and management (RMMM) steps incur additional project cost. For example, spending the time to "backup" every critical technologist costs money. Part of risk management, therefore, is to evaluate when the benefits accrued by the RMMM steps are outweighed by the costs associated with implementing them. In essence, the project planner performs a classic cost/benefit analysis. If risk aversion steps for high turnover will increase both project cost and duration by an estimated 15 percent, but the predominant cost factor is "backup," management may decide not to implement this step. On the other hand, if the risk aversion steps are projected to increase costs by 5 percent and duration by only 3 percent, management will likely put all into place.

For a large project, 30 or 40 risks may be identified. If between three and seven risk management steps are identified for each, risk management may become a project in itself! For this reason, we adapt the Pareto 80-20 rule to software risk. Experience indicates that 80 percent of the overall project risk (i.e., 80 percent of the potential for project failure) can be accounted for by only 20 percent of the identified risks. The work performed during earlier risk analysis steps will help the planner to determine which of the risks reside in that 20 percent (e.g., risks that lead to the highest risk exposure). For this reason, some of the risks identified, assessed, and projected may not make it into the RMMM plan—they don't fall into the critical 20 percent (the risks with highest project priority).

WebRef

A voluminous archive containing all entries from the ACM Forum on Risks to the Public can be found at **catless.ncl.ac.uk/Risks.**

Risk is not limited to the software project itself. Risks can occur after the software has been successfully developed and delivered to the customer. These risks are typically associated with the consequences of software failure in the field.

Software safety and hazard analysis [LEV95] are software quality assurance activities (Chapter 26) that focus on the identification and assessment of potential hazards that may affect software negatively and cause an entire system to fail. If hazards can be identified early in the software engineering process, software design features can be specified that will either eliminate or control potential hazards.

25.7 The RMMM Plan

A risk management strategy can be included in the software project plan or the risk management steps can be organized into a separate *Risk Mitigation, Monitoring and Management Plan.* The RMMM plan documents all work performed as part of risk analysis and is used by the project manager as part of the overall project plan.

Some software teams do not develop a formal RMMM document. Rather, each risk is documented individually using a *risk information sheet* (RIS) [WIL97]. In most cases, the RIS is maintained using a database system, so that creation and information entry, priority ordering, searches, and other analysis may be accomplished easily. The format of the RIS is illustrated in Figure 25.4.

Once RMMM has been documented and the project has begun, risk mitigation and monitoring steps commence. As we have already discussed, risk mitigation is a problem avoidance activity. Risk monitoring is a project tracking activity with three

Figure 25.4

Risk information sheet [WIL97]

Risk information sheet			
Risk ID: P02-4-32	Date: 5/9/04	Prob: 80%	Impact: high

Description:
Only 70 percent of the software components scheduled for reuse will, in fact, be integrated into the application. The remaining functionality will have to be custom developed.

Refinement/context:
Subcondition 1: Certain reusable components were developed by a third party with no knowledge of internal design standards.
Subcondition 2: The design standard for component interfaces has not been solidified and may not conform to certain existing reusable components.
Subcondition 3: Certain reusable components have been implemented in a language that is not supported on the target environment.

Mitigation/monitoring:
1. Contact third party to determine conformance with design standards.
2. Press for interface standards completion; consider component structure when deciding on interface protocol.
3. Check to determine number of components in subcondition 3 category; check to determine if language support can be acquired.

Management/contingency plan/trigger:
RE computed to be $20,200. Allocate this amount within project contingency cost. Develop revised schedule assuming that 18 additional components will have to be custom built; allocate staff accordingly.
Trigger: Mitigation steps unproductive as of 7/1/04

Current status:
5/12/04: Mitigation steps initiated.

Originator: D. Gagne	Assigned: B. Laster

primary objectives: (1) to assess whether predicted risks do, in fact, occur; (2) to ensure that risk aversion steps defined for the risk are being properly applied; and (3) to collect information that can be used for future risk analysis. In many cases, the problems that occur during a project can be traced to more than one risk. Another job of risk monitoring is to attempt to allocate origin (what risk(s) caused which problems throughout the project).

SOFTWARE TOOLS

Risk Management

Objective: The objective of risk management tools is to assist a project team in defining risks, assessing their impact and probability, and tracking risks throughout a software project.

Mechanics: In general, risk management tools assist in generic risk identification by providing a list of typical project and business risks, providing checklists or other "interview" techniques that assist in identifying project specific risks, assigning probability and impact to each risk, supporting risk mitigation strategies, and generating many different risk-related reports.

Representative Tools[4]

Riskman, developed at Arizona State University (www.eas.asu.edu/~sdm/merrill/riskman.html), is a risk evaluation expert system that identifies project-related risks.

Risk Radar, developed by SPMN (www.spmn.com), assists project managers in identifying and managing project risks.

RiskTrak, developed by RST (www.risktrac.com), supports the identification, analysis, reporting, and management of risks throughout a software project.

Risk+, developed by C/S Solutions (www.CS-solutions.com), integrates with Microsoft Project to quantify cost and schedule uncertainty.

X:PRIMER, developed by GrafP Technologies (www.grafp.com), is a generic Web-based tool that predicts what can go wrong on a project and identifies root causes for potential failures and effective countermeasures.

25.8 SUMMARY

Whenever a lot is riding on a software project, common sense dictates risk analysis. And yet, most software project managers do it informally and superficially, if they do it at all. The time spent identifying, analyzing, and managing risk pays itself back in many ways: less upheaval during the project, a greater ability to track and control a project, and the confidence that comes with planning for problems before they occur.

Risk analysis can absorb a significant amount of project planning effort. Identification, projection, assessment, management, and monitoring all take time. But the effort is worth it. To quote Sun Tzu, a Chinese general who lived 2500 years ago, "If you know the enemy and know yourself, you need not fear the result of a hundred battles." For the software project manager, the enemy is risk.

4 Tools noted here do not represent an endorsement, but rather a sampling of tools in this category. In most cases, tool names are trademarked by their respective developers.

REFERENCES

[AFC88] *Software Risk Abatement,* AFCS/AFLC Pamphlet 800-45, U.S. Air Force, September 30, 1988.

[BOE89] Boehm, B. W., *Software Risk Management,* IEEE Computer Society Press, 1989.

[CHA89] Charette, R. N., *Software Engineering Risk Analysis and Management,* McGraw-Hill/Intertext, 1989.

[CHA92] Charette, R. N., "Building Bridges over Intelligent Rivers," *American Programmer,* vol. 5, no. 7, September, 1992, pp. 2–9.

[DRU75] Drucker, P., *Management,* W. H. Heinemann, 1975.

[GIL88] Gilb, T., *Principles of Software Engineering Management,* Addison-Wesley, 1988.

[GLU94] Gluch, D. P., "A Construct for Describing Software Development Risks," CMU/SEI-94-TR-14, Software Engineering Institute, 1994.

[HAL98] Hall, E. M., *Managing Risk: Methods for Software Systems Development,* Addison-Wesley, 1998.

[HIG95] Higuera, R. P., "Team Risk Management," *CrossTalk,* U.S. Dept. of Defense, January 1995, pp. 2–4.

[KAR96] Karolak, D. W., *Software Engineering Risk Management,* IEEE Computer Society Press, 1996.

[KEI98] Keil, M., et al., "A Framework for Identifying Software Project Risks," *CACM,* vol. 41, no. 1, November 1998, pp. 76–83.

[LEV95] Leveson, N. G., *Safeware: System Safety and Computers,* Addison-Wesley, 1995.

[SEI93] "Taxonomy-Based Risk Identification," Software Engineering Institute, CMU/SEI-93-TR-6, 1993.

[THO92] Thomsett, R., "The Indiana Jones School of Risk Management," *American Programmer,* vol. 5, no. 7, September 1992, pp. 10–18.

[WIL97] Williams, R. C., J. A. Walker, and A. J. Dorofee, "Putting Risk Management into Practice," *IEEE Software,* May 1997, pp. 75–81.

PROBLEMS AND POINTS TO PONDER

25.1. Provide five examples from other fields that illustrate the problems associated with a reactive risk strategy.

25.2. Describe the difference between "known risks" and "predictable risks."

25.3. Add three additional questions or topics to each of the risk item checklists presented at the SEPA Web site.

25.4. You've been asked to build software to support a low-cost video editing system. The system accepts digital video as input, stores the video on disk, and then allows the user to do a wide range of edits to the digitized video. The result can then be output to DVD or other media. Do a small amount of research on systems of this type, and then make a list of technology risks that you would face as you begin a project of this type.

25.5. You're the project manager for a major software company. You've been asked to lead a team that's developing "next generation" word-processing software. Create a risk table for the project.

25.6. Describe the difference between risk components and risk drivers.

25.7. Develop a risk mitigation strategy and specific risk mitigation activities for three of the risks noted in Figure 25.2.

25.8. Develop a risk monitoring strategy and specific risk monitoring activities for three of the risks noted in Figure 25.2. Be sure to identify the factors that you'll be monitoring to determine whether the risk is becoming more or less likely.

25.9. Develop a risk management strategy and specific risk management activities for three of the risks noted in Figure 25.2.

25.10. Attempt to refine three of the risks noted in Figure 25.2 and then create risk information sheets for each.

25.11. Represent three of the risks noted in Figure 25.2 using a CTC format.

25.12. Recompute the risk exposure discussed in Section 25.4.2 when cost/LOC is $16 and the probability is 60 percent.

25.13. Can you think of a situation in which a high-probability, high-impact risk would not be considered as part of your RMMM plan?

25.14. Describe five software application areas in which software safety and hazard analysis would be a major concern.

Further Readings and Information Sources

The software risk management literature has expanded significantly over the past decade. DeMarco and Lister (*Dancing with Bears,* Dorset House, 2003) have written an entertaining and insightful book that guides software managers and practitioners through risk management. Moynihan (*Coping with IT/IS Risk Management,* Springer-Verlag, 2002) presents pragmatic advice from project managers who deal with risk on a continuing basis. Royer (*Project Risk Management,* Management Concepts, 2002) and Smith and Merritt (*Proactive Risk Management,* Productivity Press, 2002) suggest a proactive process for risk management. Karolak(*Software Engineering Risk Management,* Wiley, 2002) has written a guidebook that introduces an easy-to-use risk analysis model with worthwhile checklists and questionnaires supported by a software package.

Schuyler (*Risk and Decision Analysis in Projects,* PMI, 2001) considers risk analysis from a statistical perspective. Hall (*Managing Risk: Methods for Software Systems Development,* Addison-Wesley, 1998) presents one of the more thorough treatments of the subject. Myerson (*Risk Management Processing for Software Engineering Models,* Artech House, 1997) considers metrics, security, process models and other topics. A useful snapshot of risk assessment has been written by Grey (*Practical Risk Assessment for Project Management,* Wiley, 1995). His abbreviated treatment provides a good introduction to the subject.

Capers Jones (*Assessment and Control of Software Risks,* Prentice-Hall, 1994) presents a detailed discussion of software risks that includes data collected from hundreds of software projects. Jones defines 60 risk factors that can affect the outcome of software projects. Boehm [BOE89] suggests excellent questionnaire and checklist formats that can prove invaluable in identifying risk. Charette [CHA89] presents a detailed treatment of the mechanics of risk analysis, calling on probability theory and statistical techniques to analyze risks. In a companion volume, Charette (*Application Strategies for Risk Analysis,* McGraw-Hill, 1990) discusses risk in the context of both system and software engineering and suggests pragmatic strategies for risk management. Gilb (*Principles of Software Engineering Management,* Addison-Wesley, 1988) presents a set of "principles" (which are often amusing and sometimes profound) that can serve as a worthwhile guide for risk management.

Ewusi-Mensah (*Software Development Failures: Anatomy of Abandoned Projects,* MIT Press, 2003) and Yourdon (*Death March,* Prentice-Hall, 1997) discuss what happens when risks overwhelm a software project team. Bernstein (*Against the Gods,* Wiley, 1998) presents an entertaining history of risk that goes back to ancient times.

The Software Engineering Institute has published many detailed reports and guidebooks on risk analysis and management. The Air Force Systems Command pamphlet AFSCP 800-45 [AFC88] describes risk identification and reduction techniques. Every issue of the *ACM Software Engineering Notes* has a section entitled "Risks to the Public" (editor, P. G. Neumann). If you want the latest and best software horror stories, this is the place to go.

A wide variety of information sources on software risk management is available on the Internet. An up-to-date list of World Wide Web references can be found at the SEPA Web site: **http://www.mhhe.com/pressman.**

CHAPTER

26 QUALITY MANAGEMENT

KEY CONCEPTS

The software engineering approach described in this book works toward a single goal: to produce high-quality software. Yet many readers will be challenged by the question: What is software quality?

Philip Crosby [CRO79], in his landmark book on quality, provides a wry answer to this question:

> The problem of quality management is not what people don't know about it. The problem is what they think they do know . . .
>
> In this regard, quality has much in common with sex. Everybody is for it. (Under certain conditions, of course.) Everyone feels they understand it. (Even though they wouldn't want to explain it.) Everyone thinks execution is only a matter of following natural inclinations. (After all, we do get along somehow.) And, of course, most people feel that problems in these areas are caused by other people. (If only they would take the time to do things right.)

Some software developers continue to believe that software quality is something you begin to worry about after code has been generated. Nothing could be further from the truth! *Quality management* (often called *software quality assurance*) is an umbrella activity (Chapter 2) that is applied throughout the software process.

Quality management encompasses (1) a software quality assurance (SQA) process; (2) specific quality assurance and quality control tasks (including formal technical reviews and a multitiered testing strategy); (3) effective software engineering practice (methods and tools); (4) control of all software work products

QUICK LOOK

What is it? It's not enough to talk the talk by saying that software quality is important. You have to (1) explicitly define what is meant when you say "software quality," (2) create a set of activities that will help ensure that every software engineering work product exhibits high quality, (3) perform quality control and assurance activities on every software project, (4) use metrics to develop strategies for improving your software process and, as a consequence, the quality of the end product.

Who does it? Everyone involved in the software engineering process is responsible for quality.

Why is it important? You can do it right, or you can do it over again. If a software team stresses quality in all software engineering activities, it reduces the amount of rework that it must do. That results in lower costs, and more importantly, improved time-to-market.

What are the steps? Before software quality assurance activities can be initiated, it is important to define "software quality" at a number of different levels of abstraction. Once you understand what quality is, a software team must identify a set of SQA activities that will filter errors out of work products before they are passed on.

What is the work product? A *Software Quality Assurance Plan* is created to define a software team's SQA strategy. During analysis, design, and code generation, the primary SQA work product is the formal technical review summary report. During testing, test plans and procedures are produced. Other work products associated with process improvement may also be generated.

How do I ensure that I've done it right? Find errors before they become defects! That is, work to improve your defect removal efficiency (Chapter 22), thereby reducing the amount of rework that your software team has to perform.

and the changes made to them (Chapter 27); (5) a procedure to ensure compliance with software development standards (when applicable), and (6) measurement and reporting mechanisms.

In this chapter, we focus on the management issues and the process-specific activities that enable a software organization to ensure that it does the right things at the right time in the right way.

26.1 Quality Concepts[1]

Controlling variation is the key to a high-quality product. In the software context, we strive to control the variation in the generic process we apply and the quality emphasis that permeates software engineering work.

Variation control is the heart of quality control. A manufacturer wants to minimize the variation among the products that are produced, even when doing something relatively simple like duplicating DVDs. Surely, this cannot be a problem—duplicating DVDs is a trivial manufacturing operation, and we can guarantee that exact duplicates of the software are always created.

Or can we? We need to ensure the tracks are placed on the DVDs within a specified tolerance so that the overwhelming majority of DVD drives can read the media. The disk duplication machines can, and do, wear and go out of tolerance. So even a "simple" process such as DVD duplication may encounter problems due to variation between samples.

But how does this apply to software work? How might a software development organization need to control variation? From one project to another, we want to minimize the difference between the predicted resources needed to complete a project and the actual resources used, including staff, equipment, and calendar time. In general, we would like to make sure our testing program covers a known percentage of the software, from one release to another. Not only do we want to minimize the number of defects that are released to the field, we'd like to ensure that the variance in the number of bugs is also minimized from one release to another. (Our customers will likely be upset if the third release of a product has 10 times as many

---

1 This section, written by Michael Stovsky, has been adapted from "Fundamentals of ISO 9000," a workbook developed for *Essential Software Engineering,* a video curriculum developed by R. S. Pressman & Associates, Inc. Reprinted with permission.

defects as the previous release.) We would like to minimize the differences in speed and accuracy of our hotline support responses to customer problems. The list goes on and on.

26.1.1 Quality

The *American Heritage Dictionary* defines *quality* as "a characteristic or attribute of something." As an attribute of an item, quality refers to measurable characteristics—things we can compare to known standards such as length, color, electrical properties, and malleability. However, software, largely an intellectual entity, is more challenging to characterize than physical objects.

Nevertheless, measures of a program's characteristics do exist. These properties include cyclomatic complexity, cohesion, number of function points, lines of code, and many others discussed in Chapter 15. When we examine an item based on its measurable characteristics, two kinds of quality may be encountered: quality of design and quality of conformance.

Quality of design refers to the characteristics that designers specify for an item. *Quality of conformance* is the degree to which the design specifications are followed during manufacturing.

> **"People forget how fast you did a job—but they always remember how well you did it."**
>
> **Howard Newton**

In software development, quality of design encompasses requirements, specifications, and the design of the system. Quality of conformance is an issue focused primarily on implementation. If the implementation follows the design and the resulting system meets its requirements and performance goals, conformance quality is high.

But are quality of design and quality of conformance the only issues that software engineers must consider? Robert Glass [GLA98] argues that a more "intuitive" relationship is in order:

$$\text{user satisfaction} = \text{compliant product} + \text{good quality} + \text{delivery within budget and schedule}$$

At the bottom line, Glass contends that quality is important, but if the user isn't satisfied, nothing else really matters. DeMarco [DEM99] reinforces this view when he states: "A product's quality is a function of how much it changes the world for the better." This view of quality contends that if a software product provides substantial benefit to its end-users, they may be willing to tolerate occasional reliability or performance problems.

26.1.2 Quality Control

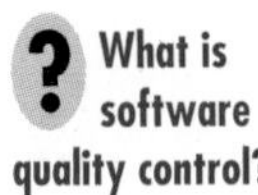
What is software quality control?

Variation control may be equated to quality control. But how do we achieve quality control? Quality control involves the series of inspections, reviews, and tests used throughout the software process to ensure each work product meets the requirements placed upon it. Quality control includes a feedback loop to the process that created the work product. The combination of measurement and feedback allows us to tune the process when the work products created fail to meet their specifications.

A key concept of quality control is that all work products have defined, measurable specifications to which we may compare the output of each process. The feedback loop is essential to minimize the defects produced.

26.1.3 Quality Assurance

WebRef
Useful links to SQA resources can be found at **www.qualitytree.com/links/index.htm.**

Quality assurance consists of a set of auditing and reporting functions that assess the effectiveness and completeness of quality control activities. The goal of quality assurance is to provide management with the data necessary to be informed about product quality, thereby gaining insight and confidence that product quality is meeting its goals. Of course, if the data provided through quality assurance identify problems, it is management's responsibility to address the problems and apply the necessary resources to resolve quality issues.

26.1.4 Cost of Quality

The cost of quality includes all costs incurred in the pursuit of quality or in performing quality-related activities. Cost of quality studies are conducted to provide a baseline for the current cost of quality, identify opportunities for reducing the cost of quality, and provide a normalized basis of comparison. The basis of normalization is almost always dollars. Once we have normalized quality costs on a dollar basis, we have the necessary data to evaluate where the opportunities lie to improve our processes. Furthermore, we can evaluate the effect of changes in dollar-based terms.

? What are the components of the cost of quality?

Quality costs may be divided into costs associated with prevention, appraisal, and failure. *Prevention costs* include quality planning, formal technical reviews, test equipment, and training. *Appraisal costs* include activities to gain insight into product condition the "first time through" each process. Examples of appraisal costs include in-process and interprocess inspection, equipment calibration and maintenance, and testing.

Don't be afraid to incur significant prevention costs. Rest assured that your investment will provide an excellent return.

Failure costs are those that would disappear if no defects appeared before shipping a product to customers. Failure costs may be subdivided into internal failure costs and external failure costs. *Internal failure costs* are incurred when we detect a defect in our product prior to shipment. Internal failure costs include rework, repair, and failure mode analysis. *External failure costs* are associated with defects found after the product has been shipped to the customer. Examples of external failure costs are complaint resolution, product return and replacement, help line support, and warranty work.

As expected, the relative costs to find and repair a defect increase dramatically as we go from prevention to detection to internal failure to external failure costs.

FIGURE 26.1

Relative cost of correcting an error

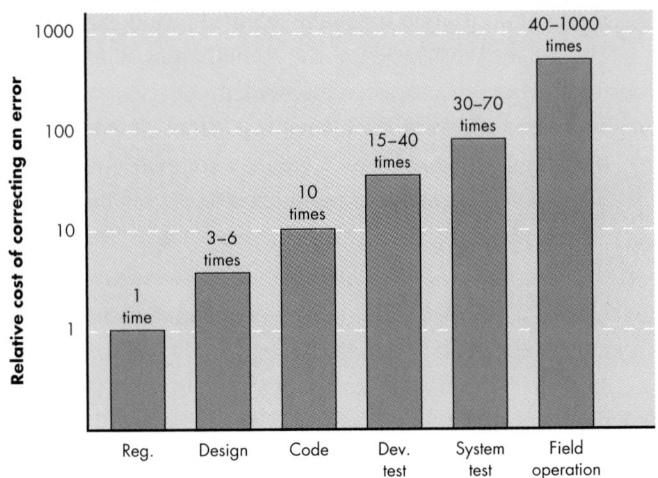

Figure 26.1, based on data collected by Boehm [BOE81] and others, illustrates this phenomenon.

> **"It takes less time to do a thing right than to explain why you did it wrong."**
>
> **H. W. Longfellow**

26.2 SOFTWARE QUALITY ASSURANCE

Even the most jaded software developers will agree that high-quality software is an important goal. But how do we define quality? A wag once said, "Every program does something right, it just may not be the thing that we want it to do."

Many definitions of software quality have been proposed in the literature. For our purposes, *software quality* is defined as:

? How do we define software quality?

> Conformance to explicitly stated functional and performance requirements, explicitly documented development standards, and implicit characteristics that are expected of all professionally developed software.

There is little question that this definition could be modified or extended. In fact, the definition of software quality could be debated endlessly. For the purposes of this book, this definition serves to emphasize three important points:

1. Software requirements are the foundation from which quality is measured. Lack of conformance to requirements is lack of quality.
2. Specified standards define a set of development criteria that guide the manner in which software is engineered. If the criteria are not followed, lack of quality will almost surely result.

3. A set of implicit requirements often goes unmentioned (e.g., the desire for ease of use and good maintainability). If software conforms to its explicit requirements but fails to meet implicit requirements, software quality is suspect.

26.2.1 Background Issues

Quality control and assurance are essential activities for any business that produces products to be used by others. Prior to the twentieth century, quality control was the sole responsibility of the craftsperson who built a product. The first formal quality assurance and control function was introduced at Bell Labs in 1916 and spread rapidly throughout the manufacturing world. During the 1940s, more formal approaches to quality control were suggested. These relied on measurement and continuous process improvement [DEM86] as key elements of quality management.

> **"You made too many wrong mistakes."**
>
> **Yogi Berra**

Today, every company has mechanisms to ensure quality in its products. In fact, explicit statements of a company's concern for quality have become a marketing ploy during the past few decades.

The history of quality assurance in software development parallels the history of quality in hardware manufacturing. During the early days of computing (1950s and 1960s), quality was the sole responsibility of the programmer. Standards for quality assurance for software were introduced in military contract software development during the 1970s and have spread rapidly into software development in the commercial world [IEE94]. Extending the definition presented earlier, software quality assurance is a "planned and systematic pattern of actions" [SCH98] that are required to ensure high quality in software. Many different constituencies have software quality assurance responsibility—software engineers, project managers, customers, salespeople, and the individuals who serve within an SQA group.

The SQA group serves as the customer's in-house representative. That is, the people who perform SQA must look at the software from the customer's point of view. Does the software adequately meet the quality factors noted in Chapter 15? Has software development been conducted according to preestablished standards? Have technical disciplines properly performed their roles as part of the SQA activity? The SQA group attempts to answer these and other questions to ensure that software quality is maintained.

26.2.2 SQA Activities

Software quality assurance is composed of a variety of tasks associated with two different constituencies—the software engineers who do technical work and an SQA group that has responsibility for quality assurance planning, oversight, record keeping, analysis, and reporting.

Software engineers address quality (and perform quality assurance and quality control activities) by applying solid technical methods and measures, conducting formal technical reviews, and performing well-planned software testing. Only reviews are discussed in this chapter. Technology topics are discussed in Parts 1, 2, 3, and 5 of this book.

The charter of the SQA group is to assist the software team in achieving a high-quality end product. The Software Engineering Institute recommends a set of SQA activities that address quality assurance planning, oversight, record keeping, analysis, and reporting. These activities are performed (or facilitated) by an independent SQA group that conducts the following activities:

? **What is the role of an SQA group?**

Prepares an SQA plan for a project. The plan is developed during project planning and is reviewed by all stakeholders. Quality assurance activities performed by the software engineering team and the SQA group are governed by the plan. The plan identifies evaluations to be performed, audits and reviews to be performed, standards that are applicable to the project, procedures for error reporting and tracking, documents to be produced by the SQA group, and amount of feedback provided to the software project team.

Participates in the development of the project's software process description. The software team selects a process for the work to be performed. The SQA group reviews the process description for compliance with organizational policy, internal software standards, externally imposed standards (e.g., ISO-9001), and other parts of the software project plan.

Reviews software engineering activities to verify compliance with the defined software process. The SQA group identifies, documents, and tracks deviations from the process and verifies that corrections have been made.

Audits designated software work products to verify compliance with those defined as part of the software process. The SQA group reviews selected work products; identifies, documents, and tracks deviations; verifies that corrections have been made; and periodically reports the results of its work to the project manager.

Ensures that deviations in software work and work products are documented and handled according to a documented procedure. Deviations may be encountered in the project plan, process description, applicable standards, or technical work products.

Records any noncompliance and reports to senior management. Noncompliance items are tracked until they are resolved.

In addition to these activities, the SQA group coordinates the control and management of change (Chapter 27) and helps to collect and analyze software metrics.

26.3 Software Reviews

Reviews are like filters in the software process workflow. Too few, and the flow is "dirty." Too many, and the flow slows to a trickle. Use metrics to determine which reviews work and emphasize them.

Software reviews are a "filter" for the software process. That is, reviews are applied at various points during software engineering and serve to uncover errors and defects that can then be removed. Software reviews "purify" the software engineering activities that we have called analysis, design, and coding. Freedman and Weinberg [FRE90] discuss the need for reviews this way:

> Technical work needs reviewing for the same reason that pencils need erasers: *To err is human.* The second reason we need technical reviews is that although people are good at catching some of their own errors, large classes of errors escape the originator more easily than they escape anyone else.

Many different types of reviews can be conducted as part of software engineering. Each has its place. An informal meeting around the coffee machine is a form of review, if technical problems are discussed. A formal presentation of software design to an audience of customers, management, and technical staff is also a form of review. In this book, however, we focus on the *formal technical review,* sometimes called a *walkthrough* or an *inspection.* A formal technical review (FTR) is the most effective filter from a quality assurance standpoint. Conducted by software engineers (and others) for software engineers, the FTR is an effective means for uncovering errors and improving software quality.

INFO

Bugs, Errors, and Defects

The goal of SQA is to remove quality problems in the software. These problems are referred to by various names—"bugs," "faults," "errors," or "defects" to name a few. Are each of these terms synonymous, or are there subtle differences between them?

In this book we have made a clear distinction between an *error* (a quality problem found *before* the software is released to end-users) and a *defect* (a quality problem found only *after* the software has been released to end-users[2]). We make this distinction because errors and defects have very different economic, business, psychological, and human impact. As software engineers, we want to find and correct as many errors as possible before the customer and/or end-user encounter them. We want to avoid defects—because defects (justifiably) make software people look bad.

It is important to note, however, that the temporal distinction made between errors and defects in this book is *not* mainstream thinking. The general consensus within the software engineering community is that defects and errors, faults, and bugs are synonymous. That is, the point in time that the problem was encountered has no bearing on the term used to describe the problem. Part of the argument in favor of this view is that it is sometimes difficult to make a clear distinction between pre- and post-release (e.g., consider an incremental process used in agile development [Chapter 4]).

Regardless of how you choose to interpret these terms, recognize that the point in time at which a problem is discovered does matter and that software engineers should try hard—*very* hard—to find problems before their customers and end-users encounter them. If you have further interest in this issue, a reasonably thorough discussion of the terminology surrounding "bugs" can be found at www.softwaredevelopment.ca/bugs.shtml.

2 If software process improvement is considered, a quality problem that is propagated from one process framework activity (e.g., modeling) to another (e.g., construction) can also be called a "defect" (because the problem should have been found before a work product (e.g., a design model) was "released" to the next activity.

FIGURE 26.2

Defect amplification model

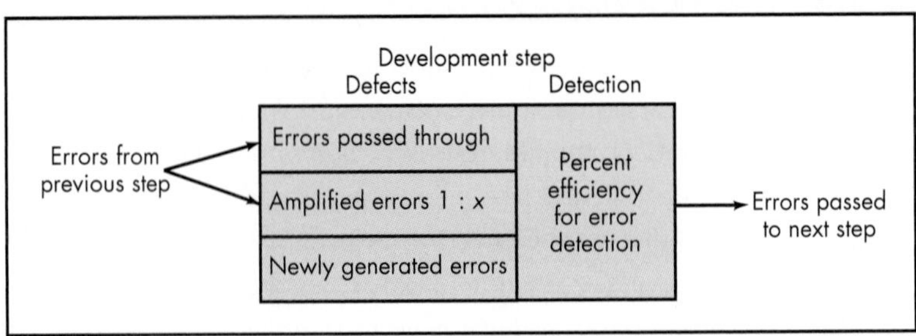

26.3.1 Cost Impact of Software Defects

The primary objective of an FTR is to find errors before they are passed on to another software engineering activity or released to the end-user.

The primary objective of formal technical reviews is to find errors during the process so that they do not become defects after release of the software. The obvious benefit of formal technical reviews is the early discovery of errors so that they do not propagate to the next step in the software process.

A number of industry studies (by TRW, NEC, Mitre Corp., among others) indicate that design activities introduce between 50 and 65 percent of all errors (and ultimately, all defects) during the software process. However, formal review techniques have been shown to be up to 75 percent effective [JON86] in uncovering design flaws. By detecting and removing a large percentage of these errors, the review process substantially reduces the cost of subsequent activities in the software process.

To illustrate the cost impact of early error detection, we consider a series of relative costs that are based on actual cost data collected for large software projects [IBM81].[3] Assume that an error uncovered during design will cost 1.0 monetary unit to correct. Relative to this cost, the same error uncovered just before testing commences will cost 6.5 units; during testing, 15 units; and after release, between 60 and 100 units.

26.3.2 Defect Amplification and Removal

A defect amplification model [IBM81] can be used to illustrate the generation and detection of errors during the preliminary design, detail design, and coding steps of a software engineering process. The model is illustrated schematically in Figure 26.2. A box represents a software development step. During the step, errors may be inadvertently generated. Review may fail to uncover newly generated errors and errors from previous steps, resulting in some number of errors that are passed through. In some cases, errors passed through from previous steps are amplified (amplification factor, x) by current work. The box subdivisions represent each of these characteristics and the percent of efficiency for detecting errors, a function of the thoroughness of the review.

3 Although these data are well over 20 years old, they remain applicable in a modern context.

FIGURE 26.3

Defect amplification—no reviews

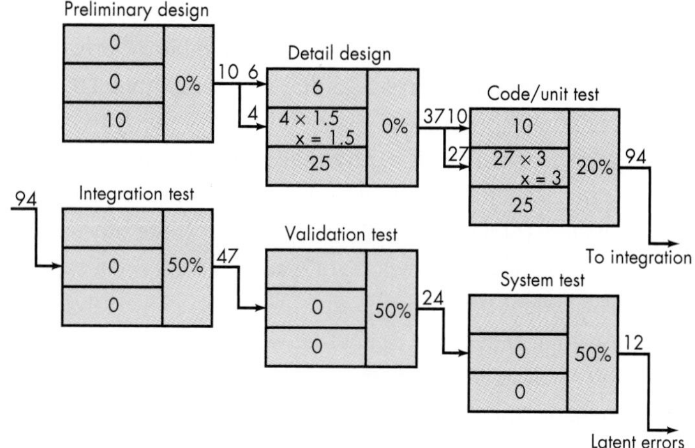

FIGURE 26.4

Defect amplification—reviews conducted

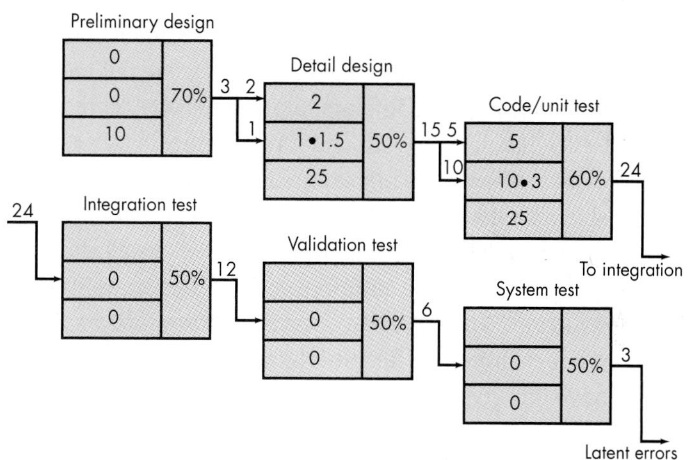

> "Some maladies, as doctors say, at their beginning are easy to cure but difficult to recognize . . . but in the course of time when they have not at first been recognized and treated, become easy to recognize but difficult to cure."
>
> **Niccolo Machiavelli**

Figure 26.3 illustrates a hypothetical example of defect amplification for a software process in which no reviews are conducted. Referring to the figure, each test step is assumed to uncover and correct 50 percent of all incoming errors without introducing any new errors (an optimistic assumption). Ten preliminary design defects are amplified to 94 errors before testing commences. Twelve latent defects are released to the field. Figure 26.4 considers the same conditions except that design and code reviews are conducted as part of each development step. In this case, 10 initial preliminary design errors are amplified to 24 errors before testing commences. Only three latent defects exist. Recalling the relative costs associated with the discovery and correction of errors, overall cost (with and without review for our hypothetical example) can be established. The number of errors uncovered during each of the steps noted in Figures 26.3 and 26.4 is multiplied by the cost to remove an error (1.5 cost units for design, 6.5 cost units before test, 15 cost units during test, and 67 cost units after release). Using these data, the total cost for development and maintenance when reviews are conducted is 783 cost units. When no reviews are conducted, total cost is 2177 units—nearly three times more costly.

To conduct reviews, a software engineer must expend time and effort, and the development organization must spend money. However, the results of the preceding example leave little doubt that we can pay now or pay much more later. Formal technical reviews (for design and other technical activities) provide a demonstrable cost benefit. They should be conducted.

26.4 Formal Technical Reviews

? When we conduct FTRs, what are our objectives?

A formal technical review is a software quality control activity performed by software engineers (and others). The objectives of an FTR are (1) to uncover errors in function, logic, or implementation for any representation of the software; (2) to verify that the software under review meets its requirements; (3) to ensure that the software has been represented according to predefined standards; (4) to achieve software that is developed in a uniform manner; and (5) to make projects more manageable. In addition, the FTR serves as a training ground, enabling junior engineers to observe different approaches to software analysis, design, and construction. The FTR also serves to promote backup and continuity because a number of people become familiar with parts of the software that they may not have otherwise seen.

> "There is no urge so great as for one man to edit another man's work."
>
> **Mark Twain**

The FTR is actually a class of reviews that includes walkthroughs, inspections, round-robin reviews, and other small group technical assessments of software. Each FTR is conducted as a meeting and will be successful only if it is properly planned, controlled, and attended. In the sections that follow, guidelines similar to those for a walkthrough (e.g., [FRE90], [GIL93]) are presented as a representative formal technical review.

WebRef
The NASA SATC *Formal Inspection Guidebook* can be downloaded at **satc.gsfc.nasa.gov/fi/fipage.html.**

26.4.1 The Review Meeting

Regardless of the FTR format that is chosen, every review meeting should abide by the following constraints:

- Between three and five people (typically) should be involved in the review.

- Advance preparation should occur but should require no more than two hours of work for each person.
- The duration of the review meeting should be less than two hours.

Given these constraints, it should be obvious that an FTR focuses on a specific (and small) part of the overall software. For example, rather than attempting to review an entire design, walkthroughs are conducted for each component or small group of components. By narrowing focus, the FTR has a higher likelihood of uncovering errors.

An FTR focuses on a relatively small portion of a work product.

The focus of the FTR is on a work product (e.g., a portion of a requirements specification, a detailed component design, a source code listing for a component). The individual who has developed the work product—the *producer*—informs the project leader that the work product is complete and that a review is required. The project leader contacts a *review leader,* who evaluates the product for readiness, generates copies of product materials, and distributes them to two or three *reviewers* for advance preparation. Each reviewer is expected to spend between one and two hours reviewing the product, making notes, and otherwise becoming familiar with the work. Concurrently, the review leader also reviews the product and establishes an agenda for the review meeting, which is typically scheduled for the next day.

In some situations, it's a good idea to have someone other than the producer walk through the product undergoing review. This leads to a literal interpretation of the work product and better error recognition.

The review meeting is attended by the review leader, all reviewers, and the producer. One of the reviewers takes on the role of the *recorder;* that is, the individual who records (in writing) all important issues raised during the review. The FTR begins with an introduction of the agenda and a brief introduction by the producer. The producer then proceeds to "walk through" the work product, explaining the material, while reviewers raise issues based on their advance preparation. When valid problems or errors are discovered, the recorder notes each.

At the end of the review, all attendees of the FTR must decide whether to (1) accept the product without further modification, (2) reject the product due to severe errors (once corrected, another review must be performed), or (3) accept the product provisionally (minor errors have been encountered and must be corrected, but no additional review will be required). The decision made, all FTR attendees complete a sign-off, indicating their participation in the review and their concurrence with the review team's findings.

26.4.2 Review Reporting and Record Keeping

During the FTR, a reviewer (the recorder) actively records all issues that have been raised. These are summarized at the end of the review meeting and a *review issues list* is produced. In addition, a *formal technical review summary report* is completed. A review summary report answers three questions:

1. What was reviewed?
2. Who reviewed it?
3. What were the findings and conclusions?

The review summary report is a single page form (with possible attachments). It becomes part of the project historical record and may be distributed to the project leader and other interested parties.

The review issues list serves two purposes: (1) to identify problem areas within the product and (2) to serve as an action item checklist that guides the producer as corrections are made. An issues list is normally attached to the summary report.

It is important to establish a follow-up procedure to ensure that items on the issues list have been properly corrected. Unless this is done, it is possible that issues raised can "fall between the cracks." One approach is to assign the responsibility for follow-up to the review leader.

> **"A meeting is too often an event in which minutes are taken and hours are wasted."**
>
> **Author unknown**

26.4.3 Review Guidelines

Guidelines for conducting formal technical reviews must be established in advance, distributed to all reviewers, agreed upon, and then followed. A review that is uncontrolled can often be worse that no review at all. The following represents a minimum set of guidelines for formal technical reviews:

Don't point out errors harshly. One way to be gentle is to ask a question that enables the producer to discover the error.

1. *Review the product, not the producer.* An FTR involves people and egos. Conducted properly, the FTR should leave all participants with a warm feeling of accomplishment. Conducted improperly, the FTR can take on the aura of an inquisition. Errors should be pointed out gently; the tone of the meeting should be loose and constructive; the intent should not be to embarrass or belittle.
2. *Set an agenda and maintain it.* One of the key maladies of meetings of all types is drift. An FTR must be kept on track and on schedule. The review leader is chartered with the responsibility for maintaining the meeting schedule and should not be afraid to nudge people when drift sets in.
3. *Limit debate and rebuttal.* When an issue is raised by a reviewer, there may not be universal agreement on its impact. Rather than spending time debating the question, the issue should be recorded for further discussion off-line.
4. *Enunciate problem areas, but don't attempt to solve every problem noted.* A review is not a problem-solving session. Problem solving should be postponed until after the review meeting.
5. *Take written notes.* It is sometimes a good idea for the recorder to make notes on a wall board, so that wording and priorities can be assessed by other reviewers as information is recorded.
6. *Limit the number of participants and insist upon advance preparation.* Two heads are better than one, but 14 are not necessarily better than 4. Keep the number of people involved to the necessary minimum. However, all review

team members must prepare in advance. Written comments should be solicited by the review leader (providing an indication that the reviewer has reviewed the material).

7. *Develop a checklist for each product that is likely to be reviewed.* A checklist helps the review leader to structure the FTR meeting and helps each reviewer to focus on important issues.
8. *Allocate resources and schedule time for FTRs.* For reviews to be effective, they should be scheduled as a task during the software process. In addition, time should be scheduled for the inevitable modifications that will occur as the result of an FTR.
9. *Conduct meaningful training for all reviewers.* To be effective all review participants should receive some formal training. The training should stress both process-related issues and the human psychological side of reviews.
10. *Review your early reviews.* Debriefing can be beneficial in uncovering problems with the review process itself. The very first product to be reviewed should be the review guidelines themselves.

> **"It is one of the most beautiful compensations of life, that no man can sincerely try to help another without helping himself."**
>
> **Ralph Waldo Emerson**

Because many variables (e.g., number of participants, type of work products, timing and length, specific review approach) have an impact on a successful review, a software organization should experiment to determine what approach works best in a local context. Porter and his colleagues [POR95] provide excellent guidance for this type of experimentation.

26.4.4 Sample-Driven Reviews

In an ideal setting, every software engineering work product would undergo a formal technical review. In the real world of software projects, resources are limited and time is short. As a consequence, reviews are often skipped, even though their value as a quality control mechanism is recognized. Thelin and his colleagues [THE01] address this issue when they state:

> Inspections [FTRs] are only viewed efficient if many faults are found during the fault searching part. If many faults are found in the artifacts [work products], the inspections are necessary. If, on the other hand, only few faults are found, the inspection has been a waste of time for several people involved in the inspections[4]. Moreover, software projects which are late often decrease the time for inspection activities, which leads to a lack of

4 Of course, it can be argued that by conducting reviews we encourage producers to focus on quality, even if no errors are found.

quality. A solution would be to prioritize the resources for the inspection activities and thereby concentrate the available resources on the artifacts that are most fault-prone.

ADVICE

Reviews take time, but it's time well spent. However, if time is short and you have no other option, do not dispense with reviews. Rather, use sample-driven reviews.

Thelin and his colleagues suggest a sample-driven review process in which samples of all software engineering work products are inspected to determine which work products are most error prone. Full FTR resources are then focused only on those work products that are likely (based on data collected during sampling) to be error-prone.

To be effective, the sample driven review process must attempt to quantify those work products that are primary targets for full FTRs. To accomplish this, the following steps are suggested [THE01]:

1. Inspect a fraction a_i of each software work product, *i*. Record the number of faults, f_i found within a_i.
2. Develop a gross estimate of the number of faults within work product *i* by multiplying f_i by $1/a_i$.
3. Sort the work products in descending order according to the gross estimate of the number of faults in each.
4. Focus available review resources on those work products that have the highest estimated number of faults.

The fraction of the work product that is sampled must (1) be representative of the work product as a whole and (2) large enough to be meaningful to the reviewer(s) who does the sampling. As a_i increases, the likelihood that the sample is a valid representation of the work product also increases. However, the resources required to do sampling also increase. A software engineering team must establish the best value for a_i for the types of work products produced.[5]

SAFEHOME

SQA Issues

The scene: Doug Miller's office as the *SafeHome* software project begins.

The players: Doug Miller (manager of the *SafeHome* software engineering team) and other members of the software engineering team.

The conversation:

Doug: I know we didn't spend time developing an SQA plan for this project, but we're already into it and we have to consider quality . . . right?

Jamie: Sure. We've already decided that as we develop the requirements model [Chapters 7 and 8], Ed has committed to develop a V&V procedure for each requirement.

Doug: That's really good, but we're not going to wait until testing to evaluate quality, are we?

Vinod: No! Of course not. We've got reviews scheduled into the project plan for this software increment. We'll begin quality control with the reviews.

5 Thelin and his colleagues have conducted a detailed simulation that can assist in making this determination. See [THE01] for details.

Jamie: I'm a bit concerned that we won't have enough time to conduct all the reviews. In fact, I know we won't.

Doug: Hmmm. So what do you propose?

Jamie: I say we select those elements of the analysis and design model that are most critical to *SafeHome* and review them.

Vinod: But what if we miss something in a part of the model we don't review?

Shakira: I read something about a sampling technique [Section 26.4.4] that might help us target candidates for review. (Shakira explains the approach.)

Jamie: Maybe . . . but I'm not sure we even have time to sample every element of the models.

Vinod: What do you want us to do, Doug?

Doug: Let's steal something from Extreme Programming [Chapter 4]. We'll develop the elements of each model in pairs—two people—and conduct an informal review of each as we go. We'll then target "critical" elements for a more formal team review, but keep those reviews to a minimum. That way, everything gets looked at by more than one set of eyes, but we still maintain our delivery dates.

Jamie: That means we're going to have to revise the schedule.

Doug: So be it. Quality trumps schedule on this project.

26.5 Formal Approaches to SQA

Over the past two decades, a small, but vocal, segment of the software engineering community has argued that a more formal approach to software quality assurance is required. It can be argued that a computer program is a mathematical object [SOM01]. A rigorous syntax and semantics can be defined for every programming language, and a rigorous approach to the specification of software requirements (Chapter 28) is available. If the requirements model (specification) and the programming language can be represented in a rigorous manner, it should be possible to apply mathematic proof of correctness to demonstrate that a program conforms exactly to its specifications.

Attempts to prove programs correct (Chapters 28 and 29) are not new. Dijkstra [DIJ76] and Linger, Mills, and Witt [LIN79], among others, advocated proofs of program correctness and tied these to the use of structured programming concepts (Chapter 11).

26.6 Statistical Software Quality Assurance

Statistical quality assurance reflects a growing trend throughout industry to become more quantitative about quality. For software, statistical quality assurance implies the following steps:

? What steps are required to perform statistical SQA?

1. Information about software defects is collected and categorized.
2. An attempt is made to trace each defect to its underlying cause (e.g., nonconformance to specifications, design error, violation of standards, poor communication with the customer).

3. Using the Pareto principle (80 percent of the defects can be traced to 20 percent of all possible causes), isolate the 20 percent (the "vital few").
4. Once the vital few causes have been identified, move to correct the problems that have caused the defects.

This relatively simple concept represents an important step towards the creation of an adaptive software process in which changes are made to improve those elements of the process that introduce error.

> "20 percent of the code has 80 percent of the errors. Find them, fix them!"
>
> **Lowell Arthur**

26.6.1 A Generic Example

To illustrate the use of statistical methods for software engineering work, assume that a software engineering organization collects information on defects for a period of one year. Some of the defects are uncovered as software is being developed. Others are encountered after the software has been released to its end-users. Although hundreds of different defects are uncovered, all can be tracked to one (or more) of the following causes:

- Incomplete or erroneous specifications (IES).
- Misinterpretation of customer communication (MCC).
- Intentional deviation from specifications (IDS).
- Violation of programming standards (VPS).
- Error in data representation (EDR).
- Inconsistent component interface (ICI).
- Error in design logic (EDL).
- Incomplete or erroneous testing (IET).
- Inaccurate or incomplete documentation (IID).
- Error in programming language translation of design (PLT).
- Ambiguous or inconsistent human/computer interface (HCI).
- Miscellaneous (MIS).

To apply statistical SQA, the table in Figure 26.5 is built. The table indicates that IES, MCC, and EDR are the vital few causes that account for 53 percent of all errors. It should be noted, however, that IES, EDR, PLT, and EDL would be selected as the vital few causes if only serious errors are considered. Once the vital few causes are determined, the software engineering organization can begin corrective action. For example, to correct MCC, the software developer might implement facilitated requirements gathering techniques (Chapter 7) to improve the quality of customer communication and specifications. To improve EDR, the developer

FIGURE 26.5

Data collection for statistical SQA

Error	Total No.	Total %	Serious No.	Serious %	Moderate No.	Moderate %	Minor No.	Minor %
IES	205	22%	34	27%	68	18%	103	24%
MCC	156	17%	12	9%	68	18%	76	17%
IDS	48	5%	1	1%	24	6%	23	5%
VPS	25	3%	0	0%	15	4%	10	2%
EDR	130	14%	26	20%	68	18%	36	8%
ICI	58	6%	9	7%	18	5%	31	7%
EDL	45	5%	14	11%	12	3%	19	4%
IET	95	10%	12	9%	35	9%	48	11%
IID	36	4%	2	2%	20	5%	14	3%
PLT	60	6%	15	12%	19	5%	26	6%
HCI	28	3%	3	2%	17	4%	8	2%
MIS	56	6%	0	0%	15	4%	41	9%
Totals	942	100%	128	100%	379	100%	435	100%

might acquire tools for data modeling and perform more stringent data design reviews.

It is important to note that corrective action focuses primarily on the vital few. As the vital few causes are corrected, new candidates pop to the top of the stack.

Statistical quality assurance techniques for software have been shown to provide substantial quality improvement [ART97]. In some cases, software organizations have achieved a 50 percent reduction per year in defects after applying these techniques.

The application of the statistical SQA and the Pareto principle can be summarized in a single sentence: *Spend your time focusing on things that really matter, but first be sure that you understand what really matters!*

A comprehensive discussion of statistical SQA is beyond the scope of this book. Interested readers should see [GOH02], [SCH98], or [KAN95].

26.6.2 Six Sigma for Software Engineering

Six Sigma is the most widely used strategy for statistical quality assurance in industry today. Originally popularized by Motorola in the 1980s, the Six Sigma strategy "is a rigorous and disciplined methodology that uses data and statistical analysis to measure and improve a company's operational performance by identifying and eliminating 'defects' in manufacturing and service-related processes." [ISI03]. The term "six sigma" is derived from six standard deviations—3.4 instances (defects) per million occurrences—implying an extremely high quality standard. The Six Sigma methodology defines three core steps:

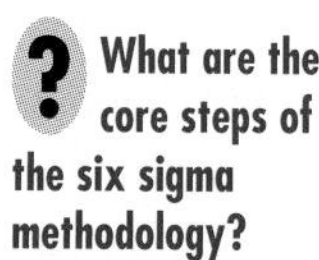

What are the core steps of the six sigma methodology?

- *Define* customer requirements, deliverables, and project goals via well-defined methods of customer communication.

- *Measure* the existing process and its output to determine current quality performance (collect defect metrics).
- *Analyze* defect metrics and determine the vital few causes.

If an existing software process is in place, but improvement is required, Six Sigma suggests two additional steps:

- *Improve* the process by eliminating the root causes of defects.
- *Control* the process to ensure that future work does not reintroduce the causes of defects.

These core and additional steps are sometimes referred to as the DMAIC (define, measure, analyze, improve, and control) method.

If an organization is developing a software process (rather than improving an existing process), the core steps are augmented as follows:

- *Design* the process to (1) avoid the root causes of defects and (2) to meet customer requirements
- *Verify* that the process model will, in fact, avoid defects and meet customer requirements.

This variation is sometimes called the DMADV (define, measure, analyze, design, and verify) method.

A comprehensive discussion of Six Sigma is best left to resources dedicated to the subject. The interested reader should see [ISI03], [SNE03], and [PAN00].

26.7 Software Reliability

Software reliability, unlike many other quality factors, can be measured directed and estimated using historical and developmental data. *Software reliability* is defined in statistical terms as "the probability of failure-free operation of a computer program in a specified environment for a specified time" [MUS87]. To illustrate, program *X* is estimated to have a reliability of 0.96 over eight elapsed processing hours. In other words, if program *X* were to be executed 100 times and require a total of eight hours of elapsed processing time (execution time), it is likely to operate correctly (without failure) 96 times.

> "The unavoidable price of reliability is simplicity."
>
> C.A.R. Hoare

Whenever software reliability is discussed, a pivotal question arises: What is meant by the term *failure?* In the context of any discussion of software quality and reliability, failure is nonconformance to software requirements. Yet, even within this definition, there are gradations. Failures can be only annoying or catastrophic. One failure can be corrected within seconds while another requires weeks or even months to correct. Complicating the issue even further, the correction of one failure may in fact result in the introduction of other errors that ultimately result in other failures.

26.7.1 Measures of Reliability and Availability

KEY POINT

Software reliability problems can almost always be traced to defects in design or implementation.

Early work in software reliability attempted to extrapolate the mathematics of hardware reliability theory (e.g., [ALV64]) to the prediction of software reliability. Most hardware-related reliability models are predicated on failure due to wear rather than failure due to design defects. In hardware, failures due to physical wear (e.g., the effects of temperature, corrosion, shock) are more likely than a design-related failure. Unfortunately, the opposite is true for software. In fact, all software failures can be traced to design or implementation problems; wear (Chapter 1) does not enter into the picture.

There has been debate over the relationship between key concepts in hardware reliability and their applicability to software (e.g., [LIT89], [ROO90]). Although an irrefutable link has yet to be established, it is worthwhile to consider a few simple concepts that apply to both system elements.

It is important to note that MTBF and related measures are based on CPU time, not wall clock time.

If we consider a computer-based system, a simple measure of reliability is *mean-time-between-failure* (MTBF), where

$$MTBF = MTTF + MTTR$$

The acronyms MTTF and MTTR are *mean-time-to-failure* and *mean-time-to-repair*,[6] respectively.

Many researchers argue that MTBF is a far more useful measure than defects/KLOC or defects/FP. Stated simply, an end-user is concerned with failures, not with the total error count. Because each defect contained within a program does not have the same failure rate, the total defect count provides little indication of the reliability of a system.

Some aspects of availability (not discussed here) have nothing to do with failure. For example, schedule downtime (for support functions) causes the software to be unavailable.

In addition to a reliability measure, we must develop a measure of availability. *Software availability* is the probability that a program is operating according to requirements at a given point in time and is defined as

$$\text{Availability} = [MTTF/(MTTF + MTTR)] \times 100\%$$

The MTBF reliability measure is equally sensitive to MTTF and MTTR. The availability measure is somewhat more sensitive to MTTR, an indirect measure of the maintainability of software.

26.7.2 Software Safety

Software safety [LEV86] is a software quality assurance activity that focuses on the identification and assessment of potential hazards that may affect software negatively and cause an entire system to fail. If hazards can be identified early in the software

6 Although debugging (and related corrections) may be required as a consequence of failure, in many cases the software will work properly after a restart with no other change.

process, software design features can be specified that will either eliminate or control potential hazards.

> "I cannot imagine any condition which would cause this ship to founder. Modern shipbuilding has gone beyond that."
> **E. I. Smith, captain of the Titanic**

A modeling and analysis process is conducted as part of software safety. Initially, hazards are identified and categorized by criticality and risk. For example, some of the hazards associated with a computer-based cruise control for an automobile might be:

- Causes uncontrolled acceleration that cannot be stopped.
- Does not respond to depression of brake pedal (by turning off).
- Does not engage when switch is activated.
- Slowly loses or gains speed.

Once these system-level hazards are identified, analysis techniques are used to assign severity and probability of occurrence.[7] To be effective, software must be analyzed in the context of the entire system. For example, a subtle user input error (people are system components) may be magnified by a software fault to produce control data that improperly positions a mechanical device. If a set of external environmental conditions are met (and only if they are met), the improper position of the mechanical device will cause a disastrous failure. Analysis techniques such as fault tree analysis [VES81], real-time logic [JAN86], or Petri net models [LEV87] can be used to predict the chain of events that can cause hazards and the probability that each of the events will occur to create the chain.

WebRef
A worthwhile collection of papers on software safety can be found at **www.safeware-eng.com/.**

Once hazards are identified and analyzed, safety-related requirements can be specified for the software. That is, the specification can contain a list of undesirable events and the desired system responses to these events. The role of software in managing undesirable events is then indicated.

Although software reliability and software safety are closely related to one another, it is important to understand the subtle difference between them. Software reliability uses statistical analysis to determine the likelihood that a software failure will occur. However, the occurrence of a failure does not necessarily result in a hazard or mishap. Software safety examines the ways in which failures result in conditions that can lead to a mishap. That is, failures are not considered in a vacuum, but are evaluated in the context of an entire computer-based system and its environment. Those readers with further interest should refer to Leveson's [LEV95] book on the subject.

---

7 This approach is similar to the risk analysis methods described in Chapter 25. The primary difference is the emphasis on technology issues rather than project related topics.

26.8 The ISO 9000 Quality Standards[8]

A *quality assurance system* may be defined as the organizational structure, responsibilities, procedures, processes, and resources for implementing quality management [ANS87]. Quality assurance systems are created to help organizations ensure their products and services satisfy customer expectations by meeting their specifications. ISO 9000 describes a quality assurance system in generic terms that can be applied to any business regardless of the products or services offered.

ISO 9000 describes what must be done to be compliant, but it does not describe how it must be done.

To become registered to one of the quality assurance system models contained in ISO 9000, a company's quality system and operations are scrutinized by third-party auditors for compliance to the standard and for effective operation. Upon successful registration, a company is issued a certificate from a registration body represented by the auditors. Semiannual surveillance audits ensure continued compliance to the standard.

ISO 9001:2000 is the quality assurance standard that applies to software engineering. The standard contains 20 requirements that must be present for an effective quality assurance system. Because the ISO 9001:2000 standard is applicable to all engineering disciplines, a special set of ISO guidelines (ISO 9000-3) have been developed to help interpret the standard for use in the software process.

WebRef

Extensive links to ISO 9000/9001 resources can be found at **www.tantara.ab.ca/info.htm.**

The requirements delineated by ISO 9001:2000 address topics such as management responsibility, quality system, contract review, design control, document and data control, product identification and traceability, process control, inspection and testing, corrective and preventive action, control of quality records, internal quality audits, training, servicing, and statistical techniques. For a software organization to become registered to ISO 9001:2000, it must establish policies and procedures to address each of the requirements just noted (and others) and then be able to demonstrate that these policies and procedures are being followed. For further information on ISO 9001, the interested reader should see [HOY02], [GAA01], or [CIA01].

Info

The ISO 9001:2000 Standard

The following outline defines the basic elements of the ISO 9001:2000 standard. Comprehensive information on the standard can be obtained from the International Organization for Standardization (www.iso.ch) and other Internet sources (e.g., www.praxiom.com).

Establish the elements of a quality management system.
    Develop, implement, and improve the system.
    Define a policy that emphasizes the importance of the system.
Document the quality system.
    Describe the process.
    Produce an operational manual.
    Develop methods for controlling (updating) documents.
    Establish methods for recordkeeping.
Support quality control and assurance.

8 This section, written by Michael Stovsky, has been adapted from "Fundamentals of ISO 9000," a workbook developed for *Essential Software Engineering,* a video curriculum developed by R. S. Pressman & Associates, Inc. Reprinted with permission.

- Promote the importance of quality among all stakeholders.
- Focus on customer satisfaction.
- Define a quality plan that addresses objectives, responsibilities, and authority.
- Define communication mechanisms among stakeholders.

Establish review mechanisms for the quality management system.

- Identify review methods and feedback mechanisms.
- Define follow-up procedures.

Identify quality resources including personnel, training, infrastructure elements.

Establish control mechanisms.

- For planning.
- For customer requirements.
- For technical activities (e.g., analysis, design, testing).
- For project monitoring and management.

Define methods for remediation.

- Assess quality data and metrics.
- Define approach for continuous process and quality improvement.

26.9 The SQA Plan

The *SQA Plan* provides a road map for instituting software quality assurance. Developed by the SQA group (or the software team if a SQA group does not exist), the plan serves as a template for SQA activities that are instituted for each software project.

A standard for SQA plans has been published by the IEEE [IEE94]. The standard recommends a structure that identifies (1) the purpose and scope of the plan; (2) a description of all software engineering work products (e.g., models, documents, source code) that fall within the purview of SQA; (3) all applicable standards and practices that are applied during the software process; (4) SQA actions and tasks (including reviews and audits) and their placement throughout the software process; (5) the tools and methods that support SQA actions and tasks; (6) software configuration management procedures (Chapter 27) for managing change; (7) methods for assembling, safeguarding, and maintaining all SQA-related records; and (8) organizational roles and responsibilities relative to product quality.

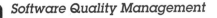

Software Tools

Software Quality Management

Objective: The objective of SQA tools is to assist a project team in assessing and improving the quality of software work product.

Mechanics: Tools mechanics vary. In general, the intent is to assess the quality of a specific work product. Note: a wide array of software testing tools (see Chapters 13 and 14) are often included within the SQA tools category.

Representative Tools[9]

ARM, developed by NASA (satc.gsfc.nasa.gov/tools/index.html), provides

9 Tools noted here do not represent an endorsement, but rather a sampling of tools in this category. In most cases, tool names are trademarked by their respective developers.

measures that can be used to assess the quality of a software requirements document.

QPR ProcessGuide and Scorecard, developed by QPR Software (www.qpronline.com), provides support for Six Sigma and other quality management approaches.

Quality Tools Cookbook, developed by Systma and Manley (www.sytsma.com/tqmtools/tqmtoolmenu.html), provides useful descriptions of classic quality management tools such as control charts, scatter diagrams, affinity diagrams, and matrix diagrams.

Quality Tools and Templates, developed by iSixSigma (http://www.isixsigma.com/tt/), describe a wide array of useful tools and methods for quality management.

TQM Tools, developed by Bain & Company (www.bain.com), provide useful descriptions of a variety of management tools used for TQM and related quality management methods.

26.10 Summary

Software quality management is an umbrella activity—incorporating both quality control and quality assurance—that is applied at each step in the software process. SQA encompasses procedures for the effective application of methods and tools, formal technical reviews, testing strategies and techniques, procedures for change control, procedures for assuring compliance to standards, and measurement and reporting mechanisms.

SQA is complicated by the complex nature of software quality—an attribute of computer programs that is defined as "conformance to explicitly and implicitly specified requirements." But when considered more generally, software quality encompasses many different product and process factors and related metrics.

Software reviews are one of the most important quality control activities. Reviews serve as filters throughout all software engineering activities, removing errors while they are relatively inexpensive to find and correct. The formal technical review is a stylized meeting that has been shown to be extremely effective in uncovering errors.

To properly conduct software quality assurance, data about the software engineering process should be collected, evaluated, and disseminated. Statistical SQA helps to improve the quality of the product and the software process itself. Software reliability models extend measurements, enabling collected defect data to be extrapolated into projected failure rates and reliability predictions.

In summary, we recall the words of Dunn and Ullman [DUN82]: "Software quality assurance is the mapping of the managerial precepts and design disciplines of quality assurance onto the applicable managerial and technological space of software engineering." The ability to ensure quality is the measure of a mature engineering discipline. When the mapping is successfully accomplished, mature software engineering is the result.

REFERENCES

[ALV64] Alvin, W. H., von (ed.), *Reliability Engineering,* Prentice-Hall, 1964.

[ANS87] ANSI/ASQC A3-1987, *Quality Systems Terminology,* 1987.

[ART92] Arthur, L. J., *Improving Software Quality: An Insider's Guide to TQM,* Wiley, 1992.

[ART97] Arthur, L. J., "Quantum Improvements in Software System Quality, *CACM,* vol. 40, no. 6, June 1997, pp. 47–52.

[BOE81] Boehm, B., *Software Engineering Economics,* Prentice-Hall, 1981.

[CIA01] Cianfrani, C. A., et al., *ISO 9001:2000 Explained,* 2nd ed., American Society for Quality, 2001.

[CRO79] Crosby, P., *Quality Is Free,* McGraw-Hill, 1979.

[DEM86] Deming, W. E., *Out of the Crisis,* MIT Press, 1986.

[DEM99] DeMarco, T., "Management Can Make Quality (Im)possible," Cutter IT Summit, Boston, April 1999.

[DIJ76] Dijkstra, E., *A Discipline of Programming,* Prentice-Hall, 1976.

[DUN82] Dunn, R., and R. Ullman, *Quality Assurance for Computer Software,* McGraw-Hill, 1982.

[FRE90] Freedman, D. P., and G. M. Weinberg, *Handbook of Walkthroughs, Inspections and Technical Reviews,* 3rd ed., Dorset House, 1990.

[GAA01] Gaal, A., *ISO 9001:2000 for Small Business,* Saint Lucie Press, 2001.

[GIL93] Gilb, T., and D. Graham, *Software Inspections,* Addison-Wesley, 1993.

[GLA98] Glass, R., "Defining Quality Intuitively," *IEEE Software,* May 1998, pp. 103– 104, 107.

[GOH02] Goh, T., V. Kuralmani, and M. Xie, *Statistical Models and Control Charts for High Quality Processes,* Kluwer Academic Publishers, 2002.

[HOY02] Hoyle, D., *ISO 9000 Quality Systems Development Handbook: A Systems Engineering Approach,* 4th ed., Butterworth-Heinemann, 2002.

[IBM81] "Implementing Software Inspections," course notes, IBM Systems Sciences Institute, IBM Corporation, 1981.

[IEE94] *Software Engineering Standards,* 1994, IEEE Computer Society, 1994.

[ISI03] iSixSigma, LLC, "New to Six Sigma: A Guide for Both Novice and Experienced Quality Practitioners," 2003, available at http://www.isixsigma.com/library/content/six-sigma-newbie.asp.

[JAN86] Jahanian, F., and A. K. Mok, "Safety Analysis of Timing Properties of Real-Time Systems," *IEEE Trans. Software Engineering,* vol. SE-12, no. 9, September 1986, pp. 890–904.

[JON86] Jones, T. C., *Programming Productivity,* McGraw-Hill, 1986.

[KAN95] Kan, S. H., *Metrics and Models in Software Quality Engineering,* Addison-Wesley, 1995.

[LEV86] Leveson, N. G., "Software Safety: Why, What, and How," *ACM Computing Surveys,* vol. 18, no. 2, June 1986, pp. 125–163.

[LEV87] Leveson, N. G., and J. L. Stolzy, "Safety Analysis Using Petri Nets," *IEEE Trans. Software Engineering,* vol. SE-13, no. 3, March 1987, pp. 386–397.

[LEV95] Leveson, N. G., *Safeware: System Safety and Computers,* Addison-Wesley, 1995.

[LIN79] Linger, R., H. Mills, and B. Witt, *Structured Programming,* Addison-Wesley, 1979.

[LIT89] Littlewood, B., "Forecasting Software Reliability," in *Software Reliability: Modeling and Identification,* (S. Bittanti, ed.), Springer-Verlag, 1989, pp. 141–209.

[MUS87] Musa, J. D., A. Iannino, and K. Okumoto, *Engineering and Managing Software with Reliability Measures,* McGraw-Hill, 1987.

[PAN00] Pande, P., et al., *The Six Sigma Way,* McGraw-Hill, 2000.

[POR95] Porter, A., H. Siy, C. A. Toman, and L. G. Votta, "An Experiment to Assess the Cost-Benefits of Code Inspections in Large Scale Software Development," *Proc. Third ACM SIGSOFT Symposium on the Foundations of Software Engineering,* Washington, D.C., October 1995, ACM Press, pp. 92–103.

[ROO90] Rook, J., *Software Reliability Handbook,* Elsevier, 1990.

[SCH98] Schulmeyer, G. C., and J. I. McManus (eds.), *Handbook of Software Quality Assurance,* 3rd ed., Prentice-Hall, 1998.

[SOM01] Somerville, I., *Software Engineering,* 6th ed., Addison-Wesley, 2001.

[SNE03] Snee, R., and R. Hoerl, *Leading Six Sigma,* Prentice-Hall, 2003.

[THE01] Thelin, T., H. Petersson, and C. Wohlin, "Sample Driven Inspections," *Proceedings Workshop on Inspection in Software Engineering (WISE'01),* Paris, France, July 2001, pp. 81–91, can be downloaded from http://www.cas.mcmaster.ca/ wise/wise01/ThelinPetersson-Wohlin.pdf.

[VES81] Veseley, W. E., et al., *Fault Tree Handbook,* U.S. Nuclear Regulatory Commission, NUREG-0492, January 1981.

Problems and Points to Ponder

26.1. Early in this chapter we noted that "variation control is the heart of quality control." Since every program that is created is different from every other program, what are the variations that we look for and how do we control them?

26.2. Is it possible to assess the quality of software if the customer keeps changing what it is supposed to do?

26.3. Quality and reliability are related concepts but are fundamentally different in a number of ways. Discuss them.

26.4. Can a program be correct and still not be reliable? Explain.

26.5. Can a program be correct and still not exhibit good quality? Explain.

26.6. Why is there often tension between a software engineering group and an independent software quality assurance group? Is this healthy?

26.7. You have been given the responsibility for improving the quality of software across your organization. What is the first thing that you should do? What's next?

26.8. Besides counting errors and defects, are there other countable characteristics of software that imply quality? What are they, and can they be measured directly?

26.9. A formal technical review is effective only if everyone has prepared in advance. How do you recognize a review participant who has not prepared? What do you do if you're the review leader?

26.10. Some people argue that an FTR should assess programming style as well as correctness. Is this a good idea? Why?

26.11. Review the table presented in Figure 26.5 and select four vital few causes of serious and moderate errors. Suggest corrective actions using information presented in other chapters.

26.12. Research the literature on software reliability, and write a paper that describes one software reliability model. Be sure to provide an example.

26.13. The MTBF concept for software is open to criticism. Can you think of a few reasons why?

26.14. Consider two safety critical systems that are controlled by computers. List at least three hazards for each that can be directly linked to software failures.

26.15. Acquire a copy of ISO 9001:2000 and ISO 9000-3. Prepare a presentation that discusses three ISO 9001 requirements and how they apply in a software context.

Further Readings and Information Sources

Books by Moriguchi (*Software Excellence: A Total Quality Management Guide,* Productivity Press, 1997) and Horch (*Practical Guide to Software Quality Management,* Artech Publishing, 1996) are excellent management-level presentations on the benefits of formal quality assurance programs for computer software. Books by Deming [DEM86], Juran (*Juran on Quality by Design,* Free Press, 1992), and Crosby ([CRO79] and *Quality Is Still Free,* McGraw-Hill, 1995) do not focus on software, but are must reading for senior managers with software development responsibility. Gluckman and Roome (*Everyday Heroes of the Quality Movement,* Dorset House, 1993) humanizes quality issues by telling the story of the players in the quality process. Kan (*Metrics and Models in Software Quality Engineering,* Addison-Wesley, 1995) presents a quantitative view of software quality.

The ISO 9001:2000 quality standard is discussed by Cianfani and his colleagues (*ISO 9001:2000 Explained,* second edition, American Society for Quality, 2001) and Gaal (*ISO 9001:2000 for Small Business: Implementing Process-Approach Quality Management,* St. Lucie Press, 2001). Tingley (*Comparing ISO 9000, Malcolm Baldrige, and the SEI CMM* for Software, Prentice-Hall, 1996) provides useful guidance for organizations that are striving to improve their quality management processes.

Books by George (*Lean Six Sigma,* McGraw-Hill, 2002), Pande and his colleagues (*The Six Sigma Way Fieldbook,* McGraw-Hill, 2001), and Pyzdek (*The Six Sigma Handbook,* McGraw-Hill, 2000) describe Six Sigma, a statistical quality management technique that leads to products that have very low defect rates.

Radice (*High Quality, Low Cost Software Inspections,* Paradoxicon Publishers, 2002), Wiegers (*Peer Reviews in Software: A Practical Guide,* Addison-Wesley, 2001), Gilb and Graham (*Software Inspection,* Addison-Wesley, 1993) and Freedman and Weinberg (*Handbook of Walkthroughs, Inspections and Technical Reviews,* Dorset House, 1990) provide worthwhile guidelines for conducting effective formal technical reviews.

Musa (*Software Reliability Engineering: More Reliable Software, Faster Development and Testing,* McGraw-Hill, 1998) has written a practical guide to applied software reliability techniques. Anthologies of important papers on software reliability have been edited by Kapur et al. (*Contributions to Hardware and Software Reliability Modelling,* World Scientific Publishing Co., 1999), Gritzalis (*Reliability, Quality and Safety of Software-Intensive Systems,* Kluwer Academic Publishers, 1997), and Lyu (*Handbook of Software Reliability Engineering,* McGraw-Hill, 1996).

Hermann (*Software Safety and Reliability,* Wiley-IEEE Press, 2000), Storey (*Safety-Critical Computer Systems,* Addison-Wesley, 1996) and Leveson [LEV95] continue to be the most comprehensive discussions of software safety published to date. In addition, van der Meulen (*Definitions for Hardware and Software Safety Engineers,* Springer-Verlag, 2000) offers a complete compendium of important concepts and terms for reliability and safety. Gartner (*Testing Safety-Related Software,* Springer-Verlag, 1999) provides specialized guidance for testing safety critical systems. Friedman and Voas (*Software Assessment: Reliability Safety and Testability,* Wiley, 1995) provide useful models for assessing reliability and safety.

A wide variety of information sources on software quality management is available on the Internet. An up-to-date list of World Wide Web references can be found at the SEPA Web site: **http://www.mhhe.com/pressman.**

CHAPTER

27 CHANGE MANAGEMENT

KEY CONCEPTS

Change is inevitable when computer software is built. And change increases the level of confusion among software engineers who are working on a project. Confusion arises when changes are not analyzed before they are made, recorded before they are implemented, reported to those with a need to know, or controlled in a manner that will improve quality and reduce error. Babich [BAB86] discusses this when he states:

> The art of coordinating software development to minimize . . . confusion is called configuration management. Configuration management is the art of identifying, organizing, and controlling modifications to the software being built by a programming team. The goal is to maximize productivity by minimizing mistakes.

Change management, more commonly called *software configuration management* (SCM or CM), is an umbrella activity that is applied throughout the software process. Because change can occur at any time, SCM activities are developed to (1) identify change, (2) control change, (3) ensure that change is being properly implemented, and (4) report changes to others who may have an interest.

It is important to make a clear distinction between software support and software configuration management. Support is a set of software engineering activities that occur after software has been delivered to the customer and put into operation. Software configuration management is a set of tracking and control activities that are initiated when a software engineering project begins and terminate only when the software is taken out of operation.

QUICK LOOK

What is it? When you build computer software, change happens. And because it happens, you need to manage it effectively. Change management, also called software configuration management (SCM), is a set of activities designed to manage change by identifying the work products that are likely to change, establishing relationships among them, defining mechanisms for managing different versions of these work products, controlling the changes imposed, and auditing and reporting on the changes made.

Who does it? Everyone involved in the software process is involved with change management to some extent, but specialized support positions are sometimes created to manage the SCM process.

Why is it important? If you don't control change, it controls you. And that's never good. It's very easy for a stream of uncontrolled changes to turn a well-run software project into chaos. For that reason, change management is an essential part of good project management and solid software engineering practice.

What are the steps? Because many work products are produced when software is built, each must be uniquely identified. Once this is accomplished, mechanisms for version and change control can be established. To ensure that quality is maintained as changes are made, the process is audited; and to ensure that those with a need to know are informed about changes, reporting is conducted.

What is the work product? A *Software Configuration Management Plan* defines the project strategy for change management. In addition, when formal SCM is invoked, the change control process produces software change requests, reports, and engineering change orders.

How do I ensure that I've done it right? When every work product can be accounted for, traced, and controlled; when every change can be tracked and analyzed; when everyone who needs to know about a change has been informed—you've done it right.

A primary goal of software engineering is to improve the ease with which changes can be accommodated and reduce the amount of effort expended when changes must be made. In this chapter, we discuss the specific actions that enable us to manage change.

27.1 Software Configuration Management

The output of the software process is information that may be divided into three broad categories: (1) computer programs (both source level and executable forms); (2) work products that describe the computer programs (targeted at both technical practitioners and users), and (3) data (contained within the program or external to it). The items that comprise all information produced as part of the software process are collectively called a *software configuration.*

If each configuration item simply led to other items, little confusion would result. Unfortunately, another variable enters the process—*change.* Change may occur at any time, for any reason. In fact, the First Law of System Engineering [BER80] states: "No matter where you are in the system life cycle, the system will change, and the desire to change it will persist throughout the life cycle."

> **"There is nothing permanent except change."**
>
> **Heraclitus, 500 B.C.**

What is the origin of these changes? The answer to this question is as varied as the changes themselves. However, there are four fundamental sources of change:

? What is the origin of changes that are requested for software?

- New business or market conditions dictate changes in product requirements or business rules.
- New customer needs demand modification of data produced by information systems, functionality delivered by products, or services delivered by a computer-based system.
- Reorganization or business growth/downsizing causes changes in project priorities or software engineering team structure.

- Budgetary or scheduling constraints cause a redefinition of the system or product.

Software configuration management is a set of activities that have been developed to manage change throughout the life cycle of computer software. SCM can be viewed as a software quality assurance activity that is applied throughout the software process. In the sections that follow, we examine major SCM tasks and important concepts that help us to manage change.

27.1.1 A SCM Scenario[1]

A typical CM operational scenario involves a project manager who is in charge of a software group, a configuration manager who is in charge of the CM procedures and policies, the software engineers who are responsible for developing and maintaining the software product, and the customer who uses the product. In the scenario, assume that the product is a small one involving about 15,000 lines of code being developed by a team of six people. (Note that other scenarios of smaller or larger teams are possible but, in essence, there are generic issues that each of these projects face concerning CM.)

At the operational level, the scenario involves various roles and tasks. For the project manager, the goal is to ensure that the product is developed within a certain time frame. Hence, the manager monitors the progress of development and recognizes and reacts to problems. This is done by generating and analyzing reports about the status of the software system and by performing reviews on the system.

? What are the goals of and the activities performed by each of the constituencies involved in change management?

The goals of the configuration manager are to ensure that procedures and policies for creating, changing, and testing of code are followed, as well as to make information about the project accessible. To implement techniques for maintaining control over code changes, this manager introduces mechanisms for making official requests for changes, for evaluating them (via a Change Control Board that is responsible for approving changes to the software system), and for authorizing changes. The manager creates and disseminates task lists for the engineers and basically creates the project context. Also, the manager collects statistics about components in the software system, such as information determining which components in the system are problematic.

For the software engineers, the goal is to work effectively. This means engineers do not unnecessarily interfere with each other in the creation and testing of code and in the production of supporting documents. But, at the same time, they try to communicate and coordinate efficiently. Specifically, engineers use tools that help build a consistent software product. They communicate and coordinate by notifying

1 This section is extracted from [DAR01]. Special permission to reproduce "Spectrum of Functionality in CM Systems by Susan Dart [DAR01], © 2001 by Carnegie Mellon University is granted by the Software Engineering Institute.

There must be a mechanism to ensure that simultaneous changes to the same component are properly tracked, managed, and executed.

one another about tasks required and tasks completed. Changes are propagated across each other's work by merging files. Mechanisms exist to ensure that, for components which undergo simultaneous changes, there is some way of resolving conflicts and merging changes. A history is kept of the evolution of all components of the system along with a log with reasons for changes and a record of what actually changed. The engineers have their own workspace for creating, changing, testing, and integrating code. At a certain point, the code is made into a baseline from which further development continues and from which variants for other target machines are made.

The customer uses the product. Since the product is under CM control, the customer follows formal procedures for requesting changes and for indicating bugs in the product.

Ideally, a CM system used in this scenario should support all these roles and tasks; that is, the roles determine the functionality required of a CM system. The project manager sees CM as an auditing mechanism; the configuration manager sees it as a controlling, tracking, and policy making mechanism; the software engineer sees it as a changing, building, and access control mechanism; and the customer sees it as a quality assurance mechanism.

27.1.2 Elements of a Configuration Management System

In her comprehensive white-paper on software configuration management, Susan Dart [DAR01] identifies four important elements that should exist when a configuration management system is developed:

- *Component elements*—a set of tools coupled within a file management system (e.g., a database) that enable access to and management of each software configuration item.
- *Process elements*—a collection of procedures and tasks that define an effective approach to change management (and related activities) for all constituencies involved in the management, engineering, and use of computer software.
- *Construction elements*—a set of tools that automate the construction of software by ensuring that the proper set of validated components (i.e., the correct version) has been assembled.
- *Human elements*—to implement effective SCM, the software team uses a set of tools and process features (encompassing other CM elements).

These elements (to be discussed in more detail in later sections) are not mutually exclusive. For example, component elements work in conjunction with construction elements as the software process evolves. Process elements guide many human activities that are related to SCM and might therefore be considered human elements as well.

Most software changes are justified, so there's no point in complaining about them. Rather, be certain that you have mechanisms in place to handle them.

27.1.3 Baselines

Change is a fact of life in software development. Customers want to modify requirements. Developers want to modify the technical approach. Managers want to modify the project strategy. Why all this modification? The answer is really quite simple. As time passes, all constituencies know more (about what they need, which approach would be best, how to get it done and still make money). This additional knowledge is the driving force behind most changes and leads to a statement of fact that is difficult for many software engineering practitioners to accept: *Most changes are justified!*

A *baseline* is a software configuration management concept that helps us to control change without seriously impeding justifiable change. The IEEE (IEEE Std. No. 610.12-1990) defines a baseline as:

> A specification or product that has been formally reviewed and agreed upon, that thereafter serves as the basis for further development, and that can be changed only through formal change control procedures.

A software engineering work product becomes a baseline only after it has been reviewed and approved.

Before a software configuration item becomes a baseline, change may be made quickly and informally. However, once a baseline is established, we figuratively pass through a swinging one-way door. Changes can be made, but a specific, formal procedure must be applied to evaluate and verify each change.

In the context of software engineering, a baseline is a milestone in the development of software. A baseline is marked by the delivery of one or more software configuration items that have been approved as a consequence of a formal technical review (Chapter 26). For example, the elements of a design model have been documented and reviewed. Errors are found and corrected. Once all parts of the model have been reviewed, corrected, and then approved, the design model becomes a baseline. Further changes to the program architecture (documented in the design model) can be made only after each has been evaluated and approved. Although baselines can be defined at any level of detail, the most common software baselines are shown in Figure 27.1.

Be sure that the project database is maintained in a centralized, controlled location.

The progression of events that lead to a baseline is also illustrated in Figure 27.1. Software engineering tasks produce one or more SCIs. After SCIs are reviewed and approved, they are placed in a *project database* (also called a *project library* or *software repository* and discussed in Section 27.2). When a member of a software team wants to make a modification to a baselined SCI, it is copied from the project database into the engineer's private workspace. However, this extracted SCI can be modified only if SCM controls (discussed later in this chapter) are followed. The arrows in Figure 27.1 illustrate the modification path for a baselined SCI.

27.1.4 Software Configuration Items

A software configuration item is information that is created as part of the software engineering process. In the extreme, a SCI could be considered to be a single section of

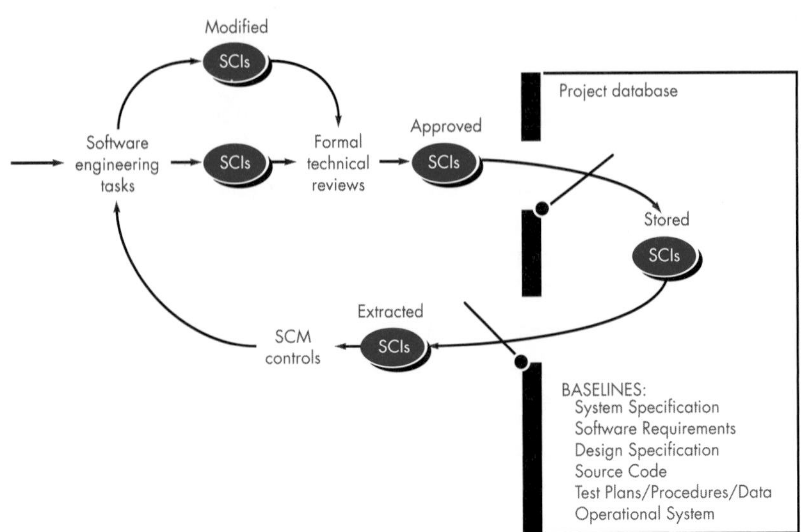

FIGURE 27.1 Baselined SCIs and the project database

a large specification or one test case in a large suite of tests. More realistically, a SCI is a document, a entire suite of test cases, or a named program component (e.g., a C++ function or a Java applet).

In addition to the SCIs that are derived from software work products, many software engineering organizations also place software tools under configuration control. That is, specific versions of editors, compilers, browsers, and other automated tools are "frozen" as part of the software configuration. Because these tools were used to produce documentation, source code, and data, they must be available when changes to the software configuration are to be made. Although problems are rare, it is possible that a new version of a tool (e.g., a compiler) might produce different results than the original version. For this reason, tools, like the software that they help to produce, can be baselined as part of a comprehensive configuration management process.

In reality, SCIs are organized to form configuration objects that may be cataloged in the project database with a single name. A *configuration object* has a name, attributes, and is "connected" to other objects by relationships. Referring to Figure 27.2, the configuration objects, **DesignSpecification, DataModel, ComponentN, SourceCode** and **TestSpecification** are each defined separately. However, each of the objects is related to the others as shown by the arrows. A curved arrow indicates a compositional relation. That is, **DataModel** and **ComponentN** are part of the object **DesignSpecification.** A double-headed straight arrow indicates an interrelationship. If a change were made to the **SourceCode** object, the interrelationships enable a software engineer to determine what other objects (and SCIs) might be affected.[2]

2 These relationships are defined within the database. The structure of the database (repository) is discussed in greater detail in Section 27.2.

FIGURE 27.2 Configuration objects

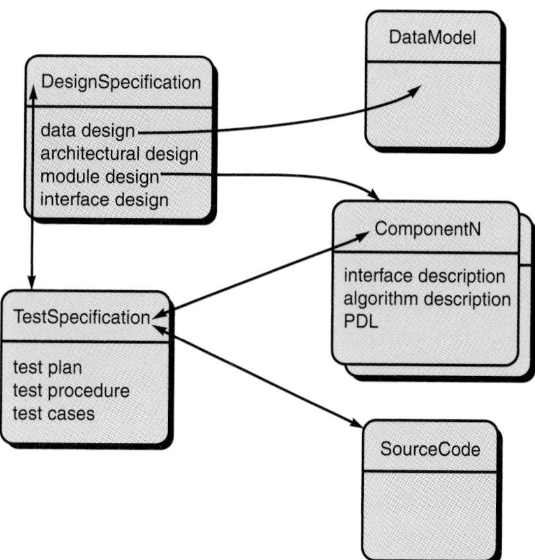

27.2 The SCM Repository

In the early days of software engineering, software configuration items were maintained as paper documents (or punched computer cards!), placed in file folders or three-ring binders, and stored in metal cabinets. This approach was problematic for many reasons: (1) finding a configuration item when it was needed was often difficult; (2) determining which items were changed, when and by whom was often challenging; (3) constructing a new version of an existing program was time consuming and error-prone; (4) describing detailed or complex relationships between configuration items was virtually impossible.

Today, SCIs are maintained in a project database or repository. Webster's Dictionary defines the word *repository* as "any thing or person thought of as a center of accumulation or storage." During the early history of software engineering, the repository was indeed a person—the programmer who had to remember the location of all information relevant to a software project, who had to recall information that was never written down, and reconstruct information that had been lost. Sadly, using a person as "the center for accumulation and storage" (although it conforms to Webster's definition) does not work very well. Today, the repository is a "thing"—a database that acts as the center for both accumulation and storage of software engineering information. The role of the person (the software engineer) is to interact with the repository using tools that are integrated with it.

27.2.1 The Role of the Repository

The SCM repository is the set of mechanisms and data structures that allow a software team to manage change in an effective manner. It provides the obvious functions of a database management system, but in addition, the repository performs or precipitates the following functions [FOR89]:

? What functions are implemented by a SCM repository?

- *Data integrity* includes functions to validate entries to the repository, ensure consistency among related objects, and automatically perform "cascading" modifications when a change to one object demands some change to objects related to it.
- *Information sharing* provides a mechanism for sharing information among multiple developers and between multiple tools, manages and controls multiuser access to data, and locks or unlocks objects so that changes are not inadvertently overlaid on one another.
- *Tool integration* establishes a data model that can be accessed by many software engineering tools, controls access to the data, and performs appropriate configuration management functions.
- *Data integration* provides database functions that allow various SCM tasks to be performed on one or more SCIs.
- *Methodology enforcement* defines an entity-relationship model stored in the repository that implies a specific process model for software engineering; at a minimum, the relationships and objects define a set of steps that must be conducted to build the contents of the repository.
- *Document standardization* is the definition of objects in the database that leads directly to a standard approach for the creation of software engineering documents.

To achieve these functions, the repository is defined in terms of a meta-model. The *meta-model* determines how information is stored in the repository, how data can be accessed by tools and viewed by software engineers, how well data security and integrity can be maintained, and how easily the existing model can be extended to accommodate new needs. For further information, the interested reader should see [SHA95] and [GRI95].

27.2.2 General Features and Content

WebRef
Examples of commercially available repositories can be obtained at **www.software.hp.com/products/SCMGR or otn.oracle.com/documentation/repository.html.**

The features and content of the repository are best understood by looking at it from two perspectives: what is to be stored in the repository and what specific services are provided by the repository. A detailed breakdown of types of representations, documents, and work products that are stored in the repository is presented in Figure 27.3.

A robust repository provides two different classes of services: (1) the same types of services that might be expected from any sophisticated database management system and (2) services that are specific to the software engineering environment.

A repository that serves a software engineering team should (1) integrate with or directly support process management functions; (2) support specific rules that govern the SCM function and the data maintained within the repository; (3) provide an

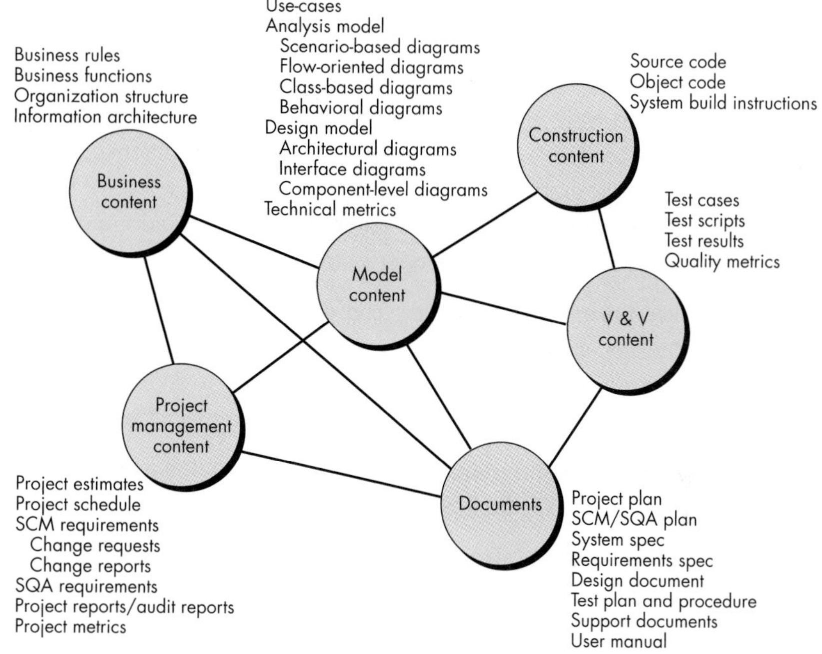

FIGURE 27.3 Content of the repository

interface to other software engineering tools; and (4) accommodate storage of sophisticated data objects (e.g., text, graphics, video, audio).

27.2.3 SCM Features

To support SCM, the repository must have a tool set that provides support for the following features:

The repository must be capable of maintaining SCIs related to many different versions of the software. More important, it must provide the mechanisms for assembling these SCIs into a version-specific configuration.

Versioning. As a project progresses, many versions (section 27.3.2) of individual work products will be created. The repository must be able to save all of these versions to enable effective management of product releases and to permit developers to go back to previous versions during testing and debugging.

The repository must be able to control a wide variety of object types, including text, graphics, bit maps, complex documents, and unique objects like screen and report definitions, object files, test data, and results. A mature repository tracks versions of objects with arbitrary levels of granularity; for example, a single data definition or a cluster of modules can be tracked.

Dependency tracking and change management. The repository manages a wide variety of relationships among the configuration objects stored in it. These include relationships between enterprise entities and processes, among the parts of an application design, between design components and the enterprise information architecture, between design elements and other work products, and so on. Some of these relationships are merely associations, and some are dependencies or mandatory relationships.

The ability to keep track of all of these relationships is crucial to the integrity of the information stored in the repository and to the generation of work products based on it, and it is one of the most important contributions of the repository concept to the improvement of the software development process. For example, if a UML class diagram is modified, the repository can detect whether related classes, interface definitions, and code components also require modification and can bring affected SCIs to the developer's attention.

Requirements tracing. This special function provides the ability to track all the design and construction components and deliverables that result from a specific requirements specification (forward tracing). In addition, it provides the ability to identify which requirement generated any given work product (backward tracing).

Configuration management. A configuration management facility keeps track of a series of configurations representing specific project milestones or production releases.

Audit trails. An audit trail establishes additional information about when, why, and by whom changes are made. Information about the source of changes can be entered as attributes of specific objects in the repository.

27.3 The SCM Process

The software configuration management process defines a series of tasks that have four primary objectives: (1) to identify all items that collectively define the software configuration; (2) to manage changes to one or more of these items; (3) to facilitate the construction of different versions of an application; and (4) to ensure that software quality is maintained as the configuration evolves over time.

A process that achieves these objectives need not be bureaucratic and ponderous, but it must be characterized in a manner that enables a software team to develop answers to a set of complex questions:

? What questions should the SCM process be designed to answer?

- How does a software team identify the discrete elements of a software configuration?
- How does an organization manage the many existing versions of a program (and its documentation) in a manner that will enable change to be accommodated efficiently?
- How does an organization control changes before and after software is released to a customer?
- Who has responsibility for approving and ranking changes?
- How can we ensure that changes have been made properly?
- What mechanism is used to appraise others of changes that are made?

FIGURE 27.4
Layers of the SCM process

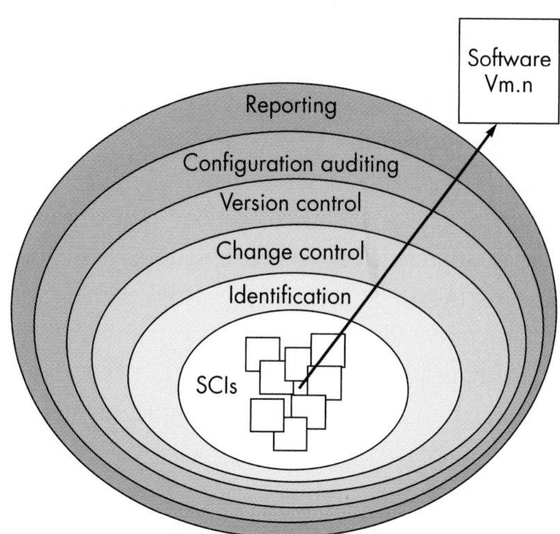

These questions lead us to the definition of five SCM tasks—identification, version control, change control, configuration auditing, and reporting—illustrated in Figure 27.4.

Referring to the figure, SCM tasks can be viewed as concentric layers. SCIs flow outward through these layers throughout their useful life, ultimately becoming part of the software configuration of one or more versions of an application or system. As an SCI moves through a layer, the actions implied by each SCM process layer may or may not be applicable. For example, when a new SCI is created, it must be identified. However, if no changes are requested for the SCI, the change control layer does not apply. The SCI is assigned to a specific version of the software (version control mechanisms come into play). A record of the SCI (its name, creation date, version designation, etc.) is maintained for configuration auditing purposes and reported to those with a need to know. In the sections that follow, we examine each of these SCM process layers in more detail.

27.3.1 Identification of Objects in the Software Configuration

To control and manage software configuration items, each should be separately named and then organized using an object-oriented approach. Two types of objects can be identified [CHO89]: basic objects and aggregate objects.[3] A *basic object* is a unit of information that has been created by a software engineer during analysis, design, code, or test. For example, a basic object might be a section of a requirements specification, part of a design model, source code for a component,

3 The concept of an aggregate object [GUS89] has been proposed as a mechanism for representing a complete version of a software configuration.

or a suite of test cases that are used to exercise the code. An *aggregate object* is a collection of basic objects and other aggregate objects. Referring to Figure 27.2, **DesignSpecification** is an aggregate object. Conceptually, it can be viewed as a named (identified) list of pointers that specify basic objects such as **DataModel** and **ComponentN.**

Each object has a set of distinct features that identify it uniquely: a name, a description, a list of resources, and a "realization." The object name is a character string that identifies the object unambiguously. The object description is a list of data items that identify the SCI type (e.g., model element, program, data) represented by the object, a project identifier, and change and/or version information.

The interrelationships established for configuration objects allow a software engineer to assess the impact of change.

Configuration object identification can also consider the relationships that exist between named objects. For example, using the simple notation

Class diagram <part-of> analysis model;
Analysis model <part-of> requirements specification;

we create a hierarchy of SCIs.

In many cases, objects are interrelated across branches of the object hierarchy. These cross structural relationships can be represented in the following manner:

Even if the project database provides the ability to establish these relationships, they are time-consuming to establish and difficult to keep up-to-date. Although very useful for impact analysis, they are not essential for overall change mangagement.

data model <interrelated>data flow model;
data model <interrelated>test case class m;

In the first case, the interrelationship is between a composite object, while the second relationship is between an aggregate object (**DataModel**) and a basic object (**TestCaseClassM**).

The identification scheme for configuration objects must recognize that objects evolve throughout the software process. Before an object is baselined, it may change many times, and even after a baseline has been established, changes may be quite frequent.

27.3.2 Version Control

A "make" facility enables a software engineer to extract all relevant configuration objects and construct a specific version of the software.

Version control combines procedures and tools to manage different versions of configuration objects that are created during the software process. A version control system implements or is directly integrated with four major capabilities: (1) a project database (repository) that stores all relevant configuration objects; (2) a *version management* capability that stores all versions of a configuration object (or enables any version to be constructed using differences from past versions); (3) a *make facility* that enables the software engineer to collect all relevant configuration objects and construct a specific version of the software. In addition, version control and change control systems often implement an *issues tracking* (also called *bug tracking*) capability that enables the team to record and track the status of all outstanding issues associated with each configuration object.

> "Any change, even a change for the better, is accompanied by drawbacks and discomforts."
>
> **Arnold Bennett**

A number of version control systems establish a *change set*—a collection of all changes (to some baseline configuration) that are required to create a specific version of the software. Dart [DAR91] notes that a change set "captures all changes to all files in the configuration along with the reason for changes and details of who made the changes and when."

A number of named change sets can be identified for an application or system. This enables a software engineer to construct a version of the software by specifying the change sets (by name) that must be applied to the baseline configuration. To accomplish this, a *system modeling* approach is applied. The system model contains: (1) a *template* that includes a component hierarchy and a "build order" for the components that describes how the system must be constructed, (2) construction rules, and (3) verification rules.[4]

A number of different automated approaches to version control have been proposed over the last two decades. The primary difference in approaches is the sophistication of the attributes that are used to construct specific versions and variants of a system and the mechanics of the process for construction.

SOFTWARE TOOLS

The Concurrent Versions System (CVS)

The use of tools to achieve version control is essential for effective change management. The *Concurrent Versions System* (CVS) is a widely used tool for version control. Originally designed for source code, but useful for any text-based file, the CVS system (1) establishes a simple repository, (2) maintains all versions of a file in a single named file by storing only the differences between progressive versions of the original file, and (3) protects against simultaneous changes to a file by establishing different directories for each developer, thus insulating one from another. CVS merges changes when each developer completes her work.

It is important to note that CVS is not a "build" system; that is, it does not construct a specific version of the software. Other tools (e.g., *Makefile*) must be integrated with CVS to accomplish this. CVS does not implement a change control process (e.g., change requests, change reports, bug tracking).

Even with these limitations, CVS "is a dominant open-source network-transparent version control system [that] is useful for everyone from individual developers to large, distributed teams" [CVS02]. Its client/server architecture allows users to access files via Internet connections, and its open source philosophy makes it available on most popular platforms.

CVS is available at no cost for Windows, Macintosh, and UNIX environments. See www.cvshome.org for further details.

---

4 It is also possible to query the system model to assess how a change in one component will impact other components.

27.3.3 Change Control

The reality of change control in a modern software engineering context has been summed up beautifully by James Bach [BAC98]:

> Change control is vital. But the forces that make it necessary also make it annoying. We worry about change because a tiny perturbation in the code can create a big failure in the product. But it can also fix a big failure or enable wonderful new capabilities. We worry about change because a single rogue developer could sink the project; yet brilliant ideas originate in the minds of those rogues, and a burdensome change control process could effectively discourage them from doing creative work.

Bach recognizes that we face a balancing act. Too much change control, and we create problems. Too little, and we create other problems.

> **"The art of progress is to preserve order amid change and to preserve change amid order."**
> **Alfred North Whitehead**

It should be noted that a number of change requests may be combined to result in a single ECO and that ECOs typically result in changes to multiple configuration objects.

For a large software engineering project, uncontrolled change rapidly leads to chaos. For such projects, change control combines human procedures and automated tools. The change control process is illustrated schematically in Figure 27.5. A *change request* is submitted and evaluated to assess technical merit, potential side effects, overall impact on other configuration objects and system functions, and the projected cost of the change. The results of the evaluation are presented as a *change report,* which is used by a *change control authority* (CCA)—a person or group who makes a final decision on the status and priority of the change. An *engineering change order* (ECO) is generated for each approved change. The ECO describes the change to be made, the constraints that must be respected, and the criteria for review and audit.

The object(s) to be changed can be placed in a directory that is controlled solely by the software engineer making the change. A version control system (see the CVS sidebar) updates the original file once the change has been made. As an alternative, the object(s) to be changed can be "checked out" of the project database (repository), the change is made, and appropriate SQA activities are applied. The object(s) is (are) then "checked in" to the database and appropriate version control mechanisms (Section 27.3.2) are used to create the next version of the software.

Confusion leads to errors—some of them very serious. Access and synchronization control avoid confusion. Use version and change control tools that implement both.

These version control mechanisms, integrated within the change control process, implement two important elements of change management—access control and synchronization control. *Access control* governs which software engineers have the authority to access and modify a particular configuration object. *Synchronization control* helps to ensure that parallel changes, performed by two different people, don't overwrite one another [HAR89].

Some readers may begin to feel uncomfortable with the level of bureaucracy implied by the change control process description shown in Figure 27.5. This feeling is

FIGURE 27.5
The change control process

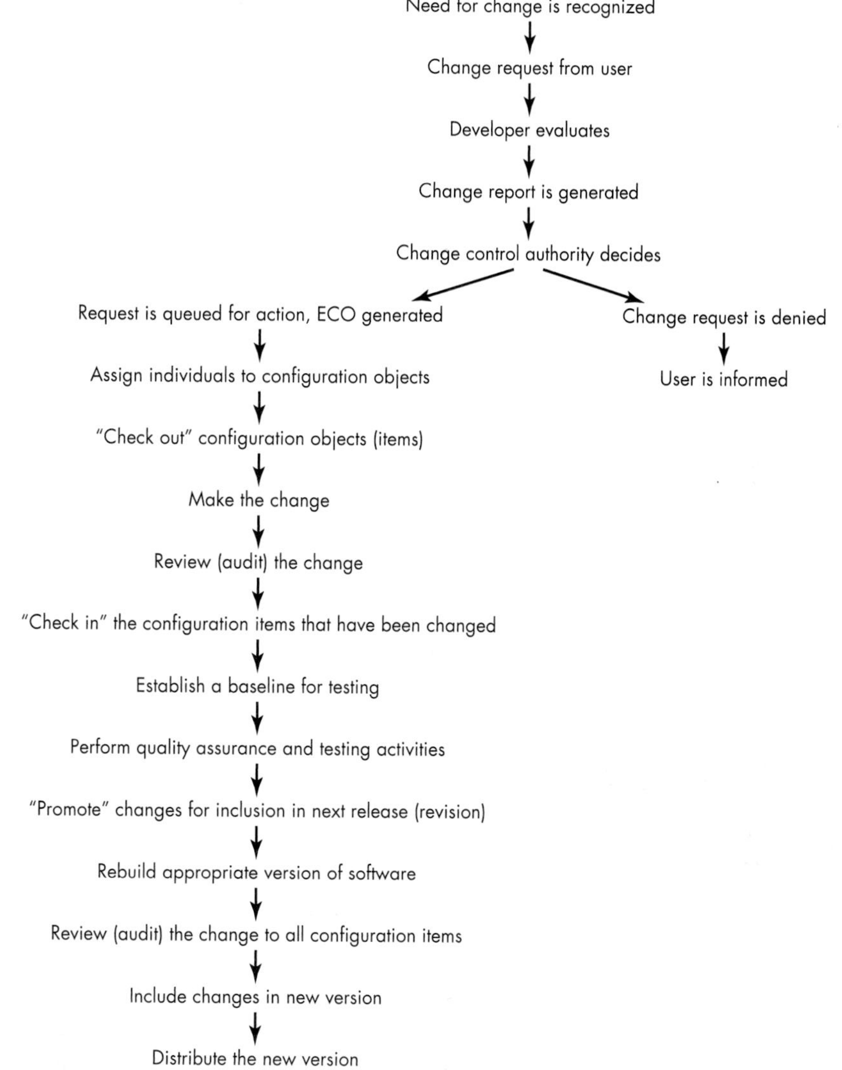

> **ADVICE** *Opt for a bit more change control than you think you'll need. It's likely that too much will be the right amount.*

not uncommon. Without proper safeguards, change control can retard progress and create unnecessary red tape. Most software developers who have change control mechanisms (unfortunately, many have none) have created a number of layers of control to help avoid the problems alluded to here.

Prior to an SCI becoming a baseline, only *informal change control* need be applied. The developer of the configuration object (SCI) in question may make whatever changes are justified by project and technical requirements (as long as changes do not affect broader system requirements that lie outside the developer's scope of work). Once the object has undergone formal technical review and has been approved, a baseline can be created.[5] Once a SCI becomes a baseline, *project level change control* is implemented. Now, to make a change, the developer must gain approval from the project manager (if the change is "local") or from the CCA if the change affects other SCIs. In some cases, formal generation of change requests, change reports, and ECOs is dispensed with. However, assessment of each change is conducted, and all changes are tracked and reviewed.

When the software product is released to customers, *formal change control* is instituted. The formal change control procedure has been outlined in Figure 27.5.

> **"Change is inevitable, except for vending machines."**
>
> **Bumper sticker**

The change control authority plays an active role in the second and third layers of control. Depending on the size and character of a software project, the CCA may be composed of one person—the project manager—or a number of people (e.g., representatives from software, hardware, database engineering, support, marketing). The role of the CCA is to take a global view, that is, to assess the impact of change beyond the SCI in question. How will the change affect hardware? How will the change affect performance? How will the change modify the customer's perception of the product? How will the change affect product quality and reliability? These and many other questions are addressed by the CCA.

SAFEHOME

SCM Issues

The scene: Doug Miller's office as the *SafeHome* software project begins.

The players: Doug Miller (manager of the *SafeHome* software engineering team) and Vinod Raman, Jamie Lazar, and other members of the product software engineering team.

The conversation:

Doug: I know it's early, but we've got to talk about change management.

Vinod (laughing): Hardly. Marketing called this morning with a few "second thoughts." Nothing major, but it's just the beginning.

Jamie: We've been pretty informal about change management on past projects.

Doug: I know, but this is bigger and more visible, and as I recall . . .

Vinod (nodding): We got killed by uncontrolled changes on the home lighting control project . . . remember the delays that . . .

Doug (frowning): A nightmare that I'd prefer not to relive.

Jamie: So what do we do.

Doug: As I see it, three things. First we have to develop—or borrow—a change control process.

Jamie: You mean how people request changes?

Vinod: Yeah, but also how we evaluate the change, decide when to do it (if that's what we decide), and how we keep records of what's affected by the change.

5 A baseline can be created for other reasons as well. For example, when "daily builds" are created, all components checked in by a given time become the baseline for the next day's work.

Doug: Second, we've got to get a really good SCM tool for change and version control.

Jamie: We can build a database for all of our work products.

Vinod: They're called SCIs in this context, and most good tools provide some support for that.

Doug: That's a good start, now we have to . . .

Jamie: Uh, Doug, you said there were three things . . .

Doug (smiling): Third—we've all got to commit to follow the change management process and use the tools—no matter what, okay?

27.3.4 Configuration Audit

Identification, version control, and change control help the software developer to maintain order in what would otherwise be a chaotic and fluid situation. However, even the most successful control mechanisms track a change only until an ECO is generated. How can we ensure that the change has been properly implemented? The answer is twofold: (1) formal technical reviews and (2) the software configuration audit.

The formal technical review (presented in detail in Chapter 26) focuses on the technical correctness of the configuration object that has been modified. The reviewers assess the SCI to determine consistency with other SCIs, omissions, or potential side effects. A formal technical review should be conducted for all but the most trivial changes.

A *software configuration audit* complements the formal technical review by addressing the following questions:

? What are the primary questions that we ask during a configuration audit?

1. Has the change specified in the ECO been made? Have any additional modifications been incorporated?
2. Has a formal technical review been conducted to assess technical correctness?
3. Has the software process been followed, and have software engineering standards been properly applied?
4. Has the change been "highlighted" in the SCI? Have the change date and change author been specified? Do the attributes of the configuration object reflect the change?
5. Have SCM procedures for noting the change, recording it, and reporting it been followed?
6. Have all related SCIs been properly updated?

In some cases, the audit questions are asked as part of a formal technical review. However, when SCM is a formal activity, the SCM audit is conducted separately by the quality assurance group. Such formal configuration audits also ensure that the correct SCIs (by version) have been incorporated into a specific build and that all documentation is up-to-date and consistent with the version that has been built.

Develop a "need to know" list for every configuration object and keep it up-to-date. When a change is made, be sure that everyone on the list is notified.

27.3.5 Status Reporting

Configuration status reporting (sometimes called *status accounting*) is a SCM task that answers the following questions: (1) What happened? (2) Who did it? (3) When did it happen? (4) What else will be affected?

The flow of information for configuration status reporting (CSR) is illustrated in Figure 27.5. Each time a SCI is assigned new or updated identification, a CSR entry is made. Each time a change is approved by the CCA (i.e., an ECO is issued), a CSR entry is made. Each time a configuration audit is conducted, the results are reported as part of the CSR task. Output from CSR may be placed in an on-line database or Web site, so that software developers or maintainers can access change information by keyword category. In addition, a CSR report is generated on a regular basis and is intended to keep management and practitioners appraised of important changes.

SOFTWARE TOOLS

SCM Support

Objective: SCM tools provide support to one or more of the process activities discussed in Section 27.3

Mechanics: Most modern SCM tools work in conjunction with a repository (a database system) and provide mechanisms for identification, version and change control, auditing, and reporting.

Representative Tools[6]

CCC/Harvest, distributed by Computer Associates (www.cai.com), is a multiplatform SCM system.

ClearCase, developed by Rational (www.rational.com), provides a family of SCM functions.

Concurrent Versions System (CVS), an open source tool (www.cvshome.org), is one of the industry's most widely used version control systems (see earlier sidebar).

PVCS, distributed by Merant (www.merant.com), provides a full set of SCM tools that are applicable for both conventional software and WebApps.

SourceForge, distributed by VA Software (sourceforge.net), provides version management, build capabilities, issue/bug tracking, and many other management features.

SurroundSCM, developed by Seapine Software (www.seapine.com), provides complete change management capabilities.

Vesta, distributed by Compac (www.vestasys.org), is a public domain SCM system that can support both small (<10 KLOC) and large (10,000 KLOC) projects.

A comprehensive list of commercial SCM tools and environments can be found at www.cmtoday.com/yp/commercial.html.

27.4 Configuration Management for Web Engineering

In Part 3 of this book, we discussed the special nature of Web applications and the Web engineering process that is required to build them. Among the many characteristics that differentiate WebApps from conventional software is the ubiquitous nature of change.

Web engineering uses an iterative, incremental process model (Chapter 16) that applies many principles derived from agile software development (Chapter 4). Using this

6 Tools noted here do not represent an endorsement, but rather a sampling of tools in this category. In most cases, tool names are trademarked by their respective developers.

approach, an engineering team often develops a WebApp increment in a very short time period via a customer-driven approach. Subsequent increments add additional content and functionality, and each is likely to implement changes that lead to enhanced content, better usability, improved aesthetics, better navigation, enhanced performance, and stronger security. Therefore, in the agile world of Web engineering, change is viewed somewhat differently.

Web engineers must embrace change, and yet a typical agile team eschews all things that appear to be process-heavy, bureaucratic, and formal. Software configuration management is often viewed (albeit incorrectly) to have these characteristics. This seeming contradiction is remedied not by rejecting SCM principles, practices, and tools, but rather by molding them to meet the special needs of Web engineering projects.

27.4.1 Configuration Management Issues for WebApps

? What impact does uncontrolled change have on a WebApp?

As WebApps become increasingly important to business survival and growth, the need for configuration management grows. Why? Because without effective controls, improper changes to a WebApp (recall that immediacy and continuous evolution are the dominant attributes of many WebApps) can lead to unauthorized posting of new product information; erroneous or poorly tested functionality that frustrates visitors to a Web site; security holes that jeopardize internal company systems; and other economically unpleasant or even disastrous consequences.

The general strategies for software configuration management (SCM) described in this chapter are applicable, but tactics and tools must be adapted to conform to the unique nature of WebApps. Four issues [DAR99] should be considered when developing tactics for WebApp configuration management—content, people, scalability, and politics.

Content. A typical WebApp contains a vast array of content—text, graphics, applets, scripts, audio/video files, forms, active page elements, tables, streaming data, and many others. The challenge is to organize this sea of content into a rational set of configuration objects (Section 27.1.4) and then establish appropriate configuration control mechanisms for these objects.

People. Because a significant percentage of WebApp development continues to be conducted in an ad hoc manner, any person involved in the WebApp can (and often does) create content. Many content creators have no software engineering background and are completely unaware of the need for configuration management. As a consequence, the application grows and changes in an uncontrolled fashion.

Scalability. The techniques and controls applied to a small WebApps do not scale upward well. It is not uncommon for a simple WebApp to grow significantly as interconnections with existing information systems, databases, data warehouses, and portal gateways are implemented. As size and complexity grows, small changes can have far-reaching and unintended affects that can be problematic. Therefore, the rigor of configuration control mechanisms should be directly proportional to application scale.

Politics. Who "owns" a WebApp? This question is argued in companies large and small, and its answer has a significant impact on the management and control activities associated with WebE. In some instances Web developers are housed outside the IT organization, creating potential communication difficulties. Dart [DAR99] suggests the following questions to help understand the politics associated with WebE:

? **How do I determine who has responsibility for WebApp CM?**

- Who assumes responsibility for the accuracy of the information on the Web site?
- Who assures that quality control processes have been followed before information is published to the site?
- Who is responsible for making changes?
- Who assumes the cost of change?

The answers to these questions help determine the people within an organization who must adopt a configuration management process for WebApps.

27.4.2 WebApp Configuration Objects

WebApps encompass a broad range of configuration objects—content objects (e.g., text, graphics, images, video, audio), functional components (e.g., scripts, applets), and interface objects (e.g., COM or CORBA). WebApp objects can be identified (assigned file names) in any manner that is appropriate for the organization. However, the following conventions are recommended to ensure that cross-platform compatibility is maintained: filenames should be limited to 32 characters in length, mixed-case or all-caps names should be avoided, and the use of underscores in file names should be avoided. In addition, URL references (links) within a configuration object should always use relative paths (e.g., ../products/alarmsensors.html).

All WebApp content has format and structure. Internal file formats are dictated by the computing environment in which the content is stored. However, *rendering format* (often called *display format*) is defined by the aesthetic style and design rules established for the WebApp. *Content structure* defines a content architecture; that is, it defines the way in which content objects are assembled to present meaningful information to an end-user. Boiko [BOI02] defines structure as "maps that you lay over a set of content chunks [objects] to organize them and make them accessible to the people who need them."

27.4.3 Content Management

Content management is related to configuration management in the sense that a content management system (CMS) establishes a process (supported by appropriate tools) that acquires existing content (from a broad array of WebApp configuration objects), structures it in a way that enables it to be presented to an end-user, and then provides it to the client-side environment for display.

> "Content management is an antidote to today's information frenzy."
>
> **Bob Boiko**

The most common use of content management system occurs when a dynamic WebApp is built. Dynamic WebApps create Web pages "on-the-fly." That is, the user typically queries the WebApp requesting specific information. The WebApp queries a database, formats the information accordingly, and presents it to the user. For example, a music company provides a library of CDs for sale. When a user requests a CD or its e-music equivalent, a database is queried, and a variety of information about the artist, the CD (e.g., its cover image or graphics), the musical content, and sample audio are all downloaded and configured into a standard content template. The resultant Web page is built on the server-side and passed to the client-side browser for examination by the end-user. A generic representation of this is shown in Figure 27.6.

The collection subsystem encompasses all actions required to create, acquire, and/or convert content into a form that can be presented on the client side.

In the most general sense, a CMS "configures" content for the end-user by invoking three integrated subsystems: a collection subsystem, a management subsystem, and a publishing subsystem [BOI02].

FIGURE 27.6

Content management system (CMS)

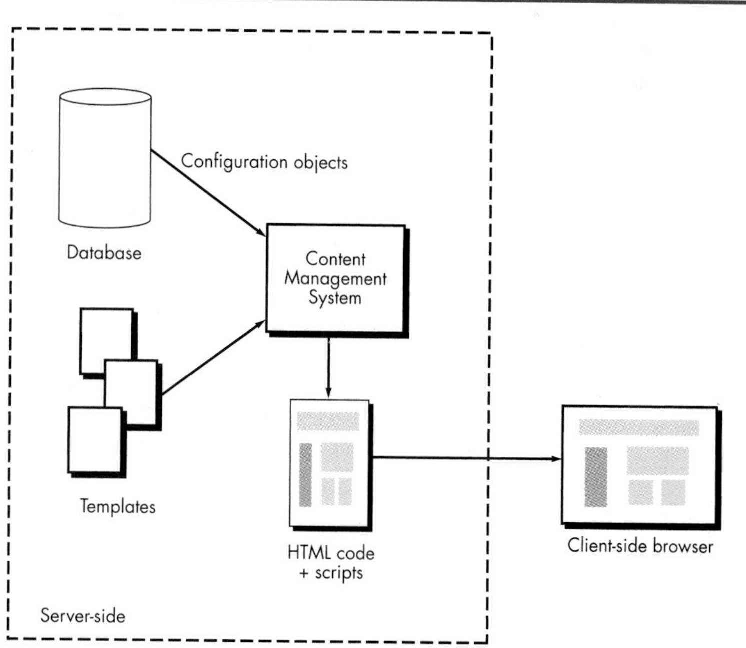

The management subsystem implements a repository for all content. Configuration management is performed within this subsystem.

The collection subsystem. Content is derived from data and information that must be created or acquired by a content developer. The *collection subsystem* encompasses all actions required to create and/or acquire content, and the technical functions that are necessary to (1) convert content into a form that can be represented by a mark-up language (e.g., HTML, XML), and (2) organize content into packets that can be displayed effectively on the client side.

The management subsystem. Once content exists, it must be stored in a repository, cataloged for subsequent acquisition and use, and labeled to define (1) current status (e.g., is the content object complete or in development), (2) the appropriate version of the content object, and (3) related content objects. Therefore, the *management subsystem* implements a repository that encompasses the following elements:

- *Content database*—the information structure that has been established to store all content objects.
- *Database capabilities*—functions that enable the CMS to search for specific content objects (or categories of objects), store and retrieve objects, and manage the file structure that has been established for the content.
- *Configuration management functions*—the functional elements and associated workflow that support content object identification, version control, change management, change auditing, and reporting.

In addition to these elements, the management subsystem implements an administration function that encompasses the metadata and rules that control the overall structure of the content and the manner in which it is supported.

The publishing subsystem extracts content from the repository and delivers it to client-side browsers.

The publishing subsystem. Content must be extracted from the repository, converted to a form that is amenable to publication, and formatted so that it can be transmitted to client-side browsers. The *publishing subsystem* accomplishes these tasks using a series of templates. Each *template* is a function that builds a publication using one of three different components [BOI02]:

- *Static elements*—text, graphics, media, and scripts that require no further processing are transmitted directly to the client-side.
- *Publication services*—function calls to specific retrieval and formatting services that personalize content (using predefined rules), perform data conversion, and build appropriate navigation links.
- *External services*—provide access to external corporate information infrastructure such as enterprise data or "back-room" applications.

A content management system that encompasses each of these subsystems is applicable for major Web engineering projects. However, the basic philosophy and functionality associated with a CMS are applicable to all dynamic WebApps.

SOFTWARE TOOLS

Content Management

Objective: To assist software engineers and content developers in managing content that is incorporated into WebApps.

Mechanics: Tools in this category enable Web engineers and content providers to update WebApp content in a controlled manner. Most establish a simple file management system that assigns page-by-page update and editing permissions for various types of WebApp content. Some maintain a versioning system so that previous versions of content can be achieved for historical purposes.

Representative Tools[7]

Content Management Tools Suite, developed by interactivetools.com (www.interactivetools. com/), is a suite of content management tools that focus on content management for specific application domains (e.g., news articles, classified ads, real estate).

ektron-CMS300, developed by ektron (www.ektron.com), is a suite of tools that provides content management capabilities as well as Web development tools.

OmniUpdate, developed by WebsiteASP, Inc. (www.omniupdate.com), is a tool that allows authorized content providers to develop controlled updates to specified WebApp content.

Tower IDM, developed by Tower Technologies (www.towertech.com), is a document processing system and content repository for managing all forms of unstructured business information—images; forms; computer-generated reports; statements and invoices; office documents; e-mail and Web content.

Additional information on SCM and content management tools for Web engineering can be found at one or more of the following Web sites:

Web Developer's Virtual Encyclopedia (www.wdlv.com), *WebDeveloper* (www.webdeveloper.com), Developer Shed (www.devshed.com), *webknowhow.net* (www.webknowhow.net), or WebReference (www.webreference.com).

27.4.4 Change Management

The workflow associated with change control for conventional software (Section 27.3.3) is generally too ponderous for Web engineering. It is unlikely that the change request, change report, and engineering change order sequence can be achieved in an agile manner that is acceptable for most WebApp development projects. How then do we manage a continuous stream of changes requested for WebApp content and functionality?

To implement effective change management within the "code and go" philosophy that continues to dominate WebApp development, the conventional change control process must be modified. Each change should be categorized into one of four classes:

Class 1—a content or function change that corrects an error or enhances local content or functionality.

Class 2—a content or function change that has impact on other content objects or functional components.

7 Tools noted here do not represent an endorsement, but rather a sampling of tools in this category. In most cases, tool names are trademarked by their respective developers.

FIGURE 27.7

Managing changes for WebApps

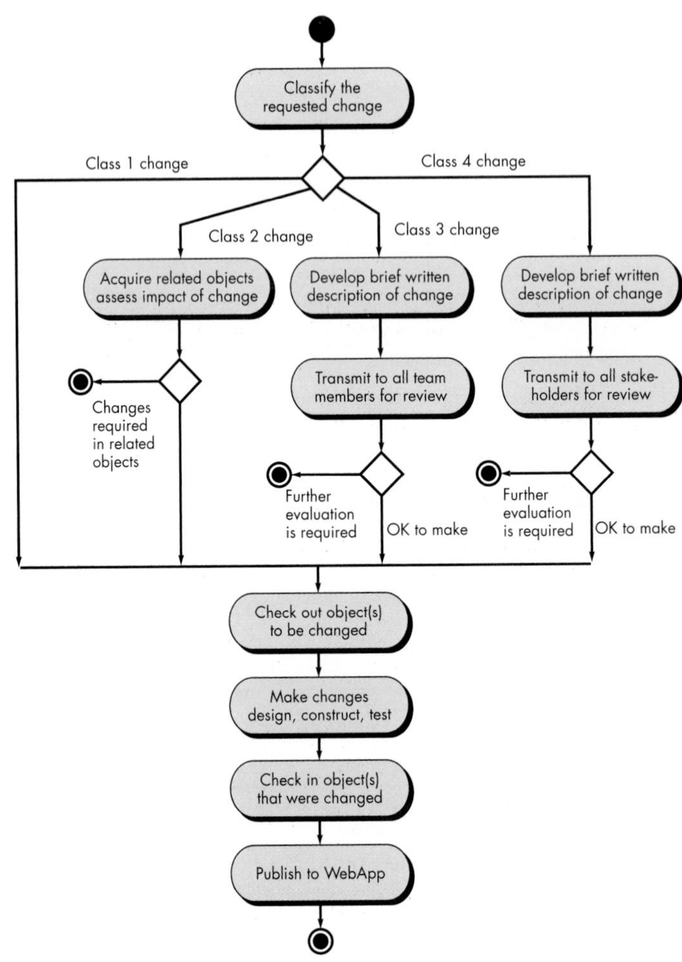

Class 3—a content or function change that has broad impact across a WebApp (e.g., major extension of functionality, significant enhancement or reduction in content, major required changes in navigation).

Class 4—a major design change (e.g., a change in interface design or navigation approach) that will be immediately noticeable to one or more categories of user.

Once the requested change has been categorized, it can be processed according to the algorithm shown in Figure 27.7.

Referring to the figure, class 1 and 2 changes are treated informally and are handled in an agile manner. For a class 1 change, the Web engineer evaluates the impact of the change, but no external review or documentation is required. As the change is made, standard check-in and check-out procedures are enforced by configuration repository tools. For class 2 changes, it is incumbent on the Web engineer to review the impact of the change on related objects (or to ask other developers responsible for those objects to do so). If the change can be made without requiring significant changes to other objects, modification occurs without additional review or documentation. If substantive changes are required, further evaluation and planning are necessary.

Class 3 and 4 changes are also treated in an agile manner, but some descriptive documentation and more formal review procedures are required. A *change description*—describing the change and providing a brief assessment of the impact of the change—is developed for class 3 changes. The description is distributed to all members of the Web engineering team who review it to better assess its impact. A change description is also developed for class 4 changes, but in this case, the review is conducted by all stakeholders.

SOFTWARE TOOLS

Change Management

Objective: To assist Web engineers and content developers in managing changes as they are made to WebApp configuration objects.

Mechanics: Tools in this category were originally developed for conventional software, but can be adapted by Web engineers to make controlled changes to WebApps.

Representative Tools[8]

ChangeMan WCM, developed by Serena (www.serena.com), is a one of a suite of change management tools that provide SCM capabilities.

ClearCase, developed by Rational (www.rational.com), is a suite of tools that provides full configuration management capabilities for WebApps.

PVCS, developed by Merant (www.merant.com), is a suite of tools that provides full configuration management capabilities for WebApps.

Source Integrity, developed by mks (www.mks.com), is a SCM tool that can be integrated with selected development environments.

27.4.5 Version Control

As a WebApp evolves through a series of increments, a number of different versions may exist at the same time. One version (the current operational WebApp) is available via the Internet for end-users; another version (the next WebApp increment) may be in the final stages of testing prior to deployment; a third version is in development and represents a major update in content, interface aesthetics, and functionality. Configuration objects must be clearly defined so that each can be associated with the appropriate version. In addition, control mechanisms must be

8 Tools noted here do not represent an endorsement, but rather a sampling of tools in this category. In most cases, tool names are trademarked by their respective developers.

established. Dreilinger [DRE99] discusses the importance of version (and change) control when he writes:

> In an *uncontrolled* site where multiple authors have access to edit and contribute, the potential for conflict and problems arises—more so when these authors work from different offices at different times of day and night. You may spend the day improving the file *index.html* for a customer. After you've made your changes, another developer who works at home after hours, or in another office, may spend the night uploading their own newly revised version of the file *index.html,* completely overwriting your work with no way to get it back!

This situation should sound familiar to every software engineer as well as every Web engineer. To avoid it, a version control process should be established.

1. *A central repository for the WebApp project should be established.* The repository will hold current versions of all WebApp configuration objects (content, functional components, and others).
2. *Each Web engineer creates his or her own working folder.* The folder contains those objects that are being created or changed at any given time.
3. *The clocks on all developer workstations should be synchronized.* This is done to avoid overwriting conflicts when two developers make updates that are very close to one another in time.
4. *As new configuration objects are developed or existing objects are changed, they are imported into the central repository.* The version control tool (see discussion of CVS earlier in this chapter) will manage all check-in and check-out functions from the working folders of each Web engineer.
5. *As objects are imported or exported from the repository, an automatic, time-stamped log message is made.* This provides useful information for auditing and can become part of an effective reporting scheme.

The version control tool maintains different versions of the WebApp and can revert to an older version if required.

27.4.6 Auditing and Reporting

In the interest of agility, the auditing and reporting functions are deemphasized in Web engineering work. However, they are not eliminated altogether. All objects that are checked into or out of the repository are recorded in a log that can be reviewed at any point in time. A complete log report can be created so that all members of the Web engineering team have a chronology of changes over a defined period of time. In addition, an automated e-mail notification (addressed to those developers and stakeholders who have interest) can be sent every time an object is checked in or out of the repository.

INFO

SCM Standards

The following list of SCM standards (extracted in part from www.12207.com) is reasonably comprehensive:

IEEE Standards	**standards.ieee.org/catalog/olis/**
IEEE 828	Software Configuration Management Plans
IEEE 1042	Software Configuration Management
ISO Standards	**www.iso.ch/iso/en/ISOOnline.frontpage**
ISO 10007-1995	Quality Management, Guidance for CM
ISO/IEC 12207	Information Technology—Software Life Cycle Processes
ISO/IEC TR 15271	Guide for ISO/IEC 12207
ISO/IEC TR 15846	Software Engineering—Software Life Cycle Process—Configuration Management for Software
EIA Standards	**www.eia.org/**
EIA 649	National Consensus Standard for Configuration Management
EIA CMB4-1A	Configuration Management Definitions for Digital Computer Programs
EIA CMB4-2	Configuration Identification for Digital Computer Programs
EIA CMB4-3	Computer Software Libraries
EIA CMB4-4	Configuration Change Control for Digital Computer Programs
EIA CMB6-1C	Configuration and Data Management References
EIA CMB6-3	Configuration Identification
EIA CMB6-4	Configuration Control
EIA CMB6-5	Textbook for Configuration Status Accounting
EIA CMB7-1	Electronic Interchange of Configuration Management Data
U.S. Military Standards	**www-library.itsi.disa.mil**
DoD MIL STD-973	Configuration Management
MIL-HDBK-61	Configuration Management Guidance
Other standards	
DO-178B	Guidelines for the Development of Aviation Software
ESA PSS-05-09	Guide to Software Configuration Management
AECL CE-1001-STD rev.1	Standard for Software Engineering of Safety Critical Software
DOE SCM checklist	cio.doe.gov/ITReform/sqse/download/cmcklst.doc
BS-6488	British Std., Configuration Management of Computer-Based Systems
Best Practice—UK	Office of Government Commerce: www.ogc.gov.uk
CMII	Institute of CM Best Practices: www.icmhq.com

A *Configuration Management Resource Guide* provides complementary information for those interested in CM processes and practice. It is available at www.quality.org/config/cm-guide.html.

27.5 Summary

Software configuration management is an umbrella activity that is applied throughout the software process. SCM identifies, controls, audits, and reports modifications that invariably occur while software is being developed and after it has been released to a customer. All information produced as part of software engineering becomes part of a software configuration. The configuration is organized in a manner that enables orderly management of change.

The software configuration is composed of a set of interrelated objects, also called software configuration items, that are produced as a result of some software engineering activity. In addition to documents, programs, and data, the development environment that is used to create software can also be placed under configuration control. All SCIs are stored within a repository that implements mechanisms and data structures to ensure data integrity, provides integration support for other software tools, supports information sharing among all members of the software team, and implements functions in support of version and change control.

Once a configuration object has been developed and reviewed, it becomes a baseline. Changes to a baselined object result in the creation of a new version of that object. The evolution of a program can be tracked by examining the revision history of all configuration objects. Basic and composite objects form an object pool from which versions are created. Version control is the set of procedures and tools for managing the use of these objects.

Change control is a procedural activity that ensures quality and consistency as changes are made to a configuration object. The change control process begins with a change request, leads to a decision to make or reject the request for change, and culminates with a controlled update of the SCI that is to be changed.

The configuration audit is an SQA activity that helps to ensure that quality is maintained as changes are made. Status reporting provides information about each change to those with a need to know.

Configuration management for Web engineering is similar in most respects to SCM for conventional software. However, each of the core SCM tasks should be streamlined to make it as lean as possible, and special provisions for content management must be implemented.

References

[BAB86] Babich, W.A., *Software Configuration Management,* Addison-Wesley, 1986.

[BAC98] Bach, J., "The Highs and Lows of Change Control," *Computer,* vol. 31, no. 8, August 1998, pp. 113–115.

[BER80] Bersoff, E.H., V.D. Henderson, and S.G. Siegel, *Software Configuration Management,* Prentice-Hall, 1980.

[BOI02] Boiko, B., *Content Management Bible,* Hungry Minds Publishing, 2002.

[CHO89] Choi, S.C., and W. Scacchi, "Assuring the Correctness of a Configured Software Description," *Proc. 2nd Intl. Workshop on Software Configuration Management,* ACM, Princeton, NJ, October 1989, pp. 66–75.

[CVS02] Concurrent Versions System Web site, www.cvshome.org, 2002.

[DAR91] Dart, S., "Concepts in Configuration Management Systems," *Proc. Third International Workshop on Software Configuration Management,* ACM SIGSOFT, 1991, download from: http://www.sei.cmu.edu/legacy/scm/abstracts/abscm_concepts.html.

[DAR99] Dart, S., "Change Management: Containing the Web Crisis," *Proc. Software Configuration Management Symposium,* Toulouse, France, 1999, available at http://www.perforce.com/perforce/conf99/dart.html.

[DAR01] Dart, S., *Spectrum of Functionality in Configuration Management Systems,* Software Engineering Institute, 2001, available at http://www.sei.cmu.edu/legacy/scm/tech_rep/TR11_90/TOC_TR11_90.html.

[DRE99] Dreilinger, S., "CVS Version Control for Web Site Projects," 1999, available at http://www.durak.org/cvswebsites/howto-cvs/howto-cvs.html.

[FOR89] Forte, G., "Rally Round the Repository," *CASE Outlook,* December 1989, pp. 5–27.

[GRI95] Griffen, J., "Repositories: Data Dictionary Descendant Can Extend Legacy Code Investment," *Application Development Trends,* April 1995, pp. 65–71.

[GUS89] Gustavsson, A., "Maintaining the Evolution of Software Objects in an Integrated Environment," *Proc. 2nd Intl. Workshop on Software Configuration Management,* ACM, Princeton, NJ, October 1989, pp. 114–117.

[HAR89] Harter, R., "Configuration Management," *HP Professional,* vol. 3, no. 6, June 1989.

[IEE94] *Software Engineering Standards,* 1994 edition, IEEE Computer Society, 1994.

[JAC02] Jacobson, I., "A Resounding 'Yes' to Agile Processes—But Also More," *Cutter IT Journal,* vol. 15, no. 1., January 2002, pp. 18–24.

[REI89] Reichenberger, C., "Orthogonal Version Management," *Proc. 2nd Intl. Workshop on Software Configuration Management,* ACM, Princeton, NJ, October 1989, pp. 137–140.

[SHA95] Sharon, D., and R. Bell, "Tools That Bind: Creating Integrated Environments," *IEEE Software,* March 1995, pp. 76–85.

[TAY85] Taylor, B., "A Database Approach to Configuration Management for Large Projects," *Proc. Conf. Software Maintenance—1985,* IEEE, November 1985, pp. 15–23.

Problems and Points to Ponder

27.1. Why is the First Law of System Engineering true? Provide specific examples for each of the four fundamental reasons for change.

27.2. What are the four elements that exist when an effective SCM system is implemented? Discuss each briefly.

27.3. Discuss the reasons for baselines in your own words.

27.4. Assume that you're the manager of a small project. What baselines would you define for the project, and how would you control them?

27.5. Use UML aggregations or composites (Chapter 8) to describe the interrelationships among the SCIs (configuration objects) listed in Section 27.1.4.

27.6. Design a project database (repository) system that would enable a software engineer to store, cross-reference, trace, update, and change, all important software configuration items. How would the database handle different versions of the same program? Would source code be handled differently than documentation? How will two developers be precluded from making different changes to the same SCI at the same time?

26.7. Research an existing SCM tool, and describe how it implements control for versions and configuration objects in general.

27.8. The relations <part-of> and <interrelated>represent simple relationships between configuration objects. Describe five additional relationships that might be useful in the context of a SCM repository.

27.9. Research an existing SCM tool and describe how it implements the mechanics of version control. Alternatively, read two or three of the papers on SCM and describe the different data structures and referencing mechanisms that are used for version control.

27.10. Using Figure 27.5 as a guide, develop an even more detailed work breakdown for change control. Describe the role of the CCA and suggest formats for the change request, the change report, and the ECO.

27.11. Develop a checklist for use during configuration audits.

27.12. What is the difference between a SCM audit and a formal technical review? Can their functions be folded into one review? What are the pros and cons?

27.13. Briefly describe the differences between SCM for conventional software and SCM for WebApps.

27.14. What is content management? Use the Web to research the features of a content management tool and provide a brief summary.

Further Readings and Information Sources

Lyon (*Practical CM,* Raven Publishing, 2003, available at www.configuration.org) has written a comprehensive guide for CM professionals that includes pragmatic guidelines for implementing every aspect of a configuration management system (updated yearly). Hass (*Configuration Management: Principles and Practice,* Addison-Wesley, 2002) and Leon (*A Guide to Software Configuration Management,* Artech House, 2000) provide useful surveys of the subject. White and Clemm (*Software Configuration Management Strategies and Rational ClearCase,* Addison-Wesley, 2000) present SCM within the context of one of the more popular SCM tools.

Mikkelsen and Pherigo (*Practical Software Configuration Management: The Latenight Developer's Handbook,* Allyn & Bacon, 1997) and Compton and Callahan (*Configuration Management for Software,* VanNostrand-Reinhold, 1994) provide pragmatic tutorials on important SCM practices. Ben-Menachem (*Software Configuration Management Guidebook,* McGraw-Hill, 1994), and Ayer and Patrinnostro (*Software Configuration Management,* McGraw-Hill, 1992) present good overviews for those who need further introduction to the subject. Berlack (*Software Configuration Management,* Wiley, 1992) presents a useful survey of SCM concepts, emphasizing the importance of the repository and tools in the management of change. Babich [BAB86] provides an abbreviated, yet effective treatment of pragmatic issues in software configuration management. Arnold and Bohner (*Software Change Impact Analysis,* IEEE Computer Society Press, 1996) have edited an anthology that discusses how to analyze the impact of change within complex software-based systems.

Berczuk and Appleton (*Software Configuration Management Patterns,* Addison-Wesley, 2002) present a variety of useful patterns that assist in understanding SCM and implementing effective SCM systems. Brown, et al. (*Anti-Patterns and Patterns in Software Configuration Management,* Wiley, 1999) discuss the things not to do (anti-patterns) when implementing an SCM process and then consider their remedies.

Buckley (*Implementing Configuration Management,* IEEE Computer Society Press, 1993) considers configuration management approaches for all system elements—hardware, software, and firmware—with detailed discussions of major CM activities. Rawlings (*SCM for Network Development Environments,* McGraw-Hill, 1994) considers the impact of SCM for software development in a networked environment. Bays (*Software Release Methodology,* Prentice-Hall, 1999) presents a collection of best practices for all activities that occur after changes are made to an application.

As WebApps have become more dynamic, content management has become an essential topic for Web engineers. Books by Addey and his colleagues (*Content Management Systems,* Glasshaus, 2003), Boiko [BOI02], Hackos (*Content Management for Dynamic Web Delivery,* Wiley, 2002), Nakano (*Web Content Management,* Addison-Wesley, 2001) present worthwhile treatments of the subject.

A wide variety of information sources on software configuration management is available on the Internet. An up-to-date list of World Wide Web references can be found at the SEPA Web site: **http://www.mhhe.com/pressman.**

PART

Five

ADVANCED TOPICS IN SOFTWARE ENGINEERING

In this part of *Software Engineering: A Practitioner's Approach,* we consider a number of advanced topics that will extend your understanding of software engineering. In the chapters that follow, we address the following questions:

- What notation and mathematical preliminaries ("formal methods") are required to formally specify software?
- What key technical activities are conducted during the cleanroom software engineering process?
- How is component-based software engineering used to create systems from reusable components?
- What technical activities are required for software reengineering?
- What are the future directions of software engineering?

Once these questions are answered, you'll understand topics that may have a profound impact on software engineering over the next decade.

CHAPTER

28 FORMAL METHODS

KEY CONCEPTS

Software engineering methods can be categorized on a "formality" spectrum that is loosely tied to the degree of mathematical rigor applied during analysis and design. For this reason, the analysis and design methods discussed earlier in this book fall at the informal end of the spectrum. A combination of diagrams, text, tables, and simple notation is used to create analysis and design models, but little mathematical rigor has been applied.

We now consider the other end of the formality spectrum. Here, a specification and design are described using a formal syntax and semantics that specify system function and behavior. The specification is mathematical in form (e.g., predicate calculus can be used as the basis for a formal specification language).

In his introductory discussion of formal methods, Anthony Hall [HAL90] states:

> Formal methods are controversial. Their advocates claim that they can revolutionize [software] development. Their detractors think they are impossibly difficult. Meanwhile, for most people, formal methods are so unfamiliar that it is difficult to judge the competing claims.

In this chapter, we explore formal methods and examine their potential impact on software engineering in the years to come.

QUICK LOOK

What is it? Formal methods allow a software engineer to create a specification that is more complete, consistent, and unambiguous than those produced using conventional methods. Set theory and logic notation are used to create a clear statement of facts (requirements). This mathematical specification can then be analyzed to improve (or even prove) correctness and consistency. Because the specification is created using mathematical notation, it is inherently less ambiguous than informal modes of representation.

Who does it? A specially trained software engineer creates a formal specification.

Why is it important? In safety-critical or mission-critical systems, failure can have a high price. Lives may be lost or severe economic consequences can arise when computer software fails. In such situations, it is essential that errors are uncovered before software is put into operation. Formal methods reduce specification errors dramatically and, as a consequence, serve as the basis for software that has very few errors once the customer begins using it.

What are the steps? The notation and heuristics of sets and constructive specification—set operators, logic operators, and sequences—form the basis of formal methods. Formal methods define the data invariant, states, and operations for a system function by translating informal requirements for the problem into a more formal representation.

What is the work product? A specification represented in a formal language such as OCL or Z is produced when formal methods are applied.

How do I ensure that I've done it right? Because formal methods use discrete mathematics as the specification mechanism, logic proofs can be applied to each system function to demonstrate that the specification is correct. However, even if logic proofs are not used, the structure and discipline of a formal specification will lead to improved software quality.

28.1 Basic Concepts

The Encyclopedia of Software Engineering [MAR94] defines formal methods in the following manner:

> A method is formal if it has a sound mathematical basis, typically given by a formal specification language. This basis provides a means of precisely defining notions like consistency and completeness, and more relevantly, specification, implementation and correctness.

The desired properties of a formal specification—consistency, completeness, and lack of ambiguity—are the objectives of all specification methods. However, the use of formal methods results in a much higher likelihood of achieving these ideals. The formal syntax of a specification language (Section 28.4) enables requirements and design to be interpreted in only one way, eliminating ambiguity that often occurs when a natural language (e.g., English) or a graphical notation must be interpreted by a reader. The descriptive facilities of set theory and logic notation (Section 28.2) enable clear statement of facts (requirements). To be consistent, facts stated in one place in a specification should not be contradicted in another place. Consistency is ensured by mathematically proving that initial facts can be formally mapped (using inference rules) into later statements within the specification.

> "Formal methods have tremendous potential for improving the clarity and precision of requirements specifications, and in finding important and subtle errors."
>
> **Steve Easterbrook et al.**

Completeness is difficult to achieve, even when formal methods are used. Some aspects of a system may be left undefined as the specification is being created; other characteristics may be purposely omitted to allow designers some freedom in choosing an implementation approach; and finally, it is impossible to consider every operational scenario in a large, complex system. Things may simply be omitted by mistake.

Although the formalism provided by mathematics has an appeal to some software engineers, others (some would say, the majority) look askance at a mathematical view of software development. To understand why a formal approach has merit, we must first consider the deficiencies associated with less formal approaches.

28.1.1 Deficiencies of Less Formal Approaches[1]

The methods discussed for analysis and design in Parts 2 and 3 of this book make heavy use of natural language and a variety of graphical notations. Although careful application of analysis and design methods coupled with thorough review can and does lead to high-quality software, sloppiness in the application of these methods can create a variety of problems. A system specification can contain contradictions, ambiguities, vagueness, incomplete statements, and mixed levels of abstraction.

Although a good document index cannot eliminate contradictions, it can help to uncover them. Consider creating an index for specifications and other documents.

Contradictions are sets of statements that are at variance with each other. For example, one part of a system specification may state that the system must monitor all the temperatures in a chemical reactor while another part, perhaps written by another person may state that only temperatures occurring within a certain range are to be monitored.

Ambiguities are statements that can be interpreted in a number of ways. For example, the following statement is ambiguous:

> The operator identity consists of the operator name and password; the password consists of six digits. It should be displayed on the security VDU and deposited in the login file when an operator logs into the system.

In this extract, does the word *it* refer to the password or the operator identity?

Vagueness often occurs because a system specification is a very bulky document. Achieving a high level of precision consistently is an almost impossible task.

> **"Making mistakes is human. Repeating 'em is too."**
>
> **Malcolm Forbes**

Incompleteness is one of the most frequently occurring problems with system specifications. For example, consider the functional requirement:

> The system should maintain the hourly level of the reservoir from depth sensors situated in the reservoir. These values should be stored for the past six months.

ADVICE

Effective formal technical reviews can eliminate many of these problems. However, some will not be uncovered. Be on the lookout for deficiencies during design, code, and test.

This describes the main data storage part of a system. If one of the commands for the system was

> The function of the AVERAGE command is to display on a PC the average water level for a particular sensor between two times.

and assuming that no more detail was presented for this command, the details of the command would be seriously incomplete. For example, the description of the command does not include what should happen if a user of a system specifies a time that was more than six months before the current hour.

1 This section and others in the first part of this chapter have been adapted from work contributed by Darrel Ince for the European edition of the fifth edition of *Software Engineering: A Practitioner's Approach.*

Mixed levels of abstraction occur when very abstract statements are intermixed randomly with statements that are at a much lower level of detail. While both types of statements are important in a system specification, specifiers often manage to intermix them to such an extent that it becomes very difficult to see the overall functional architecture of a system.

28.1.2 Mathematics in Software Development

Mathematics has many useful properties for the developers of large systems. One is that it can succinctly and exactly describe a physical situation, an object, or the outcome of an action. A specification of a computer-based system can be developed using specialized mathematics in much the same way that an electrical engineer can use mathematics to describe a circuit.[2]

Mathematics supports abstraction and thus is an excellent medium for modeling. Because it is an exact medium there is little possibility of ambiguity. Specifications can be mathematically validated for contradictions and incompleteness, and vagueness can be eliminated. In addition, mathematics can be used to represent levels of abstraction in a system specification in an organized way.

Finally, mathematics provides a high level of validation when it is used as a software development medium. It is possible to use a mathematical proof to demonstrate that a design matches a specification and that program code is a correct reflection of a design.

28.1.3 Formal Methods Concepts

The aim of this section is to present the main concepts involved in the mathematical specification of software systems, without encumbering the reader with too much mathematical detail. To accomplish this, we use a few simple examples.

Example 1: a symbol table. A program is used to maintain a symbol table. Such a table is used frequently in many different types of applications. It consists of a collection of items without any duplication. An example of a typical symbol table is shown in Figure 28.1. It represents the table used by an operating system to hold the names of the users of the system. Other examples of tables include the collection of names of staff in a payroll system or the collection of names of computers in a network communications system.

KEY POINT
A data invariant is a set of conditions that are true throughout the execution of the system that contains a collection of data.

Assume that the table presented in this example consists of no more than *MaxIds* members of staff. This statement, which places a constraint on the table, is a component of a condition known as a *data invariant*—an important idea that we shall return to throughout this chapter.

2 A word of caution is appropriate at this point. The mathematical system specifications that are presented in this chapter are not as succinct as a mathematical specification for a simple circuit. Software systems are notoriously complex, and it would be unrealistic to expect that they could be specified in one line of mathematics.

FIGURE 28.1

A symbol table

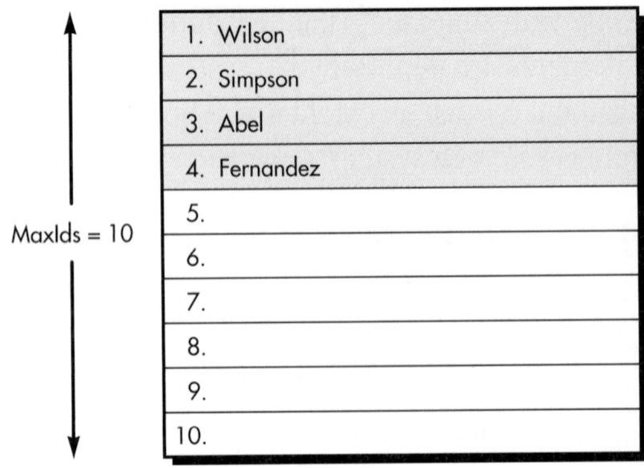

Another way of looking at the notion of state is to say that data determines state. That is, you can examine data to see what state the system is in.

A data invariant is a condition that is true throughout the execution of the system that contains a collection of data. The data invariant that holds for the symbol table just discussed has two components: (1) that the table will contain no more than *MaxIds* names and (2) that there will be no duplicate names in the table. In the case of the symbol table program, this means that no matter when the symbol table is examined during execution of the system, it will always contain no more than *MaxIds* staff identifiers and will contain no duplicates.

Another important concept is that of a *state.* Many formal languages, such as OCL (Section 28.5) , use the notion of a state as it was discussed in Chapters 7 and 8; that is, a system can be in one of several states, each representing an externally observable mode of behavior. However, a different definition for the term *state* is used in the Z language (Section 28.6). In Z (and related languages), the state of a system is represented by the system's stored data (hence, Z suggests a much larger number of states, representing each possible configuration of the data). Using the latter definition in the example of the symbol table program, the state is the symbol table.

The final concept is that of an *operation.* This is an action that takes place within a system and reads or writes data. If the symbol table program is concerned with adding and removing staff names from the symbol table, then it will be associated with two operations: an operation to *add* a specified name to the symbol table and an operation to *remove* an existing name from the table.[3] If the program provides the facility to check whether a specific name is contained in the table, then there would be an operation that would return some indication of whether the name is in the table.

Three types of conditions can be associated with operations: invariants, preconditions, and postconditions. An *invariant* defines what is guaranteed not to change. For example, the symbol table has an invariant that states that the number of elements is always less than or equal to *MaxIds.* A *precondition* defines the circum-

3 It should be noted that adding a name cannot occur in the *full* state and deleting a name is impossible in the *empty* state.

FIGURE 28.2

A block handler

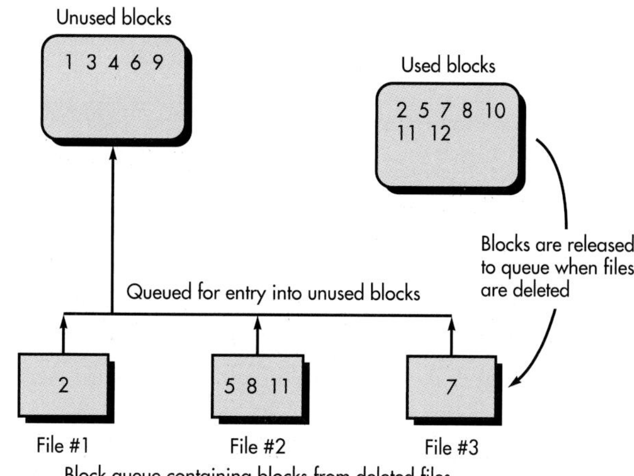

stances in which a particular operation is valid. For example, the precondition for an operation that adds a name to the staff identifier symbol table is valid only if the name that is to be added is not contained in the table and also if there are fewer than *MaxIds* staff identifiers in the table. The *postcondition* of an operation defines what is guaranteed to be true upon completion of an operation. This is defined by its effect on the data. In the example of an operation that adds an identifier to the staff identifier symbol table, the postcondition would specify mathematically that the table has been augmented with the new identifier.

ADVICE

Brainstorming techniques can work well when you must develop a data invariant for a reasonably complex function. Have each member of the software team write down bounds, restrictions, and limitations for the function and then combine and edit.

Example 2: a block handler. One of the more important parts of a computer's operating system is the subsystem that maintains files created by users. Part of the filing subsystem is the *block handler.* Files in the file store are composed of blocks of storage that are held on a file storage device. During the operation of the computer, files will be created and deleted, requiring the acquisition and release of blocks of storage. To cope with this, the filing subsystem will maintain a reservoir of unused (free) blocks and keep track of blocks that are currently in use. When blocks are released from a deleted file they are normally added to a queue of blocks waiting to be added to the reservoir of unused blocks. This is shown in Figure 28.2. In this figure, a number of components are shown: the reservoir of unused blocks, the blocks that currently make up the files administered by the operating system, and those blocks that are waiting to be added to the reservoir. The waiting blocks are held in a queue, with each element of the queue containing a set of blocks from a deleted file.

For this subsystem the state is the collection of free blocks, the collection of used blocks, and the queue of returned blocks. The data invariant, expressed in natural language, is:

- No block will be marked as both unused and used.

- All the sets of blocks held in the queue will be subsets of the collection of currently used blocks.
- No elements of the queue will contain the same block numbers.
- The collection of used and unused blocks will be the total collection of blocks that make up files.
- The collection of unused blocks will have no duplicate block numbers.
- The collection of used blocks will have no duplicate block numbers.

Some of the operations associated with the data invariant are: *add()* a collection of blocks to the end of the queue, *remove()* a collection of used blocks from the front of the queue and place them in the collection of unused blocks, and *check()* whether the queue of blocks is empty.

The precondition of the first operation is that the blocks to be added must be in the collection of used blocks. The postcondition is that the collection of blocks is now found at the end of the queue. The precondition of the second operation is that the queue must have at least one item in it. The postcondition is that the blocks must be added to the collection of unused blocks. The final operation—checking whether the queue of returned blocks is empty—has no precondition. This means that the operation is always defined, regardless of what value the state is. The postcondition delivers the value *true* if the queue is empty and *false* otherwise.

In the examples noted in this section, we introduce the key concepts of formal specification. But we do so without emphasizing the mathematics that are required to make the specification formal. In Section 28.2, we consider these mathematics.

28.2 Mathematical Preliminaries

To apply formal methods effectively, a software engineer must have a working knowledge of the mathematical notation associated with sets and sequences and the logical notation used in predicate calculus. The intent of the section is to provide a brief introduction. For a more detailed discussion the reader is urged to examine books dedicated to these subjects (e.g., [WIL87], [GRI93], and [ROS95]).

28.2.1 Sets and Constructive Specification

A *set* is a collection of objects or elements and is used as a cornerstone of formal methods. The elements contained within a set are unique (i.e., no duplicates are allowed). Sets with a small number of elements are written within curly brackets (braces) with the elements separated by commas. For example, the set

{C++, Smalltalk, Ada, COBOL, Java}

contains the names of five programming languages.

The order in which the elements appear within a set is immaterial. The number of items in a set is known as its *cardinality.* The # operator returns a set's cardinality. For example, the expression

$$\#\{A, B, C, D\} = 4$$

implies that the cardinality operator has been applied to the set shown with a result indicating the number of items in the set.

What is constructive set specification?

There are two ways of defining a set. A set may be defined by enumerating its elements (this is the way in which the sets just noted have been defined). The second approach is to create a *constructive set specification*. The general form of the members of a set is specified using a Boolean expression. Constructive set specification is preferable to enumeration because it enables a succinct definition of large sets. It also explicitly defines the rule that was used in constructing the set. Consider the following constructive specification example:

$$\{n : \mathbb{N} \mid n < 3 \bullet n\}$$

This specification has three components, a signature, $n : \mathbb{N}$, a predicate $n < 3$, and a term, n. The *signature* specifies the range of values that will be considered when forming the set; the *predicate* (a Boolean expression) defines how the set is to be constricted; and, finally, the *term* gives the general form of the item of the set. In the example above, $\mathbb{N}$ stands for the natural numbers; therefore, natural numbers are to be considered. The predicate indicates that only natural numbers less than 3 are to be included; and the term specifies that each element of the set will be of the form n. Therefore, this specification defines the set

$$\{0, 1, 2\}$$

When the form of the elements of a set is obvious, the term can be omitted. For example, the preceding set could be specified as

$$\{n : \mathbb{N} \mid n < 3\}$$

ADVICE

Knowledge of set operations is indispensable when formal specifications are developed. Spend the time to familiarize yourself with each, if you intend to apply formal methods.

All the sets that have been described here have elements that are single items. Sets can also be made from elements that are pairs, triples, and so on. For example, the set specification

$$\{x, y : \mathbb{N} \mid x + y = 10 \bullet (x, y^2)\}$$

describes the set of pairs of natural numbers that have the form (x, y^2) and where the sum of x and y is 10. This is the set

$$\{(1, 81), (2, 64), (3, 49), \ldots\}$$

Obviously, a constructive set specification required to represent some component of computer software can be considerably more complex than those noted here. However, the basic form and structure remain the same.

28.2.2 Set Operators

A specialized symbology is used to represent set and logic operations. These symbols must be understood by the software engineer who intends to apply formal methods.

The $\in$ operator is used to indicate membership of a set. For example, the expression

$$x \in X$$

has the value *true* if x is a member of the set X and the value *false* otherwise. For example, the predicate

$$12 \in \{6, 1, 12, 22\}$$

has the value *true* since 12 is a member of the set.

The opposite of the $\in$ operator is the $\notin$ operator. The expression

$$x \notin X$$

has the value *true* if x is not a member of the set X and *false* otherwise. For example, the predicate

$$13 \notin \{13, 1, 124, 22\}$$

has the value *false.*

The operators $\subset$, and $\subseteq$, take sets as their operands. The predicate

$$A \subset B$$

has the value *true* if the members of the set A are contained in the set B and has the value *false* otherwise. Thus, the predicate

$$\{1, 2\} \subset \{4, 3, 1, 2\}$$

has the value *true.* However, the predicate

$$\{HD1, LP4, RC5\} \subset \{HD1, RC2, HD3, LP1, LP4, LP6\}$$

has a value of *false* because the element RC5 is not contained in the set to the right of the operator.

The operator $\subseteq$ is similar to $\subset$. However, if its operands are equal, it has the value *true.* Thus, the value of the predicate

$$\{HD1, LP4, RC5\} \subseteq \{HD1, RC2, HD3, LP1, LP4, LP6\}$$

is *false,* and the predicate

$$\{HD1, LP4, RC5\} \subseteq \{HD1, LP4, RC5\}$$

is *true.*

> "Mathematical structures are among the most beautiful discoveries made by the human mind."
> **Douglas Hofstadter**

A special set is the empty set ∅. This corresponds to zero in normal mathematics. The *empty set* has the property that it is a subset of every other set. Two useful identities involving the empty set are

$$\varnothing \cup A = A \text{ and } \varnothing \cap A = \varnothing$$

for any set *A*, where ∪ is known as the *union operator,* sometimes known as *cup;* ∩ is the *intersection operator,* sometimes known as *cap.*

The union operator takes two sets and forms a set that contains all the elements in the set with duplicates eliminated. Thus, the result of the expression

{Filel, File2, Tax, Compiler} ∪ {NewTax, D2, D3, File2}

is the set

{Filel, File2, Tax, Compiler, NewTax, D2, D3}

The intersection operator takes two sets and forms a set consisting of the common elements in each set. Thus, the expression

$$\{12, 4, 99, 1\} \cap \{1, 13, 12, 77\}$$

results in the set {12, 1}.

The set *difference operator,* \, as the name suggests, forms a set by removing the elements of its second operand from the elements of its first operand. Thus, the value of the expression

{New, Old, TaxFile, SysParam} \ {Old, SysParam}

results in the set {New, TaxFile}.

The value of the expression

{a, b, c, d} ∩ {x, y}

will be the empty set ∅. The operator always delivers a set; however, in this case there are no common elements between its operands, so the resulting set will have no elements.

The final operator is the *cross product,* ×, sometimes known as the *Cartesian product.* This has two operands which are sets of pairs. The result is a set of pairs where each pair consists of an element taken from the first operand combined with an element from the second operand. An example of an expression involving the cross product is

$$\{1, 2\} \times \{4, 5, 6\}$$

The result of this expression is

$$\{(1, 4), (1, 5), (1, 6), (2, 4), (2, 5), (2, 6)\}$$

Notice that every element of the first operand is combined with every element of the second operand.

A concept that is important for formal methods is that of a *powerset.* A powerset of a set is the collection of subsets of that set. The symbol used for the powerset operator in this chapter is $\mathbb{P}$. It is a unary operator that, when applied to a set, returns the set of subsets of its operand. For example,

$$\mathbb{P}\,\{1, 2, 3\} = \{\varnothing, \{1\}, \{2\}, \{3\}, \{1, 2\}, \{1, 3\}, \{2, 3\}, \{1, 2, 3\}\}$$

since all the sets are subsets of {1, 2, 3}.

28.2.3 Logic Operators

Another important component of a formal method is *logic:* the algebra of true and false expressions. The meaning of common logical operators is well understood by every software engineer. However, the logic operators that are associated with common programming languages are written using readily available keyboard symbols. The equivalent mathematical operators to these are

$\wedge$	and
$\vee$	or
$\neg$	not
$\Rightarrow$	implies

Universal quantification is a way of making a statement about the elements of a set that is true for every member of the set. Universal quantification uses the symbol, $\forall$. An example of its use is

$$\forall\, i, j\!: \mathbb{N} \bullet i > j \Rightarrow i^2 > j^2$$

which states that for every pair of values in the set of natural numbers, if i is greater than j, then i^2 is greater than j^2.

28.2.4 Sequences

A sequence is a mathematical structure that models the fact that its elements are ordered. A sequence *s* is a set of pairs whose elements range from 1 to the highest-number element. For example,

{(1, Jones), (2, Wilson), (3, Shapiro), (4, Estavez)}

is a sequence. The items that form the first elements of the pairs are collectively known as the *domain* of the sequence, and the collection of second elements is known as the *range* of the sequence. In this book, sequences are designated using angle brackets. For example, the preceding sequence would normally be written as ⟨Jones, Wilson, Shapiro, Estavez⟩.

Unlike sets, duplication in a sequence is allowed, and the ordering of a sequence is important. Therefore,

$$\langle \text{Jones, Wilson, Shapiro} \rangle \neq \langle \text{Jones, Shapiro, Wilson} \rangle$$

The empty sequence is represented as $\langle\ \rangle$.

A number of sequence operators are used in formal specifications. Catenation, $\frown$, is a binary operator that forms a sequence constructed by adding its second operand to the end of its first operand. For example,

$$\langle 2, 3, 34, 1 \rangle \frown \langle 12, 33, 34, 200 \rangle.$$

results in the sequence $\langle 2, 3, 34, 1, 12, 33, 34, 200 \rangle$.

Other operators that can be applied to sequences are *head, tail, front,* and *last.* The operator *head* extracts the first element of a sequence; *tail* returns with the last $n - 1$ elements in a sequence of length n; *last* extracts the final element in a sequence; and *front* returns with the first $n - 1$ elements in a sequence of length n. For example,

$$\begin{aligned} &head\ \langle 2, 3, 34, 1, 99, 101 \rangle = 2 \\ &tail\ \langle 2, 3, 34, 1, 99, 101 \rangle = \langle 3, 34, 1, 99, 101 \rangle \\ &last\ \langle 2, 3, 34, 1, 99, 101 \rangle = 101 \\ &front\ \langle 2, 3, 34, 1, 99, 101 \rangle = \langle 2, 3, 34, 1, 99 \rangle \end{aligned}$$

Since a sequence is a set of pairs, all set operators described in Section 28.2.2 are applicable. When a sequence is used in a state, it should be designated as such by using the keyword *seq.* For example,

$$\begin{aligned} &FileList : seq\ \text{FILES} \\ &NoUsers : \mathbb{N} \end{aligned}$$

describes a state with two components: a sequence of files and a natural number.

28.3 Applying Mathematical Notation for Formal Specification

To illustrate the use of mathematical notation in the formal specification of a software component, we revisit the block handler example presented in Section 28.1.3. To review, an important component of a computer's operating system maintains files that have been created by users. The block handler maintains a reservoir of unused blocks and will also keep track of blocks that are currently in use. When blocks are released from a deleted file they are normally added to a queue of blocks waiting to be added to the reservoir of unused blocks. This has been depicted schematically in Figure 28.2.[4]

A set named *BLOCKS* will consist of every block number. *AllBlocks* is a set of blocks that lie between 1 and *MaxBlocks.* The state will be modeled by two sets and a sequence. The two sets are *used* and *free.* Both contain blocks—the *used* set

---

4 If your recollection of the block handler example is hazy, please return to Section 28.1.3 to review the data invariant, operations, preconditions and postconditions associated with the block handler.

? How can I represent states and data invariants using the set and logic operators that have already been introduced?

contains the blocks that are currently used in files, and the *free* set contains blocks that are available for new files. The sequence will contain sets of blocks that are ready to be released from files that have been deleted. The state can be described as

$$used, free: \mathbb{P}\ BLOCKS$$
$$BlockQueue: seq\ \mathbb{P}\ BLOCKS$$

This is very much like the declaration of program variables. It states that *used* and *free* will be sets of blocks and that *BlockQueue* will be a sequence, each element of which will be a set of blocks. The data invariant can be written as

$$used \cap free = \varnothing \wedge$$
$$used \cup free = AllBlocks \wedge$$
$$\forall\ i: \mathrm{dom}\ BlockQueue \bullet BlockQueue\ i \subseteq used \wedge$$
$$\forall\ i, j: \mathrm{dom}\ BlockQueue \bullet i \neq j \Rightarrow BlockQueue\ i \cap BlockQueue\ j = \varnothing$$

WebRef
Extensive information on formal methods can be found at **www.afm.sbu.ac.uk.**

The mathematical components of the data invariant match four of the bulleted, natural-language components described earlier. The first line of the data invariant states that there will be no common blocks in the used collection and free collections of blocks. The second line states that the collection of used blocks and free blocks will always be equal to the whole collection of blocks in the system. The third line indicates the *i*th element in the block queue will always be a subset of the used blocks. The final line states that, for any two elements of the block queue that are not the same, there will be no common blocks in these two elements. The final two natural language components of the data invariant are implemented by virtue of the fact that *used* and *free* are sets and therefore will not contain duplicates.

The first operation we shall define is one that removes an element from the head of the block queue. The precondition is that there must be at least one item in the queue:

$$\#BlockQueue > 0,$$

The postcondition is that the head of the queue must be removed and placed in the collection of free blocks and the queue adjusted to show the removal:

$$used' = used \setminus head\ BlockQueue \wedge$$
$$free' = free \cup head\ BlockQueue \wedge$$
$$BlockQueue' = tail\ BlockQueue$$

A convention used in many formal methods is that the value of a variable after an operation is primed. Hence, the first component of the preceding expression states that the new used blocks (*used'*) will be equal to the old used blocks minus the blocks that have been removed. The second component states that the new free blocks (*free'*) will be the old free blocks with the head of the block queue added to it. The third component states that the new block queue will be equal to the tail of the old value of the block queue; that is, all elements in the queue apart from the first one.

A second operation adds a collection of blocks, *Ablocks,* to the block queue. The precondition is that *Ablocks* is currently a set of used blocks:

How do I represent pre- and postconditions?

$$Ablocks \subseteq used$$

The postcondition is that the set of blocks is added to the end of the block queue, and the set of used and free blocks remains unchanged:

$$BlockQueue' = BlockQueue \frown \langle \text{Ablocks} \rangle \wedge$$
$$used' = used \wedge$$
$$free' = free$$

There is no question that the mathematical specification of the block queue is considerably more rigorous than a natural language narrative or a graphical model. The additional rigor requires effort, but the benefits gained from improved consistency and completeness can be justified for many types of applications.

28.4 Formal Specification Languages

A formal specification language is usually composed of three primary components: (1) a *syntax* that defines the specific notation with which the specification is represented, (2) *semantics* to help define a "universe of objects" [WIN90] that will be used to describe the system, and (3) a *set of relations* that define rules that indicate which objects properly satisfy the specification.

The syntactic domain of a formal specification language is often based on a syntax that is derived from standard set theory notation and predicate calculus. For example, variables such as x, y, and z describe a set of objects that relate to a problem (sometimes called the *domain of discourse*) and are used in conjunction with the operators described in Section 28.2. Although the syntax is usually symbolic, icons (e.g., graphical symbols such as boxes, arrows, and circles) can also be used, if they are unambiguous.

The *semantic domain* of a specification language indicates how the language represents system requirements. For example, a programming language has a set of formal semantics that enables the software developer to specify algorithms that transform input to output. A formal grammar (such as BNF) can be used to describe the syntax of the programming language. However, a programming language does not make a good specification language because it can represent only computable functions. A specification language must have a semantic domain that is broader; that is, the semantic domain of a specification language must be capable of expressing ideas such as, "For all x in an infinite set A, there exists a y in an infinite set B such that the property P holds for x and y" [WIN90]. Other specification languages apply semantics that enable the specification of system behavior. For example, a syntax and semantics can be developed to specify states and state transition, and events, along with their effect on state transition, synchronization and timing.

It is possible to use different semantic abstractions to describe the same system in different ways. We did this in a less formal fashion in Chapter 8. Classes, data, functions, and behavior were each represented. Different modeling notation can be used to represent the same system. The semantics of each representation provides complementary views of the system. To illustrate this approach when formal methods are used, assume that a formal specification language is used to describe the set of events that cause a particular state to occur in a system. Another formal relation depicts all functions that occur within a given state. The intersection of these two relations provides an indication of the events that will cause specific functions to occur.

A variety of formal specification languages are in use today. OCL [OMG03], Z ([ISO02], [SPI88], [SPI92]), LARCH [GUT93], and VDM [JON91] are representative formal specification languages that exhibit the characteristics noted previously. In this chapter, we present a brief overview of OCL and Z.

28.5 Object Constraint Language (OCL)[5]

Object Constraint Language (OCL) is a formal notation developed so that users of UML can add more precision to their specifications. All of the power of logic and discrete mathematics is available in the language. However the designers of OCL decided that only ASCII characters (rather than conventional mathematical notation) should be used in OCL statements. This makes the language more friendly to people who are less mathematically inclined, and more easily processed by computer. But it also makes OCL a little wordy in places.

28.5.1 A Brief Overview of OCL Syntax and Semantics

WebRef
Detailed information about OCL can be found at **www-3.ibm.com/software/awdtools/library/standards/ocl.html.**

To use OCL, a software engineer starts with one or more UML diagrams—most commonly class, state, or activity diagrams. To these, we add OCL expressions that state facts about elements of the diagrams. These expressions are called *constraints*; any implementation derived from the model must ensure each of the constraints always remains true.

Like an object-oriented programming language, an OCL expression involves operators operating on objects. However, the result of a complete expression must always be a Boolean, i.e. true or false. The objects can be instances of the OCL **Collection** class, of which **Set** and **Sequence** are two subclasses.

The object **self** is the element of the UML diagram in the context of which the OCL expression is being evaluated. Other objects can be obtained by *navigating* using the · (dot) symbol from the **self** object. For example:

- If **self** is class **C,** with attribute **a,** then **self.a** evaluates to the object stored in **a.**

5 This section has been contributed by Professor Timothy Lethbridge of The University of Ottawa and is presented here with permission.

- If **C** has a one-to-many association called *assoc* to another class **D,** then **self.assoc** evaluates to a **Set** whose elements are of type **D.**
- Finally (and a little more subtly), if **D** has attribute **b,** then the expression **self.assoc.b** evaluates to the set of all the **b**'s belonging to all **D**'s.

OCL provides built-in operations implementing the mathematics described in Section 28.2, and more. A small sample of these is presented in Table 28.1.

TABLE 28.1 SUMMARY OF KEY OCL NOTATION

OCL notation	Meaning
x.y	Obtain the property y of object x. A property can be an attribute, the set of objects at the end of an association, the result of evaluating an operation, or other things depending on the type of UML diagram. If x is a Set, then y is applied to every element of x; the results are collected into a new Set.
c−>f()	Apply the built-in OCL operation f to Collection c itself (as opposed to each of the objects in c). Examples of built-in operations are listed below.
and, or, =, <>	Logical and, logical or, equals, not-equals.
p implies q	True if either q is true or p is false.
Sample of Operations on Collections (including Sets and Sequences)	
c−>size()	The number of elements in Collection c.
c−>isEmpty()	True if c has no elements, false otherwise.
c1−>includesAll(c2)	True if every element of c2 is found in c1.
c1−>excludesAll(c2)	True if no element of c2 is found in c1.
c−>forAll(elem | boolexpr)	True if boolexpr is true when applied to every element of c. As an element is being evaluated, it is bound to the variable elem, which can be used in boolexpr. This implements universal quantification, discussed earlier.
c−>forAll(elem1, elem2 | boolexpr)	Same as above, except that boolexpr is evaluated for every possible *pair* of elements taken from c, including cases where the pair consists of the same element.
c−>isUnique(elem | expr)	True if expr evaluates to a different value when applied to every element of c.
Sample of Operations Specific to Sets	
s1−>intersection(s2)	The set of those elements found in s1 and also in s2.
s1−>union(s2)	The set of those elements found in either s1 or s2.
s1−>excluding(x)	The set s1 with object x omitted.
Sample Operation Specific to Sequences	
seq−>first()	The object that is the first element in the sequence seq.

28.5.2 An Example Using OCL

In this section, OCL is used to help formalize the specification of the block handler example, introduced in Section 28.1.3. The first step is to develop a UML model. For this example we start with the class diagram found in Figure 28.3. This diagram specifies many relationships among the objects involved; however we must add OCL expressions to ensure that implementers of the system know more precisely what they must ensure remains true as the system runs.

The OCL expressions we will add correspond to the six parts of the invariant discussed in Section 28.1.3. For each, we will repeat the invariant in English and then give the corresponding OCL expression. It is considered good practice to provide English text along with the formal logic; doing so helps the reader to understand the logic, and also helps reviewers to uncover mistakes, e.g., situations where the English and the logic do not correspond.

1. No block will be marked as both unused and used.

```
context BlockHandler inv:
   (self.used->intersection(self.free)) ->isEmpty()
```

   Note that each expression starts with the keyword **context.** This indicates the element of the UML diagram that the expression constrains. Alternatively, the software engineer could place the constraint directly on the UML diagram, surrounded by braces {}. The keyword **self** here refers to the instance of **BlockHandler**; in the following, as is permissible in OCL, we will omit the **self.**

2. All the sets of blocks held in the queue will be subsets of the collection of currently used blocks.

```
context BlockHandler inv:
   blockQueue->forAll(aBlockSet | used->includesAll(aBlockSet ))
```

FIGURE 28.3

Class diagram for a block handler

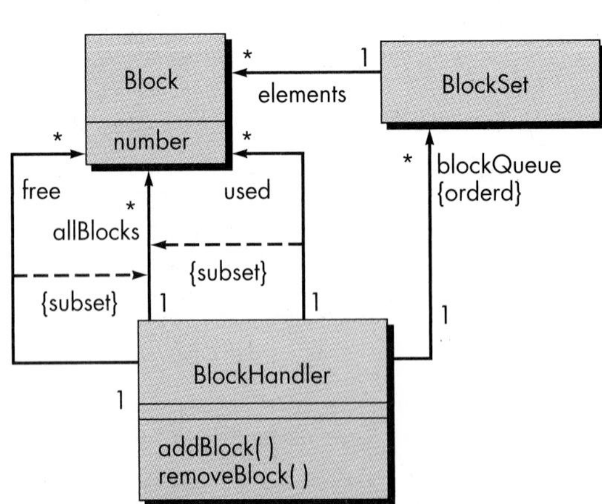

3. No elements of the queue will contain the same block numbers.

```
context BlockHandler inv:
   blockQueue->forAll(blockSet1, blockSet2 |
      blockSet1 <> blockSet2 implies
      blockSet1.elements.number->excludesAll(blockSet2.elements.number))
```

   The expression before **implies** is needed to ensure we ignore pairs where both elements are the same block.

4. The collection of used blocks and blocks that are unused will be the total collection of blocks that make up files.

```
context BlockHandler inv:
   allBlocks = used->union(free)
```

5. The collection of unused blocks will have no duplicate block numbers.

```
context BlockHandler inv:
   free->isUnique(aBlock | aBlock.number)
```

6. The collection of used blocks will have no duplicate block numbers.

```
context BlockHandler inv:
   used->isUnique(aBlock | aBlock.number)
```

OCL can also be used to specify preconditions and postconditions of operations. For example, consider operations that remove and add sets of blocks to the queue. Note that the notation **x@pre** indicates the object **x** as it existed *prior* to the operation; this is opposite to mathematical notation discussed earlier, where it is the **x** *after* the operation that is specially designated (as **x′**).

```
context BlockHandler::removeBlocks()
   pre: blockQueue->size() >0
   post: used = used@pre - blockQueue@pre->first() and
      free = free@pre->union(blockQueue@pre->first()) and
      blockQueue = blockQueue@pre->excluding(blockQueue@pre->first)

context BlockHandler::addBlocks(aBlockSet :BlockSet)
   pre: used->includesAll(aBlockSet.elements)
   post: (blockQueue.elements = blockQueue.elements@pre
      ->append(aBlockSet))and
      used = used@pre and
      free = free@pre
```

OCL is a modeling language, but it has all of the attributes of a formal language. OCL allows the expression of various constraints, pre- and postconditions, guards, and other characteristics that relate to the objects represented in various UML models.

28.6 The Z Specification Language

Z (properly pronounced as "zed") is a specification language that has evolved over the past two decades to become widely used within the formal methods community. The Z language applies typed sets, relations, and functions within the context of first-order predicate logic to build *schemas*—a means for structuring a formal specification.

WebRef
Detailed information about the Z language can be found at **www-users.cs.york.ac.uk/~susan/abs/z.htm.**

28.6.1 A Brief Overview of Z Syntax and Semantics

Z specifications are organized as a set of schemas—a boxlike structure that introduces variables and specifies the relationship between these variables. A *schema* is essentially the formal specification analog of the programming language component. In the same way that components are used to structure a system, schemas are used to structure a formal specification.

A schema describes the stored data that a system accesses and alters. In the context of Z, this is called the "state." This usage of the term *state* in Z is slightly different from the use of the word in the rest of this book.[6] In addition, the schema identifies the operations that are applied to change state and the relationships that occur within the system. The generic structure of a schema takes the form:

```
—— schemaName ————————————
    declarations
——————————————————————————
    invariant
——————————————————————————
```

where declarations identify the variables that comprise the system state and the invariant imposes constraints on the manner in which the state can evolve. A summary of Z language notation is presented in Table 28.2.

28.6.2 An Example Using Z

In this section, we use the Z specification language to model the block handler example, introduced earlier in this chapter. The following example of a schema describes the state of the block handler and the data invariant:

—— BlockHandler ————————————

$used, free : \mathbb{P}\ BLOCKS$

$BlockQueue : \text{seq}\ \mathbb{P}\ BLOCKS$

$used \cap free = \varnothing\ \wedge$

6 Recall that in other chapters *state* has been used to identify an externally observable mode of behavior for a system.

TABLE 28.2 SUMMARY OF Z NOTATION

Z notation is based on typed set theory and first-order logic. Z provides a construct, called a *schema*, to describe a specification's state space and operations. A schema groups variable declarations with a list of predicates that constrain the possible value of a variable. In Z, the schema X is defined by the form

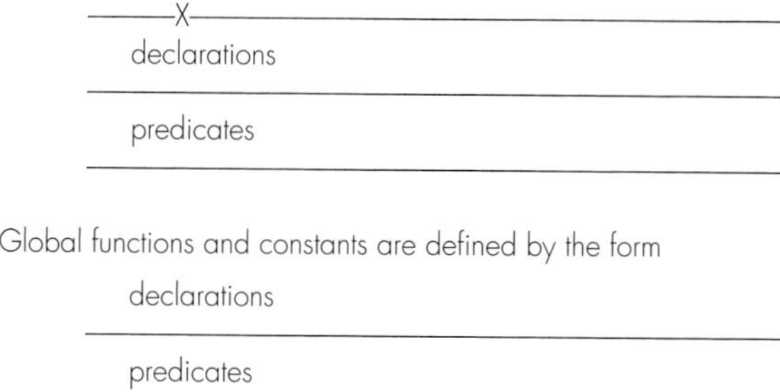

Global functions and constants are defined by the form

declarations

---

predicates

The declaration gives the type of the function or constant, while the predicate gives it value. Only an abbreviated set of Z symbols is presented in this table.

Sets:

$S : \mathbb{P}\, X$	*S* is declared as a set of *X*s.
$x \in S$	*x* is a member of *S*.
$x \notin S$	*x* is not a member of *S*.
$S \subseteq T$	*S* is a subset of *T*: Every member of *S* is also in *T*.
$S \cup T$	The union of *S* and *T*: It contains every member of *S* or *T* or both.
$S \cap T$	The intersection of *S* and *T*: It contains every member of both *S* and *T*.
$S \setminus T$	The difference of *S* and *T*: It contains every member of *S* except those also in *T*.
$\varnothing$	Empty set: It contains no members.
$\{x\}$	Singleton set: It contains just *x*.
$\mathbb{N}$	The set of natural numbers 0, 1, 2, ...
$S : \mathbb{F}\, X$	*S* is declared as a finite set of *X*s.
max (*S*)	The maximum of the nonempty set of numbers *S*.

Functions:

$f : X \rightarrowtail\!\!\!\!\!\!\!+\; Y$	*f* is declared as a partial injection from *X* to *Y*
dom *f*	The domain of *f*: the set of values *x* for which *f*(*x*) is defined.
ran *f*	The range of *f*: the set of values taken by *f*(*x*) as *x* varies over the domain of *f*.
$f \oplus \{x \mapsto y\}$	A function that agrees with *f* except that *x* is mapped to *y*.
$\{x\} \ntriangleleft f$	A function like *f*, except that *x* is removed from its domain.

Logic:

$P \wedge Q$	*P* and *Q*: It is true if both *P* and *Q* are true.
$P \Rightarrow Q$	*P* implies *Q*: It is true if either *Q* is true or *P* is false.
$\theta S' = \theta S$	No components of schema *S* change in an operation.

used ∪ *free* = *AllBlocks* ∧

∀*i*: **dom** *BlockQueue* • *BlockQueue i* ⊆ *used* ∧

∀*i*, *j*: dom *BlockQueue* • *i* ≠ *j* => *BlockQueue i* ∩ *BlockQueue j* = ∅

As we have noted, the schema consists of two parts. The part above the central line represents the variables of the state, while the part below the central line describes the data invariant. Whenever the schema specifies operations that change the state, it is preceded by the Δ symbol. The following example of a schema describes the operation that removes an element from the block queue:

——— RemoveBlocks ————————————————

Δ *BlockHandler*

————————————————————————

$\#\text{BlockQueue} > 0,$

$used' = used \setminus head\ BlockQueue \wedge$

$free' = free \cup head\ BlockQueue \wedge$

$BlockQueue' = tail\ BlockQueue$

————————————————————————

The inclusion of Δ *BlockHandler* results in all variables that make up the state being available for the *RemoveBlocks* schema and ensures that the data invariant will hold before and after the operation has been executed.

The second operation, which adds a collection of blocks to the end of the queue, is represented as

———AddBlocks————————————————

Δ BlockHandler

Ablocks? : BLOCKS

————————————————————————

$Ablocks? \subseteq used$

$BlockQueue' = BlockQueue \frown \langle \text{Ablocks?} \rangle \wedge$

$used' = used \wedge$

$free' = free$

————————————————————————

By convention in Z, an input variable that is read but does not form part of the state is terminated by a question mark. Thus, Ablocks?, which acts as an input parameter, is terminated by a question mark.

SOFTWARE TOOLS

Formal Methods

Objective: The objective of formal methods tools is to assist a software team in specification and correctness verification.

Mechanics: Tools mechanics vary. In general, tools assist in specification and automated correctness proving, usually by defining a specialized language for theorem proving. Many tools are not commercialized and have been developed for research purposes.

Representative Tools[7]

ACL2, developed at the University of Texas (www.cs.utexas.edu/users/moore/acl2/), is "both a programming language in which you can model computer systems and a tool to help you prove properties of those models."

EVES, developed by ORA Canada (www.ora.on.ca/eves.html), implements the Verdi language for formal specification and an automated proof generator.

An extensive list of over 90 formal methods tools can be found at http://www.afm.sbu.ac.uk/.

28.7 The Ten Commandments of Formal Methods

The decision to use formal methods in the real world is not one that is taken lightly. Bowan and Hinchley [BOW95] have coined "the ten commandments of formal methods" as a guide for those who are about to apply this important software engineering approach.[8]

1. *Thou shalt choose the appropriate notation.* To choose effectively from the wide array of formal specification languages, a software engineer should consider language vocabulary, application type to be specified, and breadth of usage of the language.
2. *Thou shalt formalize but not overformalize.* It is generally not necessary to apply formal methods to every aspect of a major system. Those components that are safety critical are first choices, followed by components whose failure cannot be tolerated (for business reasons).
3. *Thou shalt estimate costs.* Formal methods have high startup costs. Training of staff, acquisition of support tools, and use of contract consultants result in high first-time costs. These costs must be considered when examining the return on investment associated with formal methods.
4. *Thou shalt have a formal methods guru on call.* Expert training and on-going consulting are essential for success when formal methods are used for the first time.
5. *Thou shalt not abandon thy traditional development methods.* It is possible, and in many cases desirable, to integrate formal methods with conventional or object-oriented methods (Part 2 of this book). Each has strengths and weaknesses. A combination, if properly applied, can produce excellent results.[9]

---

7 Tools noted here do not represent an endorsement, but rather a sampling of tools in this category. In most cases, tool names are trademarked by their respective developers.

8 This treatment is a much-abbreviated version of [BOW95].

9 Cleanroom software engineering (Chapter 29) is an example of an integrated approach that uses formal methods and more conventional development methods.

6. *Thou shalt document sufficiently.* Formal methods provide a concise, unambiguous, and consistent method for documenting system requirements. However, it is recommended that a natural language commentary accompany the formal specification to serve as a mechanism for reinforcing the reader's understanding of the system.
7. *Thou shalt not compromise thy quality standards.* "There is nothing magical about formal methods," [BOW95] and for this reason, other SQA activities (Chapter 26) must continue to be applied as systems are developed.
8. *Thou shalt not be dogmatic.* A software engineer must recognize that formal methods are not a guarantee of correctness. It is possible (some would say, likely) that the final system, even when developed using formal methods, may have small omissions, minor bugs, and other attributes that do not meet expectations.
9. *Thou shalt test, test, and test again.* The importance of software testing has been discussed in Chapters 13 and 14. Formal methods do not absolve the software engineer from the need to conduct well-planned, thorough tests.
10. *Thou shalt reuse.* Over the long term, the only rational way to reduce software costs and increase software quality is through reuse (Chapter 30). Formal methods do not change this reality. In fact, it may be that formal methods are an appropriate approach when components for reuse libraries are to be created.

28.8 Formal Methods—The Road Ahead

Although formal, mathematically based specification techniques are not used widely in the industry, they do offer substantial advantages over less formal techniques. Liskov and Bersins [LIS86] summarize these in the following way:

> Formal specifications can be studied mathematically while informal specifications cannot. For example, a correct program can be proved to meet its specifications, or two alternative sets of specifications can be proved equivalent . . . Certain forms of incompleteness or inconsistency can be detected automatically.

In addition, formal specification removes ambiguity and encourages greater rigor in the early stages of the software engineering process.

But problems remain. Formal specification focuses primarily on function and data. Timing, control, and behavioral aspects of a problem are more difficult to represent. In addition, some elements of a problem (e.g., human/machine interfaces) are better specified using graphical techniques or prototypes. Finally, specification using formal methods is more difficult to learn than methods that incorporate UML notation and represents a significant "culture shock" for some software practitioners.

28.9 Summary

Formal methods provide a foundation for specification environments leading to analysis models that are more complete, consistent, and unambiguous than those produced using conventional or object-oriented methods. The descriptive facilities of set theory and logic notation enable a software engineer to create a clear statement of facts (requirements).

The underlying concepts that govern formal methods are (1) the data invariant, a condition true throughout the execution of the system that contains a collection of data; (2) the state, a representation of a system's externally observable mode of behavior, or (in Z and related languages) the stored data that a system accesses and alters; and (3) the operation, an action that takes place in a system and reads or writes data to a state. An operation is associated with two conditions: a precondition and a postcondition.

Discrete mathematics—the notation and heuristics associated with sets and constructive specification, set operators, logic operators, and sequences—forms the basis of formal methods. Discrete mathematics is implemented in the context of formal specification languages, such as OCL and Z. These formal specification languages have both syntactic and semantic domains. The syntactic domain uses a symbology that is closely aligned with the notation of sets and predicate calculus. The semantic domain enables the language to express requirements in a concise manner.

A decision to use formal methods should consider startup costs as well as the cultural changes associated with a radically different technology. In most instances, formal methods have highest payoff for safety-critical and business-critical systems.

References

[BOW95] Bowan, J. P., and M. G. Hinchley, "Ten Commandments of Formal Methods," *Computer,* vol. 28, no. 4, April 1995.

[GRI93] Gries, D., and F. B. Schneider, *A Logical Approach to Discrete Math,* Springer-Verlag, 1993.

[GUT93] Guttag, J. V., and J. J. Horning, *Larch: Languages and Tools for Formal Specification,* Springer-Verlag, 1993.

[HAL90] Hall, A., "Seven Myths of Formal Methods," *IEEE Software,* September 1990, pp. 11–20.

[HOR85] Hoare, C.A.R., *Communicating Sequential Processes,* Prentice-Hall International, 1985.

[ISO02] *Z Formal Specification Notation—Syntax, Type System and Semantics,* ISO/IEC 13568:2002, Intl. Standards Organization, 2002.

[JON91] Jones, C. B., *Systematic Software Development Using VDM,* 2nd ed., Prentice-Hall, 1991.

[LIS86] Liskov, B. H., and V. Berzins, "An Appraisal of Program Specifications," in *Software Specification Techniques,* N. Gehani and A. T. McKittrick (eds.), Addison-Wesley, 1986, p. 3.

[MAR94] Marciniak, J. J. (ed.), *Encyclopedia of Software Engineering,* Wiley, 1994.

[OMG03] "Object Constraint Language Specification," in *Unified Modeling Language,* v2.0, Object Management Group, September 2003, download from www.omg.org.

[ROS95] Rosen, K. H., *Discrete Mathematics and Its Applications,* 3rd ed., McGraw-Hill, 1995.

[SPI88] Spivey, J. M., *Understanding Z: A Specification Language and Its Formal Semantics,* Cambridge University Press, 1988.

[SPI92] Spivey, J. M., *The Z Notation: A Reference Manual,* Prentice-Hall, 1992.

[WIL87] Wiltala, S. A., *Discrete Mathematics: A Unified Approach,* McGraw-Hill, 1987.

[WIN90] Wing, J. M., "A Specifier's Introduction to Formal Methods," *Computer,* vol. 23, no. 9, September 1990, pp. 8–24.

[YOU94] Yourdon, E., "Formal Methods," *Guerrilla Programmer,* Cutter Information Corp., October 1994.

Problems and Points to Ponder

28.1. Review the types of deficiencies associated with less formal approaches to software engineering in Section 28.1.1. Provide three examples of each from your own experience.

28.2. The benefits of mathematics as a specification mechanism have been discussed at length in this chapter. Is there a downside?

28.3. You have been assigned to a team that is developing software for a fax modem. Your job is to develop the "phone book" portion of the application. The phone book function enables up to *MaxNames* people to be stored along with associated company names, fax numbers, and other related information. Using natural language, define

a. The data invariant.
b. The state.
c. The operations that are likely.

28.4. You have been assigned to a software team that is developing software, called *Memory-Doubler,* that provides greater apparent memory for a PC than physical memory. This is accomplished by identifying, collecting, and reassigning blocks of memory that have been assigned to an existing application but are not being used. The unused blocks are reassigned to applications that require additional memory. Making appropriate assumptions and using natural language, define

a. The data invariant.
b. The state.
c. The operations that are likely.

28.5. Develop a constructive specification for a set that contains tuples of natural numbers of the form (x, y, z^2) such that the sum of x and y equals z.

28.6. The installer for a PC-based application first determines whether an acceptable set of hardware and system resources is present. It checks the hardware configuration to determine whether various devices (of many possible devices) are present, and determines whether specific versions of system software and drivers are already installed. What set operator could be used to accomplish this? Provide an example in this context.

28.7. Attempt to develop an expression using logic and set operators for the following statement: "For all x and y, if x is the parent of y and y is the parent of z, then x is the grandparent of z. Everyone has a parent." Hint: Use the function $P(x, y)$ and $G(x, z)$ to represent parent and grandparent functions, respectively.

28.8. Develop a constructive set specification of the set of pairs where the first element of each pair is the sum of two nonzero natural numbers and the second element is the difference between the same numbers. Both numbers should be between 100 and 200 inclusively.

28.9. Develop a mathematical description for the state and data invariant for Problem 28.3. Refine this description in the OCL or Z specification language.

28.10. Develop a mathematical description for the state and data invariant for Problem 28.4. Refine this description in the OCL or Z specification language.

28.11. Using the OCL or Z notation presented in Tables 28.1 or 28.2, select some part of the *SafeHome* security system described earlier in this book and attempt to specify it with OCL or Z.

28.12. Using one or more of the information sources noted in the references to this chapter or in Further Readings and Information Sources, develop a half-hour presentation on the basic syntax and semantics of a formal specification language other than OCL or Z.

Further Readings and Information Sources

In addition to the books used as references in this chapter, a fairly large number of books on formal methods topics have been published over the past decade. A listing of some of the more useful offerings follows:

Bowan, J., *Formal Specification and Documentation using Z: A Case Study Approach,* International Thomson Computer Press, 1996.

Casey, C., *A Programming Approach to Formal Methods,* McGraw-Hill, 2000.

Clark. T., et al. (eds.), *Object Modeling with OCL,* Springer-Verlag, 2002.

Cooper, D., and R. Barden, *Z in Practice,* Prentice-Hall, 1995.

Craigen, D., S. Gerhart, and T. Ralston, *Industrial Application of Formal Methods to Model, Design and Analyze Computer Systems,* Noyes Data Corp., 1995.

Harry, A., *Formal Methods Fact File: VDM and Z,* Wiley, 1997.

Hinchley, M., and J. Bowan, *Applications of Formal Methods,* Prentice-Hall, 1995.

Hinchley, M., and J. Bowan, *Industrial Strength Formal Methods,* Academic Press, 1997.

Hussmann, H., *Formal Foundations for Software Engineering Methods,* Springer-Verlag, 1997.

Jacky, J., *The Way of Z: Practical Programming with Formal Methods,* Cambridge University Press, 1997.

Monin, F., and M. Hinchley, *Understanding Formal Methods,* Springer-Verlag, 2003.

Rann, D., J. Turner, and J. Whitworth, *Z: A Beginner's Guide,* Chapman and Hall, 1994.

Ratcliff, B., *Introducing Specification Using Z: A Practical Case Study Approach,* McGraw-Hill, 1994.

Sheppard, D., *An Introduction to Formal Specification with Z and VDM,* McGraw-Hill, 1995.

Warmer, J., and A. Kleppe, *Object Constraint Language,* Addison-Wesley, 1998.

Dean (*Essence of Discrete Mathematics,* Prentice-Hall, 1996), Gries and Schneider [GRI93], and Lipschultz and Lipson (*2000 Solved Problems in Discrete Mathematics,* McGraw-Hill, 1991) present useful information for those who must learn more about the mathematical underpinnings of formal methods.

A wide variety of information sources on formal methods is available on the Internet. An up-to-date list of World Wide Web references can be found at the SEPA Web site: **http://www.mhhe.com/pressman.**

CLEANROOM SOFTWARE ENGINEERING

KEY CONCEPTS

The integrated use of conventional software engineering modeling (and possibly formal methods), program verification (correctness proofs), and statistical SQA have been combined into a technique that can lead to extremely high-quality software. *Cleanroom software engineering* is an approach that emphasizes the need to build correctness into software as it is being developed. Instead of the classic analysis, design, code, test, and debug cycle, the cleanroom approach suggests a different point of view [LIN94]:

> The philosophy behind cleanroom software engineering is to avoid dependence on costly defect removal processes by writing code increments right the first time and verifying their correctness before testing. Its process model incorporates the statistical quality certification of code increments as they accumulate into a system.

In many ways, the cleanroom approach elevates software engineering to another level. Like the formal methods presented in Chapter 28, the cleanroom process emphasizes rigor in specification and design, and formal verification of each design element using correctness proofs that are mathematically based. Extending the approach taken in formal methods, the cleanroom approach also emphasizes techniques for statistical quality control, including testing that is based on the anticipated use of the software by customers.

When software fails in the real world, immediate and long-term hazards abound. The hazards can be related to human safety, economic loss, or effective operation of business and societal infrastructure. Cleanroom software engineering is a process model that removes defects before they can precipitate serious hazards.

QUICK LOOK

What is it? How many times have you heard someone say, "Do it right the first time"? That's the overriding philosophy of cleanroom software engineering—a process that emphasizes mathematical verification of correctness before program construction commences and certification of software reliability as part of the testing activity. The bottom line is extremely low failure rates that would be difficult or impossible to achieve using less formal methods.

Who does it? A specially trained software engineer.

Why is it important? Mistakes create rework. Rework takes time and increases costs. Wouldn't it be nice if we could dramatically reduce the number of mistakes (bugs) introduced as the software is designed and built? That's the premise of cleanroom software engineering.

What are the steps? Analysis and design models are created using box structure representation. A "box" encapsulates the system (or some aspect of the system) at a specific level of abstraction. Correctness verification is applied once the box structure design is complete. Once correctness has been verified for each box structure, statistical usage testing commences. The software is tested by defining a set of usage scenarios, determining the probability of use for each scenario, and then defining random tests that conform to the probabilities. The error records that result are analyzed to enable mathematical computation of projected reliability for the software component.

What is the work product? Black-box, state-box, and clear-box specifications are developed. The results of formal correctness proofs and statistical use tests are recorded.

How do I ensure that I've done it right? Formal proof of correctness is applied to the box structure specification. Statistical use testing exercises usage scenarios to ensure that errors in user functionality are uncovered and corrected. Test data are used to provide an indication of software reliability.

29.1 The Cleanroom Approach

The philosophy of the "cleanroom" in hardware fabrication technologies is really quite simple: It is cost- and time-effective to establish a fabrication approach that precludes the introduction of product defects. Rather than fabricating a product and then working to remove defects, the cleanroom approach demands the discipline required to eliminate errors in specification and design and then fabricate in a "clean" manner.

The cleanroom philosophy was first proposed for software engineering by Mills, Dyer, and Linger [MIL87] during the 1980s. Although early experiences with this disciplined approach to software work showed significant promise [HAU94], it has not gained widespread usage. Henderson [HEN95] suggests three possible reasons:

1. A belief that the cleanroom methodology is too theoretical, too mathematical, and too radical for use in real software development.
2. It advocates no unit testing by developers but instead replaces it with correctness verification and statistical quality control—concepts that represent a major departure from the way most software is developed today.
3. The maturity of the software development industry. The use of cleanroom processes requires rigorous application of defined processes in all life cycle phases. Since much of the industry continues operating at relatively low levels of process maturity, software engineers have not been ready to apply cleanroom techniques.

Despite elements of truth in each of these concerns, the potential benefits of cleanroom software engineering far outweigh the investment required to overcome the cultural resistance that is at the core of these concerns.

> "The only way for errors to occur in a program is by being put there by the author. No other mechanisms are known . . . Right practice aims at preventing insertion of errors and, failing that, removing them before testing or any other running of the program."
>
> **Harlan Mills**

29.1.1 The Cleanroom Strategy

The cleanroom approach makes use of a specialized version of the incremental process model (Chapter 3). A "pipeline of software increments" [LIN94] is developed by small independent software teams. As each increment is certified, it is integrated into the whole. Hence, functionality of the system grows with time.

The sequence of cleanroom tasks for each increment is illustrated in Figure 29.1. Overall system or product requirements are developed using the system engineering methods discussed in Chapter 6. Once functionality has been assigned to the software element of the system, the pipeline of cleanroom increments is initiated. The following tasks occur:

? **What are the major tasks conducted as part of cleanroom software engineering?**

Increment planning. A project plan that adopts the incremental strategy is developed. The functionality of each increment, its projected size, and a cleanroom development schedule are created. Special care must be taken to ensure that certified increments will be integrated in a timely manner.

Requirements gathering. Using techniques similar to those introduced in Chapter 7, a more-detailed description of customer-level requirements (for each increment) is developed.

Box structure specification. A specification method that makes use of *box structures* [HEV93] is used to describe the functional specification. Conforming to

FIGURE 29.1

The cleanroom process model

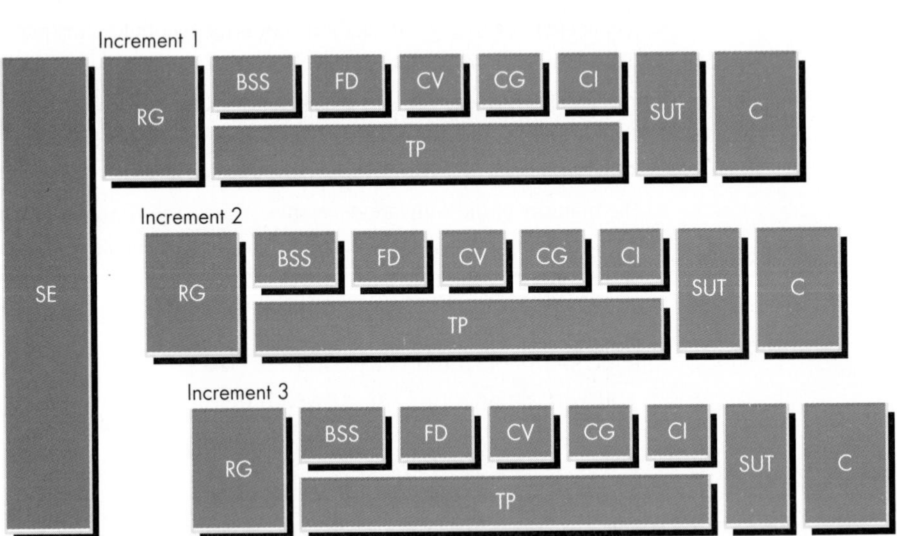

the operational analysis principles discussed in Chapters 5 and 7, box structures "isolate and separate the creative definition of behavior, data, and procedures at each level of refinement."

WebRef
An excellent source of information and resources for cleanroom software engineering can be found at **www.cleansoft.com.**

Formal design. Using the box structure approach, cleanroom design is a natural and seamless extension of specification. Although it is possible to make a clear distinction between the two activities, specifications (called *black boxes*) are iteratively refined (within an increment) to become analogous to architectural and component-level designs (called *state boxes* and *clear boxes,* respectively).

Correctness verification. The cleanroom team conducts a series of rigorous correctness verification activities on the design and then the code. Verification (Sections 29.3 and 29.4) begins with the highest-level box structure (specification) and moves toward design detail and code. The first level of correctness verification occurs by applying a set of "correctness questions" [LIN88]. If these do not demonstrate that the specification is correct, more formal (mathematical) methods for verification are used.

Code generation, inspection, and verification. The box structure specifications, represented in a specialized language, are translated into the appropriate programming language. Standard walkthrough or inspection techniques (Chapter 26) are then used to ensure semantic conformance of the code and box structures and syntactic correctness of the code. Then correctness verification is conducted for the source code.

> "Cleanroom software engineering achieves statistical quality control over software development by strictly separating the design process from the testing process in a pipeline of incremental software development."
>
> **Harlan Mills**

Cleanroom emphasizes tests that exercise the way software is really used. Use-cases provide input to the test planning process.

Statistical test planning. The projected usage of the software is analyzed and a suite of test cases that exercise a "probability distribution" of usage is planned and designed (Section 29.4). Referring to Figure 29.1, this cleanroom activity is conducted in parallel with specification, verification, and code generation.

Statistical use testing. Recalling that exhaustive testing of computer software is impossible (Chapter 14), it is always necessary to design a finite number of test cases. Statistical use techniques [POO88] execute a series of tests derived from a statistical sample (the probability distribution noted earlier) of all possible program executions by all users from a targeted population (Section 29.4).

Certification. Once verification, inspection, and use testing have been completed (and all errors are corrected), the increment is certified as ready for integration.

Like other software process models discussed elsewhere in this book, the cleanroom process relies heavily on the need to produce high-quality analysis and design models. As we will see later in this chapter, box structure notation is simply another way for a software engineer to represent requirements and design. The real distinction of the cleanroom approach is that formal verification is applied to engineering models.

29.1.2 What Makes Cleanroom Different?

Dyer [DYE92] alludes to the differences of the cleanroom approach when he defines the process:

> Cleanroom represents the first practical attempt at putting the software development process under statistical quality control with a well-defined strategy for continuous process improvement. To reach this goal, a cleanroom unique life cycle was defined which focused on mathematics-based software engineering for correct software designs and on statistics-based software testing for certification of software reliability.

KEY POINT The most important distinguishing characteristics of cleanroom are proof of correctness and statistical use testing.

Cleanroom software engineering differs from the conventional and object-oriented software engineering methods because:

1. It makes explicit use of statistical quality control.
2. It verifies design specifications using a mathematically based proof of correctness.
3. It implements testing techniques that have a high likelihood of uncovering high-impact errors.

Obviously, the cleanroom approach applies most, if not all, of the basic software engineering principles and concepts presented throughout this book. Good analysis and design procedures are essential if high quality is to result. But cleanroom engineering diverges from conventional software practices by deemphasizing (some would say, eliminating) the role of unit testing and debugging and dramatically reducing (or eliminating) the amount of testing performed by the developer of the software.[1]

In conventional software development, errors are accepted as a fact of life. Because errors are deemed to be inevitable, each program component should be unit tested (to uncover errors) and then debugged (to remove errors). When the software is finally released, field use uncovers still more defects and another test and debug cycle begins. The rework associated with these activities is costly and time consuming. Worse, it can be degenerative—error correction can (inadvertently) lead to the introduction of still more errors.

> "It's a funny thing about life: If you refuse to accept anything but the best, you may very often get it."
> **W. Somerset Maugham**

In cleanroom software engineering, unit testing and debugging are replaced by correctness verification and statistically based testing. These activities, coupled with the record keeping necessary for continuous improvement, make the cleanroom approach unique.

---

1 Testing is conducted by an independent testing team.

29.2 Functional Specificaton

Regardless of the analysis method that is chosen, the operational analysis principles presented in Chapter 7 apply. Data, function, and behavior are modeled. The resultant models must be partitioned (refined) to provide increasingly greater detail. The overall objective is to move from a specification (or model) that captures the essence of a problem to a specification that provides substantial implementation detail.

Cleanroom software engineering complies with the operational analysis principles by using a method called *box structure specification.* A "box" encapsulates the system (or some aspect of the system) at some level of detail. Through a process of elaboration or stepwise refinement, boxes are refined into a hierarchy where each box has referential transparency. That is, "the information content of each box specification is sufficient to define its refinement, without depending on the implementation of any other box" [LIN94]. This enables the analyst to partition a system hierarchically, moving from essential representation at the top to implementation-specific detail at the bottom. Three types of boxes are used:

? **How is refinement accomplished as part of a box structure specification?**

Black box. The black box specifies the behavior of a system or a part of a system. The system (or part) responds to specific stimuli (events) by applying a set of transition rules that map the stimulus into a response.

State box. The state box encapsulates state data and services (operations) in a manner that is analogous to objects. In this specification view, inputs to the state box (stimuli) and outputs (responses) are represented. The state box also represents the "stimulus history" of the black box, that is, the data encapsulated in the state box that must be retained between the transitions implied.

Clear box. The transition functions that are implied by the state box are defined in the clear box. Stated simply, a clear box contains the procedural design for the state box.

Figure 29.2 illustrates the refinement approach using box structure specification. A black box (BB_1) defines responses for a complete set of stimuli. BB_1 can be refined into a set of black boxes, $BB_{1.1}$ to $BB_{1.n}$, each of which addresses a class of behavior. Refinement continues until a cohesive class of behavior is identified (e.g., $BB_{1.1.1}$). A state box ($SB_{1.1.1}$) is then defined for the black box ($BB_{1.1.1}$). In this case, $SB_{1.1.1}$ contains all data and services required to implement the behavior defined by $BB_{1.1.1}$. Finally, $SB_{1.1.1}$ is refined into clear boxes ($CB_{1.1.1.n}$) and procedural design details are specified.

Box structure refinement and correctness verification occur simultaneously.

As each of these refinement steps occurs, verification of correctness also occurs. State-box specifications are verified to ensure that each conforms to the behavior defined by the parent black-box specification. Similarly, clear-box specifications are verified against the parent state box.

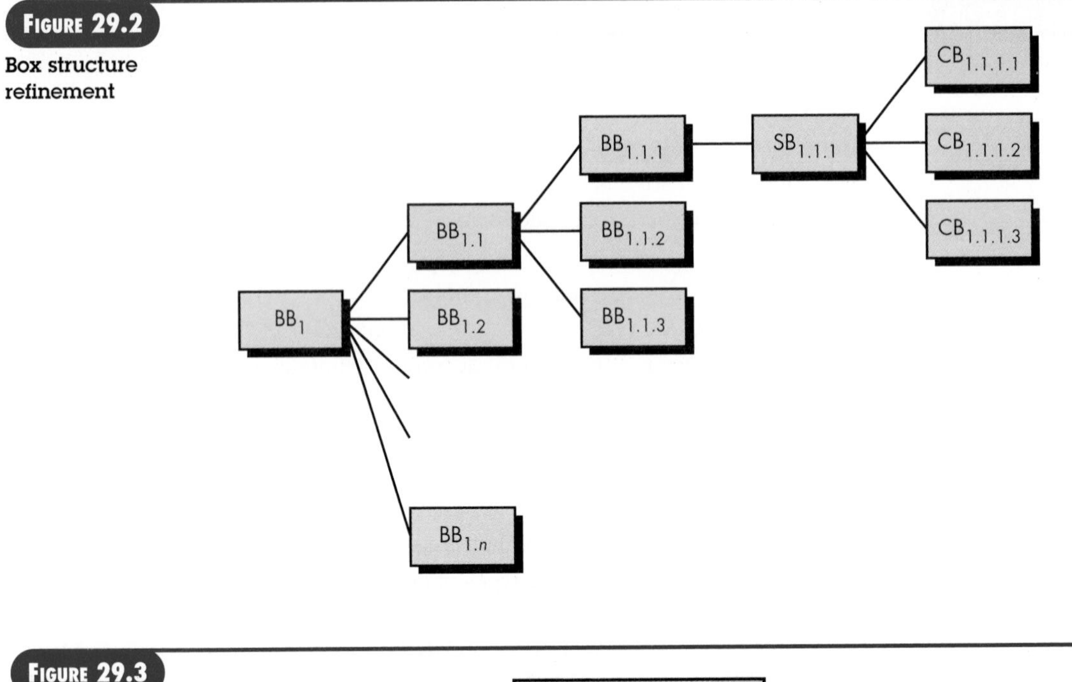

FIGURE 29.2 Box structure refinement

FIGURE 29.3 A black-box specification

S → $f: S^* \rightarrow R$ → R

It should be noted that specification methods based on languages such as OCL or Z (Chapter 28) can be used in conjunction with the box structure specification approach. The only requirement is that each level of specification can be formally verified.

29.2.1 Black-Box Specification

A *black-box* specification describes an abstraction, stimuli, and response using the notation shown in Figure 29.3 [MIL88]. The function *f* is applied to a sequence, S^*, of inputs (stimuli), *S*, and transforms them into an output (response), *R*. For simple software components, *f* may be a mathematical function, but in general, *f* is described using natural language (or a formal specification language).

Many of the concepts introduced for object-oriented systems are also applicable for the black box. Data abstractions and the operations that manipulate those abstractions are encapsulated by the black box. Like a class hierarchy, the black box specification can exhibit usage hierarchies in which low-level boxes inherit the properties of those boxes higher in the tree structure.

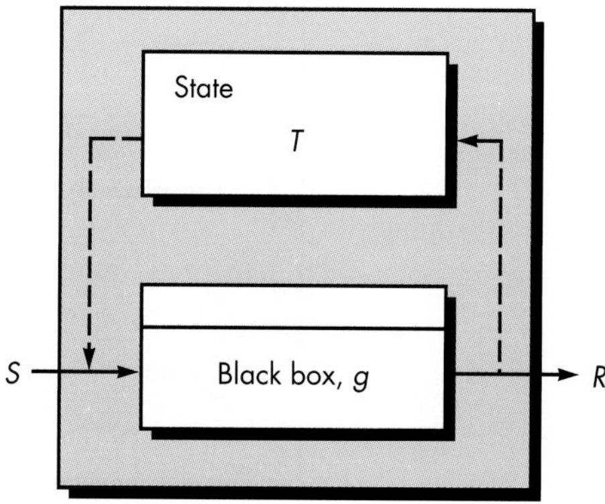

FIGURE 29.4
A state-box specification

29.2.2 State-Box Specification

The *state box* is "a simple generalization of a state machine" [MIL88]. Recalling the discussion of behavioral modeling and state diagrams in Chapter 8, a state is some observable mode of system behavior. As processing occurs, a system responds to events (stimuli) by making a transition from the current state to some new state. As the transition is made, an action may occur. The state box uses a data abstraction to determine the transition to the next state and the action (response) that will occur as a consequence of the transition.

Referring to Figure 29.4, the state box incorporates a black box. The stimulus, *S*, that is input to the black box arrives from some external source and a set of internal system states, *T*. Mills [MIL88] provides a mathematical description of the function, *f*, of the black box contained within the state box:

$$g : S^* \times T^* \rightarrow R \times T$$

where *g* is a subfunction that is tied to a specific state, *t*. When considered collectively, the state-subfunction pairs (*t*, *g*) define the black-box function *f*.

29.2.3 Clear-Box Specification

The clear-box specification is closely aligned with procedural design and structured programming (Chapter 11). In essence, the subfunction *g* within the state box is replaced by the structured programming constructs that implement *g*.

As an example, consider the clear box shown in Figure 29.5. The black box, *g*, shown in Figure 29.4, is replaced by a sequence construct that incorporates a conditional. These constructs, in turn, can be refined into lower-level clear boxes as stepwise refinement proceeds.

It is important to note that the procedural specification described in the clear-box hierarchy can be proved correct. This topic is considered in the next section.

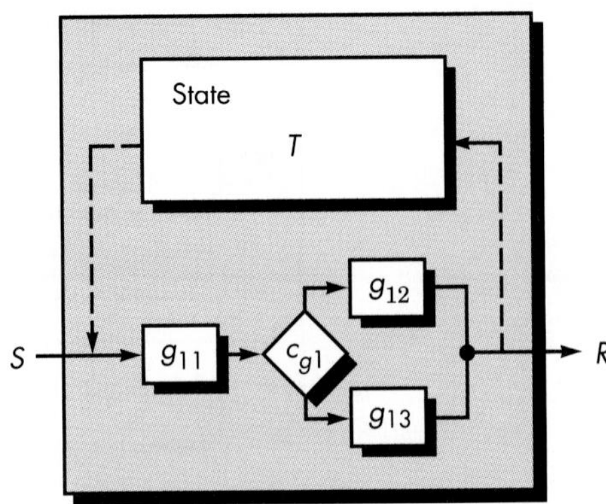

FIGURE 29.5 A clear-box specification

29.3 Cleanroom Design

The design approach used in cleanroom software engineering makes heavy use of the structured programming philosophy. But in this case, structured programming is applied far more rigorously.

Basic processing functions (described during earlier refinements of the specification) are refined using a "stepwise expansion of mathematical functions into structures of logical connectives [e.g., *if-then-else*] and subfunctions, where the expansion [is] carried out until all identified subfunctions could be directly stated in the programming language used for implementation" [DYE92].

The structured programming approach can be used effectively to refine function, but what about data design? Here a number of fundamental design concepts (Chapters 5 and 9) come into play. Program data are encapsulated as a set of abstractions that are serviced by subfunctions. The concepts of data encapsulation, information hiding, and data typing are used to create the data design.

29.3.1 Design Refinement and Verification

Each clear-box specification represents the design of a procedure (subfunction) required to accomplish a state box transition. With the clear box, the structured programming constructs and stepwise refinement are used as illustrated in Figure 29.6. A program function, *f*, is refined into a sequence of subfunctions *g* and *h*. These in turn are refined into conditional constructs (*if-then-else* and *do-while*). Further refinement illustrates continuing logical refinement.

? What conditions are applied to prove structured constructs correct?

At each level of refinement, the cleanroom team[2] performs a formal correctness verification. To accomplish this, a set of generic correctness conditions are attached

2 Because the entire team is involved in the verification process, it is less likely that an error will be made in conducting the verification itself.

FIGURE 29.6

Stepwise refinement

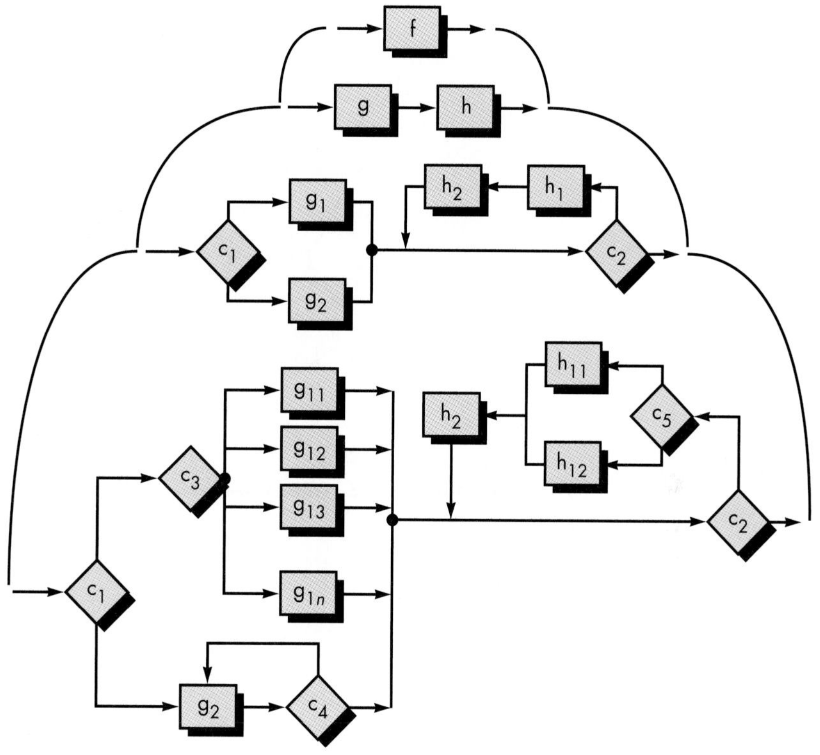

to the structured programming constructs. If a function *f* is expanded into a sequence *g* and *h,* the correctness condition for all input to *f* is

- Does *g* followed by *h* do *f?*

When a function *p* is refined into a conditional of the form, if <*c*> then *q,* else *r,* the correctness condition for all input to *p* is

- Whenever condition <*c*> is true, does *q* do *p;* and whenever <*c*> is false, does *r* do *p?*

If you limit yourself to just the structured constructs as you develop a procedural design, proof of correctness is straightforward. If you violate the constructs, correctness proofs are difficult or impossible.

When function *m* is refined as a loop, the correctness conditions for all input to *m* are

- Is termination guaranteed?
- Whenever <*c*> is true, does *n* followed by *m* do *m;* and whenever <*c*> is false, does skipping the loop still do *m?*

Each time a clear box is refined to the next level of detail, these correctness conditions are applied.

It is important to note that the use of the structured programming constructs constrains the number of correctness tests that must be conducted. A single condition

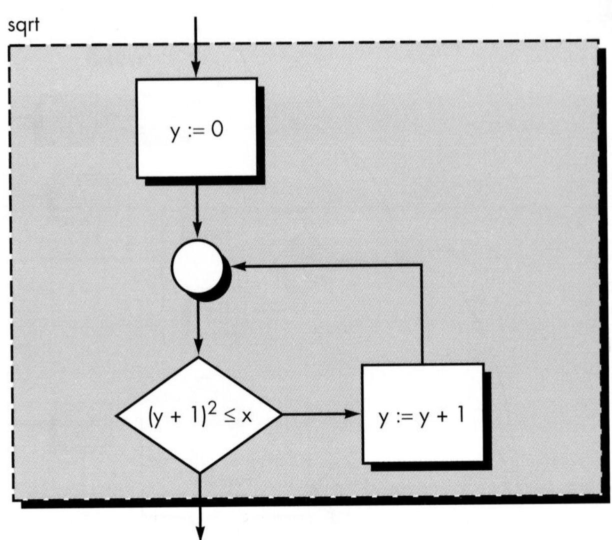

FIGURE 29.7 Computing the integer part of a square root [LIN79]

is checked for sequences; two conditions are tested for *if-then-else,* and three conditions are verified for loops.

To illustrate correctness verification for a procedural design, we use a simple example first introduced by Linger, Mills, and Witt [LIN79]. The intent is to design and verify a small program that finds the integer part, *y,* of a square root of a given integer, *x.* The procedural design is represented using the flowchart in Figure 29.7.

To verify the correctness of this design, we must define entry and exit conditions as noted in Figure 29.8. The entry condition notes that *x* must be greater than or equal to 0. The exit condition requires that *x* remain unchanged and that *y* satisfy the expression noted in the figure. To prove the design correct, it is necessary to prove the conditions *init, loop, cont, yes,* and *exit* shown in Figure 29.8 are true in all cases. These are sometimes called *subproofs.*

KEY POINT To prove a design correct, you must first identify all conditions and then prove that each takes on the appropriate Boolean value. These are called *subproofs.*

1. The condition *init* demands that $[x \geq 0$ and $y = 0]$. Based on the requirements of the problem, the entry condition is assumed correct.[3] Therefore, the first part of the *init* condition, $x \geq 0$, is satisfied. Referring to the flowchart, the statement immediately preceding the *init* condition, sets $y = 0$. Therefore, the second part of the *init* condition is also satisfied. Hence, *init* is true.
2. The *loop* condition may be encountered in one of two ways: (1) directly from *init* (in this case, the *loop* condition is satisfied directly) or via control flow that passes through the condition *cont.* Since the *cont* condition is identical to the *loop* condition, *loop* is true regardless of the flow path that leads to it.

3 A negative value for the square root has no meaning in this context.

FIGURE 29.8

Proving the design correct [LIN79]

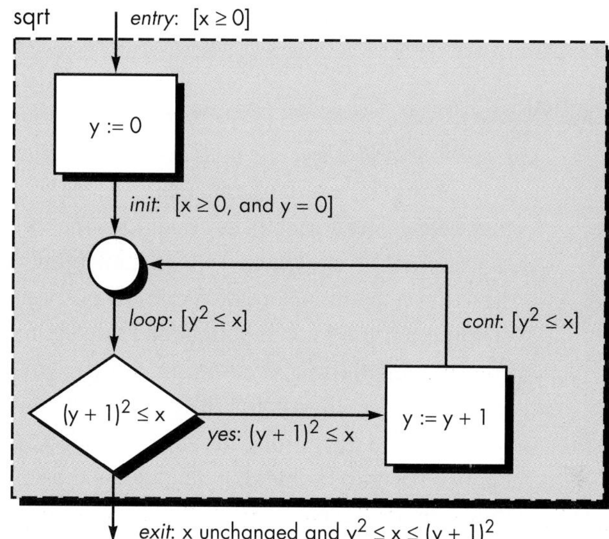

3. The *cont* condition is encountered only after the value of y is incremented by 1. In addition, the control flow path that leads to *cont* can be invoked only if the *yes* condition is also true. Hence, if $(y + 1)^2 \leq x$, it follows that $y^2 \leq x$. The *cont* condition is satisfied.
4. The *yes* condition is tested in the conditional logic shown. Hence, the *yes* condition must be true when control flow moves along the path shown.
5. The *exit* condition first demands that x remain unchanged. An examination of the design indicates that x appears nowhere to the left of an assignment operator. There are no function calls that use x. Hence, it is unchanged. Since the conditional test $(y + 1)^2 \leq x$ must fail to reach the *exit* condition, it follows that $(y + 1)^2 \leq x$. In addition, the *loop* condition must still be true (i.e., $y^2 \leq x$). Therefore, $(y + 1)^2 > x$ and $y^2 \leq x$ can be combined to satisfy the exit condition.

We must further ensure that the loop terminates. An examination of the *loop* condition indicates that because y is incremented and $x \geq 0$, the loop must eventually terminate.

The five steps just noted are a proof of the correctness of the design of the algorithm noted in Figure 29.7. We are now certain that the design will, in fact, compute the integer part of a square root.

A more rigorous mathematical approach to design verification is possible. However, a discussion of this topic is beyond the scope of this book. Interested readers should refer to [LIN79].

29.3.2 Advantages of Design Verification[4]

Rigorous correctness verification of each refinement of the clear-box design has a number of distinct advantages. Linger [LIN94] describes these in the following manner:

What do we gain by doing correctness proofs?

- *It reduces verification to a finite process.* The nested, sequential way that control structures are organized in a clear box naturally defines a hierarchy that reveals the correctness conditions that must be verified. An "axiom of replacement" [LIN79] lets us substitute intended functions with their control structure refinements in the hierarchy of subproofs. For example, the subproof for the intended function f1 in Figure 29.9 requires proving that the composition of the operations g1 and g2 with the intended function f2 has the same effect on data as f1. Note that f2 substitutes for all the details of its refinement in the proof. This substitution localizes the proof argument to the control structure at hand. In fact, it lets the software engineer carry out the proofs in any order.
- *It is impossible to overemphasize the positive effect that reducing verification to a finite process has on quality.* Even though all but the most trivial programs

FIGURE 29.9

A design with subproofs

```
[f1]                    Subproofs:
 DO                     f1 = [DO g1; g2; [f2] END] ?
  g1
  g2
  [f2]                  f2 = [WHILE p1 DO [f3] END] ?
   WHILE
    p1
  DO [f3]               f3 = [DO g3; [f4]; g8 END] ?
    g3
    [f4]                f4 = [IF p2; THEN [f5] ELSE [f6] END] ?
    IF
     p2
    THEN [f5]           f5 = [DO g4; g5 END] ?
     g4
     g5
    ELSE [f6]           f6 = [DO g6; g7 END] ?
     g6
     g7
    END
    g8
  END
 END
```

4 This section and Figures 29.7 through 29.9 have been adapted from [LIN94] and are used with permission.

Despite the extremely large number of execution paths in a program, the number of steps to prove the program correct is quite small.

exhibit an essentially infinite number of execution paths, they can be verified in a finite number of steps.

- *It lets cleanroom teams verify every line of design and code.* Teams can carry out the verification through group analysis and discussion on the basis of the correctness theorem, and they can produce written proofs when extra confidence in a life- or mission-critical system is required.
- *It results in a near zero defect level.* During a team review, every correctness condition of every control structure is verified in turn. Every team member must agree that each condition is correct, so an error is possible only if every team member incorrectly verifies a condition. The requirement for unanimous agreement based on individual verification results in software that has few or no defects before first execution.
- *It scales up.* Every software system, no matter how large, has top-level, clear-box procedures composed of sequence, alternation, and iteration structures. Each of these typically invokes a large subsystem with thousands of lines of code—and each of those subsystems has its own top-level intended functions and procedures. So the correctness conditions for these high-level control structures are verified in the same way as are those of low-level structures. Verification at high levels may take, and well be worth, more time, but it does not take more theory.
- *It produces better code than unit testing.* Unit testing checks the effects of executing only selected test paths out of many possible paths. By basing verification on function theory, the cleanroom approach can verify every possible effect on all data, because while a program may have many execution paths, it has only one function. Verification is also more efficient than unit testing. Most verification conditions can be checked in a few minutes, but unit tests take substantial time to prepare, execute, and check.

It is important to note that design verification must ultimately be applied to the source code itself. In this context, it is often called *correctness verification.*

29.4 Cleanroom Testing

The strategy and tactics of cleanroom testing are fundamentally different from conventional testing approaches. Conventional methods derive a set of test cases to uncover design and coding errors. The goal of cleanroom testing is to validate software requirements by demonstrating that a statistical sample of use-cases (Chapter 7) have been executed successfully.

> "Quality is not an act, it is a habit."
>
> Aristotle

29.4.1 Statistical Use Testing

The user of a computer program rarely needs to understand the technical details of the design. The user-visible behavior of the program is driven by inputs and events that are often produced by the user. But in complex systems, the possible spectrum of input and events (i.e., the use-cases) can be extremely wide. What subset of use-cases will adequately verify the behavior of the program? This is the first question addressed by statistical use testing.

ADVICE

Even if you decide against the cleanroom approach, it's worth considering statistical use testing as an integral part of your test strategy.

Statistical use testing "amounts to testing software the way users intend to use it" [LIN94]. To accomplish this, cleanroom testing teams (also called *certification teams*) must determine a usage probability distribution for the software. The specification (black box) for each increment of the software is analyzed to define a set of stimuli (inputs or events) that cause the software to change its behavior. Based on interviews with potential users, the creation of usage scenarios, and a general understanding of the application domain, a probability of use is assigned to each stimuli.

Test cases are generated for each set of stimuli[5] according to the usage probability distribution. To illustrate, consider the *SafeHome* system discussed earlier in this book. Cleanroom software engineering is being used to develop a software increment that manages user interaction with the security system keypad. Five stimuli have been identified for this increment. Analysis indicates the percent probability distribution of each stimulus. To make selection of test cases easier, these probabilities are mapped into intervals numbered between 1 and 99 [LIN94] and illustrated in the following table:

Program stimulus	Probability	Interval
Arm/disarm (AD)	50%	1–49
Zone set (ZS)	15%	50–63
Query (Q)	15%	64–78
Test (T)	15%	79–94
Panic alarm	5%	95–99

To generate a sequence of usage test cases that conform to the usage probability distribution, random numbers between 1 and 99 are generated. Each random number corresponds to an interval on the preceding probability distribution. Hence, the sequence of usage test cases is defined randomly but corresponds to the appropriate probability of stimuli occurrence. For example, assume the following random number sequences are generated:

13-94-22-24-45-56
81-19-31-69-45-9
38-21-52-84-86-4

5 Automated tools may be used to accomplish this. For further information, see [DYE92].

Selecting the appropriate stimuli based on the distribution interval shown in the table, the following use-cases are derived:

AD–T–AD–AD–AD–ZS
T–AD–AD–AD–Q–AD–AD
AD–AD–ZS–T–T–AD

The testing team executes these use-cases and verifies software behavior against the specification for the system. Timing for tests is recorded so that interval times may be determined. Using interval times, the certification team can compute mean-time-to-failure. If a long sequence of tests is conducted without failure, the MTTF is low and software reliability is likely to be high.

29.4.2 Certification

The verification and testing techniques discussed earlier in this chapter lead to software components (and entire increments) that can be certified. Within the context of the cleanroom software engineering approach, certification implies that the reliability (measured by mean-time-to-failure, MTTF) can be specified for each component.

The potential impact of certifiable software components goes far beyond a single cleanroom project. Reusable software components can be stored along with their usage scenarios, program stimuli, and probability distributions. Each component would have a certified reliability under the usage scenario and testing regime described. This information is invaluable to others who intend to use the components.

? How do we certify a software component?

The certification approach involves five steps [WOH94]:

1. Usage scenarios must be created.
2. A usage profile is specified.
3. Test cases are generated from the profile.
4. Tests are executed and failure data are recorded and analyzed.
5. Reliability is computed and certified.

Steps 1 through 4 have been discussed in an earlier section. In this section, we concentrate on reliability certification.

Certification for cleanroom software engineering requires the creation of three models [POO93]:

Sampling model. Software testing executes *m* random test cases and is certified if no failures or a specified numbers of failures occur. The value of *m* is derived mathematically to ensure that required reliability is achieved.

Component model. A system composed of *n* components is to be certified. The component model enables the analyst to determine the probability that component *i* will fail prior to completion.

Certification model. The overall reliability of the system is projected and certified.

At the completion of statistical use testing, the certification team has the information required to deliver software that has a certified MTTF computed using each of these models.

A detailed discussion of the computation of the sampling, component, and certification models is beyond the scope of this book. The interested reader should see [MUS87], [CUR86], and [POO93] for additional detail.

29.5 Summary

Cleanroom software engineering is a formal approach to software development that can lead to software that has remarkably high quality. It uses box structure specification (or formal methods) for analysis and design modeling and emphasizes correctness verification, rather than testing, as the primary mechanism for finding and removing errors. Statistical use testing is applied to develop the failure rate information necessary to certify the reliability of delivered software.

The cleanroom approach begins with analysis and design models that use a box structure representation. A "box" encapsulates the system (or some aspect of the system) at a specific level of abstraction. Black boxes are used to represent the externally observable behavior of a system. State boxes encapsulate state data and operations. A clear box is used to model the procedural design that is implied by the data and operations of a state box.

Correctness verification is applied once the box structure design is complete. The procedural design for a software component is partitioned into a series of subfunctions. To prove the correctness of the subfunctions, exit conditions are defined for each subfunction and a set of subproofs is applied. If each exit condition is satisfied, the design must be correct.

Once correctness verification is complete, statistical use testing commences. Unlike conventional testing, cleanroom software engineering does not emphasize unit or integration testing. Rather, the software is tested by defining a set of usage scenarios, determining the probability of use for each scenario, and then defining random tests that conform to the probabilities. The error records that result are combined with sampling, component, and certification models to enable mathematical computation of projected reliability for the software component.

The cleanroom philosophy is a rigorous approach to software engineering. It is a software process model that emphasizes mathematical verification of correctness and certification of software reliability. The bottom line is extremely low failure rates that would be difficult or impossible to achieve using less formal methods.

References

[CUR86] Curritt, P. A., M. Dyer, and H. D. Mills, "Certifying the Reliability of Software," *IEEE Trans, Software Engineering,* vol. SE-12, no. 1, January 1994.

[DYE92] Dyer, M., *The Cleanroom Approach to Quality Software Development,* Wiley, 1992.

[HAU94] Hausler, P. A., R. Linger, and C. Trammel, "Adopting Cleanroom Software Engineering with a Phased Approach," *IBM Systems Journal,* vol. 33, no.1, January 1994, pp. 89–109.

[HEN95] Henderson, J., "Why Isn't Cleanroom the Universal Software Development Methodology?" *Crosstalk,* vol. 8, No. 5, May 1995, pp. 11–14.

[HEV93] Hevner, A. R., and H. D. Mills, "Box Structure Methods for System Development with Objects," *IBM Systems Journal,* vol. 31, no.2, February 1993, pp. 232–251.

{LIN79] Linger, R. M., H. D. Mills, and B. I. Witt, *Structured Programming: Theory and Practice,* Addison-Wesley, 1979.

[LIN88] Linger, R. M., and H. D. Mills, "A Case Study in Cleanroom Software Engineering: The IBM COBOL Structuring Facility," *Proc. COMPSAC '88,* Chicago, October 1988.

[LIN94] Linger, R., "Cleanroom Process Model," *IEEE Software,* vol. 11, no. 2, March 1994, pp. 50–58.

[MIL87] Mills, H. D., M. Dyer, and R. Linger, "Cleanroom Software Engineering," *IEEE Software,* vol. 4, no. 5, September 1987, pp. 19–24.

[MIL88] Mills, H. D., "Stepwise Refinement and Verification in Box Structured Systems," *Computer,* vol. 21, no. 6, June 1988, pp. 23–35.

[MUS87] Musa, J. D., A. Iannino, and K. Okumoto, *Engineering and Managing Software with Reliability Measures,* McGraw-Hill, 1987.

[POO88] Poore, J. H., and H. D. Mills, "Bringing Software Under Statistical Quality Control," *Quality Progress,* November 1988, pp. 52–55.

[POO93] Poore, J. H., H. D. Mills, and D. Mutchler, "Planning and Certifying Software System Reliability," *IEEE Software,* vol. 10, no. 1, January 1993, pp. 88–99.

[WOH94] Wohlin, C., and P. Runeson, "Certification of Software Components," *IEEE Trans. Software Engineering,* vol. SE-20, no. 6, June 1994, pp. 494–499.

Problems and Points to Ponder

29.1. If you had to pick one aspect of cleanroom software engineering that makes it radically different from conventional software engineering approaches, what would it be?

29.2. How do an incremental process model and certification work together to produce high-quality software?

29.3. Using box structure specification, develop "first-pass" analysis and design models for the *SafeHome* system.

29.4. Develop a box structure specification for a portion of the PHTRS system introduced in Problem 8.10.

29.5. A bubble sort algorithm is defined in the following manner:

```
procedure bubblesort;
var i, t, integer;
begin
repeat until t=a[1]
        t:=a[1];
        for j:= 2 to n do
            if a[j-1] > a[j] then begin
                t:=a[j-1];
                a[j-1]:=a[j];
                a[j]:=t;
                end
endrep
end
```

Partition the design into subfunctions, and define a set of conditions that would enable you to prove that this algorithm is correct.

29.6. Document a correctness verification proof for the bubble sort discussed in Problem 29.5.

29.7. Select a program component that you have designed in another context (or one assigned by your instructor), and develop a complete proof of correctness for it.

29.8. Select a program that you use regularly (e.g., an e-mail handler, a word processor, a spreadsheet program), and create a set of usage scenarios for the program. Define the probability of use for each scenario, and then develop a program stimuli and probability distribution table similar to the one shown in Section 29.4.1.

29.9. For the program stimuli and probability distribution table developed in Problem 29.8, use a random number generator to develop a set of test cases for use in statistical use testing.

29.10. In your own words, describe the intent of certification in the cleanroom software engineering context.

Further Readings and Information Sources

Prowell et al. (*Cleanroom Software Engineering: Technology and Process,* Addison-Wesley, 1999) provide an in-depth treatment of all important aspects of the cleanroom approach. Useful discussions of cleanroom topics have been edited by Poore and Trammell (*Cleanroom Software Engineering: A Reader,* Blackwell Publishing, 1996). Becker and Whittaker (*Cleanroom Software Engineering Practices,* Idea Group Publishing, 1996) present an excellent overview for those who are unfamiliar with cleanroom practices.

The Cleanroom Pamphlet (Software Technology Support Center, Hill AF Base, April 1995) contains reprints of a number of important articles. Linger [LIN94] produced one of the better introductions to the subject. The Data and Analysis Center for Software (DACS) (www.dacs.dtic.mil) provides many useful papers, guidebooks, and other information sources on cleanroom software engineering.

Linger and Trammell ("Cleanroom Software Engineering Reference Model," SEI Technical Report CMU/SEI-96-TR-022, 1996) have defined a set of 14 cleanroom processes and 20 work products that form the basis for the SEI CMM for cleanroom software engineering (CMU/SEI-96-TR-023).

Michael Deck of Cleanroom Software Engineering (www.cleansoft.com) has prepared a bibliography on cleanroom topics. Many are available in downloadable format.

Design verification via proof of correctness lies at the heart of the cleanroom approach. Books by Stavely (*Toward Zero-Defect Software,* Addison-Wesley, 1998), Baber (*Error-Free Software,* Wiley, 1991), and Schulmeyer (*Zero Defect Software,* McGraw-Hill, 1990) discuss proof of correctness in considerable detail.

A wide variety of information sources on cleanroom software engineering is available on the Internet. An up-to-date list of World Wide Web references can be found at the SEPA Web site: **http://www.mhhe.com/pressman.**

CHAPTER

COMPONENT-BASED SOFTWARE ENGINEERING 30

KEY CONCEPTS

In the software engineering context, reuse is an idea both old and new. Programmers have reused ideas, abstractions, and processes since the earliest days of computing, but the early approach to reuse was ad hoc. Today, complex, high-quality computer-based systems must be built in a very short time and demand a more organized approach to reuse.

Component-based software engineering (CBSE) is a process that emphasizes the design and construction of computer-based systems using reusable software "components." Clements [CLE95] describes CBSE in the following way:

> [CBSE] is changing the way large software systems are developed. [CBSE] embodies the "buy, don't build" philosophy espoused by Fred Brooks and others. In the same way that early subroutines liberated the programmer from thinking about details, [CBSE] shifts the emphasis from programming software to composing software systems. Implementation has given way to integration as the focus. At its foundation is the assumption that there is sufficient commonality in many large software systems to justify developing reusable components to exploit and satisfy that commonality.

But a number of questions arise. Is it possible to construct complex systems by assembling them from a catalog of reusable software components? Can this be accomplished in a cost- and time-effective manner? Can appropriate incentives be established to encourage software engineers to reuse rather than reinvent? Is

QUICK LOOK

What is it? You purchase an entertainment system and bring it home. Each component has been designed to fit a specific audio-video architecture—connections are standardized, and communication protocol has been preestablished. Assembly is easy because you don't have to build the system from hundreds of discrete parts. Component-based software engineering (CBSE) strives to achieve the same thing. A set of prebuilt, standardized software components are made available to fit a specific architectural style for some application domain. The application is then assembled using these components, rather than the discrete parts of a conventional programming language.

Who does it? Software engineers apply the CBSE process.

Why is it important? It takes only a few minutes to assemble the home entertainment system because the components are designed to be integrated with ease. Although software is considerably more complex, it follows that component-based systems are easier to assemble and therefore less costly to build than systems constructed from discrete parts. In addition, CBSE encourages the use of predictable architectural patterns and standard software infrastructure, thereby leading to a higher-quality result.

What are the steps? CBSE encompasses two parallel engineering activities: domain engineering and component-based development.

Domain engineering explores an application domain with the specific intent of finding functional, behavioral, and data components that are candidates for reuse. These components are placed in reuse libraries. Component-based development elicits requirements from the customer; selects an appropriate architectural style to meet the objectives of the system to be built; and then (1) selects potential components for reuse, (2) qualifies the components to be sure that they properly fit the architecture for the system, (3) adapts components if modifications must be made to properly integrate them, and (4) integrates the components to form subsystems and the application as a whole. In addition, custom components are engineered to address those aspects of the system that cannot be implemented using existing components.

What is the work product? Operational software, assembled using existing and newly developed software components, is the result of CBSE.

How do I ensure that I've done it right? Use the same SQA practices that are applied in every software engineering process—formal technical reviews assess the analysis and design models, specialized reviews consider issues associated with acquired components, testing is applied to uncover errors in newly developed software and in reusable components that have been integrated into the architecture.

management willing to incur the added expense associated with creating reusable software components? Can the library of components necessary to accomplish reuse be created in a way that makes it accessible to those who need it? Can components that do exist be found by those who need them?

Even today, software engineers grapple with these and other questions about software component reuse. We look at some of the answers in this chapter.

30.1 Engineering of Component-Based Systems

WebRef
Useful information on CBSE for WebApps can be found at **www.cbd-hq.com.**

On the surface, CBSE seems quite similar to conventional or object-oriented software engineering. The process begins when a software team establishes requirements for the system to be built using conventional requirements elicitation techniques (Chapter 7). An architectural design (Chapter 10) is established, but rather than moving immediately into more detailed design tasks, the team examines requirements to determine what subset is directly amenable to *composition,* rather than construction. That is, the team asks the following questions for each system requirement:

- Are commercial off-the-shelf (COTS) components available to implement the requirement?
- Are internally developed reusable components available to implement the requirement?
- Are the interfaces for available components compatible within the architecture of the system to be built?

The team may attempt to modify or remove those system requirements that cannot be implemented with COTS or in-house components.[1] If the requirement(s) cannot be changed or deleted, software engineering methods are applied to build those new components that must be developed to meet the requirement(s). But for those requirements that are addressed with available components, a different set of software engineering activities commences: qualification, adaptation, composition, and update. Each of these CBSE activities is discussed in more detail in Section 30.4.

In the first part of this section, the term *component* has been used repeatedly, yet a definitive description of the term is elusive. Brown and Wallnau [BRO96] suggest the following possibilities:

- *Component*—a nontrivial, nearly independent, and replaceable part of a system that fulfills a clear function in the context of a well-defined architecture.
- *Run-time software component*—a dynamic bindable package of one or more programs managed as a unit and accessed through documented interfaces that can be discovered in run time.
- *Software component*—a unit of composition with contractually specified and explicit context dependencies only.
- *Business component*—the software implementation of an "autonomous" business concept or business process.

In addition to these descriptions, software components can also be characterized based on their use in the CBSE process. In addition to COTS components, the CBSE process yields:

- *Qualified components*—assessed by software engineers to ensure that not only functionality, but performance, reliability, usability, and other quality factors (Chapter 26) conform to the requirements of the system or product to be built.
- *Adapted components*—adapted to modify (also called *mask* or *wrap*) [BRO96] unwanted or undesirable characteristics.
- *Assembled components*—integrated into an architectural style and interconnected with an appropriate infrastructure that allows the components to be coordinated and managed effectively.
- *Updated components*—replacing existing software as new versions of components become available.

1 The implication is that the organization adjusts its business or product requirements so that component-based implementation can be achieved without the need for custom engineering. This approach reduces costs and improves time to market, but it is not always possible.

30.2 The CBSE Process

The *CBSE process* is characterized in a manner that not only identifies candidate components but also qualifies each component's interface, adapts components to remove architectural mismatches, assembles components into a selected architectural style, and updates components as requirements for the system change [BRO96]. The process model for component-based software engineering emphasizes parallel tracks in which domain engineering (Section 30.3) occurs concurrently with component-based development.

Figure 30.1 illustrates a typical process model that explicitly accommodates CBSE [CHR95]. *Domain engineering* creates a model of the application domain that is used as a basis for analyzing user requirements in the software engineering flow. A generic software architecture provides input for the design of the application. Finally, after reusable components have been purchased, selected from existing libraries, or constructed (as part of domain engineering), they are made available to software engineers during component-based development.

The *analysis* and *architectural design* steps defined as part of *component-based development* (Figure 30.1) can be implemented within the context of an *abstract design paradigm* (ADP) [DOG03]. An ADP implies that the overall model of the software—represented as data, function, and behavior (control)—can be decomposed hierar-

Figure 30.1

A process model that supports CBSE

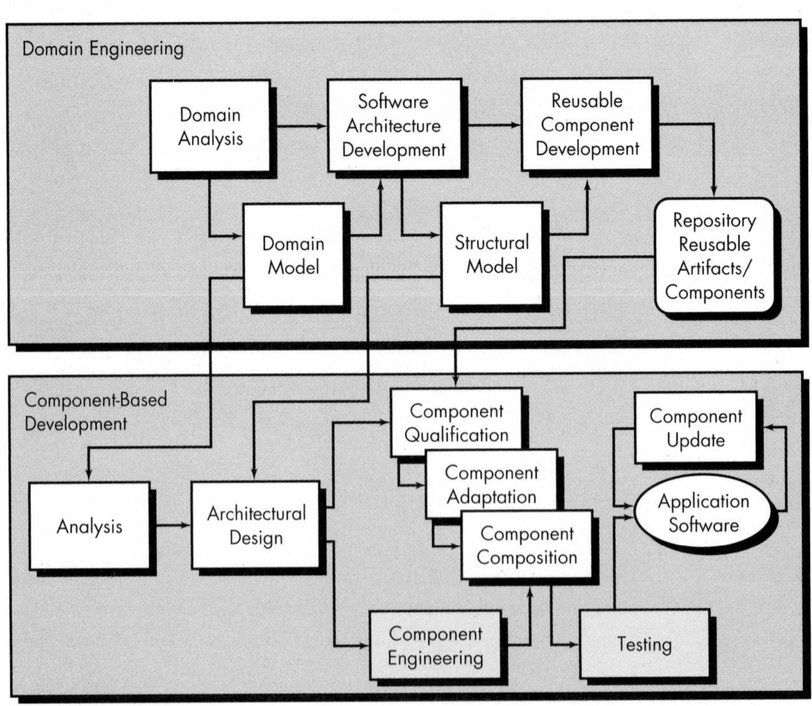

chically. As decomposition begins, the system is represented as a collection of architectural frameworks, each composed of one or more design patterns (Chapter 10). Further refinement identifies the components that are required to create each design pattern. In an ideal context, all of these components would be acquired from a repository (*component qualification, adaptation,* and *composition* activities apply). When specialized components are required, *component engineering* is applied.

30.3 Domain Engineering

The intent of *domain engineering* is to identify, construct, catalog, and disseminate a set of software components that have applicability to existing and future software in a particular application domain. The overall goal is to establish mechanisms that enable software engineers to share these components—to reuse them—during work on new and existing systems. Domain engineering includes three major activities—analysis, construction, and dissemination.

> **"Domain engineering is about finding commonalities among systems to identify components that can be applied to many systems, and to identify program families that are positioned to take fullest advantage of those components."**
>
> **Paul Clements**

It can be argued that "reuse will disappear, not by elimination, but by integration" into the fabric of software engineering practice [TRA95]. As greater emphasis is placed on reuse, some believe that domain engineering will become as important as software engineering over the next decade.

ADVICE *The analysis process we discuss in this section focuses on reusable components. However, the analysis of complete COTS systems (e.g., e-commerce apps, sales force automation apps) can also be a part of domain analysis.*

30.3.1 The Domain Analysis Process

The overall approach to domain analysis is often characterized within the context of object-oriented software engineering. The steps in the process are defined as:

1. Define the domain to be investigated.
2. Categorize the items extracted from the domain.
3. Collect a representative sample of applications in the domain.
4. Analyze each application in the sample and define analysis classes.
5. Develop an analysis model for the classes.

It is important to note that domain analysis is applicable to any software engineering paradigm and may be applied for conventional as well as object-oriented development.

? What components identified during domain analysis will be candidates for reuse?

Although the steps just noted provide a useful model for domain analysis, they provide no guidance for deciding which software components are candidates for reuse. Hutchinson and Hindley [HUT88] suggest the following set of pragmatic questions as a guide for identifying reusable software components:

- Is component functionality required on future implementations?

- How common is the component's function within the domain?
- Is there duplication of the component's function within the domain?
- Is the component hardware dependent? If so, does the hardware remain unchanged between implementations or can the hardware specifics be removed to another component?
- Is the design optimized enough for the next implementation?
- Can we parameterize a nonreusable component so that it becomes reusable?
- Is the component reusable in many implementations with only minor changes?
- Is reuse through modification feasible?
- Can a nonreusable component be decomposed to yield reusable components?
- How valid is component decomposition for reuse?

For additional information on domain analysis, see [ATK01], [HEI01], and [PRI93].

30.3.2 Characterization Functions

It is sometimes difficult to determine whether a potentially reusable component is in fact applicable in a particular situation. To make this determination, it is necessary to define a set of domain characteristics that are shared by all software within a domain. A domain characteristic defines some generic attribute of all products that exist within the domain. For example, generic characteristics might include the importance of safety/reliability, programming language, concurrency in processing, and many others.

A set of domain characteristics for a reusable component can be represented as $\{D_p\}$, where each item, D_{pi}, in the set represents a specific domain characteristic. The value assigned to D_{pi} represents an ordinal scale that is an indication of the relevance of the characteristic for component *p*. A typical scale [BAS94] might be

1: Not relevant to whether reuse is appropriate.

2: Relevant only under unusual circumstances.

3: Relevant—the component can be modified so that it can be used, despite differences.

4: Clearly relevant, and if the new software does not have this characteristic, reuse will be inefficient but may still be possible.

5: Clearly relevant, and if the new software does not have this characteristic, reuse will be ineffective and reuse without the characteristic is not recommended.

WebRef
Useful information on domain analysis can be found at **www.sei.cmu.edu/str/descriptions/deda.html.**

When new software, *w,* is to be built within the application domain, a set of domain characteristics is derived for it. A comparison is then made between D_{pi} and D_{wi} to determine whether the existing component *p* can be effectively reused in application *w.*

Even when software to be engineered clearly exists within an application domain, the reusable components within that domain must be analyzed to determine their applicability. In some cases (hopefully, a limited number), "reinventing the wheel" may still be the most cost-effective choice.

30.3.3 Structural Modeling and Structure Points

When domain analysis is applied, the analyst looks for repeating patterns in the applications that reside within a domain. Structural modeling is a pattern-based domain engineering approach that works under the assumption that every application domain has repeating patterns (of function, data, and behavior) that have reuse potential.

Each application domain can be characterized by a structural model (e.g., aircraft avionics systems differ greatly in specifics, but all modern software in this domain has the same structural model). Therefore, the structural model is an architectural style (Chapter 10) that can and should be reused across applications within the domain.

McMahon [MCM95] describes a *structure point* as "a distinct construct within a structural model." Structure points have three distinct characteristics:

? What is a structure point, and what are its characteristics?

1. A structure point is an abstraction that should have a limited number of instances. In addition, the abstraction should recur throughout applications in the domain. Otherwise, the cost to verify, document, and disseminate the structure point cannot be justified.
2. The rules that govern the use of the structure point should be easily understood. In addition, the interface to the structure point should be relatively simple.
3. The structure point should implement information hiding by isolating all complexity contained within the structure point itself. This reduces the perceived complexity of the overall system.

A structure point is analogous to a design pattern that can be found repeatedly in applications with a specific domain.

As an example of structure points as architectural patterns for a system, consider the domain of software for alarm systems. This domain might encompass systems as simple as *SafeHome* (discussed in earlier chapters) or as complex as the alarm system for an industrial process. In every case, however, a set of predictable structural patterns are encountered: an *interface* that enables the user to interact with the system, a *bounds-setting mechanism* that allows the user to establish bounds on the parameters to be measured, a *sensor management mechanism* that communicates with all monitoring sensors, a *response mechanism* that reacts to the input provided by the sensor management system, and a *control mechanism* that enables the user to control the manner in which monitoring is carried out. Each of these structure points is integrated into a domain architecture.

It is possible to define generic structure points that transcend a number of different application domains [STA94]:

- *Application front end*—the GUI including all menus, panels, and input and command editing facilities.
- *Database*—the repository for all objects relevant to the application domain.
- *Computational engine*—the numerical and nonnumerical models that manipulate data.
- *Reporting facility*—the function that produces output of all kinds.
- *Application editor*—the mechanism for customizing the application to the needs of specific users.

Structure points have been suggested as an alternative to lines of code and function points for software cost estimation [MCM95]. A brief discussion of costing using structure points is presented in Section 30.6.2.

30.4 Component-Based Development

Component-based development (CBD) is a CBSE activity that occurs in parallel with domain engineering. Using analysis and architectural design methods discussed earlier in this book, the software team refines an architectural style that is appropriate for the analysis model created for the application to be built.[2]

Once the architecture has been established, it must be populated by components that (1) are available from reuse libraries and/or (2) are engineered to meet custom needs. Hence, the task flow for component-based development has two parallel paths (Figure 30.1). When reusable components are available for potential integration into the architecture, they must be qualified and adapted. When new components are required, they must be engineered. The resultant components are then "composed" (integrated) into the architecture template and tested thoroughly.

30.4.1 Component Qualification, Adaptation, and Composition

As we have already seen, domain engineering provides the library of reusable components that are required for component-based software engineering. Some of these reusable components are developed in-house, others can be extracted from existing applications, and still others may be acquired from third parties.

Unfortunately, the existence of reusable components does not guarantee that these components can be integrated easily or effectively into the architecture chosen for a new application. It is for this reason that a sequence of component-based development activities is applied when a component is proposed for use.

---

2 It should be noted that the architectural style is often influenced by the generic structural model created during domain engineering (see Figure 30.1).

Component qualification. Component qualification ensures that a candidate component will perform the function required, will properly "fit" into the architectural style specified for the system, and will exhibit the quality characteristics (e.g., performance, reliability, usability) that are required for the application.

? **What factors are considered during component qualification?**

The interface description provides useful information about the operation and use of a software component, but it does not provide all of the information required to determine if a proposed component can, in fact, be reused effectively in a new application. Among the many factors considered during component qualification are [BRO96]: application programming interface (API); development and integration tools required by the component; run-time requirements, including resource usage (e.g., memory or storage), timing or speed, and network protocol; service requirements, including operating system interfaces and support from other components; security features, including access controls and authentication protocol; embedded design assumptions, including the use of specific numerical or non-numerical algorithms; and exception handling.

Each of these factors is relatively easy to assess when reusable components that have been developed in-house are proposed. However, it is much more difficult to determine the internal workings of COTS or third-party components because the only available information may be the interface specification itself.

Component adaptation. In an ideal setting, domain engineering creates a library of components that can be easily integrated into an application architecture. The implication of "easy integration" is that (1) consistent methods of resource management have been implemented for all components in the library, (2) common activities such as data management exist for all components, and (3) interfaces within the architecture and with the external environment have been implemented in a consistent manner.

In addition to assessing whether the cost of adaptation for reuse is justified, the software team also assesses whether achieving required functionality and performance can be done cost-effectively.

In reality, even after a component has been qualified for use within an application architecture, conflicts may occur in one or more of the areas just noted. To avoid these conflicts, an adaptation technique called *component wrapping* [BRO96] is often used. When a software team has full access to the internal design and code for a component (often not the case when COTS components are used) *white-box wrapping* is applied. Like its counterpart in software testing (Chapter 14), white-box wrapping examines the internal processing details of the component and makes code-level modifications to remove any conflict. *Gray-box wrapping* is applied when the component library provides a component extension language or API that enables conflicts to be removed or masked. *Black-box wrapping* requires the introduction of pre- and post-processing at the component interface to remove or mask conflicts. The software team must determine whether the effort required to adequately wrap a component is justified or whether a custom component (designed to eliminate the conflicts encountered) should be engineered instead.

Component composition. The component composition task assembles qualified, adapted, and engineered components to populate the architecture established for an application. To accomplish this, an infrastructure must be established to bind the components into an operational system. The infrastructure (usually a library of specialized components) provides a model for the coordination of components and specific services that enable components to coordinate with one another and perform common tasks.

Among the many mechanisms for creating an effective infrastructure is a set of four "architectural ingredients" [ADL95] that should be present to achieve component composition:

? **What ingredients are necessary to achieve component composition?**

Data exchange model. Mechanisms that enable users and applications to interact and transfer data (e.g., drag and drop, cut and paste) should be defined for all reusable components. The data exchange mechanisms not only allow human-to-software and component-to-component data transfer but also transfer among system resources (e.g., dragging a file to a printer icon for output).

Automation. A variety of tools, macros, and scripts should be implemented to facilitate interaction between reusable components.

Structured storage. Heterogeneous data (e.g., graphical data, voice/video, text, and numerical data) contained in a "compound document" should be organized and accessed as a single data structure, rather than a collection of separate files. "Structured data maintains a descriptive index of nesting structures that applications can freely navigate to locate, create, or edit individual data contents as directed by the end user" [ADL95].

Underlying object model. The object model ensures that components developed in different programming languages that reside on different platforms can be interoperable. That is, objects must be capable of communicating across a network. To achieve this, the object model defines a standard for component interoperability.

Because the potential impact of reuse and CBSE on the software industry is enormous, a number of major companies and industry consortia have proposed standards for component software:

WebRef
The latest information on CORBA can be obtained at **www.omg.org.**

OMG/CORBA. The Object Management Group has published a *common object request broker architecture* (OMG/CORBA). An *object request broker* (ORB) provides a variety of services that enable reusable components (objects) to communicate with other components, regardless of their location within a system.

WebRef
The latest information on COM can be obtained at **www.microsoft.com/COM.**

Microsoft COM. Microsoft has developed a *component object model* (COM) that provides a specification for using components produced by various vendors within a single application running under the Windows operating system. COM encompasses two elements: COM interfaces (implemented as COM objects) and a set of mechanisms for registering and passing messages between COM interfaces.

WebRef
The latest information on Javabeans can be obtained at **java.sun.com/products/javabeans/docs/.**

Sun JavaBeans Components. The JavaBeans component system is a portable, platform independent CBSE infrastructure developed using the Java programming language. The JavaBeans component system encompasses a set of tools, called the *Bean Development Kit* (BDK), that allows developers to (1) analyze how existing Beans (components) work, (2) customize their behavior and appearance, (3) establish mechanisms for coordination and communication, (4) develop custom Beans for use in a specific application, and (5) test and evaluate Bean behavior.

Which of these standards will dominate the industry? There is no easy answer at this time. Although many developers have adopted one of the standards, it is likely that large software organizations may choose to use all three standards, depending on the application categories and platforms that are chosen.

INFO

Object Request Broker Architecture

Client/server systems are implemented using software components (objects) that must be capable of interacting with one another within a single machine (either client or server) or across the network. An *object request broker* (ORB) is "middleware" that enables an object residing on a client to send a message to a method that is encapsulated by an object residing on a server. In essence, the ORB intercepts the message and handles all communication and coordination activities required to find the object to which the message was addressed, invoke its method, pass appropriate data to the object, and transfer the resulting data back to the object that generated the message in the first place.

CORBA, COM, and JavaBeans implement an object request broker philosophy. In this sidebar CORBA will be used to illustrate ORB middleware.

The basic structure of a CORBA architecture is illustrated in Figure 30.2. When CORBA is implemented in a client/server system, objects on both the client and the server are defined using an *interface description language* (IDL), a declarative language that allows a software engineer to define objects, attributes, methods, and the messages required to invoke them. To accommodate a request for a server-resident method by a client-resident object, client and server IDL stubs are created. The stubs provide the gateway through which requests for objects across the c/s system are accommodated.

Because requests for objects across the network occur at run time, a mechanism for storing the object description must be established so that pertinent information about the object and its location are available when needed. The interface repository accomplishes this.

When a client application must invoke a method contained within an object elsewhere in the system, CORBA uses dynamic invocation to (1) obtain pertinent information about the desired method from the interface repository, (2) create a data structure with parameters to be passed to the object, (3) create a request for the object, and (4) invoke the request. The request is then passed to the ORB core—an implementation-specific part of the network operating system that manages requests—and the request is fulfilled.

The request is passed through the core and is processed by the server. At the server site, an object adapter stores class and object information in a server-resident interface repository, accepts and manages incoming requests from the client, and performs a variety of other object management functions. At the server, IDL stubs that are similar to those defined at the client machine are used as the interface to the actual object implementation resident at the server site.

30.4.2 Component Engineering

As we noted earlier in this chapter, the CBSE process encourages the use of existing software components. However, there are times when components must be engineered. That is, new software components must be developed and integrated with

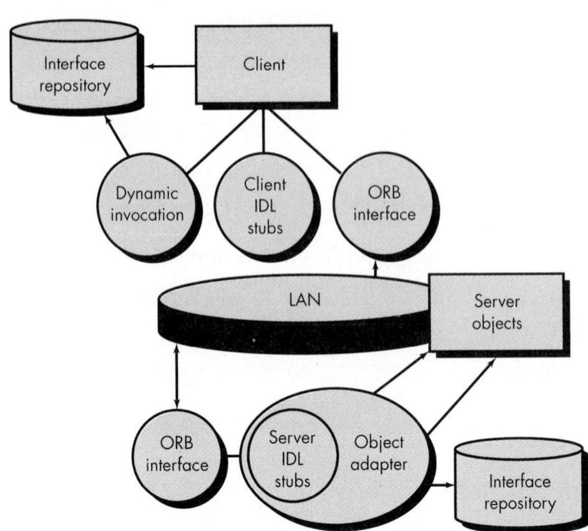

FIGURE 30.2 The basic CORBA architecture

existing COTS and in-house components. Because these new components become members of the in-house library of reusable components, they should be engineered for reuse.

Nothing is magical about creating software components that can be reused. Design concepts such as abstraction, hiding, functional independence, refinement, and structured programming, along with object-oriented methods, testing, SQA, and correctness verification methods, all contribute to the creation of software components that are reusable.[3] In this section we will not revisit these topics. Rather, we consider the reuse-specific issues that are complementary to solid software engineering practices.

30.4.3 Analysis and Design for Reuse

The analysis model is analyzed to determine those elements of the model that point to existing reusable components. The problem is extracting information from the requirements model in a form that can lead to "specification matching."

If specification matching yields components that fit the needs of the current application, the designer can extract these components from a reuse library (repository) and use them in the design of new systems. If design components cannot be found, the software engineer must apply conventional or OO design methods to create them. It is at this point—when the designer begins to create a new component—that *design for reuse* (DFR) should be considered.

As we have already noted, DFR requires the software engineer to apply solid software design concepts and principles (Chapter 9). But the characteristics of the ap-

3 To learn more about these concepts, see Parts 2 and 5 of this book.

DFR can be quite difficult when components must be interfaced or integrated with legacy systems or with multiple systems whose architecture and interfacing protocols are inconsistent.

plication domain must also be considered. Binder [BIN93] suggests a number of key issues[4] that form a basis for design for reuse:

Standard data. The application domain should be investigated and standard global data structures (e.g., file structures or a complete database) should be identified. All design components can then be characterized to make use of these standard data structures.

Standard interface protocols. Three levels of interface protocol should be established: the nature of intramodular interfaces, the design of external technical (nonhuman) interfaces, and the human/machine interface.

Program templates. The structure model (Section 30.3.3) can serve as a template for the architectural design of a new program.

Once standard data, interfaces, and program templates have been established, the designer has a framework in which to create the design. New components that conform to this framework have a higher probability for subsequent reuse.

30.5 Classifying and Retrieving Components

Consider a university library. Tens of thousands of books, periodicals, and other information resources are available for use. But to access these resources, a categorization scheme must be developed. To navigate this large volume of information, librarians have defined a classification scheme that includes a Library of Congress classification code, keywords, author names, and other index entries. All enable the user to find the needed resource quickly and easily.

Now, consider a large component repository. Tens of thousands of reusable software components reside in it. But how does a software engineer find the one she needs? To answer this question, another question arises: How do we describe software components in unambiguous, classifiable terms? These are difficult questions, and no definitive answer has yet been developed. In this section we explore current directions that will enable future software engineers to navigate reuse libraries.

30.5.1 Describing Reusable Components

A reusable software component can be described in many ways, but an ideal description encompasses what Tracz [TRA90] has called the *3C model*—concept, content, and context.

The *concept* of a software component is "a description of what the component does" [WHI95]. The interface to the component is fully described and the semantics—represented within the context of pre- and postconditions—are identified. The concept should communicate the intent of the component.

4 In general, DFR preparations should be undertaken as part of domain engineering (Section 30.3).

The *content* of a component describes how the concept is realized. In essence, the content is information that is hidden from casual users and need be known only to those who intend to modify or test the component.

The *context* places a reusable software component within its domain of applicability. That is, by specifying conceptual, operational, and implementation features, the context enables a software engineer to find the appropriate component to meet application requirements.

To be of use in a pragmatic setting, concept, content, and context must be translated into a concrete specification scheme. Dozens of papers and articles have been written about classification schemes for reusable software components (e.g., [LUC01] and [WHI95] contain extensive bibliographies). The methods proposed can be categorized into three major areas: library and information science methods, artificial intelligence methods, and hypertext systems. The vast majority of work done to date suggests the use of library science methods for component classification.

Figure 30.3 presents a taxonomy of library science indexing methods. *Controlled indexing vocabularies* limit the terms or syntax that can be used to classify an object (component). *Uncontrolled indexing vocabularies* place no restrictions on the nature of the description. The majority of classification schemes for software components fall into three categories:

Enumerated classification. Components are described by a hierarchical structure in which classes and varying levels of subclasses of software components are defined. The hierarchical structure of an enumerated classification scheme makes it easy to understand and to use. However, before a hierarchy can be built, domain engineering must be conducted so that sufficient knowledge of the proper entries in the hierarchy is available.

FIGURE 30.3

A taxonomy of indexing methods [FRA94]

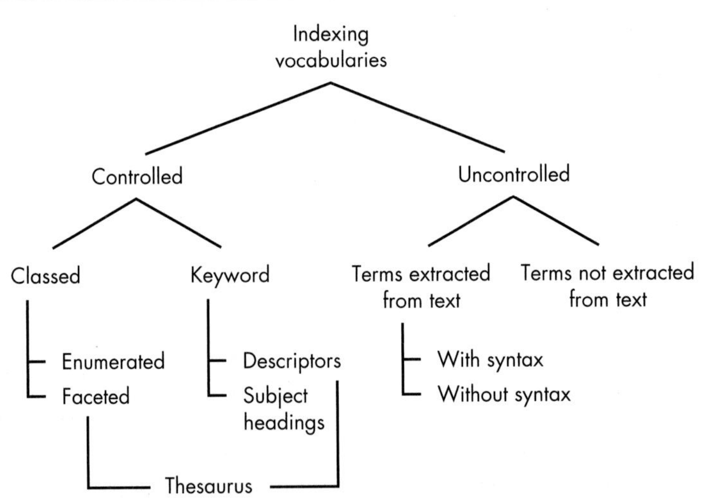

Faceted classification. A domain area is analyzed and a set of basic descriptive features are identified. These features, called *facets,* are then ranked by importance and connected to a component. A facet can describe the function that the component performs, the data that are manipulated, the context in which they are applied, or any other feature. The set of facets that describe a component is called the *facet descriptor.* Generally, the facet description is limited to no more than seven or eight facets.

Attribute-value classification. A set of attributes is defined for all components in a domain area. Values are then assigned to these attributes in much the same way as faceted classification. In fact, attribute value classification is similar to faceted classification with the following exceptions: (1) no limit is placed on the number of attributes that can be used, (2) attributes are not assigned priorities, and (3) a thesaurus function is not used.

Based on an empirical study of each of these classification techniques, Frakes and Pole [FRA94] indicate that there is no clear "best" technique and that "no method did more than moderately well in search effectiveness. . . ." It would appear that further work remains to be done in the development of effective classification schemes for reuse libraries.

30.5.2 The Reuse Environment

Software component reuse must be supported by an environment that encompasses the following elements:

- A component database capable of storing software components and the classification information necessary to retrieve them.
- A library management system that provides access to the database.
- A software component retrieval system (e.g., an object request broker) that enables a client application to retrieve components and services from the library server.
- CBSE tools that support the integration of reused components into a new design or implementation.

Each of these functions interact with or is embodied within the confines of a reuse library.

The reuse library is one element of a larger software repository (Chapter 27) and provides facilities for the storage of software components and a wide variety of reusable work products (e.g., specifications, designs, patterns, frameworks, code fragments, test cases, user guides). The library encompasses a database and the tools that are necessary to query the database and retrieve components from it. A component classification scheme (Section 30.5.1) serves as the basis for library queries.

Queries are often characterized using the context element of the 3C model described earlier in this section. If an initial query results in a voluminous list of

WebRef
A comprehensive collection of resources on CBSE can be found at **http:// www. cbd-hq.com/.**

candidate components, the query is refined to narrow the list. Concept and content information are then extracted (after candidate components are found) to assist the developer in selecting the proper component.

A detailed discussion of the structure of reuse libraries and the tools that manage them is best left to sources dedicated to the subject. The interested reader should see [FIS00] and [LIN95] for additional information.

SOFTWARE TOOLS

Component-Based Development

Objective: To aid in modeling, design, review, and integration of software components as part of a larger system.

Mechanics: Tools mechanics vary. In general, CBD tools assist in one or more of the following capabilities: specification and modeling of the software architecture; browsing and selection of available software components; integration of components.

Representative Tools[5]

ComponentSource (www.componentsource.com) provides a wide array of COTS software components (and tools) supported within many different component standards.

Component Manager, developed by Flashline (www.flashline.com), "is an application that enables, promotes, and measures software component reuse."

Select Component Factory, developed by Select Business Solutions (www.selectbs.com/products), "is an integrated set of products for software design, design review, service/component management, requirements management, and code generation."

Software Through Pictures-ACD, distributed by Aonix (www.aonix.com), enables comprehensive modeling using UML for the OMG model driven architecture—an open, vendor-neutral approach for CBSE.

30.6 ECONOMICS OF CBSE

WebRef
A variety of articles providing guidelines for CBD and COTS-based systems can be found at **www.sei.cmu.edu.**

Component-based software engineering has an intuitive appeal. In theory, it should provide a software organization with advantages in quality and timeliness. And these should translate into cost savings. But are there hard data that support our intuition?

To answer this question we must first understand what actually can be reused in a software engineering context and then what the costs associated with reuse really are. As a consequence, it is possible to develop a cost/benefit analysis for component reuse.

30.6.1 Impact on Quality, Productivity, and Cost

Considerable evidence from industry case studies (e.g., [ALL02], [HEN95], [MCM95]) indicates substantial business benefits can be derived from aggressive software reuse. Product quality, development productivity, and overall cost are all improved.

Quality. In an ideal setting, a software component that is developed for reuse would be verified to be correct (see Chapter 29) and would contain no defects. In

5 Tools noted here do not represent an endorsement, but rather a sampling of tools in this category. In most cases, tool names are trademarked by their respective developers.

reality, formal verification is not carried out routinely, and defects can and do occur. However, with each reuse, defects are found and eliminated, and a component's quality improves as a result. Over time, the component becomes virtually defect free.

In a study conducted at Hewlett Packard, Lim [LIM94] reports that the defect rate for reused code is 0.9 defects per KLOC, while the rate for newly developed software is 4.1 defects per KLOC. For an application that was composed of 68 percent reused code, the defect rate was 2.0 defects per KLOC—a 51 percent improvement from the expected rate, had the application been developed without reuse. Henry and Faller [HEN95] report a 35 percent improvement in quality. Although anecdotal reports span a reasonably wide spectrum of quality improvement percentages, it is fair to state that reuse provides a nontrivial benefit in terms of the quality and reliability for delivered software.

Productivity. When reusable components are applied throughout the software process, less time is spent creating the plans, models, documents, code, and data that are required to create a deliverable system. It follows that the same level of functionality is delivered to the customer with less input effort. Hence, productivity is improved. Although percentage productivity improvement reports are notoriously difficult to interpret,[6] it appears that 30 to 50 percent reuse can result in productivity improvements in the 25–40 percent range.

The cost to develop a reusable component is often greater that the cost to develop a component that is specific to one application. Be sure that there will be a need for the reusable component in the future. That's where the payoff is realized.

Cost. The net cost savings for reuse are estimated by projecting the cost of the project if it were developed from scratch, C_s, and then subtracting the sum of the costs associated with reuse, C_r, and the actual cost of the software as delivered, C_d.

C_s can be determined by applying one or more of the estimation techniques discussed in Chapter 23. The costs associated with reuse, C_r, include [CHR95]: domain analysis and modeling, domain architecture development, increased documentation to facilitate reuse, support and enhancement of reuse components, royalties and licenses for externally acquired components, creation or acquisition and operation of a reuse repository, and training of personnel in design and construction for reuse. Although costs associated with domain analysis (Section 30.3) and the operation of a reuse repository can be substantial, many of the other costs noted here address issues that are part of good software engineering practice, whether or not reuse is a priority.

30.6.2 Cost Analysis Using Structure Points

In Section 30.3.3, we defined a structure point as an architectural pattern that recurs throughout a particular application domain. A software designer (or system engineer) can develop an architecture for a new application, system, or product by defining a domain architecture and then populating it with structure points. These structure points are either individual reusable components or packages of reusable components.

6 Many extenuating circumstances (e.g., application domain, problem complexity, team structure and size, project duration, technology applied) can have a profound impact on the productivity of the project team.

Even though structure points are reusable, their qualification, adaptation, integration, and maintenance costs are nontrivial. Before proceeding with reuse, the project manager should understand the costs associated with the use of structure points.

Since all structure points (and reusable components in general) have a past history, cost data can be collected for each. In an ideal setting, the qualification, adaptation, integration, and maintenance costs associated with each component in a reuse library is maintained for each instance of usage. These data can then be analyzed to develop projected costs for the next instance of reuse.

As an example, consider a new application, *X*, that requires 60 percent new code and the reuse of three structure points, SP_1, SP_2, and SP_3. Each of these reusable components has been used in a number of other applications, and average costs for qualification, adaptation, integration, and maintenance are available.

To estimate the effort required to deliver *X*, the following must be determined:

$$\text{overall effort} = E_{new} + E_{qual} + E_{adapt} + E_{int}$$

where

E_{new} = effort required to engineer and construct new software components (determined using techniques described in Chapter 23)

E_{qual} = effort required to qualify SP_1, SP_2, and SP_3

E_{adapt} = effort required to adapt SP_1, SP_2, and SP_3

E_{int} = effort required to integrate SP_1, SP_2, and SP_3

The effort required to qualify, adapt, and integrate SP_1, SP_2, and SP_3 is determined by taking the average of historical data collected for qualification, adaptation, and integration of the reusable components in other applications.

30.7 Summary

Component-based software engineering offers inherent benefits in software quality, developer productivity, and overall system cost. And yet, many roadblocks remain to be overcome before the CBSE process model is widely used throughout the industry.

In addition to software components, a variety of reusable artifacts can be acquired by a software engineer. These include technical representations of the software (e.g., specifications, architectural models, designs), documents, patterns, frameworks, test data, and even process-related tasks (e.g., inspection techniques).

The CBSE process encompasses two concurrent subprocesses—domain engineering and component-based development. The intent of domain engineering is to identify, construct, catalog, and disseminate a set of software components in a particular application domain. Component-based development then qualifies, adapts, and integrates these components for use in a new system. In addition, component-based development engineers new components that are based on the custom requirements of a new system.

Analysis and design techniques for reusable components draw on the same principles and concepts that are part of good software engineering practice. Reusable components should be designed within an environment that establishes standard data structures, interface protocols, and program architectures for each application domain.

Component-based software engineering uses a data exchange model, tools, structured storage, and an underlying object model to construct applications. The object model generally conforms to one or more component standards (e.g., OMG/CORBA) that define the manner in which an application can access reusable objects. Classification schemes enable a developer to find and retrieve reusable components and conform to a model that identifies concept, content, and context. Enumerated classification, faceted classification, and attribute-value classification are representative of many component classification schemes.

The economics of software reuse are addressed by a single question: Is it cost effective to build less and reuse more? In general, the answer is yes, but a software project planner must consider the nontrivial costs associated with the qualification, adaptation, and integration of reusable components.

References

[ADL95] Adler, R.M., "Emerging Standards for Component Software, *Computer,* vol. 28, no. 3, March 1995, pp. 68–77.

[ALL02] Allen, P., "CBD Survey: The State of the Practice," *The Cutter Edge,* March, 2002, available at http://www.cutter.com/research/2002/edge020305.html.

[ATK01] Atkinson, C., et al; *Component-Based Product Line Engineering with UML,* Addison-Wesley, 2001.

[BAS94] Basili, V. R., L. C. Briand, and W. M. Thomas, "Domain Analysis for the Reuse of Software Development Experiences," *Proc. of the 19th Annual Software Engineering Workshop,* NASA/GSFC, Greenbelt, MD, December 1994.

[BIN93] Binder, R., "Design for Reuse Is for Real," *American Programmer,* vol. 6, no. 8, August 1993, pp. 30–37.

[BRO96] Brown, A. W., and K. C. Wallnau, "Engineering of Component-Based Systems," *Component-Based Software Engineering,* IEEE Computer Society Press, 1996, pp. 7–15.

[CHR95] Christensen, S. R., "Software Reuse Initiatives at Lockheed," *CrossTalk,* vol. 8, no. 5, May 1995, pp. 26–31.

[CLE95] Clements, P. C., "From Subroutines to Subsystems: Component-Based Software Development," *American Programmer,* vol. 8, No. 11, November 1995.

[DOG03] Dogru, A., and M. Tanik, "A Process Model for Component-Oriented Software Engineering, *IEEE Software,* vol. 20, no. 2, March/April 2003, pp. 34–41.

[FIS00] Fischer, B., "Specification-Based Browsing of Software Component Libraries," *J. Automated Software Engineering,* vol. 7, no. 2, 2000, pp. 179–200, available at http://ase.arc.nasa.gov/people/fischer/papers/ase-00.html.

[FRA94] Frakes, W. B., and T. P. Pole, "An Empirical Study of Representation Methods for Reusable Software Components," *IEEE Trans. Software Engineering,* vol. SE-20, no. 8, August 1994, pp. 617–630.

[HEI01] Heineman, G., and W. Councill (eds.), *Component-Based Software Engineering,* Addison-Wesley, 2001.

[HEN95] Henry, E., and B. Faller, "Large Scale Industrial Reuse to Reduce Cost and Cycle Time," *IEEE Software,* September 1995, pp. 47–53.

[HUT88] Hutchinson, J. W., and P. G. Hindley, "A Preliminary Study of Large Scale Software Reuse," *Software Engineering Journal,* vol. 3, no. 5, 1988, pp. 208–212.

[LIA93] Liao, H., and Wang, F., "Software Reuse Based on a Large Object-Oriented Library," *ACM Software Engineering Notes,* vol. 18, no. 1, January 1993, pp. 74–80.

[LIM94] Lim, W. C., "Effects of Reuse on Quality, Productivity, and Economics," *IEEE Software,* September 1994, pp. 23–30.

[LIN95] Linthicum, D. S., "Component Development (a Special Feature)," *Application Development Trends,* June 1995, pp. 57–78.

[LUC01] deLucena, Jr., V., "Facet-Based Classification Scheme for Industrial Software Components," 2001, can be downloaded from http://research.microsoft.com/ users/cszypers/events/WCOP2001/Lucena.pdf.

[MCM95] McMahon, P.E., "Pattern-Based Architecture: Bridging Software Reuse and Cost Management," *Crosstalk,* vol. 8, no. 3, March 1995, pp. 10–16.

[ORF96] Orfali, R., D. Harkey, and J. Edwards, *The Essential Distributed Objects Survival Guide,* Wiley, 1996.

[PRI93] Prieto-Diaz, R., "Issues and Experiences in Software Reuse," *American Programmer,* vol. 6, no. 8, August 1993, pp. 10–18.

[POL94] Pollak, W., and M. Rissman, "Structural Models and Patterned Architectures," *Computer,* vol. 27, no. 8, August 1994, pp. 67–68.

[STA94] Staringer, W., "Constructing Applications from Reusable Components," *IEEE Software,* September 1994, pp. 61–68.

[TRA90] Tracz, W., "Where Does Reuse Start?" *Proc. Realities of Reuse Workshop,* Syracuse University CASE Center, January 1990.

[TRA95] Tracz, W., "Third International Conference on Software Reuse—Summary," *ACM Software Engineering Notes,* vol. 20, no. 2, April 1995, pp. 21–22.

[WHI95] Whittle, B., "Models and Languages for Component Description and Reuse," *ACM Software Engineering Notes,* vol. 20, no. 2, April 1995, pp. 76–89.

[YOU98] Yourdon, E. (ed.), "Distributed Objects," *Cutter IT Journal,* vol. 11, no. 12, December 1998.

Problems and Points to Ponder

30.1. One of the key roadblocks to reuse is getting software developers to consider reusing existing components, rather than reinventing new ones (after all, building things is fun!). Suggest three or four different ways that a software organization can provide incentives for software engineers to reuse. What technologies should be in place to support the reuse effort?

30.2. Although software components are the most obvious reusable "artifact," many other work products produced as part of software engineering can be reused. Consider project plans and cost estimates. How can these be reused, and what is the benefit of doing so?

30.3. Do a bit of research on domain engineering and flesh out the process model outlined in Figure 30.1. Identify the tasks that are required for domain analysis and software architecture development.

30.4. How are characterization functions for application domains and component classification schemes the same? How are they different?

30.5. Develop a set of domain characteristics for information systems that are relevant to a university's student data processing.

30.6. Develop a set of domain characteristics that are relevant for word-processing/desktop-publishing software.

30.7. Develop a simple structural model for an application domain assigned by your instructor or one with which you are familiar.

30.8. What is a structure point?

30.9. Acquire information on the most recent CORBA or COM or JavaBeans standard and prepare a three- to five-page paper that discusses its major highlights. Get information on an object request broker tool and illustrate how the tool achieves the standard.

30.10. Develop an enumerated classification for an application domain assigned by your instructor or one with which you are familiar.

30.11. Develop a faceted classification scheme for an application domain assigned by your instructor or one with which you are familiar.

30.12. Research the literature to acquire recent quality and productivity data that support the use of CBSE. Present the data to your class.

Further Readings and Information Sources

Many books on component-based development and component reuse have been published in recent years. Heineman and Councill [HEI01], Brown (*Large Scale Component-Based Development,* Prentice-Hall, 2000), Allen (*Realizing e-Business with Components,* Addison-Wesley, 2000), Herzum and Sims (*Business Component Factory,* Wiley, 1999), and Allen, Frost, and Yourdon (*Component-Based Development for Enterprise Systems: Applying the Select Perspective,* Cambridge University Press, 1998) cover all important aspects of the CBSE process. Apperly and his colleagues (*Service- and Component-Based Development,* Addison-Wesley, 2003), Atkinson [ATK01], and Cheesman and Daniels (*UML Components,* Addison-Wesley, 2000) discuss CBSE with a UML emphasis.

Leach (*Software Reuse: Methods, Models, and Costs,* McGraw-Hill, 1997) provides a detailed analysis of cost issues associated with CBSE and reuse. Poulin (*Measuring Software Reuse: Principles, Practices, and Economic Models,* Addison-Wesley, 1996) suggests a number of quantitative methods for assessing the benefits of software reuse.

Dozens of books describing the industry's component-based standards have been published in recent years. These address the inner workings of the standards themselves but also consider many important CBSE topics. A sampling for the three standards discussed in this chapter follows:

CORBA

Bolton, F., *Pure CORBA,* Sams Publishing, 2001.

Doss, G. M., *CORBA Networking With Java,* Wordware Publishing, 1999.

Hoque, R., *CORBA for Real Programmers,* Academic Press/Morgan Kaufmann, 1999.

Siegel, J., *CORBA Fundamentals and Programming,* Wiley, 1999.

Slama, D., J. Garbis, and P. Russell, *Enterprise CORBA,* Prentice-Hall, 1999.

COM

Box, D., K. Brown, T. Ewald, and C. Sells, *Effective COM: 50 Ways to Improve Your COM- and MTS-Based Applications,* Addison-Wesley, 1999.

Gordon, A., *The COM and COM+ Programming Primer,* Prentice-Hall, 2000.

Kirtland, M., *Designing Component-Based Applications,* Microsoft Press, 1999.

Tapadiya, P., *COM+ Programming,* Prentice-Hall, 2000.

Many organizations apply a combination of component standards. Books by Geraghty and his colleagues (*COM-CORBA Interoperability,* Prentice-Hall, 1999), Pritchard (*COM and CORBA Side by Side: Architectures, Strategies, and Implementations,* Addison-Wesley, 1999), and Rosen and his colleagues (*Integrating CORBA and COM Applications,* Wiley, 1999) consider the issues associated with the use of both CORBA and COM as the basis for component-based development.

JavaBeans

Asbury, S., and S. R. Weiner, *Developing Java Enterprise Applications,* Wiley, 1999.

Anderson, G., and P. Anderson, *Enterprise Javabeans Component Architecture,* Prentice-Hall, 2002.

Monson-Haefel, R., *Enterprise Javabeans,* third edition, O'Reilly & Associates, 2001.

Roman, E., et al., *Mastering Enterprise Javabeans,* 2nd ed., Wiley, 2001.

A wide variety of information sources on component-based software engineering is available on the Internet. An up-to-date list of World Wide Web references can be found at the SEPA Web site:
http://www.mhhe.com/pressman.

CHAPTER

REENGINEERING 31

KEY CONCEPTS

In a seminal article written for the *Harvard Business Review,* Michael Hammer [HAM90] laid the foundation for a revolution in management thinking about business processes and computing:

> It is time to stop paving the cow paths. Instead of embedding outdated processes in silicon and software, we should obliterate them and start over. We should "reengineer" our businesses: use the power of modern information technology to radically redesign our business processes in order to achieve dramatic improvements in their performance.
>
> Every company operates according to a great many unarticulated rules . . . Reengineering strives to break away from the old rules about how we organize and conduct our business.

Like all revolutions, Hammer's call to arms resulted in both positive and negative changes. During the 1990s, some companies made a legitimate effort to reengineer, and the results led to improved competitiveness. Others relied solely on downsizing and outsourcing (instead of reengineering) to improve their bottom line. Organizations with little potential for future growth often resulted [DEM95].

During this first decade of the twenty-first century, the hype associated with reengineering has waned, but the process itself continues in companies large and small. The nexus between business reengineering and software engineering lies in a system view.

QUICK LOOK

What is it? Consider any technology product that has served you well. You use it regularly, but it's getting old. It breaks too often, takes longer to repair than you'd like, and no longer represents the newest technology. What to do? If the product is hardware, you'll likely throw it away and buy a newer model. But if it's custom-built software, that option may not be available. You'll need to rebuild it. You'll create a product with added functionality, better performance and reliability, and improved maintainability. That's what we call reengineering.

Who does it? At an organizational level, reengineering is performed by business specialists (often consulting companies). At the software level, reengineering is performed by software engineers.

Why is it important? We live in a rapidly changing world. The demands on business functions and the information technology that supports them are changing at a pace that puts enormous competitive pressure on every commercial organization. Both the business and the software that supports (or is) the business must be reengineered to keep pace.

What are the steps? Business process reengineering (BPR) defines business goals, identifies and evaluates existing business processes, and creates revised business processes that better meet current goals. The software reengineering process encompasses inventory analysis, document restructuring, reverse engineering, program and data restructuring, and forward engineering. The intent of these activities is to create versions of existing programs that exhibit higher quality and better maintainability.

What is the work product? A variety of reengineering work products (e.g., analysis models, design models, test procedures) are produced. The final output is the reengineered business process and/or the reengineered software that supports it.

How do I ensure that I've done it right? Use the same SQA practices that are applied in every software engineering process—formal technical reviews assess the analysis and design models, specialized reviews consider business applicability and compatibility, and testing is applied to uncover errors in content, functionality, and interoperability.

BPR often results in new software functionality, whereas software reengineering works to replace existing software functionality with better, more maintainable software.

Software is often the realization of the business rules that Hammer discusses. As these rules change, software must also change. Today, major companies have tens of thousands of computer programs that support old business rules. As managers work to modify the rules to achieve greater effectiveness and competitiveness, software must keep pace. In some cases, this means the creation of major new computer-based systems.[1] But in many others, it means the modification or rebuilding of existing applications.

In this chapter, we examine reengineering in a top-down manner, beginning with a brief overview of business process reengineering and proceeding to a more detailed discussion of the technical activities that occur when software is reengineered.

31.1 Business Process Reengineering

Business process reengineering (BPR) extends far beyond the scope of information technologies and software engineering. Among the many definitions (most somewhat abstract) that have been suggested for BPR is one published in Fortune magazine [STE93]: "the search for, and the implementation of, radical change in business process to achieve breakthrough results." But how is the search conducted, and how is the implementation achieved? More important, how can we ensure that the "radical change" suggested will in fact lead to "breakthrough results" instead of organizational chaos?

> "To face tomorrow with the thought of using the methods of yesterday is to envision life at a standstill."
> **James Bell**

1 The explosion of Web-based applications and systems discussed in Part 3 of this book is indicative of this trend.

31.1.1 Business Processes

A business process is "a set of logically related tasks performed to achieve a defined business outcome" [DAV90]. Within the business process, people, equipment, material resources, and business procedures are combined to produce a specified result. Examples of business processes include designing a new product, purchasing services and supplies, hiring a new employee, and paying suppliers. Each demands a set of tasks, and each draws on diverse resources within the business.

Every business process has a defined customer—a person or group that receives the outcome (e.g., an idea, a report, a design, a product). In addition, business processes cross organizational boundaries. They require that different organizational groups participate in the "logically related tasks" that define the process.

As a software engineer, your work occurs at the bottom of this hierarchy. Be sure, however, that someone has given serious thought to the levels above. If this hasn't been done, your work is at risk.

In Chapter 6, we noted that every system is actually a hierarchy of subsystems. A business is no exception. Each business system (also called a *business function*) is composed of one or more business processes, and each business process is defined by a set of subprocesses.

BPR can be applied at any level of the hierarchy, but as the scope of BPR broadens (i.e., as we move upward in the hierarchy), the risks associated with it grow dramatically. For this reason, most BPR efforts focus on individual processes or subprocesses.

> "As soon as we are shown something old in a new thing, we are pacified."
>
> **F. W. Nietzsche**

31.1.2 A BPR Model

WebRef
Extensive information on BPR can be found at **www.brint.com/BPR.htm.**

Like most engineering activities, business process reengineering is iterative. Business goals and the processes that achieve them must be adapted to a changing business environment. For this reason, there is no start and end to BPR—it is an evolutionary process. A model for business process reengineering is depicted in Figure 31.1. The model defines six activities:

Business definition. Business goals are identified within the context of four key drivers: cost reduction, time reduction, quality improvement, and personnel development and empowerment. Goals may be defined at the business level or for a specific component of the business.

Process identification. Processes that are critical to achieving the goals defined in the business definition are identified. They may then be ranked by importance, by need for change, or in any other way that is appropriate for the reengineering activity.

Process evaluation. The existing process is thoroughly analyzed and measured. Process tasks are identified; the costs and time consumed by process tasks are noted; and quality/performance problems are isolated.

FIGURE 31.1

A BPR model

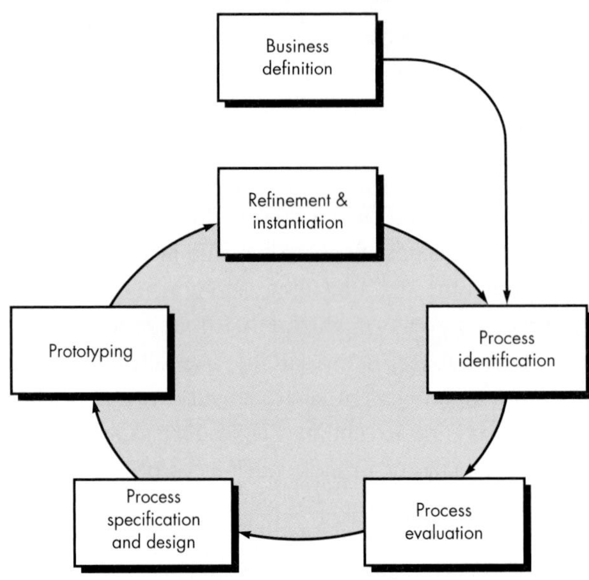

Process specification and design. Based on information obtained during the first three BPR activities, use-cases (Chapter 7) are prepared for each process that is to be redesigned. Within the context of BPR, use-cases identify a scenario that delivers some outcome to a customer. With the use-case as the specification of the process, a new set of tasks are designed for the process.

Prototyping. A redesigned business process must be prototyped before it is fully integrated into the business. This activity "tests" the process so that refinements can be made.

Refinement and instantiation. Based on feedback from the prototype, the business process is refined and then instantiated within a business system.

These BPR activities are sometimes used in conjunction with workflow analysis tools. The intent of these tools is to build a model of existing workflow in an effort to better analyze existing processes. In addition, the modeling techniques commonly associated with business process engineering activities (Chapter 6) can be used to implement the first four activities described in the process model.

SOFTWARE TOOLS

Business Process Reengineering (BPR)

Objective: The objective of BPR tools is to support the analysis and assessment of existing business processes and the specification and design of new ones.

Mechanics: Tools mechanics vary. In general, BPR tools allow a business analyst to model existing business processes in an effort to assess workflow inefficiencies or functional problems. Once existing problems are identified, tools allow the analyst to prototype and/or simulate revised business processes.

Representative Tools[2]

Extend, developed by ImagineThat, Inc. (www.imaginethatinc.com), is a simulation tool for modeling existing processes and exploring new ones. Extend provides comprehensive "what if" capability that enables a business analyst to explore different process scenarios.

e-Work, developed by Metastorm (www.metastorm.com), provides business process management support for both manual and automated processes.

IceTools, developed by Blue Ice (www.blueice.com), is a collection of BPR templates for Microsoft Office and Microsoft Project.

SpeeDev, developed by NimbleStar Group (www.numblestar.com), is one of many tools that enable an organization to model process work flow (in this case, IT work flow).

Workflow tools, developed by MetaSoftware (www.metasoftware.com), incorporates a suite of tools for workflow modeling, simulation, and scheduling.

A useful list of BPR tool links can be found at http://www.donald-firesmith.com/Components/Producers/Tools/BusinessProcessReengineeringTools.html.

31.2 Software Reengineering

The scenario is all too common: An application has served the business needs of a company for 10 or 15 years. During that time it has been corrected, adapted, and enhanced many times. People approached this work with the best intentions, but good software engineering practices were always shunted to the side (due to the press of other matters). Now the application is unstable. It still works, but every time a change is attempted, unexpected and serious side effects occur. Yet the application must continue to evolve. What to do?

Unmaintainable software is not a new problem. In fact, the broadening emphasis on software reengineering has been spawned by a software maintenance problems that have been growing in size for more than 40 years.

31.2.1 Software Maintenance

Over three decades ago, software maintenance was characterized [CAN72] as an "iceberg." We hope that what is immediately visible is all there is to it, but we know that an enormous mass of potential problems and cost lies under the surface. In the early 1970s, the maintenance iceberg was big enough to sink an aircraft carrier. Today, it could easily sink the entire navy!

The maintenance of existing software can account for over 60 percent of all effort expended by a development organization, and the percentage continues to rise as more software is produced [HAN93]. Uninitiated readers may ask why so much

2 Tools noted here do not represent an endorsement, but rather a sampling of tools in this category. In most cases, tool names are trademarked by their respective developers.

maintenance is required and why so much effort is expended. Osborne and Chikofsky [OSB90] provide a partial answer:

> Much of the software we depend on today is on average 10 to 15 years old. Even when these programs were created using the best design and coding techniques known at the time [and most were not], they were created when program size and storage space were principle concerns. They were then migrated to new platforms, adjusted for changes in machine and operating system technology and enhanced to meet new user needs—all without enough regard to overall architecture. The result is the poorly designed structures, poor coding, poor logic, and poor documentation of the software systems we are now called on to keep running. . . .

Another reason for the software maintenance problem is the mobility of software people. It is likely that the software team (or person) that did the original work is no longer around. Worse, subsequent generations of software people have modified the system and moved on. Today, there may be no one left who has any direct knowledge of the legacy system.

As we noted in Chapter 27, the ubiquitous nature of change underlies all software work. Change is inevitable when computer-based systems are built; therefore, we must develop mechanisms for evaluating, controlling, and making modifications.

> **"Program maintainability and program understandability are parallel concepts: the more difficult a program is to understand, the more difficult it is to maintain."**
>
> **Gerald Berns**

KEY POINT Software maintenance encompasses four activities: error correction, adaptation, enhancement, and reengineering.

Upon reading the preceding paragraphs, a reader may protest: "But I don't spend 60 percent of my time fixing mistakes in the programs I develop." Software maintenance is, of course, far more than "fixing mistakes." We may define maintenance by describing four activities [SWA76] that are undertaken after a program is released for use. *Software maintenance* can be defined by identifying four different activities: corrective maintenance, adaptive maintenance, perfective maintenance or enhancement, and preventive maintenance or reengineering. Only about 20 percent of all maintenance work is spent "fixing mistakes." The remaining 80 percent is spent adapting existing systems to changes in their external environment, making enhancements requested by users, and reengineering an application for future use. When maintenance is considered to encompass all of these activities, it is relatively easy to see why it absorbs so much effort.

WebRef An excellent source of information on software reengineering can be found at **www.reengineering.net.**

31.2.2 A Software Reengineering Process Model

Reengineering takes time, costs significant amounts of money, and absorbs resources that might be otherwise occupied on immediate concerns. For all of these reasons, reengineering is not accomplished in a few months or even a few years. Reengineering of information systems is an activity that will absorb information technology resources for many years. That's why every organization needs a pragmatic strategy for software reengineering.

A workable strategy is encompassed in a reengineering process model. We'll discuss the model later in this section, but first, some basic principles.

Reengineering is a rebuilding activity, and we can better understand the reengineering of information systems if we consider an analogous activity: the rebuilding of a house. Consider the following situation.

You have purchased a house in another state. You've never actually seen the property, but you acquired it at an amazingly low price, with the warning that it might have to be completely rebuilt. How would you proceed?

- Before you can start rebuilding, it would seem reasonable to inspect the house. To determine whether it is in need of rebuilding, you (or a professional inspector) would create a list of criteria so that your inspection would be systematic.
- Before you tear down and rebuild the entire house, you would be sure that the structure is weak. If the house is structurally sound, it may be possible to "remodel" without rebuilding (at much lower cost and in much less time).
- Before you start rebuilding, you would be sure to understand how the original was built. Take a peek behind the walls. Understand the wiring, the plumbing, and the structural internals. Even if you trash them all, the insight you'd gain would serve you well when you start construction.
- If you begin to rebuild, you would use only the most modern, long-lasting materials. This may cost a bit more now, but it would help you to avoid expensive and time-consuming maintenance later.
- If you decide to rebuild, you would be disciplined about it. Use practices that would result in high quality—today and in the future.

Although these principles focus on the rebuilding of a house, they apply equally well to the reengineering of computer-based systems and applications.

To implement these principles, we apply a software reengineering process model that defines six activities, shown in Figure 31.2. In some cases, these activities occur in a linear sequence, but this is not always the case. For example, it may be that reverse engineering (understanding the internal workings of a program) may have to occur before document restructuring can commence.

The reengineering paradigm shown in the figure is a cyclical model. This means that each of the activities presented as a part of the paradigm may be revisited. For any particular cycle, the process can terminate after any one of these activities.

Inventory analysis. Every software organization should have an inventory of all applications. The inventory can be nothing more than a spreadsheet model containing information that provides a detailed description (e.g., size, age, business

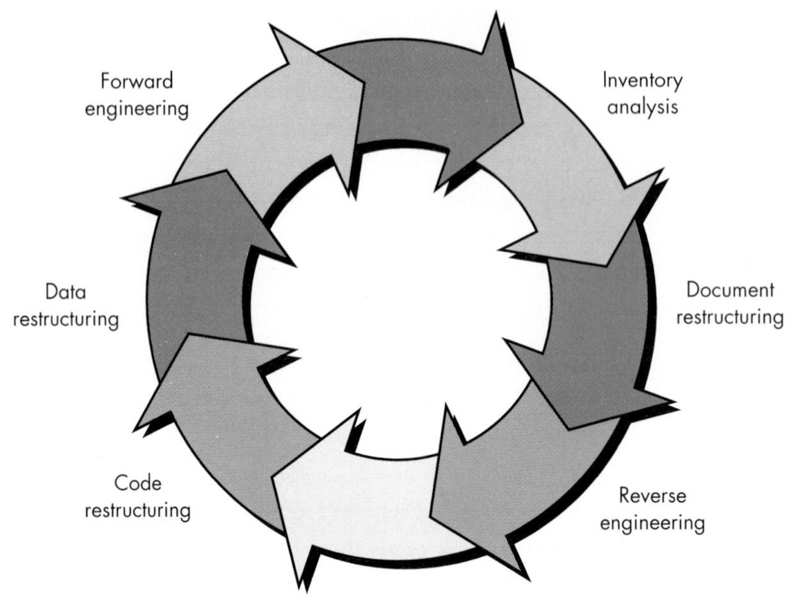

FIGURE 31.2 A software reengineering process model

If time and resources are in short supply, you might consider applying the Pareto principle to the software that is to be engineered. Apply the reengineering process to the 20 percent of the software that accounts for 80 percent of the problems.

Create only as much documentation as you need to understand the software, not one page more.

criticality) of every active application. By sorting this information according to business criticality, longevity, current maintainability, and other locally important criteria, candidates for reengineering appear. Resources can then be allocated to candidate applications for reengineering work.

It is important to note that the inventory should be revisited on a regular cycle. The status of applications (e.g., business criticality) can change as a function of time, and as a result, priorities for reengineering will shift.

Document restructuring. Weak documentation is the trademark of many legacy systems. But what do we do about it? What are our options?

1. *Creating documentation is far too time consuming.* If the system works, we'll live with what we have. In some cases, this is the correct approach. It is not possible to recreate documentation for hundreds of computer programs. If a program is relatively static, is coming to the end of its useful life, and is unlikely to undergo significant change, let it be!
2. *Documentation must be updated, but we have limited resources.* We'll use a "document when touched" approach. It may not be necessary to fully redocument an application. Rather, those portions of the system that are currently undergoing change are fully documented. Over time, a collection of useful and relevant documentation will evolve.
3. *The system is business critical and must be fully redocumented.* Even in this case, an intelligent approach is to pare documentation to an essential minimum.

Each of these options is viable. A software organization must choose the one that is most appropriate for each case.

Reverse engineering. The term *reverse engineering* has its origins in the hardware world. A company disassembles a competitive hardware product in an effort to understand its competitor's design and manufacturing "secrets." These secrets could be easily understood if the competitor's design and manufacturing specifications were obtained. But these documents are proprietary and unavailable to the company doing the reverse engineering. In essence, successful reverse engineering derives one or more design and manufacturing specifications for a product by examining actual specimens of the product.

Reverse engineering for software is quite similar. In most cases, however, the program to be reverse engineered is not a competitor's. Rather, it is the company's own work (often done many years earlier). The "secrets" to be understood are obscure because no specification was ever developed. Therefore, reverse engineering for software is the process of analyzing a program in an effort to create a representation of the program at a higher level of abstraction than source code. Reverse engineering is a process of *design recovery*. Reverse engineering tools extract data, architectural, and procedural design information from an existing program.

WebRef
An array of resources for the reengineering community can be obtained at **www.comp.lancs.ac.uk/projects/RenaissanceWeb/.**

Code restructuring. The most common type of reengineering (actually, the use of the term reengineering is questionable in this case) is *code restructuring*.[3] Some legacy systems have a relatively solid program architecture, but individual modules were coded in a way that makes them difficult to understand, test, and maintain. In such cases, the code within the suspect modules can be restructured.

To accomplish this activity, the source code is analyzed using a restructuring tool. Violations of structured programming constructs are noted, and code is then restructured (this can be done automatically). The resultant restructured code is reviewed and tested to ensure that no anomalies have been introduced. Internal code documentation is updated.

Data restructuring. A program with weak data architecture will be difficult to adapt and enhance. In fact, for many applications, data architecture has more to do with the long-term viability of a program that the source code itself.

Unlike code restructuring, which occurs at a relatively low level of abstraction, data structuring is a full-scale reengineering activity. In most cases, data restructuring begins with a reverse engineering activity. Current data architecture is dissected, and necessary data models are defined (Chapter 9). Data objects and attributes are identified, and existing data structures are reviewed for quality.

3 Code restructuring has some of the elements of "refactoring," a redesign concept introduced in Chapter 4 and discussed elsewhere in this book.

When data structure is weak (e.g., flat files are currently implemented, when a relational approach would greatly simplify processing), the data are reengineered.

Because data architecture has a strong influence on program architecture and the algorithms that populate it, changes to the data will invariably result in either architectural or code-level changes.

Forward engineering. In an ideal world, applications would be rebuilt using an automated "reengineering engine." The old program would be fed into the engine, analyzed, restructured, and then regenerated in a form that exhibited the best aspects of software quality. In the short term, it is unlikely that such an "engine" will appear, but vendors have introduced tools that provide a limited subset of these capabilities that addresses specific application domains (e.g., applications that are implemented using a specific database system). More important, these reengineering tools are becoming increasingly more sophisticated.

Forward engineering, also called *renovation* or *reclamation* [CHI90], not only recovers design information from existing software, but uses this information to alter or reconstitute the existing system in an effort to improve its overall quality. In most cases, reengineered software reimplements the function of the existing system and also adds new functions and/or improves overall performance.

31.3 Reverse Engineering

Reverse engineering conjures an image of the "magic slot." We feed a haphazardly designed, undocumented source listing into the slot and out the other end comes a complete design description (and full documentation) for the computer program. Unfortunately, the magic slot doesn't exist. Reverse engineering can extract design information from source code, but the abstraction level, the completeness of the documentation, the degree to which tools and a human analyst work together, and the directionality of the process are highly variable.

The *abstraction level* of a reverse engineering process and the tools used to effect it refers to the sophistication of the design information that can be extracted from source code. Ideally, the abstraction level should be as high as possible. That is, the reverse engineering process should be capable of deriving procedural design representations (a low-level abstraction), program and data structure information (a somewhat higher level of abstraction), object models, data and/or control flow models (a relatively high level of abstraction), and UML class, state and deployment diagrams (a high level of abstraction). As the abstraction level increases, the software engineer is provided with information that will allow easier understanding of the program.

The *completeness* of a reverse engineering process refers to the level of detail that is provided at an abstraction level. In most cases, the completeness decreases as the abstraction level increases. For example, given a source code listing, it is relatively easy to develop a complete procedural design representation. Simple design repre-

FIGURE 31.3

The reverse engineering process

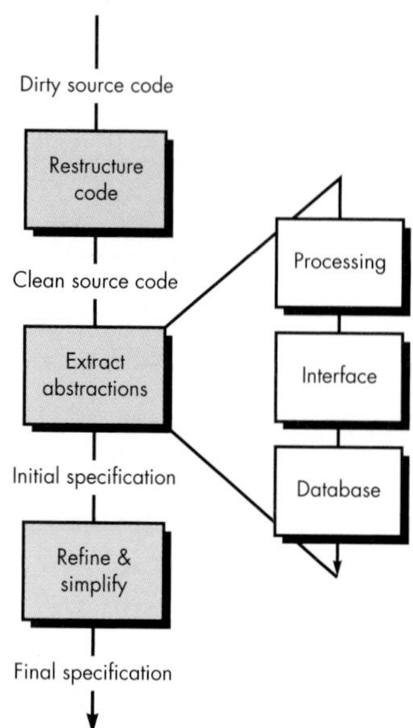

sentations may also be derived, but it is far more difficult to develop a complete set of UML diagrams or models.

KEY POINT

Three reverse engineering issues must be addressed: abstraction level, completeness, and directionality.

Completeness improves in direct proportion to the amount of analysis performed by the person doing reverse engineering. *Interactivity* refers to the degree to which the human is "integrated" with automated tools to create an effective reverse engineering process. In most cases, as the abstraction level increases, interactivity must increase or completeness will suffer.

If the *directionality* of the reverse engineering process is one-way, all information extracted from the source code is provided to the software engineer who can then use it during any maintenance activity. If directionality is two-way, the information is fed to a reengineering tool that attempts to restructure or regenerate the old program.

The reverse engineering process is represented in Figure 31.3. Before reverse engineering activities can commence, unstructured ("dirty") source code is restructured (Section 31.4.1) so that it contains only the structured programming constructs.[4] This makes the source code easier to read and provides the basis for all the subsequent reverse engineering activities.

The core of reverse engineering is an activity called *extract abstractions*. The engineer must evaluate the old program and from the (often undocumented) source code, develop a meaningful specification of the processing that is performed, the user interface that is applied, and the program data structures or database that is used.

4 Code can be restructured using a *restructuring engine*—a tool that restructures source code.

WebRef
Useful resources for "design recovery and program understanding" can be found at **wwwsel.iit.nrc.ca/projects/dr/dr.html.**

31.3.1 Reverse Engineering to Understand Data

Reverse engineering of data occurs at different levels of abstraction and is often the first reengineering task. At the program level, internal program data structures must often be reverse engineered as part of an overall reengineering effort. At the system level, global data structures (e.g., files, databases) are often reengineered to accommodate new database management paradigms (e.g., the move from flat file to relational or object-oriented database systems). Reverse engineering of the current global data structures sets the stage for the introduction of a new system-wide database.

Seemingly insignificant compromises in data structures can lead to potentially catastrophic problems in future years. Consider the Y2K problem as an example.

Internal data structures. Reverse engineering techniques for internal program data focus on the definition of classes of objects. This is accomplished by examining the program code with the intent of grouping related program variables. In many cases, the data organization within the code identifies abstract data types. For example, record structures, files, lists, and other data structures often provide an initial indicator of classes.

Database structure. Regardless of its logical organization and physical structure, a database allows the definition of data objects and supports some method for establishing relationships among the objects. Therefore, reengineering one database schema into another requires an understanding of existing objects and their relationships.

The following steps [PRE94] may be used to define the existing data model as a precursor to reengineering a new database model: (1) build an initial object model, (2) determine candidate keys, (3) refine the tentative classes, (4) define generalizations, and (5) discover associations (use techniques that are analogous to the CRC approach). Once information defined in the preceding steps is known, a series of transformations [PRE94] can be applied to map the old database structure into a new database structure.

31.3.2 Reverse Engineering to Understand Processing

Reverse engineering to understand processing begins with an attempt to understand and then extract procedural abstractions represented by the source code. To understand procedural abstractions, the code is analyzed at varying levels of abstraction: system, program, component, pattern, and statement.

The overall functionality of the entire application system must be understood before more detailed reverse engineering work occurs. This establishes a context for further analysis and provides insight into interoperability issues among applications within the system. Each of the programs that make up the application system represents a functional abstraction at a high level of detail. A block diagram, representing the interaction between these functional abstractions, is created. Each component performs some subfunction and represents a defined procedural abstraction. A processing narrative for each component is developed. In some situations, system,

program, and component specifications already exist. When this is the case, the specifications are reviewed for conformance to existing code.[5]

> "There exists a passion for comprehension, just as there exists a passion for music. That passion is rather common in children, but gets lost in most people later on."
>
> **Albert Einstein**

Things become more complex when the code inside a component is considered. The engineer looks for sections of code that represent generic procedural patterns. In almost every component, a section of code prepares data for processing (within the module), a different section of code does the processing, and another section of code prepares the results of processing for export from the component. Within each of these sections, we can encounter smaller patterns; for example, data validation and bounds checking often occur within the section of code that prepares data for processing.

For large systems, reverse engineering is generally accomplished using a semi-automated approach. Automated tools are used to help the software engineer understand the semantics of existing code. The output of this process is then passed to restructuring and forward engineering tools to complete the reengineering process.

31.3.3 Reverse Engineering User Interfaces

Sophisticated GUIs are now de rigueur for computer-based products and systems of every type. Therefore, the redevelopment of user interfaces has become one of the most common types of reengineering activity. But before a user interface can be rebuilt, reverse engineering should occur.

To fully understand an existing user interface, the structure and behavior of the interface must be specified. Merlo and his colleagues [MER93] suggest three basic questions that must be answered as reverse engineering of the UI commences:

? How do I understand the workings of an existing user interface?

- What are the basic actions (e.g., keystrokes and mouse clicks) that the interface must process?
- What is a compact description of the behavioral response of the system to these actions?
- What is meant by a "replacement," or more precisely, what concept of equivalence of interfaces is relevant here?

Behavioral modeling notation (Chapter 8) can provide a means for developing answers to the first two questions. Much of the information necessary to create a behavioral model can be obtained by observing the external manifestation of the existing interface. But additional information necessary to create the behavioral model must be extracted from the code.

---

5 Often, specifications written early in the life history of a program are never updated. As changes are made, the code no longer conforms to the specification.

It is important to note that a replacement GUI may not mirror the old interface exactly (in fact, it may be radically different). It is often worthwhile to develop new interaction metaphors. For example, an old GUI requests that a user provide a scale factor (ranging from 1 to 10) to shrink or magnify a graphical image. A reengineered GUI might use a slide-bar and mouse to accomplish the same function.

SOFTWARE TOOLS

Reverse Engineering

Objective: To help software engineers understand the internal design structure of complex programs.

Mechanics: In most cases, reverse engineering tools accept source code as input and produce a variety of structural, procedural, data, and behavioral design representations.

Representative Tools[6]

Imagix 4D, developed by Imagix (www.imagix.com), "helps software developers understand complex or legacy C and C++ software" by reverse engineering and documenting source code.

Understand, developed by Scientific Toolworks, Inc. (www.scitools.com), parses Ada, Fortran, C, C++, and Java "to reverse engineer, automatically document, calculate code metrics, and help you understand, navigate and maintain source code."

A comprehensive listing of reverse engineering tools can be found at http://scgwiki.iam.unibe.ch:8080/SCG/370.

31.4 Restructuring

Software restructuring modifies source code and/or data in an effort to make it amenable to future changes. In general, restructuring does not modify the overall program architecture. It tends to focus on the design details of individual modules and on local data structures defined within modules. If the restructuring effort extends beyond module boundaries and encompasses the software architecture, restructuring becomes forward engineering (Section 31.5).

Restructuring occurs when the basic architecture of an application is solid, even though technical internals need work. It is initiated when major parts of the software are serviceable and only a subset of all components and data need extensive modification.[7]

31.4.1 Code Restructuring

Code restructuring is performed to yield a design that produces the same function as the original program but with higher quality. In general, code restructuring techniques (e.g., Warnier's logical simplification techniques [WAR74]) model program logic using Boolean algebra and then apply a series of transformation rules that yield restructured

6 Tools noted here do not represent an endorsement, but rather a sampling of tools in this category. In most cases, tool names are trademarked by their respective developers.

7 It is sometimes difficult to make a distinction between extensive restructuring and redevelopment. Both are reengineering.

Although code restructuring can alleviate immediate problems associated with debugging or small changes, it is not reengineering. Real benefit is achieved only when data and architecture are restructured.

logic. The objective is to take "spaghetti-bowl" code and derive a procedural design that conforms to the structured programming philosophy (Chapter 11).

Other restructuring techniques have also been proposed for use with reengineering tools. A resource exchange diagram maps each program module and the resources (data types, procedures, and variables) that are exchanged between it and other modules. By creating representations of resource flow, the program architecture can be restructured to achieve minimum coupling among modules.

31.4.2 Data Restructuring

Before data restructuring can begin, a reverse engineering activity called *analysis of source code* must be conducted. All programming language statements that contain data definitions, file descriptions, I/O, and interface descriptions are evaluated. The intent is to extract data items and objects, to get information on data flow, and to understand the existing data structures that have been implemented. This activity is sometimes called *data analysis* [RIC89].

Once data analysis has been completed, *data redesign* commences. In its simplest form, a *data record standardization* step clarifies data definitions to achieve consistency among data item names or physical record formats within an existing data structure or file format. Another form of redesign, called *data name rationalization,* ensures that all data naming conventions conform to local standards and that aliases are eliminated as data flow through the system.

When restructuring moves beyond standardization and rationalization, physical modifications to existing data structures are made to make the data design more effective. This may mean a translation from one file format to another, or in some cases, translation from one type of database to another.

SOFTWARE TOOLS

Software Restructuring

Objective: The objective of restructuring tools is to transform older unstructured computer software into modern programming languages and design structures.

Mechanics: In general, source code is input and transformed into a better structured program. In some cases, the transformation occurs within the same programming language. In other cases, an older programming language is transformed into a more modern language.

Representative Tools[8]

DMS Software Reengineering Toolkit, developed by Semantic Design (www.semdesigns.com), provides a variety of restructuring capabilities for COBOL, C/C++, Java, FORTRAN 90, and VHDL.

FORESYS, developed by Simulog (www.simulog.fr), analyzes and transforms programs written in FORTRAN.

Function Encapsulation Tool, developed at Wayne State University (www.cs.wayne.edu/~vip/RefactoringTools/), refactors older C programs into C++.

plusFORT, developed by Polyhedron (www.polyhedron.com), is a suite of FORTRAN tools that contains capabilities for restructuring poorly designed FORTRAN programs into the modern FORTRAN or C standard.

8 Tools noted here do not represent an endorsement, but rather a sampling of tools in this category. In most cases, tool names are trademarked by their respective developers.

31.5 Forward Engineering

A program with control flow that is the graphic equivalent of a bowl of spaghetti, with "modules" that are 2000 statements long, with few meaningful comment lines in 290,000 source statements and no other documentation must be modified to accommodate changing user requirements. We have the following options:

? What options exist when we're faced with a poorly designed and implemented program?

1. We can struggle through modification after modification, fighting the implicit design and source code to implement the necessary changes.
2. We can attempt to understand the broader inner workings of the program in an effort to make modifications more effectively.
3. We can redesign, recode, and test those portions of the software that require modification, applying a software engineering approach to all revised segments.
4. We can completely redesign, recode, and test the program, using reengineering tools to assist us in understanding the current design.

There is no single "correct" option. Circumstances may dictate the first option even if the others are more desirable.

Rather than waiting until a maintenance request is received, the development or support organization uses the results of inventory analysis to select a program that (1) will remain in use for a preselected number of years, (2) is currently being used successfully, and (3) is likely to undergo major modification or enhancement in the near future. Then, option 2, 3, or 4 is applied.

This *preventative maintenance* approach was pioneered by Miller [MIL81] under the title *structured retrofit.* This concept is defined as "the application of today's methodologies to yesterday's systems to support tomorrow's requirements."

At first glance, the suggestion that we redevelop a large program when a working version already exists may seem quite extravagant. Before passing judgment, consider the following points:

Reengineering is a lot like getting your teeth cleaned. You can think of a thousand reasons to delay it, and you'll get away with procrastinating for quite a while. But eventually, your delaying tactics will come back to cause pain.

1. The cost to maintain one line of source code may be 20 to 40 times the cost of initial development of that line.
2. Redesign of the software architecture (program and/or data structure), using modern design concepts, can greatly facilitate future maintenance.
3. Because a prototype of the software already exists, development productivity should be much higher than average.
4. The user now has experience with the software. Therefore, new requirements and the direction of change can be ascertained with greater ease.
5. Automated tools for reengineering will facilitate some parts of the job.
6. A complete software configuration (documents, programs, and data) will exist upon completion of preventive maintenance.

When a software development organization sells software as a product, preventive maintenance is seen in "new releases" of a program. A large in-house software developer (e.g., a business systems software development group for a large consumer products company) may have 500–2000 production programs within its domain of responsibility. These programs can be ranked by importance and then reviewed as candidates for preventive maintenance.

The forward engineering process applies software engineering principles, concepts, and methods to recreate an existing application. In most cases, forward engineering does not simply create a modern equivalent of an older program. Rather, new user and technology requirements are integrated into the reengineering effort. The redeveloped program extends the capabilities of the older application.

31.5.1 Forward Engineering for Client/Server Architectures

Over the past few decades, many mainframe applications have been reengineered to accommodate client/server architectures (including WebApps). In essence, centralized computing resources (including software) are distributed among many client platforms. Although a variety of different distributed environments can be designed, the typical mainframe application that is reengineered into a client/server architecture has the following features:

- Application functionality migrates to each client computer.
- New GUI interfaces are implemented at the client sites.
- Database functions are allocated to the server.
- Specialized functionality (e.g., compute-intensive analysis) may remain at the server site.
- New communications, security, archiving, and control requirements must be established at both the client and server sites.

In some cases, migration to a client/server architecture should be approached not as reengineering, but as a new development effort. Reengineering enters the picture only when specific functionality from the old system is to be integrated into the new architecture.

It is important to note that the migration from mainframe to client/server computing requires both business and software reengineering. In addition, an "enterprise network infrastructure" [JAY94] should be established.

Reengineering for client/server applications begins with a thorough analysis of the business environment that encompasses the existing mainframe. Three layers of abstraction can be identified. The *database layer* sits at the foundation of a client/server architecture and manages transactions and queries from client applications. Yet these transactions and queries must be controlled within the context of a set of business rules (defined by an existing or reengineered business process). Client applications provide targeted functionality to the user community.

The functions of the existing database management system and the data architecture of the existing database must be reverse engineered as a precursor to the redesign of the database layer. In some cases a new data model (Chapter 8) is created. In every case, the client/server database is reengineered to ensure that transactions are executed in a consistent manner, that all updates are performed only by authorized users, that core business rules are enforced (e.g., before a vendor record is deleted, the server ensures that no related accounts payable, contracts, or communications exist for that vendor), that queries can be accommodated efficiently, and that full archiving capability has been established.

The *business rules layer* represents software that is resident at both the client and the server. This software performs control and coordination tasks to ensure that transactions and queries between the client application and the database conform to the established business process.

The *client applications layer* implements business functions that are required by specific groups of end-users. In many instances, a mainframe application is segmented into a number of smaller, reengineered desktop applications. Communication among the desktop applications (when necessary) is controlled by the business rules layer.

A comprehensive discussion of client/server software design and reengineering is best left to books dedicated to the subject. The interested reader should see [VAN02], [COU00], and [ORF99].

31.5.2 Forward Engineering for Object-Oriented Architectures

Object-oriented software engineering has become the development paradigm of choice for many software organizations. But what about existing applications that were developed using conventional methods? In some cases, the answer is to leave such applications "as is." In others, older applications must be reengineered so that they can be easily integrated into large, object-oriented systems.

Reengineering conventional software into an object-oriented implementation uses many of the same techniques discussed in Part 2 of this book. First, the existing software is reverse engineered so that appropriate data, functional, and behavioral models can be created. If the reengineered system extends the functionality or behavior of the original application, use-cases (Chapters 7 and 8) are created. The data models created during reverse engineering are then used in conjunction with CRC modeling (Chapter 8) to establish the basis for the definition of classes. Class hierarchies, object-relationship models, object-behavior models, and subsystems are defined, and object-oriented design commences.

As object-oriented forward engineering progresses from analysis to design, a CBSE process model (Chapter 30) can be invoked. If the old application exists within a domain that is already populated by many object-oriented applications, it is likely that a robust component library exists and can be used during forward engineering.

For those classes that must be engineered from scratch, it may be possible to reuse algorithms and data structures from the existing conventional application. However, these must be redesigned to conform to the object-oriented architecture.

31.5.3 Forward Engineering User Interfaces

As applications migrate from the mainframe to the desktop, users are no longer willing to tolerate arcane, character-based user interfaces. In fact, a significant portion of all effort expended in the transition from mainframe to client/server computing can be spent in the reengineering of client application user interfaces.

Merlo and his colleagues [MER95] suggest the following model for reengineering user interfaces:

What steps should we follow to reengineer a user interface?

1. *Understand the original interface and the data that move between it and the remainder of the application.* The intent is to understand how other elements of a program interact with existing code that implements the interface. If a new GUI is to be developed, the data that flow between the GUI and the remaining program must be consistent with the data that currently flow between the character-based interface and the program.
2. *Remodel the behavior implied by the existing interface into a series of abstractions that have meaning in the context of a GUI.* Although the mode of interaction may be radically different, the business behavior exhibited by users of the old and new interfaces (when considered in terms of a usage scenario) must remain the same. A redesigned interface must still allow a user to exhibit the appropriate business behavior. For example, when a database query is to be made, the old interface may require a long series of text-based commands to specify the query. The reengineered GUI may streamline the query to a small sequence of mouse picks, but the intent and content of the query remain unchanged.
3. *Introduce improvements that make the mode of interaction more efficient.* The ergonomic failings of the existing interface are studied and corrected in the design of the new GUI.
4. *Build and integrate the new GUI.* The existence of class libraries and automated tools can reduce the effort required to build the GUI significantly. However, integration with existing application software can be more time consuming. Care must be taken to ensure that the GUI does not propagate adverse side effects into the remainder of the application.

WebRef

A 300+ page handbook on reengineering patterns (developed as part of the FAMOOS ESPRIT project can be downloaded from **www.iam.unibe.ch/~scg/Archive/famoos/patterns/index3.html.**

> "You can pay a little now, or you can pay a lot more later."
>
> **Sign in an auto dealership suggesting a tune up**

31.6 The Economics of Reengineering

In a perfect world, every unmaintainable program would be retired immediately, to be replaced by high-quality, reengineered applications developed using modern software engineering practices. But we live in a world of limited resources. Reengineering drains resources that can be used for other business purposes. Therefore, before an organization attempts to reengineer an existing application, it should perform a cost/benefit analysis.

A cost/benefit analysis model for reengineering has been proposed by Sneed [SNE95]. Nine parameters are defined:

P_1 = current annual maintenance cost for an application
P_2 = current annual operation cost for an application
P_3 = current annual business value of an application
P_4 = predicted annual maintenance cost after reengineering
P_5 = predicted annual operations cost after reengineering
P_6 = predicted annual business value after reengineering
P_7 = estimated reengineering costs
P_8 = estimated reengineering calendar time
P_9 = reengineering risk factor ($P_9 = 1.0$ is nominal)
L = expected life of the system

The cost associated with continuing maintenance of a candidate application (i.e., reengineering is not performed) can be defined as

$$C_{maint} = [P_3 - (P_1 + P_2)] \times L \quad (31\text{-}1)$$

The costs associated with reengineering are defined using the following relationship:

$$C_{reeng} = [P_6 - (P_4 + P_5) \times (L - P_8) - (P_7 \times P_9)] \quad (31\text{-}2)$$

Using the costs presented in Equations (31-1) and (31-2), the overall benefit of reengineering can be computed as

$$\text{cost benefit} = C_{reeng} - C_{maint} \quad (31\text{-}3)$$

The cost/benefit analysis presented in the equations can be performed for all high-priority applications identified during inventory analysis (Section 31.2.2). Those applications that show the highest cost/benefit can be targeted for reengineering, while work on others can be postponed until resources are available.

31.7 Summary

Reengineering occurs at two different levels of abstraction. At the business level, reengineering focuses on the business process with the intent of making changes to improve competitiveness in some area of the business. At the software level, reengineering examines information systems and applications with the intent of restructuring or reconstructing them so that they exhibit higher quality.

Business process reengineering defines business goals, identifies and evaluates existing business processes (in the context of defined goals), specifies and designs revised processes, and prototypes, refines, and instantiates them within a business.

BPR has a focus that extends beyond software. The result of BPR is often the definition of ways in which information technologies can better support the business.

Software reengineering encompasses a series of activities that include inventory analysis, document restructuring, reverse engineering, program and data restructuring, and forward engineering. The intent of these activities is to create versions of existing programs that exhibit higher quality and better maintainability—programs that will be viable well into the twenty-first century.

Inventory analysis enables an organization to assess each application systematically, with the intent of determining which are candidates for reengineering. Document restructuring creates a framework of documentation that is necessary for the long-term support of an application. Reverse engineering is the process of analyzing a program in an effort to extract data, architectural, and procedural design information. Finally, forward engineering reconstructs a program using modern software engineering practices and information learned during reverse engineering.

The cost/benefit of reengineering can be determined quantitatively. The cost of the status quo, that is, the cost associated with ongoing support and maintenance of an existing application, is compared to the projected costs of reengineering and the resultant reduction in maintenance costs. In almost every case in which a program has a long life and currently exhibits poor maintainability, reengineering represents a cost-effective business strategy.

REFERENCES

[CAN72] Canning, R., "The Maintenance 'Iceberg'," *EDP Analyzer,* vol. 10, no. 10, October 1972.

[CAS88] "Case Tools for Reverse Engineering," *CASE Outlook,* CASE Consulting Group, vol. 2, no. 2, 1988, pp. 1–15.

[CHI90] Chikofsky, E. J., and J. H. Cross, II, "Reverse Engineering and Design Recovery: A Taxonomy," *IEEE Software,* January 1990, pp. 13–17.

[COU00] Coulouris, G., J. Dollimore, and T. Kindberg, *Distributed Systems: Concepts and Design,* 3rd ed., Addison-Wesley, 2000.

[DAV90] Davenport, T. H., and J. E. Young, "The New Industrial Engineering: Information Technology and Business Process Redesign," *Sloan Management Review,* Summer 1990, pp. 11–27.

[DEM95] DeMarco, T., "Lean and Mean," *IEEE Software,* November 1995, pp. 101–102.

[HAM90] Hammer, M., "Reengineer Work: Don't Automate, Obliterate," *Harvard Business Review,* July–August 1990, pp. 104–112.

[HAN93] Manna, M., "Maintenance Burden Begging for a Remedy," *Datamation,* April 1993, pp. 53–63.

[JAY94] Jaychandra, Y., *Re-engineering the Networked Enterprise,* McGraw-Hill, 1994.

[MER93] Merlo, E., et al., "Reverse Engineering of User Interfaces," *Proc. Working Conference on Reverse Engineering,* IEEE, Baltimore, May 1993, pp. 171–178.

[MER95] Merlo, E., et al., "Reengineering User Interfaces," *IEEE Software,* January 1995, pp. 64–73.

[MIL81] Miller, J., in *Techniques of Program and System Maintenance,* (G. Parikh, ed.) Winthrop Publishers, 1981.

[ORF99] Orfali, R., D. Harkey, and J. Edwards, *Client/Server Survival Guide,* 3rd ed., Wiley, 1999.

[OSB90] Osborne, W. M., and E. J. Chikofsky, "Fitting Pieces to the Maintenance Puzzle," *IEEE Software,* January 1990, pp. 10–11.

[PRE94] Premerlani, W. J., and M. R. Blaha, "An Approach for Reverse Engineering of Relational Databases," *CACM,* vol. 37, no. 5, May 1994, pp. 42–49.

[RIC89] Ricketts, J. A., J. C. DelMonaco, and M. W. Weeks, "Data Reengineering for Application Systems," *Proc. Conf. Software Maintenance—1989,* IEEE, 1989, pp. 174–179.

[SNE95] Sneed, H., "Planning the Reengineering of Legacy Systems," *IEEE Software,* January 1995, pp. 24–25.

[STE93] Stewart, T. A., "Reengineering: The Hot New Managing Tool," *Fortune,* August 23, 1993, pp. 41–48.

[SWA76] Swanson, E. B., "The Dimensions of Maintenance," *Proc. Second Intl. Conf. Software Engineering,* IEEE, October 1976, pp. 492–497.

[VAN02] Van Steen, M., and A. Tanenbaum, *Distributed Systems: Principles and Paradigms,* Prentice-Hall, 2002.

[WAR74] Warnier, J. D., *Logical Construction of Programs,* Van Nostrand-Reinhold, 1974.

Problems and Points to Ponder

31.1. Consider any job that you've held in the last five years. Describe the business process in which you played a part. Use the BPR model described in Section 31.1.3 to recommend changes to the process in an effort to make it more efficient.

31.2. Do some research on the efficacy of business process reengineering. Present pro and con arguments for this approach.

31.3. Your instructor will select one of the programs that everyone in the class has developed during this course. Exchange your program randomly with someone else in the class. Do not explain or walk through the program. Now, implement an enhancement (specified by your instructor) in the program you have received.

a. Perform all software engineering tasks including a brief walkthrough (but not with the author of the program).
b. Keep careful track of all errors encountered during testing.
c. Discuss your experiences in class.

31.4. Explore the inventory analysis checklist presented at the SEPA Web site and attempt to develop a quantitative software rating system that could be applied to existing programs in an effort to pick candidate programs for reengineering. Your system should extend beyond economic analysis presented in Section 31.6.

31.5. Suggest alternatives to paper and ink or conventional electronic documentation that could serve as the basis for document restructuring. (Hint: Think of new descriptive technologies that could be used to communicate the intent of the software.)

31.6. Some people believe that artificial intelligence technology will increase the abstraction level of the reverse engineering process. Do some research on this subject (i.e., the use of AI for reverse engineering), and write a brief paper that takes a stand on this point.

31.7. Why is completeness difficult to achieve as abstraction level increases?

31.8. Why must interactivity increase if completeness is to increase?

31.9. Using information obtained via the Internet, present characteristics of three reverse engineering tools to your class.

31.10. There is a subtle difference between restructuring and forward engineering. What is it?

31.11. Research the literature and/or Internet sources to find one or more papers that discuss case studies of mainframe to client/server reengineering. Present a summary.

31.12. How would you determine P_4 through P_7 in the cost-benefit model presented in Section 31.6?

Further Readings and Information Sources

Like many hot topics in the business community, the hype surrounding business process reengineering has given way to a more pragmatic view of the subject. Hammer and Champy (*Reengineering the Corporation,* HarperBusiness, revised edition, 2001) precipitated early interest with their best-selling book. Later, Hammer (*Beyond Reengineering: How the Processed-Centered Organization Is Changing Our Work and Our Lives,* HarperCollins 1997) refined his view by focusing on "process-centered" issues.

Books by Smith and Fingar (*Business Process Management (BPM): The Third Wave,* Meghan-Kiffer Press, 2003), Jacka and Keller (*Business Process Mapping: Improving Customer Satisfaction,* Wiley, 2001), Sharp and McDermott (*Workflow Modeling,* Artech House, 2001), Andersen (*Business Process Improvement Toolbox,* American Society for Quality, 1999), and Harrington et al. (*Business Process Improvement Workbook,* McGraw-Hill, 1997), present case studies and detailed guidelines for BPR.

Feldmann (*The Practical Guide to Business Process Reengineering Using IDEF0,* Dorset House, 1998) discusses a modeling notation that assists in BPR. Berztiss (*Software Methods for Business Reengineering,* Springer, 1996) and Spurr et al. (*Software Assistance for Business Reengineering,* Wiley, 1994) discuss tools and techniques that facilitate BPR.

Secord and his colleagues (*Modernizing Legacy Systems,* Addison-Wesley, 2003), Ulrich (*Legacy Systems: Transformation Strategies,* Prentice-Hall, 2002), Valenti (*Successful Software Reengineering,* IRM Press, 2002), and Rada (*Reengineering Software: How to Reuse Programming to Build New, State-of-the-Art Software,* Fitzroy Dearborn Publishers, 1999) focus on strategies and practices for reengineering at a technical level. Miller (*Reengineering Legacy Software Systems,* Digital Press, 1998) "provides a framework for keeping application systems synchronized with business strategies and technology changes." Umar (*Application (Re)Engineering: Building Web-Based Applications and Dealing with Legacies,* Prentice-Hall, 1997) provides worthwhile guidance for organizations that want to transform legacy systems into a Web-based environment. Cook (*Building Enterprise Information Architectures: Reengineering Information Systems,* Prentice-Hall, 1996) discusses the bridge between BPR and information technology. Aiken (*Data Reverse Engineering,* McGraw-Hill, 1996) discusses how to reclaim, reorganize, and reuse organizational data. Arnold (*Software Reengineering, I*EEE Computer Society Press, 1993) has put together an excellent anthology of early papers that focus on software reengineering technologies.

A wide variety of information sources on software reengineering is available on the Internet. An up-to-date list of World Wide Web references can be found at the SEPA Web site: **http://www.mhhe.com/pressman.**

CHAPTER

32 THE ROAD AHEAD

KEY CONCEPTS

In the 31 chapters that have preceded this one, we explored a process for software engineering. We presented both management procedures and technical methods, basic principles and specialized techniques, people-oriented activities and tasks that are amenable to automation, paper and pencil notation, and software tools. We argued that measurement, discipline, and an overriding focus on quality will result in software that meets the customer's needs, software that is reliable, software that is maintainable, software that is better. Yet, we have never promised that software engineering is a panacea.

As we continue our journey into a new century, software and systems technologies remain a challenge for every software professional and every company that builds computer-based systems. Although he wrote these words with a twentieth century outlook, Max Hopper [HOP90] accurately describes the current state of affairs:

> Because changes in information technology are becoming so rapid and unforgiving, and the consequences of falling behind are so irreversible, companies will either master the technology or die . . . Think of it as a technology treadmill. Companies will have to run harder and harder just to stay in place.

QUICK LOOK

What is it? The future is never easy to predict—pundits, talking heads, and industry experts not-withstanding. The road ahead is littered with the carcasses of exciting new technologies that never really made it (despite the hype) and is often shaped by more modest technologies that somehow modify the direction and width of the thoroughfare. Therefore, we won't try to predict the future. Rather we'll discuss some of the issues that you'll need to consider to understand how software and software engineering will change in the years ahead.

Who does it? Everyone!

Why is it important? Why did ancient kings hire soothsayers? Why do major multinational corporations hire consulting firms and think tanks to prepare forecasts? Why does a substantial percentage of the public read horoscopes? We want to know what's coming so we can ready ourselves.

What are the steps? There is no formula for predicting the road ahead. We attempt to do this by collecting data, organizing it to provide useful information, examining subtle associations to extract knowledge, and from this knowledge, suggest probable occurrences that predict how things will be at some future time.

What is the work product? A view of the near-term future that may or may not be correct.

How do I ensure that I've done it right? Predicting the road ahead is an art, not a science. In fact, it's quite rare when a serious prediction about the future is absolutely right or unequivocally wrong (with the exception, thankfully, of predictions of the end of the world). We look for trends and try to extrapolate them ahead in time. We can assess the correctness of the extrapolation only as time passes.

Changes in software engineering technology are indeed "rapid and unforgiving," while at the same time progress is often quite slow. By the time a decision is made to adopt a new method (or a new tool), conduct the training necessary to understand its application, and introduce the technology into the software development culture, something newer (and even better) has come along, and the process begins anew.

In this chapter, we examine the road ahead. Our intent is not to explore every area of research the holds promise. Nor is it to gaze into a "crystal ball" and prognosticate about the future. Rather, we explore the scope of change and the way in which change itself will affect the software engineering process in the years ahead.

32.1 The Importance of Software—Revisited

The importance of computer software can be stated in many ways. In Chapter 1, software was characterized as a differentiator. The function delivered by software differentiates products, systems, and services and provides competitive advantage in the marketplace. But software is more than a differentiator. The programs, documents, and data that are software help to generate the most important commodity that any individual, business, or government can acquire—*information.* Pressman and Herron [PRE91] describe software in the following way:

> Computer software is one of only a few key technologies that will have a significant impact on nearly every aspect of modern society . . . It is a mechanism for automating business, industry, and government, a medium for transferring new technology, a method of capturing valuable expertise for use by others, a means for differentiating one company's products from its competitors, and a window into a corporation's collective knowledge. Software is pivotal to nearly every aspect of business. But in many ways, software is also a hidden technology. We encounter software (often without realizing it) when we travel to work, make any retail purchase, stop at the bank, make a phone call, visit the doctor, or perform any of the hundreds of day-to-day activities that reflect modern life.

The pervasiveness of software leads us to a simple conclusion: Whenever a technology has a broad impact—an impact that can save lives or endanger them, build businesses or destroy them, inform government leaders or mislead them—it must be handled with care.

> **"Predictions are very difficult to make, especially when they deal with the future."**
>
> **Mark Twain**

32.2 The Scope of Change

The changes in computing over the past 50 years have been driven by advances in the hard sciences—physics, chemistry, materials science, and engineering. This trend will continue during the first quarter of the twenty-first century. The impact of new technologies is pervasive—on communications, energy, healthcare, transportation, entertainment, economics, manufacturing, and warfare, to name only a few.

INFO

Technologies to Watch

The editors of *PC Magazine* [PCM03] prepare an annual "Future Tech" issue that "[sorts] through all the chatter (there's a lot of it) to identify 20 of the most promising technologies of tomorrow." The technologies noted run the gamut from healthcare to warfare. However, it's interesting to note that software and software engineering have a significant role to play in every one, either as an enabler for the technology or an integral part of it. The following represents a sampling of the technologies noted:

Carbon nanotubes—with a tiny graphite-like structure, carbon nanotubes can serve as wires to transmit signals from one point to another and as transistors, using signal changes to store information. These devices show promise for use in the development of smaller, faster, lower energy, and less expensive electronic devices (e.g., microprocessors, memory, displays).

Biosensors—external or implantable microelectronic sensors are already in use for detecting everything from chemical agents in the air we breathe to blood levels in a cardiac patient. As these sensors become more sophisticated, they may be implanted in medical patients to monitor a variety of health-related conditions or attached to a soldier's uniform to monitor the presence of biological and chemical weapons.

OLED displays—An OLED "uses a carbon-based designer molecule that emits light when an electric current passes through it. Piece lots of molecules together and you've got a superthin display of stunning quality—no power-draining backlight required." [PCM03] The result—ultra-thin displays that can be rolled up or folded, sprayed onto a curved surface, or otherwise adapted to a specific environment.

Grid computing—this technology (available today) creates a network that taps the billions of unused CPU cycles from every machine on the network and allows exceedingly complex computing jobs to be completed without a dedicated supercomputer. For a real-life example encompassing over 4.5 million computers, visit http://setiathome.berkeley.edu/.

Cognitive machines—the 'holy grail' in the robotics field is to develop machines that are aware of their environment, that can "pick up on cues, respond to ever-changing situations, and interact with people naturally" [PCM03]. Cognitive machines are still in the early stages of development, but the potential (if ever achieved) is enormous.

WebRef
For predictions about the future of technology and other matters, see **www.futurefacing.com.**

Over the longer term, revolutionary advances in computing may well be driven by soft sciences—human psychology, sociology, philosophy, anthropology, and others. The gestation period for the computing technologies that may be derived from these disciplines is very difficult to predict, but early influences have already begun (e.g., the communities—an anthropological construct—of users that are an off-shoot of peer-to-peer networks).

The influence of the soft sciences may help mold the direction of computing research in the hard sciences. For example, the design of future computers may be guided more by an understanding of brain physiology than an understanding of conventional microelectronics.

In the shorter term, the changes that will affect software engineering over the next decade will be influenced by four simultaneous sources: (1) the people who do the work, (2) the process that they apply, (3) the nature of information, and (4) the underlying computing technology. In the sections that follow, each of these components—people, the process, information, and the technology—is examined in more detail.

32.3 People and the Way They Build Systems

The software required for high-technology systems becomes more and more complex with each passing year, and the size of resultant programs increases proportionally. The rapid growth in the size of the "average" program would present us with few problems if it wasn't for one simple fact: As program size increases, the number of people who must work on the program must also increase.

Experience indicates that as the number of people on a software project team increases, the overall productivity of the group may suffer. One way around this problem is to create a number of software engineering teams, thereby compartmentalizing people into individual working groups. However, as the number of software engineering teams grows, communication between them becomes as difficult and time consuming as communication between individuals. Worse, communication (between individuals or teams) tends to be inefficient—that is, too much time is spent transferring too little information content, and all too often, important information "falls into the cracks."

> **"Future shock [is] the shattering stress and disorientation that we induce in individuals by subjecting them to too much change in too short a period of time."**
>
> **Alvin Toffler**

If the software engineering community is to deal effectively with the communication dilemma, the road ahead for software engineers must include radical changes in the way individuals and teams communicate with one another. E-mail, Web sites, and centralized video conferencing are now commonplace as mechanisms for connecting a large number of people to an information network. The importance of these tools in the context of software engineering work cannot be overemphasized. With an effective electronic mail or instant messaging system, the problem encountered by a software engineer in New York City may be solved with the help of a colleague in Tokyo. In a very real sense, focused chat sessions and specialized newsgroups become knowledge repositories that allow the collective wisdom of a large group of technologists to be brought to bear on a technical problem or management issue.

Video personalizes the communication. At its best, it enables colleagues at different locations (or on different continents) to "meet" on a regular basis. But video also provides another benefit. It can be used as a repository for knowledge about the software and to train newcomers on a project.

> **"The proper artistic response to digital technology is to embrace it as a new window on everything that's eternally human, and to use it with passion, wisdom, fearlessness and joy."**
>
> **Ralph Lombreglia**

More and more "nonprogrammers" are building their own (small) applications. This on-going trend is likely to accelerate into the future. Should these "civilians" apply the technology discussed in this book? Probably not. But they should adopt an agile software engineering philosophy, even if they don't adopt the practice.

The evolution of intelligent agents will also change the work patterns of a software engineer by dramatically extending the capabilities of software tools. Intelligent agents will enhance the engineer's ability by cross-checking engineering work products using domain-specific knowledge, performing clerical tasks, doing directed research, and coordinating human-to-human communication.

Finally, the acquisition of knowledge is changing in profound ways. On the Internet, a software engineer can subscribe to newsgroups that focus on technology areas of immediate concern. A question posted within a newsgroup precipitates answers from other interested parties around the globe. The World Wide Web provides a software engineer with the world's largest library of research papers and reports, tutorials, commentary, and references in software engineering.

If past history is any indication, it is fair to say that people themselves will not change. However, the ways in which they communicate, the environment in which they work, the way in which they acquire knowledge, the methods and tools that they use, the discipline that they apply, and therefore, the overall culture for software development will change in significant and even profound ways.

32.4 The "New" Software Engineering Process

It is reasonable to characterize the first two decades of software engineering practice as the era of "linear thinking." Fostered by the classic life cycle model, software engineering was approached as a linear activity in which a series of sequential steps could be applied in an effort to solve complex problems. Yet, linear approaches to software development run counter to the way in which most systems are actually built. In reality, complex systems evolve iteratively, even incrementally. It is for this reason that a large segment of the software engineering community is moving toward agile, incremental models for software development.

Agile, incremental process models recognize that uncertainty dominates most projects, that timelines are often impossibly short, and that iteration provides the ability to deliver a partial solution, even when a complete product is not possible within the time allotted. Evolutionary models emphasize the need for incremental work products, risk analysis, planning and then plan revision, and customer feedback. In many instances, the software team applies an "agile manifesto" (Chapter 4) that emphasizes "individuals and interactions over processes and tools; working software over comprehensive documentation; customer collaboration over contract negotiation, and responding to change over following a plan" [BEC01].

> **"The best preparation for good work tomorrow is to do good work today."**
>
> **Elbert Hubbard**

Object technologies, coupled with component-based software engineering (Chapter 30), are a natural outgrowth of the trend toward incremental and evolutionary process models. Both will have a profound impact on software development productivity and product quality. Component reuse provides immediate and compelling benefits. When reuse is coupled with CASE tools for application prototyping, program increments can be built far more rapidly than through the use of conventional approaches. Prototyping draws the customer into the process. Therefore, it is likely that customers and users will become much more involved in the development of software. This, in turn, may lead to higher end-user satisfaction and better software quality overall.

The rapid growth in network and multimedia technologies (e.g., the exponential increase in WebApps over the past decade) is changing both the software engineering process and its participants. Again, we encounter an agile, incremental paradigm that emphasizes immediacy, security, and aesthetics as well as more conventional software engineering concerns. Modern software teams (e.g., a Web engineering team) often meld technologists with content specialists (e.g., artists, musicians, videographers) to build an information source for a community of users that is both large and unpredictable. The software that has grown out of these technologies has already resulted in radical economic and cultural change. Although the basic concepts and principles discussed in this book are applicable, the software engineering process must adapt.

32.5 New Modes for Representing Information

Over the history of computing, a subtle transition has occurred in the terminology that is used to describe software development work performed for the business community. Forty years ago, the term *data processing* was the operative phrase for describing the use of computers in a business context. Today, data processing has given way to another phrase—*information technology*—that implies the same thing but presents a subtle shift in focus. The emphasis is not merely to process large quantities of data but rather to extract meaningful information from this data. Obviously, this was always the intent, but the shift in terminology reflects a far more important shift in management philosophy.

When software applications are discussed today, the words *data* and *information* occur repeatedly. We encounter the word *knowledge* in some artificial intelligence applications, but its use is relatively rare. Virtually no one discusses *wisdom* in the context of software applications.

Data is raw information—collections of facts that must be processed to be meaningful. Information is derived by associating facts within a given context. Knowledge associates information obtained in one context with other information obtained in a different context. Finally, wisdom occurs when generalized principles are derived from disparate knowledge. Each of these four views of "information" is represented schematically in Figure 32.1.

To date, the vast majority of all software has been built to process data or information. Software engineers are now equally concerned with systems that process

FIGURE 32.1

An "information" spectrum

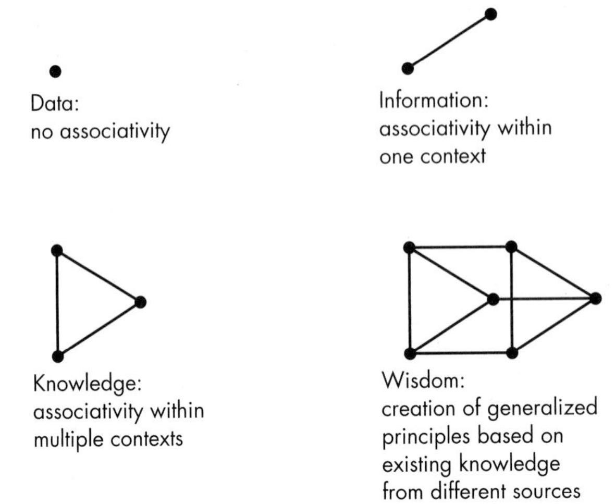

knowledge.[1] Knowledge is two-dimensional. Information collected on a variety of related and unrelated topics is connected to form a body of fact that we call *knowledge.* The key is our ability to associate information from a variety of different sources that may not have any obvious connection and combine it in a way that provides us with some distinct benefit.

> "Wisdom is the power that enables us to use knowledge for the benefit of ourselves and others."
>
> **Thomas J. Watson**

To illustrate the progression from data to knowledge, consider census data indicating that the birthrate in 1996 in the United States was 4.9 million. This number represents a data value. Relating this piece of data with birthrates for the preceding 40 years, we can derive a useful piece of information—aging "baby boomers" of the 1950s and early 1960s made a last gasp effort to have children prior to the end of their child-bearing years. In addition "gen-Xers" began their childbearing years. The census data can then be connected to other seemingly unrelated pieces of information. For example, the current number of elementary school teachers who will retire during the next decade, the number of college students graduating with degrees in primary and secondary education, the pressure on politicians to hold down taxes and therefore limit pay increases for teachers.

All of these pieces of information can be combined to formulate a representation of knowledge—there will be significant pressure on the education system in the United States in the first decade of the twenty-first century, and this pressure will

1 The rapid growth of data mining and data warehousing technologies reflect this growing trend.

continue for over a decade. Using this knowledge, a business opportunity may emerge. There may be significant opportunity to develop new modes of learning that are more effective and less costly than current approaches.

The road ahead for software leads to systems that process knowledge. We have been processing data using computers for over 50 years and extracting information for more than three decades. One of the most significant challenges facing the software engineering community is to build systems that take the next step along the spectrum—systems that extract knowledge from data and information in a way that is practical and beneficial.

32.6 Technology as a Driver

The people who build and use software, the software engineering process that is applied, and the information that is produced are all affected by advances in hardware and software technology. Historically, hardware has served as the technology driver in computing. A new hardware technology provides potential. Software builders then react to customer demands in an attempt to tap the potential.

The road ahead for hardware technology is likely to progress along two parallel paths. Along one path, hardware technologies will continue to evolve at a rapid pace. With greater capacity provided by traditional hardware architectures, the demands on software engineers will continue to grow.

But the real changes in hardware technology may occur along another path. The development of nontraditional hardware architectures (e.g., carbon nanotubes, EUL microprocessors, cognitive machines, grid-computing) may cause radical changes in the kind of software that we build and fundamental changes in our approach to software engineering. Since these nontraditional approaches are only now maturing, it is difficult to determine which will have broad-based impact and even more difficult to predict how the world of software will change to accommodate them.

The road ahead for software engineering is driven by software technologies. Reuse and component-based software engineering offer the best opportunity for order of magnitude improvements in system quality and time to market. In fact, as time passes, the software business may begin to look very much like the hardware business of today. There may be vendors that build discrete devices (reusable software components), other vendors that build system components (e.g., a set of tools for human/computer interaction), and system integrators that provide solutions (products and custom-built systems) for the end-user.

Software engineering will change—of that we can be certain. But regardless of how radical the changes are, we can be assured that quality will never lose its importance and that effective analysis and design and competent testing will always have a place in the development of computer-based systems.

INFO

Technology Trends

J. P. Cripwell Associates (www.jpcripwell.com), a consulting firm specializing in knowledge management and information engineering, discusses five technology drivers that will influence technology directions in the coming years:

Combination technologies. When two important technologies are merged, the impact of the merged result is often greater than the sum of the impact of each taken separately. For example, GPS satellite technology, coupled with on-board computing capability, coupled with LCD display technologies has resulting in sophisticated automobile mapping systems. Technologies often evolve along separate paths, but significant business or societal impact occurs only when someone combines them to solve a problem.

Data fusion. The more data we acquire, the more data we need. More importantly, the more data we acquire, the more difficult it is to extract useful information. In fact, we often need to acquire still more data to understand (1) what data are important; what data are relevant to a particular need or source, and what data should be used for decision making. This is the data fusion problem. J. P. Cripwell uses an advanced automobile traffic monitoring system as an example. Digital speed sensors (in the roadway) and digital cameras sense an accident. The severity of the accident must be determined (via camera?). Based on severity, the monitoring system must contact police, fire, or ambulance; traffic must be rerouted; media (radio) must broadcast warnings; and individual cars (if equipped with digital sensors or wireless communication) must be informed. To accomplish this, a variety of decisions, based on data acquired from the monitoring system (data fusion), must be made.

Technology push. In years past, a problem surfaced and technology was developed to solve it. Because the problem was evident to many people, the market for the new technology was well-defined. Today, some technologies evolve as solutions looking for problems. A market must be pushed to recognize that it needs the new technology (e.g., mobile phones, PDAs). As people recognize the need, the technology accelerates, improves, and often morphs as combination technologies evolve.

Networking and serendipity. In this context networking implies connections between people or between people and information. As the network grows, the likelihood of synergy between two network nodes (e.g., people, information sources) also grows. A chance connection (serendipity) can lead to inspiration and a new technology or application.

Information overload. A vast sea of information is accessible by anyone with an Internet connection. The problem, of course, is to find the right information, determine its validity, and then translate it into practical application at a business or personnel level.

32.7 The Software Engineer's Responsibility

Software engineering has evolved into a respected, worldwide profession. As professionals, software engineers should abide by a code of ethics that guides the work that they do and the products that they produce. An ACM/IEEE-CS Joint Task Force has produced a *Software Engineering Code of Ethics and Professional Practices* (Version 5.1). The code [ACM98] states:

> **WebRef**
> A complete discussion of the ACM/IEEE code of ethics can be found at **seeri.etsu.edu/Codes/default.shtm.**

> Software engineers shall commit themselves to making the analysis, specification, design, development, testing and maintenance of software a beneficial and respected profession. In accordance with their commitment to the health, safety and welfare of the public, software engineers shall adhere to the following Eight Principles:
>
> 1. PUBLIC—Software engineers shall act consistently with the public interest.

> 2. CLIENT AND EMPLOYER—Software engineers shall act in a manner that is in the best interests of their client and employer consistent with the public interest.
>
> 3. PRODUCT—Software engineers shall ensure that their products and related modifications meet the highest professional standards possible.
>
> 4. JUDGMENT—Software engineers shall maintain integrity and independence in their professional judgment.
>
> 5. MANAGEMENT—Software engineering managers and leaders shall subscribe to and promote an ethical approach to the management of software development and maintenance.
>
> 6. PROFESSION—Software engineers shall advance the integrity and reputation of the profession consistent with the public interest.
>
> 7. COLLEAGUES—Software engineers shall be fair to and supportive of their colleagues.
>
> 8. SELF—Software engineers shall participate in lifelong learning regarding the practice of their profession and shall promote an ethical approach to the practice of the profession.

Although each of these eight principles is equally important, an overriding theme appears: a software engineer should work in the public interest. On a personal level, a software engineer should abide by the following rules:

- Never steal data for personal gain.
- Never distribute or sell proprietary information obtained as part of your work on a software project.
- Never maliciously destroy or modify another person's programs, files, or data.
- Never violate the privacy of an individual, a group, or an organization.
- Never hack into a system for sport or profit.
- Never create or promulgate a computer virus or worm.
- Never use computing technology to facilitate discrimination or harassment.

Over the past decade, certain members of the software industry have lobbied for protective legislation that [SEE03]:

1. Allows companies to release software without disclosing known defects;
2. Exempts developers from liability for any damages resulting from these known defects;
3. Constrains others from disclosing defects without permission from the original developer;
4. Allows the incorporation of "self-help" software within a product that can disable (via remote command) the operation of the product;
5. Exempts developers of software with "self-help" from damages should the software be disabled by a third party.

Like all legislation, debate often centers on issues that are political, not technological. However, many people (including this author) feel that protective legislation, if improperly drafted, conflicts with the software engineering code of ethics by indirectly exempting software engineers from their responsibility to produce high-quality software.

32.8 A Concluding Comment

It has been 25 years since the first edition of this book was written. I can still recall sitting at my desk as a young professor, writing the manuscript (by hand) for a book on a subject that few people cared about and even fewer really understood. I remember the rejection letters from publishers, who argued (politely, but firmly) that there would never be a market for a book on "software engineering." Luckily, McGraw-Hill decided to give it a try,[2] and the rest, as they say, is history.

Over the past 25 years, this book has changed dramatically—in scope, in size, in style, and in content. Like software engineering, it has grown and (I hope) matured over the years.

An engineering approach to the development of computer software is now conventional wisdom. Although debate continues on the "right paradigm," the importance of agility, the degree of automation, and the most effective methods, the underlying principles of software engineering are now accepted throughout the industry. Why, then, have we seen their broad adoption only recently?

The answer, I think, lies in the difficulty of technology transition and the cultural change that accompanies it. Even though most of us appreciate the need for an engineering discipline for software, we struggle against the inertia of past practice and face new application domains (and the developers who work in them) that appear ready to repeat the mistakes of the past.

To ease the transition we need many things—an agile, adaptable, and sensible software process; more effective methods; more powerful tools; better acceptance by practitioners and support from managers; and no small dose of education and "advertising." Software engineering has not had the benefit of massive advertising, but as time passes, the concept sells itself. In a way, this book is an "advertisement" for the technology.

You may not agree with every approach described in this book. Some of the techniques and opinions are controversial; others must be tuned to work well in different software development environments. It is my sincere hope, however, that *Software Engineering: A Practitioner's Approach* has delineated the problems we face, demonstrated the strength of software engineering concepts, and provided a framework of methods and tools.

As we move into the twenty-first century, software has become the most important product and the most important industry on the world stage. Its impact and im-

2 Actually, credit should go to Peter Freeman and Eric Munson, who convinced McGraw-Hill that it was worth a shot.

portance have come a long, long way. And yet, a new generation of software developers must meet many of the same challenges that faced earlier generations. Let us hope that the people who meet the challenge—software engineers—will have the wisdom to develop systems that improve the human condition.

References

[ACM98] ACM/IEEE-CS Joint Task Force, *Software Engineering Code of Ethics and Professional Practice,* 1998, available at http://www.acm.org/serving/se/code.htm.

[BEC01] Beck, K., et al., "Manifesto for Agile Software Development," http://www.agilemanifesto.org/.

[BOL91] Bollinger, T., and C. McGowen, "A Critical Look at Software Capability Evaluations," *IEEE Software,* July 1991, pp. 25–41.

[GIL96] Gilb, T., "What Is Level Six?" *IEEE Software,* January 1996, pp. 97–98, 103.

[HOP90] Hopper, M. D., "Rattling SABRE, New Ways to Compete on Information," *Harvard Business Review,* May–June 1990.

[PAU93] Paulk, M., et al., *Capability Maturity Model for Software,* Software Engineering Institute, Carnegie Mellon University, 1993.

[PCM03] "Technologies to Watch," *PC Magazine,* July 2003, available at http://www.pcmag.com/article2/0,4149,1130591,00.asp.

[PRE91] Pressman, R. S., and S. R. Herron, *Software Shock,* Dorset House, 1991.

[SEE03] The Software Engineering Ethics Research Institute, "UCITA Updates," 2003, available at http://seeri.etsu.edu/default.htm.

Problems and Points to Ponder

32.1. Get a copy of this week's major business and news magazines (e.g., *Newsweek, Time, Business Week*). List every article or news item that can be used to illustrate the importance of software.

32.2. One of the hottest software application domains is Web-based systems and applications. Discuss how people, communication, and process have to evolve to accommodate the development of "next generation" WebApps.

32.3. Write a brief description of an ideal software engineer's development environment circa 2010. Describe the elements of the environment (hardware, software, and communications technologies) and their impact on quality and time to market.

32.4. Review the discussion of the agile, incremental process models in Chapter 4. Do some research, and collect recent papers on the subject. Summarize the strengths and weaknesses of agile paradigms based on experiences outlined in the papers.

32.5. Attempt to develop an example that begins with the collection of raw data and leads to acquisition of information, then knowledge, and finally, wisdom.

32.6. Provide specific examples that illustrate one of the eight software engineering ethics principles noted in Section 32.7.

Further Readings and Information Sources

Books that discuss the road ahead for software and computing span a vast array of technical, scientific, economic, political, and social issues. Sterling (*Tomorrow Now,* Random House, 2002) reminds us that real progress is rarely orderly and efficient. Teich (*Technology and the Future,* Wadworth, 2002) presents thoughtful essays on the societal impact of technology and how changing culture shapes technology. Naisbitt, Philips, and Naisbitt (*High Tech/High Touch,* Nicholas Brealey, 2001) note that many of us have become "intoxicated" with high technology and that the "great irony of the high-tech age is that we've become enslaved to devices that were supposed to give us freedom." Zey (*The Future Factor,* McGraw-Hill, 2000) discusses five forces that will shape human destiny during this century. Canton (*Technofutures,* Hay House, 1999) discusses how technology will transform business in the twenty-first century. Robertson (*The New Renaissance: Computers and the Next Level of Civilization,* Oxford University Press, 1998) argues that the computer revolution may be the single most significant advance in the history of civilization.

Broderick (*Spike,* Forge, 2001) discusses the impact of emerging technologies. Dertrouzos and Gates (*What Will Be: How the New World of Information Will Change Our Lives,* Harper-Business, 1998) provide a thoughtful discussion of some of the directions that information technologies may take in the first few decades of this century. Barnatt (*Valueware: Technology, Humanity and Organization,* Praeger Publishing, 1999) presents an intriguing discussion of an "ideas economy" and how economic value will be created as cyber-business evolves. Negroponte's *(Being Digital,* Alfred A. Knopf, 1995) was a best seller in the mid-1990s and continues to provide an interesting view of computing and its overall impact.

Kroker and Kroker (*Digital Delirium,* New World Perspectives, 1997) have edited a controversial collection of essays, poems, and humor that examines the impact of digital technologies on people and society. Brin (*The Transparent Society: Will Technology Force Us to Choose Between Privacy and Freedom?* Perseus Books, 1999) revisits the continuing debate associated with the inevitable loss of personal privacy that accompanies the growth of information technologies. Shenk (*Data Smog: Surviving the Information Glut,* HarperCollins, 1998) discusses the problems associated with an "information-infested society" that is suffocating from the volume of information that software produces.

Brockman (*The Next Fifty Years,* Vintage Books, 2002) and Miller and his colleagues (*21st Century Technologies: Promises and Perils of a Dynamic Future,* Brookings Institution Press, 1999) have edited a collection of papers and essays on the impact of technology on social, business, and economic structures. For those interested in technical issues, Luryi, Xu, and Zaslavsky (*Future Trends in Microelectronics,* Wiley, 1999) have edited a collection of papers on probable directions for computer hardware with an emphasis on nanotechnologies. Hayzelden and Bigham (*Software Agents for Future Communication Systems,* Springer-Verlag, 1999) have edited a collection that discusses trends in the development of intelligent software agents.

As software becomes part of the fabric of virtually every facet of our lives, "cyberethics" has evolved as an important topic of discussion. Books by Spinello (*Cyberethics: Morality and Law in Cyberspace,* Jones & Bartlett Publishers, 2002), Halbert and Ingulli (*Cyberethics,* South-Western College Publishers, 2001), and Baird and his colleagues (*Cyberethics: Social and Moral Issues in the Computer Age,* Prometheus Books, 2000) consider the topic in detail. The U.S. government has published a voluminous report on CD-ROM (*21st Century Guide to Cybercrime,* Progressive Management, 2003) that considers all aspects of computer crime, intellectual property issues, and the National Infrastructure Protection Center (NIPC).

Kurzweil (*The Age of Spiritual Machines, When Computers Exceed Human Intelligence,* Viking/Penguin Books, 1999) argues that within 20 years, hardware technology will have the capacity to fully model the human brain. Borgmann (*Holding on to Reality: The Nature of Information at the Turn of the Millennium,* University of Chicago Press, 1999) has written an intriguing history of information, tracing its role in the transformation of culture. Devlin (*InfoSense: Turning Information into Knowledge,* W. H. Freeman & Co., 1999) tries to make sense of the constant flow of information that bombards us on a daily basis. Gleick (*Faster: The Acceleration of Just About Everything,* Pantheon Books, 2000) discusses the ever-accelerating rate of technological change and its impact on every aspect of modern life. Jonscher (*The Evolution of Wired Life: From the Alphabet to the Soul-Catcher Chip—How Information Technologies Change Our World,* Wiley, 2000) argues that human thought and interaction transcend the importance of technology.

A wide variety of information sources on future directions in software-related technologies and software engineering is available on the Internet. An up-to-date list of World Wide Web references can be found at the SEPA Web site:

http://www.mhhe.com/pressman.

INDEX